The Life of Nelson A. Rockefeller

Worlds to Conquer 1908–1958

Also by Cary Reich

Financier: The Biography of André Meyer

The Life of Nelson A. Rockefeller

Worlds to Conquer 1908–1958

Cary Reich

Doubleday
New York London Toronto Sydney Auckland

PUBLISHED BY DOUBLEDAY
a division of Bantam Doubleday Dell Publishing Group, Inc.
1540 Broadway, New York, New York 10036

DOUBLEDAY and the portrayal of an anchor with a dolphin
are trademarks of Doubleday, a division of
Bantam Doubleday Dell Publishing Group, Inc.

All photos courtesy of the Rockefeller Archive Center, unless otherwise noted.

Library of Congress Cataloging-in-Publication Data

Reich, Cary.
The life of Nelson A. Rockefeller : worlds to conquer, 1908–1958 / Cary Reich.
— 1st ed.
p. cm.
Includes index.
1. Rockefeller, Nelson A. (Nelson Aldrich), 1908–1979. 2. Vice-Presidents—United States—Biography. 3. Governors—New York (State)—Biography. I. Title.
E748.R673R55 1996
973.925092
[B]—DC20 96-14718
CIP
ISBN 0-385-24696-X

Printed in the United States of America

November 1996

First Edition

1 3 5 7 9 10 8 6 4 2

To Karen

CONTENTS

Introduction

COMBINATIONS

What a great President he would have been! How he would have ennobled us! What an extraordinary combination of strength and humanity, decisiveness and vision!
—Henry Kissinger, "Words of Commemoration," Memorial Service for Nelson Aldrich Rockefeller, February 2, 1979

He irritated the shit out of a lot of people. It was a combination of things: all that wealth, that opportunism, that arrogance, rolled up together. . . . Sure, there are other arrogant politicians, there are other rich politicians, there are other opportunistic politicians. But where do you get such a gorgeous combination of them as in this one figure?
—William Rusher, conservative commentator and publisher

More than a decade and a half after his death, and two decades after he departed public life, the invocation of Nelson A. Rockefeller's name still conjures up a host of powerful, distinct images.

First, there is the image of his progressive and profligate New York governorship, with Rockefeller as a latter-day Cheops, building such monuments as the State University and the billion-dollar South Mall in the capital, introducing a multitude of far-reaching programs, and bequeathing to the state's taxpayers an awesome mountain of debt.

Then there is the storied "Rocky": garrulous, backslapping, eye-winking, offering a gravelly "Hi ya, fella" to one and all and tossing any manner of ethnic treats down his cast-iron gullet. And, in vivid counterpoint to that, there is the imperial Nelson Rockefeller, commanding limitless wealth, presiding over his magnificent Georgian manor house in the very private 3,500-acre family preserve in Westchester—merely one of his five residences—and assembling one of the twentieth century's great private art collections.

And, of course, for many, the image that first comes to mind is the one engendered by his mysterious, much-gossiped-about demise: that of a lusty septuagenarian, meeting his maker while, apparently, in *hysteria libidinosa* with a lady almost half a century his junior.

In history, Rockefeller has left his mark as the perennial Man Who Would

Be President, an object lesson in the limits of what money can buy. No politician of his era, it is commonly agreed, was better equipped, by temperament and background, for the presidency; none had as formidable a machine at hand to realize his dream. But three times he tried, and three times he failed. In the end, the closest he would come to the White House was a brief lame-duck turn at the vice presidency.

But probably the most enduring and pervasive view of Rockefeller is steeped in irony, for it is the one cherished by his adversaries, American conservatives, for whom it has been a precious talisman passed on from one generation of the right wing to the next: the Rockefeller of "Rockefeller Republicanism," that reviled and discredited amalgam of tax-and-spend big government liberalism and avid internationalism. It is a totem of seemingly undiminished potency, as witness its use as a conservative rallying cry against the prospective presidential candidacy of General Colin Powell, a reputed Rockefeller Republican. "If he should get the nomination," warned one conservative activist, "it would be as if Ronald Reagan had never lived and Nelson Rockefeller never died." (Another conservative spokesman saw fit to remind his audience that Rockefeller, the general's supposed ideological mentor, was "a conspicuous philanderer.")

This power, the power to fire up the most incendiary political passions at the mere mention of his name, is ample testimony to the grip that Nelson Rockefeller—vintage progressive, unabashed spender, master builder, thwarted presidential contender, "conspicuous philanderer"—continues to hold on the popular imagination. One way or another, he is still with us.

He was born into awesome wealth, a fortune so vast that his very family name was synonymous with stupendous sums. And yet, throughout his life, he exhibited the relentless drive of the self-made man: he was every bit the go-getter, a patrician Sammy Glick. Asked once by an interviewer what he would have done if he hadn't been born into fortune, Rockefeller instantly replied, "I would think of making one." Possessed of boundless reserves of energy, soaring ambition, and an unshakable will, Rockefeller would have achieved great things regardless of his material circumstances. "He was interested in accomplishing," reflects his brother David, "and he spent a lot of time in seeing where he wanted to go, and then developing a strategy to get there. In other words, things did not happen by accident in his life."

"His life was dedicated to moving ahead," says his onetime aide William Alton, who had known Rockefeller since boyhood. "There was always a mission, something to be done. He was always building, building, building."

Those associated with Rockefeller over the years tend to describe him in terms usually reserved for hustlers from the Lower East Side tenements. "He was a fighter, a real scrapper right from the start," remarks commentator Thomas Braden, who first came into Rockefeller's orbit in the early 1940s. "It's hard to believe that a guy with all the natural advantages Nelson had would be remembered as someone who overcame obstacles, but that's how I remember him. That was his strength, the thing I always admired."

Every domain he entered was a new world to conquer, every realm something to be subjugated to his will—starting with his very own family. From his earliest years he strove to dominate the Rockefeller empire. While his siblings were great strivers in their own right—one the world's preeminent commercial banker, another among America's most successful venture capitalists, another a philanthropist of global renown and the prime mover behind Lincoln Center—rarely did any of them dare to challenge his supremacy.

And as it was for the Rockefellers, so it would be, for almost a generation, for the state of New York. "Nothing stands in Rockefeller's way," his political contemporary U.S. senator Jacob Javits would say. "Nothing. He always gets what he wants."

And so, too, would it be for the coterie of men and women—many of them illustrious figures in their own right—who would serve Nelson Rockefeller. No less a personage than Henry Kissinger—who owed much of his ascension in public life to Rockefeller's sponsorship—would complain that "the problem with Nelson was that he was such a dominant personality, and he tended to draw you into his orbit, and he tended to become all-consuming. So it was very hard to keep your identity with him."

"I think Rockefeller got interested in politics," opines his longtime conservative foe, *National Review* publisher William Rusher, "because it was one of the few things in the world that resisted his approach."

Surely precious little else did. In Nelson Rockefeller's world, no gratification was ever deferred for long, no whim ever went unsatisfied—be it in art, in automobiles, in real estate, or in women. Expressing admiration for a rare replication in tapestry of one of Picasso's masterworks, he thought it would be grand if the artist's other masterpieces were similarly rendered for him in cloth—with the artist himself supervising, of course. Picasso obliged. Coveting a yellow Phantom Five Rolls-Royce, and finding that the company had made only one and it wasn't for sale, he bought a gray Phantom instead and contrived to paint it yellow. When the manufacturer refused to go along, Rockefeller had his agents hire a former Royal Air Force intelligence operative to sneak into the Rolls-Royce garage and scratch a paint chip from the yellow vehicle, so that the exact shade could be analyzed and reproduced.

Flying one night over Mount Rushmore in his private plane, Rockefeller asked his traveling companion, "Have you ever seen Mount Rushmore?" When the man said no, Rockefeller said, "Just a minute," and picked up a phone on the plane. Suddenly, beneath them, the presidential likenesses were bathed in spotlights.

Then there was the time Rockefeller played host to the national conference of governors and decided to fete his guests at the Metropolitan Museum of Art—in the days when parties at the august institution were strictly forbidden. A Rockefeller assistant met with museum director Thomas Hoving, and, the aide recalls, "Hoving kept telling us how impossible it was, you can't possibly put chafing dishes there, and all that. Finally, I told Hoving that as far as Nelson was concerned, nothing was impossible. And he just sighed and said, 'Well, if that's what Nelson wants . . .' "

Having his way in all things, he seemed like a veritable King of New York. Never did he approach his private plane on the tarmac when it wasn't poised for takeoff, propeller churning. Never on a rainy day did he have to ask for his topcoat; no sooner did he raise his arms than the coat would be slipped over them. "Rockefeller was a royal presence," admits one of his political foes. "The whole aura was overwhelming." And not just for New York pols. Once, the Earl of Mountbatten, mentor of Prince Philip and Prince Charles, became embroiled in a vigorous dispute with Rockefeller at his Pocantico Hills estate. "But, Your Majesty," Mountbatten remonstrated, before he caught himself.

The grandeur of Rockefeller's surroundings—the Manhattan triplex whose fireplaces were decorated by Matisse and Léger, the Pocantico Hills estate with its Calders, Moores, and David Smiths filling the porches and manicured lawns, the Seal Harbor, Maine, residence hovering over the granite outcroppings like a great beached schooner—added further to the regal aura. Even other Rockefellers stood in awe. On one occasion brother David was touring the private underground gallery architect Philip Johnson designed for Nelson beneath Kykuit, the main house at Pocantico, where Nelson resided. Taking in corridor upon corridor of Picassos and Chagalls, Motherwells and Warhols, David heaved a great sigh. "Only Nelson," he said, "could live like this."

Constitutionally immune to embarrassment, Rockefeller was particularly unembarrassed by his wealth. Asked once by a southern U.S. senator why so many rich politicians were liberals, he replied, "Because of a guilt complex. I have to tell you, I have no guilt complex."

"How's it feel to be rich?" a young girl asked him on the campaign trail. "Fine!" Rockefeller replied with gusto. "How's it feel to be good-looking?"

While his wealth per se never troubled him ("Being a Rockefeller never bothers me," he once remarked), taking the measure of his fortune sometimes gave him pause. On a visit to East Berlin, Rockefeller was confused and flustered when the East German guard at Checkpoint Charlie asked, "How much money do you have?" Finally, one of his aides leaned over and clarified things: "Governor, what he means is, how much money do you have *on* you?"

He was always keenly aware of the unique power his money commanded. Wealth, he told an interviewer in 1971, is "a tool. It can be used constructively . . . if you use it badly, it can cut you, like a sharp tool."

Never did he shy from wielding this power, barbed as it was. "He had none of the hangups about wealth or being a Rockefeller that some of his brothers had," noted his son Steven. "He rather gloried in it. He thoroughly enjoyed the power and the freedom that the money gave him."

His career is, among other things, a study in the unabashed use of a great fortune to secure influence. With his fortune, he was able to lure some of the country's best minds into his web; with his fortune, he ingratiated himself with occupants of the White House; with his fortune, he won elections.

Unhesitant about deploying his own private resources, he proved equally unhesitant about deploying the state of New York's. "If he wanted to spend money, money was no object," says Louis Lefkowitz, his attorney general and four-time running mate. "If he wanted something done, he did it. He had ideas all the time, and they were good ideas. He'd spend money, sure, but he'd give you something for your money."

Indeed he did; no governor in the Empire State's history—in fact, probably no governor in *any* state's history—produced as much in bricks and mortar, in blacktop and concrete, for the citizenry. In the course of its fifteen-year run, his administration gave the state 90,000 new low- and moderate-income housing units; 200 water treatment plants to curb pollution; 23 new state mental health facilities; and helped construct or expand 109 voluntary and municipal hospitals. Rockefeller boasted that the state built four and a half miles of highway for every day he was in office; among the great road-building enterprises of his regime were the Adirondack Northway, connecting the remote northeast of the state with Canada, and the completion of the Long Island Expressway.

Unquestionably, Rockefeller's proudest achievement was the vast expansion of the State University system: from 38,000 students on 28 campuses when he took over to 246,000 students on 71 campuses when he left, all brought off with typical Rockefeller panache (among the architects he recruited to design the new units were such world-class figures as I. M. Pei, Philip Johnson, and Edward Durell Stone). But the monument that made the most indelible mark on the public consciousness was not SUNY, but the South Mall in Albany, the soaring billion-dollar marble-clad government complex that gave new life to the much-maligned capital city, and, some said, new meaning to the word "megalomania."

Aside from bestowing upon the state these edifices, Rockefeller's dynamism and largesse engendered other profound changes in the Empire State. His administration midwifed the creation of the Metropolitan Transportation Authority, rescuing the vital commuter railroads serving New York City from total collapse. It offered record amounts of financial aid to private and public college students. It saved the Adirondack Park from commercial and residential blight (as well as creating 55 new state parks). It set the pattern for government arts funding through the state Council on the Arts. And it oversaw the explosive growth of health care for the needy through the new federal-state Medicaid program; no state was as generous (at its peak Medicaid covered 45 percent of New York residents), and no state would be so overwhelmed by the program's skyrocketing costs.

What this all added up to, in the words of U.S. senator Daniel Patrick Moynihan, was "the last great moment of expansive government in New York." The bill for this final flourish was truly staggering. On Rockefeller's watch, state spending more than quadrupled, while the state's debt grew from a mere $900 million in 1959 to $3.4 billion in 1973—and, on top of that, there was another $6.7 billion in debt undertaken through various fiscal gimmicks. Rockefeller's budgetary excesses not only triggered a state credit crisis in the mid-1970s but undoubtedly set the stage for the monumental fiscal crisis that brought New York City to the brink of bankruptcy less than two years after he left office.

Rockefeller expressed not the slightest remorse about what he had wrought. "I have too much to do to waste my time with regrets," he told one close adviser. So it was, as well, with the two great controversies that shadowed his final years in office: the inflexible, "lock 'em up for life" antidrug laws and the bloody, brutal retaking of the Attica state prison. The only major mistake he would own up to about Attica was that he hadn't sent in the state troopers sooner.

To many, the actions of his last years seemed a calculated rejection of his past liberalism, a shift rightward to propitiate the Nixon White House and the ascendant conservative wing of the GOP. But those who worked for him, those who knew him well, did not see any real disjuncture in his attitudes; the fundamental misperception about Rockefeller, they felt, was to regard him in the first instance as a liberal. As one aide put it, "He wasn't a liberal. He was a problem solver." True, much of the time the solution he came up with had a liberal tinge: promoting racial equality through antidiscrimination laws, broadening health coverage through a sprawling, openhanded aid program. But frequently (granted, more frequently as his frustration mounted) the answer was anything but liberal: a crackdown on "welfare chiselers," a law-and-order approach to drug use. "He took his greatest pleasure out of unraveling a problem, and if not solving it, at least finding a way around it," says his friend and counsel Oscar Ruebhausen. Which philosophical direction the solution came from mattered little.

Rockefeller's liberal reputation was further belied by his hawkishness. For the most part forgotten now is how militant and stridently anti-Communist he was; his rhetoric made not only John F. Kennedy but Richard Nixon seem like mushy peaceniks by comparison. He was against disarmament, against nuclear test ban treaties. In the late 1950s, he made America's defense inadequacies a national cause célèbre, fomenting talk of a supposed "missile gap." In the early 1960s, he was a prime instigator of the country's fallout shelter mania.

His stridency, however, was not rooted, as it was for so many others, in McCarthyesque anti-Red paranoia, but in the exigencies of Cold War geopolitics. "I'm a great believer in power," he once said, and in his mind power translated into preparedness. Yet at the same time Rockefeller was convinced the war had to be waged on nonmilitary fronts, that the Cold War was as much a battle for "hearts and minds" as it was for zones of containment. Thus he also emerged as America's staunchest advocate of foreign aid, particularly aid to the developing world, whose backward economies he saw as ripe for Communist inroads. In the same breath, he could speak of building more H-bombs *and* of fighting smallpox and boosting rice harvests.

His was a conception of America's mission directly descended from the doctrines of Teddy Roosevelt: that of a puissant, all-encompassing imperium, preserving the world order with both brawn and beneficence.

"Father was not a sophisticated intellectual," notes Rockefeller's oldest son, Rodman, "but he was an idea man. He liked ideas: nice, big, fat ideas that he could get his hands around." And here was the biggest of ideas: all that he lacked was the launching pad for it, a platform that could only be found in the Oval Office of the President of the United States.

Near the end of his life, Rockefeller was asked what he wished most he might have done. His reply was terse and unhesitant. "Been President," he said.

Never was there any question that he coveted the job. Asked by a newsman once how long he had this craving, Rockefeller answered, "Ever since I was a kid. After all, when you think of what I had, what else was there to aspire to?"

About his predecessor, Thomas E. Dewey, a local political boss once remarked, "It's a funny thing with this guy. Every time he runs for President, he gets reelected governor." The same would hold true for Rockefeller—only Dewey, at least, won his party's nomination. Had Rockefeller been nominated, there was a better than even chance—at least in 1960 and 1968—that he would have been elected. But the nod from the Republican Party eluded him; the grail was always just beyond his grasp.

Rockefeller would retrospectively offer various reasons for his failure. He was too preoccupied with the business of being governor; he lacked "sufficient singleness of purpose." But there was always more to it than that. His presidential bids had a wayward, lurching quality to them, so utterly and strangely at odds with the turbocharged smoothness of his gubernatorial runs. All too often, the candidate was mired in a slough of indecision—again, bizarre and unfathomable behavior for a man who so evidently lusted for the prize.

When Winston Churchill was in the political wilderness, it was said of him, "Mr. Churchill carries great guns, but his navigation is uncertain." Much the same could be said of Nelson Rockefeller.

Victimized by his own vacillation and by the inchoate character of his campaigns, Rockefeller was equally the victim of a force seemingly beyond his control: the rise of the right wing of the Republican Party. It was Rockefeller's misfortune that GOP conservatism hit its stride in the 1960s, at the very time he was bidding for the presidency. Yet, in one of history's sublime twists, Rockefeller may well have been instrumental in the right's ascendancy. Indeed, it would be fair to say that conservatism would not have advanced so relentlessly had it *not* been for Nelson Rockefeller. In Bill Rusher's words, "Every movement needs a villain. For the GOP right, Nelson Rockefeller was it." He was cast perfectly for the part: an arrogant, aristocratic East Coast internationalist, a tax-and-spend pro-civil rights liberal who was clearly on the side of big government. The more vehemently he stood up to the right wing, the more he condemned their philosophy and their tactics, the more the conservative movement coalesced. Hatred of Nelson Rockefeller, for the right, became a uniquely binding force.

The final, mordant irony of Rockefeller's life in politics is this: while he never achieved the Age of Rockefeller, he may well have brought about the Age of Reagan.

Even in his failure, Nelson Rockefeller was among the most compelling figures in twentieth-century America. There was a rambunctious, Barnum-like quality to the man, all trombones and calliopes. Everything about him was in boldface: his life and, as it happened, his death.

So much of his life, public and private, was played out before us—his extravagant governorship, his futile presidential bids, his divorce and remarriage, the search for his lost son in New Guinea—that he seemed virtually a man without secrets, an impression bolstered by his CinemaScopic personality. But his intimates and aides knew better. Even after decades of association, they found much about the man that was inscrutable, much that was self-contradictory. For all his extroversion and bonhomie, there remained a cold, impenetrable inner core.

"He could be ruthless, as well as the most compassionate person," reflects Ruebhausen. "He could be caring and callous. You name the contradiction, he had it."

"Looking at Nelson was like looking up close at an elephant. A lot of us saw a piece of the elephant, and some saw more of the elephant than others. But none of us ever saw the entire elephant."

It is the aim of this work to see Nelson Rockefeller whole: to ponder the immense strengths and search for the inner, insidious flaws—what his childhood crony William Alton describes as "the grain of sand in the bar of steel." As any proper biography would, this work will sift for clues in the shards of his past lives. But unlike most other biographies, it will treat those past lives not just as raw quarries to be mined, or as mere preludes to the grander later career. For in Nelson Rockefeller's case—perhaps uniquely in his case, among our era's great political figures—the past was more than prologue, but a wondrous story in itself.

Long before he became a professional politician, long before he was the gravelly-voiced Rocky of blintzes and backslaps, Nelson Rockefeller was a powerhouse on the national and international stage. Before he was thirty he was the driving force at his family's spectacular new real estate venture, Rockefeller Center, as well as that other fledgling New York landmark, the Museum of Modern Art. Before he was forty he had spearheaded American policy toward Latin America during World War II as FDR's Coordinator of Inter-American Affairs, and had played a pivotal role in shaping the postwar order at the United Nations organizing conference—almost single-handedly capsizing the whole conference when his demands were not met.

By the time he was fifty Rockefeller had influenced policy making by two other U.S. Presidents. He was the prime mover behind Harry Truman's Point Four program of aid to the developing world. As an adviser to Dwight Eisenhower, he put forward the first reorganization of the federal government since the New Deal; later, as Eisenhower's deputy, he choreographed the dramatic "Open Skies" initiative at the 1955 summit, arguably the United States' greatest Cold War propaganda coup. After his exit from the White House, Rockefeller marshaled the country's finest minds for the postwar era's most sweeping study of America's future, a study that would help shape the nation's strategic thinking for years to come.

All this was accomplished by Nelson Rockefeller before he spent a single day in the governor's chair in Albany.

So much of what would define the politician to come was already on view in the younger Rockefeller. Consuming ambition. Superhuman energy and boundless, infectious enthusiasm. Heedlessness about cost. Far-reaching, enlightened social consciousness. A talent for manipulation, for stroking, for strategic alliances—and a readiness to resort to underhanded ploys to achieve his ends (a trait he shared with his great role model, FDR).

He was, indeed, political long before he was in politics. At Rockefeller Center, where he attained supremacy by ousting the management team that had overseen the Center from the beginning. At the Museum of Modern Art, where he overpowered and undermined the museum's driving creative force, director Alfred Barr. And, in perhaps the greatest political test of all, within his own family, where he engaged in supreme emotional gamesmanship with the imperious Rockefeller patriarch, his father, John D. Rockefeller, Jr.

The story of Nelson Rockefeller's first fifty years, then, is both a foreshadowing and a full-blooded saga in its own right: a saga of manipulation and betrayal, of grandiose feats and humiliating setbacks, of visions of glory and a better world, and of acts of supreme cynicism and calculation. It is the story of what happens when unimaginable wealth, uninhibited enthusiasm, and unparalleled energy are put in the service of one man's relentless ambitions.

It is the story, as well, of consequences: for the larger world he would shape, for his family, for the men and women who were his advisers, his acolytes, his lovers—and, not least, for himself.

Part One

Early Riser

One

July 1908

In the early summer of 1908 all of America was caught up in the imminent contest for the presidency. People talked of delegate counts and of party platforms, but mostly they talked of an old firehorse of a candidate who had failed over and over in his quest for his life's dream, the White House. Now he was at it again, mounting his third attempt at the elusive grail.

His name was William Jennings Bryan.

The phenomenon known as Bryanism, with its appeals to populist fervor, to disaffected farmers and downtrodden city dwellers, had blazed across the country in the closing years of the old century and the first years of the new one. Now only the faint embers of the great cause remained. But Bryan the man still was a force to be reckoned with. And as the Democratic Party gathered in Denver, eager to nominate him for the third time, America's monied class eyed the spectacle with unalloyed dread.

No one on the American political scene, it could be said, dreaded Bryan and Bryanism more than did Senator Nelson W. Aldrich.

In his twenty-six years in the U.S. Senate, Aldrich had come to be the archdefender and prime power broker of the great trusts and combines that dominated the country's economy. He championed high tariffs, hard money, and a sound banking system. The muckraking press—coming into its own as a force in American public opinion—viewed the Rhode Island senator as nothing less than the grand vizier of rapacious capitalism. Lincoln Steffens called him "the arch-representative of protected, privileged business."

Inciting the muckrakers to a special frenzy was the well-known fact that Aldrich had managed to become a multimillionaire himself in the course of his three decades in the Senate—thanks to his timely dealings in the shares of Providence trolley companies. Those trades, it turned out, were facilitated by a loan to Aldrich from the Sugar Trust, and the fortuitous intervention of J. P. Morgan & Co., which arranged the sale of the trolley lines to the New Haven Railroad. (Aldrich, not surprisingly, was an intimate of Pierpont Morgan himself.)

Aldrich weathered the attacks on his politics and on his person with the implacable sangfroid that was his trademark. "Deny nothing, explain nothing," was his favorite maxim, and he heeded it every day he was in the Senate. The depth and breadth of his influence on that legislative body was undeniable. His was the first and last word on any bill affecting money and business, and on much else besides. A master of parliamentary procedure who savored the parry and thrust of legislative maneuvering, Aldrich, Majority Leader for seventeen years, was the gatekeeper for the country's legislative agenda. Employees in the Capitol referred to him as "the General Manager of the Senate." Steffens described him quite simply as "the boss of the United States."

For Aldrich, however, much seemed to be changing by the summer of 1908. Under constant attack by progressive Senator Robert La Follette of Wisconsin and others during the previous two sessions of Congress, Aldrich finally had to yield to them that spring and modify an important currency bill. The old guard that had been Aldrich's bulwark was dying out, and the younger senators were unwilling to blindly, unquestioningly follow his lead. It was even said that if Aldrich did not give in, the presidential nomination of President Theodore Roosevelt's handpicked successor, William Howard Taft, might be in jeopardy.

More and more, Aldrich's thoughts turned to Indian Oaks, the ninety-nine-room château he had built overlooking Narragansett Bay on Warwick Neck. He talked of leaving the Senate after his term expired in 1912. He would be seventy years old then, he told friends; he was entitled to a rest and meant to have it.

The old lion was plainly tired of being the newspapers' favorite whipping boy, tired of all the caricatures of him as the corporation senator and the champion of the trusts. For now he would soldier on, because Taft would need his help. But the power that had been his for so long—the power to make government an instrument of the great engine of commerce—was clearly ebbing.

The summer of 1908 was also not the best of times for John D. Rockefeller.

Progenitor of the Standard Oil trust, with a fortune that dwarfed all the mighty fortunes of the Gilded Age, Rockefeller was in retirement now. The business of Standard was now overseen by his longtime lieutenant, John Archbold; Rockefeller had not made an appearance at Standard's headquarters at 26 Broadway in lower Manhattan in eleven years. The handling of the family fortune was entrusted to his only son, John Jr., and it was Junior (as the younger Rockefeller had been known in and out of the family since adolescence) who, along with the dynamic Baptist minister Frederick T. Gates, was building the family's great philanthropic edifices. The senior Rockefeller could presumably spend most of his time at his country estate at Pocantico Hills, in New York's Westchester County, or one of his many other residences, indulging his new passion for golf, and watching his net worth continue to mount to staggering dimensions. Some $200 million at the turn of the century, the fortune would burgeon to just under $1 billion by 1913—or $14 billion in 1996 dollars.

But Rockefeller could enjoy little of this. Since the dawn of the new century he and Standard Oil had been under unremitting attack. First there were the muckrakers, most notably Ida Tarbell, whose *History of the Standard Oil Company,* published as a magazine serial in 1902, documented the monopolist practices and heavy-handed tactics Rockefeller and his associates employed to build the company. Then the government, spurred by President Roosevelt's outcry against "the malefactors of great wealth," moved in, unleashing a barrage of lawsuits against the company. The ultimate aim of the litigation was nothing less than the breakup of Standard Oil.

By midsummer 1907 the federal government had seven different suits pending against Standard, and in June 1908 federal prosecutors mounted plans for a new attack on Standard in the Chicago courts, aimed at extracting fines of up to $68 million from the corporation. Although the company's attorneys voiced confidence that they could beat back any attempt to dissolve the company, there was little doubt that Standard's days as sole master of the nation's petroleum supplies were numbered.

And yet, in the midst of this legal fusillade, Rockefeller—ascetic, iron-willed, serene in his certainty that all he had done was right and proper—went about his life seemingly unperturbed by the clamor and the controversy. "Let the world wag," was his typically sanguine advice to his son—even as process servers lay in wait for him outside his townhouse in New York and his Forest Hill estate in Cleveland. The pleasant, unruffled retirement he had so assiduously arranged for himself was rapidly falling to pieces.

For seven years now the families and the fortunes of the bull-like senator from Rhode Island and the spindly, calculating oil baron had been linked.

The bond had been forged in October 1901 with the marriage of Junior to Aldrich's eldest daughter, Abby. Given the reputations of the fathers, the nuptials were greeted as a veritable royal wedding of capitalism, and the press duly recounted the pilgrimage of notables of the day to the ceremony at Warwick Neck. The muckrakers tended to paint the marriage in a more sinister light. "Thus," wrote David Graham Phillips, "the chief exploiter of the American people is closely allied by marriage with the chief schemer in the service of their exploiters."

But in truth the marriage had none of the earmarks of an arranged union of wealth and power. The courtship had lasted a full four years, dating back to Junior's days at Brown, all because of Junior's indecision about whether Abby truly was the right woman for him. (What he feared, he confessed years later, was "marrying someone and finding out later that I loved someone else more.") Inculcated by his parents with a stern Baptist ethic, he prayed every night of those four years for divine guidance in the matter. In the end, it was not the Almighty's intervention but his mother's gentle prodding that finally swung the balance. "Of course you love Miss Aldrich," she told him. "Why don't you go and get her?"

Junior proceeded to meet with Senator Aldrich, aboard the senator's yacht in Newport Harbor, to formally request his daughter's hand. The senator was said to have been immensely amused when young Rockefeller went on to detail his financial prospects.

It was only after they were wed that the straitlaced, repressed Junior truly allowed his love for Abby to blossom. His ardor, as evidenced by his letters to her during their separations, often glowed with white-hot intensity. "How happy you made me that night, darling," he wrote her two years into their marriage, "in the radiance of your young womanhood, so beautiful, so fascinating, so loving, and so long the one object of my passionate desires. . . . What a beautiful night that was, darling. We were oblivious of all else except each other and our great love."

Their first child, Abby (quickly nicknamed "Babs"), arrived in 1903. Then, on March 21, 1906, came a son, John 3rd, whose birth was celebrated on front pages and in editorial columns across the country. "Richest Baby in History" was the headline in the *Boston Post*. The coverage was often barbed; the *New York Journal*, for one, noted that the baby's namesake "is forced to put a curb upon his eagerness to view his grandson for fear of process servers, who lurk in wait for his advent in the State of New York."

In the early summer of 1908 Abby was expecting their third child. The names had been selected well in advance. A girl would be named Laura, after Junior's mother. A boy would be named after the senator.

The first two children had been born in the master bedroom of the family's townhouse on West 54th Street in Manhattan. But Abby's physician, Allen Thomas, always spent his summers on Mount Desert Island, off the coast of Maine. Rather than change doctors, Abby and Junior decided to follow him there. They would find accommodations in the island's most celebrated community, Bar Harbor.

Bar Harbor was still then what it had been since the 1890s: a locale that each year vied with Newport for the title of summer social capital of the United States. Each summer the leisure class of the eastern seaboard would make the long trek up the Maine coast, many coming by yacht; one of the season's grand traditions was the arrival of the armada from the New York Yacht Club, led by the club's commodore, J. Pierpont Morgan, in his steam vessel *Corsair.* Once nestled into what they whimsically called their "cottages," the elite embarked on the full sweep of divertissements: long afternoons of croquet, attended by silver-salver-laden butlers; horse shows at Robin Hood Park; golf and, in the evening, *tableaux vivants* at the town's social epicenter, the Kebo Valley Club. And there were nonpareil dinner parties: one of the great Bar Harbor houses was renowned for its dining table, which sank through the floor to the kitchen below between courses, only to rise again with the next course perfectly presented.

The Rockefellers positioned themselves well to take advantage of this florid social scene, renting one of the town's larger residences, the Sears Cottage, then owned by Washington newspaper publisher Edward McLean and his wife. But they seem to have kept mostly to themselves. Junior's stern Baptist upbringing had bred a pronounced distaste for the high life—abetted, no doubt, by his family's proscription against alcoholic beverages. And Abby was caught up in the excitement and stress of the imminent new arrival.

It was, in fact, a lonely interval for Abby. Junior spent much of his time back in New York, overseeing the finishing touches on the grand manor house he was building for his father on the Pocantico Hills estate. In a letter to him on June 29, Abby wrote openly of her loneliness, and how it had rendered her unable to sleep. She consoled herself with little domestic details, such as putting the new baby's bassinet together with the help of a maid. "It is so pretty," she wrote, "I wish that I could have the dear little new one safely tucked up in it when you arrived next week."

As the due date approached, she found that the slightest effort tired her. But, in writing her husband, she could barely contain her anticipation. "I am getting very anxious to *see* the new baby," she gushed in a July 2 letter. "It is so strange to have an unknown quantity with one all the time." She and the two children, she added, were counting the days—three and a half—before Junior's return to Bar Harbor.

Finally, having dutifully put in a full workweek, Junior set off by train on Saturday evening, July 4, for Bar Harbor. He arrived the next afternoon at the Sears Cottage, with the plan in mind of spending the next two weeks there with his wife and children, including the new one.

And the baby dutifully obliged. In a bedroom of the Sears Cottage, on a cool, rainy Wednesday, July 8, at 12:30 P.M., Abby delivered nine-and-a-quarter-pound Nelson Aldrich Rockefeller. The devoted Junior had a double reason to be delighted: it was his father's sixty-ninth birthday.

John D. Rockefeller had celebrated his birthday quietly at his rambling old home, Forest Hill, in Cleveland. He went off on a brief automobile ride in the morning, after spending but an hour on business. When newspapermen came to call, he cordially told them that he was in fine health and expected to live to see many more birthdays. That afternoon he sat down to read the congratulatory telegrams—in the midst of which was the cable from Junior advising him that he was a grandfather once more.

The senior Rockefeller was in a buoyant mood. The next day, he even did something quite out of the ordinary for John D. Rockefeller: he spoke in public, addressing a Baptist student group from nearby Western Reserve College. The oil tycoon's rare utterances were front-page news, to which was appended another dispatch from the Rockefeller front: the word from Bar Harbor that a third child had been born to John D. Rockefeller, Jr., and his wife.

But the tidings of the Rockefeller family were buried by banner headlines heralding the momentous event of the day: the nomination by the Democrats of William Jennings Bryan for the presidency. The orator from the Plains—embodying all that was galling to Senator Nelson Aldrich and to John D. Rockefeller—simply would not, could not, stop seeking the great prize.

Bryan would lose once again that November. But his legacy lived on. Populism would be transmuted into progressivism, and its champion would be Teddy Roosevelt, who had stepped aside in favor of Taft in 1908. Four years later, Roosevelt's third-party candidacy would doom Taft's attempt at reelection, and create a schism in the Republican Party whose effects would echo down the decades—and come to haunt the life of the baby born to the Rockefellers that summer.

Barely two weeks after his arrival at Bar Harbor, Junior was on his way back to New York. Aboard the train to Portland, Maine, the first leg of the trip, he penned some sentimental words to Abby: "And so sweetheart, I am off and away again. I am sorry as ever to leave you but glad the baby has come, is so well and that you are so well." Then he toted up all they had accomplished in those two weeks; among other things, he noted in a singular burst of jocosity, "we have sold much real estate, perhaps enough to pay for the baby."

But even in the afterglow of joy in his wife and burgeoning family, Junior could not help but feel the inexorable tug of duty, and frame his happiness in terms of a balance sheet. "These weeks have been happy and restful," he concluded, "and although I hate to leave you and exchange a state of idleness for insistent and forced industry, I must not begrudge to pay the price for my rest."

As the train rumbled through the hamlets along the Maine coast, Junior felt the full weight of the great fortune settle once again on his shoulders.

Two

The Family Foundation

John D. Rockefeller, Jr., seemed to live his whole life on the verge of implosion. Stern and cheerless as a youth, he grew into a stiff and unspontaneous man to whom few pleasures came easily. "He was constantly, indefatigably, at work," writes his sympathetic biographer Raymond Fosdick. "Life to him meant work, and relaxation was largely an escape to a different type of work."

His taut, relentless temperament took its toll. In 1904, seven years after he had gone to work in his father's office, Junior, at age thirty, suffered a nervous collapse. Unable to work, he repaired with his wife and baby daughter to the South of France, where he spent six languid months recovering. It would be many months after his return to New York before he could resume a full-time schedule.

This was not the first time Junior had suffered a breakdown. At seventeen he had gone into seclusion for almost a year at the Forest Hill estate to treat what the family delicately described as a "nervous condition." Nor, apparently, would it be the last. In 1922 he checked himself into a sanitarium in Battle Creek, Michigan, after suffering excruciating headaches. The doctors diagnosed his condition as "auto-intoxication" brought on by strain.

His grinding, dutiful character was certainly in large measure the product of his Baptist upbringing, which even Junior would later acknowledge was "narrow and confining." His father's frequent absences meant that it was young John's mother, Cettie, who was the dominant force in the household. Pious, didactic (she "talked to us constantly about *duty,*" Junior would recall), Cettie gently but firmly imposed her moralistic principles on her five children (Junior was the only boy). "Everything centered around the home and the church, and there was nothing else," Junior remarked later. "We had no childhood friends, no school friends."

The children's isolation was no doubt reinforced by the long list of worldly vices they were compelled to abjure: among them, cardplaying, dancing, theater, and opera. (Junior did not attend his first dance until he was well into college.) At ten, well before such sins could have entered his young head, Junior took the pledge to abstain from alcohol, tobacco, and profanity.

Above all, the children were warned about vanity, a sin to which their wealth naturally made them more than susceptible. Cettie went to great, sometimes absurd lengths to enforce those warnings: compelling young John to wear his sisters' remade hand-me-downs until age eight, requiring the children to share a single bicycle. She once proudly confided to a neighbor, "I am so glad my son has told me what he wants for Christmas, so now it can be denied him."

While some children might have struggled to break out of this Baptist straitjacket, Junior was perfectly content to live within the rules: attending the prayer meetings, reciting the temperance slogans, keeping with the most exacting rigor his accounts ("Practicing the violin at $.05 per hour; Killing flies at $.02 per fly") just as his father had before him.

Ironically, given his flinty public persona, it was John D. Senior who was the sole liberating, spontaneous force in the household. While almost the equal of Cettie in piety, Senior made room in his life for game playing, for storytelling at the dinner table, for vigorous outdoor pursuits. "He taught us everything," Junior would recall, "how to skate, swim, ride, drive horses, and we were never so happy as when we were with him." His father "never told us what not to do. He was one with us."

But it was also Senior who saddled his son with the most awesome obligation of all: the burden of the Rockefeller name and the Rockefeller fortune. From an early age Junior was made to understand that in time, as the only son, those burdens would be his to bear; Junior, for his part, readily accepted the charge. "I took responsibility early," he would later say, "and like my parents I was serious."

When Junior finally left home at eighteen to go to Brown University, many of the prohibitions of his youth were discreetly cast aside. He learned to dance, he attended football games, and he even (once) smoked a pack of cigarettes. (He remained, however, a steadfast teetotaler.) But his sense of mission, his acute feeling of obligation to his father, remained firmly intact. "My one thought from the time I was a boy was to help my father," he said. "I knew from the beginning I was going into his office."

He could not, however, have possibly imagined how much he would be on his own when he finally reported to work at 26 Broadway in October 1897. Senior had made good on his vow to retire and was no longer coming into the office, even though he retained the title of Standard Oil president. What's more, he had left without carving out any clear role for his son. "Father never said a word to me about what I was to do in the office before I began to work there," Junior recalled in 1920. "Moreover, he did not say anything on the subject to anyone else in the office, so far as I have ever learned."

Floundering under the weight of his sense of obligation, Junior did everything from filling the inkwells to doling out the staff paychecks. But gradually his dogged attention to detail brought more and more of his father's affairs under his purview. And it wasn't long before he showed himself a worthy successor to the senior Rockefeller as a bargainer. When the indomitable J. P. Morgan was seeking the family's Mesabi iron ore properties to complete his assemblage of what was to become U.S. Steel, it was Junior who went head-to-head with the financier. "Well, what's your price?" Morgan demanded, to which Junior coolly replied, "I think there must be some mistake. I did not come here to sell. I understand you wished to buy." Morgan wound up with the properties, but at a stiff cost. When Rockefeller Senior was told of the encounter, he cackled, "Great Caesar, but John is a trump!"

But the prospect of a life in business soon began to pall on the younger Rockefeller. Standard Oil was his father's creation, and there was little he could do to add to its grandeur; what's more, a bevy of longtime Rockefeller lieutenants were already firmly in command of the trust. Far more alluring to Junior were his father's philanthropic activities, which were just beginning to gather momentum under the stewardship of the Reverend Frederick T. Gates. Philanthropy would fulfill two of Junior's most fundamental needs: to be of use to his father and to bring his mother's Baptist precepts to bear on the world.

Gates had grand designs in mind for the Rockefeller fortune, and it fell to Junior to be the point man in carrying them out. As Junior later described their respective roles, "Gates was the brilliant dreamer and creator. I was the salesman—the go-between with Father at the opportune moment. Gates did the heavy thinking, and my part was to sell his ideas to Father."

Together, in the opening years of the new century, Junior and Gates forged some of the philanthropic world's most imposing organizations. There was the Rockefeller Institute for Medical Research (later to be known as Rockefeller University), whose accomplishments in the century's first decade included the sanitization of New York City's milk supply and the discovery of a serum for cerebrospinal meningitis. Then there was the General Education Board, a wide-ranging institution that over the years poured resources into everything from higher education for blacks to the eradication of hookworm in the South. Finally, in 1913, there was the creation of the family's mightiest charitable instrument, the Rockefeller Foundation, endowed with $182 million of Senior's money.

These institutions, and the many others Junior was to create, represented more than simply a monumental recycling of Rockefeller wealth. By dint of their influence, they came to magnify the family's impact on American life. And their good works inevitably would serve to overcome the taint that had afflicted the Rockefeller name. Junior would never admit as much, but it was hard not to see this motive at work, no matter how unconscious it might have been. The self-expressed aim of his life was to serve his father. And by making the Rockefeller name synonymous with medical advances and with education, rather than with the insatiable rapaciousness of the oil trust, Junior was undoubtedly rendering his father the greatest service of all.

The one great setback in this campaign—and a potentially devastating one, at that—was the Ludlow massacre of 1914. What began as a labor uprising in the Colorado mining camps of the Rockefeller-controlled Colorado Fuel and Iron Company had taken a tragic turn, when strikebreaking militiamen mowed down scores of workers. The discovery in the rubble the next day of the bodies of two women and eleven children sparked a paroxysm of national outrage against the Rockefellers.

In the early days of the uproar, Junior made matters worse for the family by defending the company's brutal tactics and insisting that he and his father were mere shareholders who had nothing to do with Colorado Fuel and Iron's day-to-day management. But as the heat of a congressional probe intensified, and as the death threats against his family mounted, Junior made the most abrupt about-face of his career. He took personal responsibility for the situation, brought in as advisers the prominent Canadian politician (and future Prime Minister) Mackenzie King and public relations sage Ivy Lee, and sought an accommodation with the miners. In the company of King, Junior toured the Ludlow site, shared dinner with the miners in their homes, and met face-to-face with employee representatives. He and King came up with a landmark industrial relations plan that set up a system of elected worker representation and established formal grievance procedures. The plan was overwhelmingly endorsed by the workers.

Ludlow was truly a rite of passage for Junior. While still very much his father's son, Junior had firmly and decisively broken away from Senior's hidebound nineteenth-century attitudes toward labor relations, and much else besides. In the public mind, the Rockefellers were actually coming to be identified with progressivism—that movement that was anathema to doughty old Senator Aldrich. It was an amazing transformation, as breathtaking in its own way as the building of Standard Oil. And the achievement was all Junior's.

He began to distinguish himself from his father in other ways. Whereas the height of Senior's cultural experience was the Sunday-evening hymn singing, Junior came to enjoy classical music and fine art. He quietly acquired a world-class collection of Renaissance tapestries (including the renowned Unicorn Tapestries) and seventeenth-century Ming Dynasty porcelain. As he once rather defensively explained his porcelain collecting to his skeptical father, "I have never squandered money on horses, yachts, automobiles or other foolish extravagances. . . . This hobby, while a costly one, is quiet and unostentatious and not sensational."

Junior also became capable of the grand seigneurial gesture to those who served him well, lavishing on them gifts of cash and other precious commodities. Grateful to a Seal Harbor, Maine, physician for his ministrations to the family over the years, Junior told the doctor he would be happy to bestow upon him any gift the physician thought appropriate. The doctor promptly requested a Rolls-Royce. And not just any Rolls-Royce—but one "built high enough so that people don't have to bend over to get in." Junior unblinkingly obliged, ordering the strange vehicle custom-built from the factory. "It looked like a house on wheels," says someone who saw the car tooling around Seal Harbor in the twenties.

Yet as far as Junior had come, his personality remained a tightly constricted one. He marveled, for instance, at his associates' ability to call one another by their first names. As Fosdick observed, "There was a kind of formality about him, a tendency toward reticence, which to some who knew him seemed to surround him like a cloud."

In raising his children, there would be no breach of the Baptist creed ingrained in him by his parents. Sundays would be devoted to family gatherings and prayer. Tobacco and alcohol would be strictly forbidden. Accounts would be kept, and spendthrift habits would be broken. Above all, the children would always be reminded that they were Rockefellers and that their wealth and good name were a sacred trust.

Fortunately for the children, Abby Aldrich Rockefeller was around to leaven all this.

If life to Junior was a great sack of burdens to be slung over one's shoulder and borne as best one can, to Abby it was a cornucopia, spilling a glittering array of pleasures and temptations at one's feet. The somber mien, the iron self-discipline, the monochromatic formality that marked her husband were nowhere in evidence in Abby. She was whimsical, intuitive, fond of gay colors and outlandish hats festooned with lilies of the valley.

While Junior, growing up, took little delight in his wealth, Abby was taught by the senator to savor hers. A connoisseur of rare books, Renaissance art, and fine rugs, Senator Aldrich inculcated in his children a passion for collecting—a passion that made its way through the generations to his grandson and namesake. Abby's tastes were further refined during several grand tours of Europe, with the senator leading his family through a dizzying succession of museums and galleries.

Abby could not take anything quite as seriously as Junior did. She went through none of the soul-searching that beset him during their courtship. While he agonized for four years over the question of marriage, she simply went on to entertain other suitors.

It was not long into their engagement before Junior realized that Abby did not exactly share his sober sense of fiscal responsibility. He gave her a substantial sum of money as a wedding present, hoping that she would buy some memento of their forthcoming union. A few days later she calmly informed him she no longer had the money. "You see," she said, "I gave it away."

In the course of their honeymoon, he gently suggested that she keep a weekly expense account. "I won't!" Abby snapped back, and that was that.

She was equally emphatic during their honeymoon about the limits of her marital subservience. "Do you know, John," she said, "that if you should ever strike me, I should leave you?" He protested that he wouldn't dream of striking her, to which she replied, "I'm just warning you of what would happen if you ever did."

Thoroughly smitten, Junior gladly overlooked such effusions. He simply couldn't believe his good fortune. As he would recall years later, "She was so gay and young and so in love with everything that I kept wondering why she had ever consented to marry a man like me." And Abby, for her part, was equally in love. A quarter century after her marriage, in a letter to one of her sons, she summed up her devotion to Junior this way: "I am happy and contented wherever your father happens to be. He always means home to me."

Each made subtle concessions to the other's whims and personality. Under Abby's influence, Junior became a bit more sociable, a bit more tolerant of galas and dinner parties. Abby, in turn, tried to mute her unbridled enthusiasm and chattiness, although sometimes she was forced to resort to extreme measures to do so. In the midst of one trip, she wrote one of her sons that "your father is afraid that I shall become intimate with too many people, and will want to talk to them, so generally we eat in what I call the old people's dining room where he feels I am safer."

Not surprisingly, the raising of their children became a yin-yang affair, with Abby's motherly solicitude and natural buoyancy counterbalancing Junior's stiff-necked sanctimony.

Required each day to recite a favorite Bible verse from memory, the children were quietly coached by their mother, who would write out the verses for them on five-by-eight index cards. And when they retreated from their father's study after his regular Saturday morning review of their accounts, the children knew they could find solace in Abby's sitting room across the hall, where a soothing word—and cookies and milk—could always be found.

But for all of Abby's mitigating influence, it was Junior's dictates that still prevailed. The weekly accounting of income and outgo still had to be meticulously maintained (by the children if not by Abby). The Sabbath rules—no games, no reading, just prayer and churchgoing and hymn singing—were rigorously adhered to (although when the children got older they were allowed a game of tennis on Sunday afternoons). And family rituals were scrupulously observed—the most important of which were Sunday afternoon dinners with John D. Senior at Pocantico, with the boys decked out in Eton suits with stiff collars.

Junior's preaching of household economy would have its effect on Abby: she would instruct the maids to darn the family's frayed curtains, rather than replace them, and she would invariably wait for January white sales to purchase new linen. And Abby, in turn, would cultivate a frugal strain in her children. "I am glad you have saved twelve dollars for your Christmas presents," she wrote one of them. "I will go shopping with you, and if we are careful, I am sure we can make it do."

As a youth, Junior had to press and mend his own clothes, and he was determined to inculcate such everyday skills in his children—even if, as adults, they never would have occasion to use them. Once a week, for instance, dinner was prepared not by the Rockefeller kitchen staff but by the children, who would do everything from sifting flour to dicing vegetables. And in these practices, too, Abby became as watchful as her husband. Once, Nelson was assigned the chore of weeding a flower garden at Pocantico. A groundskeeper came along and offered to help, but Nelson sadly shook his head. "No, you better not," he said. "Mother will probably come along to check." He was right; she did.

As they slogged away at these exercises in frugality, Nelson and his siblings—Babs and John and the later children, Laurance and Winthrop and David—were not unmindful of their true circumstances. All around them was the physical evidence of what growing up a Rockefeller really meant—most obviously in the homes in which they dwelled, homes that transcended mere luxury.

First, there was their New York City townhouse at 10 West 54th Street. A nine-story limestone monolith Junior built for his family in 1913, the house had bedrooms for each of the children, guest suites, living quarters for the servants, a gymnasium, an infirmary, two drawing rooms, a music room, an art gallery, and a rooftop playground complete with squash court. Just about the only unimposing aspect of this residence was the neighborhood, which was rapidly losing out in chic to upper Fifth and Park avenues, thanks to the saloons and cheap shops sprouting up beneath the nearby Sixth Avenue elevated subway line.

Then there was the family's summer refuge on the coast of Maine, the Eyrie. Captivated by his summers in Bar Harbor, Junior decided in 1910 it was time to own a home of his own there. He purchased a sixteen-acre property in the nearby, more isolated hamlet of Seal Harbor, and proceeded to vastly expand the already massive 65-room house that stood there. Over time the number of rooms in the place grew to 107; the house eventually had 2,280 windows, 44 fireplaces, 22 bathrooms, and two elevators. Lush gardens, highlighted by two eighth-century T'ang period Chinese pagodas, adjoined the residence, which had a commanding view of the Atlantic.

Finally, there was the Rockefeller "country" seat, Pocantico Hills. Just north of Tarrytown, New York, a mere thirty miles from New York City, the Pocantico estate was so enormous—some 3,500 acres—that it seemed an Elysian dream world to its inhabitants. Junior and Abby's house on the estate, a Norman English-style residence they renamed Abeyton Lodge, was a modest dwelling compared with their other homes. But a short walk away was the Georgian manor house called Kykuit (Dutch for "lookout"), which Junior built for his father, with its eighteenth-century tiered gardens, sunken brooks, Greek statuary, and adjoining Japanese teahouse. And for the children, diversion could be found at the Playhouse, a rambling Tudor-style two-story building that housed a bowling alley, billiard room, squash court, indoor tennis court, and indoor swimming pool—not to mention the outdoor tennis court, croquet court, and nine-hole golf course that could be found in the back. Yet the most sublime pleasures Pocantico afforded were its vast rambles and riding paths through woods and meadows, and its awe-inspiring vistas of the Hudson River, glistening in the spring sunlight.

But as sumptuous as these homes seem, they truly were not, in Junior's mind, gestures of extravagance. In their expansiveness, solidity, and seclusion, they were fortresses—places designed to shield his family from the outside world. The homes were expressions of Junior's concept of family, a concept he had derived from his parents. (It was John D. Senior, in the midst of his empire building, who had written his wife, Cettie, "I feel more than ever . . . the world is full of Sham, Flattery and Deception; our home is a haven of rest and freedom.")

Ultimately, these domiciles—self-contained, enduring, discreet in their self-indulgence—were also expressions of Junior's never-ending preoccupation with what being a Rockefeller *meant*. It was a preoccupation that would leave its mark on all his children.

Each of the Rockefeller children would come to grips in his or her own way with the rigorous terms of their upbringing.

The oldest child, and the lone daughter, Babs, would grow to hate and fear her father. In her later years she would describe her childhood rituals with bitter scorn, sarcastically remembering the sight of "the fannies waving" during the morning prayers. She painfully recalled the ways in which Junior picked apart her report card, tearing her down without ever raising his voice. And her feelings about Abby were not much better. Babs felt herself constantly under Abby's most critical scrutiny, a scrutiny that continued even after Babs had children of her own. Babs's daughter, Abby O'Neill, remembers that "she gave my mother a hard time as to whether or not we were learning our manners properly and sat properly and dressed properly and behaved properly. Instead of supporting my mother, she undermined her confidence."

Babs's response to her home environment was to rebel, doing everything she possibly could to get under Junior's skin. She sloughed off on her schoolwork. She kept sloppy accounts. She started smoking at fifteen. She necked with her beau (and future husband), David Milton, on the grounds of Pocantico, in full view of the staff. She drove her car recklessly and accumulated a raft of speeding tickets.

The oldest son, John 3rd, on the other hand, couldn't have been more dutiful. A shy, somber, awkward boy, with the lean, long-faced look of old John D., he seemed to have been cut from exactly the same cloth as his father. His accounts were always in perfect order; he was frugal to a fault. As a small boy he could frequently be found at the lake in Central Park, playing alone with his toy sailboat, talking not with the other children but with policemen and park officials. His seriousness was so overwhelming that his parents began to worry about it. Even Junior came to believe that his son might be a little *too* reserved. When young John was nine years old, Junior wrote to his schoolmaster, "He is such a taciturn boy that it is difficult always to know from him just what his physical condition is."

The sons who came after Nelson—Laurance, then Winthrop, then David—also tended to fall in line uncomplainingly with their parents' rules and commands. While self-discipline and frugality did not come nearly as easy to them as it did to their older brother John, they learned to accommodate themselves to their father's demands. Rebellion was simply not in their natures.

But Nelson was different. Physically, with his broad nose and thrusting chin, he was more Aldrich than Rockefeller.* And temperamentally as well, the exuberant Aldrich strain was far more noticeable in him than in his siblings. For Nelson, the temptation to test the limits of his father's strictures, to probe and poke at the rules, was always there. But unlike Babs, he had a positive genius for getting away with it. Nelson could rebel without seeming rebellious. He could diligently attend to the Rockefeller rituals, while stealthily subverting them at the same time.

In the formidable family edifice his father and grandfather had built, it was a very special talent.

*The resemblance to his mother grew more and more marked as he grew older. Nelson Rockefeller in his fifties appeared to be the male twin of his mother at the same age. A similar phenomenon was often noted between Franklin D. Roosevelt and his mother, Sara.

Three

A Most Unruly Little Boy

Young Frederick Warburg, the son of financier Felix Warburg, was serving as a lunchroom monitor at the Lincoln School, a private school near Columbia University. Patrolling the cafeteria, he came upon one of his fellow students engaged in the act of placing pats of butter on his knife and catapulting them to the ceiling. Warburg admonished the boy: "You don't do that sort of thing at home, do you?"

"Yes I do," little Nelson Rockefeller snapped in reply.

Indeed he did. In the muffled sanctum of the dining room in the 54th Street townhouse, amid the somber Victorian furnishings, Nelson was a master of food throwing. When his parents weren't around, the rolls or the butter balls would fly, often landing right between the eyes of their intended victim. When his parents were around, it was all more artful, more surreptitious. A sibling would be about to put a piece of cookie or bread in his mouth when a sudden flick of Nelson's fingers would send the morsel clear across the table.

Prankishness and high spirits were always bubbling over in the sturdy little boy; he seemed perpetually caught up in a whirlwind of mischief and activity. "Nelson is so full of life he doesn't know what to do with himself," a family servant wrote when the boy was thirteen—by way of advising Abby that Nelson's latest diversion was destroying a hornet's nest on the Pocantico grounds, in the course of which he was stung in the face.

Nothing could ever happen fast enough for Nelson; impatience was constantly gnawing away at him. When the time came for the boys to be taught marksmanship, Nelson went over to the firing range at the estate, shot for a while, and then asked the instructor, "Can I beat my brothers?" When he was told that he couldn't yet, and that he would have to practice to catch up with them, he left and never returned.

Assigned the task of learning the cello, Nelson sawed away at it for a while, without much success, and then decided he would rather learn the piano instead. The cello, he announced, was too slow an instrument for his temperament.

"Nelson is having great struggles with his reading," the children's longtime nurse, Florence Scales, wrote Abby when he was seven. Exasperated, she declared that "I do believe myself that the child could read if he would put his mind on it." Yet, for all that, she goes on to say that "he is just as fascinating as ever and I haven't the heart to scold him when he wiggles and loses his place and asks all sorts of questions in the middle of a sentence."

There was, indeed, a winsome, disarming quality about Nelson that perennially won him forgiveness for his misdeeds and shortcomings. When he was chastised, he would earnestly declare that he had learned his lesson and would be much, much better from then on. He never sulked, never shifted blame, never whined.

He won adults over with, among other things, his generosity. Gestures which, on the part of other children, might have seemed calculating and cloying were, in Nelson's case, taken as genuine expressions of his outgoing nature. At Christmastime, for instance, the other Rockefeller children would be caught up in making their lists of what they wanted from Santa Claus. Nelson, however, would be preoccupied instead with deciding what gifts he would be giving to the others.

He also had a knack for surprising, and sometimes frustrating, his overseers with an occasional display of what lay beneath the layers of tomfoolery. Scales would attempt to teach him poetry, and Nelson would clown around, "apparently not paying a bit of attention to what I am trying to teach him. Then all of a sudden when I get stern with him I find that he knows it perfectly and what is more he remembers it."

Above all, what was captivating about young Nelson was the sheer joy and exuberance he brought to the household. It was a quality that seemed to come directly from Abby, and none of her other children had it in such a pure and unadulterated form.

His boyhood letters to his mother, written to her during Abby's periodic journeys abroad with Junior, offer ample testimony to his unbounded effervescence. "I have been going to dancing school with Jimmy. I like it very much," he wrote in one letter. "Tomorrow [Aunt Lucy] is going to take John, Laurance and I to the movie (The Three Musketeers). It will be great. Everything is lovely here." And in another: "I had lots of fun at the opera. We had a box and it was great. I think it would have been better if they had sung in a language that you could understand but the costumes and acting was great."

As Abby's personal secretary, A. L. Kelly, once told her, "You can count on Nelson's having a good time anywhere."

Much as Junior might take some private pleasure in Nelson's high spirits, so reminiscent of his wife's, certain rules and standards had to be maintained. So when Nelson began to play to one of his brothers at the dinner table (Laurance was his most frequent accomplice), Nelson was moved to the other end of the table. And when that didn't have any effect, he was excused—and, on occasion, spanked.

As far as Junior was concerned, Nelson simply had some bad habits that had to be broken. He included among these his son's left-handedness. Time after time, he urged the boy to switch his spoon or fork from the left to the right hand, but the hectoring didn't work. Finally, Junior one day slipped a rubber band over Nelson's left wrist, tied one end of a string to the rubber band, and held the other end of the string in his hand. Each time Nelson picked up a utensil with the left hand, Junior yanked on the string. This tactic was only partly successful; Nelson became ambidextrous, doing most things with his right hand, but playing tennis left-handed, and learning to write with either hand.

Most of all, what Junior would not brook was any deviation from the fundamental tenets of the code that had governed his own life. Those tenets were both spiritual (scrupulous churchgoing and strict observance of the Sabbath) and temporal (diligence and thrift being among the paramount virtues). "We looked to God for guidance on our moral conduct, and to Father for guidance on our fiscal conduct," his son Laurance observed many years later. The net effect, said Laurance, was that the children felt forever on trial, forever shadowed by the disapproving scrutiny of God and Father.

Not that Nelson didn't try, in mild ways, to subvert the code. He never cared for the family's Sunday-night hymn singing; when he was compelled to undergo the ritual, he would sing off-key. One Sunday morning, he hid a pet rabbit in Abby's muff before going to church; she played along with the joke, and sat through the whole service with the quivering animal tucked away.

But there was little Nelson could do about his father's unyielding emphasis on thrift and fiscal responsibility. Everything had been systematized. Each child was given an allowance to start of thirty cents a week; if his or her accounts withstood the scrutiny of Junior's weekly audit, the child would be rewarded with a five-cent raise. But if for some reason the books didn't balance, a five-cent penalty was levied. It was also understood that a third of the allowance would be saved, and another third would go to charity. In short, the Rockefeller children never had much candy money, a fact that was well known among their set. One of David's classmates once complained about his allowance, and the boy's father told him, "You find out what David Rockefeller gets, and I'll see if I can match it." The father never heard a word of protest about the allowance after that; his bemused son had learned that David's thirty cents a week was seventy cents less than he was getting.

Childhood was to a great extent an exercise in double-entry bookkeeping for the Rockefellers. Rewards and penalties were precisely calibrated. Nelson, along with his siblings, was taught this lesson at a tender age. One of his earliest letters was a "contract" he drew up between himself and his mother; in his elementary school scrawl he wrote, "If I don't miss one day of school this year I get $1.00."

Even the children's Sunday afternoon walks with Junior around the grounds of Pocantico, or in the woods behind the Eyrie, were regulated. "They were a very severe business, those walks," recalls someone who, as a young girl, was invited to join them. "Everyone had to march in single file, and you were punished if you broke out of the line." To those who stayed in line and completed the walk, Junior bestowed awards: lumps of maple sugar that he kept in his coat pockets.

Virtue was never its own reward in the Rockefeller house; almost every activity had a price tag attached. If the children caught mice in the attic, they were paid five cents a mouse. Flies brought in ten cents a hundred. And they were paid a nickel for every pair of shoes they shined.

Probably the most flagrant example of Junior's monetary carrot-and-stick was his standing offer of $2,500 to each child who abstained from smoking until the age of twenty-one. The offer had only middling success. Of the six children, only Nelson, David, and Laurance collected.

The effect of all this was that the heirs to America's greatest fortune grew up scrounging for cash like street urchins. On the day of a big summer dance in Maine, for instance, Nelson could be found laboriously catching rose bugs in his mother's garden. His parents would pay him fifty cents for each one hundred bugs, enough to cover a couple of ice-cream sodas. If he was really pressed, Nelson would covertly borrow from the help.

But far from feeling oppressed by this byzantine reward system, Nelson positively flourished in it. Once, believing his boys were not getting enough exercise, Junior urged them to take long walks around Pocantico, and offered to pay them at the rate of ten cents a mile. Nelson and Laurance did so much walking that Junior soon owed them $15 apiece. In a letter to his absent father, Nelson advised him that "you had better come back soon or we will put you in bankruptcy."

It wasn't long before young Nelson's abundant energies were channeled into formulating new ways to supplement his meager allowance. His grandest childhood scheme was rabbit breeding. In partnership with Laurance, he borrowed male and female rabbits from the Rockefeller Institute for Medical Research, then sold their progeny back to the institute at a healthy profit (as much as $13 for eight rabbits, or $180 in 1996 terms).

Nelson's rabbit business was very much in keeping with what one of the

Rockefeller brothers once described as their "do-it-yourself childhood. We were taught to be self-reliant when we were very young and self-sufficient too." Junior and Abby stressed initiative and resourcefulness. Their children learned to mend their own clothes and to cook their own meals, to make their maple syrup and maple sugar from the sap each child had arduously drawn from the trees on the Pocantico grounds. It was as though the bevy of butlers, governesses, tutors, housemaids, and cooks who surrounded them did not exist. Or, at least, did not exist for the couple of hours each week that the children spent learning these household skills. While it all smacked a bit of Marie Antoinette playing at being a milkmaid, these lessons did serve their larger purpose: to convince the young Rockefellers that they were competent in their own right, and not just creatures of the family's vast support system.

The boys' most ambitious demonstration of self-reliance was their construction of a cabin in the Maine woods. Nelson and older brother John conceived the idea in the summer of 1920, when Nelson was twelve and John fourteen. Helped by brother Laurance, they cleared a site, chopped down trees and trimmed them, and yoked two Shetland ponies to a rig of ropes and pulleys to haul the logs into place. The boys finished the job by putting on a shingled roof, fitting latched windows and a split-log door, and installing a working fireplace. The cabin served as a hideaway for several summers. (Revisiting the site more than thirty years later, Nelson poked around the ruins of the cabin and bragged, "It was a big project for us. Even then we always had some big project going.")

Barely three months before the boys embarked on their construction venture, they had vividly experienced the other, less self-sufficient side of being a Rockefeller.

Joining their parents and sister Babs (the youngest children, Winthrop and David, stayed home), they ventured forth on a two-month cross-country railroad journey that would take them through the Rockies, up and down the state of California, and to the Pacific Northwest. They traveled in a style befitting their wealth and station. The family had its own private railroad car, the Pioneer, which was hitched to the rear of the trains that took them westward. The Pioneer was outfitted in the best *grand luxe* style, with its own dining room, observation room, porch, five staterooms, and servants' quarters. Attending the Rockefellers was a three-man crew: a porter, a waiter, and a cook. The family's retinue included an associate from Junior's office, a medical doctor from the Rockefeller Institute, a French maid for Abby, and a young Englishwoman to chaperone Babs.

The accommodations and the entourage were not all that distinguished this trip from the ordinary vacation jaunt. The journey was a rite of homage to Rockefeller traditions and Rockefeller power. In Cleveland the family visited the old homestead of Junior's youth, Forest Hill, and Cettie's grave (the matriarch had died five years earlier). In Chicago they dined with the president of the Rockefeller-endowed University of Chicago. In Omaha they were greeted by the president of the Union Pacific Railroad, who attached his private car to theirs, invited the family to dinner, and treated the children to a tour of the engine repair shop and a ride in the engine.

And at every stop, the family was hounded by packs of newspapermen. Rarely had the Rockefeller children, up to then, ventured from their well-guarded sanctuaries; the press fairly salivated at the chance to glimpse America's wealthiest family at play. As John 3rd noted in his diary, "All along on our trip newspaper photographers were after us trying to take pictures of us, and reporters were after Father trying to get interviews with him." The wary Junior eventually struck a deal with the reporters: he would grant them interviews if they would agree to leave his children alone.

The journey gave the Rockefeller children a good taste of the pleasures that unbounded wealth and influence could command. But the ever-wary Junior was careful not to make such indulgence a habit. Later trips were considerably less elaborate, and Junior, as was his wont, made sure his sons earned their keep. As Laurance once recalled, "One of us paid the bills, another looked after the luggage, another would run the errands; and each of us was paid weekly for the job."

During a visit to Yellowstone National Park, Junior treated his sons to an elaborate display of haggling with the park superintendent over the cost of the Rockefellers' private cars. "I dislike being overcharged just because of who I am," Junior grumbled. The superintendent, Horace Albright, walked away from the encounter convinced that the whole thing had been staged by Junior as a lesson in penny-pinching for his boys.

Another such demonstration by Junior during that trip was vividly recalled by Nelson years later: "We had two rooms, we children, and there was a bath in between, and they had charged him for two double rooms with baths. I'll never forget his arguing with the clerk that it was one bath and two rooms and not two baths and two rooms." Nelson remembered his acute embarrassment about the episode, and his father's explanation that "if we don't do this, then other people won't feel they can do it because they might be embarrassed to do it, and people will take advantage."

The wild oscillations on these trips between a cosseted lifestyle and didactic parsimony, between grand self-indulgence and spartan self-restraint, were typical of the schizoid upbringing endured by Nelson and his siblings.

All around them—in the eighteenth-century gardens at Pocantico, in the Ming Dynasty porcelains their father was collecting, in the servants fluttering about with hushed footsteps—was the physical evidence of the immense wealth into which they had been born. Yet they were taught to ignore this evidence, to conduct their lives as though the fortune was a mere delusion.

Their young lives, as a result, were dotted with some amazing contradictions, at least in the eyes of those outside the family. A boyhood friend of Nelson's, William Alton, was often a summer guest of the family at the Eyrie in Maine. He remembers the formality of the place—"we had to dress for dinner almost every night"—and the level of service there, akin to that of a first-class hotel. "You'd take off your pajamas in the morning, and put on your tennis clothes, and when you came back after tennis the pajamas would be gone. They washed them and folded them and had them back to you at the end of the day. The same thing with your tennis clothes; you'd leave them on the bed, and come back later, and they would be washed and folded. And in the evening they'd take out your nightclothes and turn down your bed."

Yet Alton also remembers what happened when the boys one summer decided they wanted to buy a Victrola. "They were all sitting around trying to figure out how much they were going to spend for it. Mr. Rockefeller was leading the discussion, and he was weighing the question carefully on all sides. It became a great ordeal for them." After prolonged agonizing, the boys got their phonograph.

A Lincoln School classmate, Sheldon Stark, vividly describes the first time he was invited by Nelson to dinner at the Rockefeller townhouse on 54th Street. "We were the only ones there except for the servants in the back room," relates Stark. "When I walked in, Nels said to me, 'Come on, I want to show you something.' We walked up the stairs, and stopped at a mid-floor landing. There was a solid wall on one side and a banister on the other. Nels pushed a certain place on the wall, and the wall began to slide open. Then a blast of cold air hit us. We looked inside a room, and there, on the walls around the whole room was an Aubusson tapestry. The room was air-conditioned just for that tapestry." (And that was in the 1920s, when air-conditioning was a costly, rarely used amenity.)

But the same Nelson Rockefeller whose father spared no expense to preserve a priceless tapestry in his home was also the Nelson Rockefeller who was constantly scrounging money from Stark and other friends. "He never had any money in his pocket," says Stark. "He would borrow from anybody who was around."

Junior would be the first to acknowledge the incongruity of all this. But in his mind, the contradictions were an inevitable outgrowth of his heartfelt desire for normality for his children. He knew, of course, that there could be no such thing as a normal childhood for the heirs of John D. Rockefeller. But that didn't stop him from pursuing whatever stratagems he could to approach that illusory goal.

He worked vigilantly, and successfully, to shield his children from the spotlight of the press. It was not until 1922 that an article focusing on one of the Rockefeller scions appeared; the occasion was Nelson's hospitalization after an accident with an air rifle at Pocantico. (He had aimed the rifle at the ground, but the BB shot ricocheted off the lawn and hit him in the right leg.) During the family's travels, Junior sometimes resorted to a pseudonym (Davison, his middle name, was a popular choice) to put off nosy local reporters.

Junior was always security-conscious, particularly after Ludlow. He employed a watchman to patrol outside the 54th Street home, and kept a pistol—a Smith & Wesson .38—in his office. But he eschewed the shadowing of his children by bodyguards, then the practice of some of his wealthy contemporaries. "Certainly the thought that bodyguards were necessary, or even advisable, was never entertained by mother and father," Winthrop once recalled. "They were determined that we should lead normal lives."

Junior and Abby seemed to show none of the jitteriness about their children that lesser-heeled parents were constantly displaying. A schoolmate of Nelson's, the distinguished historian James T. Flexner, remembers that "my mother and father were very apprehensive about their children, and they were amazed at the amount of freedom Abby gave her children to roam around, to swim, even at the risk of life and limb."

This freedom was most visibly flaunted by the rebellious Babs, who would often be found in the local ice-cream parlor near the Pocantico estate, smoking her cigarettes while nibbling on a sundae. But Nelson also took full advantage of the latitude his parents gave him. He would roller-skate fearlessly along the sidewalks of Manhattan, dodging pedestrians as he glided past the great mansions on upper Fifth Avenue.

Among his skating partners was classmate Sanderson Vanderbilt, a poor relation of the monied clan who later became a prominent writer for *The New Yorker.* One day Nelson and Sandy decided to visit their friend Tom Prideaux, who was living at a fashionable Upper East Side apartment-hotel. They skated right into the lobby, went up to the desk, and asked the concierge if they could see Mr. Prideaux. When the concierge asked, "Who shall I say is calling?" Nelson replied, "Mr. Rockefeller and Mr. Vanderbilt." Muttering assorted imprecations, the concierge shooed them away.

But at the same time that Junior and Abby were trying to inject a semblance of normalcy into their children's lives, they also were not letting them forget that they were Rockefellers and that they bore some special responsibilities.

At every turn, young Nelson and his siblings were reminded of that burden. During World War I, for instance, they were instructed to plant Victory gardens on the Pocantico grounds (Nelson proudly harvested $112 worth of produce), and they scrupulously adhered to the wartime rationing of meat and sugar. Abby moved a Red Cross bandage unit into the basement of the 54th Street house, and each of the children, appropriately dressed in white uniforms, lent a hand in producing the bandages.

Abby never missed an opportunity to extol her husband's virtues to the children. After the war, she even went so far as to commission and privately print a volume entitled "The War Work of John D. Rockefeller Jr." solely for the children's edification. In the introduction she explained, "Your father is so modest, so unassuming and often so doubtful of his own ability, that I question if you will ever hear from his lips of his ceaseless toil, his unending sacrifice of time and often of comfort during the war. Like many a soldier, he never reached the front but the results of his efforts did, and were a blessing to the American and Allied armies."*

Junior's rectitude and good works indeed set a rather daunting example for the children. By the time Nelson reached adolescence, his father, now the total overseer of the family fortune, had emerged as the world's preeminent philanthropist. The range of Junior's activities was mind-boggling. He funded the restoration of the palace of Versailles. He financed a museum in Jerusalem to house priceless artifacts of biblical times. He rebuilt the library of Tokyo's Imperial University, destroyed in the earthquake of 1923. He financed the construction of New York's magnificent Riverside Church. He anonymously backed Margaret Sanger's Birth Control Clinical Research Bureau. He purchased and donated much of the land (some 11,000 acres) needed to establish Acadia National Park on Mount Desert Island, the site of his Seal Harbor retreat.

The children were eyewitnesses to some of this. On a trip to France with their parents they inspected the damage done to Reims cathedral in the war. Late in his life, Nelson could recall climbing up a ladder in the cathedral to pick up some of the shattered glass off the ledge of a rose window. His father ended up financing the repairs. "Wherever we went," Nelson would remember, "if something needed to be rebuilt because of the war or a national disaster, he would always help."

As the children grew up, the public's memories of Ludlow and the Standard Oil trust faded. The great oil monopoly had been broken up by court decree, and the Rockefellers no longer ran its affairs. The family, thanks to Junior, was now extolled for its munificence, rather than reviled for its greed.

The children were taught to hallow their grandfather, the progenitor of both the fortune and the precepts that ruled their lives. To the youngsters, however, he was more than a family totem; he was a spry, puckish figure who played blindman's buff with them at Kykuit and told rambling, silly stories at their Sunday dinner visits. As they grew older, they would play golf with him on the nine-hole course he built on the Kykuit lawn, and come around for a

*Abby somewhat overstated the case. Junior's principal contribution to the war effort was to coordinate the efforts of such morale-boosting service organizations as the Young Men's Christian Association and the Knights of Columbus. Source: Raymond Fosdick, *John D. Rockefeller, Jr.*, p. 404.

game of Numerica, an arcane card game to which he was addicted. They found him more fun to be with than their own father, and, in the way of grandchildren, sometimes used him to circumvent their parents' decrees. Spying her brothers toiling in the garden to earn a few extra nickels of allowance, Babs sniffed that it wasn't worth the bother. "I can always get a dollar from Grandfather," she said.

Just as the elderly tycoon had invested all his hopes in his son, so, too, did he now build his dynastic dreams around his grandsons. Naturally, the greatest part of the burden fell on the eldest son and namesake. In a Christmas letter to fifteen-year-old John 3rd, the old man wrote, "We look to you for great and good and valiant service, walking in the footsteps of your dear father. So equip you for this service and quit you like a man."

Although his older brother bore the brunt of the family's expectations, Nelson had more than his fair share. Part of the pressure was self-created; he made much of the fact that he and his grandfather Rockefeller had the same birthday. "He always thought it had some symbolic significance," his brother David recalls. And even without this sense of destiny, the family pressure to make something of himself, to live up to his father's shining example, left its mark on him.

As Abby exhorted him in a letter when he was just thirteen, "I am eager that you shall be *much* above the ordinary in character and achievement. The world needs fine men, there is great work waiting to be done. I want you to train yourself to meet any opportunity the future may hold in store for you."

But Nelson, for much of his childhood, seemed little inclined to do that.

In the same letter, Abby vented her utter frustration with him. "If you can only train yourself now to concentrate and to stop fooling except in play time," she scolded him, "you will do yourself an endless service for which you will be thankful for the rest of your life."

"Learn to use your brains *now,*" she warned, "before it is too late."

Year after year, the story is the same: Nelson would accomplish so much, if only . . . In 1915, when he was seven, nurse Scales reported to Abby, "I had Nelson read to me for 15 minutes today and he really does very well but he is very careless and so eager to get to the story." Eight years later, Scales wrote Abby, "Nelson will have to do some good work if he hopes to keep up with the ninth grade. He will never *hurt* himself studying, I am sure." "The best thing that can happen to Nelson," another governess told Abby then, "is to have plenty of work which he *must* do."

Every now and then, when the spirit moved him, Nelson could apply himself. Frustrated by constantly losing to Laurance at chess, Nelson brought his mind to bear on the game, and soon found himself beating Laurance half the time. As he explained to his nurse, "I made up my mind to think hard and more slowly and find that was the thing I needed." In relating this story to

Abby, the nurse added, "I then told Nell that I believed he would find that the same thing would work in his school work. Many of his mistakes are only carelessness."

Some of Nelson's learning difficulties could be attributed to reading problems: his eyes tended to transpose letters. Many years later, this would be diagnosed as dyslexia, but during his youth, he was simply classified as a slow reader.* The eyesight problem also may have had something to do with his egregious spelling errors, although Abby, who noted that her children all had this difficulty, attributed it to an inherited Aldrich family trait.

But unquestionably the biggest obstacle to Nelson's studies was his restless energy. Darting from his rabbit pen to his Victory garden, roller-skating down bustling Manhattan streets, fiddling with his wireless to pluck a jazz concert from the airwaves (he insisted on listening to the radio while he did his homework), hurriedly downing vast quantities of chocolate cake and malted milk, Nelson dashed through childhood in a blur, shirttails flying, ash-blond hair askew. He simply couldn't, wouldn't sit still.

"Perhaps there is a little bit too much Aldrich in us and not enough Rockefeller," Abby once sighed to her children. And of none of them was this more true than Nelson. In a family bound by the obligations of a mighty fortune on one side and Junior's Baptist precepts on the other, Nelson was a rule-bending life force, his vigor energizing, frustrating, intimidating all those around him. "He was just too much for Junior," remarks his boyhood friend Bill Alton.

He was also, even as a youngster, too much for his brothers. This was especially so for the dour, dutiful John 3rd, whose shyness and social awkwardness contrasted so vividly with the ebullience of his younger brother. "Nelson dances very well. I am rotten," John once mournfully recorded. On another occasion John ruefully noted, "Nelson always makes a big hit." As if John's self-consciousness about their differences was not bad enough, Nelson would sometimes inadvertently rub it in. When John once almost suffered a serious rope-climbing accident in boarding school, Nelson wrote to sympathize, and then went on to point out how he had just set the rope-climbing record at the Lincoln School.

As the middle son, two years younger than Nelson, Laurance was not nearly as threatened as John by his brother's personality. Instead, Laurance came to idolize Nelson. Alert and spirited in his own right (albeit prone to periods of sickliness), Laurance soon became, as he once put it, Nelson's "partner in crime." They shared a room in the 54th Street house, and were

*The problem continued to plague him decades later, when he became a public figure. "I have a terrible time," he once confessed to his chief speechwriter, Hugh Morrow. "I can't see a whole word. I have to go through it syllable by syllable. If I just glance at something I get it mixed up. I have no confidence in reading." Source: Unpublished Hugh Morrow interview, Persico Papers, SUNY Albany.

natural allies in everything from rabbit breeding to giggling at the dinner table. Disliking their given names, they gave each other new, more manly ones: Laurance became "Bill," and Nelson became "Dick." (While "Dick" never stuck, Nelson went on addressing Laurance as "Bill" for the rest of his life, much to the puzzlement of those who worked for the New York governor.)

Alone among the brothers, the quick-witted Laurance had a knack for cutting Nelson down to size. As Nelson once recalled, "He could always put the rapier right through me with a twist." But these gibes seemed to only strengthen their bond.

It fell to Winthrop to bring out the crueler aspects of Nelson's exuberance. Four years his brother's junior, Winthrop was always the odd man out. He tended, from an early age, to see himself as a victim. When he was seven he noticed that the window in his room had bars in front of it, and his brothers' windows didn't (the reason being that Winthrop's window led to a fire escape). He became convinced that the bars were there to imprison him.

Given his sensitivity, and his tendency toward pudginess, it was not terribly surprising that he became the frequent butt of his brothers' jokes. Even John 3rd joined in; he would crack that you could *see* little Winthrop getting fatter every day. But Winthrop's most merciless tormentor was Nelson. Aided and abetted by Laurance, Nelson took an almost sadistic pleasure in making his little brother's life miserable.

He would trip Winthrop, and pull his chair out from under him. He called him "Wissy-Wissy," a nickname Winthrop detested. He would get on a seesaw with Winthrop, then jump off and let his brother crash to the ground. Swearing he would never do such a thing again, Nelson would convince Winthrop to get back on the seesaw—only to repeat the trick one more time, to Nelson's immense giggly delight. After Nelson pulled this stunt on him three times in a single morning, the infuriated Winthrop grabbed a pitchfork and stabbed his brother in the knee. Ever the impartial arbiter, Junior spanked both boys after the incident.

When Winthrop fell ill with a kidney ailment, Nelson and Laurance lost no opportunity to remind him that a young cousin, also named Winthrop, had died of a kidney disease. "Two cousins, both the same name, same disease," they would chant. "Killed him. How are you feeling today?"

During their summers in Maine, Winthrop was barred from the hideaway cabin his older brothers had built. And when other amusement was lacking, Nelson and Laurance would take Winthrop into the woods, tie him to a tree, and run away.

When he reached adulthood Winthrop would try to be philosophical about his treatment at the hands of his brothers, even going so far as to call it a character-building experience. "I believe," he once said, "that the teasing I got from Laurance and Nelson—and their very direct methods of curbing me when I lost control of my temper—did help me to keep it under control in later years."

But the scars were deep, and lasting. Showing a visitor around the Seal Harbor homestead in the late 1950s, Winthrop took his guest for a drive through the hemlock forest behind the house. Suddenly Winthrop stopped the car and pointed to a spot deep within the darkest recesses of the hemlocks. "Do you see that tree way down there?" he said. "That's where Nelson and Laurance used to kick me and tie me up and leave me."

Just how to channel Nelson's energy—to harness it, and keep it under some measure of control, without quashing it—was a question that would preoccupy Junior and Abby throughout Nelson's childhood. The matter came to a head early, when a decision had to be made about the boy's education.

Nelson, like his brother John before him, had been enrolled in the Roger Ascham School, a small coeducational institution on East 79th Street. But Ascham covered only the early grades. The question remained as to where Nelson would receive the rest of his education leading up to college.

In John's case, Junior had chosen to send him to the Browning School, the same progressive Manhattan school that Junior had attended. (Babs, it should be noted, was put on a more traditional girls' school track, first attending Brearley, then Chapin.) Browning, in its early days, had largely been bankrolled by the Rockefellers: Junior, his cousins, and some friends were the only students. The school had grown since then, but it was still overseen by Junior's beloved old headmaster, John A. Browning.

But when Nelson's time came, Junior and Abby decided not to enroll him in Browning. In part this was because it was clear that the aging headmaster would be retiring soon, and Junior was not entirely comfortable with his chosen successors. In larger measure, however, it was because a dramatically new concept in American education was taking shape—a concept funded by Rockefeller money. And Junior and Abby were eager to have their boys take part in it.

The idea was the brainchild of Abraham Flexner, a distinguished educator who worked for the Rockefeller-backed General Education Board. Flexner was thoroughly caught up in the new doctrine of progressive education promulgated by Columbia University's John Dewey. What Flexner had in mind was nothing less than a school that would embody Dewey's precepts, as well as those of like-minded educational reformers. The school would encourage scientific thinking and intellectual curiosity, and shun all forms of rote learning. It would downplay examinations and grades in favor of more free-form yardsticks of growth. It would emphasize the emerging modern social sciences, and spurn Latin and Greek.

The institution, to be called the Lincoln School, would, in short, be an ongoing educational experiment in the guise of a private school.

This concept had immense appeal to Junior and Abby. Abby was perennially eager to experiment, and Junior, for all his rigidity, was completely in favor of new approaches to education (the GEB's whole raison d'être, after all, was to be an agent for such change). They particularly appreciated the fact that Lincoln would be a radical departure from the traditional prep school, with its cloistered atmosphere and homogeneous student body. Lincoln was intended to be coeducational, with students from a kaleidoscope of backgrounds, and would be based right in Manhattan. Obsessed with the unachievable notion of normality for his children, fearful that they would grow up to be rich, self-indulgent snobs, Junior saw the Lincoln School as a democratic alternative to the prep school path.

And so while his peers were dispatched to Groton or St. Paul's, to be initiated into the mysteries of the anointed, Nelson Rockefeller roller-skated up Fifth Avenue to the Lincoln School.

Four

Lincoln's Lessons

The Lincoln School began its first classes on September 24, 1917, in cramped quarters on Park Avenue between 66th and 67th streets. Among the 116 boys and girls who filed in on that opening day was Nelson Rockefeller, about to enter the third grade.

The school, which would educate its students from the early grades all the way up through high school, was established as a unit of Columbia University's Teachers College. The GEB agreed to fund Lincoln's annual deficit in the early years and gave Teachers College a $3 million endowment for the new school. When it became clear after just three years that Lincoln had outgrown the Park Avenue space, the GEB spent $1.25 million to erect a massive seven-story home for the school on 123rd Street and Morningside Avenue, a few blocks from the Columbia campus.

Flexner decided that he would not run Lincoln himself. Instead, he brought in Otis Caldwell from the University of Chicago to be its first director. But Flexner's guiding hand could be seen in everything from the shaping of the curriculum to admissions policy to the selection of teachers. And always lurking behind the scenes was the dour, demanding figure of John D. Rockefeller, Jr., whose money paid for this whole edifice and who would eventually send his four youngest sons there.

The composition of the student body was certainly in keeping with what he and Abby had in mind. There were hardly any blue bloods, and the ethnic and social backgrounds of the youngsters covered a broad spectrum. A good number of the students were the children of Columbia professors. Unlike the tonier prep schools, Lincoln admitted Jewish children in more than token numbers—although Lincoln adhered to a secret policy of keeping its Jewish percentage of the student body at 20 percent, a number roughly equal to the proportion of Jews in New York City at the time. (When Caldwell, under pressure to admit more Jewish students, nervously asked one of Junior's top aides in 1925 if he was right in adhering to those restrictions, the aide said that he "thoroughly approved" the Jewish quota.)

Diversity at the Lincoln School had its limits in other ways. Despite frequent assertions in later years that Lincoln admitted black students, there were no blacks in Nelson's class. Nor does anyone who attended the school during his time recall the presence of any, save for the brief appearance of a black girl sometime in the early grades.

With its tuition set initially at $200 to $250 a year—not cheap, by 1917 standards, but not exorbitant either—Lincoln was a natural magnet for the children of upwardly mobile middle-class parents. "It was a good intellectual *bon bourgeois* school," recalls James Flexner, Abraham's nephew, who was a year behind Nelson at Lincoln. While there was a smattering of scholarship students—whose financial aid was well hidden from their fellows—and representatives of the monied gentry (the Rockefellers, as well as various German Jewish families), by and large the student body was from the vast middle tier of the New York community.

What the families of Lincoln School students—from the Rockefellers on down—had in common was the quest for something different, something unique for their children. And *that* was a promise on which Lincoln totally delivered.

From the start, the Lincoln School had the air of a grand, free-form experiment, in which the elements of American education were extracted and tossed about and recombined in protean variety. None of the old techniques and benchmarks applied; the teachers would have to devise their own curricula, write their own textbooks, and formulate their own methods of judging achievement. The faculty's motto, in the words of one instructor, was to "try anything once and see if it works."

Instead of viewing each subject in isolation, the Lincoln School's teachers took an interdisciplinary approach, in which the boundaries between math and science and literature were thoroughly smeared. The third grade, for example, focused all its attention on the study of boats. History was learned by studying the great seagoing civilizations, math by solving problems related to boat making. The students partook of literature by reading classic tales of the sea, built models of boats for their industrial arts training, and studied music by learning the "Volga Boat Song" and old Gaelic lullabies.

By the rigid standards of the prep schools, with their time-honored codes of conduct and tradition of martial discipline, Lincoln was a singularly relaxed and accommodating place. Unlike at the prep schools, says another of Nelson's classmates, Stephen Duggan, "there wasn't that sense of competition. You had a great sense of friendliness and kidding around. A *lot* of kidding around; I can certainly remember that."

To be sure, life at Lincoln wasn't a total carnival. Contrary to the popular lore about the school, there were exams and grades (although Lincoln didn't adopt the standard A-to-F system until 1925, preferring until then a gentler, more graduated approach). And because Lincoln was Lincoln, its students found themselves guinea pigs for every new testing technique that came down the pike. The Stanford-Binet intelligence test—soon to be the standard IQ exam—was tried out and refined at Lincoln.

But for the most part, students at Lincoln led stimulating, unpressured lives. School, for them, was a daily adventure, something to be eagerly anticipated and savored. It was, in many respects, an educational environment that was tailor-made for young Nelson Rockefeller.

Each weekday morning, when the weather was fair enough, Nelson and Laurance would strap on their roller skates in the doorway of the 54th Street mansion and coast over to Fifth Avenue, to begin their daily commute to the Lincoln School. When the school was on Park and 67th, they would skate all the way up; when it was relocated farther north, they skated as far as Fifth and 93rd ("though we often settled for 79th Street," Laurance remembers). Then the limousine that was puttering close behind them, trailing them from the time they left their home, would slow to a halt, and the boys would clamber in for the ride the rest of the way uptown. But once they entered the school building, the Rockefeller boys became just two more Lincolnians, careering through the hallways, plunging into the array of activities the school had to offer.

Nelson, characteristically, charged through Lincoln more breathlessly than most. He performed gamely in Lincoln theatricals, winning kudos for his portrayal of an obstreperous frog in a sixth-grade operetta. He wrote a short story with a canine hero, based on his favorite work of juvenile fiction, *Wolf the Storm Leader*. He dutifully plugged away at the cello, and competed with somewhat greater enthusiasm for a school medal in parade-ground drumming. He developed an interest in biology—inspired, no doubt, by his experiments in rabbit breeding. He became enchanted with photography, and began taking photos for school publications.

A classmate remembers the grade school Nelson as a "jolly, noisy little boy." What he most decidedly was *not* was a student. Partly it was a question of intellectual limitation. ("You know, I don't have a very high IQ," Nelson would confess to a friend later in life. Asked how he knew that, he replied, "I took one of those tests in school and found out.") Partly, it was the dyslexia, which made not only reading a chore but math as well; he had great difficulty adding and subtracting because he mixed up the columns of numbers. But mostly, his troubles could be traced to his study habits, the perennial bane of his governesses' existence. Sitting still for more than five minutes, poring over a textbook, was for Nelson a superhuman feat.

But the glory of Lincoln, for a student like Nelson, was that it tolerated and accommodated such behavior. Rather than grind away at weaknesses, Lincoln catered to strengths—which, in Nelson's case, tended to be in the realm of athletics. He excelled in a host of gymnastic events: rope climbing, broad jumping, the hundred-yard dash. His greatest school achievements were at intramural track meets. After attending one competition, Abby, glowing with maternal pride, reported on Nelson's victories to son John: "In the rope climbing test he did wonderfully, getting up to the top of the rope about three or four seconds before anyone else. He also jumped I should say 18 inches further than any of the other boys, and in both of these events, he helped his side to win. The whole thing was extremely interesting and I found myself getting almost as excited as the boys."

Nelson also became an enthusiastic soccer player—making up with brute force and energy what he may have lacked in finesse. A teammate, his friend Bill Alton, remembers that "Nelson was just a steamroller. He'd go after the ball, and if anybody was in the way, he'd knock them aside. Straight ahead was all he knew." It was a style of play truly indicative of the kind of boy Nelson was—and of the man he was to become.

While other, stricter schools might have tried to rein in Nelson's bubbly, expansive personality, free and easy Lincoln let it come to the fore. "He had a good time in everything he did. He was a happy kid," says Pauline Falk, who was in Laurance's class, two years behind Nelson. The hearty claps on the back, the comradely arm around the shoulders, the unbounded bonhomie—all those mannerisms and traits of the adult Nelson Rockefeller were already in full flower at the Lincoln School. "My memory of him at Lincoln is of someone with tremendous physical vitality," relates James Flexner. "He charged around everywhere." And Alton recalls how Nelson "would laugh his way around problems. He'd pat you on the back, and there was never any problem. Nelson wouldn't let there be a problem."

The ebullient Nelson had a knack for making his fellow students feel at ease around him, for bridging the vast chasm in means and social standing. When the students entertained each other in their apartments, Nelson would invariably be found in the kitchen, washing dishes. "It wasn't a show-offy kind of thing," notes Tom Prideaux. "It was perfectly natural."

The Rockefeller aura was also dispelled by the sorry state of Nelson's allowance, and his occasional entreaties for a loan. Duggan recalls lending Nelson a nickel for the bus. "That was a big moment for me," he says. "I remember coming home and telling my parents that I had just given Nelson Rockefeller a nickel to get home."

There was, indeed, very little of the air of affluence about Nelson. His clothes were nondescript, and his shirttails were forever fluttering outside his trousers. At the end of the school day, when he and Laurance were old enough to travel on their own, they would join their classmates for the ride home on the Fifth Avenue bus, munching Eskimo Pies and horsing around as the bus made its slow, lurching way downtown.

All this made Nelson immensely popular with his classmates. Bubbly, athletic, eager to please, he seemed the very prototype of that evergreen paradigm, the all-American boy. But with one critical difference: he was a Rockefeller.

As Flexner points out, "There was always the truth of the situation, which was that Rockefeller money financed the school." Try as they might, there was no way to really camouflage the fact that the Rockefellers were the Lincoln School's first family.

Every now and then, the reality of who they were intruded on the boys' serene time at Lincoln. Playing with fellow students in Morningside Park across the street, one of the Rockefeller boys was called over by a stranger. "I understand the Rockefellers send their children here," the man said. "Can you point them out to me?" The Rockefeller boy huffily replied, "They don't like to be pointed out," and ran away.

Nevertheless, if Nelson and his brothers wanted to build friendships with their fellow students, they had no choice but to give them a glimpse of their rarefied lifestyle. Having friends over for dinner, for example, meant bringing them to the 54th Street townhouse. The friends were appropriately awestruck by the experience. Says Stephen Duggan, "I still remember that formal dining room, and being so impressed with all the butlers and maids around. Holy Jehoshaphat! Oh, what a big deal that was for us kids."

It wasn't long before outings with the Rockefellers became part of the Lincoln School experience. Each fall, for example, Junior and Abby would invite their children's classmates to Pocantico for the weekend. The youngsters would go camping in a cabin on one of the estate's ponds, cooking out and frolicking under the watchful eye of Lincoln's athletic director, "Chief" Gucker. And sometimes Nelson's class would go en masse, as Junior's guests, to an event at Madison Square Garden: the circus or a hockey match. They would have dinner, attended by butlers, at the 54th Street house, then pile into chauffeur-driven cars for the drive to the arena. Eyeing the convoy of limousines, a goggle-eyed youngster named Thomas Tierney stammered at one of the chauffeurs, "Exactly how many cars do the Rockefellers own?"

For a few students—those who became especially close to Nelson or his brothers—the curtains shrouding the Rockefeller clan parted even wider. Such was the case with Bill Alton.

Alton had attained some celebrity of his own when he became the youngest Eagle Scout in the United States. The achievement caught the eye of the

Rockefeller family. As Alton recalls, "The Rockefellers were always interested in people that had accomplished something. From there on out, Nelson sort of took me under his wing."

Soon Alton was not only dining with the Rockefellers at 54th Street but vacationing with them as well. He gazed with adolescent wonder on the scene. One summer, there was a cruise on the Great Lakes: "Henry Ford met the boat at one point, and took us to lunch. In Duluth the head of U.S. Steel met us with his private train and took us to see the mines of Hibbing." At Seal Harbor, there were the scurryings of servants at his beck and call, the leisurely lunches at the Jordan Pond House, the Saturday evening dances hosted by the Edsel Fords and the Atwater Kents. "The Kents had a yacht with a full orchestra on it anchored in the harbor. You'd take a speedboat to get out there." And there were the not infrequent appearances of celebrities on the Rockefellers' doorstep; Alton remembers playing water polo one weekend with Charles Lindbergh.

At one point, Junior asked Alton to serve as a companion for the lonely Winthrop. Alton can still recall Junior's discomfort when the time came, at summer's end, to figure out how much Alton might be paid for this service.

Young Alton also got a telling glimpse of Rockefeller power. He once told Nelson that what he really wanted to do that summer was work in a national park; Nelson suggested that Junior might be able to help. "Father will write a letter for you," he said. But when Junior dispatched the letter to the appropriate official at the National Park Service, he received, to his disbelief, a curt reply advising him there were no openings.

"It was the kind of thing Mr. Rockefeller wouldn't take," Alton relates. "So he wrote to the Secretary of the Interior and expressed his displeasure. The secretary got in touch with the fellow and made it clear to him it wasn't a matter of whether he liked it or not. Well, you should have seen the next letter the fellow sent to Mr. Rockefeller.

"I worked in Glacier National Park that summer."

For all his formidable family connections, Nelson's social associations at Lincoln showed not a trace of snobbery. One of his best friends there was Sheldon Stark, a Jewish boy from Brooklyn who had little in common with Nelson save a mutual affinity for soccer. He invited Stark to the 54th Street house and for weekends at Pocantico; Stark even went to church on Sunday morning with the Rockefeller family. "We liked each other instantly," Stark recalls. "It amazed me that he was so natural around me."

While there were cliques at Lincoln, the most prominent of which was a coterie that called itself "the Informal Crowd," Nelson steered clear of them. The closest he came to cliquishness was his tendency to hang out with fellow athletes like Stark, Alton, and Ted Martin.

He also didn't have very much to do with school politics, despite the fact that Lincoln was a very political place. "My friends and I were running a real Tammany Hall-type political machine there at the time," notes Flexner. "I would have been quite conscious of it if Nelson wanted to take part, but I don't remember him being involved in that at all."

Nelson's one great foray into the Lincoln political scene was his election as eighth-grade class chairman. In that capacity he oversaw the drafting of a class constitution, one of whose provisions was that all eighth-graders must strictly obey the class chairman. He did, however, generously allow the class chairman to be impeached "if he disobeys one of the important laws of the constitution, if he says anything against God or his country, or if he plays hookey."

After that experience, Nelson limited his officeholding to the athletic arena. Lincoln's intramural sports program divided the student body into two teams, the Oranges and the Blues; in his senior year Nelson was elected captain of the Blues. He also became chairman of the school's Athletic Council, which laid out Lincoln's athletic program for the year.

But that was the total extent of Nelson's political activity at Lincoln. He simply had far more pressing things on his mind—athletically, academically, and romantically.

"Nelson, it seems to me, is changing every day," the frazzled nurse Florence Scales wrote to Abby in 1923, when he was not yet fifteen. "He is such a queer combination of a dear little boy, a tough big boy, and a manly youth. I never quite know how to take him. . . . He is a most lovable boy but in a trying age."

In truth, the adolescent Nelson was probably not much more trying than any other rambunctious teenager, and in many ways a lot less so. Unlike his brooding older brother, Nelson seemed utterly devoid of adolescent angst. For him, puberty simply marked a transition from one set of amusements and diversions to a different set. He began to show an interest in his clothes, eagerly visiting the family's tailor of choice, De Pinna's, and insisting on wearing a favorite suit day after day. He took to manicuring his nails. He indulged his curiosity about jazz, listening for hours to his gramophone or wireless and snapping up favorite piano rolls at the Aeolian Hall.

At fifteen, he entered into a new passion: motorcars. All the Rockefeller boys obtained licenses at that age, taking advantage of the state of Maine's looser age requirements. Their first cars were "red bugs": four-seated buckboards with red wooden-slat sides and puttering, low-powered motors. The boys would circumnavigate the Pocantico estate in these vehicles, as well as use them to travel to the nearby village. Nelson, unsurprisingly, always seemed a bit more reckless than his brothers. He once earned a stern reprimand from Abby when he was caught zipping around the statuary near his grandfather Rockefeller's manor house.

When he turned seventeen, his parents presented him with a more substantial vehicle: a sporty Ford roadster. Not leaving well enough alone, Nelson proceeded to festoon the car with a variety of horns. The Ford, to his immense delight, became the talk of Seal Harbor that summer. "He took it to the village the other day to do an errand," Abby reported to daughter Babs, "and when he came out of the shop there were about twenty men standing around it, looking it over. He says that it is impossible to leave it for a moment without its collecting a crowd. I think he enjoys the excitement."

In the fall, Nelson took the roadster back to New York City, where he used it to shuttle his three brothers and himself to and from the Lincoln School. Anticipating his parents' objections, he cited frugality—always a useful point with Junior—to justify himself. "You see," he wrote them, "it saves us forty cents a day on bus fares."

The roadster created as big a sensation at Lincoln as it did back in Seal Harbor. Nelson's fellow students were generally not in a position to commute to school in their own vehicles—let alone in a machine as souped-up and glistening as the Ford. Considering how hard the Rockefellers worked to maintain their low profile and blend in with the rest of the student body, the conspicuousness of Nelson's car was a stunning breach of the family's precepts. The car declared, in the loudest, most unmistakable tones, that Nelson Rockefeller was a special presence among them.

And yet while the other students envied the vehicle, they did not seem to resent it. The car's owner had so won them over that a mere plaything like the Ford was not about to dent their affection for him. Besides, he was a Rockefeller, and they took it for granted that a Rockefeller would have some expensive toys.

Still, the roadster revealed something about Nelson, something that was just beginning to bubble to the surface as he moved through adolescence. A certain show-off quality, bordering on arrogance, was starting to manifest itself. Far from playing down his Rockefeller identity, Nelson seemed to be reveling in it. He gloried in being the center of attention. The lessons in humility that Junior and Abby ground into him from an early age certainly had had their impact. But they simply had not been enough.

Abby was duly alarmed. She saw these qualities emerging not just in Nelson but in her other children as well. At one point she warned son John, "I have felt for some little time that you and Nelson and Babs were assuming a rather superior air about people and places and things that was not justified or becoming." And of all the children, it was clearly Nelson who most exhibited this "superior air."

Perhaps the most telling indication of this was the time Nelson was driving around New Haven and asked a policeman for directions to the Yale Bowl. The policeman flagged down a passing motorcycle patrolman, and Nelson was given an escort to the stadium. Relating the tale in a letter to John 3rd,

Nelson exulted, "Now if that is not pretty swift I would like to know. Think, when I arrive in a town I have the officer meet me and show me around. That kind of stuff *goes big with me.*"

To the girls of Lincoln, Nelson's roadster merely added to his already considerable appeal. "Everyone thought he was terribly handsome," remembers Linda Storrow. "All the girls had crushes on him."

But for the teenaged Nelson, there was really only one girl at Lincoln: his classmate Geraldine Chittolini.

A frisky, alluring ash-blonde, Chittolini had a formidable reputation as the class flirt. "She was by far the most attractive girl in the school," says Flexner, who harbored a certain passion for her himself. "She was not a great beauty, but she was very come-hitherish. She flirted enough with me that I was aggrieved when she chose Nelson."

Aside from her obvious charms, there was considerable substance to Chittolini. The daughter of a violin dealer, she was utterly engrossed in the world of music. She attended her first opera when she was six, and she had come to know well the many conductors and singers who visited her parents' home. She also was an accomplished athlete, breaking school records in the high jump and starring as a forward on the girls' basketball team. And Chittolini was possessed of a breezy, serene self-confidence that made her all the more attractive.

Chittolini entered Lincoln School in the ninth grade, and it wasn't long before she and Nelson became an item. Nelson would hang around the girls' hallway lockers, looking for a chance to chat with her. Classmates would sometimes encounter the two of them in an empty classroom, completely absorbed in each other.

Nelson's parents were well aware of the relationship, and he went to great lengths to reassure them that the affair wasn't distracting him from his studies. "Gerry and I have been ever so good," he wrote to them at one point. "We have not wasted one minute in school. In fact, I hardly see her any more. To make up I have been to see her three times on Sunday. She is still as sweet as ever, but I promise you I am not letting it interfere with my studies in the least bit!"

But sometime in the fall of his senior year, Nelson abruptly severed the relationship. Their Lincoln classmates were never told exactly what happened, but strongly suspected that someone—probably Nelson's parents—had put a stop to it. There were even whispers that Nelson had wanted to marry Geraldine. The way the story went, his parents, aghast at the prospect of a Rockefeller scion wedding the daughter of a violin dealer—and an Italian Catholic violin dealer at that—barred him from ever seeing her again.

But in fact it was Nelson himself who took the initiative. His parents' possible disapproval of the relationship may have been lurking in his subconscious when he did so, but there is little doubt that Nelson, and Nelson alone, made the decision.

Junior and Abby were vacationing in Cannes when Nelson advised them about what had happened. "I guess the affair between Gerry and I is about over," he wrote. "She had changed a powerful lot since last year, and to my mind it was not for the better. I did my best to show her and get her to take a different viewpoint, but it was all in vain. We have not fallen out or anything of the kind but I just explained to her how I felt and we are just as good friends as ever but that [sic] all. Of course there is nothing bad about her, it is just her general attitude, but I will tell you about it when you get back."

Presumably, he told them, when they got back, exactly what it was about her "general attitude" to which he took such exception. There is no further reference to the breakup in his correspondence, and the precise reasons for it remain mysterious. It is not clear just how Gerry had changed. Perhaps she did indeed want to force the issue of marriage ("I did my best to show her and get her to take a different viewpoint"). Perhaps Nelson—anticipating his parents' objections—came to see how unsuitable, how unacceptable in their eyes such an intimate tie, so early in his life, would be.

The one explanation Nelson gave outside the family for what had happened came in a cryptic remark Nelson made to one of his aides decades later. Describing how he felt compelled to buckle down to his studies at Lincoln, Nelson said, "I even had to tell my girl—I had a very heavy girl—I had to call that off. . . . I just told her, 'Look, I want to go to college. I just can't do it this way.' "

While this comment does not shed any light on what might have been different about Gerry, it does offer a plausible reason for the breakup. Great things were expected of Nelson, and the progress of his studies was hardly consistent with achieving them. Gerry Chittolini represented a monumental distraction—a distraction that he could ill afford as college loomed. Nelson's already acute sense of obligation—to his family, to their expectations, and to his own hopes for himself—prevailed.

For the first time in his life, Nelson had to contend with the warring imperatives of passion and career. This time, career won out.

But there were also hints of that other, more elusive motivation for the breakup: the need to make a match that would be more acceptable to his parents. The hints come later in the same letter to his parents in which Nelson advises them that he and Gerry have split. He details, with considerable gusto, all the invitations he has received from eager young ladies to dances during the Christmas vacation period. "I have also received four or five Deb. coming-out invitations," Nelson says. "I have excepted [sic] nearly all of them so far." The girls in question were, it should be noted, of considerably bluer blood than Gerry.

The sort of pressure Nelson was feeling at the time was indicated by a document his father drafted less than a year earlier. Entitled "Memorandum of the Choice of a College," it spelled out the criteria Junior expected his boys to use when selecting a school. As was typical with Junior, the memo took on a preachy, pedantic tone, and was as much a declaration of what he demanded of his sons as it was a helpful guide.

"I covet for my boys scholarly attainment in school and college," Junior's memo intoned. "By that I do not mean standing at the head of their classes, but being well up in the upper half. . . . By natural endowment and through the opportunities open to them they ought to rank well above the average. This I confidently expect. Mediocrity ought not to satisfy them, any more than it does me."

By those lofty standards, Nelson was well on his way to abject failure as he approached college age. His grades at even a permissive school like Lincoln were distinctly mediocre. He needed additional, before- or after-school tutoring in Spanish and math, and his spelling remained atrocious. Spanish was his particular bête noire; his D's in the subject were enough to cause any Ivy League admissions officer to blanch.

Junior observed Nelson's plight with mounting apprehension. As far as Junior was concerned, there could be only one reason why his son was doing so badly: Nelson's utter unwillingness to apply himself.

To document this, he went so far as to ask Nelson, in the middle of his junior year, to record in a little notebook exactly how long he spent on each subject every day. After painstakingly compiling the results with a bookkeeper's precision, Junior sent them on to Nelson's Lincoln School class adviser, Charles W. Finley. "You will see that the average time spent on his lessons each day for the five days was, for the first week, two hours and fifteen minutes, for the second week two hours and twenty minutes," he advised Finley. "Nelson fully agrees that this is not adequate." To remedy this, Junior told Nelson that in the next semester he would have to study during his "idle periods" in school. More importantly, Junior reported to Finley, "he has agreed not to operate the radio or his phonograph at all from Monday morning until after school Friday each week."

Nevertheless, there was little improvement that next semester. Nelson still kept his study log, and Junior regretfully informed Caldwell that "the record does not indicate any material change in the amount of time spent on his lessons."

As his senior year approached, Nelson was told he would have to spend the summer undertaking remedial work in Spanish. Upon his return to Lincoln in the fall, he was given a three-hour exam on his summer studies. "Nelson's work was such," Caldwell reported to Junior's aide Charles Heydt, "that it was quite impossible to give him a passing grade." As a last resort,

Caldwell asked Nelson to come in at eight-thirty three mornings a week for special work in the subject.

But nothing helped. For Nelson, the poor showing in Spanish had dire consequences: it meant that he might never make it into Princeton, where he hoped to join his brother John. Finally, after a long talk with Caldwell and Finley, Nelson agreed that the best course would be to just drop Spanish and forgo his chance at Princeton. He struggled to put the best face on the decision in a letter to his parents: "By stopping the Spanish I am able to walk in the morning which is great because I needed the exercise badly."

With the great Spanish millstone out of the way, Nelson could focus on those subjects in which he had a fighting chance of improvement. And this time, he was determined not to blow the opportunity. Settling down to his books, Nelson single-mindedly brought his grades up to college standards. He learned that by harnessing his powers of concentration, he could even overcome the dyslexia (which then was still regarded as a "reading problem"). "I was told that if I worked harder I could make it," he reflected years later. "And that was absolutely true."

As his grades improved, Nelson settled on a new choice of college: Dartmouth. Smaller and less demanding academically than Princeton or Harvard, Dartmouth also had the considerable advantage, for the easily distracted Nelson, of its isolated setting in Hanover, New Hampshire. But perhaps Dartmouth's most considerable virtue, for Nelson, was his father's enthusiasm for the school. Junior had a high opinion of its president, Ernest M. Hopkins, who just happened to be a trustee of the Rockefeller Foundation. (Among Hopkins' virtues, as Junior once remarked, was that he was the only college president who had never asked him for money.) In fact, Junior had prodded John 3rd to attend Dartmouth rather than Princeton, which Junior viewed as a singularly elitist place. By choosing Dartmouth, Nelson would surely restore himself to his father's good graces.

And Dartmouth, in turn, was delighted to have him. Hopkins had come to know Nelson on Mount Desert Island, where the Dartmouth president had a summer house of his own (albeit in Manset, a distinctly down-market part of the island). The Hopkins and Rockefeller families frequently exchanged visits during the long, languid August afternoons.

It was hardly surprising, then, that Nelson's initial visit to Hanover in the fall of his senior year had the air of a state occasion. Accompanied by an entourage that consisted of Caldwell and friends Shelly Stark and Ted Martin, both of whom also aspired to Dartmouth, Nelson was formally received by President Hopkins and then given a tour of the verdant campus. Stark and Martin had no illusions about why they had been asked along; they were merely suitable foils for the crown prince.

This fact was underscored during the long overnight train ride to Hanover aboard the Boston & Maine Railroad. Sitting in the drawing-room car, Caldwell painstakingly went over the boys' chances of admission. He didn't believe Martin would have much of a problem. As for Stark, there was the delicate matter of his religion. "You know, Sheldon," he said, "you *are* Jewish, and there's a quota." Only with Nelson was there virtually no discussion. His admission, it seemed, was a foregone conclusion.

For Nelson, the legacy of Lincoln was unquestionably a positive one—not so much because of what the school did for him, but because of what it *didn't* do. It didn't bridle his vibrant personality with draconian regulations and inflexible requirements. It didn't promote the elitist attitudes and the social and intellectual homogenization associated with the prep schools. (In fact, so isolated was Nelson from the prep school milieu that he would later venture to say, "The only times I ever felt shy or uncomfortable were at certain society affairs when I didn't know the boys who were from the better prep schools. I didn't fit into their group.")

If Lincoln was not quite the melting pot its admirers envisioned, the school did manage to bring Nelson into contact with a diversity of ethnic backgrounds and social strata. He and his brothers learned to judge people on merit, not on the basis of their class backgrounds.

Perhaps Lincoln's most important intellectual bequest to Nelson was the training it gave him in looking at problems with an independent, eclectic eye. As Flexner points out, "The school got us to think for ourselves; that was its real point. We learned never to take anything on authority."

For a young man born into immense wealth, destined to be cosseted by a network of aides and advisers and hired hands, no lesson could be of more value.

Five

PRINCE OF HANOVER

In the middle of his senior year at Lincoln, Nelson hatched a plan for a summer bicycle excursion in France with his brother John. The two boys would travel on their own; there would be no companions, no chaperones, no bodyguards. Trying to sell his wary father on the scheme, Nelson argued that the trip would improve his French. When that ploy didn't do the trick, Nelson leveled with his father. It was time, he told Junior, that he and John learned to manage things on their own. Everything in their lives up to then had been planned for them. As a result, Nelson contended, he and John were not getting the experience and sense of independence that would come from handling matters themselves and learning from their own mistakes.

It was an argument that had a certain resonance with Junior, so long in the shadow of his own father. Half convinced that he should give the boys the go-ahead, Junior wrote to Lincoln School director Otis Caldwell about the scheme. He and Abby, he said, had been worried about what would happen if the boys fell ill during their trip. But that concern was dispelled by the thought that Nelson and John could be supplied the name of a "splendid English doctor" in Paris; they could also, he said, contact the head of the Standard Oil Company there "if any situation developed which they could not deal with."

Caldwell wholeheartedly endorsed the trip, and went to great lengths to reassure Junior about what the schoolmaster gingerly referred to as "situations which would hold dangers for a good many boys who would be on their own in France." Nelson and John, he said, "will not knowingly get into such situations, and will probably extricate themselves promptly if they find they are in such places. I believe they are thoroughly honorable in this matter."

Thus assured that neither the boys' health nor their chastity was in jeopardy, Junior agreed to the journey. Nelson and John mapped out a two- to three-week trip that would take them through Normandy, Brittany, and the Loire Valley. They would travel well armed: Nelson would have in hand $500 in traveler's checks, and John would carry on his person a $500 letter of credit.

With all the arrangements set, Nelson spent one last weekend with his school friends Ted Martin and Tad Bullock at a small house Martin had in Montauk, at the easternmost tip of Long Island. Late on Sunday the threesome clambered into Nelson's Ford for the long ride back to the city. Spotting a tempting straightaway, Nelson opened the throttle and passed a car parked on the side of the highway. He thought nothing of it—until a motorcycle patrolman emerged from behind the car, and gave chase.

Nelson described the rest of the scene this way to his parents:

> Naturally, I got a ticket. After he was all through writing it out, I called him over and told him I was sorry I couldn't come to court as I was sailing. He said that was all right that Ted could come in my place. Then I told him that I didn't want it to go in my name as the papers would be liable to get hold of it. He said it had to go down in the book but he thought that if Ted came around and saw him before the trial he would be able to fix it up by putting Ted's name in instead of mine. He asked if I was trying to hide my arrest from my father and I said no, I would tell you. . . . We parted friendly. He was a nice fellow!

Left unsaid is just what sort of special consideration the "nice fellow" might require to "fix it up." To Nelson, the bargain is eminently acceptable: his friend will bear the responsibility in his stead, and he will set sail for Europe, free of any unpleasant publicity. It does not seem to occur to him that there might be something wrong with all this. Perhaps he was merely naive. Or perhaps he was again displaying that nonchalant aristocratic arrogance that was so worrisome to Abby.

Nelson did make a clean breast of the situation in this note to his parents. But, significantly, the letter was written on board the SS *Aquitania,* when he and John were already well on their way across the Atlantic.

Setting off on their bicycles as soon as they debarked in Le Havre, Nelson and John took in a picture postcard view of France: the lush Normandy countryside, the old cobbled byways of Rouen, Mont-St.-Michel, the châteaus of the Loire. The ever-cheerful Nelson encountered "nothing but nice people," although he was somewhat discomfited by the Gallic temperament. "Everybody rushed about, making a lot of noise which I don't think is very becoming to the French," he recalled to his parents. "They get all excited." John served as treasurer for the trip, and maintained a tight grip on the purse strings—although Nelson did cajole him into coughing up fifty francs for some etchings of Rouen that Nelson fancied. It was probably his first purchase of art.

The boys did not disappoint Caldwell. There were no embarrassing incidents, no surrender to "dangerous situations." The closest they came to dissipation was on Nelson's birthday, when they went to a café–movie house and spent half the night drinking lemonade and watching Pola Negri in an American movie.

While they stayed in first-class hotels, the brothers managed to remain quite solvent, thanks to John's thrift. They returned in late July with $180 of the original $500 in traveler's checks, and the letter of credit still untendered in John's pocket. To end their journey on a note of frugality, they booked their return voyage aboard a freighter—a fact that was duly noted, and played up, by the press.

Arriving in New York on July 26, they loaded their belongings into a taxicab waiting at the pier. Upon entering the cab, they noticed that the meter already registered three dollars. When they quizzed the driver about this, he brusquely told them he had been hailed by the steamship company and had been sitting there for an hour and a half. John paid the fare, but a few days later he asked the Rockefeller family office to look into the matter. "I hate to make a fuss over three dollars, but I also hate to get gypped by a taxi driver," he told a functionary. Unable to get anywhere with the cab company, John suggested to the aide that he get in touch with a certain second deputy police commissioner, John Daly, who had evidently been useful to the Rockefellers in the past. "I think that it would be rather fun to see it through," young John chirped.

But John's fun had some tragic repercussions. Daly promptly located the cabbie and revoked his hack license. Four months later, the family office was told that the driver, married and with three children, was destitute, having been unable to find work since. Realizing their blunder, the Rockefellers appealed to Daly to reverse his decision. It is not known if he ever did.

The incident was a chilling reminder of the Olympian power the family wielded. The merest wave of a hand, however unconscious, could send some poor mortal hurtling to his doom. Practically everything a Rockefeller did had consequences. For Nelson, who just a few months earlier had blithely arranged for a friend to be his surrogate in court, it was a lesson still to be learned, and learned again.

In late September, Nelson Rockefeller, newly arrived at the leafy Hanover campus, picked up a copy of the student newspaper, *The Dartmouth,* and read the following welcome to the freshman class:

> You have come to a college that is distinct, unique and without parallel. It is an institution wherein you will get four years of "college" in its most concentrated form—it offers you no women, very little wine, and no song but of its own brewing. It offers you nothing of the maze of cosmopolitan things, nothing of those gay and worldly things which mean so much to life in other colleges. In winter it is raw, windy, and the air is filled with snow; in spring it is slushy and mushy . . .

Having laid out this appetizing prospect, the newspaper went on to describe what Dartmouth *did* offer: "that vague and precious thing called 'Hanover atmosphere' . . . the opportunity to make friends—friends which have their equal nowhere else."

To be sure, Dartmouth offered more than hail-fellow-well-met camaraderie. Under Hopkins' iron rule, the school had attained a first-class, albeit somewhat unorthodox, academic reputation; unlike other Ivy League schools, Dartmouth discouraged faculty research, preferring that its instructors concentrate on the classroom.

Still, it was not scholarship for which the college was best known. The hallmarks of the Dartmouth experience were the three F's: fellowship, fraternities, and football. The latter was the fulcrum for nearly all of campus life from September to the Christmas break, with the high point the annual Harvard-Dartmouth tussle, when nearly the entire school descended on Boston for the match and the pregame black-tie ball at the Copley Plaza Hotel.

And there was always the lure of the outdoors. The Dartmouth Outing Club maintained a network of cabins and trails in the nearby White Mountains, to which students would repair on weekends—when there was precious little else to do in isolated Hanover. More freshmen signed up for the Outing Club than for any other campus organization.

Not that Dartmouth men were immune to less wholesome pursuits. They regularly slipped across the Connecticut River to nearby Norwich, Vermont, to patronize the local bootlegger, Joe Kilmer. It was said that Kilmer and Hopkins had a gentleman's agreement that as long as Kilmer sold the students good liquor and not rotgut Hopkins would refrain from prosecuting him. And for those in need of "companionship," there was the so-called college whore, who would make the rounds of the dormitories plying her trade.

Such comforts, however, did little to mitigate the sense of complete isolation that Dartmouth men felt. Small wonder, then, that the high points of the school year were the occasions when that isolation was breached: the Harvard-Dartmouth game, with its attendant Boston revelries, and the annual snow-and-ice extravaganza known as Winter Carnival. Eligible young women from throughout the Northeast descended on Hanover for the festivities, which included a carnival ball, skating and skiing races and exhibitions, fraternity dances, and a grand torchlight parade presided over by the Queen of the Snows. Much rye was consumed at the carnival, and many romances initiated, and even consummated.

When this winter idyll had run its course Dartmouth resumed its essential character: a place of pristine charm, of hardy fellowship and high spirits, where academia was perennially taking a back seat to more outgoing pursuits. It would not be a place to which young Nelson Rockefeller would have a great deal of difficulty adjusting.

Less than a week after their arrival, the 600-man class of 1930 was subjected to its first Dartmouth ritual: the annual freshman-sophomore rush. Gathering on the quadrangle, the two classes contended for possession of two footballs. The clash vaguely resembled a rugby scrum, but with looser rules—and 1,200 players. "Sweating and pushing," *The Dartmouth* reported, "the 1930 men tried to dislodge the two balls from enemy territory. . . . Whistles were heard in the midst of the panting mass." At the center of the panting mass, shirt torn, face encrusted with dirt, was Nelson Rockefeller.

Nelson, in fact, was the mastermind behind the freshman strategy. "He had us organized," recalls classmate Francis Horn. "I was way over on the left side, coming like this"—he makes a thrusting move with his hand—"and there was another group all the way on the right. And Nelson took a third group right up the center." The strategy worked: the freshmen recovered both balls and prevailed.

For the first, but hardly the last time, Nelson eagerly demonstrated that he could mix it up with the best of his fellows. It was as though he wanted to instantly erase, with his sweat, any impression his classmates had that he might hold himself above them. Of course, he *was* a special case; Nelson gave ample proof of that, as soon as he arrived, by calling on President Hopkins (needless to say, everyday freshmen did not have audiences with the president).

But the great leveler—for Nelson as well as for the rest of the wide-eyed newcomers—was the mountain of indignities traditionally heaped on Dartmouth freshmen by their betters, the sophomores. The first of these was the annual ritual known as Delta Alpha, in which Nelson and his classmates paraded around in baby costumes—giant diapers, bonnets, and rattles—before Dartmouth's opening football game against the hapless Norwich College.

To set themselves apart for the rest of the year, the freshmen were compelled to wear green beanies. They were also expected to adhere to a plethora of other rules about their dress and comportment. Among them: "No knickers or golf socks will be tolerated on freshmen." "Keep off the grass. Freshmen may only leave the paths when accompanied by an upperclassman."

At every turn, Nelson found himself beset by some arcane hazing ritual. Just as he would settle in for the evening, he would be aroused by sophomore shouts of "Class of '30 out—'30 out!" and be forced to file into the hallway.

Then he and his fellow freshmen would have to entertain the upperclassmen—singing songs, telling jokes, performing stunts. When the entertainment met with the sophomores' disapproval—and it invariably did—Nelson and the others were whacked on their backsides with wooden paddles.

If a sophomore in his dormitory needed some furniture moved, or his rugs beaten, Nelson and his classmates would be called upon to perform the service. Other freshmen soon noticed that Nelson was summoned more often than they were. No sophomore, it seemed, could resist having a Rockefeller at his beck and call, ready to perform the most menial task.

Nelson bore all this with his usual good cheer—although he complained to his parents about the lack of sleep ("I haven't had six hours for the last three days"). Perhaps it was his weariness with the hazing that led him, after just a few weeks at Hanover, to ask Junior and Abby if it would be okay to leave the campus during the weekends. Possibly he could go to Boston, and possibly even back to Pocantico. His parents, though, wouldn't hear of it. Replied Abby, "It would make a very bad impression on the college, both faculty and students, to have you spend two Sundays away in the first month that you are there. The boys who cannot afford to go will feel restless and envious and the professors will not feel that you are taking your work very seriously."

So Nelson stayed, and endured.

Even though Nelson shared in the torments of freshman hazing, he managed to escape certain other privations. Other, less well-off freshmen settled into Dartmouth's older, tumbledown dormitories. But Nelson secured lodgings at Hitchcock, the school's most expensive and (comparatively speaking) most luxurious dorm. The rooms at Hitchcock, in fact, were actually suites, consisting of one or two substantial bedrooms and a large living room with a fireplace.

For all their spaciousness, the rooms at Hitchcock were unfurnished—as were all the other dormitory rooms at Dartmouth back then. This meant a brisk business for the local furniture stores. Nelson, however, had his furnishings shipped over from Pocantico. Among other items, Abby sent him Chinese carpets to be laid in front of the fireplace.

Nelson shared his accommodations with three other boys. Two were his old buddies from Lincoln, Shelly Stark and Ted Martin. The other was a new acquaintance, John French. French's presence there was hardly accidental. The groundwork for it had been meticulously laid by Abby months before her son arrived at Hanover.

John was the son of Mary M. Billings French, a kindred socialite with whom Abby served on the board of the YWCA. No sooner had the two grandes dames determined that both their sons were entering Dartmouth than they began plotting, with the calculation of Old World matchmakers, to bring the two boys together. That summer Abby invited the Frenches to spend some time at Pocantico, and Nelson and John got along well enough, despite the vast differences in their personalities. Quiet, thoughtful, and studious, French was the utter antithesis of his rambunctious new friend. But that seemed exactly what lay behind Abby's maneuvers: she was counting on young French to mute Nelson's exuberance and maybe even inculcate some better study habits.

When Nelson and John got through their first few months at Hitchcock in relative harmony, Abby was immensely pleased, but her satisfaction was tempered by the knowledge that Stark and Martin were still around. For one reason or another, she felt that her son's Lincoln School friends were not suitable companions now that Nelson was a college man. She began dropping not so subtle hints that perhaps Nelson and John should find other lodgings of their own. "The way will come for you to room together, just wait," she ventured to her son. "I have quite a strong feeling that Ted and Shelly would be quite as happy either together or with some older boys whom they may choose."

Nelson, ever eager to please his mother, readily took the hint. By the second semester, he and John French had moved to new accommodations at Hitchcock, leaving Stark and Martin to find other roommates.*

"There is only one thing that I want to urge you to do," Abby told Nelson on the eve of his departure for Dartmouth. "And that is to start right in from the very first day to study. If you don't get behind in your lessons I am sure that everything will go well with you."

Chastened by his brinkmanship at Lincoln, and goaded by John French's example, Nelson followed his mother's advice. Arising at 7 every morning, he would hit the books from 8 to 10 A.M., and again in the evening after an early supper, until about 9. Spelling was as big a bugaboo as ever; to appease his anxious father, Nelson would underline, in his letters home, all the words he wasn't certain about, and promise to look them up later. (The trouble was that most of the words that were misspelled hadn't been underlined by Nelson.)

Nelson relied on more than just study habits to see him through. From the outset, he worked assiduously at ingratiating himself with his teachers. He talked in early October about becoming better acquainted with his physics professor: "As soon as we get well started, I'm going around to see him some

* Martin would leave Dartmouth after his freshman year to attend Harvard. As for Stark, he and Nelson drifted apart, although they played on the college soccer team together. But the two youths would remain linked in a way that Stark would only learn about years later, upon going through his father's papers: Junior, it seems, paid for Stark's Dartmouth tuition. Stark's father, an attorney, was squeezed financially, and had written Junior for help. Junior gave it, albeit grudgingly, complaining—based on what Nelson was telling him—that young Stark wasn't doing enough to help himself. Source: Stark interview; Junior letter to Otis Caldwell, April 10, 1929, JDR Jr. Educational Interests Box 61, RAC.

evening," he confided to his parents. "You see, my idea has been to get to know the teachers as soon as possible. . . . I felt I would get more out of the courses if there was more of a personal relationship between the teacher and I." The freshman Nelson arranged to dine not only with the professors but with the professors' families—impressing faculty wives with, among other things, his eagerness to help with the dishes. As one of his professors put it, "He was a real smoothie."

Whether by dint of his study habits or his charm, Nelson managed to obtain more than acceptable grades that first semester. His parents, needless to say, were overjoyed. "We are still rejoicing over the good marks that you made in your exams," Abby wrote him in late October, wiring her secretary to send him "a box of good things from New York" as a reward. At the same time, as mothers are wont to do, she chided him for missing meals: "No engine can continue to run at high pressure unless regularly stoked."

That Nelson was running at high pressure, there was little doubt—and not simply because of his attention to schoolwork. In his first months at Dartmouth, he signed on for a full round of extracurricular activities. Indulging his fascination with photography, he joined the Camera Club and the staff of the college's picture magazine, *The Pictorial.* He tried out for, and made, the soccer team. He joined the school's Chapel Committee, critiquing the Sunday services and making suggestions for improving them. And he became chairman of the freshman "informals," a weekly gathering for songs, speeches, and entertainment. The informals gave Nelson his first taste of actually *running* something in public on his own. He fully savored the experience. "I've lost my feeling of incompetency," he told his parents, "of not being able to handle a job without relying on someone else. In other words, if something has to be done . . . I feel that I'm fully capable of doing it."

The informals also offered him his first exposure to public speaking. "I'm losing my fear of standing up before a crowd and saying what I've got to say, for I have to preside," he advised his parents.

The spring brought the freshman year's grandest distraction, the fraternity rushes. The same upperclassmen who had so sadistically tormented the freshmen just a few months earlier were now eagerly vying for their friendship, crowding into their rooms, imploring them to attend the fraternities' open houses.

For Nelson, who found himself besieged by as many as fifteen callers in a single evening, the fraternity rush period was a vexatious time. His parents—Abby in particular—were pushing him to join a fraternity. But the endless visits by upperclassmen, the deluge of open-house invitations, posed a worrisome threat to his newfound study habits. John French, who perhaps because of his proximity to Nelson encountered a similar volume of solicitations, was equally unsettled. Comparing notes one day, they decided to vent their discomfort in a letter to *The Dartmouth.*

Their letter pleaded for restraint in the open houses and in the incessant visits to freshman dorms. "The way it is now, the upperclassmen drop in any time and stay for indefinite periods. . . . Could not one or maybe two evenings a week, say from 8 to 9, be set aside for these visits?" And, concluding on a skeptical note, French and Nelson suggested that since no plan "eliminating the enormous wastage of time involved" had been found, "does it not point out that some radical defect exists in the fraternity system?"

The missive created a predictable stir not only on the campus but well beyond it; the *New York Herald Tribune,* pouncing on a Rockefeller tidbit, ran an item on Nelson's grievances. Given the influence and irascibility of fraternities at Dartmouth, the controversy would have been expected to permanently mark Nelson and French for ostracism. But, in fact, nothing of the sort occurred. The suitors continued to call, and soon Nelson found himself bowing to the inevitable and, despite his misgivings, thoroughly enjoying the ritual. "Tonight I am going to the following fraternities—Alpha Delta Phi, Psi Upsilon and Sigma Alpha," he told his parents. "I'm really getting to know an awful lot of fellows going around this way and if it didn't take up so much time it would be great."

In the end, Nelson and John French, erstwhile critics of the fraternity system, pledged with the toniest, most exclusive fraternity of them all, Psi Upsilon. The standouts of the class—the go-getters, those destined to be president of the class or editor of the newspaper or captain of the football team—invariably were members of Psi U.

The talk of a "radical defect" now forgotten, Nelson Rockefeller settled into his proper place in the campus establishment.

In dress and manner, Nelson was virtually indistinguishable from the other 2,000-odd students in Hanover. He wore the ubiquitous Dartmouth garb of the day: green wool crew-neck sweater, corduroy trousers, and, when the winter chill set in, plaid ski jacket and knit ski cap. If anything, Nelson seemed determined to dress down, even on those occasions when fancier attire was the rule. At Dartmouth concerts, for instance—where the likes of Sergei Rachmaninoff or Pablo Casals would perform—formal wear was expected. "But not Nelson," relates Horn. "I remember him appearing in the usual dirty corduroys and sweater, with the corduroys all too obviously torn. He wore the same sweater and the same corduroys for four years, I'm sure."

As was the case at Lincoln, Nelson was perennially hard up for cash. Junior provided him with $1,500 a year for school expenses—a decent but hardly extravagant sum for a Dartmouth undergraduate in the 1920s. (The scuttlebutt at the school was that Junior had asked Hopkins what a respectable allowance would be. When Hopkins told him, Junior said, "Well, I'll give Nelson half that.") Just as he did at Lincoln, Nelson would hustle his classmates for the odd bit of change. "He was always good for the dough," one lender remarked. And every now and then he would amuse his classmates with some bizarre exercise in petty thrift, such as when he purchased his fraternity picture; told that he could have it framed for fifty cents more, he bought it unframed, figuring he could frame it himself for less.

So squeezed was Nelson that he even briefly held down a job as a waiter in one of the boardinghouses where Dartmouth upperclassmen customarily took their meals. Nelson gave the job up after it was gently pointed out to him that he might be denying employment to someone a bit more needy.

Yet Nelson from time to time also indulged in some acts of extravagance—acts that, in their own way, were outgrowths of his exuberant personality. Eager to pursue his hobby of photography, he purchased the finest camera equipment. And once, when Laurance came to visit one snowy weekend, Nelson met him at the train station with a horse-drawn sleigh.

It wasn't long before Nelson's classmates recognized that he was anything but an effete aristocrat. A fraternity brother, Lee Chilcote, once challenged Nelson to a wrestling match in the living room of Psi U house. Chilcote, a two-time city high school champion back in Cleveland, thought he would have an easy time. "But," he recalls, "I could not pin Nelson Rockefeller. It was an even match; neither one of us won. I'll tell you, he was tough."

Nelson plunged with gusto into the manly, outdoorsy activities that defined the Dartmouth experience. As a member of the Outing Club, he braved high winds and numbing cold in ascents of the White Mountains, huddling with his fellow climbers for shelter in the club's cabins. A fellow Camera Club member, Robert Keene, remembers Nelson "shooting during a blizzard when we were climbing up Mount Washington one time, when we were all pretty much hanging by our toenails." One spring, he awed his hiking companions by retrieving some duck hawk eggs from a mountain ledge, hanging from a tree to accomplish the feat, seemingly unfazed by the thousand-foot drop beneath him.

And always, there was that air of bouncy, irrepressible boyishness about him, that sense, in the words of one classmate, that "he majored in having a good time." And when the time came around, in the spring of his sophomore year, for a brawl with the freshmen, Nelson was once again in the front line. He managed to hold off the freshman charge by grabbing a fire hose and dousing the attackers; the battle escalated after that, to the point that the Hanover police had to be called to restore order. Nelson came away from the scramble proudly sporting a black eye. The tussle, and Nelson's role in it, made the Boston newspapers: "John D., Jr., Son Mauled in Fight," read the *Boston Herald*'s headline.

He also pitched in when the campus was confronted with a far graver matter a few months earlier. A brutal flood had raged through the nearby town of White River Junction in early November, with the White and Connecticut rivers rising more than thirty feet in just twelve hours. The deluge ripped down huge steel bridges, devastated countless homes, and took its toll in human lives. Heeding an American Red Cross appeal, Dartmouth dispatched over 800 students to the besieged town to clean up, salvage, and restore.

Nelson was one of the first to board the Boston & Maine Railroad flatcars bound for White River Junction. For two days he shoveled mud out of homes, buried the carcasses of animals swept along by the raging tide, and pushed wheelbarrows laden with river silt and gravel cleared from the town's streets.

And once again the media latched on to the story. Photographers and newsreel cameramen rushed to the town to catch the rescue effort—and get a shot of a young Rockefeller joining in. "Once they caught sight of Nelson," remembers his classmate Charles Widmayer, "he was all they focused on."

Yet for all the ways that Nelson exemplified the Dartmouth man, there were other aspects that broke with the norm. He did not partake of the expected vices—smoking cigarettes and drinking Joe Kilmer's bootleg rye. He abstained from the raunchy scene at Hanover's sole movie theater, the Nugget, where students spiced up the current silent attraction by interjecting filthy dialogue and asides and hurling peanuts at the screen. For all his boisterousness, says fraternity brother Chilcote, "Nelson was never raucous. He was never out of order."

Indeed, there were times when Nelson could even have been described as prissy. He and French installed flower boxes outside their dormitory windows. French thought the flowers would kill any chances they had of getting into a fraternity; instead, the flower boxes became a Dartmouth fad.

Following his family's best Baptist tradition, Nelson landed a position teaching Sunday school at the White Church on the campus. His class consisted of eight- to ten-year-old girls. Each Sunday, Nelson would walk after class through the campus, holding hands with his charges—to the accompaniment of whistles and catcalls from his Dartmouth classmates.

Nelson also stood aloof from the football mania that besieged the college each autumn. On the weekends when the Dartmouth team went on the road, Nelson was one of the few souls left on the campus; he would go for walks in the woods or join a few other boys for hikes to the Outing Club cabins in the mountains.

There was, of course, one other important way in which Nelson set himself apart from his peers: the cultivation of his special relationship with President Hopkins. "Hopkins wasn't too accessible to undergraduates," notes Widmayer, who went on to write a book on the Hopkins years. "He got together with them occasionally, but, on the whole, he was kind of a revered figure that students looked up to." Access, however, was never a problem for Nelson. Photographing a baseball game from atop the grandstand one Saturday afternoon, Nelson spotted Hopkins walking by and hailed him. Hopkins clambered up, and for the next two hours he sat with Nelson, sharing peanuts, telling stories, and watching the game. The president would reciprocate such gestures by inviting Nelson to dinner parties at his home; Nelson would usually be the only student present.

Not surprisingly, Hopkins would write to Junior of his son's progress in the rosiest of terms. "A man becomes a priceless member of the college who shows the disposition and the capacity to think things out himself," Hopkins advised Junior at the end of Nelson's freshman year. "It is a great gratification to me that Nelson is so definitely one of this sort."

Nelson's special status was a fact of life at Dartmouth. For all his efforts to come off as just an ordinary guy, the royal aura still clung to him. Alone among the student body, he was a public figure.

Struggling to evade the publicity, which he rightly feared would bring down his father's wrath, Nelson turned to John French for help. As a result, French served as a human shield for Nelson for the rest of their time at Dartmouth. "Johnny French was assigned to watch out that Nelson not be photographed by news photographers," relates Keene, an aspiring news photographer himself. "He'd jump in the way if he saw it happening. He spoiled many pictures of Nelson."

As a campus celebrity, Nelson inevitably attracted a coterie of classmates mesmerized by the Rockefeller name and the storied fortune. "I felt sorry for Nelson," says classmate James Wiggin. "There were always a lot of people hanging around him, associating with him, because he had money." The hangers-on ranged from an obscure outcast (he belonged to no fraternity) named Victor Borella, who had dropped out of school for a while to earn a living, to the confident, well-connected Bob Bottome, an incipient Big Man on Campus himself.

They could be described as his friends, except that the friendship lacked any real element of intimacy. Rather, the relationship seemed thoroughly utilitarian on both sides: for varying reasons, they were useful people for him to know, because of what they could do for him in his myriad campus activities, just as he would be, now and in the future, useful for them.

Those who knew him well at Dartmouth question whether he really had friends there, with the possible exception of John French. Bill Alton, who at Nelson's behest followed him to Dartmouth, declines to characterize himself as a friend, and doubts that anyone else would fit that description either. "Because to be a friend, you're someone that he would ask out just to be with," says Alton. "And Nelson didn't do that. I doubt if he ever had a real friend. Even then his life was dedicated to moving ahead, and he always had something in the back of his mind, he always had a purpose. And he would tuck people away, like a squirrel would hide nuts, to come back to them at some later time." He tucked away Borella, and Bottome, and numerous others whom he met at Dartmouth. They would all come to serve his purposes in the years to come.

As he moved through his second year at Dartmouth, Nelson continued to shine academically. His grade point average in the first semester soared to 3.75, putting him in the top 3 percent of his class. Junior and Abby got the good news directly from President Hopkins. An ecstatic Abby wrote Nelson that she "really and truly nearly shed tears of joy" when she heard. "Of course," she said, "I have always realized that you had a good mind but I feared (a little) that you might never, or at least for some time, know what you could do with it and that you might not feel the need of training and disciplining it by hard study."

Nonetheless, fretful mother that she was, she couldn't help worrying that perhaps he was driving himself too hard. One letter from her that spring was particularly shrill: "Please! Please! Take care of yourself! Go to bed early! Get lots of exercise! Good food! Fresh air! Cut out evening committees! Don't talk to too many boys! You probably know what most of them think by this time anyway!"

Abby had some reason for concern; her son's schedule was overloaded, as usual. There was lots of soccer: Nelson not only challenged for a starting berth on the Dartmouth team but captained the class of '30 squad in the college's interclass tournament. There was his photography: making still lifes and scenic shots his specialty, he took charge of the art pictures at *The Pictorial*. And, in the spring, he ran for, and was elected, vice president of the sophomore class.

But somehow, Nelson managed to juggle it all, and produce exemplary grades to boot. After years of coasting, he seemed to be finally measuring up to his parents' vaulting expectations.

His performance was, to some extent, an act of contrition. The previous summer he had run seriously afoul of his father on the critical issue of his accounts. It seems that he had run up a bill of $80 for new photographic equipment and somehow had forgotten to tell Junior about it. Just as was the case the previous summer, his memory was conveniently restored as soon as he boarded a steamer bound for a European vacation.

Nelson drafted a letter to Junior while en route. The letter's misspellings may well have exasperated Junior as much as his son's confessions.

> Dear Pa,
>
> This is just a little note to tell you something which I wanted to tell you while we were on the boat, but found very difficult to do so. As you can guess it deals with accounts.
>
> I have a bill at "Herbert & Hughstons" for approximately eighty dollars.

I didn't tell you of it before because—well I guess you can see why. But I knew I should tell you and I kept putting it off, until now I have to use this roundabout way. It is a bill that has been accumulating for photographic stuff, including a camera. I swaped in two camaras and got two other ones of much more sutable models. I was unable to pay for one, but not the other, therefore I have this bill left over. It also covers most of my outfit for the summar.

All my connections with accounting and accounts have been discraceful so far. I have said I was going to improve but have only gotten worse. I appologise which does no good I know and now I give you my word as a gentilman that you will have no more trouble with me in that line. You may be doubious about this statement and I'll admit it sounds improbable, but you shall see.

Again I bet your pardon for all the time I have wasted for you.

Your loving son,
Nelson

Junior's response was to blame himself for Nelson's reluctance to come forward. "My chief regret was that my attitude in our several talks was apparently such as to make you hesitate to tell me what you wrote," he advised his son. "Forgive me for letting my temporary disappointment so show in my manner as to chill you and hold you aloof." Immensely relieved, Nelson dashed off a note to his father from the Hotel Bristol in Berlin that fairly overflowed with self-flagellating remorse.

. . . I feel more ashamed than ever about not having told you about my other expenditures. It was darn nice of you to give me an ally of escape by saying it was your attitude, but I'm afraid it's not that, but my cowerdness. I've been trying to fight that in myself for quite a while now, but every once and a while just when I get in a tight place I do the easy thing like a coward instead of being a man. It's worried me quite a bit, but I'm still fighting it.

As to your attitude in the situation, I think you were really over lenient, as I deserve no sympathy under the conditions . . .

You know I really don't think I deserve any credit for my change in attitude toward my work during the last two years. I think rather I should be condemed for not coming round to a sensible viewpoint sooner and having wasted so much of my time and your energy and money in bringing me to the right way of thinking. And if you looked a little further into the situation with a broader vision, one would clearly see that any good traights or desirable characteristics that we may have are not the results of our own achievements. But the credit should be laided to your and mother's strivings and uncompairable example of living. You know the old saying, "Like father, like son." . . .

His abject apologies and undertakings notwithstanding, Nelson lapsed again when he returned to Dartmouth in the fall. Once more, he dispatched a groveling note to Junior. "I think this time I've learned a lesson, not only in accounting, that I will never forget," Nelson wrote. "I feel more strongly than ever now your generosity and bigness of spirit. I'm afraid I did not deserve the generous treatment with which you delt with me, but I shall try to make myself worthy of it in the future. I trust that this time actions will speak louder than words . . ."

They didn't. Three weeks later Abby told Nelson that a notice had just come from the bank that he had overdrawn his account by $10, and she had made good on the shortfall herself. She hadn't mentioned the incident to his father, she said, "because I know that it would disappoint and grieve him."

It was the old pattern of Nelson's childhood, writ larger now. Nelson would transgress, apologize, promise never to make the same mistake again—and then make it. Junior no doubt had long since come to see the value of Nelson's promises, but he seemed to have an infinite capacity for swallowing them. The sincerity, the self-abnegation, and, above all, the transparently fawning quality in Nelson's prose appeared to weave a certain spell on Junior. Once again, Nelson displayed an ineffable knack for playing to his father.

In his junior year at Dartmouth, Nelson took some other steps that were bound to ingratiate him with his father. He switched his major from political science (the favorite of his mother, no doubt in memory of the late Senator Aldrich) to economics, a more practical specialty for a Rockefeller scion. And, for his honors thesis in economics, he chose for a subject none other than the formation and growth of the Standard Oil Company, under the farsighted leadership of John D. Rockefeller, Sr.

Nelson asked his father if it might be possible to interview the old man—by that time a skeletal figure beloved of the newsreels for his jovial dispensing of dimes to one and all. "I was thinking the other day that Grandfather has never mentioned the Company to us, nor has he ever told us anything about his stupendous work in organizing the Company and leading it for so many years," Nelson told Junior. A session with his grandfather, he said, "would be an outstanding and unforgettable experience in our lives."

Delighted with Nelson's interest, Junior promised to take the matter up with the elder Rockefeller. In the meantime, he sent him an unpublished manuscript of a biography of Senior by W. O. Inglis. The adulatory, family-commissioned manuscript was gratefully received and devoured by Nelson. "It was thrilling!" he enthused to his father. "For the first time I felt that I really knew Grandfather a little—got a glimpse into the power and grandeur of his life. . . . I sincerely feel that I got more out of reading that book than I did out of any other course last semester."

Nelson never did get to interview his grandfather. The old man apparently had no desire to rehash his life and times, even for a blood relative. But with the Inglis material as his primary source, Nelson proceeded to fashion a thesis that was bound to bring contented smiles to the faces of both father and grandfather. The paper was nothing less than a spirited, point-by-point defense of the elder Rockefeller's business tactics and, for the most part, an unalloyed glorification of the Standard Oil Company.

Dismissing as "a hardy fiction" the charge that the company forced out its competitors, Nelson maintained that none of them were coerced into selling out to Standard Oil. "These companies," he asserted, "were treated with extreme fairness and in many cases with generosity." Similarly, he treated as a gross canard the idea that Standard gained its monopoly power "through local price discrimination, bogus independents and espionage." Never, he insisted, did the company do anything unlawful.

The Standard Oil that Nelson saw was the Standard Oil as his grandfather wanted it to be seen: a super-efficient engine of economic growth that brought order to the primitive, chaotic petroleum business. True, the Standard monopoly produced unnaturally high oil prices—but without those high prices "the industry most likely would not have developed nearly as fast."

Nelson's thesis was also a celebration of John D. Rockefeller's homely virtues—those very same virtues that Nelson had been taught to prize since his earliest days. He unfurled examples of his grandfather's abhorrence of waste, his painstaking attention to detail, his unwavering vision; when a fire broke out in one of his refineries, Nelson related, and others dashed around to battle the flames, "Mr. Rockefeller could be seen with paper and pencil, making plans for the rebuilding.

"You may wonder why so much time has been devoted to such unimportant details," Nelson wrote. "But it is these little things on the inside of the Company which, when put together, mount up so far." The lines could have been lifted verbatim from one of Junior's lectures.

The thesis, despite many misspellings, was given an A.

Nelson's junior year was a dizzying swirl. He was elected to Green Key, an honor society whose many functions included ushering at football games and arranging for the Winter Carnival entertainment. He bounded around Hanover taking photographs for *The Pictorial.* He choreographed an Outing Club photo exhibit (featuring many of his own pictures) at Winter Carnival. He finally won a starting job (and a letter) on the soccer team, excelling at left fullback.

An unofficial member of the campus aristocracy since the day he arrived at Dartmouth, Nelson was officially certified as such by the time his junior year was over. He was tapped to be a member of Casque & Gauntlet, an honor society that was the Dartmouth equivalent—in prestige if not in mystique—of Yale's Skull and Bones.

Casque & Gauntlet maintained its own residence hall, and Nelson moved there in his senior year. But he didn't desert John French: his old roommate had also been tapped by C&G.

French, in fact, had broken through his shyness and emerged as an even bigger man on campus than Nelson. He was elected editor of *The Dartmouth,* and at the end of his junior year he was also elected president of Palaeopitus, the senior class's governing committee. Nelson had been elected to one of the twelve positions on Palaeopitus as well; that in itself was considered a singular achievement. "To be elected to Palaeopitus was *the* honor at Dartmouth," notes Widmayer. French had simply gone Nelson one better.

As Nelson and French went through school together, their friendship became tinged with a certain sense of rivalry. Nelson, who would get up as early as five in the morning to hit the books, was intensely jealous of his roommate's seemingly effortless academic success. "He never went to class and he never studied," Nelson would remark years later. "He read Charles Beard's *The Rise of American Civilization* the night before the exam and got an 'A.' " Nelson, for his part, took credit for French's emergence as a campus figure. "I really carried him socially in college," Nelson would remark years later.

French's junior year triumphs may have made the sting of Nelson's one great setback that year that much more painful. In March, Nelson announced he was running for the class presidency. It was a four-way race; the other candidates were Bob Bottome, Roland Booma, and Alden Smith. (French ran for class secretary.) Nothing much is known about the campaign, except the outcome. Nelson lost to Booma, the son of a shoe worker.

Looking back, some of Nelson's classmates say a certain hidden resentment of Nelson may have figured in his defeat. "People said to themselves, 'Why should I vote for someone who has so much money?' " recalls Chilcote. Nelson's chumminess with President Hopkins and his occasional standoffishness may not have sat well with the electorate either.

The junior class didn't know it at the time, but they would soon be given one more reason to resent Nelson Rockefeller. In early April, Hopkins unveiled another of his innovations: the senior fellowship program. The five fellows, handpicked by the president, would be given absolute freedom to study whatever they pleased in their senior year. These senior fellows need not worry about exams, or grades, or attendance: all those strictures would be lifted. The fellows' graduation would be guaranteed. They would not even have to pay tuition. Hopkins regarded the program as "the capstone of our honors work."

Two months later the names of the lucky five were announced. One of the five was John French. Another was Nelson Rockefeller.

Nelson's selection raised plenty of eyebrows, even among students who knew and admired him. "We all felt that Rockefeller got this because he was Rockefeller," says Francis Horn. "Although he was a good student, it was felt that there was a good deal of influence behind the choice." And Widmayer notes that "if they had really picked the very best economics student, I don't think Nelson would have been it." Furthermore, his nonscholastic activities—soccer, the Outing Club, *The Pictorial*—while impressive, were hardly extraordinary.

The truly suspicious might have seen a bit of quid pro quo behind the choice of Nelson. After all, Dartmouth's honors program had been financed by a $1.5 million grant from the Rockefeller-funded General Education Board and an "anonymous donor"; the anonymous donor turned out to be John D. Rockefeller, Jr. But that crass a trade-off would have been unthinkable on the part of the high-minded Hopkins, and it is unlikely that Junior would have stood still for it either.

What is more probable is that Hopkins *was* guilty of favoritism, but for somewhat more elevated reasons. As Widmayer, his biographer, sees it, Hopkins may well have regarded the senior fellowship as a vital formative experience for Nelson, encouraging self-reliance while exposing him to a broader range of subjects than his economics major allowed. True, many students would have benefited from such an experience. But Nelson's special status in the world made it particularly compelling that *he* benefit from it.

Hopkins insisted, in a letter to Junior, that Nelson's selection was a popular one: "The common remark of the undergraduates, in their own vernacular, has been: 'Nelson rates it and ought to have it.' " And, apparently seeking to justify his choice, the normally laconic Dartmouth president waxed effusive about Nelson's sterling qualities. "He embodies in his own person," Hopkins said, "the attitude and the spirit which we are trying to inculcate into the college as a whole."

Six

ARTS AND CRAFT

But before he began his senior fellowship year, Nelson embarked on a much different sort of formative exercise.

Along with brother Laurance, he shipped out for the summer on the hospital ship *Maravan,* bound for the farthest reaches of Labrador. The vessel set sail each year under the command of Sir Wilfred Grenfell, a British medical missionary who strived to bring modern medicine—and Christian piety—to the Eskimos and other dwellers of those remote regions. Grenfell had long been urging Junior, one of his prime backers, to send a son or two on one of the *Maravan*'s expeditions. After John demurred, the opportunity, such as it was, fell to the two younger boys.

The trip—which would be plagued by a series of calamities and ultimately cut short by an attack of appendicitis that befell Laurance—gave Nelson a firsthand view of Eskimo life. Far from broadening his horizons, his experience with the Eskimos left him unmoved and unimpressed. "They just sit around and go fishing when the spirit moves them," he wrote home. "Why, if any of them were half-way ambitious he could make some money."

Upon his return to Hanover, Nelson made known what his prime area of concentration would be during his freewheeling year as a senior fellow. The faculty expected something in economics, or possibly in his earlier major, political science. But Nelson had a surprise for them.

He would spend the year studying art.

Unorthodox though it may have been, his decision was not totally out of the blue. At Dartmouth, Nelson's artistic inclinations had been foreshadowed by his interest in photography, particularly the arty, dreamy photos of his that appeared in school publications. And under the influence of his mother, a world-class collector of Impressionist and Post-Impressionist art, he had taken to frequenting New York galleries during his intersession period.

A visit during Christmas break in his sophomore year to Abby's favorite gallery, the Downtown Gallery, turned out to be a seminal event. "I feel as if I had been introduced to a new world of beauty," Nelson wrote his mother, "and for the first time I think I have really been able to appreciate and understand pictures, even though only a little bit. I hope to continue this when I am in New York and maybe do a tiny bit of collecting myself."

(Actually, the collecting bug bit him much earlier. When he was seven and a half he wrote the following in one of his composition books: "I would like to have the Sistine Madonna. I would hang it in my dining room. I would not sell it for all the money in the world. I would not give it to the Museum. It is one of the most wonderful paintings that Raphaele painted.")

Abby was delighted by Nelson's enthusiasm. "We could have such good times going about together," she told him, in the course of sending him a Daumier lithograph from Paris. "And if you start to cultivate your taste and eye so young, you ought to be very good at it by the time you can afford to collect much."

Part of the appeal of art for Nelson was, no doubt, the special bond it forged between mother and son. Just as Abby bounded about the great museums of Europe in the company of her connoisseur father, so now could the young Nelson, namesake of the senator, share in her passion for such moderns as Braque and Matisse.

For someone as dyslexic as Nelson, art also opened a world immune to the treachery of words and sentences. It was a world of form and light, of bumps and shadows, and no great literacy was needed to dwell happily within it.

Unlike any other subject he encountered in school, art came easily and instinctively. In one of his junior year courses, the students were given a book of 125 masterpieces, showing two copies of each painting: one was the original, and the other a version that had been altered in some subtle way—a tree missing here, an arm held differently there. The students were asked to pick out the originals, and Nelson easily outscored the rest of the class. In fact, he proudly informed Abby, "I ranked in the exceptional group of all those who have taken the test throughout the country."

Nelson's concentration on art fortuitously coincided with the opening of the Dartmouth art department's commodious new building, Carpenter Hall. Aside from ample classroom space, Carpenter offered studios where both students and visiting artist/lecturers could work, a spacious top-floor gallery, and an expansive library.

Nelson rarely left the confines of Carpenter. Not only did he attend classes but he sought, and got, special tutoring from the faculty. Eager to learn about the history of art and architecture, he devoured (in spite of his dyslexia) the books his tutors recommended. "We started with the pyramids—Nelson was very interested in the pyramids—and went on from there," remembers one of his teachers, Churchill Lathrop. "He'd come into my office with some books on early medieval art, and we'd discuss them, and then I'd tell him about a very fine book about Romanesque art. A few days later, he'd be back to discuss that one."

When Nelson wasn't reading about art and talking about it, he was trying his hand at making it. In Carpenter's new studios he drew, painted, sculptured with clay, and labored at an etching press. While Nelson knew that his efforts were barely more than workmanlike, he recognized that that wasn't the point. As he would later expound, "It is unbelievable how such crude attempts can increase one's understanding of paintings."

So absorbed was Nelson in his artistic milieu that he began to openly toy with the idea of becoming an architect. Abby sought to gently discourage him: "I am glad if you feel absolutely sure," she said, "but there are lots of things to think over." A Rockefeller, she delicately hinted, might be expected to fulfill a somewhat higher calling. Once again, Nelson bowed under the weight of his family's expectations. "With the responsibilities the family had," he later explained, "I didn't see how I could justify giving way to a personal whim."

Nelson's senior year was not entirely taken up with the cultivation of his artistic sensibilities. For the first time, he set out to build his own little fiefdoms—domains in which his entrepreneurial drive began to come to the fore.

One of these fiefdoms was *The Pictorial,* the photo magazine for which Nelson had toiled since his freshman year. Nelson was one of the contenders for the job of editor-in-chief; the other was Kirt Meyer, who specialized in shooting athletic events and was regarded as a more proficient lensman. "Kirt Meyer should have been made the editor," says Eugene Zagat, then *The Pictorial*'s business manager. "But because of a deal they made between them, it was agreed that the editor would be Nelson." The deal, as Zagat recounts it, revolved around the fact that the four top *Pictorial* staffers shared in the publication's profits. Those profits could be considerable: Zagat, who served as business manager for both *The Pictorial* and the yearbook, says he netted from $7,000 to $8,000 a year between the two, as much as $72,000 in today's dollars. What Nelson offered Meyer was his share of the profits. "So Nelson became the editor," says Zagat, "and Meyer became the managing editor, and Meyer got 25 percent of the profits of the publication, and Nelson got nothing."

In a way, then, it could be said that Nelson bought his election.

The Pictorial was one of those college publications whose look and content barely changed from year to year. There were the usual shots of campus life, accompanied by cheeky captions; coverage of those seminal Hanover events, the football season and Winter Carnival; some out-of-focus nature shots; and, to round it all off, the obligatory cheesecake photo at the end of the book.

But once Nelson took charge, something extraordinary happened. *The Pictorial* took on the style and panache of a slick New York magazine. The transformation was most evident in the covers. In the past they were always the same dull Dartmouth forest green, framing the same old photos (a football player for the fall issue, a smiling lass at Winter Carnival time). Under Nelson's editorship, the background colors began to vary, and so did the photos. Instead of a gridiron star there was a shot of a student in Indian garb, peering out toward the horizon. Instead of the smiling lass, there was an ambiguous, arty photo of a pair of woman skaters—from the picture, it was hard to tell whether they were real, or a marble sculpture, or maybe even an ice sculpture.

The publication's quality, needless to say, stunned the college. "Mr. Rockefeller, as the incoming editor-in-chief of *The Pictorial,* is certainly off to a fine start with this first issue under his regime," wrote a commentator in *The Dartmouth,* who described the book as "a masterpiece of subject matter, composition, and atmosphere."

At the same time that he was boosting *The Pictorial,* Nelson was also bringing his entrepreneurial flair to bear on another organization he headed: a group known as The Arts.

Before Nelson came on the scene, The Arts—with the unenviable mission of promoting artistic interest among the distinctly unartistic Dartmouth student body—had fallen into stagnation and disrepute. The organization was perceived as having come under the sway of the school's gay element—or, as Nelson would describe them, using a favorite euphemism of the day, "light-footed tea drinkers." No one was terribly interested in what The Arts was doing, including, it appeared, the group's own meager membership.

All that changed when Nelson became president. Suddenly, the "tea drinkers" departed, and were replaced by a bevy of student big shots, including Bob Bottome, John French, and football hero Al Marsters. And, just as suddenly, The Arts became a force on campus.

Nelson began a lecture series, and rather than trot out the usual dusty academics, he went for names—the bigger, the better. Somehow, he managed to attract to Dartmouth some of the preeminent literary lights of the time: Sinclair Lewis, Carl Sandburg, Vachel Lindsay, Edna St. Vincent Millay, Thornton Wilder, Bertrand Russell. Dartmouth gained immeasurably from their visits and, not coincidentally, so did Nelson. For from the time these luminaries stepped off the train at White River Junction, Nelson was their constant aide and companion. He helped them with their luggage, checked them in at the Hanover Inn, hosted a small dinner in their honor, accompanied them to the lecture hall, and organized the reception of well-wishers afterward. The payoff for these ministrations was proximity to these great minds, the sort of proximity that was beyond the wildest dreams of most undergraduates. He could talk to Sandburg about Lincoln, to Lindsay about poetry, to Wilder about playwriting. As Nelson later pointed out, "It would be hard to estimate the value derived from such contacts." (How much he might have derived from his contact with Bertrand Russell, who used his Arts lecture to rail against big business, is an open question.)

Nelson also had a new wrinkle for The Arts in the world of painting. He discovered that some excellent reproductions of masterworks were being produced with a new German process, and he proceeded to set up exhibitions of these reproductions—with the works for sale at from one to seven dollars apiece. "In this we have hoped to encourage fellows to buy worthwhile pictures for their rooms, rather than spend the same amount of money for poor stuff as many of them do," he explained. The fascination with reproductions nested in Nelson's mind. Almost half a century later, he would be spreading the gospel again, peddling reproductions with virtually the same sales pitch he used at Dartmouth.

The Arts, for the most part, accomplished its mission: inculcating an interest in, or at least a curiosity about, things aesthetic in Dartmouth's heretofore sneering student body. But Nelson also employed the organization as a springboard for less democratic activities—pursuing, it seemed, some private, self-indulgent agenda of his own.

Nowhere was this more apparent than in his handling of a promised poetry anthology. Rather than publish a simple, inexpensively bound volume, Nelson orchestrated a lavish production worthy of a Renaissance prince. The book was bound in slate-green airplane silk, stamped with gold leaf; the paper was handmade Van Gelder, imported from Holland. The typeface was a rarely used font known as Deepdene, and a printer's mark in the form of a flame (signifying, it was said, creative energy) was stamped on the cover, endpapers, and title page. In the midst of all this opulence, the poetry was almost an afterthought.

The volume was a testament to Nelson's exquisite taste, and to his heedlessness about the cost.

Not satisfied with just this venture, Nelson undertook at the same time another gilt-edged publication, dubbed *The Five Arts.* His partner in this enterprise was another well-heeled undergraduate: Walter Chrysler, Jr., heir to the Chrysler motorcar fortune. Chrysler cut a markedly different figure at Dartmouth than did Nelson. Snobbish, ostentatious, and distinctly effeminate, Chrysler tooled around Hanover in a custom-built car that was the stuff of legend on the campus: it was said to have been fitted with a barber chair and wraparound library shelf in the back. "He was a very unpopular person," says art instructor Lathrop. "Just the opposite of Nelson, really."

But Chrysler did have a taste for fine books and an interest in publishing them, and as far as Nelson, a nascent connoisseur himself, was concerned, that was common ground enough. Chrysler became editor-in-chief of *The Five Arts,* while Nelson ostensibly stayed in the background as an adviser. But in fact Francis Horn, who served as the publication's business manager, describes Chrysler as "more of a figurehead than an active participant." Nelson, Horn says, really ran the show.

The Five Arts was promoted as an anthology of the best of Dartmouth student writing. But, as with the poetry compilation, the sumptuous presentation, rather than the prose, was the main attraction. The cover was vellum, on which was overlaid a light blue design and a black hand-drawn print. Printed on Flemish paper, the magazine was bound in book form, with board backs.

Nelson's dream was to have Edna St. Vincent Millay write the introduction to *The Five Arts,* and he was prepared to go to great lengths to accomplish that. When she arrived at Dartmouth for her Arts-sponsored lecture, he lavished his usual celebrity treatment on her and her husband. Then, after the lecture, Nelson, along with three fellow Arts officers, brought Millay and husband to one of their dormitory rooms. Once they were all safely inside, a bottle was produced. When that was finished off, there was another, and then another. Nelson, it seems, had heard about the poet's weakness for alcoholic potables and earlier in the day dispatched two of his minions to local bootlegger Joe Kilmer for $50 worth of his best mash. So it was that the son and grandson of rigid teetotalers spent a long evening plying America's greatest living poetess with hooch.

At six in the morning Nelson finally popped the question to a thoroughly inebriated Millay. "I'll think about it," she said. At nine the group left the dormitory to put Millay and husband on the train at White River Junction. "I'll think about it some more," she told Nelson in her semi-stupor just before the train pulled away.

He never did get the introduction.

In the spring of 1930, as his time at Dartmouth drew to a close, Nelson sat down to write an article about his senior fellowship year for the *Dartmouth Alumni Magazine.* Entitled "The Use of Leisure," the article is a testimonial to the freedom the fellowship afforded him: the freedom to immerse himself in the study of art, the freedom to devote himself to transforming The Arts.

As with so many other of his Dartmouth milestones, the article was given prominent play in *The New York Times.* The *Times* paid particular attention to Nelson's suggestion that more young men should be given the same freedom he was, so that they could train themselves to make more cultivated use of their leisure time in the years to come.

Nelson's essay was written as the nation teetered on the brink of the Great

Depression, and an "education in leisure" was the last thing most working men were interested in obtaining.

To be fair to Nelson, the oncoming economic upheaval was but a distant rumble at the leafy, isolated Dartmouth campus. The only indication that something untoward might be happening was *The Dartmouth*'s decision in mid-October 1929, two weeks before the Crash, to publish the closing prices of thirty representative New York Stock Exchange stocks. "*The Dartmouth* has decided to print this new service as a result of the recent nationwide interest in the ups and downs of the stock market," the paper explained.

"The Crash made very little impression on us," one of Nelson's classmates recalled. "We had no reason to question the status quo. I would think it fair to say that Nelson, along with the rest of us, accepted the existing order pretty much as it was."

So if Nelson's article could be read as a manifesto for the leisure class, his expressions were not out of keeping with the worldview at Hanover. And, as a personal testament, the piece does ring true. The senior fellowship did, as he said, give him a welcome respite from the relentless demands of family and career and allow him to nurture what would prove to be a lifelong passion. And, as the article makes clear, the fellowship gave him the freedom to pursue extracurricular ventures like The Arts and *The Five Arts* and *The Pictorial*.

Indeed, it would not be too much to say that it was the latter freedom that had the most telling impact on Nelson Rockefeller. Through those ventures, ostensibly undertaken in the name of art, Nelson was able to exercise certain aptitudes and talents that were not exactly part of the Dartmouth curriculum. Entrepreneurial drive and flair, for one thing. The extravagant perfectionism of the connoisseur. A knack for ingratiating himself with the celebrated. A zest for promotion. And a feel for politics, as shown by his deft deal making at *The Pictorial*.

It took that unfettered senior year to bring these skills and traits to the fore. And as much as anything he learned at Dartmouth, those skills and traits would define the adult Nelson Rockefeller.

When class honors were announced, Nelson was notably absent from the lists. He did not win the Barrett Cup, given to the senior judged most likely to succeed by combined vote of the sophomore, junior, and senior classes. Neither was he voted most popular, or most respected, or as having done the most for Dartmouth. The closest Nelson came was in the balloting for most versatile man, where he finished second by a huge margin. All that Nelson had done—for The Arts, for *The Pictorial*, for the soccer team—was not enough to sway his peers.

If these slights bothered him, he never showed it. To the end, he was buoyant, cheerful, eager to win the favor of his classmates. As a parting gesture to his fraternity brothers, he tried to invite twenty-one of them to Pocantico for three or four days; his parents, blanching at the prospect of such a horde, vetoed the idea.

It was the custom in those days for each graduating senior to pass around a cane, with the Dartmouth Indian head on top, on which all the student's cronies would carve their initials. Nelson went the custom one better: he carved a figure of a rocking horse, under which he boldly inscribed "Rocky."

The special ties that the Rockefellers had to Hopkins and Dartmouth, not to mention the family's largesse, were duly recognized at commencement. Nelson's father—whose latest gift, seven months earlier, was $80,000 to the medical school—was chosen to speak for all the class of 1930's parents at the annual alumni luncheon a day before commencement.

His address was studded with his usual stern, biblical-sounding warnings. "This world," Junior declared, "has no prize to offer, whether it be wealth, position, or power, that is worth having at the price of tarnished honor or guilty conscience."

A photograph taken at commencement shows father and son posing for the ritual congratulatory handshake. Straw boater in hand, Junior seems to be eyeing Nelson from behind his steel-rimmed spectacles with the slightest edge of wariness. Nelson, trim and boyish in his loose black gown, beaming his most effervescent grin, seems ready to race to the next great step in his life.

He would not have long to wait. In just six days he was due to be married.

Seven

A Main Line Wedding

Dartmouth had posed the sternest of challenges for Nelson's libido. The college's isolation forestalled any meaningful contact with the opposite sex, aside from a couple of ritualized mating events: the fall and spring fraternity open houses, Winter Carnival, the Green Key prom in the spring. And so, when he was freed from Hanover's constraints—during intersemester breaks, vacations, and other interludes—Nelson made the most of his opportunities. His brother John once borrowed Nelson's car to take a trip to Vassar. "I didn't know the road," John told him later, "but I just turned your car loose on the highway and it headed for the nearest girls' college, you have it so well trained."

Nelson's most energetic performance was turned in during a European summer trip in 1928, his first solo journey abroad. The ostensible purpose of the sojourn was to work on his French, by means of a stay with a family in the South of France. But from the moment he boarded the *Ile de France* for the Atlantic crossing, it was clear that Nelson had other priorities. In a letter home, he described a shipboard encounter with a lass who "really is a peach—full of fun, nice looking, very intelligent and has a great deal of *savoir faire*. . . . It has really made the trip across a great deal more interesting; in fact, very delightful."

In Paris, where he stayed with Abby's sister Lucy, Nelson had liaisons with, among others, a Belgian princess and an American girl with whom he spent Bastille Day in Montmartre. "We had a wonderful time," he enthused to his mother. "There certainly were some interesting sights and people to watch. . . . I think this is going to be the most profitable summer I ever spent." "I don't know much about all these girls that you have been seeing in

Paris," a bemused Abby wrote back. "I comfort myself with the thought that there is safety in numbers."

His Parisian escapades, however, did not distract him, upon his return to the States, from the principal object of his attentions: a certain young lady he had seen year after year during his family's August getaways to the Maine coast. She was a plain, awkward-looking girl, thin and very tall (at five feet ten and a half inches, she was a good inch and a half taller than he), and she was a year older than Nelson. Yet he found himself intensely attracted to her, and his various flirtations hardly dampened his ardor.

Her name was Mary Todhunter Clark. To family and friends, she was simply "Tod."

She was the very essence of Main Line Philadelphia: in her pedigree, in her upbringing, in the patrician pursuits (horseback riding, Junior League social work) in which she indulged. On her mother's side, her forebear John Roberts was one of the earliest Quaker settlers in Pennsylvania. It was on land purchased from William Penn himself that Roberts built the family homestead, Pencoyd, and it was on this ancestral plot that seven generations of Roberts descendants made their homes—including, in the early years of the twentieth century, Mary Todhunter Clark's parents, Percy and Elizabeth Roberts Clark.

The Main Line owed its very existence to her grandfather, George Roberts. As president of the Pennsylvania Railroad in the 1880s and 1890s, Roberts enticed Philadelphia's affluent to settle in communities serviced by the railroad's new commuter "Main Line." He gave those communities names that harked back to the Roberts family's Welsh ancestry: Bala and Cynwyd and Bryn Mawr. And Mary Clark was no less blessed on her father's side: great-grandfather Enoch White Clark founded one of Philadelphia's oldest private banks.

The main house of her family's Cynwyd estate, Willoughby, had the burnished quality of an English country manor: massive animal trophy heads guarding the entrance hall, a huge central staircase leading upstairs to what a family member recalls as "endless bedrooms." The outbuildings included an enormous garage for Percy Clark's collection of Packards, residences for the family's two chauffeurs, and a house for the caretaker, who, among other things, ministered to Willoughby's milk cows. There was a substantial formal garden and an apple orchard and, for the children's diversion, a charming little playhouse in which they could entertain their friends. To tend this estate the family employed gardeners and chauffeurs and a staff of servants presided over by the Clarks' longtime houseman, John Hansel.

"We grew up with a great sense of belonging," recalled Tod's first cousin Eleanor Clark French in a memoir. The family was a vast, self-contained institution. Tod was one of eight children (six of them boys), her father one of six children, and her mother one of six. With many of their relations clustered in Main Line communities (and the Roberts side dwelling a stone's throw away in other parts of the old Pencoyd demesne) the world seemed a great gaggle of aunts and uncles and cousins.

Looking back on her childhood, Tod described it as "a sunny fog." And, indeed, there was a serene, sheltered quality about it; rarely were the shadows of a harsher world allowed to intrude. Even on those occasions when the Clarks, in a charitable gesture, offered a day's frolic on one of their estates to poor city children, the young Clarks were hustled off elsewhere, for fear they would catch some disease from the indigent youngsters.

Everything about Tod's upbringing was true to Main Line form. Father was a Philadelphia lawyer (in partnership with his brother Joseph, the father of future Pennsylvania senator Joseph Clark) whose main amusement was cricket, in which he was an internationally ranked player. Mother was a grande dame of Cynwyd who enjoyed her morning jaunts into the village to chat with local shopkeepers. When the time came to send their daughters away to school, the Clarks packed them off to the Foxcroft School, the exclusive girls' academy in Middleburg, Virginia.

In the words of *Sargent's Handbook on Private Schools,* Foxcroft was an institution "where the atmosphere of the Old South . . . the well appointed stables pervades . . . and a sense of social responsibility is inculcated. It was established in 1914 by a Virginian, a hard rider, who demanded a good seat of her girls."

With a streak of the tomboy in her, and no great aptitude for academics, Tod took naturally to Foxcroft's equestrian bent. She became an accomplished horsewoman who could outride most of her male companions. And she readily absorbed all the niceties and nuances with which Foxcroft sought to prepare its charges for their lives as society belles.

After Foxcroft, Tod chose to complete the finishing process with a year at the Sorbonne to work on her deficient French. The year in Paris was a customary last fling for young ladies of Tod's station before they took their places in society. Upon her return to Cynwyd, Tod did what was expected of her: she had her formal coming-out at a tea and joined the Junior League.

The arc of her progress—Main Line to Foxcroft to the Sorbonne to the Junior League—suggests a young lady of a certain aristocratic decorum. But while hardly a rebel, Tod Clark was anything but decorous. She had a gift for mimicry, and a tart wit that she unsheathed at the slightest opportunity. When the mood struck her, she and older sister Miriam would gossip in German at the dinner table (no one was quite sure whether it was real German or some nonsense guttural tongue they made up)—a practice that drove their brothers, and later their husbands, to distraction. She loved to appear on the stage: one Junior League production saw her swaggering as Sir Dandiprat Bombas in *Snow White.*

But it was during the family's summers in Northeast Harbor, at the great shingled seaside cottage they dubbed Seaward, that Tod truly allowed her spunkiness and sense of fun to flourish. "Northeast Harbor was swarming with activity," remembers Hal Haskell, who spent boyhood summers there. And Tod partook of all of it. There was tennis on the Clarks' own court, and sunning on the Clarks' small private beach, and sailboat racing in the family's twenty-five-foot boat, the *Don Q*. "Racing was the center of the wheel," recalls Haskell. "You had three races a week, and everybody competed violently against each other. There were no holds barred."

On other days Tod would join her father for strenuous hikes on the trails of Mount Desert Island's Acadia National Park—a park whose preservation was largely due to the munificence of John D. Rockefeller, Jr. "My grandfather knew almost every trail in the park by heart," recalls Tod's nephew, James Wallis. And it wasn't long before Tod knew them too.

Northeast Harbor was also a place where Tod could give her sense of showmanship free rein. Every now and then, she and a friend would don Gay Nineties attire and travel Mount Desert Island on a bicycle built for two. And she was a regular player in the vaudeville productions that toured the island's villages and hamlets.

It was in the midst of those carefree, windblown Maine summers that she came to know young Nelson Rockefeller.

When the Rockefeller boys wanted to get away from the splendid isolation of Seal Harbor and the Eyrie, they made the two-mile jaunt west, past Bracy Cove, to Northeast Harbor. As Hal Haskell puts it, "Seal Harbor was where the Fords and the Rockefellers lived. It just didn't have the same community thing that Northeast Harbor had." Northeast was the mecca for most of the island's young people; as many as four dances a week were held there.

Nelson and his brothers inevitably found themselves drawn into the circle of the high-spirited Clarks. Laurance remembers that "Tod and her friends were all fun-loving, sort of semi-practical jokers. There was always a lot of laughter and kidding." The Clarks were not terribly impressed by the Rockefellers—"Nelson was just one of many nice boys," notes Tod's cousin Ellie. But Nelson soon won them over with his flashy Ford roadster, with its array of horns and whistles. In no time at all he was off sailing with them and camping out with the Clarks in nearby Seal Cove.

The Clarks, in turn, were given a chance to sample the pleasures of the Eyrie. "I'll always remember," says Eleanor Clark French, "Nelson used to have house parties there, wonderful house parties. There would be tennis and swimming. We'd play in the playhouse they had there, and take our meals in the big house." They would join the Rockefellers for dancing lessons in the cavernous ballroom Junior had built (one of his favorite diversions, not at all in keeping with his upbringing, was dancing). "We would go there every Thursday for our lessons," recalls French.

At some point in the midst of the dancing—or, perhaps, around the campfire at Seal Cove—Nelson began to *notice* the Clark girl. "She is always full of good fun and never dull," he told his parents. He was captivated by her energy, her athleticism, her willingness to try anything. Nelson's friend Bill Alton, who stayed with him in Seal Harbor during those summers, remembers that "he was always coming up with something to do—a hayride, or something like that—and Tod was always part of it. She'd fall into the spirit and carry out her end of it. She wasn't a shrinking violet."

Nelson's initial approaches to courtship were paragons of Victorian discretion. In 1928 he invited Tod to an Easter vacation house party at Pocantico, where she met with his father's approval. Junior termed her "an exceptionally fine girl, so bright, so clever . . . and withal such a fine spirit."

Then Nelson went off on his bachelor's foray in Europe. His romantic exploits notwithstanding, he redoubled his pursuit of Tod upon his return.

That fall, his parents invited Tod to join them and young David on a trip to Egypt they would be making in January. Clearly, the invitation was more than just a hospitable gesture; sensing their son's intentions, Abby and Junior were vetting the young woman. The trip put Nelson on an emotional roller coaster. On the one hand, he was elated that his parents were taking such interest in Tod. But on the other, he was anxious about the impression she was making—and about the attention that she might get from young Charles Breasted, who had joined his father, noted Egyptologist James Breasted, as part of Junior's entourage.

Closeted in his dormitory in snowbound Hanover, Nelson penned one worried missive after another to his parents. "I do so want to know how you all like Tod," he wrote at the journey's outset, "and whether she has been all you expected as a travelling companion, which I know she has and probably a lot more. I've been a little worried about Breasted, but I'm counting on Dave."

Word from his mother that "Mary has been a great success" and that Breasted was bedridden with a temperature of 104 did little to calm Nelson's jangled nerves. Again, he begged for reassurance:

> You don't know how glad I was that Tod went along on the trip with you. There's nobody's judgment I'd trust as much as yours, not even my own. Consequently, what you think about Tod when you get home after having had the opportunity to get really to know her—probably much better than I do—will make an awful lot of difference with me. Well, enough said, and I'm sorry to have taken so much of your time on this subject. Probably Tod's engaged to that young Breasted boy by now anyhow. But we'll hope not!

Exasperated, Abby sent back some maternal words of wisdom. "In my own life I have found that patience, much patience and a real desire to do the right thing have always led to the right solution of my problems," she wrote. "I love you too much to try and impose my will or opinion upon yours. All that Papa and I want is that *you* find and follow the right path. When we reach home can we not talk of this further?"

But far from easing Nelson's mind, this counsel sent him into another one of his paroxysms of guilt and contrition. "All of a sudden," he replied, "I realize for the first time how unutterably selfish and thoughtless I have been getting to be."

> What can I do now? I'd like to hide from everything, back out of all the complications I'm in, none of them serious, but all the results of my own selfishness. To apologize does no good. I spend half my time saying I'm sorry and I'm going right ahead and doing the same or a worst thing. To think you and Pa have gone on uncomplainingly—both of you with 100 times the number of responsibilities I have had—and purely to add to my own amusement and convenience I've left the arrangments of details and asked you both to do things for me that I have no right to ask anyone to do—much less you two who have done everything for me. . . . God alone knows how humble I feel."

He signed the letter: "Your thoughtless son, Nelson."

And yet, that spring, instead of inviting Tod, the object of all this ardor, to his fraternity house party, Nelson asked another girl. He cautioned his parents not to "think I'm forgetting Tod or have fallen for Y———." (The girl's full name was later expunged from a copy of the letter.) "Well," he went on, "I have fallen for Y——— in a sense but it doesn't effect my love for Tod in the least bit. I think I'm too young to only know and like one girl, so I periodically fall for some one—about once a year—but always giving them to understand how I feel toward Tod."

This confession did not exactly augur well for Nelson's future fidelity. At the very least, it called into question whether he was emotionally ready for a more permanent relationship.

That summer he went off on the Grenfell expedition, still consumed by thoughts of Tod. "You know," he wrote Abby on his twenty-first birthday, "I'm beginning to think that I really am in love with Tod, whatever being in love means. . . . She is the only girl that I know who measures up anywhere nearly to the standards set by you, Mum."

"But," he added, "don't get worried. I'm not going to run into anything in a headstrong way."

Barely a month later, upon his return to Maine, Nelson and Tod Clark were engaged.

Junior could hardly contain his fury. As far as he was concerned, his son was acting precipitously and unwisely. What's more, after all of Nelson's effusive assertions about how much he was relying on his parents' judgment, he hadn't bothered to even go through the motions of asking their advice on this, the most important decision of his life. Abby attempted to act as a peacemaker, but apparently to little avail.

On the train up to Hanover on the first of September, Nelson tried to gather his thoughts. He wrote Abby, thanking her profusely for her "cooperative attitude" about the engagement and for her kind treatment of Tod: "It means so much because she is coming into a new city where she doesn't know many people. Already you have made her feel at home in New York." Then he turned to the trouble he and Tod were having with Junior:

> At first, all we thought of was the fact that we both loved each other desperately and that we wanted to get married some day—our thoughts didn't get further than that. And ever since we've been realizing that it wasn't as simple as one would think. We both feel very badly that Pa feels the way he does but really we didn't mean to try and put one over on him or go counter to his wishes. And we are terribly sorry that we disappointed him so early in the game. I hope it will be the one and only time.

Nelson added that "I wrote Pa today and tried to straighten things out—do let me know if it helped matters any."

More than two and a half months went by before Junior finally relented—under prodding from his wife—and accepted the engagement. He dispatched gracious notes to the couple, going out of his way to praise Tod's fine qualities. Nelson, needless to say, was ecstatic. "I still am thrilling over Pa's wonderful letter," he wrote his mother on November 25, "but Mum, I shall always feel that if it wasn't for you things wouldn't be the way they are now." He was, he said, "the luckiest person in the world. To have you and Pa for parents, and Tod for fiancee, combined with all the wonderful breaks that I have had, is really more than one person deserves." Overwhelmed with joy, Nelson sat down five days later and expressed his gratitude all over again. Tossing another bouquet to his mother, Nelson told her that one of the reasons he loved Tod so "is because she is more like you than any girl I have ever met."

Tod wrote her own thank-you note to Junior and Abby, a note fragrant with Foxcroft politesse. "Nelson and I not only hope for your advice now but always," she said. "We look to our parents for all the guidance they can give us, and hope so to live our life together that they may be proud of us.

"You, Mr. Rockefeller, by your letter have assured me of your happiness over our engagement and that makes my happiness complete." She signed the note: "Affectionately, Mary"; Junior, as was his wont, preferred not to use nicknames.

The engagement was formally announced on December 17, and the news was promptly transmitted nationwide by the Associated Press. *The Dartmouth,* in a rare nod to Nelson's celebrity, ran the AP story on its front page.

Those of Nelson's friends and fraternity brothers who had met Tod—and not many had—were generally pleased by the news. "She wasn't much to look at," says Psi Upsilon brother Lee Chilcote. "She had a very long neck, and she was tall and ungainly. But she was a lot of fun. Really, a lot of fun." But a few privately wondered what had led Nelson to choose someone as unprepossessing as Tod. Even Bill Alton, who had come to know Tod and appreciate her joie de vivre during summers in Seal Harbor, took a somewhat jaundiced view of the match.

"Nelson was a planner in everything he did," explains Alton, looking back on what had fueled his skepticism. "He didn't just slip into something. I think in this case he had a very clear vision of the place of family. The Rockefellers were very much like royalty in those days, and who you married counted a great deal. Tod, being from the Philadelphia Main Line—well, I think she was *selected.* He maybe said to himself, 'Now this will be a good mother of my children.' At the very least, she met his requirements."

"Maybe it was the difference that appealed to him," opined his brother Laurance. "She was Main Line, imperious, hard to get perhaps. Philadelphia looked down on Rockefellers. That would be a challenge for Nelson."

There was little doubt about the depth of Nelson's passion, at least in those tempestuous months from the spring to the fall of 1929. But, as Alton suggests, Tod's allure might well have been magnified by her utter acceptability. Nelson may have been far more calculating than his father gave him credit for.

A few minutes after four o'clock in the afternoon on Monday, June 23, 1930, a limousine pulled up to the parish house of St. Asaph's Episcopal Church in Bala, and a young man clad in morning coat and striped gray trousers leapt out of the car. Bounding up the steps, he flipped his top hat into the waiting hands of the aged sexton and slapped the old man on the shoulder. "The best o' luck, sir," the sexton called out. "Oh, thank you," Nelson Rockefeller replied.

Outside the ivy-covered gray stone Gothic church, more than a thousand spectators jostled for position; each time another limousine pulled up, the throng surged forward for a better view. Some ninety policemen were on hand to hold them back and direct traffic.

Inside the vestry, Nelson paced nervously while his best man, older brother John, checked his watch. Spying the jittery groom, one of the chauffeurs whispered, "Gosh, he's just like any other kid, ain't he? Nervous as a cat in a strange attic, and wantin' to get it over with!"

At last, moments before the appointed hour of four-thirty, the bridesmaids (in lavender) and matrons of honor (in delphinium blue) formed a double line on the church steps to frame the arrival of the bride and her father.

News photographers scrambled as Tod took the hand of Percy Clark and descended from the limousine. Her bridal attire more than lived up to society expectations: a gown of ivory duchess satin, from which flowed a panel of rare old lace leading to a formal court train. (Less noticed were the flat slippers she wore so as not to tower over the groom.) She carried a bouquet of madonna lilies and orchids as she entered St. Asaph's.

The church was filled with 275 invited guests. Among them were the governor of Virginia, John G. Pollard, and Secretary of Labor James J. Davis. Also among them were some of Nelson's old friends from Dartmouth and the Lincoln School: John French and Sheldon Stark and Tom Prideaux and Bill Alton. Alton and French were given the honor of serving as ushers. Absent from the nuptials—despite rumors that persisted to the last minute that he might show up—was ninety-year-old John D. Rockefeller, Sr.

The voice of the Reverend Benjamin Bird rang from the altar as he led Nelson and Tod through their vows. Bird used the new Episcopal ceremony, in which the injunction to "obey" was omitted.

Ten minutes later, the wedding party emerged into the sunshine—and into the glare and cacophony of the swarm of feverish cameramen. Flashes popped and sputtered as the couple posed. Nelson glowed, but Tod was visibly discomfited by the tumult around her. "Oh, please do hurry," she urged the photographers as they begged for just one more shot. "Oh, please, we do have to go," she snapped. A newspaper afterward described her as "impatient and restive as a mettlesome steed under the coldly winking eyes of the cameras."

The party proceeded in their cars to Willoughby, just a mile away, where a grand reception was mounted on the lawns and veranda of the Clark estate. Despite Prohibition, the champagne flowed, much to teetotaling (and law-abiding) Junior's discomfort. Percy Clark had insisted that no daughter of his would be married without bumpers of champagne, and Percy Clark had prevailed.

Some 1,500 well-wishers waited their turns to file onto the veranda to offer felicitations to the bride, the groom, and their parents. Almost an hour and a half passed before the human tide finally abated.

Even by the elevated standard of Main Line Philadelphia, the reception was an awe-inspiring affair. "It was huge!" remembers Eleanor Clark French, who was a bridesmaid; Bill Alton recalls that "there were butlers everywhere."

Meanwhile, piled up on the second floor of the Clark home was a breathtaking display of material tributes to the newlyweds. There were eighteenth-century English silver coffeepots and tea sets, antique glass and Sèvres China, and a Chippendale bookcase crammed with rare leather-bound volumes of Shakespeare, Smollett, and Defoe. The entire second-floor hallway was lined with Early American furniture, destined for the couple's new home in Pocantico.

The Rockefellers themselves were hardly stinting in their presents. From Abby and Junior, Tod received a necklace of matching pearls, and from the absent Senior the couple received, appropriately enough, securities worth $20,000. But like any substantial Rockefeller gift, this one was carefully calibrated in a Junior-Senior consultation. It was Junior who suggested the amount, the same amount Senior had given Nelson's older sister, Babs, upon her marriage to David Milton eight years before. And it was Junior who advised Senior to split the gift in half: $10,000 to Nelson and $10,000 to Tod. While the bride customarily received all such gifts, Junior felt it prudent to make a fifty-fifty division. The sum was, after all, the first small chunk of the family's wealth that Nelson would own outright.

At the end of the day's festivities, the newlyweds drove off to nearby Princeton, where they would spend their wedding night at the Princeton Inn—an intermediate stop en route to their two-week honeymoon in Maine, at the Eyrie.

The next morning they found the news accounts of their nuptials greeting them at every turn. *The New York Times* reported the wedding on its front page. So did *The Philadelphia Inquirer.* There was no doubt about why the event was deemed so newsworthy. Nelson was the first of the Rockefeller sons to be married and, as the *Inquirer* pointed out, he was "destined one day to become one of the wealthiest young men upon the earth." For all her family's social prominence, Mary Todhunter Clark was simply the "Cynwyd Girl" who was "Wed to Scion of Rockefeller," in the words of the *Inquirer* headline.

The surge of the crowd at St. Asaph's, the fusillade of photo flashes, the front-page news coverage—these were Tod's true welcome to the world of Nelson Rockefeller.

They stayed at the Eyrie for two weeks. Just the two of them, and twenty-four servants, in Junior's 107-room "cottage."

Later that July, Nelson's old comrade-in-arms at the Dartmouth *Pictorial,* Eugene Zagat, was visiting his father's office at 45th Street and Fifth Avenue. When Zagat came downstairs, he found a calling card perched on the steering wheel of his Buick. The card was Nelson Rockefeller's.

Nelson had scratched out his name and scrawled, "Gene: We're off on a little trip around the world. Nels."

The "little trip" was a gift to the newlyweds from Junior and Abby: a nine-month excursion around the globe that would give the young couple a taste of the more exotic ports of call, as well as of the capitals of Europe. But as mapped out by Nelson, the journey was hardly a typical honeymooners' jaunt.

The trip would have its touristic elements, to be sure. But along with the sightseeing would be meetings with dignitaries and Standard Oil officials and Rockefeller Foundation representatives. The journey would be nothing less than a grand state visit by a Rockefeller crown prince to the many outposts of the family's empire. It would expose Nelson to an impressive panoply of political luminaries and world-class intellectuals. The only thing the trip would not do was give Nelson and Tod a chance to quietly bask in each other's company. Rarely would they ever be alone together.

The tone of the trip was set by the reading list Nelson put together in preparation for it—a list that included such tomes as *The Growth and Development of China.* Clearly, Nelson's mind was on matters other than romance.

The whirlwind began with their first stop in Honolulu in late July. Nelson and Tod were feted by the territory's governor, treated by the president of the Senate to what Nelson described as a "big native feast with hula dancers"—and then given a tour of a leper colony. ("It was a very interesting but depressing experience," Nelson wrote.)

From there it was on to Japan for temple visits and luncheons with ambassadors and university leaders, as well as such diversions as fishing with cormorants by torchlight under a full moon. Then the couple made their grand tour of China, a country that was benefiting much from Junior's largesse: the Rockefeller-funded China Medical Board was in the process of training a whole generation of Chinese physicians.

Their travels next took the couple to Manila, where they danced until 3 A.M. before catching a boat to the Dutch East Indies. They visited Java, Sumatra, and Bali, and as Christmas approached Nelson and Tod found themselves in Bangkok, scrambling for clothes to wear to a royal reception (their luggage had been delayed en route).

Every move Nelson and Tod made was painstakingly choreographed. Chaperoned by eager Standard Oil officials, they found their calendar filled with as many as six or seven events a day. The pace became too much, even for Nelson. "We haven't even had a meal alone for over a month," he wrote home. "We'd been making an effort to be nice to people for so long that we were just dying for a rest and a chance to be by ourselves. . . . We were at the end of our rope."

Back in Pocantico, Abby was alarmed by the photographs Nelson had sent of their visit to the ancient Cambodian capital of Angkor. "You look fairly bursting with health," she wrote her son, "but it seemed to me that Mary looked extremely thin. . . . I think you must take time in Paris to let Mary have a little rest and gain a few pounds before she gets home or people will feel that you haven't been treating her very well."

But Nelson's idea of a restful interlude was to organize a packhorse trip into the Himalayas upon their arrival in India in February. Pulling the necessary strings—he contacted the British colonial governor, who wired his aide-de-camp in Darjeeling—Nelson secured a pass to Nepal and a fur coat for Tod. They rode from sunrise to sunset, climbing to the 12,000-foot summit of Mount Landakfu, from which they had a commanding view of Mount Everest.

And, while in India, Nelson managed to pull off the ultimate coup: an audience with Gandhi. In the course of a visit Nelson and Tod made to a Mr. Sarabhai, a wealthy Indian mill owner who was one of Gandhi's advisers, Sarabhai got word that Gandhi's negotiations with the British were breaking down and that the leader might be thrown back in jail. Sarabhai resolved to return to Delhi at once, and invited Nelson and Tod to join him.

Boarding the one o'clock train to the capital, they arrived the next day at noon and headed straight to Gandhi's house. In the courtyard, the great man, clad in his white dhoti, was at work at his spinning wheel, his disciples clustered around him. When the Rockefellers were introduced to him, Gandhi nodded but did not say a word. It was his day of silence. When Nelson expressed the hope of talking to him, Gandhi penciled a note: "Come back tomorrow. I'll talk to you."

So Nelson and Tod returned the next morning, only to be told that the leader could spare just a minute or two. But, perhaps aware of what Rockefeller aid could do for his cause and his country, Gandhi invited the couple to join him for his morning walk the next day. They showed up at ten to seven, and drove out with Gandhi to an old Mogul fort on the edge of Delhi. As they strolled through the fort, Gandhi spoke of his talks with the British viceroy and his belief that at long last they might be close to an agreement. Just then, as Nelson later recounted, "the sky, which had been dark with great, heavy clouds, at that moment opened and the sun flooded the morning walk."

Eleven years later, he would describe his encounter with Gandhi in more prosaic terms: "It gave me the Indian point of view. I have a great interest in the other person's point of view. He showed no interest in me whatever."

There were other times during that trip when the "other person's point of view" flooded into the comfortable world of Nelson and Tod Rockefeller. In Japan, Nelson heard from Teruhiko Fujiyama, a Dartmouth classmate, who spoke bitterly about the anti-Japanese prejudice he was encountering among Westerners now that he had returned to his native land. During a boat ride up the Irrawaddy River in Burma in the company of some titled Europeans, Nelson and Tod winced at the racial remarks the Europeans made about the Burmese aboard the vessel. "All of these things," Nelson wrote, "left a very strong impression and one which we felt boded little good for future relations with those countries."

Only in Bangkok did Nelson see any sign of Westerners reaching out to the local population. The new American ambassador wanted to improve relations, and started out by inviting a horde of Bangkok youngsters to a Christmas ice-cream party on the embassy grounds. Nelson observed that "this unheard-of contact with the masses turned out to be a great success as a good-will gesture. But the first secretary of the embassy was horrified. He had never heard of such a thing. The sight of the striped-pants young man gingerly picking his way through the seething mass of ice-cream-happy children was a memorable one, indeed."

Steeped though he was in personal privilege, Nelson simply could not fathom the sneering colonial attitude toward the masses. His recollection of that attitude would linger, long after much else about the trip had faded from his mind.

Back in New York, Junior followed the reports of his son's adventures with mounting apprehension. What worried him was not the countries Nelson was visiting or the people he was meeting or the breakneck pace he was maintaining. What concerned Junior was his son's cavalier use of Standard Oil officials as his personal factotums—and how much those services were going to cost.

There had never been any question that Nelson could call on Standard people in case of need, just as other Rockefellers traveling overseas had done for decades. And it had been assumed that the logistical exigencies of a round-the-world tour would require some assistance from the oil company.

But as they made their way from one exotic locale to another, Nelson and Tod seemed to be going well beyond what was expected or anticipated in their dealings with Standard representatives. Everywhere they went they were surrounded by Standard people, who served as travel agents, as scheduling secretaries, and as all-around lackeys.

Unsettled by this state of affairs—possibly because it undermined the Rockefellers' public contention that they had little to do anymore with the oil companies—Junior made his displeasure known in letters back to Nelson. And, from India, Nelson responded, by way of a note to his brother John:

> Tell Pa that I don't think we are spoiling the family name with the company representatives in the Orient and that I don't think all the people wish we hadn't come, after we're gone.

John relayed Nelson's protestations of innocence to his parents:

> He said that from the beginning they had not let the [Standard Oil] men do any more for them than they could possibly help; also, that when they did insist on doing things for them, which cost them a personal expense, they gave them some form of present upon leaving, the value of which was

commensurate with the amount done for them. He said that they had felt that the Standard men were entirely satisfied with this arrangement.

It fell to John, recently installed in the family office as his father's aide-de-camp, to monitor his brother's mounting expenses. In response to one query, Nelson insisted in March, eight months into his trip, that he had only spent half the amount Junior had allotted. John passed this on to his father, who dryly observed that that "seems hardly possible."

"Do you not suppose," asked Junior, "he is failing to include the expenses met by the Standard Oil Company, which are being charged to New York, but which are, of course, a part of the trip expenses and are properly to be covered by the allowance made Nelson?"

John told his father that was exactly what was happening; Nelson seemed to have no idea that the expenses racked up by Standard Oil were being charged back to the Rockefeller family office. "As a matter of fact," said John, "when I wrote him that we were receiving bills here for Standard Oil entertaining expenses he wrote back that the reason they were so large was because they included the expenses of the Standard Oil officials who have been traveling with them. This of course is not the case."

Ironically, at the same time that he was defending his round-the-world trip expenditures, Nelson was busy ordering up yet another new car, a Lincoln convertible roadster. Brother John, the beleaguered go-between, was saddled with the task of producing a vehicle that met Nelson's very precise specifications: black, with chromium-plated wire wheels, an aluminum paint stripe down the length of the body, leather upholstery, and a tannish cloth top. And Nelson wanted the car delivered before his return, so he could hop right into it as soon as he arrived in Pocantico.

With boyish glee, Nelson confessed to his brother, "I get so excited writing about it that I don't know what to do. I really think it is going to be the smartest car in New York.

"Oh! One more thing! Can you have my initials—just plane in block letters done in the aluminum paint—on both doors. (See large diagram.)"

From Bombay, Nelson and Tod sailed to the Middle East. Then it was on to Paris for a grand get-together with bubbly Aunt Lucy Aldrich, before at long last heading home.

In New York all was made ready for the couple's arrival. Their new home on the Pocantico estate, a two-storied white shingled prerevolutionary structure known as Hawes House, had been thoroughly remodeled and redecorated during their absence by Junior and Abby. It would provide a suitable setting for all the Early American furniture Nelson and Tod had been given. In the city, an apartment on East 67th Street had been acquired; its decoration would await the newlyweds' return.

Nelson was coming home to all the accoutrements of an affluent New Yorker-about-town: a fashionable city apartment, a charming country house, and, not least, a well-schooled, socially prominent wife. All that was missing from the tableau was one small element: some idea of what it was he was supposed to do with himself.

Part Two

Taking Over

Eight

Ventures and Misadventures

The world assumed that Nelson Rockefeller had no more chance of choosing a career than did the Prince of Wales. He would unquestionably join his brother John in the family office, assisting their father in managing the Rockefellers' far-flung activities. But Nelson bridled at that assumption. Throughout his years at Dartmouth he hinted that he couldn't be counted on to docilely play the role of the dutiful son.

In a letter home during his 1928 European trip, Nelson artfully sought to uncouple his fate from John's. "I only hope that I shall grow up and live a life that will be worthy of the family name," he wrote. "I'm sure Johnny will because he already thinks and acts exactly like you, Pa. I see the likeness . . . more clearly every day. But as for myself—well, I'm a lot different and I don't think the same way."

A year later, as he journeyed northward with the Grenfell expedition, Nelson made his qualms more explicit. "Frankly, I don't relish the idea of going into some business," he informed his parents. "There is nothing very appealing or challenging about it. Just to work my way up in a business that another man has built, stepping from the shoes of one to those of another, making minor changes here and there and then finally, perhaps at the age of sixty, getting to the top where I would have real control for a few years. No, that isn't my idea of living a real life."

Nelson also didn't find terribly appealing the immediate prospect of meandering around his father's office in search of a role. "Unless I have some definite goal, I'm afraid I'll just repeat my career at college all over again. That is, going into a lot of different things, do a little in each, but not really make a success of any of them." He was thinking seriously, he said, about becoming an architect.

His parents were unruffled by Nelson's declarations. Abby suggested he think the architecture business over: "There are so many fine things that it is possible for you to do and so many things that seem necessary for some one to do." And Junior amiably assured his son that whatever the young man decided was fine with him. "So long as you earn your living in some worthwhile occupation, where there is opportunity for real service, I shall be satisfied," he said. "Fortunately, there is no haste."

Junior, meanwhile, tried to gently nudge Nelson in the proper direction by arranging for him to attend Rockefeller board meetings and strategy sessions during his intersession breaks. "The thought of having you commence to get in touch with these problems, to which I have given so much time and thought," the father said, "gives me the greatest pleasure."

But Nelson continued to waffle on the subject, right up through graduation day. While the articles on his wedding confidently reported that "Mr. Rockefeller will enter his father's office several months hence," Nelson left for his honeymoon still dropping hints that he might have other plans.

His exposure to Standard Oil people and other businessmen during his round-the-world trip served only to make him even more ambivalent about joining his father. Halfway through the trip, during a stop in Sumatra, he wrote Junior that "I'm sorry to say that seeing and hearing so much about business doesn't make me very keen to go into it. It seems to squeeze all other interests out of the men's lives that are in it. In fact, I've spent hours and hours thinking over what is really the best thing for me to do. As yet, I've come to no conclusions."

Within two months, though, he had. Casting his misgivings aside, Nelson bowed to the inevitable. The weight of family obligation was simply too great. Reporting to Junior in February on his latest communication with Nelson, John noted the following:

> Another thing he said which will be of interest to you, is that he had definitely decided not to become an architect and that he hoped to come to this office if we could find room for him.

Junior had no trouble finding room.

There was, potentially, no more exciting place in America to work in the spring of 1931 than the office of John D. Rockefeller, Jr. Taking up all of the twentieth floor of the curved, Ionic-columned Standard Oil Building at 26 Broadway, the office was the seat of the world's greatest private fortune and of the myriad enterprises and philanthropic endeavors in which the Rockefeller family was engaged.

That spring the office was bustling with an imposing array of Rockefeller ventures. It was in the process of assembling what would become Grand

Teton National Park, the magnificent expanse of snowcapped mountains and lush valleys along the Snake River in Wyoming. It was restoring Colonial Williamsburg, creating a living museum of eighteenth-century America (Junior would eventually pour $55 million into the project). It was financing the excavation of the Agora, the center of ancient Athenian political and social life. In New York City, it was overseeing the construction of Riverside Church, a splendid Gothic edifice inspired by the cathedrals of Laon and Chartres. And it was mapping out plans for a unique museum of medieval art on the northern tip of Manhattan to be known as the Cloisters.

But by far the most grandiose enterprise absorbing Junior and his associates that spring was a real estate development covering three square blocks of midtown Manhattan, just south of the family townhouse. Junior had acquired a lease on the site in 1928 from its owner, Columbia University, with the thought that part of the land would be used for a new home for the Metropolitan Opera, and the rest for skyscrapers. The opera trustees, however, refused to okay the building unless Junior paid for half its cost. A stubborn Junior decided to go ahead with the development without the opera. In the face of the deepening Depression, he brought in a team of architects to map out plans for a complex of office towers, theaters, and a broad promenade.

The drawings were now in their final stages, and leasing had begun. (The Radio Corporation of America had already signed for one million square feet in the seventy-story central tower, which would be known henceforth as the RCA Building.) Groundbreaking was just months away. Though the opera had long since pulled out, the project was still officially titled Metropolitan Square. But very soon it would bear a new name: Rockefeller Center.

Observing this panorama of activity, Nelson could do little more than wistfully press his nose up against the glass. Everywhere he turned, it seemed, the chance to become meaningfully involved was closed off to him.

What fascinated him most, particularly in view of his architectural inclinations, was the Metropolitan Square development. Recognizing this, Junior had placed Nelson on the Metropolitan Square board in 1929, when he was still at Dartmouth. But board membership counted for little, because the actual management of the enterprise—from architectural oversight to construction to leasing—was in the hands of the firm of Todd, Robertson & Todd, headed by veteran builder John R. Todd. And in almost everything else—the Grand Tetons, Colonial Williamsburg—Nelson found himself elbowed aside by Junior's formidable phalanx of advisers.

They were truly a daunting group for a twenty-two-year-old to confront. There was Colonel Arthur Woods, a former New York City police commissioner, whom Junior had hired to run the Bureau of Social Hygiene, a pioneering Rockefeller effort to grapple with such social ills as narcotics traffic and prostitution. Woods now served as Junior's majordomo and as president of Metropolitan Square. There was Thomas Debevoise, the imperious family counsel, one of the few individuals in the world on a first-name basis with Junior. There was Charles Heydt, who had started at the office the same year Junior did, 1897, and now oversaw the Rockefellers' real estate interests. There was Bertram Cutler, who had been around almost as long as Heydt (Cutler started in the office in 1901) and for years had managed the family's awesome securities portfolio. And there was Raymond Fosdick, Junior's chief philanthropic adviser and all-around confidant.

Collectively, they functioned as Junior's viceroys, tending to virtually every aspect of the Rockefeller empire. Precious little escaped their purview, precious little that an ambitious, energetic young man could call his own.

Watching over them all, of course, was the meticulous, austere little man known around the office as Mr. Junior. He was no less intimidating a presence to his sons than he was to his employees. Few casually entered his sanctum sanctorum, a dark, forbidding chamber lined with English Tudor oak paneling, dominated by a massive fireplace, and ponderously furnished with a Jacobean refectory table and chairs, Queen Anne desk, and hand-carved Elizabethan conference table. When John 3rd at one point delicately pleaded with his father to make himself a little more accessible, the elder Rockefeller tendered a characteristically starchy response.

> Either before I went abroad or after my return when I had a luncheon talk with you boys I think I said . . . that you boys would always have the first call on my time for conference about any matter that you were seriously desirous of discussing with me. To that end I suggested that you . . . feel free to let me know any time when you had such subjects that you wanted to discuss and that I would at my early convenience appoint a leisurely time for such a talk. I cannot promise to arrange for such a conference at short notice . . . but I will always set a time at your request and that too at my early convenience . . .

John, who had entered the office a year and a half before Nelson, felt himself adrift in the buttoned-up milieu their father had created. Appointed by Junior to a bevy of boards—everything from the Rockefeller Foundation to the Bureau of Social Hygiene to Riverside Church—he marked the end of his second year in the office by confiding to his diary, "I have not been working on any one thing but doing lots of smaller things. It . . . does not give one a chance to go to the bottom of anything or get very familiar with anything." Decades later, John would dryly recall that one of his primary tasks was to serve on his father's behalf as chairman of the Seal Harbor Tennis Committee and find the teaching pro each year.

Nelson would fare no better. In his first months on the job he looked over the plans for new buildings at the Rockefeller Institute (a lowly assistant business manager there was assigned to spend the day with him), reviewed a dummy of a booklet on Colonial Williamsburg, and devoted much time to determining whether the family's Lincoln should be repaired or traded in for a new model. (He recommended fixing it.) He was given the task of overseeing the construction of farm barns at Pocantico: this involved such matters as deciding whether to use white cement ("for the Pennsylvania Dutch effect") or buff cement for the pointing of the stonework, and whether to install a "milking parlor" in lieu of separate milking machines. (Nelson put himself out on a limb by approving the parlor without prior consultation with his father.)

He did have one seemingly challenging assignment: to act as his father's representative in the construction of the Cloisters. But this job was much less than it seemed. It mainly involved acting as a go-between, relaying messages from his father to the architects and vice versa. Junior, in fact, had no compunction about leaving Nelson out of key meetings about the museum's design, only informing his son by memo after the fact as to what had transpired.

Grown man though he was, Nelson couldn't help but feel that his status, in Junior's eyes, was still that of the dependent child. In every important respect, he was thoroughly under his father's thumb. Nelson's prime source of income was still the $17,000 allowance Junior gave him; his office salary was a meager $75 a week. Any trips he made had to be authorized by Junior. All hell broke loose when Nelson once went off on vacation to Mexico without consulting his father in advance.

Rarely would either John or Nelson overtly go against their father's wishes. One such instance occurred when twenty-three-year-old Nelson was invited to join the august board of trustees of New York's Metropolitan Museum of Art. The prospect was a heady one for a young man who, barely two years before, was poring over art texts as a Dartmouth undergraduate. But Junior insisted that he turn the invitation down, on the grounds that his son had no time for such added responsibility. Unfazed, Nelson accepted the post anyway.

"I realize that I am taking the responsibility upon myself against your better judgment," he advised his father. "[But] I feel that the aesthetic side of a person's life is almost as important as his spiritual development or his physical well-being." And, if that wasn't enough, Nelson had another, more pragmatic reason for accepting: "I feel that the contacts which such a position offers are not to be disregarded," he noted.

Hemmed in on all sides by Junior's advisers, shuffled from one inconsequential task to another, John 3rd went about his business stoically, unwilling or unable to break away from the path his iron-willed father laid out for him. Nelson, on the other hand, bristling with energy, simply could not find it in him to tolerate the constricted compass of his father's office. Yet true rebellion—a clean break with the office—was out of the question.

So Nelson took an entirely different tack. If he couldn't carve a meaningful place for himself in his father's empire, then he would simply create a little empire of his own.

The announcement card was dated February 1, 1932. "Fenton Benedict Turck, Jr., Webster Bray Todd and Nelson Aldrich Rockefeller announce the formation of a corporation for the purpose of serving business enterprises in the marketing and distribution of merchandise," the card read. The corporation's address was the Standard Oil Building at 26 Broadway.

For the first time, a descendant of John D. Rockefeller was going into business for himself.

The concept for this enterprise was the brainchild of Turck, a young vice president of the American Radiator Company. Believing that large corporations were not getting the full benefit from their outlays for supplies, insurance, shipping, advertising, and the like, Turck devised a complicated one-hand-washes-the-other scheme. A building materials company, say, that was after the business of a construction contractor would get the railroad that hauled its goods to send business to the contractor; the grateful contractor, in turn, would be encouraged to use the company's materials. Turck and colleagues would broker these multisided deals for a fee. The scheme had been tried out by Turck at American Radiator, with some success. Now he wanted to go out on his own with it—although he was careful to retain his position at American Radiator.

Besides Nelson, the other partner was Webster Todd, the junior Todd in the firm managing Rockefeller Center. Given Todd's connection to Rockefeller Center, as well as Nelson's, it was obvious that the threesome saw the massive project as a vast mother lode of business connections that they could assiduously mine. Among other things, the new firm could try to lure tenants to Rockefeller Center, whose rental prospects were still dicey amidst the gloom of the Depression.

Nelson sought, and obtained, his father's permission for the venture. He pledged to devote no more than half his time to the firm; the other half would be spent working for Junior, as before. If Junior had any misgivings about the new enterprise, and its potential use of Rockefeller connections, he kept them to himself. Relating Nelson's plans to patriarch John D. Senior, he explained why he gave in to Nelson: "His temperament is such that he is happier when he is creating something himself and directly responsible for its success," said Junior.

Not satisfied with just his father's approbation, Nelson sought the blessing of the founding father himself. He and Turck visited John D. at his winter retreat in Ormond Beach, Florida, and sketched out their plan. As Turck would remember, "The old gentleman got the idea in three minutes and gave Nelson his old rolltop desk at 26 Broadway. He invited us to stay on a few days and talk over details. Every morning we'd take turns reading Psalms before breakfast, which consisted of floods of orange juice."

In February the firm opened its doors as Turck & Co., perhaps in deference to Turck's senior status, or perhaps as a gesture of discretion about the Rockefeller connection. (Todd, busy helping his father, John R. Todd, with Rockefeller Center, appears to have played no more than a nominal role in the venture.) Within two months three clients were signed: Devoe & Reynolds, a paint and varnish company; Johns-Manville, the homebuilding concern; and Rockefeller Center. The Rockefeller ties were again exploited a few months later when the Chase National Bank came aboard; the Rockefellers were significant shareholders of Chase, and Nelson's uncle Winthrop Aldrich, with Junior's support, had just been named president. Two more clients were added by the fall: Consolidation Coal, then in receivership, and Ingersoll Rand.

It was soon abundantly evident that Turck & Co.'s biggest selling point was not Fenton Turck's wheeling and dealing but Nelson Rockefeller's family influence. From the outset Nelson made unabashed use of Rockefeller power. A confidential report to Nelson on the firm's progress chronicled this phenomenon. Regarding Consolidation Coal, the report noted, "Influence brought to bear through the Rockefeller family interests, such as, for example, the Chase National Bank and Rockefeller Center, Inc., has served to secure some actual business for the company, conservatively, 100,000 tons of coal, and to secure a good promise of more in the future."

Turck & Co.'s relationship with the Chase Bank was especially close. "Efforts have been made to increase accounts and deposits for the bank through the personal connections of Mr. Turck, Mr. Rockefeller, and through the influence of the business placed by Todd & Brown [Todd, Robertson's engineering subsidiary] for Rockefeller Center," the report said. "The result may be conservatively estimated as an increase of a million dollars in the deposits of the bank." The bank, in turn, "has been generous with needed information, and with assistance for our clients."

But it was on Rockefeller Center that Nelson lavished most of his attention. Freed from the hierarchical constraints of the family office, Nelson could spin out ideas at will. He began working on the notion of devoting one building in the Center to charitable, philanthropic, and nonprofit groups, and persuaded several organizations to sign binding agreements to lease space if the building was constructed. (It was never built, but several of those organizations wound up leasing other spaces in the complex.) He also conceived the idea of renting the store space on the RCA Building's ground floor to large national advertisers for exhibition purposes. To pursue the scheme (which ultimately never came off) he hired Dartmouth classmate Bob Bottome. So intent was Nelson on Rockefeller Center that he opened a Turck & Co. office uptown in the Graybar Building at 420 Lexington Avenue—an office that, conveniently enough, was provided to him rent-free by Todd, Robertson, which happened to manage the property.

Not all the firm's clients came away satisfied. Johns-Manville severed its relationship after less than a year. Nelson told Turck that a representative of the company had come to see him and "seemed rather upset." Ingersoll Rand also dropped the firm. "Apparently the contract was entered into under a misapprehension as to the nature of our services," an in-house memo noted.

Turck & Co. would end its first year only marginally profitable, with a mere $5,600 of net income. But as a launching pad for Nelson, a place where he could channel his pent-up energy, it was a complete success.

In mid-October of that year, Fenton Turck was enough at ease about the firm's prospects to take a trip to Bermuda. He jotted a wish-you-were-here letter to Nelson. "It is a perfect spot here to do a real loaf," Turck wrote.

Turck needn't have hurried back. Upon his return to New York he was informed that Turck & Co. would be reorganized as of the first of the year. The reorganization would consist of Nelson Rockefeller acquiring 100 percent of the stock. Turck and Webster Todd were out of the picture.

Turck's idyll in Bermuda, while his partner was working frenetically up north, may have had something to do with his fate. But the more likely reason for the reshuffling was the inescapable fact that nearly all of Turck & Co.'s business came about because of Nelson's Rockefeller connections.

Nelson, in other words, had transformed Turck & Co. into a vehicle for cashing in on the Rockefeller network. And for that, he hardly needed partners.

The breakup of the partnership showed that behind Nelson's glad-handing, insouciant facade, a certain ruthlessness lurked. Turck and Todd wanted to stay on, but Nelson gave them no choice. He paid Turck $3,000 for his stock, and gave Turck his share of as yet uncollected client fees. Todd was paid $2,110—exactly what he had invested eleven months earlier—plus 6 percent interest. While Turck and Todd would later describe the parting as amicable, the negotiations had their rough moments. Turck thought he was underpaid, and that the firm's contribution to Rockefeller Center hadn't been adequately recognized. Rockefeller family counsel Thomas Debevoise, in turn, threatened to dissolve the corporation rather than give in to Turck's demands.

By November 30, Turck had capitulated and resigned as the firm's president. Nelson was the new president, and he had a new name for the company: Special Work, Inc.

He promptly renegotiated the contracts with his clients, including a new retainer arrangement with Rockefeller Center: Special Work was to be paid $800 a month for its services, plus half the regular brokerage commission on all leases it closed. Chase—perhaps sensing some public relations problems if a formal agreement with Nelson became known—worked out an informal understanding in which, in Special Work's words, "this company places its facilities at the disposal of the bank and wherever possible assists in the new business activities of that institution."

Working his Rockefeller connections to the hilt, Nelson tried to bring other family-linked companies into the fold. In March he added Socony-Vacuum—the old Standard Oil of New York—to his list. He even made overtures to Colorado Fuel and Iron, the company that had brought such opprobrium to the Rockefellers when it massacred miners at Ludlow two decades before. No doubt to Junior's everlasting relief, the company and Nelson were unable to come to terms.

The Socony-Vacuum tie paid off immediately. The company promptly signed leases for two Rockefeller Center storefronts. Not long after, Nelson persuaded International Paper Co. to give Socony-Vacuum all its New York and New Jersey oil business. While he was at it, he also brokered International Paper's southern oil purchases to Standard Oil of New Jersey, and its Canadian oil purchases to Imperial Oil.

But the prime focal point for his energies remained Rockefeller Center. As he toured the construction site he could see the magnificent agglomeration of buildings taking shape, the mammoth metal skeletons sheathed in Indiana limestone as the first of the edifices neared completion. Radio City Music Hall, the triumphant concoction of impresario Roxy Rothafel, had already opened in December 1932 with a seventeen-act gala featuring everyone from Ray Bolger to Martha Graham to the Roxyettes (the future Rockettes). The RCA Building would soon be ready for occupancy, as would the RKO Building.

More than anything, Nelson yearned to be a part of it all. And with Special Work as his vehicle, he could be. Because at the same time that Todd, Robertson was signing up tenants, Nelson had his own, parallel rental operation going on at Special Work. Rather than delegate the job, he obtained a broker's license and handled it himself.

Landing commercial tenants in the depths of the Great Depression was no small feat. Yet in the course of the next year Nelson closed twenty-one leases, accounting for 110,000 square feet in the RCA and RKO buildings, and yielding average annual rental income of $286,000. Among the tenants were Special Work clients (Consolidation Coal, Socony-Vacuum), offshoots of the Rockefeller oil empire (Standard Oil of California), trade associations (New York State League of Buildings and Loans, American Petroleum Institute), and some of the nonprofit groups, such as the National Health Council, that he had once thought he could sell on a separate building.

Aside from those he signed up himself, Nelson claimed to have "assisted"

Rockefeller Center on "more than one hundred important leases." Sometimes, he said, he was the deciding factor in the negotiations; in other instances he played a more modest role.

For the most part, he coexisted peacefully enough with the Rockefeller Center renting department. But on at least one occasion, a major contretemps developed. The tenant in question was Nelson's erstwhile "client," the Chase Bank. Chase was dickering for a branch in the RCA Building, and was pressing for the most favorable possible terms: a nineteen-year lease with a rental based on the branch's deposits, capped at a maximum of $100,000 a year. The Rockefeller Center rental committee was ready to agree to those terms, albeit with considerable reluctance, when Chase, at the last minute, threw in one more demand: that no other bank, except possibly a savings bank, be allowed to open an office in Rockefeller Center.

This demand for exclusivity was simply more than the rental committee could stomach. Giving in to Chase not only would seriously hamper their efforts to rent out other space in the complex but would hold all of Rockefeller Center and its tenants hostage to a single bank. Colonel Woods, the Center's president, felt that way; so did the family's top real estate man, Charles Heydt. While John Todd was eager to rent the space to Chase, he, too, felt that exclusivity was going too far.

But on the other side, pushing for the concession, was Nelson Rockefeller. To say he had something of a conflict of interest in this situation, given Special Work's relationship with Chase, would be the grossest understatement. Indeed, the Chase executive at the other end of the bargaining table was none other than Nelson's uncle Winthrop Aldrich.

Nelson somehow enlisted the support of two of Junior's stalwarts, Debevoise and Bertram Cutler. They argued that since Chase was a Rockefeller institution, why shouldn't it get special privileges? This was too much for Heydt, who penned an angry missive to the vacationing Junior, asking him to adjudicate.

"I have no quarrel with [the Chase Bank] because they are looking out for themselves," wrote Heydt, "but we also have a duty to look out for Rockefeller Center. In this instance, I feel that it is unreasonable and unjust to you to give us an ultimatum that they will not do business except on their own terms."

Looking over Heydt's note at the Eyrie, Junior was inclined to agree with him. He relayed word to Nelson that Chase's demands were "neither fair nor good business for us." But he pointedly added that his mind was "still open."

After mulling the matter some more, Junior came up with a compromise. There was no way, he told his brother-in-law, that Rockefeller Center could grant Chase exclusivity in the lease. But, on the other hand, the two of them could have a gentleman's agreement, set forth in an exchange of personal letters between them. The agreement *would* give Chase exclusivity—but at the same time, somewhat paradoxically, it would also give Rockefeller Center the right to rent space to another bank, as long as Chase was allowed first refusal on the space.

This solution, convoluted and contradictory though it was, seemed to satisfy everyone. Chase had its branch, Rockefeller Center kept its options open—and Nelson could point to one more major lease on which he had "assisted."

What Chase knew, when it squeezed Rockefeller Center, was exactly what just about every other prospective tenant knew: the development was in trouble.

"Conditions," a report to the Rockefeller Center board noted in March 1933, "have not been ideal for making leases for office space." In fact, to say that they were abysmal would be putting it mildly. The breadlines, the bank runs, the desperate crowds milling around shuttered factories were ample testimony to what Rockefeller Center was up against. A new President was taking office, and soon he would embark on a breakneck hundred days that would lift the nation's spirits. But it would be a long time before the shards of business confidence could be patched together again, a long time before the willingness to buy and invest and, yes, sign new leases would return.

"Certain leases that had been out for execution have been held up," the board was told. "Also many active prospects from whom favorable decision was expected have taken no action. Many prospective tenants whose leases expire on their present space on the first of May have deferred decisions on new leases until April." The French and British syndicates organized to lease out space in the two buildings dedicated to those countries—La Maison Française and the British Empire Building—were unable to deliver, and Rockefeller Center was compelled to force them out and take over the renting itself. Even tenants that had already signed on were backing off from their pledges: RCA cut its commitment for a million square feet in half. In a conciliatory gesture, RCA president David Sarnoff offered to surrender the building name to General Electric if the company relocated there. General Electric declined.*

The heaviest blow of all was the bankruptcy of RKO. When the theater and movie company went into receivership in 1933 Rockefeller Center lost not only $1.2 million in annual rentals from two theaters in the complex, but $250,000 a year in rent on office space. As compensation, the Center received what Junior regarded as a rather dubious gift: a large chunk of RKO stock. Eventually, to Junior's dismay and Nelson's delight, the holding would represent a controlling interest.

*Eventually, GE *did* get its name on the building, half a century later—when it bought RCA.

Rockefeller Center was rapidly turning into a citywide laughingstock. A popular Broadway play, *As Thousands Cheer,* featured a skit in which Junior played a colossal joke on his father by giving him Rockefeller Center as a birthday present. Critics savaged the venture as a gargantuan affront to the city's sensibilities. *The New Yorker*'s Lewis Mumford railed at the "graceless hulk" that was the RCA Building, and the magazine's editor, Harold Ross, complained about having "to look at that damn thing every day of my life." And, for all the hoopla attending its gala opening, the Music Hall was turning out to be a resounding flop. To boost its prospects, the theater began supplementing its stage show with movies.

With their backs against the wall, Rockefeller Center's managers resorted to every trick in the real estate book to fill their buildings. They launched an all-out public relations blitz, trumpeting such superlatives as the "world's largest chandelier" (at the Center Theater) and the planet's biggest motion-picture screen (at the Music Hall). They leaned hard on Rockefeller family connections: the Rockefeller Foundation was persuaded to take two floors in the RCA Building, and Nelson found himself beseeching such far-flung relations as first cousin once removed Percy Rockefeller (renowned as a "stock market operator," in the words of *Fortune* magazine) to relocate to the tower.

But the most successful (and, some would later say, most desperate) tactic was the Center's offer to prospective tenants to relieve them of the burden of their present leases if they agreed to move to Rockefeller Center. The way it usually worked was that the tenant would be credited for the amount of the old lease, and would assign subletting rights to the former premises to a Rockefeller Center subsidiary, Centroc, Inc., which had been specifically formed for the purpose. To lure Shell Union Oil Corporation, for example, Rockefeller Center credited Shell with the amount of its unexpired leases in five different buildings, some with four years to run. American Cyanamid was similarly enticed from the twenty-three floors of space it was renting in the Ruppert Building on Fifth Avenue and 44th Street.

While landlords grumbled about the Center's predations, no one was willing to take on the Rockefeller colossus. But then, in early 1934, Universal Pictures was lured to Rockefeller Center with an offer to take on its space in the Heckscher Building (now the Crown Building) on Fifth Avenue and 57th Street. Infuriated, the building's owner, August Heckscher, sued Rockefeller Center for $10 million.

A feisty old entrepreneur with a bent for the speculative—at one point, convinced that oil would be discovered in Florida, he bought up thousands of acres in the uninhabitable heart of the state—Heckscher was mortgaged to the hilt on the eight buildings he owned in midtown Manhattan. He had much to lose from the Rockefeller tactics, and his suit overflowed with bitterness. He characterized Rockefeller Center as a "modern Frankenstein" stepping "through the door of special privilege into the realms of destructive competition" and charged that the Rockefeller interests were "depopulating" competing buildings through "coercion."

Heckscher's suit named Junior, John Todd, and other top officers and directors of Rockefeller Center, including Nelson Rockefeller. The suit was not specific about Nelson's involvement, and it was not clear what, if any, role he might have played in the Universal Pictures lease. But even if the Heckscher suit did not spell it out, there was no question that the rental practices he was complaining about were avidly employed by Nelson. In at least one of the leases Nelson negotiated, the deal with the National Health Council for space in the RCA Building, he induced the tenant to break its lease with a building on Seventh Avenue by offering to credit the council for the old lease's $10,000 cancellation penalty. Judging from Nelson's success as a rental agent, there were undoubtedly other such situations.

Rockefeller Center officials defended their tactics on the grounds that they were common practice in the real estate industry. But, as it turned out, this defense would never be aired in court, because the Heckscher suit never came to trial. In 1941 it was dropped, after Heckscher's death. Heckscher's last years validated the forebodings expressed in his lawsuit: overextended and squeezed by the Depression, he lost the Heckscher Building and the rest of his fortune as well.

The Heckscher suit had no real impact on Rockefeller Center's rental operation: the special deals were still being struck, by Nelson and by others. (To attract Consolidated Oil Corporation to the development, Rockefeller Center ended up buying Consolidated's entire headquarters building in lower Manhattan.) Still, it did produce a raft of discomfiting publicity that Junior would gladly have done without, publicity that had echoes of the monopolist charges that dogged his father at the turn of the century. He couldn't really blame Nelson for this; his son was simply taking advantage of an established practice among Rockefeller Center managers.

But the stirrings over the lawsuit were coming on top of another, more monumental controversy that had already swamped Junior and Rockefeller Center with a deluge of negative press. And, in this one, his enterprising second son had more than a passing role.

The trouble stemmed from Nelson's deep involvement in another budding institution the Rockefellers were sponsoring: the Museum of Modern Art.

The museum had been the pet project of Abby and a small coterie of other prominent collectors. Frustrated with the Metropolitan Museum's aloofness toward modern art, eager to compress the timespan between an artist's work and his recognition by the public, these collectors banded together in 1929 to start a new museum devoted to Impressionism and all that had come after. As its first director, they hired Alfred Barr, a young Wellesley professor with an eclectic bent and a discriminating eye. And, ironically enough, they set up its first home in the Heckscher Building. Soon, the crowds the new museum was drawing would compel a move to a Rockefeller-owned townhouse on 53rd Street and Fifth Avenue.

From the outset Nelson had been his mother's family co-conspirator in the museum, sharing in her hopes and frustrations, not the least of which was with Junior's skepticism. "I showed Papa the pictures and the gallery today," she wrote Nelson at Dartmouth in May 1929, "and he thinks that they are terrible beyond words, so I am somewhat depressed tonight." Mindful of his closeness to Abby, and his enthusiasm for the museum's mission, Nelson was singled out by the trustees, even while he was still in college, for an important role in the institution. In the spring of 1930, during his final semester at Dartmouth, he was named to the museum's new Junior Advisory Committee, a group of young art-minded New Yorkers who would be groomed as future trustees. And by June of that year, Modern Museum president A. Conger Goodyear was writing to Abby asking if it would be all right if Nelson was appointed the committee's chairman.

Abby delightedly gave her blessing, while pointing out to Goodyear that Nelson wouldn't be able to take up the reins until his return from his round-the-world honeymoon. This was fine with Goodyear, although, as Abby would later relate to her son, "Every time I see Mr. Goodyear he says in a pensive tone of voice, 'When is Nelson coming back?' I think he has great confidence in your ability to stir up that younger group."

Stir them up he did. One of the committee members, Elizabeth Cobb—niece of museum co-founder Lillie P. Bliss, and stepdaughter of Conger Goodyear—recalls the group's meetings under Nelson as raucous free-for-alls: "We were told by the trustees that they wanted us to criticize them. So we thought that was a wonderful idea: we loved criticizing them. We'd have meetings that would go on all morning, break up for lunch and come back again. We'd sit on the floor, and hold up our hands when we wanted to speak because we all wanted to speak. We were very excited about it."

The group came by its intellectual feistiness rather naturally. Among its members were George Gershwin (whose interest in art, both as a collector and as a fledgling painter, nearly matched his devotion to music) and two well-heeled, highly opinionated young aesthetes, Edward Warburg and Lincoln Kirstein, who at Harvard had organized the influential Society of Contemporary Art. Also on the committee was a lanky young modern architecture buff named Philip Johnson.

It was quickly apparent that this assemblage of egos would not be content to merely advise and criticize. Speaking for them all, Nelson told the trustees, "We feel there is a real opportunity for a contribution on our part, and we do not want to be just the members of an important-sounding committee."

What the group most wanted to do something about was the museum's perceived disinterest in American artists. "The opening exhibitions were all

European," Cobb recalls. "We criticized the trustees very severely for not doing enough for American artists. Of course, we were in the Depression then, and we thought we could do something to help those artists."

"So," relates Cobb, "finally the trustees said to us, 'All right, go ahead, put on a show.' "

The job of organizing the show landed in the lap of Lincoln Kirstein. To showcase the artists, he came up with the novel idea of asking each one to execute a mural—or, at least, his or her idea of a section of one.

There was, it turned out, considerable calculation behind Kirstein's murals idea. At the very moment the exhibition was mounted, Rockefeller Center was in the process of selecting artists to execute murals in the RCA Building lobby. Kirstein saw the murals show as a way of positioning American artists to get those commissions. For Nelson, who served on the committee overseeing the Center's artwork, the show offered one more wedge in his struggle for influence at Rockefeller Center. (The exhibition's catalogue, in fact, was partly underwritten by Rockefeller Center managing agent John Todd.)

With the iconoclastic Kirstein as impresario, the murals exhibition was bound to be provocative. But just how provocative would not be evident to the trustees until their first advance viewing of the mural panels. To the utter horror of Goodyear, Samuel Lewisohn, and the other affluent directors, several of the pictures were heavily ideological in content, with a marked tilt to the left. A Ben Shahn mural depicted the Sacco and Vanzetti trial, including an unflattering portrayal of the esteemed Harvard University president Abbott Lawrence Lowell, chairman of the panel that upheld the pair's guilt. And another work, entitled " 'Us Fellas Gotta Stick Together'—Al Capone," showed the gangster with several of his "cronies": Henry Ford, President Herbert Hoover, J. P. Morgan, and John D. Rockefeller, Sr.

As the trustees took all this in with speechless stupefaction, Lewisohn—who normally slept through the meetings—opened his eyes and cracked, "And I thought the museum needed money!"

The appalled trustees pressed for the removal of the offending works from the exhibition. "I cannot help feeling," argued Singer sewing machine magnate Stephen Clark, "that we might jeopardize the whole future of the Museum if we should show pictures which would be so offensive to so many of our supporters." Shaken and surprised by the uproar—he seems to have had no idea that the murals would be so controversial—Nelson immediately offered to either remove the pictures or have the artists change the caricatures in question. But when Kirstein was dispatched to negotiate with the artists, he found them as adamant as the trustees. One artist warned of a suit, and others threatened to rally all the show's artists to withdraw their works and exhibit them in a protest show somewhere else.

Worried now about the firestorm of publicity that would descend on the museum—and himself—if that threat was carried out, a frantic young Nelson retreated to the sanctuary of the Rockefeller family office. His father's key advisers agreed that the best course would be to let the show go on. But Junior was not so easily swayed; all he could see were the most dire repercussions, for Nelson and for the family. He laid out his foreboding in a letter to the family counsel, Thomas Debevoise:

> The point which Nelson thinks insignificant and which Mrs. Rockefeller and I feel is at least deserving of the fullest consideration is this: What effect will it have on Nelson's future relations with public men like Mr. Morgan, Mr. Lowell and others, what effect will it have on the efforts of the Museum to get support from people of this class, and what effect will it have on Mrs. Rockefeller and me and the name of Rockefeller to have it publicly evident that at least Mrs. Rockefeller and Nelson, because of their official relationship to the Museum, have permitted the use of the Museum for promulgating propaganda as between the classes and against the institutions of government. This, I feel, is the real question.

To placate Morgan and the other targets of the murals, Junior told Nelson he would have to meet with the venerable gentlemen, show them photographs of the murals, and ask them what they think should be done. Nelson dutifully called on Morgan at the financier's majestic Wall Street office and apologized profusely for the offending artwork. Morgan, who had just recruited Nelson to the Metropolitan Museum board, was jovial about the whole matter, and told the downcast young man that the best course would be to simply hang the pictures as inconspicuously as possible and be done with them. Unable to meet with Lowell, Nelson dispatched a letter expressing his mortification: "We have been caught in a very embarrassing situation and there is no way out of it." Lowell, too, agreed that the show should be mounted.

Armed with these assurances, Nelson secured the support of Debevoise and the family's renowned public relations adviser, Ivy Lee. Stephen Clark rescinded his objections, and Goodyear, who had threatened to resign over the affair, now gave his grudging approval to the exhibition.

And so, on May 2, 1932, the show *Murals by American Painters and Photographers* opened at the Modern. The critics were far from kind. "The exhibition is so bad as to give America something to think about for a long time," wrote *The New York Times,* while the *New York Herald Tribune*'s critic hissed: "In sheer, dismal ineptitude the exhibition touches bottom."

Privately, museum director Alfred Barr seemed to agree. When a Dallas museum inquired about mounting the exhibition after its New York run, Barr deflated the idea: "Many of the pictures are scarcely worth sending around except as illustrations of how not to paint a mural." But with Nelson, the director—no political naif—mouthed a much more upbeat line. The critics, he told Nelson, "missed the point." He urged him not to be discouraged.

Barr need not have bothered. Having come this far, Nelson was not about to be deflected by a few critical barbs. Elated by the public response to the exhibition—almost 14,000 had seen it in a little over three weeks—he pushed the trustees to extend at least part of the show through the summer (the exhibition was scheduled to run only until the end of the month). He also talked up the idea of circulating the show among other museums, the very idea that so appalled Barr. "It seems to me," Nelson wrote his mother, "that . . . educationally [the exhibition] is very important and I don't think the Museum has anything to be ashamed of in sponsoring it."

It soon became clear just why he was so eager to tout it. In late June he invited Barr and Colonel Arthur Woods, the family chief of staff, who was serving as president of Rockefeller Center, to join him for lunch to discuss "the recent murals exhibition and the possibility of some of these artists doing work for Rockefeller Center."

Nelson got nowhere in his efforts to bring the museum muralists to Rockefeller Center. But far from retreating, he simply switched tactics. Instead of promoting unknown young Americans, he would champion an artist of world-class stature, a muralist of impeccable reputation—and an artist whose work his mother knew and adored.

Abby Aldrich Rockefeller was a connoisseur of truly catholic tastes, collecting everything from Cubists to cigar-store Indians. But none of her affinities was as incongruous as her patronage of the flamboyant Mexican artist Diego Rivera. A dedicated Communist who viewed his work as agitprop as well as art, a contentious paranoid who would stand on his scaffold with pistols strapped to his waist, the hulking, moon-faced Rivera was truly an unlikely object of a doyenne's affections. But Abby loved his murals, sprawling cinematic frescoes populated by *bandoleros* and sombreroed peasants and bristling with primitive force. Even his anticapitalist tirades, put forth in his work through imagery and caricatures that made the MOMA murals seem positively tepid by comparison, were taken in stride and perhaps even savored by Abby. So enchanted was she by a Mexico City mural that depicted her own father-in-law, along with Henry Ford and J. P. Morgan, partaking of a dinner of gold coins and ticker tape that she asked Rivera to make a copy for her.

Abby was instrumental in organizing a monumental Rivera one-man show at the Museum of Modern Art in December 1931 that did much to affirm the artist's worldwide reputation. She seemed hardly daunted by the gloomy frescoes Rivera executed specially for the show; entitled *Frozen Assets,* they depicted scenes of Depression-wracked New York, including a dreary hall filled with sleeping unemployed men. By that time, a passion for Rivera was in vogue among the country's cognoscenti: he was lionized throughout a 1930 visit to California, during which he delighted San Francisco art lovers by painting three murals there (including one in which the artist's posterior was prominently featured). And in May 1931 he received his biggest commission yet: a $25,000 grant from Edsel Ford, Henry's son, to paint a "Portrait of Detroit" on the walls of the Detroit Institute of Art's inner court.

Considering Rivera's renown, and Abby's copious affection for the man and his work, it was not at all surprising that Nelson blithely ignored the artist's penchant for outrageousness and began promoting him as a prospective muralist for the RCA Building. The idea of dressing up the building's lobby with murals had been the inspiration of architect Raymond Hood; the murals would complement the sculptures (portraying such uplifting themes as "Gifts of Earth to Mankind" and "The Spirit of Progress") planned for the Rockefeller Center building exteriors. Two accomplished, albeit conservative, painters, Frank Brangwyn and José María Sert, had already been signed on for some of the lobby walls. But the showpiece wall—the one opposite the building's main entrance on Rockefeller Plaza—would be reserved for an artist of international stature.

Hood and John Todd journeyed to Paris to woo Matisse (who turned them down flat) and Picasso (whom they found impossible to even track down). Finally, at Nelson's urging, and with Junior's grudging approval, Rivera was approached. "Although I do not personally care for much of his work," Junior told Hood, "he seems to have become very popular just now and will probably be a good drawing card." Rivera accepted in October 1932—but only after insisting that his fresco be in color, not black, white, and gray as the architects had wanted. Nelson clearly felt Rivera was doing Rockefeller Center a favor by accepting the $21,000 commission. When the negotiations were at last concluded, he wrote the artist, "May I take this opportunity to again tell you how much my mother and I appreciate your spirit in doing this mural under the existing circumstances."

Like the other Rockefeller Center artists, Rivera was given a portentous theme: in his case, "Man at the Crossroads Looking with Hope and High Vision to the Choosing of a New and Better Future." From Detroit, where he was beginning work on the Institute of Art mural, he sent back a vague sketch, along with a lengthy verbal description of what he intended. The description was rife with socialist imagery. One panel, he said, "will show the Workers arriving at a true understanding of their rights regarding the means of production. . . . It will also show the Workers of the cities and the country inheriting the earth." Other parts of the mural would be peopled by more workers, and peasants, and unemployed workmen in a breadline.

Despite these hints that Rivera had more in mind for his fresco than simply a bevy of Adonises marching toward the sunrise, Todd and Hood and, ultimately, Junior himself approved the Rivera sketches. According to one of Rivera's assistants, when Hood was shown the final drawing by Rivera, he glanced at it only cursorily before signing it. Handed the contract by Hood, Rivera flipped it to the last page and signed. "You better have your lawyer see it," said Hood, whereupon Rivera replied, "You signed my sketch without looking it over. You trust me, I trust you!"

In Detroit, meanwhile, a storm was brewing over the Institute of Art frescoes. "Señor Rivera," fulminated one educator, "has foisted on Mr. Ford and the museum a Communist manifesto." Throughout the city, ministers mounted pulpits to denounce the Rivera mural for its alleged lampooning of the Holy Family and for its "slattern" and "grossly sensual" nude figures.

Groping for support, the institute turned to its sister museum and Rivera sponsor, the Museum of Modern Art. The trustees, however, were wary of getting involved, until Nelson spoke up in Rivera's defense, persuading the board that at the very least it should allow someone at the museum to issue a statement backing the institute and its embattled mural.

With the tumult in Detroit still reverberating around him, Rivera arrived in New York in mid-March 1933 to begin work on the RCA Building. As a gaggle of reporters and photographers looked on, he mounted the metal scaffolding and went over the charcoal outline of his sketches that his assistants had laid out on the 1,000-square-foot wall. Then the painting began, thirty square feet at a time, with the planks on the scaffolding lowered day after day as more of the wall was covered. Often Rivera and his assistants (one of whom was Ben Shahn) would work through the night.

In a matter of days the first section of the mural was revealed: a panorama of airplanes, death rays, and bayonet-wielding soldiers wearing gas masks. Then the next section became clear. It was a May Day demonstration in Red Square, with kerchief-clad women singing as the Red Flag-waving procession passed Lenin's tomb. One of his assistants, Lucienne Bloch, noted in her diary that "Diego had been expelled from the Communist Party three years earlier for refusing to toe the line. He wanted desperately to return to the fold, but on his own terms. So it is to prove to them that he is not afraid of any capitalists that he paints the Moscow May Day with gusto and with plenty of Venetian red."

Two days later Rivera completed the section beneath the war scene. It was a constellation of floating microbes: syphilis, gonorrhea, tuberculosis. To get the germs right, Rivera consulted slides at New York Hospital and Brooklyn Jewish Hospital, and pored over medical texts while he stood on the scaffolding, brush in hand.

Far from laboring in secrecy, Rivera, ever the showman, delighted in welcoming visitors to his work-in-progress. One day Abby Rockefeller herself arrived and cheerfully climbed the scaffold. Scrutinizing the Moscow May

Day parade, she pronounced it the finest part of the mural yet. At other times, Tod Rockefeller would show up, and so would Nelson. Taking in all that was visible so far—the Moscow May Day marchers, the gas masks and death rays, the venereal-disease germs hovering over cardplaying, gin-swilling society ladies—they were just as enthusiastic as Abby. Bloch noted in her diary on April 19, "Nelson R. called on Diego, is crazy about the fresco!"

Then, five days later, the *New York World-Telegram* hit the stands with a headline that blared, "RIVERA PAINTS SCENES OF COMMUNIST ACTIVITY AND JOHN D. JR. FOOTS BILL." The article gleefully catalogued the mural's sensational elements: "Germs of infectious and hereditary social diseases . . . so placed as to indicate them as the results of a civilization revolving about night clubs . . . a Communist demonstration . . . The dominant color is red—red headdress, red flags, waves of red." It quoted Rivera: "Mrs. Rockefeller said she liked my painting very much," he said. "Mr. Rockefeller likes it too."

The next day the *Telegram* followed up with another article in which various Communist Party functionaries derided Rivera for not going *far enough* with the RCA Building mural. "He has not portrayed to me the brutality, the starvation and the hunger as it really exists," one said. Whether it was because of this goading, or out of pique with the earlier *Telegram* attack, Rivera decided to up the ante. He asked his assistants to obtain a photograph of Lenin, and began sketching out a new tableau for his fresco. A soldier, a worker, and a Negro farmer would be shown holding hands with the Soviet leader.

A quarter of a century later, in a newspaper interview, one of Rivera's assistants, Stephen Dimitroff, said that "all of us, including Rivera's wife [Frida Kahlo, a painter in her own right], begged him not to include the portrait [of Lenin]. But he insisted it made good composition."

On April 30, the day the RCA Building at last opened its doors to the public, Rivera worked furiously on his Lenin panel. "Diego painted him without his cap," Bloch noted. "Now there's no doubt about who is up there!"

Four days later, Rivera received a letter from Nelson Rockefeller:

> While I was in the No. 1 building at Rockefeller Center yesterday viewing the progress of your thrilling mural I noticed that in the most recent portion of the painting you had included a portrait of Lenin. The piece is beautifully painted but it seems to me that his portrait appearing in this mural might very seriously offend a great many people. If it were in a private house it would be one thing, but this mural is in a public building and the situation is therefore quite different. As much as I dislike to do so, I am afraid we must ask you to substitute the face of some unknown man where Lenin's face now appears.
>
> You know how enthusiastic I am about the work which you have been doing and that to date we have in no way restricted you in either subject

or treatment. I am sure you will understand our feeling in this situation and we will greatly appreciate your making the suggested substitution.

Rivera summoned his friends and aides to his side. Shahn threatened to walk off the job if the Lenin portrait was changed. Fearing the worst, Frida urged Bloch to photograph the fresco as soon as possible.

Finally, Rivera sent Nelson his reply. The head of Lenin, he asserted, had been included in the original sketch he had given Hood (in fact, it was nowhere indicated in the sketch, or in Rivera's verbal plan). Lenin, the artist declared, had to stay. However, he was willing to offer a compromise: counterbalancing the Soviet leader would be a portrait of Lincoln, surrounded by abolitionists like John Brown and Harriet Beecher Stowe.

Should he be compelled to remove Lenin, Rivera warned, "rather than mutilate the conception, I should prefer the physical destruction of the conception in its entirety."

On May 9 Rivera was back at his scaffold, but beneath him the lobby had the ominous air of an encampment on the eve of battle. Uniformed and plainclothes guards patrolled the halls, challenging anyone who came near the mural. Then, at six o'clock, managing agent Hugh Robertson strode into the lobby, asked Rivera to come down from the scaffold, and handed him a check for the balance of his $21,500 fee. Rivera's services would no longer be required.

Within moments an army of workmen ascended to the fresco and nailed heavy canvas sheets over it, obscuring every inch of it from view. Rivera was surprisingly buoyant. *"Maintenant,"* he shouted to his assistants, *"c'est la bataille!"*

His words proved instantly prophetic: by nine o'clock, a crowd of three hundred protesters had gathered outside the building, bearing placards reading "Save Rivera's Art," and scuffled with police called in to break up the march. The Rivera affair was front-page news the next day, and went on making headlines in the days that followed, as artists and writers banded together to voice solidarity with Rivera. The Rockefeller action was likened to Nazi book burning, and at a Columbus Circle rally Communists yelled, "We want Rockefeller with a rope around his neck!" The business community, meanwhile, rallied to the Rockefellers' support. The National Association of Manufacturers wrote to congratulate Nelson for his "courageous and patriotic" rejection of "subversive propaganda." General Motors, which had contracted with Rivera for a mural at its building at the Chicago Century of Progress Exposition, announced that it was terminating the commission.

Although it had not been Nelson who called Rivera off his scaffold (he was conveniently out of town at the time), it was Nelson who was identified in the public mind as Rivera's antagonist. He even was the subject of a bit of doggerel in *The New Yorker* penned by E. B. White (in which an anguished

Nelson explains to Rivera, "And though your art I dislike to hamper, I owe a *little* to Gamper").

For Nelson, it was all publicity of the most unwelcome sort. He had been cast in the role of puritanical censor, a particularly uncomfortable position for a young man who fancied himself a budding modern art connoisseur and who just months before had vigorously defended Rivera in the Detroit brouhaha. Yet what was most unsettling about the whole business was that it could have so easily been foreseen and avoided. It was as though Nelson had learned nothing from the uproar over the museum murals show a year earlier, and as though he knew nothing about the proclivities of the artist he was so anxious to retain. True, Rivera had given no indication until the very end that he would be featuring Lenin in his mural. But well before the image of Lenin went up, Nelson had looked on approvingly at the Moscow May Day scenes and the floating venereal-disease microbes, elements that would have sparked outrage even if Lenin never entered the picture.

Once again, as in the murals show, Nelson had allowed his radical artistic sensibilities, his eagerness to make an impact on Rockefeller Center, and his unbridled enthusiasm to overwhelm his better judgment. But unlike the murals show, a few apologies this time would not be enough.

All the rest of that year the Rivera mural lay hidden behind its canvas shroud, as Nelson and the Rockefeller Center architects and managers agonized over what to do with it. Finally, Nelson proposed a solution that would seemingly satisfy both the Rivera partisans and the conservative faction at the Center: the fresco would be donated to the Museum of Modern Art. To pay for the move, he suggested that the museum sell tickets to see the mural. Although the Rockefeller Center managers were willing to go ahead with the scheme, the museum's trustees apparently balked. Having gone through the storm over the murals show, and having witnessed the furor the Detroit fresco created, they perhaps were not willing to suffer through a repeat performance.

Late one cold February evening in 1934, Lucienne Bloch and Steve Dimitroff, Rivera's assistants, were strolling through midtown Manhattan after taking in a movie. On a whim, they decided to look in on the RCA Building. The doors were locked, but as the couple turned to leave they noticed about a dozen fifty-gallon oil drums near the entrance, heaped with what looked like small chunks of plaster. Peering into the drums, they discovered to their horror that the plaster chunks were the smashed-up shards of Diego Rivera's mural.

Nine months earlier, Rivera had told Nelson, in his fusillade of verbiage, that he would prefer the piece's "physical destruction" to its mutilation. Rockefeller Center had now taken him up on his preference.

Speaking out in Mexico City, Rivera called the mural's destruction "an act of cultural vandalism." Outraged New York artists labeled it "art murder" and organized a downtown protest rally that was attended by 1,000.

Describing the affair to old John D. Senior in Florida, Junior made it plain that he heartily approved of the mural's smashing. "The picture was obscene and, in the judgment of Rockefeller Center, an offense to good taste," he told his father. "It was for this reason primarily that Rockefeller Center decided to destroy it."

A chastened Nelson said nothing as the workmen hauled off the debris that had once been the Rivera mural, the mural he had so proudly contracted for and urged along. There was no talk now of artistic integrity, no championing of Rivera's vision. The only course left for Nelson was to fall in line with his father's wishes. Too much lay ahead for him, too much was at stake, to do otherwise.

Nine

Power Play

On April 24, 1932, at Doctors Hospital in New York, a son was born to Tod and Nelson Rockefeller. The jubilant father wired the happy news to John D. Rockefeller, Sr., in Daytona Beach, Florida: "Your great-grandson arrived this morning. Nelson."

The glad tidings were welcomed by Junior, albeit with a touch of sardonic amusement. "It seems difficult to think of Nelson as a father," Junior confided to Senior the next day. "I fancy his own son will always find him more like a brother."

Aside from the normal flush of paternal joy, Nelson could take special pride in the arrival of little Rodman Clark Rockefeller. The first of the brothers to marry, Nelson was now also the first to produce a male heir. (Babs by then had had two daughters.) And for a family with a dynastic imperative, this was hardly a trivial achievement. Nelson wasted no time underscoring the theme, arranging the appropriate "four generations" photo with his father and grandfather. The implication in the family was unmistakable: Nelson was on his way to supplanting his still unmarried older brother John as crown prince.

Ever since his return to New York from his honeymoon, Nelson seemed eager to establish his primacy in family matters. At a Pocantico birthday party for Senior in 1931, it was Nelson who was the master choreographer, assembling his siblings in various groupings as they posed for photographs with the patriarch. And Nelson jumped at every opportunity to cultivate his grandfather, trekking down to Florida to golf with him and treasuring whatever pearls of wisdom the old man was willing to dispense. Well aware of Junior's reverence for his father, Nelson avidly recounted for him the details of every meeting.

"We went to Grandfather's for lunch today," he wrote Junior in August

1932. "Afterwards he took me aside and we had a little talk for half an hour or so. He certainly is an extraordinary man, about the finest I know. There are few people that I really admire as being an all-round success, but he leads the list. His point of view and outlook on life are so perfectly grand. And what a sense of humor!"

More than any of his siblings, Nelson nurtured a sense of manifest destiny about the Rockefeller family, a sense of the power they could collectively wield. "My chief desire," he told Abby, "is that we as a family should ultimately develop into a closely-knit, effective group." To that end, he began to display a paternalistic preoccupation with the ups and downs of his sister and brothers. In notes to Abby, he chronicled their doings with the approving air of a schoolmaster relating the progress of his charges. "Johnny is showing more confidence and poise every day," he told his mother at one point. "Sis is coming along very fast and beginning to take her part in things. An example is the fact that she has invited the Advisory Committee of the Museum to have their next meeting at her apartment and she is going to pour tea. That is something she wouldn't have thought of doing two years ago."

Nelson was unsparing in his criticism of the hapless Winthrop, who was stumbling through Yale, but pronounced himself "tickled to death" by a report that Winthrop was doing better. In words that might have been plucked straight from the mouth of Junior, Nelson declared to his mother that "the present progress which Winnie is making is the source of almost as much pride to me as I know it is to you." (Not long afterward Winthrop dropped out.)

And then there was the instance when Nelson's brotherly solicitude threatened to turn into something more sinister.

In the summer of 1932 Nelson was planning to travel up to Seal Harbor. So was Blanchette Hooker, the comely debutante whom his brother John was ardently courting. The plan was for Blanchette to sojourn at the Eyrie so that she and John might put their relationship on a more serious footing. Hearing of Blanchette's visit, Nelson phoned and suggested they might drive up together.

Blanchette accepted the offer, and the next day joined Nelson for what she thought would be a long but leisurely drive to Boston, and thence to Maine. But instead, Nelson drove the car onto the New York-to-Boston ferry, for an overnight cruise. The Boston night ferry was a notorious venue for illicit assignations, and a shiver went down Blanchette's spine when they boarded it. When they entered the dining room later for dinner, Blanchette was further mortified to see Abby's brother Winthrop and his family at a nearby table, eyeing her and Nelson with evident curiosity. As it happened, nothing more of moment occurred that evening—owing, perhaps, to Uncle Winthrop's obvious presence.

Debarking the next morning, Nelson and Blanchette began the long drive up to Seal Harbor. The journey turned out to be a lot longer than Blanchette expected; thanks to several breakdowns en route, she and Nelson did not arrive at the Eyrie until seven-thirty that evening, an hour and a half late for dinner. They were greeted with the frostiest of stares by Junior, Abby, and John. "Nelson," Abby icily informed her son, "Tod has supper waiting for you."

The next day, Abby summoned Blanchette to her sitting room. There, as Blanchette would later delicately recall, Abby talked to her "about Nelson."

Once John had calmed down, the courting proceeded apace, and by summer's end the couple announced their engagement. Blanchette and Tod, meanwhile, hit it off instantly, and initiated a lifelong friendship. Nothing more was said about the Boston ferry, or about exactly what Nelson had in mind that evening. But late in her life, when Blanchette was asked to reflect on Nelson, her thoughts were still clearly tinged by that incident. Blanchette would describe him as "one of those men who is full of power and excitement and who could not get along without women. In many ways he was the jewel of the family, in other ways always remained a naughty boy. He was just a little out of hand all the time."

It was around that period—when Nelson was still struggling to secure a beachhead in his father's office—that Tod and Nelson's schoolboy friend Bill Alton happened to chat about Nelson's future. "We talked about where we thought he would end up," remembers Alton. "Our conclusion was that we thought he would either be President or Secretary of State."

Tod, who by then had settled comfortably into the role of society wife and mother, had already taken the full measure of her husband's ambitions. Perhaps it was the bustle of their honeymoon, with the cavalcade of potentates and business leaders, that convinced her. Or perhaps there was for her, as there was for Alton, simply a sense of inevitability about the arc of her husband's career, a feeling that the boundless energy, properly harnessed, might one day achieve great things.

No one had a keener understanding of his ambition, of the raw hunger for success that possessed him, than Nelson himself. And, to an extent that would have shocked those who knew him only as a bubbly go-getter, he was deeply troubled—even haunted—by that hunger. Hardly anyone knew how tormented he was. But Abby knew. In a singular moment of introspection, he unburdened himself in an exchange of letters with her in the early spring of 1933.

Responding to a note from his mother (which has since been lost), Nelson was ruthlessly, painfully self-analytical:

> I can . . . assure you that you can't be any more worried about me than I am myself. I find life just as perplexing and pointless as Laurance

does, only as I have a driving force in me, and a happy-go-lucky nature, I keep on going. . . .

But first to take up the matters you discuss.

1. I agree with you that I talk too much about the family and that I lack sympathy. These two points, I will try and correct.

2. I don't agree with you that I should talk more about myself and what I'm doing. I make a definite effort not to as it would probably be exceedingly boring, and talking about one's self is man's greatest weakness, and a sign of conceit. Lord knows I have enough trouble fighting down conceit.

3. I think that you give me too much credit when you say you don't think that I really am hard and unfeeling. I'm sorry to say that I am both of these, not naturally, but by schooling myself to be. That sounds strange, but I think it is true. It is a result of my overpowering ambition. If one is going to get very far in this world one must be impersonal and not waste one's emotional strength on irrelevant things. The result has been that I take a pretty cold attitude about most things. Your answer will probably be that I have been unfeeling about important things as well as about unimportant things. I think you are right. But I think it is just because I am inexperienced. I still feel that to take a cold impersonal point of view about life is very important to sound impartial judgment, and it certainly saves one from a lot of useless worrying. . . .

One of my worst troubles (which you did not mention) is my strong tendency towards a very contemptuous attitude: contemptuous of certain people as well as of certain social institutions. I guess it is a form of arrogance or conceit. . . .

Probably if I were a little more humble it would solve a good many questions. Anyway, I'll make an effort and I do appreciate your letter. If I saw the point of it all it would be somewhat simpler. But who knows, I may someday.

Don't worry Mum, we'll all stick together anyway.

Your devoted bad boy,
Nelson

P.S. I bought a swell blue hippopotamus by Carl Walters from Mrs. Halpert. Wait until you see it!

Arrogance, contemptuousness, hardness, conceit: these were the predominant qualities young Nelson Rockefeller saw in himself. He had "schooled himself" to be hard and unfeeling, all in the service of his "overpowering ambition." No foe of Nelson would ever offer a more cutting analysis of his personality.

On the other hand, this confessional, with its existential overtones ("If I saw the point of it all"), had a somewhat overblown, hand-wringing quality— as though Nelson was angling for reassurance from his mother that he really wasn't as bad as all that. And, indeed, having witnessed her son's tendency to self-flagellation in the past, Abby was not unduly alarmed by this missive. Deftly, she sought to calm him down, though not without offering some motherly admonitions:

> You are not the only one in the family who talks too much about family affairs, we all do!!! I really believe that you have sympathy but often fail to express it sometimes! . . .
>
> What you take to be conceit, seems to me to come more from a certain sureness of your own opinion. You think quickly, often with no basis of knowledge or facts, you form a judgment and express it strongly, then sometimes you are wrong and may have caused trouble. The trouble is that through your family connection you have a certain power, but the same connection has robbed you of experience. Time will cure this difficulty. . . .
>
> I say again that you are not hard. It is good to look at life objectively. There is no need of letting the other fellow make a fool of you. It is great to be ambitious, it is one of the things that raises us above the animals, but honesty must go with it. . . .

Abby also saw fit to tack on this word of warning: "One more thing. I am sure that too much money makes people stupid, dull, unseeing and uninteresting. Be careful . . ."

Busy as he was with Special Work, with renting Rockefeller Center, and with the Museum of Modern Art, Nelson was eager to venture into one more sphere: public service. He had rarely spoken openly about his interest in that world. However, it was always assumed, in his circle of intimates and associates, that some involvement in public service—if not in his grandfather Aldrich's calling of politics—was in the offing. The issues of the day fascinated him, just as they fascinated Junior, who had long shown a reformist zeal in such matters as prostitution, public health, and population control. "Father didn't have the political side at all; Nelson took that more from his grandfather Aldrich," reflects David Rockefeller. "But I think that Father imbued in him, as he did, really, in all of us, a sense that one has obligations that are commensurate with one's opportunities. I think that Nelson took that very seriously." His concerns were already much on display in the course of his honeymoon, with its strange conjunction of sybaritism and social consciousness. And, beyond those concerns, Nelson's outgoing, all-embracing personality—not to mention his perennial surfeit of energy—seemed to make his involvement in public affairs all but inevitable.

For starters, something modest would do, something low-profile that would allow him to gain some experience.

Late in 1932 Nelson journeyed to Port Chester, not far from the Rockefeller family seat at Pocantico Hills, to meet with Westchester County Republican chairman W. L. Ward. "Boss" Ward had an iron grip on public jobs in the county, and he had witnessed just about every entreaty in the books, but his astonishment must have been considerable when he found a young Rockefeller at his doorstep beseeching him for a position. After thinking it over, Ward suggested an appointment to the Westchester County Board of Health.

The position would expose Nelson to some challenging public health problems; more to the point, as far as Ward was concerned, Nelson's appointment might convince the Rockefellers to help subsidize the sagging county health budget. "This county has been good to you," Ward growled at Nelson. "Now it is up to you to do something for us."

After his first meeting, in February 1933, Nelson declared himself "only a novice." Nevertheless, he soon proved himself something more than that in coping with the board's efforts to squeeze the Rockefeller purse. Invited by the county health commissioner to tour the ramshackle health center in Tarrytown, Nelson declined, fearing that the tour would merely be a prelude to an approach to Junior.

Once he made it clear that his appointment would not bring the county a windfall, Nelson could settle in and engross himself in the board's work. He was fascinated by the range of issues: in his first year alone, the board tackled the problem of raw milk (barring its sale) and expanded the county's prenatal and venereal-disease clinics.

His service on the board would inspire an abiding interest in public health, an interest that would resonate throughout his later government career. (He continued to serve on the board, on and off, until 1953.) But of far more immediate moment was the precedent the position set. For the first time, a Rockefeller had stepped into the spotlight of public service.

His prime focus, however, remained Rockefeller Center. Unfazed by the Rivera imbroglio, Nelson enthusiastically sought to insert himself in anything and everything affecting the Center, even if the jobs he came up with bordered on the marginal. He involved himself in the furnishing of the new Rockefeller family offices when they were moved from 26 Broadway to the RCA Building in mid-1933, haggling with the architects about everything from lighting fixtures to partitions to the linoleum contract. He was nominally in charge of the foreign buildings—the British Empire, La Maison Française, and a contemplated Italian building. The rental of those buildings, however, was thoroughly controlled by managing agent Hugh Robertson, leaving Nelson with such tasks as thanking the Italian representative on behalf of Junior for the gift of some commemorative postage stamps. ("I can't tell you how pleased my father was to receive the autographed album of Marshal Balbo's flight stamps. . . . It was a uniquely valuable souvenir.") When the time came to fire this Italian representative, it was Robertson, not Nelson, who did the dirty work.

At one point, Nelson, Philip Johnson, and the Museum of Modern Art's Alan Blackburn cooked up the idea of selling "high grade souvenirs and art objects"—including postcards—at Rockefeller Center. They went so far as to organize a corporation for that purpose, dubbed Art Incorporated. John Todd, however, was not enamored of the scheme and quashed it.

Nelson encountered even more frustration with another idea he was boosting: a restaurant-café in a temporary building on one of the Center's still vacant lots. This time, it was Junior himself who was the stumbling block: he worried that the temporary structure would be an eyesore, and that the restaurant management's "questionable reputation" would do "untold harm to the whole Rockefeller Center enterprise."

In a note to the restaurant's promoter, Nelson conceded defeat, in words that truly captured his sense of powerlessness: "Realizing the general feeling of those in whom the responsibility for Rockefeller Center rests I do not feel that I can push the matter any further." The "responsibility for Rockefeller Center," it was evident, still did not rest with him.

"I have just emerged into a new period with an entirely new line-up as far as certain of my ideas are concerned," Nelson briskly informed Junior in early July 1933.

> I went into Special Work, Inc., because I felt lost and beyond my depth in the work of this office. Special Work gave me a chance to do things on a smaller scale—where if I made mistakes it didn't make so much difference as the responsibility rested squarely on my shoulders. There is no question but that this work has been of the greatest possible value to me and I have confidence where before I was groping fearfully in the dark. However, I have come to see things more clearly in their true proportions and now realize that the activities of Special Work, Inc., are not all important. Furthermore, I am beginning to see more clearly the importance and even international significance of some of the things that take place in this office.

The purpose of the letter, Nelson went on to say, "is to tell you that Special Work is running smoothly now and will require very little of my time in the future. Therefore, I hope that I will be able to be of distinctly more assistance to you." Specifically, Nelson said his plan was "to become more familiar with all phases of your real estate interests and to avail myself of every opportunity to get acquainted with your oil, coal and banking interests."

"I am back in the fold again," Nelson cheerily assured his father.

Junior was plainly delighted to hear it. After his brief experiment with going into business on his own, the errant son was coming home.

Or so it seemed. Because the true fact of the matter was, his assertions to Junior notwithstanding, Nelson still was very much involved in Special Work. Five months after his letter to Junior, for example, Nelson was negotiating a new agreement with the chief of Consolidation Coal, "to act as the operating head of what you commonly refer to as your 'Ball Rolling Department.'" (What this amounted to was securing entrées to prospective customers.) Nelson was also talking with Socony-Vacuum about "a closer working relationship with Special Work."

Undoubtedly, Nelson was sincere about coming "back in the fold." After all, if he was to have any hope of wresting a full measure of influence over the Rockefeller empire, a rapprochement with Junior was essential. But having experienced firsthand the elusiveness of true authority in his father's duchies, Nelson was not about to abandon his separate little power base.

Special Work, it turned out, served another important purpose in the web of influence Nelson was seeking to weave.

Back in January 1933 the company had signed a contract with one of Rockefeller Center's principal architects, Wallace K. Harrison. Under the agreement, Harrison would serve as a broker for Special Work in leasing Rockefeller Center offices, and Special Work would split the brokerage commissions for those leases fifty-fifty with Harrison.

There was nothing sub rosa about the deal with Harrison; it was signed with the full knowledge of Rockefeller Center. Nonetheless, it was a curious arrangement: why, if Harrison wanted to broker offices on the side, was he doing it through Special Work, rather than directly for Rockefeller Center? The only plausible answer is that Harrison, as architect, was not permitted to act directly as a broker, but was allowed to do so "off the books," as it were, with the help of Nelson Rockefeller and Special Work.

For the thirty-seven-year-old Harrison, the arrangement offered the chance to put some badly needed extra dollars in his pocket. But the deal's significance went far beyond the brokerage fees. The pact represented the first golden link between the up-and-coming architect and the venturesome young aristocrat.

Wallace Harrison had already come a long way in his career before he met Nelson Rockefeller. Born in Worcester, Massachusetts, the son of a foundry superintendent, Harrison dropped out of high school to work as an office boy for a local building contractor. Fascinated by drafting and design, he took night courses at Worcester Polytechnic Institute, got a job as a junior draftsman at a Worcester architectural firm and, at twenty-one, landed a position at McKim, Mead & White, then America's preeminent architects. In New York he came under the influence of Harvey Wiley Corbett, a futuristic designer who was one of the early apostles of the skyscraper. After a stint in Paris studying at the Ecole des Beaux-Arts, and associations with two of the era's busiest architects, Bertram Goodhue and Raymond Hood, Harrison was invited by Corbett in 1927 to become his partner.

Barely two years later, Corbett was one of a group of leading architects asked to submit their ideas for Metropolitan Square. It was Corbett's conception—a broad promenade leading from Fifth Avenue to a plaza that would have a slender skyscraper as a backdrop—that was the nucleus of what would soon be Rockefeller Center. Thanks to Harrison's connections, not only to Corbett but to his brother-in-law David Milton, Babs Rockefeller's husband, the gangling neophyte designer found himself catapulted into a leading role in one of the era's greatest architectural projects.

Although the youngest of the team of architects laboring on Rockefeller Center, and by no means the most creative (Hood could easily claim that distinction), Harrison soon emerged as *primus inter pares.* His diplomatic and organizational skills, his Yankee solidity, and, not least, the ease with which he moved among the Rockefellers made him a mainstay of the multidimensional, logistically intimidating enterprise.

One morning in 1931, in the Todd firm's offices in the Graybar Building, Harrison was pinning some drawings to the wall when Nelson Rockefeller sauntered through the door and asked if he could help. It was the first time the two men met; Harrison recalled that Nelson "asked intelligent questions and gave the impression of a man who could get a job done. He radiated youth and confidence." Equally impressed by Harrison—and by the pivotal role Harrison was playing in Rockefeller Center's design—Nelson began regularly picking Harrison's brain about what was going on in the Center. The two would meet for midmorning repasts of marmalade and bacon on toast, washed down by lots of coffee, and chat about such things as the Center's underground arcades and the gardens planned for some of the building terraces.

They grew more and more comfortable in each other's company, both men realizing early on in their toast-and-coffee sessions how mutually beneficial their relationship could be. For Harrison, the architecturally minded young Rockefeller was a fount of future commissions and contacts. For Nelson, the upwardly mobile architect was a simpatico sounding board for his grander ideas and visions. Indeed, there were those who saw Harrison, thirteen years Rockefeller's senior, as almost a father figure to Nelson in those days. "Wally was always reaching out towards younger guys," notes Max Abramovitz, who would later become Harrison's partner. "And I think that's what flowered between them."

Harrison would earn some $4,000 a year from Special Work, a not inconsiderable sum in those Depression days. But, as he well knew, that was only a small token of what Nelson Rockefeller could offer him. The relationship promised opportunities, as Harrison later put it, "to work with great people and do beautiful buildings. For an architect, it was like being handed a meringue glacée; it was almost too easy."

As Nelson contemplated a closer working relationship with Junior, his thoughts also turned to the financial relationship between father and son.

His status as Junior's economic vassal rankled Nelson more and more. He was a married man, and a father, and an individual of presumed means. Yet he still had to approach Junior as a supplicant every time some more than trivial expense had to be paid. His vacations, his cars, even the doctor bills for the delivery of Roddy: all were costs he had to humbly ask Junior to bear.

In July 1933, on the occasion of his twenty-fifth birthday, Nelson would presumably be given $100,000 by his father, the same sum John had received on his twenty-fifth two years before. But even that healthy gift could not even begin to cover the ongoing costs of a lifestyle that included the maintenance of an Upper East Side apartment, the requisite servants, generous donations to the Museum of Modern Art, and an already burgeoning art collection.

Something, Nelson was convinced, had to be done. John and Babs, in the same predicament, thought so, too. Meeting among themselves at Pocantico that spring, the siblings decided on a direct approach to their father. They drafted a letter that paid the proper homage to their parents ("we have begun to realize how much you and Mother have done for us") and gingerly suggested that the "intimate relationship" they all had with Junior and Abby was "in jeopardy." They prayed not to be misunderstood: "We write solely because of our genuine interest in the family as such, and feel that no effort should be spared to guard its unity. . . . We do not want you to think for a minute that we are trying to get more for ourselves. Nor do we want you to get the impression that we are trying to 'cut loose' from you and Mother."

This apologetic invocation of family harmony was followed by a request for an allowance increase—an increase large enough to cover such items as "apartment rent, hospital expenses at childbirth, moderately priced cars, summer vacation expenses, including trips abroad—in short, all those things which you would be paying for us anyway."

Somewhat unctuously, the children justified the increase on the grounds that "it would relieve you of an infinite amount of detail. With your many interests and responsibilities, we do not feel that it is fair to you to take up so much of your time and strength with the minor questions involved in our current problems." It would also "free us when with you to discuss the more important and fundamental questions of life, as well as to hear of your many interesting doings." Their yearning for financial independence was mentioned only obliquely.

While Junior no doubt saw through all this verbiage, the letter nonetheless struck a responsive chord. Two decades earlier, he had found himself in much the same situation with his own father; it was only in 1917, when Junior was well into his forties, that a wary John D. Senior started transferring the bulk of his fortune to his son. Trying to strike a balance between his children's strivings and his never-ending preoccupation with the perniciousness of wealth, Junior decided the best course would be to "capitalize" their allowances. At year end 1933 he gave John, Babs, and Nelson 200,000 shares each of Socony-Vacuum stock, worth $3.2 million. The children would live on the dividends, which in 1934 would amount to $120,000.

For the first time, Nelson and his siblings were millionaires in their own right.

Yet even as he was making these gifts, Junior knew the solution was only an interim one. The Depression had sparked an all-out attack on America's wealthy families, with the likes of fiery Louisiana senator Huey Long calling for total liquidation of the great fortunes. The populist rhetoric had its effect on the Roosevelt administration, which was eager to capture some of that wealth to stimulate the dormant economy. Talk of steep hikes in income, gift, and estate taxes was in the air. If Junior was ever going to make substantial transfers of wealth to his children, now was the time.

And so, in the course of 1934, Junior set up trusts for each of his six children. Nelson, John, and Babs each received $12 million in stock (the trusts for the three younger children were, at the outset, more modestly endowed). "A substantial portion" of the trusts' income would be paid out to each of the children, and the trustees could disburse some of the principal to them as well.

The immediate effect on the Rockefeller children's wallets was dramatic. John, for one, saw his annual income rise from $150,000 in 1934 to $476,000 in 1935, thanks to the trust's earning power. Nelson presumably saw much the same jump in his fortune.

It was those trusts—to be spoken of reverently in family councils forevermore as the " '34 Trusts"—that would be the backbones of the children's wealth, as Junior transferred more and more stock to them over the years. The trusts assured the Rockefeller heirs financial independence, at least—even if so much else in their lives, from their jobs to their Pocantico homes, remained firmly under Junior's control.

Nelson had no trouble finding uses for his newfound fortune.

In the spring of 1934 he acquired a new apartment at 810 Fifth Avenue, at 62nd Street. The address, just north of the posh Sherry-Netherland, Pierre, and Plaza hotels, was tony, and the views of Central Park, across the street, were breathtaking. His family was larger now—a girl, Ann, was born in May—but that had very little to do with the move. It was simply time for grander quarters, both for living and for all the entertaining he planned to do.

Nelson asked Harrison to redesign the space, and the two plunged headlong into the project, leaving Tod to do little more than play the part of bemused bystander. For the flooring, Nelson acquired nothing less than eighteenth-century French parquet, and Harrison was faced with the task of integrating the antique planks with modern timbers. Rococo moldings evocative of Louis XIV were designed by Harrison for the apartment's walnut paneling and window surrounds. To oversee the furnishings, Nelson and Harrison recruited Jean-Michel Frank, one of the outstanding French designers of the period, who commissioned one-of-a-kind pieces, including lamps and upholstery, from such artists as Alberto Giacometti and Christian Bérard.

Eyeing this lavish mise-en-scène, Abby Rockefeller was appalled. Inspecting a mantel by French sculptor Gaston Lachaise, she admonished Nelson, "My own feeling is that nothing else in that room will count. Your furniture will look—in my humble opinion—as if it were trying to associate with people it didn't like." She had complained about it to Harrison and gotten nowhere. "Mr. Harrison's reasons seemed to be that he felt he must be original. Of course I like being different, but I see no point in sacrificing one's comfort and pleasure on the altar of originality."

But that was just the point. The apartment was never meant to be just another comfortable Fifth Avenue abode, crammed with chintz and mahogany. It was to be a fully integrated expression of its owner's already highly refined aesthetic sensibility, as well as a work of art that would properly showcase other works of art. And, as Abby must have intuited, it would be something more: a physical statement, in walnut and bronze, of the owner's status as a New York grandee.

Nelson Rockefeller was barely twenty-six years old at the time.

"If you start to cultivate your taste and eye so young," his mother had written him when he was in college, "you ought to be very good at it by the time you can afford to collect much." Now that he could afford it, Nelson was utterly uninhibited about indulging his well-cultivated taste. Even before his windfall, he had already set the stage for an impressive, and eclectic, collection. During his honeymoon trip, he scoured villages in the Dutch East Indies for primitive carvings—some of which, he was later to learn, were German-made knockoffs. In the course of his monthlong 1933 vacation in Mexico, he was introduced to the glories of pre-Columbian art, and he began acquiring both antique pieces and folk art. And, thanks to his mother's influence, Nelson had bought American Expressionist works by Pascin, Kuniyoshi, and others.

Now, with his augmented resources, Nelson could truly become a *collector.* Fascinated by Cubism and the Fauves, he sought out works by Picasso, Braque, Matisse, and Léger. Passionate about sculpture ("I always liked forms of art where I could feel the artist, feel the material," he would later say), he acquired pieces by Lachaise and Elie Nadelman. A purchase of an Alexander Calder stabile, "Spiny," piqued his interest in that artist as well; decades later, he would commission Calder to execute a twelve-foot-high version of "Spiny" for the Pocantico gardens.

Nelson could also now freely support his mother's pride and joy, the Museum of Modern Art. The year 1934 marked a critical juncture for the museum. One of its founders, Lillie Bliss, had died three years earlier, and bequeathed her magnificent collection to the institution—provided that the museum amass by March 1, 1934, an endowment fund sufficient to assure its permanence. The target amount set by her executors was $1 million.

Alfred Barr considered acquisition of the Bliss works absolutely imperative: it would be the museum's first significant permanent collection. With the Bliss collection in hand, he argued, New York can "look London, Paris, Berlin, Munich, Moscow and Chicago in the face so far as public collections of modern art are concerned." And as far as Nelson was concerned, even more was at stake. "If we are not able to secure the endowment," he warned, "it will be an indication to many that the Museum has lost the confidence of the public and no longer justifies their support."

In an all-out quest for the million dollars, Nelson and the other trustees scrounged and wheedled contributions from financiers and foundations. But as the deadline loomed, they were still well short of the goal. Then Lillie Bliss's brother, Cornelius, let it be known that he would consider $600,000 sufficient—and an eleventh-hour $100,000 contribution, from an anonymous source, put the museum over the top. The Bliss collection, and MOMA's future, was secure.

The evening after the pivotal anonymous donation was announced, Nelson escorted fellow trustee Eliza Bliss, Lillie Bliss's niece, to her Upper East Side home. As their taxicab wended its way through Central Park, Bliss prodded Nelson to confide to her the identity of the mystery donor. "Come on," she said, "tell me. You must know."

As she remembers the scene, "He turned into a stone statue; that's the only way I can describe it. He sat in the corner of the taxi and didn't look at me." Finally, when they emerged from the park at 72nd Street, he turned to Bliss and said, "All right, I'll tell you if you give me your word that as long as my mother is alive you'll never tell a living soul." Bliss made the vow, and Nelson slumped back in his seat. "I gave the hundred thousand dollars," he said. "You see, I just came into my money."

He turned again to Bliss. "You know," he went on, "my mother is so crazy for this museum to really mean something to people, and for people to love modern art as much as she does. I just feel it would mean a great deal more to her if it came from somebody out there than if she knew it came from me."

He now had the trappings of power, but not the power itself. As Nelson took stock of what stood in the way, there was no obstacle more formidable than John R. Todd, the chief managing agent of Rockefeller Center.

A hard-bitten powerhouse with a taste for expensive cigars, the sixty-seven-year-old Todd was used to having his way in everything from building contracts to the preparation of his lunchtime eggs Benedict at the University Club. (When his wife, during a western railroad trip, expressed a sudden desire to see the Grand Canyon, Todd had the train rerouted to accommodate her.) His doggedness and tenacious bargaining brought him to the top ranks of the New York real estate business, despite his widely known contempt for the architectural profession. ("For an architect, you show almost human intelligence" was a favorite utterance of Todd's.) He built the Graybar Building and the Cunard Building, cowing contractors, architects, workmen, and tenants alike with his imperious, autocratic manner.

When Junior was looking for someone in 1929 to oversee Rockefeller Center—someone who would ride herd on the architects and engineers, award the contracts, supervise the construction, find the tenants, and operate the buildings—he turned, to no one's surprise, to John Todd. And Todd, for the most part, had delivered. By 1934 four buildings, along with Radio City Music Hall and the Center Theater, totaling three million square feet of space, were open for business, and two more were set to open in 1935. The architectural team managed to work in harmony, the construction work by and large proceeded smoothly. And the special elements that were already making Rockefeller Center a landmark—the sunken plaza, the gilded statue of Prometheus, the swank deco Rainbow Room atop the RCA Building—were all in place and drawing crowds. No one was joking about Rockefeller Center anymore.

Grasping from the start Junior's keen interest in every aspect of the development, Todd assiduously kept him informed, accommodating Rockefeller's frequent appearances at construction sites, gold-plated folding ruler in hand. And Junior, for his part, seemed well satisfied with Todd and his associates. The assorted setbacks the development had encountered—the rental struggle (by 1934 leases were picking up), troubles with the theaters, the Rivera flap—could not be blamed on Todd. There was little to carp about, and much to praise, concerning his job. "In spite of almost insuperable economic obstacles," Junior wrote Todd, "you and your splendid organization have gone forward with dauntless courage and boundless resourcefulness."

Any challenge to Todd, in short, would seem to have about as much chance of success as foisting a mug of beer on the teetotaling Junior. And Nelson Rockefeller knew that as well as anyone. If he was to get anywhere, he would have to try a different approach.

When he "returned to the fold" in the spring of 1933, he told his father he wanted to undertake a study of the family office, and make some "constructive suggestions" about how it should be run. Junior readily agreed. What better way, after all, was there for Nelson to reinject himself into the family business than to survey the whole of it?

Nelson presented his "preliminary" report to Junior in late August, after vetting it with John. The gist of it was that the office had to have clearer divisions of authority—and that the Rockefeller brothers, as they came of age, ought to have more definitive roles in the family's activities.

He laid out an organization chart in which each of the departments—investments, real estate, philanthropies, etc.—would come under the purview of a Rockefeller son, in "close association" with a staff expert. Nelson's plan was nothing less than a radical shift in authority from the hired hands—and, implicitly, from Junior—to the brothers.

As Nelson no doubt expected, Junior rejected the scheme out of hand. But all the talk about efficiency and clearer lines of command had a certain appeal to the fastidious Junior. He told Nelson he should go on with his study and make an intensive survey of each area, one at a time. Nelson could start, they agreed, with Rockefeller Center.

"The time has come when Rockefeller Center ought to be on a more definite, clear-cut, departmentalized basis," Junior told his counsel and confidant Thomas Debevoise. "I do not think we can look to Mr. Todd alone to bring about that result."

But before Nelson could get very far in his Rockefeller Center study, he shifted his attention to the management of the family office itself, and the Pocantico estate. (It is not clear whether the shift was Junior's idea or Nelson's.) He found both places beset by miscommunication and blurred lines of authority that often pitted one brother against another. Nelson's solution: give John complete authority over both the estate and the office.

The proposal was certain to strengthen the alliance between the brothers. And, not coincidentally, it also cleared the way for Nelson to assume his own potential sphere of influence: Rockefeller Center.

Although Junior was willing to go along with Nelson's plan, he began to bristle at his sons' aggressive pursuit of power and their eagerness to shove his old retainers aside. Seeking to make peace, Nelson and John penned a Christmas note to their father. "From your reaction to our endeavors we are often concerned lest you may think we suggest this or do that in order directly or indirectly to promote our own ends," they wrote. "However it may appear on the surface, this is the farthest from our thoughts we can assure you."

The apologetic missive had its intended effect. "All the money in the world could not have bought for me a Christmas present as acceptable as your beautiful letter of December 18th," Junior told his sons, adding that he would be "glad at a convenient time to discuss with you the one or two minor matters that have given you concern."

For Nelson, the new year of 1934 brought a fortuitous power vacuum at the top of the Rockefeller Center hierarchy. Colonel Woods, the president, was ill, and to fill the role of acting chief executive the board chose Albert Scott, a civil engineer who served as the Center's vice president. This scrambling of positions gave Nelson all the pretext he needed to re-launch his study of

Rockefeller Center. In early August he came up with his recommendation: that the Center's long-dormant executive committee be reconstituted as an active, decision-making body. The committee would have three members: brother John, family investment chief Barton Turnbull, and himself. Together, they would oversee the managing agents, meeting with John Todd and his partners weekly for full reports on the Center's activities.

There was no mistaking the import of what Nelson was proposing. John Todd would finally be under his thumb.

But Nelson had not reckoned on the reaction of Debevoise. Fed up with all the machinations ("There has been so much talk recently that I do not see how anyone has had time to do his work," he grumbled), Debevoise came out squarely on the side of the managing agents. "They have done a stupendous job," the family counsel declared, "and have not only kept us out of trouble but done the best kind of work for us in all our relationships."

If Junior had to make the choice, it was clear to Debevoise that the Center's officers and directors "could be much more readily replaced than the Managing Agents."

Dubbed by the brothers the "Prime Minister," the cautious, unbending Debevoise was as close to an alter ego as Junior had in the office. Sometimes the counsel's rectitude surpassed even his boss's: upon hearing that a cocktail café was planned for the sunken plaza, Debevoise pronounced the scheme "unthinkable," only to learn, to his horror, that Junior had heartily approved the restaurant. But in the matter of Todd & Co., Debevoise found himself backed 100 percent by Junior. A new executive committee was indeed created, with Nelson as one of the members, but shorn of the overriding power he had so ardently sought. Woods retired and Scott resigned, leaving the Rockefeller Center presidency vacant. Junior was in no hurry to fill the job.

Seeing the writing on the wall, Nelson concluded he had no choice but to beat a strategic retreat. It seemed like the ideal time to learn something about the banking business.

Just after Thanksgiving, Nelson joined his uncle Winthrop Aldrich and other Chase officers for a swing through the southern and western United States to drum up new clients for the bank. Nelson served in the lowly role of secretary and trip manager. Despite this, Nelson informed his father that he was, as usual, "having the most marvelous time imaginable."

Upon his return, Nelson settled into the role of part-time trainee banker (he continued to spend half his time at Rockefeller Center). The only aspect of Chase that really interested Nelson was the foreign department, and in June 1935 he arranged to spend the summer working at the bank's branches in London and Paris.

In the course of this European sojourn he and Tod resumed the imperial lifestyle that had marked their honeymoon. They played tennis with royal relations, rode in a coach-and-four, and feted Chase and Standard Oil executives at lavish dinners. Nelson appeared to have learned precious little about banking in the course of all this, but he did come away from his Paris visit impressed with a sleek new French automobile. When he returned to the States, he phoned his Seal Harbor neighbor Edsel Ford and arranged to have the body of one of the cars imported and specially mounted for him on a Ford chassis.

Nelson may have been lying low, but in his months of self-exile he never lost sight of his ultimate goal. Just after New Years 1935 he lunched with John and finalized their private accord about the divvying up of the family empire. John would oversee the philanthropies, Colonial Williamsburg, the family office, and Pocantico; Nelson would take charge of Rockefeller Center. It was not without considerable reluctance that John gave up Rockefeller Center. More than any of the other areas, he told Nelson, it was "on the firing line." But he bowed, as always, to the force of his brother's avidity. As John reported in his diary afterward, "Nels said that very definitely he would be keen to be chief executive officer, and pointed out that he felt this position could best be filled by a member of the family in view of the Managing Agents' general attitude."

Several months later, Nelson arranged a lunch at the Rainbow Room with Junior to press his case again. John, who joined them near the end of the lunch, found their father as unyielding as ever. "Father seemed to so completely misunderstand our point of view," he related in his diary, "that I really felt as if we were discussing two different questions."

But not very long after, Nelson managed to turn Thomas Debevoise around. Just how Nelson accomplished this is somewhat murky; perhaps, as some would later suggest, Debevoise simply woke up one day and realized it wasn't John Todd's name that was on his paycheck. Whatever the reason for the change of heart, Debevoise suddenly began loudly moaning about Todd's high-handedness. One incident in particular stood out: while Todd was in Europe that spring, Nelson enlisted the support of Todd's associates on changes in the RCA Building's rooftop patio. Upon his return, a livid Todd ordered work stopped and scrapped Nelson's plan. Siding with Nelson, Debevoise charged that Todd was "browbeating" the architects and wasting Rockefeller money.

"The whole question is this," Debevoise told Nelson. "Is Mr. Todd bigger than the organization which he helped to set up and which appeared to have his wholehearted approval? If he is, we had better let Mr. Todd run the party himself."

By early January 1936, with the managing agents' contract up for renewal, Debevoise was wondering aloud whether Todd should be dropped "entirely out of the picture." Other advisers of Junior, however, argued that it was still premature to drop the managing agents entirely. As Barton Turnbull pointed out, "dealing with tenants at 'arm's length' through an agent may have merit, particularly as the name of the landlord is 'Rockefeller.' " Junior was inclined to agree.

In the past he had always negotiated with Todd himself, man to man, and he wanted to do it this time as well. But Debevoise convinced Junior it was time to turn the bargaining over to the executive committee—which meant, in effect, turning it over to Nelson, the committee's dominant member.

At long last, Nelson had the upper hand.

Now that he had it, he had no hesitancy about squeezing Todd. He proposed contract terms that were bound to infuriate the prickly, domineering real estate man. He offered an extension that would run only a mere fifteen months, until December 31, 1937. And Nelson insisted on a substantial cut in the managers' compensation. The old contract called for payment of $450,000 a year: a $250,000 flat fee and another $200,000 as an advance against the managers' share of Rockefeller Center profits (under a complicated formula, Todd and his associates were entitled to a piece of the profits until 1952). Since there were no profits, and there weren't expected to be any for years to come, the $200,000 represented an out-of-pocket expense for Junior.

What Nelson offered Todd was a flat $350,000 a year.

At a meeting with Todd and his colleagues, Nelson heaped praise on them for their efforts ("To say that we are eternally indebted to you is putting it mildly"). Then he lowered the boom. The work today "has eased up considerably." The Center's management costs, compared with comparable buildings in the city, "seem almost preposterous." Then, as an added gibe at Todd, he mentioned that Junior and Todd had had an understanding that the manager would arrange secondary financing for Rockefeller Center (primary financing in the form of a $65 million loan from Metropolitan Life had already been provided). Todd, said Nelson, had not delivered on his commitment.

Swallowing his anger, Todd put into play his legendary bargaining prowess. Unyielding on the compensation question, he secured a continuation of the $450,000-a-year retainer. And he won an extra year on top of the fifteen months Nelson was offering, on the grounds that it would take that long to complete the additional Rockefeller Center buildings.

Yet even as he gained these concessions, Todd, savvy entrepreneur that he was, could see that the game was up. His apprehensions were further confirmed later that year, when Nelson pushed through the Rockefeller Center board a new organizational setup that gave board committees, not the managing agents, decision-making power over every important aspect of the Center's operations. The chairman of all the important committees—the committee on art and architecture, the committee on operations, the promotional committee—would be Nelson Rockefeller.

Finally, in April 1937, Nelson made his conclusive bid for power. He sat down in the fifty-sixth-floor family office with Debevoise, Turnbull, and brother John and won their support for naming him president and chief executive officer. But when the plan was presented to Junior, he balked; no family member, he insisted, should hold that position.

It would be another year before Nelson would finally win Junior's assent. But by then, all Junior could do was recognize a fait accompli. In fact, if not in name, twenty-nine-year-old Nelson was already acting as the boss of Rockefeller Center.

All that was left for John Todd, meanwhile, was to negotiate a graceful, and lucrative, exit, which he did. On May 23, 1938, he resigned as a manager under an agreement whereby he was to be paid $105,000 over a three-year period. His colleagues were given similar severance packages. The one exception was Hugh Robertson, with whom Nelson had an especially good relationship. Robertson was named executive manager of Rockefeller Center, becoming the Center's day-to-day operating chief. He reported to only one man: Nelson A. Rockefeller.

Four years in the making, Nelson's ascension to the top was nothing less than his first great political victory. Like the canniest of politicos, Nelson took the measure of his goal, secured his power base, forged strategic alliances, and patiently bided his time for the right moment to strike. Rather than challenge Todd immediately, he retreated to the haven of Special Work. Upon his return to the family fold, Nelson cleverly used the device of an "organizational study" as a wedge. Rebuffed, he bought time for himself courtesy of the Chase, until the moment was ripe for the coup de grace.

He displayed none of the impulsiveness that had brought on the Rivera fiasco. Instead, he had plotted his moves with infinite patience and care. Never did Nelson bluntly confront his father. Rather, he prodded and probed, issuing profuse apologies whenever he was caught overstepping himself, slipping discreetly behind the curtain as Debevoise, the "Prime Minister," won Junior over.

Having outwitted and outmaneuvered the formidable John Todd, having finally won a chunk of the Rockefeller empire, Nelson Rockefeller could truly be said to have arrived.

Ten

The Ruler of Rockefeller Center

The East River Savings Bank was about to launch its branch on the ground floor of Rockefeller Center's International Building in March 1937, and bank president Darwin James thought it would be a wonderful idea if the first depositor was a Rockefeller. Someone in the family office suggested either Nelson or Laurance (by then out of Princeton and assisting his brother with Rockefeller Center) might do the honors. When the proposition was put to Nelson, he followed protocol and sent the suggestion on to Debevoise for his reaction. The counsel's response was a swift and unambiguous "No" scrawled across Nelson's memo.

A week later the East River Bank staged its gala opening. And there to smile for the cameras and happily accept the first passbooks from Darwin James were both Nelson and Laurance Rockefeller.

A new order for the Rockefellers was plainly at hand.

"You have caught the snake in the process of changing its skin," Nelson told *Fortune* three months earlier, when the magazine trumpeted the glories of Rockefeller Center in a multipage spread. He was talking about the Center's transition from a construction project to an ongoing enterprise, but he might just as well have been describing his personal metamorphosis. No longer was he the apprentice, obligingly deferring to the better judgment of elders like Debevoise and Todd, of "those in whom the responsibility for Rockefeller Center rests," to use the meek words he had uttered just three years before. Now he was the unquestioned master of the awesome limestone forest springing up all around him. He ruled Rockefeller Center.

While both his reserved father and his shy elder brother blanched at the prospect of public appearances, Nelson gloried in them. Glad-handing came naturally to him; he genuinely *enjoyed* ribbon cutting and ceremonial observances, no matter how banal the circumstances. Even before his ascendance in the Rockefeller Center hierarchy, he was always available, in the words of one commentator, to "open bunny gardens in the Sunken Plaza, dedicate wisteria exhibits and skating rinks, present certificates and gold buttons to outstanding construction workers, and so on." His exuberant personality found its ideal outlet in this city within a city, where promotional pizzazz leavened the monumentality of the Machine Age architecture, where an art deco nightclub in the clouds and a sunken skating rink just steps from Fifth Avenue held all of New York (not to mention prospective tenants) in thrall. If Rockefeller Center was the ultimate expression of Depression-bound New York's resilience and energy and optimism, then Nelson Rockefeller, resilient and energetic and brimming with optimism, was its perfect spokesman.

He leapt at every opportunity to talk up the Center and what it had brought to the city. He gave a fifteen-minute radio address on WJZ, urging other real estate owners to follow the Rockefeller lead and launch a "concentrated program of reconstruction" in New York. Before going on the air, Nelson tried to get parks commissioner Robert Moses—already fully engaged in the mammoth public works programs that would transform the metropolis—to join him on the program, but Moses declined. Nelson went ahead on his own, and his speech—his first major pronouncement in the public arena—made headlines. No longer was he described in the newspapers as a "Rockefeller heir" or a "Rockefeller scion." Now he was simply "Nelson A. Rockefeller," a "very dominant factor in the development of Rockefeller Center," in the words of the *Herald Tribune*.

His zest for promotion played itself out in other ways. He became the principal backer of the *Rockefeller Center Magazine,* a money-losing publication chronicling the Center's doings. And Nelson fostered one of Rockefeller Center's biggest public relations coups, the Sidewalk Superintendents Club. The idea had come to him when his father, trying to spy the progress of one of his buildings from the vantage point of a truck ramp, was shooed away by a watchman. ("Keep moving, buddy," the guard told a startled Junior. "You can't stand around loafing here.") Nelson thought it was high time that all those other curious bystanders, straining for a view through cracks and knotholes, had a more civilized perch. He erected a special platform for their use and heralded it with a press release announcing the formation of the Sidewalk Superintendents Club. Soon badges and membership cards were issued to the "superintendents," and branches of the club sprouted across the country. A *Life* magazine executive wrote Hugh Robertson that "three loud cheers" should go "to the person who had the marvelous public relations instinct to think of the idea."

Yet, at the same time, Nelson also showed that he had not entirely forgotten the lessons in caution ingrained in him by his father and by the family's counselors. When the magazine *Today,* inspired by Nelson's radio talk, tried to do a full-fledged profile of him, Nelson persuaded the publication's owner, fellow millionaire Vincent Astor, to squelch the piece. "For several reasons I was extremely anxious not to have an article appear," he told Astor. (Given that this was the summer of 1936, when he was in the midst of his climactic bid for power at Rockefeller Center, the reasons are fairly obvious.)

His caution extended to the RCA Building's entrance lobby wall, still blank three years after Diego Rivera's mural was hacked away. Nelson quietly acceded to the commissioning of José María Sert, the bombastic muralist whose work already appeared elsewhere in the lobby. Sert painted a vista of muscle-bound giants mounting the scaffolding around Rockefeller Center, with Abraham Lincoln and Ralph Waldo Emerson aiding them in their labors. The fresco was pure shlock, as Nelson must have been among the first to recognize. But it was inoffensive shlock, and it filled up the wall, and by 1937 that was all that really mattered.

The Rockefeller Center complex was still not complete when Nelson took control that year. Three more towers had yet to be built, and Nelson moved swiftly to get them underway.

The first was a fifteen-story structure just north of the RCA Building whose prime tenant would be the Associated Press. The building possessed little of the grandiloquent style of its brethren; it was a commercial structure, pure and simple, designed with one eye on cost-efficiency and the other on the needs of the tenants. The one exalted touch was the Isamu Noguchi stainless-steel sculpture, "News," that Nelson commissioned for the entrance (in time it would be regarded as the finest work of art connected with the Center). By February 1938, before the Associated Press Building was even finished, Nelson was proudly advising his father that it was a complete success: "This is the first time that any building in Rockefeller Center shows a profit."

Next off the drawing board was a tower south of the RCA Building, between 49th and 50th streets. Prospects for this structure were not nearly as good as for the AP Building. As Nelson confidentially advised Junior, "I should say frankly that if we were approaching this on the basis of an outside investment we certainly would not give the matter serious consideration. However, in view of the current carrying charges and the necessity for the completion of Rockefeller Center, the construction of this building, it seems to me, is an extremely sound step for us to take."

Originally, the plan was for the edifice to be another one of the Center's international theme buildings, Holland House, with the Dutch government occupying offices there. But the Dutch were never more than token tenants, and it was only after the burgeoning Eastern Air Lines—in which Laurance was a significant investor—made the building its headquarters that the tower became viable.

The final Rockefeller Center skyscraper was to be erected on Sixth Avenue, next door to the struggling Center Theater. The site would soon be clear of the elevated train line's shadow (the city was set to demolish the elevated in early 1939), but the neighborhood still had a raffish, Dead End tone. Finding tenants would not be easy. But then Nelson and Hugh Robertson resurrected the ploy that had so infuriated old August Heckscher. They approached the U.S. Rubber Company about moving from its headquarters on Columbus Circle. The only trouble was, U.S. Rubber wasn't a tenant at Columbus Circle; it actually owned the building. So Rockefeller Center obligingly purchased the whole building, and U.S. Rubber happily signed a lease for eleven floors in the new Sixth Avenue structure.

Nelson spurred one more piece of Rockefeller Center construction. This was a six-story (three below ground) parking garage on 49th Street, behind the Eastern Air Lines Building. Nelson contended that the garage would help lure tenants and ease the area's traffic congestion; skeptics retorted that the facility was a sure money loser. Acknowledging that the garage was at best a break-even proposition, Nelson thought he could (literally) pump up profits by selling gas and oil inside. That notion never came off, but the garage stayed. Although it would never be a great profit spinner, it was, as Nelson foresaw, one more amenity rounding out the colossal development.

Finishing up Rockefeller Center was not enough for Nelson. He was eager to expand the project's boundaries, to make more of it than his father or the original architects had intended.

For several years now, Junior's representatives had been stealthily snapping up properties north of Rockefeller Center, properties as far north as West 55th Street. The idea was to hold on to these parcels in the event Junior wanted to extend the private street running through Rockefeller Center northward to his 54th Street mansion, erecting new buildings all along the way.

As a member since 1933 of the committee overseeing his father's real estate investments, Nelson was well aware of how much of this property his father owned—and what could be done with it. In 1935 he talked up the concept of building an apartment house on a West 54th Street lot, across the street from his father's and grandfather's homes. The prospect of a residential complement to Rockefeller Center appealed to Junior. That, plus the hope of finding a channel for the energies of his restless second son, led him to okay the idea, and put Nelson in charge.

Nelson did not hesitate to ballyhoo the enterprise. He described it as "the only major apartment construction in the center of Manhattan in the past six years" and flaunted the family connection in his advertising—dubbing the project "The Rockefeller Apartments" and billing it as "Owned by John D. Rockefeller, Jr."

The apartments, designed by Wally Harrison's new firm, were intended to be modest pieds-à-terre. But once Nelson and Harrison sunk their teeth into it, the project turned out to be anything but modest, in either design or execution.

The Rockefeller Apartments would consist of twin twelve-story buildings, one on 54th Street, the other on 55th Street, with a private garden in between. To bring more light and air into the units, costly semicircular bay windows would be cantilevered out from the wheat-colored brick facade. Among the other exceptional features were wood-burning fireplaces in the living rooms and bedrooms equipped with silent ventilators.

In no time at all, construction costs rose from the original estimate of $1.6 million to $1.8 million. Of this, $1.1 million was financed by a Chase mortgage; the rest came straight out of Junior's pocket. Nelson assured him it was worth it; the apartments' costly fittings, he told Junior, placed them "in a class by themselves as far as competition is concerned." The public seemed to agree; the buildings were fully rented even before their scheduled October 1936 opening. And the critics who had been so doleful about Rockefeller Center pronounced the apartments a triumph. Lewis Mumford described them as "the most brilliant and most successful example of modern architecture in the city."

Profits, however, were another matter; in the first year the apartments were to yield a mere $11,000. Yet far from being daunted by this, Nelson talked of erecting still more apartment buildings north of Rockefeller Center, nestling them around a department store he would build on Fifth Avenue. These grand designs put him, for the first time, at loggerheads with his brother John. With some vehemence, John argued that residential construction was a foolish undertaking. "It would not seem," he cuttingly advised Junior, "as if the net return compared very favorably with other available investments such as Government notes." About the only reason John could see for going ahead was to provide "experience for members of the family"—a thinly veiled reference to Nelson.

Junior agreed. There would be no more Rockefeller Apartments. (Ultimately, in 1945, the 54th Street and 55th Street towers would be sold for $1.7 million, or $100,000 less than they cost to build.)

But Nelson had other ideas for his father's undeveloped property. New York's flamboyant mayor, Fiorello La Guardia, was pushing for a grand municipal art center that would include a symphony hall, an opera house, and a new home for the Museum of Modern Art. In the spring of 1936 Nelson suggested to La Guardia that the two blocks north of Rockefeller Center would be an ideal home for such a center. The Center's private street, Rockefeller Plaza, could be extended to 53rd Street, and the art center complex could run along its western flank. To the east would be new headquarters for William Paley's

Columbia Broadcasting System, paralleling archrival RCA's foothold in Rockefeller Center itself. At the end of the private street, completing the axis of Rockefeller institutions, would be the Museum of Modern Art.

La Guardia's Municipal Art Committee quickly endorsed the scheme, and Harrison's firm was retained to draw up plans for the opera building, the centerpiece of the development. But neither Nelson nor the mayor had reckoned on the obstinacy of "21," the fashionable onetime speakeasy that happened to be located directly in the path of the projected private street. The club's owners flatly refused to sell their townhouse. The dream of a municipal art center lingered through 1938, when the ubiquitous Robert Moses came up with an alternate plan that would have located the complex further west. By then, though, La Guardia had lost interest, and the arts complex idea drifted into oblivion—only to be revived, on an even grander scale, two decades later as Lincoln Center for the Performing Arts.

Nelson did secure one aspect of his master plan. In early 1936, Junior gave the Museum of Modern Art his property on the north side of West 53rd Street, the property that marked the terminus of the projected private street. While the extended street would never be built, a new museum—a fitting home for Abby's beloved Modern—would be.

There seemed no end to the designs and schemes spinning out of Nelson's mind, no limit to the energy gushing through the myriad worlds in which he played. Still not yet thirty, he already was a superb specimen of that New York genus known as the "operator": a telephone-wielding networker adept at picking brains, cutting deals, and moving mountains. He adroitly cultivated other movers and shakers like Robert Moses and David Sarnoff, entertaining them at lunch at what was now his house aerie, the Rainbow Room.

Savoring his family's pivotal role at RKO—thanks to the large stock holding that had come their way when the bankrupt movie company defaulted on its Rockefeller Center lease—Nelson injected himself into the company's reorganization efforts. Emissaries in Hollywood kept him posted on RKO's affairs, and in the summer of 1937 he was in on machinations to bring David O. Selznick to RKO as production boss; when that came to naught his representatives talked to Samuel Goldwyn. Finally, Nelson and Sarnoff (whose RCA was still a major RKO shareholder) lured George Schaefer from United Artists with a fat three-year deal.

No idea was too far-fetched for Nelson to consider. Take, for example, his encounter with "art diver" Jane Fauntz. Fauntz wrote him in May 1936 about the possibility of staging an Olympic diving exhibition in a "smart glass pool"—in the Rainbow Room. She described herself as a "former United States champion diver who has done exhibition diving at the 'Streets of Paris' and the Arizona Biltmore Hotel. I am very feminine and have the reputation of being the most graceful diver ever to become prominent in the Sporting World."

No doubt attracted by her femininity, Nelson responded to the overture and met with Fauntz, inviting her to lay out her idea over lunch at the Rainbow Room. The lunch went well; in her thank-you note the next day, she dropped the "Dear Mr. Rockefeller" formality and addressed him as "Nelson":

> Had simply a bang up time yesterday—thank you again—You are such enjoyable company—I think your [sic] mighty swell, I do.
>
> I'd certainly like to see that startling idea of yours work out, Nelson. It would be so darned unusual and very effective with beautiful lighting. You said you were a promoter so get busy and promote. As for old "Promiscuous," the golden gent in the fountain—perhaps he'd like someone to talk to for company—he looks rather lonesome.

Fauntz went on to tell Nelson she was contemplating diving in a tank in Macy's to commemorate National Swim for Health Week. "But if you think for a moment that my appearing diving in a department store would detract from the dignity of this possibility at Rockefeller Center (and personally I do) I shall dismiss the idea completely."

Nelson had actually entertained the notion of a diving exhibition by Fauntz in the Center's sunken plaza. Perhaps it was the risqué imagery of her note—such as her allusion to the Prometheus fountain by another name—that brought him to his senses. He fired off a telegram: "Just returned to find your letter Stop Afraid no chance of working out scheme in sunken Plaza Stop Sorry."

But Fauntz was not so easily dissuaded. Pronouncing herself "lower than a duck's instep," she penned an impassioned plea to Nelson to reconsider. "Do you suppose," she asked, "you could put on a pair of false whiskers, and a red ribbon across your chest and pass for a foreign ambassador? I wish you could drop in and talk to me about this, or we could go on a picnic in the Central Park zoo."

Whether Nelson put on the false whiskers and dropped in on Fauntz, or whether he joined her for the Central Park picnic, is not known. But not long after her note, he asked John Roy, the manager of the Rainbow Room, to see if he could get Fauntz a booking at another club, the French Casino. Roy tried, but failed, and soon Jane Fauntz, "art diver," was heard from no more.

Just days after Christmas 1937 flyers began popping up all over Rockefeller Center: in the hallways, in the rest rooms, in the underground freight garages. They were addressed to the Center's employees:

Rockefeller Center is one of the *very* few buildings in which the Employees are as yet not organized.

DON'T STAND ALONE!!

In *Union* there is Strength.

The handouts were distributed by the Building Maintenance Craftsmen, an American Federation of Labor affiliate that was seeking to organize the 1,100 mechanics, carpenters, electricians, cleaning people, and the like who kept the vast complex going. One organizing meeting had already been held at the Hotel Victoria; another was slated for early January. The Building Maintenance Craftsmen definitely meant business.

To underscore the situation's seriousness, Rockefeller Center's electrical workers walked off their jobs in mid-February, and other workers threatened to follow suit. While hardly a crippling walkout (it was over in a week and a half), the strike, with its processions of resolute pickets blocking the majestic building entrances, was a potent demonstration of union muscle and an ominous threat of even greater disruptions ahead.

The labor unrest was the first true crisis to confront Nelson since he effectively took command of Rockefeller Center. And, from his family's point of view, it was absolutely the worst sort of crisis imaginable, evoking as it did shades of Ludlow and his father's struggle to master the grim legacy of the camps. That history—coupled with the elemental fact of union power in the 1930s—meant that any hard-line resistance to the workers was utterly out of the question. The issue at hand for Nelson was not whether to allow unions into Rockefeller Center, but on what terms they would be permitted to enter.

And just as his father had to overcome John D. Senior's Neanderthal attitudes about his workers, so too did Nelson now have to overcome Junior's somewhat antiquated paternalism. Junior loudly mistrusted "outside representation," preferring the harmonious "family relationship" of a company-sponsored union; "employers and employees are partners, not enemies," he intoned. Laudable as these sentiments were, they were fundamentally irrelevant to Depression-era industrial relations, in which hard-nosed bargaining, not harmonious feelings, governed the relations between management and labor.

Further complicating matters were the bitter jurisdictional wars raging within the labor movement, wars not only between unions but between the two mighty associations which vied for their allegiance, the AF of L and the Congress of Industrial Organizations. Those hostilities made the initial negotiating sessions a minefield for any employer—let alone an employer as prestigious and publicly visible as Rockefeller Center.

This, then, was the thorny situation confronting Nelson and Hugh Robertson when they sat down for the first time with their formidable opposite numbers: Thomas Murray, president of the AF of L's Building Trades Council, the master group for all the unions potentially representing Center employees, and Joseph Blek, president of the Building Maintenance Craftsmen, the union that had done all the early organizing.

Nelson did not enter the session unarmed. He had sought out the advice of experts, including that of Standard Oil of New Jersey president Walter Teagle. But the coaching that had meant the most to him, that had convinced him that he could make his way through the thicket of jurisdictional issues, came not from economists or industrialists, but from a feisty, diminutive, politically wired dynamo named Anna Rosenberg.

A Budapest native who emigrated to the United States when she was ten, Rosenberg had never let her gender, nor very much of anything else, stand in her way. Barging into the back rooms of New York politics, she became a Tammany Hall player while still in her twenties, at the same time cultivating a talent for labor negotiation. Her skills in both arenas brought her to the attention of New York governor Franklin Roosevelt. As President, he named Rosenberg regional director of the National Recovery Administration, where she made a name for herself with such high-profile stunts as climbing down into a New York subway tunnel during a 1930s strike by subway electricians. Rosenberg's indomitable nature was already the stuff of legend, as were her contacts. *The New Yorker* in 1938 described her as "a kind of switchboard through which enemies can make connections."

As one of her longtime clients, renowned advertising man William Benton, would later comment, "There never was a story, an illustration, that was more appropriate to Anna Rosenberg than the Scottish line 'Where MacGregor sits, there is the head of the table.' Where Anna sat, there was the head of the table."

Two decades earlier, Junior had turned to Canadian politician W. L. Mackenzie King to help him out of the Ludlow morass. Now, displaying the same facility for picking the right brain at the right time, Nelson called on Anna Rosenberg.

With Rosenberg as his mentor, Nelson engineered an ingenious solution to his labor problem. A single union, the Building Maintenance Craftsmen, would represent all of Rockefeller Center's employees; the need to negotiate separately with up to a dozen different craft unions would be eliminated. Anxious to organize the Center's workers with as little fuss as possible, and to foreclose any initiative by the CIO, the Building Trades Council's Murray readily agreed to this approach. The one potential stumbling block was the state's Labor Relations Board: would it be willing to quickly and quietly certify the AF of L unit as the authorized representative of the Center workers? If it didn't—if, for instance, the board called for hearings—Nelson feared "the whole thing might go to pieces."

Once again, he took his dilemma to Anna Rosenberg. And once again she came through for him. She phoned the state board's counsel, who happened to be "one of her boys," as she put it. The counsel hemmed and hawed; Rosenberg pounded away. Finally, he relented. The union could have its certification. There would be no hearings, and no publicity, just as she wished.

Two days later, Rockefeller Center and the union signed their contract. At Nelson's behest, the Building Trades Council kept the lid on publicity. As Nelson proudly informed his father, who was in London at the time, "The following day only a small notice appeared in the papers, the most important being the Tribune, and there it only appeared on the third page."

Efficiently, almost stealthily, labor peace had been achieved at Rockefeller Center.

Junior was immensely gratified by the outcome, and his son's direct role in it. "You were very wise in making connections with the labor leaders yourself, and getting into such good personal relations with them," he wrote Nelson. "You now have first-hand knowledge of the men we are dealing with. . . . The closer we keep in touch with these men, the better."

Those "good personal relations" would be carefully nurtured by Nelson in the years to come. The word was passed from Tom Murray to his fellow building trades leaders: Nelson Rockefeller was someone we could deal with. One of those who got the word was the president of the AF of L's New York State federation, a rising star of organized labor named George Meany. Meany would remember, and so would many others in the labor movement.

To cement those relationships, Nelson named a new industrial relations director for Rockefeller Center: Victor Borella, a member of his old Dartmouth circle. Borella came from a working-class background himself—at one point, he had been forced to drop out of Dartmouth to earn a living—and was completely at ease with the pugnacious cigar chompers who bossed the unions. He also had Nelson's utmost trust, a factor that weighed not inconsiderably in the labor leaders' estimation of both Borella and Nelson.

But the most momentous connection Nelson made in the course of those early labor negotiations was with the spirited, savvy Anna Rosenberg. He had never met anyone like her: tenacious, street-smart, with a web of contacts that permeated the innermost depths of City Hall and ranged up to the highest levels in Washington. Probably more than anyone he had ever met, she had a gift for slicing through rhetoric and posturing and getting to the heart of a matter. As her son Thomas, who worked for her for years, would recall, "If she was brought into a situation, she would say very simply, 'Do you want to settle this or don't you? You have two choices. You can take a strike, and if you want to take it it's none of my goddamn business, or do you want to settle this thing? If you want to settle it, here's what I suggest to you. Boom, boom, boom.' "

Thoroughly feminine—she fancied glittering gold bracelets and flowery hats and possessed a daunting collection of French perfumes—Rosenberg nonetheless could storm into a room and pound tables with the best of them. (Some years later, representing the movie companies, she confronted the then very left-wing president of the Screen Actors Guild, Ronald Reagan. "Ah," he greeted her, "the stalking horse of the capitalists." "Listen, Mr. Reagan," she shot back, "do you want to trade a lot of bullshit or do you want to get this thing settled?")

Now that the union contract had been signed, Nelson had no obvious reason for Rosenberg's services. But he knew that he wanted her in his orbit, to advise him, to make the occasional pivotal connection, to be his link to the liberal Democratic establishment that controlled the White House. And so, beginning in that year of 1938, he put Rosenberg on retainer, paying her (through the medium of Special Work, now renamed Corporate Research, Inc.) the substantial sum of $6,000 a year.

It would, very soon, prove to be one of the soundest investments he ever made.

The last rivet of the fourteenth and final building of Rockefeller Center, the U.S. Rubber Building on Sixth Avenue and 48th Street, was set to be driven on November 1, 1939. Nelson determined that this would be more than just a mechanical exercise attended by a handful of sweaty foremen. It would be a gala event, a grand celebration of Rockefeller Center, with speechmaking and marching bands, all broadcast nationwide on the National Broadcasting Company radio network. And the centerpiece of the occasion would be the driving of that last rivet—not by some anonymous steelworker, but by the procreator of it all, John D. Rockefeller, Jr.

So it was that some four hundred guests gathered in the bunting-festooned lobby of the U.S. Rubber Building that November 1, listening to the martial airs of the Seventh Regiment Band as the procession of luminaries mounted the speakers' platform. Then the crowd was hushed. NBC was on the air. And standing at the microphone, his hair meticulously coiffed, his richly textured three-piece suit neatly draping his trim form, was the master of ceremonies, Nelson A. Rockefeller.

"The driving of the last rivet at Rockefeller Center is like speaking the last word of a story," he began. "A story of planning and building, of advances and setbacks, of the unexpected, the unforeseen."

After speeches by other eminences connected with the Center—including La Guardia and union leader Tom Murray—it was Junior's turn. "It is perhaps difficult for a son to introduce his father," Nelson remarked. "So many things you want to say and can't say." His father, he told the radio audience, "has always had a suppressed desire to drive a rivet," and now it was time for him to drive the last one at Rockefeller Center. Slipping his hands into work gloves (but leaving on his pinstriped suit coat), Junior approached the bare steel girder and was handed a pneumatic drill. Then, with foreman M. L. Carpenter steadying the drill, Junior pushed through the rivet amidst the glitter of flashbulbs and the whir of newsreel cameras.

It was Junior's day. But anyone who glimpsed the poised young man at the podium making small talk with La Guardia, palling around with the union leaders, and adroitly taking command of the microphone could have little doubt whose day it really was.

In the public mind, Rockefeller Center was now as much Nelson's project as it was his father's. *Forbes* magazine was among many to take note. "Radio City has become the strongest magnet for visitors to New York," the magazine commented. "The genius who has made Rockefeller Center uniquely attractive is Nelson A. Rockefeller, second son of John D. Jr. Keep your eye on him."

Eleven

PLAYING POLITICS

A tide of bobbing top hats and a sea of mink and ermine filled West 53rd Street on a sparkling May evening in 1939, the vast swell converging on a stark white marble-and-glass building a few steps from Fifth Avenue. Few of the thousands who flooded into its lobby had seen the likes of such a structure: a flat, unornamented rectangular box, surmounted by a floating, portholed roof—New York's first example of the "international," Bauhaus style. The interior was just as avant-garde: huge panes of plate glass through which a sculpture garden could be espied, sleek chairs and other furniture by such modernist masters as Marcel Breuer and Alvar Aalto. Dazzling and iconoclastic, this was the new, permanent home of the Museum of Modern Art.

The cream of the city's society, along with various worthies from the political, artistic, and literary worlds, elbowed and jostled each other for breathing space on that opening night. Mayor La Guardia was there, as were Mrs. Vincent Astor and Mrs. Cornelius Vanderbilt (but not Mrs. Nicholas Murray Butler, wife of the Columbia University president, who took one look at the crush and headed right home, muttering, "You couldn't drag me in there"). Salvador Dali showed up, as did Constantin Brancusi and Jo Davidson and Lillian Gish and Katherine Anne Porter.

After taking in the scene, the throng found themselves herded downstairs, to the museum's auditorium. With Lowell Thomas as master of ceremonies, the proceedings were broadcast nationwide on the Columbia Broadcasting System. Edsel Ford and La Guardia spoke. And then, through the magic of radio, the voice of Walt Disney, live from Hollywood, filled the hall, paying tribute to the museum's hallowing of the motion picture as an art form.

Finally, the radio hookup switched to Washington, and the audience heard the unmistakable patrician tones of the President of the United States. "We are dedicating this building to the cause of peace and to the pursuits of peace," Roosevelt declared, hailing the museum as "a citadel of civilization" because "in encouraging the creation and enjoyment of beautiful things we are furthering democracy itself."

After this peroration, Thomas called up to the auditorium microphone the new president of the Museum of Modern Art: Nelson A. Rockefeller.

Nelson was alternately glib—joking with Thomas about whether there were moths in one of the museum's most controversial works, Méret Oppenheim's "Fur-Lined Teacup"—and hortatory, declaiming on the museum's mission to spread the gospel of contemporary art. And, as the cognoscenti in the audience were quick to note, he omitted any word of praise for or even reference to his fellow trustees, the most notable of whom was his predecessor, A. Conger Goodyear. (Nelson later apologized for the omission, blaming it on the constraints of the radio broadcast.)

The evening was a crowning moment for the ten-year-old museum, marking its transition from a precocious showplace to a basilica for the new artistic establishment, an institution with, as one commentator put it, "a national reputation and national responsibilities." And, equally, the opening was one more turn in the national spotlight for the museum's effusive young president.

Just as he would do six months later at the Rockefeller Center last-rivet ceremony, Nelson had turned an institutional celebration into a personal coming-out party. The event landed him on the cover of *Time* magazine, beaming at the nation with natty self-confidence. To the ears of the coast-to-coast broadcast audience, he shared the stage with the President of the United States.

He had climbed to the pinnacle of his father's great creation, Rockefeller Center. Now Nelson had made his way to the top of his mother's, the Museum of Modern Art. But he had not waited to assume the presidency before leaving his mark on the museum. All along—virtually from the moment Nelson returned to New York from his honeymoon—the institution had come under the sway of his drive and exuberance.

Years later, Nelson would observe, "I learned about politics at the Museum of Modern Art." It would be fairer to say that the museum gave him one more arena in which to practice and to hone the political skills and stratagems that came so naturally to him.

He had entered the museum in 1931, as we have seen, as the golden boy, the dynamo who would bring new verve and spunk to the councils of the monied elite who governed the institution. Mobilizing his Junior Advisory Committee, he more than lived up to that promise with his murals show. The controversy and consternation that exhibition sparked did little to tarnish his aura. By early 1932 he was a full-fledged trustee; by 1934 he was chairman of the finance committee.

Despite its well-heeled core of patrons, the Modern was desperately scrounging for funds in those days, and Nelson quickly emerged as its most inveterate scrounger. At one point he came up with a scheme to squeeze large pledges out of the museum's core supporters, payable over twenty-five years—with the museum charging 5 percent interest each year on the unpaid balance. Abby would be faced with the biggest levy, some $300,000; George Gershwin would be asked for $25,000, while Nelson himself (who had not yet come into his money) would pledge $15,000. Nothing came of his idea, because the museum was soon faced with the far more immediate problem of drumming up a $1 million endowment to meet the terms of the Lillie Bliss bequest.

More than any other trustee, Nelson shouldered the burden of building that endowment, importuning magnates like Felix Warburg, pulling strings to get the mighty Metropolitan Museum involved in the fund-raising quest for its sister institution. Thanks to his efforts—and his own timely, anonymous $100,000 contribution—the endowment, the Bliss bequest, and, some would say, the future of the museum were secured.

Looking back on those early years, his fellow trustee Eliza Cobb (Lillie Bliss's niece) has no difficulty assaying Nelson's importance. "I think it's fair to say that if it hadn't been for Nelson, the museum might never have gotten off the ground," she says. "His interest, his enthusiasm, his enormous attention to the place attracted people and got them excited about things.

"He always would say—it would be his philosophy—'We've got to put on a show.' And somebody would say, 'But we haven't got any money to put on a show.' And he'd say, 'Well, put it on anyway. We'll get the money afterwards.' And, of course, if he said it, people would have confidence and they would go ahead and put it on. And somehow he got the money."

Above all, in those formative years, Nelson stood squarely behind the museum's guiding genius, Alfred Barr. An obscure Wellesley College art professor when he was tapped, to much surprise, as MOMA's first director in 1929, Barr was frail, contentious, and cranky. Yet it was Barr's unerring taste and his eclectic vision of what a modern art museum should be that was the institution's great propulsive force. "This is not a traditional museum," Barr told one new employee in 1935. "This is a continual opening night; this is a three-ring circus." And the gaunt, tightly wound young director was the ringmaster, orchestrating one blockbuster show after another. There was the Van Gogh exhibition in October 1935, drawing 125,000 to the museum in just six weeks. There were trendsetting surveys of Cubism and Abstract Art and, nine months later, of Dada and Surrealism (where the notorious fur-lined teacup made its first appearance). These shows, along with such unorthodox forays as the Machine Art exhibition, put Barr's museum firmly on the cultural map.

Barr also played another, less publicized role: that of a personal art adviser to the trustees. And no trustee picked Barr's brain more than Nelson Rockefeller. As Nelson's collection took shape, Barr was always available to educate, to counsel, and to prod.

But as much as the trustees respected Barr, they also found him a maddeningly impossible person to deal with. Edward Warburg remembers that "his nose was out of joint on practically every damn issue. At a board meeting you'd say, 'Well, Alfred, what do you think?' and his usual response would be 'Well, it's about time somebody asked me.' "

Unwilling to loosen his grip on every aspect of the museum's operations—the shows, the catalogues (most of which he wrote himself), the assembling of its permanent collection—he would agonize over niggling details, while letting vital administrative issues pile up. "He would spend weeks deciding how the lettering should be of the word 'Men' over the men's room," says Warburg. Neurotic and neurasthenic, Barr struggled with chronic insomnia, among other ailments; at one point, to help him recover, Abby arranged for him to go off on a one-year European sabbatical. "When he came back," recalls Cobb, "he said he still couldn't sleep, and could he have two more weeks?"

Barr's behavior drove even the regally tolerant Abby Rockefeller to distraction. "Why," she once asked James Flexner, "is Mr. Barr so *terribly* difficult in every way?"

But it was the Modern's president, Conger Goodyear, who was the most enraged by Barr. "Toughie" Goodyear, as he was known, was a Buffalo lumberman whose gruff military bearing seemed to make him uniquely ill suited to preside over a temple of the avant-garde. Yet he had got along well with the grandes dames who had organized the museum; believing (as was all too often the case in those days) that the institution would be taken seriously only if a man was at the helm, they asked Goodyear to be president. Eager to make his mark in New York society, Goodyear happily agreed. Remarks Warburg, "They used to say about Kitty Miller, who was very much in the social scene in England, that on Armistice Day, when there were two minutes of silence, you could hear her climbing. Conger was very much the same way."

For the ladies' sake, Goodyear tolerated Barr—but just barely. And Barr, in turn, treated Goodyear with thinly veiled condescension. For an institution still in its formative years, the mixture was a dangerously volatile one.

Rather than stand by and wait for the explosion, Nelson chose to engage in a bit of internal intrigue.

In April 1933 he wrote to his mother at the Homestead resort in Hot Springs, Virginia, that he had been talking with museum executive director Alan Blackburn about the idea of Abby assuming the presidency. Blackburn, he said, had confided that "if it had not been for you last year he thought Alfred would have gone to pieces long before he did and he has been very much worried about the coming year because he does not feel that Alfred, under Mr. Goodyear's leadership, will last much longer."

Nelson signed off with this promise: "I'll have you in the chair before you come back."

Horrified, Abby fired back a cease-and-desist missive. "I feel like saying, as the young woman did when she received a proposal, 'This is so sudden!' I had no idea that you were really serious when you talked with me in New York about my becoming president of the Museum. I took it more or less as a joke. Do you think it proper for a son to go around campaigning for his mother's promotion in office?" If Nelson was so intent on making a change, then perhaps, she said, he should approach trustee Stephen Clark, the Singer sewing machine heir, about becoming president.

Clark, however, wasn't interested. Undaunted, Nelson continued to weave his web. Seizing on a vague statement by Goodyear that the museum's officers should be changed every five years, he approached Goodyear about switching Abby from treasurer to vice president so that she would be in a position to succeed him. "I think she could be persuaded to take the office," Nelson assured Goodyear, "although she knows nothing about this 'conspiracy' on my part, which is probably just as well."

Ignorant of her son's further machinations, Abby agreed to the switch. But her health—she suffered from high blood pressure and other cardiovascular ailments—truly did not permit her to take on the presidency, although Nelson expressed the hope that he could change her mind. In the meantime, Goodyear stayed on. Clark still adamantly refused the job, and Nelson was too busy with his simultaneous power struggle at Rockefeller Center to make his own bid.

Nonetheless, if Nelson wasn't prepared to take on the Modern presidency yet, he managed to acquire an imposing grip on the museum's affairs. By 1935 he was chairman of the finance committee, the endowment committee, and the nominating committee. Even Abby felt this was going too far. "It does not seem wise to me that Nelson should be Chairman of all of the important committees of the Museum," she complained to Goodyear. "It does not seem to me it is conducive to a happy or successful future for the Museum."

But having stepped into the museum's power vacuum, Nelson was not about to be dislodged. And, in 1936, his influence was augmented even further when he was named chairman of the three-man committee to oversee the Modern's new building (the other members were Barr and Goodyear).

The appointment made eminent sense. It was Nelson, after all, who had first issued the call for a move from the cramped West 53rd Street townhouse the museum had occupied since 1932. He envisioned the Modern's new, permanent home as part of the municipal arts center that he was cooking up with La Guardia. From his father's properties north of Rockefeller Center he assembled the land on which the new museum would stand. (The Modern, in fact, bought the land from Junior, but this "purchase" was hardly a purchase at all, since the money for it came from a gift from Abby.)

The financial logic behind Nelson's appointment was also inescapable: there was little doubt that the Rockefellers would be bearing the lion's share of the building costs. That indeed proved to be the case: Junior, Abby, and Nelson together ended up paying $750,000, close to 60 percent of the total building fund contributions.

To serve as chief architect, the Modern board named one of its own members, Philip Goodwin, a gentlemanly neoclassical designer of the Beaux Arts school. Barr, however, had grave reservations about Goodwin's appointment; the only fitting architect of the Modern's new home, as far as he was concerned, was a world-class apostle of the architectural new wave. The names that came to mind were Walter Gropius and Mies van der Rohe.

But Nelson Rockefeller had other ideas.

In May 1936, Barr sailed on the SS *Normandie* for a three-month European business trip. Among the items on his agenda were approaches to Mies, Gropius, and Dutch architect J. J. P. Oud about "collaborating" with Goodwin on the new building. While Oud and Gropius weren't interested, Mies, to Barr's utter delight, was eager to accept the commission. But just as Barr was preparing to relay the happy news to New York, a series of urgent letters arrived from the museum. Goodwin, it seemed, was apoplectic about Barr's overtures to the Europeans and threatened to resign from the job if he was forced to accept one as his "collaborator." Rather than stand up to him, the building committee—Nelson and Goodyear—had affirmed Goodwin's appointment and named a young, relatively obscure young architect named Edward Durell Stone to assist him.

Stone had worked on Radio City Music Hall, and Nelson had come to know him when he produced displays for the Museum of Science and Industry in Rockefeller Center. "One day," Stone would recall, "I overheard Wally [Harrison] say to Nelson, 'What about Ed?' I didn't know what the hell was going on." Soon after, Stone got word that he would be working with Goodwin on the new Museum of Modern Art.

Over in Paris, Barr was utterly incredulous at this turn of events. Nelson had assured him, before he left, that no final, ironclad decision on Goodwin's co-architect would be made before the end of the summer. Now, behind Barr's back, he had engineered a fait accompli.

Hearing that Junior and Abby, with David in tow, were also visiting Paris, Barr sought an immediate meeting with the museum's doyenne at her suite in the Hotel Crillon. "I do not believe that Nelson would want to abandon the Museum to Mr. Goodwin and Mr. Stone," he told her, "if he knew that Mies van der Rohe was available." Abby agreed, and fired off a cable to Nelson, urging him to delay action on the architects. Barr, meanwhile, penned long, anguished letters to Goodyear and Goodwin. "When I left New York, Nelson was definitely in favor of Mies," he wrote Goodyear. "He seems to have changed his mind for reasons which I do not clearly understand."

Goodyear's cabled reply was blunt:

> TOO LATE TO CONSIDER ANY EUROPEAN ARCHITECT STOP GOODWIN USING STONE STOP GREATLY PLEASED WITH PRELIMINARY PLANS STOP NELSON CABLING MRS ROCKEFELLER FULLY

A livid Barr wired Nelson that he was resigning from the building committee: "As member presumably concerned with buildings architectural quality cannot share responsibility committees action especially with Mies available." But he might as well have saved the transatlantic cable fees; Nelson was utterly immovable.

There were many reasons why Nelson would risk Barr's ire and commit what Barr regarded as a supreme act of double-dealing. The most obvious one was his unwillingness to offend Goodwin, a fellow trustee. But arguably a far more compelling factor was the availability of the talented, hungry young Edward Durell Stone. Here was someone with whom Nelson had already worked, an architect with whom Nelson could have the same sort of artistic symbiosis that he had already developed with Wally Harrison. What it probably came down to in the end was that Mies would have been Barr's architect, while Stone, surely, was Nelson's.

Ironically, the design that Goodwin and Stone came up with was as true to Bauhaus principles as anything the European architects might have produced. Even such renowned skeptics as Lewis Mumford hailed MOMA's new home; *Architectural Forum* pronounced it "a thoroughly distinguished addition to the best modern architecture has produced." Today the structure endures as a jewel of the New York cityscape.

It hardly seemed coincidental that two days before the new building's gala opening, Nelson Rockefeller was at last elevated to the MOMA presidency—just in time to bask in the praise and pageantry that accompanied the grand event. As Eliza Cobb points out, "The presidency was a natural step for him to take. It was just a question of when he took it." Just as John Todd accepted the inevitable two years before at Rockefeller Center, so now did A. Conger Goodyear. "Sometimes his mother has stressed Nelson's youth as a detriment," Goodyear said at a trustees dinner to celebrate the changing of the guard, "but I can't agree that youth is any handicap."

Barr, meanwhile, continued to sulk. He considered the opening-night extravaganza "undignified" and in "thoroughly bad taste" and bristled at Nelson's jocular references to "Fur-Lined Teacup." "That the president of an art museum should make fun publicly of a work of art by a serious artist," he fumed to a colleague, "I consider a pretty cheap and unnecessary conniving with the public's desire to laugh at anything it can't understand at first glance . . . the same kind of 'fun' was made of the work of Van Gogh, Cézanne and Whistler some fifty years ago."

Nelson may have been Barr's staunchest defender in the past. But he served notice, in the architects controversy, that he was not about to yield to the fusillades of the museum's mercurial director. Now that he was president, Nelson would make Conger Goodyear seem like a model of forbearance by comparison.

Determined to work around Barr and streamline the Modern's operations, Nelson brought in time-and-motion experts. Their presence sent shivers through the staff. "It was just *awful,*" remembers Barr's deputy, Dorothy Miller. "To suddenly have these people peering into everything you were doing, to have them snooping through your files—it was a terrible blow to the staff." Barr was contemptuous of the efficiency experts, but, as his wife Marga would later write, "Alfred had not foreseen the consequences of their reports. Now, Nelson Rockefeller has bypassed Alfred's authority as director of the museum and has played havoc with its central nervous system."

Without Barr's knowledge or consent (he was once again in Paris at the time) Nelson proceeded to fire executive director Thomas Mabry and publications director Frances Collins, along with a number of men on the maintenance staff. (Collins' dismissal was apparently triggered by her prankish printing of a mock invitation to the opening of the "Museum of Standard Oil.") Several key staffers wired Barr with their support, offering to join him in a resignation en masse. Barr told them to sit tight, and then dispatched a heated telegram to Abby in Seal Harbor: "Profoundly shocked by purges. Staff morale seriously undermined during past month by insecurity and even more by loss of faith in capacity to maintain standards and ideals. No word from Nelson. Do you want me to stay. Need your personal advice and support."

But Abby, this time, stood squarely behind her son. "Executive Committee unanimously voted drastic reduction of budget," she wired Barr, "which necessitates reorganization of museum work. This was done after much study and serious consideration. Personally feel that you have no reason for anxiety. Think first step has been taken towards smoothly running, efficient, harmonious institution in every way better for you."

Upon his return to New York, Barr simply shrugged off the resignation talk and went on about his business. It was plain to the staff, as one member put it, that "he didn't have any power any more."

Still another bitter blow to the director came soon afterward, when Nelson forced the resignation of John McAndrew, the head of the museum's architecture department, amidst the scaling down of the entire unit. Nelson simply said he found McAndrew "incompatible."

Privately railing at Nelson's high-handed moves, Barr expressed the fear that the museum was cultivating amiable mediocrities, "as if organization was an end in itself." Yet, once again, he felt himself incapable of bucking Nelson.

Curiously, the director's personal relationship with Nelson seemed utterly unaffected by the stormy doings at the museum. They still eagerly chitchatted about art and artists, still swapped notes on pieces that were becoming available (Barr would order paintings and store them in the MOMA basement until Nelson decided whether he wanted them), and they still spent hours together hanging and rehanging the works in Nelson's collection. In their mutual passion for modern art they found a spiritual bond. As Barr would later admiringly remark, "Nelson needs art more than any man I know." And for all his problems with Barr's administration of the museum, Nelson's immense respect for Barr's discernment and sure sense of the museum's mission never ebbed.

Perhaps because of these sentiments, Barr never blamed Nelson for the denouement of his turbulent directorship: his dismissal from the job in 1943. The villain in his eyes was Stephen Clark, who would succeed Nelson when the latter went off to wartime service in Washington. "Stephen Clark was the person responsible, not Nelson," says Miller. "He was infinitely jealous of Alfred Barr's knowledge of art, and he couldn't bear to have someone around who knew as much or more than he did." But, jealous though he may have been, the fact of the matter was that Clark encountered much the same frustration with Barr's executive skills that Goodyear, and Nelson, and Abby had experienced. All Clark did was administer the final coup de grace.

It was not Stephen Clark who had isolated Barr and undermined his position—by bringing in efficiency experts, by purging his staff, by undercutting his authority in such pivotal matters as the selection of the new building's architect. It was Nelson Rockefeller.*

The same relentless ambition Nelson brought to bear on the museum and on Rockefeller Center was now also trained on his personal surroundings.

His apartment was already a showcase for sculpture by Lachaise, andirons by Giacometti, and rugs by Christian Bérard. In 1938 he purchased the apartment below, and he determined that this duplex setting offered an opportunity for originally commissioned art on an even grander scale.

The huge new living room on the lower floor had two fireplaces, for which Wallace Harrison designed graceful wood rococo mantels that reached almost to the ceiling. Nelson wanted murals for those mantels: paintings that would

*Actually, the long-run result of all this, for both Barr and the museum, was not at all unhappy. Barr stayed on at the museum as an advisory director; later, he was given the title of director of collections. Freed at last from his administrative burdens, he could concentrate on that which he did best: building MOMA's permanent collection, mounting shows, and bringing his authoritative presence to bear on artistic scholarship.

be executed specifically for the space and would be inset directly into Harrison's paneling, mimicking its sinuous curves.

To paint those murals, Nelson commissioned Henri Matisse and Fernand Léger.

Working in Paris from full-scale drawings of the fireplaces, Matisse produced a painting he called "La Poésie": four languid female figures, executed in the lyrical, sensuous style that marked Matisse's output during the 1930s. Léger, meanwhile, actually came to New York and painted his mural right in Nelson's living room. Day after day, Nelson stood in rapt fascination as Léger's mural revealed itself. The finished work was more abstract than Matisse's—vaguely plantlike forms were splayed across the canvas—and far less restful. But Nelson loved it, so much so that he promptly asked Léger if he might stay a little longer and do murals for the marble circular staircase connecting the two floors and for the hallways—much as a lesser mortal might ask a housepainter to touch up a closet while he was at it. Léger agreed.

That same year, Nelson also decided to expand his quarters up in Pocantico. He and Tod now had five children—a son, Steven, was born in 1936, and twins, Michael and Mary, arrived in 1938—and their colonial residence, Hawes House, was overloaded. Feeling the need for additional space to accommodate his visitors, Nelson asked for, and received, Junior's permission to build a guest house. The elder Rockefeller, however, undoubtedly was taken aback by the conception Wally Harrison and Nelson came up with, a design utterly alien to the country-manor look prevailing on the rest of the estate. Bauhaus, it seemed, was coming to Pocantico.

The guest house would consist of two small fieldstone pavilions: a rectilinear building for the bedrooms and a round structure for the living room, the two buildings connected by a single roof. To let in light between the buildings, Nelson and Harrison decided a cutout in the roof was needed. To design the cutout, they once again commissioned Fernand Léger. The distinctiveness of the guest house was further enhanced by such ultramodern touches as floor-to-ceiling electrically operated windows that opened upon a semicircular swimming pool in the back. But undoubtedly the house's most unusual feature was a living-room pond fed by water from the outdoor pool.

The Hawes Guest House, as it was known, turned out to be merely a prelude to another, far more majestic undertaking two years later. Nelson was eager to build a house of his own at Seal Harbor, and he had located a suitably dramatic site, a rocky granite outcropping that commanded a spectacular Atlantic vista. Stalking the property with Harrison one day, Nelson drove two wooden stakes into the soil. Here, he told the architect, was where he wanted his picture window. The rest was up to Harrison.

The design Harrison came up with melded beautifully with the roughhewn, natural grandeur of the site. The house, of wood and fieldstone, would be a sprawling concave curve, or, to be more precise, two concave curves, the larger one, containing most of the living quarters, facing the forest, the smaller one, consisting of the living room, jutting out into the sea. A dining area would be perched on the massive coastal rocks, while below a stony stairwell would lead to a swimming pool literally scooped out of the granite; the pool would be filled by the onrushing tide. To further the house's nautical lines, Harrison designed a conical tower, rising from the home's seaward side like a ship's mast, in which drenched sails could be hung to dry.

When it was all done, when Nelson had planted stone Japanese lanterns around the house as a finishing touch, he invited his father over for a look. Junior had watched the work in progress with mounting apprehension, dreading the appearance of this Bauhaus apparition in his beloved Acadia. But what he saw—a structure that both respected and surmounted its environment, a wood and stone homage to the enduring Maine coast—took his breath away.

Upon his return to the Eyrie, he sat down and wrote his son a letter:

> As you well know, I have spoken often with some skepticism in regard to your house. . . . In view of this attitude on my part I hope you realized how completely captivated I was by the place and how abjectly I apologized for my skepticism. . . . It is beautiful in its location and the marvelous views which it commands.

Nelson dubbed his new home The Anchorage. The name was evocative of his love of the sea and of sailing, a love that had deepened since his boyhood runs on the *Jack Tar.* That affection prompted him to make some other substantial investments in his Maine lifestyle.

In the late 1930s a new class of racing yachts, known as International One Design, came on the market. Anxious to bring the vessels to Mount Desert Island, Nelson organized a syndicate of fifteen local buyers, contacted the shipyard in Norway, and had it ship the boats across the Atlantic. Nelson bought two of the racing sloops and gave one to Tod's older sister Miriam and her husband, Philip Wallis.

Nelson named his boat the *Queen Mary*—alluding to both his wife and the great ocean liner—and began arranging races with its sister vessels. His enthusiasm for the sport, however, did not quite make up for his lack of aptitude at it. "He was about as bad a sailor as I ever saw," recalls Harold Haskell, who purchased one of the Norwegian boats. "I can remember one summer I raced against him fifteen times and beat him fifteen times.

"He wasn't a born sailor, but there was more to it than that. His mind was always on other things."

One by one, the old symbolic cornerstones of the Rockefeller empire were passing from the scene.

There was the death, from sheer old age, of John D. Rockefeller, Sr., on May 23, 1937, at age ninety-seven. He had outlived not only all his business rivals but also the muckraking fervor that had once dogged his footsteps. By the time of his demise, Rockefeller Senior was best known as a bent, wizened figure who handed out dimes for the newsreel cameras. To Junior, who until the very end made regular pilgrimages to the old man's warm-weather hideaway in Ormond Beach, Florida, he remained an object of utmost devotion and veneration, the family's spiritual core. Although Junior had run the family's affairs for almost forty years, it was only now, at sixty-three, that he could truly regard himself as the Rockefeller patriarch.

Then, a year later, there was the demolition of both Junior's massive 54th Street townhouse and the smaller one next door that Senior had occupied. With the children grown, Junior and Abby felt no need for such sprawling premises, and they moved to a Park Avenue co-op. The land on which these homes stood was sold to the Museum of Modern Art, which would use it for its restful sculpture garden.

At around the same time Abeyton Lodge, the rambling Pocantico structure that had also been home to Junior and his brood, was bulldozed as well. Upon the death of his father, Junior had succeeded, in true baronial fashion, to Senior's Georgian manor house, Kykuit. Unwilling to maintain two such formidable homes, Junior opted to simply tear his former residence down. His distinctly unsentimental, utilitarian view of the family's domain would not be lost on his children.

The leveling of these antiquated structures could serve as a metaphor for the transition the Rockefeller family was undergoing. In the locus of power, the suite of offices in 30 Rockefeller Plaza that the family coyly referred to as Room 5600, the old was gradually (albeit grudgingly) making way for the new, as one son after another sought to stake out his turf. The directory downstairs now listed it as the "Office of the Messrs. Rockefeller."

It would not be long before the media began to take notice. As the 1930s drew to a close, a succession of feature articles in magazines and newspapers appeared on "The Rockefeller Boys" (that in fact was the title of articles in *The Saturday Evening Post* and *The New York Times Magazine*). The pieces described the roles the sons were playing, marveled that their immense wealth had not yet gone to their heads, and portrayed each son in capsule terms akin to those used for the Seven Dwarfs. There was John the high-minded, Nelson the rambunctious, Laurance the laconic, Winthrop the amiable ("a friendly young koala" was the way the *Post* described him), and David the studious. Within the Rockefeller empire, "each fits into his niche as though he had been carved there," observed the *Times Magazine*.

The sons were in fact distinct characters, each one coming to terms in his own way with his awesome birthright. After his early struggles, John was finally finding his own voice in the philanthropic world, supporting such pet causes as birth control (he became the primary donor to Margaret Sanger's Research Bureau) and the fight against juvenile delinquency. Laurance, who took over his grandfather's seat on the New York Stock Exchange, was a budding venture capitalist; he was already a principal backer of Eddie Rickenbacker's Eastern Air Lines and was a key investor in the aircraft company an ambitious young engineer named James McDonnell was putting together.

Winthrop's path was the most problematic. Tossed out of Yale after he was caught showering with a young lady in his room, he set off for the oil fields of Texas to find himself. There, the grandson of the greatest oilman of them all labored as a common roustabout, digging ditches, repairing pipelines, mixing mud. He lived on his laborer's wages, slept in a boardinghouse, and learned to drink like a field hand. It was a life of grit and of brawn, and Winthrop's sturdy six-foot-three-inch frame was more than up to the challenge. But after three years of this, he faced the inevitable summons to New York to rejoin the white-collar world. He trained at Chase for a year, then was named vice chairman of the big master charity known as the Greater New York Fund. Winthrop's fund-raising work, however, was overshadowed in the public mind by his nocturnal activities: he became a regular at such hot spots as the Stork Club and El Morocco, swilling martinis as he gazed into the eyes of such eligible Broadway starlets as Mary Martin.

David, meanwhile, lived a life that was positively monastic by comparison. The chubby, studious little boy had grown into a slightly pudgy intellectual young man, graduating cum laude from Harvard and doing postgraduate work at both Harvard and the London School of Economics before earning his Ph.D. in economics at the University of Chicago in 1940. In the course of his studies he had a taste of the political life when he served briefly as an intern in the office of Mayor La Guardia. But it was banking, not politics, that attracted him. A career at the family bank, the Chase, beckoned.

The notion that these five disparate personalities could be welded into a unified force had long been on Nelson's mind. Back in 1934, he had confided to his mother that "my chief desire is that we as a family should ultimately develop into a closely knit, effective group." Of all Junior's sons, he was most caught up in the vision of Rockefeller power: the band of brothers, sallying forth to change the world with their energy, their resourcefulness, their ideas—and, of course, their billions.

"I can honestly say," Nelson told an interviewer in 1938, "that none of us has ever had a feeling of actually being rich—that is, of having a lot of money. What we did find out was that we had inherited a lot of responsibilities towards both the family and the world at large." For all his meanderings from the family fold, none took that sense of mission as seriously as did Nelson.

As brother David remembers, "He felt there were great opportunities for our generation, and that we had a better chance to be successful both as individuals and collectively if we worked together. He took the lead in getting us as a group to have regular meetings, what we called Brothers' Meetings."

It was at the first of these meetings, in late 1939, that Nelson turned his siblings' attention to the philanthropic realm. The brothers, he argued, should coordinate their giving, rather than diffuse their donations' power through individual contributions. At Nelson's instigation, the five agreed that they should form their own fund as the vehicle for their collective philanthropy.

By September 1940 the brothers had signed a "partnership agreement"—with the enthusiastic blessing of their father—and by the end of the year a certificate of incorporation for the new Rockefeller Brothers Fund was filed in Albany.

But no sooner had Nelson accomplished this than the gravest of threats loomed to the brothers' future unity. Looking forward to the day, not too far off, when Rockefeller Center would turn into the black, Junior began musing aloud about the possibility of donating his stock in the complex to the Rockefeller Institute for Medical Research. The idea alarmed Nelson; he already saw Rockefeller Center, not yet a decade old, as an essential element of the Rockefeller heritage, a sort of corporate heirloom that ought to be handed down from one generation to the next.

He told his father that he ought to leave the Center in trust for the family. (According to one account, Nelson even threatened to resign as president if the Rockefeller Institute became the owner.) John 3rd recorded in his diary that "Nelson presented his point of view well but did not change Father's point of view." What Nelson did achieve, however, was a stalemate: his father put the notion of donating the stock on the back burner. The Center's fate, for the time being, would remain unresolved.

At much the same time that this drama was being played out, another institution closely identified with the Rockefellers, an institution to which Nelson and most of his brothers had deep sentimental ties, was under siege, its future hanging in the balance. Once again Nelson was at the center of the struggle.

This battle—the battle to save the Lincoln School—was about educational policy, and about money. But most of all, for Nelson at least, it was about politics.

In the years since Nelson graduated, one authority after another hailed the Lincoln School as an educational experiment that actually worked. Despite the ravages of the Depression, and the school's location at the edge of Harlem, enrollment remained strong; for a core of upper-middle-class parents, Lincoln was still a desirable alternative to the prep school experience for their children. The school's alumni were among its greatest proponents. When

Nelson's son Rodman reached school age, he was unhesitatingly sent off to Lincoln.

Yet for all this, the Lincoln School was an institution under fire as the 1930s drew to a close. The threat did not come from hidebound academic critics, but from the school's own proprietor, Teachers College of Columbia University. Lincoln had never had a truly independent existence of its own; from the start it had been operated by Teachers College, under a $3 million grant from the Rockefeller-sponsored General Education Board. Teachers College's control, however, most of the time seemed more a matter of legal record than anything else. With the GEB and John D. Rockefeller, Jr., as its angels, Lincoln could pretty much steer its own progressive course.

But that began to change in 1937. The GEB decided to remove its restrictions from the Lincoln School endowment, which meant that as of 1939 Teachers College would not have to use the money to finance Lincoln. The school would be totally at the mercy of Teachers College. Lincoln could no longer look to the GEB for support, and it certainly couldn't turn to Junior, who even while his sons were attending the school had come to harbor serious doubts about its educational approach. By the 1930s his coolness toward the institution had long since congealed to frost.

For Teachers College, the Lincoln endowment was a particularly tempting plum. The college had been running substantial deficits for years; by 1938, its cumulative deficit stood at over $600,000. A sizable chunk of this was due to the consistent losses registered at the other school operated by the college, Horace Mann. Having unrestricted access to Lincoln's $3 million would certainly go a long way toward easing the college's financial burden.

The temptation for Teachers College was too great to resist. It soon was evident that what the college had in mind was a merger of Horace Mann and Lincoln, a merger in which the unique experimental character of Lincoln would almost certainly be lost.

Lincoln School parents were quick to mount the barricades; to defend their interests, in the spring of 1939 they elected a five-member committee, including Nelson Rockefeller. Despite his many other concerns that spring—among them the running of Rockefeller Center and his imminent presidency of the Museum of Modern Art—Nelson plunged into the Lincoln controversy. Fresh from his union victories at Rockefeller Center, he was convinced he could broker a solution here as well.

He soon demonstrated that, being Nelson Rockefeller, he could pull strings and marshal resources in ways no other parent could. At his own expense, he commissioned a four-man advisory group, whose members included the Connecticut state education commissioner, to study the situation and come up with proposed solutions. And he swung the formidable apparatus of Room 5600 into action, directing the family's financial experts, headed by Junior's longtime aide Arthur Packard, to look over the college's numbers.

Taking note of the publicity the Lincoln contretemps was generating, Junior and Tom Debevoise determined that even more help was needed. Debevoise approached a young Milbank, Tweed partner, John Lockwood, about serving as Nelson's counsel. The lanky, bespectacled Lockwood possessed an impeccable legal pedigree: a graduate of Harvard Law School, where he edited the law review, he had gone on to clerk for Justice Oliver Wendell Holmes. His family friendship with Debevoise had gained him entrée to Milbank, Tweed. With Lockwood just four years older than Nelson, a certain attorney-client rapport might be expected; at the same time, the young lawyer had Debevoise's implicit trust. Lockwood would recall that "my role was to help Nelson in any way he needed, and to keep him out of trouble if I could."

Lockwood's arrival couldn't have been timelier, because the situation was becoming more and more highly charged. At commencement on June 2, Lincoln's progenitor, Abraham Flexner, entered the fray, with a speech that was nothing less than a battle cry.

"Long may the Lincoln School continue to enjoy the independence which it has enjoyed up to this time," Flexner declared. "Its work is not yet done. Until its work is done, the integrity of its endowment is absolutely sacred."

Despite his insistence that he was on their side, some parents were starting to become suspicious of Nelson's role. Probably the most suspicious of all was PTA president J. B. W. (Jack) Woods, an accountant who was adamantly opposed to any accommodation with Teachers College. Many parents, he warned Nelson, "feel that your goodwill and honesty are being imposed upon in order that plans for a change for the worse may be perfected behind the scenes."

The uneasiness was hardly allayed by the report of Nelson's advisory group in late November. The study recommended the merger of Lincoln and Horace Mann, while suggesting that the schools broaden their mission from what it caustically described as "college preparation for the economically and socially favored." As for the endowment, the report asserted that Teachers College "bears no legal obligation and no moral obligation to continue the Lincoln School."

Many parents regarded the study as a veritable endorsement of the Teachers College position. An infuriated Jack Woods insisted that Nelson, with all his clout, could solve the whole problem by "affirmative action" instead of encouraging "through silence or otherwise" Teachers College's subjugation of the school. Nelson replied that he didn't have that kind of influence.

But in fact Nelson had a lot more power over the situation than he was letting on. Enough power, for instance, to summon Teachers College dean James Russell and provost Michael Del Manzo to his Rockefeller Center office late in 1939 in an effort to cut a deal. Nelson was willing to concede the merger of Lincoln and Horace Mann, as long as the surviving entity was called the Lincoln School and all the income from the endowment was earmarked for its use. In addition, he wanted an independent board of trustees to govern the school.

Russell and Del Manzo, for their part, were sufficiently willing to kowtow to Nelson's wishes that they began submitting drafts to him of Del Manzo's imminent report—due in January—on Lincoln School's future. Perusing one such draft at Pocantico one Sunday afternoon, Nelson found it so unsatisfactory that he ripped it to shreds. Del Manzo obediently started over again. "I don't want to let Mr. Rockefeller down," he later told Lockwood.

The meetings with the Teachers College officials began to resemble treaty negotiations, with Nelson attended by a retinue of educational advisers, attorneys, and public relations counselors. At these sessions, Russell and Del Manzo irritated Nelson by raising, sotto voce, what they considered the *real* problem at both Lincoln and Horace Mann: the schools had too many Jewish students (Jews made up 39 percent of the student body). Lincoln's experimental program, they insisted, was hurt by this lack of diversity; what's more, even the Jewish parents were complaining that the school was becoming too Jewish. (No mention was made of the principal reason why Lincoln attracted so many Jews: the rampant anti-Semitism that prevailed at the other prestigious prep schools.) Nelson, however, quickly squelched all further talk of the "Jewish problem."

By early January, Nelson had worked out a deal close to the one he had earlier proposed. Lincoln and Horace Mann would merge, with the combined entity to bear the Lincoln name. An independent board of overseers would be created—although that board, significantly, would be an advisory rather than a governing body. As for the endowment, Teachers College pledged to devote it to Lincoln—but for its "extra-normal" and "experimental" activities, not the school's day-to-day operations.

The deal violated Nelson's mandate from his fellow parents to preserve Lincoln as a separate, distinct entity. But Nelson felt his agreement was all anyone could expect under the circumstances.

What he had not fully bargained on was the ire of Lincoln parents about his secret diplomacy. Even before the deal became public, Nelson was pilloried by fellow parents for his "defeatist attitude." The fix was in, one man charged, and Nelson was out to "railroad" his agreement through the PTA.

Nelson bristled at these attacks, warning his committee about succumbing to "minority pressure groups." His boyish ebullience evaporated; he displayed the wary, defensive air of a man under siege. On a sheet of notepaper, he scribbled a memo to himself on "Groups to Watch Out For": among them were "Progressive Education Enthusiasts," "Flexner," "Woods & group," and "Jews."

As he girded himself for a further barrage, Nelson concluded that he had had enough of the whole business. Closeting himself with his advisers at the University Club on January 13, he decided to resign immediately from the parent committee. His resignation letter—carefully crafted over breakfast at his apartment the next day with Packard, Lockwood, and a public relations man—was dispatched to Lincoln School parents and teachers. Copies were also hand-delivered to the major New York newspapers and to the national wire services, all of which had been closely following the "merger row," as one paper described it.

Nelson made no attempt to camouflage why he was quitting. "For some time everything the Committee has done and every plan it has made have been criticized," his letter read, "and the opposition to it has become so bitter that its continued usefulness is at least problematical. This criticism and opposition have to a large extent centered on me."

A deluge of letters from parents and teachers followed, urging Nelson to reconsider. Among the Lincoln parents importuning Nelson was Judge Samuel Rosenman, one of President Roosevelt's key advisers and speechwriters. But even Rosenman couldn't get Nelson to budge.

Meanwhile, the parental outrage over his compromise plan meant that it was for all intents and purposes dead on arrival. Teachers College, though, was determined to bring the merger about. In November the trustees approved a new plan that contained a few more concessions, mostly in the direction of Horace Mann (such as naming the new school the Horace Mann–Lincoln School). This hardly placated Lincoln parents, who proceeded to take the whole issue to court. The suit dragged on for two years, to no avail; the courts ruled that Teachers College could do what it pleased.

Abraham Flexner's dire prophecy of 1939—that with the merger "no human ingenuity can prevent the practical extinction of the Lincoln School"—was sadly borne out. Nine years later, citing continued financial difficulties, Teachers College closed the Lincoln School for good.

Did Nelson Rockefeller sell out the Lincoln School? Or did he, as he would always later maintain, wage a valiant but doomed battle to save it?

There is no question that Nelson wanted to preserve the school, believing, as he said in his resignation letter, that it "has been and can continue to be an invaluable instrument in the development of progressive education." And he was convinced that the only way to save Lincoln was to negotiate; Teachers College, in his view, held all the cards. Proceeding from that premise, all that he could do was extract concessions from Teachers College about the school's identity, its endowment, and its governance. And this, as far as Nelson was concerned, he did accomplish.

Nevertheless, in exercising realpolitik from the outset, Nelson was probably conceding far too much. While it cannot be assumed that had Nelson taken a hard line Teachers College's Del Manzo and Russell would have folded, certainly Nelson could have tried—and, given the deference accorded him by college officials ("I don't want to let Mr. Rockefeller down," Del Manzo had said), he might well have turned them around.

Instead, he chose to accommodate *them.* And he did so in ways that bordered on the improper, given his position as the ostensible advocate for the Lincoln parents. Saddled with an unambiguous mandate by the parents to maintain Lincoln as a "separate entity," he completely ignored this directive and accepted the merger as a fait accompli.

He could, of course, justify this conduct on the grounds that it was in the service of a greater good, the preservation of the Lincoln School. But he did not seem to realize that the central concession he made at the outset—his acceptance of the merger—rendered moot all his maneuvering. His stratagems, in fact, actually sealed the Lincoln School's doom. For the first time, but hardly the last, he was so caught up in his machinations that he had lost touch, fatefully, with what was fundamental.

The battle for the Lincoln School would leave a lasting mark on Nelson Rockefeller—although for reasons that are not at all apparent from the facts of the case.

Its impact stemmed from the way Nelson perceived the confrontation, not just at the time he was immersed in it, but as he would look back on it in the years to come. In his mind, the battle would come to be regarded not so much as a struggle to preserve the school, but as an elemental clash between his own forces of moderation and reason and the vanguard of a subversive educational left wing, in the person of Jack Woods.

Here, for instance, is how Nelson described the Lincoln affair to a sympathetic biographer some two decades later:

> The point is that Rockefeller believed it was important to save Lincoln School. He worked out a program for that purpose, but . . . was frustrated at every turn. . . . Rockefeller was sure the main reason was the action of a few Communists and fellow travelers who outtalked him, outwaited him and outmaneuvered him. Rockefeller was convinced that their purpose had nothing to do with education but was to discredit the Dean of Teachers College, an outspoken anti-Communist.

Nelson's recollections were even more black-and-white when he spoke of the Lincoln School affair to another interviewer in 1961: "We had a hundred meetings. The Communists out-witted and out-maneuvered us. Finally they licked us. They closed the school. Teachers College was afraid to oppose them. Later I learned that I had three Communists or fellow travelers on my committee."

Nelson's view of Woods had some basis in fact. Woods was indeed a Communist, according to attorney Arthur Bullowa, who represented Woods and the parents in their court battle (and who, coincidentally, was a Lincoln classmate of Nelson's). "He told me so himself," says Bullowa. "He was sent to Alcatraz during the First World War as a conscientious objector."

But Bullowa dismisses as "nonsense" the idea that the opposition to Teachers College was some sort of Communist plot. "There were a number of parents in the PTA of known liberal views," he says, "and it is very easy to say they were Communists, but the only person I knew who was entitled to that distinction was Jack Woods." And even Woods, he notes, described his Communist affiliation in the past tense.

Although Nelson was careful not to make a public issue of Woods's views, Woods knew that he knew. "It was lurking in the background," remembers his daughter Mary Woods. "My father felt that Nelson Rockefeller was trying to discredit him because he was quite a left-wing fellow."

Still, the question of whether Woods was truly a Communist and whether the Lincoln School opposition was Communist-inspired is almost beside the point. What is important here is that Nelson Rockefeller believed this to be so. Perhaps he did not make much of an issue of it at the time, but as the years passed, his opinions hardened into absolute, adamantine certitude.

He would, in fact, come to describe the Lincoln School battle as a turning point in his life. It inspired him, he would say, to begin a serious study of modern Communism. He delved into *Das Kapital,* and started handing out copies of Marx's tome to his associates. He pondered not just Communist theory, but Communist methods. His earliest lessons in those methods, he firmly believed, came from the president of the Lincoln School PTA. "That experience made a deep impression on me," he said years later. "I learned how the Communists wreck free institutions—what they're trying to do to this country."

For the first time, young Nelson Rockefeller had acquired an ideological compass.

Part Three

To Washington

Twelve

El Príncipe de Gasolina

One evening a week, in a Greenwich Village townhouse, they gathered: a clique of well-tailored, accomplished uptown gentlemen, some young, some middle-aged. They called themselves "The Group." Later, when their purposes became apparent, they would describe themselves, only semi-ironically, as "The Junta."

Their host was Beardsley Ruml, an outsized, cigar-smoking bon vivant who spun out new ideas with each exhalation of his Montecristo. (Among his inspirations would be the concept of the withholding tax; he called it "pay-as-you-go," and it soon became standard governmental practice.) Ruml had worked for a time in the Rockefeller philanthropic enterprises, where he pushed for funding of the emerging social sciences. But his penchant for the high life, among other reasons, had led him to take his fertile mind elsewhere. He was now treasurer of R. H. Macy, the department store company.

His guests had equally impressive pedigrees. Jay Crane, the treasurer of Standard Oil of New Jersey, was a regular. So were Wally Harrison and Rockefeller Center manager Hugh Robertson. Sometimes Robert Hutchins, the dynamic young president of the University of Chicago, would join The Group, as would renowned advertising man William Benton. And a constant presence at Group meetings was the taciturn head of the Chase Bank's foreign department, Joseph Rovensky.

But the central figure at these gatherings since they began in 1938, the lodestar around whom the other members of The Group revolved, was Nelson Rockefeller. Despite The Group's pretensions to serve as a colloquium where the weightiest of world issues could be discussed, what it really did was act as an advisory council for the edification of a single individual—a sort of private, informal Council on Foreign Relations for the benefit of one man. From the interplay of these minds would come intellectual capital that Nelson could harvest and invest as confidently as his grandfather had invested the financial capital of the petroleum industry.

When he was a boy Nelson's mother had counseled him to seek out the advice of his "superiors": the people who knew more than he did about whatever field of endeavor he was pursuing. From his school days onward he had heeded her words, cultivating one sage mentor after another: Ernest Hopkins at Dartmouth, Wally Harrison in architecture, Alfred Barr in art. He also had his father's example. Junior was a master at assembling a brain trust, pulling into his orbit such diverse wise men as Mackenzie King, Abraham Flexner, and Raymond Fosdick.

But the other, less praiseworthy side to this reliance on others was a princely tendency—exhibited by Nelson over and over in his young life—to have surrogates handle his dirty work. He let his friend Ted Martin bear the burden of a traffic ticket in his stead; at Rockefeller Center, it was Hugh Robertson, not Nelson, who handled the unpleasant task of calling Diego Rivera down from his scaffold. Then there was the time a deranged individual showed up in the lobby of Nelson's old apartment building on 67th Street, demanding to speak to the Rockefeller heir. Nelson dispatched his neighbor Simon Flexner, the elderly director of the Rockefeller Institute, to chase the man away.

At the meetings of The Group, however, such tendencies never came to the fore. The atmosphere was collegial; the talk, high-minded. Far from the placid confines of the townhouse drawing room, the world in 1938 had begun descending into what Churchill called "the dark gulf." Each day brought new intimations of the conflagration to come. Long into the night, The Group argued about the crisis, and what the United States should do about it. Yet the perspective from which they viewed it was not that of the trembling war zones in Western Europe and Asia. Rather, their focus was southward, on Latin America.

The reason they took this point of view was simple: while other regions of the world were points of curiosity for Nelson Rockefeller, Latin America was an object of passion.

It was art that had first led him south of the border, in 1933. His fascination with such modern Mexican painters as Rivera and Orozco drew him to Mexico, where he spent a month exploring the country's wealth of pre-Columbian artwork. Awed by the experience, Nelson attempted upon his return to interest the Metropolitan Museum in co-sponsoring, with New York's Museum of Natural History, a series of South American archaeological digs. The idea went nowhere: the Metropolitan hierarchy hadn't the slightest interest in pre-Columbian art. Far from discouraging him, the rejection only intensified his commitment to the artwork and the culture that produced it.

Two years later, faced with the decision of how to invest the windfall that had come his way from the 1934 trust, Nelson chose to put part of it into the stock of Creole Petroleum, the Venezuelan subsidiary of Standard Oil of New Jersey. It was a shrewd investment: the prolific oil fields of Lake Maracaibo had turned Venezuela into the world's second-biggest oil producer (after the United States), and the greatest part of that production was controlled by Creole. But from the outset Nelson regarded his stake as more than just a lucrative annuity. He arranged his election to the Creole board of directors and enrolled himself in a Berlitz course in Spanish. He dreamed of making a grand tour of Creole properties—and of the vast continent that lay beyond.

His struggles at Rockefeller Center, however, led him to hold that dream in abeyance. But in the spring of 1937, with his grip on the Center at last secure, he could finally indulge his fantasy. The trip would be no modest fact-finding junket; rather, it would be a monumental odyssey on the order of his round-the-world honeymoon. Only this time he would be accompanied by an entourage: Tod, her cousin Eleanor Clark (to keep Tod company), brother Winthrop, Jay Crane from Standard, and Chase's Rovensky. The group would travel, via chartered aircraft, from Venezuela to Brazil, then on to Argentina and across the Andes to Chile and Peru, on up the west coast to the Panama Canal. In all, the journey would take almost two months.

At every stop, they were treated with the pomp and deference accorded the most exalted of visiting dignitaries. Provincial governors and oil company officials greeted them at the airport, and the group was regularly granted the finest hospitality the country had to offer.

The VIP treatment gave Nelson and his party a somewhat rarefied—and detached—view of their surroundings. "We met people in government and people in the oil business," Eleanor Clark French notes, "but we were never shown anything poor."

It was only when he was out in the countryside that Nelson could truly drink in the exoticism of this strange new world around him. In Venezuela his party cruised along the Orinoco River in a ninety-foot oil company steamer, and Nelson thrilled to the sights and sounds of the tropical jungle through which they passed: the dense overhanging growth of the swamps, the cackling monkeys and flame-colored birds, the alligators undulating along the riverbanks, and the Indians—veritable *National Geographic* pages come to life. "They live in little palm leaf huts," he wrote of the natives, "wear practically no clothes and paddle around in hollowed out logs."

And always alongside his official agenda was his private art agenda. The young collector swooped down on the local markets, acquiring a cornucopia of native handicrafts of all varieties—the good, the bad, and the ugly. In the ancient Inca city of Cuzco, in the Peruvian mountains, Nelson walked away with vast armloads of woolen blankets and serapes. In another town, one of his companions was offered a hideous travel bag festooned with alligator claws. "I won't buy it," the man told the vendor, "but I'll bet you sell it before the day is over." A few hours later, he wasn't the least surprised when a beaming Nelson tramped into the hotel lobby with the grotesque bag flung over his shoulder.

In Peru, Nelson became entranced by archaeologist Julio César Tello's recent discovery of more than one hundred mummy bundles, dating back to before 800 A.D., in the tombs at Paracas. When Tello informed him that the Peruvian government was refusing to finance the preservation of the bundles, Nelson brought the matter to the country's President, offering to pay for the preservation work himself if the government would provide a permanent home for the collection. The President agreed, and the bundles were saved.

Nelson embraced his Latin experience with an ardor startling even to those who were well accustomed to his enthusiasms. Something about that world—its people, its culture, its physical grandeur—touched a resonant chord in him. Quite possibly, as some of his intimates were later to observe, he saw the Latin temperament—with its unabashed effusions of emotion, its hearty shoulder claps and fervent bear hugs (*abrazos,* they called them)—as a reflection, in primary colors, of his own. "Nelson loved the Latin Americans," Wallace Harrison would comment. "They made him feel human: the warm, human gestures, the touching. Nelson wanted to express himself in this way, a way which could not easily be done with North Americans."

Yet at the same time he was hardly blind to the bleaker aspects of the region. He did not have to look any further than Creole's own Venezuelan outposts to see the yawning gap between the native population and the *yanquis* who were exploiting their resources. The Creole camps were self-contained compounds, shielded by barbed-wire fences, utterly isolated from their surroundings. The company furnished its own power and imported its own food. Its managers treated the natives with a supercilious disdain reminiscent of the worst of the British Raj. Few of them even bothered to learn Spanish. Meanwhile, outside those compounds squatter towns had sprung up, towns bereft of schools and sewers and even fresh water. Those towns were a glaring, everyday reminder of the hard facts of Venezuelan life: that some 70 percent of the country was illiterate, 60 percent lived in houses of straw and sticks with dirt floors, and only 32 percent of the population was employed.

Somehow, despite his cosseted lifestyle and his omnipresent Standard Oil chaperones, these brutal facts crept into Nelson Rockefeller's consciousness. As exhilarated as he was by his South American experience, the memory of the barbed wire, and of the squalor that lay just beyond it, was ineffaceable.

When word reached Nelson of his grandfather's death, he cut his trip short and scrambled to book sleeper berths on a flight back to New York. But what he had seen in Venezuela still preyed on his mind. Not long after his return, he asked if he could address the annual conference of Standard of New Jersey's top managers.

Some three hundred Standard executives, gathered from all over the globe, sat in stunned silence as this fresh-faced Rockefeller heir lectured them on their social responsibilities. "The only justification for ownership," he told them, "is that it serves the broad interest of the people. We must recognize the social responsibilities of corporations and the corporation must use its ownership of assets to reflect the best interests of the people. If we don't, they will take away our ownership."

Coming from almost anyone else, such a warning might have been waved away. But coming from a Rockefeller, it could not be ignored. Among those who took it most seriously were two top Creole officials, Arthur Proudfit and Henry Linam. Linam, for one, was that rarest of birds, an oil company manager who spoke Spanish, who lived in the native section of Caracas rather than the North American colony, and who sent his children to Venezuelan schools. All this made him uncommonly receptive to Nelson's words.

Within a year, the warning took on the character of a prophecy, when Venezuela doubled its oil royalty and served notice on the oil companies, in the words of one commentator, that "the old days were over." With the specter of expropriation hovering over the company, Linam and Proudfit (who would soon become Creole president) set in motion changes that would, in time, transform Creole's image in Venezuela. For starters, a dozen Berlitz instructors were dispatched to Venezuela to teach Creole executives—*all* of them—Spanish. Accepting responsibility for the squatter towns, Creole provided them with medical assistance, and began working with the state government to get the towns water, sewers, schools, and the other rudiments of modern society. Advanced job training and education in Creole-run schools was offered to the illiterate native oil workers and their families: by the late 1940s the workers' illiteracy rate was slashed from 82 percent to 12 percent. A little more than a decade after Nelson first roused the company to action, Creole was regarded as a paragon of corporate citizenship.

Nelson returned to Venezuela in March 1939. If his first trip had the air of a royal visit, this one seemed more like a full-blown political campaign. Gladhanding his way across the oil fields, Nelson chatted with the drillers, in his rapidly improving Spanish, about their work; so casual was he that he was sometimes mistaken for a new field superintendent getting to know his crew. He blithely paid calls on local newspaper editors who were lambasting the activities of the man they labeled *El Príncipe de Gasolina*. "I'm Nelson Rockefeller and I'd like to meet your editor," he chirped as he bounded into the city room.

Most Venezuelans were charmed by the insouciant millionaire. But not everyone was. One of the biggest skeptics was Rómulo Betancourt, a newspaperman-cum-political activist who decried Nelson's "specious, hypocritical" comments about improving the lot of the Venezuelan people. "After looking over his vast oil properties," Betancourt tartly mused, "he will return to his office atop Rockefeller Center, to the warm shelter of his home, to resume his responsibilities as a philanthropist and Art Maecenas. Behind him will remain Venezuela producing 180 million barrels of oil for the Rockefellers. . . . Behind him will remain Venezuela with its half million children without schools, its workers without adequate diets."

Despite such tirades, Nelson was fast gaining a reputation as a uniquely simpatico figure in the fractious world of inter-American relations. When the oil companies later that same year were faced with Mexican government expropriation of their wells, they sought Nelson's help in heading off the threat. Nelson did not waste time going through channels; instead he arranged to meet one-on-one with Mexico's President, Lázaro Cárdenas, at the presidential hideaway in Jiquilpan de Juárez.

Nelson took pains to disavow any personal connection with the oil companies; he was merely speaking, he told the President, as a "layman." His presentation, however, was hardly that of a layperson; he laid out for Cárdenas a detailed, thirteen-point program to resolve the dispute. Nelson's formula fell far short of the outright expropriation Cárdenas was demanding. It made the Mexican government little more than a minority partner of the foreign oil companies. Cárdenas rejected the proposal outright.

The President made it plain that the issue was not about economics but about national pride. Expropriation, he told Nelson, would restore the nation's self-respect. "We must retain ownership even if the oil has to stay in the ground," insisted Cárdenas. "Better that than for the people to lose their dignity." He refused to budge, even when Nelson raised the specter of "very serious" repercussions, including intervention by the U.S. government. Finally, having exhausted all his arguments, Nelson gave up.

His encounter with Cárdenas underscored for the young man a pivotal concept: that in Latin America "dignity" was a quality not just of individuals but of nations. No outsider could hope to get anywhere in the region without paying homage to this essential attribute. How well Nelson understood this would be amply demonstrated in the years ahead.

Nelson, meanwhile, was eager to be more than merely the oil companies' goodwill ambassador to Latin America. It was time, he resolved, to play a more intensive and more direct role there.

The initial inspiration had come from his talks with another Latin American President, Eleázar López Contreras of Venezuela, during the visit earlier in 1939. López Contreras lamented the absence of a first-class hotel in Caracas; the best the capital had to offer was the Majestic, a tumbledown Victorian heap where guests customarily had to turn their shoes over in the morning to shake out the scorpions. The President had tried to interest foreign investors in building a new hotel, but those he approached were only interested if a gambling casino could be attached. Turning Caracas into Monte Carlo south was not what López Contreras had in mind.

Nelson was intrigued. It was not that great a leap from building Rockefeller Center to building hotels. Such a project would help Caracas, would help the oil companies (which for want of adequate hotel space were accommodating their visitors in an elaborate system of guest houses), and would help diversify the oil-dependent Venezuelan economy. It would, as he wrote Creole's Linam, "contribute to the general good will and understanding which you have so ably developed to date."

Within months Nelson had set the wheels in motion. A holding company, Compañía de Fomento Venezolano (Company for Venezuelan Development), was formed to own the stock in the new hotel. To man this Venezuelan beachhead, he dispatched a team of aides to Caracas, including his Dartmouth classmate Robert Bottome and Edward "Hutch" Robbins, a Dartmouth graduate who, more importantly, was a cousin of Franklin Roosevelt (Robbins' grandmother was Roosevelt's aunt Cassie, the fun-loving sister of FDR's mother, Sara). Another Dartmouth alumnus, Carl Spaeth—who had been the quintessential Big Man on Campus during Nelson's time there—was lured from his teaching post at Yale Law School to join the Caracas group. And the ever-ready Wallace Harrison got the architectural commission.

Although he knew that he and his family would have to provide the core of the financing, Nelson was determined to bring in other investors. He approached all the big oil companies doing business in Venezuela, and all agreed to stakes in the hotel (the largest investment, of course, came from Standard of New Jersey and its Venezuelan affiliates, Creole and Lago Petroleum). He also tried to line up local investors; despite these efforts, only 16 percent of the shares would be owned by Venezuelan nationals.

The biggest individual investors, inevitably, were Nelson and his loyal brother Laurance. Nelson ended up funneling $300,000 into the Fomento holding company, and Laurance $100,000. After chatting with his older brothers, David also wanted to join the venture, and asked his father's advisers to channel $100,000 from his trust to Fomento. Horrified, the wise men endeavored to talk him out of it, but the best they could do was to get him to cut the investment to $50,000.

From the outset, there were abundant warnings that the shareholders shouldn't expect much in the way of a return. One of Laurance's advisers suggested to him that the hotel "would be profitable only as an advertisement for this Venezuelan city which now lacks a hotel worthy of the name. . . . If it is looked upon as a scheme for profit, however, I venture to say that there will be not a few headaches."

As it was, there were headaches enough. "Opportunism characterizes the programs of all politicians," Spaeth told Nelson, "but I have the feeling that it can be found in larger quantities here than in most countries." One of the foremost opportunists was López Contreras himself, who obligingly made it known to Nelson's emissary that "if we were having any difficulty in finding property, he was most anxious to make his own available to us for purchase." The offer was politely rebuffed, because an attractive site—owned, as it turned out, by a provincial governor—had already been located. It was an old hilltop hacienda in the Los Cabos district on the outskirts of the city, and it commanded stunning views of Caracas and the surrounding mountains.

For this site, Harrison designed a structure that reconciled structural integrity and tropical languor. Within the earthquake-proof walls, open-air corridors let cooling breezes flow through the rooms' louvered doors. Each bedroom would have a private balcony, with terra-cotta overhangs offering protection from the seasonal torrential downpours. On the building's stucco exterior—painted in the national colors of red, yellow, and blue—grilles were installed on which tropical flowers could grow. And, to accommodate the late-afternoon people-watching proclivities of the local matrons, a covered walkway with a seating area was incorporated into the hotel entrance.

The Hotel Avila, as it would be known, was destined to be the talk of Caracas. Yet even before the first foundations were dug, Nelson was dreaming of more. He envisioned Fomento as a broad-based development enterprise, diversifying into everything from water drilling to asphalt mining to low-cost housing. Fomento, he enthused to a friend, could be "of real assistance in connection with the general development of the country, which is short on management and venture capital but long in natural resources."

Nelson found himself the subject of a Venezuelan guessing game as speculation mounted about his next move. One rumor circulating in the highest government circles was that he would build a huge charity hospital staffed with the country's best physicians.

Adding urgency to the rumors was the war situation and its potentially chilling effect on the Venezuelan economy. "Almost every day," Spaeth wrote Nelson from Caracas in June 1940, "newspaper editorials refer to the distressed condition of the coffee and cocoa industries, the difficulties with oil exports, the dependence upon importation of foods." And as one European nation after another fell victim to the Nazi onslaught in those bleak opening months of 1940, the specter of German influence in the Western Hemisphere began to loom. "Already German commercial houses dominate important parts of Venezuelan business," Spaeth advised. Although Venezuelan businessmen "are emotionally sympathetic with the cause of the democracies, they feel that their economic interests can be put into a separate compartment."

It was imperative, Spaeth suggested, for both the American government and American business to move swiftly to head off those German inroads. And Fomento could be an important weapon in that fight.

"You have no idea how timely your letter of June 10th was," Nelson wrote in reply. "It was almost as though you had some psychic power and had anticipated events that were to take place up here." Those very themes—the war's impact on Latin America and the threat of Nazi influence—had long been debated by The Group in Beardsley Ruml's townhouse. Now, in late spring 1940, the denouement of the discussions was at hand. And what was involved were possibilities much, much more momentous than Fomento.

Thirteen

The Way In

It was back at Christmastime 1938, in the course of a congratulatory note from Beardsley Ruml to his old friend Harry Hopkins, the newly appointed Secretary of Commerce, that Ruml dropped the following hint:

> If you are to be in New York soon, I think it would be well worth while for you to spend about two hours at leisure with Nelson Rockefeller to hear his views on U.S. commercial relations with South America, a subject on which he is well informed and very much interested. N.R. would esteem it a privilege and I should be delighted to arrange.

As Ruml well knew, Hopkins was more than just another cabinet member; he was Franklin Delano Roosevelt's prized troubleshooter and confidant, someone whose access to the President could be gauged by the fact that he now lived in the White House itself, his bedroom just across the hall from the President's own. For what Nelson Rockefeller was after was more than just a colloquy on inter-American relations; he sought an entrée, for himself and for his ideas, to the Oval Office. Ruml's intercession with Harry Hopkins was but one step in a long, persistent, and quiet campaign to get it.

And Latin America was the key. It was an area about which Rockefeller was knowledgeable and for which he had a special passion. With the administration's attentions focused on the crisis in Europe, it was also an area suffering from profound neglect. The Group's deliberations could produce a program that would fill that policy vacuum. The issue, in short, was there for the plucking, and no one was in a better position to do so than Nelson Rockefeller.

That he was ready to do so then, and in the anxious months ahead, there could be little doubt. As absorbing as the presidency of Rockefeller Center was, the job's true challenges—the planning, construction, and rental of the last elements of the complex—would soon be history. And no matter how much authority Nelson had, there was no escaping the reality that the ultimate control remained firmly in the grip of his father. The Museum of Modern Art offered Nelson another venue in which he could exercise his executive skills, in the service of the art he so dearly loved. But as glamorous and enthralling as the work there was, it was, at best, a sideline. His South American business ventures—the Hotel Avila, the Creole directorship, the prospects of further investments through Fomento—would utterly engage his attention, but they all had a certain transitory quality about them. For Nelson Rockefeller, business had always been, and would always be, a stopover en route to his grander destination.

Nelson's campaign to make his mark in Washington had begun in earnest some seven months before Ruml's letter, in the spring of 1938. That was when Anna Rosenberg entered his life. She had been an unofficial member of Roosevelt's brain trust since his days as governor of New York, and she enjoyed an enviable access to the chief executive; it was probably better, in fact, than that of most of Roosevelt's cabinet. Now, in the wake of her intervention in the Rockefeller Center labor dispute, she was Nelson Rockefeller's paid adviser. And the most prized aspect of her advice was her ability to pick up the phone and get through to FDR.

Which is what she did in the summer of 1938. Nelson, she told the President, was someone he ought to get to know. He was, she assured Roosevelt, "sympathetic. He feels quite differently from some of the other members of his family." (This was an allusion to the family's traditional down-the-line support of the Republican Party, including financial backing of FDR's 1936 opponent, Alfred Landon. Nelson had never, at least in public, given anyone any reason to believe he did not share his family's political views. In fact, he contributed $33,000 to Landon's campaign, the most of any of the brothers.) If the President met the young man, she assured FDR, they didn't have to talk about anything special—just "business and things in general." The main thing, said Rosenberg, was to have Nelson fall under the spell of the formidable Roosevelt charm.

Roosevelt, for his part, was agreeable to such a seduction, and suggested that Rosenberg bring Nelson up to his home in Hyde Park sometime. For one reason or another that meeting never took place, but the irrepressible Rosenberg doggedly stayed on the case. In March 1939 she phoned the White House again, telling one of FDR's aides that "the President wanted to see Nelson Rockefeller sometime." She had been looking, she said, for a legitimate excuse to bring Nelson to Washington, and now she had one: the gala opening, in two months' time, of the Museum of Modern Art's new building.

It was Rosenberg, it turned out, who came up with the idea of inviting FDR to speak at the event, via a nationwide radio hookup. The invitation, she concluded, offered a perfect pretext for a Roosevelt-Rockefeller encounter.

Four days later, Nelson Rockefeller was ushered into the Oval Office for the first time. There is no record of what he discussed with the President, but Roosevelt readily accepted the speaking invitation. In and of itself this was a considerable coup for Nelson and the museum, leaving aside what it might betoken for the young man's future relationship with the President. Nelson's expressions of gratitude, both before and after the event, were profuse. "We have had so many enthusiastic letters and comments about your speech," he wrote the President afterward, "that I could not resist the temptation of writing you a note to again express our appreciation."

But Nelson did not leave it at that. Yet another reason to contact the President was found a few weeks later, when a House subcommittee began investigating the Works Progress Administration's federal arts projects. Nelson dispatched to the subcommittee chairman a long, impassioned defense of the WPA program, and mailed a copy of his letter to Roosevelt. The President responded with an amiable "Dear Nelson" note, which expressed his frustration with Congress's benighted view of federal support of artists. "Unfortunately, there are too many people who think that this type of white collar worker ought to be put to digging ditches like anybody else," FDR lamented. "We need all the help we can get to educate the Congress and the nation!"

Interchanges about art, however, could only carry Nelson so far. He wanted to get beyond the petty pretexts and bring the weightier issues he was grappling with—the Latin American issues—to the President's attention. Ruml's approach to Harry Hopkins a few months earlier was a start; Hopkins, in response, had expressed a general interest in meeting Nelson, although he seemed far more interested in getting together with Ruml again on the latter's next trip to Washington.

Nelson soon sought out the help of other well-wired intermediaries, the most notable of which was Thomas G. Corcoran. "Tommy the Cork," as he was known in the White House, or "White House Tommy," as he was known outside it, was already the stuff of Washington legend: a fast-talking attorney and political operator par excellence whose influence pervaded every level of the administration. In the words of one commentator, "Smart people who want to get action at headquarters ignore the regular secretariat, overlook the Cabinet and cultivate the acquaintance of White House Tommy. He can get things done."

At around the same time Ruml was contacting Hopkins, Nelson was journeying to Washington to confer with Corcoran. They met at the Hay-Adams Hotel, across Lafayette Square from the White House. Nelson laid out for Corcoran his ideas about Latin America and the plan he wanted to present to the President—a plan in which government and business would work in concert to promote inter-American relations. Just what Corcoran might have offered to do for Nelson is not clear, but the two stayed in touch. "I am looking forward to the opportunity of discussing the plan with Harry Hopkins when he has a spare moment," Nelson wrote Corcoran in early March 1939. "In the meantime, I have had very reassuring indications here in New York of a willingness and desire to cooperate if the plan goes through."

But for the duration of 1939, and on into the spring of 1940, the summons to meet Harry Hopkins did not come.

The world, meanwhile, shuddered at the force of the Nazi onslaught in the first spring thaw of 1940. One by one the nations of Western Europe fell: first Denmark, then Norway, then the Netherlands and Belgium. By the end of May the British had evacuated Dunkirk and on June 14 the German Army entered Paris. The new British Prime Minister, Winston Churchill, pleaded with Roosevelt for military aid. Faced with a strong core of isolationist sentiment in Congress, the President responded cautiously. But with only the will of the British people standing in the way of a total Nazi stranglehold on Europe, Roosevelt knew that America's own security was now at stake. "If we go down," Churchill had warned him, "you may have a United States of Europe under Nazi command far more numerous, far stronger, far better armed than the new [world]." And then, the President's military planners were suggesting, Hitler's next strikes would be against South America and the Caribbean—possibly as soon as that autumn.

Pockets of pro-Nazi sentiment could already be found throughout the hemisphere. The most blatant support was in Argentina, where Army and nationalist factions were openly pro-Hitler. But the Argentinians were hardly alone. In late May the Uruguayan government foiled an attempted Nazi coup. Meanwhile, in Chile and Brazil, influential German minorities, and an admiring military caste, rallied to the Axis cause. Brazilian President Getulio Vargas, himself a dictator, scorned the "sterile demagogy of political democracy" as he explored closer ties with the Nazi regime, including an arms deal with the mighty Krupp manufacturing empire.

Suddenly, Latin America moved to the forefront of American strategic thinking. "We must concentrate on the South American situation," said U.S. Army chief of staff George Marshall, after a May 22 meeting with the President. Secret talks were initiated with the Latin American military, and a congressional resolution approved the sale of coastal guns and ships to Latin governments.

An economic war worried Roosevelt and his advisers as much as a military one. At an April 18 news conference he spoke of potential Nazi inroads into South American commerce and speculated about a "Germania Corporation" that would subjugate the United States' neighbors as surely as the Wehrmacht subjugated Western Europe. Of more immediate concern was the fragility of South American economies; with their traditional European export markets cut off by the hostilities, many of those economies were hanging by a thread. If there ever was a time for the United States to live up to the President's Good Neighbor policy—a policy that heretofore had been more public relations than substance—this was it.

All at once, there was a premium on fresh ideas about inter-American relations. Now, in June 1940, Harry Hopkins was at last eager to hear what Nelson Rockefeller had to say.

He asked Rockefeller and Ruml to put their thoughts in a memo. Getting together with The Group, they hammered out a four-page draft and then requested a meeting with Hopkins to personally present it to him. Hopkins told them to come right down.

On the afternoon of Friday, June 14 the carefully turned-out young millionaire and his garrulous cigar-chomping associate presented themselves at the White House gate. They were ushered into the residential part of the executive mansion and shown directly into Harry Hopkins' bedroom. It was where the chronically ill Hopkins—he had had two-thirds of his stomach removed in a cancer operation two years earlier—conducted much of his business those days.

Hopkins greeted his guests and then, sinking into a chair, asked Rockefeller to read his memo out loud. Point by point, Rockefeller laid out his program: The United States should undertake emergency measures to buy up surplus Latin American commodities. Tariffs should be reduced or even eliminated. Business and government should cooperate on a plan to encourage hemisphere investment. External debts should be refinanced, possibly by converting them into domestic currency obligations. The U.S. diplomatic presence in the region should be substantially increased. A "vigorous program" of cultural, educational, and scientific exchange should be initiated.

To coordinate all this, Rockefeller proposed that the President appoint two committees—an interdepartmental panel and a small advisory committee of private individuals. And those committees, he said, "should be served by a proper executive. In view of the importance of the work to be done, it is suggested that this executive be appointed to one of the vacancies among the president's administrative assistants."

Rockefeller then pulled out of his briefcase his June 10 letter from Carl Spaeth in Caracas. The letter, he said, "illustrates very well the possibilities of the situation," and he thought Hopkins might like to look it over. Besides its advocacy of a more sweeping role for Fomento—"now is the time for American capital to push ahead in Venezuela," Spaeth said—the letter called for a broad program of American grants-in-aid to help develop South American infrastructure.

Hopkins skirted over the issue of financial aid and zeroed in instead on Fomento itself. Perhaps, he mused, it might be possible to set up companies of that sort throughout Latin America—companies that would closely cooperate with the U.S. government to protect American trade. Fomento would be an ideal model. Might it be possible, he wondered, for Rockefeller to set up a Fomento in every country south of the border within the next three months?

Rockefeller told Hopkins how very flattered he was by the suggestion—and then deftly sidestepped the question. He most definitely had not come to the White House to talk about Fomento.

They returned to his memo. Hopkins was enthusiastic. It couldn't have come at a better time, he told Rockefeller and Ruml. Four different departments—State, Treasury, Agriculture, and Commerce—were each working on their own hemisphere programs, and he feared that the friction between them would scuttle any chance for a coordinated scheme. He liked the memo's comprehensive approach to the problem. It was high time, he said, that the administration pulled the whole thing together. Rockefeller's memo was exactly the tool he needed to do that.

Hopkins would be spending the next day with the President on the Navy yacht *Potomac,* he said, and he would show FDR the memo. What he would suggest to Roosevelt, intimated Hopkins, was a conference of the four cabinet officers involved, at which the President would instruct them to prepare a comprehensive program along the lines the memo suggested. The meeting could take place as early as Monday.

In the meantime, Hopkins added, perhaps Rockefeller could prepare a list of suggested names for his private sector advisory committee.

Two hours after their meeting began, Rockefeller and Ruml emerged from Hopkins' bedroom, heady with the exhilaration of the moment. The session had gone better, much better, than they had dared imagine. Hopkins had seized on their proposals and would be presenting them to the President—not next month, not next week, but the very next day. Their memo might well provide the framework for a new U.S. approach to Latin America. And somewhere in that new order there might well be a role for Nelson Rockefeller.

They returned to New York to await the outcome of what they had set in motion.

The next day, aboard the *Potomac,* Hopkins showed Roosevelt the memo. As Hopkins had foreseen, it was just the spur the President had been looking for. Roosevelt dictated a letter to the secretaries of State, Agriculture, Treasury, and Commerce, telling them he wanted the "combined judgment" of those departments about a Latin program in "specific form"—and he wanted it on his desk by the following Thursday. "I am enclosing," said FDR, "a copy of one of the many memoranda I have received relating to this subject." The memorandum was Rockefeller's.

On Monday, June 17, the four cabinet members—Cordell Hull of State, Henry Wallace of Agriculture, Henry Morgenthau of Treasury, and Hopkins—gathered in Hull's office. Also present was Hull's number two, Undersecretary Sumner Welles. Hull began the meeting by reading aloud the memorandum. "I don't know who prepared it," he snapped afterward, "but whoever did apparently is not familiar with the things we are already doing." Wallace asked Hopkins who drafted the memo; "Nelson Rockefeller," Hopkins replied. (Pride of authorship notwithstanding, Rockefeller was distressed when he heard later that Hopkins had mentioned his name. He feared that the other cabinet officers' well-known resentment of Hopkins' high-handedness would rub off on him.)

For all their grousing, the secretaries had no choice but to comply with the President's request. Three days later, they forwarded their joint program to the White House. The program's centerpiece was the creation of an Inter-American Trading Corporation which would purchase and distribute the hemisphere's surplus commodities. This was precisely what Rockefeller had suggested in his memo: that surpluses "should be pooled and disposed of by single management." The next day, the President formally proposed the inter-American cartel.

As satisfying as this development was, it fell far short of the sweeping hemispheric program Rockefeller had called for. What, for instance, had happened to his idea of an advisory committee? Once again, Rockefeller turned to Rosenberg. Moving swiftly, she phoned the White House and arranged a meeting with FDR himself. She brought with her to the meeting a list of suggested appointees to Rockefeller's advisory committee.

Roosevelt heard Rosenberg out and told her he was thoroughly enthusiastic about the advisory committee idea. What's more, he had every intention of naming Rockefeller to the committee. First, though, he had to resolve a slight problem: Sumner Welles, it seemed, was still upset about the way Rockefeller had "butted into the situation" through Hopkins. Roosevelt would be talking to Welles and he hoped to iron out some of the ill will.

Rosenberg's report of her conversation with the President left Rockefeller discouraged. "It is simply tragic," he complained to Spaeth, "that at a time like this there can be such friction and indecision between the various departments in Washington. Every day that is lost seems to me to weaken the possibility of our taking effective action."

Finally, at the end of June, Roosevelt made it known he was naming a special assistant to grapple with the government's entire Latin American program. This assistant was a wealthy New Yorker with impeccable ties to the business world, a man of energy and ideas who was eager to bring his talents to Washington.

His name was James Forrestal.

A wily, self-made dynamo, Forrestal had risen to the pinnacle of Wall Street as president of Dillon, Read & Co. But as he moved into his late forties he began experiencing a midlife restlessness; utterly driven by his work, he craved new challenges. When Roosevelt sought to reinvigorate his administration with fresh blood from the hitherto despised business community, Forrestal was a ready recruit to the ranks of presidential assistants.

Arriving at the White House in June 1940, Forrestal found himself lacking any clearly defined job. Then suddenly, in late June, the President handed him the Latin American portfolio. Roosevelt told newsmen that Forrestal would "act as my legs and ears on the coordination of this particular program—just for me." One more element of Rockefeller's proposals—the designation of a presidential assistant who would oversee the inter-American effort—had come to pass. But Rockefeller himself had been left in the cold.

Forrestal easily managed to contain his excitement about his new assignment; Latin America was a subject he knew and cared little about. What fascinated him were issues of military strategy and intelligence and preparedness, and it was to those areas that he shifted the focus of his job. He reviewed British intelligence intercepts of communications between Latin Americans and German and Italian agents and took the measure of Axis infiltration of the Southern Hemisphere. And he launched an all-out effort to construct airstrips throughout South America, enlisting Pan American Airways as a U.S. government front.

Still, Forrestal recognized that there were other, less cloak-and-daggerish matters he had to attend to, and in early July he phoned Nelson Rockefeller: would Rockefeller be willing to come down to Washington for a chat? What about? Rockefeller asked. Well, said Forrestal, he wanted to talk to him about producing movies in Latin America. Forrestal had been talking to Hollywood producer David Selznick about a film on Simón Bolívar, and Selznick thought he should confer with Rockefeller about it.

Since co-producing a Simón Bolívar movie was not exactly the role Rockefeller envisioned himself playing, he asked Forrestal, ever so politely, if this might be part of some larger scheme for dealing with hemisphere relations. "I don't know," replied Forrestal. "I'm just trying to gather all the ideas I can and this is one of the possibilities." Rockefeller then casually mentioned that he had been involved in a group that had put together a report for Harry Hopkins; had Forrestal seen it? No, he hadn't, the presidential aide answered, but he guessed he could get a copy from Mr. Hopkins.

The conversation left Rockefeller profoundly disillusioned with, as he put it, the "confusion and lack of leadership" in Washington. Forrestal, the official in charge of Latin American policy, had not even seen his memo—the very memo that had accelerated the government's thinking about Latin America.

Retracing his talk with Forrestal, Rockefeller was at a loss to figure the man out. "Frankly," he confided to Spaeth, "my reaction was that he did not have a grasp of the tremendous significance and importance of the whole relationship and that he was rather confused and was grasping at straws."

But Forrestal, in reality, had a far shrewder command of the situation than Rockefeller perceived. He had brought with him to Washington his most trusted aide at Dillon, Read, Paul Nitze, and—unbeknownst to Rockefeller—Nitze was in the process of studying the government's whole Latin American policy-making apparatus. As Nitze recalls, "I went around town and talked to everybody about what the nature of the problem was. And I finally came to the conclusion that there weren't many people in the State Department who had a sense for action. They were more interested in talking and listening and reporting, rather than being operators. They weren't interested in taking a problem and defining it, and deciding who should do what with it, and getting it done." Nitze knew, and Forrestal knew, that what the President wanted now was action: someone who could get the job done, someone who was an operator.

Forrestal and Nitze also realized that that operator would not be James Forrestal. Forrestal had no desire to get involved in inter-American economic affairs; at best, he saw himself as a White House overseer, whose involvement in those issues would be transitory. (Indeed, Forrestal may already have had an inkling that a new, more tempting assignment awaited him: appointment as Undersecretary of the Navy.)

And so, while Forrestal was making vague, rambling chitchat with Nelson Rockefeller, Paul Nitze was already laboring to create a new mechanism for dealing with the Latin American problem. Working with another young Roosevelt adviser, James Rowe, Nitze drew up the outline of a new position: Coordinator of Inter-American Affairs. This coordinator would choreograph the government's Latin American initiatives, working with—but outside of—the existing departments and agencies. Ironically, at the same time Nitze had come up with this plan, an interdepartmental committee of experts, created by the cabinet in response to the President's call for a Latin program, had come up with much the same scheme. Under this plan, however, the coordinator would be a creature not of the White House but of the departments: he would report to a permanent cabinet committee on inter-American affairs. The distinction was a crucial one.

The creation of a coordinator, separate from the State Department, was bound to appeal to the President. Roosevelt had always been disposed toward setting up new agencies to tackle the nation's problems. As Walter Lippmann observed, "When anything went wrong, Roosevelt wouldn't change the man, he'd set up another office." And, in the case of the State Department, he had even fewer inhibitions than usual about doing so. Dealing with State, he is said to have once cracked, "is like watching an elephant become pregnant.

Everything's done on a very high level, there's a lot of commotion, and it takes twenty-two months for anything to happen." He found himself constantly prodding Hull, to no avail, on issues ranging from relief aid for the war-ravaged Chinese to Mussolini's dealings with Japan. Often he bypassed the secretary entirely, prompting Hull to complain, in his lisping Tennessee twang, about "that man across the street who never tells me anything."

FDR, then, couldn't have been more pleased when Forrestal broached the coordinator concept to him. The only real issue for Roosevelt was who would get the job. Forrestal had pulled together a list of twenty names. Nelson Rockefeller's name, however, was not at the top. Instead, Forrestal's first choice was William Clayton, the president of the cotton brokerage firm of Anderson-Clayton. Clayton had extensive experience in international trade, and his company had been doing business for years in South America. Forrestal knew him well, and thought he would be an ideal choice.

FDR, however, thought otherwise. Clayton, he informed Forrestal, had been a member of the Liberty League, an anti-New Deal business group. What's more, he had heard that Clayton had contributed $25,000 to Roosevelt's Republican opponent in 1940, Wendell Willkie. (Clayton would later insist that FDR was only half right; while he did indeed belong to the Liberty League, he never contributed to the Republican campaign.) "We can't have him," he told Forrestal with dismissive firmness.

Next on the list was Ferdinand Eberstadt, a brilliant, iconoclastic investment banker who, like Forrestal, was eager for government service. But FDR knew all about Eberstadt; he considered the banker too prickly and too controversial for the job. (Eberstadt was later brought into the government, as deputy director of the War Production Board, where he turned out to be every bit as controversial as FDR had foreseen.)

The third name down was Nelson Rockefeller. "Well," Roosevelt said after a moment's thought, "Nelson would be fine." True, he was a Republican, but he was different from Clayton; he had, the President asserted, given $25,000 to the *Roosevelt* campaign.*

(Roosevelt was apparently unaware that Nelson, along with brothers John and Laurance, had offered financial support to the Willkie campaign a little more than a month earlier. The three had drawn checks totaling $2,400 to pay for the publication and distribution of the candidate's speeches. But fortuitously, it turned out, for Nelson, the Willkie forces—worried about the Rockefeller contribution's effect on their grass-roots public image—sent the checks back. Had the contribution gone through and come to FDR's attention, it is entirely possible that Nelson would never have gotten the coordinator's job.)

* No independent corroboration, in either Roosevelt's papers or Rockefeller's, can be found for this dramatic assertion.

Roosevelt's designation of Rockefeller did not entirely please Forrestal. He admired Rockefeller's energy and drive and what he was accomplishing with Fomento. But he felt that Rockefeller was too young and inexperienced for the position, and urged the President to reconsider. FDR, though, was adamant; Rockefeller was his man. In that case, Forrestal said, they should at least bring Clayton in as Rockefeller's deputy, to add some wisdom and expertise to the operation. This suggestion was one that Roosevelt found agreeable. Smiling, he said, "Well, I guess Will will be all right for the deputy job, because *Mrs.* Clayton contributed ten thousand dollars to my campaign."

Thus it was, on the basis of campaign dollars as much as on ability, that the position of Coordinator of Inter-American Affairs was settled.

Forrestal phoned Rockefeller immediately and asked if he could come down to Washington for dinner. Rockefeller agreed, and on the evening of July 9 strode into the exclusive F Street Club, where he was greeted by both Forrestal and Nitze. Over the course of an intense five hours they laid the situation out for him. There was still no overarching administration Latin American program, and Forrestal didn't want to wait for the departments to agree on one. Immediate action was needed on such commercial issues as control of Latin American local airlines, which Forrestal feared would soon be dominated by German and Italian interests. A propaganda offensive also had to be launched to counter a relentless Axis media blitz in the Southern Hemisphere. There was no money available as yet for these programs, but Forrestal was confident the President would provide it. What was most important now was to have someone in place to organize those initiatives, and the President thought that Rockefeller was just the man to do it.

Forrestal, however, stopped short of actually offering Rockefeller a full-time position. Instead, he suggested that Rockefeller come down to Washington and "try it out" for a couple of weeks. He could sit in on interdepartmental meetings and get some of the programs off the ground. As to what would happen after that, he was vague.

Understandably, Rockefeller was confused. Not quite getting Forrestal's drift, he still harped on the need for an overall game plan and pitched once again for a presidential advisory commission to formulate it. There was no time for that, Forrestal shot back. "We must have action," he tersely told Rockefeller.

Declining to commit himself, Rockefeller asked for a few days to think it over. As he left the F Street Club late that evening, he felt his excitement about the looming opportunity shadowed by a certain trepidation about exactly what he was getting into. His misgivings about Forrestal and about the chaotic state of White House decision making continued to gnaw at him. "It certainly is disillusioning," he wrote Spaeth after the dinner, "to see the weakness and incompetence of the engine that gives the driving power to this tremendous machine."

Why had Forrestal not offered him, outright, the coordinator's job? The reason is rooted in the quirky, often mysterious workings of that White House "engine." Forrestal, according to Nitze, was still working on building a cabinet-level consensus for the new position. "His view," says Nitze, "was that it would be a disaster if he were to just get the President to sign the order. Everybody in Washington would be mad at him, and he couldn't get it organized and done." So Forrestal was meeting with Hull and Welles at State, and Morgenthau at Treasury, and Wallace at Agriculture, lining up support—even as he and Roosevelt were already discussing who would hold the post.

What was going on was a vintage Roosevelt performance: an attempt to defuse a potentially confrontational situation through finesse and through stealth. "I am a juggler," FDR once confided, "and I never let my right hand know what my left hand is doing." The maneuvering behind the Latin American job was just one more Roosevelt juggling act.

Rockefeller himself was aware of none of this; all he knew was that Forrestal seemed, in his words, "rather confused." He asked the family office to check Forrestal out with their Wall Street contacts; the aides reported back with a complimentary referral from, ironically, Ferdinand Eberstadt. They also checked with the leading light at the law firm of Sullivan & Cromwell, one John Foster Dulles, who told them that Forrestal "knew little about international relations, and nothing about South America."

By July 15, Rockefeller had tossed aside his misgivings and decided to accept the position—whatever the position was. He asked Forrestal to arrange a meeting with the President the following week; if, after talking with Roosevelt, and then with Hopkins and Welles, he was satisfied there were "no crossed wires," he would go to work the very next day.

But first Rockefeller had one more matter to attend to.

On Wednesday, July 24, a cheerful young man named George Franklin stepped off a United Airlines sleeper in Salt Lake City, Utah, and proceeded into town. He checked into Room 520 of the Utah Hotel and then dashed off to his one and only appointment in Salt Lake City: a meeting with the newly nominated Republican candidate for President, Wendell Willkie.

This "George Franklin" was actually Nelson Rockefeller, traveling solo and incognito, assuming the identity of one of his aides in Room 5600. He kept up the ruse throughout his trip: in his contacts with the hotel, with the airline, even in his thank-you note later to Willkie's secretary. It was all for Willkie's benefit, Rockefeller would later explain: "I went up the back way so I wouldn't embarrass him." But perhaps, given the prickly political climate back in Washington, Rockefeller was resorting to camouflage to protect himself as well—because he was in Salt Lake City to advise Willkie (who was in the middle of a western campaign swing) of the offer he had had from Roosevelt. It was a gesture of political civility, but it also had a practical purpose: Rockefeller wanted to be sure that Willkie was as firm a backer of a hemispheric program as Roosevelt was. "It would be very unfortunate," Rockefeller wrote an associate, "should the present administration adopt some program which would be changed by the succeeding administration should they come into power by the first of next year."

Rockefeller, in other words, sought some assurance of security—for his program and, quite probably, for himself—if Willkie took over.

Sitting down with the bluff, hoarse-voiced Indianan, Rockefeller described his uncertainty about the job offer. Willkie cut him off. "If I were President in a time of international crisis," he rumbled, "and if I asked someone to come to Washington to help me in foreign affairs and if that man turned me down—well, I don't need to tell you what I would think of him. Of course, you should go!"

Willkie offered Rockefeller all the assurance he needed. Hurriedly departing for the airport (he was in such a rush that he left his Burberry overcoat behind in his hotel room), "George Franklin" scrambled to board the next United flight back East. He was to meet that very Friday, July 26, with the President.

Before his Oval Office encounter, he talked again with Forrestal. It was good that he did, because the game plan had again changed. Forrestal had just submitted to the President a memo proposing the creation of a Commission for Pan American Affairs. This commission would consist of both government and private-sector representatives, and FDR had suggested that Rockefeller be named its chairman. Whatever gratification Rockefeller derived from seeing his commission idea finally adopted must have been tempered by the realization that this was one more strange White House change of course—and a thoroughly illogical one in view of Forrestal's dismissive comments about the commission just two and a half weeks earlier.

In any event, Rockefeller played along when he finally entered the President's office. FDR was appropriately enthusiastic about the commission's prospects, and Rockefeller was appropriately thankful for the opportunity. He asked the President if either his family's Republican loyalties or their connections to Latin American oil companies gave him pause. Roosevelt merely shrugged. "I'm not worried," he said.

It was probably not until he reported for his first day of work that Monday that Rockefeller learned the truth about the Pan American Commission: that it was but one more devious White House maneuver. Far from being sidetracked, the plans for the coordinator's office were very much alive; Forrestal and Nitze were still working on the outline of the coordinator's responsibilities. The commission, it was now apparent, was simply a convenient expedient for bringing Rockefeller into the picture until Forrestal could get all the powers that be to sign off on the new position.

Rockefeller's first task, in fact, was to help write his own job description. Drawing on Forrestal's talks with the President—FDR, Forrestal said, wanted more emphasis on the cultural and propaganda side—and helped by the legal mind of Carl Spaeth, who had flown up from Caracas to assist, Rockefeller fine-tuned Forrestal's outline. By week's end, Forrestal was sending a draft of the blueprint to Hopkins, and Rockefeller was anxiously awaiting word on its fate. "As yet the situation has not clarified itself as far as we are concerned," he wrote his aide Hutch Robbins in Caracas, "and we are not sure it will be possible for us to do a really constructive job. However, should things break the way we hope we will probably stay there [in Washington] for some time."

The charter that Forrestal sent to Hopkins gave the coordinator a sweeping mandate: to devise a program for the United States' commercial and cultural relations with Latin America and to chair the interdepartmental committee on Latin American affairs. Technically, the coordinator's office was part of the Council of National Defense, a vague, all-purpose entity that Roosevelt used as a vehicle for his preparedness measures. But the memorandum made it clear that the coordinator would have "direct responsibility to the President." Rockefeller would not be a cabinet subordinate.

Some two weeks later, on August 14, Forrestal submitted the final plan to the President. That act marked the end of Forrestal's involvement in the Latin American business; he had just been named Undersecretary of the Navy, and would move over to the Navy Department a week later. From that point on, Nelson Rockefeller was on his own.

The next day, August 15, FDR's appointments secretary, Edwin "Pa" Watson, slipped the President a note: "Forrestal asked me to inquire if the President could see Nelson Rockefeller for a minute before he left." Roosevelt said all right, he would see Rockefeller tomorrow, "for two minutes if we can run him in."

Rockefeller had his two minutes. His appointment as Coordinator of Inter-American Affairs was now official.

"I got the job the way I get all my jobs," Rockefeller would insist years later. "I thought up something that had to be done and somebody said, 'O.K., it's your idea. Now let's see you make it work.' "

"Most of the things I've done in life," he would reflect on another occasion, "have been because I've written a memo to someone suggesting someone ought to do something."

But as Rockefeller knew full well, there was a lot more to it than that.

When the appointment was announced, FDR phoned Anna Rosenberg. "Now, Anna," he said, "don't forget. If this fellow gets into trouble, he's your boy. You get him out of it."

Fourteen

GO-GETTER

From now on I imagine that you will have some confidential papers. Probably it will be better if you do not leave them about. I am sure I really don't need to tell you this.

—Abby Aldrich Rockefeller to her son Nelson, August 21, 1940

Washington, D.C., in the summer of 1940 was a city on the brink of what might be termed the greatest peacetime invasion in the history of the United States. With preparedness the new national watchword, and with Roosevelt bent on creating a "government within a government" (in the words of his budget director) to run the machinery of defense, the capital became a vast magnet for thousands of would-be civil servants, aspiring advisers and hopeful contractors. Some 50,000 new arrivals would settle in the city in the next twelve months, vying for already scarce housing, jostling one another for the attention of surly waitresses at the capital's lunch counters. Lamented the *Washington Times-Herald,* "The once sleepy southern city of charm and grace on the Potomac has burgeoned into the frenzied capital of the world. . . . Lobbyists, propagandists, experts of every species, wealthy industrialists, social climbers, inventors, ladies of uneasy virtue and pickpockets infest the city." And at the vanguard of this influx were a thousand "dollar-a-year men": private-sector executives on loan to the government to manage the transition to a war economy (in compensation for which they received the token dollar). Among this army of public-spirited Washington newcomers was Nelson Rockefeller.

Yet from the first day he reported for work in the immense rococo State Department Building, just across from the White House's West Wing, there was much to indicate that Rockefeller was more than just another dollar-a-year man. He was given the ornate suite of offices that were once occupied by Secretary of War Newton D. Baker when the War Department shared the building with State. And although his initial budget was a modest $3.5 million, he swiftly augmented it with other resources: the resources of a Rockefeller.

To begin with, he obtained an unusual letter of credit from his father. This letter instructed the family bank, the Chase, that Junior would personally guarantee loans the bank might give to persons doing business with the coordinator's office. The total amount Junior was willing to guarantee at any one time was relatively paltry ($150,000), and, in the end, the credit facility was never used. Nonetheless, it set a startling precedent: for the first time, a private individual was, in effect, personally bonding a government agency. The letter was vivid proof of how ready Nelson Rockefeller was to deploy his family's advantages in the service of his new position.

Those advantages, of course, were more than monetary. There was the far-flung network of connections, lacing its way through the cream of America's business, academic, cultural, and media establishment. Now that he was ensconced in Washington, Rockefeller immediately capitalized on this network, drawing from it a caliber of intellect and of influence that instantly gave his new agency a unique cachet.

In the course of his first months, he persuaded Joseph Rovensky to leave his position as head of the Chase Bank's foreign department and take over the coordinator's trade and finance section, and wooed James W. Young, a former top executive at the J. Walter Thompson advertising agency, to run his communications division. To oversee his motion picture division, and in effect serve as the coordinator's emissary to Hollywood, Rockefeller turned to his fellow young multimillionaire John Hay Whitney. They had come to know one another on the board of the Museum of Modern Art, where Whitney oversaw the development of the vaunted film library. Whitney had already gained a reputation as one of the film industry's most discerning and successful financiers. He had put up the money to develop the Technicolor process, and was still basking in the glory, and the profits, of his most successful venture to date: the bankrolling of *Gone With the Wind*. Hollywood had learned to take Jock Whitney seriously, and his entreaties on behalf of Rockefeller and South America would not be ignored.

Rockefeller also saw fit to add one more layer of influence. He appointed what he called his "advisory committee on policy." It consisted of his two well-connected confidants, Anna Rosenberg (his unofficial ambassador to FDR) and Beardsley Ruml (his envoy to Harry Hopkins), along with two titans of the media: Time Inc. chairman Henry Luce and legendary adman William Benton, now vice president of the Rockefeller-financed University of Chicago. The role of this committee was vague—there was some talk about "short-term and long-term planning"—and it seemed mainly designed to bring these power brokers officially into the coordinator's fold.

In the months to come, other prominent names, including CBS chairman William S. Paley and Rockefeller's fellow Dartmouth aesthete Walter Chrysler, Jr., would associate themselves with the coordinator's office (or, to use the typically Rooseveltian acronym, the CIAA). But Rockefeller knew full well that he would need more than big names; what he also had to assemble was a loyal cadre of aides: individuals whose sole mission would be to serve him and his office.

For this, Rockefeller energetically mined his past business associations. From Fomento in Venezuela came his initial core of aides: Carl Spaeth, Hutch Robbins, and John Clark, a former *Washington Post* editorial writer. Spaeth was named executive assistant, and soon afterward, when Will Clayton decided to forsake his number two position for a top job at the Reconstruction Finance Corporation, Spaeth became assistant coordinator. (All three men, not at all coincidentally, were from Dartmouth.)

It was almost inevitable, given how closely their careers thus far had been intertwined, that Wally Harrison would also join Rockefeller in Washington. The move was not immediate; Harrison still had a thriving architectural business to attend to. But within a year Harrison would leave his partnership and resettle in the capital to take over the coordinator's cultural relations unit.

Turning to another recent chapter in his life, Rockefeller brought in as his counsel John Lockwood, the young attorney who had steadfastly slogged through the Lincoln School quagmire. His cool, pragmatic handling of the Lincoln furor had impressed Rockefeller—and so, perhaps, had his knowledge of Spanish, gained during a three-month stint helping the Chase set up a Buenos Aires office. "Lockwood was very sharp," Spaeth later observed, "usually on the bearish side of things, which Nelson's enthusiastic nature needed."

But, in retrospect, the most noteworthy recruit of those early months was the man hired to run the public relations division: Francis A. Jamieson. A high school dropout from Trenton, New Jersey, Jamieson had made an early mark as an enterprising young reporter for the Associated Press; his coverage of the Lindbergh baby kidnapping won him the Pulitzer Prize in 1933. His Lindbergh scoops were facilitated by his astute cultivation of the high and mighty. When he learned that the state police were about to make an important announcement about the baby, Jamieson simply phoned New Jersey governor A. Henry Moore and persuaded him to find out from the state police chief what the announcement was going to be. When his fellow reporters gathered for the press conference, Jamieson's newsbreak—that the baby's body had been found—was already moving on the ticker.

Not very long after these heroics, Jamieson left the journalistic profession and, like many other burnt-out newsmen, switched to a less stressful career in public relations. Through his p.r. work for a fund-raising organization, he came to know Winthrop Rockefeller, who in turn introduced him to brother Nelson. Although Jamieson spurned Nelson's earlier bid to lure him to Creole

Petroleum, the Washington job was something else again. Not only did the political content of the position captivate him, but so did the possibility that the job would help persuade his girlfriend Linda Eder to marry him. (Eder's family had a farm in Colombia.) Jamieson accepted, and so did Eder; within days of their marriage they were on their way to the capital.

Surveying the lineup of luminaries Rockefeller had assembled, Jamieson told his bride, "I quake at the thought of some of the important names involved with this." But his wife already knew better; sardonic and unflappable, Jamieson was hardly the sort to quake at anyone or anything. From the very outset, his air with Rockefeller was appropriately deferential, but blunt. "If you're looking for a guy who's going to get in at nine in the morning, it's not me," he told his prospective boss at the job interview. (Jamieson preferred to saunter in at ten or ten-thirty.) Jamieson had his own style, and Rockefeller could either take it or leave it. He took it.

But it was this very style—that of a glib, chain-smoking newshound out of a Hecht-MacArthur script—that Rockefeller would soon come to prize. Rarely exposed to the street-smart, Rockefeller valued the commodity when he encountered it—as witness his instant affinity for the gritty immigrant wisdom of Anna Rosenberg. And, in Jamieson's case, as in Rosenberg's, this hard-edged quality was coupled with sound political judgment. Surrounded for the most part by a coterie of governmental novices like himself, Rockefeller needed someone who could navigate deftly through the New Deal labyrinth. Frank Jamieson—whose judgment, like his prematurely gray hair, belied his thirty-six years—was precisely that person.

Even by the hyperkinetic standards of a Washington girding for war, the Rockefeller office raised eyebrows. The brashness, the effervescence, the high-octane energy level of the newcomers both dazzled and distressed the hoary old State Department retainers who padded past the coordinator's suite. Observed *Cosmopolitan,* "Washington is shocked daily by the irrepressible activity of Rockefeller's coordination squad—but it is an electric shock."

On virtually every front covered by Rockefeller's far-reaching mandate—finance, exports, education, communications, and cultural relations—the fledgling agency was mobilizing for action. It rushed to survey Latin reserves of such strategic commodities as rubber, tin, and industrial diamonds. It secured U.S. Export-Import Bank financing of a new Brazilian steel mill. It dispatched aviation expert William Harding to study the South American air transport situation. It began laying out plans for inter-American art exhibits and an educational exchange program. It developed a program for production and distribution of 16-millimeter documentary films throughout Latin America.

Rockefeller never missed an opportunity to talk up his office's mission.

Within days of taking on his new position, he was already grandly proclaiming to the interdepartmental committee on inter-American affairs that his appointment signaled "a reorientation of the whole Latin American problem from the viewpoint of national defense." Eschewing the novice bureaucrat's customary low profile, he preached hemisphere unity to groups ranging from the *New York Herald Tribune* forum to the National Farm Institute in Des Moines, Iowa. He also began circulating to FDR and other top officials a "Weekly Progress Report" on Latin American relations—with the coordinator's efforts prominently featured.

It was hard to say what unhinged the State Department brahmins the most: Rockefeller's copious energy, his avid self-promotion—or the hearty "Hi, fella" with which he greeted visitors to his office.

Rockefeller's spirited informality extended to his domestic arrangements. He had rented an expansive Colonial house on tony Foxhall Road, just west of Georgetown. But with Tod choosing not to uproot the children so soon before the school year, Rockefeller found himself presiding over an empty domain. The prospect rattled him; as Jamieson's wife Linda notes, "Nelson had to be with somebody. He just couldn't be alone." So he invited Carl Spaeth, his wife Sheila and children, and Paul Nitze, his wife Phyllis and *their* children, to move in with him. (Now that his mentor Forrestal had moved to the Navy Department, Nitze had gone to work for Rockefeller.) Given the Washington housing situation, they all gratefully accepted.

As other staffers joined the coordinator's office, they, too, were invited to hole up on Foxhall Road until they could find suitable accommodations. At one point, Rockefeller hosted as many as fifteen house guests. This suited him perfectly, satisfying as it did two of his most elemental needs: the need for company and the need for nonstop work. With so many of his aides as housemates, there was no reason to end the day at six or seven: they could talk about Peruvian long-staple cotton imports at the Foxhall Road dinner table.

Back in New York, Junior and Abby fretted that their son was perhaps driving himself too hard. "While you have a magnificent constitution and an iron will," Junior wrote him, "neither can withstand indefinitely the strain you are putting on them."

Disarmed by Rockefeller's collegiate ebullience, Washington insiders made the same mistake so many others—at Rockefeller Center, at the Museum of Modern Art, in the Rockefeller family office—had made before them. They did not perceive the calculation and the political sensibility that were obscured by his outsized personality. Yet that aspect of Nelson Rockefeller—the shrewd, designing side—was there from the first, running like an undercurrent in a stream.

At the same time that he was glad-handing his way through the capital, Rockefeller was also discreetly establishing his own private back channels of information. Within three months of his arrival he was in contact with the controversial, well-wired columnist Drew Pearson. Pearson regularly infuriated FDR—at one point Roosevelt called him a "son of a bitch" and tried to withdraw his White House press pass—but such opprobrium did not in the least faze Rockefeller. Impressed no doubt by Pearson's impeccable sources, the young coordinator sought out the columnist's counsel—and Pearson, no doubt sensing a potential new source, was more than happy to oblige.

In late November, he prepared for Rockefeller a confidential memorandum on American diplomats in South America. The memo went down the list of principal envoys, country by country, with Pearson offering pithy comments about each man. (Ambassador to Mexico Josephus Daniels was "too kindly to be effective and rather difficult to work with"; John Muccio, first secretary in Peru, was a "hard drinker and all that goes with it"; Claude Bowers, ambassador to Chile, "doesn't work any too hard at the job but is one of the best of the political appointees.")

It was the sort of inside information to which Washington newcomers rarely had access. The possession of such a memo showed just how far from "collegiate" Rockefeller really was.

His cultivation of Drew Pearson, however, was a mere footnote compared to his early alliance with a far more highly placed source: J. Edgar Hoover.

The director of the Federal Bureau of Investigation was already one of the most storied figures in American public life. His pursuit of such fabled criminals as John Dillinger, Ma Barker, and Machine Gun Kelly had become part of Depression era mythology, with radio shows, comic books, even toys and bubble-gum cards celebrating the exploits of his fearless "G-men." As the nation moved to a war footing, Hoover's FBI did the same, shifting its focus from gangsters to suspected saboteurs and Nazi spies.

Eager to expand his empire even further, Hoover sought to broaden the bureau's counterintelligence charter to the whole of the Western Hemisphere. FBI operations were supposedly restricted to U.S. territory, but Roosevelt—appreciative of the "many interesting and valuable reports" Hoover was sending him on his political enemies—assented to Hoover's maneuver and issued a presidential directive expanding the FBI's turf. Soon hundreds of FBI agents, detailed to the new Special Intelligence Service, would be covertly planted throughout Latin America.

By the time Rockefeller came on the scene, two months after FDR's directive, the FBI's involvement was a fait accompli. It was up to Rockefeller to accommodate himself to this state of affairs—which he did, with uncommon avidity.

Just a week after his appointment as coordinator, he showed up in the office of Percy Foxworth, the man in charge of the FBI's South American operation, to propose an alliance between his new agency and the FBI. As Foxworth recounted afterward to Hoover, "Rockefeller felt that he would want to furnish us with all information coming to him (and he thought there would be considerable). . . . He then said that he would like to stay in touch with us, for the purpose of receiving the benefit of any information we received that might be of assistance to him, principally upon the question of foreign propaganda."

Rockefeller then brought up several specific projects which he thought would be of particular interest to the FBI. One was Hopkins' notion of setting up Fomento-like development companies in each of the Latin American countries. Another was an arrangement he had made with pollster George Gallup to establish an Institute of Public Opinion in South America, to survey local attitudes about the United States and other foreign powers. Both, Foxworth observed, would provide "an ideal cover for any of our men," and Rockefeller indicated he would be happy to cooperate. As Foxworth reported to Hoover, "Rockefeller said that he would be very glad to help us in placing our men with either the Institute of Public Opinion or with the developing company if we so desired." The coordinator even suggested that the FBI agents might want to write Gallup's questions.

Impressed by Rockefeller's enthusiasm, Foxworth suggested to his chief that the young man "can be of considerable value to us in the work we are undertaking." Hoover instantly agreed. On the bottom of Foxworth's memo, the director scrawled, "I want to work very closely with him."

The ideas he outlined to the FBI were among dozens fluttering across Rockefeller's desk. But at the top of the list of challenges, defining his early success or failure, was the search for some way out of the desperate economic morass in which much of Latin America now found itself.

The European war had effectively eliminated three-fifths of the region's foreign trade. Roosevelt himself estimated that the hostilities had cut those countries' exports by as much as 40 percent. Brazil was awash in coffee it could no longer export; Chile saw its markets for copper cut off by the British boycott of the continent; Argentina's warehouses were bursting with unsold wheat and meat.

The idea of an inter-American cartel to snap up these surpluses—an idea propounded by Rockefeller in his memo to Hopkins and later endorsed by the President—had already fallen victim to bureaucratic infighting. From what Rockefeller could see, the only possible alternative was for the United States itself to step into the breach. On September 26 he met with Roosevelt, bearing with him the draft of a letter for the President's signature. (Rockefeller had already mastered this essential technique for getting things done in official Washington.) The letter, addressed to the cabinet, instructed: "When buying in foreign markets for defense needs, it is my earnest desire that priority of consideration be given to Latin American products."

The President issued the letter the next day.

With this directive as the spur, U.S. defense agencies began to absorb South American materials into their stockpiles. Such strategic products as rubber, tin, industrial diamonds, and, of course, Chilean copper were bought up. And, for all his inexperience, Rockefeller displayed noteworthy tenacity in enforcing the presidential edict. When a congressional bloc opposed a proposal to allow the Navy to buy Argentine corned beef, he raced to Capitol Hill to argue his case.

In prodding the administration on Latin trade issues, Rockefeller found himself helped by an unlikely ally: Jesse Jones, the crusty, archconservative, sixty-six-year-old Texas millionaire who held down not one but two key administration positions. He had headed the Reconstruction Finance Corporation since the dawn of the New Deal. Then, in a political peace offering to the Democratic right for the purposes of the 1940 presidential campaign, Roosevelt named him Secretary of Commerce, to replace the ailing Hopkins. (The appointment prompted Ohio senator Robert Taft to observe, "I do not think with the exception of the President of the United States any man in the United States ever enjoyed so much power.") Both agencies were vital links in the trade picture; the RFC, in particular, had billions of dollars at its command to stockpile critical commodities.

Jones was perfectly comfortable commanding vast resources: he was Houston's most powerful business figure, having amassed a huge fortune in lumber, real estate, construction, and banking by the age of thirty-five. He was a newspaper magnate as well, thanks to his purchase of the *Houston Chronicle* in 1926. Despite his conservative politics, Jones was the very embodiment of the big-government philosophy of the New Deal. The contradiction never seemed to give him a moment's pause; in his own mind, he remained a fiscal conservative.

Rockefeller first met Jones at a Washington poker party. Exercising his by now well-honed talent for ingratiating himself with powerful mentors, Rockefeller would show up at Jones's immense knotty-pine-paneled office every Thursday afternoon to eagerly gather up whatever pearls of wisdom Jones was prepared to dispense. And the self-made Jones, flattered by such adulation from a young Rockefeller, was delighted to offer them. "Call me Uncle Jesse," he would say.

One piece of advice, in particular, registered with Rockefeller. "Don't ever take your problems to the President unless you have an answer that he can approve or reject," Jones told him. "He doesn't like people who leave problems on his desk."

Rockefeller had already heeded those words when he first approached

FDR about Latin American exports—with a draft of a presidential order already in hand. Now, as he sought even more help from the Oval Office, he would show how deftly he could follow Uncle Jesse's lead.

First, there was the tricky issue of Latin American shipping. With the U.S. Navy requisitioning more and more vessels that would normally be used for hemisphere trade, South America was threatened with virtual commercial isolation. In a letter to Forrestal, Rockefeller raised the prospect of "widespread suffering and possibly violent social disorder in some South American countries." But Forrestal's boss, Navy Secretary Frank Knox, was unmoved by Rockefeller's dire scenarios. The Navy's program, he said, would go on.

Two months later, with Knox still immovable, Rockefeller took the issue to "the Boss," as he now breezily called Roosevelt. Invoking the specter of tons of freight piling up on docks throughout North and South America, Rockefeller offered to FDR an FDR-style solution: formation of a committee to organize and direct all available shipping for the hemisphere. The President instantly approved the idea, and Rockefeller rushed to form the committee.

Meanwhile, one more element of Latin America's commercial bind had come to the fore: the dwindling availability of U.S. manufactured goods. Now that their European suppliers had been cut off, the United States was the Latin countries' only possible source for agricultural equipment and industrial machinery. But the U.S. defense buildup had absorbed virtually all such exports. The consequences south of the border were already disastrous: into Rockefeller's office filtered reports of Brazilian and Argentinian factory closings, with similar shutdowns also expected in Chile.

The decisive agency for untying this knot was the Office of Production Management, which set defense priorities. But the OPM's ineffectualness was already the stuff of Washington lore, starting with the fact that it was presided over by two supposedly coequal directors, General Motors executive William Knudsen and union boss Sidney Hillman. (Asked at a press conference, "Why don't you have a single responsible head?" Roosevelt replied, "I have a single, responsible head. His name is Knudsen and Hillman.") Unable to make any headway with the OPM, Rockefeller went once again to the top.

This time, what he wanted from FDR was his signature on a letter to Knudsen, directing the OPM to give Latin American needs some priority. Once more, Roosevelt agreed.

Soon afterward, yet another committee was formed: the Committee on Essential Requirements of the Other American Republics. Rockefeller was a member, and so was the State Department's Dean Acheson. But they were soon at loggerheads over the cumbersome procedures State wanted to impose. And American manufacturers, with all the domestic machinery orders they could handle, had little desire to go through the rigamarole of selling to Latin America. Nevertheless, Rockefeller's persistence did free up some of the equipment South American factories and farms so desperately needed.

Rockefeller's success with the White House in those first few months could be attributed to several factors. One was Roosevelt's own vested interest in his accomplishments; having created the coordinator's office to break through the bureaucratic logjam, FDR couldn't very well oppose Rockefeller's efforts to do just that. Another was the young coordinator's adherence to Jesse Jones's dictum: never present a problem without a solution attached.

There was also the fact that his experience in his father's service had made Rockefeller a consummate courtier. He knew instinctively, for instance, what others around the White House learned only through hard-won experience: that the chief's ideas, no matter how harebrained they sometimes were, had to be taken seriously. When the President suggested one day that what Latin America really needed was a chain of five-and-ten-cent stores à la Woolworth's, Rockefeller responded with an earnest two-page memo on such stores' prospects in the region.

Already a past master at the art of ingratiation—having honed his skills to a fine edge with Junior—Rockefeller was tireless in his devout flattery of the President. Despite his family's financial support of Wendell Willkie, Rockefeller quickly dispatched a congratulatory letter upon Roosevelt's November victory: "Your reelection yesterday constitutes the greatest vote of confidence ever given any American." After a Roosevelt radio address, Rockefeller hastened to wire the President: "Deeply moved by your powerful realistic message which has given new hope and courage to the world." And when the coordinator's cultural division decided to hand out some $80,000 in scholarships (with federal funds) to deserving Latin American students, Rockefeller asked the President if it would be all right to call them the Roosevelt Scholarships. FDR replied that he had no objection to the honor.

But what probably helped the coordinator's cause with FDR the most was his constant harping on a theme that was bound to get the President's ear: the theme of hemisphere defense against the potential Axis enemy.

Testifying before the House Appropriations Committee in January 1941, Rockefeller spelled out the threat: "Without economic stability and political independence, without a sense of security, the nations of the hemisphere will not be able to withstand the flood of insidious Axis propaganda that has swept over the entire hemisphere. This intellectual imperialism of ideas is at the moment just as serious a threat to the security and defense of our hemisphere as the possibility of a military invasion."

Thus, with a single stroke, Rockefeller had endowed his own work with an essential imprimatur: that of the strategically imperative.

At times, he would hint even more darkly at the forces menacing the hemisphere. Speaking to the National Police Academy, he warned of the Axis powers' "insidious penetration" of Latin America. "If, working from within," he said, "they could get control of a single country, the mechanism for hemisphere defense will be disrupted."

Rockefeller's warning about the enemy within was not just a rhetorical flourish. It was, in fact, a justification for yet another role he had found for his office: exorcist of this "insidious penetration."

Harry Hopkins had been the first to propose this role, just days after Rockefeller had settled into the coordinator's job. Convinced that Nazi influence was permeating much of Latin America, Hopkins suggested that Rockefeller survey the region to determine just how far, and how deeply, the German inroads ran. What particularly worried Hopkins was the possibility that Germans or German sympathizers were acting as Latin American agents for American corporations.

With this charge in hand from Hopkins, Rockefeller rapidly organized a fact-finding mission. Officially, it consisted of three men, including his trusted aide John Lockwood. Unofficially, there was one more member, whose covert participation was Rockefeller's idea: the FBI's Percy Foxworth.

The mission hopscotched through eighteen countries in three months. Part of the time, Lockwood remembers, they were tailed by a German and a Japanese. "It was very funny," he says. "At every stop, we'd go off someplace to talk, and they'd step behind a barn or something to talk." The group returned just before Christmas, and when Rockefeller saw their report he set up a meeting with Assistant Secretary of State Adolf A. Berle.

A charter member of FDR's New Deal brain trust, the diminutive, ferretlike Berle was coaxed to join State by Roosevelt in 1938. He was the department's overseer of the intelligence field—as well as a glib, energetic idea man whose overbearing manner infuriated much of official Washington. "Irascible, prickly, obnoxious, arrogant, abusive, snobbish, and elitist" were just a few of the adjectives attached to his name; "it rhymes with surly," sniped *Time.* But those who penetrated the thorny cover were rewarded with glints of a rare intellect.

Eager to make allies at State, particularly one who still enjoyed considerable access to FDR, Rockefeller diligently and deferentially sought out Berle's advice and companionship. Nevertheless, the early impression he made on Berle was hardly a favorable one: after a long dinner in September 1940, Berle concluded the young coordinator was someone with "boundless strategy and good will and only the slimmest notion of what it is all about except in the limited field of commerce—which does not take anyone very far." But before long the sheer fecundity of Rockefeller's agency, not to mention the young man's ingratiating manner, had won Berle over.

Rockefeller wanted to go public with the report on Axis infiltration in

Latin America (even though it was still preliminary), and Berle gave him a green light. The press was summoned to the coordinator's suite in the State Building; headlines the next day (often accompanied by Rockefeller's picture) trumpeted the news. "U.S. Firms' Agents Called Axis Aides," declared *The New York Times.*

The findings of Rockefeller's mission were an utter embarrassment for U.S. businesses: that "many employees of North American companies or their affiliates in Central and South America are known members of local anti-American organizations"; that many of the companies' local business agents were active Axis propagandists who were not only touting the Nazi cause but slipping confidential trade information to the Germans; that often these agents were using the American businesses' advertising dollars to spread the Nazi line.

To follow up these charges, Rockefeller's office engaged in a low-key appeal to the U.S. firms' patriotic instincts. Some 1,700 letters were sent out to companies doing business in Latin America, asking them to "review" their representation and advise the coordinator as to what changes they planned to make. The emphasis was on voluntary compliance. But when that proved insufficient, Commerce Department officials petitioned the companies in person. In the cases of the largest firms, Rockefeller called on the top executives himself.

The voluntary program proved surprisingly effective. By May 1941 Rockefeller could report that "hundreds of undesirable representatives have been replaced; hundreds more are in the process of being replaced." That the program was so successful was a tribute not only to the painstaking compilation of data by his office, but to the undoubted commercial influence of the Rockefeller name.

Still, there were some holdouts, notably the mighty General Motors Corporation. In early February 1941, Rockefeller's office advised GM that five of its Latin American car dealers were Axis sympathizers, and urged the auto company to sever its relationship with them. But GM stonewalled, citing the lack of "detailed charges" against the dealers. The company loftily declared that it was reluctant to mix business with "politics."

The dispute pitted Rockefeller against the automaker's meticulous, willful chairman, Alfred P. Sloan. Sloan informed Rockefeller in early May that *if* GM, after its own investigation, found those charges to be valid, then the company would replace the dealers—"through the process of evolution." Furthermore, he warned that GM might have trouble finding suitable local replacements—in which case, he implied, Latin America would find its supply of GM vehicles cut off.

Rockefeller, the scion of Standard Oil, was hardly about to quail before any industrialist. Nevertheless, recognizing that he lacked the firepower to stand up to Sloan, he took the matter to Harry Hopkins, who erupted with white-hot fury. "I want you to make clear to General Motors," he fumed, "that the United States government cannot be indifferent to an American firm of that prestige having agents in Latin America that we believe are carrying on pro-Axis activities."

Rockefeller then contacted Undersecretary of State Sumner Welles, who agreed to summon top GM executives to his office for a decisive confrontation. At this May 8 meeting, Welles made it clear to the executives (Sloan was not among them) that the national security was at stake. If it became known that the country's biggest automaker was refusing to cooperate, the whole anti-Axis program in Latin America would be wrecked. The GM people, however, continued to parrot the Sloan line: "We're not interested in getting involved in politics," one of the men sniffed.

"Well," Rockefeller interjected, an edge of steel in his voice, "there is one alternative. That is to make a public statement and say that of all American businessmen involved you are the only ones who haven't cooperated." Just to be sure his point hit home, Rockefeller added, "I just can't conceive how an intelligent businessman can take a position like this—especially in view of the number of stockholders in your company."

The threat—and Rockefeller's determination to make good on it—was unmistakable. The GM men snapped shut their briefcases and shuffled out of Welles's office. A few days later word came from the company that it would cooperate with the government. Sloan, however, insisted in his officious way on a formal request from the State Department. In short order, he got it.

That Sloan ultimately had little choice became evident within weeks of GM's capitulation. On May 27, fearing a German naval assault against the United States in the Atlantic, the President declared a state of national emergency. "Unless the advance of Hitler is forcibly checked now," he said, "the Western Hemisphere will be within range of the Nazi weapons of destruction." On July 17 he issued a formal blacklist of 1,800 Latin American firms deemed to be aiding Germany or Italy. Compliance was no longer a voluntary matter.

But even without the force of law behind it, Rockefeller's program had worked. By the time the blacklist was imposed, 89 percent of the U.S. companies contacted had severed their ties to pro-Axis firms. From his perch at the Navy Department, James Forrestal sent his congratulations, writing Rockefeller, "Here's at least one tangible result for which you can rightly take credit."

In the midst of his anti-Axis campaign, Rockefeller had moved his office from the Beaux Arts State Department Building to the nine-year-old Commerce Department Building a half mile away. Distinguished mainly by its immensity—through it ran five miles of corridors and thirty-two elevators—the Commerce Building was still (with the construction of the Pentagon just then getting underway) the capital's largest office structure. It offered Rockefeller ample space for his burgeoning staff. But beyond that there was the symbolic significance of the move: Rockefeller was out from under the wing of the State Department. In the cavernous halls of his new home, he could truly build a fiefdom of his own.

A visitor to his new office would be greeted by one of his six comely young secretaries. (Rockefeller's discerning taste in clerical help was already prompting Washington whispers. No less a source than *Time* magazine panted about the "brunette bombshell with a rippling voice" and the "blonde vision" in the coordinator's personal secretarial pool.) As aides bounded in and out of the chief's office, the sounds of offhand, slangy repartee could be overheard: "I've got my spies out on this." "We're really going to town on Paraguay." "This," the coordinator could be heard to moan through his open doorway, "is absolutely *graveyard.*"

When Rockefeller at last was free he would hurry out himself to greet his guest and usher him into the inner chamber. No Légers decorated the walls, no Giacomettis stood guard by the windows. To those who had heard of his vaunted reputation as a connoisseur, the office's spartan quality—not only no fine art, but no art at all—always came as a shock. All there was was a desk and a long conference table surrounded by chairs.

What the visitor might have easily missed was a small stairway that ran from Rockefeller's office to the floor below, where, in a huge windowless space once occupied by the U.S. Patent Office, a much different decor prevailed. The walls were all of corkboard, and steel runners lined their entire width, and on those runners were mounted cardboard charts. There were pie charts and bar charts, organization charts and photo-collage charts, as well as stylized maps of Latin America, populated by little locomotives and little trucks and little steel mills. Each chart was thirty by forty inches, and they stood end to end, lined up in three tiers that rose to the ceiling. When a particularly telling point had to be made, a score of these boards would be lined up on a wall to form a single, CinemaScopic map, with bigger locomotives and trucks chugging across the multihued landscape.

This room was the brainchild of Wally Harrison, newly arrived from New York. Well aware of Rockefeller's dyslexic reading problems—and, as an architect, most comfortable with the graphic form himself—Harrison began translating his reports into charts. Delighted with this medium, Rockefeller soon asked Harrison to depict other people's reports in chart form as well. Harrison assigned the task to his young assistant, George Dudley, whom Harrison had met during a short part-time stint teaching at Yale.

To facilitate the display of these visual aids, Harrison located the space downstairs and redesigned it as the coordinator's chart room. Before long the room would serve as a sort of all-purpose forum: part conference room, part theater, where progress could be reviewed, ideas could be hatched, and potential administration allies wooed by means of dramatic pictographic presentations. (It also had the allure of being the only room in the Commerce Building that was air-conditioned.)

Nothing quite like this room existed anywhere else in official Washington—not in the White House, not in the State Department, not even (yet) in the War Department. It was flashy, it was dramatic (helped along by such touches as the little staircase that led down to it), it was state-of-the-art (a projector and screen would soon be added to make Rockefeller's shows truly multimedia). In all its glory, the chart room was emblematic of the vast gulf between the slangy, snap-brimmed Rockefeller office hotshots and the homburged State Department mandarins half a mile—and seemingly half a world—away.

If anyone epitomized the fusty style and gravitas of which the Rockefeller office was the antithesis, it was Sumner Welles.

With his tall and erect bearing, his Savile Row suits, and his malacca cane, Welles was an august and imposing figure. "He conducts himself with portentous gravity and as if he were charged with all the responsibilities of Atlas," observed Interior Secretary Harold Ickes. An old family friend of Roosevelt's (he had been a page at FDR's wedding), Welles moved in the same Groton-Harvard axis and vaulted effortlessly up the ranks of the foreign service. His special area of expertise was Latin America; it was Welles who, as a foreign policy adviser to the newly elected President Roosevelt, coined the term "Good Neighbor Policy." When Welles was named Undersecretary of State in 1937, his long-standing ties to FDR gave him special entrée to the Oval Office—much to the distress of Secretary Cordell Hull. Indulging his predilection for competing lines of authority, Roosevelt built up Welles at Hull's obvious expense. In early 1940, it was Welles, not Hull, whom the President dispatched to Europe on a last-ditch peace mission. When *The New York Times*'s Arthur Krock once raised the subject of disloyalty to Hull, the hard-bitten Tennessean pointed to the door between his office and Welles's and snapped, "I've got the prime example of disloyalty right in there."

In the world of statesmen, Welles was a distinctly impassive figure, but Hull, among others, knew also of the dark side lurking behind the crimped facade. Welles was a chronic alcoholic, capable of the most compromising indiscretions when under the influence. Drunk, he would indulge his homosexual bent by seeking out lower-class partners, preferably black. In private, Hull would mock Welles's proclivities, referring to him as "my fairy."

But to the public, and to those with whom he did business, Welles projected the utmost decorousness. And, in those months when America was girding for war, the dry chill of Welles's personality was felt particularly by the effervescent Coordinator of Inter-American Affairs.

Arriving for his first appointment with Welles, Rockefeller was almost turned away by an aloof secretary who expected the coordinator to be "an older man." When Rockefeller was finally admitted into the undersecretary's presence, Welles greeted him with a stiff bow, then sat down and fixed his expressionless blue eyes on the young man, waiting for Rockefeller to utter the first words.

Despite Rockefeller's earnest offers of cooperation, Welles's distaste for the coordinator and his upstart agency was transparent. He was particularly scornful of the coordinator's plans in the cultural sector, feeling that they duplicated State's own efforts in that area. Welles was, however, willing to entertain certain limited diplomatic relations between his department and Rockefeller's agency, permitting his deputy Laurence Duggan, head of the Division of American Republics, to meet with one of Rockefeller's deputies.

Welles terminated the meeting by rising and offering another formal bow.

Far from being cowed by the haughty undersecretary, Rockefeller left the encounter determined to steer his own course. He promptly directed his aide Hutch Robbins to establish a direct liaison with the embassies of the other American republics—a gross breach of the time-honored principle that the State Department was the sole official link to foreign ambassadors.

Disparaging the reports State was willing to share with him, Rockefeller continued to cultivate his own private intelligence back channel: J. Edgar Hoover's FBI. "We finished up with the FBI data on Argentina and most of the recent material on Mexico," he wrote Hoover in October 1940. "The information to be obtained there contains a much higher percentage of pay dirt than the State Department documents." And to develop his own sources of information, he borrowed a page from the Hoover text and dispatched "observers" to eight Latin American cities, "observers" who were ostensibly working for something called the Research Division of the American Association of Advertising Agencies' Export Information Bureau. (This Research Division was in fact a coordinator's office front.) The observers were specifically instructed not to make themselves known to any of the U.S. missions in Latin America.

Rockefeller went even further in early 1941, sending two staff members, Berent Friele and Frank Nattier, to Brazil on a supposed fact-finding tour. They stopped in Rio de Janeiro—and there they remained. For the real reason for their trip, unbeknownst to State, was to establish the coordinator's first official beachhead in Latin America itself.

Rockefeller could have found no better person for the task than the Norwegian-born Friele. He had settled in Brazil in 1917 and went on to found the American Coffee Corporation, the principal procurer of Brazilian coffee for the giant A&P food chain. Fluent in Portuguese, a personal friend of Foreign Minister Oswaldo Aranha and others of the country's elite, Friele possessed two indispensable elements for his job: contacts and a wealth of local experience. Before long his activities for the Rockefeller office came to the attention of U.S. ambassador Jefferson Caffery, a shrewd, able diplomat who made little effort to conceal his displeasure.

Friele's activities, along with Robbins', were open and unquestionable provocations. Yet Welles held off making an issue of them. He was biding his time, seemingly waiting for Rockefeller to commit the one big blunder that would give Welles an unassailable pretext for reining in the young bounder.

He did not have long to wait.

In early 1941, James Young, the former J. Walter Thompson executive who was now in charge of the coordinator's communications division, came to Rockefeller with a scheme for leveraging the fabled power of advertising. The coordinator's office, through an "Inter-American Travel Committee," would purchase huge amounts of advertising space in some 350 Latin American newspapers. The ads would tout the many pleasures of travel in the United States. But their true purpose was to fill the newspapers with pro-U.S. propaganda—and to fill the coffers of Latin papers struggling to survive in the wartime economy.

Rockefeller was thoroughly captivated by the idea. He broached the plan to Assistant Secretary of State Berle, who had no objection, and in April 1941 the first torrent of travel ads hit Latin American presses.

And instantly the cries of outrage began. Some South American publishers—indignant at the implication that they could be "bought" by *yanqui* dollars—loudly refused to accept the ads. Other publishers who had not received the ads protested just as loudly at having been denied those tainted greenbacks. There was widespread anger at the fact that some of the ads were knowingly placed in pro-Axis newspapers. (Young's people thought that the ad revenues would convert them to the Allied cause.)

American ambassadors in the region, under constant pressure from the Rockefeller office to shake out pro-German business agents, were incensed at the spectacle of the office's funneling government dollars to Nazi sympathizers. The diplomats also derided the ads' sunny, "come on up" content, which seemed to mock wartime travel restrictions and the inability of most Latin Americans to afford even steamship steerage fare.

The ad campaign was building into a first-class fiasco, which played quite nicely into Sumner Welles's hands. "It was," Rockefeller would reflect long afterward, "his chance to get rid of the CIAA. And he almost did."

Welles took his case to Roosevelt. The ad business, he told the President, demonstrated how Rockefeller's freewheeling operation was mangling U.S. policy in the Southern Hemisphere. The time had come, Welles said, for young Rockefeller to be reminded just who had authority over that policy. (Welles was either unaware of or chose to ignore the fact that the ad program had been approved by Berle.) Despite his sympathy for Rockefeller's position—the whole point of creating the coordinator's office, after all, had been to break through State Department gridlock—Roosevelt felt duty-bound to support his senior diplomats. He asked Welles to draft a letter to Rockefeller, then signed it without changing a single word.

The letter from the President arrived in the coordinator's suite on April 22, 1941. A shaken Rockefeller read it again and again, so upset was he by its import. "My Dear Nelson," it began:

> As you know, it was my thought in the establishment of an Office of the Coordinator of Commercial and Cultural Relations between the American Republics that such an office was especially desirable as a coordinating organ for certain emergency measures rendered advisable by the course of events since the outbreak of the war. But in order that our foreign relations may be conducted so as to advance the security and welfare of the country, it is now more than ever essential that the Secretary of State be apprised of all Governmental undertakings, whether carried on directly by Governmental agencies or indirectly through private agencies, relating to foreign countries. . . .

The President went on to say that although he was aware of Rockefeller's "personal intentions to cooperate" with State, he had observed "impairment of our total effort, particularly in regard to activities which, while directed from within this country, are carried out in the other American republics"—an obvious allusion to the ad program. He directed Rockefeller to "institute arrangements" for ensuring that all his office's programs are "discussed fully with and approved by the Department of State, and a full meeting of minds obtained before action is undertaken or commitments are made."

Couched though it was in formalistic prose, there was little question that the letter amounted to a severe reprimand of the coordinator. Rockefeller and his top aides were haunted by the chilling implication that perhaps their upstart operation had already lost the confidence of the chief executive. "We all wondered, are we dead or aren't we?" remembers Lockwood.

Rockefeller had to know, one way or the other. He phoned Pa Watson, FDR's appointments secretary.

"Pa," said Rockefeller, "I need to see the Boss."

"Yes, Nelson," replied Watson, "you sure do! Come on over."

Roosevelt clearly was expecting the visit, and greeted Rockefeller with one of his patented megawatt smiles. He genuinely liked Rockefeller, perhaps because the young man reminded him of his own days as an eager-to-please aristocrat in the Navy Department during World War I. Nevertheless, Roosevelt made no bones about Rockefeller's predicament.

"Look, Nelson," he said, "I know that you're in a difficult situation in regard to State and I knew it was going to be tough when I set up your office. But understand this: it is up to you to get along with them because if it ever comes to a showdown between your office and State I will have no choice but to back the department and Mr. Welles."

Then, taking a deep drag on his cigarette, the President offered his acolyte some fatherly advice: "You have got to handle your problems in a way that doesn't give them an opening to take the kind of shot they've already taken at you—or to create a showdown in which I'll have to make a decision."

A chastened Rockefeller earnestly promised to heed FDR's counsel and left the Oval Office with his job—at least for the time being—still intact.

With scrupulous obeisance to form as well as substance, Rockefeller proceeded to hammer out liaison procedures between his agency and State. All projects would henceforth be submitted in writing to State for prior approval; once cleared, State would receive a steady stream of memoranda about their progress. Laurence Duggan would serve as State's principal link to the CIAA—although on "matters of basic policy" Rockefeller would go directly to Hull and Welles. As Rockefeller breezily summed up the modus vivendi, "We've worked out a formal relationship whereby we show them projects in the early stages. It slows you down, but what the hell!"

He instructed his key aides to meet once a week with Welles, and schedule regular short meetings with Duggan. "We now need to impress the State Department with results," he told his deputies, "so that they feel they cannot get on without us."

The top brass at State, for once, seemed well satisfied. Hull assured Congress in June that "nothing will be undertaken by the Coordinator's Office which is not based upon mutual agreement and thorough cooperation between the Office of the Coordinator and this Department." Even Welles was converted. In early July he told Rockefeller he was now quite pleased with the CIAA-State relationship.

Rockefeller had found himself in situations before where he had incurred the wrath of an elder. To propitiate the disapproving authority figure (usually his father) he had always resorted to the same measures he employed in this case: a regretful admission of guilt and a solemn undertaking to mend his ways in the future. And, more often than not, he soon found some means to subtly subvert his own commitments.

It had been that way in his adolescence, with all his promises of fiscal responsibility. It had been that way at Rockefeller Center, when he pledged to return to the "family fold" while simultaneously sticking with his private company, Special Work.

And it was that way now, too.

In the spring of 1941, just as Rockefeller was obediently falling into line with State, movie actor Douglas Fairbanks, Jr., embarked on an official tour of Latin America. Fairbanks, an FDR friend and pen pal who had emceed the inaugural gala three months earlier, was an emissary of the White House, not the coordinator's office. Nevertheless, the fact that he was accompanied by Rockefeller aide Hutch Robbins led to the inevitable conclusion in the diplomatic corps that the mission was a Rockefeller production.

The trip infuriated U.S. ambassadors throughout the region; they felt it demeaning for the President to be represented by the star of *The Prisoner of Zenda* and other swashbucklers. Ambassador Spruille Braden in Colombia (who had complained, after meeting Fairbanks in Rockefeller's office, that the actor "must have taken a shower bath in eau de cologne") flatly told him to stay out of the country. Braden maintained that sending a divorced man as a presidential emissary would be deeply offensive to a Catholic country.

If the ambassadors had known at the time about the principal outcome of the trip, they would have had even more reason to be outraged. In a five-page memo to Rockefeller in early June, Robbins ripped the American diplomatic presence in Latin America, charging that the U.S. missions were "ineffective" and "pathetically understaffed." By contrast, "the Axis elements have the best informed, best organized and most efficient machine existing in South America." To counteract this, Robbins urged the creation of local organizations, made up of expatriate American businessmen, to spearhead the propaganda battle against the Axis.

While Robbins took pains to point out that such organizations would act "with the full knowledge and support" of U.S. diplomats, the thrust of his proposal was unmistakable: that a new corps of American operatives—separate and distinct from the U.S. embassies—be set up in the Latin countries, under the aegis of the coordinator.

Rockefeller loved the idea. It was one more means by which he could have his own representatives sprinkled throughout Latin America. He rushed to set the wheels in motion to make it a reality.

The first step he and Robbins took—even before lining up the support of the State Department—was to get the sponsorship of Franklin Roosevelt.

As a close relation of the President, Robbins had his own connections to the White House, and he sent a copy of his report to FDR. Roosevelt saw the merit of Robbins' scheme immediately. Then, exhibiting once again his bent for making mischief with his chief advisers, Roosevelt proceeded to slip the copy to Sumner Welles. "Hutch would slay me if he knew I had let you see this," wrote the President in his July 21 cover note, "but I do so on condition you do not tell a soul and let me have this back!"

After perusing it, Welles thanked the President for sharing the report, which he found "extremely interesting, constructive and really helpful." The department would act on Robbins' proposal, "but I know you will realize that it is not an easy matter to solve promptly."

That was what Welles thought.

Roosevelt's personal interest tipped the balance. Barely two weeks later, spurred by a presidential request, a complete plan for the implementation of Robbins' scheme was formally approved by Rockefeller and Secretary of State Cordell Hull.

Henceforth, in each Latin American country, there would be the State Department's people—and there would be Nelson Rockefeller's.

Fifteen

Going to War

Ambassador to Colombia Spruille Braden was on one of his periodic visits to Washington when a phone call came from Nelson Rockefeller, inviting Braden and his wife to Sunday-evening supper at Foxhall Road. Braden begged off, but Rockefeller persisted. It wasn't just a supper, he explained; each Sunday evening he hosted a night of Latin American culture, with movies and songs. There would be plenty of Latin dignitaries, Rockefeller promised. Unable to shake off the coordinator's dogged entreaties, Braden finally agreed to come.

When Braden and his wife arrived, the sprawling house was completely dark, except for a dim light in the front hallway. They rang the bell, and Rockefeller opened the door. He led them to the left, to a darkened living room, where the movie had already started. Stumbling over the legs of guests stretched out on the floor, the Bradens squeezed into a place for themselves.

The film was a convoluted Argentinian tale about a man's desperate desire for an heir and his wife's attempt to placate him by pretending to be pregnant. It made little sense to Braden, and he sat through it glumly until the closing credits mercifully rolled across the screen. The lights were flipped back on, but no sooner did Braden and the other guests unlimber than they were shepherded back across the front hall to a study, where they were instructed to be seated once again. The songs were about to begin.

Rockefeller proceeded to hand out mimeographed booklets containing the lyrics to some fifty different Spanish songs, all of which were numbered. Then he called out a number, popped a record on the Victrola and set the needle down. "Forty-four," Rockefeller yelled. "Allá en el Rancho Grande." As the music swelled, the dulcet tones of dozens of bureaucrats and their wives filled the house, singing along in (for the most part) execrable Spanish. Braden tried not to glance at his wife, for fear that they both would burst out in disrespectful laughter. But the worst was yet to come.

"Twenty-three," Rockefeller shouted. "Expropiación." Braden was aghast when he glanced at the lyrics: the tune was a Mexican ditty penned in honor of the country's expropriation of American oil company properties. "We've expropriated the oil fields," the song ran. "Now we're going to expropriate the Atlantic Ocean." Rockefeller lustily led the singing. *"Expropiación,"* he bellowed. *"¡Expropiación!"*

Braden looked around the room in disbelief. Not only was the Coordinator of Inter-American Affairs singing this paean to anti-Americanism, but so were some of the federal government's most distinguished officials. Harold Smith, the President's budget director, was joining in, as were several senators.

But Braden was most agog at the sight of a tousle-haired man across the room. It was none other than Henry A. Wallace, the Vice President of the United States. His high-pitched Iowa twang wrapped itself around the Spanish refrain: *"Expropiación. ¡Expropiación!"*

The Sunday-evening culturefests were a regular feature at Foxhall Road, and Vice President Wallace, it turned out, faithfully attended most of them, genuinely enjoying himself. Self-taught in Spanish, Wallace over the past decade had developed a true fascination with Latin America, a fascination that rivaled Nelson Rockefeller's. The Vice President had his own collection of Latin American recorded music. Since the mid-1930s he had regularly attended a weekly luncheon club at which, over *tamales* and *frijoles,* events of the day were discussed in Spanish. He even read from a Spanish edition of the Bible each evening.

The enchantment with Latin America was but one more unusual twist in the eclectic, often unfathomable mind of Henry Agard Wallace. A true son of the Corn Belt, Wallace had worked, like his father and grandfather before him, on the family newspaper, *Wallace's Farmer.* But Wallace's interests ranged far afield of journalism, into such diverse realms as agrarian politics and plant genetics (he was a leader in the development of new strains of hybrid seed corn). His father had been Secretary of Agriculture in the Harding and Coolidge administrations, and the younger Wallace's enthusiastic backing of FDR in 1932 (a stunning break with his Republican roots) led Roosevelt to appoint him to the same job in his new administration.

As Agriculture Secretary, Wallace shaped the New Deal's multifaceted campaign to bring relief to America's Depression-stricken farmers. In Wallace, FDR saw that rarest of combinations: a skillful, tenacious administrator who was also a man of surpassing vision. Unlike Roosevelt's Vice President at the time, the acerbic old Texas pol John Nance Garner, Wallace was a passionate defender of the New Deal faith, someone who could be counted upon to hallow the Roosevelt legacy. Convinced that Wallace was a worthy successor, Roosevelt forced the dubious Democratic Party pros to accept him as his 1940 running mate. "He's a philosopher, he's got ideas," FDR assured his worried political operative James Farley. "He'll help the people think."

But Wallace's philosophy—an amalgam of socialist utopianism, agrarian populism, and benevolent internationalism by way of Thomas Jefferson, William Jennings Bryan, and Woodrow Wilson—was not destined to allay the politicians' fears. Wallace repeatedly denied he was any sort of mystic, but his fascination with such eclectica as Confucian economic doctrine, American Indian corn dances, and the aerodynamics of the boomerang soon gave him a reputation as Washington's foremost eccentric.

While his preoccupation with Latin America was at times regarded as just another idiosyncrasy, there was nothing mystical about it. His farming background had taught him the value of complementary crops, and he saw the merit of that principle writ large in the potential complementarity of U.S. and Latin American agriculture. From there it was but a short leap to the broader issues of inter-American relations, and in 1939 Wallace made the jump, calling in a speech for "cultural unity" as well as "economic reciprocity" in the Americas.

For Nelson Rockefeller, gathering up all the administration allies he could, the Vice President's commitment to Latin America was fortuitous, to say the least. Wallace was at the peak of his influence in 1941: FDR still regarded him (mystical tendencies aside) as his most likely successor. No one in the government was better positioned to serve as a counterbalance to the jaded skeptics at State.

With his usual assiduousness, Rockefeller worked his way quickly into the Vice President's good graces. Knowing of Wallace's fondness for tennis, Rockefeller invited him for top-of-the-morning doubles on the court at Foxhall Road. Before long Wallace and Rockefeller were everyday doubles partners, taking on senators, CIAA officials, and anyone else who was willing to arrive on the court at the crack of dawn to serve them out. The pair had similar tennis styles, making up in bulldog aggressiveness what they lacked in finesse.

Then there were the Sunday-evening musicales, which seemed to be aimed as much at pleasing Wallace, the Latin music buff, as at edifying the bureaucratic elite. Says Lockwood, "I attended countless sessions at Nelson's house at which we sat around and sang Latin American songs in Spanish. I never took it seriously, but I realized that, politically, keeping Henry Wallace happy was something very important to us."

When a particular native work of art caught Rockefeller's fancy, he sent it over to Wallace as a gift. "I am overwhelmed with the gift of the corn god from Oaxaca," Wallace wrote the coordinator in December 1941. "The next time you are in my office, I hope perhaps you can tell me a little more about this particular corn god."

Coordinator of Inter Amer Affairs

Rockefeller made sure the Vice President was au courant with his office's doings, filling him in with extensive memos. He kept a special eye out for what he knew to be Wallace's pet projects. Latching on to Wallace's dream of agricultural harmony in the hemisphere, Rockefeller went so far as to establish an Inter-American Institute of Tropical Agriculture under the coordinator's aegis. Such an institute, which would encourage noncompetitive tropical crops, had long been one of Wallace's most cherished concepts.

Rockefeller sometimes visited Wallace in the evenings at the latter's Washington apartment to get the benefit of the Vice President's wisdom. On one such occasion he brought with him some of his aides, who were treated to one of Wallace's more metaphysical exhibitions. The Vice President sat with his eyes closed for minutes at a time, then finally uttered, "Liberty and unity. Liberty of the individual and unity of mankind. That is the issue." He shut his eyes again, and after another long pause he suddenly opened them and said, "Corn." There was another pause, while his guests tried to figure out what to make of this. At last, the Vice President spoke again. "The rest of the world is a wheat civilization. We are a corn civilization, and so is Latin America. That is the tie that binds us. Corn." Then Wallace went back into his trance, a spent oracle, and the visitors quietly took their leave.

Walking down the hallway, the coordinator's people were caught up in an embarrassed silence. One man was struck by the unwelcome thought that if anything happened to President Roosevelt, the country would be in deep trouble. Then, as they boarded the elevator, Nelson Rockefeller spoke up.

"There are no two ways about it," he said. "That man must be the next President of the United States."

In July 1941, in what amounted to a further vote of confidence in his new Vice President, FDR named Henry Wallace to chair a new Economic Defense Board, whose members included the secretaries of State, War, Treasury, and four other cabinet members. The EDB was charged with making policy in such areas as trade, preclusive buying and international shipping and transportation. It was also charged with enforcement of the anti-Axis blacklist.

By dint of its charter, the EDB effectively usurped all of Rockefeller's activities on the commercial front. But Rockefeller was surprisingly sanguine about this development. For one thing, he had confidence in Henry Wallace. For another, he was feeling mounting frustration with those activities.

The various committees he earlier convinced the President to form to free up exports to Latin America had not broken through the logjam of defense priorities. Profiteering on scarce commodities was rampant. Inter-American shipping was paralyzed, as more and more vessels were requisitioned by the armed forces. In late May, Rockefeller pleaded with the President to intercede and stop the removal of ships from Latin American service; the President did not respond.

Hamstrung by his lack of authority, the coordinator resorted to taking his case public. In a speech dedicating the new ocean liner *Rio de Janeiro,* he warned that if America's good neighbors "do not get such products as steel, machines, and agricultural equipment, there will follow in order drastic economic contraction, social unrest, and eventually political upheaval."

With the sympathetic Wallace at the helm, the EDB represented a rare chance to break through the deadlock. Still, Rockefeller wasn't entirely at ease. One more maneuver would be needed to fully reassure him.

It took three more months to accomplish, but Rockefeller finally achieved exactly what he sought.

"Confidentially," he informed the CIAA executive committee on November 21, "we are just completing and waiting the President's approval on a merger with the Economic Defense Board." The "merger" consisted of moving the coordinator's commercial and financial division, in toto, to the EDB, where it would be dubbed the Americas division. The head of this division would be Rockefeller's assistant coordinator and confidant, Carl Spaeth.

The maneuver was, on paper at least, a masterstroke for Rockefeller. By aligning his unit with the powerful EDB, he could endow his commercial division with the governmental clout it had so sorely lacked. Yet at the same time, with his faithful aide Spaeth running the operation, it would remain under the sway of the coordinator's office.

FDR approved the merger on November 24. As an added sweetener for Rockefeller, Wallace named him to the board. Grand plans for the reconstituted commercial unit began emanating from the coordinator's suite; there was talk it would add as many as 200 people to its staff.

Rockefeller was ecstatic. He wrote EDB executive director Milo Perkins that the merger proved that "democracy can function effectively in time of crisis."

"I am sending you herewith a memorandum describing the program of the Communications Division of this office," Rockefeller wrote Wallace on April 1, 1941. But if there was any area where Rockefeller *didn't* seem to need the Vice President's help, it was "communications"—a euphemism for propaganda. Unlike the commercial side—where the coordinator was hemmed in at every turn by defense priorities and competing jurisdictions—the communications effort, and the agency's complementary initiatives in the cultural area, had a clear field.

The coordinator's mandate was unmistakable, and had come from FDR himself, who had insisted in his discussions with Forrestal that Rockefeller's marching orders strongly emphasize the cultural and propaganda side. Indeed, the bulk of the office's initial $3.5 million appropriation was earmarked for such activities as radio broadcasts, moviemaking, academic exchange programs, and traveling art exhibitions.

The coordinator's ventures ran the gamut from high culture to comic books, from all-America boosterism to avant-garde sophistication. The summer of 1941, for instance, saw CIAA-sponsored South American tours by Lincoln Kirstein's American Ballet Caravan, representing the cutting edge of contemporary dance, and by the Yale Glee Club. Tapping his art world connections, Rockefeller arranged for the Museum of Modern Art to organize a traveling exhibition of contemporary U.S. art; during that same summer the show made stops in Mexico City (drawing 1,000 visitors a day), Buenos Aires, and eight other capitals. And plans were underway for a similar exhibition of Latin American art to tour the United States.

The CIAA also sponsored a series of archaeological expeditions in seven different Central and South American countries. As was the case in art, Rockefeller's personal interest in the field gave these efforts added impetus: the very expeditions he had been vainly proposing for years to the Metropolitan Museum were now underway under the coordinator's aegis.

To promote hemisphere unity through the great American pastime of baseball, Rockefeller sent former Chicago White Sox catcher Moe Berg on a goodwill bat-and-ball tour. Berg was not your average tobacco-chewing, profanity-spewing ballplayer. An honors graduate of Princeton University and the Columbia University Law School, Berg was an accomplished linguist and philologist who spoke Spanish fluently. Berg's skills were such that Rockefeller was soon using him for more than mere instruction on catching curveballs. Berg sent reports to Rockefeller, marked "secret and confidential," on Axis influence and activities; for the better part of two years he was the coordinator's personal spy. (Much of his intelligence dealt with conditions at U.S. bases in Latin America, including graphic accounts of the GIs' sexual escapades. "Highly recommended," he wrote Rockefeller, "was a redhead in the Ideal, a little older, not the most attractive, but whose record was above reproach.") The ex-catcher liked the work so much that he moved on to Europe as a secret agent for the Office of Strategic Services—the predecessor of the Central Intelligence Agency. His assignments would include sniffing out the progress of Germany's atomic bomb project.

Of all the coordinator's cultural ventures, none could rival the potential impact of the agency's foray into the motion picture business. Art and music and sports had their discrete audiences. Only the movies could deliver the message of inter-American brotherhood to the masses.

In tapping Jock Whitney to head his motion picture division, Rockefeller had chosen well: Whitney's monumental success with *Gone With the Wind* earned him considerable Hollywood influence. A congenitally diffident man—"he carries his wealth, as he does his liquor, like an English gentleman," an associate once said—Whitney nonetheless displayed uncommon assertiveness in his new role. Shortly after taking the job, he summoned leading movie producers to a meeting in Hollywood and exhorted them to promote good relations by, among other things, giving more positive treatment to Latin American subjects and shooting more footage on location there. "Process shots, gentlemen," he declared, "are not the answer to Nazi propaganda!"

Troubled by Hollywood's tendency to typecast Latin Americans as either slimy gigolos or amiable buffoons, Whitney and Rockefeller cajoled producers into mending their ways. Their first test came with the release of *Down Argentine Way.* Not only was one of the principal characters an Argentine gigolo, and the other Argentines the butt of jokes, but the only Argentine character heard speaking any Spanish spoke with an obvious Mexican accent. When Whitney and Rockefeller confronted the producer with their objections, he agreed to rephotograph those scenes, at a cost of $40,000, before releasing the picture in Latin America.

From that point on, CIAA influence—and censorship—became a fact of Hollywood life. Whitney installed one of his people in the studios' Production Code Administration (the infamous Hays Office). This man's job was to review all scripts in advance for material potentially offensive to Latin Americans. And Whitney pressed the producers to refrain from releasing in the other American republics films that reflected badly on the United States—citing as an example Frank Capra's *Mr. Smith Goes to Washington.*

Not content to merely serve as bluenoses, Rockefeller and Whitney prodded moviemakers to undertake films centered on Latin American themes. The producers, who were eager in any case for fresh new material, were more than happy to comply. Soon MGM was preparing a Simón Bolívar bio with Robert Taylor, and 20th Century–Fox was filming *That Night in Rio* with Alice Faye and Carmen Miranda. Even Charlie Chan was pressed into service, with Fox setting a series of his adventures in South America. To promote these films, as well as Hollywood in general, personal appearance tours in Latin America were arranged for such stars as Faye and Dorothy Lamour, the sarong-clad female lead of Bob Hope–Bing Crosby movies.

But undoubtedly the Rockefeller-Whitney team's biggest coup was enlisting Walt Disney in their cause. In August 1941 Disney signed on to produce several short features for the coordinator's office, to be commercially distributed throughout the hemisphere. An added inducement for Disney was the relative lack of risk involved: the CIAA agreed to reimburse him for any losses he incurred up to $150,000.

Two Disney feature films resulted from his collaboration with the CIAA. The first, *Saludos Amigos,* was actually a collection of four cartoon shorts, including segments on Gaucho Goofy's misadventures on the Argentine pampas and Donald Duck's visit to Lake Titicaca. The second, *The Three Caballeros,* featured three "birds of a feather," to quote the title song: Jose Carioca, a well-traveled Brazilian parrot; the Mexican rooster Panchito; and the estimable Donald Duck.

Neither film was a *Pinocchio* or *Snow White,* but they fared quite respectably, both north and south of the border. Disney never had to draw on his $150,000 guarantee.

The experience with another renowned filmmaker—the mercurial, polymathic young actor-director Orson Welles—was somewhat less felicitous.

Rockefeller first came to know Welles through the Rockefeller family's continued financial stake in RKO Pictures. It was RKO that produced Welles's first films, including his masterwork, *Citizen Kane.* Rockefeller, in fact, found himself embroiled in the early 1941 prerelease controversy over *Citizen Kane.* Newspaper baron William Randolph Hearst, believing (with good reason) that the film was a thinly veiled account of his tempestuous career, enlisted his star Hollywood columnist, Louella Parsons, in an all-out campaign to blackball the movie. Parsons contacted Rockefeller and, as RKO president George Schaefer would later tell the story, threatened to run a defamatory article about John D. Senior unless *Citizen Kane* was barred from Radio City Music Hall. How Rockefeller reacted to this threat is not known. What is known is that Radio City Music Hall agreed not to show *Citizen Kane.*

Whatever ill will might have been generated by this had thoroughly vanished by the latter part of the year. Seeking yet another stellar filmmaker to lend his talents to inter-American unity, Rockefeller asked Welles if he would be willing to make a film about the annual carnival in Rio. Just as he did for Disney, Rockefeller offered (through the CIAA) to subsidize RKO's potential losses—this time up to a total of $300,000. Tantalized by the guarantee, Welles agreed. He saw this as a unique opportunity to resuscitate his idea for an anthology picture that he called *It's All True.* Welles had already filmed one segment, "The Story of Bonito the Bull," a sentimental fable set in Mexico. Another Latin American tale, based in Brazil, would make a perfect fit.

Traveling everywhere in an immense convertible heralded by a pair of motorcycle escorts, the dashing Yankee filmmaker quickly captured the imagination of his Rio hosts. But the aura of triumph faded as soon as the cameras began to roll. The movie was plagued by huge cost overruns—overruns caused in large part by Welles's extravagance and hefty personal expenses (amounting to upward of $2,500 a week), as well as by his tendency to disappear from the set for hours on end to dally with a seemingly endless supply of starstruck Rio females.

Welles soon ran afoul of local sentiment by shooting scenes in the *favelas,* the shantytown slums on the edge of the city center. The Brazilian government was horrified, and word of its distress reached Washington. A CIAA report concluded that Welles was toying with "national susceptibilities," not only by filming the *favelas* but by highlighting the black and mestizo (mixed race) roots of the samba. Brazilians were not ashamed of the Indian and black blood in their ancestry, the report pointed out, but they resented an outsider's pointing it out.

Meanwhile, any support Welles still had in Hollywood was rapidly disappearing. The advance screening of his latest film, *The Magnificent Ambersons* (shown, the director insisted, before he had a chance to complete it), had been an utter disaster; the film's dismal prospects, along with Welles's various excesses, resulted in the firing of his chief sponsor and protector, George Schaefer. When RKO's new management learned of Welles's latest Brazilian extravagance—a planned "Pan American Night" nightclub scene that would cost close to $150,000 to shoot—it pulled the plug not just on the scene but on Welles's entire relationship with the studio.

There remained the question of what to do with the incomplete *It's All True,* which cost RKO some $1.2 million before it was terminated. Both the studio and Welles explored various ways of salvaging the footage, secure in the knowledge that at least they still had the backing of the coordinator's office.

Secure, that is, until Nelson Rockefeller informed them otherwise.

At a board meeting of the Motion Picture Society for the Americas—an association of film producers the CIAA formed to further its Hollywood efforts—Rockefeller asserted that Welles and RKO had not lived up to their agreement with his office. The agreement, he said, called for a Class A picture. And those who had seen the footage, including David Selznick, informed him that what they saw simply did not add up to a feature film.

Accordingly, said Rockefeller, the CIAA's $300,000 guarantee was no longer operative.

The coordinator's withdrawal effectively was the end of the line for *It's All True* (although as late as January 1945 Welles was still trying to interest the CIAA in reviving the project).* And, while it hardly seemed so at the time, the episode proved to be a dramatic turning point in Welles's fortunes. In the minds of the movie industry's moneymen, the aborted film created an indelible impression of Welles as an unreliable, profligate eccentric, an impression that would cast a shadow on the whole of his remaining working life. Other, later projects would confirm that impression, but the first stigma came with *It's All True.*

And for this, to the end of his days, Orson Welles blamed Nelson Rockefeller. "I thought he was the one who really let me down," Welles remarked

* Salvaged and reconstructed footage of *It's All True* was finally seen by the public for the first time in late 1993, eight years after Welles's death.

decades later. "Because the movie companies you *expect* to, but I really didn't expect to be scuttled by him."

"Nobody was ever more cowardly in the world than Nelson, you know. He didn't want to be near anything that was under any kind of shadow."

Welles extracted a measure of revenge, of sorts, with his 1948 feature *The Lady from Shanghai.* The film's villain, a lawyer, hoodwinks a naive sailor, played by Welles, into a scheme that nearly destroys the sailor—re-creating Welles's perceived plight at the hands of Nelson Rockefeller. To underscore his point, Welles had the lawyer, played by Glenn Anders, call everyone "fella." "In fact," Welles would later explain, "Glenn Anders was doing a kind of a parody of Nelson Rockefeller and Glenn looked a little like him, so it was perfect!"

The Disney and Welles efforts were merely the leading edge of the coordinator's motion picture onslaught. Dozens of other, lower-profile projects were in the works, ranging from newsreels to documentaries and short subjects specially edited and translated for the Latin American market. Whitney's operation opened offices in New York and Hollywood, and the staff of the division would grow to over forty people. Kenneth MacGowan, who had produced the epic *Stanley and Livingstone,* was brought in as director of production. The CIAA intended to do more than simply goad Hollywood; it would be a filmmaker and distributor in its own right.

To help out, Rockefeller and Whitney enlisted the services of their alma mater, the Museum of Modern Art. MOMA's film library would serve as a clearinghouse for documentaries and shorts, reviewing and reediting existing films and providing new Spanish and Portuguese sound tracks for their Latin American versions. The museum would also oversee the production of new shorts and would acquire Latin films for showing in the United States.

In awarding the contract (for which no other bids were entertained) to MOMA, Rockefeller and Whitney were well aware of the opportune favor they were doing the museum. Not only would it receive $10,000 a month from the CIAA but its still nascent film library would get an immense boost. And the library, in turn, would give employment to various expatriate movie professionals: among those it hired as a translator was the soon to be celebrated Spanish director Luis Buñuel.

What MOMA ended up working with was a hodgepodge of slice-of-American-life short subjects (including one called "Better Dresses Fifth Floor"), industrial training and promotion films ("The American Can Company Silver Millions," "General Electric Excursions in Science"), and military preparedness documentaries ("Eyes of the Navy," "Soldiers of the Sky"). The coordinator's film program was roasted in the U.S. press—"Bad Films for Good Neighbors" was one headline. But to a Latin American villager for whom a moving picture was an experience akin to a miraculous visitation, even "Better Dresses Fifth Floor" looked good.

Searching for more original fare, Rockefeller and Whitney extracted a commitment from the major movie companies to produce at least twenty-four theatrical shorts glorifying the hemisphere. Suspending their critical faculties, the studios turned out such items as "Viva Mexico," "Highway to Friendship," "Gaucho Sports," and "Cuba, Land of Romance and Adventure."

Then there were the newsreels. For the Nazis, newsreels were a prime propaganda vessel, and the Germans blanketed Latin America with them. Rockefeller couldn't help noticing the contrast between the German films and the product shipped south by the American newsreel companies like Movietone and Pathé. The German newsreels were paeans to the triumphant Wehrmacht and to glorious, sunburnt Aryan youth; the American newsreels, on the other hand, depicted the United States as "a nation of flag pole sitters, polar bear bathers, and people who were utterly and completely publicity mad," in the words of a CIAA document. Coverage of Latin American events—aside from the occasional Acapulco high diver or Brazilian bathing beauty—was minimal.

Given that the newsreel studios were loath to change their formula—particularly for the commercially limited Latin American market—Rockefeller offered them a deal. If the companies agreed to pool their resources and permanently station camera crews in Santiago, Chile, and Rio de Janeiro, Rockefeller's office would pick up half the tab. These CIAA-vetted segments would then be substituted for footage that, in the coordinator's judgment, "did not necessarily further the United States hemisphere program."

Thus Latin American moviegoers were treated to such segments as "Salvage Collection in Brazil," "President of Nicaragua Visits President of Costa Rica," and "Chilean Navy on Guard in Pacific."

Hokey as all this seemed, it achieved an overwhelmingly positive response south of the border. Even the State Department was impressed. In July 1942, six months after the newsreel effort began, Ambassador Claude Bowers told Cordell Hull that "the American newsreels are the most effective form of propaganda now being sent to Chile."

Not that they were the only form of propaganda.

In August 1941 a glossy new magazine began popping up in mailboxes throughout Latin America. Titled *En Guardia* (On Guard), the publication was a much slicker, more polished production than the local periodicals. There were huge photographs (some spread out over full facing pages) and punchy, tersely written prose. The magazine, in fact, bore a considerable resemblance to *Life,* the hot new American weekly published by *Time*'s Henry Luce. This was not exactly a coincidence, for *En Guardia* had been produced with the advice and assistance of *Life*'s editors. *En Guardia,* however, was not put out by Luce, but by Nelson Rockefeller and the CIAA.

En Guardia was blatantly propagandistic: its first issue was a glorification of the U.S. Navy. Nevertheless, it was an instant hit. So popular was the magazine that copies were stolen from the mails and hawked on the streets. Within months, circulation had soared to 200,000 (eventually it would climb to over 550,000).

Perhaps the best measure of its appeal was that the Germans soon distributed a knockoff, called *De Guardia.* Dispatching a copy of the German version to the White House, Rockefeller proudly declared to FDR, "Imitation is the highest form of flattery they say!"

But the most potent news medium of all, the one medium that could instantly reach all classes and economic levels, was radio. It was also the medium that presented the most imposing obstacles to Rockefeller's efforts.

Some of those obstacles were spelled out to the coordinator by Don Francisco, the polished advertising executive who headed his radio division. Francisco set off on a fact-finding tour of Latin America in early 1941, and came back with some discouraging news. A Latin listener eager to hear U.S. radio programs had to seek out the broadcasts of one of the twelve North American shortwave stations. These stations, whose owners included CBS, NBC, and various radio manufacturers, were poorly funded public service affairs with meager programming. What's more, the odds were that this listener wouldn't even be able to pick up those stations because of their primitive, scattershot broadcasting techniques, with weak signals dispersed over a wide area. The shortwave broadcasts from Radio Berlin, on the other hand, came in loud and clear, thanks to their strong, well-targeted signals. And, to further build the audience, the Berlin broadcasts were widely advertised in Latin American newspapers; the U.S. companies wouldn't think of placing such ads.

Rockefeller, of course, was not without connections in the radio business. There were his long-standing Rockefeller Center links with NBC boss David Sarnoff. And, in the past few years, he had come to know CBS chief William S. Paley. It was through Rockefeller's offices that Paley—an avid collector and an even more avid social climber—was invited on the board of MOMA.

Vain, youthful (he was not yet forty), and desperate to outdo the more established NBC, Paley was especially susceptible to the coordinator's entreaties. Accordingly, it was to Paley that Rockefeller turned as he came to grips with his Latin radio conundrum.

Paley enthusiastically accepted the challenge. He set off on a seven-week tour of South America, accompanied by his wife and two top aides. His goal was to put together nothing less than a new network—what he called *La Cadena de las Américas* (Network of the Americas). In short order he signed up sixty-four stations in eighteen countries, presenting them with exquisitely engraved contracts to seal the deal. The CBS head's avowed intent was to fulfill his "patriotic duty" to promote "hemisphere solidarity." Making some money from the enterprise, however, was not ruled out.

The members of *La Cadena* agreed to rebroadcast CBS's shortwave transmissions. In addition, CBS would prepare a special fifteen-minute Latin American newscast that would be sent via radiotelephone to the stations.

As happy as he was with Paley's initiative, Rockefeller felt more could be done. Not content to leave things in the hands of the private marketplace, he sought more direct CIAA involvement in broadcasting—the radio equivalent, as it were, of *En Guardia.*

Soon enough, he saw his opportunity, in the form of the World Wide Broadcasting Foundation, which operated two of the twelve U.S. shortwave stations. Rockefeller agreed to pump $200,000 of CIAA money into the stations, and would get in exchange a guarantee of 700 hours a year of programming "to strengthen the bonds between the American republics." World Wide also would undertake improvements to make its transmitter the most powerful in North America.

The coordinator now had what he wanted: captive stations that would transmit, unaltered, the CIAA's message throughout the hemisphere. He told Frank Jamieson to start assembling a radio pressroom similar to those of the big American wire services—manned by the CIAA's own newswriters and Spanish-speaking commentators. The radio effort was given a start-up budget in excess of $1 million.

Nelson Rockefeller was on his way to establishing his agency's own strong presence in the radio business.

He was also on his way to a head-on collision with another strong presence: Colonel William J. Donovan.

Silver-haired, erudite, and closemouthed, fifty-eight-year-old William J. Donovan was an incorporeal figure in the corridors of power: someone whose influence was palpable even as his physical presence was maddeningly elusive. The press dubbed him FDR's "mystery man," and one of his chief mysteries was how he came to be nicknamed "Wild Bill," for he was anything but. As the *New York Sun* noted, "The nickname conveys an utterly inaccurate idea of the man. Shrewd, studious, competent, controlled, mild-mannered and soft-spoken, he is always aware of the consequences of his words and deeds. There is nothing reckless about him." Of his behind-the-scenes power, there was little question. The director of British naval intelligence reported to his superiors in 1941 that "Donovan exercises controlling influence over [Navy Secretary] Knox, strong influence over [Secretary of War] Stimson, and friendly advisory influence over the President and Hull. There is no doubt that we can achieve infinitely more through Donovan than through any other individual."

Donovan's whole life had been a saga of accomplishment. Rising from youthful poverty in Buffalo, New York, Donovan became a storied hero of the Great War as commander of the Fighting 69th. His valor in the campaign of St.-Mihiel won him the Congressional Medal of Honor. Pursuing a legal career after the war, Donovan founded one of Wall Street's most successful law firms; in the depths of the Depression he was earning half a million dollars a year. But the appeal of government service never faded: he took time out to head the Justice Department's antitrust unit in the Coolidge administration, and ran, unsuccessfully, for the governorship of New York in 1932.

When Roosevelt sought a bipartisan cast for his cabinet in 1940, he considered naming Donovan Secretary of War, but yielded to the arguments of adviser Felix Frankfurter and appointed the seventy-two-year-old Stimson instead. Nevertheless, prizing Donovan's discretion and judgment, FDR proceeded to send him off on a series of secret missions aimed at assessing the European war. The most critical of these was to London in July 1940. In a move to counter the defeatist reports of Ambassador Joseph P. Kennedy, Roosevelt asked Donovan to determine the British will to fight. Donovan's assessment of the Churchill government's resolve paved the way for the rapid escalation of U.S. military assistance.

Never lacking in vision—both for the nation and for himself—Donovan used his journeys as the springboard for an even more momentous undertaking. Convinced that America's diffused intelligence apparatus (the Army, the Navy, and the State Department all had separate intelligence units) ill served a nation girding for war, Donovan urged the President to create a single master intelligence agency. This agency would pull together the input of the various separate units, would work to counter Nazi propaganda—and would train "special operatives," otherwise known as spies. Directing it all—acting in effect as America's first spymaster—would be William J. Donovan.

Roosevelt approved the plan in July 1941. But seeking to defuse isolationist critics—who were already charging that Donovan would be the Heinrich Himmler of an American Gestapo—he gave the new agency the innocuous title of Coordinator of Information. Its role, he said, would be to "collect and analyze all information and data which may bear on national security." At the same time, the agency would serve as a worldwide propaganda arm, whose aim, in the words of *The New York Times,* was to "neutralize Germany's lie campaign against the United States."

The latter mission, of course, was exactly what Nelson Rockefeller's office was doing in Latin America.

FDR made it clear that Donovan's work "is not intended to supersede or duplicate or involve any direction of the activities of established agencies." But Rockefeller, along with the rest of official Washington, knew better than to put much stock in such assurances. Much the same presidential bromides had accompanied the creation of his own agency. It was all part of what

Stimson tartly described as "the topsy-turvy, upside-down system of poor administration with which Mr. Roosevelt runs the government."

Sensing the potential for one more round of intramural feuds, Rockefeller turned again to his most trusted ally, Anna Rosenberg. He phoned her on Monday, July 14, the very day Donovan's appointment was announced. It so happened that Rosenberg was already on the case: she had spoken with FDR on Friday and contacted Donovan the day after to let him know that the President agreed with her that there was no need to duplicate CIAA efforts. The colonel's response was to talk vaguely about the need for "a central policy" for information.

Rosenberg suggested a dinner meeting at Foxhall Road to thrash the situation out, and there she brokered a gentleman's agreement between the two coordinators. Donovan would have the whole world for his bailiwick, except for Latin America, where Rockefeller would be the sole channel for news, information, and propaganda. Relations from that evening on seemed amicable enough; when Rockefeller proceeded with his plans for CIAA "coordination committees" of American businessmen in important Latin American cities, he consulted Donovan, who joined Sumner Welles in assenting to the plan.

It was while Rockefeller was off on a late-summer hunting trip in the Yukon that Donovan began making his move. He invited several top CIAA officials, along with Duggan of State, over to his office and indicated that all international broadcasting would henceforth be funneled through his agency. Turning to Duggan, he asked, "Whom do I deal with on Latin American problems? I guess I deal with you, don't I?" To which Duggan replied, "No, I think you deal both with us and the coordinator's office." Donovan also started to backtrack on the coordination committees, suggesting that his office should have "the most important position" in regard to them.

The alarms set off by this meeting prompted Carl Spaeth (who had not yet moved to the Economic Defense Board) to seek a one-on-one encounter with the colonel. Once again, Donovan executed a deft about-face. Asked about the "misunderstandings" between his organization and the CIAA, Donovan blamed them on lower-level people. There was never any question, he said, that the CIAA bore the primary responsibility for Latin America. All he wanted was a closer liaison between Rockefeller's people and his own on the broadcasting front, and he invited the CIAA to install one of its people in his New York office, which was handling the radio work. "That way," he said, "it will be a joint undertaking."

Looking over Spaeth's memo of the meeting upon his return, Rockefeller was satisfied a confrontation had been headed off. "Fine," he scribbled across the top. "A grand job."

A little more than a month later, however, the uneasy alliance between the two agencies once again began to unravel. Donovan's radio people were alarmed by the rapid buildup of the CIAA pressroom; Jamieson told them he had lined up twenty-five newspapermen who were ready to go to work in shifts. They were also upset about the CIAA's independent negotiations with the shortwave stations, as well as with CBS and NBC, which were going on at the same time as Donovan approaches to the broadcasters. While Donovan appealed to the broadcasters' patriotism, Rockefeller appealed to their greed, offering them cash subsidies to carry CIAA programming.

"It won't work," Donovan's top radio man, Joseph Barnes, warned his chief. "We cannot conduct psychological warfare that way, without unification of command, in the first place, and unification of execution, in the second." The COI people, caught up in their martial visions of the war to come, viewed themselves as the sentinels of democracy and the CIAA as a bunch of second-rate do-gooders who were getting in the way.

At last, on October 7, Donovan took the matter up with Rockefeller. Both men dug in their heels. The confrontation convinced Rockefeller that the gentleman's agreement would soon disintegrate and that only a formal, written pact would keep Donovan at bay. John Lockwood got busy preparing drafts, but an edgy Rockefeller rejected one version after another as inadequate. Finally, after laboring all morning long on Friday, October 10, he hurried out the door, document in hand, bound for Pennsylvania Avenue.

His first stop was Sumner Welles's office. The State Department had taken a characteristically frosty view of Donovan's personal diplomacy and empire building. Compared to Donovan, Nelson Rockefeller—particularly the Nelson Rockefeller who was now scrupulously adhering to State's demands—was a veritable soul mate. Welles, accordingly, was delighted to back Rockefeller in the looming power struggle. He read over the draft and pronounced himself "more than happy to be of any service which you may feel desirable."

Rockefeller then went across the street to the White House to enlist another powerful ally, budget director Harold Smith. The budget office was increasingly leery of Donovan's operation, regarding it as a contentious, power-grabbing agency with an already excessive ($10 million) appetite for funds. The CIAA, on the other hand, was "doing a good job and we saw no reason to disturb it," recalled Smith's deputy, Bernard Gladieux. Although Smith did not commit himself immediately, it was evident that he, too, was in Rockefeller's corner.

At 9:15 Saturday morning, as Rockefeller sat by his office phone waiting to hear definitively from Smith, a hand-delivered letter arrived on his desk. It was from Bill Donovan, and dated October 9—two days earlier. In the bluntest possible language, Donovan asserted his control of all the government's international broadcasts, including the Latin American programming.

"I accept your statement that you are acting for the State Department in South America," Donovan cuttingly informed Rockefeller, "and that your plan of independent operation has met with the approval of the President. However, no such directive has been sent to me by the President, and until issued, I must continue to meet my obligation in the manner he has directed."

Donovan, the savvy old Wall Street lawyer, had trumped his younger counterpart. Not only had he beaten Rockefeller to the bureaucratic punch but he had baldly asserted presidential authority for his position—and, as well, snidely cast doubt on Rockefeller's own authority.

Just why Donovan could be so confident about his position became clear early the next week, when Rockefeller charged into the colonel's office in the State Department building. Sitting there with Donovan was the Coordinator of Information's new liaison officer: James Roosevelt, FDR's eldest son.

"Jimmy," the COI boss casually confided, had taken the opportunity on Saturday, while cruising aboard the presidential yacht, to let his father see Donovan's letter. "Of course," Donovan assured Rockefeller, "I wouldn't go to the President without you, but Jimmy thought he ought to show this to his father. And Jimmy has a message from his father."

A livid Rockefeller cut Donovan short. "I want to get this clear on policy," he fumed. "Is Jimmy here as his father's son or is he working for you? Because if he's working for you, I'd rather not deal with the office boy."

Ignoring the salvo, Donovan suggested that perhaps he ought to excuse himself and leave young Roosevelt and Rockefeller alone for a while. But Rockefeller would have none of that. "If Jimmy has a message from his father," he said, "and is working for you as you say, I want you to be here. There's enough confusion without your getting one message and my getting another." Then, pulling out a memo that summarized his position, he turned to Roosevelt. "Before you tell me what your father says, Jimmy, please read this letter. When you talked to your father did you tell him this side?" Roosevelt admitted he hadn't. "Then his answer is to only one side of the picture," Rockefeller said. "All right, go ahead and tell me his message."

The "message" was the gospel according to Bill Donovan; the President confirmed the Coordinator of Information's supremacy, as set out in Donovan's letter. Rockefeller refused to believe it. He wanted to hear the words from FDR himself, and suggested they arrange an immediate meeting with the chief executive. Young Roosevelt frowned. "No," he said, "Father's too busy to be bothered with this sort of thing. Why don't we turn it over to Judge Rosenman and let him settle the issue?" Presidential adviser and speechwriter Samuel Rosenman was by then an old hand at mediating such intramural disputes. Rockefeller, who knew Rosenman from the Lincoln School wars, agreed. "Fine," he said. "You go ahead with the arrangements if that's the way you want it, and I'll be at the meeting."

Rockefeller, though, hadn't the slightest intention of leaving the matter in Rosenman's hands. No sooner had he departed Donovan's office than he began working all his high-level contacts: Harry Hopkins, Sumner Welles, Harold Smith, Henry Wallace.

"You know," said Wallace, "what you ought to do is use the same technique Welles has used on both you and me with the President: give him something that's ready to be signed."

"You mean like this?" said Rockefeller, sliding a piece of paper from his jacket pocket.

It was a memorandum from the President to the Coordinator of Information—a memorandum that Rockefeller and his staff had just drafted. "It appears that some question has been raised as to the relation of your information and short-wave broacasting work to that of Nelson Rockefeller's organization," the memo began. "I continue to believe that the requirements of our program in the hemisphere are quite different from those of our programs to Europe and the Far East."

The memorandum would settle the matter once and for all in Rockefeller's favor. Now all he had to do was get FDR to sign it.

It was time, once again, to ring up Anna Rosenberg.

So while savvy Bill Donovan was busy preparing for a climactic meeting the following Sunday with Sam Rosenman, shipping documents to the judge's New York office, Anna Rosenberg was phoning Pa Watson for an immediate appointment with FDR.

Suspecting what was coming, Roosevelt at first refused to see her. But denying Rosenberg on one of her tears was like denying a buzz saw, and on Wednesday, October 15, she was ushered into the President's office. Methodically and emphatically, Rosenberg laid out Rockefeller's case, adding that both Harold Smith and Sumner Welles were in accord with it. FDR laughed. "You don't have to tell me about Welles," he said. "After all the trouble I've had with Nelson and Welles, now Welles is his strongest advocate in Washington!"

Rosenberg pulled out the memorandum. The President looked it over, scribbled in some minor changes, and signed it. Whatever the "message" he had sent to his son was, he was now finally and definitively coming out on Nelson Rockefeller's side.

When a copy of the signed memo landed on Bill Donovan's desk, the normally imperturbable colonel exploded. He raged at Jimmy Roosevelt, and called in another of his well-connected aides, playwright Robert Sherwood, an intimate of both FDR and Hopkins. Sherwood was ordered to write a long letter complaining about how impossible the situation was. Then, in a last-ditch effort to salvage his position, Donovan sent Sherwood's letter and a plaintive memo of his own to FDR. But the President had had enough of the controversy, and told his budget director to work out the bureaucratic niceties.

The colonel, the hero of St.-Mihiel and the Argonne, had been outflanked and outmaneuvered by the Coordinator of Inter-American Affairs.

The outbreak of war on December 7, 1941, did not stop the frenetic power jockeying within the Roosevelt administration. It merely raised the stakes.

In January 1942 delegates from the twenty-one American republics met in Rio to forge a unified position toward the Axis. After Pearl Harbor only nine Latin American countries had joined the United States in declaring war; another seven (including Mexico and Venezuela) had severed relations with the Axis powers, but stopped short of going to war. The Rio conference represented an all-out U.S. effort to rally its neighbors to its side.

The push for unity, however, was waylaid by the adamant refusal of Argentina and Chile—both still harboring influential pro-Nazi factions—to break with the Axis. Brazilian dictator Vargas, fearing a backlash by his fascist-leaning military, made it known that he would not go along with any resolution that Argentina opposed. Desperate not to walk away from the conference empty-handed, Sumner Welles, who headed the U.S. delegation, accepted a watered-down Argentinian proposal that preserved each nation's freedom of action. Welles's top aides were appalled ("Our moral leadership at the conference had been lost," Berle noted afterward), and Cordell Hull was furious. Phoning Welles from Washington, he subjected his deputy to a violent tongue-lashing punctuated with some of his choicest Tennessee expletives. "It is obvious," Berle wrote in his diary, "that now there is a breach between the Secretary and Sumner which will never be healed."

The breach involved more than just the tempestuous personal relations between the two men. It was the first manifestation of the fundamental dichotomy in the U.S. posture toward Latin America: the good-neighborly desire for inter-American harmony versus the defensive demands of total war. In principle, as Rockefeller and others had been stressing, the two aims were not contradictory. But in practice they were, as long as Argentina and Chile had pro-Nazi bents and others such as Brazil were ambivalent. The rift at the Rio conference would be played out again and again in the years to come, not just by Welles and Hull but also, momentously, by Nelson Rockefeller.

For the time being, though, Rockefeller had no problem subordinating his agency's mission to the war effort.

Mindful that some might regard the CIAA's work as peripheral, he delivered a pep talk to his top staffers three days after Pearl Harbor. They were in the "first line of defense," he told them; nothing was more important, from the defense point of view, than the job they were doing.

He framed his charge in military metaphors, as in this testimony before a House committee: "The other American republics are a vital flank of the United States. . . . This country must have confirmed allies defending that flank. . . . The other American republics are also a vital source of the materials of war. We must have confirmed allies who will produce those materials and who will help us make the weapons of modern warfare."

Rockefeller seized every opportunity to mobilize his agency in support of U.S. military objectives. One such opportunity came in November 1942, with the Allied invasion of North Africa, the armed forces' first major campaign on the other side of the Atlantic. Rockefeller was given an advance peek at the invasion plans, so that he could get a head start on choreographing a propaganda blitz. As soon as the invasion was launched, the CIAA began bombarding Latin America with news of the Allied progress and explications of the U.S. strategy. The local coordinating committees were instructed to report to Washington on local reaction, to solicit endorsements from leading Latin American figures, and to hunt for favorable newspaper editorials that could be distributed throughout the hemisphere. Reams of telegrams were sent to U.S. embassies in the region, advising them on how to trumpet the invasion. "I hate to think how many thousands of dollars were spent just on the telegrams to Cuba," recalled Spruille Braden, who had just been transferred there.

If these displays of patriotic zeal weren't enough, Rockefeller was ready to go even further.

On August 13, 1942, he sat down to lunch with President Roosevelt. "I'd like your advice on a personal matter," Rockefeller began. "I'm prepared to go into the Army now or at any time in the future—unless, as commander-in-chief, you want me to continue with my present work."

Roosevelt waved the offer aside as if it was a housefly alighting on his vichyssoise. "*I'll* let you know when I want you to go into the Army," he said, "and that will only be if there's some special job for which your experience and background will especially qualify you. In the meantime, I want you to stay right where you are. There is no one else who can undertake the work you are doing."

Roosevelt went on to recollect how, as Assistant Secretary of the Navy in the last war, he had gone to President Wilson with a similar offer and had received the same response.

And with that—a heartening reminder, from the lips of Franklin Roosevelt himself, of his indispensability to the war effort—the question of Nelson Rockefeller's military service was closed for good.

Sixteen

No Limits

"Is it wise for you to permit the recent emphasis given to your name?" one of Rockefeller's staff advisers wrote him in February 1942. "The job you have done and will do does not need emphasis—it speaks for itself. Too frequent use of your name in national publicity could be dangerous to the program and to you personally."

This advice Rockefeller blithely ignored.

Never one to shirk the limelight, he positively basked in it now that his agency had come into its own. He could, of course, justify his press clippings by pointing out that they focused public attention not just on himself but on Latin America. Still, there was no mistaking the unabashed glee with which he trumpeted the CIAA's accomplishments. The potential hazards of self-promotion—the possibility that it could yield further ammunition for his jealous rivals—seem never to have given him a moment's pause.

The apex came in April 1942, when *Life* featured Rockefeller on its cover and *The New Yorker* published a two-part profile of him. The *Life* cover photo caught the coordinator in all his youthful exuberance: eyes sparkling, smile toothy and expansive. He was the very embodiment of the energy and bravado with which an aroused, muscular America was going to war. As Rockefeller told *The New Yorker,* "I'm optimistic about South America, but you'll have to qualify that by saying I'm optimistic about everything."

Both magazines appraised his performance, mostly positively. "It now appears that Rockefeller has accomplished more in a year and a half than Herr Goebbels did in a decade," wrote *Life,* which also singled out the CIAA's success at navigating the bureaucratic minefield. "By no means the least amazing thing about Rockefeller's extraordinary organization," it said, "is the skill, directly traceable to its top man, with which it has integrated its top job with that of its collaborators."

But it was the man, not the institution, that truly captivated the publications. *The New Yorker* described him as "a wavy-haired, handsome, idealistic young man who inspires considerable hero worship in his staff." At the same time, he is "impetuous, has no patience with subtlety, and is used to acting with the directness which is instinctive in a man accustomed to power." *Life* cited his "extraordinary capacity for learning from experience and using his connections to the best advantage." Both articles told his life story in extensive (and sometimes inaccurate) detail.

Despite some reservations (*Life,* describing Rockefeller's appetite for publicity, noted that in his press releases "the lead refrain 'Nelson A. Rockefeller, Coordinator of Inter-American Affairs, announced today,' recurs so frequently as to be reminiscent of *'Mrs. Otis Regrets'* "), both portraits were upbeat. Whatever mistakes he had made in his young life were the results of his impetuousness and his serene self-confidence. "He has no interior tension," a friend was quoted as saying. "His temperament is very much like FDR's."

Above all, the reader was left with the impression that Rockefeller was a comer. "In view of the undeniable success attained by his agency, it seems likely to outlast the war and go on to bigger things," *Life* predicted. "Its founder is a good bet to do so also."

It may have been purely a coincidence, but those admiring articles just happened to have been published at a time when Nelson Rockefeller was embroiled in still another jurisdictional battle—this one even more menacing than the Bill Donovan power grab.

The source of the trouble was yet another new ingredient in the Roosevelt alphabet soup, the Office of War Information. The OWI was an attempt by Roosevelt and his budget director to come to grips with the tangle of wartime information agencies. Not only was there the CIAA and the COI, but, since late October, also something called the Office of Facts and Figures, which was supposed to oversee the dissemination of war information to the American public. (The OFF was headed by that literary jack-of-all-trades Archibald MacLeish, poet, magazine writer, and former Librarian of Congress.) Sensing that it was all getting out of hand, the budget office came up in early March 1942 with the idea of the OWI, which would centralize all the government's information activities.

Thus, for the second time in six months, Rockefeller was faced with a grave threat to his agency. Not only did he stand to lose his radio operation, but the rest of his propaganda base as well: the moviemaking, the newsreels, the newspaper feature service, and *En Guardia.* Everything would be swallowed up by the OWI.

Making the threat even more imposing was the fact that presidential confidants Sam Rosenman and Robert Sherwood were ardent backers of the consolidation (Sherwood, perhaps, because he saw himself running the new agency). Most ominous of all was the support of budget chief Harold Smith; he had been in Rockefeller's corner in the battle with Donovan, but wouldn't be this time.

Rockefeller, in fact, almost lost the battle before he knew what was happening. Adroit insiders that they were, Rosenman and Smith stealthily prepared an executive order for FDR's signature and scheduled an appointment to see him on Saturday afternoon, March 7. Rockefeller first heard of the plan earlier that day—and only because a sympathetic budget staffer, Bernard Gladieux, tipped him off. After racing over to the budget office to get a copy of the order from Gladieux, Rockefeller summoned his top aides for an urgent caucus.

"I saw the order that's been drafted and Harold Smith is taking it to the President this afternoon," he told them. "If it goes through, we might as well close up."

A pall descended on the room. Then Frank Jamieson spoke up. Who, he wondered, was on the President's schedule before Smith? A quick call to the White House yielded the information that Henry Wallace was due to have lunch with Roosevelt. Rockefeller turned to his Bolivian counselor, Enrique de Lozada, and told him to hurry to Wallace's Senate office. De Lozada arrived just as the Vice President was leaving for the White House. The CIAA man asked Wallace if he might ride over with him. As their taxicab plodded through midday Pennsylvania Avenue traffic, de Lozada laid out the situation. Wallace said he would do what he could.

Back at the office, meanwhile, Rockefeller was drafting an urgent note to the keeper of the Oval Office gate, Pa Watson, asking to see the President immediately about the information order. He cast the matter in the direst terms: "While I recognize that there is a need for propaganda directives by a central agency, the removal of this Office from operations can only be construed by me as indicating that the President has changed his concept of this work and that my job is ended."

He signed the letter and raced over to the State Department to seek the aid of another key ally, Sumner Welles. The undersecretary agreed to accompany Rockefeller to the White House. There, Welles was ushered in to see the President while Rockefeller was shunted off to meet with Rosenman and Smith. Told by them that the decision to consolidate the agencies was "final," Rockefeller exploded. "If this decision sticks," he yelled, "I'll get out."

As it turned out, his theatrics were unnecessary; nothing was final. Thanks to the last-minute entreaties of Wallace and Welles, Roosevelt decided to put off his decision on the order.

The tussle went on for three more months. Ultimately, cabinet members were dragged in: Hull to side with Rockefeller, and Attorney General Francis Biddle to side with Rosenman and Smith. For a while, Rockefeller found himself aligned with Bill Donovan, who was also fighting the consolidation, once it was clear that he would not be named to head the new agency.

On June 13, 1942, the President signed the executive order creating the Office of War Information. MacLeish's Office of Facts and Figures was absorbed into the new agency. So were Bill Donovan's propaganda operations; his covert activities, however, remained intact, and would be reconstituted, under Donovan's leadership, in the new Office of Strategic Services, the country's first full-time spy agency.

Only the CIAA remained beyond the order's reach.

As Rockefeller later told Henry Wallace, "A coordinator is someone who can keep all the balls in the air without losing his own."

As if Rockefeller hadn't reason enough to cling so tenaciously to his information role, events of those first few months of 1942 offered him an added inducement. His agency's much-touted merger with Henry Wallace's Board of Economic Warfare (the former Economic Defense Board) was disintegrating after a run of less than half a year. All his vital economic functions—the coordination of U.S. purchases of key Latin American commodities, the freeing up of U.S. exports to the south—were slipping away from him as a result. And the reason was an abrupt and wrenching deterioration in Rockefeller's relationship with his former top deputy, Carl Spaeth.

Spaeth had moved over to the BEW, as head of its Americas division, in what seemed at first like a classic Trojan horse maneuver. While nominally a BEW official, he would in fact represent the CIAA's interests from within the new agency. The organization charts said he reported to both BEW executive director Milo Perkins and to Rockefeller. But few in the executive branch had any illusions about where his true loyalties lay.

When Spaeth arrived at the BEW, however, he found the situation was hardly as clear-cut as all that. Expecting direction from either Rockefeller or Perkins, he got none from either boss. "As it turned out," recalls Paul Nitze, who joined Spaeth in the move to BEW, "we never, ever got any guidance from the two of them on any subject whatsoever. And so Carl and I decided the thing to do was to make all these decisions on our own."

"Everything was fine for a while," continues Nitze. "And then Nelson was suddenly told by somebody that we were running it without specific guidance from him. And he blew his top. He accused us of arrogating to ourselves his authority, which we had. I've never seen anybody so angry."

As far as Rockefeller was concerned, his onetime aide was trying to create a little empire of his own, independent of both the CIAA and the BEW. (As a past master of such plots himself, Rockefeller was in a position to know.) And so, in early March, the coordinator launched a campaign aimed at putting

Spaeth out of business by dissolving the merger. Rockefeller well knew that his move was self-defeating: the BEW would retain authority over such pivotal areas as export controls and commodities purchases, and by pulling out of the merger he was sacrificing his best chance to influence those areas. But this course seemed preferable to the alternative of watching them slip out of his grasp anyway, via Spaeth's machinations.

By the end of the month Rockefeller could announce to his staff that the joint BEW-CIAA operation was terminated due to "certain differences in emphasis." Spaeth, he told them, was resigning from both agencies. Oddly, in view of the hard feelings involved, Rockefeller had offered to take Spaeth back as an assistant coordinator who would serve as a liaison with the BEW, among other agencies. But Spaeth, who knew a demotion when he saw one, spurned the offer.

A week later, Rockefeller sent Spaeth a check for $2,500, "which completes my obligation covered in our verbal agreement when you resigned from Yale University to go to Venezuela, assuring you of a minimum salary of $14,000 a year." Whatever their differences, Rockefeller intended to stand by the commitments he had made when he first lured Spaeth to come to work for him.

His dealings, and his differences, with Carl Spaeth, however, were far from over. Spaeth was named U.S. delegate to the Emergency Advisory Committee for Political Defense, an inter-American body created at the January Rio conference. From his new office in Montevideo, Uruguay, he began mapping out ambitious plans to use the CPD to combat Axis propaganda in the hemisphere. In early June he proposed to his superiors at the State Department that he be allowed to borrow CIAA personnel to work on the project.

What Spaeth was planning, of course, ran head-on into what the CIAA itself was doing in the propaganda field; what's more, he had the temerity to suggest enlisting CIAA people to handle the work for him. And if all that wasn't sufficient to bring Rockefeller to the boiling point, Spaeth sought to justify his undertaking by skewering the CIAA's propaganda efforts in a memo to the State. The CIAA program, he said, "has left much to be desired. . . . There is an excess of wishful optimism."

Spaeth's acid analysis enraged Rockefeller as few such memos had ever done. He demanded an immediate meeting with Welles and Duggan, advising the latter that "in my opinion, the memo is superficial and evidences a fundamental lack of knowledge and understanding not only of the program of this Office itself but the effect which it has had on the other countries." He went even further when he saw Welles, complaining that Spaeth was overly ambitious, was unable to handle people, and lacked tact.

At the end of June, Spaeth returned to Washington for consultation, and on June 30 met with Rockefeller and his associates. The session did not go well. The next day, Spaeth wrote his former boss that "a review of our unpleasant meeting of yesterday satisfies me that it would not be helpful to you or your office for me to meet with your directing group, today or at any other time." Rockefeller gave Spaeth no quarter over the next several months, fighting Spaeth's idea every inch of the way until it died a slow bureaucratic death.

Yet for all that, some personal bond between the two men remained. When Spaeth's son Grant became gravely ill in Montevideo the following January, Rockefeller consulted top Washington physicians and cabled their advice to Spaeth—advice that greatly helped the boy's recovery and for which Spaeth was profoundly grateful.

But on another level, the political level, Rockefeller behaved quite differently. Two years later, when Rockefeller was appointed an Assistant Secretary of State, he took note of the fact that Spaeth was still in the State Department—and promptly fired him. "I thought that was carrying a feeling that one of your subordinates had been disloyal to an extraordinary length," remarks Nitze, who remained friendly with Spaeth through that period.

To some, including Nitze, what Rockefeller did was an act of supreme vindictiveness. That Rockefeller rarely appeared to harbor grudges—his attitude, when crossed, was to simply shrug his shoulders and get on with the job—made his action in Spaeth's case even more extraordinary.

But set in the context of Rockefeller's relationship with his top advisers, what happened to Carl Spaeth seems less surprising; seems, in fact, almost inevitable. Between Rockefeller and his key aides, a princely compact existed: never set in writing, hardly ever spoken of, but understood by all parties just the same. Rockefeller swept them up into his world, a world of heady challenges and infinite possibilities; assured their financial comfort and security; bonded their careers. To Wally Harrison, he offered the chance to "work with great people and do beautiful buildings"; to Lockwood and Jamieson and others, the promise was equally dazzling. In exchange for all this, Rockefeller expected nothing more, and nothing less, than loyalty: utter, absolute, and complete.

Such loyalty took its personal toll. Lockwood suffered from acute stomach pain, and spent the whole of each Sunday in bed, resting his gnawing insides for the pressure-packed week to come. Jamieson chain-smoked, the spent butts forming little hillocks in the ashtray before him. Yet whatever the cost, they stood by their stations, secure in the knowledge that if they kept their end of the bargain, Rockefeller would keep his.

Spaeth, however, had breached the compact, and there was but one fitting penalty: exile from the kingdom.

Shorn of its economic power by the dissolution of the BEW merger, the CIAA in the early months of 1942 was caught up in an identity crisis. The coordinator's adroitness in the power game had preserved its role in the information and propaganda business, but this role was not nearly enough for

Rockefeller, "the eager beaver to end all eager beavers," as Tennessee Valley Authority chairman David Lilienthal labeled him. Poring over all the possibilities landing on his desk, he engaged in a single-minded pursuit of new missions and new mandates for the CIAA. No idea was too off-the-wall, no brainstorm was too far-fetched.

One day he heard about a strange scheme some Commerce Department officials had cooked up for the construction of wooden sailing vessels. Seizing upon this as the perfect solution to the Latin shipping gridlock, Rockefeller began lobbying his connections in support of the idea. Before the Commerce people knew what hit them, it was a CIAA plan.

Rockefeller talked of building some one hundred boats in Latin American shipyards. Because they would be made of wood, they would not use up vital metal supplies; because they would be built locally, they would give a boost to Latin economies. The vessels, he suggested, could haul up to one million tons of cargo a year. Soon, what had seemed a harebrained notion was becoming a fait accompli, thanks to Rockefeller's ardent salesmanship. Sumner Welles signed off on it, and so did Navy Secretary Frank Knox. Most important of all, Jesse Jones gave his assent; it was from Jones's Reconstruction Finance Corporation that Rockefeller intended to get the $7 million to finance the shipbuilding.

And, as it happened, no idea could have been better calculated to capture the imagination of the chief executive. A lifelong yachtsman with a fancy for building toy sailboats, FDR was readily receptive to any and all nautical ventures. Not only did he endorse Rockefeller's plan, but he peppered him with suggestions on such matters as the best means for cleaning and overhauling the vessels. If anything, the President's dreams were even more grandiose than Rockefeller's; Roosevelt envisioned a great wooden armada plying the waters of the south.

And so, in the summer of 1942, with his $7 million in hand, Nelson Rockefeller set out to build his fleet. It did not take long for reality to set in. Latin American shipyards shunned the program after they found out that only a few critical components could be imported from the United States. Sail power alone was impractical, and the designs were altered to call for diesel engines. Even the goal of all-wood construction was abandoned in favor of an easier composite technique.

In the end, just two boats were contracted for, and only one small vessel was actually completed. In July 1943, exactly one year after it was launched, Nelson Rockefeller's shipbuilding program was officially scuttled.

By that time, however, he had other conceptions perking away. More importantly, he had found an ingenious mechanism to make them happen: the government corporation, à la Jesse Jones, the wily old Texas banker. Jones had not invented the device (his Reconstruction Finance Corporation was actually a creation of the Hoover administration), but he had learned to manipulate it with consummate mastery. With the outbreak of war Jones created and controlled a veritable corporate empire (the Defense Plant Corporation, the Defense Supplies Corporation, the Metals Reserve Company, to name just a few), spending billions of federal dollars.

The key advantage of the corporate form, as Jones's RFC had demonstrated, was its freedom: though nominally a U.S. government entity, a corporation was exempt from most government strictures, including the civil service code. The corporation, therefore, could enter into contracts, disburse funds, purchase supplies, and hire workers without worrying about the plethora of wartime regulations, audits, quotas, and the like. Equally advantageous, from the standpoint of the never-ending administration power struggles, was the inherent insularity of the corporation: pristine and self-contained, it was virtually immune to the encroachment of governmental rivals.

But as impervious as the corporate form was, Rockefeller managed to harden its carapace even further. Arguing that his corporations would need more freedom if they were to operate in Latin America, he persuaded the President to insert a little-noticed clause into the Appropriations Act of July 1942—a clause that allowed the coordinator's corporations to act "without regard to the provisions of law regulating the expenditure, accounting for and audit of government funds." The only window into the corporations would be annual reports Rockefeller was required to submit to the President. Thus, Rockefeller shielded his corporations from any accountability—save to himself and, once a year, to the President. It was a trick that not even Jesse Jones had been able to pull off.

With such freedom to maneuver, Rockefeller could engage in any number of new projects. And he moved with alacrity to do just that. Not only did Rockefeller use a corporation, the Inter-American Navigation Corporation, to build his wooden boats, but he also used one—with far more success—to revamp the whole Mexican railway system.

Alerted by his coordination committee in Mexico in early 1942 to the dilapidated condition of the country's railroads, he sent his old friend Walter Douglas (the former president of the Southern Pacific of Mexico) to investigate. Douglas came back with a harrowing report of tottering bridges, wheezing locomotives, and rickety track. The situation was fraught with serious security implications for the United States, since Mexico had agreed to sell the United States its entire exportable surplus of such critical war materials as zinc, lead, tin, and copper. Without a well-functioning railroad system, those materials would never be delivered.

After further surveys confirmed Douglas' findings, Rockefeller decided to act. In June 1943 he set up the Institute of Inter-American Transportation, a Delaware corporation whose avowed purpose was to assist in all means of transportation in the Western Hemisphere. In fact, its sole mission was to rehabilitate the Mexican railways—with the help of $7.5 million funneled into the corporation from the President's emergency fund. Deploying a team of sixty-four technicians, the corporation set into motion a complete overhaul of the railroad.

And then there was Prencinradio. Incorporated in July 1942, Prencinradio was, in form at least, similar to the other entities Rockefeller was establishing. It was a Delaware corporation, wholly owned by the U.S. government, with officers who were all CIAA employees. But in Prencinradio's case, there was a difference: its existence was a secret, known only to a handful of top CIAA and State Department officials.

The reason for the secrecy was this: Prencinradio was to be a conduit for "confidential" CIAA investment in Latin American media, both new and existing. The corporate format, in this case, was designed to camouflage the CIAA involvement.

Through Prencinradio, Rockefeller's campaign to influence hemisphere opinion was taking a new, more invasive tack. And its potential scope could be denoted from the new corporation's name, a contraction of *prensa* (press), *cinema,* and *radio.*

Prencinradio's initial target was the Mexican motion picture industry. The corporation provided the country's two leading studios with new motion picture equipment (via a convoluted arrangement with the Bank of Mexico to hide the source of this largesse), financed films "deemed necessary to the war effort and hemispheric solidarity," and sent down Hollywood directors and technicians to assist.

Ultimately, Prencinradio's impact on the Latin American media—except for some Mexican moviemakers—would prove to be insignificant. (Its principal impact on the coordinator's office was to embarrass it, when *The Wall Street Journal* uncovered the secret operation in May 1944.)

Its fate, however, was of little moment, for by the time Prencinradio got underway Rockefeller was focusing on a far grander design: a corporation that would offer him his most glorious raison d'être yet.

Its genesis dated back to those final tense months before America at last entered the war. Looking for a way to involve the CIAA in the defense buildup, Rockefeller had sent over to the War Department a plan for a mammoth $100 million public works program in Latin America aimed at supporting the potential U.S. military presence there. Housing, hospitals, roads, and sanitation and water supply systems would be built at "strategic and focal points."

After Pearl Harbor, Rockefeller had moved swiftly to revive his idea. Summoning his chart designers, he put together a black book that showed, through the ingenious use of transparent overlays, the health, sanitation, and food needs of the areas where the United States would locate its bases. Then, black book in hand, he headed over to the White House on December 29 to present Harry Hopkins with what Rockefeller called his "Preparedness Program for the Americas."

The program was ambitious, involving "effective disease control, water supply and sewage, hospitalization, properly trained sanitary engineers, doctors and nurses, essential food supplies." It was also very, very expensive: Rockefeller estimated total costs of $150 million, with an initial U.S. outlay of $25 million. To sell it, Rockefeller continued to frame the program as a military measure, emphasizing "the vital importance of adequate health defense."

Hidden beneath this salubrious agenda was another, somewhat more sinister one. Fascinated as ever by covert activity, Rockefeller pointed out to Hopkins the "intelligence" applications of his program. It presented, he said, "an unusual opportunity for American military personnel to get into the strategic areas of the American hemisphere" as well as an opportunity "for representatives of the United States to enter into close relations with the authorities of the countries involved . . . to take steps necessary to eliminate political opposition."

The perpetually ailing Hopkins was still in bed when Rockefeller arrived that morning. Sitting up, he studied the memo and the charts, heard Rockefeller's pitch, and then swung his feet off the bed and into a pair of slippers. He wanted to talk it over with the Boss, who was in his room next door.

Ten minutes later, he returned. "Okay," Hopkins said, "the President will make an initial allocation of $25 million."

Rockefeller's next move was to persuade Sumner Welles to introduce a resolution at the upcoming Rio conference calling for inter-American cooperation in improving health, sanitation, and food supplies. With that resolution in hand, no one could accuse the United States of unilaterally barging into other nations' domestic affairs. Meanwhile, Rockefeller also called on George Marshall, to get the Army to designate the strategic areas upon which the program would focus—and to talk about bringing a military man in to head the CIAA project. The officer Rockefeller had in mind was Colonel George Dunham, a fifty-four-year-old veteran of the Army Medical Corps and an expert on tropical diseases.

Dunham, however, would not actually work for the coordinator's office. Instead, he would be employed by a new entity, the Institute of Inter-American Affairs—yet another of Rockefeller's corporations.

No sooner had the institute got going than Rockefeller learned that one of the roles he had touted would be stripped from it. Sumner Welles had heard about the coordinator's enthusiastic suggestion that his health institute serve as an intelligence cover, and he was not amused. In March 1942 he sent Rockefeller a terse warning: "If any hint should arise in the minds of the public or of the government authorities of the other American republics that our general program of cooperation was being used as a cloak for intelligence activities, this whole program would be seriously jeopardized. . . . With this background I suggest to you that as a general policy your Office decline to entertain any proposal which may be brought forward for using the personnel connected with your Office in political, military or naval intelligence activities."

Whatever the institute's future role would be, it would not be in the spy business.

During the program's first few months, Rockefeller was having a harder and harder time arguing that a program that grappled with Latin America's intractable health and nutrition problems had some specific military objective—particularly as it became increasingly apparent that the U.S. military presence in the region would be relatively minor. He resorted to propaganda themes, claiming that his health effort would refute the charges of Axis agents that "the friendship of the United States is a matter of mere words, unsupported by deeds."

It fell to Henry Wallace, mystic and guru, to show Rockefeller a way out of his dilemma. He sat down with the young coordinator and sketched out for him, as the Vice President would later recall, "the problem of the billion and a third people located in Latin America, the Middle East, Eastern Asia, and Africa which [sic] live on the land and cannot read or write. . . . I said that the solution of this problem required a new missionary spirit, a spirit which should appeal both to church people and to business men. Nelson Rockefeller seemed to respond."

Wallace's clarion call, indeed, fell on very receptive ears. Exactly this sort of "new missionary spirit" had infused his family's charitable efforts over the decades, principally through the work of the Rockefeller Foundation. The foundation's international health division was a ubiquitous presence in public health in the developing world, doing battle against a host of virulent diseases: yellow fever, tuberculosis, malaria, typhus. Its China Medical Board had trained a whole generation of Chinese doctors. And Rockefeller himself had long been caught up in this spirit. There were glimmers of it on his honeymoon trip, with its tour of leper colonies and medical facilities, and there were larger intimations of it later in his pressuring of Creole Petroleum to improve its workers' sorry living conditions.

The mission of his new institute—*his* mission—was now clear: to aid the U.S. war effort, yes, but to go far beyond that and help the millions who, in his words, "know only poverty and hardship, without security or even a sufficient food supply." It would be the ultimate expression of the Good Neighbor Policy.

Down in Latin America, expectations of what Rockefeller would accomplish ran high—perhaps too high. In September 1942 he embarked on a whirlwind tour of the region. There were meetings with Presidents, speeches to congresses, visits to schools, factories, and national shrines. (There was also a near-disaster, when Rockefeller's plane crashed in a ditch upon landing at Pôrto Alegre on the southern coast of Brazil. He and his companions managed to walk away unhurt.)

At every stop he was showered with public acclaim—and appeals for aid. In Quito, Ecuador, Rockefeller was shown a large parcel of land made available to a school, and was given a large hint that cash was needed to acquire the property. (He told his hosts he would take it under consideration.) In Panama, President Ricardo Adolfo de la Guardia spoke to Rockefeller about establishing a school of sanitary engineering at the University of Panama. De la Guardia came away from the meeting with the impression that the coordinator would provide financial support, and plans for the school proceeded. Six months later, the Panamanians were incensed to learn that Rockefeller had quietly backed away from the project.

But if some hopes were dashed, many more were fulfilled. By early 1943 the institute was operating in fourteen countries: battling malaria, building hospitals, training doctors, constructing sewers. Floating dispensaries to distribute antimalarial drugs were traversing the Amazon River and its many tributaries. Work was beginning on a new water supply system for Chimbote, in northern Peru, and new sewers in Quito, Ecuador. In Asunción, the capital of Paraguay, where diseases ranging from hookworm to leprosy were rampant, plans were laid for a vast expansion of the health-care system.

The institute was also busy tackling a longer-term health threat: the chronic food shortages throughout Latin America. In Brazil, it distributed thousands of pounds of seed, three hundred tons of insecticides and fungicides, and 150,000 hand tools (farmers there were still planting seeds with sticks). It set up model farms in Paraguay and cooperative farm machinery pools in Peru. And, in an effort to both feed U.S. servicemen in the Panama Canal Zone and relieve local shortages, it launched an all-out campaign to boost Costa Rican food production.

In all this, the institute's key modus operandi was a new concept, the *servicio*. This was a cooperative arrangement between the institute and each country in which it operated, by which semi-autonomous units, or *servicios*, were set up within the host government. The director of each *servicio* was an institute staffer, reporting to a government ministry. This arrangement made the institute part of the country's own governmental fabric, rather than an external operation implanted from the north. The hope was that the *servicio* would eventually be manned entirely by nationals.

Just how dramatically effective these *servicios* could be was shown in Haiti. The country was beset by yaws, a syphilis-like disease that caused disfiguring and potentially disabling skin lesions. Hundreds of thousands suffered from the scourge. A ready cure was at hand—penicillin—but the country's rampant poverty and poor public health care put that treatment beyond the reach of most of the population.

The Haitian *servicio* set out to change all that. Some twenty clinics were set up in every region of the country, and mobile dispensaries prowled the remote Haitian countryside. Hearing of the cure, the people came, some trekking six to eight hours on horseback to get their penicillin injections. The institute clinics took on the aspect of a tropical Lourdes.

In the autumn of 1944 Rockefeller visited one of the yaws clinics in the hills. As his car slowly made its way along the dirt road, it caught up with a teeming procession of the infirm—some hobbling on crutches, some riding donkeys led by children—all headed for the little hut where the vials of medicine were kept.

It was a special day: the American-run clinic was to be turned over at last to Haitian doctors. Outside, one of the elders stood up and, in a quivering voice, thanked the American doctors and the people of the United States for the help they had brought his people. A cheer went up from the crowd of patients, many bearing the visible scars of the disease. As the old man sat down, Rockefeller could see that he was softly crying.

Latin America was teeming with vast, intractable problems, and there were times when Rockefeller's operation seemed intent on solving all of them. Eyeing the devastation in Ecuador's El Oro province wrought by the country's border war with Peru, the institute set out to help the beleaguered inhabitants. Vaccines, quinine, and other drugs were flown in, and rice, beans, and other staples were delivered.

When the city of Guayaquil in Ecuador was hit by an earthquake, an institute field party was on the scene the next day, providing sulfa drugs, vaccines, and a portable chlorinator, and offering engineering help in cobbling together the town's shattered infrastructure.

No enterprise was too grandiose, or improbable, for the CIAA to consider. At the urging of Brazil's President Vargas, Rockefeller talked about building a great inland waterway connecting the Amazon with Venezuela's Orinoco River, thus connecting Brazil to the Venezuelan oil fields and giving Amazonian rubber production another outlet to the sea. "It would have been something like digging half a dozen Panama Canals," one CIAA hand recalled. (The idea, after some early surveys, was quietly dropped.) Upon hearing that Ecuador was facing a llama shortage—the animals, for unaccountable reasons, had stopped breeding—Rockefeller dispatched a veterinary scientist who solved the shortage through artificial insemination.

"Some of their ideas were utterly wild," recalled John Cabot, then head of Central American affairs at the State Department. "I remember one meeting when Nelson Rockefeller wanted, in effect, to take over the whole educational system of El Salvador. We didn't think that was a very good idea. We were afraid that it would cause quite a row sooner or later when the El

Salvadorans discovered that their little children were being educated by Americans."

By 1943, a little more than a year after Rockefeller had first presented his charts to Harry Hopkins, the coordinator's health, food, and related activities grouped under the rubric "basic economy" had supplanted the propaganda efforts as the CIAA's principal thrust. That year $12.6 million would be spent on "basic economy," versus $11.4 million for information. The "new missionary spirit" preached by Wallace was now the CIAA's guiding ethic.

Yet somehow, Rockefeller still managed to justify his do-good campaign in terms of the war effort. Bubonic plague was battled in Ecuador because the United States might station troops on the coast. Malaria was fought in Brazil because the disease impacted key rubber-producing areas. Challenged by Sumner Welles as to what his Amazon waterway project had to do with the war, Rockefeller invoked the specter of Nazi submarine marauders on the Brazilian coast and the threat to rubber and petroleum supplies.

Nonetheless, skeptics abounded. In 1943, a congressional delegation visited U.S. air bases in Latin America to size up the situation firsthand, and found, no doubt to their astonishment, that what Rockefeller had been telling them was true. His programs *had* helped the war effort. "Too much credit," they concluded, "cannot be given for this achievement, for it has probably resulted in saving the lives of many thousands of American boys."

Among his critics, however, the notion persisted that Rockefeller had grabbed hold of the now defunct New Deal—with all its governmental largesse and social engineering—and brought it to Latin America. FDR's conservative foes had a new target. Their brief was summed up thusly by *New York Daily News* columnist John O'Donnell: "In his handling of billions of U.S. cash, young Mr. Nelson Rockefeller will be shown up as a socially-minded young person whose inability to appreciate the value of one shiny dime is responsible for those violent seismographic disturbances reported in the vicinity of the grave of his revered grandfather, John D." It was Nebraska's Republican senator Hugh A. Butler who took it upon himself to do the showing up. Butler was a prototypical midwestern isolationist, a study in ornery insularity and hidebound conservatism. He opposed lend-lease. He opposed the extension of the Draft Act. He opposed the repeal of the Neutrality Act. He opposed, and tried to abolish, Social Security. He relished any opportunity to puncture the New Deal.

In the summer of 1943 Butler embarked on a two-month fact-finding tour of Latin America, and returned with a trunkful of tales chronicling the "hemispheric handout," as he put it. These he put forward simultaneously in a *Reader's Digest* article (bearing the steamy title "Our Deep Dark Secrets in Latin America") and in a 179-page report to the Senate.

Butler fulminated about such dubious CIAA projects as road building in Honduras ("There are fewer than 3,500 automobiles in the entire country") and the stocking of Venezuelan lakes and streams with game fish. He contended that the agency was plowing huge sums into health and sanitation projects, with only paltry assistance from the Latin Americans themselves. He alleged that the "handouts"—shielded by a "cloak of secrecy"—totaled some $6 billion. And in the end, he was convinced, it will all be for naught. "No doubt they will put up with almost anything while we are footing the bill, but it seems equally probable that they will throw the whole collection of imported ideas out the window as soon as the spending stops."

No sooner was Butler's attack aired than the coordinator's supporters rallied to his defense. Henry Wallace denounced the report as "a shocking slur." Senator Kenneth McKellar of Tennessee, the powerful chairman of the Appropriations Committee, blasted Butler and two associates who accompanied him on the trip as "a triumvirate of the most monumental and erroneous guessers that the world has ever known." McKellar went on to bestow verbal garlands on Rockefeller, praising his "indomitable energy."

Unwilling to leave it at that, Rockefeller issued an exhaustive 26-page statement that, among other things, set out to demolish Butler's $6 billion price tag (his own office, Rockefeller said, had been allotted only $80 million over the previous three fiscal years).

The Butler uproar soon blew over, and Rockefeller went on about his business. Yet privately his aides admitted that, notwithstanding the senator's multitudinous errors, there was a certain validity to Butler's core complaint: that Rockefeller was setting out to introduce some version of the New Deal to Latin America. As Frank Jamieson noted, "It was his own belief that it was for the best long-term interest of democratic free governments to take so-called New Deal social advances to Latin America during the war."

"An advantage that we had in that respect," said Jamieson, "was the fact that to many people Rockefeller was 'safe,' or conservative. Behind that facade we were able to operate."

The facade, however, was beginning to crumble. True conservatives were starting to see him not as his grandfather's heir, but as FDR's. For the first, but hardly the last time, Nelson Rockefeller was branded a free-spending liberal.

Seventeen

Pull and Haul

With teams of scientists, physicians, and technicians dispatched throughout Latin America, with a vast news-gathering operation churning out feature articles, radio broadcasts, newsletters, and a glossy monthly magazine, with offices in New York, Washington, and Hollywood and outposts all over the hemisphere, Nelson Rockefeller's CIAA had become a big-time federal agency. By June 1943 it employed 1,413 people. And while the operation retained much of its youthful exuberance, it inevitably succumbed to the pressures and patterns endemic to any burgeoning governmental empire.

There were meetings upon meetings, fueled by a surfeit of like-sounding committees whose ostensible mission was to get a handle on the office's overall program. Thus, the CIAA had at one and the same time a Policy Committee and an Administration Committee and a Directive Council, all supposedly dedicated to charting the agency's direction. In practice, none of them did; the coordinator preferred to reserve the question of direction for himself. Part of the problem was Rockefeller's tendency to emulate his Oval Office mentor and resolve "problems of human nature," as Rockefeller delicately put it, by creating more and more committees, rather than permit messy confrontations. But essentially Rockefeller genuinely liked meetings; he enjoyed the interplay, the ebb and flow of ideas, the "natural pull and haul," in his words.

Despite his backslapping informality, Rockefeller became a distant figure to most of those who worked for his agency, a leader known only by the ubiquitous "NAR" acronym dotting interoffice memoranda. Like the Sun King, he was shielded by phalanxes of courtiers, the Lockwoods and the Jamiesons and the Harrisons, counselors whose prudence braked his congenital impulsiveness. (That much, at least, was nothing new. Be they known as "associates" or as a "junta," the advisers were as integral a part of Rockefeller's operating style as they had been for his father and grandfather before him.)

In his retinue, pride of place belonged—as it had since he first arrived in Washington—to the irrepressible Anna Rosenberg. She had a wartime job of her own now: New York regional director of the War Manpower Commission. But she still made herself available to Rockefeller on a myriad of matters, ranging from White House access to speechwriting. And whenever there was a critical meeting on the CIAA's future path, Rosenberg was in attendance, a dominating figure as always.

In Rosenberg's presence, Rockefeller reverted to the persona of eager apprentice. Phyllis McGlincy, Rosenberg's longtime secretary, remembers that "on Saturday mornings he used to come into our office on West 42nd Street. She would sit at a conference table with him and go over his speeches. I remember, because I always had to stay late to do the typing. They had a very close relationship. It was always Nelson this and Nelson that."

During her meetings with FDR, she never failed to put in a plug for Rockefeller. Once, she even told Roosevelt she thought Rockefeller would one day sit in the White House. "Please, Anna," FDR jocularly replied, "at least have him wait until I am out of here."

All his years in Washington, all the slogging through bureaucratic quagmires, had not changed Rockefeller's pace: it was still as breathless and headlong as ever. He drove himself to work each morning at eight o'clock and made a point of stopping along the way to pick up staff members who were on his route. It would have been a much-appreciated gesture—had it not been for the gray hairs and heart palpitations engendered along the way. "He drove as if he were piloting a Parisian taxicab," one of his regular passengers recalled. "He drove too fast. He drove too close to other cars. The rest of us were always cringing and mentally putting on the brakes. He didn't seem to give a damn. But he never had an accident. The only trouble I recall was that one day he ran out of gas and, when we got some from a filling station, he didn't have a cent in his pocket to pay for it."

Rockefeller began each weekday playing his sunrise round of tennis with Henry Wallace and perhaps a senator or two. His 8:30-to-6:30 office schedule was honeycombed with appointments, and evenings were spent either plowing through two hefty briefcases or else "entertaining" in a fashion that was simply an extension of his work. (The Spanish sing-alongs were his idea of a relaxing night.)

Although Rockefeller seemed as robust as ever, the pace and the pressures were beginning to wear him down. He suffered from sinus trouble and amassed a wide variety of pills and nose medications. The state of his health frequently alarmed his anxious mother. "Nelson has lost thirty pounds in the last two years and he looks very pale, very tired and very thin," she told his brother Winthrop in April 1944. "Papa and I were greatly disturbed about him and finally persuaded him to see Dr. Todd who said he was really in good condition but that he was anemic and needed a rest."

To unwind, he repaired to Pocantico, when the infrequent opportunity arose. (Not every Pocantico visit, though, was a retreat. Rockefeller sometimes dragged aides along for a working weekend in the sylvan setting, and he once hosted a party in the playhouse for seventy-five Latin American officials, with the group traveling to the estate in a car-and-bus motorcade accompanied by a noisy police escort.) There, he could once again indulge in the intimate mother-son tête-à-têtes he so prized. On one such occasion Abby recorded that "after breakfast we settled down to another good talk and you know that Nelson and I have most amusing conversations, both being very frank and outspoken people. But our affection for and understanding of each other keeps us from having our feelings hurt, no matter what may be said."

More than ever, Nelson was Abby's favorite among her six children, the closest of them all to a true soul mate. He shared the feisty Aldrich spirit, and she exulted in their arguments as much as she did in their quieter times. As she once put it, in an apothegm that neatly summed up her family's salient characteristics, "Laurance puts you off, Papa doesn't like arguing, John wouldn't think of arguing, but Nelson loves it."

Still, as in the old days, there were times when that affection and understanding were sorely tried. No matter what lofty station Nelson now occupied, the old cycle of revolt-and-contrition continued. In conversations with his parents, he would assert himself, then step back and offer up the same profusion of apologies as when he was a penitent teenager.

"I can't tell you how badly I feel about the sorrow I know I have caused you by what I said in our talks," he wrote Junior at year end 1942. "I know that this time again I have failed you—please forgive my clumsiness and the sadness I have brought you—particularly at Christmas time when you and Mother were so sweet and came all the way down to Washington to be with us. . . . What I said came from the bottom of my heart as do all my feelings for you and Mother. . . . The fact that it was so poorly expressed is something I sincerely regret. I only hope that someday I'll learn."

Exactly what triggered this outburst is not known, but in any case the cause is probably not as important as Rockefeller's abject response to it. For all his triumphs in the public arena, he still saw fit to deny his worthiness in the eyes of his parents.

These episodes aside, his sojourns at Pocantico, and especially the time he spent at his mother's side, offered him some rare moments of respite and comfort. Such was not the case at his other home front, on Foxhall Road.

———

By the fall of 1941 the boarders had moved out of the house and Tod and the five children had moved in. High-pitched squeals filled the hallways; "Slow—Children" signs lined the long driveway.

The children's time with their busy father was measured out as sparingly as vials of some precious balm. Access, for the most part, was governed by certain daily rituals. In the early morning, when he wasn't occupied on the tennis court with Henry Wallace, the older children would join him for his daily calisthenics, after which the family would all gather at the breakfast table. There, in a ceremony more than a little reminiscent of the breakfasts of Nelson's youth, they would all join in prayers and Bible reading. Then Rockefeller would engage the kids in table talk—not about their schoolwork or their toys or their playmates, but about world affairs. (A newspaper cartoon dubbed the Rockefeller family breakfasts "Oatmeal Seminars.")

This colloquy completed, Rockefeller would grab his briefcase and bound off to the car. Evenings and weekends were even more constricted, what with Rockefeller's chockablock schedule of meetings and business dinners and homework. Time, however, would always be found to attend to another hoary Rockefeller family ritual, the weekly review of the children's accounts. Only in the summers, during the annual August retreat to Maine, did the children get an unbounded dose of their father's vitality. They would sail the *Jack Tar* and camp out on Shingle Island, bunking overnight in a wooden cabin (not just any old cabin, though, but one Rockefeller asked architect Harmon Goldstone, a Harrison associate, to design).

With Rockefeller such an absent figure, the full burden of child rearing was borne by Tod. It was a role she relished. There was the expected retinue of nurses and servants, but they were helpers, not substitutes. Unlike the usual run of society matrons, who contented themselves with a peck on the cheek before heading off to their garden parties and bridge games, Tod was always there for her children: to mediate their quarrels, to help with their schoolwork, to chauffeur them to skating rinks and swimming lessons. "She was totally devoted to the children," recalls her cousin Eleanor Clark French, "and they to her."

At the same time, Tod also attended to her duties as hostess of her husband's various gatherings, particularly those Sunday-night evenings of Latin culture. She watched the movies, joined in the sing-alongs, oversaw the dinner service—and led the other ladies in discreetly retiring to the kitchen or to a parlor while their men debated the state of inter-American affairs.

But those who observed Tod closely could see that there were certain limits to her sense of wifely duty. "She didn't put on any graciousness that she didn't have," remembers Frank Jamieson's wife, Linda. "If she was sleepy, or she was bored by all the people that Nelson would have on a Sunday evening in Washington, she'd just say so." The acerbic tongue of her youth had not deserted her, however frequently it was held in check.

In her youth, though, her snappish side was leavened by her lively sense of fun and prankishness, the qualities that had first drawn Nelson to her. With her children she was still that way. But outside her family, she rarely showed that sparkle any longer. What the world saw, instead, was a flinty, stubborn doyenne: "stiff, terribly stiff, and absolutely determined," was the way one female contemporary remembered her.

Bill Alton, who had known Tod since Nelson first started courting her, noticed the change when he went down to stay with them in 1942 while trying to resolve his draft status. "Tod was not much fun anymore. She was very serious and long-faced and just very *heavy*. She had lost her enthusiasm, her joie de vivre."

The contrast with her chipper, effusive husband was starker than ever. Their relationship, which always contained an element of incongruity, now appeared increasingly unfathomable.

Inexorably, as if conforming to some natural law, the relationship did erode. In such matters, cause and effect are so intertwined they become a single strand, so it is impossible to say what happened first, the change in Tod or the change in the relationship. Only one thing is certain: while the transformation may have been years in the making, it first became perceptible during the war.

Nelson's innate inconstancy—the trait that led him to date someone else in college even as he professed his devotion to Tod—came to the fore. His eye wandered, and alighted on the cluster of comely secretaries working in his office. One, in particular, caught his attention: Janet Barnes. She was intelligent, sprightly, and attractive; she was also married (her husband, Tracy Barnes, would later become a top figure in the Central Intelligence Agency) and was Nelson's cousin by marriage (her stepfather was Abby's brother Richard). Neither of the latter conditions deterred Nelson in the slightest. Barnes was one of the regulars on Rockefeller's morning shuttle, and it was not long before he sought her company on more than a commutation basis. She apparently was pleased to offer it.

"They had quite a fling," says Barnes's half brother, Richard Aldrich. "It was, well, quite a problem in the family."

Janet Barnes may not have been a blood relation, but she was a relation, and that fact overwhelmed whatever upper-class tolerance there may have been for Rockefeller's peccadilloes. Within the Aldrich family, a certain degree of waywardness was accepted. Nelson's uncle (and Barnes's step-uncle) Winthrop Aldrich, the stolid president of the Chase Bank, was well known for his wandering eye. In the 1950s, when he served as U.S. ambassador to Great Britain, it would be whispered of him that "Winthrop Aldrich arrived at the Court of St. James's with a closed mind and an open fly."

But Nelson's affair with Janet Barnes was apparently just too much. "The family really came down hard on them," says her stepbrother. Discreetly, but firmly, the Aldriches brought a halt to the "fling"—but not to Rockefeller's roving ways.

The frenetic expansion—in size and in scope—of the coordinator's office was the subject of continued consternation in the Beaux Arts corridors of the State Department and in its embassies and legations. Despite his *entente cordiale* with Sumner Welles, Rockefeller and the CIAA were still widely distrusted within the ranks. And that distrust only deepened as the burgeoning coordinator's office planted deeper and deeper roots—by means of the *servicios* and the coordinating committees—throughout Latin America.

The *servicios,* those cooperative arrangements between Rockefeller's health institute and the host countries, existed entirely outside the normal diplomatic framework. Yet American embassies still found themselves saddled with monitoring the comings and goings of the coordinator's technicians. And what was especially galling to the diplomatic corps was how much better paid those technicians were, compared to themselves.

Rockefeller's coordination committees were also arousing the professional diplomats' concern. Set up to involve expatriate American businessmen in the CIAA program, the committees were now established in sixty-seven cities throughout Latin America. While their principal avowed role was to facilitate CIAA propaganda efforts—arranging local rebroadcasts of CIAA radio programs, organizing screenings of CIAA-produced films, planting CIAA-generated articles in local newspapers—they also served another, less explicit purpose: to act as Rockefeller's intelligence and "antisubversion arm" in the Latin countries. It was not a role that was officially sanctioned; in fact, a State Department memorandum of April 22, 1942, expressly forbade the committees from "independent reporting or investigating of political subjects." Nevertheless, a memo to Rockefeller two months later from assistant coordinator John McClintock—who was overseeing the committees—made it clear that intelligence was still part of their charge. "The Committees," McClintock reported, "have been active in connection with the operation of the blacklist, the supplanting of Axis firms, the prevention of sabotage, and the checking of subversive activity."

The nebulous nature of the committees' mission was not all that discomfited the State Department. The composition of the committees—with members culled from the biggest American businesses, including Standard Oil, General Electric, and National City Bank—was also worrisome. As State's top Latin America hand, Laurence Duggan, warned Welles, "They have very definite ideas as to what our general policy should be, and in general their ideas have been the most reactionary."

That Rockefeller sought out big business's help should have come as no surprise. Despite the congressional caricatures of him as a New Dealer in a double-breasted suit, he remained an unreconstructed advocate of private enterprise and the American capitalist way of life. "Whenever anybody had a new idea," one of his staff members said, "Rockefeller's first reaction was to ask whether it would hurt business—not his own personal business, mind you, but the business community generally."

Many of the ideas he touted were as beneficial to business as they were to the Allied cause. His avid exporting of American films and radio shows created a new potential postwar market for the entertainment industry. In early 1942 he pushed for the forced takeover of Axis-influenced telephone companies in Latin America by "hemisphere interests," a policy that was bound to benefit such hemisphere giants as American Telephone & Telegraph and International Telephone & Telegraph. The proposal was brushed off by Welles, who advised Rockefeller that "as a matter of policy the Department does not favor a monopolistic control by United States interests of telecommunication facilities in the other American republics."

To be sure, Rockefeller had his eye out as much for overall hemisphere economic development as he did for the interests of U.S. business. His health program, his food program, his road building and railway reconstruction all were targeted not just at short-term war needs but also at the long-run economic security of the Latin American people. By May 1943 he was sketching out an ambitious ten-year plan for Latin development involving $3.5 billion of investment by both U.S. business and the U.S. government. The formula of benevolent capitalism that he had embraced before the war, through his Fomento holding company, was still very much on his mind.

But the benevolence was strictly of the Big Brother variety; there was never any question that the United States would call the shots. Indicative of his thinking was his irate reaction to an August 1944 interagency memo on development policy in the Americas. Next to the memo's proposal that the United States should make its expertise available "upon request" of the Latin countries, he furiously scribbled, "That doesn't sound like leadership."

The coordination committees, in Rockefeller's scheme of things, were another potential instrument of U.S. leadership.

Many of the U.S. ambassadors in the south, eager to maintain their own ties to the American business colony, docilely accepted the committees. But a few of the more prominent envoys openly bridled at the CIAA incursion. The most notable, and trenchantly outspoken, of these was George Messersmith in Mexico.

Rockefeller had a relatively free hand in Mexico under Messersmith's genial predecessor, Josephus Daniels, FDR's World War I Navy Department boss. But all that changed when the feisty, opinionated Messersmith arrived on the scene. In his long foreign service career, Messersmith had acquired a formidable reputation for grit and determination. As U.S. consul general in Berlin in the 1930s, he stood up to the Nazis and was one of the few American diplomats to openly criticize their persecution of the Jews. Later, as ambassador to Cuba, he warned Cuban officials that "they will find it is a very difficult thing to wear me down," and went on to prove it. Now, about to turn sixty, he was bringing those bulldog qualities to bear on the most prestigious posting of his career.

Duggan had warned him about Rockefeller. "Nelson is not a very clear thinker," he pointed out. "He is inclined to generalize, be vague, and blur the edges. That is why I have urged from the beginning that you be as precise as possible with him and commit to writing any arrangements arrived at in order to avoid later ambiguity."

Messersmith tried to do just that—and was astonished by the mandate Rockefeller was asserting for himself. "I have just had a letter from Nelson Rockefeller," he wrote Duggan in July 1943, "which has made me as mad as a hatter. . . . The obvious intent is to endeavor to set up an organization here, eventually, similar to the one which they have in Rio de Janeiro; in other words an independent or practically semi-independent organization."

The testy Messersmith was not about to supinely accept Rockefeller's incursions. He formed his own coordination committee, and made it known that from now on he would control the flow of CIAA propaganda. In one wing of the embassy residence, he set up a movie theater—complete with plush seats and a bar—to hold advance screenings of Rockefeller's films. He took over the distribution of all CIAA publicity material and withheld items he deemed unsuitable.

All this was too much for Rockefeller, who flew down to Mexico City to see if he could reach an accommodation with the rebellious ambassador. But Messersmith was obdurate, leaving Rockefeller no choice but to brandish his ultimate weapon. "Either we are going to run our own program in Mexico without interference from the embassy, or we are going to pull out," he warned. "And if we have to pull out of Mexico, you can be sure that we will explain why we did it." Messersmith, who had faced down the likes of Hermann Göring, was unimpressed.

Eventually, after high-level intervention by the State Department, a compromise of sorts was worked out. The coordinator would continue to operate in Mexico, while Messersmith would retain his right to approve the activities. Such projects as the Mexican railway mission proceeded—but always under Messersmith's watchful eye. As Frank Jamieson recalled, "He never let us fully operate without interference."

Rockefeller's standing with State was not helped by a very public flap over another one of his programs: the food supply effort.

The CIAA was combating malnutrition in northern Brazil, revolutionizing the primitive agriculture of Peru, and bringing bountiful harvests to the countries of Central America. But along the way the effort had become one more victim of intramural rivalry, this time not only with State but with the Agriculture Department. Agriculture had its own unit, the Office of Foreign Agricultural Relations, whose mission was much the same as the CIAA's—and which viewed the coordinator's program as an outright usurpation of its authority. By May 1943 Agriculture was demanding—with the support of State—that the coordinator's initiative be totally taken over by its own office.

The prospect of a confrontation with not just one but two departments was more than Rockefeller was prepared to undertake. In July he made it known he would yield to Agriculture's ultimatum.

Rockefeller's surrender infuriated James Le Cron, the director of the CIAA program. Le Cron, a longtime associate of Henry Wallace, decided to resign in protest, and to do so in the loudest, most attention-getting way possible. On September 3 he drafted a long letter of resignation that castigated State for its "interference, obstruction, delay and unintelligent dictation" of his program. The letter was gentler on Rockefeller, but did not completely spare him: Le Cron accused his boss of bypassing him in cutting his deal with Agriculture.

Rockefeller looked over the letter and blanched. "You're not going to make this public, are you?" he asked Le Cron—to which Le Cron replied that that was exactly what he had in mind.

"Oh, don't do that," Rockefeller remonstrated. "We will have more trouble with the State Department. It's bad enough now. They'll just get their back up and it will be very bad."

Le Cron, however, stood firm. He dispatched copies of his letter to all the principal newspapers and wire services and, for good measure, he sent a copy over to Harry Hopkins at the White House.

The next day "Le Cron Quits CIAA" made the front page of *The New York Times.*

Whether it was because of the public embarrassment engendered by Le Cron, or simply because of some second thoughts, Rockefeller quickly backtracked from his accord with Agriculture. The CIAA remained in the food and agriculture business. But the difficulties with State persisted. In early 1944, at the insistence of the American ambassador, the food effort in Nicaragua was halted. State tried to terminate the program in Brazil as well, until a last-ditch appeal by Rockefeller to Cordell Hull gained a stay of execution. (The program, however, was drastically curtailed.)

By then, it was obvious to all that the wartime rationale for the CIAA food initiative—and for many others as well—was increasingly flimsy. The Allies were winning the war, and with America's attention riveted on the decisive battles in the Pacific and in Europe, the Latin "theater" seemed more and more like an inconsequential sideshow. Rockefeller was vulnerable now, more so than at any time since his prewar skirmishes with Bill Donovan, and his rivals at State knew it.

Adding acutely to his sense of vulnerability was the sudden resignation, in August 1943, of his most highly placed supporter in the department: Sumner Welles.

A volatile conjunction of Welles's drinking, his homosexuality, and the machinations of Cordell Hull did the undersecretary in. The precise instrument of his downfall was his behavior three years earlier aboard the presidential train returning from the funeral of House Speaker William Bankhead. An intoxicated Welles, upon retiring to his compartment, summoned several Pullman porters and propositioned them. The incident was swiftly hushed up, but word of it leaked out anyway. FDR heard about it from J. Edgar Hoover, but chose to ignore it—until Hull, with the active connivance of another Welles antagonist, former ambassador William Bullitt, spread the story of Welles's improprieties around Capitol Hill. Faced with the looming threat of a Senate investigation, a visibly upset FDR had no choice but to ask for the undersecretary's resignation.

After years of putting up with his deputy's haughty insubordination, Hull at last had his revenge. Never very far from his backwoods Tennessee roots, Hull had said of his victory over another administration adversary, a decade earlier, "I cut the son-of-a-bitch's throat from ear to ear." Now he had done the same with Sumner Welles.

With his ally Welles out of the picture, Rockefeller felt a new need to ingratiate himself with Hull—not that he hadn't been working that angle all along. In April 1943 he commemorated the Good Neighbor Policy's tenth anniversary by sending photographic reproductions of the secretary's formal portrait to all the Latin American ambassadors. He forwarded another of the reproductions to Hull's wife, enclosing this effusive letter: "There is no man who is more beloved, both here and throughout the Hemisphere, than Mr. Hull. . . . We are indeed fortunate as a nation to have a man with his integrity and vision in these times." Hull responded with a clipped thank-you note, but Mrs. Hull was more appreciative, describing the coordinator's gesture as "the most inspiring and generous thought I have ever known."

Now that Hull's supremacy in the department was unchallenged, Rockefeller's sycophancy went into overdrive. When Hull returned from a critical meeting of Allied Foreign Ministers in Moscow in November 1943, Rockefeller was at the airport to welcome him home. Afterward, he dashed off a letter to the secretary: "I can't tell you what a thrill I got when the wing of your great army plane swung out over the President's car and came to rest in front of the hangar, the door opened, and you stepped out, returning from the most significant trip that any American has made since the start of the war. . . . You have brought new hope and confidence into the hearts of the people in every home in this country."

Rockefeller did not have to exert himself quite as much with Welles's successor as undersecretary, Edward R. Stettinius, Jr. They shared a background of affluence (Stettinius' father was a J. P. Morgan partner) as well as precocious success: at thirty-seven, Stettinius was chairman of U.S. Steel. And, like Rockefeller, Stettinius was recruited into the government by Harry Hopkins, serving as priorities director in the Office of Production Management and then as head of the lend-lease program.

Stettinius' boosterish enthusiasm, his bouncy eagerness to tackle problems, was also akin to Rockefeller's, although he appeared much older, largely because of his shock of prematurely gray hair. If there were any qualities that set the two men apart, they were cunning and guile: Stettinius was as naive and uncalculating as he seemed, while Rockefeller was anything but. Consequently, in their early relations it was Rockefeller who played the role of the savvy, hard-boiled operator showing the ropes to Stettinius, the befuddled novice. When Stettinius came under fire at OPM, Rockefeller urged him to write a letter to the President threatening resignation unless he was given more power. (The tactic, after all, had worked for Rockefeller.) Stettinius, however, declined to go that far. "They are going to take care of me," he blandly told Rockefeller, referring to the White House. "I have confidence they will." As it turned out, he was right; "they" gave him lend-lease.

By any measure, Stettinius was a wan successor to the imperious Welles. He lacked Welles's decades of foreign policy experience, his crisp, authoritative point of view, his haughty self-confidence. On the other hand, Stettinius prided himself on his administrative skills and his ability to build consensus: talents, to be sure, that were sorely needed in the halls of State. And his tactful disposition would at least assure some semblance of harmony in the department's upper reaches for the first time in years. But all that was not enough to overcome the initial impression of him as a figure hopelessly out of his depth, someone scarcely able to fill Sumner Welles's bench-made shoes.

Welles's departure was not the only high-level upheaval to affect Nelson Rockefeller that summer. The other involved two of the coordinator's most revered mentors and trusted cohorts: Henry Wallace and Jesse Jones.

Wallace and Jones had been at loggerheads ever since the war began. There were ideological reasons for their animus (Wallace was as far left of the Democratic center as Jones was to the far right of it) and personal ones. But mostly, their conflict was about power: they presided over conflicting duchies. Wallace's Board of Economic Warfare had wide-ranging authority to procure strategic materials for the American war machine. Jones, at the same time, ran a vast network of government corporations—including the Defense Supplies Corporation and the Metals Reserve Company—that was doing the exact same thing. Neither official evinced any desire to cooperate with the other, and both were more than ready to take their gripes about the other public.

By July 1943 FDR had had enough. Refusing to side with one or the other, he came down hard on both. Jones was stripped of all authority over wartime procurement. Wallace's BEW was reconstituted as the Office of Economic Warfare, with economist Leo T. Crowley as its head. The moves would be devastating to both Wallace and Jones. Never again would Jones wield the same untrammeled authority; by January 1945 he was out of the cabinet and out of the government. And Wallace's rebuff marked the beginning of a breach with FDR that would culminate in Wallace's ouster from the Democratic ticket, in favor of Harry S. Truman, in 1944.

With his two mainstays suddenly bereft of power, Rockefeller had more reason than ever to feel isolated.

Through much of Latin America, Nelson Rockefeller had achieved heroic stature. He was the man who put food on the tables of starving Peruvians, who cured Haitians of the disfigurement of yaws, who gave hoes and seed to struggling Brazilian farmers, who brought clean water and modern sewers to Paraguay. In Nicaragua, babies were named after him; his was the third most popular foreign namesake, right behind Franklin Roosevelt and Winston Churchill.

He had proved, once and for all, that there was more to the Good Neighbor Policy than pious rhetoric. In the words of one Mexican diplomat, "Today, for the first time in the history of the Western Hemisphere, we of Latin America may confidently clasp the open hand extended to us by a President of the United States." This achievement was Nelson Rockefeller's.

His was a wartime agency, and much of what it did in its early days—the torrents of propaganda, the blacklist, the aviation and shipping initiatives—related to the war effort. But, at the same time, the war also served as a pretext for achieving the grander aims of Henry Wallace's "missionary spirit."

Often, out of political necessity, he had to camouflage those goals. But he chafed at the camouflage, and as the war progressed, and his agency's impact on Latin America intensified, he became more open about his long-run aims. By early 1944, in testimony before the House Appropriations Committee, Rockefeller was touting the significance of the CIAA program from the "point of view of laying foundations for economic development and the expansion of markets based on a rising standard of living" after the war. He even rewrote his initial mandate, claiming that when his office started in 1940 its original objective was to "secure the cooperation and collaboration of the American republics in increasing the general welfare of the peoples of these countries."

With his larger objectives out of the closet, Rockefeller grew bolder about attaining them. He created a new department of economic development within the CIAA, under his aide John McClintock. Its sweeping charter included assisting the Latin republics in the development of their natural resources, removing trade barriers, and furthering industrialization.

He and his aides began talking about longer time frames for their programs—time frames that would not necessarily be congruent with the duration of the war. About the health program, General Dunham declared, "In no instances have we ever considered that there would be any time limit on the work we are doing in any of the Latin American countries."

Out of these diverse appeals a consistent theme emerged: that, following the war, the coordinator's programs, if not the coordinator's office itself, should become a permanent part of the government landscape.

Any doubt about what Rockefeller had in mind was dispelled in January 1944, when he sent a memo to Stettinius urging the retention of a "permanent inter-American affairs agency" that would carry out a "well-rounded, dynamic action program."

Rockefeller wanted to make his creation a lasting one. But Cordell Hull had other ideas.

Hull realized that an abrupt cutoff of the CIAA programs might have a disastrous effect on inter-American relations. What he had in mind was a gradual, "orderly" conclusion—but a conclusion nonetheless.

Just how intractable the Tennessean and the rest of the State hierarchy could be about this became clear to Rockefeller later that same month. The issue was the future of his coordination committees. Rockefeller wanted to keep them in business after the war, to help advance the economic development process. "The wealth of manpower and experience," he told Stettinius, "is an asset which should be preserved." He advised the undersecretary that he planned to send McClintock on a tour of Latin America at the end of the month to meet with the committees and plot out their future.

Stettinius, however, made it plain to Rockefeller that the department did not envision *any* postwar role for the committees. If McClintock wanted to visit Latin America for some other reason, that was fine, but if the reason for his trip was to discuss the committees' future, then "I find myself unable to approve it."

Rockefeller sent McClintock off anyway; the purpose of his trip would be "to discuss and study the economic development problems of the other American republics." Nevertheless, State officials were suspicious—and with good reason, in view of the fact that those businessmen with whom McClintock planned to discuss development were the very same businessmen who were members of the coordination committees. Consequently, when McClintock arrived at his first stop, Rio de Janeiro, he was greeted by the U.S. ambassador with an unpleasant surprise: a State Department order barring McClintock from any discussions with businessmen, be they Latins or Americans. Rockefeller vociferously protested the order, but to no avail.

If the message State was sending the coordinator somehow eluded him, it would come in loud and clear in the months ahead. On May 9 a new interdepartmental committee on hemisphere economic development was set up. It seemed to fulfill all of Rockefeller's aspirations on the development front: not only would it map out development policy but it would consider how the U.S. government could work with Fomento corporations, those engines of growth that were Rockefeller's own prewar inspiration.

Wielding the power of this committee, the coordinator could make the United States a permanent protagonist in the transformation of Latin America. It soon became apparent, however, that this power would never be Rockefeller's to wield. To his utter horror, he learned that State and Leo Crowley's Foreign Economic Administration (the latest incarnation of the old Board of Economic Warfare) had agreed that the latter should chair the new committee. The CIAA, which had taken the lead on hemisphere issues since before the war, would be shunted to a backseat role. What's more, the new group's far-reaching mandate effectively precluded the CIAA from any economic development activities of its own.

The State Department, after years of trying, had finally found a mechanism for squeezing out Nelson Rockefeller.

Later in May 1944, some two hundred delegates from the twenty-one American republics gathered in New York for a convocation of Rockefeller's Inter-American Development Commission, which he had chaired since November 1940. The purpose of the conference was to hammer out proposals for sparking economic growth in the hemisphere. But what the meeting rapidly turned into was a lionization of Nelson Rockefeller.

Speaker after speaker showered him with encomiums. The Pan American Society presented him with its gold medal, in recognition of his efforts toward inter-American unity and cooperation. At the end of the conference, Bill Benton, who chaired the U.S. delegation, stood up and announced that he now knew two words in Spanish: *"Señor Rockefeller,"* because "in every Spanish speech, the refrain throughout is *Señor Rockefeller."*

Observing this spectacle, with boundless pride, were Rockefeller's father and mother. Abby's special moment came at a tea Mrs. Cornelius Vanderbilt hosted for the delegates. Nelson brought over one Latin emissary after another to his mother, and, she related, "each and every one of them told me how very fond they were of Nelson, what a good job he had done and how much he meant to them and to the problem of continuing good relations between the countries."

Junior watched his son accept the gold medal and listened in awe to the expressions of affection and devotion. Afterward, he penned his son a note fairly overflowing with paternal bliss.

"When you started on this work," the father wrote, "and many people said to me, 'Yes, but it is impossible,' you will recall that my answer always was, 'It may be impossible but it is necessary.' Because you believed it was necessary and vital, you have made it possible and, by grinding, unremitting, indefatigable hard work, have brilliantly turned the impossible into the possible. . . .

And so," Junior concluded, "with a heart full of pride, joy and gratitude, I say: 'Well done, my son, you have wrought a good work. . . . you have brought added credit to the family name.' "

From Junior, there could be no higher praise.

Yet the considerable satisfaction Rockefeller derived from his parents' pride was diluted by the realization that his moment of triumph was a last hurrah. He watched as one resolution after another was adopted by the conference, knowing that he and his agency would have no power to implement any of them. The single greatest exponent of the inter-American movement had been reduced to the status of a much-admired, oft-praised figurehead.

In June, Rockefeller returned to Pocantico for a two-week rest. "Personally," Abby wrote her son Winthrop, "I think two weeks will only scratch the surface. Both Papa and I really feel quite anxious about him. I wish the democrats [sic] would put him out. It might save his health."

The unending frustration of his situation seemed to be wearing him down. His hay fever returned in full force; there were times when he could hardly speak. Abby was right: the two weeks barely helped. Two months later, when she saw him again in Maine, she was appalled at her son's condition. "I never saw anyone look quite so miserable as Nelson," she recorded.

Upon his return to the capital after Labor Day, he fired off a letter to Hull in which he raged against the "indecisive and dilatory manner in which the Department deals with problems vitally affecting the collaboration of the Americas." His complaints were noted, and ignored.

For the first time Rockefeller talked about leaving the government, no later than the following June. In a mid-November interview, he described his plans for the gradual liquidation of his agency. "Rather than have someone kick the props from under it," he said, "we want to take it down in an orderly manner."

About all Rockefeller could hope for to change the depressing scenario was some extraordinary occurrence, some drastic event that would upend the status quo.

Which was exactly what happened.

Shortly after the November election, with Roosevelt returned to office for a fourth term, his Secretary of State checked himself into Bethesda Naval Hospital. The seventy-three-year-old Hull was ill, and utterly exhausted, worn out not only from the demands of the job but from years of Rooseveltian maneuvers. As he put it to one of his deputies, Breckinridge Long, he was "tired of intrigue . . . tired of being bypassed . . . tired of being relied upon in public and ignored in private."

On November 27, after a visit to the hospital by FDR, Hull's resignation was announced. He would be succeeded not by his first choice for the job—former South Carolina senator (and perennial vice presidential contender) James Byrnes—but by his undersecretary, Edward Stettinius. Despite his own deteriorating physical condition, Roosevelt was more intent than ever on holding on to the foreign policy reins at a time when the future, postwar world would be shaped. It was clear he wanted as secretary someone of utmost loyalty and maximum pliability, someone content to let FDR and Harry Hopkins call the shots. Stettinius—a "decent man of considerable innocence," in the words of one of his aides, Charles Bohlen—more than filled the bill.

Seeking to inject some new blood into the department, Stettinius asked for, and got, the President's permission to purge the top ranks. (The only holdover would be that consummate brahmin, Dean Acheson.) Five new assistant secretaries were nominated, along with the new undersecretary, veteran diplomat Joseph Grew. They included FDR's old favorite Archibald MacLeish (to oversee the department's information and cultural activities) and William Clayton, who had gone on from his brief stint at the coordinator's office to become Jesse Jones's right-hand man.

But far and away the most prominent name on Stettinius' list was that of the man selected as Assistant Secretary of State for Latin America: Nelson A. Rockefeller.

Rockefeller could not be said to have directly campaigned for the job. Nonetheless, in the course of pushing for a permanent inter-American agency back in January, he had also urged Stettinius to designate a special undersecretary who would "integrate all the activities of the Department re Latin America both political and economic." Eight months later, when he vented his frustration in his letter to Hull, he reiterated the idea. "This person," he said, "will not only have the authority to direct and integrate all the work of the Department in this area, but also will express the policy and give clearance to the other agencies of the Government on behalf of the Department."

Once again, Nelson Rockefeller had proposed a job for which he just happened to be the ideal candidate.

Rockefeller certainly had some important boosters: not only Harry Hopkins but also George Marshall. Back in January, in a conversation with Henry Wallace, Marshall had extolled Rockefeller's work and opined that "the Latin American situation could be straightened out if Nelson Rockefeller could be made assistant secretary of state for Latin America."

All this helped tip the scales in Rockefeller's favor. But what was unquestionably the decisive factor was the President's own high regard for Rockefeller's work. That much was made plain in a chat Rockefeller had with Pa Watson. "It was the boss who wanted you," confided Watson, "not the new Secretary."

The President, in fact, had been contemplating appointing Rockefeller to the job since earlier in the year. In a chat with Henry Morgenthau back in March, he remarked, "The trouble is ever since Sumner Welles left, we really have nobody of importance in the State Department who can handle South

America. The only person who might do it is Rockefeller. Maybe we will make Rockefeller an assistant secretary."

The reasons for FDR's esteem were not hard to fathom. Rockefeller had single-handedly kept the Good Neighbor Policy afloat. Ever mindful of his legacy, Roosevelt was appropriately grateful for his young coordinator's stewardship of one of its most vaunted elements.

The President had never been reluctant to show his appreciation. Time after time, when there was a showdown, FDR sided with Rockefeller. Now, when Nelson Rockefeller most needed a boost, FDR had once again delivered.

Expecting a grilling on his activities as coordinator, Rockefeller prepared intensively for his confirmation hearings. But his appearance, on December 12, was the briefest of all the hearings on assistant secretary nominees. The senators were far more interested in quizzing Clayton on his allegedly anti-New Deal views and MacLeish about the meaning of his poems. Anointed with extravagant senatorial praise, Rockefeller walked out of the hearing room virtually unquestioned and unscathed. Along with all the other nominees, he was confirmed December 19.

In little more than a month he had gone from the brink of political obsolescence to a position of unassailable authority over Latin American policy. The minions of the State Department, with whom he had to plead and kowtow for over four years, were now thoroughly under his thumb. With only a weak and untested Secretary of State to stand in his way, he at last had the freedom, and the power, to turn the tide of inter-American relations.

Part Four

Unity of the Americas

Eighteen

CHANGING COURSE

For Edward Stettinius, the changing of the guard at State was not to be a muted affair, but rather an occasion marked by all the ruffles and flourishes his venerable department could muster. It was as though he sought to confer instant legitimacy—upon himself as well as his new aides—by means of pomp and ceremony.

The swearing-in of his six deputies took place in the large conference room adjoining the secretary's office. As Acheson would acerbically recall, "It resembled a mass baptism. Stettinius, snow-capped and episcopal, flanked by the protocol officer holding a Bible, received the line of initiates. Grouped near them were their wives, garbed in fur and identified by one or more orchids." After each man took the oath—accompanied by the popping of flashbulbs by the news photographers crowded into the chamber—the assemblage moved across the hall to the department's stately diplomatic reception room. There, as the movie cameras rolled, Stettinius brought each of his aides to the microphone to say a few words.

All this, however, was merely a prelude to the festivities to come. At Constitution Hall, the whole department was gathered to greet the new arrivals. The scarlet-coated Marine Band played as Rockefeller and his confreres mounted the stage. One veteran foreign service officer cracked that he hadn't seen such organized spontaneous fervor since Ed Stettinius had been head cheerleader at the University of Virginia.

It was a rousing, soul-stirring welcome, just the sort of brassy reception that Rockefeller loved. And what he must have especially savored was the symbolism of it: four and half years after they grudgingly acknowledged his presence, the minions of State were on their feet for Nelson Rockefeller.

If Rockefeller ever needed proof of his standing in Latin America, he found more than enough of it in the joyous, effusive reaction to his new assignment.

The Panamanian press called him an upholder of "Bolívar's ideal" of hemisphere solidarity, while Brazilian radio greeted the news with "maximum satisfaction." Mexican radio labeled him "the first friend of our country—we should all be grateful for his appointment." At a Caracas dinner party hosted by former Venezuelan President López Contreras for the ex-President of Colombia, the assembled Latin dignitaries "were all as happy as though they themselves had made the appointment," U.S. ambassador Frank Corrigan reported to Rockefeller.

Among the most enthusiastic was *La Fronda,* the newspaper mouthpiece of the Argentinian junta. It was especially pleased that Norman Armour, the former U.S. ambassador who was Rockefeller's predecessor as State's top Latin America hand, was no longer on the scene. "Mr. Armour has always been an enemy of our country," the paper declared. "His tendentious and false reports influenced in no small degree the mind of Mr. Hull in determining the absurd, grossly aggressive policy which the Secretary followed toward our country." Rockefeller's appointment, *La Fronda* predicted, "will greatly clear the atmosphere."

"It is very pleasant and interesting to me to address his letters now to 'Hon. Nelson A. Rockefeller,' " Abby related to her son Winthrop. "I had such a nice talk with Nelson last night and he seemed happier and calmer and more like himself than I have known him to be for a long time. He said that at last he had lost his feeling of frustration and he was able to plan and go ahead with the program in a way that had not been possible for him during the past year."

In his lofty new position Rockefeller could truly grasp the levers of power and achieve all that had eluded him as coordinator. No longer did he have to shuffle papers over to State for approval, to beseech its bureaucrats for a decision, to defer to its wisdom when a program of his intersected with some element of "policy." *He* controlled the papers and the bureaucrats now; *he* made the policy.

Needless to say, it was the CIAA that was the most immediate beneficiary of Rockefeller's new station in government. He had left the ever-faithful Wally Harrison in charge of the agency, and together they plotted the operation's future course. Suddenly, all talk of an "orderly liquidation" and of taking down the scaffolding was dropped.

To skeptical congressmen, who pressed him on when the CIAA would be winding up its affairs, Harrison pointed out Rockefeller's earlier commitment to dissolve the agency had an important caveat attached: to wit, it would be done "if it was the will of the President and the Congress." Somehow, no one had noticed this loophole before, and Rockefeller certainly had never drawn anyone's attention to it.

The State Department's official position now was that it would be "most unfortunate" if the CIAA's activities ceased with the end of the war.

Rockefeller was never much for gentle transitions, and his switch to State was no exception. He moved quickly to put his personal stamp on his new surroundings. An elaborate dining-room set was installed in his new office, so that he might properly entertain Latin American dignitaries. He began scouting out locations for his chart room, displaying particular interest in the burnished old State Department library (much to the alarm of the department's librarian).

Among the matters to which he had to attend was the question of what to do about his salary. There were no dollar-a-year men in the State Department; Rockefeller was legally obliged to accept a salary. He asked Lockwood if he could assign his wages to an "entertainment fund" for the use of people in his office, but Lockwood said he couldn't do that. The money was his by act of Congress, and he couldn't assign it to anyone. So Rockefeller quietly accepted his first government paycheck.

His inner circle included some familiar faces: John Lockwood, Frank Jamieson. But the new assistant secretary also felt the need of a right-hand man who knew the department ropes and was experienced in the ins and outs of Latin American policy. His choice proved to be a fateful one. He was Avra M. Warren, fifty-one, recently returned from an assignment as special envoy to Bolivia.

Warren had devoted a quarter century to the foreign service, dutifully hopscotching from one posting to the next, from Cap Haitien to Nairobi to St. John's, Newfoundland. He came under the sway of Sumner Welles, and Welles's specialty—Latin America—became Warren's. His rise up the diplomatic ranks, if not swift, was steady—and not without controversy. In the early years of the war he ran the State Department's visa division, and was given the task of ruling on the admissibility of European refugees, including thousands of persecuted Jews. Along with his superior, Breckinridge Long, Warren became identified with State's dilatory, obstructionist approach to the refugee problem. In Warren's eyes, as in Long's, concerns about "subversives" among the refugees far outweighed any humanitarian concerns.

Eventually, Warren was yanked from that hot seat and named ambassador to the Dominican Republic. It was not long before he struck up a friendship with Dominican strongman Rafael Trujillo, even going so far as to enroll his son in the dictator's military academy.

Warren's next role, in Bolivia, merely bolstered his image as a diplomat of pronounced right-wing sympathies. A pro-Axis military junta had overthrown the government there in December 1943, and Hull refused to recognize the new regime. It fell to Warren to broker a settlement whereby the junta agreed to expel pro-Axis elements in exchange for U.S. recognition. Despite Warren's assurances that the regime had reformed itself, the junta continued to terrorize its opponents, torturing and murdering the former Foreign Minister who signed the country's declaration of war against the Nazis. According to a December 1944 report to Stettinius by the U.S. ambassador to Chile, Claude G. Bowers, all those whom Warren earlier identified as pro-Nazi remained in power. Later, as Rockefeller's deputy, Warren would glibly dismiss further allegations about Bolivia.

Warren's accommodating attitude toward the Bolivian junta (not to mention his friendship with Trujillo) was indicative of a mind-set locked into realpolitik and untroubled by the absence of such democratic niceties as free elections and an untrammeled, unjailed opposition. He was energetic and mentally agile, prone to quick decisions and rapid action: all qualities, along with his experience, that Nelson Rockefeller esteemed.

This was the man, and the mind-set, that the new assistant secretary had chosen to be his guide through the thicket of Latin American policy.

Not that he had forgotten about his other mentors—notably Adolf Berle, one of his few consistent allies within State all those years. Berle was one of the casualties of the Stettinius shakeout, but Rockefeller was determined not to leave his old friend out in the cold. He arranged for Berle's appointment as ambassador to Brazil, replacing Jefferson Caffery.

In talking up the job, Rockefeller intimated to Berle that he would serve as more than just another envoy. The Rio embassy, he said, would be one of the pivotal points from which hemisphere policy was to be made; together, he and Berle could work to reshape that policy. With that commitment (and a Rockefeller promise that once the war in Europe ended he could come home) in hand, Berle accepted the position.

The rest of the ambassadorial corps—those not handpicked by Rockefeller—was more of a problem. The suspicion with which he was viewed for over four years would not be allayed overnight. Nevertheless, Rockefeller did his best to make amends with some of the harder cases, such as Spruille Braden. The young assistant secretary had barely settled into his new office when he was bombarded by requests from Braden to be brought up from Havana for consultation. Braden wanted to talk to Rockefeller and to Stettinius—and he particularly wanted to have a "long conversation" with FDR.

Rather than brush off Braden's missives, Rockefeller went all out to satisfy the prickly envoy. He arranged all the meetings Braden desired, including the session with the President.

Eager as he was to please, Rockefeller also felt the need to swiftly assert his authority over the diplomats—to make it plain that he was no pushover. This led to one notable confrontation early on with his old nemesis, George Messersmith. Messersmith was summoned to Washington by the President to chat about FDR's plans for postwar Germany (there was talk that the ambassador might serve as the top U.S. diplomat there). The veteran envoy was used to dealing on a firsthand basis with the President; Roosevelt, in fact, encouraged direct feedback from his ambassadors, to the everlasting consternation of Hull. Thus, Messersmith saw nothing out of order in flying to Washington and conferring with the President without deigning to consult with, or even inform, his superiors across the street at State.

When he returned to the Metropolitan Club after his morning White House meeting, however, Messersmith found a message waiting for him to phone Nelson Rockefeller immediately. The ambassador returned the call, and was told, in the chilliest, most peremptory tones, that Rockefeller wanted him to come over to his office at once.

The assistant secretary greeted him with uncharacteristic stiffness and formality, his bearing more than a little reminiscent of that of the departed Sumner Welles.

"I understand you've been to see the President this morning," Rockefeller began.

"That's correct," replied Messersmith.

"Don't you know that there's a rule that no ambassador or chief of mission is to see the President without the previous knowledge and consent of the Secretary or myself?"

"No, I didn't," said Messersmith. "Just who made this rule?"

"Ed did," answered Rockefeller. "You should not have gone to see the President without seeing Ed and me."

This was more than Messersmith could take. Barely checking his fury, he informed the assistant secretary that ambassadors were not only the representatives of the department but personal emissaries of the President. Any President could insist on a one-to-one relationship with an ambassador, and *this* President was quite often inclined to do so. "I hope the President doesn't know about your new rule," Messersmith said, "because he would be very annoyed."

The last thing Rockefeller needed, in his first weeks on the job, was a run-in with the President. So he did the only prudent thing: he passed the buck to Stettinius.

Messersmith then stomped over to the secretary's office and gave Stettinius the same half-hour lecture he had delivered to Rockefeller on the traditions and procedures of the department. Wilting almost instantly, Stettinius ventured that perhaps "Nelson and I have proceeded a little bit too fast," and they would henceforth forget about their rule.

Ever conscious of turf, Rockefeller unhesitantly carved out huge chunks of it for himself in his new job. His survival instincts honed by his battles with the likes of Bill Donovan, Rockefeller knew that naked self-assertion was the sine qua non for success in this administration. Stettinius' uncertain grip on the tiller only made the task that much easier, and more essential.

Rockefeller wasted no time declaring himself the utter and complete master of Latin American policy. Appearing before the House Appropriations Committee, he made it clear that "the final responsibility for whatever goes on in the Western Hemisphere whether in the economic, cultural or any other way, I will have."

This proclamation did not sit well with his fellow assistant secretaries whose jurisdictions existed on functional, rather than geographical, lines. Taking particular offense was the department's new cultural and information czar, Archibald MacLeish. Upon reading the House testimony, MacLeish dispatched an enraged memo to Stettinius.

"I dare say Nelson did not mean 'final responsibility' literally," MacLeish fumed. "Nevertheless, the repetition does indicate that he feels that his authority in the Western Hemisphere is final not only in political, but in economic and in cultural and informational matters also. This is in conflict with the order of reorganization and very decidedly in conflict with my understanding. I imagine that you will feel as I do that the fog in Nelson's mind ought to be removed before it produces a collision."

He went on to warn Stettinius that if MacLeish were asked the same question at *his* upcoming appearance before the House committee, "my answers will have to be quite different from Nelson's."

With the threat of such public disunity in the air, Stettinius had no choice but to rein in Rockefeller. The setback, however, was a paltry one. For even if he was denied formal recognition of his supremacy, Rockefeller retained de facto preeminence through his control of the political agenda—and through his sheer, overwhelming vigor. In the face of this whirlwind, all MacLeish and the others could do was grumble and stand back.

From his first days on the job, one issue above all others dominated Rockefeller's thinking: the question of what to do about Argentina. For three years it had been the bane of Latin American policy, an intractable problem that had riven the State Department and confounded the foreign service's finest minds. Now it was Rockefeller's turn to grapple with it.

Throughout the war years, while its neighbors rallied in varying degrees to the Allies' side, Argentina stood implacably aloof, refusing during most of that period to even break relations with the Axis powers. With an army whose officers were openly enamored of the German war machine, and with a government dominated by a profascist right wing, the country was a veritable Axis citadel in the Western Hemisphere. The German embassy in Buenos Aires served as the Nazi spy center for the whole of the hemisphere, tracking Allied ship movements and controlling a network of agents infiltrating other

Latin American governments. The Nazis subsidized newspapers, publishing houses, and movie theaters, and employed Argentine holding companies as fronts to hold dollar assets in the United States. They were "a state within a state," in the words of the U.S. ambassador. In the face of all this activity, the government was mute, preferring to concentrate its energies on rounding up suspected "Communists" and stamping out prodemocratic organizations.

The country's political scene was as tempestuous as ever, with coups and conspiracies the order of the day. One general after another rose to power, only to be supplanted, after a brief reign, by a younger, more ruthless military rival. In their terror tactics, each regime seemed determined to outdo its predecessor: phones were tapped, mail was seized, and suspected "subversives" were dispatched, without trial, to concentration camps in Patagonia. The Argentine rulers resembled their German counterparts in other ways, with anti-Semitic politicians occupying key positions of power and Jewish newspapers suspended from publication.

While Argentina's authoritarian excesses might be ignored by the United States, its tolerance of Axis activities could not. Cordell Hull, in particular, seethed at the country's behavior. Its refusal to join most of the hemisphere in breaking with the Axis at the January 1942 Rio conference infuriated the Secretary of State; the stalking of Argentina became a crusade for him. And the renegade nation usually gave him ample justification for his ill will. When many of the country's leading citizens, in October 1943, presented the government of Pedro Ramírez with a petition calling for a return to democracy and a closer alliance with the rest of the hemisphere, the signers found themselves the targets of harsh reprisals, including dismissal from their jobs. Three months later, faced with an American threat to seize all his country's assets in the United States, Ramírez finally buckled under and agreed to break relations with the Axis. For this transgression Ramírez was promptly booted out of office in yet another military coup.

The new President was General Edelmiro Farrell, Ramírez' Minister of War. But the true power was wielded by his charismatic deputy, Colonel Juan Domingo Perón. A swashbuckling six-footer given to strutting about with his pistol stuffed in his belt, Perón was the very essence of the *caudillo,* the dashing, proud military strongman. As bad as the previous Argentine regimes were in U.S. eyes, Peron's held the promise of being infinitely worse. Not only was he an admirer of German and Italian "social democracy" but, in his sideline as a military historian, he was an avowed disciple of the German concept of all-out militarism: *Das Volk in Waffen,* the Nation in Arms. He soon confirmed everyone's worst forebodings by calling, in a June 1944 speech, for a mobilization of his country's armed forces to combat "odious imperialism."

Hull took Perón's statements as a virtual declaration of war. He refused to recognize the Farrell-Perón government, and recalled the U.S. ambassador, urging America's allies to do likewise. "If Argentina goes on the way it is headed," he warned, "then after the war it will become a refuge of every Axis and fascist scoundrel who can get there. . . . To aid the Argentine Government is to aid the Axis powers in the present war."

FDR tended to view the situation in somewhat less apocalyptic terms. "You make a bad face at the Argentinians once a week," he told Stettinius. "You have to treat them like children." He impishly enjoyed egging Hull on about Argentina, just to see his Secretary of State's bilious reaction. Nevertheless, he fully backed Hull's measures.

The state of affairs, however, presented numerous quandaries for American policy makers. For one thing, the British were markedly unenthusiastic about supporting the U.S. position. Not only did Britain have long-standing business and cultural ties to the Argentine (in Buenos Aires' smart set, it was still de rigueur to be Anglophilic) but the British were highly dependent on Argentine beef supplies. It was only grudgingly that Churchill agreed to recall his ambassador. "I do not see what we expect to get out of the Argentines by this method," he complained to Roosevelt, "and I do not myself see where this policy is leading to."

The United States' jittery hemisphere allies also felt themselves in a box. Utterly dependent on U.S. economic and military aid, they had no choice but to go along with Hull's demands. Yet they were also fearful of antagonizing the newly militant Argentines. Having witnessed the allegedly Argentine-fomented coup in Bolivia, and having ogled the intimidating display of armaments at Argentina's annual independence day parade in July, much of Latin America was left to wonder just how steep a price they would have to pay for their loyalty to Cordell Hull's foreign policy.

Seeking to break through this impasse, Mexico's tall, courtly Foreign Minister, Ezequiel Padilla, proposed an inter-American conference to discuss the Argentine controversy. Of all Latin America's diplomats, Padilla was by far the most sympathetic to the United States: he spoke a fluent English, had studied law at Columbia University, and had adopted such Yankee pastimes as golf and poker. Throughout the war, beginning with the 1942 Rio conference, Padilla had been a steadfast and eloquent ally.

But Hull flatly rejected the Mexican's initiative; as far as the crusty secretary was concerned, such a meeting would be a charade. Padilla, however, continued to press his point, and in late October 1944 the Argentines—seizing on Hull's intransigence as a way of driving a wedge into inter-American solidarity—themselves called for a conference. Hull dug in his heels. "Argentina," he snapped, "can go to hell!"

Adding another discordant ingredient to this sour stew was that summer's Dumbarton Oaks conference, at which the Allied powers laid the groundwork for the postwar United Nations. The Latin American nations had not been invited to this parley, but they expected to at least be consulted by the United States; when their views were ignored, they reacted with profound anger and bitterness.

It was into this tangle of wounded pride, of spiraling doubts and mounting apprehension that Nelson Rockefeller stepped in his first days as Assistant Secretary of State for Latin America. Of all the daunting tasks confronting American policy makers as the world war drew to a close, few were thornier, and none less enviable, than those which Rockefeller faced.

But he was eager and ready to take them on. Those very issues, in fact, had preoccupied him well before his appointment came through.

As coordinator, he was fully versed in the special difficulties posed by the Argentines. His coordination committee in Buenos Aires was beset by government censorship. And some of his closest allies in the administration, people like Henry Wallace and Adolf Berle, were among Argentina's most outspoken critics. Wallace in early 1944 pushed for economic sanctions, warning of "a great peril to the democratic cause in Latin America through Argentina."

Perhaps because of the influence of Wallace, Rockefeller early on took a similar hard line. In January 1944, before Argentina's break with the Axis and the ensuing Farrell-Perón coup, he told Wallace the United States and Britain should boycott Argentine beef. Rockefeller said he was disgusted with the whole situation: with the British for temporizing and with Hull for delaying clear-cut action.

But by July, when Hull *had* taken action, Rockefeller's thinking had changed. He still clung to his idea of a meat boycott and had his staff prepare a paper showing how the United States could make up the British shortfall without much of an impact on American meat rationing. ("Serious political instability" in Argentina would result from such a boycott, the staff suggested.) Yet he was also captivated by Padilla's proposal for an inter-American conference to resolve the whole issue.

Coupling the two ideas, Rockefeller sent Hull a memo suggesting a carrot-and-stick approach that would both demonstrate Allied resolve and restore the sense of hemispheric cooperation and unity. The secretary, however, gave Rockefeller's brainstorm short shrift: Hull was as immovable as ever about the notion of a conference. As for the meat boycott, he flatly reminded Rockefeller that 1944 was an election year, and anything that might remotely affect the supply of beef to America's tables was politically suicidal.

The rebuff, coming on top of all his other frustrations with the State Department at the time, left Rockefeller feeling profoundly disheartened. He saw Hull's imperiousness as a scourge that was eating away the core of the inter-American alliance—the alliance he had been struggling, as coordinator, for four years to shape. And in his thinking, the preservation of the inter-American system took precedence over the isolation of the antidemocratic, Axis-leaning Argentines.

No longer was Rockefeller in concert with Henry Wallace's views on the Argentine menace. Instead, he saw as the far greater menace the potential rebirth of unilateral American "big stick" diplomacy in the standoff. He was convinced that the nonrecognition of Argentina was a "negative" policy that would ultimately prove counterproductive, as the Latin American masses came to hail the Argentines for standing up to the Colossus of the North. Freezing out Argentina—and forcing its neighbors to follow suit—would only solidify that country's rabid nationalism and make the Perón government that much more difficult to dislodge.

All this represented an important watershed in Rockefeller's thinking. Yet the turnabout was not as dramatic as it might first appear. Throughout his years as coordinator, Rockefeller had learned to accommodate himself to military juntas, one-party states, and dictators: to Somoza in Nicaragua, Trujillo in the Dominican Republic, Batista in Cuba, and Vargas in Brazil. Whatever misgivings he harbored were subordinated to a greater good: winning the war. Now, with the conflict almost over, he was merely shifting to a new greater good: solidifying and making permanent the great inter-American alliance.

In early September 1944 he wrote to Hull again, but this time he urged the secretary to eschew any "punitive measures" against Argentina, and instead simply let "internal forces" in the country take their course.

The memo was to no avail. Hull would not shift one inch from his stand.

Among some of his aides, however, there was a growing feeling that perhaps Padilla's proposed inter-American conference might not be such a bad idea after all. In early September the Latin American division concluded that such a meeting was "desirable," "to relieve the strain which our relations with the other American Republics are now undergoing."

It was the Argentines themselves who brought matters to a head on October 27 with *their* proposal for a conference. Rockefeller immediately fired off a note to Hull urging that the United States accept the offer. This would have had the same negligible effect as all Rockefeller's previous pitches, had it not been for one thing: Hull was now in the hospital. With the obdurate secretary out of the picture and with the more amenable Stettinius in charge, State's opposition to a meeting suddenly melted away.

But the type of meeting Stettinius and his Latin American hands envisioned was not exactly what Rockefeller, or the Argentines, had in mind. The conference would discuss "hemispheric postwar problems," to make up for the Latin nations' exclusion from the Dumbarton Oaks talks. The discussion of Argentina would merely be the last item on the agenda—and the Argentines would be entirely barred from the conference. So the principle of inter-

American consultation would be observed, without any change in the tough U.S. position. As Stettinius advised FDR, "Until there is a real turnover in Buenos Aires, the department will do everything possible to maintain quarantine to the full extent in the political relations and to the maximum extent in economic relations."

Despite the aggrieved cries from Buenos Aires, Padilla and the rest of the Latin American Foreign Ministers swiftly fell into line behind the U.S. plan. (They really had no choice; if they wanted a conference, this was their only chance.) A meeting on war and peace would be held in Mexico City around February 1—and the Argentines would have to stay home.

It was the planning for this conclave that dominated Rockefeller's agenda when he arrived at the State Department in mid-December 1944. He wasted no time: within days of taking office, he had invited three Latin American ambassadors to lunch at Foxhall Road to discuss Argentina and the conference.

The ambassadors gave him a rapid education in the pitfalls that awaited. The conference, they warned, would have to discuss the Argentina issue, and when it came up it would fracture the meeting. Most of Argentina's neighbors were too fearful of armed retaliation and of "another Bolivia" to join in a U.S. hard line. The only possible way out of this conundrum, said one envoy, was for the United States to agree to "an inter-American basis for solving problems of peace and security," including the question of Argentina.

To the ambassadors' disbelief, Rockefeller was instantly agreeable to the idea. "I believe," he told them, "that the United States may be prepared to proceed along those lines."

It was a bold and potentially foolhardy commitment for any diplomat to make, let alone one who had been on the job less than a week. In effect, Rockefeller was pledging to surrender the U.S. position on Argentina to the deliberations of an inter-American body. It was a commitment Cordell Hull had adamantly refused to undertake, which was why he repeatedly spurned Padilla's calls for a conference. And while Stettinius was more agreeable to a hemisphere parley, his position on Argentina—with its talk of continued "quarantine"—seemed as unyielding as Hull's.

But Rockefeller was breezily confident that he could turn U.S. policy around and secure his seemingly impossible inter-American objective. He would accomplish it the way he always accomplished the impossible: with a direct pitch to FDR.

On January 3, Edward Stettinius visited the White House to bring the President up to date on preparations for the upcoming Yalta summit. Accompanying the secretary was Nelson Rockefeller, who had absolutely nothing to do with the Yalta conference, but who thought he might take the opportunity to brief Roosevelt on another, somewhat lesser, meeting in Mexico City.

The President's physical decline—his loss of weight, his increasing feebleness—was alarming his closest associates. But on that day, he seemed more like the old FDR: relaxed, focused, in good spirits.

Rockefeller sat silently while Stettinius went over the summit issues. When his turn to speak finally came, Rockefeller pulled out two memoranda for the President to peruse.

The first was headed "Suggested U.S. Policy Toward Latin America." It formally proclaimed that it was the intention of the United States to cooperate with the other American republics in such fields as public health, nutrition and food supply, education and economic development. This agenda just happened to coincide with that of the coordinator's office; what Rockefeller was doing was embedding these considerations permanently in U.S. policy. The declaration not only made these economic and social issues a top priority at the Mexico City conference, but effectively ensured a postwar afterlife for Rockefeller's prized programs.

Roosevelt gave the policy an instant okay.

The other memo dealt with Argentina. It laid out two alternative scenarios that the Argentines might follow in light of the Mexico City conference. One was a continuation of their old belligerent ways, with "further aid and comfort to the enemy" and menacing gestures toward their neighbors. The other was a total reversal in course: "a drastic change in internal policy, followed by steps designed to qualify her for readmission to the American family of nations."

If Argentina followed the first path, then, Rockefeller argued, its isolation should go on—but, at the same time, the United States should be prepared to give "military and economic guarantees" to the country's wary neighbors.

But if Argentina mended its ways, then the United States, he suggested, should be prepared to join with the other American republics in granting it diplomatic recognition. He proceeded to define exactly what steps the Argentines would have to take for that to happen. The Farrell-Perón regime would have to cede control to an interim government—overseen by the Argentine Supreme Court—which would end the state of siege and promptly call elections. The country's break with the Axis had to be reaffirmed, "leading to a declaration of war," and Argentina had to initiate a total crackdown on Nazi influence, including dissolution of Axis organizations and jailing of Axis individuals.

At first glance, Rockefeller's prescriptions seemed eminently in keeping with past U.S. policy. But the critical departure was that for the first time the United States was willing to spell out the measures Argentina had to take to reingratiate itself with the hemisphere. Hull had persistently refused to do so, convinced that the slippery Argentines would figure out ways to superficially comply while in actuality maintaining their pro-Axis bent. And, as recently as November 12, Stettinius had reaffirmed that position.

Rockefeller, however, had long regarded this posture as emblematic of U.S. intransigence; if there was ever to be a way out of the impasse, the United States had to say *something* about what it expected.

Roosevelt listened attentively to the presentation, nodding his head in approval from time to time. Stettinius was silent, letting his assistant secretary make his case. It was not clear whether he truly understood where Rockefeller was leading the President and himself.

FDR wanted to know how Rockefeller would determine Perón's willingness to comply with all those measures. Rockefeller replied that he hoped to send an emissary—Rafael Oreamuno, a former Costa Rican ambassador who was now one of his top advisers—to Buenos Aires to meet with the strongman himself. The President approved of the mission.

Roosevelt held on to Rockefeller's memo; he evidently wanted to study it further. Two weeks later, upon another visit to the White House, Stettinius and Rockefeller retrieved the memo, with the presidential imprimatur, "OK FDR," scrawled on the bottom.

With that stroke of the pen, America's stance toward Argentina was irrevocably altered.

While Stettinius may not have appreciated what Rockefeller's memo portended, others in the State Department certainly did. The department's division of River Plate affairs, which oversaw relations with Argentina and its neighbors, adamantly refused to sign on to the memo, charging that it was a total break with past policy. The Perón government, it warned, was "deliberately pursuing a course that is neither one thing nor the other" and would go on doing so.

But upon his return from the White House, Rockefeller had an all-purpose answer to those who second-guessed his new direction. "My instructions come from the President," he said. "If you want to change this policy, you will have to take it up with him."

A week later, Rockefeller was back in the Oval Office. This time he brought a guest: Eduardo Santos, the former President of Colombia. The appointment had not been easy to secure. Rockefeller had to plead with Pa Watson to overrule other presidential aides who insisted FDR was too busy with Yalta to waste time with a Latin American official.

Santos, it turned out, had more in mind than a courtesy call. As an obviously fatigued Roosevelt listened, he described an ongoing arms race in Latin America—made possible by the United States' lend-lease aid. Some nations were spending up to a third of their income on the military, not to defend against the Axis, but to counter possible aggression from their neighbors. Not only was this arms race entrenching the continent's military dictatorships but it was diverting scarce resources from the region's *real* problems: illiteracy, poverty, hunger, and disease.

The only hope, Santos said, was a revival of Woodrow Wilson's idea of a mutual guarantee of borders, a sort of regional antiaggression pact. "Do you think," he asked, "that you or Secretary Stettinius might mention such an idea at the Mexican conference?"

FDR demurred. He agreed wholeheartedly with Santos' concerns, but thought it would be "more appropriate" if Colombia or some other Latin American country, rather than the United States, took the lead. If they introduced such a resolution, then the United States would be happy to support it. Besides, he said, there was the whole issue of defining aggression. Roosevelt felt it was more than menacing words and gestures. "In my opinion," he said, "aggression would be when an armed man crosses the frontier from one country to another."

Santos didn't dispute that. Plainly delighted with Roosevelt's offer of support, he indicated that Colombia could indeed propose the idea, and that Venezuela could probably be persuaded to co-sponsor it. Roosevelt was happy to hear it. "This is a wonderful example of cooperation in the Western Hemisphere," he said—adding that he would bring up the issue at Yalta. As his visitors departed, the frail figure raised his hand in salute. "God bless you!" he said.

The meeting put in place yet another piece of Rockefeller's Mexico City mosaic: a presidential commitment to some sort of hemisphere defense alliance. It would give the Latin Americans one more reason not to worry about Argentina—and one more reason to put their faith in inter-American unity. That this pledge might conflict with another, more overarching commitment—to the global peacemaking organization known as the United Nations—seemed not to have bothered FDR, nor Nelson Rockefeller, in the slightest.

Shortly after this latest breakthrough, a letter arrived on Rockefeller's desk from James I. Miller, an influential American businessman in Buenos Aires. Miller's advice in the past had been sought out by Hull and Rockefeller, and now he was writing about reports he was hearing that Rockefeller was softening the U.S. line on Argentina—"that if certain Argentine Government officials would resign you would favor recognition of the present regime."

"If this Government is recognized by the United States," he warned, "it will be considered here as a tremendous victory for the military clique, and it would strengthen its position to the point where this country would be condemned to a Fascist military dictatorship for the next ten years or more.

"Perón has no intention of holding free elections; there will be no elections, in my opinion, unless he is certain that he himself will be elected president of the country."

The softening, however, continued.

On January 10 Rockefeller gained Stettinius' assent to a change in the U.S. economic policy toward Argentina. This new policy lifted curbs on U.S. imports of "essential" war materials from Argentina, and permitted certain hitherto restricted exports to that country as well on a quid pro quo basis. To attract Argentine exports of much-needed vegetable oils, for instance, the United States might have to send Argentina larger shipments of petroleum.

The necessities of the war effort—"the requirements of the United States and the United Nations for speedy victory"—were cited by Rockefeller as the principal justification for the change. Almost as an afterthought, he mentioned that the easing might also help the United States "regain a realistic economic base for our political policy toward Argentina."

The dawn of this "realistic" attitude would not escape the other nations in the hemisphere, hitherto compelled to toe the tough U.S. line. It made the U.S. diplomatic isolation of Argentina that much more indefensible—which was probably exactly what Rockefeller had in mind.

At the same meeting that he won this concession, Rockefeller suffered a setback on another front. Looking ahead toward the upcoming organizing conference of the United Nations, Stettinius told his aides that only those nations that had declared war on the Axis would be permitted to attend the conference and join the postwar body. This meant, he informed Rockefeller, that the six Latin states (excluding Argentina) that had still not declared war would have to be brought into line, and soon.

These six—Ecuador, Paraguay, Peru, Chile, Uruguay, and Venezuela—had severed relations with the Axis after the Rio conference, but declined to go any further. Never, in the course of the war, had the United States pressed the point, in part because of the American military's reluctance to extend its line of defense too far. And despite their technical neutrality, these nations had rendered a wide range of assistance to the Allied cause—permitting the United States to set up military bases on their territory, rounding up Axis spies, supplying the Allies with strategic materials. Theirs was a far different type of neutrality than that of Argentina.

Rockefeller pointed all this out to Stettinius, stressing the humiliation these governments would feel at being forced to comply with this eleventh-hour change of direction. But Stettinius was insistent on the matter, both out of his own convictions and because FDR himself was insistent on the matter. Back in mid-November the President had told Stettinius that it was "entirely proper" that only those nations that declared war should be invited to attend the UN conference. In the end, a somewhat face-saving tack was agreed upon: Stettinius would ask the President to write an informal letter to the head of each country, requesting the declaration.

The disagreement between the secretary and Rockefeller was the first indication that the two men were operating with a set of vastly different priorities. As one of Stettinius' top aides, Joseph E. Johnson, would later put it, "Ed Stettinius made up his mind that he was going down in history as the guy who established the United Nations. Nelson Rockefeller had made up *his* mind that he was going to move up the ladder as the guy who re-created the inter-American system." That these two visions were often incompatible, if not mutually exclusive, would very soon become painfully apparent.

Stettinius and Rockefeller arrived at the White House on Thursday, January 18, with the proposed agenda for the Mexico City meeting in hand. (Due to the Yalta parley, scheduled to begin February 4, the start of the Latin American conference was pushed back to February 25.) The conference would consider both the future world organization (expecting Latin governments to fall in line, the agenda listed "General Support for Dumbarton Oaks" as an item) *and* the further development of the inter-American system. Santos' concern—the "joint guarantee of boundaries"—was included as well, as was consideration of the economic and social problems that perennially plagued the hemisphere.

The final agenda item—"Other Matters of General and Immediate Concern to the Participating Governments"—was where Argentina would presumably be discussed.

FDR approved the agenda in toto. Totally caught up now in the preparations for Yalta—he would begin the long journey on January 22, two days after his fourth inauguration—he left all further planning for Mexico City in the hands of Rockefeller. Stettinius would also be out of the way; he was accompanying the President to the Crimea, and would fly from there directly to the Latin American conference.

Before he left, however, Stettinius held one more staff meeting to discuss the inter-American parley. The talk turned to Argentina, and Rockefeller proceeded to unleash a bombshell: he was now *against* bringing the issue up at the conference. The reason for his startling turnabout, he said, was that "we have no really good case against Argentina. Of course, we can't admit that, because everyone thinks we have a tremendous case." Because the U.S. case was so weak, Rockefeller insisted, America would suffer a tremendous loss of prestige in a showdown.

He elaborated on his thinking in a letter he wrote the same day to George Messersmith. If Argentina were put on the agenda, he said, everyone would assume that "we have some ingenious formula worked out which would be expressed in a formal resolution. Under the existing circumstances, we of course have no such formula. If we should have a weasel-worded resolution or no resolution at all . . . everybody would say that the conference had been a failure."

Just three months earlier, Rockefeller had been beating the drums for an inter-American conference to discuss Argentina. Now, out of the blue, he was saying that the inter-American conference should discuss everything *but* Argentina. What had happened in the interim to cause this about-face was the radical transformation he had wrought in the nature of the convocation. As he was choreographing it, the meeting promised to be a grand celebration of hemisphere unity, where the nations would enter into solemn commitments to jointly resolve their economic, social, and security problems. The last thing he needed was the irascible Argentine bull upending the proceedings.

And so, in the endless department brainstorming sessions leading up to the Mexico City gathering, the question of Argentina, on which the whole region's attention was riveted, was hardly mentioned at all.

But try as he might to turn his back on the issue, the Argentine conundrum continued to dog him.

A key Argentine opposition leader, Julio González Iramain, arrived in Washington to plead his case with Rockefeller. "What is it that you want from the United States?" Rockefeller asked González.

"We want no money, no arms," the opposition leader answered. "We want only the continued nonrecognition of Argentina."

Rockefeller excused himself; he had to see Stettinius. When he returned, he assured González, "Don't worry. There will be no recognition of the Argentine colonels."

Before he left the United States, Iramain distributed a report detailing the incarceration and grisly torture of political foes by the Argentina junta—a campaign "encompassing the worst characteristics of the Spanish Inquisidores and the German Gestapo," in the words of *The New York Times.*

American public opinion, decidedly skewed against the Argentines since the beginning of the war, was further solidified by the publicity given Iramain's report. In the public mind, the image of the Argentinian regime as a brutal, menacing fascist dictatorship was as sharply etched as ever. And this image was repeatedly confirmed by impartial observers—including, notably, Rockefeller's friend Adolf Berle.

In early February, Berle visited Buenos Aires and was granted an audience with Perón. The new ambassador concluded that Perón had "completely fascized the life of the country; there is no tangible opposition in sight. The bulk of the country is against him, but as they are silenced and cowed, nothing is going to happen."

Perón's despotic ways, and the military buildup he was setting in motion—

a buildup that clearly threatened the country's neighbors—led Berle to favor tough measures. The Mexico City conference, he decided, had "to build a high wall around Argentina . . . making it plain to Perón that any military adventures will mean trouble at once, and lots of it . . ."

At Yalta, in the midst of all the discussions laying out the shape of postwar Europe, the matter of Argentina came up.

Over dinner one evening, Stalin began harping on the country's unfriendliness and its pro-Axis leanings. Was anything, he demanded, going to be done to punish Argentina? A flustered Roosevelt responded that the Argentine people were good; unfortunately, "there are some bad men in power at the moment."

Stalin found this answer utterly unsatisfactory. "If Argentina was in this section of the world," he said, "I would see that she was punished."

Roosevelt then managed to change the subject, and the Argentine question was not brought up again. But Stalin had made his point.

The Big Three, meanwhile, set a deadline of March 1 for nonbelligerent nations to declare war on the Axis. Any country that had not acted by that date would be barred from the United Nations conference, now slated to begin at the end of April.

As the Mexico City meeting loomed closer, certain changes could be observed in the position of Juan D. Perón and his government. The country's two most notorious anti-American newspapers were banned. Foreign Minister Orlando Peluffo was forced out on the grounds that he was pro-Nazi. And the government announced that a "state of tension" now existed in its relations with Germany.

It was with some hopefulness, then (however flimsy its foundations might be), that Nelson Rockefeller's emissary, Rafael Oreamuno, arrived in Buenos Aires in mid-February, just days before the Mexico City conference was to begin. After going through security checks (a military junta can never be too careful) Oreamuno was whisked into the presence of Perón himself, at his office in the Ministry of War.

The Argentine leader listened incredulously as Oreamuno broached Rockefeller's idea of turning the reins over to the president of the Supreme Court, in anticipation of elections. "That would be like turning the government over to a corpse," said Perón, alluding to the Supreme Court president's feeble physical condition. Under no circumstances, he told the emissary, would he accept such a plan. "It would be unfaithful to the nation and would result in a complete loss of the work done since the revolution," he said. "In any case, the Army would veto it."

On the other hand, he vowed that "fair and democratic elections" would indeed be held before the end of October, elections that would "restore a constitutional and democratic life to our people."

Then, waxing grandiloquent, Perón pledged Argentina's complete cooperation with anything asked of it by the other American states—so long, of course, as there is "no motive to humble the governing body or the country." He dismissed the apprehensions about his country's military might as without foundation; Argentina's arms industry, he insisted, was moribund due to the lack of steel, nickel, and aluminum. As for the characterizations of his regime as Nazi or fascist-inspired, they were "unreasonable and preposterous."

The interview was as notable for what Perón didn't promise as what he did. He did not make any specific commitment to crack down on Axis agents and Axis influence (beyond his vague promise to cooperate with the rest of the hemisphere). Nor did he express any intention to lift the country's state of siege. Oreamuno, as it happened, did not press him on either point, despite the fact that they were on the list of Rockefeller's conditions.

In his cable to Rockefeller afterward, Oreamuno counseled a "realistic" stance. The Army was firmly in control, he said, and while elections will be held, "it may be presumed that elections will give the Presidency for the coming six years to Perón." At the same time, he conveyed this cautionary assessment of the Argentine leader: "It is desirable at the outset to emphasize the intelligence and shrewdness of Perón and that one cannot determine at first meeting when or whether he is telling the truth or is sincere."

On the eve of Rockefeller's February 16 departure for Mexico City, an envelope arrived at the State Department from J. Edgar Hoover. The department, in preparation for the conference, had asked the FBI for any documentary evidence it could provide on Argentine collaboration with the Axis. Hoover was now happy to provide this data.

The dossier the bureau compiled was voluminous and detailed. It included evidence that Argentina's arrest of some of the notorious Axis agents was a sham (many were promptly released, and others were never apprehended); that high Argentine officials, including Perón, collaborated with German agents in undermining the governments of neighboring countries, including Chile and Brazil; and that Perón and the Germans were behind the December 1943 coup in Bolivia. Copies of intercepted communications were provided.

It was, in short, the "case" against Argentina that Rockefeller had claimed was so elusive. The material was there for him—if he chose to use it.

Nineteen

Chapultepec

The inter-American conference was a Nelson Rockefeller production, and he imbued it with his hyperkinetic style even before the opening gavel. For the trip down to Mexico City, he chartered (at his own expense) a plushly outfitted DC-3, and invited a formidable throng of Latin American ambassadors to join him. Also accompanying Rockefeller was a phalanx of aides: Avra Warren and John Lockwood and Frank Jamieson and Wally Harrison, among others. And, to attend to Rockefeller's more corporeal needs, Dr. Kenneth Riland of New York, an osteopath who had been a house physician at U.S. Steel, where he ministered to Ed Stettinius' aching back. Hearing of the wonders of a Riland massage, Rockefeller began using him as well. Henceforth, he would not attempt any business trip of consequence without Riland in attendance to relieve his muscular—and sometimes psychological—tension. Riland was a good listener as well as a good masseur.

At the same time that the Rockefeller party was heading south, another group from the State Department was en route in a somewhat more leisurely fashion, via railroad. They took the train because their leader, Leo Pasvolsky, absolutely refused to fly. And they had long since learned it was best not to question anything Leo Pasvolsky wanted.

The fifty-two-year-old Pasvolsky served as special assistant to the secretary, in charge of postwar planning. His principal task, and his passion, was the forging of the global peacekeeping union to be known as the United Nations. To that task he brought considerable academic skills: before entering government in the late 1930s he had been a longtime fellow at the Brookings Institution and the author of numerous works on international relations. And he also brought the worldliness of the émigré: he had escaped czarist Russia as a youth and become a U.S. citizen in 1911, at age eighteen.

A squat, mustachioed, pipe-puffing figure, Pasvolsky carried about him an air of supreme intellectual authority. "The brain that walked like a man," was one derisive description of him. Said his aide Joseph E. Johnson, "He reminded me of the third little pig in Disney's version of that fairy tale—the one whose house could not be blown down." Yet he was also a pragmatist and a canny political infighter. Recruited by Hull to advise on trade issues, he soon became a confidant of the flinty secretary; when Hull began looking ahead to the structure of the postwar world, it was to Pasvolsky that he instinctively turned for ideas and counsel.

Though Hull was now gone, Pasvolsky remained to carry on their quest for a world organization. He had been the intellectual wellspring behind Dumbarton Oaks, and ever since had been intensively involved in plans for the great conference at which the world body would at last be organized.

But first, he had to attend to Mexico City. He had barely countenanced the idea of an inter-American conclave. As far as Pasvolsky was concerned, it was at best a distracting sideshow, and at worst a potential threat to all his grander designs. Unable to head the meeting off, he was determined to limit the damage. As his train clattered through the Great Plains, Pasvolsky sat wreathed in pipe smoke in his private car, mulling the dangers that lay ahead.

Stettinius, meanwhile, was winging his way to the Mexico meeting from Yalta.

En route, he stopped in Rio de Janeiro for a preconference tête-à-tête with President Vargas. Despite his suspicions of Argentina, Vargas expressed the hope that it might somehow be permitted to attend the meeting. But Stettinius waved away this notion as "off beam . . . we do not wish to stoop to that position at this time." The United States, he told Vargas, already had much evidence "relative to sabotage, to smuggling, to clandestine radical activity." In view of that, he felt there was no point in being too hasty about welcoming Argentina back into the inter-American fold.

The delegation sent by the United States to Mexico City was one of the largest entourages ever dispatched to an international conference. Besides the two official delegates (Stettinius and Rockefeller) there were thirty-three "advisers," six "special assistants to the delegates," and twenty-two "technical officers." In all, after counting in translators, press officers, stenographers, and clerical help, the American mission totaled 107: at least three times the size of any other nation's retinue.

This imposing assemblage was partly a reflection of Rockefeller's grandiose aspirations for the conference. But it was equally a manifestation of the assistant secretary's shrewd political calculus. He had persuaded both Tom Connally, chairman of the Senate Foreign Relations Committee, and Warren Austin, the committee's most influential Republican, to attend the conference; two prominent members of the House Foreign Affairs Committee were also invited. Thus, Rockefeller assured the conference of a sympathetic hearing in Congress. The U.S. military was equally well represented: among the brass in attendance were General Stanley D. Embick of the Joint Chiefs of Staff, and Rear Admiral Harold C. Train of the Navy.

The ranks of the "advisers" also included an odd potpourri of American business and labor officials, including Rockefeller's old friend George Meany of the American Federation of Labor. Rounding out the delegation were, as well, top officials from every U.S. government agency that might have some conceivable interest in Latin America. Commerce, Treasury, Leo Crowley's Foreign Economic Administration—all were more than amply represented. No one, but no one, would have any cause to complain to Nelson Rockefeller that they were left out.

Awaiting the arrival of Stettinius' plane on February 20, most of the American horde whiled away the hours playing poker and indulging in the soothing ministrations of Dr. Riland. Rockefeller, however, had no time for such diversions. There were too many pieces to be put into play.

One of these was furthering his relationship with James Reston, the enterprising young correspondent of *The New York Times.* Reston's beat was the postwar order, and he already had infuriated Stettinius by printing top-secret details of the Dumbarton Oaks talks. Despite this, the press-savvy Rockefeller recognized that Reston's could well be the authoritative word on the success of the conference, and so he hastened to fill him in on the directions in which the conclave was likely to go. The result was a scene-setting article on February 19 that reflected, in unattributed fashion, Rockefeller's current approach to Argentina: "Those who are responsible for 'steering' the conference would like to keep the Argentine discussion on as broad a base as possible and if they have their way it is likely that all the cross-currents and discussion of this issue will end with a broad declaration favoring the return of democratic principles to Argentina and the appointment of a committee to watch developments there." It was the same line Rockefeller had privately been taking for weeks: Argentina should be downplayed as much as possible.

On the evening of the nineteenth, Rockefeller—accompanied by Avra Warren and several other aides—went to dinner at the American embassy. Among George Messersmith's other guests were two top Mexican officials, Manuel Tello and Campos Ortiz. After dinner the question of Dumbarton Oaks was brought up. The United States wanted the conference to formally endorse the Dumbarton Oaks proposals, but many Latin nations—still miffed at not being consulted in the first place—were not inclined to do so. What would happen, wondered one of the guests, if the conference issued a report critical of Dumbarton Oaks? Would the United States try to block it?

Those questions had been preying on Leo Pasvolsky's mind for weeks, and they partly explained why he had such trepidation about the inter-American parley. To have this conference—a conference the United States actively promoted—issue complaints about Dumbarton Oaks would amount to a direct repudiation of the agreements the United States had struck with the other great powers, agreements that were the very linchpins of the planned international organization. The intricate mechanism of a new world order, the mechanism fashioned piece by piece at Dumbarton Oaks and at Yalta, could well fall apart. To avoid this calamity, Pasvolsky was willing to allow individual Latin ministers to vent their spleens—as long as the conference as a whole did not issue a critical report.

But Leo Pasvolsky was not at this dinner; Nelson Rockefeller was. And Nelson Rockefeller had other ideas. He flatly told his fellow dinner guests that State had considered the matter, and would indeed permit the conference to promulgate a critical report, along with resolutions suggesting modifications of the Dumbarton Oaks accord. The United States, he said, would then transmit the whole package to its wartime partners. Rockefeller was unequivocal on the matter: this, he said, was the *decided* policy of the United States.

The guests left the embassy impressed with this turnabout in the American position, and none were more impressed than the Mexicans. Mexico had many problems with the Dumbarton Oaks plan, but had been reluctant to disrupt the conference by raising them. Now the Assistant Secretary of State was practically *encouraging* the Mexicans to make Dumbarton Oaks an issue. In so doing, he was plainly trying to mollify his aggrieved Latin American friends—even at the cost of compromising the position of his own government, the government for which he worked, with the other major powers. It was, for a newly minted Assistant Secretary of State, the riskiest of gambits.

At 1:45 the next afternoon the big C-54 transport plane bearing Edward Stettinius and his party at last touched down in the brilliant, arid sunshine of Mexico City. After the obligatory remarks before the cameras and microphones, the group headed for the Hotel Genève, where Stettinius and Rockefeller had accommodations across the hall from one another. The largest hotel in Mexico, the Genève combined an opulent Spanish colonial style with Anglo-Saxon efficiency: it advertised itself as "the ONLY hotel in Mexico under the personal management of Canadians and Americans."

Once settled in, Stettinius summoned Rockefeller, Messersmith, Pasvolsky, and other top aides to his suite. Distracted until recently by Yalta, the Secretary of State was just getting around to reviewing the composition of the U.S. delegation—and he was utterly astonished by what he saw. All those advisers, and technical officers, and translators: it was just too much, he moaned. But, in the face of Rockefeller's energetic defense of his handpicked entourage, the travel-weary Stettinius yielded.

Rockefeller, however, was mute when Stettinius stopped at one name on the list: that of their mutual osteopathic friend, Dr. Riland. The secretary bluntly told Rockefeller he was "extremely displeased" to note Riland's presence.

Stettinius then asked Rockefeller what was being done about Argentina. Padilla, who would serve as conference president, had it all under control, the assistant secretary assured him. The Mexican Foreign Minister will squelch any discussion of Argentina until the end of the meeting, and then defuse the issue by appointing a committee to study the matter. Argentina would *not* sidetrack the conference.

The next morning a caravan of official vehicles wended its way up the six-lane boulevard known as the Paseo de la Reforma to the outskirts of the city, finally entering a vast, lush park. Driving past trailing vines and profusions of tropical flowers, the convoy snaked up a high winding road, through groves of ancient *ahuehuete* trees, some dating to the time of Montezuma. At the top of the hill, past monumental iron gates decorated with bronze martial figures, the vehicles finally reached their destination: the castle of Chapultepec, site of the Inter-American Conference on Problems of War and Peace.

Chapultepec (Aztec for Grasshopper Hill) was the site of Montezuma II's summer palace. The castle, begun in 1783 by the Spanish viceroy, went through a succession of reconstructions and incarnations as the country passed from ruler to ruler. A getaway for the viceroy, it served as a fortress under Santa Anna and was the scene of the climactic battle of the Mexican-American War in 1847.

The castle attained its apogee of grandeur under the ill-fated Emperor Maximilian, who—with the eager collaboration of his Empress Carlota—rebuilt it as a semi-tropical Versailles. The walls of the salons were covered with Gobelin tapestries, the bedchambers and anterooms were studded with Louis XV furnishings. The country's later revolutionary governments grafted their own symbols onto the grandiose setting: at the bottom of the castle's grand staircase a fresco was executed depicting Mexico's great revolutionists. The palace served as the Mexican presidential residence until the 1930s, when the sumptuous surroundings proved too much for the ardently egalitarian Cárdenas.

And so the castle stood, a monument to both colonial excess and passionate nationalism, a relic in which the baroque, heroic, and lachrymose strains in the national character freely intermingled. As the conference delegates' cars slowed to a halt, they passed tiled fountains and pergolas bright with flowers, as well as a memorial sculpture of a weeping woman: "Mexico Mourning Her Slain Sons." Once inside the cool of the palace, the delegates entered a reception room, rich with pink satin brocade, that had once been Carlota's boudoir.

From the first session on Wednesday morning, February 21, it became apparent that this conference would frustrate the best efforts of Nelson Rockefeller, or anyone else, to keep it within bounds.

This session was supposed to be a sedate meeting of the steering committee, made up of the nineteen Foreign Ministers. They would elect the conference president (Padilla), organize committees, and then adjourn to await the formal opening of the conclave that evening at the Mexican Chamber of Deputies. Some of the ministers—including, apparently, Stettinius—thought the session would be private. But when they arrived at the meeting place, the palace's Jewel Room, a narrow rectangular chamber some one hundred fifty feet long and no more than forty feet wide, they were confronted with absolute bedlam. More than 1,000 people, including newsmen, photographers, and assorted hangers-on, were crammed into the room, jostling for position and taking up every conceivable inch of space. An endless din filled the room, and when the loudspeakers failed just minutes after the opening gavel, the ministers found themselves shouting just to be heard by their colleagues at the other end of the table.

The first order of business, Padilla's election, proceeded uneventfully enough. But then the Paraguayan ambassador to Washington, Oelso Veláquez, rose and stunned the assemblage by immediately bringing up the matter of Argentina. It should not be the last item on the agenda, said Veláquez, but the *first,* and he offered a motion to that effect.

All eyes turned to Padilla. The Mexican pointed out that all the participants had previously agreed to discuss Argentina last. Another delegate from Mexico, Castillo Najera, then stood up and suggested that the Paraguayan motion be referred to the steering committee. The other committee members, however, rejected that maneuver. They voted to stick to the original agenda, with Argentina the concluding item.

Padilla had prevailed, but only for the moment. It was already obvious, to the crowd that packed the room as well as to the ministers, that the Argentina issue could not be shunted off to parliamentary limbo forever.

It became even more obvious that evening, at the ceremonies formally launching the conference.

The lavishly gilded Chamber of Deputies was awash in a cascade of illumination as the beams of floodlights circled the room and flashbulbs erupted. In the tangle of bodies jostling for places in the galleries, a group of Mexican military cadets made their way to the forefront. They were brandishing the Argentine flag.

At the rostrum stood Mexico's President, Manuel Avila Camacho, greeting the delegates with exhortations to collaborate in building a permanent peace and a sound economic future. There were allusions to Dumbarton Oaks, with assertions by the Mexican President that Latin America had "the right as well as the responsibility" to offer its own proposals.

Then he brought up Argentina. The Argentines had "a cordial place in our thoughts and affection," Avila Camacho said. "Deploring their absence, and hoping that circumstances will soon give us the satisfaction to see them officially associated with the present efforts, I salute the delegations here," he declared. The comments were greeted with an ovation—the only one the President's speech elicited.

Afterward, there was much speculation about the drift of Avila Camacho's remarks. "There is a growing feeling here," said the *Times*'s Reston, "that the conference is only at the beginning of its trial with Argentina."

Unable to keep the Argentine matter bottled up any longer, Stettinius and Rockefeller searched for a way out of their Gordian dilemma.

They had in hand reports of some recent meetings various intermediaries had with Perón. One account—relayed to Mexico City by the U.S. embassy in Bogotá, Colombia—described conversations within the previous two weeks between Perón and the Acting Foreign Minister of Colombia, Gustavo Santos. Perón told Santos he was willing to accept anything, without restrictions, in order to become reconciled with the United States and the other American nations—so long as Argentine "decorum" (another of his euphemisms for national pride) was preserved. Any loss of "decorum," he warned, would result in his fellow officers marching in from their barracks and cutting him to pieces. He would rather die at the hands of the *"Señores Americanos"* than suffer such a fate.

The Argentine strongman then specifically asked Colombia to shepherd the efforts toward his country's rehabilitation at the Mexico City meeting. He accompanied this request with dire warnings: that if his reconciliation attempts were not accepted the present government would be replaced by an even more militantly nationalist one, that complete chaos could ensue, that the Communists might step into the vacuum and take control and then use Argentina as a base for expansion throughout South and Central America.

Even if the United States discounted these overtures, they were bound to come to the attention of the other American states and wreak havoc at the conference. There were indications that Colombia might indeed press Argentina's case at the conference; Colombian President Alfonso López unequivocally told the U.S. ambassador that something had to be done about Argentina at Mexico City.

Reviewing their options, Stettinius and Rockefeller decided they could no longer downplay the issue. Instead, they would do what the State Department had never before been prepared to countenance: they would take Juan Perón at his word. If Perón was truly serious about meeting U.S. conditions, they would propose those conditions and put the ball back in his court.

A top-secret cable was prepared for transmission to Roosevelt. In it, Stettinius explained the turnabout this way: "The Argentines seem prepared to desert the Axis and join the good neighbors. They have considerable support in their maneuvering but so far we have been able to hold the line. However, I am convinced that we should take decisive action promptly in order to maintain the initiative. As Argentina meets conditions on which I believe there is a consensus of opinion, we can insure the unity of the Americas. Otherwise, while Mexico City on the surface might appear to be a success to hemispheric unity, yet basically there would be quicksands that would undoubtedly begin to shift before the Conference is over."

The conditions Stettinius and Rockefeller proposed were that Argentina declare war immediately on Germany and Japan; that it join an inter-American committee to combat subversion; that it disperse its troops along the Brazilian and Chilean borders to allay the suspicions of its neighbors; and that Argentina subscribe to all the resolutions of the Mexico City conference. Significantly, there was no longer any insistence on democratic elections or on turning the government over to the Supreme Court; Stettinius was at last willing to accept, as he told FDR, that "Perón is going to remain in the Argentine whether we like it or not."

Once those conditions were agreed to, Argentina would be invited to send representatives to Mexico City, and at the end of the conference each of the American republics would announce that it was resuming normal relations with the country.

Rather than issue those terms publicly, Stettinius and Rockefeller chose to use a more discreet channel. Peru's Foreign Minister, Manuel Gallagher y Canaval, would privately approach the Argentine government with the offer. Nothing would be made public until the Argentines accepted.

The proposal was relayed to FDR aboard the USS *Quincy,* still en route from Yalta, on February 23, and on February 25 he wired back his okay. Gallagher went ahead with the plan.

Despite the attention the press was giving his role—*Time* described the conference as "the test of Nelson Rockefeller's long and earnest efforts to win Latin American friendship"—Rockefeller endeavored, uncharacteristically, to remain in the shadows. He chaired no committees, made no speeches, gave no on-the-record interviews. He may well have been the meeting's most influential player, but, at least in the early days, he left no footprints in his wake.

In the afternoon of February 23, Stettinius gave his first Chapultepec press conference. He reviewed some innocuous proposals the United States would be making, deflected questions about Argentina, and introduced his principal aides.

"I know we should not adjourn," Stettinius said, "without asking Mr. Rockefeller to say something to you."

Rockefeller approached the microphone. "Pleasure to be here," he said, and walked away.

In his backroom machinations, Rockefeller received help from a familiar source: the FBI.

The bureau by now was well established in Mexico City; it even had operatives planted in the city's telephone department. Each morning FBI agents reported to Rockefeller and Warren on the doings in the rest of the diplomatic community. And at the outset of the conference, the agents sent Rockefeller a warning: his hotel suite was bugged. The bureau could install a device that would vibrate and break up the recordings, but it couldn't do it right away, so Rockefeller had best be careful.

The FBI well knew the impact this disclosure would have on Rockefeller: since 1943 agents had been checking his home and office phones for wiretaps once a month, at Rockefeller's request. It was not clear just what led Rockefeller to believe his phones might be tapped. Most likely, his fears were simply a by-product of his own conspiratorial bent and taste for the covert; like others caught up in the intelligence subculture, he was somewhat paranoid about becoming a victim of it himself. When he moved over to State it was suggested that the FBI checks be discontinued, on the grounds that no other assistant secretary received such a service. Rockefeller, however, was adamant, and the monthly phone checks continued.

Duly warned in Mexico City, Rockefeller proceeded to exercise appropriate wariness, even going so far as to watch what he said in restaurants, because the FBI also advised him that some of the tables were wired. When Latin diplomats visited his suite, he took them out on the terrace—and, sotto voce, explained to them why. His whispered cautions were a sublime display of diplomatic one-upmanship, sure to discombobulate the most seasoned envoy, and Rockefeller loved to watch the flabbergasted expressions on his guests' faces when he confided the warnings from his friends at the FBI. As he would later recall, "This was the kind of G-man stuff that everybody has an interest in. They were impressed that I knew about it, and they were impressed that I told them about it."

Friday, February 23, was "resolutions day," when a deluge of proposals—covering everything from the rights of man to the abolition of censorship—descended upon the conference. But only one resolution truly stood out: Colombia's antiaggression resolution, the proposal that ex-President Santos had vetted with FDR a month earlier.

The Colombian resolution effectively expanded the Monroe Doctrine—which set up a shield against the designs of nonhemisphere powers—to cover inter-American aggression as well. There was little doubt in anyone's mind as to just whom this new doctrine was aimed at.

The press was quick to report U.S. support, and even encouragement, of the resolution. Nevertheless, as the American delegation began to digest the Colombian verbiage, a quiver of foreboding was felt in certain quarters about the potential blank-check commitment of U.S. military power and about what it would all mean for the future world peacekeeping organization. Among those who voiced their concern was Leo Pasvolsky.

Rockefeller, however, was determined to push the resolution through. He had midwifed the proposal since his first conversations with Santos: wangling time with FDR and making sure that Roosevelt signed off on the idea. The resolution, in his eyes, would seal the postwar inter-American alliance, engaging the United States in a permanent commitment to the security of the hemisphere. Not only would it alleviate the pervasive fear of Argentina but it would also counter another, less openly discussed apprehension: the fear of Communism.

Worries about Communist inroads had long haunted the Latin American ruling class, and now that the war was ending the specters seemed chillingly close at hand. As Laurence Duggan would note, "The sweep of the Red Army through Poland and East Prussia produced more shivers than admiration among the ruling caste of Latin America. The triumvirate of landowner, priest, and Army officer which had held power in most of the Latin American republics for the past four hundred years trembled in its boots. . . . Soviet victory frightened them as the Nazi conquests never had."

At the heart of the Latin anxiety about Dumbarton Oaks was their nervousness about the Soviet clout in the new world body. Small wonder, then, that the Colombian resolution was so instantly, and gratefully, acclaimed by the delegates: it offered a means to neutralize that clout, at least in the hemisphere. In Duggan's words, "The Latin American oligarchs wanted an inter-American peace system so effective that there would be no need for the proposed world organization to take a hand in the political disputes of this hemisphere."

Rockefeller, well aware of Great Power sensitivities, scrupulously refrained from citing, or even elliptically alluding to, the Communist menace. But then again, there was no need to. He found it sufficient to invoke the dream of hemisphere unity; the delegates, in their own minds, could fill in the rest.

And now that the measure was on the table, there was no way he would allow it to be deflected.

Throughout that weekend—while Stettinius relaxed at a hideaway in the nearby resort town of Cuernavaca—Rockefeller worked tirelessly to move the resolution along, securing the vital endorsement of the U.S. Joint Chiefs of Staff. Wary of the nebulous world organization, the chiefs were eager to cement regional military alliances, particularly in the hemisphere. General Embick declared himself solidly in favor of the Colombian doctrine.

By Monday afternoon, the redrafted resolution was sent to the conference committee on inter-American organizations for approval—the final step before it was formally ratified by the entire conference. It now bore a title that reflected the significance its sponsors attached to the measure: "The Declaration of Chapultepec."

Earlier that day, Senator Warren Austin made his first appearance at the conference. The sixty-seven-year-old Austin, an old Vermont country lawyer, was an internationalist and a fervent supporter of the new world peacekeeping organization. Long cultivated by State, Austin was vital to the administration's hopes for bipartisan support of the postwar order.

Austin was assigned to Committee III: the committee that would be reviewing the Chapultepec Declaration. The next morning the senator listened attentively as one speaker after another heaped accolades on the resolution. Shuffling through his papers, Austin searched for a copy of this declaration; he knew absolutely nothing about it. The only copy available was in Spanish, and Austin hadn't the slightest idea what it said. With mounting irritation, he watched the Cuban delegate rise and call for approval of the resolution by acclamation.

Austin asked to be recognized. Struggling to be as polite as possible, he said he was in sympathy with the declaration's aims but, under the circumstances, he couldn't possibly vote for it, because no English text was available. He respectfully requested postponement of the vote, at least until he could review the text and confer with his colleague Senator Connally, who was due to arrive the next day.

The committee agreed to the postponement—but only until eleven o'clock the next morning.

A furious Austin immediately called a meeting of U.S. officials involved in the committee, including Nelson Rockefeller. The resolution, he fumed, was a "bombshell" which had caught him totally unawares; now he was expected to come back the next morning and vote for it, before Connally had even had a chance to see it. Rockefeller offered to move the vote back a day, to March 1, and tried to explain to Austin how the resolution had come about, recounting the story of Santos' meeting with FDR. But Austin cut him short. This declaration, he curtly pointed out, was a peacetime guarantee, not a wartime one, and therefore was up to the Congress, not the President, to provide.

As far as Austin was concerned, the declaration, as it stood, was "completely unacceptable." It effectively allowed a majority of Latin American states to commit U.S. armed forces to regional conflicts, whether the United States wanted to go in or not; if Argentina, for instance, attacked Uruguay, all it took were the votes of eleven Latin American nations to force the United States into the war. This, for Austin, was utterly beyond the pale. "Gentlemen," he said, "this is a matter of the responsibilities of the Senate of the

United States. We cannot commit United States forces without a very special constitutional action."

Pasvolsky then chimed in. "Aren't these questions the same issues that will come up when we discuss the world organization?" he asked. "Shouldn't they be discussed first in regard to the world organization, before we get into how they would apply in an inter-American system?" Austin agreed. Pasvolsky, in effect, was moving toward tabling the whole matter until the United Nations conference two months hence.

The meeting broke up with Austin volunteering to try his hand at a redraft that would take care of his objections. As the officials went their separate ways, Rockefeller was bristling, his anger directed not at Austin but at Pasvolsky. Glaring at the rotund aide, Rockefeller snapped, "If you're going to work against the agreed position of our delegation and the agreed position of the State Department, you better go back to Washington. I'm responsible to the secretary for the conduct of the United States delegation here."

Since when was all this agreed to? Pasvolsky might have replied. (That meeting, in fact, was the first open discussion the U.S. delegation had had of the Colombian resolution.) But, exercising a wise forbearance, Pasvolsky said nothing, and went on his way.

Rockefeller's defensiveness about the Chapultepec Declaration was understandable: it was now the vessel of all his hopes for the conference. Without it, he would have little to show for his months of arduous preparation except agreeable bombast and a grab bag of toothless resolutions.

That much was even more apparent when he heard his fellow assistant secretary Will Clayton's anxiously anticipated economic speech on February 27. Clayton's economic, or "E," area of State had been lukewarm from the start about the Mexico City meeting, and Clayton's tepid speech aptly reflected those doubts. While acknowledging Latin America's concerns about its postwar plight, Clayton offered next to nothing in the way of tangible programs to alleviate them.

Even the upbeat Stettinius had to acknowledge afterward that there was "some disappointment" among the Latin American delegates "that Mr. Clayton had not made more substantial commitments." One Latin commentator sniped that Clayton had plagiarized "a good speech made by Theodore Roosevelt before 1910."

Clayton's "tendency to understate and under-promise," as Stettinius put it, may have made political sense, but it proved a bitter disappointment for those hoping for relief, not rhetoric, from the Colossus of the North.

And, on top of that, there was more bad news from Argentina.

Peru's Gallagher was still awaiting a response to his overture. But on February 26 Perón gave an interview to the Associated Press in which he all but ruled out any declaration of war against Germany. With his usual verbal flourish, he asserted that such a declaration, "on grounds palpably insufficient, tardily recognized and opportunistic would alienate our friends in this country and other American republics and give our foes an opportunity to heap scorn on us."

Asked what steps were needed to restore harmony with the United States, Perón declared, "You must not demand that we go to war against anybody. You must learn to understand the Argentines—their practical sense as well as their sense of proportion and their sense of pride."

In the salons of Chapultepec, meanwhile, the growing restiveness with the United States was becoming manifest. And the American who felt it most was not Nelson Rockefeller, but Pasvolsky.

A special committee had been appointed to deal with the Dumbarton Oaks proposals, and Pasvolsky thought he had struck a satisfactory deal with the committee chairman, Venezuelan Foreign Minister Caracciolo Parra-Pérez: the various nations' views on Dumbarton Oaks would be collected, and Parra-Pérez would draft a thirty-page summary, pointing up the issues on which a consensus had emerged. There would be no critical resolutions and no attempt to force a conference stance on the Dumbarton Oaks plan—except to generally endorse it.

Several prominent delegates, however, bridled at this accommodation and, at a committee meeting, lashed out at Pasvolsky. Gustavo Guttiérrez of Cuba said that a summary was something "a college student or a Foreign Office stooge could equally well accomplish." Roberto Córdova of Mexico insisted that at the very least the consensus should be presented as the American republics' "minimum" and "indispensable" demands, and offered a resolution to that effect.

Clearly taken aback by the Latins' fiery rhetoric, Pasvolsky replied that the use of such terms as "minimum" and "indispensable" would be thoroughly undesirable. Córdova, though, was adamant. "The Mexican delegation feels there must be a resolution," he said. "Otherwise people will wonder how the conference could take so much time and accomplish nothing."

Senator Connally's train, scheduled to arrive at midday on February 28, was running late. Rather than wait for his colleague, Austin set to work that morning on the troublesome language in the Chapultepec Declaration.

It was not long before a solution presented itself. The declaration would be divided into two parts. The first part would apply only for the duration of the war, and was essentially the peacekeeping framework envisioned by the Latin states, with an important proviso tacked on: nations would be required to act cooperatively against an aggressor, but only "subject to their constitutional processes." For the United States, this meant the President could take action using his war powers.

The second part continued this framework after the war, but only if a treaty to that effect was signed. Since this treaty would have to be approved by the Senate, there would be no blank-check commitment of the U.S. military. What's more, because the Senate also had to approve the plan for the new world organization, the regional mechanism created by the treaty could be made subordinate to the world body.

Austin circulated his reworking to the delegations of Colombia, Uruguay, and Brazil, all of whom were involved in the original resolution; none had any problems with it. By day's end, Rockefeller confidently told the *Times*'s Reston, "It's in the bag"—and proceeded to leak the details of the new resolution. All that remained to be done, he advised Reston, was for Connally to give his imprimatur upon his arrival that afternoon.

It was indicative of Tom Connally's power that Stettinius cut short his afternoon meetings to hasten to the train station to greet the Texan. Looking every inch the prototypical senator, with his black silk bow tie and his wavy locks curling over his high starched collar, Connally had been one of Congress's most formidable figures for over a decade and a half. A canny, cautious politico, Connally was heartily distrusted by some of the more ardent New Dealers such as Henry Wallace, who once described him as "in some respects . . . the lowest type of senator we have. . . . He is essentially a demagogue with no depths of perception, no sense of the general welfare, and no interest in it." No one, however—from FDR down—dared question his clout.

Not very long after Connally had settled into his hotel room, Rockefeller came calling, declaration text in hand. The senator waved it away. "I'm too tired right now," he snorted. "I'm not reading *anything* today." The assistant secretary persisted, whereupon Connally fixed upon him his most withering glower. "Don't try to rush me, young man," he warned.

Rockefeller retreated from the room, beset, for once, with a frisson of panic. The *Times,* he knew, would be describing the amended resolution the next morning as a done deal; when Connally saw the story he would be fuming. The whole carefully crafted resolution might well blow up in a puff of senatorial pique. Scrambling for a phone, he called Reston and begged him to kill the story. "Sorry," the reporter said. "It's already in print in New York."

The next morning Rockefeller received word that the paper indeed had gone with the story—on page one. The only saving aspect of the article was that it mentioned Connally would be "studying" the new resolution. At least Reston hadn't written that Connally had approved it—as the newspaperman might well have if he had taken Rockefeller's flip comments at face value.

As a concession to Connally, the conference committee agreed to postpone consideration of the Chapultepec Declaration one more day, to March 2.

Both Connally and Austin had been invited to join the rest of the U.S. delegation at a March 1 luncheon in Cuernavaca hosted by Mexico's Economy Minister. They went along, and afterward stayed on at Stettinius' hideaway to work on the draft.

Upon their return to the city that evening, the senators were telling reporters that they had reached full agreement on the resolution. There would be some changes in Austin's draft, Connally said, but nothing substantial, and he believed they would be acceptable to the other American republics.

This was enough for Rockefeller. Finally seeing his opening, and determined to head off any further frittering by Pasvolsky and his cohorts, the assistant secretary prepared a cable to the President seeking FDR's approval of the declaration. By ten o'clock that same evening—after Rockefeller had phoned Stettinius, still in Cuernavaca—the memo, marked "secret and personal," and bearing the secretary's signature, was on its way to the embassy code room, for transmission to Washington. The next morning, the response was wired from the White House: the President had approved.

Considering the importance of the declaration as an expression of U.S. and hemisphere policy, Stettinius' role in shaping it was a curiously passive one.

From the outset, he unquestioningly accepted Rockefeller's assertion that the antiaggression policy was what FDR wanted, based on the assistant secretary's account of the meeting with Santos. Stettinius left it to Pasvolsky to raise the issue of how this policy would fit in with the new world body, and to Austin to pose the very real potential political and constitutional conflicts. His involvement in the revisions—once he abdicated them to the two senators—was perfunctory.

It was true that there were other matters that preoccupied him during the Mexico City meeting, most notably the Yalta accords and the upcoming United Nations conference in San Francisco. But it could also be said that his disengagement was part of his operating style: he truly believed in delegation, even when it came to policy making. This style, however, had its price. Tugged from one position to the next by his zealous aides, he found himself caught up in a welter of contradictions and last-minute reversals (as witness Argentina).

Observing Stettinius' performance at Chapultepec, Messersmith concluded that he was "completely beyond his depth. He was depending very largely for counsel on Nelson Rockefeller. . . . He seemed to be completely unaware of the fact that the decisions with regard to the meeting were really being made by Connally and Austin . . . and a few of us working with them." Wrote Berle in his diary, "His cheerful ignorance remains the amazement of all hands."

For Rockefeller, this ignorance proved highly convenient, to say the least. And, to assure his boss's placidity, he endeavored to slather him with praise at every opportunity.

On February 28, as the tussle over the declaration was coming to a head, Rockefeller took the time to drop Stettinius "just a few lines to tell you what a wonderful impression you have been making here among all the delegates and in the press throughout the Americas.

"The fact that you were willing to take the time to come to Mexico City and stay throughout the Conference will be one of the turning points in the future of the unity of the Americas. It means a great deal to me personally to be associated with you in this work."

On March 3 the amended declaration, now known as the "Act of Chapultepec," was formally presented to the conference for approval. Praise from the Latin American delegates was universal, and Tom Connally gratified the Latin Americans by speaking forcefully in favor of the measure. It was, he said, "one of the greatest state papers in the world," a new Monroe Doctrine backed by all the Americas instead of just the United States.

Rockefeller sent a cable to Santos in Colombia: "Your dream has been realized and the Act of Chapultepec rises as one of the great milestones in the path of advance towards peace and security of the peoples of the hemisphere. History will record your vision."

The U.S. press, which had hitherto characterized the State Department's efforts in Mexico City as bumbling, ill prepared, and ill conceived, had its viewpoint magically transformed by the passage of the act. "Stettinius' Aides Lauded in Mexico" was the headline in the *Times*: "The State Department's new 'team' has had its first real test at the Inter-American Conference and the general impression here is that it has done pretty well. . . . Mr. Rockefeller particularly has had a personal success. He has been friendly, patient, and quick to anticipate crises and to get to the proper people about them."

The act, indeed, was a triumph for Rockefeller. It cemented the inter-American alliance, the great cause for which he had been working since he entered public life. It was a decisive victory over Pasvolsky and his internationalist faction, who regarded the United States' hemisphere neighbors as little more than squawking, squabbling children getting in the way of the Great Powers' designs. And it virtually guaranteed that whatever else happened, this conference—*his* conference—would be seen as a majestic success.

All that stood in his way now was the issue of Argentina—still, eleven days into the conference, as combustible a matter as ever.

It was at the end of the meeting's second week that Rockefeller finally heard from Gallagher about the overtures to Argentina. "You won't believe this," Gallagher told him. "Perón has turned it all down."

At the outset of the conclave, Rockefeller probably would have felt some relief at this news. But as the conference wore on, the agitation among the delegates for an Argentine breakthrough was growing. And with the conference rapidly working through the 150-odd resolutions on the table, the day of reckoning—when, with all other business disposed of, Argentina would be brought up—was approaching.

That weekend, he and Padilla struggled for a solution to the Argentine conundrum, searching for some mechanism, some formula that would defuse the controversy before it sent verbal shrapnel flying through Chapultepec's gilded halls.

In his own backroom negotiations, meanwhile, Leo Pasvolsky had been unable to sidetrack the specific Latin criticisms of Dumbarton Oaks. The best he could do was water down the language (there was no talk about "minimum" and "indispensable" conditions) and throw in a clause making it clear that the United States was not a party to this critique.

And so the Latins had their say about Dumbarton Oaks—just as Nelson Rockefeller had privately assured them they would. It was now left to Pasvolsky to see to it that the infection was confined to Mexico City.

By the end of the weekend, Padilla had come up with a way out of the Argentina impasse, and Rockefeller thought it might work.

The Perón regime would be asked to meet two conditions: to declare war on the Axis and to abide by the decisions of the Chapultepec conference. By agreeing to the latter, Argentina would assure other nations it was not simply going through the motions of a war declaration, since many of the Chapultepec resolutions dealt with the war effort. Most importantly, Argentina would have to sign the Act of Chapultepec, thus committing itself to the regional peacekeeping alliance.

If Argentina agreed to those terms, it would be welcomed back into the American family of nations.

The terms, in fact, were not very different from those conveyed by Gallagher. The key distinction was that they were now gathered under the all-purpose rubric of the Mexico City conference. Even Argentina's staunchest partisans would have a hard time arguing that it shouldn't submit to the same conditions and accords to which all its hemisphere brethren had subscribed.

But the principal stumbling block remained: Argentina had to declare war.

Nonetheless, Rockefeller moved quickly to transform Padilla's concepts into language the conference could consider. For this, he turned to Berle. Meanwhile, an outline of the Padilla formula was leaked to Reston, and the

Times printed the terms on Tuesday, March 6, even as Berle was still laboring over the language—and before Stettinius had a chance to inform the President of this latest change of course. (The leak was later explained by Rockefeller as an attempt to test the waters of U.S. public opinion.)

That evening six Latin diplomats gathered in Rockefeller's hotel suite to go over Berle's draft. One of them, Alberto Lleras Camargo of Colombia, was an old newspaperman, and before long he doffed his jacket, grabbed a typewriter, and began banging out new versions of the resolution. Soon the floor was littered with discarded drafts.

While the Latins argued over phraseology, Berle and Rockefeller stepped outside for some air, walking along one of the boulevards until they came upon a small park. At last, free of the squabbling Latin Americans, Berle felt he could unburden himself to Rockefeller on Argentina. Berle had willingly done Rockefeller's bidding, but he harbored serious misgivings about the direction in which his friend was going.

"I don't believe you should negotiate with the Argentines; certainly not now," Berle told him. "Be cool toward them. Let them wait.

"This conference has been a great success. You're now sitting on top of the world. It would be a political error to rush into any negotiations with Perón and, anyway, I don't believe you can change Perón. He is completely cynical."

Rockefeller listened pensively. Finally, after a few moments' silence, he spoke up. "Thanks," he said. "I'll think about it. But I believe unity of the Americas means a lot."

It was not until midnight that the final draft rolled out of Lleras Camargo's typewriter. Rockefeller grabbed it and ran out the door. He wanted to show it to Padilla immediately.

The finished product bore scant resemblance to anything Berle, the former Columbia Law School professor, might have written. Orotund declamations rumbled through paragraphs laden with diplomatic filigree. The resolution praised the "notable contributions" Argentina has made to the "juridical and political heritage of the continent" and solemnly declared that "the unity of the Nations of America is indivisible and that the Argentine Nation is and always has been an integral part of the Union of American Republics."

Every turn of phrase seemed calculated to play up to the hypersensitive "national dignity" of the Argentines. There were no references to Argentina's misdeeds; instead, the conference merely "deplored" that the country had "not found it possible to take steps that would allow it to participate" in the Mexico City conference. The resolution expressed the "hope" and the "desire" that Argentina would adhere to the conference accords, particularly the Act of Chapultepec. It left the "final act" of the conclave open to signing by the Argentines and empowered Padilla to communicate this to the country's government.

The draft did *not* demand outright that Argentina declare war on the Axis. The closest it came to this was to hope that the country would orient its policy to achieve "incorporation" into the United Nations. (In point of fact, the only way it could achieve this would be to declare war.)

At the same time, the resolution was equally vague about what would happen if Argentina complied with all these Pan-American hopes and desires. Nowhere was there any promise of diplomatic recognition, let alone sponsorship for a seat in the new world organization. Even the faintest implication of a quid pro quo was absent.

Padilla looked all this over and pronounced himself pleased with the draft.

The next morning, chairing a meeting of the U.S. delegation, Rockefeller presented the draft resolution on Argentina. It immediately came under fire from Clayton: the resolution, he insisted, had to go beyond its polite verbiage and require a declaration of war by the Argentines. Rockefeller tried to defend the waffling on the declaration issue by pointing out that four countries already considered part of the United Nations had merely declared a state of belligerency, not a state of war; why should Argentina be held to a higher standard?

Austin, however, was still concerned about public opinion in the United States. At the very least, he said, "in our statements to the public we should emphasize that in order to satisfy the terms of the resolution Argentina should declare war."

But Rockefeller was not even willing to go that far.

"At the risk of being accused of appeasement," he said, "I want to emphasize that it is our desire that Argentina should come into the family of nations, and this resolution has been worded in such a way as to make this possible. In commenting on it, we would be doing ourselves a disservice if we emphasize the need that Argentina declare war, even though those sort of comments would be popular."

There it was: an admission by Rockefeller that what he wanted now was an all-out rapprochement with the wayward nation. The genteelly worded resolution was not meant to be an ultimatum, but an enticement, an alluring invitation to rejoin the family and restore the precious "unity of the Americas."

This position was infinitely more accommodating than any the United States had taken before. In fact, it so happened that it was more accommodating than the viewpoint currently held by Rockefeller's boss, the Secretary of State.

Later that morning Stettinius showed up at the meeting of the delegation steering committee, and vigorously agreed with Austin that the resolution should be construed that Argentina *must* declare war before she could be admitted to the family of nations.

"It is my opinion that we should not even open the door a crack until she declares war," he said. That, he insisted, was the attitude which all the delegates would take when they went home.

Rockefeller did not respond.

That afternoon the press gathered for an off-the-record briefing on the Argentine resolution. Stettinius stayed only long enough to greet the reporters and praise Rockefeller's work, before turning the floor over to his assistant secretary.

"We have here something which the Americas as a group can stand together on and subscribe to," Rockefeller said. "For the first time we have got a unified position which eliminates all this maneuvering and moving around."

Going over what the resolution *meant,* as opposed to what it said, he pointed out that "we do not in this document indicate or commit ourselves to recognize the Argentine government."

Then he addressed the issue of the war declaration. No, he said, "the declaration of war is not stated as such." Instead, the resolution focused on the requirement that the Argentines "put themselves in a position to subscribe to the United Nations declaration." When a reporter asked, "That can't be done without war, can it?" Rockefeller replied, "I don't think it can be."

Thus, Rockefeller was already backing away from the stance he had taken that morning. He wasn't emphasizing the need to declare war, but he wasn't ducking it either. Having judged just how far out on the limb he had left himself, he elected, prudently, to climb down.

The Perón regime, meanwhile, was offering Rockefeller some well-timed encouragement that his conciliatory approach might actually work.

Pressed by foreign correspondents for his views on the Mexico City proceedings, Argentine Foreign Minister César Ameghino issued a statement indicating his government was sympathetic to many of the sentiments expressed there. Though couched in the usual bombast of Peronista prose, the statement was seen by many of the correspondents as a definite prelude to Argentine compliance with the Mexico City accords.

The next day, March 8, the inter-American conference ended as it began: with the blinding glare of newsreel floodlights, the clamor of spectators filling the balconies, and the drone of cigar-chomping delegates conducting their private transactions while a succession of speakers held forth from the podium.

The scene this time was not the Chamber of Deputies, but the so-called "lounge" of Chapultepec Castle. As usual, the physical setting bore a certain rococo formality, with old Spanish paintings adorning the walls and even the little bar area in the back closed off by a huge antique Spanish folding screen depicting angels bringing the tablets of the Ten Commandments to earth.

As Padilla made his way down the crowded aisle, he stopped to chat with Rockefeller. Then, mounting the podium, the Mexican Foreign Minister read through the final acts of the conference—including the resolution on Argentina. All were loudly approved.

One delegate after another then rose to shower compliments on Padilla and Stettinius. Finally, the American Secretary of State offered a motion praising Padilla's good works. It passed by acclamation amid a torrent of applause.

Stettinius said he hoped he would see them all in San Francisco, just a few weeks hence.

As the delegates exited into the brilliant sunshine of the castle courtyard for the last time, their mood was one of elation. Lleras Camargo declared that the conference's cooperative spirit surpassed that of "any other Pan-American occasion." The Chilean Foreign Minister pronounced it the "most constructive conference ever held in America."

The initial press reaction coming in was equally enthusiastic. *The New York Times* praised the conference as "the most successful meeting ever held by the American Republics." Even Argentina's *La Prensa* saw fit to conclude that "beyond all doubt, the Conference of Chapultepec will pass into history as the most transcendental of all the Pan-American meetings from 1889 to date."

Amidst the euphoria, not many commentators ventured to question the longer-term implications of the conference's decisions. Not many were sagacious enough to perceive that by sanctioning a separate security zone in the Western Hemisphere, the Act of Chapultepec was setting a far-reaching precedent. The danger, as *Washington Post* columnist Barnet Nover was one of the few to notice, was that "the Act of Chapultepec will provide an excuse for the setting up of other regional arrangements similar in form but very different in spirit from the American type . . . based not on the sovereign equality of the States inhabiting the region but on the unchallenged supremacy of one nation, with the other States reduced to the status of puppets and satellites."

The consequences of this act, Nelson Rockefeller's act, would be felt in San Francisco, and beyond.

Rockefeller's utter joy at the conference's success prompted an endless effusion of hyperbolic praise for everyone associated with the conference. As usual, much of it was aimed at his superior. At the final meeting of the U.S. delegation he again (for at least the third time) expressed his gratitude for Stettinius' willingness to spend two weeks in Mexico City; it was, Rockefeller said, "the fundamental basis for the success of the conference." All the members of the U.S. contingent, the assistant secretary added, felt "inspired" by Stettinius' leadership.

Surrounded by newsmen upon his return to Washington aboard Stettinius' Air Force transport plane, Rockefeller paid tribute to the huge delegation he had assembled. "It was a tremendous help having the Senators and Congressmen as well as representatives of labor, business and agriculture along with us." And he happily tossed some kudos the journalists' way as well. The forty-eight reporters who covered the conference, he said, had done a "magnificent job—their work was an important feature of the conference."

As for himself—well, he modestly told the reporters, "I am very well pleased with the conference."

Twenty

Welcoming the Pariah

Resettled at last in his Washington office, after over a month and a half of globe-trotting, Stettinius took a moment to send over a note to his assistant secretary:

> Dear Nelson,
>
> You have been through a long strain and I hope you will not fail to take some time off just as soon as you can possibly arrange to do so to get rested up from the ordeal at Mexico City.
>
> Again my congratulations to you for your great accomplishment there.
>
> Faithfully,
> Ed

But a salubrious rest was the last thing Rockefeller had in mind for himself. The conference itself may have adjourned, but the endgame was just beginning.

He was still preoccupied with Argentina, to the exclusion of virtually all the other business crossing his desk. With the Perón regime still dithering about its response to the Mexico City resolution, the assistant secretary feared that the Argentines would start "shopping around" among the American states for the most favorable interpretation of the resolution and use that interpretation to drive a wedge in the Americas' united front. To head that off, he met with the Argentine chargé d'affaires in Washington, Rodolfo García Arias.

There was no question, Rockefeller told García, that Argentina would have to declare war. At this, García visibly blanched. His government, he said, would be willing to declare war on Japan, but would find it embarrassing "at this late date" to declare war on Germany.

Afterward, Rockefeller sought out Brazilian Foreign Minister Pedro Leão Velloso, who was visiting Washington. It was not enough, they agreed, for the Mexico City resolution to speak for itself; there now had to be common ground on what it exactly meant.

They summoned the Latin American ambassadorial corps to a meeting that Thursday, March 15, at Blair House, just across from the White House. In a matter of hours, the group—impelled by Rockefeller's sense of urgency—produced a memorandum that, by comparison with the prolix opus produced at Chapultepec, was a model of clarity and concision.

The memorandum laid out the three conditions Argentina would have to meet to comply with the Mexico City resolution. First, a declaration of war against Germany and Japan; second, conformity and compliance with the "principles and declarations" of the Chapultepec conference; third, signing the final act of the conference.

If the Argentine government met all three, then, the memo said, it would "be recognized by the Governments of the American Nations." Furthermore, "the United States as the depository state will request that Argentina be invited to sign the Joint Declaration of the United Nations."

Thus, the American states for the first time put on the table the quid pro quos they were reluctant to spell out in Mexico City. The first—diplomatic recognition—was straightforward enough. But the other was somewhat more convoluted. Signing the Joint Declaration of the United Nations was a necessary first step toward an invitation to the San Francisco organizing conference of the new world organization; only nations that had signed it were permitted to participate in the conference and then join the world body. Complicated as the diplomatic formula was, there was no mistaking its import: Argentina, the pariah state, would be on its way to its conclusive breakthrough, admission to the UN conference, the final seal of acceptance by the international community.

Acting on his own authority, Rockefeller had pledged the United States to a major foreign policy commitment. True, he could claim that the real commitment was undertaken in Mexico City and that the memorandum merely "interpreted" it. But the fact of the matter was—as Rockefeller well knew—that the Mexico City resolution, with its intricate verbal scaffolding, had been deliberately framed to avoid any ironclad quid pro quos. Now, with the work of a single afternoon, he was moving beyond the vague equations and locking the United States into a definitive bargain with the Argentines.

This latest maneuver was of a piece with his handling of the Argentina issue all along, dating back to his original memo to FDR in early January. At each step along the way, Rockefeller presented his proposals as merely a restatement or refinement of the existing policy, rather than any radical change. Yet every step—the January memo, the Oreamuno mission to Perón, the Gallagher overtures, the Mexico City resolution—pushed the United States further and further from its original implacable opposition to the Perón regime. It was, if nothing else, a masterful demonstration of incremental policy making: how a major turnaround could be accomplished with only the faintest nudges of the rudder.

All that was needed now, to seal the matter once and for all, was the imprimatur of the sole unassailable arbiter. As soon as he left the Blair House meeting Rockefeller phoned the White House and secured an appointment for the very next day, March 16.

It was a wan, emaciated FDR who greeted the assistant secretary in the Oval Office. Rockefeller was shocked by the physical deterioration of the man since he had last seen him two months earlier. The pallid, frail, exhausted figure seemed little more than a skeletal shell. "It was as though the fires had gone out," Rockefeller would later recall.

Nonetheless, FDR showed a brief spark of animation as Rockefeller recounted the goings-on at the Mexico City conference. When Rockefeller talked about what had happened with Argentina, the President seemed interested and even amused.

The assistant secretary then pulled out his memorandum, describing, as he did so, the meeting at Blair House. Roosevelt looked the memo over, scrawled "OK FDR" on top, and handed it back. For a few, brief moments the President was his old loquacious self, as he expounded on the importance of the Western Hemisphere. Then he sank back in his chair, spent, and Rockefeller quickly expressed his thanks and left.

As it happened, Rockefeller was back at the White House the next evening, when he and Tod were among a group of eighteen invited to celebrate the President and Mrs. Roosevelt's fortieth wedding anniversary. The party broke up shortly after eleven, with the President making it known he planned to sleep until noon the next day. It was Rockefeller's final glimpse of Franklin D. Roosevelt.

Much later, when the full ramifications of Rockefeller's deed became apparent, he was accused of deliberately taking advantage of the President's enfeebled physical and mental condition. Veteran diplomat Charles Bohlen, who accompanied Roosevelt to Yalta and was at the White House virtually every day during those last weeks, leveled the charge against Rockefeller in his memoirs. "Roosevelt," wrote Bohlen, "signed the memo without fully realizing its intent."

The accusation, while understandable, probably does Rockefeller a disservice. It fails to take into consideration the fact that Rockefeller's meeting with the President was totally consistent with his normal modus operandi over the years, which was to go over the heads of his superiors and secure FDR's assent to an action. While there was no question Rockefeller was fully aware of the President's impaired condition, it would be a stretch to say that Rockefeller deliberately planned his visit to make the most of that condition. Whatever the President's state, Rockefeller would have been in the Oval Office, memo in hand, eagerly soliciting the magical "OK FDR."

As to whether Roosevelt truly understood the memo's import, that was quite another matter. By permitting Argentina to sign the United Nations declaration, Roosevelt was reneging on the clear agreement he made with Joseph Stalin at Yalta little more than a month earlier: the agreement that only nations that had declared war by March 1 would be allowed to sign the declaration and go to San Francisco. There was no mistaking Stalin's vehemence on the subject of the Argentines at Yalta, and little question that the deadline was largely aimed at keeping them out. In fact, Harry Hopkins, who was at Roosevelt's side throughout the conference, told Cordell Hull later that he had overheard FDR twice promise Stalin to bar Argentina.

Considering the significance Roosevelt attached to the Yalta commitments, it would seem highly unlikely that he would consciously turn his back on one of them just weeks after the parley. Certainly, an FDR fully in command of his faculties would not. Bohlen, then, was probably half right: Roosevelt could not have "fully realized" the implications of the document Rockefeller handed him. He almost certainly would never have signed it if he had.

The same day he met with Roosevelt, Rockefeller received a letter from María Rosa Oliver, an Argentinian who had worked for him in the coordinator's office. The letter had taken almost three weeks to reach Rockefeller; it had been sent via Montevideo, Uruguay, because of Oliver's distrust of the security of the Argentine mails.

Oliver hoped her letter would be seen by Rockefeller before the Mexico City meetings began, "because we Argentines democratic and friendly to the United Nations fear that in said reunion it would be decided to recognize the government of General Farrell." Recognition, she warned, would enable the regime "to import machinery and necessary material to carry out their enormous armament plan. . . . The fascist sector of the Argentine Army has decided to convert this country into the greatest war power of Latin America and into the leader of Latin American nationalism. . . . In other words," she said, "to recognize the Government of Farrell would be a terrible 'faux pas,' whose first victim would be the Argentine people and the next victim, America as a whole."

Rockefeller routed the letter to Avra Warren for a reply.

No longer uncertain about the Mexico City resolution's meaning, the Perón regime finally had to make a move.

Given the flow of events in Europe, there didn't seem to be much to decide. Allied forces were crossing the Rhine, and on March 7 the U.S. First Army had captured Cologne. With the Red Army sweeping toward Berlin from the east, *Götterdämmerung* for the Nazis was at hand.

Yet for all that, the Argentine cabinet still waffled, intimidated, as always, by the diehard pro-Nazi camp. Feelers were sent out to Washington as to whether a declaration of war against Japan alone would suffice; no, the Argentines were told, it wouldn't.

At last, on March 27, after the seventh cabinet meeting on the subject, President Farrell announced that Argentina was declaring war on the Axis. "The decision has been taken. That is all that I have to say," he commented as he hurried away from newspapermen. Presidential secretary Gregorio Tauber, left behind to elaborate on the announcement, was visibly shaken, and pronounced each word of the proclamation with difficulty.

The twisted wording of the declaration showed how hard it was for the generals to stomach. Argentina was declaring war on Japan, and on Germany "in its capacity as an ally of Japan." To the end, the junta was determined to make any hostilities against Germany simply an incidental factor.

Later that day, Argentine radio announced that the government was "ready and prepared" to carry out the Chapultepec resolutions.

The public reaction to the news, both in Argentina and in the United States, was hardly one of elation. Argentine opposition groups feared the moves would merely solidify the Perón regime's grip, while the government's supporters were embittered at having been forced into a declaration of war.

Newspapers in the United States took a skeptical view of the whole affair. The *New York Herald Tribune* dismissed the declaration as "a ritualistic performance, intended to qualify Argentina for membership in the United Nations. It did not alter the character of the 'colonels' government' in Buenos Aires."

The Washington Post urged the U.S. government to proceed warily, for fear of repeating "the Bolivian fiasco, when the State Department accepted what it knew to be window dressing as a real transformation." The paper called for the appointment of a "representative committee of inquiry" to check on Argentina's behavior.

Rockefeller, however, hadn't the slightest intention of appointing any committees of inquiry. Now that he had the Argentine declaration in hand, all his efforts were focused on speeding up—not slowing down—the readmission of Argentina into the family of American states.

He arranged a meeting of the Pan American Union's governing board on March 31, to consider whether Argentina would now be permitted to sign the

Mexico City conference's final act. The PAU, the cooperative body to which all the American states, including Argentina, belonged, had been given that authority by the conference; now, at Rockefeller's urging, the union's board unanimously agreed that Argentina should, indeed, be allowed to sign. With that signature on the Mexico City document, the third and final condition in the memo Roosevelt had approved would be met.

Now there were, seemingly, no further obstacles in the way of the next step: recognition by the American republics of the Farrell-Perón regime. Rockefeller moved swiftly to bring about what, just months before, would have been unthinkable. That morning, even before he went over to the Pan American Union, he gained Stettinius' assent that if "everything proceeded in a satisfactory manner" recognition would be granted on April 9. Later, he buttonholed various Latin American ambassadors and obtained their agreement on the April 9 date.

That evening, Rockefeller appeared on a national radio broadcast to explain the turnabout on Argentina. "We believe," he said, "on the developments to date, that the Argentine government has reoriented its position both on the war and with regard to the American security system."

Then he addressed the issue of the Argentine dictatorship. He came out, he said, on the side of nonintervention in the internal affairs of the other American states. "It is up to the people of each country to work out their internal problems as long as they don't interfere with the peace and security of their neighbors," he maintained.

"You can't superimpose democracy by force from the outside," Rockefeller argued. "It must grow up from the people."

Earlier that day, from the embassy in Rio de Janeiro, Adolf Berle sent a telegram—not to his friend Nelson Rockefeller, but to Edward Stettinius. Argentina's signature on the Mexico City document should not, "repeat not," be deemed sufficient reason to reestablish relations, Berle pleaded, "unless and until a probatory period has elapsed."

Much the same advice was cabled to Stettinius by Edward Reed, the U.S. chargé d'affaires in Buenos Aires. "I am firmly convinced," he said, "that a deferment of recognition publicly explained on grounds that other American countries are awaiting concrete evidence of implementation of war declaration and adherence to Act of Mexico would do more good than harm."

But if it was "concrete evidence" that was needed, Rockefeller felt he had plenty of it. Since the March 27 war declaration, Argentina had taken a number of measures to prove its good faith. Among them: the suspension of fifteen pro-Axis newspapers, the announced takeover of Axis firms' assets, the internment of Japanese diplomatic and consular officers, and the imprisonment of Austrian industrialist Fritz Mandl, who had shifted his activities to Argentina at the beginning of the war.

In senior staff meetings at State, the decision to reestablish relations with Argentina on April 9 was reaffirmed—notwithstanding the protestations of Berle and Reed. There would be no turning back.

Stettinius, however, was insistent that recognition did *not* automatically commit the United States to sponsor Argentine admission to the UN conference. That commitment, he said, would wait "until there was agreement that from a world as well as a hemispheric point of view it was warranted."

On Sunday morning, April 8, Stettinius spent a half hour with Rockefeller going over the recognition announcement. Afterward, the secretary jotted this note on their conversation: "He [Rockefeller] has definitely committed himself in pressing the matter of the Argentines not being allowed to sign the United Nations Declaration and will be satisfied with the recognition statement. . . . I talked with Warren about the same thing."

The next day—the day the United States and the other American republics at long last resumed full diplomatic relations with Argentina—a buoyant Nelson Rockefeller took his seat at Stettinius' daily senior staff meeting. The assistant secretary was "convinced," he said, that Perón would follow through on the war declaration "in good faith and not merely pro forma." He spoke of a "new relationship" between Argentina and the rest of the hemisphere; the era of friction and hostility was "definitely over." He expected elections to be held in the fall, and expressed certainty about the result: the victory of Perón.

Stettinius listened to Rockefeller's cheery prognosis, and then reiterated what was clearly his own principal concern: that recognition "did not involve any commitment on our part to favor Argentina's signature of the United Nations declaration." Stettinius had been with FDR at Yalta; he knew all about Stalin's vehemence on this issue and Roosevelt's promises to the Soviet leader. And he knew, and feared, what might happen if the United States were to back away from those promises.

In the face of Stettinius' pronouncement, Rockefeller maintained a discreet silence. Wary of taking any action that might jeopardize recognition, he chose not to make an issue of the memorandum in his files—the memorandum in which Rockefeller had undertaken just such a commitment, and on top of which was scrawled, in a faltering hand, "OK FDR."

So Stettinius was in no hurry to act on Argentina's behalf, and Rockefeller, on April 9, was not inclined to push for it. First, Rockefeller wanted his statement of recognition. And, on that day, he got it: the United States would "resume normal diplomatic relations with Argentina."

And then, on April 12, Franklin D. Roosevelt fell into a coma and died in Warm Springs, Georgia.

Rockefeller shared the national grief for the fallen leader, but in his case the sense of loss was a keenly personal one. Roosevelt was a mentor, an adviser, and a role model: a monumental figure whose impeccable political instincts, seductive charm, and superhuman drive served as a template for the young man's aspirations. FDR had shown how a Hudson Valley aristocrat could both capitalize on and transcend his background, could outfox the ward heelers and command the devotion of sharecroppers and slum dwellers. Over the years, Rockefeller had actually spent relatively little time with the President: a lunch here, a handful of Oval Office meetings there. Yet no one in Rockefeller's life, save his parents, had left more of a mark on him.

Many in the administration now felt cast off from their moorings, but few had more reason to feel that way than Rockefeller. At so many pivotal junctures in the past five years, when disaster loomed, Roosevelt had reached out his strong right arm and pulled the floundering young bureaucrat to safety. In a pinch, Rockefeller knew he could always show up at FDR's desk with a memo and trust in the *deus ex machina* of the presidency—in the form of the all-powerful "OK FDR"—to confound his rivals. Now, the bulwark was gone. Like most of his peers in the executive branch, Rockefeller hardly knew Harry S. Truman.

While a shocked Washington shuddered through the changing of the guard, the Farrell-Perón regime was busy demonstrating just what its "good faith" actually meant.

The day after Roosevelt's death, Foreign Minister Ameghino summoned the American chargé, Reed. Ameghino had just heard that Rockefeller was requesting the help of Argentine naval vessels in Atlantic fleet patrols, similar to the assistance that British and Brazilian vessels were already providing. If what the United States had in mind, said Ameghino, was patrols by Argentine war vessels in their home waters, or escorts of Argentine merchant vessels as far as Trinidad, the Buenos Aires government would be happy to comply. But if the United States meant that Argentina should send her ships to engage in combat with the enemy—well that, huffed Ameghino, was another matter.

Argentina could not consider such a request, he said, until its position vis-à-vis the United Nations had been "reclarified."

The country's supposed crackdown on Axis-controlled businesses, meanwhile, was proving as illusory as its military presence.

On April 13 Rockefeller's aide John McClintock sent him a memo outlining the possibilities of economic cooperation with Argentina. McClintock pointed out that the regime's current attitude toward Axis firms was that it would merely veto transactions it deems undesirable, "the Axis owners continuing to initiate and, in general, control all transactions."

Shedding even more light on the Argentine ambivalence was a meeting a

U.S. embassy official had a few days later with Luis Fiore, the man in charge of the crackdown against Axis businesses. Fiore confided that his agency's program had actually moved more rapidly *before* rather than after the declaration of war. So frustrated was Fiore that he privately urged the United States to continue its blacklist of Axis-oriented firms in his country—at least until the Argentine government showed more willingness to take matters into its own hands.

As usual, the regime was far more interested in cracking down on internal dissent. On April 14 the government enacted a decree prescribing severe penalties for acts "against the security of the state." Henceforth, the dissemination of any news considered detrimental to the government would be punishable by imprisonment.

The reports of Argentine recalcitrance exposed the dubiousness of Rockefeller's Argentine policy. For weeks he had been brandishing his Blair House memo, invoking its clauses as if they were Holy Writ. Yet anyone who read the memo could see that it required Argentina to *comply* with the anti-Axis principles of Mexico City—not just give them lip service. If it could be shown that Argentina was not complying, then the whole platform of Rockefeller's policy—the platform on which he had based recognition, and much else to come—would slide right out from under him.

Some emergency buttressing was needed, and for that, Rockefeller turned to Avra Warren.

In the late afternoon of April 18, two U.S. Army Air Corps B-17 Flying Fortresses touched down at the Palomar military airfield outside of Buenos Aires. In the first plane were Warren and various aides; in the second were American military brass from the Caribbean Defense Command, including the Caribbean unit's commanding general, George Brett.

The American delegation, augmented by Vice Admiral William Munroe, chief of the South Atlantic fleet, whose flagship, the USS *Omaha,* was docked in Buenos Aires harbor, was greeted by a large contingent of Argentine officials headed by Perón himself. A military guard of honor presented arms; the two national anthems were played; and expressions of goodwill, personal and official, were offered by both sides.

While the military men conferred on cooperation, Warren called on Perón, Farrell, and others in the hierarchy. He heard Argentine appeals for fuel and rubber, Argentine promises of full economic cooperation with the war effort, and Perón's complaints about his "bad press." But there was a curiously formalistic air to Warren's program; it was almost as though he was traveling as a head of state, not as a State Department fact finder. He seemed more intent on building bridges to the regime than on pressuring it for reforms.

The mission's most substantive talks with Perón, in fact, were not undertaken by Warren but by Rockefeller's old friend and emissary Rafael

Oreamuno, who had arrived on his own from Washington. It was through Oreamuno that Perón conveyed his solemn assurance to Rockefeller that his government could be counted on to fulfill its commitments. "We have assumed very definite obligations and we shall comply with them faithfully," Perón declared. "When it was 'no,' it was 'no.' Now it is 'yes,' and it means fully that, 'yes.' "

Perón now offered the naval assistance that his Foreign Minister, days before, had said was impossible. He did not link it to the issue of the UN, and downplayed the whole question of the San Francisco conference, insisting that Argentina's attendance was of more importance to the United States than to his own government. And, once again, he assured Oreamuno that he would hold elections, "as clean and democratic as humanly possible."

But most of the time, Perón blustered about his enemies: in the U.S. embassy (he accused the American military attaché of conspiring with those trying to overthrow his government) and among the political dissidents, who he was certain were plotting a coup. "We shall fall upon them with great severity," he promised. "No one will be shot, we don't do that here, but we shall punish them very severely."

When the time came for the Warren group to depart, Perón was on hand at the Palomar airfield to see them off. He pulled Oreamuno aside as he was about to board the B-17. "Tell Mr. Rockefeller we are grateful," he said, "and show him this memorandum, which I have prepared for your confidential use."

The memorandum reiterated Perón's appeals for rubber and trucks, and beseeched Rockefeller to curb U.S. support of exiled Argentine dissidents through the embassy in Montevideo. It was well larded with fulsome tributes to Warren: "We are now convinced that the men who come to us from the United States are of two different types: those who are our friends and win our hearts and those who are not our friends. The Warren Mission has shown itself to belong to the first type."

Warren, for his part, pronounced himself equally pleased, and was even more enthusiastic in his phone conversations with Rockefeller. "The situation in Argentina is developing in a very satisfactory way," Rockefeller announced at a senior staff meeting after one such chat, and ventured to say that "we are getting more effective and more prompt cooperation from Argentina than from any other Latin American government."

But what Rockefeller and Warren pronounced "very satisfactory" would strike almost any other rational observer as palpably the opposite. All Warren actually came away with—save the commitment to naval assistance—were the usual woolly Argentine promises, accompanied by a long list of Argentine requests for rubber, fuel oil, and other matériel.

Regarding the Mexico City resolutions, Warren observed in his written report on the trip, "It is not believed that the Government has yet thoroughly considered nor is it prepared to apply many of the resolutions."

The Warren mission, in other words, did not find the evidence of compliance that was necessary to make Rockefeller's Blair House memo operative. But this could only be discerned through a careful reading of Warren's well-hedged report. And, in any case, the report was not submitted to Stettinius until April 26—the day after the San Francisco conference had begun.

And even before Warren submitted his report—even before his arrival in Buenos Aires—Rockefeller was proceeding as if Warren's positive findings were a foregone conclusion. Blithely assuming that Argentina was doing all that was required of it, he began pressing Stettinius to keep the other end of the bargain: sponsorship of the country's admission to the UN conference.

Rockefeller had carefully bided his time on the issue, waiting until recognition had gone through before making his move on the conference. At last, on April 17, while Warren was still en route to Buenos Aires, the assistant secretary submitted a memorandum urging U.S. sponsorship. The other Latin nations, he reported, were demanding Argentina's admission; it was only with considerable difficulty, he said, that he was restraining them from taking some potentially embarrassing action on Argentina's behalf. He wasn't sure he could restrain them very much longer.

Stettinius was meeting with British Foreign Secretary Anthony Eden later that day, and he invited Rockefeller to sit in and make his case. "If Eden is agreeable," Stettinius told Rockefeller, "then I'll go along." So Rockefeller presented his arguments to the two secretaries—with less than stellar results. His recollections of the encounter, decades later, were particularly acerbic: "It was the most fascinating meeting I've ever seen. Here are these two frightened and mousey guys, they don't know what to do, and they had just won the war!" His private assessment of Stettinius, never very favorable to begin with (despite the obsequious public accolades), plummeted to a new low. Stettinius, he would later say, "was a terrific handshaker, but he just simply could not make a big decision." He "was lost as soon as Roosevelt died."

Eden, however, did not totally foreclose consideration; he agreed to take the Argentine matter up with the Soviet and Chinese Foreign Ministers when he met with them on April 20. This hardly appeased Rockefeller. He wanted Stettinius and the United States to take the lead, and pressed his case again at the secretary's April 18 senior staff meeting. There, he found three of his fellow assistant secretaries—Acheson, MacLeish, and veteran diplomat James Dunn—firmly aligned against him. Until there was more evidence of Argentina's good faith, they argued, the United States should do nothing further on the country's behalf.

Rockefeller pointed to the Blair House agreement initialed by FDR: "There is a commitment," he said, "which had been approved by the President." But Stettinius, for once, stood his ground. "I accept your judgment of what the commitment was," he told Rockefeller, "but I don't think any further action should be taken until I talk the matter over with the other three Foreign Ministers."

Well, said Rockefeller, in that case, "if the Soviet Foreign Minister asks what our position is, you can say, 'This government has agreed with the Latin American republics to support the Argentine request.' " But Stettinius was unwilling to go that far. "Any indication of our support of such a request," he sternly reminded his assistant, "will require President Truman's approval."

If it was Truman's approval that was needed, then Rockefeller would get it.

Retreating to his office, Rockefeller summoned his aides and began hammering out a memorandum to the President. The memo quickly summarized the background of the Argentine situation, including Hull's position, and cited the Mexico City resolution and the subsequent Blair House memorandum (a copy of the document, initialed by FDR, was attached). It then went over all that followed: the declaration of war, the reestablishment of full diplomatic relations.

Argentina, the memo asserted, had taken "a series of steps" to reorient its policy "toward the war and the Americas." "In view of the above steps and our belief that Argentina is acting in good faith"—a belief based on Warren's glowing reports—Truman was asked to put into effect the last phase of the Blair House agreement.

Before April 12, Rockefeller would have raced over to the White House himself with the memo and obtained speedy presidential approval. But the pathways of power were now forever altered; there was no special relationship with Harry Truman. As he came to grips with the awesome burdens of the presidency, Truman was relying on his cabinet secretaries, not assistant secretaries, for counsel. If Rockefeller's memo was to reach Truman's desk, it would have to be via the good offices of Edward Stettinius.

Stettinius agreed to show the memo to the President during their meeting on April 20, if the paper was ready by then. Rockefeller made sure that it was.

Truman read through the three-page memo, and put it down—utterly unconvinced. Though he had little experience with Latin American policy, he shared Cordell Hull's profound distrust of the Argentines. He felt definitely, he told Stettinius, that they had not "worked their way back" as yet, despite Rockefeller's assurances of Argentine "good faith."

Stettinius then reminded the President of the Blair House memo and the "OK FDR" on it. This gave Truman pause.

"Well," he finally said, "if President Roosevelt made a commitment, then I want it carried out. But I hope we can find some way to get around it."

The next day Stettinius met with Eden and Eden's top deputy, Sir Alexander Cadogan, and told them about Truman's reaction. As far as Stettinius was concerned, it had confirmed his own predisposition about the Argentine issue. He had promised Rockefeller he would raise the matter with the other Foreign Ministers, and he would do so—but, he told the British aides, "I am not prepared to make the request on behalf of Argentina or to sponsor the request."

The three men agreed among themselves to block, for the time being, Argentina's admission to the conference.

Whatever else was said about Juan Perón, he could never be accused of pandering to world opinion. On April 21, the day of Warren's departure, Perón celebrated his new understanding with the United States by launching wholesale arrests of civilian and military opposition leaders. Among the sixty-seven caught up in the dragnet were an ex-Argentine President, an ex-Finance Minister, various influential newspapermen, and the former head of the Argentine Olympic Committee. Many were staunch supporters of the Allied cause.

"The men who led Argentina into corruption and fraud shall not again prostitute the government and administration," Perón declared.

In Rio de Janeiro, word of the arrests left Adolf Berle profoundly depressed. "If we had kept our shirts on," he wrote in his diary, "the situation would probably have reversed itself. Now we are in the position of having to work with a government which is jailing the people who have stood by us through thick and thin. This is a case where Nelson Rockefeller, with the best intentions in the world, showed his inexperience."

Rockefeller's troubles, however, had nothing to do with inexperience. After five years of Washington maneuvering, he could hardly be considered a greenhorn. Rather, the root of his problem was his dogged, unswerving commitment to that abstract concept "the unity of the Americas." For the sake of that unity he was willing to overlook Juan Perón's excesses, to gloss over his fascist bent, to accept, uncritically, his vows of cooperation and reform. For the sake of that unity Rockefeller pounced on Warren's flimsy findings as ample justification for Argentina's admission to the UN conference. Rockefeller was determined to bring Argentina back into the hemisphere fold as a full partner, and nothing—not the arrests, not Big Power politics, not even the fate of the San Francisco conclave—would stand in his way.

He was unable or unwilling to perceive the myriad other factors—political, practical, moral—at work. That Americans who sacrificed blood and treasure battling overseas dictators were not about to countenance the appeasement of an Axis-leaning dictatorship in their own hemisphere was something he either discounted or simply failed to comprehend. That a stolid, unyielding insistence on Argentina's participation would put the United States at odds with the Soviets and jeopardize the entire United Nations conference was, seemingly, of little consequence to him.

There had been other times in his life when he fastened on the blinders in his single-minded pursuit of an objective. It had happened with the Rivera mural at Rockefeller Center, when, to the very end, he was naively oblivious of Rivera's revolutionary intentions. It had happened in the Lincoln School battle, when in his haste to cut a deal he failed to perceive that he was sealing the school's doom. It had happened countless times in his youth and even, perhaps, in his marriage.

There was nothing inherently malevolent about this trait: it was an outgrowth of the irrepressible enthusiasm that propelled him through life. In much of what he had already accomplished in his precocious career—and in much to come—this single-mindedness served him well. But the lack of perspective, the heedlessness of consequence also had its costs: for Rockefeller, for those around him, and, sometimes, for the body politic he served.

It was that way with Argentina, and it would be that way, again and again, in the tempestuous years to come.

Berle was not the only Rockefeller intimate who saw the portents of disaster in the Argentina issue. Frank Jamieson was worried, and so was John Lockwood. "Nelson's a goner on this one," Lockwood thought to himself.

Jamieson had seen through Warren's rose-colored tidings from Buenos Aires. The shrewd ex-newspaperman figured that Warren had set off on his trip "rather anxious to find that Perón had lived up to his obligations" and had made sure his conclusions did not disappoint. As far as Jamieson was concerned, Warren's optimism was leading their boss straight into a quagmire.

In a meeting with Rockefeller and Warren, Jamieson gave full vent to his misgivings. He questioned whether Perón really was fulfilling his obligations, no matter what Warren said.

The push to bring Argentina to San Francisco was, Jamieson felt, the wrong issue at the wrong time. His advice was to go slow: to hold off on sponsoring Argentina's admission early in the conference, and maybe jettison the whole pro-Argentine initiative entirely. To do otherwise, he warned Rockefeller, "might jeopardize the success of the conference."

But Rockefeller was immovable; he was locked into his support for the Argentines. His sole focus now was on the stratagems needed to achieve Argentine admission. As he ticked off possible ploys, Jamieson's frustration mounted. "You just can't do these things," Jamieson finally blurted out.

With that, Rockefeller's eyelids suddenly drooped and he trained a frigid, impassive stare on his aide. It was, one witness to the encounter remembered, Rockefeller's "steel shutter look—you know, those steel shutters would come crashing down and just freeze you in your tracks." The look was unsettling both for its suddenness and for what it intimated: it was, for a few brief seconds, a window into the implacable ambition that lay within.

"I don't want you to tell me why I can't do it," Rockefeller said. "I want you to tell me *how* I can do it."

From the list of deputies Stettinius planned to take with him to San Francisco, Nelson Rockefeller's name was conspicuously absent. Whether he was excluded because Stettinius didn't see the need for his presence (it was Pasvolsky's show, after all) or because the secretary didn't want to hear any more about Argentina, the fact remained that the omission was no clerical error.

But anyone who thought Rockefeller would meekly accept the snub and stay home had not reckoned on his determination—or his private resources.

Whether he was part of Stettinius' official retinue or not, Rockefeller would be going to San Francisco.

Once again, as he did for the Mexico City conference, he chartered at his own expense a plushly outfitted private aircraft. And once again, he invited as his guests a veritable Who's Who of Latin American diplomacy, including the Foreign Ministers of Cuba, Ecuador, and Bolivia.

The plane was one of the first to arrive at San Francisco for the conclave. Reporters, hungry for the first crumbs of news about the conference, surrounded Rockefeller as he stepped down the gangway.

All he would say was "Everything is swell."

Then he and his guests headed for their lodgings in the city. Stettinius and the rest of the American delegation would be staying at the Fairmont atop Nob Hill, but Rockefeller, still operating as an unofficial freelance, decided to make his home the St. Francis in Union Square—the headquarters of the Latin delegations.

His choice of lodging said much about Rockefeller's priorities and allegiances in San Francisco.

Twenty-one

NINETEEN VOTES

Even for a city steeped in raffish spectacle, a city that took the robber barons of Nob Hill and the inebriated cutthroats of the Barbary Coast in equal stride, the United Nations peace conference presented a tableau of infinite wonderment. There was the kaleidoscopic array of exotic attire on view each day in the hotel lobbies, the fezzes and the turbans and the flowing white desert robes of the Saudi Arabian sheikhs (which, hotel valets unhappily learned, required daily pressing). There were the comings and goings of the Soviet delegation, with a phalanx of burly, chain-smoking security men shielding the phlegmatic Foreign Minister, Vyacheslav Molotov, from public view. There were the U.S. Army cars and the gray U.S. Navy buses that now commandeered the principal streets, ferrying the delegates to their meeting places. (The cars were driven by local ladies who, according to one correspondent, "were chosen for their pulchritude as well as driving ability.") And there was the vast army of journalists that descended on the city's watering holes: by the conference's first day, more than 1,800 newsmen and photographers had registered, and hundreds more were still waiting for their press passes. (It was perhaps for their benefit that the saloon nearest the conference site displayed a freshly lettered sign on its walls: "During the peace conference please do not loiter. Hurry along.")

In this cacophonous scene Nelson Rockefeller strode briskly, confidently, as though he had personally choreographed the entire extravaganza. Although still quite unofficial and uncredentialed, he acted from the moment he arrived like one of the conference's grandees. Choice hotel rooms in San Francisco were at a premium, but Rockefeller somehow managed to obtain a plush suite on the fourth floor of the St. Francis, overlooking Union Square Park. The suite included both a nice-sized living room and a formal dining room, where he promptly began entertaining Latin delegates for breakfast. He also found rooms, and office space, elsewhere in the hotel for his aides and secretaries.

He and his party quickly became the bane of the St. Francis staff, thanks to their overwhelming demands on room service—and meager tips.

From the outset, Rockefeller took as his personal charge the care and feeding of the Latin American delegations. Unhappy with the St. Francis' valet service, he contacted Rear Admiral Harold Train, who had represented the U.S. Navy at Chapultepec and was doing the same at San Francisco. Might the Navy help, he asked Train, in getting the Latins' laundry done? Train was happy to oblige. For the duration of the conference, the Latin American laundry was handled by the Treasure Island Naval Station in San Francisco Bay.

There was someone else Rockefeller made sure to look up when he arrived in San Francisco: Edward Tamm, the FBI's chief operative at the conference.

Although the bureau furnished a bodyguard for Stettinius, the main function of the large squad of agents at the conference was not security. It was, said an internal memo, "the gathering and dissemination of intelligence." In other words, the FBI was there to spy on the foreign delegations for the edification of the State Department—and, for good measure, to snoop on the U.S. delegation, for the private enlightenment of J. Edgar Hoover.

Rockefeller was well aware of what the FBI was up to. Far from disapproving it, he wanted to secure a place for himself in the intelligence loop. He made it clear to Tamm that he and Warren would be the chief conduits of FBI intelligence to the State Department, including to Stettinius.

In view of Rockefeller's extensive cooperation with the FBI in the past, Tamm was willing to go along with this arrangement. Privately, however, he had his doubts as to how long it would last, as he confided to Hoover: "If this works out, it will be fine, until Stettinius and Rockefeller are again at swords' points, and then we will have to develop another contact."

The friction between the secretary and the assistant secretary was avidly chronicled by Tamm in his communiqués to the FBI director. The situation, said Tamm, was "explosive": "It was anticipated that within a few days there would be a complete 'blow-up' between these two. Mr. Rockefeller had made tentative plans to return to Washington immediately in the event of an open break with Mr. Stettinius although he was counseled not to withdraw from the Conference because of the possibility of unfavorable publicity."

But in the meantime, at least until the expected blowup, Tamm would do all he could to help Rockefeller. Hearing that the assistant secretary did not have a ticket for the conclave's opening session, Tamm obtained one of the tickets for the FBI's own private box, prepared a blue guest credential with Rockefeller's name on it, and hurried over to the St. Francis to hand the passes over to Rockefeller. Upon his arrival, however, he learned that Rockefeller had obtained a seat through other means. Tamm proceeded to personally destroy the blue FBI guest credential, bearing Rockefeller's name, because, he told Hoover, "I was apprehensive about having it around."

A soaking spring rain blew in from the Pacific late that afternoon of April 25 as the dignitaries filed in to the San Francisco Opera House for the official opening of the United Nations conference. The opulent 3,500-seat Opera House, with its sea of red plush seats and its majestic sunburst chandelier, offered an appropriately august setting, and its theatricality was augmented by the stage set: four gold columns, symbolic of the Four Freedoms, between which were arrayed, in a semicircle, the flags of the forty-six participating nations.

Precisely at 4:30 P.M. a U.S. military honor guard marched onto the platform, to the tune of martial airs from an offstage orchestra, and crisply turned about-face as the day's principals mounted the stage. Stettinius led the way, followed by California governor Earl Warren, San Francisco mayor Roger Lapham, and Alger Hiss, the State Department aide and onetime New Deal wunderkind who was serving as secretary-general of the conference.

With spotlights (covered, for better cosmetic effect, with blue filters) playing on his silvery hair, Stettinius strode to the microphone and announced, "The conference is now convened."

After a minute of silent meditation, he introduced the President of the United States. Via radio from Washington, Truman reminded the delegates, in the most solemn terms, of their mission. "This conference," the President declared, "will devote its energies and its labor exclusively to the single problem of setting up the essential organization to keep the peace. You are to write the fundamental charter."

After the President's ten-minute talk, Stettinius, Warren, and Lapham took their turns at the podium, welcoming the delegates and expressing their hopes for the gathering. The addresses were greeted with perfunctory applause—indicative, to many, of the mood of somber, edgy uncertainty that enshrouded the conference.

There were also intimations of the confusion that was to come. When the orchestra, during one of the intervals, tried to lighten the atmosphere with a swinging "Lover, Come Back to Me," some of the delegates leaped to their feet, believing this was a sister nation's national anthem.

Throughout the opening ceremonies, the eyes of delegates and newsmen darted to the ninth row of the orchestra section, where Molotov sat utterly motionless, listening to his interpreter's staccato translation. Over the next several weeks, for as long as the parley lasted, the Soviet Foreign Minister promised to be the most watched, and most gossiped about, figure at the conference.

"Aggressive to the point of combativeness, quick to disagree, voluble, and inflexible"—that was how Hiss, who dealt with him at Yalta, described Molotov. But the stolid old Bolshevik could also charm, as Walter Lippmann learned when he met Molotov for the first time in San Francisco. Expecting to encounter an implacable technocrat, Lippmann was surprised to find that "in real life . . . He has the physical toughness of a peasant and the manners of a French academic."

Ever the enigma, Molotov indeed could come across as bullying one moment and prissy the next. "He had small, almost dainty features like a doll's," Stettinius observed in his diary, "and his inscrutable, cheerful expression made him look rather like a Buddhist idol. . . . To a casual observer he might have passed as a greengrocer."

The conference's fate, in the view of many, lay in this "greengrocer's" hands. If Molotov was satisfied, then the conference was a success; but if Molotov was unhappy, if he beat a premature retreat to the airport, as some feared he might, then all the hopes of the conferees for a new postwar order would vanish in the mists of San Francisco Bay.

As the United Nations meeting began, the signs were not good. Molotov had just come from Washington and a calamitous Oval Office meeting with Harry Truman. At issue was the future of Poland. The Red Army was in control there and had installed a government (the so-called Lublin government) that Western observers feared would be little more than a puppet regime. At Yalta, Roosevelt and Churchill had extracted from Stalin what they thought was a commitment to incorporate democratic forces, including Polish exiles in London, in the new government. Stalin also promised to hold "free and unfettered elections," perhaps within a month.

But even before Roosevelt's death, it was already evident that the Soviets would not live up to their commitments. When Truman took office, the Polish question was at the top of the mound of foreign policy issues confronting him. His advisers were split; some, such as the venerable Henry Stimson, urged caution, while others, including Forrestal, argued for a showdown. Truman shied from issuing an ultimatum, but resolved to make his displeasure quite clear when Molotov came to call.

The President did just that at the April 23 encounter—and his blunt language left the normally composed Molotov ashen and stammering. "I have never been talked to like that in my life," he blurted out.

"Carry out your agreements," Truman replied, "and you won't get talked to like that."

Molotov flew off immediately to San Francisco, still smarting from the confrontation. His composure had returned by the time he sat down with Stettinius the next day; he was once again the browbeating Molotov of Yalta, insistently harping on his own set of demands. ("Throughout these days," Stettinius would note in his diary two days later, "I was reminded of the meaning of Molotov's name: 'The Hammer.' ")

At the top of the list, ironically, was another of the Yalta agreements. Stalin wanted Byelorussia (White Russia) and the Ukraine, both Soviet republics, to have their own independent memberships in the new world body, and Churchill and Roosevelt—eager to buy his cooperation on other matters—acceded to the demand. But the United Nations conference still had to approve the new members, and Molotov worried that the United States and Britain were going to renege. If that were to happen, he warned, "I would have to go home."

Stettinius assured him that the Allies would keep their end of the bargain. They simply needed a little time to line up the support of the other countries.

Molotov then raised the issue of whether the two republics, once admitted, would be able to participate in the conference. Stettinius, however, insisted that that was another matter entirely, and was not covered by the Yalta accord. (In fact, the question was raised at Yalta, but was left unresolved.) Molotov, for the time being, did not press the issue.

Stettinius left the meeting knowing his conference would go nowhere unless he could deliver on his pledge. And for that, he needed votes. Suddenly, Stettinius gained a new appreciation for the hitherto unwanted presence of Assistant Secretary Nelson A. Rockefeller.

Rockefeller had been spending most of his time, in the days before the conference opened, drumming up support for Argentina. He made the rounds of the St. Francis, and reported to Undersecretary of State Grew in Washington the unsurprising consensus view of the Latin American delegates: the Americas had to live up to their commitment and support Argentina's presence at the conference.

His chances of getting anywhere, however, seemed nil—until the issue of the two Soviet republics came to the fore.

It was all a matter of numbers, simple and incontrovertible. There were forty-six nations represented at the conference. Nineteen of them were in Latin America. If the United States wanted the Soviets' resolution to pass, the support of those nineteen was essential.

Ever since Chapultepec the theoretical prospect of a unified Latin American bloc at the San Francisco conference had loomed. But only one man was in a position to tame the fractious elements of the coalition, to build a consensus, to see to it that the votes were really there. Only one man, in other words, was in a position to keep the conference from disintegrating. And that was the man who was regarded as an unnecessary impediment by Leo Pasvolsky and the other UN policy planners at State.

Now, overnight, their perspective had changed.

Rockefeller knew he could deliver the votes. But he also knew they would come at a price. And the price was an invitation to Argentina.

On the morning of April 25 the U.S. delegation met for the first time. It was a group more notable for its bipartisan cast than for anything else; its members were handpicked by FDR to avoid the partisan sniping that had torpedoed Woodrow Wilson's League of Nations. Most prominent of the delegates were Arthur Vandenberg, the Senate Foreign Relations Committee's ranking Republican, a onetime isolationist who had undergone a recent conversion to the internationalist cause, but who harbored an intense suspicion of the Russians; Sol Bloom, the House Foreign Affairs Committee chairman, a dapper Brooklyn native and former theatrical producer whose principal claims to fame were the hootchy-kootchy shows at the 1893 Chicago World's Fair; Harold Stassen, the erstwhile "boy governor" of Minnesota, now on leave from the U.S. Navy (he was addressed as "Commander Stassen"); and Tom Connally.

The intellectual firepower came, for the most part, not from the delegates but from the roster of advisers to the delegation. Aside from Pasvolsky and veteran assistant secretary James Dunn, there was the influential editor of *Foreign Affairs,* Hamilton Fish Armstrong, and the astute, well-connected John Foster Dulles, Wall Street lawyer and chief foreign policy adviser to the Republican establishment. (Roosevelt had been against having Dulles at the conference; "he'll just mess everything up," he complained, but yielded in the name of bipartisanship.)

The universal concern, at that first meeting, was with the issue of the Soviet republics. Stassen worried that failing to push through their membership "would result in the failure of the conference." The U.S. ambassador to the Soviet Union, Averell Harriman, predicted that "Molotov would probably pack up and go home" if his demands were thwarted. And Dunn warned that if the United States didn't follow through on its Yalta commitment, "our position with respect to other agreements reached at Yalta would be very weak"—a chilling allusion to the Polish situation.

With one dire scenario after another filling the air, Rockefeller saw his moment. He broke into the discussion to tersely point out that there was no way the Latin American states would vote for the Russian proposal "unless Russia relaxes its position on Argentina. If the United States wants the Latin American votes for the Russian proposal there would have to be a settlement of the Argentinian question."

Stettinius excused himself: he had another meeting to attend. As soon as he left, Rockefeller seized the opportunity of his boss's absence to make his point again, this time even more insistently. "We should not forget," he said, "that we have to carry this out with the American republics, and if we want to put the proposal through, we will have to get their votes. And I think the only way we could get their votes is to give in to their desires on Argentina."

The others, however, found the prospect of linking one unsavory concession to another one less than appetizing. Both Connally and Armstrong noted that, given American public opinion about Argentina, the linkup would provoke a storm of outrage. Connally said he didn't even like the idea of Argentina joining the world body as a member, let alone sitting at the conference.

Only Dulles seemed to appreciate the realpolitik behind Rockefeller's words. Without Latin American support, the conference might well vote down the Soviet proposal, and, said Dulles, "if the conference votes down the proposal there is every reason to expect a blow-up. Then the Russians will accuse us of having sent Nelson Rockefeller around to tell the Latin American governments to vote against the proposal." Like it or not, the Argentinian question had to be dealt with.

But Leo Pasvolsky, among others, was still resistant. "The admission of Argentina to the conference will not help us," he warned.

Facing off with his old adversary one more time, Rockefeller was emboldened to brusquely issue a warning of his own. "I cannot be held responsible for delivering the vote if nothing is done on Argentina," he said.

Rockefeller's activities—from his unauthorized appearance, complete with retinue, in San Francisco, to his stubborn refusal to rally Latin American support unless Argentina was part of the deal—bordered on rank insubordination. But Stettinius, already overwhelmed by events, was helpless to do anything about it: his assistant secretary, by dint of his control of the Latin votes, was now an indispensable player at the conference.

By the time the delegation met again that evening, the secretary had reluctantly come to the conclusion that the Argentina question had to be addressed, just as Rockefeller said.

But Stettinius also knew that even if he was wavering, Truman wasn't. The President was still dead set against the admission of Argentina to the new world body. If Stettinius was to have any hope of turning Truman around, he would have to present him with a delegation consensus in favor of the concessions.

So he left it to Harold Stassen to propose a compromise. The conference would agree to make both the two Soviet republics and Argentina initial members of the world organization—and would grant them seats at the conference during the parley's third week.

In the face of Rockefeller's persistence—and Stettinius' obvious unwillingness to take his deputy on—the other delegation members wilted. First Bloom, then Connally fell in line behind the Stassen approach. Only Vandenberg remained opposed; he didn't want *any* deal that would give the Soviets the extra seats.

Stettinius said he would phone the President the first thing in the morning with word of the delegation's sentiments.

Truman was willing to give the Soviets all they wanted in regard to the two republics. But when Stettinius brought up Argentina, the President let loose a hefty dose of old-fashioned Missouri venom. That country, he barked, "doesn't deserve to be elected a member of the United Nations. . . . While most of the United Nations were suffering for the common cause, she was standing aside, if not helping the enemy."

However, after Stettinius brought up the salient facts—that the Argentine matter and the fate of the two republics were now inextricably linked—Truman relented. He would go along with the admission of Argentina and the republics to the conference, at "a later date," as well as support the immediate inclusion of the two republics in the world organization's initial membership, as agreed at Yalta.

He left open the question of whether Argentina would also be made a member of the organization. And Truman was absolutely adamant on one point: no matter what else happened, Argentina should not be permitted to sign the United Nations declaration. The declaration—which officially made Argentina part of the wartime alliance—was purely a formality. But Truman felt it would be an insult to the spirit of the declaration and the many nations that shed blood on its behalf to see Argentina's signature on the document.

Rockefeller had no problem with that proviso. The only reason he wanted Argentina to sign the declaration was to gain an invitation to the conference. If Argentina could accomplish that without the declaration, it was all the same to him, and to the Argentines.

He assured Stettinius the Latin delegations would not object to Truman's stipulation.

The next morning—Friday, April 27—the conference steering committee, made up of the heads of all forty-six delegations, met to consider the admission of Byelorussia and the Ukraine to the new international organization. No objections—from the Latin Americans or from any other quarter—were heard. The motion passed unanimously.

Molotov then stood up and demanded that both republics be immediately seated at the conference itself. In response, Lleras Camargo of Colombia suggested referring the question to the conference executive committee. Molotov was agreeable—as long as the committee submitted its report no later than the next day. There were no objections, and Camargo's motion was approved.

Molotov, however, was not through. He asked for the immediate admission of Poland—the Poland of the Lublin government—to the conference as well. When Stettinius and Eden spoke out vociferously against this, the steering committee decided to let the Big Three hash the matter out among themselves.

There was no mention at all of Argentina in the course of the meeting. The Latin nations held their due bills, merely waiting for Rockefeller's signal to tender them.

Upon his return to his suite at the Fairmont, Stettinius put through a call to Cordell Hull at the Bethesda Naval Hospital in Washington.

Though still bedridden, Hull was a member of the U.S. delegation to the conference, and his successor made a point of phoning him early each evening to brief him on developments. That evening, Stettinius steeled himself to talk about that sorest of subjects for his predecessor: Argentina.

Groping for the best way to frame his question, Stettinius asked Hull if he would be "badly upset" if Argentina was seated at the conference.

According to Stettinius' later account, Hull replied he wouldn't like it—but indicated that he would not oppose the move as long as Argentina was not allowed to be a party to the United Nations declaration.

But as Hull himself later told the story, he said no such thing: "I was separated by a continent from the American delegation at San Francisco, and it was never suggested that I should vote on any project at the conference. Had I been present and voting on the question of admitting Argentina at that time to the United Nations organization, I would have voted against it."

Afterward, Stettinius and the rest of the U.S. delegation took stock of the position in which they found themselves. By engineering conference approval of Molotov's resolution on the two republics, they had headed off a Soviet walkout. The work of the conclave, however, was still in suspended animation, since the Soviets refused to go along with the organization of committees unless the republics were included—and that meant invitations to the two to the conference. The private trade-off that Truman approved—invitations to the republics and to Argentina at an unspecified later date—was already untenable.

Once again, Rockefeller found it necessary to remind the delegation of the necessary quid pro quos. The Latin Americans, he pointed out, had thus far refrained from making Argentina an issue because "they did not wish to disturb the possible success of the conference." But if the Soviets pushed for the seating of the two republics, then the Latins would feel "duty-bound" to insist on the same for Argentina.

The conference, in other words, would go nowhere unless the Latin American demands were met.

On Saturday evening, Stettinius brought together the Big Four Foreign Ministers—Eden, Molotov, T. V. Soong of China, and himself—at his Fairmont penthouse suite to hear out the Latin Americans. Rockefeller was present, but said nothing. The Latin nations—represented by the Foreign Ministers of Chile, Brazil, Venezuela, and Mexico—would speak for themselves.

Predictably, it was Mexico's Padilla—eloquent, polished, every inch the urbane diplomat—who took the floor to present their case.

All the Latin countries, he began, had been "glad to vote" for the admission of Byelorussia and the Ukraine. Now he also wanted to bring up a commitment that the Latin American nations had, to Argentina.

Padilla described the conditions laid out in Mexico City. "Argentina," he said, "has fulfilled these conditions." On that basis, Argentina was now expecting "the other republics to keep their share of the bargain."

"I hope," he concluded, "that Mr. Molotov would find it possible to agree to this."

Molotov, though, was not inclined to be so agreeable. As soon as Padilla sat down, the Soviet demanded, "How would it be understood if we were to invite Argentina to attend this conference and not Poland? I think it would be very difficult to explain since Poland has suffered so much in this war and had been the first country to be invaded, whereas Argentina had, in effect, helped the enemy."

It was typical Molotov one-upmanship: linking the admission of Poland, rather than the two republics, to the Argentine question. Without an invitation to Poland, he could not agree to one for Argentina.

On that note of stalemate, with the fate of the conference still hanging in the balance, all the parties agreed to leave the matter to the executive committee to resolve on Monday.

Still hoping that Molotov would drop his objections to Argentina, Stettinius settled on one last ploy to appease him. When the question of invitations to the two Soviet republics came up—it was the first item on the executive committee's agenda—the United States would support the motion, and urge its allies to do the same.

So when the thirteen-member executive committee gathered that Monday morning, the Soviet motion sailed through unanimously. Then Padilla stood up and offered his motion on Argentina. All eyes turned to Molotov, who asked to be recognized.

Once again, he brought up Poland. If the Polish government in Warsaw was rejected by the conference because it was not representative of the people, then, he argued, the Farrell-Perón regime should be rejected for the same reason. And if the policies of the Argentine government were *not* considered relevant to inviting Argentina, then these same considerations should not be used to keep the Polish government out.

Stettinius replied that the Polish matter was a separate issue, a question of the Yalta agreements. Argentina, he said, had fully complied with the requests of its sister republics; in view of that, the United States agreed with their insistence that it was entitled to an invitation.

Molotov then sought the shelter of delay, asking that the Argentine question be referred to the conference's four sponsoring powers. This motion, however, was defeated, clearing the way for a final committee vote on the Argentine invitation. It was approved nine to three, with one abstention. The identical scenario was played out later that morning at the steering committee meeting, with identical results.

Molotov, however, was just warming up. The press was notified that the Soviet Foreign Minister would see them at his hotel, the St. Francis, at 2:45 P.M. Some four hundred newsmen crowded into the hotel ballroom to hear the diplomat—appearing this time as the soul of reason—make his arguments for public consumption. He was only asking, he said, that "this invitation be postponed a few days and all the members of the conference be given time to study the question."

From there it was over to the Opera House, for the conference's plenary session, which Anthony Eden gaveled to order promptly at 3:30 P.M. Guillermo Belt, Cuba's ambassador to the United States, reported on the votes of the executive and steering committees. When Eden asked if there were any objections, Molotov rose and, interpreter in tow, strode to the stage.

Speaking extemporaneously, his words and manner trimmed of their usual bombast, he adopted a dry, sardonic approach. Everybody knew, he said, that Argentina had played a very important role in the war—in support of our enemies. He quoted Cordell Hull's December 1944 charge that Argentina was the hemisphere's fascist headquarters and similar excoriations of the country by Roosevelt.

It was true, he added, that these statements were made some time ago, and he had been told that there had been some changes since. But he thought it was only wise to hold up the invitation until the conference had a chance to study those changes.

By the time he sat down, Molotov's cogent arguments and low-key appeals for time had won him some support among the European delegations. Belgian Foreign Minister Paul Henri Spaak told the gathering Molotov had made "a reasonable and legitimate request."

Nevertheless, Molotov still did not have the votes—particularly with the United States pushing so forcefully for the Argentines. His motion to delay was roundly defeated, thirty-one to four. Argentina, along with the two Soviet republics, would be invited immediately to participate in the conference. Poland would not.

Exhausted and hoarse from days of lobbying, but exultant nonetheless, Rockefeller phoned his mother to tell her the news. "We've had a great tussle," he said, "but things have come through successfully." The Latin American countries, he bubbled, "have been simply magnificent." They "stood up for their rights and their opportunities for future development." While concerned about Stettinius' unwillingness to meet with the press—Rockefeller said he had finally prevailed upon him to give an interview the next morning—he was nonetheless full of praise for his boss's performance. Stettinius, he told Abby, was doing a "magnificent" job. He had shown "great ability, character and firmness and stood up for what he felt to be the rights of the democracies."

At the same time, Rockefeller acknowledged his own role in stiffening the secretary's backbone. He has been "backing up Ed Stettinius," he informed Abby, "helping to try to prevent his being pushed around by certain groups who are very demanding."

In other, more public, quarters, the reviews of Stettinius' performance, and Rockefeller's, were not nearly as favorable.

The Washington Post blasted Stettinius' "inept handling" of the Argentine situation and State's "bush-league diplomats." "The moral sense of onlookers has been affronted" by their efforts on Argentina's behalf, the *Post* declared. "At the hands of the amateurs of the State Department," sneered the paper, "this kind of blundering is worse than criminal, for the consequences may be grievous."

Walter Lippmann was equally worried about the "dangerous consequences" of Stettinius' actions. The naked display of voting clout by the United States and its Latin allies, Lippmann warned, "will diminish the authority" of the new world organization. In allowing their votes to be marshaled in this way, he opined, "the American republics were badly advised. . . . They have called attention dramatically to the fact that the voting power of the Americas is out of all proportion to their political weight in the world."

Lippmann's column, in fact, was only a muted expression of his private convictions about this turn of events. The Argentine showdown, he was convinced, was a watershed event in U.S.-Soviet relations. "I remember being there when it happened and feeling this was an ominous thing for the future," he mused five years later. "If we were going to use that kind of a majority to dominate things, we were going to run into *iron* resistance to anything else from the Russians."

Within the U.S. delegation, there was little rejoicing over the Argentine vote. Some delegation members were convinced that Molotov, despite his defeat, had scored a clear propaganda coup with his remarks—particularly with his

Admiring the new arrival: a doting John D. III, Abby, and Babs welcome baby Nelson.

John D. Rockefeller, Junior and Senior.

The children of Junior and Abby, circa 1918, dressed for their weekly visit to Senior at Kykuit: from left, Winthrop, Nelson, Babs, John, Laurance, and, in the foreground, toddler David.

Nelson with rabbit, his first venture in free enterprise. *(Photo courtesy of UPI/Corbis-Bettmann)*

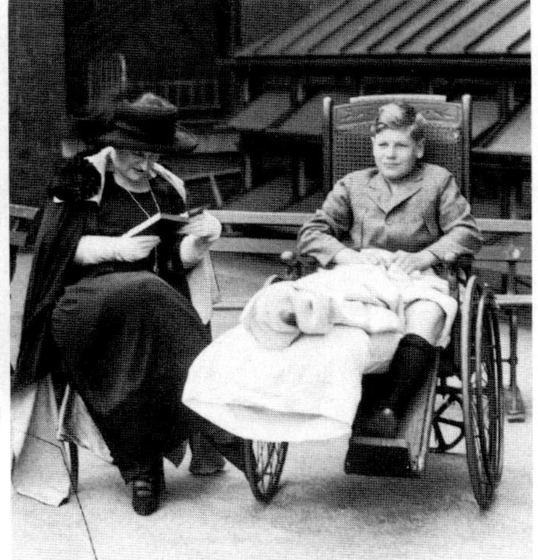

Injured by a ricochet from his air rifle, Nelson enjoys the ministrations of his devoted mother. *(Photo courtesy of UPI/Corbis-Bettmann)*

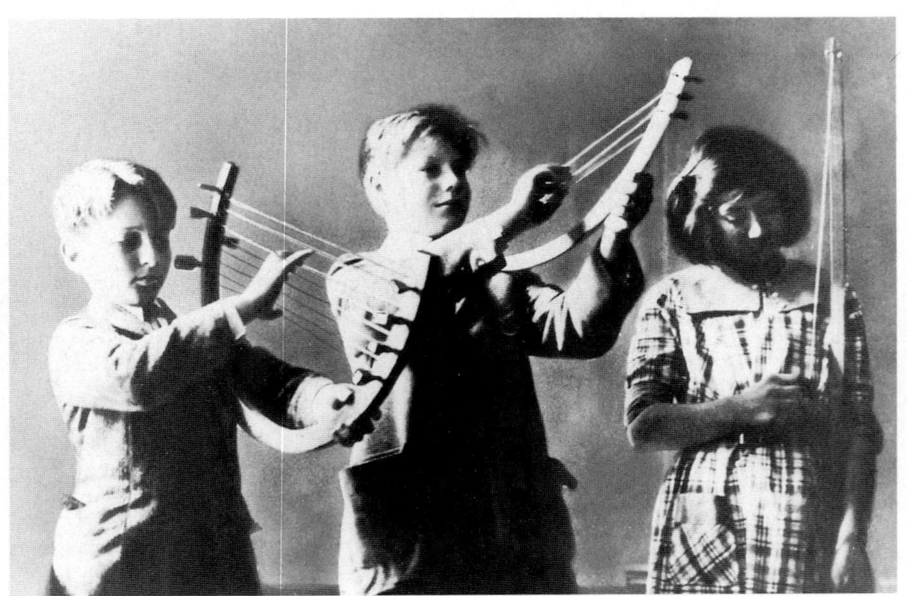

Nelson at the Lincoln School. "A jolly, noisy little boy," one classmate recalled.

Graduation day at Dartmouth, 1930. In his time there, Nelson displayed a precocious entrepreneurial flair—but lost his bid for the senior class presidency. *(Photo courtesy of UPI/Corbis-Bettmann)*

Six days after his graduation, Nelson wed Mary Todhunter Clark, a product of Philadelphia's Main Line. The contrast in their reaction to the spotlight is already evident. *(Photo courtesy of UPI/ Corbis-Bettmann)*

Coming into his own at Rockefeller Center: In his early years at his father's epic development, Nelson tended mainly to the ceremonial . . . *(Photo courtesy of Rockefeller Archive Center, © Wendell MacRae)*

. . . but it was not long before he had engineered the ouster of the center's managers and put himself in charge of the great complex. *(Photo courtesy of Rockefeller Archive Center, © Wendell MacRae)*

Diego Rivera at work on his ill-fated mural at 30 Rockefeller Plaza. "Nelson is crazy about the fresco!" Rivera's assistant noted in her diary. *(Photo courtesy of UPI/ Corbis-Bettmann)*

Nelson and Tod with their brood at their Pocantico Hills homestead, Hawes House: Rodman, infant twins Michael and Mary, Steven, and Ann.

The budding collector. By his late twenties, he was amassing a world-class array of Cubists and Fauves—and had persuaded Matisse and Léger to decorate his apartment's fireplaces. *(Photo courtesy of UPI/Corbis-Bettmann)*

En route to Latin America. "I'm optimistic about South America," he told one interviewer, "but you'll have to qualify that by saying I'm optimistic about everything."

The Coordinator of Inter-American Affairs, in his renowned chart room with key aides: among them, John Lockwood (fourth from left), Wallace Harrison (to right of Rockefeller), and, in the foreground, Paul Nitze (left) and Frank Jamieson (right). *(Photo by Myron Davis, Life* magazine, © Time Inc.)

Reviewing copy for his slick propaganda magazine, *En Guardia,* with Jamieson (left) and Percy Douglas (center). *(Photo by Myron Davis, Life* magazine, © Time Inc.)

The "eager beaver to end all eager beavers," typically at work on three things at once.

Sharing a ceremonial moment with Brazilian dictator Getulio Vargas and family, and scooping up a Vargas offspring while he is at it.

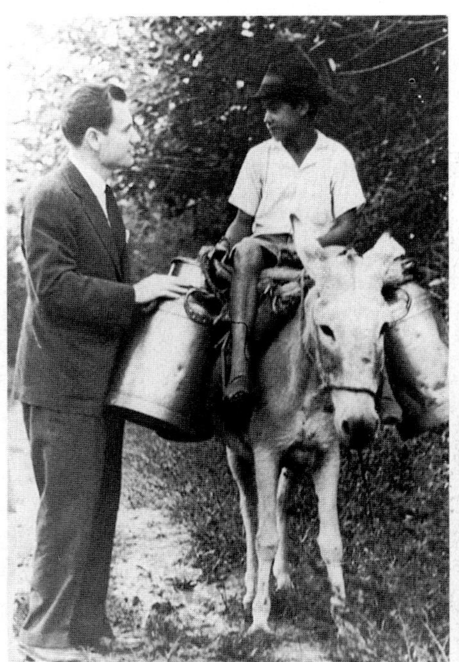

Coordinator Rockefeller's empathy for the downtrodden of Latin America triggered an array of health, sanitation, and food-supply programs south of the border.

A Latin from Manhattan: The Coordinator pursues a personal Good Neighbor Policy. His partner is unidentified.

With Secretary of State Edward Stettinius at the Chapultepec conference, 1945. Of Stettinius, a deputy would observe, "His cheerful ignorance remains the amazement of all hands."

Meeting—some would say conspiring—with Latin delegates at the United Nations conference in San Francisco, May 1945.

Rockefeller confers with Stettinius and a baleful Senator Arthur Vandenberg during the UN parley. Rockefeller's machinations with Vandenberg, behind Stettinius's back, would almost wreck the conference.

quotations from Hull and FDR—and pondered how best to counteract the negative publicity. For others, the concerns ran deeper: by backing Argentina, they feared, the United States had ceded the moral high ground to the Soviets for the duration of the conference.

Only one member of the American contingent, aside from Rockefeller, was truly delighted with the outcome and immensely pleased with its implications. This was Arthur Vandenberg, the hulking, bushy-browed senator from Michigan.

Vandenberg was renowned among Capitol Hill insiders for his keen sense of self-importance (he "could strut sitting down" was the way one reporter put it) as well as his isolationist views. He had passionately opposed FDR's pre-Pearl Harbor aid to the Western Allies, labeling lend-lease a "crime" and "suicide." But in early 1945 Vandenberg underwent a conversion of sorts, openly endorsing the new world order laid out at Dumbarton Oaks. The speech landed him on the cover of *Time* and boosted his 1948 presidential hopes—which, suggested some cynics, was why he made it in the first place.

In the ensuing months, however, Vandenberg's brief flirtation with internationalism gave way to his rabid distrust of the Soviet regime. He hailed Truman's hard line with Molotov over Poland: "This is the best news in months," chirped Vandenberg. "FDR's appeasement of Russia is over." By the time he arrived in San Francisco his views on the Soviets had thoroughly calcified; he felt nothing but foreboding about the new world organization. "I don't know whether this is Frisco or Munich," he remarked on the conference's opening day.

His doleful mood was instantly dispelled by the tussle over Argentina. He was immensely gratified by the Latin American bloc's confrontation with the Soviets, and elated at what it augured for the future. Molotov, he wrote in his diary, had "done more in four days to solidify Pan America against Russia than anything that ever happened. . . . We shall see the results in subsequent events in this Conference."

Far from sharing his fellow delegates' apprehensions about the Latin bloc, Vandenberg was positively jubilant about the prospect of this mass of votes thwarting the Soviets at every turn. Suddenly, he had a whole new view of Latin America—and of Nelson Rockefeller. Suddenly the Latin Americans were, in Vandenberg's words, "our only friends," "the one group of states we could count on."

The burly senator now regarded Rockefeller as an indispensable ally in his battle against the Soviets and their machinations. So confident was he of the assistant secretary that when the U.S. delegation decided not to push for a committee chairmanship for the Argentines, Vandenberg grudgingly went along after he saw that Rockefeller would not make a fuss. It was, Vandenberg said, a "lousy" decision, but if Rockefeller was agreeable he would accept it.

"Anything," the senator said, "that pleased Mr. Rockefeller on this question would satisfy me."

Throughout the wrangle over Argentina's admission, Rockefeller had insisted he was merely an agent, a go-between conveying the sentiments of the Latin American republics. It was *they,* the Latin republics, who had dug in their heels on Argentina, *they* who had risen up in unison against the Soviets, *they* who had linked their votes on White Russia and the Ukraine to the Argentine matter.

There were those in the U.S. delegation, however, who suspected that Rockefeller was more than a mere messenger—that the spontaneous Pan-American movement on Argentina's behalf was, in fact, orchestrated from the start by Rockefeller himself.

Among the skeptics was Edward Stettinius. On April 27, when the crisis was at full boil, Stettinius wrote in his diary: "Nelson Rockefeller undoubtedly had been responsible for bringing the situation to the point where the nineteen Latin American republics probably would not vote for the two new Soviet Republics being seated until Argentina was also admitted to the Conference." He chose, however, not to confront Rockefeller with his suspicions.

That those suspicions had some basis in fact was shown by some of the confidential statements of the Latin ministers themselves. When a reporter asked one of them whether they planned to stage a demonstration when Argentina arrived, the minister replied, "Of course, there will be no such thing. You see, this was done very reluctantly by so many delegates."

Then there was the remark of Alberto Lleras Camargo, the chain-smoking Colombian Foreign Minister, to a State Department official who was bringing him the English translation of the speech Lleras was about to deliver in support of the Argentines. "Nothing good will come of this speech," Lleras grumbled in Spanish. Then why, the State official asked, was he making it? Lleras shrugged his thin shoulders and said, through the cigarette smoke, "What do you think? Nelson asked me to do it."

On May 3 Henry Wallace paid a visit to Cordell Hull at Bethesda Naval Hospital. Wallace found Hull pale but alert—and frothing at the mouth about Nelson Rockefeller. "Little Rockiefeller," he called him—"Little Rockiefeller" was to blame for the whole Argentine mess. From the time he arrived as assistant secretary, Hull groused, he had gone out of his way to appease Argentina. And Avra Warren was just as guilty. Hull had nothing but disgust and disdain for both of them.

That evening, Wallace hosted a dinner party at his home. Among the guests was a rising young political star from Illinois, Adlai Stevenson, just back from San Francisco, where he worked under Archibald MacLeish. Eager to hear more about what went on at the conference, Wallace asked Stevenson to stay after the other guests had left.

Stevenson gave the former Vice President a full recounting of the events leading to Argentina's invitation. As Wallace noted in his diary, Stevenson "said the Russians were right with regard to Argentina and that many people in the State Department realized this to be the case. It happened, however, that Nelson Rockefeller placed the unity of the hemisphere above the unity of the world and that he felt it was more important to bring in Argentina than to work out a satisfactory world formula. The only conclusion I could reach from Stevenson's statement was that we had definitely entered into an era of power politics—with the U.S. on one side and Russia on the other."

By the time he finally saw Stevenson to the door, Wallace—who still nurtured hopes that the wartime alliance could be perpetuated—was deeply depressed about the future.

As it happened, Rockefeller was in Washington that very day, though not at Henry Wallace's. He had hurriedly flown back from San Francisco to testify before a House Appropriations subcommittee on behalf of his division's annual budget.

At Rockefeller's request, not only were members of the subcommittee present, but others on the full committee as well, along with any members of the Senate Foreign Relations Committee who were in town. It was an unusual request, betokening something out of the ordinary about his testimony.

Rockefeller quickly came to the point. What he wanted, he told the lawmakers, was a $2 million increase in his appropriation. The Bureau of the Budget, he said, had cut the proposed increase out, because he was unable to explain to them in any detail how the money would be used. But because the need was so urgent, he wanted to share with the congressmen the *real* reasons he wanted the money—the reasons he somehow couldn't disclose to the budget office.

There were subversive activities going on in the hemisphere, he told the lawmakers—left-wing, Communist subversive activities. The committee, he knew, would want something to be done about those activities, and *that* was why he needed the $2 million: to combat this subversion.

Rockefeller then chronicled the achievements of his division thus far on that score. He boasted that they had fashioned a firm twenty-one-nation bloc against the Soviet Union. What's more, through this bloc his division had seen to it that Argentina was admitted to the San Francisco conference. Argentina's presence was vital, he said, because it was the number one anti-Soviet republic south of the border.

Rockefeller's testimony—aired at a time when the U.S.-Soviet alliance was still intact—left those who heard it thunderstruck. In essence, he was drawing up a new militant mission for his division and for the State Department.

Hemisphere unity, his great goal, was in this light not an end in itself, but a means to a larger objective: the creation of a solid anti-Soviet front. And the fight for Argentina's admission to the conference was not about keeping the promises of Mexico City, but about maintaining a strong anti-Communist bulwark in the hemisphere.

The assistant secretary's testimony amounted to a manifesto—and a startling confession by Rockefeller of his true motivations. Still, there is some reason to wonder how much of it represented bedrock conviction and how much was simply a calculated effort to squeeze more money out of the congressmen by telling them what they wanted to hear. After all, never before, as coordinator or as assistant secretary, had he invoked the Soviet threat as a rationale—not at Chapultepec (although some of the Latin delegates were certainly receptive to such arguments), or, for that matter, at San Francisco.

On the other hand, there is no question that Rockefeller believed in Communist conspiracies and considered himself an aficionado of Communist subversive techniques, dating back to the brouhaha at the Lincoln School. (In the controversy's wake, it should be remembered, he handed out copies of *Das Kapital* to his friends.) He was also undoubtedly influenced by the tutelage of J. Edgar Hoover and Avra Warren (the same Avra Warren who had worked to exclude wartime European refugees on the basis of their "subversive" sentiments) and by the staunch anti-Communism of the Latin American elite. And Rockefeller had good reason to hold his tongue during the war years: given the exigencies of the wartime alliance, the utterance of strong anti-Soviet views would have been politically suicidal.

Whatever led him to his new position—be it conviction or calculation or some mix of the two—there was no question where it left him in the ideological spectrum. Among those in the U.S. government who were already hunkering down for the start of the Cold War, Nelson Rockefeller was in the vanguard.

The reverberations from his testimony were limited: the committee had met secretly, in executive session, and there was no press distribution of his remarks. Nonetheless, whispers about them began to waft through official Washington. Among those who got the word was Henry Wallace. Still reluctant—despite all he had already heard—to think the worst of his onetime administration ally, Wallace sought to check out the rumors with his own Capitol Hill sources. To his utter dismay, he learned the gossip was true: Rockefeller had indeed given such testimony.

One of Wallace's administration informants urged him to bring the matter up with Truman, but Wallace declined. (After Wallace's demurral, the official took the information to Harry Hopkins.) The former Vice President was still having trouble digesting the implications. If what he was hearing was true, he observed, "Rockefeller—in his vigorous endeavor to get hemispheric unity—will provoke the type of world disunity which will inevitably produce war."

Rockefeller also used the occasion of his congressional testimony to call, for the first time, on Harry Truman.

Accompanied by Undersecretary Grew, Rockefeller briefed the President on the San Francisco meeting and the vote on Argentina. Considering that a week earlier Rockefeller had not even been part of the official delegation (though now he was formally designated an "adviser"), the session with the President was a signal achievement.

As he departed the White House, Rockefeller offered the waiting reporters words of praise for Stettinius and "the magnificent job he has been doing at the conference."

Rockefeller's endorsement was no accident. All week long Stettinius had been taking heat in the press for the Argentine decision. The uproar added fuel to the growing speculation that the secretary's days were numbered. Walter Lippmann, even before the conference, had called for Stettinius' replacement, not on the grounds of his performance, but because the secretary, under the Constitution, was now next in line for the presidency, and Lippmann didn't feel he was up to the job.

Rockefeller was also well aware that the shakier Stettinius' position was—particularly if that shakiness had something to do with Argentina—the more vulnerable the assistant secretary was as well. So by praising Stettinius, he was, indirectly, taking some heat off himself.

To further shore up their position, Rockefeller took some time while in Washington to draft a statement explaining State's posture on Argentina. He handed it to Grew, hoping that the undersecretary would publicly release it. But before Grew went ahead, he prudently phoned Stettinius in San Francisco. It was a good thing he did, because Stettinius, when he heard about Rockefeller's statement, blew up.

There will *not* be any such release, he firmly instructed Grew. If anyone asked, Stettinius wanted it emphasized that it was only under duress that the Argentines were accommodated: "If that action had not been taken the conference would not have continued." And, he added, "we will be very sure that Argentina does not sign the United Nations Declaration."

For most of the civilized world, that week, the first week of May 1945, was a time of prayer and jubilation. On May 2, Berlin fell, and on May 7 the German high command at last surrendered to the Allied armies at a brick schoolhouse in Reims, France. The next morning, cities and towns and villages throughout the Western world were engulfed in the joyous celebration of V-E Day.

In Buenos Aires, however, the streets were ominously still. A state of martial law was declared as soon as the final German capitulations became known. Civilians were warned to stay off the thoroughfares, which were patrolled by mounted policemen armed with Mausers and sabers. The Perón regime was bent on suppressing any and all demonstrations triggered by the Allied triumph; the demonstrators, the generals feared, might start calling for democracy, and that would pose a danger to the state.

The diplomatic thaw Rockefeller set in motion, meanwhile, continued apace. The regime prepared for the arrival in mid-May of a new American ambassador: Spruille Braden, late of Cuba and, before that, of Colombia.

Braden was surprised by his appointment. While he knew Argentina well from his prediplomatic days in the mining business and spoke fluent Spanish, the cantankerous, no-nonsense reputation he had earned in his previous postings was not likely to sit well with the hypersensitive Perón government. Braden, in fact, wondered if his appointment had been forced on Stettinius and Rockefeller by FDR shortly before his death.

Still, the very fact of Braden's arrival was a breakthrough for the Perón regime. Coming on top of the invitation to San Francisco, it was another giant step up the ladder of legitimacy.

From his perch in Rio, Adolf Berle shuddered at the prospect. Having observed the events in San Francisco with mounting dread—both for the fate of Argentine democracy and for his old friend Rockefeller's political future—Berle feared the worst. Yet he felt bound by the ties of both duty and friendship to try to intervene one last time. Fortunately, he had at his side John McClintock, Rockefeller's longtime aide, who had just returned from Argentina and was utterly appalled by what he saw.

Together they drafted a telegram to Rockefeller. It was imperative, they said, that he minimize any political advantage Perón would gain from the San Francisco invitation. And the way to do that, they suggested, was to have the President send the new ambassador a tough letter of instruction—a letter that would be made public.

The presidential directive would underscore certain Argentine obligations under the Mexico City pact, notably an adherence to democratic principles and the pledge of nonintervention in sister republics' affairs. And it would instruct the ambassador to pay particular attention to the regime's resort to torture.

The letter, in short, would retake the moral high ground: telling the Argentine government, in unsparing, unequivocal terms, that the San Francisco vote was *not* a blanket endorsement of its actions.

Berle sent off the telegram on May 1. He was not hopeful. The situation, he confided, "looks past praying for."

He was right. Four days later, from San Francisco, Rockefeller cabled his chilling response.

"I have discussed matter fully here," he said, "and in view of all the circumstances we feel it is inadvisable to proceed along these lines."

Twenty-two

In Self-defense

Upon his return to San Francisco, Rockefeller found the Latin American delegations in an uproar. The issue was the Act of Chapultepec, the one great achievement of his Mexico City conference.

It so happened that while he was busy in Washington, Stettinius and Pasvolsky had negotiated an agreement with the Soviet Union, Britain, and France on the powers of the new world organization's Security Council. The accord gave the council unquestioned supremacy over all "regional arrangements"—with one notable exception. Regional alliances forged to repel any renewed aggression by the Axis powers were exempted; this description conveniently applied to the bilateral security pacts the Soviets were busily cementing throughout Eastern and Western Europe. But in their zeal to mollify the Soviets, Stettinius and Pasvolsky completely ignored the regional arrangements in their own hemisphere. There was no exception for the Act of Chapultepec.

When word of the agreement reached the Latin Americans early on Saturday, May 5, they exploded in rage. Two representatives, Lleras Camargo and Cuba's Guillermo Belt, were dispatched to find Pasvolsky and make their displeasure known. Accompanying the Latin diplomats, when they finally caught up with their quarry, were Avra Warren and John Lockwood.

What disturbed them, the Latins maintained to Pasvolsky, was not the regional arrangements clause per se, but its interaction with the veto the Big Powers reserved for themselves in the Security Council. By making the Chapultepec alliance subordinate to the council, the United States was placing the inter-American enforcement machinery at the mercy of any one of those veto-wielding powers. A potential aggressor in the hemisphere, contended

Camargo, could shop around for the support of one of the Big Five and then "proceed with impunity."

It was soon apparent that while they talked about the Big Five, Belt and Camargo were really concerned about only one: the Soviet Union. They invoked the specter of stepped-up Soviet-inspired Communist activity in the hemisphere ("political infiltration from abroad") and even raised the possibility of an attack against the United States through Latin America—an attack the Latin countries would be helpless to forestall because of the Soviet veto. With the Russians exerting a stranglehold over the inter-American alliance, Camargo warned, the hemisphere could be the scene of World War III.

These dire prognostications left Pasvolsky profoundly unmoved. The *real* danger, he told Camargo and Belt, came from the regional alliances—it was those alliances that posed the true threat of another great war. The United States could not abandon its commitment to the world organization in favor of regional groupings. As for the veto, the Latin Americans would just have to assume that the Great Powers would act in good faith.

Apprised later that day of this disastrous dialogue, Rockefeller contacted one of Stettinius' assistants about an immediate meeting with the boss. But Stettinius sent back word that he was exhausted and wasn't seeing anyone that weekend. He suggested that Rockefeller meet with Pasvolsky or Dunn instead.

Knowing that a session with the immovable Pasvolsky was pointless, Rockefeller decided on another tack. He phoned his newfound booster, Arthur Vandenberg, and invited him over to his suite at the St. Francis for dinner. Rockefeller caught the senator at an opportune moment; the new regional arrangements clause, said Vandenberg, "had bothered me all day."

Over dinner, Vandenberg blustered about his role at the conference as the self-appointed scourge of the Soviets. FDR, he claimed, had named him to the delegation at the last minute because the President wanted someone the Soviets couldn't intimidate. "You are the only man the Russians fear," he recalled FDR telling him.

When the senator was through with his soliloquy, Rockefeller proceeded to lay out the problems with the regional arrangements. Was it a coincidence, the assistant secretary wondered, that the Pasvolsky denunciations of regional pacts just happened to find favor with the Russians, whose own arrangements would continue untrammeled? And the British and French—did they support the new clause because they feared, for some reason, inter-American cooperation?

Vandenberg required little persuasion. The problem, as he saw it, was to come up with a formula that would preserve "legitimate regional arrangements" like Chapultepec without undermining the organization that he liked to call the "Peace League." Since the only "legitimate regional arrangement" that concerned Rockefeller and him was the Act of Chapultepec, why not tack on another clause that would exempt Chapultepec from the Security Council override, just as the Russians' pacts were exempted?

This idea, as far as Rockefeller was concerned, was splendid. Now all they had to do was sell it to Stettinius. And the way to accomplish that, he and Vandenberg agreed, was to have Vandenberg write the secretary a letter. Parking himself on a sofa, with one of his trademark stogies clenched between his teeth, with Rockefeller sitting beside him in one armchair and Rockefeller's secretary seated in another, the senator began to dictate.

As the pungent scent of Vandenberg's *supremo* filled the room, the draft of the letter took shape. Together, the senator and Rockefeller polished and pruned it. The document they crafted was terse, precise—and blunt. "I am greatly disturbed," wrote Vandenberg, "lest we shall be charged with a desertion (1) of our Pan American obligations at Chapultepec and (2) of the Monroe Doctrine. The former is a threat to the Pan American solidarity which becomes increasingly indispensable to our own safety. The latter is a threat to confirmation of the entire San Francisco charter by the Senate of the United States."

Having brandished his ultimate weapon—rejection of the charter by the Senate—Vandenberg went on to suggest that all this could be headed off merely by adding the Act of Chapultepec to the arrangements that were exempted. This would not, he insisted, encourage other regional blocs or endanger the new "Peace League," because Chapultepec was simply "the expression of a continuous inter-American policy for more than a century."

It was not until after midnight that the final version of the letter, marked "Top Secret," was typed and handed to the senator. He intended to deliver it personally to Stettinius that very morning.

Edward Stettinius undoubtedly could think of far more pleasant ways to start Sunday morning than receiving Arthur Vandenberg in his living room. And his mood was not exactly lightened by the note, with its ostentatious "Top Secret" markings, that Vandenberg handed him. Still, the secretary managed to maintain his equanimity. He promised to circulate copies of the letter immediately to the other members of the delegation as well as to the advisers.

Within hours, however, "hell broke loose," Vandenberg noted in his diary. Stettinius—irate about what he undoubtedly saw as yet another instance of rank insubordination—phoned Rockefeller and demanded to know if he had written the Vandenberg letter. Rockefeller insisted he hadn't, which, strictly speaking, was true (glossing over his active incitement of, and collaboration with, the letter writer).

There was no mistaking the letter's import: if the Latin Americans didn't get their way, Vandenberg would scuttle the United Nations Charter in the Senate.

A furious John Foster Dulles confronted Rockefeller face-to-face.

"That letter," he exclaimed, "could wreck the conference."

"Well," Rockefeller weakly replied, "I didn't write it. Van wrote it."

But Dulles saw right through the denial. "You've hoodwinked the senator," he seethed. "You've taken a man I was sent out here to keep from doing some goddamn fool thing, and you've gotten us into a real pickle."

That evening a small group caucused in the bedroom of one of the U.S. advisers, Isaiah Bowman, the president of Johns Hopkins University. Among the participants were several high-ranking representatives of the U.S. military, including Assistant Secretary of War John McCloy and General Embick of the Joint Chiefs, along with Hamilton Fish Armstrong and Bowman. They were there to hear Rockefeller out.

Rockefeller did not speak much of hemisphere solidarity or of moral obligations. Fear of the Soviets: *that,* Rockefeller made it plain, was the essential reason why the Act of Chapultepec must be preserved. Once again, as he had earlier in the week before Congress, Rockefeller spoke about security concerns, about how "a new era, with new forces, is upon us." There were Communist riots in Montevideo when Berlin fell. Communist Germans, he warned, could incite riots in Latin America through the networks of German agents still in place. Some Latin American countries even feared that the U.S.S.R. might invade the Western Hemisphere to put the "fascist" Argentina in its place.

For the military men, ever distrustful of the world organization, Rockefeller's litany was a bracing antidote to all the "one world" talk they had been hearing for the past two weeks. Embick chided "idealists" like Armstrong who were unaware of the need for strong U.S. defenses based in the Western Hemisphere. And McCloy related a conversation he had just had with Stimson, the venerable Secretary of War. Stimson, said McCloy, endorsed the Vandenberg-Rockefeller approach of offsetting the Soviets' bilateral treaties with the Act of Chapultepec. "Stimson," he said, "is heartily in favor of alliances."

For the military planners, as for Rockefeller, the Act of Chapultepec was less about good neighbors than it was about good allies.

By the time the full U.S. delegation met the next morning, the battle lines were clearly drawn. On one side, speaking up for Chapultepec, were Rockefeller, Vandenberg, and McCloy. On the other side was the full array of State Department internationalists, led by Pasvolsky and Dunn, such key advisers as Dulles and Armstrong, and, significantly, Republican Harold Stassen, who told the meeting that "to adopt Senator Vandenberg's amendment would be to destroy the organization." The normally stoic Pasvolsky was especially impassioned. If the regional approach were to be adopted, he said, then "the world organization is finished." Ultimately, said Pasvolsky, "we will convert the world into armed camps and end up with a world war unlike any we have yet seen."

Rockefeller had little in the way of firepower to counter Pasvolsky's sallies. (He chose not to broach his apprehensions about the Soviets to this group.) The best he could do was speak of the "word of honor" the United States had given its Latin American neighbors, and remind the delegates that the initiative for the Act of Chapultepec had come from FDR in his meeting with Santos of Colombia. Vandenberg, meanwhile, hinted darkly about "reservations" he would bring up when the charter came to the Senate for approval.

Caught in the middle of the crossfire, as usual, was Stettinius—though there was little doubt about which way he was leaning. Having negotiated the new regional arrangements clause with the Soviets, he was loath to tear it up and start all over again. He pointed out to the delegation that Molotov had called on him late Saturday evening and fully accepted the language. "I don't see how I can go to Mr. Molotov and make an about-face," he said. He seemed especially irritated by his assistant secretary's constant prodding. When Rockefeller suggested that he take the matter up with Molotov at that afternoon's meeting of the Big Five Foreign Ministers, Stettinius shot back that he most definitely would *not* do so.

Reluctantly, the secretary agreed to one concession, urged by Stassen: he would meet with groups of Latin American Foreign Ministers in his Fairmont suite, to hear their grievances. "Out of the doghouse and into the penthouse," quipped Vandenberg.

It was not much of an opening, but Rockefeller made the most of it. Scrambling to round up his ministers, he had them at the door of Stettinius' suite promptly at nine o'clock the next morning. The day was foggy and drizzly, and as Stettinius showed them into his living room he bantered about the lack of sunshine. "The sunshine," responded Padilla, to much laughter, "is in our hearts."

Their hearts, in fact, were filled with anything but sunlight.

The Bolivian ambassador to the United States, Víctor Andrade, warned that if the current language went through, "the whole inter-American system disappears and the solidarity of the republics will be broken." Cuba's Belt invoked the Red menace: "An international party exists in Latin America. It takes its orders from Moscow. Why put such an advantage in the hands of this party?" And his views were echoed by Lleras Camargo. "Clearly," said the Colombian, "Russia's purpose is to intervene in Latin America via domestic action."

By now, it was obvious that there was more to the Act of Chapultepec than the sentimental longing for inter-American unity. The driving force behind the act was paranoia about the Russians, pure and simple.

The meeting ended as bleakly as it began, with a glum summing-up by Chilean Foreign Minister Joaquin Fernández y Fernández. Latin Americans, he feared, would conclude from the proceedings that within thirty days of Roosevelt's death the whole inter-American system was being abandoned.

The following morning, Rockefeller's secretary, Susan Herter, phoned Stassen's. Would the Commander be free to dine with Mr. Rockefeller that evening? When Stassen's secretary put down the phone to ask her boss, Herter could hear his voice in the background. "Oh no," he said, "he'll get me in the same trap he got Vandenberg. I don't want any part of this." The secretary returned to the phone and reported that, regrettably, the Commander was not free.

Later that day, however, Stassen told Stettinius of Rockefeller's invitation. Stettinius, more wary than ever of his assistant secretary, thought Stassen should go. "This way," said Stettinius, "we'll find out what he's planning to do next." And so Stassen rang up Rockefeller and informed him that he was available after all.

When they sat down together, Rockefeller deployed one of his favorite bargaining tactics: he spoke about everything but the subject at hand. He asked Stassen about his youth, about his early political career, about his experiences as the nation's youngest governor. Finally, Stassen couldn't stand it any longer. "Don't you want to talk about this Security Council thing?"

"Well, all right." Rockefeller shrugged diffidently.

"I've been thinking about it," Stassen went on, "and I have a little draft of something in my pocket."

Stassen's draft was an entirely new approach to the problem, built around the notion of self-defense. As Stassen saw it, a nation's inherent right of self-defense could be construed to include its involvement in mutual security pacts like Chapultepec, where an attack on one was considered an attack on all. So if the new organization's charter specifically guaranteed the right of self-defense, it was effectively allowing action under the Chapultepec Act, immune from any veto.

This time, it was Rockefeller's turn to register amazement. He had arranged the dinner in the vague hope he could turn Stassen around; now he was finding that Stassen was actually tossing in his lap a solution to the whole regional arrangements conundrum. "My God, Harold," Rockefeller exclaimed, "you've got it."

The two men began working on refining the language. Just to make things crystal clear, a second clause was added: "In the application of this provision the principles of the Act of Chapultepec and of the Monroe Doctrine are specifically recognized."

Stassen's memo was submitted to the delegation at its meeting the following evening, May 10. Stettinius, who no doubt had been apprised by Stassen of Rockefeller's collaboration in the memo, asked Rockefeller what he thought. "It's interesting," Rockefeller said, acting as though it was the first he'd seen of the proposal. "But I'll need more time before I can make any decision on it." Just as with the Vandenberg letter, he found it impossible to confess to his backstage, string-pulling role.

The delegation decided to let the advisers—Rockefeller, Armstrong, Pasvolsky, Dulles, et al.—hash out Stassen's plan, Vandenberg's, and others on the table, and somehow come up with a compromise.

To critics already disgusted with the handling of the whole Argentine affair, already fed up with the way the pouting Latin Americans were dominating the conference agenda, the Chapultepec controversy was the last straw.

"Let us hope," sighed Walter Lippmann, "that none of our Latin-American neighbors will place us in the position of having to choose between solidarity with them, which we cherish so highly, and the strategic realities of security for ourselves and for the world which we can forget only at our peril."

The Washington Post accused the Latin Americans of sending "a flying wedge into the very soul of the world organization." And the paper knew exactly whom to blame for the Latin uprising. "The Chapultepec institution seems to have no leadership, except the leadership provided by the State Department's Nelson Rockefeller, Avra Warren and Señor Padilla of Mexico. This is the trio who are heading the so-called Latin bloc. . . . The trio have put the American delegation in a tizzy."

The Chapultepec imbroglio served to amplify the grumblings about the hapless Stettinius. He was blamed for not anticipating the problem and heading it off before the conference even began—although the responsibility for that lapse, in the first instance, belonged to his assistant secretary for Latin America, who evidently was so preoccupied with Argentina that he did not see the crisis coming.

Vandenberg, in his diary, complained that "Stettinius does *not* have a seasoned grasp of foreign affairs. He rarely contributes to our policy decisions. We improvise as we go along. Stettinius is not *really* Secretary of State. He is *really* 'General Manager' of the State Department (which is a totally different thing). Incidentally, he is the *best* 'General Manager' I ever saw. He *gets things done.* But I am afraid that is his chief idea—just to 'get things done.' "

Still, to some astute observers, just "getting things done" at this tempestuous, intrigue-filled conference was no inconsiderable feat. There were those who wondered where the conclave would be if Stettinius was more arbitrary, more self-assured, and less willing to smother his own ego and his own preconceptions in the interest of advancing the new world organization. They watched in admiration as he smoothed Vandenberg's perpetually ruffled feathers. Armstrong would recall one delegation meeting when "Vandenberg came in and said, 'Really, I think this whole thing is over. This is not working.

I think we'd better go back to Washington. The Senate will never take what's going to come out of this.' And Stettinius said, 'Now what side of the bed did you get out of this morning, you old bear.' He just jollied him along, jollied him along. They talked and talked, and he calmed Vandenberg down." Averell Harriman would later describe Stettinius as "one of the most underrated American secretaries of state that we have."

But those views were distinctly in the minority. The prevailing image of him at the conference was of a bumbling, uncertain figure, the hapless hotel manager in a French farce. He seemed to grope from meeting to meeting, dependent on the whispered promptings of his aides and the wad of index cards—his "script"—he always carried with him. (One U.S. delegate said he felt "humiliated" watching his Secretary of State refer constantly to the cards in the course of a meeting with Anthony Eden.) A member of the American contingent told a Canadian friend his delegation was adopting as its motto "What'll I do? What'll I say?" after Stettinius' perennial refrain to his advisers.

"He is a total misfit as Secretary of State," one of his top aides, Charles Darlington, confided to his wife two weeks into the conference. "At one meeting he turned to Leo [Pasvolsky] and me who were sitting behind him and said, 'If I say anything wrong, kick me in the ass!' This, mind you, is the Secretary of State!"

Visibly unsettled by the precariousness of his position and the renewed press attacks—and no doubt aware of much of what was said about him behind his back—Stettinius had less and less patience for Rockefeller and his Latin friends and their incessant demands. He startled the U.S. delegation at its next meeting on May 11 by launching into an all-out diatribe against the Latin Americans.

"The time has arrived," he said, "when we must not be pushed around by a lot of small American republics who are dependent on us in many ways—economically, politically, militarily. We must provide leadership."

Rockefeller, as taken aback as anyone else by his boss's outburst, tried to pacify him his usual way: through flattery. He assured Stettinius that the secretary has already given "the right kind of leadership." The Latin American's attitudes, he went on, merely reflected their concern about developments that might weaken the inter-American system. This concern "made them say things they ordinarily would not say."

But Stettinius, on this day, was having none of it. The Latin Americans, he said, had come to his suite and declared they had lost faith in the conference. They wanted to "build a fence around the hemisphere." And that, as far as he was concerned, was unacceptable. "We have come to this conference to create an international organization," he said, an uncharacteristic edge of steel in his voice, "and we will not be deviated from that course."

The group then turned to the new regional arrangements clause the advisers had hammered out the night before. It was, essentially, a reworking of Stassen's self-defense formula—with the Act of Chapultepec specifically mentioned. The Security Council's power to act was preserved—but so was the right of the American states to take their own hemisphere defense measures.

Stettinius, who just moments before had fulminated about the Latins' loss of faith, reacted surprisingly calmly to the new proposal—even though it was a major concession to Latin American obstinacy. Rather than rise up in indignation, he returned to his old conciliatory, get-things-done self. After canvassing the opinion of the others at the meeting, and finding a consensus willing to go along with the new formula, Stettinius agreed to run it by Truman, and then the other Big Five powers.

After days of nonstop wrangling and cajolery, Rockefeller could finally glimpse victory on the horizon. All that stood in the way was resistance from one of the Big Five—or a wildcat move by the Latin American states to push through their own regional arrangements measure. He would rely on Stettinius to take care of the former. As for the Latin Americans, he had already taken steps to ensure there would be no surprises from that quarter. What those steps were, he dared not describe to anyone but his closest associates.

On the evening of May 9, and again on May 11, five men gathered in Room 840 of the Palace Hotel at the invitation of Rockefeller's aide and confidant John Lockwood. Joining Lockwood were his assistant William Tapley Bennett, two Army lieutenants on military leave from their jobs at the State Department, and two agents of the FBI.

Lockwood called the group together because there was a job—a very confidential job—he wanted them to do. The men would all be issued "gray" credentials, designating them as "Liaison Officers of the Delegation of the United States of America." They would use these passes to get into conference committee meetings, and their task at the meetings was to take note of any attempt by a delegate "to introduce measures contrary to the policy of the Big Four." The "liaison officers" would also keep their eyes and ears open for any hint of a collaboration between different groups of delegates.

What Lockwood was mainly interested in was the activities of the Latin American delegates. He especially wanted to know about any attempts by them to institute regional arrangements or to try to limit the Big Five's veto power in the Security Council.

Each man was to report orally to Lockwood at the close of the business day; he also expected written reports the following day. And the whole detail would meet each morning at 9:30 in Lockwood's room in the Palace Hotel.

Lockwood explained the reason for this whole arrangement in fairly innocuous terms: "one section of the State Department doesn't know what the other section is doing," and he needed coverage of the committee meetings to "keep advised of current trends and developments."

Nonetheless, his instructions laid special emphasis on the sub rosa, back-door elements of the work, bespeaking intentions that were hardly so innocent or straightforward. He asked the FBI agents, for instance, to dictate their daily reports at the bureau's San Francisco office, rather than to Lockwood's secretaries, because he didn't want his clerical help to know about the agents' connection with him.

All the reports would go to Avra Warren—at whose behest, according to Lockwood, the whole setup was initiated. Warren and he would be the *only* State Department officials aware of their little spy network. Lockwood was especially emphatic that their boss, Nelson Rockefeller, did *not* know of the arrangement.

Their marching orders in hand, Lockwood's cadre went off on their assignments, silently ferreting out the intentions of the Latin American delegations.

That Nelson Rockefeller truly was unaware of any of this seems impossible.

In the first place, it is hardly likely that such trusted aides as Warren and, especially, Lockwood would have embarked on so risky a scheme—a potential diplomatic calamity had it ever become known—without Rockefeller's okay. Second, the arrangement's use of FBI agents was altogether in keeping with the intelligence links that already existed in San Francisco among Rockefeller, Warren, and the FBI—links which Rockefeller himself was instrumental in establishing.

Finally, there is this memo sent by Stanley J. Tracy, one of the agents in charge of the FBI's San Francisco presence, to J. Edgar Hoover at the end of the conference: "Several times recently, Messrs. Nelson Rockefeller and Avra Warren, both separately and together, have expressed to me their high regard for and appreciation of the intelligence that has been furnished to them since the beginning of this Conference." Tracy reported that at one point Rockefeller even threw his arms around him and exclaimed, "The FBI is marvelous" because of the information it was providing him.*

*One of the bits of information Rockefeller would later claim to have obtained had nothing to do with the Latin Americans. In the midst of the 1964 New Hampshire primary campaign, he described how FBI agents visited him one morning during the conference and told him, "We have the goods on Alger Hiss." His explosive recollections caused Hoover to order up an internal investigation, which found no evidence that Rockefeller was ever so apprised, or was given the FBI's dossier on Hiss's alleged Communist ties. Rockefeller, however, did have one verifiable link to the Hiss case: in 1949 he was questioned by FBI agents in connection with their investigation. Exactly why he was sought out, and what he told the agents, is not known. Source: FBI internal memo, W. A. Branigan to W. C. Sullivan, January 11, 1964; Memo to J. Edgar Hoover, February 14, 1949, FBI Files.

Rockefeller went so far as to put his gratitude in writing, in a letter to Tracy on July 4:

> I wish to tell you again personally, as well as on behalf of the Department, how much the helpful information, which you and members of your staff made available to us throughout the San Francisco Conference, is appreciated.
>
> You know better than anyone the effective use we were able to make of this information in preventing some situations which might have proved to be most detrimental to the outcome of the Conference.

Ironically, at around the same time Lockwood was setting up his intelligence apparatus, Rockefeller was learning, in a particularly embarrassing way, that he himself was entrapped by some snooping.

U.S. military code breakers, it seemed, were busy throughout the conference intercepting the other delegations' communications back home (thus showing the limits of American idealism, even during a peace parley). One of the messages they picked up was from the Peruvians, who reported some disparaging comments Rockefeller had made to them about the Russians. The remarks in the intercept were brought to the attention of Stettinius. Infuriated by this latest impropriety of his assistant secretary, he confronted Rockefeller.

"There's nothing of significance in this message," Rockefeller protested. "I think somebody's giving you a song-and-dance."

But for Stettinius, it wasn't the message's content that was the issue here. "You talk too much anyhow with these people," he exploded. "Goddamn it, you've got to be careful."

Restricting his contacts with the Latin Americans, however, was not something Rockefeller would easily countenance. Instead, he resorted to a different expedient. He told some of the Latin delegates that he had reason to believe the *Soviets* were reading their messages; his advice to the delegates was to take care not to include any matters they did not want the Russians to read.

From that point on, there were no more embarrassing intercepts.

The Latin Americans never did find out that the *real* spying was done by the United States—and, particularly, by their great friend Nelson Rockefeller.

"I don't see a thing wrong with it," Harry Truman told Stettinius, when the Secretary of State phoned him with the new regional arrangements formula. "It sounds very good to me."

But the sailing was far less smooth at the Big Five meeting in Stettinius' living room on Saturday afternoon, May 12. The Soviet objections, raised by the ambassador to the United States, Andrei Gromyko (Molotov had returned to the U.S.S.R., peaceably, three days earlier), were to be expected. But what was completely unanticipated was the visceral reaction of Anthony Eden. "He hit the roof," Dulles recounted later.

"I am frank to say I dislike it intensely," railed Eden after he looked over the draft. "Either we have a world organization or we don't." He warned that he would not be able to sign any world organization charter that included such a provision—because, he sneered, "it would make it a Latin American document."

As the two sides thrashed out their differences, it became apparent that what really bothered Eden was the singling out of Chapultepec. If exceptions were to be made, he wanted Britain to have the same freedom of action—free of a Soviet veto—in its sphere of influence.

By the time the U.S. delegation next met, on Monday morning, Vandenberg had concluded that maybe it would be better, after all, if Chapultepec wasn't specifically mentioned. The Arab League, for one thing, would demand a similar mention, and that, said Vandenberg, would be "poison to the Jews."

Of course, he added, the elimination of the reference would only be agreeable to him if it was agreeable to "Mr. Rockefeller and the Latin Americans." Rockefeller, in response, said nothing.

And so, that same afternoon, the Latin Foreign Ministers were shepherded once again to Stettinius' penthouse. They listened sullenly as Stettinius begged them once more to subordinate their concerns to the broader goals of the conference. He went on to read aloud the new regional arrangements draft, *sans* any reference to Chapultepec. Vandenberg then stood up and expounded on the problems of mentioning Chapultepec; we would be doing nothing for that pact, he said, "if in addition we have to include with it the names of a number of other agreements. It would almost ruin the unity of our undertaking if that should happen." Instead, he ventured to make the Latins an offer. He would guarantee that the Senate Foreign Relations Committee, in its report to the full Senate on the charter, would specifically spell out that the self-defense section applies to Chapultepec. "The Senate of the United States," he thundered, "will nail this down so nobody on earth can misunderstand it."

It was now the Latin diplomats' turn to respond, and Lleras Camargo took the lead. He spoke in cool, measured tones, in marked contrast to the stentorian locution of Vandenberg, and used his persuasive style to put across a thoroughly obdurate viewpoint. "It is essential," he said, "that the Act of Chapultepec be mentioned in order to assure that there be no question of its consistency with the principles of the charter." As for Vandenberg's offer, it might satisfy the United States, but it would not affect the rest of the world's interpretation of the provision.

If the United States and Latin America understood one another, Vandenberg shouted in reply, "it doesn't matter what attitude other countries take."

But the Latin delegates were unbending. "The American republics," said Padilla, "will not be internationally reassured unless the Act of Chapultepec is mentioned."

As he listened to all this, Stettinius' exasperation with the stubborn Latin Americans again began to build. He pointed out to them that there was not much time to work out a compromise. The American republics would have to decide "whether they wanted world organization or whether they wanted regional organization."

Vandenberg, now as fed up with the Latins' inflexibility as Stettinius was, seconded the secretary's remarks.

With both sides digging in their heels, it fell to Rockefeller to try to bridge the gap. He asked if Vandenberg would be willing to give his assurances in writing, and Vandenberg said he definitely would. This affirmation seemed, at least momentarily, to break the ice; Cuba's Belt said it was just what he wanted.

The next day Stettinius showed up for the 9 A.M. meeting of the U.S. delegation still tense and petulant, and listened with mounting ire as Rockefeller launched into one more recitation of the Latin American grievances. "The difficulty is that they feel that our promises might be carried out or they might not be carried out," the assistant secretary was saying. "They are concerned about whether the secretary is speaking for the President and whether he is voicing the foreign policy of this government."

Finally, Stettinius had had enough. "In spite of the obvious hazards to the world organization," he snapped, "you keep tenaciously and exclusively advocating the limited Latin American viewpoint."

All eyes turned to Rockefeller.

"I personally have stood for nothing but what was in the interest of the United States," the assistant secretary sputtered. "I favor only what is in our interests."

This time, Stettinius was determined not to let him off the hook. "Well, then," Stettinius said, "are you also willing to say that the world organization is a matter of primary interest to us?"

"Yes, I do," Rockefeller answered. "It is essential for our interests."

"Then," Stettinius continued, "could you get our Southern friends to say this?"

"Yes, I can," Rockefeller replied.

His point made, Stettinius went on with the meeting.

A new stratagem had been proposed by State's Dunn the night before. Since the Chapultepec Act would not take effect in any case until a treaty was signed by the American states, he suggested that in exchange for dropping references to Chapultepec in the charter, the United States could signal its willingness to hold a treaty conference soon. In that way, the Latin ministers could return home with something to show for their labors—and the

United States could avoid the messiness of an actual mention of Chapultepec in the charter itself.

Stettinius had resisted this idea. To have the United States announce a regional treaty conference while the world organization was still being fashioned would, he feared, amount to an instant vote of no confidence in the new world body.

But as so often happened, Stettinius chose not to put up a fight. The only point about which he remained adamant was that this treaty conference *not* be announced while the UN conclave was still going on. There would be just a private exchange of letters between himself and, say, Padilla, disclosing plans for the parley.

He then phoned Truman and ran through the strategy, including the plans to drop the references to Chapultepec in exchange for a treaty conference that autumn. "Nothing wrong with that," the President said.

With the President's approval in hand, Stettinius steeled himself for another meeting with the volatile Latin Americans. Hopefully, it would be the last.

That afternoon in his living room, Stettinius disclosed the new U.S. plan to the Latin Foreign Ministers. He emphasized that what he had to say was private. Then he presented the proposal for a treaty conference, adorning the plan with fulsome avowals of faith in the Good Neighbor Policy and the inter-American system.

The ministers asked Stettinius when word of the conference could be released. Not until after the San Francisco meetings were over, the Secretary of State replied. "How can we explain this to our people?" Belt of Cuba demanded. Without the disclosure of the trade-off for dropping mention of Chapultepec, he said, everyone would think they had abandoned the inter-American system.

Once again, a U.S. proposal seemed headed for the dustbin. Then Tom Connally stood up.

What happened next was vividly recounted by Stettinius in his diary:

> He reminded the group how very greatly we need to depend on confidence in each other, and he said, "You know the United States is not going to let *any* nation interfere in the Western Hemisphere." Gradually gaining momentum, his voice became louder and he gestured dramatically, as if he had forgotten that he was talking in a living room in San Francisco to a small group, but was on the Senate floor or perhaps at a political rally. . . . "I appeal to you. Trust us!" he proclaimed. "*We* are in the Western Hemisphere just as much as you are. We *cain't* do it alone. You've got to help us harmonize this with the International System." He had been more operatic than any of the Latins during the Conference; they ap-

peared to appreciate the speech and greeted its conclusion with sustained applause.

Single-handedly, through sheer stem-winding eloquence, the Texas senator had broken through the Latin American intransigence.

Lleras Camargo asked to be recognized, and said that so far as he was concerned, there was no need of any additional assurances or documents. The word of the secretary, Senator Connally, and the other members of the American delegation was enough for him.

Later that afternoon, Stettinius presented the new regional arrangements language to the other representatives of the Big Five. The revisions received a warm response, with Lord Halifax, the British ambassador to the United States, praising the "ingenuity and industry" of the U.S. delegation. Gromyko, however, insisted he would have to consult with his government about them.

But a few days later, after some minor quibbles, the Soviets agreed to the new clause.

It became Article Fifty-one of the United Nations Charter: "Nothing in the present Charter shall impair the inherent right of individual or collective self-defense . . ." And, before long, it would assume an importance in the postwar world transcending any of the designs of Rockefeller or Vandenberg or the Latin Americans.

They had sought this clause because it would give the regional security arrangements envisioned at Chapultepec a legal basis outside the United Nations. And so it did. Under Article Fifty-one, an inter-American treaty conference was held (though not, as it turned out, until 1947) and a mutual defense accord—soon known as the Rio Pact—was signed.

But soon Article Fifty-one was serving other uses. Under its umbrella, a succession of other Cold War alliances—the North Atlantic Treaty Organization, the Warsaw Pact, the Southeast Asia Treaty Organization—were created. Article Fifty-one made all of them possible.

The dire warnings of Pasvolsky and the other internationalists were vindicated: the Act of Chapultepec would serve as a template for a host of regional combinations, all given legitimacy by Article Fifty-one. And, just as Pasvolsky had feared, the net effect was to hobble the peacekeeping authority of the United Nations, to render it a helpless bystander to the bloody conflicts to come. These regional alliances, not the UN, would be the bastions of the postwar world order.

This outcome was not at all unwelcome to the viziers of the Cold War. They came to regard Article Fifty-one as an unalloyed blessing, a veritable foundation stone for the citadels of the free world. John Foster Dulles, who had been so enraged by Vandenberg's letter, later described the provision as "of incalculable value." Without it, he observed, "the Soviet Union would have had an unlimited right to prevent organization of effective defense agreements against its own possible aggression." One evening during the 1950s, Dulles, now Secretary of State, found himself sitting next to Nelson Rockefeller at an official banquet. "I owe you an apology," Dulles said. "If you fellows hadn't done it, we might never have had NATO."

In a letter to Rockefeller in 1949, the fervently anti-Communist Arthur Vandenberg looked back on what they had wrought with considerable satisfaction. "As our foreign policy debates develop from month to month—now centering around the North Atlantic Pact—it becomes more and more evident that Article 51 of the U.N. Charter is the key provision as far as effective hope for organized peace is concerned," Vandenberg observed.

And no one would ever see fit to question that without Nelson Rockefeller—without his determination, his brazenness, and his guile—there would never have been an Article Fifty-one.

Twenty-three

ENDGAME

With two major victories under his belt, Nelson Rockefeller was in a celebratory mood. On the evening of May 15, just hours after the climatic meeting with the Latin American ministers in Stettinius' suite, he served as toastmaster at a San Francisco Press Club dinner in honor of Ezequiel Padilla, and in the ensuing days he hosted two cocktail parties for the Latin American delegations: the first at the exclusive Bohemian Club, the second at a private home. The guest list included not only Stettinius and the rest of the official U.S. contingent but prominent Latin and U.S. journalists and a cross section of the local elite. Stettinius observed in his diary that his assistant secretary was no longer the "pale and intense" figure of the past two weeks: he had "relaxed considerably."

A meeting with the Latin Foreign Ministers the evening of May 20 was, recounted Stettinius, "a regular love feast with everyone congratulating each other." Among those present was the Argentine minister; in a private moment, Rockefeller whispered to Armstrong, "I think we're going to find Argentina *very cooperative* from now on."

The next morning, after barely squeezing in a few hours of sleep, an ebullient Rockefeller phoned his mother at 6:30 (California time) to fill her in on all that had happened over the past few breathtaking days.

Elated though he was, Rockefeller did not loosen his iron grip on the Latin delegations. The biggest crises may have passed, but Rockefeller still was the ringmaster of the Latin American bloc—a bloc whose existence he continued to publicly deny.

He was an omnipresent player at committee meetings, even though officially he had no business attending those meetings. Sitting directly behind the Latin American ministers, he could be seen whispering instructions to Cuba's Belt, or, when he wanted to be more discreet, circulating his wishes through another minister's aide. It was all so obvious that whenever Associated Press correspondent Flora Lewis spotted Rockefeller entering the Veterans Building, where the committee sessions were held, she would whisper out of the side of her mouth, "Cracking the whip."

Although Rockefeller usually displayed obeisance to diplomatic niceties and protocol, his intercessions were sometimes embarrassingly direct. On one occasion, the youthful Costa Rican Minister of Development was told by one of Rockefeller's aides that a committee meeting the Costa Rican was chairing had to be postponed because Rockefeller wasn't ready for it. The minister was incensed; he was the chairman of the committee, and a representative of a sovereign country, he sputtered, and was not accustomed to taking orders in such a manner. Ultimately, he was persuaded that it might be in his best interest, as well as his committee's, if the meeting was rescheduled.

Rockefeller's influence over the Latin Americans was palpably clear. Yet when it did not suit his purposes to use that influence, he could baldly fall back on his old argument that he was merely a go-between, a conduit for the views of the hemisphere.

Such was the case with one of the most pivotal issues the conference faced: the question of veto power.

At Yalta the Big Three powers had agreed to give themselves a veto over any economic and military sanctions by the new world body's Security Council. But in San Francisco (as at Chapultepec) the smaller nations voiced their outrage at the preemptive role of the Great Powers. Then the Soviets further inflamed matters by insisting that the veto applied not just to the use of force but to any effort at peacekeeping by the Security Council—and, furthermore, that even the very *discussion* of a dispute could be vetoed.

"The 'veto' is bad enough under any circumstances," groused Vandenberg in his diary. "But when it can stop the whole process of peaceful inquiry, it becomes at this point utterly indefensible."

"Most of the South American countries," he added, "threaten to bolt unless it is changed."

Indeed, fresh from their victory on the regional arrangements question, the Latin Americans were again wielding their numerical strength to squeeze the Big Powers.*

* Ironically, it may have been these displays of Latin muscle, particularly in the battle over Argentina, that solidified the Soviets' resolve on the veto. As Laurence Duggan noted, "The trend of the conference probably strengthened Soviet determination to uphold the veto power as a safeguard against being outvoted by a group of small states." Source: Duggan, *The Americas*, pp. 121–22.

The United States had "sweat blood to satisfy the Latin Americans," Stettinius icily observed at a May 22 delegation meeting; it was now time they gave the United States some backing and support. And Connally was even pithier. "We're up against a buzz saw here," he said, "and unless Mr. Rockefeller can gather up four or five Latinos we're going to get the hide licked off of us." As Connally and the others continued to lash out at the Latin American ingrates, Rockefeller groaned, "Why did I ever come to this meeting?"

"I was not speaking of you," Connally shot back, "only of your satellites."

Rockefeller, though, was not disposed to gather up his "Latinos." Suspicious as always of the Soviets, he shared the Latin Americans' apprehensions about the veto. Yet he also realized he was now under the gun to round up Latin support.

To deflect the pressure, he called together his advisers after the meeting and drafted a memo to Stettinius expressing his anxieties about the veto and urging the secretary to seek modifications in the veto power, even if this meant a direct appeal to Stalin himself. "If after we have exhausted every possibility along these lines we cannot bring about a change, then and only then will we be in a logical position to appeal to the small nations for the support of this Yalta agreement."

The memo, however, did little to ease the pressure on him to bring the Latin delegates to heel. When an exasperated Stettinius asked him point-blank whether the Latin Americans would unanimously support Yalta, Rockefeller finally yielded; he allowed as to how he *thought* he could get all their votes.

As it happened, Rockefeller did not have to make good on this commitment, because soon the U.S. delegation, and the whole conference, was embroiled in an all-out tussle over the veto provisions. At issue was the Soviet demand that even preliminary discussions by the Security Council could be blocked by a veto. This went beyond what the United States thought was agreed upon at Yalta and was more than even Stettinius and Connally could stomach. The Great Powers were deadlocked, and the only way out was (as Rockefeller had suggested) a direct appeal to Stalin himself. Fortunately, one of the few American officials Stalin still esteemed—frail, exhausted Harry Hopkins—was already in Moscow, trying to patch up the burgeoning differences between the two superpowers. As a result of Hopkins' entreaties, the Soviet leader relented.

The only stumbling block that remained was the continued groundswell among the smaller nations, including the Latin Americans, for even more restrictions on the veto. Australia had offered an amendment to that effect, and an anxious Stettinius wanted to know from Rockefeller just which way the Latins were leaning. The assistant secretary assured him there was nothing to worry about; five Latin American states would abstain from the vote on the Australian amendment, and the rest would all go along with the United

States. And when the final vote on the veto came, only Colombia and Cuba would abstain.

But as far as Stettinius was concerned, an abstention offered meager consolation; this was not at all the show of inter-American solidarity he had expected Rockefeller to produce. Rockefeller replied that he had taken the position—with which, he said, he was certain the secretary agreed—that the United States "did not intend to club the small powers into line."

Stettinius, who was well aware that his assistant secretary clubbed small powers into line every day, could barely contain his fury. "The time has come," he snapped, "for you to take more vigorous action."

In response, Rockefeller summoned up a hauteur that verged on outright defiance. "I am taking the course," he said, "which in my opinion is best suited to the interest of the United States in the long run."

And that course was to let the Latin Americans go their own way—on this issue at least. The result was even worse that Rockefeller foresaw. In the final vote on the veto provisions, nine Latin nations (including Argentina) abstained; Colombia and Cuba did not abstain, but voted no. It was a startling rebuff from the United States' hemisphere allies.

By that time, Stettinius was already a man on the edge. Day after day, fresh rumors about his imminent dismissal and possible successors swept through the conference corridors. Rockefeller and Warren joined in the buzz; they tossed around names of likely candidates, and agreed that the best choice would be Warren Austin.

In Stettinius' agitated state, one issue, above all, was the focus of his frustration and despair. That was the Argentina mess, a diplomatic and public relations disaster for which he had, mostly, Nelson Rockefeller to thank.

Stettinius had never really recovered from the relentless press assault on his role in engineering Argentina's admission to the conference. Nothing could have been better calculated to undermine his already tenuous hold on his job than the editorialists' castigation of his "ineptitude" and "criminal blundering" in the Argentine affair. He felt himself libeled. In none of the attacks was there any cognizance of what he was convinced were the true facts of the case: that he had been caught in a squeeze play by the Latin American delegations, and had he not yielded, the whole conference might have run aground.

The Secretary of State was determined to clear his name. Earlier, he had turned down Rockefeller's request to issue a statement explaining the U.S. position. But as the full force of the newspaper attacks hit home, Stettinius changed his mind. He phoned Rockefeller and instructed his assistant secretary to arrange some sort of public statement describing what really happened.

But this story, the Stettinius version of events—with its allusions to Latin

American coercion—was not a tale Rockefeller was eager to tell. Dodging the request, Rockefeller assured Stettinius that he was "unduly alarmed" and that no one was condemning him personally. But if Stettinius wanted to pursue the matter, Rockefeller would see what he could do.

And then Rockefeller let the matter slide, hoping his overwrought boss would soon calm down.

But he underestimated Stettinius' resolve—not to mention his determination to hold on to his job. In late May, Stettinius decided it was time to give a radio report to the nation on the progress of the United Nations conference. The broadcast would give him the opportunity to tout the conclave's accomplishments—and, along the way, explain himself on Argentina.

He entrusted the speech to Archibald MacLeish, bypassing Rockefeller entirely. It was only after the draft was completed—on May 25, three days before the talk was scheduled—that Rockefeller was shown a copy.

Mercifully, the speech did not go into a blow-by-blow account of the Argentina vote. But, from Rockefeller's perspective, what he read was bad enough. The text made plain Stettinius' loathing of the Perón regime: "I wish to make clear that the vote of the United States did not constitute an endorsement of all the policies of the present Argentine Government. With many of the policies pursued by that Government, including some which have been pursued since Argentina declared war on Germany and Japan, both the Government and people of the United States have no sympathy."

By voting to admit Argentina, Stettinius would declare, the United States "has in no way abandoned its position that Argentina is to be expected to do much more than she has done so far to carry out the commitments of the Mexico City Declaration."

This, of course, was exactly the opposite of what Rockefeller had been saying for weeks. Rockefeller's line was that Argentina was fulfilling its commitments; his assurances on that score were the key to the reestablishment of relations with the country, and all that followed. Now Stettinius, in effect, was recanting this position: Argentina had to do "much more than she has done so far."

Sensing that all he had worked for was in danger of unraveling, Rockefeller tried desperately to head off the speech. He and his aides swiftly crafted a memo to the secretary, warning that the proposed remarks "would be an attack by the U.S. upon the internal policies of the government in Argentina," a departure from the principle of nonintervention "that has been the cornerstone of the Good Neighbor Policy."

Then, perhaps judging that this broadside would only stiffen the secretary's resolve, Rockefeller toned it down to a more measured entreaty: "I feel that it would be wiser to make no reference to Argentina in the broadcast on Sunday night. A statement at this time with regard to decisions already taken and publicly explained perhaps would only have the effect of reviving a controversy. Any statement which could be made would have to be defensive in tone."

Any chance Rockefeller had of changing Stettinius' mind was at best slim. It soon receded even further, thanks to a certain cantankerous patient at Bethesda Naval Hospital, over three thousand miles away.

Cordell Hull—back to his normal weight and close to his normal energy—was receiving visitors now, and on May 26 he saw Arthur Krock, the Washington bureau chief of *The New York Times.* What was on the former Secretary of State's mind was the UN conference—specifically, what had happened with Argentina. Hull railed at how the United States supported "and even led" the movement to seat "the Fascist government of Argentina which had aided the Germans throughout, is still aiding them and has not repented." Not only had this support discouraged the prodemocratic forces in the country but, charged Hull, it had dangerously and unnecessarily alienated the Soviet Union.

For this turn of events, Hull blamed Stettinius—but he blamed Nelson Rockefeller and Avra Warren even more. Rockefeller and Warren, he told Krock, had "deceived the President about the real conditions in Argentina, after the Warren mission," and it was on this "false representation" that Truman had agreed to Argentina's invitation to the conference.

Hull was so upset that he hinted that he might make a public statement of his own on the whole Argentine matter once the conference was over.

Somehow, word of Hull's diatribe reached his successor in San Francisco. Stettinius immediately phoned Undersecretary Grew in Washington and instructed him to personally deliver a copy of the imminent radio address to Hull at the hospital. If Hull saw the draft, said Stettinius, "it might satisfy him and dispose of the whole incident."

Hull looked over the text. Gratified that the State Department was at long last backing away from its disastrous course, he assured Grew he no longer needed to make his own statement.

The radio address Stettinius delivered from the Fairmont the evening of May 28 was slightly gentler than the original (the damning call for Argentina to do "much more than she has done so far" was deleted). But the gist had not changed. It was still an expression of distaste for the Argentine government—and a warning that the United States expected the regime to fulfill "all of her commitments."

For the first time—out of his sense of personal grievance and, no doubt, in the interest of self-preservation—Edward Stettinius was distancing himself from Nelson Rockefeller's foreign policy.

Four days later, atop *The New York Times*'s front page, a banner headline blared: "ALL FREEDOM FOUND ENDED IN ARGENTINA."

Correspondent Arnaldo Cortesi in Buenos Aires detailed a Perón government "campaign of intimidation by wholesale arrests of prominent citizens and severe measures against any newspaper that dared to raise its voice in protest."

"Things have happened in Buenos Aires recently," said Cortesi, "that exceed anything that this correspondent can remember in his seventeen years' experience in fascist Italy."

A *Times* editorial, entitled "Argentine Volcano," lambasted the regime even further. "Instead of living up to the pledges assumed at Mexico City, Argentina has even nullified some of the steps she had taken toward a more democratic government prior to the Mexico City Conference."

The next day *The Washington Post* checked in, using the *Times* article to once again excoriate the State officials it held responsible for the Argentine fiasco. "Mr. Cortesi provides a shocking epilogue to the Stettinius-Rockefeller-Warren shenanigans," the paper editorialized. "We don't know whether the heroes of the San Francisco exploit think themselves smart or merely cynical. All we know is that that bloc they have built up is built upon sand."

The same day, the paper's news pages reported on an informal conversation President Truman had with a group of Latin American newsmen following his weekly press conference. When the reporters asked him how he felt about the Argentine situation, Truman replied, "I am not very happy about it."

Smarting from the newspaper salvos, and feeling more and more isolated, Rockefeller and Warren turned for consolation to the one camp where they knew they could find sympathy: the FBI.

"Messrs. Warren and Rockefeller are 'pretty much in the dumps' and are anxious to get away this afternoon," an internal bureau memo reported. To cheer them up, Stanley Tracy, now their principal FBI contact in San Francisco, drove them to a retreat an hour's drive north of San Francisco, where the threesome spent the whole of Saturday night and most of Sunday.

Both Rockefeller and Warren seemed, to Tracy's eyes, considerably worried. Rockefeller told his companions flatly that he might be "out." And, as he was doing increasingly these days, he viewed his troubles through a Cold War lens. He and Warren expressed concern that Truman did not really understand Communist tactics and how the Russians operate. Rockefeller thought it would be a "grand thing" if J. Edgar Hoover were to educate Truman on that score, and he asked Tracy if he thought Hoover would be amenable to this. But Tracy demurred; he didn't see how in the world Hoover could do such a thing. Rockefeller agreed that he probably couldn't, which was a shame, since "the director is the only one who really knows the picture."

They also talked about a subject they knew was close to Hoover's heart: the future worldwide intelligence role of the FBI. The bureau and its archrival, Bill Donovan's OSS, were already jostling for supremacy in the postwar framework. Rockefeller and Warren offered to help line up the Army and Navy behind the FBI, through their contacts with the likes of General Embick and Admiral Train.

"Messrs. Rockefeller and Warren," the FBI memo on the meeting recorded, "agreed the Director's position is absolutely sound and correct with reference to any move on our part to enter the world picture."

No sooner had Rockefeller returned to the conference fray than he was confronted by his own private intelligence reports indicating that the situation in Argentina was every bit as bad as—and in some ways worse than—Cortesi had painted it. Not only were the arrests continuing but the government was beset by internal schisms, with Perón bitterly complaining about "the unpatriotic and disloyal people who only want elections when there are so many fundamental questions to solve."

The economy, Rockefeller learned, was wracked by soaring inflation rates, commodity shortages, and rampant stock market speculation.

Yet the engine of normalization that Rockefeller had set in motion continued to grind out concessions to the Argentine regime. On June 10 the United Press reported that the United States was about to supply Argentina with 500,000 tons of fuel oil—raising the country's consumption to close to prewar levels, at a time when America's own fuel supplies were still tightly rationed. In exchange, Argentina agreed to sell to the United States its surplus vegetable oil.

Word of the deal infuriated the rest of Latin America, which had been told just days earlier by the United States that their fuel allocations could not be increased. The Brazilians were especially incensed. What particularly galled them was that Argentina had just proposed a deal in which Brazil would supply it with 10,000 rubber tires in exchange for gasoline—the very gasoline that the United States had just shipped to Buenos Aires, the very gasoline the United States had denied its longtime ally.

Brazil's ambassador to the United States, Carlos Martins, collared Rockefeller and, in a singularly acrimonious session, informed him that while they had been friends for years, he was now through with him. The State Department's word, as far as Martins was concerned, was no longer good.

The rupture with Brazil not only pointed up the fragility of Rockefeller's inter-American alliance but showed that his policy of rapprochement with Argentina, far from cementing that alliance, was actually fracturing it.

The Washington Post seized upon the oil deal with Argentina as one more example of the incomprehensibility of U.S. policy in Latin America. "By making hostility to the United States pay, we seem to be trying to turn our friends into our enemies," the newspaper pointed out on June 15.

"Congress should take up this and other problems in connection with our affairs in Latin America while we still have any prestige left."

Congress, it appeared, was not taking the *Post*'s suggestion lightly. Two days later, Drew Pearson was reporting on his radio broadcast that the Senate Foreign Relations Committee planned to investigate the whole Argentine situation—particularly why the United States decided to recognize the Perón-Farrell regime. The probe, said Pearson, was a bipartisan affair; among its backers was Warren Austin. The senators planned to call both Stettinius and Rockefeller to testify.

Once again, Rockefeller endeavored to reassure his boss. "My personal feeling," he wrote Stettinius, "is that it would be a most opportune and helpful thing should this action be taken by the Senate, particularly if the hearings were to be open. Our case is a very strong one and one which in the long run is going to reflect tremendous credit, in my opinion, on you and the Department."

At that moment, with newspapers calling for his head, senators mulling an investigation, and his Latin American friends muttering about betrayal, Nelson Rockefeller threw a party. Not a cocktail party, not a dinner party, but a *party*: the biggest, swankest, showiest, most opulent bash of the conference. The June 18 gala had been in the works for weeks, and Rockefeller was not about to let his Argentine angst throw it off course.

The setting was the St. Francis Yacht Club on San Francisco Bay, a mile from the Golden Gate Bridge. Gathering on the yacht club terrace for cocktails, the guests—Foreign Ministers and ambassadors, senators and congressmen, select journalists, and assorted California glitterati—took in the magnificent sweep of the bay at sunset. The crowd then headed inside, to a room adorned with a profusion of roses, begonias, peonies, and, at the tables, white sweet peas. The buffet was, exclaimed one guest, "a sight for point-rationed eyes," with immense platters of turkey, ham, and Columbia red salmon.

Painstaking care had been taken in the seating arrangements, so as not to offend delicate diplomatic sensibilities. But all those plans were instantly upset with the arrival of the evening's featured entertainment: Carmen Miranda, Hollywood's "Brazilian Bombshell." Storming into the dining room just as the guests were about to be seated, she declared her intention to sit between the Brazilian Foreign Minister and Nelson Rockefeller. Told by a Rockefeller aide that that was impossible, Miranda waved the pest away and proceeded to rearrange all the place cards at the three head tables.

The discombobulation she caused was forgotten as soon as she took the floor, accompanied by her full orchestra and her sister Aurora (who had appeared in the CIAA-sponsored Disney film *The Three Caballeros*). With her trademark fruit-festooned hat balanced atop her head, Miranda ran through a medley of her movie hits, swaying with the samba beat from table to table, electrifying the room with her outlandish mannerisms and *picante* personality.

"I should doubt that a more cosmopolitan social gathering ever assembled in this country outside of Washington or perhaps New York," one guest observed. The gala was a tribute to the discernment, the influence—and the limitless means—of the host. It is safe to say that no other assistant secretary would have had the nerve, let alone the wherewithal, to have thrown such a revel.

It was a good time for grand gestures and raised champagne glasses. At long last, two months after the work commenced, the delegates espied the completion of their task. A charter for the new world organization—a charter that was the product of confrontation, compromise, bluster, intrigue, and plain old grunt work—was at hand. A postwar peacekeeping framework, flawed and wobbly though it was in its particulars, would indeed emerge from its scaffolding.

All that remained, save some last-minute tidying-up, was the final act: the signing ceremony, now slated for June 26. It would be a memorable event, a celebration of peace and global brotherhood after the long years of blood and devastation. President Truman himself would appear, to sign the document on behalf of the United States.

As the preparations for the closing festivities proceeded apace, Rockefeller busied himself with some last-minute stroking of his Latin American friends. He offered the use of his Foxhall Road house in Washington to Brazilian Foreign Minister Velloso once the conference was over (Rockefeller himself planned to head up to Pocantico). And he invited Velloso and Padilla to join Stettinius on board the secretary's military plane back to the capital—without bothering to ask Stettinius first. When the secretary found out about the invitations, he phoned Rockefeller and peevishly informed him there was no room on the plane for the two Latin Americans. No problem, Rockefeller replied; Stettinius merely had to pick out two less important people on his flight, and Rockefeller would find room for them on *his* plane.

Velloso and Padilla flew with Stettinius. Once again, Rockefeller's unique personal resources had come through.

On June 21 one of Truman's aides, George Allen, arrived in San Francisco, ostensibly to help plan the President's visit. He immediately sought out Stettinius, and as the two men sat in the Fairmont penthouse Allen doled out gobs of praise for the job the secretary had done in the past two months. In fact, Stettinius had performed so well that "the only thing that can happen to you is something bigger than secretary of state."

Stettinius saw right through the blarney. Allen was there to sound him out about a resignation, and to dangle another position as a consolation prize. The position Allen talked about was chief U.S. representative in the new world organization. Stettinius was noncommittal, but the handwriting was on the wall. "Tell me one thing," he said, as he gazed out the window at the glistening bay. "Do you think the President has made a commitment to Byrnes?"

"I think he has," Allen replied.

"So do I," said Stettinius. "If he has, the sooner the better."

Stettinius now learned from Allen that the commitment to name James Byrnes Secretary of State, in fact, had been made by Truman within days of FDR's death—largely to assuage Democratic leaders' fears about the presidential succession, now that Stettinius was next in line. So as not to disrupt the San Francisco conference, Truman decided to have Stettinius remain in place for the duration—and to keep him in the dark about his plans.

Were he a free agent today, Allen told Stettinius, the President would undoubtedly want him to stay on. But a promise was a promise, and Truman felt honor-bound to carry it out.

The announcement would not be made until Stettinius' return to Washington on June 27, a day after the closing of the conference. But even before Truman's arrival, word of the switch was already leaking to the delegation. Despite the perennial grousing about Stettinius, the change was not universally welcomed.

It was not that anyone questioned Byrnes's credentials. On the contrary, Byrnes was a consummate Washington insider: a seven-term congressman, former South Carolina senator, and Supreme Court justice, he had stepped down from the Court to become FDR's War Mobilization Director, earning the appellation "assistant president for the home front." After narrowly losing out to Truman in his bid for the vice presidency, Byrnes had been Hull's first choice to succeed him as Secretary of State. Even though Roosevelt passed him over for the job, he wanted him at his side at Yalta. It was Byrnes who served as the chief explicator of the Yalta accords before Congress and the public.

But to know Byrnes, at least in the view of old pros like Connally and Vandenberg who had served with him in the Senate, was not necessarily to like him or trust him. Beneath the patina of South Carolina gentility lay the soul of a downtown Irish pol, in their humble opinion.

Connally, when he heard the news, feared for the worst. "He's a fellow who likes to fix things up on the side," the senator grumbled. "He thinks he's a sight cleverer than he is."

With as grave a sense of moment as when they commenced their work two months earlier, the delegates filed into the Veterans Auditorium at the stroke of noon on June 26 for the signing of the United Nations Charter. Each country took its turn at the blue-draped table on which the document rested, each delegation posing proudly for the battery of newsreel cameras.

Later, at the final plenary session at the Opera House, the delegates listened as Truman extolled their achievement, an achievement that, he earnestly hoped, would keep the world "free from the fear of war."

The sentiments of the assemblage were aptly expressed by Britain's Lord Halifax. "We may all feel," he told his fellow delegates, "that we have taken part, as we may hope, in one of the great moments of history."

Three thousand miles from this august scene, rumors of an imminent housecleaning—touched off by the news of Stettinius' resignation—brought the State Department to a virtual standstill. "It is said that we shall all be fired except Clayton and Grew," Dean Acheson wrote in his diary. "It is said that Grew will certainly be fired." MacLeish walked into Acheson's office and asked whether he should resign before the following Monday, because he had heard that Byrnes planned to fire both him and Rockefeller. Acheson dissuaded him: "One should not hurry mounting the tumbril," he counseled.

Beset by the rumors, and thoroughly exhausted by the cumulative tensions and high-wire negotiating of the past weeks, Rockefeller repaired for some succor and relief to his sylvan citadel, Pocantico.

There, he confessed to his mother that he really didn't know what was going to happen to him. He mused in a disoriented way about his next step. If he really was tossed out of the State Department, then he would go ahead and do what he always wanted to do: join the Army. It was only Roosevelt's insistence that he remain where he was that had kept him from enlisting before. Maybe there was a place in the Pacific where he could be of service . . .

Listening to this desultory monologue, Abby concluded that it really was time her son "got out of Washington."

Before he left, she insisted that he sit for a formal portrait; she wanted wartime portraits of all her sons. Afterward, when she saw the result, she was sorry she asked. "I am not sure whether the trouble is with the portrait or in Nelson," she wrote. "He was simply exhausted after the San Francisco conference and I think I made a great psychological mistake in asking him to have his portrait painted when he was so tired."

"Anyway," she added in her usual chipper fashion, "if he gets thrown out of the State Department and goes into the Army as he says he is going to do, I will then have a chance to get him painted in uniform, which would please me immensely."

His mood was not improved upon his return to Washington. Waiting for him there was the latest issue of *The New Republic*. Its cover article was entitled "Young Nelson Rockefeller."

"Whatever usefulness he may have," argued the author, Helen Fuller, "Nelson Rockefeller, on the basis of his past record and his present expressed attitudes, cannot be trusted with the making of our Latin American policies." Fuller gave short shrift to his accomplishments as coordinator, zeroing in instead on his track record as assistant secretary—particularly with regard to Argentina. In San Francisco, she charged, "Nelson Rockefeller stood out in plain view of the conference as the most active and determined proponent of rushing through Argentine admission, regardless of the feelings of the other nations involved." His motives, said Fuller, might have remained in doubt, had it not been for his May congressional testimony justifying support for Argentina as a bulwark against Communism.

"This plain speaking," contended Fuller, "could leave no doubts as to what Nelson Rockefeller and his associates were up to." Rockefeller was determined to preserve the mostly right-wing status quo and forge an alliance "with the new industrial class which has fattened on the war."

Shrill though it was, the *New Republic* piece was bound to give added ammunition to those who might be pressing Byrnes for his ouster.

Byrnes, however, was in no hurry. Right after his swearing-in on July 3, he announced that he had asked the Bureau of the Budget to conduct a thorough investigation of the structure of his department. "Until I receive that report," he said, "and have an opportunity to study it and make such personal inquiry as I deem advisable no change in personnel will be made."

On June 30, Juan Perón summoned U.S. ambassador Braden to his office in the Casa Rosada. Unlike their previous encounters since Braden's arrival in Buenos Aires—when Perón greeted Braden with warm *abrazos* and effusive professions of friendship—the Argentine leader received his guest frigidly, without even a handshake. "Sit down," he snapped.

"There is a movement and movements to overthrow me," Perón began, "and we will not stand for it. If these groups try anything we will fight in the streets and blood will flow."

That was very interesting, Braden replied, but what did that have to do with Argentine–United States relations?

"It has to do with them because your journalists form a part of these movements."

Braden protested that the American reporters had nothing to do with the opposition, but Perón was adamant. His supporters, he went on, were "enraged" by the attacks on the regime in the U.S. press: so enraged that "in their fanatical adoration for me they are entirely capable of murdering Cortesi [the *New York Times* correspondent] or anyone they think stands in their way."

Shuddering in disgust and disbelief at Perón's only faintly veiled threat, Braden made it clear that any attack on Cortesi or any other correspondent would have "serious repercussions on friendly relations between Argentina and the U.S." To this, Perón responded that of course he knew who these fanatics were and would keep them under observation. But he "could not guarantee that some fanatic from the country would not kill Cortesi and then commit suicide."

As soon as he emerged, shaken, from this interview, Braden contacted Cortesi and the other American reporters and offered them sanctuary in the U.S. embassy. Then he fired off a cable to his superiors in Washington: "Perón's astonishing outburst . . . confirms he is dangerous . . . I recommend that Dept. read riot act to Argentine Ambassador and I be instructed specifically and in detail to make similar protest here."

Braden's missive was quickly brought to the attention of Byrnes. In one of his first acts as Secretary of State, Byrnes dispatched a telegram to his ambassador: "You are instructed to call on Colonel Perón and to state that this Government takes a very grave view of the implications in Colonel Perón's statement that the lives of American citizens and representatives of reputable American newspapers are in danger and that they cannot be protected by the Argentine Government; that this government expects the Argentine Government to give categorical assurances that they will take all requisite measures to guard the safety of the American correspondents . . ."

Had all this happened even a month earlier, Rockefeller might have pooh-poohed the whole affair as so much empty posturing by Perón. He might have repeated his customary words of caution about interference in another country's internal affairs. But this time there were no such admonitions. Perhaps it was because of the precariousness of his own position, and the realization that the policy drift, under Byrnes, was now moving away from him. Or perhaps it was a recognition that in heedlessly threatening American nationals and the American press, Perón had finally stepped over the line.

Whatever the reason, the first faint notes of a new tune could be heard from the assistant secretary. Instead of restraining Braden or cautioning him, Rockefeller phoned the ambassador and pronounced himself "simply delighted" with how Braden was handling the situation.

Byrnes went off in mid-July to Potsdam, for the first Allied summit conference since the victory in Europe, leaving Rockefeller and the rest of State's top echelon in bureaucratic limbo. Rockefeller tried to wax philosophical, but his appearance told a different tale. Haggard and thin, his closely tailored clothes now drooping on his usually robust frame, Rockefeller so alarmed his mother during a visit later in the month to Pocantico that she ordered him to get some new clothes—and a haircut. "I told him I suspected him of trying to look like Senator Connally. . . . His clothes hang on him and no matter how good looking they may be, he still looks somewhat like a tramp. He promised me solemnly to go to the tailors the next time he is in New York."

For all his recent setbacks, for all the public sniping he had endured, Rockefeller did not want to give up his job. The whole thrust of policy was now counter to his own inclinations, yet he still wanted to be on the inside, influencing, nudging—and, perhaps, rebuilding his eroded stature.

Never one to mope, Rockefeller forged ahead with the gritty resolve of someone determined to hold on. The first step was to try to make amends with the man whose opinion Byrnes revered above all others: Cordell Hull.

It took a certain degree of brazenness for Rockefeller, after all that had transpired with Argentina and the UN conference, to dare to approach the crusty Tennessean, now finally released from the hospital. But, as he had demonstrated so often before, Rockefeller was not easily embarrassed about anything. (This, after all, was the man who had blithely requested a little extra work from Léger, as long as the artist was hanging around his Fifth Avenue apartment.) He approached a likely go-between, Thomas Blake, a State Department official who was a family friend of Hull's. Sitting in Blake's office, Rockefeller asked him to phone Hull then and there and ask for an appointment on Rockefeller's behalf. Blake obliged, and then held out the receiver so Rockefeller could hear Hull's response.

"You can tell the young whippersnapper to go to hell!" roared the former Secretary of State.

With that door slammed in his face, Rockefeller shifted gears and settled on an entirely different approach. He would make a speech on the Argentine situation, a speech that would frankly express the United States' growing concern about the Perón regime. He was the logical official to deliver such an address, he told Grew on July 31, because of the reservoir of goodwill he had built up in Latin America over the years: "There are many things which I can say which might be subject to misinterpretation or as a departure from the Good Neighbor Policy were they voiced by one not as closely associated with the inter-American scene."

The speech would give the State Department the opportunity to deliver a blunt public warning to Perón. That the talk might also redound to the benefit of the man who delivered it—might identify him with the critics of the regime, might rehabilitate his reputation, and might enable him to retake the policy lead—was both obvious and unsaid, at least by Rockefeller.

"I feel very strongly that the sooner this statement is made the better," he advised Grew. But Grew was in no hurry to okay such a controversial move; he suggested that Rockefeller hold off until Byrnes's return from Potsdam.

So Rockefeller bided his time, enlisting support for his proposal from others at the department, and meeting privately with Argentines who gave him vivid accounts of the regime's defensiveness and isolation. "Business, agriculture, the universities and the responsible press all are opposed to

Perón," one businessman told him. "The only solution to the Argentine problem is free elections. But free elections will be impossible as long as Perón remains in power."

All this had been evident for months. Indeed, nothing this man recounted to Rockefeller was very different from what the Argentine opposition, among others, tried, in vain, to tell him that spring, before the momentous decisions of Mexico City and San Francisco were set in motion. Back then, Rockefeller was unwilling to listen. Now, suddenly, he was a good deal more receptive.

His next move was to contact Braden in Buenos Aires. Advising the ambassador of his planned speech, Rockefeller asked for data on Argentina's failure to crack down on the Axis: how the regime had given the directors and officers of Axis firms free rein, how Japanese and German schools and social organizations were still going strong. Once again, it was information that he could have readily obtained for months now, but in which he showed little interest prior to Byrnes's arrival. Indeed, it was precisely the sort of information that Molotov had requested when he urged a delay in admitting Argentina to the San Francisco conference.

Meanwhile, there were reports that certain unnamed "influential" figures on Capitol Hill—presumably Vandenberg and Connally—were pushing for Rockefeller's retention as assistant secretary. Defending Rockefeller's record, these supporters maintained that in backing Argentina he was merely carrying out administration policy and the wishes of the U.S. delegation in San Francisco. (The talk of a Senate probe had long since fallen by the wayside.)

Nevertheless, the prevailing word in the capital was that Byrnes would ax Rockefeller, as well as Grew, MacLeish, and other high officials, as soon as he returned from Potsdam.

But as it happened, Byrnes had more critical issues on his mind upon his return. On August 5 a single bomb from an American airplane virtually obliterated Hiroshima and on August 9 another cataclysmic weapon was unleashed on the seaport city of Nagasaki. Five tense days later, the Japanese surrendered.

The next afternoon, as jubilant crowds filled the streets around the State Department, Dean Acheson sat down for what he described as "a rambling talk" with Byrnes. The secretary wanted Acheson to be his undersecretary, replacing Grew. Byrnes then went on to outline his other plans. Will Clayton would stay, and so would Jim Dunn. MacLeish, he said, had already tendered his resignation, and it had been accepted. And Nelson Rockefeller's resignation would be accepted as well.

But Byrnes chose not to call in Rockefeller immediately. First, he wanted to line up his successor: none other than Spruille Braden.

Braden was in bed with a cold when Byrnes phoned. The ambassador reacted hesitantly to Byrnes's offer. He didn't want to supplant Rockefeller, he told Byrnes; he didn't want "Nelson to feel that I had been gunning for his job." Byrnes assured him that shouldn't be a concern. Rockefeller, he said, was already out.

But Rockefeller remained in ignorance, still anxiously waiting word of his fate, still planning his great expiatory speech on Argentina. On August 17 he penned a rueful note to MacLeish: "I have just gotten word of the White House announcement that your resignation has been accepted, and I feel very badly—although there are certain advantages to knowing one way or the other!"

He read the pile of cables from Braden documenting the mounting unrest in Buenos Aires: the celebrations of the Allied victory that were suppressed by the military with tear gas; the reports of beatings and shootings by Perónist gangs, with 50,000 turning out to mourn the victims; the student-teacher strikes at two universities.

Finally, after several futile efforts to see Byrnes, he sent over to him a draft of his planned speech. "Events in Argentina of the last few days indicate that it is of the utmost importance to make this statement now," he advised the secretary, "and I would appreciate it if I might see you in reference to this."

Byrnes at last saw him on August 23. Rockefeller was just pulling out his draft when Byrnes cut him short. "Frankly," said the secretary, "there's no use talking. The President is going to accept your resignation."

As much as he had been bracing for it, the news still came as a blow. Then, as if oblivious to what Byrnes had said, Rockefeller tried to return to the subject of his speech. "Well, Mr. Secretary," Rockefeller said, "I have given you a speech on Argentina which I am going to make tomorrow night."

Byrnes stared at him disbelievingly. Didn't the man get it?

Curtly, he pointed out to Rockefeller that there would be no speech, because Rockefeller was no longer Assistant Secretary of State.

A wounded Rockefeller set his jaw and stared stonily at Byrnes. He would give the address anyway, he informed the secretary. His dismissal "will free me to make the kind of speech I would like to make as a private citizen and to tell the true story."

It was a defiant gesture, born as much out of Rockefeller's pent-up frustration as out of his compulsion to tell the story.

Rather than call the young man's bluff, Byrnes elected to concede him the point. "All right," he said, "the President won't accept your resignation until after your speech."

The next evening in Boston, at a dinner of the Pan American Society of Massachusetts and Northern New England, Rockefeller delivered his speech. It was easily the toughest—and most eloquent—address of his five-year public service career.

He spoke of the commitments Argentina had made to the Mexico City accords, commitments the United States accepted at face value, "making it clear—as we did—that we expected full performance." But now it was time "to face up to the facts—to look squarely at the record." And that record, as Rockefeller showed in copious detail (all supplied by Spruille Braden), was abysmal. "Too often the action has appeared to be reluctant. Too often steps have been begun or promised and not carried through to completion. The fact remains that many vital commitments in which Argentina joined with her American neighbors still remained unfulfilled by her government."

But Rockefeller distinguished between the Argentine government and the Argentine people. The people, in their "spontaneous manifestos," were voicing their disgust with the regime and their longing for a constitutional government. He expressed confidence that, in time, their will would prevail.

The speech was hardly a mea culpa, but, by the same token, it was not an apologia for past policies either. What was most striking was its tone: harsh and unsparing ("all the hateful methods of fascism were imposed on the Argentine people"), full of polemic touches that would have made Cordell Hull (to whom Rockefeller paid tribute in the speech) proud.

Its great flaw was its timing. Had it been delivered even six weeks earlier, the speech would have been hailed as a bold change of course, a decisive break from Rockefeller's past unwillingness to speak out, to intervene. But coming when it did, the address was derided as the assistant secretary's "off-key swan song"—his "last diplomatic backflip," in the words of one commentator. What praise there was was slight, and often sardonic. Among the Argentine opposition, a U.S. embassy official noted, the attitude was that "at last Mr. Rockefeller has attempted to atone in small part for his sins of appeasement."

The very next morning, Byrnes announced Rockefeller's resignation and the appointment of Spruille Braden to take his place.

Still acting as though the reality of his removal hadn't quite sunk in, Rockefeller requested—and received—an audience with President Truman.

He didn't want to resign, he told Truman. South America was just too important, and there was still much to be done. He wanted to finish the job, if Truman would allow him to.

"Harry was very decent about it," Rockefeller would later reminisce. "He told me I'd done a good job. But he fired me."

"He fired me," he repeated wonderingly. All those years later, he still could not believe it.

"I feel as though a great burden has been lifted from my shoulders," Rockefeller told his mother over the phone after his resignation was announced. Observed Abby, "His voice sounded more buoyant than I had heard it for a long time." As soon as he wrapped things up in Washington, he informed her, he would head up to Pocantico for a few days and from there go on to Seal Harbor.

But when he at last walked through the doors of Kykuit on August 29, he hardly appeared his usual vigorous, exuberant self. "Poor dear," Abby related to Winthrop, "he looked perfectly exhausted, rather as if he had been run over by a steamroller—which seems to me exactly what has happened to him, the steamroller being the Democratic Party." (Now that her son was no longer in the government, Abby felt free to indulge her dyed-in-the-wool Aldrich Republicanism.)

"Your father and I feel that probably Nelson is getting out of Washington just in time to save him from a nervous breakdown."

He told his mother he would be going up to Maine for two weeks, and would be taking two of his children with him. As Abby recounted, "Nelson has decided that he has been away from the children so much for the last five years that this will be a marvelous opportunity to really get to know them."

The only problem was that the Seal Harbor house was already shut for the season and the servants discharged. Abby groaned at the thought of Nelson, the erstwhile majordomo of Latin American policy, playing homemaker and cook for two weeks. She consoled herself with the thought that "they probably will be asked out to lunch and dinner a great deal and they can always go to the Seaside Inn where the food is very good."

Part Five

Luke in the Service of God

Twenty-four

The Next Conspiracy

Nelson Rockefeller did not join the Army.

Instead, after his brief Seal Harbor sojourn, he did what he would always do during the transitional periods of his life: return to the family office, to the sanctuary of 30 Rockefeller Plaza's fifty-sixth floor.

First, there were some matters in Washington to which he had to attend. He lent the Foxhall Road house to his old friend Bill Benton, who had just been appointed to MacLeish's old job at State. "Do you also want the five servants and the chauffeur?" he asked Benton; Benton did. Rockefeller even went so far as to give Benton's children his children's places at the exclusive Sidwell Friends School. Finding openings at choice Washington private schools, he explained, is "the toughest problem you face in Washington."*

He also wielded what clout he had left to help brother Winthrop, who had contracted hepatitis during his combat tour in the South Pacific. Responding to Abby's pleas to somehow get Winthrop home, he contacted his "very great friend," the Surgeon General, who assured Rockefeller he would send orders down the line to bring Winthrop back to the States. If, for some reason, the Surgeon General didn't follow through, Rockefeller promised his mother, he would take further steps to "interest those even higher up." Soon enough, Winthrop was whisked to a hospital bed in San Francisco.

*This was not the first time Rockefeller generously offered the use of his homes to influential friends, nor would it be the last. Two months earlier, he had given Harry Hopkins use of the Fifth Avenue apartment while Hopkins and his wife were house hunting in New York. And in 1947, after Benton had vacated the Foxhall Road home, Rockefeller offered the house to the new Secretary of State, George Marshall, who gladly accepted. Sources: NAR to Mrs. NAR, July 9, 1945, NAR DOS Box 18, RAC; Marshall to NAR, April 29, 1947, Marshall Papers, George Marshall Foundation.

And Rockefeller had to respond to all the letters that poured in after his resignation. Old friends and associates professed their shock at the news. Galo Plaza, Ecuador's ambassador to the United States, termed it "an American tragedy." Representative Charles Eaton, a member of the San Francisco delegation, was "grieved beyond words"; Rockefeller's work with the Latin Americans at the conference, Eaton maintained, "made the charter possible."

Even those with whom he had various fallings-out sent words of consolation. "Though I did not agree with the Argentine business," wrote Adolf Berle, "everyone who knows you realizes that the course you took was chosen from the highest motives of patriotism, and inspired by a desire to protect the inter-American experiment."

But perhaps no note was more heartening—or helpful—than that sent to Junior by one of Rockefeller's first Washington mentors, James Forrestal, now Secretary of the Navy. "Of all the people I have seen in government," said Forrestal, "except possibly Bob Patterson, the Undersecretary of War, I know of no one who has worked harder or more conscientiously—and I may add, in my own opinion, more effectively.

"I hope this will not be the terminus of his public activity."

To the ever-demanding Junior—with whom Rockefeller would again now have to come to terms—such high praise was rare balm for the soul. "What happiness this letter brings to Mamma and me you can hardly imagine," he told his son. "That we know it to be so well-deserved only increases our joy in its receipt."

It was the irrepressible Beardsley Ruml who, as much as anyone, helped launch Rockefeller's Washington career. And now, five years later, Ruml was checking in again, as chipper as ever. "Well," he wrote Rockefeller four days after the firing, "I hope all this means that you are coming back to New York pretty soon and that we can resume the conspiracy where we left off. I do not mean that we will necessarily be conspiring about the same things, but there certainly will be two or three little matters that we may be able to take a crack at."

Delighted to hear from his once and future adviser, Rockefeller responded with much of his old verve. "I shall always feel that I owe the opportunity which I have had during the past five years largely to you," he replied. "It has been a great experience and I am all set to start the next conspiracy!"

Not that Rockefeller needed much prompting to set off on conspiracies. Never given to brooding, he approached his life's crises by simply plunging ahead into a fresh round of activities; it was this kinetic quality, as much as what he accomplished with it, that defined the man. "I cannot picture him static, standing quietly," observed Frank Jamieson's wife, Linda. "He was always in motion."

"I'm a great believer in having a purpose," Rockefeller would say. "If you have a sense of purpose and direction, that gives meaning to life. . . . I've always had a purpose."

As he resettled into civilian life, he seemed as directed and driven as ever. One evening, he and Tod showed up at the Jamiesons' apartment, where the other guests were James "Scotty" Reston and his wife. "After dinner," remembers Linda, "Nelson just pulled up a chair and sat face-to-face with Scotty. He was someone Nelson wanted to talk to, and that was it. That was the evening. That was the real purpose."

The New York City he returned to was as well suited to his adrenaline level as was the Washington of five years before. Free at last from its wartime constraints, New York was a swaggering, self-confident metropolis, the pinnacle of the free world.

Never had the city, with its gleaming skyscrapers and its prodigious department stores, its ceaseless traffic and its resplendent nightlife, seemed so imperial. Never had it seemed such a mecca, with the troopships regularly disgorging onto the bustling West Side piers hordes of servicemen home at last, safe at last, from the war.

While the Empire State Building was New York's most identifiable symbol, it was Rockefeller Center that was truly the city's pride and joy: the place that epitomized the city's brio and cosmopolitanism, its vibrant admixture of brashness and epic grandeur. Setting foot once again in its limestone precincts, crossing again the private street that ran through its heart, Nelson Rockefeller was a prince returned to a glittering, refulgent domain.

And then he stepped out of the elevator, onto the fifty-sixth floor.

There to greet him was the familiar old black factotum, perched behind the reception desk, reading his Bible. The walls were still their dull, institutional beige and green, the carpet still red, the furniture the same stodgy red and black leather. All the people were the same, fixed, like a *tableau vivant*, in the very same places they occupied when he had left the office five years before. There was the birdlike septuagenarian Robert Gumbel, his father's executive assistant and self-styled "office boy," burrowing away at his rolltop desk. There was Thomas Debevoise, the dour "Prime Minister," and Bertram Cutler and Barton Turnbull, aging guardians of the family fortune.

And, in the southwest corner, frozen in his somber Jacobean inner sanctum, was seventy-one-year-old John D. Rockefeller, Jr., as commanding as always, as intimidating as ever.

For Nelson Rockefeller, brimming with energy, accustomed to dealing with Presidents and cabinet members on the highest matters of state, the return to these quarters was instantly deflating. All around him were the reminders that this was his father's office, and his father's empire, reminders of the controlling presence that he had escaped when he went to Washington.

Yet whatever sense of letdown he experienced was fleeting. Supremely confident as always, he knew that time—the sheer, unstoppable momentum of generational change—was on his side.

He was not the only Rockefeller scion to return to the office that fall. Laurance was back from a four-year stint in the Navy, where he spent most of his time crisscrossing the United States as an aircraft production troubleshooter. John 3rd was also just out of the Navy, having served in a Washington desk job coordinating policies in occupied territories. David was returning from Paris, after over three years in Army intelligence in North Africa, Italy, and southern France. And once he was fully recovered, Winthrop—the only one of the brothers to actually see combat duty—would be coming back too.

All of the brothers, not just Nelson, were returning to the family fold with a new sense of independence and self-reliance born of their wartime experiences. None would be content any longer to be mere acolytes of their father or to obediently heed the injunctions of his aides. Each wanted to pursue his own field of operations, with his own offices and his own staff. As one senior family adviser would ruefully recall, "They descended on the office like an avalanche." (To distinguish among all these Rockefellers, the brothers were referred to in the office by their first names: Mr. Nelson, Mr. Laurance, etc., a plantation-style nomenclature that some family office hands would always find unsettling.)

It was Nelson, as always, who led the way. To accommodate the brothers and their staffs, he proposed to his father a complete remodeling of the floor's east wing. (The new offices would house four of the brothers; John 3rd decided to stay near his father in the west wing.) The Rockefeller Foundation would be moved down to the fifty-fifth floor to make room. To no one's surprise, Wally Harrison was tabbed to be the architect.

Bowing to the inevitable, Junior gave his assent, barely blanching as the project's costs rose well over his son's initial estimates. Nelson assured him that "we have done everything possible" to keep the costs down, "but, frankly, we have been unsuccessful."

When the work was finally completed, it was readily apparent why the costs had escalated. The renovation bore Harrison's modernist stamp: slightly curved corridors, blond wood paneling, doors set flush with the walls, Scandinavian modern furniture. It was hardly the showiest job, but set against the fuddy-duddy institutional air of Junior's west wing, the new offices looked like a veritable Bauhaus fantasyland.

Taking his father on a tour of the new facilities, Nelson couldn't help beaming. At the end, he turned to Junior. "Gee, Pa," he said, "isn't this all impressive?"

His nonplussed father fixed him with a quizzical stare. "Nelson," he replied, "whom are we trying to impress?"

Several months earlier, when he was still in Washington, Nelson had met with John and Laurance to discuss their postwar roles in the family empire. They agreed to act "as if the slate was clean," with each brother to decide anew where he wanted to devote his energies. Nevertheless, each one now found himself gravitating to exactly the same pursuits that had attracted him before the war: John to philanthropy, Laurance to venture capital investing, and Nelson to Rockefeller Center and the Museum of Modern Art.

The leadership of these institutions was now virtually Nelson's as of right, and in both cases he eagerly assumed the mantle. In October 1945 he was elected chairman of Rockefeller Center, and the next year he resumed his presidency of the museum. But with both institutions now heading into a seemingly secure middle age, neither job was the challenge it once was. No longer did he have to spend much time trying to fill Rockefeller Center. "As you can well imagine," the Center's president, Turnbull, wrote him in January 1946, "we are not pressing tenants at this time to sign up—they are pressing us."

To fill his plate, Nelson took on a series of volunteer civic roles that were entirely outside the family's usual sphere of influence—but which fully befit his new stature as a national figure in his own right. He became chairman of the Victory Clothing Committee's New York City campaign, in which capacity he oversaw the collection of over three million pounds of clothing for distribution in war-ravaged Europe. To assist, he brought together an influential, if variegated group, consisting of R. H. Macy boss Jack Straus, Anna Rosenberg, and Wild Bill Donovan, among others.

Then he assumed the chairmanship of the United Jewish Appeal's nonsectarian community committee of New York. This was hardly the first time the Rockefellers had supported Jewish philanthropies: Junior, at the urging of Felix Warburg, had been a major financial backer of Jewish agricultural settlements in the Soviet Union in the 1920s. But it was far and away the most visible, and potentially controversial, Rockefeller involvement in Jewish affairs; the UJA campaign was a principal source of funds for the tidal wave of displaced Jews seeking a new homeland in Palestine.

Nelson had taken the UJA position at the urging of Felix's son Edward, his old comrade-in-arms at MOMA. His contacts with Jewish leaders, however, were already extensive, thanks undoubtedly to Anna Rosenberg's formidable connections to the Jewish labor movement. He was on good terms with both David Dubinsky, president of the International Ladies' Garment Workers' Union, and Jacob Potofsky, head of the Amalgamated Clothing Workers; the latter was a wartime guest at Nelson's Foxhall Road home. (Years later, when the three men were honored for their civic endeavors by the Urban League, Potofsky remarked, "I am glad to see a reunion of that fine firm with that good old American name of Dubinsky, Potofsky and Rockefeller!")

It was Rockefeller who initiated the contact with the UJA. He asked

Warburg, then the organization's chairman, to come see him, and staggered Warburg by offering $320,000 in contributions on the spot: $100,000 jointly from the Rockefeller brothers, $100,000 from Nelson himself, $100,000 from his father, and another $20,000 from his mother. He didn't understand, he told Warburg, why the UJA solicited only Jews; there should be a nonsectarian campaign as well. Not one to miss such a golden opportunity, Warburg agreed with him, and asked him if he would be willing to head it. Rockefeller accepted on the spot.

That Rockefeller was totally sincere and steadfast in these charitable endeavors there was never any doubt. Vera Goeller, whom he had recruited from City Hall to assist in his civic involvements, recalls that "he raised a tremendous amount of money" for the UJA and that he spent Christmas Eve 1945 huddling with the Victory Clothing Committee. (He did commit one notorious faux pas in his UJA work, hosting a luncheon of his committee at the University Club, which at the time excluded Jews. To make matters worse, the main course was ham.)

Yet it was hard, given his obvious political ambitions, not to discern other motives for this flurry of civic activity. Certainly, in the case of the UJA, his calculation was apparent: it was he who had approached Warburg, and not the other way around, a distinctly rare state of affairs for a Rockefeller. And what he stood to gain from these endeavors was obvious. The sheer visibility of his role, his identification with good causes, and—not least—the extensive connections with the city's movers and shakers would serve him well, whatever political road he chose to take.

At the same time that he was avidly asserting his presence in New York City life, he was also casting furtive backward glances at his former colleagues in Washington and the larger sphere of inter-American affairs he had left behind.

Everything his successor, Spruille Braden, did seemed aimed at repudiating Rockefeller's legacy. In late September, at Braden's urging, the President announced the United States was postponing the inter-American conference to implement the Chapultepec accords—thus backing away from one of the key commitments Rockefeller had undertaken in San Francisco. The reason cited was the continued upheaval in Argentina. Then Braden ordered an all-out investigation of Argentina's connivance with the Nazis. To head this probe, he brought back to the department, as his special assistant, Rockefeller's old nemesis, Carl Spaeth.

The damning findings were made public in February 1946, in what became known as the *Blue Book*. The report was issued just two weeks before the long-awaited Argentine elections—a fact that Perón seized upon in denouncing U.S. interference in the country's affairs. Indeed, it was exactly the sort of unilateral U.S. intervention that Rockefeller had always decried. Whether because of the *Blue Book,* or in spite of it, Perón won the election handily.

Meanwhile, within days of Rockefeller's departure from Washington the first steps were taken toward dismantling his creation, the coordinator's office. Over the next nine months most of its functions were transferred to the State Department. On May 20, 1946, the office was permanently shut down.

Rockefeller watched this procession of events with mounting exasperation. Somehow, in spite of everything, he thought his old colleagues would still take his views into account, would still solicit his help. As he would later recount, "I felt pretty well informed on Western Hemisphere affairs. I'd just come back from San Francisco and we'd gotten support of the Latins on all the important issues. I thought that I would be consulted. I *never* got a call from *anybody* in the State Department. I've got to say that was the one period in my life when I *really* was upset."

His friends, sensing his hurt, searched for ways to get him some recognition from official Washington. Anna Rosenberg and Bill Benton began orchestrating a campaign to secure for him one of the government's highest civilian awards, the Medal of Merit. Such influential stalwarts as Warren Austin and Sumner Welles were asked to weigh in with their support (Austin wrote an effusive letter of recommendation, but Welles declined to help).

But all the work was for naught. In Washington, Rockefeller was still a discredited figure, a pariah. The bid for a medal went nowhere.

For Rockefeller, a residue of bitterness would always remain. "I learned my lesson," he reflected late in his life. "After that, I recognized that you do your best, you get satisfaction out of doing it, and then forget it. Don't look for thanks, for praise, for appreciation, except what's inside of you, for the job you've done."

Nevertheless, even if the current administration wasn't listening, there were still myriad ways for a Rockefeller to have an international impact.

In early 1946 he was asked by New York mayor William O'Dwyer to join a committee of civic leaders intent on convincing the United Nations to make its permanent home in New York City. Chaired by the redoubtable parks commissioner Robert Moses, the panel also included *New York Times* publisher Arthur Hays Sulzberger, IBM chairman Thomas Watson, Rockefeller's uncle Winthrop Aldrich, and Wally Harrison.

Attracting the UN to New York would, O'Dwyer felt, "be the one great thing that would make New York the center of the world." The organization was already settling into temporary quarters—an old Sperry gyroscope plant in Lake Success, Long Island—and Moses wanted to lure the UN a few miles west, to Flushing Meadows Park in Queens, site of the 1939 World's Fair.

The UN's site selection committee, however, was less than enamored of the site; as far as the members were concerned, it was nothing more than a malodorous swamp. They were far more attracted by bids from Philadelphia, which was offering a ten-square-mile tract, and San Francisco. A deadline of December 11, 1946, was set for the final decision, and as it loomed closer, Philadelphia was the clear front-runner. So confident was the city that it had already begun condemning land for the site.

Rockefeller had gone off to Mexico City in early December, to attend the inauguration of Mexican President Miguel Alemán, and from there he went to Texas for a week of hunting and camping. Two days into his Texas interlude, he received an urgent phone call from Harrison and Frank Jamieson. Jamieson had just been informed by their friend at the *Times*, Reston, that it looked like Philadelphia would win out—unless New York came up with an eleventh-hour alternative to Flushing Meadows.

Rockefeller canceled the rest of his vacation and flew back at once to the city. Harrison met him at La Guardia Field on Sunday, December 8, and together they headed immediately to Lake Success and a meeting with UN Secretary-General Trygve Lie. When they arrived at the headquarters they were asked by the guard for their passes; they didn't have any. "Listen," said Nelson, "I am Mr. Rockefeller." "*Everybody* is Mr. Rockefeller," replied the guard. "Beat it." Rockefeller and Harrison wound up looking for a pay phone to contact Lie and get past the guard.

Joining Lie for the meeting was Warren Austin, who had succeeded Stettinius as head of the American delegation, O'Dwyer, and Moses. Lie and Austin confirmed Reston's tip: New York's only chance was if an alternative to Flushing Meadows could be found. Then they mentioned X City.

X City was the grand design of the flamboyant, chronically overextended real estate mogul William Zeckendorf. Envisioning a metropolitan complex that would dwarf even Rockefeller Center, Zeckendorf had acquired some seventeen acres in Manhattan along the East River north of 42nd Street. It was not exactly prime real estate: much of the property, a grungy neighborhood known mainly for its slaughterhouses, was purchased for a relative pittance.

Zeckendorf planned to level the site and erect an immense, seven-block-long platform above First Avenue. On that platform he would build a complex of apartment houses, office towers, and a six-thousand-room hotel—along with a yacht marina, a heliport, and even a new home for the Metropolitan Opera. It was an incredibly ambitious undertaking, even for Zeckendorf, and to design it he hired the man who had made Rockefeller Center a reality a decade earlier: Wally Harrison.

Harrison had an affinity for the high-living Zeckendorf, perhaps because the tycoon had much in common with another one of his clients. Zeckendorf, he would later say, was "like Nelson—ready to act, to do the thing." Drawings were prepared, but then Zeckendorf encountered his usual snag: he was having trouble coming up with the money. At breakfast with his wife one day in early December, he read a newspaper account of the debate over the UN site. A gust of inspiration rushed through his head. "Marion," he announced, "I'm going to put those bastards on the platform!"

He contacted O'Dwyer, who immediately broached the idea to Moses and Lie. The Secretary-General called it a "wildly remote" prospect—but one that could turn the tide in New York's favor.

Zeckendorf's proposition intrigued Rockefeller when it was laid out for him that Sunday evening in Lake Success. But when he reviewed it the next day with Harrison, he concluded that the deal would be too costly; Zeckendorf had acquired the property for $6.5 million, and would undoubtedly want a lot more in recompense.

Rockefeller, instead, had another idea. He would offer the United Nations Pocantico Hills.

At noon a day later, less than twenty-four hours before the UN's deadline, he brought together his closest aides—Jamieson, Lockwood, and Harrison—and brother Laurance. Exploring the Pocantico option, Laurance—loyally obliging as ever to his brother's desires—offered his tract of two hundred twenty acres on the northwest part of the estate, a parcel known as Rockwood Hall, that Junior had given him less than a year earlier. They then phoned John 3rd, who was visiting the Colonial Williamsburg site; reluctantly, John agreed to donate his property as well. Winthrop was in Venezuela, but David was en route uptown from Wall Street, and when he arrived the question was put to him as well. "Couldn't I give money instead?" he sputtered. Told that money alone wouldn't do, he went along.

Still, the one vote that could overrule all the others—that of the laird of Kykuit, John D. Rockefeller, Jr.—had yet to be heard from. And Junior's assent was far from a sure thing. Nelson was asking him to surrender a sizable piece of his cherished domain, the vast estate he had so assiduously assembled and groomed over four decades. His home would be spared, but the 3,300 acres over which he presided would be drastically diminished—perhaps by as much as a third.

What's more, in at least one previous instance, Junior had shown himself notably unsympathetic to Nelson's designs for the UN. Several months earlier, Nelson had eagerly offered Rockefeller Center's Center Theater for a General Assembly meeting. In his enthusiasm, he glossed over the fact that the theater already was leased for other purposes. When this little complication was pointed out to him, he sheepishly approached his father, who had the sole power to abrogate the lease. Junior refused to do so. The affair, remembered Jamieson, "became a source of personal embarrassment to Nelson because he found he could not deliver on his offer."

Nelson met his father for lunch and broached the Pocantico idea. Despite his sentimental attachment to the property, Junior was willing to go along—

perhaps because he doubted the UN would ever accept such a remote site, more than an hour's drive from the city. To make up for the land that the family would retain, he and Nelson agreed they would have to secure options on property adjacent to the estate. Returning to his office after lunch, Nelson spread out maps of the area on the cocoa-colored carpet and phoned the family's local real estate broker—William J. Yates in Ossining—to start rounding up the options.

By seven that evening, Nelson had put together a two-thousand-acre site: a thousand from the family, a thousand through Yates. He phoned Austin with the offer. The senator, however, was not encouraging: he did not believe the UN would be interested in any site that was not in the city itself.

Shortly afterward, Junior phoned, and Nelson presented the situation to him. The UN didn't want Pocantico. Only X City would do. There was a moment's silence, as Nelson's aides clustered anxiously around his desk. Suddenly, Nelson's eyes twinkled and his face lit up with an enormous grin. "Why, Pa!" he exclaimed. "That's most generous." He cupped his hand over the receiver and whispered, "He wants to know how much that site along the East River would cost! He wants to give it to them! Wally, how much do you think it would take to get it?" Harrison guessed about eight and a half million dollars. Nelson conveyed the information to his father. All right, then, Junior said, he would donate the eight and a half million, but on one condition: that the gift be totally free of any gift tax. Years before, when he had donated a library to the League of Nations, he had been socked with a huge federal tax liability, and he bristled at going through that again.

The next step, with barely twelve hours left before the UN decision, was to find Bill Zeckendorf. The task fell to Harrison, who finally tracked him down at a familiar haunt: the Monte Carlo, a nightclub owned and operated by Zeckendorf's firm.

When Harrison arrived, the portly real estate magnate was holding forth in a back room, gaily quaffing champagne to celebrate his wedding anniversary and the birthday of one of his partners. Nervously ("I tried to assume an air of nonchalance, but I couldn't make it," Harrison recalled) the architect pulled from his pocket a map of the X City site. "The United Nations," he said, "wants an option on the property."

Zeckendorf was happy to hear it; as far as he was concerned, it had all been his idea to start with. "Anything they want to pay," he said, would be fine with him. Harrison mentioned eight and a half million, whereupon Zeckendorf grabbed the map, stretched it out on the table, circled the area in question with his pen, and scrawled "8,500,000 to U.N. Dec. 10 for 30 days," signing his name underneath.

Harrison stuffed the map back in his pocket, left the Monte Carlo, and walked up the street to the St. Regis Hotel to find a pay phone. When he told Nelson the good news, Nelson jubilantly instructed him to pick up a bottle of champagne on his way back to the office. After he put down the phone, Harrison rummaged through his pockets, and suddenly realized that the man who had just concluded one of New York's most monumental deals had all of a dollar and eleven cents on him. He returned to Rockefeller Plaza empty-handed, and Nelson ended up sending down to '21' for two bottles of the bubbly.

Much still had to be done. They had to contact Robert Moses, to get assurances that the city would cede its rights to streets and bulkheads within the site. At one-thirty in the morning, Austin was phoned at his room at the Pennsylvania Hotel; it would be up to the senator to present the offer of the Manhattan site the next morning, as well as to secure the necessary assurances from Washington about Junior's tax liability. He told Nelson to meet him at eight-thirty with the legal papers.

John Lockwood, meanwhile, puzzled over the map, with its scribbled notations. As he remembers, "Harrison came back with this goddamn thing in his hand, and Nelson said, 'Here, Johnny, what is it?' and I said, 'I don't know. It's certainly not anything which you can take and say you've got something. I don't see anything here which you can present to your father.' "

Nevertheless, promptly at seven-thirty the next morning, Nelson and his weary compatriots showed up at Junior's Park Avenue apartment for breakfast, documents in hand. Lockwood presented Junior with a contract studded with "ifs"—primarily because the skeptical attorney doubted whether Zeckendorf really owned the whole site.

Junior signed all the papers. It was a moment fraught with historic resonance, and not a little familial resonance as well. As his son was heading out the door for the meeting with Austin, Junior suddenly reached up and grabbed at Nelson's coat. "Will this make up for the Center Theater?" he whispered.

Two hours later, at Lake Success, Warren Austin stood up and announced the Rockefeller offer. Elated by this development, the UN's site committee voted overwhelmingly to accept the gift. The UN would be in New York City after all—thanks to Bill Zeckendorf's foresight, Junior's generosity, and, not least, Nelson Rockefeller's dogged unwillingness to lose the world body to another locale.

Over drinks that night at his apartment with Tod and some friends, Nelson was, if not blasé, then rather matter-of-fact about his achievement. "I just couldn't imagine that they would let it be anywhere else," he said.

Whatever satisfaction he might have felt was no doubt tempered by the realization that nothing would have happened without Junior's helping hand. Indeed, the UN struggle only underscored the incontrovertible fact that the family fortune, and all the apparatus that went with it, was still firmly in Junior's septuagenarian grip.

Every day brought fresh reminders of this state of affairs. When Nelson asked his aides to extract a memo from Gumbel's files, they were firmly rebuffed by the self-styled "office boy"; if Mr. Nelson wanted the memo, said Gumbel, he would have to personally secure his father's permission. "Well," Nelson said, when told of this, "I guess I'll have to ask Father."

As Lockwood once reflected, "Mr. Rockefeller, Jr., was like a sun and the boys like the planets. If one of them got too close, he got burned; if he got too far away, he spun into space."

But for five years now, Nelson Rockefeller had been the center of his own universe; he was not about to fall back into the role of a satellite. And so, with the same purposefulness that he brought to the office remodeling, he set out to upend the office power structure—and create a new Rockefeller constellation.

The first tactic he used was to implant his own people in key positions. He brought Frank Jamieson in as the family's first full-time public relations adviser. While Jamieson was supposed to represent the entire family, there was little question where his ultimate allegiance lay. Pointed out Lockwood, "The public relations position was crucial because whoever controlled him was effectively the leader of the family. And it was always clear that Frank worked for Nelson first and the rest of the brothers second."

Then, striking even closer to the seat of power, Nelson began maneuvering to replace the aging family counsel, Tom Debevoise, with his own candidate: Lockwood (or "Johnny Lock," as Nelson was now wont to breezily call him). Debevoise's position was already eroding, partly due to his age, partly due to his drinking. "A two-martini man," Lockwood remembers. "I finally said I wouldn't have lunch with him, because he pressed it on you so hard. He used to go to sleep every day after lunch. And because of the drinking, he made a couple of big goofs."

"Nelson," says Lockwood, "sensed that the time was right to move, and he moved." With Debevoise's deputy, Vanderbilt Webb, professing a desire to return to the practice of law, the way was clear for Lockwood's appointment. And Junior, as aware as anyone of Debevoise's gaffes, was willing to go along with the choice—even in the face of last-minute lobbying by Debevoise to name, instead, a more seasoned attorney, Sinclair Hamilton.

In times past, Junior would have gladly heeded his old *consigliere*. But these were different times. "I don't think my sons are going to accept anyone that's that much older than they are," he advised Debevoise. The matter was closed.

Lockwood accepted the position, but with one important stipulation: that he be permitted to continue as a Milbank, Tweed partner, with an office outside Room 5600. "I don't think it's in your interest or your children's interest for me to be a one-client lawyer," he told Junior. He would be far more effective, he argued, if he could be exposed to a broader base of problems and clients. Thus, Lockwood preserved a modicum of independence from the Rockefeller machine. He would devote his life to the Rockefellers' interests. But, in his own mind at least, he would never be their vassal.

Shortly after Lockwood's appointment, Junior took him aside. "Mr. Lockwood," he said, "I want you to help me understand my sons." There was no longer any question that the balance of power was shifting. From now on, Junior would have to do what he could to accommodate it.

During those early postwar years, Junior continued to transfer chunks of his vast wealth to his children. From 1943 to 1947, he gave them gifts totaling some $55 million. The largest gift—over $15 million—went to John; Nelson's share was $12.6 million. That Junior had no intention of treating his offspring equally was shown by his meager transfers to Babs and Winthrop: each was given a paltry half million dollars.

The treatment of Babs reflected the moralistic Junior's disapproval of her divorce from David Milton in 1943, as well as his disappointment over her seeming lack of interest in philanthropy. As for Winthrop, his fascination with café society (upon his return from the war, he went back to his nightclubbing ways) was profoundly upsetting to Junior, who had invested so much psychic energy in ensuring that his sons wouldn't turn into rich wastrels. Even Winthrop's sterling war record did not redeem him in Junior's eyes.

While the overall gifts were impressive, and certainly heightened the brothers' feeling of financial independence, they hardly affected Junior's control of the family fortune: in all, the transfers represented barely a sixth of his prewar fortune. And the asset in his portfolio that promised the most lucrative postwar rewards—his ownership of Manhattan's greatest urban treasure, Rockefeller Center—remained Junior's, and Junior's alone.

For the most part, there was little Nelson and his brothers could do to accelerate Junior's financial bequests. But Rockefeller Center was something else again.

The possibility that the Center might not be unobtainable had been raised by Junior himself before the war, when he contemplated donating the complex to his medical research philanthropy, the Rockefeller Institute (a prospect that aroused Nelson's impassioned opposition). Seeing an opening, Nelson in the ensuing years tried several times to induce his father to revisit the question of the Center's future. Writing from Washington in 1942, he asked Junior whether he had given any further consideration to "the matter we discussed in Williamsburg over a year ago, concerning the ultimate disposition of Rockefeller Center stock."

Junior put off the question while his sons were away, but by the time they returned to the family fold he evinced a new willingness to discuss it. For one thing, he was now facing huge new outlays to modernize the Center with such postwar wonders as air conditioning and fluorescent lighting. For another, his attorneys were warning him about dire estate tax consequences if he should die with the Rockefeller Center stock still in his portfolio. What's more, many of the development's key tenants, including RCA and Time-Life, were now pressed for space; to hold them Rockefeller Center would have to undergo a new round of costly expansion (construction of new corporate headquarters for Standard Oil of New Jersey was already underway).

For all these reasons, Junior was receptive when Nelson suggested the sale of Rockefeller Center—not to the Rockefeller Institute, but to the Rockefeller brothers. Says Laurance, "He tried to make Father understand that it really wasn't his money, and that he was responsible for sharing it. And that was hard for Father to understand. But progressively he did."

The one major obstacle was the cost: the book value of Junior's shares was $55 million (coincidentally the same amount Junior had bestowed on his children in gifts). On the other hand, while the development was now making money (it had been in the black since 1943), the stock's true value was depressed by the huge load of indebtedness the Rockefeller Center company carried: $95 million, one-third owed to Metropolitan Life, the other two-thirds owed to Junior himself. Recalls David Rockefeller, "The value of the stock was very low, and Nelson pointed this out, and said, given the tax situation, wouldn't it make sense if we bought the stock from Father at the appraised value."

The "appraised value," thanks to the indebtedness, turned out to be a mere $2.2 million. And it was for that amount that Junior sold Rockefeller Center—the jewel of the family empire, on which he had lavished years of toil and tens of millions of dollars—to his sons in early 1948.

Nelson, however, was not content to leave matters rest at that. Once he had secured this bargain, he tried to instantly boost its depressed value—by having Junior forgive the father's share of the debt. But *that* accommodating, Junior wasn't. (Debt forgiveness would have required Junior to pay the gift tax that he so loathed.) He insisted that the debt—all of it—would have to be repaid.

Nelson yielded the point—for the time being. But, as with the question of the sale of the Center, he would reopen the issue again and again. Finally, in 1952, Nelson secured his father's agreement to a new scheme of his. Instead of forgiving the debt, Junior would transfer it to the Rockefeller Brothers Fund, the collective charitable vehicle the brothers had established in 1940. "Nelson talked to us about it first," says David, "and then he persuaded Father that it made sense." It was a masterstroke. Henceforth, the Rockefeller brothers would, in essence, be repaying themselves, funding their philanthropic ventures with the vast profits from Rockefeller Center—the monumental urban agglomeration they had purchased for just $440,000 apiece.

The awesome ramifications of these maneuvers would soon enough be apparent, as the boom in Manhattan real estate values turned Rockefeller

Center into a virtually priceless commodity. As Laurance dryly points out, "Father did a lot better for us than he'd ever intended, I'll tell you that. I don't think he had any idea at all Rockefeller Center would be as big as it was."

"He used to say he was much more concerned we'd have too much than he was we'd have too little. Well, taking that statement in context"—Laurance smiles—"he would have been shocked."

As much as it was a financial coup, the transfer of Rockefeller Center was a symbolic breakthrough: the handing down, from one generation to the next, of the family's most visible asset. It was tangible certification that the brothers were now powers in their own right—and that Junior's half century of hegemony over the family and its fortune was at an end.

In the wrangling with their father, Nelson's brothers were more than happy to have Nelson take the lead. As David explains, "For many of these issues, he was the one who would have been most successful in persuading Father. I think Nelson saw very clearly what he wanted, and he was articulate and effective in presenting things to Father, with considerable force. I think he used a certain toughness in his arguments, saying to Father that 'we're now at an age and stage where we're in a position to do things that you were able to do at a comparable age, and it's important that you give us these opportunities.' I think he put it pretty strongly."

Nelson was clearly less intimidated than his brethren by Junior's forbidding presence, less likely to quail when confronted by the tight-lipped scowl. "I'm not sure that 'intimidated' is the right word," says David, "although certainly the rest of us might have been more hesitant to broach things quite as directly."

As his brothers sought to find places for themselves in the family empire in those postwar years, it was always Nelson who led the way. Once again, as before the war, he was laying claim to the position of de facto number one son. "He was flailing about after the war," remembers Susan Herter, one of his secretaries at the time. "He saw himself as the ringmaster or cruise director of the family. It seemed clear to *him* what roles everyone should play, even if it wasn't at all clear to *them* that those should be their roles."

While his brothers were often willing to defer to his assertiveness, they were hardly compliant pawns. When Nelson, for instance, tried to bring Lockwood into the biweekly brothers' meetings, "he was told in no uncertain terms that I wasn't to come," Lockwood recalls. Each brother—with the notable exception of Winthrop—was establishing his own realm, with his own cadre of aides, regardless of whatever plans Nelson had for him. "There were moments of terrific competition and jockeying for position among the brothers in those early days," said Lockwood.

John 3rd focused his energies on the family's old philanthropic bastion, the Rockefeller Foundation, struggling to force it out of its ivory tower and tackle more problems of the real world, particularly population control. Laurance was setting up the family's new venture capital arm, Rockefeller Brothers, Inc., and making a host of seed investments in nascent high-technology companies. David—fresh from his overseas experience in Army intelligence—was starting his career at the family bank, the Chase. Already an inveterate globe-trotter, he found a congenial position in the bank's foreign department, and soon would be running all the Chase's Latin American business.

Only Winthrop floundered. After his bout with hepatitis, he did not leave the Army until October 1946. He rejoined the Socony-Vacuum oil company in a humdrum, paper-shuffling position, taking far more interest in his various charitable endeavors, including work on the new New York University medical center. But most of his energies were reserved for his nocturnal activities, much to the discomfort of his family. Winthrop's wooing of musical comedy star Mary Martin caused his alarmed brothers to call in the ubiquitous Anna Rosenberg for counsel. "It was decided that no Rockefeller should marry a woman who was famous for singing 'My Heart Belongs to Daddy' in a mink coat," recalls publicist Tex McCrary, a close friend of Winthrop's who was a rival for Martin's affections.

Deflected from Martin, Winthrop merely moved on to an even more notorious alliance: on Valentine's Day 1948, with Laurance the only family member in attendance, Winthrop married aspiring blond starlet Barbara "Bobo" Sears. The upwardly mobile Bobo, the daughter of a Lithuanian immigrant coal miner (her real name was Jievute Paulekiute), had just shucked her first husband, aristocratic Bostonian Richard Sears. Junior swallowed hard and accepted the marriage, solidifying his son's finances by adding $6 million to his 1934 trust. Within eighteen months, the hard-drinking glamour couple—now with a son, Winthrop Paul—were separated, after Winthrop locked his bride out of their Park Avenue duplex.

Winthrop's misadventures aside, there was an air of irresistible dynamism about the Rockefeller brothers in those postwar years. Eager to marshal their collective influence in the new world that was shaping itself before their eyes, to tap the limitless possibilities that the awesome fortune afforded them, they were poised to reinvent the concept of Rockefeller power. In their grandfather's time the Rockefellers represented economic power, the breathtaking clout of the Standard Oil trust; in their father's era, the family commanded philanthropic power, the ability to deploy vast wealth in the service of a greater good. Now, in the third generation, because of the brothers' diverse interests and ambitions, the power would be more multifaceted, and more pervasive, penetrating, as one commentator would soon write, "almost every area of life—cultural, economic, political, religious, scientific."

Still, as each of the brothers strode into the world, it was always evident that the other four were a half step behind Nelson. In John's case, it was a matter of his own diffident personality. Despite a formidable drive that was often camouflaged by his retiring persona, John was congenitally unable to assert himself over his siblings. For Laurance, it was not a question of self-confidence; he was already displaying that capacity in spades in his bold venture capital activities. Rather, his utter devotion to Nelson put him constantly in a position of deference to his older brother's wishes. Not that he couldn't be frank, even caustic with Nelson at times; with his stiletto wit, Laurance still was the one person who could bring his overbearing brother down to earth. But ultimately, his love for the brother who still called him "Bill," their private childhood nickname, sealed his support for Nelson.

Nelson's primacy could be seen in smaller, mundane ways around the office, as well as in the larger matters. One man who joined the family staff during that period, Kershaw Burbank, remembers once being asked by John 3rd to get some information for one of John's studies from some of the senior Room 5600 staff members. But when he approached them, Burbank was told, "We're working on something for Nelson. Tell John to wait."

"I thought this was just dreadful, this was sacrilege," Burbank recalls. "But I soon found out that Nelson did run the show."

While in large measure, Nelson's dominance was due to the sheer force of his personality, it was also a reflection of the fact that, more than any of his siblings, he cherished the notion of a Rockefeller destiny. Even in his youth, he had had a vision of the family as a collective force. Now, with the means at hand to achieve these dreams, his family consciousness was more acute than ever, extending to the next generation. He began having lunches with the eldest member of that generation, Babs's nineteen-year-old daughter Abby. "He wanted to have everybody take on all of the family obligations," she says. "So he and I began talking about how we could create a structure for the next generation to be able to stay together and share both financial and philanthropic and other experiences."

"There was no question that Nelson wanted to continue the family as an entity, as a unit," Abby continues. "I think he felt it had strength not only for him but for us. But I think he also saw it as—well, power base may be too strong a term—but as an important platform and group that he wanted to keep together." The preservation of the Rockefeller monolith, he knew, was crucial to the achievement of his own larger ambitions.

In taking the part of family unifier, Nelson was assuming a role that, in the normal course of dynastic affairs, would have been played by the eldest son. John 3rd was silent about this further act of usurpation, but his wife, Blanchette, was not. Blessed with a serene aristocratic demeanor, she nonetheless possessed the core of inner fiber that seemed a common denominator among the Rockefeller wives. One family adviser remembers her sniping that "John's problem was that he should have been the second son, and Nelson should have had to bear the weight of being John D. Rockefeller III." Nelson, she felt, was getting a free ride: all of the glory and self-satisfaction of being the family leader, and none of the angst.

Just as his brothers had learned to live in Nelson's shadow, so, too, did his wife and five children.

They had all learned to adjust—albeit sometimes with difficulty—to the arc of his career. The family was well settled into Washington life and then, recalls the eldest child, Rodman, "he came home over a weekend and announced that we were going back to New York. We were all absolutely horrified. It was the end of our world to go back to New York. We didn't know a soul. And my younger brothers had never really been in New York. I had, at least, gone through the third grade or something there. We didn't know what to expect."

Their transition was somewhat eased by the family's means and by the familiar rhythms of a Rockefeller lifestyle. The children found places in exclusive private schools—with the Lincoln School in shambles, Buckley was now the school of choice for the boys, Brearley for the girls—and reacclimated themselves to the plush Fifth Avenue apartment. Each Saturday morning, their chauffeur would drive the brood up to Pocantico, and each Sunday night their father would drive them back into town in his sporty maroon Lincoln Zephyr (his favored vehicle among the five that he owned).

The family rituals, wherever the children were, remained much the same. The children would begin their mornings by joining their father for exercises in his dressing room. "We all did push-ups, sit-ups, and chin-ups," the second oldest boy, Steven, would recall. Afterward, there were the family breakfasts—the one meal that their father could regularly be expected to attend—accompanied by Bible readings and sober discussions of world affairs. Certain rules had to be obeyed—or else. Steven would later note, "Our lives were actually highly regulated. If you didn't show up in time for a meal, you didn't get it. Bells were rung and then you had five minutes to show up. If you didn't make it, you didn't get fed."

The Rockefeller tradition of personal bookkeeping—which had so bedeviled Nelson in his own youth—was nonetheless scrupulously maintained by him. The children's accounts were regularly reviewed; "if they didn't balance, we wouldn't get our allowance," said Steven. And a spirit of entrepreneurial self-reliance was as strenuously ingrained in the children as it had been instilled in Nelson when he was a boy. As Tod would recall, "If they wanted extra money they had the privilege of earning it—raking leaves or shining shoes. The children in the family have always shined their own shoes."

Despite these regulations, Nelson's children often displayed a certain rambunctiousness and free-spirited quality. It was in the genes, as much from Tod as from Nelson. Both Ann and Steven exhibited a youthful wanderlust; of

Ann, her grandmother Abby complained, "She has got into her mind that she would like to run away and is seeking adventure, and she really doesn't care with whom she goes, she just wants to go." Steven once disappeared into the vast grounds of Pocantico, carrying his favorite toy train. He traveled several miles, following the pony trails, before one of the caretakers finally caught up with him.

Of all Nelson's children, the cheekiest was undoubtedly young Michael. He would cross-examine the servants. "Why do you grin so much?" he asked one bemused waitress. While his grandmother fretted that he would hurt the help's feelings, she found his curiosity forgivable: "I really think it is only because he is so very observing and is really interested to know why people look and act the way they do." The youngster, she confessed, "intrigues me enormously. He looks so little and so frail and is so penetrating. I don't believe he misses a thing that goes on." Of the children, he was the most like his father—a factor, no doubt, in Abby's fascination with him.

The children were given leeway to roam, but only up to a point. And like other young Rockefellers, they were carefully shielded from public scrutiny. When Rodman appeared in a school production of "The Dance of the Saber Tooth Tiger," news photographers were barred from the premises—although one tabloid did manage to file a report on his performance.

Nelson's concern about the children was heightened when, just two months after the return to New York, he received a possible kidnapping threat. He immediately was on the phone to his good friend J. Edgar Hoover, who sent a special agent over to investigate. Not content with those measures, Nelson brought all the children down to the New York FBI office for fingerprinting.

In the years to come, Nelson's security worries would not abate.* Given his track record, it was no surprise: this was, after all, the same man who regularly had his phone swept for wiretaps by the FBI. He would repeatedly express his apprehensions to Hoover and to the agents in the New York office. At one point, in the early 1950s, Nelson even visited the New York bureau to explore the possibility of training his daughters in "defense tactics." He dropped the idea when the agents warned him that the risks outweighed the benefits.

"He was a strong father, and a disciplinarian," remembers Rodman, "but at the same time, he did spend a lot of time with his children—within the

*In the Rockefeller clan, Nelson was not the only one to worry about personal security. Junior and his sons all owned pistols, although it is not clear whether any of them carried the guns on their persons (John 3rd did, however, acquire a "quick-draw holster" in 1941). Junior did not give up his gun permit until he was eighty-two. Nelson owned four pistols, the most of anyone in the family. Source: Family Pistol Permit File, RAC.

framework of his time commitments." The latter, however, was an omnipresent factor, whether Nelson was in or out of office. As Lockwood remarks, "Nelson was primarily then focused on whatever it was he was doing, and, if you will, *showing off* to his children." He did, however, find novel ways of spending time with his offspring (if often in the context of "showing off"). When he attended the inauguration of Mexican President Miguel Alemán in 1946, for example, he brought fourteen-year-old Rodman along, and he took the boy with him on subsequent business trips to Latin America as well. Nelson wanted to share his world with his son, that larger world in which he was so compulsive a player. "He wanted me to get the feel of it, and gain the sense of what he was doing, and the excitement of what he was doing," says Rodman.

All along, there was a certain seesaw quality to Nelson's relationship with his children: periods of intense involvement interspersed with long spells of benign neglect. "I don't think it's so much a matter of the time a parent spends with his children as it is the integrity of his relationship with them," he would later explain. To his children, their father seemed more like a beloved high-spirited uncle, popping in and out of their lives as the spirit moved him, than a day-to-day daddy.

When he was on the scene, they found themselves swept up in his force field. "His presence was always something that we felt keenly when he was around," remembered Steven. "His comings and goings were always marked by either the presence or absence of that energy and enthusiasm. His return, his arrival at the house was always something of an event.

"He liked the excitement that his arrival would create. He liked to be warmly welcomed, and he loved it when as young children we would run out to greet him. Everyone got a big hug." The children addressed him as "Daddy" and "Pops," but the boys also playfully called him "Chief"—and he, just as playfully, called them "Chief" or "Chiefie" right back.

All this made for a somewhat dichotomous upbringing for the five Rockefeller progeny. "He either was with you or he wasn't there at all," notes their cousin Abby O'Neill, Babs's daughter. "Nelson would either be telling them they were the greatest people on earth and they had done the most marvelous thing or ignore them entirely. He didn't nurture them—just be there on a daily basis to say, 'What problem do you have today? How can we work on this?' "

The nurturing, instead, was left, as it always had been, to Tod.

Although she gave her children a full measure of attention, Tod was no homebody. Upon her return to New York, she plunged into a full round of society activities: membership in the Cosmopolitan Club, fund-raising, and volunteer work for various civic and philanthropic endeavors, most notably her favorite cause, the Bellevue School of Nursing, for which she served on the board of managers (she would eventually be the board's president).

But while the contours of her life were that of the prototypical Fifth Avenue matron, Tod Rockefeller managed, in her own quiet, idiosyncratic way, to subvert the details. Rather than nestle in the rear of a limousine, she drove herself around town in Nelson's old Ford roadster. She disdained haute couture: "dressmakers," she complained, "stick pins in you." And, in a singular, unpublicized act of rebellion against her class, she enrolled in 1946 in the Liberal Party, the distinctly left-of-center party dominated by New York's clothing workers unions.

The dour public persona she had long since adopted remained firmly in place. Only her family and intimates saw the sardonic wit and the wry playfulness kept hidden behind the mask. Each year, to celebrate her wedding anniversary, she would enjoy a raucous night on the town with her bridesmaids. One year, the whole party attended a Broadway show attired in the same outfits they wore to the nuptials (all except Tod, who thought wearing her wedding gown might be a bit much). At another anniversary bash, she took the floor to dance a mean Charleston.

If the Fifth Avenue apartment, with its Matisse and Léger decorations and Jean-Michel Frank furniture, was Nelson's domain, then Hawes House, their 1750s white clapboard farmhouse on the Pocantico grounds, was very much Tod's. "It was the kind of unpretentious upbringing she wanted for her children," says Lockwood. "She wanted to not bring them up in this imperial palace, which I can understand. But Nelson—Nelson *loved* the palaces."

Furnished in period antiques, Hawes House had a cozy, *gemütlich* air; the only piece of modern art in the place was a Calder wire figure of John D. Rockefeller, Sr., playing golf which sat on the living-room mantelpiece. An old cobbler's bench, topped with a vase full of fresh-cut flowers, stood in the center of the living room. The family and guests took their meals at a narrow old pine table: for Tod, a refreshing change from the formality of their Manhattan digs. "People can really get close to each other when they sit at it," she said. The only drawback was the unruly young Rockefellers' tendency to kick each other under that narrow table.

The bucolic aspects of Pocantico well suited Tod's outdoorsy nature ("I'm just a country girl," she would say). An avid gardener, she could often be found in her sunbonnet tending her zinnias and lilies. And the miles of horse trails on the estate gave her ample scope to indulge her love of riding—although she frequently tangled with Junior's officious stablemaster, Joe Plick. On one famous occasion, she was roundly bawled out by Plick when she and a friend took a pair of horses out in the rain without Plick's authorization. Junior fully backed his man up.

For Tod, this was the one surpassing drawback of Pocantico: it was Junior's country seat, and Junior made the rules. More than any of the other Rockefeller wives, she bridled at his strictures. Somehow, she could never quite accept the fact that Pocantico was not a rambling park to be democratically enjoyed by its residents but a dynast's manor, governed by his arbitrary regulations. Once she brought her children over to Kykuit to wade in the rainbow pools there. Junior, grossly offended by this violation, ordered her and the children out.

Not that Tod didn't have her own imperious side. Those who worked for her, both in Pocantico and in the city, often found her stiff and demanding, unyielding on even the smallest matters. The widow of an architect who worked with her on Hawes House remembers the stories he would tell about Tod: "You couldn't change her mind. If there was some little thing, she would fight you on it to the end." Tod's secretary lived downstairs from this couple in Manhattan, and they would hear much the same tales from her. People in the family office learned to tread warily around Tod. "I used to send my secretary uptown to see her about some things, but after a while I couldn't do it anymore," one man recounts. "Tod was so caustic that she drove the poor woman to tears."

"No one in the entire family ever bawled me out as much as Mrs. Nelson," remembered Pocantico's longtime caretaker, Tom Pyle. But Pyle came to respect her, both for her determination and for her willingness to admit mistakes, even to the help. She once laced into Pyle when the family's pet cocker spaniel disappeared; as far as she was concerned, Pyle wasn't moving fast enough. When the dog was found, Tod wrote him a note of apology.

While she would never be serene, Tod did seem to find a point of equilibrium in her life now. She had a busy city calendar, and a full country life, and the demands and joys of raising five children. It all appeared to balance so nicely that the absence of one element in the equation could scarcely be detected. She knew what was missing, and so did Nelson. But not many others did.

To his family Nelson Rockefeller was an evanescent presence: one moment a vivid, palpable force, the next a smiling blur, en route to the next stop in his career. But to his aides and advisers, there was nothing transitory about Rockefeller. From morning till night, he was the one central fact in their lives, the great dynamo who swept them all up into his energy field, filling their days with his plans and schemes.

The core group—those whom he considered his principal sources of aid and counsel—was unchanged since the war. There was Jamieson, and Lockwood, and the ever-faithful Wally Harrison. After leaving the coordinator's office, where he had stepped into Rockefeller's shoes after Rockefeller left for the State Department, Harrison moved adroitly to rebuild his architectural practice. Now he was fast coming into his own as a world-class architect. In January 1947 he was appointed director of planning for the new UN headquarters—in effect, the architect-in-chief, presiding over a team of international designers that included such stellar names as France's Le Corbusier and Brazil's Oscar Niemeyer.

But even as his work on the UN was gaining him global renown (he would make the cover of *Time* in 1952), Harrison was still securely fixed in Nelson Rockefeller's orbit. Just as they did before the war, the two would often meet in midmorning at a coffee shop behind the Prometheus statue in Rockefeller Plaza. Over their favorite repast of bacon rolls (a hard roll split, slathered with marmalade, and stuffed with bacon strips) they would mull whatever new scheme Rockefeller was contemplating.

"Wally by nature was sympathetic," notes his partner Max Abramovitz. "He always listened. Sometimes he'd even mouth something you'd said to him, as if he said it." But in Harrison's case, sympathy did not equate with sycophancy; he was fully capable of letting Rockefeller know when one of his ideas was off-the-wall. Frank Jamieson—who also possessed that rare capacity—once said, "One good thing about Wally: when things got down to something serious, in conferences, Wally was one of the few people who could say no to Nelson."

They shared many affinities: for modern architecture, for modern art (Harrison was also a collector, and a painter as well), and, above all, for grand designs. "There was nothing niggling or petty about either Nelson or Harrison," says architect Harmon Goldstone, who worked with both men. "They thought in very broad terms, and other people followed up and swept up after them." Harrison, like Rockefeller, was governed by great strokes of intuition, rather than plodding, step-by-step syntheses, and could be equally cavalier about the consequences. "Well," he said once, when presented with a design, "let's go ahead with it, and if we don't like it, we'll tear it down and build it over." He was only half joking. Yet, at the same time, this tendency was tempered by a strong strain of Yankee practicality. As Beardsley Ruml would remark, "In this world you can find all the brilliant minds you want, but the Wally Harrisons—brilliant people who are also completely reliable—are a rare commodity."

There were many who regarded Harrison as riven by inner conflict. On the one hand, he possessed a distinct bohemian streak; it was said that he was never happier than padding around his studio at his Huntington, Long Island, house, dressed in T-shirt and a soiled pair of trousers held up by a rope belt, looking for all the world like a middle-aged artiste. On the other hand, there was a side of him that was drawn to power and to the powerful, that savored proximity to the world's movers and shakers. It was this inclination, this corporate side of Harrison, that would often overwhelm and subjugate his bohemian side. And it was this inclination that, as much as anything, explained why Harrison—for all his own career triumphs—was forever in Nelson Rockefeller's thrall.

Despite Harrison's considerable success in his own right, he was always willing to accept his patron's largesse. In 1948 Rockefeller provided him with an apartment in Laurance's Fifth Avenue building, just steps away from Rockefeller's own abode. Not only was the apartment free of charge—the lease was signed by one of Rockefeller's subsidiary corporations—but Harrison was given a reserve of up to $20,000 to renovate and furnish it.

Rockefeller would also help with the painful, and costly, matter of Harrison's mentally ill only child, Sarah. In 1950 he set up a trust fund to pay for her medical bills and institutionalization.

The relationship between Harrison and Rockefeller would always be a complex, multihued affair. It revolved around many factors, but not the least of them were the material blessings Rockefeller offered, and Harrison readily accepted. In that respect, Wally Harrison the world-class architect would be no different than the many lesser figures who would serve Nelson Rockefeller. For him, and for them, the scent of money and power simply could not be resisted. He was more than willing to be bound by the golden chain.

Beyond the inner circle was the retinue of fixers and intellectual gurus who were forever floating around Nelson Rockefeller, people like Ruml and Anna Rosenberg, people whose exact roles were never well defined, but who always had the boss's ear.

Rockefeller had never forgotten the debt he owed to Anna Rosenberg. At the end of the war, when Rosenberg was struggling to get back on her feet in the private sector, Rockefeller was approached by Bill Benton with a proposition: each of them would give her two years' pay in advance in exchange for her services. Rockefeller agreed immediately. "Bill," he said, "I want to tell you right now that everything I've amounted to here in Washington, everything I feel I've achieved here in Washington, I owe to Anna Rosenberg."

Rosenberg was richly recompensed: Rockefeller paid her $12,000 annually in 1945 and 1946 alone. For that sum, she not only advised Jamieson on public relations problems but performed such sundry services as buying gifts on Rockefeller's behalf for his mother's birthday. (Abby was well aware of what was going on. "Look," she told Rosenberg, "Nelson is going to give me some candy for my birthday. He does it every year. Would you please be sure he doesn't give me this awful brand?") Rosenberg liked to tell the story of one visit to Pocantico when, at Nelson's behest, she smuggled in six bottles of booze, so that Nelson and his brothers could circumvent Junior's strict ban of alcoholic beverages from the premises. No sooner had she settled into her room than Nelson was knocking on the door, brothers in tow. "Did you bring it? Did you bring it?" he asked. "I hadn't been there ten minutes," quipped Rosenberg, "and I had all of them in my bedroom."

Rosenberg's overbearing manner—punctuated by the jangling bracelets that announced her presence—was a constant irritant to others in Rockefeller's inner circle. Yet Rockefeller, still profoundly grateful for all she had done for him during the war, would brook no criticism of her. "No matter how arrogant she got," says one longtime aide, "he was always very respectful and deferential to her."

Aside from such familiar faces as Rosenberg, there was an assortment of lesser-known characters who flitted around Room 5600, ready to do Rockefeller's bidding. Some were old Rockefeller cronies, like his Lincoln School and Dartmouth classmate Bill Alton. Others were new arrivals, part of his stockpile of talent, people he tucked away "like a squirrel hiding nuts," in Alton's words.

Among those Rockefeller tucked away was Tom Braden. A tall, wiry Dartmouth college senior, Braden was editor of the daily paper, *The Dartmouth,* when Rockefeller met him during a 1940 visit to the campus for his tenth anniversary class reunion. Someone suggested to Rockefeller that Braden was a young man of promise, and so Rockefeller sauntered into the newspaper office—still wearing his green class of 1930 cap—and introduced himself. The next thing Braden knew, he was sitting behind a desk at Rockefeller Center.

"I don't know what he had in mind," says Braden. "I think he probably had in mind no more than that he seemed to like me, and he'd heard good things about me, and so he hired me. But if he had things for me to do, I was not smart enough or old enough to understand what the hell they were. I must have wasted my time there for nearly a year."

When war broke out, Braden went off to join the British Army, and later worked in Bill Donovan's OSS. But Rockefeller had not forgotten him. After the war Braden had settled into a teaching position at Dartmouth when Rockefeller again reached out to him. This time he planted Braden in the Museum of Modern Art, as executive secretary. Braden still gropes to describe exactly what he did there. "I guess the job was . . . the job was . . . oh, dear. It's hard to explain." Eventually, Braden would drift off again, when Donovan recruited him to start something called the American Committee for a United Europe—a front for the Central Intelligence Agency, the postwar incarnation of Donovan's OSS. Rockefeller, always happy to advance the anti-Soviet cause, approved. Soon afterward, Braden joined the CIA itself, heading its propaganda operation. He and Rockefeller stayed in close touch. When the time came for Braden's next move, Rockefeller would be there for him again.

The profusion of aides, advisers, and shadowy influences in Rockefeller's office did not exactly make for a harmonious team. "You had to look over your shoulder all the time," says Alton. "There were people there who knew how to cut your throat." But soon enough, his minions came to realize that Rockefeller not only tolerated these intramural rivalries—he probably cultivated them in the first place.

It was a page out of the FDR textbook: keeping one's deputies at loggerheads with each other in order to foster some sort of creative tension. Yet while partly inspired by Roosevelt's example, Rockefeller also was influenced by the practices of his own father. Junior ran a tight ship, but he had always been careful not to vest too much authority in any single aide. Throughout his office, a careful system of checks and balances was maintained. The more diffuse the power was, the less chance for abuse—or for becoming overly dependent on any one man. All the Rockefeller sons had learned this lesson from their father, and all would heed it, but none more so than Nelson. "I never knew anyone who was more street-wise, in an organizational sense, than Nelson," notes Alton. "He was very protective of himself. He didn't want to be afraid of anyone cutting him off at the knees."

That self-protective instinct had further been honed by his wartime struggles—particularly by what he perceived as the treachery of his top aide, Carl Spaeth. As Rockefeller confided to one of his associates years later, "I learned from that experience never to put your entire trust in any one person." And so there would never be one preemptive source of counsel, one all-powerful chief of staff for Nelson Rockefeller. Jamieson, Lockwood, Harrison would each exert his influence, but none would dominate. Instead, the lines of influence would run out in a dozen crisscrossing directions, and multiply into an impenetrable lattice in the coming years, all in the service of the web spinner at the center of it all.

It would soon fall to one person to make order out of this chaotic arrangement, to make it work for, not against, Rockefeller's interests. Fortunately for Rockefeller, he found someone more than equal to the task: Louise Robbins, the widow of his former aide Hutch Robbins.

Louise Robbins' story epitomized the enduring loyalty Rockefeller displayed to the people in his inner circle—loyalty that they, in turn, more than reciprocated. She was a woman of exquisite breeding, a character out of an Edith Wharton novel. Born to the patrician Auchincloss family, (her grandfather was Colonel Edward House, President Woodrow Wilson's top adviser), she attended the Foxcroft School, the tony Virginia boarding school whose other graduates included Tod Rockefeller. After Foxcroft, she married the equally well-connected Robbins, whose relations included the Roosevelts of Hyde Park.

Hutch Robbins became one of Rockefeller's key operatives in his prewar Venezuelan investment company, and it was then that Louise first caught Rockefeller's eye. Her pluck and willingness to uncomplainingly put up with the equatorial climate won his admiration; he went so far as to write Hutch a note about how impressed he was "by the spirit and enthusiasm with which your wife has approached this new venture." Despite the responsibility of three young children, she was always game and willing to travel.

But soon tragedy began to stalk her. During their time in Venezuela, the Robbinses' daughter died of infantile paralysis. And not very long afterward she lost Hutch. Rather than sit out the war in Washington with Rockefeller's operation, Hutch Robbins had joined the Army Air Corps. In 1942, on a mission, it was said, behind enemy lines in Italy, he was killed. With her well-composed life suddenly shattered, Louise visited with Rockefeller—he was in the hospital for treatment of a carbuncle—to talk things over. He offered her a job. Says Susan Herter, "She took over the financial stuff, the social-personal stuff. She was a friend of all the members of the family, so that was easy."

The position, with its instant and total immersion in Rockefeller's helter-skelter world, rescued her from her sorrow. "Louise once told me that he probably saved her from insanity by offering her the job," says Kershaw Burbank, one of her friends in the family office. "After all, she'd never done any work before. She was an Auchincloss, brought up with lots of money and nothing to do."

She repaid Rockefeller's kindness with utter fealty to him. When Rockefeller returned from Washington, Louise came with him, and soon was functioning as his chief secretary and administrative assistant. Never less than totally poised, she juggled his crazy-quilt schedule and incessant demands with complete aplomb. Her remarriage in 1947 to one of Laurance Rockefeller's top aides, Allston Boyer, did not affect her dedication to her job, and to Nelson Rockefeller, in the slightest.

While her duties seemed clear enough, Louise Boyer occupied an enigmatic, hard-to-define position in the Rockefeller constellation. She was more than a mere secretary: she attended meetings in Rockefeller's place, and proffered him advice on his business dealings. Her bearing remained thoroughly regal, "the complete personification of the Long Island patrician WASP," in Herter's words. Fashionably thin, Louise was always meticulously attired in tailored outfits from Henri Bendel. She occupied a social plane considerably loftier than that of her co-workers. "Louise was accepted into the high echelons of the Rockefeller family," points out Vera Goeller. "She was on the same social level as them."

Her apparent wealth, her personal connections, her soigné appearance only made her complete devotion to Nelson Rockefeller—a devotion that verged on self-abnegation—that much more puzzling to her colleagues. "I must say," says Burbank, "there were times I wondered, 'Why this dedication?' Because she had a family, she had money. But everything, *everything,* was secondary to her work for him."

The dedication had its roots in her gratitude for the hand he extended her in 1942, a hand that pulled her from the abyss. But in the end, her devotion transcended even that. It can only be explained by a remark that another one of his aides made many years later. "Nelson Rockefeller," he said, "gave you the feeling that you had become part of an enterprise larger than yourself." This was no less true for Louise Auchincloss Boyer than it was for Frank Jamieson or Wally Harrison or all the other faithful retainers still to come.

Twenty-five

MIRACULOUS MANDARIN

On a balmy, languorous springtime day in Rio de Janeiro in November 1946, the city was stirred, for once, not by the breezes caressing Sugar Loaf, but by the presence of a visitor—someone whose arrival sparked an uncommon whirl of activity in this most sybaritic of cities. Nelson Rockefeller was back, for his first visit as a private citizen, and all of Rio seemed to jump to his rhythm.

Accompanied by Tod, Frank Jamieson, and Berent Friele—the Norwegian coffee merchant who had represented Rockefeller's interests in Brazil since the early days of the CIAA—Rockefeller hurtled breathlessly through the capital, working all his old contacts, making new ones, and savoring the praise showered upon him for his good works as Franklin D. Roosevelt's coordinator. Despite the flurry of resentment engendered by his pro-Argentine tilt at the State Department, Rockefeller remained a sainted figure in Brazil, revered as a living symbol of the inter-American alliance.

A new regime was in power now: after a fifteen-year reign, Getulio Vargas had been ousted in late 1945, replaced, in a democratic election, by his former War Minister, General Eurico Dutra. But the new government was as respectful of Rockefeller as its predecessor. It warmly received him and awarded him the Order of the Southern Cross, in recognition of his efforts on behalf of Brazilian-American friendship.

Rockefeller reciprocated the hospitality by throwing a gala cocktail reception for four hundred guests. In a shrewd public relations gesture, he made sure to invite old Vargas people as well as the new movers and shakers—thus demonstrating that he was both commendably loyal and above politics. When Vargas' daughter and son-in-law arrived, Rockefeller rushed up to them and welcomed them effusively.

The excitement generated by Rockefeller was not simply due to his renown or his wartime prestige. He had come to Rio with a mission, and it was the mission, as much as the man, that set the capital abuzz. Rockefeller was in the process of setting up something he called the American International Association. In his own words, its goal would be nothing less than to "help people throughout the world to help themselves to overcome illiteracy, poverty, disease, and nationalistic hatred." AIA would resurrect the lofty social welfare aims of the defunct coordinator's office, but this time use the machinery of private enterprise, and the largesse of the Rockefellers, to accomplish its goals. And AIA's maiden ventures, he announced, would be in Brazil.

Small wonder, then, that Brazilians regarded him with almost mystical reverence. One newspaper there, *Correio da Noite,* captured the feeling about him: "A young, educated millionaire like Nelson A. Rockefeller could lead an adventurous and idle life. But he prefers to found companies, distribute wealth, and feed whole generations. . . . In his evangelical activities he seems to be almost a Luke in the service of God."

One by one, the country's woes were presented to him, in the hopes that this Luke might render a miraculous transformation. He was shown the *favelas,* the corrugated shantytowns that blighted the hills overlooking Rio's beaches and were perennial reminders of the squalor that shadowed the city's splendor. He was told of an attack of cholera that was threatening to wipe out Brazil's entire hog population. He was reminded of the country's endemic food shortages and of the primitive farming techniques that were to blame.

To the supplicants, Rockefeller offered not vague gestures of encouragement, but solid promises of help. He undertook to obtain the vaccine needed to stem the hog cholera epidemic; within days, a leading U.S. Army veterinary specialist was en route with a planeload of the serum. To deal with the food problems, Rockefeller agreed to bankroll a fledgling Brazilian company that was producing a new, super-prolific strain of hybrid seed corn. He talked about setting up a national network of farm co-ops, about building a mammoth fertilizer plant at Santos, on the coast between Rio and São Paulo, about importing 10,000 trucks from the United States to streamline farm product distribution.

By the time Rockefeller finished up his whirlwind visit, his head was teeming with the possibilities for his new organization. And, in the vast land he left behind, the farmers looked up to the skies and waited for the manna to fall.

The concept of an AIA had been incubating since Rockefeller's coordinator days, but it was only after he returned to New York after his firing from the State Department that the scheme was dusted off. A month after his return, Rockefeller discussed the idea with Eugene Holman, president of Standard

Oil of New Jersey, Creole Petroleum's parent company. "He is generally favorably inclined," Rockefeller reported to Frank Corrigan, the U.S. ambassador to Venezuela, "and we talked along the lines of a Foundation spread over the hemisphere as a whole and not just in Venezuela."

Impelled by his belief that the deep-seated problems of Latin America had only barely been touched by the coordinator's office, Rockefeller sketched out a program of uniquely rarefied objectives. "1-Ignorance 2-Poverty 3-Illness," he wrote on a legal pad; atop another page he scribbled the homily "Under heaven there's but one family." He seemed possessed by a particularly virulent strain of the family's Baptist philanthropic impulse.

Yet Rockefeller's motivation was not purely altruistic. Eyeing the growing rivalry between the U.S. and Soviet systems for the hearts and minds of the Third World, Rockefeller saw his foundation as a vital weapon in the capitalistic arsenal. As he put it, the United States could maintain its preeminence only if the world's downtrodden came to understand that "their best interests and opportunity for the future are identified with our country and our way of life."

Perhaps for that reason, he felt that his foundation's status as a privately funded entity would be only transitional; within three years of its start-up, he told his associates, he would seek financing from the U.S. Congress. In a vague, wishful way, he was laying out a blueprint for the resurrection of the CIAA—or at least of some of its programs. Only this time, instead of countering the Nazi threat, his foundation would meet the challenge of the Soviets.

The operation he expected to do this was, in his original conception, a strange two-headed creature, part capitalistic enterprise, part eleemosynary institution. It would create and foster Latin American business ventures, and somehow those ventures would root out "poverty, hunger, sickness, and ignorance." In essence, it was a melding of his prewar Fomento enterprise and the high-minded Rockefeller Foundation.

"Nelson had a hard time adjusting himself to the fact that business and charity are two different things," recalls Lockwood. Typical of his confused mind-set was his search for a name for his organization that would signify its broader purposes: at one point he toyed with calling it the People's Foundation before settling on the only slightly less lofty American International Association for Economic and Social Development. And, over Lockwood's objections, Rockefeller insisted on including a "statement of principles" in AIA's July 1946 certificate of incorporation.

The murky grandeur of his ambitions also came through in a letter he wrote to Junior that April explaining his new venture. With his usual deft sense of the themes that would most deeply touch his father, Rockefeller cloaked his new enterprise in the mantle of family tradition. "Now more than ever before," he said, "it is important that we as a family carry on with the courage and vision that led you and Grandfather to pioneer new fields and blaze new trails." Laying his obsequiousness on with a trowel, he asked his father to serve as chairman of AIA, because "you more than anyone have become a symbol to people throughout the world that democracy and the capitalistic system are interested in their well-being." Junior (as Nelson no doubt expected) declined the offer—but appreciated the sentiments in which it came wrapped.

Rockefeller did not hit up his father for funds (Junior, however, did volunteer to try to obtain some financing for AIA from the Rockefeller Foundation). Instead, he turned to his brothers. At a brothers meeting in late 1946, John 3rd recorded in his diary, "He said that he was himself putting up one million dollars as capital and wondered if the four of us would together make up an equal amount. We said that we would." To his siblings, Nelson confided that he was so enthusiastic about his new development venture that "he was now relatively less interested in getting back into politics."

But even as he was firming up family support, Rockefeller was succumbing to Lockwood's complaints about his grand design and its awkward amalgam of business and charity. "You have to realize," Lockwood told him, "that in our Christian world, during the week you make money, and on the weekend you go to church and you give it away. But it's two different processes." By year end 1946 Rockefeller had yielded to his attorney's pleas to set up two companies: a "Sunday" institution for his do-good activities, AIA, and a "weekday" company for his business ventures, which would be known as the International Basic Economy Corporation.

Nevertheless, Rockefeller was still insistent that even this weekday enterprise had to have an overarching social purpose. Just as in the case of AIA, a "preamble" was attached to IBEC's certificate of incorporation. The company, declared this preamble, would "promote the economic development of various parts of the world," would "increase the production and availability of goods, things and services useful to the lives or livelihood of their peoples," and would "better their standards of living."

All this was too much for the authorities of the state of New York. The deputy secretary of state felt the declaration improper; it would, he said, mislead the public into thinking that IBEC wouldn't be run for a profit. It was only after much cajoling by Rockefeller's lawyers that he allowed the preamble to stand. The statement of principles, they argued, was "perfectly consistent with a profit-making enterprise."

For AIA and IBEC's initial theaters of operations, Rockefeller chose Brazil and Venezuela. Brazil was selected because of its vast untapped economic potential, because of its strategic value to the United States, and, not least, because it was the country with which Rockefeller's key Latin American operatives, Berent Friele and Kenneth Kadow, were most familiar. (Kadow was the head of the coordinator's food supply program in Brazil.)

As for Venezuela, it had the advantage of Rockefeller's long-standing interest and involvement, dating back to his days on the Creole Petroleum board. More decisively, it had the foreign oil companies and their immense resources—resources that Rockefeller was eager to tap.

When Rockefeller first broached his idea to the oil companies in September 1945, they seemed to welcome the initiative. Behind his back, though, they sneered. One Standard Oil of New Jersey executive warned that the foundation would be seen as nothing more than a "North American Santa Claus."

It wasn't long, however, before events in Venezuela inspired an instant attitude adjustment. In late October of that year, the left-of-center Acción Democrática party seized power. The leader of the new ruling junta was Rómulo Betancourt—the same Rómulo Betancourt who had vehemently denounced Nelson Rockefeller as a hypocritical oil mogul before the war. For years Betancourt had inveighed against the oil companies' untrammeled influence over his country's economy. Now, at last—after spending most of his political career in exile or in hiding—he had the power to do something about it.

Betancourt pushed through a barrage of new laws—the most important of which, from the oil companies' perspective, was an increased tax on their revenues. Henceforth, the government would share those revenues on a fifty-fifty basis with the petroleum giants. Given the vast sums Venezuela's oil industry was yielding—total revenues, by 1948, would soar above $800 million—the new arrangement could hardly be called devastating; it reduced oil company profits from the obscene to the merely exorbitant. (In 1947, despite handing a huge chunk of its revenues to the government, Creole still managed to earn $130 million.) Nonetheless, the foreign companies had good reason to fear that Betancourt would go even further. He talked about creating a government-owned oil company and a state refinery. For the oil giants, Betancourt's Venezuela was looming as another Mexico, another country where nationalistic fervor would drive them to the wall.

Rockefeller's plans, in that light, seemed an absolute godsend. They offered the oil companies the chance to demonstrate to the new regime that the companies were not simply rapacious capitalists draining the country of its lifeblood and offering nothing in return. Consequently, the companies now regarded Rockefeller's scheme as a sound business move—at least for themselves. It would, said one Standard of New Jersey executive, result in "greater security for present investments and greater possibility for expansion."

The companies, though, had no interest in funding some broad hemisphere program. They wanted to funnel their investments into the only Latin American country that mattered to them, Venezuela. And so Rockefeller obligingly created an IBEC subsidiary, the Venezuelan Basic Economy Corporation. It would be VBEC, not IBEC as a whole, that the oil companies would finance.

Rockefeller was looking for $15 million from the oil companies—$10 million for VBEC and $5 million for AIA—and $15 million was exactly what he got. The largest sum, $8 million, came, not surprisingly, from Creole; Caribbean Petroleum, the subsidiary of Royal Dutch Shell, was next largest with $4.25 million, and Mene Grande Petroleum, the Gulf Oil operation, contributed $3 million. Socony-Vacuum, with the smallest stake of all the majors in Venezuela, chipped in a token $120,000. All the pledges were payable over a five-year period, and the investors were free to drop out after a year.

The oil companies attached only one significant condition: they wanted the Venezuelan government to participate financially in VBEC as well, through the government-owned development corporation, the Corporación Venezolana de Fomento (not to be confused with Rockefeller's prewar private Fomento venture). This participation would solidify their partnership with the government and assure the Venezuelan public that VBEC was not just another *yanqui* plot to bleed the country.

Rockefeller, as it happened, needed no convincing on that score. He intended all along to bring in the Venezuelan government as a partner. In fact, he planned to travel soon to Venezuela, just as he had to Brazil, to iron it all out personally, *mano a mano,* with Rómulo Betancourt.

In Venezuela, as in Brazil, IBEC did not have to look far to find a central, defining mission. For Venezuela, as for Brazil, the most critical national need was food. But in Venezuela the need was more acute—and, in many ways, more unfathomable.

"Venezuela," an IBEC internal document noted, "exhibits the paradox of a nation with one of the highest per capita government revenues in the world, while two-thirds of its population has a sub-standard level of living." Past governments chose to lavish the oil wealth on monumental urban public works projects, while letting the country's agricultural sector slide. (What the country really needed, former President López Contreras had told Rockefeller before the war, was a first-class hotel.) As a result, the nutritional profile of the average Venezuelan was on a par with that of India and other basket-case economies. Deficiency diseases like beriberi were rampant—at a time when the government was piling up a half billion dollars in foreign exchange reserves.

Unable to sustain itself, the country was forced to import close to 50 percent of its food requirements by the end of World War II. The consequence, predictably, was rampant inflation. Bread was thirty cents a loaf, chicken $1.80 a pound, four times their cost in the United States. For the

Caracas elite, whose pockets were swollen with booty from the oil boom, this was no problem. But for the vast majority of Venezuelans, it spelled disaster.

To look into this catastrophe and figure out what IBEC could do about it, Rockefeller dispatched to Venezuela in late February 1947 his staff economist, Stacy May. Another of Rockefeller's old Dartmouth contacts (May had been one of his economics professors), May had served as the War Production Board's director of planning and statistics; his chief wartime accomplishment was the exchange of vital munitions information between Great Britain and the United States. A portly, genial scholar, May was not the most scintillating character to be around. "Stacy was a wonderful human being," remarks another of his former students, "but he was also the dullest person imaginable." Just why Rockefeller was employing this fiftyish distinguished economist was, at first, a mystery—but with the onset of the Latin American ventures the reasons were now eminently clear. With his academic background and his war production experience, May combined keen analytical skills and a strong problem-solving bent. He seemed just the man to flesh out Rockefeller's amorphous intentions and to give IBEC the intellectual underpinnings on which the superstructure could be built.

What May found in his Venezuelan travels were strategic bottlenecks throughout the economy, bottlenecks that prevented food, even when it was produced, from reaching the population at a reasonable price. Poor transportation and the lack of refrigeration kept such staples as fresh milk and fish from the marketplace. Inefficient, rapacious wholesalers and retailers raised prices all along the distribution chain.

In the wake of May's findings, Rockefeller decided VBEC would concentrate on "increasing the supply and improving distribution facilities of basic foods with the aim of lowering costs to the consumer." And he wanted VBEC to make a profit doing it.

The profit motive was figuring more and more in Rockefeller's thinking as the plans for IBEC were mapped out—not as an end unto itself, but for its multiplier effect. Evangelical as ever about the wonders of capitalism, he saw IBEC as a pathfinder, blazing new business trails in the underdeveloped world so that less daring investors might follow. IBEC's activities, he insisted, had to be set up "on a sound paying basis which will attract other private capital and management to undertake similar activities." He told a newspaper reporter, "It's got to pay—or else!"

But he didn't doubt for a moment that it would pay. After all, he already had one Venezuelan success story under his belt: the Hotel Avila, the breezy, orchid-bedecked hilltop lodging he had built in Caracas before the war. If there was any project that validated his business instincts, it was that one.

To be sure, the Avila had been a struggle, pitting Rockefeller's faith in the venture against the naysayers—the most vocal of whom was his own father. Plagued by construction cost overruns, shadowed by the outbreak of the war, the Avila seemed a doomed enterprise even before its scheduled opening in the summer of 1942. Faced with the potential bankruptcy of his Venezuelan holding company, Rockefeller was forced into the painful necessity of beseeching Junior for funds—money he needed to complete the hotel and to pay off the angry Venezuelan investors. The alternative—turning the edifice over to his creditors and leaving the Venezuelans high and dry—would have been an unthinkable embarrassment for the man who was then in his full flush of glory as Coordinator of Inter-American Affairs.

Grudgingly, Junior agreed to the transfusion, but only to protect "the family name and prestige," in his words. He didn't believe his sons should be in the hotel business, and was appalled to find Nelson dropping the whole problem in his lap. In exchange for the bailout, he extracted a commitment from his son to unload the hotel. Or so he thought.

Two years later, the Avila was still in the family's hands. When Junior reminded his son of his promise and pressured him to finally sell the hotel, Nelson balked. The Venezuelans, he said, had been complaining that he had never once visited the hotel; in fact, he hadn't even been to Venezuela in four years. "For me at this time, therefore, to dump the stock," he told Junior, "might be taken as an additional evidence of a coolness for Venezuela, which frankly might have very unfortunate repercussions because of my position in the Government." Besides, he added, "my personal feeling is that the hotel will be more successful after the war than it is now, owing to the tourist trade."

To Nelson's relief, Creole Petroleum, still the second-largest investor in the hotel, intervened; the oil company blanched at seeing the hotel stock dumped at a huge loss. The sale was postponed for two years. And during that hiatus, all of Nelson's high hopes for the project were fulfilled. With the war's end, the hotel's tourist and business traffic burgeoned, just as he had foreseen, and its nightclub became a favored watering hole of the Caracas elite. By 1946 the Avila was solidly in the black.

Early the next year, Junior's advances to the hotel company—which totaled $312,000—were repaid in full. He was forced to eat a hefty slice of crow, but he professed himself "delighted" with this turn of events.

A few months later, control of the hotel was transferred to IBEC. The Avila served not just as a profit spinner but as an exemplar: a reminder to Nelson Rockefeller of the wonders that could be wrought in Latin America with a little grit and determination.

The Avila experience was also a reminder (as if Rockefeller needed any) of the perils of bringing Junior into the picture.

It explains why Rockefeller pointedly did *not* ask his father to contribute to the new venture, but asked his brothers. By the time IBEC was ready to get off the ground, each of the four had agreed to buy $300,000 worth of IBEC common stock. Rockefeller himself committed for $1.5 million, giving him a majority of the common.

On a Friday evening in June 1947, Rockefeller—accompanied by his son Roddy and Frank Jamieson—boarded one of the sparkling new planes of Venezuela's Aeropostale national airline. He was off to Caracas to see Rómulo Betancourt, to nail down the Venezuelan government's participation in VBEC—and to quell the opposition to his plans that was already bubbling to the surface. Whereas the Brazilians regarded him as an economic savior, the Venezuelan view of him was considerably less flattering. VBEC was lambasted as merely the latest devious mechanism with which Rockefeller and the oil companies could exert control over the country's economy. Among other things, there were loud calls for a cap on VBEC's profits.

As soon as he touched down in Caracas, Rockefeller, with his son and Jamieson in tow, rushed off to a meeting with top oil company officials. The companies were jittery about the mounting uproar over VBEC. Desperate to calm the waters, the oil executives suggested to Rockefeller that maybe a dividend limitation might not be such a bad idea after all.

At this, Rockefeller exploded. He berated the oilmen for forgetting what it was that made private enterprise work. "Unless we have management control and freedom to use earnings as we see fit," he snapped, "then frankly I think in the long run we will be doing the future development of Venezuela a disservice rather than a service. While we might be able to do a job based on limited dividends, nobody else will try." Furthermore, he warned them of the ultimate pitfall, for them, of such an accommodation: "Sooner or later, the government will move in on the oil companies with a similar regulation."

If the government insisted on a dividend cap, Rockefeller said, he would simply pack up his bags and leave the next day.

The oilmen, having found themselves in the unlikely position of getting a lecture on free enterprise from this ostensible "Santa Claus," quickly capitulated. They would back Rockefeller up 100 percent.

Thus armed, Rockefeller went off to prepare for his encounter, the next day, with Betancourt.

But even left-wing reformers need a day of rest, and that Sunday was so sparkling that Betancourt couldn't bear to think about business. Instead, he invited Rockefeller out for the day to his country house. There, the energetic millionaire played *bolos* on the lawn with the chauffeur and a waiter to the amusement of the sunbathing President, chatted up the ladies, and generally tried to act as though he had all the time in the world. He was determined, he said later, "not to take the initiative or show any anxiety."

The next afternoon, in town, the two men at last got down to cases. "I've taken the liberty of preparing a few notes," Rockefeller began, and it took him all of forty-five minutes to go over them. He laid out his plans to solve the nation's food shortage by setting up fisheries, milk companies, food wholesalers, and the like. He spoke of his hopes that the Venezuelan people would have a stake in all these businesses. And he asked to proceed untrammeled by government restraints.

When Rockefeller had finished, the President settled his arms over his ample midsection and offered his response. If VBEC was just any ordinary business, Betancourt said, then of course it would be entitled to make any profit it could. But the oil company money behind VBEC made it a "special situation." What's more, the type of work it was undertaking made it a form of public service, and just as public utilities in the United States were limited to a fixed return—say, 6 percent—so should VBEC.

Rockefeller had a ready rejoinder for both of Betancourt's arguments. If the oil company money prejudiced VBEC's ability to operate on a "sound business basis," he said, "then I will either return their money or dissolve VBEC and invest directly"—in which case he would have to proceed much more slowly. As for the "public utility" aspect, he suggested that if, like the utilities in the United States, Betancourt "was willing to fix the price of fish and other foods so that we would be guaranteed a six percent income, that was okay with me, because then there would be no risk." Of course, added Rockefeller, no one else would be attracted to invest in the Venezuelan fish business on that basis. "You would be automatically killing the very initiative and driving force which Venezuela needs so badly if she is to solve her economic problems."

After two and a half hours, the meeting broke up. Then, over the next day and a half, Rockefeller and Betancourt's aides were closeted in a virtually nonstop round of talks. The Venezuelans continued to hammer on such issues as capital gains—why should VBEC have them?—and Rockefeller found himself giving his private enterprise lecture over and over again.

In the end, Rockefeller's tenacity—and his not very veiled resolve to pull out completely if he didn't get his way—won out. No restrictions were placed on VBEC's capital gains or dividends, although Rockefeller did pledge to reinvest the "major portion" of the earnings in expansion of his Venezuelan businesses (in fact, he had never intended to do otherwise). The Venezuelan government development company, the Fomento, would take a 50 percent interest in each company VBEC started; ultimately, Fomento would sell its shares to the Venezuelan public. And Rockefeller, for his part, promised that Venezuelan investors would control a majority of each of VBEC's companies within ten years of their start-up.

On June 19, the final agreement was signed, and a jubilant Rockefeller headed off to the airport. But he left behind a government that was clearly ambivalent about the whole arrangement, that still distrusted Rockefeller and his oil company allies, and that was determined, somehow, to have the last word.

There would be nothing niggling or circumspect about Rockefeller's program in Venezuela, nothing to disabuse the public of the notion that he was, in one magazine's words, "a young Lochinvar riding in on a bankroll." The nation's food shortage demanded a heroic effort, and Rockefeller felt himself, and his bankroll, up to the task.

Virtually overnight several new VBEC companies were formed. Just as Rockefeller had promised Betancourt, a fishing company, dubbed PESCA, was started. Fresh fish was scarce everywhere but in the coastal towns; the average Caracas resident consumed less than seven pounds of it a year. Rockefeller's people believed that with modern production and storage methods, consumption could easily quintuple.

Soon the PESCA operation was overrunning the little east coast village of Puerto La Cruz, leaving the locals gaping in wonder. A refrigerated barge for making ice showed up in the harbor one day, along with two sleek Florida-built fishing boats. Then came the Quonset huts: prefabricated dwellings for the employees who would soon be trooping in. Before long, the din of jackhammers and cement mixers echoed through the town, as workers began construction of a huge cold-storage plant and a concrete pier.

At the same time, Rockefeller's food wholesaling operation, CADA, was gearing up. Plans were drawn up for two giant warehouses: one in Caracas and the other in Maracaibo, in the heart of the oil fields. The oil companies agreed to use CADA to supply their commissaries. And CADA began to look into establishing retail stores: as many as a half dozen in Caracas alone.

The milk business, meanwhile, was also getting VBEC's attention. A joint venture was formed with Golden State, a big San Francisco dairy company, to establish a milk plant in Valencia, one of Venezuela's prime cattle areas. But the venture stalled when Fomento objected; the government wanted VBEC to set up shop in "virgin territory," a prospect that VBEC officials feared would be financially disastrous.

Rounding out VBEC's alphabet soup of food companies (Rockefeller was proving to be as fond of acronyms as his mentor FDR) was PACA, the farming company. VBEC envisioned starting or acquiring as many as twenty-five farms in five years—not to squeeze out the native farmers, of course, but to demonstrate what modern agricultural techniques could accomplish. For starters, PACA snapped up three properties: Central Bolívar, southwest of Lake Maracaibo; Agua Blanca, a twenty-thousand-acre farm about one hundred miles east of the lake; and Monte Sacro, an estate in the Chirgua Valley that was once owned by the great "liberator" himself, the George Washington of Latin America, Simón Bolívar.

At Agua Blanca and Monte Sacro, the principal crops would be corn, rice, potatoes, and beans, and hogs would be raised. But at Central Bolívar, the prime focus would be on beef cattle—not just because this was what Venezuela needed but because of Nelson Rockefeller's fascination with cattle ranching.

His interest had blossomed with his friendship with Texas cattle baron Robert Kleberg, master of the huge King Ranch. Rockefeller loved to slip off to Texas, to hunt and camp on the King spread—as he was doing in late 1946, when Jamieson and Harrison summoned him back to New York to deal with the UN crisis. There were times now when he even talked about retiring at fifty-five and settling down to a life as a Texas rancher.

"He kind of romanticized about being a rancher," says John Camp, who ran IBEC's early Venezuelan operations before moving on to AIA. "He had all this attire—cowboy boots, a ten-gallon hat, the whole thing. And he was a good horseman. When he was at the Venezuela ranch, he'd love to get everybody together to go riding off into the mountains."

In his discussions with Kleberg, he confided his plans for IBEC, and the two men talked about some sort of joint venture. That didn't pan out, but Rockefeller did end up buying some prime breeding stock—Santa Gertrudis bulls—from his friend for the Venezuelan ranch. (It was the first time the prized cattle had ever been exported from the United States.)

More than any of the other IBEC companies, the farm operation held an abiding grip on Rockefeller's imagination. He loved to ride among the herds, to view the sea of cattle that grazed in his eight-thousand-acre domain. So entranced was he that he seemed to pay little attention to certain disturbing details: such as the fact that the Central Bolívar site was on low ground and was prone to flooding, or that the heat of the dry season could wilt the rich pastures and kill the cattle.

"Who is silly enough to believe for one minute that the great Rockefeller is interested in raising pigs?" sniped one Venezuelan left-wing newspaper. "This whole farm business of his doesn't amount to a hill of beans. It is just a scheme to get hold of future oil lands."

Throughout Venezuela's farm country, there was grumbling and gossip about what the young New York tycoon was up to. In the state of Zulia, home of the Central Bolívar farm, the Rural Society called on the government to close down Rockefeller's operation, on the grounds that the "high-powered North American enterprise" would soon drive the local farmers out of business.

Acutely sensitive to the "monopolist" charge—so redolent of the outcry against his grandfather—Rockefeller resolved to head off the groundswell. He flew down again to Venezuela, bringing with him a coterie that included his most trusted advisers: Jamieson, Harrison, Anna Rosenberg. Upon landing at the airport at La Guaira, the group boarded a convoy of jeeps for the arduous two-hour trip up steep, winding mountain roads to Caracas. There to accompany the convoy was an armed guard; Rockefeller's life, it seemed, had been threatened. Halfway up the mountains, the procession suddenly ground to a halt, and everyone was ordered out of the jeeps. It turned out to be a false alarm. While the rest of his party shuddered, Rockefeller appeared blissfully unconcerned about the threat. "If you let that sort of thing stop you," he told one of his companions, "you'll never accomplish anything."

In Caracas, thousands of left-wingers, flourishing "Down with Rockefeller" banners, filled the central square. *El Nacional,* the country's largest daily paper, charged that he was out to "monopolize food and its distribution in all Venezuela . . . to become dictator of the market."

But Rockefeller stoically shrugged off the cascade of vituperation that greeted his arrival, just as he had shrugged off the death threats. He was there on a mission, and he was determined to fulfill it. Single-mindedly, he prepared himself for the main event of his trip: his confrontation with the farmers of Zulia.

They gathered at the town hall in Maracaibo, in such numbers that the building could not accommodate them all. Rather than turn the throng away, the meeting was moved outside to a nearby illuminated tennis court. Rockefeller listened to the litany of charges: that VBEC would drive prices so low that the entire farm population would be ruined. That the company would then swoop down and buy up the bankrupt properties for pennies. That it was all a plot by the oil companies to control the nation's food supply.

Finally, when the farmers had said their piece, Rockefeller stood up. Speaking entirely in Spanish, he looked into the intent, sun-creased faces around him.

He wanted, first off, to address the "monopolist" allegations. The purpose of VBEC's farms, he argued, was not to dominate food production, but to demonstrate the impact of modern techniques. "The only way we can do any good for Venezuela is to demonstrate to you farmers that if you adopt modern methods you can increase production and the entire countryside will benefit—not just the farmers but the merchants and the consumers."

And he insisted that his people had much to learn from *them* about local soil conditions and the like. The relationship between VBEC and the farmers would have to be a true partnership. "If we have your help and if you have our help, we can progress."

By the end of that long evening on the tennis court, Rockefeller was convinced that he had defused the hostility toward VBEC. It was a defining moment—not so much for Nelson Rockefeller the businessman as for Nelson Rockefeller the budding politician. For that night in Maracaibo was really the first time Rockefeller had faced the masses, the first time he had been confronted with the challenge of swaying them to his side. Whether or not he succeeded is almost beside the point. What is important is what he took away from the encounter: a conviction that, in a crunch, he could go straight to the people and win them over with the facts.

Barely two months into its operations, the oil companies started to hear disquieting reports about VBEC. There were complaints about the callowness of the people Rockefeller was sending down to Venezuela—many of whom were former eager beavers from his Washington days—and the lack of coordination. The ample compensation packages Rockefeller was providing his people also did not go unnoticed. At the Central Bolívar farm, for instance, the three top managers were each getting $2,100 a month, including a $667 living allowance. "If VBEC can pay such staggering salaries to men who will be working under and reporting to the VBEC officials one wonders what the VBEC officials themselves are receiving," said a report to Mene Grande Petroleum president Chester Crabbe in August 1947.

While the oil company investors in VBEC were inclined to be tolerant of some shakedown period mistakes—especially given Rockefeller's vaulting ambitions—they didn't hesitate to make their early worries known in face-to-face meetings with him. Those concerns, Rockefeller conceded to one of his deputies, were "interesting": "they reflected very much those of our own finance committee, who are equally concerned with our overhead expenses both here and in the field, and don't see the prospect of earnings to carry this overhead for many years to come." He freely admitted his own culpability. "I have been so preoccupied with the promotional aspect of our effort that, frankly, I haven't given the attention I should have to the size of the overhead or the details of the structure itself."

To atone for this, he decided to send someone down from New York to survey the problem. His choice for the job, though, seemed only to underscore his offhandedness: the man he sent was his old chum Bill Alton, who knew little about finance and less about Venezuela.

Nevertheless, Alton toiled away at his task diligently, and, in the end, presented Rockefeller with a report that made the oil company critiques seem models of restraint by comparison. He found a "considerable lack of adherence to normal business practices" at VBEC, with "no accounting systems set up for any of the subsidiary companies, nor an adequate system for VBEC." And Alton saw staff excesses that were worse than even the oil companies suspected. Among the array of questionable expenses were parties for staff members and cars and chauffeurs for every principal VBEC executive.

The excesses Alton uncovered in Venezuela, however, were mere extensions of the budgetary recklessness going on in New York, right under Rockefeller's nose. "I don't remember how many staff we had in New York, but it was a big staff," recalls Alton. "We'd have these committee meetings all the time, and there would be the legal people and the public relations people and the operational people and the administrative people, and everyone would be playing at being big business big shots."

As Alton saw it, the root of the problem was Rockefeller himself: all his capitalistic rhetoric notwithstanding, he set a tone that "profits weren't that important."

"You just thought of limitless money," Alton says. "You didn't know how much Nelson had to spend, how long this thing could run. And there is nothing worse than trying to operate without knowing the bottom financial line. You simply had to take Nelson's word for it that he knew how much he had, and that the money didn't make any difference."

To anyone who had tracked Rockefeller over the years, this was hardly a surprising development. The same heedlessness that had made his youthful accounts a perennial mess, and that had later gained him a reputation in Washington as one of FDR's most profligate underlings, was evident now in IBEC. It wasn't that Rockefeller didn't understand the importance of budgets and of running his businesses on a businesslike basis; this necessity had been ground into him by his father and reinforced by his experience at Rockefeller Center. It was simply that he could not, in the end, reconcile this discipline with his prodigious energy and his grandiose schemes.

He promised, after meeting with his oil company investors, to "see where we can tighten up." But no one took the promise seriously—least of all Rockefeller himself.

Tightening up, indeed, was the last thing Rockefeller had in mind. Propelled by his vision of IBEC as the economic salvation of Latin America, he seemed bent on setting in motion as many ideas as possible.

Itching to solve Latin America's chronic housing shortage, he seized upon one of his and Wally Harrison's brainstorms: that through modern road-building methods, low-cost concrete housing could be provided.

Harrison and his deputy, George Dudley, figured out how it could be done—with giant cranes setting cast concrete slabs into place—and one day took their plans and their models to Rockefeller. "Nelson said, 'Good, good, swell, swell, swell,' " recalls Dudley. "We had a saying that if you didn't hear more than seven 'swells,' he didn't really like the idea, so we kept track of how many, and there were enough. And then he said, 'Okay, we'll have a corporation.' He was really corporation-happy at that point. He said, 'Wally, you'll be chairman, and George, you'll be president.' Afterward I went downstairs to Scribner's bookstore and asked, 'Do you have a book on what a corporation is?' "

Thus was the IBEC Housing Corporation born.

Then, rightly concluding there was no point in building homes unless there were adequate roads to reach them and adequate power to energize them, Rockefeller started yet another corporation, IBEC Technical Services. Its mission: to hire itself out as an all-purpose consultant on Latin America's infrastructure problems. Despite his ongoing commitment to the United Nations headquarters project, Harrison agreed to take on this task for Rockefeller as well, serving as Technical Services' president. Perhaps it was because Rockefeller made the job more than worth his while, paying him a handsome $20,000 a year, plus a $5,000 expense account.

In Brazil, meanwhile, Rockefeller strove to live up to the populace's expectations, albeit on less than the messianic scale that was first envisioned. (In Brazil, unlike Venezuela, he did not have the oil companies' bankrolls to fall back on.) He formed an agricultural services company, EMA, that would provide Brazilian farmers, on a contract basis, with the mechanized equipment—tractors, plows, harvesters, and the like—they so badly needed.

Soon, there were as many Rockefeller acronyms afoot in Brazil as there were in Venezuela. Aside from EMA, there was SASA (the hybrid seed corn company), HELICO (a helicopter crop-dusting enterprise), and SAFAP (a hog-raising operation).

Yet even with all these wheels spinning, Rockefeller hungered for more. His mind teemed with new ideas, new possibilities, new ways to leverage the IBEC concept. Hearing of a new process that would use natural gas, rather than coal, to produce pig iron, he financed a pilot plant in Bayway, New Jersey, to investigate the process—hoping that it might be the first step toward developing a Venezuelan steel industry, using the natural gas of the oil fields.

He was just as interested in another potential use for all that natural gas: the manufacture of dry ice. The promoter of this scheme was the unsinkable Bill Zeckendorf, whose fecund, if somewhat scattershot, mind found a ready audience in the southeast corner of Room 5600. "Zeckendorf had a new idea every day," remarks one of Rockefeller's advisers, "and Nelson loved ideas." Zeckendorf persuaded Rockefeller to invest $25,000 in the dry ice company he had just started, Carbonic Products, Inc. The two men also began talking about the possible sale of the Avila Hotel to Zeckendorf's real estate operation, Webb & Knapp. (Though nothing, in the end, would come of these initiatives, the Zeckendorf-Rockefeller link was now firmly established. When Rockefeller started looking at a possible recapitalization of Rockefeller Center, it was Zeckendorf who emerged as his principal outside adviser.)

Even Zeckendorf's concoctions would look like paragons of financial prudence compared with some of the other schemes Rockefeller was eagerly pursuing. One of them would have financed the emigration of impoverished Southern Europeans across the Atlantic, resettling the émigrés around the Amazon headwaters in northeastern Peru. "He was going to move people from Southern Europe, like Sicilians, finance them to go to Peru, and the Peruvians would supply the land, and he would supply the capital, and the manpower would come from these migrants," recounts Bill Alton, who worked on the project. The plan was ultimately dropped when, says Alton, "we began to dig into it, and we discovered that invariably the people who would only go someplace if they were financed were the people who were not successful at anything they did."

But no sooner would one brainstorm fizzle than another would pop up in its place. A new Venezuelan hotel venture in Maracaibo and Puerto La Cruz. A fish-drying machine invented by frozen food impresario Clarence Birdseye. A tuna cannery in Pago Pago.

"Nelson Rockefeller," one of his business associates remarked in early 1948, "is having more fun than anyone I know."

Indeed, in the months since its founding, IBEC had taken on a truly multiplicitous role in Nelson Rockefeller's life. It was a business. It was an economic crusade. And, not least, it was a playground.

Twenty-six

A Bigger Program

On the first Friday in April 1948 doughty old Abby Aldrich Rockefeller donned one of her trademark flower-festooned hats and joined her son Nelson for the drive up from New York to Pocantico. Just back from her annual winter sojourn with her husband at the Arizona Inn in Tucson, Abby was relaxed and refreshed, and immensely looking forward to celebrating her return with a grand family reunion that weekend at the estate.

Catching her breath as they sped along the winding Saw Mill River Parkway, Abby spoke with Nelson about art: about some young American printmakers whose work she was interested in, about the new recognition art was gaining in America, and about the latest goings-on at the Museum of Modern Art. Abby was proud of all the museum had accomplished, and delighted that her son was again so much involved in its direction. Although he could still exasperate her, Nelson remained the favorite of her six children: the one whose zest for life and art most mirrored her own. Abby doted on all his achievements, even as she lamented the distancing his busy life necessitated. (She sometimes joked about his "secretariat" and about how difficult it was for even her to penetrate his palace guard.)

As they passed through the filigreed gates guarding the family manor, she could see, to her joy, that the spring flowers in the gardens around Kykuit were already in full, glorious bloom—the perfect backdrop for a blissful family weekend. The whole Rockefeller brood turned out to greet her: the children, the spouses, the eighteen grandchildren. (Only Winthrop's Bobo was absent, pleading illness.)

For Abby, the next two days would be all that she could have wished for. Watching the youngsters frolic around the Playhouse, sharing confidences with her children, strolling the grounds with her daughters-in-law, the grande dame fairly glowed with maternal contentment. "I've never been so happy in my life," she said.

On Sunday evening she rode back to town with David, holding her newest grandchild, David's Peggy, in her lap. She made a point of stopping off to look in on Bobo; despite the high-society titters about the marriage, Abby had steadfastly stood by Winthrop and his bride, and had done her best to welcome the coal miner's daughter into the family.

She returned with Junior to their apartment at 740 Park Avenue, looking ahead to a busy week in town. But early the next morning Abby awoke feeling ill. An alarmed Junior summoned the family doctor. As the physician was examining her and inquiring about her symptoms, her head suddenly fell back on the pillow. Abby Aldrich Rockefeller was dead, at seventy-three, of a heart attack.

"Father was terribly hard hit, the end coming so suddenly and so completely out of the blue," John 3rd recorded in his diary. Although Abby had suffered for years from high blood pressure and, in the parlance of the day, a "tired heart," she had not seemed particularly unwell. During that last weekend at Pocantico, in fact, she appeared positively robust, exuberantly mapping out her plans for the future.

Devastated by his loss, Junior insisted that she be cremated immediately—that very day. As David's wife, Peggy, noted, "It was as though he could not deal with the mourning period, but rushed it through. 'Take this blow away,' he was crying." To help their father through the night, Nelson and John stayed over at 740 Park.

Less visibly shattered than his father, Nelson was nonetheless equally staggered by his mother's sudden demise. "I can remember Father coming in through the elevator door at 810 Fifth Avenue," his son Steven would recall. "He was absolutely ashen white. I don't think I've ever seen Father so deeply shaken." She had been far more than simply a parental figure for him: she was a friend, a confidante, a source of solace, the one person in the world with whom he felt completely at ease in unburdening himself. Whenever the strains of his onrushing career became too great, he would repair to Kykuit, to the drawing room just to the right of the entryway, where she would pour his tea and hear out his frustrations. Their relationship was light and spontaneous, without all the emotional baggage he seemed to carry into every encounter with his father. Caring, supportive, wise, fully cognizant of his weaknesses and yet still unabashedly adulatory, Abby fulfilled a unique role for Nelson. "If you went into his bedroom or study," noted Steven, "there was a picture of one woman: Abby Aldrich Rockefeller." Her passing left a profound void in his life.

It was only after a great public outcry that Junior at last—more than a month and a half after his wife's death—agreed to hold a memorial service in

Riverside Church. And another month would pass before he could finally bring himself to commit her ashes to the gravesite on the Pocantico grounds. Kneeling over the myrtle-carpeted ground by the twin headstones he and Abby had erected six years before, Junior, assisted by his five sons, mingled the ashes with the earth.

The loss of Abby plunged the aged patriarch into depths of emotional despair he had not experienced since his breakdowns decades earlier. With a black shawl draped around his slight frame, he prowled the hallways of Kykuit, inconsolable. One day, supposedly for relief, he invited the whole staff of Room 5600 to Kykuit; as he showed them around the house and gardens, he spoke incessantly of Abby and how much she meant to him.

To mitigate his loneliness, his daughters-in-law Tod and Blanchette took turns staying with him at Bassett Hall, the charming wood-framed dwelling he and Abby had lovingly restored on the grounds of Colonial Williamsburg. In time, the pall lifted, but he seemed rooted in a permanent state of denial—a state that had some bizarre manifestations. The Rockefeller grandchildren, for instance, continued to receive presents from their grandmother Abby. And in April 1950, upon the second anniversary of his wife's death, Junior sent this note to John and Blanchette: "The lovely calla lilies which you sent me on April 5th, bringing as they did loving thoughts from you and the children, gave me the greatest of pleasure and were, I know, equally enjoyed by Mama, in whose sitting room they were placed. To you all we send our thanks and our love."

To Junior, Abby, his life's companion, was still at his side.

While Junior dealt with Abby's death by fantasizing that it never happened, Nelson coped through total immersion in his bustling Latin American activities. That fall he traveled again to Brazil, this time accompanied by David, and basked in the adulation that still engulfed him every time his chartered DC-3 touched down.

David remembers in particular one stop they made, in a little town called Mococo, in the state of São Paulo: "You would have thought that Nelson was running for mayor of Mococo. They gave him a sort of parade, and he rode on a tractor through the town, waving at everybody, while everyone cheered enthusiastically. . . . He certainly showed his natural flair for politics. He could have been elected to almost anything in Brazil."

As keen as ever about the prospects of the farming and ranching business, Rockefeller looked over coffee plantations and cattle ranches. What particularly intrigued him were the possibilities of the Mato Grosso, the vast virgin territory in the country's interior. On the spot, he decided to snap up a huge tract—some 1,000 square miles—for himself, in partnership with a prominent Brazilian financier, Walther Moreira Salles. Once again, he envisioned a magnificent ranch, populated by the offspring of Bob Kleberg's Santa Gertrudis herds.

When Rockefeller last zigzagged around Brazil, two years before, he had generated lofty hopes for an agricultural renaissance, fostered by Rockefeller know-how and Rockefeller money. Now, he felt it was incumbent upon him to at least make a start at meeting those impossible expectations through his philanthropic organization, AIA. He arrived in Brazil with a plan, and with a place in mind to carry it out: Minas Gerais, homeland of the destitute *favela* dwellers of Rio. Historically rich in natural mineral resources—its abundance of gold, diamonds, iron, and manganese had given the state its name, Portuguese for "General Mines"—Minas Gerais had never fulfilled its equally rich agricultural potential. Its farmers, poorly trained and primitively equipped, scratched out meager livings from the soil. If ever there was an ideal proving ground for Rockefeller's methods, Minas Gerais was it.

This was doubly true because of the designs of the state's governor, Milton Campos. A longtime foe of the Vargas regime, Campos was a tireless activist for rural development, creating a New Deal-style array of programs to lift his state's impoverished farmers out of the mire. His enthusiasm for big-picture, bootstrap plans was, if anything, equal to Rockefeller's.

Campos, in fact, was waiting at the airport to greet the American when he at last touched down at Belo Horizonte, the state's capital. Wasting no time on formalities, Rockefeller breathlessly outlined his scheme to Campos as they drove together to the hotel. He proposed the creation of something called ACAR—in English, the Association of Credit and Rural Assistance—in which Rockefeller's American International Association and the state of Minas Gerais would be partners. ACAR would secure financial help for the farmers, in the form of cheap bank loans, and, at the same time, offer them a wide range of technical assistance to bring them into the twentieth century.

Campos, clearly delighted that Rockefeller had chosen to single out his state for his largesse, needed no persuading. The two men shook hands on the deal. Less than two months later—with none of the bluster that characterized the Venezuelan accord—a formal agreement was signed in Belo Horizonte's Palace of Liberty.

For all his probusiness rhetoric, Rockefeller had never ceased to regard FDR's New Deal as a role model, and ACAR was a perfect case in point. Its inspiration was Roosevelt's Farm Security Administration, which strove to better the lot of Depression-stricken small farmers through cheap credits. And to run ACAR, and AIA as a whole, he hired the FSA's most diehard liberal, associate director Robert Hudgens.

Hudgens was wary of Rockefeller, and before he accepted the job consulted an old friend, James Le Cron—the same James Le Cron who had resigned in a huff as director of the CIAA food program. While Le Cron had misgivings about some of Rockefeller's aides, characterizing Jamieson and Lockwood as "holder-backers," he had few qualms about the man himself. "He is genuinely interested in Latin America," he advised Hudgens, "and I think would like to achieve a kind of a halo for himself and his family through doing some worthwhile things. Considering his background he is remarkably enlightened."

He had only one word of warning about Rockefeller: "He is not a fighter and will yield if the going gets tough."

Willing to accept Rockefeller's commitment at face value, Hudgens signed on, and soon was making ACAR an FSA redux. To establish ACAR as a visible presence in every farm community in the state, Hudgens cooked up a concept that was soon dubbed "the man, the girl, and the jeep." The man was an agricultural expert, the girl a home economist, and the jeep the conveyance that propelled them over the rough backcountry roads. Despite some clucking over morality concerns, the advice these teams dispensed was eagerly soaked up by the citizenry. Much of it, to be sure, was shockingly rudimentary. "Simple things, like you should boil your water," recalls one old AIA Brazil hand, Harry Bagley. "And you can't defecate any longer on the ground here by the kitchen, you have to go up in the hills and make a hole and you've got to cover it and throw lime in there. They didn't know these things."

ACAR's New Deal pedigree was coming through: the service was concerned not just with farmers' livelihood but with their lives. It set out to provide them with basic medical and dental care, much like the FSA did in remote U.S. farm areas in the 1930s. And ACAR was strikingly open-minded about what farmers did with their loans: on average, 13 percent was spent on such home improvements as plumbing, repairs, sewing machines, and electricity.

Yet ACAR's liberality did not affect its solvency: every single loan it made its first year was repaid on time. By almost every measure, ACAR was a striking success, both as a financial operation and as a do-good organization dedicated to improving the farmers' careworn lives.

Within Minas Gerais, support for ACAR never waned: Campos' successor as governor, Juscelino Kubitschek, was as ardent a booster of ACAR as Campos was. So impressed was he with Rockefeller's program that when Kubitschek was elected President of Brazil in 1956, one of his first acts was to seal an agreement with Rockefeller for a nationwide ACAR program, through a partnership between Rockefeller's AIA and the federal government.

In its formative years, ACAR did not appear to be a huge drain on Rockefeller's resources. His initial agreement with Minas Gerais called for an AIA contribution of $75,000 a year in the first three years, with the state bearing an equal share of the financial burden. (The actual farm loan funds were provided by Brazilian banks.) Nevertheless, by late 1948, with his Latin American commitments piling up at an astonishing clip—all those new IBEC ventures, not to mention spur-of-the-moment purchases of 1,000-square-mile farms—Rockefeller felt a bit pressed.

Seeking some family help, he turned to brother John. With his broad philanthropic interest in the Third World and his mounting frustration with the Rockefeller Foundation, John was particularly susceptible to Nelson's pitch. He agreed to donate to AIA enough Socony-Vacuum stock to cover a full third of ACAR's cost in the three-year period.

While John's assistance kept ACAR afloat, Nelson needed more—much, much more—if he wanted to realize his broader aims for AIA. Not only was expansion in Brazil envisioned, along with a full-scale effort on similar lines in Venezuela, but also the spread of AIA's agricultural programs to other Latin American countries. The oil companies had agreed to contribute $5 million to AIA—but all that money was earmarked for Venezuela.

To get AIA the wherewithal, Rockefeller and Hudgens began making the rounds of corporate America, appealing to their boardroom consciences. But Rockefeller soon came to grips with the unsettling realization that his own involvement, far from being a plus, was a distinct hindrance. On their way out of a meeting with a top Coca-Cola executive, Rockefeller turned to Hudgens and said, "You know what that man is thinking now? He is thinking to himself, 'I'm not going to put my money into something that's going to prove that Nelson Rockefeller is a world-wide philanthropist.' "

In the end, only one truly viable alternative presented itself: the one that Rockefeller had envisaged when he first sketched out AIA on a legal pad three years earlier. Somehow, the U.S. government would have to adopt Rockefeller's program—or at least some version of it—as its own.

Rockefeller had tried his best to stay on good terms with the Truman White House, sending the President a gushing handwritten note of congratulations upon his come-from-behind victory in 1948: "No man in the political history of this country has ever shown more courage or greater understanding of the American people." But any program of the sort Rockefeller had in mind would have to be initiated by the State Department. And, in the ranks of State, Rockefeller was still an outcast, still the meddler who had almost scuttled the United Nations conference.

But then, in a providential stroke, an unlikely instrument of intervention surfaced, in the person of one Benjamin Hardy.

A soft-spoken newspaperman from Georgia who got his start working for his family's small-town paper, Ben Hardy had worked during the war for the CIAA in Brazil, serving as one of Frank Jamieson's public information minions. When the coordinator's office shut down, he moved over to State to do speechwriting in the office of public affairs. But he continued to keep in touch with his former colleagues, and sometime in the postwar period—probably through Jamieson—he was brought together with Nelson Rockefeller.

In their conversations, Rockefeller harped on one subject: AIA. While he proudly touted his organization's importance and achievements, he also made clear to Hardy that, as it was, AIA could attain only limited goals; what was needed in the developing world was a much bigger program.

Rockefeller's words struck a responsive chord in Hardy. An unabashed enthusiast, dating back to the coordinator days, of his former employer's agricultural and social welfare programs, he truly believed in their broader mission.

Although not the most highly placed State official, Hardy was, from his speechwriter's perch, well positioned to catch the department's drift. One day in late November 1948 he got hold of a memo circulated to State's higher-ups by presidential assistant Clark Clifford. Clifford was working on Truman's inaugural address, and wanted some ideas from State that would turn the speech into "a democratic manifesto addressed to the peoples of the world, not just to the American people."

The memo had sparked little feedback from top State officials, and the request was languishing in the netherworld between the "In" and "Out" stacks when Hardy came upon it. Seeing an opening, he hammered out a memorandum to his boss, Francis Russell, the director of the public affairs office. The President, Hardy argued, should "take full advantage of the opportunity presented by the almost universal yearning for better conditions of life throughout the world" and announce in his address "a dramatic, large-scale program that would capture the imagination of the peoples of other countries." At the heart of this program would be social and economic assistance to the developing world—specifically, the wielding of U.S. resources and technical know-how to solve those nations' most chronic ills.

What Hardy was proposing was, in essence, a reworking of the AIA idea, along the more sweeping lines that Rockefeller suggested—with the U.S. government footing the bill. The memo was not scripted by Rockefeller, but it might as well have been, so pervasive was his influence throughout.

Hardy even hit on some of Rockefeller's favorite Cold War themes. He presented his program as picking up where the United States' massive European recovery plan—the celebrated Marshall Plan—left off. And, like the Marshall Plan, it was rooted in the new geopolitical realities. His program, said Hardy, would be "a potent weapon in the current struggle," part of the "democratic campaign to repulse Communism and create a decent life for the peoples of the earth."

Hardy's memo was long on ringing phrases, but short on details; all that, he said, could be developed afterward. The vagueness didn't help his cause.

When Russell passed along the memo to Undersecretary Robert Lovett, who was serving as acting secretary with the recent hospitalization of Secretary Marshall, Lovett kicked it right back with a curt note saying the plan "needed study."

"I'm not sure this is a good idea," Lovett added, "but I'm quite sure that it's not appropriate for an inaugural address."

That should have ended the whole matter. But Hardy, exhibiting incredible gutsiness for a mid-level government bureaucrat, refused to let his plan die. Daring to go around his superiors, he picked up the phone and called the White House.

He reached another of Truman's assistants, George Elsey, who was also working on the inaugural address, and asked if he could see him right away. Elsey had never met Hardy, but assuming it was some official matter, told Hardy to come on over.

Hurrying into Elsey's office in the east wing, Hardy handed him a copy of his memo and launched into an impassioned pitch for his technical assistance idea. He voiced his frustration with the State Department bureaucracy, which he was certain would smother his plan under layers of studies. Intrigued by Hardy's presentation, Elsey promised to see what he could do—and to keep the visit confidential.

As soon as the State aide left, Elsey headed over to Clifford's office with the memo. Clifford was as impressed as Elsey was. As he later related, "One reading convinced me that . . . this was the solution to our dilemma: while we had a speech in search of an idea, Hardy had an idea in search of a speech."

But when Clifford tried to wangle some support for the idea from Lovett and his cohorts (without giving away Hardy's visit), he ran into a stone wall. "Insufficient planning and analysis," was the word that came back. A disgusted Clifford, more than ever convinced that the Hardy program was his speech's missing ingredient, decided to ignore the objections. Ten days before the inauguration, he and Elsey began crafting an address focused on four points—with the Hardy plan as point number four.

When the draft was finally shown to Truman, the President zoomed in on that fourth point. He loved it. As far as Truman was concerned, it was of a piece not only with the Marshall Plan but with the emergency aid he had extended to Greece and Turkey in 1947, aid that he considered a critical bulwark against Soviet expansion. The more Truman mulled over the idea, the more excited he became about the possibilities. He ran on about how U.S. assistance could transform the Tigris-Euphrates Valley into a modern Garden of Eden and a granary for the whole of the Near East. The concept appealed not only to the Cold Warrior in him, but to the old Missouri farmer as well, still in awe of the transformation wrought by such government programs as the Tennessee Valley Authority.

Four days before the inauguration, a copy of the speech was shown to Dean Acheson, who was about to replace the ailing Marshall as Secretary of State. Acheson pronounced the address "splendid." Nonetheless, the diehards in the department, led by Lovett, continued to plead for withdrawal of the fourth point. The President, as contemptuous as ever about the "striped pants boys" at State, instructed his aides to ignore them. The fourth point—still clandestinely referred to, in the White House inner circle, as "Hardy's idea"—would stand.

Now President of the United States in his own right, the newly sworn-in Harry Truman stood before the multitudes at the U.S. Capitol and (for the first time at a presidential inaugural) before the television cameras. Reading from a loose-leaf notebook on the lectern in front of him, his breath frosting in the crystalline January air, he laid out the challenge.

The United States and its allies, he declared, were once again to be tested—this time by the "false philosophy" of Communism. It was up to the United States to stand up to that philosophy, to "undertake new projects to strengthen a free world." Then he launched into his four points, the four principal aspects of "our program for peace and freedom."

Point One was "unfaltering support for the United Nations." Point Two was support for world economic recovery, including continued backing of the Marshall Plan. Point Three was the ongoing effort to create a collective security alliance among the North Atlantic powers—what would soon be known as the North Atlantic Treaty Organization.

Finally, there was Point Four: "We must embark on a bold new program for making the benefits of our scientific advances and industrial progress available for the improvement and growth of underdeveloped areas."

"More than half the people of the world are living in conditions approaching misery," said the President. "Their food is inadequate. They are victims of disease. Their economic life is primitive and stagnant." To alleviate these afflictions, Truman called for a cooperative effort with American business, private capital, agriculture, and labor to "help the free peoples of the world, through their own efforts, to produce more food, more clothing, more materials for housing, and more mechanical power to lighten their burdens."

This was not, the President insisted, "the old imperialism—exploitation for foreign profit." Rather, it was "a program of development based on the concepts of democratic fair-dealing."

The great national program that was Nelson Rockefeller's vague dream three years earlier was at last coming to pass.

Just as Clark Clifford had foreseen, nothing the President said that day stirred as much interest, or garnered as many kudos, as the global aid plan. It was hailed as an act of international humanitarianism, an affirmation that the awesome power of the United States could be a source of good as well as of destruction. A " 'Fair Deal' Plan for the World" was what *The Washington Post* called the scheme. Soon the program, for want of any catchier appellation, was referred to simply by its place in Truman's speech: it was Point Four.

Reading the text of the address with unbounded satisfaction, Rockefeller dashed off a note to the President:

> Your inauguration speech will live as one of the great declarations of our times. It evidences a world statesmanship that will give new hope to the peoples of all lands.
>
> To me, a most significant and farsighted concept is embodied in your fourth point. I sincerely believe, in outlining that point, you have blocked out the basis of the future foreign policy of the United States.

At the same time, Rockefeller was well aware that without the intervention of one unsung figure, that fourth point would never have seen the light of day. He knew all about Ben Hardy's memo; Hardy had slipped a copy to Frank Jamieson. Rockefeller gave Hardy full credit for the breakthrough: "He certainly has done a wonderful job for our country and the world," he told Jamieson.

Left unsaid was the fact that had it not been for Rockefeller's influence on Hardy, the whole chain of events might never have been set in motion.

For all the worldwide enthusiasm with which it was greeted, Point Four was still more slogan than substance. Quizzed by reporters, a week after the inauguration, about the plan, Truman was unable to offer any specifics. All he could say was that he had asked Acheson to get to work on it. "I can't tell you what is going to take place, where it is going to take place, or how it is going to take place," he snapped. "I know what I want to do."

Left to the devices of the reluctant bureaucrats at State, Point Four was soon bogged down in "planning" minutiae. When the program was finally unveiled six months later, it called for an initial outlay of a mere $45 million—a pittance compared with the billions spent on the Marshall Plan. And even that modest sum was too much for many congressional skeptics, who derided the program as "just another give-away plan."

Point Four was in need of all the friends it could get. And among those most eager to race to its rescue was Nelson Rockefeller.

He pounced on every opportunity to publicly affirm his support for the program—and to make that support known to Harry Truman. Using his position as chairman of the National Conference of Christians and Jews, Rockefeller asked to call on the President in connection with Brotherhood Week. He was granted the meeting—and spent as much time talking with Truman about Point Four as about brotherhood. Afterward, Rockefeller told a colleague that it was clear that Truman's objectives "coincide with ours 100 percent."

Dropping any pretense of Republican partisanship, Rockefeller praised Point Four in terms that went beyond even the most ardent assertions of its Democratic backers. It was, he claimed, the most "provocative" concept since the atomic bomb, because it brought "a renewal of faith and hope that free peoples can work together." Point Four, in fact, might turn out to be "one of the most significant foreign policy declarations of our time." He went so far as to begin work (with the aid of two ghostwriters) on a book, *The U.S. and the World,* that would make the case for the program.

It was almost as if he had authored the plan himself—which, more or less, he had.

His immersion in Point Four had not diminished Rockefeller's involvement in his own private-sector contribution to the cause. Indeed, more than ever now, IBEC was commanding his attention, entrancing him with its limitless possibilities. IBEC Technical Services, his flashy effort to revolutionize Latin American infrastructure, was in full swing. It had contracts to study a new highway between Caracas and La Guaira, the capital's sea and air outlet; to explore the possible expansion of the port of La Guaira; and to look into a new airport for São Paulo. And the company's prospects in Venezuela were instantly improved by yet another government upheaval there. In November 1948, a military clique alarmed by Betancourt's reforms staged a coup that sent Betancourt and other Acción Democrática leaders into exile. Demonstrating once again his flexibility about the region's internal politics, Rockefeller overlooked the fact that the coup had deposed a democratically elected government, and immediately began doing business with the new regime.

His avidity was no doubt enhanced by the shift in emphasis dictated by the new leadership under Major Marcos Pérez Jiménez. The Betancourt government's grass-roots, share-the-wealth campaign was out; big-ticket public works programs were back in. For Rockefeller's technical services unit—dedicated as it was to big-ticket projects—it was an ideal environment in which to operate.

Within six months after the military takeover, Rockefeller was talking with the new government about giant irrigation projects, about highway construction, about power plants. He was particularly intrigued by the means with which the government planned to finance this construction. Rather than tap directly into its oil revenues, it would issue bonds collateralized by the oil wealth.

By then, Rockefeller had identified the perfect executive to spearhead IBEC Technical Services' initial efforts in Venezuela and Brazil: Robert Moses, New York's master builder himself.

More than any other individual in the twentieth century, "Robert Moses shaped New York," declared his biographer, Robert Caro: shaped the great city's highways, its bridges and tunnels, its public housing, its parks. Who better, then, to plan serpentine highway projects in Latin America than the man who built virtually all of New York's magnificent parkway system? Who better to organize a mammoth public works program than the man who for close to thirty years had masterminded nearly every great public construction project in the city? And who better to map out plans massively financed by bonds than the man who wrote the book on public authority financing in New York State?

And Moses was willing. The lure was not the challenge of operating in a new sphere—he had more than enough challenges in his home base—but the money Rockefeller dangled before him. He would pay Moses a huge $100,000 consulting fee. Despite his princely personal style, Moses was always financially strapped. "For all the years of his adult life, he had been short of money," Caro observed. It was the currency of power that he was interested in; refusing to compromise that power, he did not cash in on it as other men might have. An easy $100,000, earned without any risk to his clout or reputation, had an immense appeal.

Moses took Rockefeller's money. But, as it turned out, he did not pocket much of it, preferring instead to distribute most of the fee to his aides, his *muchachos,* as he called them—as Caro noted, "to buy other men who could help him in his New York work."

Accompanied by five of the *muchachos,* Moses flew down to Caracas. Among the *caraqueños* his magisterial ways earned him instant notoriety. The morning after his arrival, one of the country's top ministers came to call on Moses at his hotel; Moses received him in his bathrobe.

To Moses, any transportation problem had but one solution: highways, more and more of them. And he didn't hesitate to impose his distinctive vision on Caracas, brushing aside local idiosyncrasies, offering up a plan that was virtually identical to the Moses textbook approach in New York. The much-needed superhighway between Caracas and La Guaira, he suggested, "should be a toll project constructed by an independent public authority" and financed by revenue bonds: the very framework he had popularized in New York. (Moses paid scant attention to how these bonds could be sold, given that the local capital market was not exactly Wall Street.) Traffic congestion in Caracas, he declared, "can be relieved by the construction of a system of expressways and boulevards leading from the business district of the city toward the outlying areas, together with appropriate feeders." What the city needed, in other words, was a Cross Bronx Expressway.

Moses filed his report, collected his fee, and returned to the far more fulfilling business of mapping out New York's postwar transportation grid. Meanwhile, Rockefeller's IBEC operatives were saddled with the unenviable task of figuring out what to do with his master plan. The centerpiece, the Caracas–La Guaira superhighway, was soon mired in bureaucracy and plagued by intractable financial problems; an IBEC pitch for help from the new World Bank went nowhere. Eventually, a toll road was built, but long after IBEC's involvement in the project was terminated.

Moses went on one more mission for Rockefeller, to São Paulo in 1950. He produced a sweeping city plan which, among other things, called for construction of a main highway artery right through the middle of town—much like the roads he was then envisioning building through the heart of Manhattan. The Brazilian authorities were impressed enough by Moses to invite him back, at their own expense. He would later claim that São Paulo stuck "fairly close to the plan set forth in our report."

But there was something about Moses' work in São Paulo that caused Nelson Rockefeller—hitherto one of his biggest boosters—to be leery of the master builder. Discussing Moses' report with his close associates, Rockefeller told them that "Mr. Moses should be watched on the contract level" by Rockefeller's lawyers. Exactly what he thought Moses was up to on the "contract level" was not clear. But indisputably a new note of wariness had entered into the relationship between these two pile-driving characters; there would be no more fat IBEC fees for Moses. And, in the years to come, that note would build slowly, inevitably, into a fateful crescendo.

In an open field in Norfolk, Virginia, a giant thirty-five-ton crane—used during World War II to lift wrecked aircraft off landing strips—stood poised like a prehistoric behemoth waiting to strike. Perched on a metal platform between the crane's huge wheels (each one as tall as a man), beaming for photographers as he clutched the controls that set this colossus in motion, was a proud, excitedly expectant Nelson Rockefeller. Another of his businesses, IBEC Housing, was, literally, about to get off the ground.

Norfolk was the first real-world test of the mass-production processes Harrison had devised. Rockefeller contracted with the city's housing authority to build 204 low-rent ($45 a month) two-family units that would take advantage of low-rate Federal Housing Administration mortgages. If the process worked close to home in Norfolk, Rockefeller was ready to export it to Latin America.

The whole system—a veritable housing production line—had been carefully plotted out by Harrison. The giant crane would lift massive steel forms into place over precast floor slabs. Concrete would then be poured into these forms; twenty-four hours later, the crane would pick up the forms, leaving behind concrete walls, and then hoist into place, over those walls, a precast concrete roof. All that would be needed then, to make this dwelling habitable, was some painting, the installation of fixtures, electrical and plumbing connections, and the mounting of doors and windows. With that, the first IBEC houses would be ready for occupancy.

Someone asked Rockefeller if the crane was difficult to operate. "Nothing to it," he replied. "A child could run it." And just to show how easy it was, he began pushing some buttons on the control panel. The huge machine shuddered, lurched, and swung into the side of a half-built house, knocking down a cement mixer and jolting a worker off his perch. Utterly unfazed, Rockefeller surrendered the controls to a professional operator and climbed down from the platform.

The colossal cranes, the rumbling cement mixers, the houses sprouting overnight in the open field: once again, another of Rockefeller's fantasies was indulged, thanks to IBEC. This was the builder's fantasy, the urge to shape, to alter, and to leave behind testaments in steel, wood, and concrete (even if he couldn't run the cranes himself). Prosaic as the IBEC Housing product was—just a squat, unadorned box, a featureless antiseptic shell—it still fired Rockefeller's imagination. Wherever housing was needed, wherever it was in short supply because of cost or materials or lack of know-how, he could bring his cranes and cement trucks and work his twenty-four-hour miracle.

But as he spun his dreams of superhighways and supershelters, Rockefeller also found himself contemplating the tribulations plaguing his ongoing IBEC enterprises.

The IBEC farms were beset by a series of calamities, the roll call of which had an almost biblical ring. There were armyworms. There were diseased chickens. There were sterile hogs.

The hogs were special hybrids, flown down to Brazil from Minnesota, to breed with the native swine and produce a meatier, more prolific strain. But something happened on the flight; when the pigs arrived, nearly all were sterile.

The chickens IBEC was raising in Venezuela were infected first by a form of pox and then by an attack of pullorum. In late 1948, the whole flock had to be destroyed.

As for the worms: they infested the corn crop of one of IBEC's Venezuelan farms, Agua Blanca, and three separate doses of insecticide were needed to beat them back. And just as that menace was receding, the Monte Sacro farm was attacked by a different type of worm, immune to the insecticide that did in the Agua Blanca worms. The entire corn crop was ruined.

Perhaps worst of all were the floods that washed over the Central Bolívar farm in Venezuela, followed by a brutally hot dry season that killed the farm's prize cattle and turned the soil to dust.

Within a year of their start-up, IBEC's farms—at least the ones in Venezuela—were looking like losing propositions. The early fears voiced by local farmers—that the mighty Rockefeller, abetted by the oil companies, would force them from the land—now seemed laughable. If anyone was on the brink of being forced out, it was Nelson Rockefeller.

The most endemic plague of them all in Venezuela—corruption—was further afflicting Rockefeller's IBEC enterprises.

Rockefeller was savvy enough in the ways of Latin America to know how the wheels were greased. But, from the outset, he was determined that any business with which he was identified would be utterly beyond reproach. Among other things, this meant that IBEC would not indulge in the traditional Latin American practice of payoffs to newspapers and newspapermen to ensure favorable coverage. Scruples played a part in this decision, but it was also a matter of practicality. "If the Venezuelan papers ever learned that Rockefeller was willing to pay to get his story in the papers," Jamieson explained, "we would have very little coverage without paying."

"Typically, in Venezuela at Christmastime," remembers John Camp, "you were supposed to send gifts to people in the government, particularly those who give you permits for different things. The income tax people, the customs people. But Nelson sat down with us, right at the beginning, and said, 'We're not going to give any gifts at any time.' "

For the most part, IBEC got away with this hard-line stance; even the most venal customs officer or the slimiest newspaper editor was intimidated by the Nelson Rockefeller mystique. "If it were Joe Zilch," admitted Jamieson, "we might not have been able to carry out that policy."

But what Rockefeller hadn't counted on was the petty corruption that pervaded everyday Venezuelan life, corruption that wasn't a matter of bald-faced bribes but of systemic thievery—carried out in many cases by one's own agents and employees. From this corruption, not even IBEC was immune.

For instance, on the first day IBEC's milk plant was open for business, a farmer arrived with milk cans in tow. When he placed the cans on the scales, fish began leaping out of them onto the scales. "Obviously," says former VBEC executive Edward Kimball, who was on the scene throughout those early days, "he had stopped at the nearest stream, and dumped the cans in the water so he could have more milk for sale. So I asked the man, 'Why does this milk have fish in it?' And he said, 'You know, I had some cows down by the lake, and they've sort of been acting funny.' "

Even worse was the scam pulled on IBEC by the fishermen of Puerto La Cruz. To boost their efficiency, IBEC had equipped their small vessels with motors and iceboxes. But when the fishery division began tallying their catch, it was startled to find the totals actually declining. Upon investigation, the management learned the reason why. Instead of wasting their time fishing, the men were happily using their swift IBEC-powered boats to smuggle contraband.

Rockefeller and his IBEC aides had also misjudged other aspects of the Venezuelan mentality.

All along they had assumed that if they could bring enough fish to market, there would be plenty of demand. But they discovered there weren't even enough buyers for the smaller catches that the smuggling fishermen were bringing in. What the IBEC planners had not reckoned on was the finickiness of the Venezuelan consumer. Decades of bad fish had driven home the lesson that the only fish worth buying was a fish with its head still on, so that the buyer could see the glisten in its eyes that was the mark of freshness. Presented with the cleaned, precut frozen IBEC fish, the consumer turned away. Where was the head?

Misjudgments of a different sort plagued the food wholesaling venture, CADA. The company cut its profit margins, in the high-minded hope that reduced prices would be passed on by retailers to the consumers. But the retailers properly assumed the CADA people were *loco,* and pocketed the profits themselves—normal enough behavior in a country where anything less than a 25 percent margin was considered scandalous.

When he began VBEC, Rockefeller had set out two objectives. One was to increase the supply and improve the distribution of foods "with the aim of lowering costs to the consumer." Two years into his great experiment, the supply had not increased, and the distribution had certainly not improved. And the consumer's costs were as high as ever.

The other was to put his enterprises on "a sound paying basis." And that goal now looked even more out of reach than the first. The cost of Rockefeller's good intentions had never seemed dearer.

The bad news was delivered to him on July 1, 1949. One of Rockefeller's financial people, William Machold, reported to him that as of April 30, VBEC had a cumulative deficit of $1.7 million, and that figure was expected to grow by another $600,000. VBEC's common stock—all of which was owned by IBEC and thus, indirectly, by Rockefeller and his brothers—was "without book value," according to Machold, meaning a loss on paper of some $1 million. What's more, Machold judged it likely that VBEC's preferred stock—representing the $10 million the oil companies had thus far sunk into the venture—would be "additionally impaired."

Yet it was imperative now, for VBEC's continued solvency, that the oil companies be asked to throw good money after bad. Machold predicted that VBEC would run out of cash during the first quarter of 1950, unless the oil companies kicked in the $2.7 million they had earlier agreed to provide by that date. (Those commitments were described as "tentative, but not firm.")

"It should be realized now," Machold advised Rockefeller, "that further substantial sums may have to be invested in VBEC to bring about a sound reorganization of VBEC's subsidiaries. Otherwise, some of VBEC's activities face the prospect of costly liquidation."

Day after day, Rockefeller sat in on meetings where the sorry state of IBEC's finances was hashed out. Accustomed to spirited brainstorming sessions where new ideas popped up like spring daisies, he was now forced to slog through interminable balance sheets and listen to the numbing drone of his accountants. He tried to seem engaged, but those who knew him well could see behind the facade. Bill Alton remembers sitting through one of those meetings when his eyes and Rockefeller's suddenly met. "I could tell, just from that look, that he was just acting a part. He was really bored to pieces."

But bored though he was, he knew he had to do something to placate the oil companies, something to induce them to contribute the $2.7 million they had promised. Rockefeller did not relish the prospect of seeing the enterprises in which he had invested so much of his energy, his money, and above all his reputation meet an unseemly, publicly embarrassing demise. Not only was he risking personal and family humiliation, but also a possibly fatal undermining of his campaign for Point Four. For Point Four to truly succeed, Rockefeller was now saying to all who would listen, it would have to engage a partnership between government and business, between public and private capital. How would it look for his own ventures to flounder and fail at a time when he was trying to rally other businessmen to follow his lead?

He could blame his Venezuelan problems on naiveté, on a misreading of the ingrained local ways and conditions. He could blame them on the armyworms, the floods, and the weeds. But, at the same time, he could not ignore the contribution of swollen overheads, of lax accounting, and, above all, of the profligate atmosphere that he himself had promoted. Two years earlier the oil companies, and his own finance committee, had warned Rockefeller about the overhead and the receding likelihood of ever generating enough earnings to carry it. Bill Alton had confirmed the warnings and cited the egregious examples of waste. Yet Rockefeller, caught up in the fever of expansion and "promotion," as he called it, had paid all this little heed. IBEC's corporate banner was still a blank check.

Now, at last, Rockefeller took action—though not the precipitous kind that so many were urging. He turned to his trusty utility man, John Lockwood, and asked the lawyer to serve as IBEC's executive vice president. To judge just how bad things were, Lockwood flew down to Caracas and, like Alton before him, was appalled at what he found. The lawyer had no confidence in the man Rockefeller had tapped to run VBEC after Camp was shifted to AIA: his old Dartmouth classmate, and later Venezuelan coventurer, Bill Coles. Said Lockwood, "Coles is a persistent amateur—which is what is the trouble with much of VBEC."

Upon his return to New York, Lockwood consulted regularly with Rockefeller about IBEC's troubles. But Lockwood was also reporting to someone else. Each day, the attorney would make his way from the east wing of the fifty-sixth floor to the west wing. There, he was admitted into the hushed baronial quarters of John D. Rockefeller, Jr.

His mourning at an end, Junior was once again bringing his rigorous presence to bear on the denizens of Room 5600. His associates had kept him posted on the misfortunes of IBEC. But he wanted to know more, and so he asked Lockwood to come by each day to brief him.

Lockwood may have been Nelson's man, but, along with everyone else in that office, he was still Junior's employee. He had no choice but to satisfy the old man's curiosity. "I had to explain *everything* to him," Lockwood recalls. "What the figures showed, what we were doing."

The gray, spectral eye of Junior was gazing down on IBEC. But to what end, no one really knew.

The oil companies were placated by Lockwood's presence, but just barely. They agreed to comply with their commitments for 1949—but only on the condition that the new funds be used solely for existing IBEC programs.

No sooner had that hurdle been negotiated, however, than Rockefeller was faced with another: what to do about the other party in the three-way VBEC alliance, the Venezuelan government.

When the government development agency, Fomento, signed its deal with VBEC, the agency thought it had pulled off a tremendous coup: forcing the great Rockefeller to surrender a stake in his businesses to the Venezuelan people. But now it discovered that the great Rockefeller was nothing more than an overenthusiastic young promoter of dubious business acumen. Far from reaping immense gains, Fomento found itself mired in the quicksand of his shaky enterprises.

The political pressures on Fomento were mounting. Viewed as an inefficient vestige of the ousted Betancourt regime, Fomento was described by pro-junta newspapers as a "white elephant" that had to be reined in. Particularly suspect was its "reliance on foreigners." With VBEC also under fire from the conservative press for its "paper promises," Fomento's future course was clear. It had to find some way of severing its ties to Rockefeller.

In a last-ditch effort to allay their concerns, Rockefeller flew down to Venezuela to meet with the new Development Minister and the new head of Fomento. He guided them on a personal tour of the Monte Sacro farm, and as they sat down to drinks at the hacienda he spoke grandly of all his plans: for a canning and quick-freeze plant, for a seed company, for a hog operation, for a lumber company on the Agua Blanca property. With a dazzling display of salesmanship, Rockefeller endeavored to create the impression of a thriving, ever-growing enterprise. "What financial squeeze?" he seemed to be saying.

Actually, Rockefeller's hyperbolic patter was not totally off base. As the troubled year of 1949 was wending to a close, there was reason for optimism about at least some of IBEC's enterprises.

The milk company, INLACA, was starting to live up to its promise to revolutionize Venezuelan dairy consumption. Its Valencia plant brought cheap pasteurized milk, for the first time, to the populace. Packed in paraffin-coated cardboard cartons (instead of more fragile bottles), the milk was an instant success with consumers who traditionally had to make do with powdered milk.

Not everyone was happy about INLACA's arrival. In one town, a left-wing agitator implored the population, "Don't buy that milk. It's no good. It comes from a capitalist." But the local INLACA salesman corrected him. "Oh no, señor," he said. "It's good milk. It's *Rockefeller* milk."

The food wholesaling operation, meanwhile, finally hit on a successful formula. Shedding its reticence, the company decided to introduce to Venezuelans the new retailing concept that was sweeping the United States: the supermarket.

The first store, dubbed Todos ("Everything"), opened in the oil city of Maracaibo in December. It featured all the amenities that were so alluring to American consumers: ample parking, air conditioning, a huge selection, even a soda fountain. Above all, it promised—and delivered—low prices, on average 10 percent less than what other stores were charging.

Determined to get it right this time, IBEC hired a savvy manager: Richard Provost, a veteran food retailer with experience in both the United States and Mexico. And Provost came through for IBEC. In its first year, Todos posted sales of $3.3 million and a net profit of almost $300,000.

Down in Brazil, IBEC had a winner in its hybrid seed corn company, Sementes Agroceres (SASA). A severe drought hit central Brazil in 1949, laying waste to farms throughout the region—except those that planted SASA's hardy seeds. The result was an unprecedented demand for SASA's product; so strong was it that the company had to ration the next year's seeds.

But all the talk about IBEC's promise, all of Rockefeller's hearty *abrazos* and heady forecasts, did not budge the Venezuelan officials. They still wanted out. At the tony country clubs in Caracas' elite Paraiso district, there was buzzing about the possible bankruptcy of Rockefeller's companies, about an *escándalo* (scandal). Fearing the worst, the government pushed for an immediate settlement.

Fomento's total stake in Rockefeller's ventures was close to $4.5 million. Even assuming Rockefeller could negotiate a buyout at something less than that figure, he still faced a multimillion-dollar exposure. And what with the further IBEC demands on his bankroll—he was thinking, for instance, of bailing out the Venezuelan farm company by buying some of the farms himself—it was a sum he would be hard pressed to provide. He had already sunk $6.4 million of his own funds into IBEC. To go much further would be to stretch his own finances to the limit.

Rockefeller could not turn to the oil companies; they had lived up to the letter of their commitment, but would not put in a penny more. Neither could he approach his brothers, whose total investment in the company now stood at $1.5 million. His ego, his sense of himself as the leader of his generation, simply would not countenance anything that smacked of a rescue effort by his siblings.

There was, as he looked around, only one ready source for the millions he would need to buy out Fomento. It was the one source he had always been loath to tap, the one source that was bound to have emotional, if not financial, strings attached. But now he had no choice. He would have to go to John D. Rockefeller, Jr., for help.

Once again, Nelson pulled out his old memo-writing tool bag. This time, though, in addition to wielding his familiar levers of ingratiation and appeals to family pride and honor, he had a new device to suit his purposes: the national interest. He would invoke the grander purposes of Point Four.

Because of Point Four, he informed his father in a February 7, 1950, letter, "there has been a growing interest in Congress and the press throughout the country" in IBEC's and AIA's activities. "Increasingly our work has been held up as an example of what could be done under the Point Four program by private enterprise. . . . I feel an increasing sense of responsibility for myself and on behalf of the family in connection with Point Four and the development of a national policy in this field of international cooperation."

It was against this red-white-and-blue backdrop that Nelson explained the financial conundrum in which he now found himself. "A much publicized failure of one of our companies," he pointed out, "with a substantial default in an obligation to the Venezuelan Government might not only have an unfortunate effect on the business standing of the family, but also on the development of the Point Four concept. Under the circumstances, I don't feel that I can follow a course which would be natural under normal business procedures"—in other words, to tell Fomento to get lost. It was his duty to the country to come to terms with the Venezuelans.

He sought to minimize the cost—"This Venezuelan situation may involve $1,000,000, at the outside possibly $2,000,000, on my part"—and to dispel the notion that IBEC was foundering. Of its nineteen subsidiary companies, he expected ten to be in the black this year; there were only four in seriously bad shape.

Then came the pitch. Nelson wanted to set up a "guarantee fund" to guard against any contingencies. "I have additional funds of my own but not quite enough to make things absolutely sure against all future possibilities." To finance this guarantee fund, he wished to sell his $4.4 million in IBEC preferred stock to Junior.

Having been briefed for months by Lockwood on IBEC's condition, Junior was ready, more than ready, to deal with Nelson's request.

Nevertheless, he treated his son's supplication with the same exacting circumspection he applied to all the serious appeals that had come across his desk over the years. He asked for figures, and more figures, from Lockwood. Then he phoned Nelson and went over a long list of questions, which elicited, in response, a further lengthy and detailed memorandum.

At last, seventeen days after he received his son's request, Junior sent over to the east wing his response.

"You well know," he began, "that from the outset I have been wholly sympathetic with the purpose and ideals which you have sought to carry out and attain, the national and international significance of which I have recognized from the start." Nelson's work "has commanded my admiration and made me very proud of you."

This admiration, however, did not stop Junior from second-guessing his son's business approach. "I, because older and with the experience of the years, would have started with fewer enterprises in fewer countries in a smaller way and on a more conservative basis."

> Very naturally, you have felt that time was of the essence of the matter and that it was important to start a number of enterprises in a number of localities and countries because of the pressing need for the wider extension of the principle if your experiments proved it to be sound, practical and workable. The price you are paying for speeding up the process of experiment has been a large turn-over in top management and both the actual and prospective loss of sums of money much greater than would have been the case had the experiment been made on a smaller investment basis.
>
> The experience which you have gotten from the past few years is invaluable, although it may prove to be costly. . . .

This was vintage Junior: a little doff of his hat to his son's praiseworthy intentions, followed by an artfully framed, thoroughly didactic scolding. Then, with a tidy note of resignation—"What has happened, has happened. . . . The question is what to do from now on"—he proceeded to present the financial situation as *he* saw it, which was not at all the way Nelson saw it. Taking his rapier to IBEC's balance sheet, Junior showed that it was not, as his son suggested, $1 million to $2 million that was needed, but $2.5 million—

followed by another $2.2 million if all of Fomento's investments were redeemed.

Having set Nelson straight on that, Junior came to the point: "I cannot consistently make available to you by gift, directly or indirectly, monies to be used as venture capital." To do so "would be a disservice rather than a service." He would, however, offer his son a loan of $2.5 million "due in ten years with interest at 4% payable semi-annually." (This was twice the prime rate.) "My purpose in making this proposal," explained Junior, "is to save you personally from the possibility of criticism on the part of the Venezuelan Government and the oil companies or from loss of prestige in the business world."

> I realize that this is far from what you have hoped I would do. I know that you would have liked me to evidence my belief in you and in your objectives by granting fully your request. Nothing would have given me greater satisfaction than to have done just that if I could have brought myself to believe that to do so would be in your ultimate interest. But I do not believe that it would be either to your benefit or in the interest of the achievement of your purpose, that I should do so.

It was hard to judge which made Nelson angrier—the rebuff itself or the pedantic, for-your-own-good manner in which it was carried out, so reminiscent of the admonitory lectures of his youth. That he was angry, there was no doubt. When he recounted to his associates what had happened, his eyes narrowed into the steely slits that were always the surest expression of his displeasure. (In later tellings, he would make Junior sound even meaner than he actually was, reporting that his father had insisted, as a condition of the loan, that he liquidate IBEC. But Junior, in fact, had not attached any conditions to the loan.)

Once again, as in the Avila Hotel venture, his father had demonstrated an utter lack of faith in him. And once again, as in the Avila, Nelson was grittily determined to prove to his father that he was wrong.

Summoning up all the self-control he could muster, Nelson thanked Junior for his offer, but respectfully declined it. He would find the money some other way. If he had to borrow the money, then he would borrow it from a bank.

Which is precisely what Rockefeller did. For the first time in his life, he applied for a bank loan—not just one, but several. And despite IBEC's dicey prospects, the banks to which he applied, in New York and São Paulo, were more than happy to oblige a Rockefeller.

At the same time, he sent Lockwood to Caracas to negotiate with Fomento—to try to somehow whittle down the government's financial demands. Lockwood managed to squeeze out an agreement whereby Fomento's VBEC positions would be bought out for a mere $1.3 million. Only $1 million of that would have to be put up by Rockefeller himself; the rest would come from VBEC and its subsidiaries.

Free, at least for the moment, from his most burdensome financial pressures, Rockefeller could finally take a step back and strategize IBEC's future. By any reasonable business standard, pruning, retrenchment, and consolidation would appear to be the order of the day.

But, as usual, Nelson Rockefeller had his own ideas about what was reasonable.

In July, he visited Venezuela and Brazil, and by the time he finished he was as effervescently optimistic about IBEC's prospects as he ever was. The milk company, he reported, "is going to town. There is a wonderful group there. The plant has been expanded—a new piece of machinery every day. I don't see any ceiling on this company." He wanted to expand it "as rapidly as business justifies." He also wanted to open new supermarkets "just as fast as experience, management and funds permit."

Rockefeller was bullish on almost everything. IBEC Housing, for all its technical achievements, had yet to get off the ground in Latin America, but "I'm confident that when they get over the hump with one or two contracts, this company will really roll." IBEC Technical Services had lost $250,000 in its first four years in business, but "it seems to have finally found its stride." Even the beleaguered fish and farming companies were looking up. "It seems to me that the financial drain should be stopped pretty soon," Rockefeller said. "There have been a lot of tough breaks but I don't think they were too unfortunate." Everything, in short, was just fine: "The relations with the oil companies are wonderful; also the government and the ambassador."

Just months before, many of his companies were on the brink of bankruptcy, virtually insolvent. And, his rosy assessments notwithstanding, many of them were still not out of the woods. But while Rockefeller conceded the need for a "well-thought-out financial policy for the future," he did not allude to cutbacks or retrenchment or anything that remotely hinted at a pruned balance sheet.

Instead, he talked about expansion and about bringing to life still more new enterprises.

He talked about doing real estate deals in São Paulo with Bill Zeckendorf. About starting a hybrid seed–insecticide–fertilizer company in Venezuela. About producing men's shirts in Brazil in partnership with the Manhattan Shirt Company. About working with David and the Chase Bank to organize a joint investment banking venture in Brazil.

Rockefeller seemed bent on showing that his was not a struggling, wheezing company, but one with all the vibrance and vitality of its founder. He wanted to prove it to the world. But, most of all, he wanted to prove it to his father.

Twenty-seven

DEBACLE

The cacophony of male voices resounded through the dining room at 810 Fifth Avenue, bouncing off the silver salvers and tureens, fluttering the plumes of candle flame. Seated around the table on a Thursday evening in late September 1950 was a cross section of America's corporate elite—industrialists, publishers, investment bankers—interspersed with various of the host's close associates (Lockwood, Harrison, brother David). As the demitasse cups were filled and the humidors passed, Nelson Rockefeller rose, thanked them all for coming, and explained his purpose in bringing the group together. He wanted to talk about the President's Point Four program: specifically, how the business community could work with the government to push the plan forward.

The executives listened with barely concealed restiveness as Rockefeller made his by now well-rehearsed pitch for a private sector–public sector partnership to aid the developing world. Around the dinner table, his appeal was met first with respectful silence, and then with a slow crescendo of disputation. Hardly favorably disposed to Harry Truman to begin with, the business leaders were not inclined to subsidize another Democratic giveaway program.

Rockefeller listened to their arguments, and parried them with his own impassioned rhetoric about the Communist menace and the urgent need to counter it not just militarily but economically. He was playing to his guests, but most of all, he was playing to one guest: a tall, lean, urbane figure, crisply attired in a bespoke English suit, who took in the proceedings attentively, but with a certain arid, bemused detachment. It was for the benefit of this man, really, that Rockefeller had arranged the whole evening. He was W. Averell Harriman, special assistant to the President, and on his finely tailored shoulders rested the future of Point Four—and much else that the profoundly ambitious Harriman considered of far greater moment.

Like Rockefeller, Harriman had been born into immense wealth, Robber Baron wealth: in his case, the vast fortune accumulated by his father, the ruthless railroad magnate E. H. Harriman. And, like Rockefeller, Harriman had relentlessly striven all his life to leverage his patrimony into power and influence on his own terms.

But all Rockefeller had accomplished in his career so far could not match what Harriman—seventeen years his senior—had achieved in his.

Nothing Rockefeller had done in the business world could approach what Harriman had done. Harriman was a pioneering investor in the infant aviation industry, and, in the depths of the Depression, he had revitalized the great railroad his father had built, the Union Pacific: it was Harriman who introduced high-speed, high-style streamlined trains to America's rail lines. Seizing the potential of the newly fashionable sport of skiing (and seeking a destination that would attract new passengers to the Union Pacific), Harriman created, from scratch, the Sun Valley ski resort in the Idaho Rockies. Soon his Sun Valley was an American St. Moritz, attracting to its slopes Errol Flynn, Ernest Hemingway, William Paley—and Nelson Rockefeller.

Harriman's international business achievements also dwarfed Rockefeller's. While still in his twenties, Harriman had assembled the world's largest merchant fleet and was known as "the Steamship King." And, less than a decade after the Russian revolution, he became one of the few Western capitalists to dare do business in the Soviet Union, negotiating face-to-face with Leon Trotsky. Although Harriman's mining operations in the Caucasus were a failure, they set the stage for the larger career that lay ahead.

Under the sway of his liberal older sister Mary, a friend of the Hyde Park Roosevelts, Harriman turned Democrat and accepted a series of New Deal positions. And just as Rockefeller was to do, he cultivated an entrée with the socially minded Harry Hopkins. With Hopkins' backing, Harriman was propelled into the heights of wartime diplomacy, serving as FDR's personal emissary to the Churchill government ("he was in 1941 the most important American in England," observed Harriman's biographer, Rudy Abramson) and as the principal negotiator of lend-lease aid to the Soviet Union. In October 1943 he was named U.S. ambassador to Russia, and for the duration of the war he was a key supporting player at all the momentous Allied parleys, including Yalta.

While Rockefeller found himself frozen out by the Truman administration, Harriman suffered no such fate. Throughout the postwar period he held a succession of enviable, high-profile posts: ambassador to Great Britain, Secretary of Commerce, and, most dramatically, on-the-spot coordinator of Marshall Plan aid to Europe. When Harriman, at his own request, was recalled to

Washington in mid-1950 to serve as the President's special assistant, his worldwide prestige—as presidential envoy, éminence grise, and now instrument of European recovery—was never greater. His sole deficiency was his personality: as frigid and as astringent as a shaken gin martini. "He was not inconsiderate," remarked a wartime aide. "He was just no good at human relations."

Undoubtedly, it was Harriman's Marshall Plan experience that led Truman to hand him the Point Four portfolio upon his return to the capital. But before he could give Point Four much more than a moment's thought, Harriman found himself distracted by a far more pressing matter: the invasion of South Korea by Communist forces on June 25.

With Truman grittily determined, as he put it, "that whatever had to be done to meet this aggression had to be done," the capital was once again on a war footing. Eager to tap his new assistant's tested skills as a go-between, the President dispatched Harriman in early August to Tokyo to meet with the imperious commander of the U.S. forces, General Douglas MacArthur, and learn of his plans for a counterattack. MacArthur dazzled the envoy with his plans for a surprise amphibious landing that would outflank the enemy from behind and win the war in a single stroke. An enthusiastic Harriman urged Truman to back the general's stratagem. A month later, on September 15, the 1st Marine Division began the attack on Inchon. The North Koreans were swiftly routed and driven from the South.

But the war was far from over. On September 27, the day before Harriman sat down to dinner at 810 Fifth Avenue, the White House endorsed MacArthur's new objective: to send his troops across the 38th parallel, the border between North and South, and wipe out the whole North Korean Army.

With all this on Harriman's mind, Point Four had receded to a faint dot on the policy horizon, the least of the manifold concerns bearing down upon him. If he appeared less than fully engaged by the dialogue after dinner, it was with good reason.

But Point Four had fallen between the policy-making cracks even before the crisis in Korea.

Partly, this was because of continued State Department hostility. Despite his early professions of support, Acheson was privately skeptical about the whole idea. As he later put it, "We were really making a lot out of nothing, and I tried to blow it up so it had more intellectual content than even I thought it really had." By the spring of 1950, White House aide George Elsey, weary of Acheson's foot-dragging, sniped, "It seems to me that a 'bold new program' is necessary to get our bold new program out of the mud."

The principal resistance to Point Four, however, came from Congress. Led by conservative senator Robert Taft, the Republicans castigated the program as a "global WPA" and an "international boondoggle." When conservative

Democrats seconded the GOP complaints, the administration was forced to slash its already modest Point Four request by $10 million. Point Four was finally signed into law on June 5, 1950, but its meager $35 million budget instantly deflated most expectations. In the words of one disheartened American diplomat, "No action by the United States could be better calculated to injure our prestige abroad."

Emaciated, unloved, Point Four seemed an orphaned initiative. Almost no one was rising to its defense any longer. No one, that is, except Nelson Rockefeller.

Preoccupied though he was with the ups and downs of IBEC, Rockefeller had not lost sight of the larger social ills he had set out to conquer when he sketched out his manifesto five years earlier. Poverty, disease, hunger: even a flourishing IBEC, it was now clear, could do little in the short term about these ills. As for his philanthropic vehicle, AIA, its already tight resources were constricted that much further by Rockefeller's single-minded drive to restore IBEC's fortunes. AIA, Rockefeller concluded, was simply too small an operation to have much of an impact; so discouraged was he by its prospects, and the financial drain it represented, that he was even contemplating shutting AIA down.

More than ever, he was convinced that "this field is a government field." More than ever, he was certain that Point Four was the answer.

In the face of congressional scorn and State Department indifference, Rockefeller had sought to identify himself even more closely with the program—and to make his commitment known to Harry Truman. Upon his return from his early-summer swing through Brazil and Venezuela, Rockefeller met on July 24 with Truman. The two men spoke about Point Four, and they spoke about Korea. The Latin Americans, Rockefeller reported, were foursquare behind the President; he suggested that the President might want to acknowledge their support in a speech. "If you just take off your hat to these people, they will be pleased," he said. "If you want me to, I could put together a few thoughts for you that might be helpful if you make such a speech."

Truman was noncommittal and suggested that Rockefeller take the idea up with Acheson, whom Rockefeller was seeing later that day. But Acheson was equally lukewarm; in the course of their conversation, the secretary deftly deflected Rockefeller's suggestion.

When he got back to New York, Rockefeller pulled out a legal pad and began setting down some thoughts. What he was writing, however, was not a speech on Korea, but something else again: a "Memorandum on Groups Subject to Communist Infiltration." "In the less industrialized countries of the world," Rockefeller wrote, "communism seems to attract supporters largely from two groups: the so-called 'intellectuals' and from among those in the low income groups. Widespread poverty, sickness and hunger naturally play into the communist agitators' hands."

Exactly what led Rockefeller to go off on this tack is unclear: there is no record that he suggested such a memo to either Truman or Acheson. But for some reason, after his meetings in Washington, Rockefeller felt compelled to underscore the strategic component of Point Four, the notion that it was the first line of defense against the Communist menace.

Whatever led him to reemphasize that rationale, Rockefeller was unquestionably playing to the tenor of the times. There was a mounting national hysteria about the Communist threat, a paranoia that the Korean War—with its imagery of Red hordes relentlessly advancing on the bastions of freedom—only heightened. The enemy was everywhere. Six months earlier, Alger Hiss, once one of the State Department's shining lights, had been sentenced to five years in prison for perjury in connection with charges he had passed secret documents to a courier for a Communist spy ring. Then, in February, a bilious, lackluster senator from Wisconsin, Joseph McCarthy, stirred a national furor by alleging that State harbored a score of "card-carrying Communists."

The emphasis on Point Four as a security measure also neatly played to the predispositions of the official who would be shepherding Point Four. Averell Harriman's years of firsthand dealing with the Kremlin had sowed in the ex-ambassador a profound distrust of the Soviets and a pervasive concern about Red expansionism. For the chronically suspicious, ever-vigilant Harriman, foreign aid—including Point Four—was just another weapon in the West's arsenal.

He was not looking for a government job: that was what Rockefeller told his White House contacts in early July when they set up his meeting with Truman. And at the time there wasn't any job to be had anyway.

But two months later, all that had changed. On September 8, the President signed an executive order creating an International Development Advisory Board. The board was to render him advice on the best ways of achieving the objectives of Point Four. Serving on this panel would be representatives of business, labor, agriculture, public health, education, and voluntary agencies. The board needed a chairman, and it would be up to Averell Harriman to find one.

So that was how Harriman came to accept Nelson Rockefeller's invitation to dinner at 810 Fifth Avenue three weeks later. Both Harriman and his host understood the evening's subtext: it was an audition. As Rockefeller vigorously proselytized for Point Four, he was, as it were, displaying his wares; all his other guests were foils and bystanders, background figures at the rehearsal. And for his part, Harriman, behind his unemotive pose, was ready to be impressed. Caught up now in Korea and a dozen other high-level crises, he was more than happy to have at least one of his burdens lifted.

A door to power had opened, and Rockefeller wasted no time hustling himself through it. Nothing gave him pause: neither his own checkered past with the Truman administration nor the utter indifference, verging on contempt, to Point Four of Acheson and the other mandarins at State, in whose hands the program's fate still rested. All Rockefeller could see were the shimmering possibilities: the prospect of bringing his bootstrap initiatives to the forefront of national policy, and the prospect that after five years in the political wilderness, he would once again have a chance to shape that policy. Not for the first time, and surely not for the last, he raced past the complications that hovered in the wings. The allure of the "inside" was impossible to resist.

The word came from Harriman that the job was his if he wanted it, and Rockefeller quickly began preparing himself for a meeting with Truman to discuss the possibility. Eager as he was to accept the position, there were certain points he felt it imperative to lay on the table with the President. He would like to take the job on a six-month basis, with the understanding that "if I feel I can't live up to his expectations I would step out." He wanted to be able to continue with his own ventures, IBEC and AIA. He wanted to view the work as nonpartisan and pledged to remain "strictly out of politics myself"—although the President should be aware of his family's long-standing Republican ties. And finally, he "would want to feel that I could come to him directly once in a while." The trump card of access, the card he had played so successfully with Roosevelt, had to be his.

He met with the President on the first of November, a day of record-breaking eighty-five-degree heat in the capital. In the course of their half hour together, he found Truman completely agreeable to all that he requested. The AIA and IBEC involvement could go on; the President would provide a confidential note expressly confirming that. And Rockefeller would be assured of access to Truman, access that would be specifically mentioned in the letter of appointment.

For Truman, the day proved eventful, and not because of his meeting with Nelson Rockefeller. That afternoon, while the President was napping at Blair House (his residence while the White House was undergoing reconstruction), he narrowly escaped assassination when two Puerto Rican nationalists opened fire on his guards in front of the building. By the time the fusillade ended, one of the would-be assassins was dead, as was one of the President's guards.

At his press conference the next afternoon, reporters clamored for details of the assassination attempt. Finally, when all the questions on the subject were spent, one of the newsmen asked about Nelson Rockefeller's visit earlier in the day.

"I asked him to become director of the implementation of the Point Four program and he said he would be very happy to do it," the President replied. "He has actually been putting Point Four in operation down in South America and he has done a wonderful job."

Asked if this meant that Rockefeller would become operating head of the program, Truman said, "It is not set up yet and the title is not settled, but what I would call him is the managing director."

In fact, the President had erred; Rockefeller had not been appointed director of anything. He was simply chairman of an advisory board. But at that point almost no one, least of all Nelson Rockefeller, was paying very much attention to the distinction.

Even before Rockefeller was formally sworn in, the State Department began maneuvering to head him off. It created something called the Technical Cooperation Administration to oversee all the technical assistance programs—agricultural, medical, educational, and engineering—the U.S. government offered to underdeveloped nations.

By setting up the TCA, State was putting in place the structure for a large aspect of Point Four—even though supposedly part of the Rockefeller committee's mandate was to come up with such a framework.

It was plain that Rockefeller had been served notice: he would not have a tabula rasa for his dreams.

When he took his new position, Rockefeller outlined, for his own benefit, the functions of the chairman. His role, he resolved, would be "very quiet, gathering information, seeing people Washington, U.N., learn what problems are, what is being done, who's in field. No suggestions . . . Relations with Board and Department very quiet and slow. Gradually crystallize ideas along with the thinking of people in key positions."

Having learned over the years, the hard way, the cost of his unbridled enthusiasm, he was struggling to rein himself in—to adopt a low-key approach that was completely at odds with his instincts. At this, he was only partly successful.

As always, he was constitutionally incapable of attacking any project without an arsenal of minds at the ready. Even his trusted standbys—Lockwood, Jamieson, Harrison—would not be enough. For a vast project such as this, a project with global reach, he needed more firepower.

And so he assembled a team of top-flight economists, plucked from academia and the private sector, who would work under Stacy May. He brought in men who had worked on the recent Hoover Commission on government reorganization and who were thoroughly conversant with the byzantine byways of the State Department. And he recruited some veteran wordsmiths, individuals who were accustomed to translating economic abstractions into politically palatable prose. Among these was the savvy political analyst and pollster Samuel Lubell.

With the U.S. government only willing to pay at the rate of $50 a day, pulling such an elite group together to work full-time on the project might have been an impossible feat—were it not for the resources of a Rockefeller. As it turned out, some number of these experts—perhaps all of them—were richly compensated out of Rockefeller's own pocket. Lubell, for one, received $5,000 from Rockefeller for his work.

To fill the role of counsel to the board, Rockefeller turned to another outsider (presumably because Lockwood was still so preoccupied with IBEC). He was Oscar M. Ruebhausen, a thirty-eight-year-old partner of Debevoise, Plimpton & McLean. Ruebhausen had some tangential connections to Rockefeller: Tom Debevoise's son was senior partner of his firm, and Ruebhausen was a Dartmouth graduate, class of 1934. But the principal link was through David Rockefeller: he and Ruebhausen saw one another a lot socially, owing to the long-standing friendship between their wives. When Nelson told his brother he was looking for a young lawyer who was experienced in Washington *and* a Democrat (to give the staff the proper bipartisan balance), David suggested Ruebhausen.

He proved to be a sterling choice. Meticulously groomed, preternaturally calm, Ruebhausen was the very model of the polished boardroom attorney. Yet he also possessed the hard-nosed practicality and the broad worldview that Rockefeller wanted in his lawyers. Ruebhausen had earned his Washington spurs during the war working for lend-lease and then as chief counsel of the Office of Scientific Research and Development, the agency charged with the initial development of the atomic bomb. His involvement with nuclear energy continued after the war: he was now chairing the New York State Bar Association committee on atomic energy. He was the rare attorney who was as comfortable in the realm of high technology as he was in the world of contracts and codicils.

With this sizable professional staff at his command, Rockefeller would seem to have enough resources for his task. But, on top of this staff, Rockefeller overlaid a whole other layer of "consultants," individuals who were part of his extended network of contacts. They included Admiral Lewis Strauss, a longtime partner of the Kuhn, Loeb investment banking firm and former member of the Atomic Energy Commission, who was now serving as a financial adviser to the Rockefeller brothers. And, to boot, there was Rockefeller's usual kitchen cabinet of thinkers: Harrison and Jamieson and Adolf Berle and Beardsley Ruml.

In all, Rockefeller had thirty-one people working, part- or full-time, on his study: people who were accomplished lawyers, bankers, economists, engineers, and educators in their own right. And that was not counting his twelve fellow members of the board.

The board was a distinguished enough group, albeit lacking anyone who could remotely rival the chairman in horsepower. The members who came closest were Harvey Firestone, the chairman of Firestone Tire and Rubber, and Rockefeller's redoubtable New York labor union ally Jacob Potofsky. There was a smattering of educators (Michigan State College president John Hannah, Virginia State College president Robert Daniel), a former Surgeon General of the United States, the president and editor of *The Progressive Farmer,* and the engineer who had been the chief designer of the Grand Coulee and Hoover dams.

Endeavoring to stick to his "very quiet and slow" game plan, Rockefeller went out of his way to accommodate the board. The members were treated royally, with their meetings often taking place at Radio City Music Hall, in the sumptuous art deco suite that Donald Deskey designed for the hall's original impresario, Roxy Rothafel. Far from being the steamroller everyone expected, Rockefeller was a paragon of restraint, cheerfully allowing each of his fellow members to run on about his or her personal hobbyhorse.

"Nelson was extraordinarily deferential to everybody," remembers Ruebhausen. "Whenever anyone spoke he would say, 'Splendid. Marvelous. Wonderful idea.' And then, 'Staff, please incorporate that in the next draft,' or 'Please take a note of that, and we'll work on it.' And I would say to myself, 'This is a stupid idea. What are we going to do with *that?*' I'd be sitting there, the newest staff person, thinking about Nelson, 'This person is not a very bright guy. He's never getting to the issues that are really crucial.' "

But Ruebhausen would see, soon enough, the cunning that lay behind Nelson Rockefeller's amiable facade.

The glimmer of insight came when the first drafts of the report, prepared by Sam Lubell, were circulated. The board members picked at this and that, until a frustrated Lubell finally snapped. "Look," he said, "I can write anything, and I can write it well, but you've got to tell me what it is you want me to write. And before I can write anything, I need some answers." He proceeded to tick off a host of unresolved questions. "Thank God," Ruebhausen remembers thinking at that moment, "someone has finally come to grips with the issues." And immediately, he recalls, "the whole commission was excited and responsive. But in conflict. And then Nelson cut in and said, 'A great deal of progress has been made and we've got lots of things to consider,' and he adjourned the meeting early."

As the board members departed, Rockefeller beckoned to his staff to stay. The doors to the Rothafel suite were closed, and Rockefeller fixed his granite gaze on Lubell. "Sam," he said, "I've been working for six months to bring this commission together, and in five minutes you've destroyed the entire work I've accomplished in six months. I never want you, ever, to do that again. Now," he sighed, "I will have to rebuild the consensus in this commission." He stood up, gathered his papers, and left the room.

"Suddenly," relates Ruebhausen, "I saw his method. I saw what Nelson was doing. He knew that if we sharpened the issues too precisely, it would be impossible for him to get a report with total concurrence; he'd get dissents. It's only by blurring the areas where they disagreed, and focusing on the areas where they could agree, that he could build a consensus."

By sidestepping controversy, and by granting his members their little victories, Rockefeller was clearing the way for a greater triumph to come. He knew, even if his fellow board members didn't, exactly where he was going.

He had known, in fact, from the very start, before a single session of his board had taken place.

Meeting with his inner core of advisers on November 16, two weeks after Truman had handed him the job, Rockefeller made it clear what *he* thought the key points of the final report should be. The report, he told the group, should aim at achieving "a dynamically expanding, interdependent world economy." It should emphasize the role of private enterprise, and point up the steps that should be taken to spur greater private investment in the underdeveloped world. And, most notably, it should call for "the centralization or coordination under an effective government agency of the U.S. foreign economic policy—the Joint Chiefs of Staff approach."

Only, he argued, through centralization, could the United States mount an effective worldwide economic offensive. The problems were just too complex, the present setup just too diffuse. There had to be a central coordinator, a single agency charged with the implementation of foreign economic policy.

And the State Department, immersed as it was in the myriad complications of Korea and the Cold War, could not be that agency. As Rockefeller put it, "The scope of the work is so great that the State Department must be relieved of the burden."

To "relieve" State, a new agency should be created. Into this new organization would be folded all the existing foreign economic agencies: the Economic Cooperation Administration, which administered the Marshall Plan; the Technical Cooperation Administration; and the Institute of Inter-American Affairs, the last artifact of the wartime CIAA, which still had its *servicios* throughout Latin America.

To underscore the importance of this new agency, its director would report directly to the President.

The actors may have changed, and the theater may have moved, but the script was a familiar one. From the talk about "coordination" to the fervent declaration that only a new agency, cutting across the existing government lines, could do the job, the production was reminiscent of one first mounted in Washington in the spring of 1940.

In 1940, it had started with a memo to Harry Hopkins. Now, a decade later, Rockefeller was employing the same device, to much the same ends—albeit this time with an official imprimatur via the International Development Advisory Board.

And was he, as in 1940, writing a job description for himself? Never, in all his conferences with his advisers, was there the barest whisper about Rockefeller's personal ambitions. Nonetheless, among his cadre of aides, the unstated assumption was, in Ruebhausen's words, that "he visualized a central agency run by someone like himself."

In the weeks that followed, Rockefeller and his advisers refined the concept of the proposed new agency—and significantly broadened its powers. Not only would it take charge of all the government's foreign assistance programs, but it would oversee the traffic in strategic goods and resources between the United States and the developing world. It would screen all requests for vital U.S. exports—seeing to it that the underdeveloped countries get essential materials—and assure America's defense forces of an ongoing supply of critical resources. Thus, it would replicate the functions of the Roosevelt administration's Office of Economic Warfare, on top of all its "do good" activities.

This concept was very much in keeping with Rockefeller's contention that Point Four was no Santa Claus program, but part and parcel of a Cold War continuum. He spoke of the interrelation of "political, psychological, economic and military aspects. Freedom and well-being can only be met if all four of these forces are used on an integrated basis in support of overall U.S. objectives."

Once in a while, in Rockefeller's private councils, a dissenting voice would be heard; usually, it was the earthy baritone of Frank Jamieson. Over and over, Jamieson warned about overemphasizing Point Four's role in the struggle against Communism. Instead, he felt the report should stress that "a dollar spent for development is worth ten dollars spent for military preparedness."

Whenever Jamieson made this point, Rockefeller would heartily agree: it fit in with his conviction that Communist influence fed on hunger and misery and that only by attacking these elemental problems could the threat be averted. "We should tone down the talk about freedom," he told his advisers early on. "Freedom is a luxury which the hungry do not worry about."

Yet as the weeks wore on, the talk about freedom continued, and the rhetoric about the East-West conflict grew ever more strident. Partly, this was because Rockefeller had Averell Harriman looking over his shoulder—specifically, Harriman's aide Richard Johnson. Johnson monitored Rockefeller's deliberations closely, even attending some of the board meetings, and his hard-line influence was palpable. "In November–early December," he reported to

Harriman, "the thinking of the Rockefeller Committee, as a group, was pretty much in the restricted terms of a more effective plan and organization to carry out economic aid for foreign development. . . . By the middle of January, thinking of the Committee began to move clearly toward more emphasis on broad U.S. strategy in regard to the East-West struggle."

Rockefeller found himself intellectually riven, torn between his grandiose development ideas and the gray imperatives of the Cold War. World events were exerting an inexorable pressure: the Korean War was continuing to escalate, and by mid-December the President had declared a state of national emergency. In the end, the Cold War emphasis won out—not simply because of Korea or because of Harriman's influence, but because Rockefeller, at heart, was a true believer in the primacy of the struggle.

He did much to evidence this belief. At one meeting of the board, a TCA official raised the question of whether the U.S. technicians in the field—the people whose role ostensibly was to render agricultural and health and sanitation advice to the developing world—should also be used for intelligence purposes. Rockefeller skirted the intelligence issue, but strongly suggested that the TCA should work closely with America's defense agencies to "support defense installations or the production of strategic and critical materials."

On another occasion, board member John Savage—the engineer who had worked on the Hoover and Grand Coulee dams—showed Rockefeller some reports he had prepared on dam-building prospects in Turkey and China. Rockefeller was impressed—so much so, he told Savage, that "I shall see that these two reports are delivered, as soon as we are through with them, to the Central Intelligence Agency." Shortly afterward, Savage was advised that a representative of the CIA's San Francisco office would soon be in touch.

Still, much of what was percolating through the board had only the faintest relationship to the Cold War and Western defense. Rockefeller was an avid booster of something called a World Development Authority: an international agency that would, in cooperation with the World Bank, help fund—through no-interest loans—vital public works projects in the developing world. He also latched on to an idea promoted by World Bank president Eugene Black for a new International Finance Corporation. Aimed at stimulating private enterprise in underdeveloped countries, the IFC would provide loans to and make equity investments in needy companies; like the WDA, it would be financed through government contributions, with the United States taking the lead role in its creation.

While all this still smacked of government handouts, Rockefeller was careful also to emphasize the role of the private sector. Only large-scale private investment, he argued, could provide the huge amounts of capital needed for development. He prodded his task forces to come up with a package of incentives, including tax breaks, that would encourage U.S. companies to make foreign investments.

It was not just personal conviction, however, that entered into his private enterprise thrust, but politics as well. If he was to sell his program to a wary Congress, he needed big business on his side.

Salesmanship, indeed, had been as much on Rockefeller's mind as substance.

"I think the time has come to work out a plan for organized promotion on the whole Point Four program," Rockefeller memoed Jamieson on December 20—when completion of the board's report was still more than two months away.

And when the talk turned to promotion, it inevitably centered on the master promoter himself. "NAR without question is the logical personage to sell Point Four to Congress, the public and business," concluded Fred Gardner, who had been put in charge of the "selling problem" by Jamieson. "He is the logical one to carry the ball in public, even though he is not a member of the Administration."

Rockefeller had been carrying the ball even before his appointment by Truman, so it was no great challenge for him to continue to do so. From the moment he accepted the chairmanship, he thought of his charter in adman's terms: the program, he would say, should combine a Democratic heart with a Republican head.

Before he had a report in his hand, before he even had a coherent set of proposals, Rockefeller was trekking to Washington to line up congressional support. He sought out such diehard Point Four foes as Senator Harry F. Byrd, Senator Eugene Millikin, and Senator Taft, and tried to win them over with arguments about the nation's defense needs. Taft, for one, was sufficiently persuaded that he agreed to review the Rockefeller group's recommendations with the President, off the record, and consider possible legislation. Given the Ohio senator's past excoriations of Point Four, it was a major concession.

But none of these efforts—with Taft, with others in Congress, with business leaders—would count for anything unless Rockefeller could sell his plan to the administration that was sponsoring it. And, as he was fast learning, that sales job would be the toughest one of all.

The first indication of just how tough it would be came in early January. Sensing that the President's men had a paucity of ideas for the State of the Union message, Oscar Ruebhausen proposed that "we might be helpful to the cause and the President if we could give him some ideas." Rockefeller thought this was a great suggestion and assigned the task to Ruebhausen and May.

A week later, Ruebhausen sent a four-page draft to Truman's general counsel, Charles Murphy, strongly reaffirming the importance of Point Four and describing it as "a new frontier" which can "promote human well-being and political and social freedom." Ruebhausen's draft also sounded the national emergency alarm: "today, the tapping of new sources of strategic materials is a matter of urgent national necessity."

But when the President stood before Congress on January 8, he made no reference to any "new frontier," no reference to Point Four. There was a cursory comment about aiding the struggling peoples of the Near East, Africa, and Asia and helping the economic growth of Latin America—but how, or why, was never explored.

Rockefeller did not have to wait long to sound out the President's true feelings. A meeting with the President had been on the schedule for weeks now, and on January 17 Rockefeller was ushered into the Oval Office.

To his great relief, Rockefeller found that Truman's enthusiasm for Point Four had not diminished in the slightest. In fact, the President was downright voluble on the subject, going on about several projects related to power and irrigation in which he had a special interest. Seeing the opportunity to test the waters on the key element of his plan, Rockefeller sketched out for Truman his idea for a single economic agency. Truman seemed to buy it. As Rockefeller related to Harvey Firestone afterward, the President "is in complete agreement as to the need for centralization in the foreign economic field." Rockefeller also tried out on Truman his World Development Authority concept. The idea was a new one to him, the President said, but it should be explored.

Rockefeller left Truman's office completely elated. "During the course of our entire conversation," he reported, "the President's comments and attitude clearly indicated his tremendous interest and faith in the Point Four program."

Soon all the gears Rockefeller had set in motion were clicking smoothly into place. His staff was churning out the initial drafts of the report, and the board members—after some quibbling about language and points of emphasis—were duly signing off on it. Every single one of the initiatives that Rockefeller and his staff had formulated was approved: the soft-loan development authority, now dubbed the International Development Authority; the IFC; the tax incentives for private business; and, most dramatically, the creation of an Overseas Economic Administration, commanding a budget of over $500 million—an agency whose chief, the overseas economic czar, would report directly to the President. The game plan Rockefeller had laid out three months earlier had been followed to the letter.

The only thorn in his side was Harriman's man, Richard Johnson, who continually hectored Rockefeller and the board to toughen up the report's anti-Communist slant. For once, Rockefeller found himself on the defensive; he bristled at the notion that he, of all people, should have his anti-Communist credentials questioned. Responding to one of Johnson's harangues, an annoyed Rockefeller suggested that it would be better if the program was *for* the people of the underdeveloped world, rather than *against* something—Communism. Johnson replied that it was indeed for something: "the dignity and freedom of the individual and the kind of life we know in the West."

After one of their set-tos, Johnson fired off a memo to Harriman insisting that the Rockefeller report should kick off an "economic offensive" against the Soviet bloc that will "eventually break the hold of Soviet imperialism." Four days later, Johnson sent a copy of his memo to Rockefeller, with this cover letter: "I gave this to Averell after your last Board meeting, and he asked me to encourage you in every way possible to move along the lines indicated."

Aside from their problems with the report's slant, Harriman's people also privately carped at some of the recommendations. The proposed IFC and International Development Authority, one aide advised Harriman, "are in the category of 'bright ideas' not at all thought through and, I suspect, politically very unpalatable."

These objections came out in the open at the February 24 meeting of Rockefeller's board, when Johnson tried to kill the development authority plan, charging that such a blatant giveaway might jeopardize support for the whole program in the executive branch and Congress. But Rockefeller refused to yield; the authority, he argued, would be the most significant feature of the report. As on every other crucial point, the board fell in line behind the chairman. The authority proposal remained.

This victory notwithstanding, Rockefeller was an experienced enough operator to see the knives that lay in wait for him in Washington. To head off his attackers, he resorted to his ultimate deterrent: a meeting with the President.

Three days later, he was in the Oval Office; Rockefeller had been given all of fifteen minutes to make his case. He warned the President that "there would be a certain number of controversial items in the report." This didn't appear to concern Truman. "If we don't reach out for something new," he replied, "we will never move forward." Reluctant to press Truman on specifics without the actual report in his hand, Rockefeller left the room with that assurance, and no other, in his pocket.

In one climactic all-night session at the Carlton Hotel in Washington, Rockefeller, his staff, and his board hammered out the final version of the report. And with them, throughout, was the baleful saber-rattler, Richard Johnson.

By then, Rockefeller had resigned himself to Johnson's influence. He knew that all the presidential pats on the back meant nothing unless he could line up the support of Johnson's boss, Truman's trusted lieutenant, Averell Harriman. Says Ruebhausen, "It was clear to me, even from my lowly position, that *Averell* was the target Nelson was working on. It wasn't the board that was a problem for Nelson; it was Averell. It was *Averell* that he was trying to persuade with his report."

The final version kept all of Rockefeller's key initiatives intact—but firmly lodged them within the strategic framework dictated by Harriman and his aides. The call to arms is sounded in the report's opening paragraphs: "The Advisory Board feels that strengthening the economies of the underdeveloped regions and an improvement in their living levels must be considered a vital part of our own defense mobilization. . . ."

Rockefeller was satisfied with the end product—and so was Richard Johnson. He dashed off this note to Harriman: "Good report completed this week. Have been able to keep Nelson Rockefeller and his Board 'on the track.' "

With his report now in hand, Rockefeller could turn his full attention to what was arguably his favorite part of the work: the sales job.

He set out to choreograph every aspect of the report's promotion, beginning with its transmission to the President. Truman was vacationing at the U.S. Naval Station at Key West, and Rockefeller intended to fly down to Florida to personally hand him the first copies of the report. Truman would then send Rockefeller an effusive letter of thanks—a letter that Rockefeller himself would compose.

Jamieson warned Rockefeller about the latter part of his plan: "It is poor taste to suggest that somebody write you a flattering letter, and to accompany it with a draft." Rockefeller, however, was insistent, and sent on to the White House a draft that expressed Truman's "deepest personal appreciation for the task which your Board has accomplished and the leadership which you have contributed to it."

White House aides signed off on the meeting with the President at Key West. But when Harriman got wind of it, he intervened. It was he, Averell Harriman, who had set the report in motion, and therefore it was he, Averell Harriman, not Nelson Rockefeller, who would present it to Harry Truman.

Rockefeller accepted the rebuff calmly: what else could he do? Packing up forty copies of the report, he dispatched them to Harriman in Washington, along with a note of thanks to Harriman for taking the trouble to deliver the report to the President.

The "Rockefeller Report," as it was quickly dubbed, was made public on March 11, and garnered page one attention across the country. As might be expected, the press zeroed in on the proposal for a giant new federal agency, commanding "billions in private capital and lesser government funds in a vast expansion of President Truman's Point Four program," in the words of *The*

New York Times. Once again—to Frank Jamieson's great annoyance—"Rockefeller" and "billions" were linked in the public mind.

"They laughed at Henry Wallace when he recommended a bottle of milk for every Hottentot," sneered the *Toledo Blade.* "Now the scion of the personifier of American capitalism is pushing the same notion—and recommending we spend $4,500,000,000 a year to put it over."

Yet the flurry of attention, pro and con, was short-lived; the nation was riveted by the far more dramatic events in Korea. The Eighth Army, in retreat since a massive Red Chinese counterattack in late November, was now on the offensive again, and was just two days away from retaking the South Korean capital of Seoul. A potential confrontation was brewing between Truman and an insubordinate Douglas MacArthur, who was openly pressing for an all-out war against Red China. Overwhelmed by the onrush of history, Rockefeller's report seemed doomed to the public policy remainder bin.

But an obscure fate was not what Rockefeller had in mind for his handiwork. Mobilizing his public relations forces, he mapped out a sweeping campaign to heighten public awareness of the report, to make his proposals the focus of a national debate. He arranged a series of speaking engagements before elite, opinion-making groups, including the Council on Foreign Relations and the Economic Club of New York. He set up a Citizen's Committee for International Development, tapping his young acolyte Tom Braden (who was already knee deep in his work with the CIA) to run it; Braden, in turn, enlisted the support of Rockefeller's old World War II nemesis, Bill Donovan, who agreed to serve on the committee.

And Rockefeller convinced Simon & Schuster to publish a paperback edition of the report, to be entitled *Partners in Progress.* Simon & Schuster's interest in the project was no doubt whetted by his willingness to purchase half of the 20,000-copy first print run, at thirty-seven cents a copy. (S&S also tried to get Rockefeller to pay for the book's advertising, but there he drew the line.) Rockefeller ended up buying 14,000 copies—nearly all of which wound up in storage at 30 Rockefeller Plaza.

On April 9, a month after the report was issued, Harriman finally got around to sending Rockefeller a congratulatory note. "I have heard nothing but favorable comment," he wrote, "and I am sure that it will have an important influence on the steps our Government will take in the future."

Those assurances notwithstanding, Rockefeller and his fellow board members would learn soon enough just how little influence they would actually have. A week after Harriman's note, they trekked to Washington to meet with various administration officials, including Assistant Secretary of State Willard Thorp. It was Thorp who, decisively and unequivocally, lowered the boom on Rockefeller's expectations.

The administration, Thorp made it clear, did not propose to set up the single Overseas Economic Administration urged in the report. As far as State was concerned, close cooperation among the existing agencies would suffice; he did not think the situation was nearly as disorderly as Rockefeller and company had painted it.

Rockefeller listened grimly to Thorp's discourse and then responded with a voice tinged with scorn. The American people, he said, were looking for a program of international development along the lines of what the President had laid out in his inaugural address. "They were confused when all they could find, in what the department referred to as Point Four, was a very limited concept of technical assistance."

"The business groups in particular," he said, with an air of dismissive authority, "are not satisfied with the present program and with the structure to carry it out."

His petulant outburst got him nowhere. State's opposition to his proposals was implacable.

While Rockefeller now had some idea of the opposition his idea for a new super-economic agency was engendering, he did not really know the full extent of it.

As soon as he received the report, Truman had forwarded copies to all the members of his cabinet. On March 16, in response, Secretary of Commerce Charles Sawyer sent the President a six-page letter that thoroughly savaged Rockefeller's idea.

A new agency, Sawyer charged, would compromise the authority of the State Department—would, in fact, humiliate the department. There would be, in effect, "two State Departments representing our government." Rockefeller's program, as a result, "will not create unity; it will create disunity."

Of equal moment was Truman's response to the Sawyer missive. "I think your analysis was a good one," he wrote the Commerce Secretary. "I am not so sure that I am in complete agreement of any further Bureaus independent of the regular Cabinet offices."

The President's foreign aid package was at last presented to Congress on May 24. Scanning the text of the presidential message, Rockefeller found that it sounded many of the same notes as his report. "The condition of the people in the underdeveloped areas would be a matter of humanitarian concern even if our national security were not involved," the President declared, in the course of calling for $400 million of economic aid for the developing world (not counting Korea)—close enough to the $500 million the Rockefeller report had requested.

But Rockefeller searched in vain for any more specific reference to his proposals. There would be no new agency created to carry out the aid program. Instead, the Economic Cooperation Administration would be in charge of the aid to most of the world, except Latin America, where economic assistance would be handled by the TCA—which would continue under State Department auspices.

Rockefeller's other proposals did not fare any better. There was no mention, in the President's message, of any incentives—tax or otherwise—to private industry for developing country investment. Nor was there any reference to the International Development Authority or the International Finance Corporation. Those ideas, as well, had ended up on the cutting-room floor.

All along, Rockefeller had known it would not be easy to get his ideas past the self-protective functionaries at State. But he had counted on the considerable influence of his White House patron, Averell Harriman, to push his proposals through. Now he knew how misplaced his confidence in Harriman had been.

Harriman was supportive enough in their meetings and frequent communications. But, in the clinches, he was completely unwilling to use his muscle to overpower the disabling force of State. His aides urged him to press the Rockefeller recommendations vigorously with the President and with Acheson. Harriman, however, elected not to do so—perhaps because he was reluctant to take on Acheson, his old Yale classmate. Adopting his customary pose of icy detachment, Harriman allowed the State Department objections to prevail.

Loath to acknowledge defeat, unwilling to walk away from his months of arduous effort, Rockefeller settled on a new strategy. If he couldn't influence the White House from the inside, then he would pressure it from the outside—through a direct appeal to the public.

And so, throughout June 1951, he barnstormed the country to plug his report, appearing at any elite venue that would have him, campaigning as indefatigably as the most ardent seeker of high office. During a West Coast swing, Rockefeller spoke at Los Angeles Town Hall, Stanford University, the San Francisco Chamber of Commerce, the San Francisco Press Club, the Portland Chamber of Commerce, and the Seattle Chamber of Commerce.

In contrast to his carefully scripted appearances of the past, he often spoke extemporaneously; it was as if he feared that any evidence of coaching, any glance at a text, might dilute the power of his message. Rambling and disjointed though they were, his speeches nonetheless had a sledgehammer eloquence and a persuasive power that was notably absent from his more polished performances. He spoke movingly about the near-starvation conditions in much of Asia, places where average food consumption was 20 percent below the UN's minimums, where the average life span was thirty years. And those, he said, "are the people upon whom we depend for seventy-three percent of the imports of our essential raw materials."*

Rockefeller also took his crusade to Congress. Armed with his usual array of charts, he testified before the House Foreign Affairs Committee. At the request of the administration, he appeared as a private citizen, not as a government representative—indicative of just how determined the White House now was to distance itself from his proposals. He came away from his Capitol Hill appearances with renewed hopes. "Frankly," he wrote the members of his advisory board, "I am more optimistic as to the outcome of a sound program in the field of international development at the present time than I have been for some months. There is real interest in Congress."

Congress *was* interested—but for peculiarly political reasons of its own.

On August 2, as Congress continued to debate the foreign aid package, Senators Alexander Smith of New Jersey and Leverett Saltonstall of Massachusetts introduced legislation to create a single cabinet-level agency that would administer all aid: military, economic, and technical. The bill was ostensibly inspired not only by Rockefeller's proposal but by a similar plan suggested by the Committee of the Present Danger, a panel of eminent private citizens chaired by Harvard president James B. Conant that was pushing for aggressive measures to meet the Soviet threat. But, in fact, its true motivation was the virulent Republican animus toward Dean Acheson. Excoriated for his support of old friend Alger Hiss, condemned for the "sellout" of China, accused of harboring Communists and fellow travelers in the State Department, blamed for the "Korean death trap" (in Joe McCarthy's words), and, not least, resented for his foppish superciliousness, Acheson was a lightning rod for all the pent-up rancor of a party long out of power.

In the face of these attacks, Truman stood staunchly by his embattled Secretary of State. Unable to dislodge Acheson, his adversaries tried the next-best thing: diluting his power. The Rockefeller and Conant reports offered an ideal mechanism to do just that.

As ardently as he hoped for a superagency, Rockefeller could not help having considerable misgivings about the congressional initiative. Aside from the bill's dubious political provenance, he found it hard to swallow the coupling of military and economic aid in the proposed agency. During his testimony in July, he had come out firmly against such a link: "I do not see how the military program can be handled efficiently by an economic agency," he

*So convincing was Rockefeller during a television appearance, on Eleanor Roosevelt's program, that Harriman was moved to write him, "Based on your performances before the cameras I think there's a great career waiting for you on TV." Seven years later, Harriman would learn, to his everlasting regret, how accurate his prophecy was. Source: Harriman to NAR, April 12, 1951, Harriman Papers Box 288, LC.

said. To mix the agency up directly in military assistance would, he believed, fatally compromise its mission in the developing world.

The White House, adamantly opposed to such a new aid setup, vowed to fight the Senate plan. But as the foreign aid bill lurched through Congress, the push for a new agency became part and parcel of the negotiations. At the end of September a compromise was reached: a new agency would, indeed, be established. Dubbed the Mutual Security Administration, it would take over from the Economic Cooperation Administration in Europe and would control all U.S. foreign aid, military and economic, throughout the world—with the exception of the Point Four technical assistance programs, which would remain in State Department hands.

While the new agency had a passing skeletal resemblance to the organism Rockefeller had envisioned, its animating spirit was utterly different. As one analyst pointed out, the difference between the old ECA and the MSA is "the difference between economic recovery and military preparedness." Economic development was purely an afterthought. The MSA's principal thrust was not to advance the well-being of the developing world, but to dole out the funds needed to maintain free world security. It would have nothing, really, to do with Point Four, which would remain in State Department purdah.

Far from a victory for Rockefeller's ideas, the congressional compromise was a disheartening convolution of them.

If the MSA was light-years away from Rockefeller's conception, it was totally compatible with Averell Harriman's.

He had, after all, always seen military and economic aid as two sides of a single coin. All along, through his aides, he had prodded the Rockefeller panel to view their mandate in terms of the East-West confrontation. To Harriman, the new agency was not a perversion, as it was to Rockefeller, but a useful, inevitable crystallization of policy.

It was hardly unexpected, then, that in the talk about who would run the MSA one name came to the fore: Averell Harriman. Or that on October 10, Truman confirmed the speculation and named Harriman the new foreign aid czar.

Thus, in a matter of weeks, Rockefeller not only saw his proposals contorted or abandoned, but witnessed his supposed protector—the man who had stood by impassively while the twisting and gutting was going on—amble in to triumphantly pick up the pieces.

His only thought now was to resign.

He phoned Potofsky and asked if the union boss was free for lunch. They met at Longchamps, and there Rockefeller broached his intention to quit the board. "We discussed the handling of the resignation," Potofsky remembered.

Potofsky's principal concern was "to make sure that there was no scandal attached to the Truman administration as a result of that resignation."

Rockefeller, however, wasn't sure he *didn't* want to make an issue of his resignation: to use it to call attention to the administration's shoddy handling of the report and to the uncertain fate of Point Four.

In the end, it was not Potofsky who dissuaded Rockefeller from creating a cause célèbre, but John Lockwood. The attorney doubted that a noisy resignation "would be advancing the cause which caused you to accept the nomination in the first place. My instinctive feeling is that you would run a greater risk of harming that cause by making the public more confused than it is now about the whole subject and thereby of torpedoing what there is in the way of foreign aid."

Heeding Lockwood's advice, Rockefeller settled on a tepid resignation letter. He was stepping down, he would explain to the President, because his assignment was completed, and because "I feel I can now best serve the program of international economic development by again concentrating on the role of private initiative in this field of international cooperation."

On October 31, he went to the White House to personally hand the letter to Harry Truman.

Rockefeller departed the Point Four committee with his reputation and his honor intact. The press did not probe the reason for his resignation, choosing to accept at face value his explanation that he merely wanted to return to the private sector. Only Rockefeller, his intimates, and a small cadre of White House aides comprehended the full extent of his failure and frustration. Only that small circle understood how far short he had fallen.

It was a quiet debacle, a debacle that stirred hardly a ripple in official Washington—but a debacle nonetheless. And for this unhappy outcome, Nelson Rockefeller, at bottom, had no one but himself to blame.

Once again—as in IBEC and, earlier, in the Argentine fiasco—Rockefeller was a victim of his own unwavering enthusiasm. Indomitably determined to push through an agenda and a program, he blinded himself to the larger realities.

From the outset, he had misjudged the administration's enthusiasm for Point Four, forgetting the program's haphazard genesis (as a last-minute stopgap in a presidential speech) and misreading the depth of the White House's commitment—particularly the depth, and nature, of Averell Harriman's commitment.

He then compounded his difficulties by fastening upon the most politically nettlesome idea imaginable: the creation of an entirely new cabinet-level agency. The proposal totally failed to take into account the volatile swirl of jealousies and allegiances in an embattled administration. No matter how neutrally the idea was framed, it could not but be seen as a reproach to

Acheson and a diminution of his authority. Given those circumstances, and given his unswerving loyalty to his Secretary of State, there was no way Truman would ever endorse Rockefeller's prescription.

There was also the not inconsiderable obstacle of the program's price tag. Despite Rockefeller's zealous efforts to highlight the private-sector aspects, media attention was bound to be focused on a new, big-budget agency: the developing world's Santa Claus. Inevitably, his other proposed creations, the World Bank-administered IFC and IDA, would be seen as part of the give-away, and assailed as such by Congress.

But Rockefeller's most fundamental error was his misreading of the national mood. Caught up in the state of emergency proclaimed by the President, mesmerized by the fulminations of Joe McCarthy, the country couldn't care less about broad-gauge development issues. Rockefeller's attempts to dress up his report in martial garb—with all the talk about stemming Communist inroads in the developing world—were for naught. Despite his energetic salesmanship, any semblance of a meaningful constituency for his proposals—even among the businessmen and intelligentsia to whom he directly appealed—was lacking.

He felt if he could present his case to an informed public, his program could be saved. The informed public, however, had other things on its mind.

Despite the Rockefeller Report's quick interment, the Point Four program was hardly extinct. Though a far cry from the grandiose operation Rockefeller envisaged, the program, under the Technical Cooperation Administration, continued to dispense advice, training, and assistance in thirty-five countries. And the TCA set the stage for a similar, much more ballyhooed initiative a decade later: the Kennedy administration's Peace Corps.

What's more, in time several of Rockefeller's proposals would be exhumed and take on new life in a less hostile environment. The IFC and IDA ideas were dusted off in the late 1950s, and both became (and still are) important elements of the World Bank's operations.

In years to come, then, Rockefeller could savor some small measure of vindication.

But in November 1951 all there was was the acrid taste of his failed dream, and the galling reminder that he remained on the outer edge of influence.

Twenty-eight

DIVERSIONS

When his Point Four report was first issued back in March, Rockefeller toasted the event with caviar and champagne at his apartment. The celebration, however, was a very private one—with only one guest, one of his assistants at IBEC, who happened to be a comely, long-legged, twentyish lady friend. And the apartment was not his art-filled residence at 810 Fifth Avenue, but another one Rockefeller kept eight blocks south, in a stolid limestone townhouse on 54th Street.

There was much that could be said about this apartment, and much more that could—and would—be said about the young lady Rockefeller was sharing champagne with that evening.

The townhouse, at 13 West 54th Street, had figured before in Rockefeller family history. Erected in 1896, along with its next-door twin at number 15, it was Junior and Abby's first New York residence after their marriage. Three of their first four children (Nelson excepted) were born there. Four stories high, with a steep flight of steps leading from the street to the front door, the building was distinguished by the ornate stone scrollwork over the windows and the barrel-like facade of the lower two floors, creating an impression of solidity and permanence well suited to a Rockefeller domicile.

The house was conveniently just across the street from John D. Senior's brownstone, and, in fact, it was Senior who purchased the property for his son. Junior added various improvements, including an Otis elevator, a central vacuum-cleaning system, and, later, a new top floor to accommodate a playroom and nurses' quarters for his growing family. A visitor remembered the house as "a very homey place, with a big lion's skin rug on the ground floor as you came in the front door." But as comfortable as he was with it, by 1910

Junior felt the house was no longer adequate to his needs. Two years later he began construction across the street of the immense nine-story mansion that would be his city residence for most of the next three decades.

But he did not dispose of 13 West 54th. Perhaps Junior kept the property for sentimental reasons; more likely, it fit his pattern of holding all the real estate he could get his hands on in the vicinity, a pattern that proved supremely wise when Rockefeller Center was later developed. Rather than let the structure lie fallow, he converted it into an apartment building, and so it remained through the early 1940s. While hardly the neighborhood's most distinguished apartment dwelling (that distinction belonged to the Rockefeller Apartments Nelson had built just down the block), the building was soundly upper-middle-class. Apartments rented for the then-pricey rate of $150 a month, with "valet and maid service available."

Nelson had his eye on the building for years, and in 1944 queried his father about donating it to the Museum of Modern Art, whose rear garden occupied the site of the now demolished family mansion across the way. Junior wasn't interested, but Nelson persisted. In June 1946, he brought up the matter again with his father; this time, though, Nelson wanted it not for MOMA, but for himself. Exactly what he told his father about his proposed use of the building is not known; no doubt, it had something to do with his need for more space for his new enterprises. Whatever his arguments were, they were instantly persuasive. Three weeks later, Junior agreed to give Nelson 13 West 54th. Nelson gratefully wrote his father that the property "means a great deal to me for two reasons: first, because of its family associations, and secondly, because of its usefulness."

Now that he was the owner, Nelson moved rapidly to evict the current occupants. (One aggrieved tenant complained to the family office that "Mr. Nelson Rockefeller . . . seeks to put me and other tenants in the street so that he may realize some vaguely defined cultural purpose.") But on that front, there were limits to even what a Rockefeller could accomplish; it would be five years before the last of the tenants were out.

Initially, he kept some of the private apartments for the use of young aides, like Tom Braden, who needed living space. But over time, the townhouse was rebuilt (under Wally Harrison's supervision) to suit Rockefeller's purposes: part office space, part pied-à-terre.

On the second floor, he outfitted a dining room, for the benefit of his own private luncheon club, whose only other members were his brothers, Harrison, Beardsley Ruml, and Adolf Berle. "The theory," noted Berle in his diary, "is that anybody can drop in to lunch there and discuss a few subjects from time to time. Nobody is to be invited as lunch guests without the consent of two members." The idea, said Berle, was to create "a center for a very small and singularly esoteric group of serious thinkers"—albeit thinkers "whose tangential contacts run into many billions of dollars." They would discuss everything from the philosophy of the Rockefeller Foundation "to drilling oil wells or making fresh water out of sea water and irrigating the Sahara Desert"—and afterward, in a nice homespun touch, gather in the kitchen to wash the dishes. Eventually, the co-conspirators landed on an appropriate nickname for their meeting place: "Cell 13."

But there was one part of 13 West 54th that was even more exclusive. Decorated with plush furniture arranged around a fireplace, bathed in soft light, this was the sanctuary of the owner: a place for beluga and champagne, and an evening *à deux* with certain guests.

Rockefeller had acquired the townhouse on 54th Street for office space and for his gatherings of "serious thinkers." But he had also acquired it for this.

As Rockefeller that evening laid out the accompaniments—the small bowls of chopped egg and chopped onion, the lemon wedges and toast points—his guest confessed that she had never eaten caviar before. Nor, she said, had she ever had champagne. Rockefeller seemed vastly amused by this admission; it fit in so neatly with her frequent assertions that she was just an unsophisticated, untutored waif out of Anderson, Indiana.

Those who worked with her in Rockefeller's office would also have been amused. For Joan Braden, née Joan Ridley, was, in their estimation, anything *but* the corn-fed ingenue she made herself out to be.

She had certainly grown up in genteel enough circumstances. Her maternal grandfather was the town banker, prosperous enough to send young Joan off to a California vacation every winter with her mother and grandmother, and her father served as the bank's president and later worked for General Motors. Like other young ladies of means, she was enrolled in a horsey finishing school, going on from there to Northwestern University. By then, she was also enjoying the advantages of her sprightly good looks. As a college homecoming queen, she traveled to the Kentucky Derby in a private railway car, finding herself doted on by middle-aged executives eager to explain to her the principles of sound business.

She spent the summer before her senior year in a volunteer program in Mexico, learning Spanish and digging latrines in the villages. One of her fellow student volunteers was Jean Wallace, the Vice President's daughter. When Wallace, as the daughter of the esteemed Henry Wallace, was invited one day to attend a reception the Mexican President was throwing for the visiting Coordinator of Inter-American Affairs, she asked her friend Joan Ridley to come along. There, Ridley met Nelson Rockefeller for the first time. "I spoke to him for maybe two minutes," she recalls. But Ridley remembered that encounter two years later when, newly arrived in New York, she leaned out the window of her apartment and mused on what she would do in the big city. She would, she resolved, go to work for Nelson Rockefeller.

Ridley phoned Room 5600, and was put in touch with one of Rockefeller's secretaries, who informed her there was an opening: Mr. Nelson was looking for someone to file the papers he had just brought back from Washington. But a file clerk job was not what Ridley had in mind; with her economics degree from Northwestern and fluency in Spanish, she thought she could do better for herself. Ridley turned the offer down. A week later, she picked up the phone in her apartment, and found Nelson Rockefeller on the other end. "He said he understood why I didn't want this job, and would I like to reconsider," she relates. "He understood why I thought this was boring, but he was sure if I came that within a month or so there would be other things. Somehow, with people like that it's hard to say no. So I said yes."

Whether it was Ridley's résumé that sparked Rockefeller's intervention or some recollection of her charms, the young lady soon found herself installed in Rockefeller's corner suite, with her desk directly in front of Louise Boyer's. Each morning, on his way in, Rockefeller would playfully rumple Ridley's short auburn hair. "It was friendly," she says, "without being . . ." She lets the phrase hang. "He would stand by my desk and laugh. So we sort of became friends quickly."

When Boyer took a month off after her remarriage in 1947, Rockefeller asked Ridley to fill in—sorting through his mail, juggling his phone calls, minding his schedule. Determined to arrive in the office before her boss, Ridley took to coming in earlier and earlier—only to find that no matter how early she showed up, Rockefeller was always in ahead of her. "It drove me nuts," she recalls. "So one day I got in at seven, and he was already there, and he laughed, and said, 'Don't you think we ought to stop this? Why don't I stop at your house and we'll walk down together?' So we did."

"It was about this time," she says, "that I started calling him Nelson."

Ridley was hardly the first secretary with whom Rockefeller had struck up an extraprofessional relationship.

During the war there was his rather intimate friendship with Janet Barnes, his Aldrich cousin (by marriage), a relationship that so alarmed the family that they felt compelled to intervene.

Then there was Susan Cable.

Like Ridley, Cable had had an affluent midwestern upbringing (her father was a stockbroker, and the Cables' circle included Stephen Clark, the Woolworth heir and former MOMA chairman). And, like Ridley, Cable had a command of Spanish, a talent that (abetted by her family connections) earned her a position in the coordinator's office when she was eighteen. By the time Rockefeller had moved on to the State Department, Cable was his number one secretary, accompanying him to the Chapultepec and UN conferences; it was Cable who took dictation during the meeting between Rockefeller and Arthur Vandenberg that resulted in Article Fifty-one.

Almost from the beginning, there was a personal flavor to their relationship. "Certainly, in the early years, I was surrogate daughter and he was surrogate father," Cable—now Susan Herter—recalls. "Here was a young thing that didn't know what the hell she was doing, and he was so very nice and protective." She came to regard him as her "best friend . . . he certainly shaped my life more than anybody else."

But over the years she drew down a discreet curtain whenever anyone tried to probe further into the connection. "A lot that has been said about a lot of people is not true," Cable remarks, "and I don't want to get more specific than that."

Upon Rockefeller's return to New York after the war, Cable found her role altered. Professionally, she was soon eclipsed by Louise Boyer, and personally, some felt, by Joan Ridley. She was assigned to handle Rockefeller's dealings with MOMA, and in December 1948 she left his employ. "I think I resigned," she says, "but in retrospect I'm not sure I wasn't fired. By that time there were a lot of other people in there, and I think I was very cross that instead of being the only person, there were all these other people in there." Yet her loyalty to Rockefeller was unshaken, as was, in his fashion, his to her. "In that kind of a relationship," Herter says, "of course there's enormous affection and gratitude and respect. And probably lots of problems too. But he always tried to keep everybody in his orbit."

While there may have been whispers about Susan Cable, she was never regarded with suspicion by Rockefeller's palace guard. Not so with Joan Ridley.

There was something about Ridley's manner—at times wide-eyed, at times coquettish—something sensually *insinuating* that set the antennae quivering, particularly those of the other females in the office. "Joan was a very pretty young girl, a very sexy young girl with a beautiful bosom," remembers one woman who worked for Rockefeller in those years. "She wore clothes that were provocative, and she had a manner about her that was very provocative, there was no question about it."

Says another, "I disliked her. I just felt she was deceitful. Oh, we were pleasant enough with each other, but there was just something about Joan I didn't like."

Among her office mates, there was a tendency to view Ridley as the encircling vulture—and Rockefeller as her innocent, unsuspecting prey. "I thought he was quite moral," recollects one of his female subordinates. "In the office, he was absolutely dignified, and there was just no sign that he liked the girls. I would defend him against a lot of the rumors. When someone would say something, I'd say, 'No, it isn't so.' "

"I worked very closely with him for maybe seven years," says Bill Alton, "and I never, ever thought that he was playing around."

Yet Ridley would later insist that it was Rockefeller who was always the instigator—although she was hardly an unwilling subject. His initial overtures were innocent enough. "One night he said to me, 'Would you like to go to the Modern and meet schoolteachers from around the country? Tod can't come.' I said I'd be delighted."

Then, one night, when they were working late, Rockefeller asked if they might go back to her apartment for dinner. Ridley was agreeable, even though it turned out that all she had in the cupboard was a box of shredded wheat. Rockefeller was unfazed; as he wolfed down the shredded wheat, he pronounced it the best he had ever eaten.

A few days later, he expressed his intention of reciprocating her hospitality. Thus began their evenings at the house on 54th Street.

They were there early one night, when, as Ridley would later tell the story, she informed him that she had to go to a party. Might she use his shower? By all means, he replied. She was busily showering when the curtain suddenly parted and an unclothed Rockefeller stepped in to join her. She leaped out of the tub, trailing a puddle of water, grabbing for a towel, while her accommodating host stood there laughing.

Maybe, she would later opine, taking a shower in Rockefeller's apartment was not such a good idea. "Hindsight and experience tell me that alone with a man, a woman who decides to take a shower is asking for trouble. She is being suggestive. She wants him to respond. Nelson did."

But, she goes on, "the fact is that on that particular evening, taking a shower was as natural as saying may I use your bathroom? I was innocent. I was not being suggestive. The innocence was."

The innocently suggestive Ridley found herself further shocked when Rockefeller leaned over to her in the office one day and said, "Joanie, I want you to know that Tod and I have an agreement that we will never get divorced but will live our own separate lives."

"Why are you telling me this?" Ridley asked.

"Because," said Rockefeller, "we're working together, and I think working together and sleeping together are the same thing. They're part of a whole."

Rockefeller's erotic equation "horrified" her, she would later say. "I was so young then, so deep in my belief in the institution of marriage. And he had children."

He continued to coax her. They had, she says, "long conversations" on the subject, in the course of which she maintained that "nice girls don't sleep with men who were married to somebody else and married men shouldn't be trying to get them to do so."

"Nelson laughed," she says.

Then it happened that, in a rare moment away from Rockefeller, Ridley met his young protégé Tom Braden. Before long Ridley and Braden were seeing each other, and she felt compelled to inform Rockefeller of this new turn in her love life. "He was furious," she recalls. "It showed a side of him that I had never seen. Whenever Nelson was mad, his eyes would get very deep-eyed, and they became very small. It was almost scary."

"Goddamn it," Rockefeller fumed, "you'll marry him."

Which, soon enough, was what happened. It was during one of their 54th Street rendezvous that Ridley informed Rockefeller of her engagement to Tom Braden—who, of course, was occupying another apartment in the same townhouse at the time, thanks to Rockefeller's largesse.

"Fortunately," she says, "the walls were thick," because Rockefeller did not exactly express his felicitations. "How could you do this?" he hollered. Then, she says, he proceeded to mutter threats: " 'I'll send him to Mexico, I'll send him to Rome, I'll see that Tom never gets another job, I'll do this, I'll do that.' I was scared." When she told her fiancé later about the threats, he shrugged them off. "Don't be silly," Braden said. "It's not going to happen."

On December 18, 1948, Joan Ridley and Tom Braden were married. Rockefeller, who had managed to regain his composure, attended the wedding.

He acted, in fact, as though the marriage had never taken place. Not only did he continue to employ the couple (Joan worked with him on IBEC, Tom represented him at MOMA); he continued to invite her to after-hours meetings at 54th Street—invitations she readily accepted.

Tom Braden put up with those get-togethers, but was pushed to the limits of marital tolerance when his wife came home one day with a watch encased in a gold bracelet: a little gift from Nelson. "I was furious," Braden recalls. "I spent two or three days in mind-searing jealousy because of it."

"I got over it pretty fast, thank God." Joan, with his assent, kept the watch.

His wife's relationship with Rockefeller "did worry me from time to time in the first year of our marriage," Braden now says. "Although I'm reluctant to admit it, even now." Thinking back on it, he suspects it was one reason why he eagerly snapped up Bill Donovan's offer to leave Rockefeller's employ and go to work on the Committee for a United Europe. Says Braden, "It may have entered my head when I went to work for Donovan that it would be a good idea for me to get out of this inevitably jealousy-making relationship."

He got out—but his wife stayed in. And the whispers continued.

Asked four decades later about her relationship with Nelson Rockefeller, Joan Braden snarls at the rumors that have pursued her all those years.

"I've heard how much he wanted to marry me," she says. "There are people who are actually saying that one of my children is *his* child. You'd just look at him and you'd see it isn't true." (She does admit to phoning Rockefeller from the hospital the evening the child—her oldest, David—was born. Rockefeller would be the boy's godfather.)

But when she is pressed on the question of just how intimate she was with Rockefeller—whether, in the course of all those quiet evenings on West 54th Street, their relationship was ever physically consummated—she issues something less than an absolute denial. "I don't know what you mean by 'intimate.' We had a close relationship, certainly. I never really thought of him as being Nelson Rockefeller. I just adored working with him and talking to him and being with him." She is at a loss, she says, to find the proper term for their relationship. "It really is something different than friendship, and it's something different than affair, and . . . it's difficult." Asked if they were lovers, she replies, "Certainly not in the standard sense."

The persistence of Joan Braden's presence—the sense that, marriage or no marriage, she was still circling over her quarry—distinctly troubled Rockefeller's palace guard. "She became a problem," recalls someone who worked for him during that period. "The story was that she had an unrequited passion, and people worried that she was going to make *claims* or something." That the exact opposite might be the case—that it was Rockefeller who was the pursuer—was still, to most of his loyal retinue, a completely implausible notion.

Much as they may have wanted her to disappear, Joan Braden stuck around, as did her husband, Tom. Although he no longer worked for Rockefeller, Tom kept in touch with his former boss during his tenure at the CIA. Braden once tried to involve Rockefeller in an agency front operation, and Rockefeller was eager to do it, until an appalled Frank Jamieson stepped in and told Braden to get lost. "He accused me of dealing behind his back," says Braden.

When Braden, in 1954, decided to leave the CIA and try his hand at newspaper publishing, Rockefeller was there once again to help out. The *Oceanside Blade Tribune,* a small Southern California newspaper, was for sale for $500,000, and Braden approached Rockefeller about putting up $80,000. Overcoming a long-standing family scruple about investing in the media ("Father has always asked us not to invest in publications," he told Braden), Rockefeller agreed to put up the money. "Tom," he said, "I'll help you any way I can." A year later, with the paper in financial trouble, Braden went to Rockefeller again—or rather, Joan Braden did. Over a private picnic lunch with Rockefeller, she broached her husband's problems—and came away with another $50,000.

Rockefeller's involvement in Braden's paper was kept secret; to disguise his ownership, his stock was transferred to his relatively obscure do-good operation, AIA. Not until twenty years later, under the glare of scrutiny during his vice presidential confirmation, would Rockefeller's aid to Braden—and the deliberate camouflaging of it—finally, and embarrassingly, become known.

(Braden sold the paper in 1966 for $1.6 million. A year later, he showed up in Albany to deliver a check to Rockefeller repaying his investment with interest. Rockefeller was puzzled. "Why did Tom pay back that money?" he asked Joan over lunch a week later. "Nobody else ever has.")

While Tom went on to make a name for himself in journalism, Joan achieved a peculiarly Washingtonian renown as a hostess and favorite dinner companion of the rich and powerful, an intimate of the Kennedys and consort to such luminaries as Joseph Alsop and Robert McNamara. She became a contemporary Madame de Staël: a woman who lured the most influential figures of the age to her salon, attracting them with the bounty of her table, the spiritedness of the company, and, not least, the mystique of her sensuality. As Braden herself would write, "Men assume, I don't know why, that I must know all these mysteries and techniques that are said to touch the passions." And the fountainhead of this mystique would be her enduring relationship with Nelson Rockefeller.

Her protestations of innocence notwithstanding, there are those who suggest that Joan Braden adroitly cultivated the innuendos. A magazine editor remembers going to a party at Pocantico and walking around the grounds with Braden. "She pointed out a cupola, and said to me, 'This is where Nelson and I would have our romantic interludes.' I didn't know what to make of it. I suppose she was trying to impress me."

Whether there were, indeed, "romantic interludes" or whether, as Rockefeller loyalists would have it, Braden was simply making the most of an unrequited passion, certain facts about the relationship are virtually indisputable. First, that Rockefeller and Braden spent a great deal of time in one another's company, both before and immediately after her marriage. And second, that the liaison, whatever form it ultimately took, transcended the normal bounds of a working relationship (unless one considers after-hours rendezvous over caviar and champagne in a private apartment just a normal working day).

Vamp or naif, seductress or seduced, Joan Braden offered Rockefeller something he could not find in his other apartment eight blocks to the north.

Not that there weren't plenty of other diversions.

Rockefeller was as assiduous a collector as ever, often taking Joan Braden with him on his gallery-hopping rounds. "He would pick out pictures that weren't particularly valuable but were ones that he liked," she recalls. So large was his collection becoming (it numbered some 240 pieces by then) that he retained an expert, Carol Uht, to catalogue it. Uht would later serve as his full-time curator.

Making his way up Madison Avenue on a Saturday, Rockefeller would stop in at favorite galleries and pick up a Henry Moore sculpture here, a Picasso drawing there, as casually as ordinary folk might acquire socks and suspenders. Visiting dealer Sidney Janis one Saturday afternoon, Rockefeller had finished making some purchases in Janis' back room and was on his way out when the dealer stopped with him in front of a large Jackson Pollock hanging in the front of the gallery. "There's something for your collection," Janis said. Rockefeller sized up the canvas, said "You're right," and snapped up the picture on the spot.

As always, much of his collecting was keyed to his symbiotic relationship with the Museum of Modern Art. Alfred Barr was his unofficial agent, sniffing out finds in the market—in the hopes that Rockefeller, in due course, would donate the pieces to the museum. On one occasion, when Rockefeller failed to land a $6,500 Braque that he wanted, Barr located another work by the artist. It cost more than twice as much, but Barr urged Rockefeller to buy it, because, the curator confessed, "it is quite unlike any Braque in the museum collection."

And, along with his fellow trustees, Rockefeller cannily learned to take advantage of the promotional cachet of MOMA: the likelihood that once works were exhibited by the museum, their value would skyrocket. Prior to the opening of MOMA's first major exhibition of Abstract Expressionism in 1952, he acquired seven of the paintings, including three de Koonings, a Motherwell, and a Gorky. Thanks to the MOMA hoopla, their value quickly soared.

Yet Rockefeller was no slave to artistic fashion. He had come to trust his own taste, to watch for the jolt of aesthetic pleasure that a favorite work gave him. While he avidly acquired the Abstract Expressionists, for instance, he had no use for Surrealists like Dali and Magritte; they were too "intellectual" for him. "I like strong, simple painting without a message," he would explain. "I'm not very excited about complicated psychological problems as presented in painting. I prefer stronger, simpler things." For that very reason—because of the strength and simplicity of the medium—Rockefeller found himself acquiring more and more sculpture.

Aside from Barr and his loyal longtime deputy Dorothy Miller, Rockefeller now had someone else at the museum looking out for him: René d'Harnoncourt. A garrulous, hulking six-foot-six-inch Viennese whose special expertise was American Indian folk art, d'Harnoncourt had helped Rockefeller put together exhibitions for the coordinator's office. Enthusiastic about d'Harnoncourt's eye, as well as about his silken diplomatic skills, Rockefeller brought him to MOMA in 1944. Five years later, Rockefeller engineered d'Harnoncourt's appointment to the long-vacant position of museum director.

Thanks largely to d'Harnoncourt's enthusiastic prodding, Rockefeller vastly expanded his holdings of primitive and pre-Columbian art. "Nelson loved nothing better than to go around with René at any off moment they could get together and buy in the primitive field," remembers old MOMA hand Porter McCray. "And Nelson's beautiful collection of Mexican folk art was largely the work of René."

"When Nelson was tired," recalls former MOMA trustee Eliza Cobb, "he used to call up René and tell him he needed to pull himself together again, so René would bring up some primitive art, something he hadn't seen yet. And looking at it would reinvigorate him."

Rockefeller found everything about art supremely relaxing: the buying of it, the viewing of it, even the hanging of it. One of his favorite weekend pastimes was to walk around his apartment, hammer in hand, front pockets bulging with nails and picture hooks, rearranging the display of his collection. His nephew James Wallis remembers helping him one morning lift a very heavy Picasso. "It was an eighth of an inch mishung, and it was bothering him, he told me, for several months, but he hadn't had time to rehang it. So in go the nails into some beautiful paneling on the wall. Fortunately, my aunt wasn't around to raise hell."

He became so proficient at picture hanging that he offered his services to friends. "When I moved into this building in 1950," says Cobb, "he came and hung all my pictures for me. He should have been a curator, you know. He could have installed a whole show all by himself."

Another of his extravagant diversions was sailing. His deficiencies as a seaman did not crimp his style; as keen as ever about the sport, Rockefeller poured more and more money into augmenting and outfitting his little armada of luxury vessels.

As a Christmas present one year, he gave Tod a boat: a seventy-one-foot racing yacht they named the *Nirvana.* He had purchased it from their old Northeast Harbor friend Hal Haskell, who had competed with it in several Bermuda races. Adding some amenities, Rockefeller turned the *Nirvana* into more of a cruising than a racing vessel (although Rodman and Steven would later race it). "She was very large," remembers Wallis. "You needed a captain or two on board." The *Nirvana* was Rockefeller's second racing yacht; he still owned the *Queen Mary,* the International One Design yacht he had ordered from Norway in the late 1930s.

Far and away the most unusual vessel in Rockefeller's little fleet was a surplus Royal Navy minesweeper and coastal patrol boat, stripped of its military hardware and converted into a pleasure yacht. He christened it the *Dragon Lady,* after the femme fatale in the comic strip "Terry and the Pirates."

During the Northeast Harbor races in July and August, Rockefeller used the *Dragon Lady* as a tender, with as many as twenty guests sleeping on board. "It was very comfortable," recalls one guest. "We would race all day and all get together at night." In the mornings, the smell of sizzling bacon would rouse his shipmates; on deck, with his stove set up on the circular platform that once swiveled the antiaircraft battery, they would find Nelson Rockefeller, wielding his spatula.

While his neighbors in Maine caught these glimpses of Rockefeller's unabashed lifestyle, it was only in his New York City residence at 810 Fifth Avenue that the grandeur achieved full flower.

Even though his ménage now sprawled over three full floors of 810 Fifth, there was never enough room for all his art. Whole walls were lined with showcases displaying his burgeoning collection of primitive works: African necklaces, Inca feather headdresses, pre-Columbian stone figures. Elsewhere in the triplex Italian Futurist masterworks vied with Cubist paintings for scarce space in his rotating exhibition.

The apartment's top floor was a penthouse—reached from the rest of the apartment by a staircase—which Rockefeller had turned into a private study. When he realized that a stone balustrade blocked his view of Central Park from his desk, he had a raised platform built over the normal flooring. With that bit of elevation, he and his guests could now enjoy the verdant panorama.

Rockefeller would indeed go to considerable lengths to guard his views. Directly across the street from 810 Fifth Avenue, on the south side of 62nd Street, was the Knickerbocker Club, one of the city's most elite private clubs. Its Georgian limestone and red brick clubhouse, designed by Delano & Aldrich, the same firm that had produced Kykuit, was considered one of the city's architectural gems. But in the postwar years financial problems began to plague the hoary institution, and there was talk that the club might find relief only by vacating the premises and selling it off to any number of developers who covetously eyed the choice Fifth Avenue corner site.

This was very bad news for Rockefeller. The last thing he wanted to see was the classic old clubhouse demolished to make way for a monumental high-rise—a high-rise that would cut off his views to the south, and much of his daylight. As a member of the club, he was well aware of the institution's financial plight and knew that the only way out might be the sale of the clubhouse. Determined to head off the developers, Rockefeller took the only course of action that, to him, made sense.

He bought the Knickerbocker Club himself.

By 1953, title to the Georgian mansion had passed into his hands. The club remained there, the membership preserved forevermore from any threat to their exclusive haven—and Nelson Rockefeller preserved forevermore from any threat to his views.

As exacting and as self-indulgent as he was in the grander aspects of his life—his homes, his boats, his art—Rockefeller exhibited a strange indifference to other matters of personal taste. His clothes were as rumpled and ill-fitting as ever. Jacob Potofsky, the clothing workers' union boss, was so appalled by the condition of Rockefeller's attire that he once offered to take up a collection for him.

Rockefeller was equally insensible in matters of fine dining. "Nelson had no taste in foods whatever," says his former public relations aide Kershaw Burbank. "He loved to work through lunch, and whether we were in his office or on his plane, he'd say, 'We'll have something served in here.' And it was always a tuna fish sandwich. Whether it was on the plane or anywhere else." Eventually, Frank Jamieson was heard to moan, "You know, I could stand it, I could live through that tuna fish sandwich if only Nelson every day wouldn't turn around with a broad grin and say, 'Isn't it great, Frankie?' "

His fellow MOMA trustee Edward Warburg once experienced a full dose of Rockefeller obliviousness when Nelson invited him to a game of tennis at Pocantico. "The first thing I noticed," recollects Warburg, "was that the court was in the most shocking shape. It hadn't been groomed in weeks. And secondly, the balls that they were using had obviously just been taken away from the dogs. There wasn't any nap left on them. And so I said, 'Nelson, look, if you don't mind, before we play, you grab hold of one side of this roller, and I'll grab hold of the other, and let's roll this court.' 'Yeah,' he said, 'it does need it. The gardener's been away for a while.' And then I said, 'I've got a special present for you: six new tennis balls. The ones you're playing with—Nelson, give those back to the Smithsonian.' "

Warburg was in for another surprise when he went to shower in the Playhouse afterward. "There was only one faucet in the shower: cold," he says. "Somehow I felt that they could have gotten a second pipe in there."

Rockefeller's chronic indifference to mundane necessities extended, as well, to the matter of pocket money. His wallet was as empty now as it was in his Dartmouth days. "He never carried money," recalls Laurance. "He just didn't like to feel money in his pocket, the way most people do."

After an evening together, he and Joan Braden would share a cab, and, she says, "Nelson either had no money, or he had a hundred-dollar bill. He'd give me the hundred, and I'd say, 'No, Nelson, I can't.' So we argued a lot. Finally, one night, he did that narrowing of the eyes, and he said, 'Look, Joanie, money means nothing to me. My time does. Do not argue with me about a cab.' "

The clothes, the weathered tennis balls, the empty wallet were the marks of a man who, more often than not, was too caught up in the breakneck pace of his life to notice.

That pace rarely slackened. There was, for instance, the maiden voyage of the *Dragon Lady*. Excited about this new toy, Rockefeller couldn't wait to take it up to Seal Harbor. Departing New York City's City Island, where the boat was kept in the off-season, he decided to head straight up the Atlantic Coast to Mount Desert Island, and brought along Wally Harrison, Frank Jamieson, and a few other friends for company.

Day after day, fierce storms battered the vessel. The captain, a grizzled old sea dog named Henry Conary, wanted to head for a safe harbor until the worst of the weather blew over. But even as the driving rain coursed over his yellow slicker, Rockefeller, exhilarated by the whole experience, insisted they press on. One storm-tossed night, he merrily announced he was preparing dinner and disappeared into the galley. A few minutes later, a mad scramble for fire extinguishers ensued when the stove burst into flames.

At last, an exasperated Conary took Harrison aside. In his pithy Down East way, he asked the question that Harrison and a host of others had been puzzling over for years.

"What's a-pepperin' him, anyway?"

Perhaps it was his genetic restlessness. Or perhaps it was his unfulfilled ambition. But whatever was a-pepperin' him, in the early 1950s it could not be sated or stilled—not by all the artwork that was piling up in storage, not by all the new yachts churning up sea spray, not by the visitors whose company he shared on 54th Street.

"The trouble with Nelson," Adlai Stevenson remarked at the time, "is that he has so many ideas, and they're so wonderful, but when you call him the next day about one of them he's on to something else or off to Venezuela." Rockefeller's focus darted from one project to the next, from one grand design to the next. It was not that he was shallow or superficial in his pursuits: once a problem or a possibility caught his eye, he would pursue it with uncommon tenacity and thoroughness. Rather, his was a case of an engine perpetually in overdrive, an engine that could be harnessed in a dozen directions and still not lose any of its propulsive power.

"He goes a little like a mad man from daybreak until dusk and then he wants to talk things over with the experts until midnight," reported one associate in the course of one of Rockefeller's Venezuelan trips. The only time this man saw his boss show any sign of strain was in the course of another of Rockefeller's interminable postdinner meetings in his hotel room. "After a while, Nelson folded his arms on the table and put his head down on his arms. I thought, well, at last, I've seen him get tired. But about that time, he said, 'Just keep on talking. I'm listening.' "

"He never stopped," says someone else who worked for him back then. "He'd have all his memos read by eight in the morning, and then come into the office. By four-thirty, you didn't mess with him: he was tired and ready to go home. But he was only ready to go home and freshen up for the set of players that were coming for the evening, all of whom tied into something else he was doing. He loved having multiple interests—huge multiple interests."

Invariably, he gravitated to people of similar bent, people who tossed off ideas like Fourth of July fusillades, people who didn't fritter their talents away on the messy details—and who wouldn't dream of second-guessing themselves. As brother Laurance would note, "Nelson's philosophy was, well, let's start, and, you know, nine times out of ten, you'll find a way. And the people who want to know how they're going to finish, before they start, which most reasonable people want to do, they never get very far."

The philosophy explains why, in those years, he was so drawn—despite his brothers' misgivings—to that definitive idea man Bill Zeckendorf.

By the early 1950s Zeckendorf was America's greatest real estate developer, a flamboyant dynamo whose vision encompassed everything from sprawling new suburban shopping malls to the redevelopment of New York's Park Avenue. A *New Yorker* cartoon said it best: a father and his young son are surveying the Manhattan skyline from a penthouse terrace. "Someday, my boy," says the father, "all this will belong to Mr. William Zeckendorf."

Brimming with ideas, but chronically short of capital, the rotund Zeckendorf could always count on a receptive audience in Nelson Rockefeller's wing of 30 Rockefeller Plaza. There were straightforward proposals—a Denver housing project, for example—as well as wilder ventures, such as Zeckendorf's scheme for transforming Venezuelan natural gas into a huge dry ice industry. But whatever the deal was, Rockefeller could be counted on to embrace it.

He thought Zeckendorf was a genius, and was eager to involve him in his own operations. He approached the developer about studying São Paulo for IBEC Technical Services. And he retained him as a consultant on the refinancing of Rockefeller Center. The two men would meet as often as three times a week.

As their dealings intensified, Zeckendorf complained that the family power structure was too hidebound, too inflexible. One day he said to Rockefeller, "Nelson, if we're going to do business together, you've got to get rid of Milbank, Tweed." It was an astonishing demand; not only was Milbank the long-standing family firm, but John Lockwood was Rockefeller's most trusted counsel. But, astonishingly, Rockefeller acceded to it, at least insofar as his dealings with Zeckendorf were concerned. Henceforth, it was Oscar Ruebhausen, not Lockwood, who would deal with the developer.

"Zeckendorf had a new idea every day," remarks Ruebhausen, "and Nelson loved the ideas, and the whole family knew he loved the ideas, and the only protection they had was the poor membrane that I provided—or so they thought." With no naysayers in his way, Rockefeller steered the family interests into one Zeckendorf scheme after another. The Rockefellers helped bankroll a sprawling 2,500-acre industrial and distribution center on the site of an old ranch between Dallas and Fort Worth. They joined with Zeckendorf in buying the Railway Express building in midtown Manhattan. And, at Zeckendorf's urging, Nelson purchased—for IBEC—Saks Fifth Avenue: not the department store itself, but the Fifth Avenue building, across the street from Rockefeller Center, in which the main store was housed. (The idea was to give IBEC's earnings a quick boost through a rapid resale of the property.)

Then, one day, Zeckendorf came to Rockefeller with his latest brainstorm: the purchase of the Chrysler Building, New York's second-tallest structure. This time, the brothers, and their financial advisers, said enough was enough. The Rockefellers pulled out of the deal, on the grounds that they should be doing no more than one deal with Zeckendorf at a time. Zeckendorf ended up turning elsewhere for backing—and reaped a tidy profit when he resold the building in the late 1950s.

"The brothers were afraid of Zeckendorf," says Ruebhausen. "They thought he was overexposed." Nelson's son Rodman would later share his uncles' misgivings. "I remember, when I was in business school, I did an analysis of Zeckendorf's company. I came to the conclusion that it was worth minus two dollars per share. And I remember trying to think, now, how am I going to tell my father this?"

In the future, when Nelson's mind was elsewhere, the family would gradually disengage itself from the tangle of Zeckendorf investments—well before the collapse they feared came to pass (which it did in the mid-1960s). But as long as Nelson was a power and a presence in Room 5600, he would never say no to Bill Zeckendorf.

Rockefeller had good reason to be simpatico with Bill Zeckendorf. After all, he was running an overextended, overreaching business himself.

Indeed, even Zeckendorf's most rose-colored reveries were hardly a match for Rockefeller's unshakably optimistic pronouncements about IBEC. "I don't see any ceiling on this company . . . the financial drain should be stopped pretty soon . . . the relations with the oil companies are wonderful": that was what Rockefeller was saying in late 1950, when he had last taken stock of the company, before the Point Four report distracted him.

But, as always, his hopeful assessments proved ill-founded, particularly in regard to the Venezuelan operations. The company was hemorrhaging everywhere. Its farming and fishing operations were expected to lose another $300,000 in 1952; the fish company would need a loan of $140,000 just to keep it in business. All told, the fishing, farming, and food warehouse units had lost over $10 million since their inception three years earlier. Even the highly regarded milk companies were still in the red, although they were expected to climb out within a year.

To keep VBEC afloat, Rockefeller would have to take some hitherto unmentionable measures. To shore up the farming company, he shut down the disease-ridden chicken farm, turned the Agua Blanca plantation over to the Venezuelan government, and took over the Monte Sacro ranch as his personal estate. He finally bit the bullet on the fishery, folding the operation after receiving a succession of gloomy prognoses from his managers.

At the same time, he resorted to a variety of expedients to bolster IBEC's tremulous finances, such as the Zeckendorf-promoted purchase of the Saks building. Then, in early 1952, Rockefeller steered IBEC into the oil business, forming the Avila Oil Company, with IBEC holding 51 percent of the shares—although the bulk of the financing would actually come from Rockefeller and his brothers. Later that year, Avila Oil began acquiring acreage: not in Latin America, but in the safer terrain of Texas and Oklahoma.

Yet even as he struggled to right his foundering vessel, Rockefeller retained his boundless faith in the course he had set. In a mid-1952 interview with the *Christian Science Monitor,* there was a touch of mea culpa in his assessment of IBEC: "It was a case of too much too soon rather than too little too late," he conceded. But he was philosophical about his losses. "Money lost in this was money honestly spent in attempting to solve problems," he said. "And I think we have found the answer to all those problems or are on the way."

"I would say in each one of the cases we learned the answers the hard way. But considering the problems that needed to be faced, if we hadn't done it this way it would not have been done at all."

Oscillating, as always, between his do-good instincts and a hard-nosed business posture, Rockefeller was now sounding more like the heart-of-gold capitalist for whom profits were merely incidental. "I think we have accomplished a basic objective," he said. "We didn't pick areas just because we could make an easy profit, but areas important to the Venezuelan economy. . . . we had social objectives with capitalistic incentives rather than straight business aims."

On the other hand, he was willing to concede that some retooling of the IBEC concept might be in order. The company's future, he opined, might be in investment banking: acting as a middleman in mobilizing local capital, rather than starting up new companies itself.

In late 1951, IBEC had set up just such an investment banking concern in Brazil. The Inter-American Finance Corporation was a joint venture of IBEC, the Chase Bank, and fourteen of the leading Brazilian commercial banks. If it worked in Brazil, then IBEC might extend the concept throughout Latin America. That way, Rockefeller said, "we can multiply efforts along constructive lines rather than taking on all the problems of setting up new companies ourselves."

Not that he was scuttling IBEC's businesses. Far from it: excited about the quick success of his supermarkets, Rockefeller pushed for expansion, not just in Venezuela, but in Puerto Rico, Colombia, Peru, and Brazil. There was talk, as well, about establishing milk companies throughout Latin America.

But then, in the spring of 1952, Rockefeller was buffeted by another financial blow. First Creole, and then the other oil companies, served notice on him that they had had enough. They wanted out of VBEC.

With a sympathetic military regime now in power, the companies no longer felt the need to placate the politicians with demonstrations of good citizenship. VBEC was now viewed strictly as a business proposition: a money-losing business proposition over which they had little control, whose proprietor was now talking about embarking on a new round of costly expansion.

The companies had invested $12.8 million in VBEC, and they knew there was no way they could come out whole. Nonetheless, they expected at least the $4.2 million par value of their preferred stock.

In the negotiations, Rockefeller's representatives tried to deflate the stock's value. VBEC's earnings outlook, they contended, did not "justify the belief that dividends can be expected soon or regularly." (This assessment was, to say the least, somewhat at odds with Rockefeller's optimistic public pronouncements.)

The oil companies, however, would not budge. They wanted $4.2 million.

Thus, for the second time in two years, Rockefeller was confronted with a costly buyout. The last time, he had gone to banks for the money. But in view of IBEC's uncertain financial picture—and his ambitious expansion plans—further loans would be a very expensive affair. The debt would weigh down IBEC's balance sheet for years to come.

Loath to put up the money himself, or ask his brothers for it, Rockefeller came around to the same solution that he had initially come up with two years before. He would go to his father.

To do so, of course, would be to risk the same humiliation he had suffered two years earlier, the same admonitions, the same pious lectures. Plus, there was this added element of abasement: the knowledge, sure to be rubbed in, that it was his father, not he, who had been vindicated by IBEC's recent performance.

Nonetheless, spurred by the awareness that this was the only reasonable way he could keep his dreams going, Rockefeller swallowed his pride, ignored his past wounds, and approached the patriarch.

And this time, Junior's response was very different. Instead of grudgingly offering his son a personal loan at exorbitant terms, as he did in 1950, he now agreed to purchase the oil companies' preferred stock—for the $4.2 million they were asking.

As a further gesture of beneficence, Junior would not hold on to the stock; rather, he would donate it to the Museum of Modern Art.

Given Junior's past stoniness, and his persistent second-guessing of IBEC, the turnabout was extraordinary. (To be sure, there were those who saw a sardonic twist in the gift to MOMA. In the words of one family aide, "It was as if he was telling Nelson, 'I'm going to make sure you manage this asset properly, by giving shares of it to your favorite museum.' ")

Objectively, Junior's switch is hard to explain; it is doubtful that Nelson could have been any more persuasive in 1952 than he was in 1950. Nor is it likely that Junior had forgotten his profound reservations about bailing his son out.

In the end, there was really only one plausible explanation. Junior's attitude had changed, because Junior had changed. Between 1950 and 1952, he had found a new wife.

She was Martha Baird Allen, the widow of an old friend and Brown classmate, attorney Arthur M. Allen of Providence, Rhode Island. A trim, sprightly woman, she was a former concert pianist who had trained with the renowned Artur Schnabel in Berlin. The Allens owned a cottage in Seal Harbor, and during their summers there often visited with Junior and Abby. So it was not at all surprising that after her husband died in May 1950, Martha Allen found Junior among the good friends offering words of comfort. Consolation very soon led to courtship; in Martha's animated presence, the doleful fog that had enveloped Junior since his own spouse's death quickly lifted. Acting with an impulsiveness that must have positively astonished his inner circle, Junior cast off his mourner's garb and married Martha Baird Allen on August 16, 1951, at the bride's Seal Harbor home. His eldest son served as best man; Nelson and David were also present. The groom was seventy-seven, the bride fifty-six.

Over the years, the accepted family line on Junior's remarriage to a woman two decades younger was that it was warmly welcomed by his offspring. As John Ensor Harr and Peter J. Johnson write in their authoritative family chronicle, *The Rockefeller Century,* "There was no jealousy or resentment among Junior's children. Their father was happy and the strain of worrying about his loneliness was over."

But that is not how some longtime family retainers remember the situation. "First of all, the brothers were stunned, because here was this man who kept speaking of Abby as if she were still alive, and then suddenly, one day, he just announced he was marrying Martha Baird," remembers one man who worked for the brothers. "They were very upset. And there was concern about the money."

John Lockwood has much the same recollection. "I don't think there's any doubt that when they realized he was going to marry her they were appalled." In fact, he recalls that the brothers even made an attempt, through an intermediary, to dissuade Martha from going through with the nuptials.

Once they realized there was nothing they could do about it, the brothers adjusted themselves rapidly to the new familial state of affairs. And none was more rapid in the turnaround than Nelson. He warmly welcomed his stepmother into the family, sent her flowers, expressed delight about all she was doing for his father. Soon he was calling her "Aunt Martha," and all his siblings followed suit.

To be sure, Martha made it easy for them. "She was a lovely person," says Lockwood, "and she was very devoted to Mr. Rockefeller." Martha was the prototypical Rockefeller wife, with nary a trace of glitz or gold digger about her. And there was no mistaking the sublime happiness she brought to Junior, the contentment and ease he found as she joined him for a horse-and-buggy ride on the carriageways of Acadia or entertained him after dinner with selections from Chopin on the Eyrie's baby grand.

It also did not take the brothers long to realize that far from hindering the transfer of wealth and power to the next generation, Martha's arrival was actually facilitating it. Their father was mellower, sunnier, less dogmatic—and more receptive to the propositions his sons brought to him. The idea of easing Nelson's IBEC burden was no longer dismissed out of hand. And neither was the infinitely more delicate, personally more poignant matter Nelson brought before him: the question of what was to be done with his beloved Pocantico estate.

The fate of Pocantico had been much on Junior's mind in recent years. He knew all about the stiff inheritance taxes that would be levied if the property was still in his hands at the time of his death. The only way to avoid those taxes would be to pass on ownership of the property to his children before he died.

By the spring of 1949, Junior's lawyers had formulated a plan. A corporation, wholly owned by Junior, would be organized, to which Junior would transfer ownership in Pocantico. He would then sell his shares in the corporation to his sons—while retaining operating control of the heart of the estate as a "legal life tenant." (His daughter Babs, long estranged from her father, no longer lived on the estate and had no desire to get involved in it.) In this way, Junior would avoid not only inheritance taxes but gift taxes as well. At the same time, he would continue to rule over the opulent Georgian main house, Kykuit, and the lush grounds and gardens that surrounded it, including the nine-hole golf course and the Playhouse, the baronial gathering place for three generations of Rockefellers.

The plan made eminent financial sense. But Junior, who had only recently surrendered control of Rockefeller Center to his sons, was in no hurry to lose this last visible vestige of his dominion—to become the tenant of his sons.

Nelson, on the other hand, warmly embraced the transfer plan. As in all the other touchy matters relating to his father, he eagerly took the lead in pressing the issue in family councils. When the transaction stalled, he could barely conceal his annoyance.

Nelson added some wrinkles of his own to the master plan. He wanted to separate ownership of the core 250 acres of the estate—the Park, as it was known in family parlance—from the rest of the 2,500 acres, the so-called open space. (The open space really was not open at all, but fenced off like all the rest of the property.) Much of the original open space—almost 1,000 acres of it—was, in fact, already owned by the brothers; both John 3rd and David had their homes there, and Nelson and Laurance owned additional pieces. The terrain covered by the Park, meanwhile, included Kykuit, the Playhouse, Nelson's house, and Laurance's.

Nelson's idea was to have the new corporation own the open space (that is, the 2,250 acres not already owned by the brothers individually), while putting the Park in the hands of a family partnership. This arrangement would head off the "endless tax problems" he had been warned the family faced if a corporation owned the core estate. Nelson then wanted to recast the corporation as a separate real estate operation. Not only would there be tax advantages to such a setup, but profits as well that could offset the costs of maintaining the estate. In one memo, he envisioned the corporation leasing remote portions of the Pocantico property to farmers, and even building "some low-cost housing"—possibly with FHA mortgages. (No doubt IBEC Housing would have been brought in to do the job.)

Whatever reservations there may have been about this aspect of Nelson's plan, the overall tax advantages of the corporation scheme were compelling. In June 1951 the legal papers were drawn up for the first aspect of the plan: Junior's transfer of title to Pocantico to the new corporation, Hills Realty Company. But even that first step was too much for Junior. He pointedly asked his old friend and counsel Thomas Debevoise (who from the beginning had helped steer the transaction) if, by signing those papers, he would be forced to go through with the rest of the plan; Debevoise assured him he wouldn't, that he was "in absolute control of the situation." He then asked Debevoise if he could dissolve the corporation and take the property back, if that was his whim. Again, Debevoise guaranteed him he could. It was only after getting those assurances—and pointedly instructing Debevoise to repeat them to Nelson—that Junior put his pen to the documents.

By the following spring, the now remarried Junior was faced with the next step in the design: the sale of the Hills Realty shares to his sons. Once again, he balked. As he tartly observed to Debevoise, "I presume I should make this sale for every reason and there is really no reason why I should not go forward with it. On the other hand, I still have the foolish feeling that it is pleasant to own the house in which I live." Once again, his pen hovered over the papers—but, in the end, he signed. Hills Realty was now in the hands of his sons, and Nelson was now the president of Hills Realty.

As was the case with Rockefeller Center, Junior's five sons somehow managed to acquire the Pocantico property for an astonishingly low sum: $760,295. The 2,500 choice acres on the Hudson, Kykuit, the Playhouse, the formal gardens and golf course, a dozen other houses (including Nelson's and Laurance's), the vast Coach Barn (three times the size of Kykuit) where the estate's carriages and cars were stored, numerous other outbuildings: all that for $760,000, or $152,000 per brother.

Again, as in Rockefeller Center, there were numerous explanations for the bargain price: Junior's life tenancy, which limited any alternative use of the property; the astronomical cost of maintaining such an estate. Nevertheless, by almost any objective standard, the price was stupefyingly low. After all, Pocantico's assessed value, as of 1949, was $3.6 million; its total book cost to Junior, as of that date, was in excess of $7.5 million.

But the only standard that really mattered was that of the U.S. Treasury—and, just as it did with Rockefeller Center, the government accepted the Rockefellers' depressed valuation.

It would be another two years (1954) before the final piece of the Pocantico transfer—the sale by Hills Realty of the inner estate, the Park, to the brothers—was put in place. The brothers paid Hills Realty (in effect, themselves) $311,000 for the heart of Pocantico. But unlike the earlier Hills deal, in which each of the five brothers took an equal stake, the purchase of the Park was skewed quite differently.

Winthrop, for one thing, chose not to participate at all. Wearied by the tempestuous breakup of his marriage, determined to carve out a new life for himself far from the public eye, he had quit New York in 1953 and resettled on a mountaintop in Arkansas, there to devote himself to cattle ranching (the ranchman fantasy was one he had long shared with Nelson). Even before then, he hardly spent any time at Pocantico. When he did make the occasional visit, he would stay in a Marcel Breuer-designed guest house just inside the main gate, as if to emphasize the emotional distance he felt from his family—and his eagerness to be near an exit.

Winthrop's withdrawal left the other four brothers to divide up shares of the Park. The division, however, turned out to be far from equal. Nelson took a 38.5 percent stake, Laurance 30.75 percent, David 23 percent, and John just 7.75 percent. The variation was supposed to reflect the extent to which each brother expected to make use of the property. With houses inside the Park, Nelson and Laurance had the biggest interest in it, while John, whose Fieldwood Farm was miles away from the main estate, had the least.

Yet it was hard not to see a larger pattern in the distribution of Park shares: the pattern of Nelson's aspirations within the family. By taking the largest share of the estate, Nelson was, in effect, positioning himself to succeed his father as laird of Kykuit.

Those aspirations were underscored by another family financial transaction at the time: the recapitalization of Rockefeller Center. Laurance had devised a plan that would have the brothers sell part of their holdings in the Center to their 1934 trusts; in addition, the trusts would purchase a new $5 million issue of Rockefeller Center stock. (The plan, among other things, revealed how incredible a bargain the brothers had struck when they bought the Center for $2.2 million in 1948. Two independent appraisals in 1954 set the Center's market value at $40 million.)

All the brothers were equally entitled to purchase a piece of the new stock for their trusts. But the ever-loyal Laurance, citing "all that Nelson has done for the Center" over many years, urged his siblings to allow Nelson to snap up the entire new stock issue. The others agreed.

For Nelson's trust, the investment was hardly the most prudent financial move, since it would be years before the debt-encrusted Center could pay dividends. But financial considerations were almost beside the point. With the new investment, Nelson now had a bigger piece of Rockefeller Center than any of his brothers—just as he now had the largest share of the other family crown jewel, the Pocantico estate. His dominant position in his generation was now more than a matter of attitude and anecdote. It was a confirmable fact.

Junior, meanwhile, reluctantly settled into his new status as his sons' tenant. As ambivalent as ever about the whole transaction, he saw fit to send them a memo shortly after the ownership transfer took place.

The memo cited, verbatim, various communications, particularly to and from Nelson, regarding Junior's future use of the estate. It quoted Nelson's "promise and commitment that none of us shall interfere or attempt to interfere in any way with the rights reserved by you . . . so that you will have during your life complete freedom in the enjoyment and use of the estate." And it quoted John Lockwood's letter that Nelson's assurances were "legal, binding and enforceable agreements according to their terms."

Junior offered no comment about these statements; he was simply compiling them, he tersely informed his sons, "for my own information."

The memo, in fact, was not so much a parental missive as it was a legal barricade, thrown up by Junior to ward off any further predations by Nelson. It spoke volumes about where they stood toward one another: In the fifth decade of their relationship, the great old benefactor, at seventy-eight, still did not entirely trust his second son.

Part Six

Influencing Ike

Twenty-nine

Back Inside

In October 1951, having just disengaged himself from any further involvement with the administration of Harry S. Truman, Nelson Rockefeller arrived for a meeting at Jock Whitney's Manhattan apartment. The diffident Whitney, in the years since the war, had quietly emerged as a significant behind-the-scenes player in New York State Republican politics, fostering GOP progressivism by bankrolling such middle-of-the-road candidates as the young Jacob Javits. Seated serenely at his desk at his 630 Fifth Avenue office (the same desk used by his grandfather John Hay, Theodore Roosevelt's Secretary of State), with Seurat's "L'Ile de la Grande Jatte" behind him, Whitney was the most patrician of power brokers. Yet no one who entered that office would deny his clout. His support was selective, but once proffered, it was wholehearted and significant. As Rockefeller would later say of Whitney, "His effectiveness in politics lies in moving in, concentrating, hitting hard, moving on."

Now Whitney was moving on to the biggest political game of all: the race for the presidency. With the contest less than a year away, Whitney and other moderate Republicans were desperately maneuvering for a candidate who could beat back the challenge of Robert Taft's conservative wing, a candidate who could erase the memories of the humiliating 1948 defeat of the moderates' last best hope, Thomas E. Dewey.

There was no mystery about the identity of this designated savior. He was Dwight D. Eisenhower, the revered supreme Allied commander of World War II. Now serving in Paris as commanding general of NATO forces, Eisenhower had consistently rebuffed efforts to draw him into the political arena—while deftly (and some would say calculatingly) leaving the door always slightly ajar. In the words of one of his biographers, Stephen E. Ambrose, "He did not seek the Presidency, but he so successfully managed his public and private life that, more than any other candidate in American history, save only George Washington, the Presidency sought him."

Not even the pledges of support by Dewey and his estimable political machine could draw Ike out of his bunker. "I don't know why people are always nagging me to run for President," Eisenhower complained. "I think I've gotten too old." So dodgy was Eisenhower that he refused to even discuss his party affiliation, leading some Democrats—Truman among them—to hope that he might be *their* party's standard-bearer in 1952.

But with the election year looming, and with Taft, "Mr. Republican," harvesting delegates by the bushel, Whitney and the others in the Draft Eisenhower movement could no longer play a waiting game. They sent General Edwin Clark, an international business consultant who had served on Eisenhower's wartime staff, to Paris to sound out his old chief once and for all. Pressed for a commitment, Eisenhower agreed to provide Clark with a letter that would, for the first time, indicate his willingness to accept the Republican nomination.

Now Clark sat in Jock Whitney's apartment, the five-page letter in hand. There to listen to his account of his meeting with Eisenhower were Rockefeller, Whitney, Whitney's business partner James Brownlee, and Senator James Duff of Pennsylvania, who was ready and eager to get the Eisenhower bandwagon rolling. The letter was to be kept strictly confidential; in fact, immediately after the meeting, it was placed in a safe-deposit box to which only Clark and Brownlee had access. Nonetheless, every man there understood its import: with the general's assent in writing, the drive for Eisenhower's nomination could, at last, begin in earnest.

Unlike Whitney, Rockefeller up to then was a virtual cipher when it came to Republican Party affairs. Aside from joining his father and brothers in what amounted to a ritualistic family tithe for the GOP (each brother contributed $6,000 to the party in 1950), Rockefeller had shown little interest in wading into Republican politics. His aloofness was not a matter of preference, but of pragmatism: as a high officeholder under FDR, and an aspiring one under Truman, he simply could not afford to identify himself too closely with the party out of power. On the other hand, he was always careful not to totally forsake his Republican roots; before accepting the coordinator's job, he made sure to clear it with Wendell Willkie.

But by the fall of 1951, Rockefeller plainly had little to lose, and much, much to gain, by aligning himself with the GOP in general and Eisenhower in particular. With the Truman administration mired in Korea and beset by scandals, the upcoming election promised to break the Democrats' two-decade-long grip on the White House—assuming the right candidate could be found. And Rockefeller joined Jock Whitney and Tom Dewey in believing that the party could not do any better than Dwight Eisenhower.

Rockefeller himself had had little contact with Eisenhower. The family member most deeply involved in the early wooing of Eisenhower for the presidency was not Nelson, but his uncle, Chase Bank president Winthrop Aldrich. A longtime intimate and financial backer of Dewey (so much so that in the 1950 gubernatorial campaign Dewey was tarred with the epithet "Chase Bank Dewey"), Aldrich shared the New York governor's conviction that the only hope for their brand of internationalist Republicanism was an Eisenhower candidacy. As a Dewey emissary, Aldrich had met with Eisenhower in Paris in May 1951 in an effort to prod the general along.

As for Nelson, there is no evidence he was enmeshed in the Eisenhower boomlet before that October 1951 meeting at Whitney's apartment. And even in the succeeding months, when the campaign apparatus began to take shape, Rockefeller seems to have participated mainly through surrogates. One such surrogate was Arthur Vandenberg, Jr., son of the senator, who had been working for Rockefeller at IBEC; in February 1952 Vandenberg became chairman of Citizens for Eisenhower. Another was Vera Goeller, Rockefeller's aide for local civic affairs; Goeller helped manage New Yorkers for Eisenhower.

Nowhere, in the long list of eminent Americans who signed on for the Citizens for Eisenhower movement, could be found the name of Nelson Rockefeller. It was as if, even at that late date, he could not bring himself to drop the bipartisan mask that had been so much a part of his political persona over the previous dozen years.

In early 1952, he was approached by publicist Tex McCrary, a friend of Jock Whitney's and one of the early boosters of Eisenhower's candidacy. The raffish McCrary had gained national renown with *The Tex and Jinx Show,* a radio (and later television) talk show he hosted with his glamorous wife, Jinx Falkenburg. In a typically outlandish maneuver to whip up enthusiasm for Ike—and spur the general's entry into the race—McCrary planned to stage a huge "I Like Ike" rally at New York's Madison Square Garden, with a star-studded list of participants.

Seeking financing for the event, he visited Rockefeller. "I'd appreciate it," said McCrary, "if you'd give me $25,000 for the rally." "Let me think about it," Rockefeller replied. When McCrary heard no further from Rockefeller, he went to Whitney for the money instead.

The closest Rockefeller came to public political entanglement during those months was in his capacity as America's number one advocate of global development aid. Still stewing over the Truman administration's handling of his Point Four report, Rockefeller now felt free to toss off the kid gloves and launch a full-bore attack on Truman's aid policies. In one speech, he lambasted the administration's "short-term emergency" approach, accused it of giving only "lip service" to the private sector, and assailed the linking of military aid and economic cooperation through Harriman's Mutual Security Administration as "disastrous."

When, in the first week of July, the moment of truth arrived for the Eisenhower movement—the climactic battle with the Taft forces at the Chicago convention—Rockefeller was there, albeit strictly as a sideline observer. He watched as Dewey and his aides masterfully triumphed in caucuses and floor fights, steering their candidate to a decisive first-ballot victory over the Ohio senator. And he witnessed the fervid wrath of the Taft supporters, denied what they once thought was a sure victory by their old mustachioed nemesis from New York. Eisenhower, they seethed, was nothing but a Dewey stooge. "Sink Dewey!!" read one Taft handbill. "Twice he led us down the road to defeat and now he is trying the same trick again hidden behind the front of another man."

And behind Tom Dewey, Taft's people charged, was "the same old gang of eastern internationalists and Republican New Dealers who ganged up to sell the Republican Party down the river in 1940, in 1944, and in 1948."

"Eastern internationalists": it was conservative code for the likes of Jock Whitney and John Foster Dulles and Winthrop Aldrich—and Nelson Rockefeller.

"Just back from convention," Rockefeller wrote a Latin American friend on July 11. "It was thrilling. Wish you had been there. Outcome gives new hope for the future."

Caught up now in the adrenaline rush of a presidential campaign, Rockefeller was ready to forsake his bystander's role and pitch in. But Tom Dewey had other ideas. Still firmly in command of the Eisenhower campaign apparatus—it was Dewey who had engineered the selection of California senator Richard M. Nixon as Ike's running mate—Dewey had no intention of letting Rockefeller's amateur exertions interfere with his well-calibrated machine. According to top Dewey aide John Burton, Rockefeller tried on at least three occasions to carve out a place for himself on the Eisenhower team. Each time he was rebuffed by the New York governor.

The freeze-out left Rockefeller frustrated and uncharacteristically surly. "He was obviously miffed and sort of unhappy at not having something really to sink his teeth into," remembers Frank Jamieson's wife, Linda. "We went with him once to a Republican Party dinner, and he just was not his big, open expansive self at all. He seemed a little petty—not to me, but to the waiter. Which was not at all usual."

Unable to storm in through the front door, Rockefeller tried entering from the side. Tapping his always ample think-tank resources, he assembled a group of economists to survey the nation's problems and come up with suggested speeches for the candidate. "I got him some of the best writers in the country," Rockefeller would later boast, "and he used a lot of our material in the campaign." But exactly how much Rockefeller's economists contributed is impossible to ascertain, since aside from his claim there is no extant record anywhere of their involvement.

Still, there was no question that in some fashion Rockefeller helped, as evidenced by Eisenhower's reply to Rockefeller's congratulatory telegram after the general's landslide victory. The "Dear Nelson" note expressed thanks for Rockefeller's "personal assistance." It was of great help to him and his staff, Eisenhower said, and he was deeply appreciative.

If there was one thing the new President-elect could be sure of, it was that Rockefeller's "personal assistance" would not end with election day. He would continue to be of help—whether or not that help was actually solicited. No sooner had the votes been tallied than Rockefeller was summoning his staff economist, Stacy May, to his office. He wanted May to produce a memo on the budget problems facing the incoming administration, a memo that Rockefeller could send over to Ike and his budget director.

New Presidents needed new ideas. And Nelson Rockefeller, as always, stood ready to provide them.

The great job shuffle now began, as a generation of frustrated Republicans scrambled for positions in the first GOP administration in two decades. All eyes were on the Commodore Hotel, where Eisenhower and his transition team had set up shop, and where a cavalcade of aspiring worthies braved a gauntlet of newsmen and photographers to pay homage to the President-elect.

From a distance, Rockefeller found himself caught up in the commotion. Traveling in Brazil on business two weeks after the election, he told reporters he had been sounded out about returning to his old position as Assistant Secretary of State for Latin American Affairs. He wasn't sure, he said, whether he would accept the job.

Exactly how real that offer was was open to question, since Eisenhower at that point was only just getting around to naming his Secretary of State, the redoubtable John Foster Dulles. And Dulles, with his elephantine memory, was not likely to have forgotten Rockefeller's renegade antics at the San Francisco UN conference. In any event, the talk about a Rockefeller return to State soon fizzled.

Then, on November 24, another balloon surfaced about Rockefeller's future—this one having nothing to do with an administration position. Walter Winchell ran the following item in his *New York Daily Mirror* column: "Nelson Rockefeller's pals are sure he would be interested in Dewey's job . . ."

It seemed preposterous, another one of Winchell's gossip-hound fantasies. Rockefeller, after all, had still never run for a single elective office.

But one of Dewey's top operatives, Herbert Brownell, perceived that there was more than a small grain of truth in what Winchell was writing. Brownell had just been treated to a firsthand glimpse of Rockefeller's ambitions—and knew that Winchell, if anything, was understating the situation.

Brownell, a former Republican national chairman, was a savvy Manhattan corporate lawyer with an unparalleled grasp of state and national politics, and had been Dewey's chief strategist in all his gubernatorial and presidential races. Though his star had dimmed after the 1948 debacle, it was burnished anew by his performance on behalf of Eisenhower: astutely working the delegate caucuses and the convention floor, Brownell deserved much of the credit for ensuring Ike's first-ballot victory.

Prizing Brownell's contacts and political expertise, Eisenhower had given him a position of extraordinary influence in the transition. It was Brownell, along with General Lucius Clay (the hero of the Berlin airlift and one of Eisenhower's most trusted friends), who was in charge of sifting through all the possible appointees.

Soon after the election, Brownell was invited by Rockefeller to lunch, ostensibly to celebrate the Eisenhower triumph. They met in the swank, art deco surroundings of the Roxy suite at Radio City Music Hall, where Rockefeller served glasses of Dubonnet (the sweet French aperitif wine that was now Rockefeller's cocktail of choice) and what Brownell remembers as "a rather meager lunch."

Rockefeller then revealed that he had more on his mind than merely a celebratory toast. Brownell braced himself for the inevitable pitch for an Eisenhower appointment—and was startled when Rockefeller went off on a totally different tack.

He wanted, he said, to run for President someday. And he wanted Brownell to manage his political affairs.

Rockefeller went on to paint, Brownell recalls, a "rosy view" of his chances. And then, says Brownell, "he led me up the mountaintop, describing all the perquisites and so forth that he could offer me," including "directorships in prestigious corporations."

Overwhelmed as he was by the offer, Brownell told his host he had no choice but to turn it down. He informed Rockefeller that he had already been tapped by Eisenhower as his Attorney General; the appointment was set, although the formal announcement had not yet been made. "Therefore, I was out of politics for the foreseeable future, and there was nothing I could do about it."

Rockefeller fully understood; "it was all very friendly," says Brownell. But, for that one brief moment, the curtains had parted to expose Rockefeller's ambition, and Brownell could see that it was every bit as vaulting—and every bit as calculating—as the relentless force that drove Tom Dewey.

Dwight Eisenhower was still two months away from entering the White House, and Nelson Rockefeller was already planning the succession.

For the time being, though, Rockefeller had to focus on the essential business at hand: carving out some sort of role for himself in the new administration in Washington.

And as it happened, that goal had also been the object of his calculation. The groundwork for his new position had already been laid, weeks before election day: not at the Eisenhower headquarters at the Commodore or at 30 Rockefeller Plaza, but at Temple University in Philadelphia.

In mid-October, while the nation's attention was riveted on the campaign's climactic days, Temple launched a series of studies of the workings of the executive branch of the federal government. The Temple studies were aimed at revisiting the proposals of the Hoover Commission, a presidential panel appointed by Truman three years earlier to uncover ways of streamlining the federal bureaucracy. Under the chairmanship of former President Herbert Hoover, the commission had produced an exhaustive set of recommendations that for the most part had died on the vine, the victim of a political tug-of-war between Truman and the Congress.

That Temple, rather than some vaunted Ivy League school, had chosen to undertake the project was no surprise: the college's president, Robert L. Johnson, was chairman of the Citizen's Committee on the Hoover Report. Johnson made it known that he would direct the study himself, on a "nonpartisan basis." And although the project would involve as many as nineteen different task forces, it would not, he promised, cost the school a penny, because it would be financed by a special fund, "subscribed by public-spirited citizens."

Johnson did not disclose it at the time, but one of his principal benefactors was Nelson A. Rockefeller. (He may actually have been the only backer; no other names ever came to light.) Indeed, Rockefeller's involvement in the project ran even deeper than that. Not only did he finance the Temple studies, but, as he later told the story, he had instigated them in the first place—at the personal behest, he insisted, of Dwight D. Eisenhower.

During the campaign, Rockefeller recounted, Eisenhower had confidentially asked him to think about the problem of federal organization and administration. The Republicans had made federal waste and mismanagement one of the principal issues of their campaign, and Eisenhower had pledged to "take out of the files the unfulfilled plans of the Hoover Commission" and enact them. For the candidate, this was more than campaign rhetoric; the ex-general, accustomed to tidy chains of command, had long been appalled by the slipshod organization of the executive branch under FDR and Truman. Knowing of Rockefeller's intimate experience with the Roosevelt and Truman bureaucracies, and of his recent studies of them for the Point Four report, Eisenhower thought Rockefeller was a natural for the assignment.

Rather than directly deploy his considerable resources for the task, Rockefeller chose to endow the project with a "nonpartisan," academic cast by bringing Johnson and Temple into the picture. The academic cover, however, was paper-thin. A fair chunk of the Temple report would be written by Rockefeller's minions; Stacy May, for example, was assigned the job of pulling together the foreign policy study, based on notes that Rockefeller himself had dictated. And Rockefeller personally recruited outside experts to work on the project. One of these was Bernard Gladieux, a Ford Foundation official who was one of Rockefeller's key Budget Bureau allies in the World War II turf wars.

Gladieux had always thought of Rockefeller as "a good administrator, a public interest-oriented person, but without any ambition himself in the political sphere." But as they worked together on the studies for Eisenhower, Gladieux came to perceive Rockefeller's more grandiose agenda. "It began to filter through to me that he wanted to be President himself one of these days," Gladieux observed, "maybe possibly following Ike." While Gladieux did not doubt that Rockefeller's interest in the reorganization project was sincere, "Nelson, I'm sure in his own mind, thought this might be the wedge, the port of entry for his own ambitions."

Four weeks after the election, on November 30, Rockefeller's role was at last formalized by Eisenhower. The President-elect named him chairman of a new Special Committee on Government Organization.* The other members would be Eisenhower's younger brother Milton, the president of Pennsylvania State University; and Arthur Flemming, the former director of the Office of Defense Mobilization and now president of Ohio Wesleyan University. They were given the broadest possible mandate: to study and make recommendations on the operation and structure of the executive branch. The White House, the cabinet, the subsidiary agencies: all fell within the purview of Rockefeller's committee, which would use the Temple studies as source material.

For Rockefeller, the appointment was an enviable consolation prize. It was not a cabinet position, or a White House position, but the job gave him a pivotal role in the shaping of the new government—and the much-coveted direct access to the President-elect. It wasn't a top-level appointment, but it was the next-best thing to one. As his friend Adolf Berle pointed out to him, "A second-string job would limit you too much; the first-string jobs are obviously spoken for by the contending factions; this is an excellent independent stance."

That this position was not an end in itself, but merely a stepping-stone to more exalted terrain for Rockefeller, was glaringly obvious to everyone. Reporting on the appointment, *Newsweek* noted that "Rockefeller has never

*That same day, Eisenhower also rewarded another member of Nelson's family, his uncle Winthrop Aldrich, tapping Aldrich to be his ambassador to the Court of St. James's.

allowed vast inherited wealth to interfere with his driving, competitive ambition to get ahead himself."

As soon as he heard the news, the director of the Central Intelligence Agency, General Walter Bedell Smith, stormed into the office of his assistant director, Allen Dulles (John Foster's brother). "Dulles," snapped Smith, "Ike is about to appoint that goddamn Communist from New York."

It was a measure of those Red-baiting times, when Joe McCarthy was still on the rampage and blacklists stalked the intelligentsia, that even an unreconstructed capitalist like Nelson Rockefeller could be accused (however offhandedly) of being a Communist. In truth, Smith didn't really believe he was; when word of his crack got back to Rockefeller, an abashed Smith retracted the remark. And, in case anyone had any doubt about it, Rockefeller passed the FBI's "loyalty check" of administration appointees with flying colors.

But others with whom he was associated were not so fortunate. When word got out that Bernard Gladieux was working for the Rockefeller committee, the conservative media pounced, rehashing old allegations that Gladieux had sabotaged loyalty investigations when he was at the Commerce Department. The day after the stories broke, Rockefeller called Gladieux up to his Rockefeller Center office. "You've seen these stories?" Rockefeller asked. Gladieux said he had, and didn't know what to do about them. "Well," said Rockefeller, "I don't care about the stories or anything else, but what makes me sore was that Foster Dulles was just up here." The incoming Secretary of State, he said, was furious. "Nelson," fumed Dulles, "how can you take on a man like this? How can you do this to Ike?"

"It just made me mad," Rockefeller told Gladieux. "It's none of his damn business. So," he went on, "what do you want me to do? I'll go to Ike. I'll issue a press release. I'll do anything you ask of me."

Gladieux was touched by Rockefeller's offer; at the same time, he realized the uproar was a monstrous diversion Rockefeller would just as well do without. Gladieux thanked him, but said that under the circumstances it might be best for everyone if he quietly withdrew. Recalled Gladieux, "I think Nelson was genuinely sorry, but also relieved."*

While Gladieux might go away, the loyalty issue, as a national phenomenon, wouldn't. Rather than ignore the issue, the Rockefeller committee chose to come to grips with it. Among its initial recommendations, at its very first meeting with Eisenhower on December 21, was the establishment of a presidential commission on loyalty and security. Such a commission was needed,

* Rockefeller also went to bat for other old associates who had come under McCarthyite fire. When his Lincoln School and Dartmouth chum Sheldon Stark, now a radio and television writer, found himself blacklisted, he asked if Rockefeller would write a note testifying that Stark was a loyal American. Unhesitatingly, Rockefeller did so. Source: Stark interview.

Rockefeller and his colleagues argued, because "many good citizens are alarmed" not only by the threat of internal subversion but by "some of the methods which have been pursued in attempting to combat the condition"—methods that "may involve an invasion of our basic liberties." In essence, the commission would be a presidential response to McCarthy's Senate witch-hunt.

The proposal came to naught; after that December 21 meeting, there would be no further mention of it. For reasons that historians are still debating, Eisenhower chose to ignore McCarthy ("I will not get in the gutter with that guy," he told an aide) and to turn a blind eye to his excesses. The new administration would never mount a serious counteroffensive. It would take other forces—notably, the Army-McCarthy Senate hearings in the spring of 1954—to bring down the senator from Wisconsin.

Within days of his formal appointment, Rockefeller outlined for his fellow committee members the panel's principal functions. It would pull together divergent thinking, put the material in usable form for the President, help in enlisting congressional support—and "avoid publicity at all times."

Aside from the brief flurry over Gladieux, the committee was an eminent success at the latter task. There were no press releases, no interviews, and, remarkably, no leaks. Rockefeller's group operated totally in the shadows—a singular feat, considering the press's ravenous hunger for tidbits on the new administration's plans.

During those first weeks, Rockefeller was keenly aware of the President-elect's wishes: both in regard to publicity and in regard to his committee's first round of proposals. Knowing that Eisenhower wanted a strong, military-style chain of command in the White House, headed by the assistant to the President, Governor Sherman Adams of New Hampshire, Rockefeller's panel produced a blueprint that called for exactly that setup. Thus, the pattern of an all-powerful presidential chief of staff was established, a pattern that would, ironically, come back to haunt Rockefeller much later in his political lifetime.

(In a further bid to ingratiate himself with Sherman Adams, Rockefeller offered him the use of his house on Foxhall Road. But the flinty, no-nonsense Adams, appalled by the home's immensity, as well as the Cubist art hanging all around the place, respectfully declined, saying he had found accommodations elsewhere.)

Then there was the matter of the Federal Security Agency. This sprawling bureaucracy, created by FDR in 1939, had under its wing the vast Social Security system, the Food and Drug Administration, the Public Health Service, and the Office of Education. Yet despite its 38,000 employees, its $4.6 billion budget, and its pervasive influence on the health and security of the population, the FSA still lacked cabinet status.

For years, Truman had repeatedly tried to upgrade the FSA to a cabinet department, only to meet with the adamant opposition of congressional Republicans who saw this new department as a precursor of the welfare state. Now, Eisenhower was privately making it known that he agreed with Truman. In fact, when he named Texas newspaper publisher Oveta Culp Hobby his FSA administrator, he assured her that she would soon preside over a new cabinet-level Department of Public Welfare.

Whether or not Rockefeller knew about the President-elect's commitment to Hobby, he made sure that the plans for a new department—which he dubbed the Department of Health, Education, and Social Security—moved to the top of the reorganization stack.

That was the easy part. What lay ahead for Rockefeller and his committee was the far more contentious question of what to do about foreign affairs—a matter made all the more arduous by the prickly personality and formidable defenses of John Foster Dulles.

It was apparent from the first that Dulles would not brook any diminution of his role as grand master of U.S. foreign policy. On the other hand, Dulles was receptive to some new arrangement that might spare him the bureaucratic tedium that was part and parcel of the secretary's job. In a speech earlier in the year, Dulles, diehard anti-Communist though he was, actually spoke enviously of the lot of the Soviet politburo: "They are, in the main, free of bureaucratic and public relations responsibilities, so that they have time to think." Before his nomination, Dulles confided to his Sullivan & Cromwell partners that "I don't think I really want to be Secretary of State. . . . The job I would like to have would be head of the planning group—to plan foreign policy."

In his early meetings with the Rockefeller panel, Dulles explored ways in which his ivory tower longings might be realized. At one point, they pondered creating some sort of "supracabinet" post for Dulles that might free him from humdrum management concerns. That idea was quickly tossed aside; Dulles wanted to be Secretary of State too badly, and feared that no other position would carry the necessary power and prestige.

Nonetheless, the exploration went on. At the committee's first meeting with Eisenhower on December 21, Rockefeller relayed Dulles' wish that State, somehow, be relieved of operational responsibilities so that it could focus strictly on policy making. Eisenhower listened, but offered no response.

Then, over the next several weeks, Rockefeller and his group came up with a formula that they thought might partially satisfy Dulles. Coincidentally or not, it was also a formula that suited Rockefeller's purposes as well.

The rudiments had been sketched out by Rockefeller as early as November 3, when he was still operating under the cover of the Temple studies. In a memo for the Temple report, he outlined a proposed Department of International

Cooperation. This department would oversee "people-to-people relations, economic and financial, cultural and informational." These functions would all be taken over from the State Department—although the new agency would still be "subject to policy guidance from State." In its initial conception, this department (presided over by a Secretary for International Cooperation) seemed like nothing less than a global version of his World War II coordinator's office.

In the ensuing weeks, after his meetings with his committee and with Dulles, Rockefeller's plan underwent a metamorphosis. The idea of a new cabinet department was scuttled. Instead, the new scheme set up two separate subcabinet agencies. One, the United States Information Agency, would take over the information functions of State, including the Voice of America. The other, the Foreign Economic Operations Agency (later to be called the Foreign Operations Administration), would oversee the United States' economic and financial relations with other countries.

This new agency's bailiwick would include foreign aid, relief and refugee assistance, and technical assistance programs. It would promote private foreign investment and trade, supervise export controls, and handle procurement of strategic materials. The agency's head would be appointed by and report directly to the President.

"When these changes have been made effective," a Rockefeller committee memo noted, "we envision the Secretary of State, freed of administrative burdens, being better able to discharge his prime responsibility of formulating an effective, far-visioned foreign policy." Thus, John Foster Dulles' longings would be fulfilled.

And so would Nelson Rockefeller's. For the Foreign Economic Operations Agency he was proposing was nothing more than a reworking of the Overseas Economic Administration of the *Partners in Progress* Point Four report. Using Dulles' desires for administrative relief as a lever, Rockefeller would catapult his program—the program that Harry Truman had spurned—to center stage in the administration of Dwight Eisenhower.

Rockefeller unveiled his plan, along with other aspects of his reorganization program, at a full-dress meeting of the President-elect and his cabinet designees at the Commodore on January 13. It was his first chance to show off his panel's progress, and he made the most of it, wheeling out charts, displaying a virtuosic command of the federal bureaucracy, skipping effortlessly from the challenges of foreign policy making to the tribulations of the Bureau of Land Management. He apologized for not meeting yet with every member of the cabinet; he would see them all, he promised, by the following week.

Six days later, on the eve of the inauguration, Rockefeller and his committee sat down with Dulles. While Dulles had "no opinion" on the transfer of the information functions from State, he was all for the move of the foreign economic operations to a new agency. He would not stand in the way of Rockefeller's program.

As of January 20, with Eisenhower now in the White House, Rockefeller's committee had a more impressive designation: it was now officially the President's Advisory Committee on Government Organization, part of the executive office of the President. And for Rockefeller, his committee's move to Washington meant a homecoming. Seven and a half years after he had left, he was back in the rambling, antique confines of the building next door to the White House that had once housed State (before its postwar move to Foggy Bottom) and now was known simply as the Executive Office Building.

He took over an unused suite of offices from the Office of Defense Mobilization and filled it with a staff hastily assembled from the Budget Bureau, the Civil Service Commission, and the ODM—all of whom worked at the chairman's tempo and in the chairman's breezy style. Meetings were very informal, small groups sitting around in shirtsleeves, batting issues around over lunch. Rockefeller was the leader, but, as one staffer remembered, it was a leadership style that "let you run with the ball and come back with the answers." The work, for all of them, occupied virtually every available evening—and most weekends.

His staff were not the only ones subjected to Rockefeller's hyperkinetic ways. One Saturday in mid-February, he brought together the President, the Vice President, the top White House staff, *and* the whole cabinet to hear his latest reorganization plans. Ike, whose devotion to leisure and the links was already becoming the stuff of Washington legend, was not at all pleased. According to the meeting's minutes, "It was suggested that it was desirable to avoid holding future meetings involving many of the Cabinet members on weekends."

The bustling atmosphere in Rockefeller's office became even more frenetic when, on February 18, one more reorganization assignment was heaped on him. Secretary of Defense Charles Wilson named him chairman of a seven-member panel that would study the overall structure of his department and its relation to the individual armed services.

The impetus for the study was the still nebulous chain of command in the department, which had been forged by Truman out of the old War and Navy departments. On the one hand, there was the Defense Secretary and his civilian underlings, the secretaries of each of the individual armed services; on the other hand, there was the military superstructure presided over by the Joint Chiefs of Staff. The internal tug of war became a political cause célèbre during the Korean conflict, when the civilian authorities were vilified for allegedly undermining the esteemed commander in the field, Douglas MacArthur. Then, too, there was an ongoing concern about interservice rivalries in the nuclear age, prompting some to call for an outright merger of the services.

Of all the reorganization issues piled on Rockefeller's shoulders, none were more politically volatile than these. The fact that the White House was now occupied by a former military man—a military man who comprehended, as well as anyone, the foibles of the current command structure—only intensified the pressures on Rockefeller and his panel.

To defuse some of the potential criticism, Rockefeller deftly arranged to have three military icons serve as consultants to his panel: General George Marshall; Admiral Chester W. Nimitz, former Chief of Naval Operations; and General Carl Spaatz, former Air Force chief of staff. With those three giving their distinguished input, no one could complain that the services' point of view was not adequately represented.

But unquestionably the most influential member of the committee was former Defense Secretary Robert Lovett, who complained convincingly about the secretary's inadequate authority and the Joint Chiefs of Staff's absorption in minutiae, at the expense of their broader planning mission. (Surprisingly, he found a ready ally in Nimitz, who offered the dramatic proposal that the secretary serve as Chairman of the Joint Chiefs.) Lovett was staunchly in favor of service unification—as was the Chairman of the Joint Chiefs, General of the Army Omar N. Bradley, who also served on the panel.

Rockefeller, however, wanted to take a less controversial course, one that would avoid the fearsome political minefield that any unification plan was bound to encounter. (Having no vested interest in the outcome one way or another, he could afford to stake out the middle ground.) In the end, his moderate view prevailed. The committee moved in many of the directions Lovett suggested: affirming the supremacy of the Defense Secretary, reinforcing the authority of the three civilian service secretaries who were his direct subordinates, removing all command functions from the Joint Chiefs so that they could concentrate on strategic planning. But it stopped short of an outright call for unification.

Wilson and Rockefeller went together to the White House to brief Eisenhower on the committee report. "Now, Nelson," said Wilson, "you're more familiar with this than I am, so you better present the details to the President." Eisenhower took it all in, and pronounced himself satisfied with the outcome. On April 29, he sent to Congress a detailed plan for Defense Department reorganization, which in almost every particular followed the lines of the Rockefeller committee report. Although the plan was denounced in some quarters as a move toward creeping unification—there were warnings about a "Prussian general staff" approach at the Pentagon—it was generally hailed as a shrewd and progressive program that acted in the "overall national interest rather than the particular desires of the individual services," in the words of the *New York Herald Tribune.*

The Defense reorganization plan gained swift congressional approval. Nonetheless, even Rockefeller recognized that the plan was just a patchwork of compromise that sidestepped the critical issues: interservice rivalry and the lack of a coherent, unified strategic framework at the Pentagon. Sooner, rather than later, those issues would have to be addressed.

In contrast to his frustrating experiences with the Truman administration, Rockefeller now had the satisfaction of seeing one proposal of his after another enacted into law by a compliant Republican Congress. First off the mark was the transformation of the Federal Security Agency into the Department of Health, Education, and Welfare. The proposal had drawn fire from the all-powerful American Medical Association, which feared that it would somehow lead to that dreaded scourge "socialized medicine." It was only after a long lunch with Rockefeller, Flemming, and Hobby that the AMA president was placated and agreed to back the bill. With that, the legislation sailed through Congress, and on April 11 the newly sworn-in secretary, Oveta Culp Hobby, was welcomed to her office with sprays of lilacs, courtesy of Nelson A. Rockefeller.

In due course, the new agencies conceived by Rockefeller's panel, the USIA and the Foreign Operations Administration, sprang to life (the latter absorbing and supplanting the Mutual Security Administration, Averell Harriman's former bailiwick). A score of his committee's more modest recommendations were also rapidly put into place. While, all in all, the changes wrought by the Rockefeller panel were far less sweeping than those called for by the earlier Hoover Commission (Hoover himself dryly observed that Rockefeller's proposals "avoid contentious issues"), they did represent the first successful effort at rationalizing the federal government since the dawn of the New Deal.

By late April, Rockefeller and his cohorts had reached the conclusion that their work was done. All that remained was follow-through, which they felt could be handled by the Budget Bureau. They wrote to the President, noted that "our major assignments have been carried out," and suggested that he abolish the committee.

But Eisenhower had other ideas. He saw reorganization not as a one-act play, as Rockefeller evidently did, but as a saga that would run for the duration of his administration. Within twenty-four hours, he dispatched an informal note to Rockefeller:

> For the moment at least, I think it would be very unwise for me to accept the recommendation of the Committee that I dissolve it and discharge it from any further responsibility in connection with reorganization.

I am quite ready for you to allow it to lie quiescent for the moment, but I should like to have another long talk with you before I do anything so drastic as to "let you off the hook."

Have a good week end.

After their "long talk," Rockefeller agreed to keep his committee in business. He had little choice; it was practically a presidential edict.

Still, this was hardly the sort of presidential appointment his rampant ambition craved. Other men might view the chairing of such a presidential advisory board as the capstone of their careers. For Rockefeller, it was little more than so much brick and mortar on the way to a grander edifice.

His service on the board had won him Eisenhower's confidence, but that confidence had led to nothing substantial. If he harbored any hopes that he might take over the new Foreign Operations Administration—the agency spawned by his own vision, dating back to Point Four—those hopes were quickly dashed. Since the FOA would succeed and absorb the Mutual Security Administration, the administration thought it only fair to give the FOA directorship to the man who was already running the MSA: the distinguished Republican officeholder (and Rockefeller's reluctant UN conference ally) Harold Stassen.

The FOA job, in any case, would soon prove to be something less than the powerhouse position Rockefeller had sketched out. In Rockefeller's conception, the FOA director would "report jointly" with the secretaries of State and Defense to the President, making the FOA chief their virtual coequal. But in the final draft of the plan approved by Eisenhower, the FOA director was clearly subordinate to the Secretary of State. To assure this, the secretary was given the statutory authority to "advise with the President concerning the appointment and tenure of the director." Thus, Dulles could, practically speaking, hire and fire the FOA chief at will.

At the end of the day, the Dulles who was so eager to surrender his "operational" burdens gave way to the Dulles who jealously guarded every iota of his power.

His Washington ambitions thwarted once again, Rockefeller returned to New York to retrace the steps he had started to take just after election day.

On April 23, the day after Rockefeller's attempt to back out of the reorganization committee, his office in Room 5600 sent over a set of incorporation papers to the New York secretary of state in Albany. The filing was for a new foundation: something to be called the Government Research Foundation, Inc. Its directors would be Nelson A. Rockefeller, Wallace K. Harrison, Francis A. Jamieson, John E. Lockwood, and Arthur H. Vandenberg, Jr. The foundation's president and managing director was to be Frank C. Moore, the lieutenant governor of New York.

The revelation that Moore, widely touted as a possible successor to Dewey in 1954, was stepping down from the state government to run this nonprofit entity was page one news. Did it mean, reporters wondered, that Dewey had decided to go for a fourth term? Did it mean that Moore and the governor were at odds? (Moore denied it.) Did it mean that Moore had been won over by a fancy compensation offer from Rockefeller? (All Moore would say was that his new salary would be "satisfactory.")

And just what was the Government Research Foundation anyway? At his Rockefeller Center office, Rockefeller issued a press release that endeavored to explain.

The foundation, he said, was devoted to "advancing and improving the science of government and the administration of public affairs." It would conduct studies on "the organization, power, operations and relationships of local, state and Federal Government."

The idea had been inspired, he said, by his work on the President's Advisory Committee, which had convinced him that more research was needed on the interrelationship of the municipal, county, state, and federal governments.

And there was no better man to look into those relationships, he was convinced, than Moore. Indeed, no one in the state of New York was more thoroughly steeped in the art of government than fifty-seven-year-old Frank Moore. For eight years the elected state comptroller, until Dewey handpicked him for the state's number two job, the mustachioed Moore had an unequaled mastery of state finances and all the essential arcana (school aid formulas, local debt limits) that went with it. In over thirty years in public service, he had been a part of government at virtually every level from the village to the statehouse.

"He was a student of government, a man of high ideals and impeccable integrity," remembers his longtime associate Lawrence Murray. Despite the cloud of speculation that enveloped Moore's resignation, Murray, who was Moore's executive assistant at the time, maintains there was nothing terribly mysterious about the decision. Moore was tired of government service; it was only with the greatest reluctance that he succumbed to Dewey's entreaties to run for lieutenant governor in 1950. "And from the day he took office," says Murray, "he was trying to get out of it." (So distasteful did Moore find his new post that he insisted that his aides still address him as "Comptroller," not "Lieutenant Governor.")

Moore mulled various escape routes, but each time he came close to accepting an outside offer, Murray, who handled his public relations, put his foot down. "Frank," he would tell him, "I can't sell it."

As Murray tells the story, "One day, Nat Goldstein, who was then the attorney general, came to Moore and said, 'I want to introduce you to a fellow named Nelson Rockefeller who is interested in doing something in government.' One word led to another, and then Moore started talking to me about this. If he undertook to head up a foundation to do research in government that would be financed by Nelson Rockefeller, what did I think of that? I said, 'I can sell *that.* I have to write the words carefully, but I can sell it.' "

Moore did not want to completely sever his involvement with state government. He insisted on retaining his memberships in various state commissions, including the position he particularly prized, membership on the board of trustees of the nascent State University of New York. To this, Rockefeller was completely agreeable; it was not in his interests to cloister his star acquisition.

The Government Affairs Foundation* would be, as the press releases indicated, a study center for intergovernment relations. But what the press releases did not say was that the foundation would also serve as an academy: an academy with but one pupil, its patron and founder, an academy that would immerse him in state and local government, just as surely as his meetings with The Group immersed him in Latin America on the eve of World War II. Moore would be his new Beardsley Ruml: a shrewd, well-connected mentor who could educate and facilitate.

"Frank Moore," relates Murray, "had a philosophy that whenever you got into a meeting on a very important subject, you better know more about the whole thing than anybody else in the room, and you had better do your homework."

By hiring Frank Moore, Nelson Rockefeller was doing his.

Rockefeller wanted to proceed with his education deliberately. But there were others—his old friends in the Liberal Party, particularly party stalwart Adolf Berle—who were more interested in a crash course. They wanted him to run for mayor of New York City in 1953.

Berle conferred with him about the mayoral race sometime that spring—probably soon after Rockefeller's return to New York. Rockefeller did not dismiss it out of hand. Like many other aspirants, he was undoubtedly attracted by the prospect of a race against the lackluster incumbent, Vincent Impellitteri, who had taken over after William O'Dwyer's abrupt departure, in the face of imminent scandal, to the U.S. ambassadorship in Mexico City. If ever there was a political year to throw caution to the winds and to speed up a personal timetable, it was 1953.

And so Rockefeller pondered Berle's proposition. And while he did, and while he welcomed Frank Moore to the ranks of his advisers, he heard from Oveta Culp Hobby.

Surveying her vast domain, the new Secretary of Health, Education, and Welfare had one priority above all others: to find an undersecretary who

*Formerly the Government Research Foundation; the foundation changed its name in July 1953.

would help her manage the great, unwieldy amalgam. She needed someone who would be unintimidated by the huge bureaucracy, someone who grasped the full scope of the department's influence, and someone who could push its program through Congress. No one she knew of fit the bill, in all those respects, better than Nelson Rockefeller.

The job of HEW Undersecretary, she told him, was his if he wanted it.

Rockefeller's brain trust—Jamieson, Lockwood, et al.—were not impressed by the offer and advised him to reject it. For one thing, it was far afield from his principal area of expertise, and his principal passion, foreign affairs. For another, it was a subordinate position. Had the department been State or Defense, that might not have mattered. But to be number two in a newly formed, second-level department like HEW hardly befit someone of Rockefeller's stature.

Yet, for all that, Rockefeller was tempted. He did not see HEW as such alien turf. "This is something I've been interested in all my life," he remarked. His family, after all, had long made health and education problems among their principal philanthropic targets. And he himself was well versed in health issues, as a result of his two decades of service on the Westchester County Board of Health. (With the exception of the war years, he had diligently held on to that position, though he usually sent surrogates to its meetings.) What's more, much of his later work as coordinator was devoted to health and education issues. (Some of the critics of his "giveaways" at the CIAA might say that he was immersed in "welfare" there as well.)

He also, he said, felt a certain sense of obligation to the new department. "I'm responsible for creating this baby," he told his aides. "I have a responsibility for seeing to it that it succeeds." He dismissed the notion that HEW was of secondary importance to the administration. It was vital, he felt, for the Republicans to shake off their hard-hearted Hoover era image and demonstrate that they were as concerned with social ills as the Democrats. To accomplish that, the administration badly needed a successful HEW.

These factors, in his mind, more than offset the bruised ego that was inherent in a deputy's role. But the motive that may have been the most decisive for him was one he didn't talk about: after eight years of exile, the yearning to be back in the government, to be back in the thick of it, was too great to resist. Undersecretary of HEW might not have been the ideal position for him, but it was a position, and in the absence of anything better, he was not inclined to spurn it.

As his brother Laurance later remarked, "Harry Emerson Fosdick once preached a sermon entitled, 'Life Is Making the Most of Second Best.' I believe life taught Nelson that sermon."

Eschewing the slow, calculated political course epitomized by the Government Affairs Foundation (though the foundation, under Moore, would remain a going entity), setting aside the chancy exercise of a mayoral race, Rockefeller opted for immediate, and certain, gratification. He accepted Hobby's offer.

"Of course, this leaves a hole in the possibilities for Mayor of New York," Adolf Berle wrote him when he heard the news. "For the city's sake, I am sorry you are out of it. For you personally, however, there would have been more heartbreaks than happiness."

Acknowledging neither the heartbreaks nor the happiness, Rockefeller, in reply, offered his apologies. "I feel in a way as though I had run out on you in connection with the City's problems, but there are some impelling reasons which made me feel that I should take this job."

His friends accepted those reasons, but still had a hard time visualizing Nelson Rockefeller as Oveta Culp Hobby's number two. As Berle noted, "I had hoped you would insist on the top job, because in this situation your own political stature is higher than that of your immediate chief, but you know the situation and can estimate it. It would have been nicer to have you in State—but there are several good reasons for not doing that until later on."

To those who expected great things from Rockefeller, the HEW job could only be regarded as a way station, a place to bide his time while awaiting the call to more stellar locales. "I have always thought you had a major chance to become Secretary of State," Bill Benton wrote him. "I hope your present decision will help you toward that end."

Rockefeller might share those hopes. But for now, his focus would be limited to health, education, welfare, and Oveta Culp Hobby.

Thirty

The Acting Secretary

In a Texas culture renowned for spawning strong, resilient women, Oveta Culp Hobby was one of the strongest.

Co-owner with her husband, former governor William P. Hobby, of the *Houston Post,* the city's second-largest paper (after Jesse Jones's *Chronicle),* Oveta Hobby was deemed one of the town's ten most powerful figures—the only woman who could stand shoulder to shoulder with the city's oil moguls and bank barons. Although she ostensibly shared the *Post* duties with her husband, there was little doubt about who really held the reins.

Oveta Hobby's iron resolve was always the hallmark of her character. Growing up in the small central Texas town of Killeen, some seventy miles north of the state capital of Austin, she spurned moviegoing and other youthful diversions, preferring to bury herself in her schoolwork. The only childhood game anyone remembered her playing was "church," where she could show off her formidable knowledge of the Bible, which she had read cover to cover three times by age thirteen.

When her father, Isaac Culp, a fiery prohibitionist lawyer, was elected to the Texas legislature in 1919, he took fourteen-year-old Oveta with him to Austin. She sat beside her father day after day, thoroughly entranced by the political life around her. From that point on, even school seemed a waste of time. Four years later, rather than enter the University of Texas, Oveta Culp found herself a job at the capitol. Within two years, though she was still not old enough to vote, she was appointed the legislature's parliamentarian.

Seeking to be more than a professional bystander, she ran for the legislature in her own right in 1930, but her stern personality proved less than appealing to the voters. Her opponent denounced her as a "parliamentarian and a Unitarian" and she lost handily. She soon found some consolation in her relationship with the recently widowed Hobby; in 1931, despite the twenty-seven-year gap in their ages, they were married.

Although she bore him two children, Oveta had no intention of leading the garden club life of a Houston matron. No sooner had her husband bought the *Post* (from their friend Jesse Jones) than Oveta installed herself on the business side, shaking up both the advertising and circulation departments. After that, she turned her attention to the paper's radio station, KPRC, making a clean sweep there as well. At the same time, she continued to dabble in Texas politics.

With the outbreak of World War II, Washington beckoned. She persuaded the War Department (with the help, some would say later, of her Texas Democratic connections) that it needed a Women's Interests Section in its public relations effort—and that Oveta Culp Hobby was just the person to run it. When chief of staff George Marshall, seeking to ease his manpower burden, decided to form a Women's Auxiliary Army Corps, he asked Hobby to be its first director. Thus Oveta Culp Hobby, at thirty-six, became the highest-ranking woman in America's war effort.

Ignoring the benighted chortling that greeted the new distaff unit (at her first press conference reporters demanded to know what color underwear her recruits would be issued), Hobby determinedly molded the WACs, as the corps was soon known, into an important cog in the country's fighting machine. Her 100,000 women would handle virtually the entire gamut of noncombatant duties.

Striding purposefully through the War Department, trimly clad in her dress uniform and her trademark visored "Hobby hat," Oveta Hobby cut an imposing figure. She insisted on strict military discipline, complete with salutes and rigid adherence to rank, and bristled whenever her male counterparts violated her finely tuned code of etiquette. The department, she asserted, "will have to get used to the idea of treating WACs as officers, rather than as women."

Hobby brusquely dismissed any suggestion that her troops be accorded special treatment because of their gender. When some of her underlings balked at being shipped overseas, Hobby refused to intervene: "They're in the Army and they're soldiers and if they are needed they are going," she declared. By the same token, she reacted like an enraged lioness whenever the Army's Neanderthal policies conflicted with her notions of equality. Upon learning that women with out-of-wedlock pregnancies would be dishonorably discharged (for "Pregnancy Without Permission"), she argued that male soldiers who fathered illegitimate babies should be similarly drummed out of the service. The red-faced generals agreed to change the regulations: from then on, the women were given honorable discharges, and medical care to boot.

Her zeal in organizing and promoting the WACs won her many admirers, among them Dwight Eisenhower, and earned Hobby the Army's Distinguished Service Medal—making her the first woman to be so honored.

In July 1945 she left the WACs to return to her life as a newspaper magnate and Houston grande dame. But even as she settled into presiding over the *Post* and a twenty-seven-room mansion, Hobby found the lure of politics irresistible. In 1952 she was spurred into action by the candidacy of her old supporter Eisenhower. Even though Hobby, like her husband, was a Democrat, she unabashedly plunged into the bitter internecine battle between Taft and Eisenhower forces in Texas. Along with an outright endorsement of Ike on the front page of her newspaper, she blanketed the state with some 400,000 "nonpartisan" political primers that abetted the Eisenhower strategists' grass-roots campaign. Her efforts were critical in swinging the Texas delegation to the general—which, in turn, paved the way for his first-ballot nomination.

After his election, a grateful Eisenhower, looking to add at least one woman to his all-male inner circle, turned to Oveta Hobby. Perhaps in a nod to her organizational skills in the WACs, he tapped her to head the sprawling, unwieldy Federal Security Agency—even though Hobby had virtually no experience with the complex issues with which the agency was grappling. All she could say, upon accepting the appointment, was that "I'm in favor of people having security and I hope I can help."

No one seemed to care very much about her halting command of the issues, at least in her first few months on the job. Instead, there was considerable fascination with such elements of the Hobby style as the double-handled calfskin bag she personally designed to carry her business papers, her purse, and a Book of Common Prayer. There was much talk, too, about her feat of decorating her eight-room apartment in the capital in just nine days, complete with rare Chinese antiques and a Matisse. And her comely appearance (at forty-eight, she looked like a gracefully aging high-fashion model) always attracted attention, particularly when she was garbed in the full-length brocade evening gowns by Valentina that she favored for her evenings out.

In a cabinet larded with gray lawyers and paunchy businessmen, Oveta Hobby was a singular figure: a rare splash of color and chic in the monochromatic Eisenhower landscape.

"She was very feminine in her appearance and all, but you had the feeling there was a solid iron core there," recalled labor leader Nelson Cruikshank, who dealt extensively with Hobby. "It wasn't all softness and pink."

The bows and brocade could never quite conceal the flinty determination that had propelled her from Killeen. The same reporters who gushed about her recherché charm were treated to a good dose of Hobby's astringent side at her very first press conference as the new Secretary of Health, Education, and Welfare.

Asked by one newsman if she would deny she was now "a full-fledged Republican," Hobby shot back, "You ask me a specific question and I'll give you a specific answer." She loftily dismissed another political inquiry as "not a proper one."

The testiness came naturally to Hobby, but it was also symptomatic of the gnawing insecurity she felt in her new position. "She was way over her head," said Cruikshank. "It was just too big a job for her, and too complex." The old Federal Security Agency hands sensed it as well. William Mitchell, who had been with the department since the dawn of Social Security and now was deputy commissioner, observed that "Mrs. Hobby was extremely timid and uncertain—certainly at the beginning and to a certain extent during the entire period of her administration."

On the face of it, it seemed incredible that a woman who had run a big-city newspaper and built, from scratch, a vital unit of the U.S. armed forces, a woman who had held her own with imperious generals and rough-and-ready oilmen, could be overwhelmed and intimidated by anything. Incredible, that is, until one took the measure of the intricate, sprawling network of fiefdoms which Hobby now found herself running.

There was the awesome Social Security system, shepherding a $17 billion trust fund for almost 70 million Americans, and disbursing $4 billion a year in payments—a system that was still, two decades after its inception, under fire from diehard Republican critics; the Public Health Service, championing medical research through its own National Cancer Institute and National Institutes of Health, and through some $130 million a year in grants to hospitals; the Office of Education, now on the firing line as the nation grappled with the escalating school needs of the postwar baby boom; and the Food and Drug Administration, guardian of food and drug purity. And there were the myriad other endeavors the department directed or subsidized, whose scope testified to the federal government's commitment to the needy and handicapped: the Office of Vocational Rehabilitation, the Children's Bureau, the American Printing House for the Blind, the Columbia Institution for the Deaf, St. Elizabeth's Hospital for the mentally ill.

Attached to this huge federal edifice was a vast beehive of special interests, prodding and petitioning and pressuring the department on all sides. Social Security had organized labor as its watchdog, while the Public Health Service had to grapple with the potent American Medical Association, among others. The Food and Drug Administration was the perennial target of the pharmaceutical companies and the food manufacturers. As for the Office of Education, it had nothing less than the entire educational establishment, public and private, to contend with.

As capable as she was, nothing in Oveta Culp Hobby's experience prepared her for all this. She had no background in health issues, no background in education issues, no background in welfare issues (save the matters relating to these areas that came before her with the WACs). The demands of her wartime position were intense and unrelenting, but, compared to what she faced now, blissfully straightforward. With the WACs, there was, really, just a single constituency she had to please and persuade: the generals. Here, at HEW, there were scores of constituencies, scores of fiefdoms.

And, with the WACs, Hobby at least had a clear, unambiguous sense of her mission. In the new administration of Dwight D. Eisenhower, there was no such clarity.

Eisenhower could never get HEW's name right; he would refer to it as "Health, Welfare and What-Not." And this confused appellation was emblematic of the murky position of the department in his administration. On the one hand, HEW was the veritable incarnation of the welfare state that Republicans had incessantly reviled for over twenty years. On the other hand, such enterprises as Social Security and the FDA were now mainstays of American life, sacred cows that only the most diehard GOP fundamentalists dared pillory. By quickly elevating the department to cabinet status—and ignoring the warnings that the move would lead to socialized medicine and other abominations—Eisenhower was freely acknowledging this fact. What's more, during the campaign he had pledged to "improve and extend" the Social Security program to the millions of workers—farmers, domestic workers, the self-employed—who were still left out of the system.

But that was as far as Eisenhower was willing to go in the way of hard-and-fast commitments. The rest was left for Hobby to infer and divine from the scattered clues the President left in meetings and in public pronouncements. Was her mission to hew to Republican gospel: maintain the status quo, halt the spread of big government, and contribute to a balanced budget? Or was it to come up with new programs that would address what she acknowledged was "a growing concern today over the problems of education, health and social security"?

Adrift, uncertain, she often in those early days found herself stumbling. At one cabinet meeting, she proudly announced that HEW could make significant budget cuts, which pleased Eisenhower no end—until he learned that aid to education was one of the areas she was trimming. "I am amazed at the thought of an education cut," he fumed. "This is the most important thing in our society." He told Hobby that "every liberal—including me—will disapprove." A confused Hobby, on that day at least, was forced to come to terms with a "liberal" Eisenhower. What the next day would bring, she could only guess.

Struggling to get on top of the situation, Hobby, characteristically, buried herself in her work. She regularly put in ten-hour weekdays and five hours on Saturdays (the afternoons were set aside for her coiffures at Elizabeth Arden).

"She couldn't exercise her power and influence until she had gone through a tremendous amount of training," noted Mitchell. Yet all the hours of self-education still weren't enough. In her uncertainty, a vacillating Hobby, harking back to her military days, fell back on her chain of command—and on a torrent of memoranda and paperwork. The memos, recalled Mitchell, "had to go through eighty-seven hands."

For once in her life, the proud, supremely competent Oveta Culp Hobby found herself overwhelmed. But, to her credit, rather than continue to stumble along, she took a decisive step. She reached out for a strong, potentially overpowering number two.

One day in late May 1953, Nelson Rockefeller leaned out of a window at the HEW Building and watched as his name was stenciled onto a parking place below. "Well," he said to an aide standing with him, "I guess that means I'm in."

He wasn't in quite yet; he still had to be confirmed by the Senate. But the confirmation hearing on June 5 lasted all of ten minutes, and the only areas about which he was asked, after he read his opening statement, were his age, his educational background, and his connection with Rockefeller Center.

Six days later, in Hobby's office, he was sworn in as Undersecretary of HEW. A photo of the ceremony shows a youthful Rockefeller barely suppressing a grin as he takes the oath, while Tod and Hobby, looking like two dour, somewhat edgy maiden aunts, witness the proceedings.

The new position meant a return, after an eight-year hiatus, to the eighteen-acre estate on Foxhall Road—but not before some considerable improvements were made. The white frame and brick house was repainted and redecorated, and newly air-conditioned throughout. The already substantial swimming pool was enlarged, and the grounds were spruced up with new plantings, including a forty-foot tree that would help block out the view of neighboring houses. Despite all this work, the house would never be the family homestead it was during the war. The children were all off at college or boarding school; in fact, two weeks after his father's swearing-in, the oldest, Rodman, a junior at Dartmouth, wed Barbara Ann Olsen, a student at Wellesley.

Before moving into Foxhall Road again, Rockefeller took one other important step. He contacted his friends at the FBI and arranged for them to install "countermeasure devices" on his phone lines—that is to say, devices to foil potential wiretaps. Rockefeller was as anxious now as he was in his State Department days to prevent phone taps, although it was hard to imagine just who (the AMA? the American Federation of Labor?) might be interested in spying on an HEW Undersecretary. Perhaps it was simply force of habit, or perhaps it was a matter of his habitual cloak-and-dagger inclinations once again coming to the fore—even in as incongruous a setting as HEW. And, after all, as a past beneficiary of sub rosa activities, Rockefeller was in some position to know how pervasive they were in the capital.

From the first day he stormed through HEW's main entrance on Independence Avenue, Nelson Rockefeller moved with purposeful vigor, as though he had been working in the building for years. Oveta Hobby struggled to mold herself to suit her new situation; Rockefeller remolded his surroundings to suit himself.

For starters, he wanted a bigger conference room, and he equipped the larger room, out of his own pocket, with a long conference table and chairs. It quickly became known why he wanted such an expansive setting: he meant to make it his chart room.

Convinced, from his days as coordinator, of the potency of visual aids—a conviction heightened by his own dyslexia and his preference for the visual over the verbal—Rockefeller resolved to have a chart facility at HEW that was the equal of the one at the CIAA. Not only did he transform the conference space into a multimedia display facility, but he took over the adjoining room for use as a staging area, from which the charts, mounted on tracks, could be rolled in and out.

The expenditures for the chart shows startled HEW hands. "We just weren't used to spending money like that," said one. There was some grumbling from the White House, and later from Congress, about the expense, but Rockefeller had his way.

Rockefeller also wanted his own staff of handpicked assistants. Right after his arrival at HEW, he summoned Hobby's deputy Rufus Miles to his office, and handed Miles a list of bright young aides he wanted to hire. Miles began to expound on the department's budgetary constraints, but Rockefeller cut him off. "Do it," he commanded.

Five of the names on that list, Miles would later recall, were those of attractive young women.

One of them was Donna Mitchell, who had worked for Rockefeller on the President's Advisory Committee. Another was a lively recent Duke University graduate named Nancy Hanks, a friend of Mitchell's whom Mitchell had brought onto the Advisory Committee staff. In both cases, Rockefeller had more in mind than mere decoration. Mitchell would work on policy papers. And Hanks would serve as an all-around aide-de-camp—a Washington Louise Boyer.

Hanks and Mitchell were new faces in the Rockefeller retinue. But another of his prospective hires was a more familiar presence: Joan Braden.

Braden had moved to the capital a year earlier when her husband took on his position as Allen Dulles' deputy at the CIA. She remained in Rockefeller's employ: he hired her to run the Washington office of a nebulous venture called Hands Across the Sea, whose main purpose, she would later realize, was to give her something to do and keep her in the fold.

In June 1953 Braden was in a Washington hospital, having just given birth to her third child. She awoke and groggily focused on a familiar beaming personage at the foot of the bed: not her husband, Tom, but Nelson Rockefeller. After enthusing about her new baby girl, Rockefeller came to the point. "I know, Joanie, what you're going to say, but I need you and I want you to come back to work for me."

"Now I know you want to nurse her," he went on, "so how about after Labor Day?" Still in a daze, Braden said yes, and Rockefeller bounded off to his next appointment.

Much as was the case back in the 1940s, Rockefeller's comely staff raised many an eyebrow in the capital. One day, Mitchell remembers, a female newspaper reporter visited Rockefeller at HEW and asked him bluntly why he had so many women on his staff. "Well, I'll tell you," Rockefeller smoothly replied, "I find that when a woman has reached a level of competence, and she's been able to rise in this world, then she's got to be more intelligent than most anybody else around her. Besides," he added with a chuckle, "they're cheaper."

To Hanks, Rockefeller offered another explanation as to why he surrounded himself with women aides. "I have never liked to have a man assistant, and I don't want one now," he said. "I think that sometimes they create the feeling of jealousy or something with the other men lower in the department. . . . I figure that a smart, young, and attractive girl could do for me what I need and not cause this feeling."

The catch was that they had to be "smart, young, and attractive." The women he hired, says Mitchell, were indeed often overachievers—"but he usually made sure they were pretty darn good-looking, too." And the fact remained that while he put great trust in them and truly esteemed their abilities—far more than was the norm in the 1950s—these women never rose to a status higher than a sort of super majordomo or executive assistant. They could be Louise Boyer, but they could never be Frank Jamieson.

Rockefeller brought in a few men, too.

With Social Security at the top of the department's agenda, he saw the need for an assistant secretary who could work with him on the legislative program. There were plenty of veterans of the Social Security wars in the department whose expertise he could have tapped. But instead, Rockefeller turned to his legal confidant Oscar Ruebhausen. Could Ruebhausen come to Washington for a while?

Ruebhausen couldn't, but he recommended a young partner at Debevoise, Plimpton named Roswell Perkins. Perkins had not only a fine, meticulous legal mind but also impeccable Republican credentials, having worked in the Eisenhower campaign. With the White House putting increasing pressure on Hobby to fill high-level openings with stalwart Republicans, Perkins' selection couldn't have been more opportune. And there was no question about Perkins' eagerness to work for Rockefeller; earlier in 1953, he had been one of the young Republicans urging Rockefeller to run for New York mayor.

So it was that in a department full of wizened professionals—some of whom had lived and breathed Social Security issues since the system's inception twenty years earlier—Rod Perkins, twenty-seven, was tapped as Rockefeller's point man on Social Security.

"It was to be a sixty-day consultancy, a crash operation, reporting to him and Mrs. Hobby," says Perkins. "But I didn't emerge from Washington until nearly three and a half years later."

Another of Rockefeller's recruits was Hal Haskell, his old sailing cohort from Northeast Harbor. Independently wealthy in his own right (his father was a principal figure at Du Pont Chemical), Haskell was dabbling in some business ventures when the call came through from Rockefeller. The job Rockefeller had in mind for him was brand-new: Haskell would be secretary of the HEW department council, an assemblage of the top people in all of HEW's subsidiary agencies. The council was an early attempt by the perennial coordinator, Rockefeller, to coordinate the work of all those fiefdoms. It would be Haskell's job to organize the daily meetings of this council, at which department heads were expected to make presentations on their activities. Haskell's arrival on the scene was a signal to the rank and file: a signal of the new undersecretary's determination to control and choreograph the department. "He hadn't been over there but a month before everybody knew who the *Acting* Secretary of HEW was," says Donna Mitchell. "If you wanted anything done, you went to Nelson."

Yet at those daily briefings, it was always Hobby who was the chairperson, and Hobby who asked most of the questions (although some suspected that Rockefeller briefed her on the questions beforehand). As assertive as he was behind the scenes, Rockefeller was scrupulously careful not be seen to be usurping his boss's authority. No decision was reached without consulting her; no initiative was taken that had not been vetted with her first; no contacts were made with Congress or the executive branch of which she had not been apprised.

"Nelson was superb," remembers Perkins. "He was very respectful, very supportive, courteous, deferential. When he wanted to make a point, he would say, 'Well, now, Oveta, I wonder whether we should consider this.' And in private conversation, there were many times when he would say something to me like 'Look, we've got to reframe this, or do something that will put it more in line with what the secretary is looking for.'

"When we'd go up to Capitol Hill," continues Perkins, "he always, before Senate committees, would do everything to make it clear that she was the boss, and that he was there to help. Including lighting her cigarettes."

Rockefeller's friends took in this spectacle with slack-jawed wonderment.

"I've never seen anyone struggle or strain as much as he did to preserve the ultimate deferential protocol," remembers Oscar Ruebhausen. "It was not easy for him at all." Not only were his friends astonished at his performance but so was the White House. Presidential special assistant Kevin McCann would later observe that "the unusual thing about Nelson Rockefeller in those days, in my opinion, was his insistence on subordinating himself to Oveta, and not moving out into the front of the HEW picture."

Rockefeller seemed bent on dispelling, once and for all, the reputation as a conniving renegade that had followed him from the State Department. And, at least in his early months at HEW, he succeeded beyond anyone's expectations.

Rockefeller had not long settled into his job before he found Hobby laying off on him what was arguably the most onerous of her tasks: jettisoning the Democratic holdovers at HEW and finding capable Republicans to take their place.

All the departments, not just HEW, were coming under tremendous pressure from GOP operatives to do so. Eisenhower may have grumbled that he was "sick and tired" of hearing the patronage complaints, but the clamor for jobs did not abate.

HEW, as the most visible holdover of the New Deal, was an especially choice target for Republican apparatchiks. Many of its top tier of officeholders owed their appointments to Franklin Roosevelt; indeed, in the case of the Social Security Administration, a good number had been part of the formative years of their agency. Adding to the Social Security operation's vulnerability was the incessant drumbeat of criticism from such GOP hard-liners as Nebraska congressman Carl Curtis, who saw a golden opportunity now to fundamentally change the system.

Inside the department there were whispers that Curtis had sent over to Hobby a list of the top Social Security officials he wanted fired. Whether or not there was such a list, by the time Rockefeller arrived, Hobby had already made one dramatic move, ousting the revered longtime Social Security commissioner Arthur Altmeyer, who had presided over the system since its birth in 1935.

Now it was up to Rockefeller to spur the shake-up, which was another reason why he brought in the politically wired Hal Haskell. "Nelson made me the patronage guy because I knew politics," says Haskell. "He kept pushing me to hire Republicans."

But first, openings had to be created; a purge was in order. "The heads just had to roll," recalled one Social Security veteran. "They needed those jobs."

One day Rockefeller called the deputy Social Security commissioner, William Mitchell, to his office. "Bill," he said, "I'm very sorry to have to impart this news, but the Republican National Committee and the White House people have become so insistent that we are going to have to take you out of the job." Rockefeller didn't want Mitchell to follow Altmeyer out the door, and promised to find another position for him, but at the same time he made it plain that Mitchell had to vacate his present job because it had been identified as one "to be filled by people active in Republican circles."

Mitchell, a career civil servant who had diligently worked his way up the Social Security Administration ladder, was outraged. Rockefeller, he recalled, "was pretty callous about the situation," pointing out to Mitchell that he didn't have too many years until retirement, so he had best adapt himself to "whatever was worked out." In the meantime, because Rockefeller didn't as yet have a new commissioner lined up, Mitchell could remain the acting chief.

With Altmeyer gone, and Mitchell soon to be shunted aside, there remained in place one last mainstay of the system, one individual who had been present at the creation and had nurtured Social Security since its inception: Wilbur D. Cohen. His title (technical adviser to the commissioner) barely reflected his stature and influence; no one in America, save Arthur Altmeyer, had a greater command of the system's inner workings. As Illinois senator Paul H. Douglas once remarked, "A Social Security expert is a man with Wilbur Cohen's telephone number." It was Cohen, along with Altmeyer and FDR's Labor Secretary, Frances Perkins, who had drafted the original Social Security Act in 1935, and it was Cohen who had guided every major change in the law since through the Congress.

But any hope that Cohen's eminence, or his obscure title, might shelter him soon proved misplaced. Like Altmeyer and Mitchell before him, Cohen got the word that he would have to resign. But unlike Altmeyer and Mitchell, Cohen, at forty, still had his whole career ahead of him. He bluntly refused to step down—setting up a potentially embarrassing confrontation for Rockefeller.

It was at this point that organized labor, in the person of the rotund, cigar-chomping new president of the American Federation of Labor, George Meany, inserted its formidable presence.

For labor, Social Security was nothing less than a sacred covenant between government and the working class that was beyond politics. Ever vigilant in the system's defense, organized labor cast a wary eye on the first Republican administration to get hold of the program. And when HEW began jettisoning such stalwarts as Altmeyer and Cohen, the unions' gravest apprehensions were confirmed. With the high priests expelled from the temple, there was no telling what blasphemies might follow.

It was time, Meany decided, to draw the line. He called his top Washington operative, Nelson Cruikshank. "I want you to come over and we'll talk to Nelson Rockefeller," he said.

Cruikshank had only met Rockefeller once, but Meany and the undersecretary were already well acquainted. They first came to know one another in the 1930s, when Rockefeller was running Rockefeller Center and Meany was the president of the New York State Federation of Labor. Rockefeller's masterful negotiation of the Center's first union contract taught Meany, as it taught others in the labor movement, that Nelson Rockefeller was someone he could do business with. The two men kept in touch during Rockefeller's wartime tour in Washington. When Assistant Secretary of State Rockefeller was looking for a U.S. labor representative at the Chapultepec conference, he turned to George Meany.

Thus, the AFL leader had some reason to believe, as he and Cruikshank stepped into Rockefeller's office, that the HEW Undersecretary would listen seriously to his appeal.

Meany and Rockefeller talked a bit about old times. "Well," said Rockefeller, "you didn't come over here just to reminisce. What do you want?" Meany came straight to the point: the housecleaning at Social Security had to stop. The purge was costing the agency good people, people like Wilbur Cohen. Those people should be retained; the Social Security Administration should be kept out of politics. "We've never asked for a job or a bit of patronage in Social Security," he said, "and we never want to. But we do want to protect the career people." If Rockefeller wanted to know what labor's first concern about Social Security was, it was that.

Rockefeller listened. He could have pleaded force majeure and described the edicts he and Hobby were getting from the Republican National Committee and the White House. He could have talked about the need to placate Carl Curtis. He could have—but he didn't.

Instead, he told Meany and Cruikshank that he would do his best to stop the housecleaning. He took pains to point out that it was Mrs. Hobby who made the decisions—"but I'll see what I can do." What's more, according to Cruikshank's later account of the meeting, "Rockefeller came as close to promising as a person in public life could that there wouldn't be any appointments made in the Social Security field that were antagonistic to us."

It was a stunning capitulation and a startling commitment from a high official in a Republican administration presumed cool—if not downright hostile—to organized labor. Indeed, so remarkable was Rockefeller's undertaking that the cynical labor leaders might have been forgiven for concluding it was so much empty blather.

But Rockefeller proved to be as good as his word. A few months later, when he finally found a candidate for Social Security commissioner—John Tramburg, the Wisconsin director of public welfare—he phoned Cruikshank. "What would be your feeling about Tramburg?" asked Rockefeller. Cruikshank checked with his people in Wisconsin, who reported that he would be an excellent choice.

A dour Anna Rosenberg (between Rockefeller and former FDR confidant James Farley) looks on as Rockefeller gives a postwar talk. "Everything I've achieved here in Washington," Rockefeller remarked, "I owe to Anna Rosenberg."

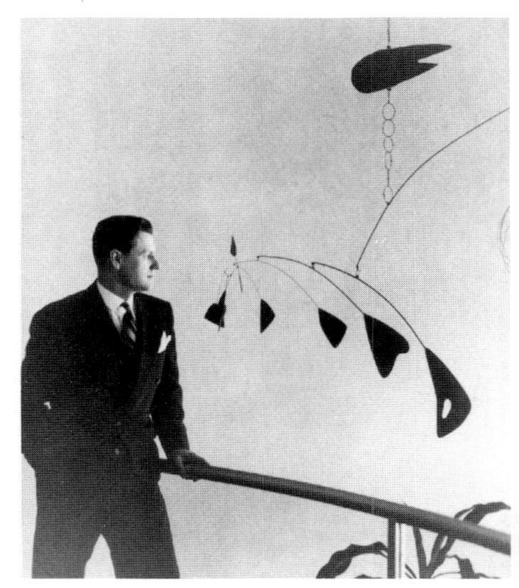

The connoisseur: scrutinizing a Calder at the Museum of Modern Art, 1948. *(Photo courtesy of Arnold Newman Photo)*

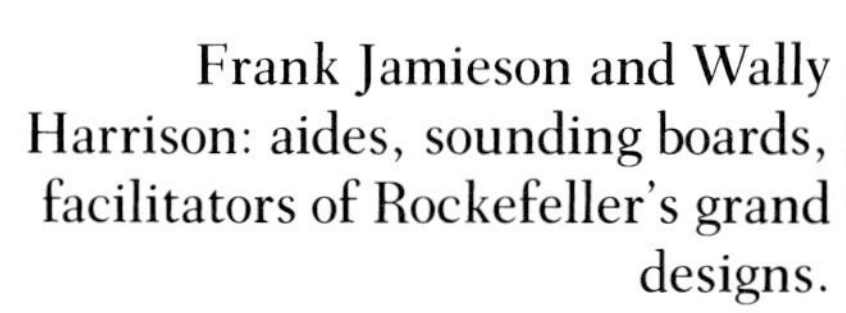

Frank Jamieson and Wally Harrison: aides, sounding boards, facilitators of Rockefeller's grand designs.

From a perch at Rockefeller Center, Rockefeller surveys the postwar skyline, including the United Nations, which owed its presence in New York to his maneuvering.

The brothers, circa 1950: Winthrop, David, Nelson, John D. III, Laurance. Nelson "saw himself as the ringmaster of the family," said an aide. "It seemed clear to *him* what roles everyone should play, even if it wasn't at all clear to *them*."*(Photo by Philippe Halsman, © Halsman Estate)*

At work in the fields of IBEC. Rockefeller had big plans for his Latin American venture, but ended up battered by big losses.

Monte Sacro, Rockefeller's hacienda in the Andes foothills of Venezuela, just one of his five homes.

Newlyweds Martha Baird Rockefeller and John D. Rockefeller, Jr., at Rockefeller Center. Appalled by their father's wedding plans, the brothers, including Nelson, tried to talk Martha out of going ahead with the nuptials.

Conferring with Harry Truman (the man in the center is unidentified). Rockefeller was the prime mover, and prime salesman, of Truman's dramatic Point Four initiative of Third World aid.

Mr. Undersecretary. Chartmeister Rockefeller tries to sell his health care plan, in the teeth of opposition from both left and right.

A winsome Nancy Hanks at the time she first went to work for Rockefeller. "He'd show her off," a colleague recalled. "She was a possession." *(Photo courtesy of Duke University Archives)*

"She became a problem." Joan Braden (left of President Eisenhower) was conspicuously present during this White House ceremony, joining Rockefeller's family and HEW Secretary Oveta Culp Hobby (seated, foreground). *(White House photo)*

Departing the Palais des Nations with Eisenhower after Ike's "Open Skies" proposal at the Geneva summit, July 21, 1955. Defying John Foster Dulles and the State Department, Rockefeller had rammed through the showstopping plan. *(Photo courtesy of UPI/Corbis-Bettmann)*

Henry Kissinger, at the time of his work on the Rockefeller brothers' reports. He resigned at least five times. *(Photo courtesy of UPI/Corbis-Bettmann)*

A handshake signifying nothing: In a bid to keep the Dodgers in Brooklyn, gubernatorial hopeful Rockefeller greets team owner Walter O'Malley at Gracie Mansion, with New York Mayor Robert F. Wagner as the man in the middle. *(Photo courtesy of Rockefeller Archive Center, © Louis Liotta)*

Pulling the right strings: Rockefeller and Assemblyman Malcolm Wilson (left) get together at a January 1958 Republican fund-raiser, through the good offices of Westchester GOP boss Herbert Gerlach (right).

As New York State Republican chairman, L. Judson Morhouse was supposed to be neutral, but behind the scenes he was Rockefeller's earliest and most energetic booster. *(Photo courtesy of Prestige Photos, Sammy Schulman)*

The "Rockettes" greet Rockefeller and spouse upon their arrival at the Rochester convention. *(Photo courtesy of Prestige Photos, Sammy Schulman)*

Breaking through the tangle—of boosters and of streamers—the nominee triumphantly makes his way to the convention podium. *(Photo courtesy of UPI/Corbis-Bettmann)*

"God must have meant Nelson to be a politician," exclaimed one awed old pro. Some vintage examples of the Rockefeller style: heading for the finish line . . . *(Photo courtesy of Prestige Photos, Sammy Schulman)*

. . . judging the bovine . . . *(Photo courtesy of Prestige Photos, Sammy Schulman)*

. . . nibbling (note the shirt) . . .
(Photo courtesy of Prestige Photos, Sammy Schulman)

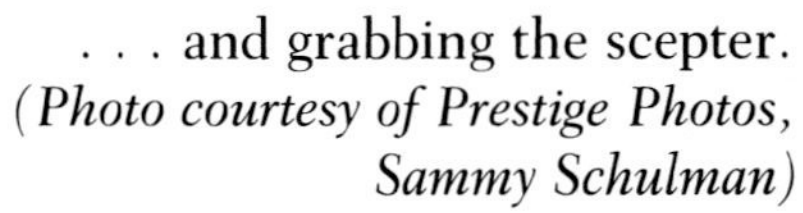

. . . and grabbing the scepter.
(Photo courtesy of Prestige Photos, Sammy Schulman)

Full Nelson: As his campaign reaches its frenetic peak, Rockefeller pumps hands in New York City's Garment District. *(Photo courtesy of UPI/ Corbis-Bettmann)*

Rockefeller found it harder to keep the other part of the bargain. The purge continued, albeit at a much-diminished pace. Mitchell kept his job as deputy commissioner, although, Mitchell would later say, this was more Tramburg's doing than Rockefeller's. (Mitchell hung on long enough to ascend to the commissionership himself in 1959.)

Wilbur Cohen was also permitted to stay on—but in a lesser capacity. He was given the vacant position of director of research and statistics, and forced to accept a $1,000 cut in pay. Formerly the department's most consulted figure, Cohen now found himself totally out in the cold. He stuck it out for three years, until finally, having had enough, he left for a teaching position at the University of Michigan.*

Cohen could have been treated better by the Hobby regime, but that was really no fault of Rockefeller's. The undersecretary had done his best; that was what he promised George Meany, and he had made good on that promise, and on others.

No one in the new administration was doing more for organized labor, and labor leaders knew it.

In its policies, as well as its personnel, this businessman's administration displayed a consistent indifference to the unions' point of view. And yet, looking back two decades later, George Meany would say that "the Eisenhower administration, in my book was by no means a bad time for labor." The reason, the sole reason, was Nelson Rockefeller. "Labor certainly made tremendous progress in health, education, medical care and things like that," said Meany. "It was because Nelson Rockefeller was running the Health, Education and Welfare Department, not Mrs. Hobby. She was the secretary, he was undersecretary, but she wasn't with it at all. . . . She just sat back and let Nelson run the show."

In catering to labor's demands, Rockefeller was treading on dangerous ground. By foiling the Social Security purge, for one thing, he was risking the wrath of the Republican Party apparatus and congressional critics like Carl Curtis. And had it become known that he was actually clearing his appointments in advance with the AFL, he would have encountered a partisan uproar that might well have driven him from office.

So why did he take those risks? Unquestionably, his craving for organized labor's support of HEW's legislative program, support that could spell the difference between success and failure in Congress, was one important factor. But there may have been another reason, having less to do with HEW than with his vaguer, more far-flung objectives.

*In 1961, with the Democrats back in power, Cohen returned to HEW, where he continued a distinguished career that was capped by his appointment as secretary in May 1968 by President Lyndon Johnson.

George Meany's gratitude, after all, was not a bad political marker to have in one's pocket.

In the midst of the uproar over the firings, it went virtually unnoticed that Rockefeller had quietly brought in his own man, Rod Perkins, to plot the future of Social Security.

The appointment of Perkins, a complete greenhorn on Social Security matters, was, if nothing else, a clever tactical move, since Perkins had no ties to any Social Security interest group, nor was he one of those career system insiders who were the bêtes noires of the program's conservative critics. Thus, anything Perkins proposed would have the benefit of an impartial viewpoint—a not inconsiderable advantage, considering how supercharged the politics of Social Security were becoming.

Under Representative Carl Curtis' pugnacious leadership, the conservatives were pressing their attack, and for once, instead of just shrill rhetoric, they had a credible alternative on the table. Put forward by the U.S. Chamber of Commerce, the plan would extend Social Security benefits immediately to all the aged in America, but at a cost: the dismantling of the whole superstructure of social insurance on which the system was built. Instead of financing benefits with contributions deducted from wage earners' paychecks—contributions that were then pooled in a trust fund, to be repaid to workers upon their retirement—the Chamber of Commerce plan would have put the system on a "pay as you go" basis, with workers taxed only enough to meet the system's current needs.

To longtime critics like Curtis, this scheme was both fair and fiscally responsible. But to the system's defenders, it was nothing less than a blueprint for the utter annihilation of Social Security. Without the cushion of a trust fund, the government would have to raise the revenues it needed each year to fund current benefits, and before long political pressures would mount to ease the tax burden by curtailing the whole program.

When Rockefeller brought Perkins on board, he left little doubt where *he* stood in the debate. Recalls Perkins: "Nelson's view was that the Republican administration had to demonstrate its concern for the individual by supporting the Social Security system, broadening it, making it better. A Republican administration couldn't be seen to be trying to turn back the clock." But it remained an open question whether Curtis' appeals for fiscal prudence, and the facile simplicity of the Chamber of Commerce plan, would strike a responsive chord in Eisenhower. Both Rockefeller and Hobby realized, said Perkins, that "if they were going to persuade President Eisenhower to oppose it, it was going to require a strong and effective articulation on their part." And that was where Perkins came in: "Nelson was very much looking to this study I was doing to help him out of the woods."

The program that Perkins formulated not only endorsed the current system but enhanced it, by increasing benefits and protecting the benefit levels of workers who become disabled. Rockefeller was delighted—it was exactly the sort of progressive approach he had in mind—and, once he had sold the report to Hobby (and Hobby, a staunch believer in the present system, needed little selling), he gave Perkins' handiwork the ultimate imprimatur: it would be translated into charts.

Then, visual aids in hand, the secretary and the undersecretary went to the White House on November 20 to make a full-dress presentation to the President and the cabinet. Hobby did most of the talking, and she proceeded to demolish the Curtis and Chamber of Commerce alternatives, decrying them as a "criminal raid on the Social Security trust fund." What her department was proposing instead, she said, was more beneficial to the aged, would have wide appeal—and was economically sound. When she finished, the cabinet broke into applause. It looked, said the President, as though the program was approved.

The presidential endorsement effectively quashed the Curtis–Chamber of Commerce initiative. But there remained the matter of shepherding the administration's program through Congress and neutralizing the inevitable salvos from Curtis. And here again, Rockefeller took the lead. He met with House Ways and Means Committee chairman Daniel Reed, who had once supported Curtis' calls for reform, and persuaded him to back the administration bill. When the time for testimony came, Rockefeller choreographed Hobby's presentations—assiduously orchestrating the cavalcade of charts—and, sometimes, took the microphone himself.

The Social Security bill wended its way through both houses, until finally on August 20, 1954—just hours before the weary Eighty-third Congress adjourned—a compromise measure was approved by voice vote. A week and a half later, in the course of a Rocky Mountain fishing trip, Eisenhower sat down at an unfinished redwood table and signed the bill into law.

"In strictly human terms," observed *The New York Times,* "this was perhaps the most significant achievement of the Administration in the 1954 session of Congress." The legislation brought ten million more Americans—farmers, farm workers, housemaids, self-employed professionals, government workers—into the system. It boosted the benefit checks of the 6.6 million persons already dependent on Social Security income. And, for the first time, it safeguarded the benefits of the disabled.

But as significant as all this was, what was even more significant was the identity of the protagonists. The strengthening of the Social Security program was, for once, the handiwork of Republicans, of Eisenhower, Hobby, and Rockefeller. As Wilbur Cohen would later point out, "for the first time in American history you could say there was truly a bipartisan support of it." The

1954 law, said Cohen, set "American social policy on a new course." Never again would the fundamental tenets of Social Security be seriously challenged.

A progressive by nature, Rockefeller wanted a Republicanism with a social conscience, a Republicanism that accepted the need for government intervention to right society's wrongs. This time, at least, he had his way.

Rockefeller notched one more key legislative victory in his first year at HEW, convincing Congress to expand federal aid for vocational rehabilitation. He seized on projections that, in the long run, the Treasury would earn ten dollars in tax revenues for every dollar it put into rehabilitation. "Every one of these people will be taken off of welfare," he exclaimed. "The government will *make* money on this!"

This performance, coming on the heels of Rockefeller's masterful lobbying for Social Security, left many of the department's old-timers awestruck. "Rockefeller instituted a revolution in the preparation of legislation," remarked one veteran official. "In the old days under FSA, we just wrote a bill and got up a stuffy letter to Congress and waited. Under Rockefeller, we spent a lot of time in preparation, getting up elaborate charts to show what we meant, and negotiating with committee chairmen on the Hill. He was ingenious in reconciling conflicting views."

He cemented the staff's allegiance by showing, as this man put it, that "he would fight for an idea." And, in making that fight, he would not hesitate to deploy his formidable network of resources, both inside and outside government—a network that HEW hands could only gape at in wonder. "He amazed me at the number of people he knew in government circles," said commissioner of education Samuel Brownell (the Attorney General's brother). "When I'd come up to discuss a problem with him, he would pick up the phone and call this person and that person, and the first thing we know, we had the information we wanted or the help we wanted."

And Rockefeller inspired loyalty with smaller gestures as well. After a team of HEW file clerks toiled long hours for several days in a row digging up data for the new budget, Rockefeller sought them out in their basement office to thank them, shaking hands all around.

Then there was the time his chart makers frantically stayed up half the night to pull together the presentation for a crucial congressional hearing the next day. "All these things had to be printed downstairs in the print shop, and run off and collated," relates Nadia Williams, an old coordinator's office chart hand who was now overseeing Rockefeller's graphics at HEW. "Everyone was up until four in the morning putting that together. And so was Nelson. He was always there when we had a rush. He'd come downstairs, and he'd make everybody feel better."

The contrast with the imperious, often remote Hobby—who insisted that her aides rise when she stepped into the room, as though this was still the WACs—could not have been starker.

And Rockefeller, intentionally or not, underscored the difference through the sheer brio with which he attacked all his activities. Playfulness was not a quality normally associated with federal undersecretaries, but playfulness was precisely the quality he brought to his job at HEW. For his birthday in 1954, his secretaries presented him with a bow tie that lit up in the dark and a propeller-topped beanie. Rockefeller donned the beanie and raced around his office suite, asking, "Is it twirling?" At the staff meeting that morning, his aides were convulsed with laughter when he arrived with his tie aglow and his beanie propeller spinning.

At Halloween, Rockefeller held a pumpkin-carving contest, and sent out a driver to pick up nine specimens. He lined them up on his big conference table, invited his aides in, and sat at the head of the table, presiding over the competition, and carving his own pumpkin in the manner of Picasso.

Suddenly, the door opened, and there was Hobby, taking in the spectacle. "Nelson," she said, "can I see you a minute?" He stepped outside, and was greeted by an angry Hobby, fuming at the notion that his secretaries could do something so unprofessional on HEW time. But it wasn't his secretaries' idea, he calmly informed her. It was *his*.

The next day, an exhibit of carved pumpkins, including Nelson Rockefeller's Picasso pumpkin, was put on display in the secretary's suite.

Rockefeller was as fulsome as ever in his public displays of deference; before Congress, the cabinet, and the press, he always yielded the floor to "Mrs. Secretary" (her preferred honorific). But these displays now had more the air of a court ceremony, a sweeping bow by a courtier before his queen. The reality of their relationship, as department insiders soon discerned, was far different.

"He was ambitious to make a name for himself, obviously," says Rufus Miles. "He sort of assumed that he had a lot more experience than she in the federal government. He assumed he should move in to take over whatever seemed to him essential and even things that were nonessential. At times he overdid it in terms of moving ahead without consulting her."

Hobby put up with his freewheeling ways for the same reason that Edward Stettinius before her had tolerated them: she needed Rockefeller—needed his persuasiveness with Congress, his gift for presentation, his adept handling of the staff, his unique ability to marshal outside expertise. And his dynamism—the very attribute that made him so troublesome—was what she prized most. Without him, she had floundered. With him, she presided over a cohesive, forward-moving department.

Still, there was no denying that a certain strained quality had entered into their relationship. "There was a standoffishness between the two," said Donna

Mitchell. "He was very diplomatic with her, but he was very forceful with her as well. She could never get her act together to be the dynamo that she had to be to get ahead of him. He was the dynamo. And he just overwhelmed her."

What overwhelmed Hobby, most of all, was the velocity and immensity of his ideas. "She was, sometimes, amused or skeptical of his grand schemes, as many were," recalls Perkins. Yet invariably, after offering her critiques, she would be swept up, as others were, by the schemes' propulsive force.

Such was the case with his great design for health care.

Ever since Harry Truman's abortive attempt to pass a national health insurance program in the late 1940s, a debate had raged about the adequacy and future viability of the country's private insurance system. While 93 million Americans had some form of health insurance, another 63 million had none. What's more, out of the United States' total annual medical bill of $9.4 billion, only $1.4 billion was covered by insurance. A single catastrophic illness could wipe out a lifetime of savings, even for an insured family.

But even the faintest suggestion of a federal insurance scheme to grapple with this problem sent Republican hard-liners into apoplectic rage. With the American Medical Association standing foursquare behind them, they railed against any program that hinted of "socialized medicine."

Eisenhower shared this revulsion (inveighing against "socialized medicine" many times in his campaign) and so did Oveta Culp Hobby. At her first press conference as HEW Secretary, she affirmed her faith in the existing system. Adequate medical care for all Americans, she was sure, could be achieved by "expanding and perfecting the system of voluntary, nonprofit, privately operated health insurance programs." She seemed inclined to do no more than fine-tune the status quo.

But that was before Nelson Rockefeller arrived on the scene.

At one of his first department meetings, Rockefeller proclaimed his special interest in health care. In his view, the administration could not sit on its hands on the health insurance issue; it had to do *something*. At the same time, he made it clear he was not talking about a nationalized system, but one that worked within the private, voluntary framework.

"He felt that the private health insurance system was basically the way to go and to build on," says Perkins. "He truly believed the government should have a limited role." (Of course, even if he didn't believe that, he would have to take that position anyway, given the Eisenhower administration's inclinations.)

What was needed, Rockefeller decided, was a task force, and he promptly set one up. It included a sizable contingent of insurance company executives, from Blue Cross, Blue Shield, Connecticut General Insurance, and the like—underscoring Rockefeller's commitment to enhance, not replace, the existing system. But it also included Rockefeller's counsel and friend Oscar

Ruebhausen, a Democrat who was a proponent of the Truman plan. Ruebhausen, however, realized that "it was impossible in the Eisenhower administration to have a federal health insurance program." So he focused, with the others, on a more middle-of-the-road course.

The plan they came up with was, if nothing else, an ingenious balancing act. It called not for federal health insurance, but for federal health *reinsurance.* The government would goad the insurance companies to broaden their coverage by setting up a reinsurance fund that would compensate them for any "abnormal losses" they suffered as a result. Initially, the government would kick in $25 million to get the program off the ground, but eventually the insurers' premium payments into the fund would, theoretically, make the program self-sustaining. Thus, the administration could solve the health care crisis—without infringing one iota on the private insurance system. Ruebhausen, for one, thought the whole thing smacked of excessive gimmickry—he called it the "Rube Goldberg reinsurance plan"—but Rockefeller couldn't have been happier.

The program was swiftly incorporated into legislation, and the plan was for Eisenhower to unveil it in a special message to Congress in January 1954. So stealthily did Rockefeller move that the first whiff the cabinet had of the plan was when Eisenhower sent around a draft of the speech for comment. Treasury Undersecretary Marion Folsom was aghast at the scheme, which he saw creating a huge bureaucracy to police every single insurance policy, and so was his boss, George Humphrey. "He hit the ceiling," said Folsom. They took their concerns to budget director Joseph Dodge, who was much less worried: "It'll never get through the Congress anyhow," he assured them.

Whatever Treasury's anxieties were, they were set aside by Eisenhower, who put his stamp of approval on the Rockefeller plan. "I think he assumed that this was one way you could do something without getting the government involved," explained Folsom. "I don't think he thought much beyond that point."

Although many of the leading insurers were lined up behind the plan, it remained to be seen what the most potent medical lobby of them all, the AMA, would do once the bill was introduced. Rockefeller and Hobby didn't have to wait long. On April 5, the organization issued a blistering condemnation of the reinsurance scheme, proclaiming it an "opening wedge" for socialized medicine. The association made it plain that it didn't want the federal government playing *any* role—even this modest one—in health insurance.

Meanwhile, on the other end of the spectrum, organized labor and other supporters of national health insurance were slamming the HEW plan for not going far enough.

To counter the opposition from the right, Rockefeller orchestrated a series of endorsements of the plan by the big insurance companies, culminating in a White House luncheon for insurance executives with the President in mid-

May. He also offered to amend the bill to specifically disclaim any federal intention to regulate the insurance business. And, in a last-ditch bid to go over the heads of the special-interest groups, he arranged for Hobby to appear on national television to appeal for public support of the reinsurance program.

But all his exertions counted for little. The reinsurance plan was doomed. And what sealed its fate was not the lobbying of the AMA, but the long shadow of Texas politics.

The endgame began when organized labor tried to cut a deal with HEW for labor backing of the scheme. Fearing that the concessions to the unions might further rile the AMA, Rod Perkins hemmed and hawed and finally, according to the AFL's Cruikshank, broke off the talks, curtly informing the labor leaders that the bill could be passed without their support. Infuriated AFL officials, determined now to kill the bill, decided to play their hole card: the deep-rooted enmity they knew that Sam Rayburn, the House Democratic leader and former Speaker, felt toward his fellow Texan Oveta Culp Hobby.

Rayburn, it seemed, found Hobby's defection to the Eisenhower camp an unforgivable sin, a betrayal of the Texas Democratic organization that had nurtured her career. "They felt they had made her," related Cruikshank: propelling her from clerical obscurity in the Texas legislature, greasing the business wheels that brought her and her husband control of the *Houston Post,* greasing the political wheels to get her the appointment to the WACs.

The AFL's Capitol Hill lobbyist, Andrew Biemiller, went to see "Mr. Sam," and after the meeting confidently assured Cruikshank, "Don't worry about their passing this bill." Henceforth, when labor's supporters in Congress asked Biemiller how they should vote on the health care bill, he simply told them, "Follow Mr. Sam. We have no position."

"Sam put the word out that this was one he was personally interested in," recalled Cruikshank, "and he wanted to kill it and kill it hard." And kill it hard he did. When the reinsurance bill came before the House on July 14, it was quashed by an overwhelming vote of 238 to 134—just hours after GOP leaders had predicted easy passage. And leading the way in vituperation was the normally taciturn Sam Rayburn: the reinsurance plan, he declared, was "a blundering, stupid way" to start a health program.

The coalition that defeated the bill, noted Cruikshank, was "the most curious combination of right-wing reactionaries and left-wing liberals that you ever saw." The right-wing fell in behind the AMA. The left-wing followed Mr. Sam.

Eisenhower reacted angrily to the setback. His fingers pounding on his desktop, he fumed to reporters that "the people that voted against this bill just don't understand what are the facts of American life."

"This," he vowed, "is only a temporary defeat. This thing will be carried forward as long as I am in office."

But the administration's attempts to revive the program in the next session of Congress quickly fizzled: the opposition was simply too entrenched, and Rayburn's influence too persuasive. Rockefeller's health insurance plan expired, a victim of special-interest antagonism and plain old Texas vengeance.

Rockefeller knew in 1954 that something had to be done about the health care squeeze. But with his failure, the crisis would be left to another generation, four decades later, to grapple with.

Despite the defeat, Rockefeller had not lost faith in the reinsurance plan's underlying premise: that a well-coordinated, programmatic synergy between big business and big government offered the best hope of remedying the nation's social ills. He was that rarest of birds in the Eisenhower administration aviary: a committed capitalist who was also a committed government interventionist.

Rockefeller was convinced that this happy melding of the public and the private would have eased America's health care burden. And he was equally convinced it was the answer to a crisis every bit as daunting: the widening gap between America's educational needs and its educational means.

With the postwar baby boom in full swing, the country was now faced with the task of educating the legions of youngsters descending on its schools. Throughout America, parents and school authorities were confronted with the appalling truth: there were not enough qualified instructors to teach the baby boomers, and not enough school buildings and classrooms, and unless something drastic was done, the shortfall would only get worse in the decade ahead. The number of new teachers had actually declined 21 percent since 1951, and overcrowded elementary school classes—many with forty or more students—were the rule. By one 1954 reckoning, the country had not produced enough new elementary school teachers that year to cover all the additional classes opening that fall—let alone enough to ease the overcrowding.

Just as pressing was the need for physical facilities to house these hordes. "Communities everywhere report that they simply cannot build schools fast enough to keep up with the increasing population," observed *The New York Times*. According to commissioner of education Samuel Brownell, the nation in March 1954 was short 340,000 elementary and secondary school classrooms. Constructing enough buildings to meet this need would cost $10 to $12 billion. And, he added, "this does not provide for the oncoming increased enrollment." One blue-ribbon advisory panel estimated that as many as 950,000 new classrooms would be needed over the next decade—at a total cost of $32 billion.

Local school districts gamely struggled to keep up, but found themselves swamped by the sheer magnitude of the demands. To the school boards, to their communities—and to an increasing number of their elected representatives—there seemed but one way out of the bind: a massive program of federal assistance.

The federal government, however, for all of Eisenhower's rhetoric about the importance of education, was wary about getting involved. Brownell repeatedly sounded the alarm about the nation's needs, but was inclined to leave the whole matter in the hands of the states and localities, insisting that they "have fiscal resources and legal authority to spend much more for school construction than they do." Budget director Joseph Dodge contended that federal aid would actually "slow down the total rate of school construction. Many school districts would hang back in the hope of getting some Federal money, if not in one year than in another."

Joining in the shrugs, at least initially, was Nelson Rockefeller. He went along with Brownell's judgment that the only response of the federal government should be a White House conference on education, at which various proposed remedies could be discussed—an idea that merely postponed the federal day of reckoning. He agreed with Brownell that the problem should be kept "within the framework of state and local responsibility."

Congress, however, faced with the clamor from constituents, was not prepared to be nearly so standoffish. In the course of 1954, bills were introduced in both houses calling for as much as $1 billion in federal aid for school construction over a two-year period. The administration could no longer sidestep the issue; it was under mounting pressure to come up with a concrete alternative to the congressional schemes. The task of finding one landed, as so much else did, on Rockefeller's desk.

And Rockefeller, in turn, rummaged through his formidable network of expertise. "Perhaps Nelson's greatest genius," Rod Perkins reflected years later, "was to identify a problem and get the best minds to work on it that he could find. He harnessed good minds probably as well as anyone in political history." In this case, the best mind he could find, someone familiar with every nuance of educational financing, was already working for him, up in New York: the former state comptroller and lieutenant governor, Frank Moore.

Brainstorming the school construction dilemma with Moore and Perkins, Rockefeller was not content to just pore over the usual financial routes. Once again, he brought up the possibilities of the private sector. Says Perkins, "Nelson's mind began to move immediately toward the question of how you harness private capital into all of this. He wanted to know, 'Why isn't it possible to utilize the financing structures of our whole capital-raising system to build schools?' "

This spin on the problem sent the discussion off in a direction for which even the supremely savvy Moore was unprepared. He consulted with some investment banker friends, and they in turn suggested he get in touch with an attorney they knew, an expert in municipal finance who had acquired a reputation, among Wall Street cognoscenti, as an innovative thinker. The attorney's name was John N. Mitchell.

A balding, close-lipped man of saturnine countenance, the forty-one-year-old Mitchell seemed hardly the sort to innovate anything. Yet as a partner in the little-known firm of Caldwell, Trimble & Mitchell, he had achieved a singular breakthrough in the staid, settled world of public finance. It came in the arena of public housing, when many states were confronted with voter resistance to bond issues that would finance the projects. Since voter approval was required under the state constitutions, the states were at a dead end—until Mitchell stepped in with a brilliant scheme for circumventing the electorate. The states would set up public corporations to issue the housing bonds, which would be backed not by the states' own credit, but by the rental income of the housing units. Since the bonds were not state obligations, no voter approval was required.

Mitchell denied the idea was his. Actually, he said, "I cribbed it from Wisconsin," which for years had a separate corporation financing public works around the state. And, in fact, Mitchell's brainchild was nothing more than an elegant reworking of the already well-worn public authority device, whereby states set up separate authorities (like New York's Triborough Bridge and Tunnel Authority) to build bridges and tunnels with bonds backed by toll revenues. But Mitchell alone had seen the potential versatility of the corporation concept, the multiplicity of uses to which it could be put by enterprising government officials.

Now Frank Moore was presenting him with a new challenge: how to tap the capital markets to bankroll the nation's school construction needs. And as Mitchell twirled the problem around in his supple mind, he concluded there was a way his magical conception could be put to work here as well.

The states, he suggested, could set up school building authorities. Those authorities would issue bonds, construct schools, and then rent them to local school districts on a lease-purchase basis (that is, the school districts would obtain ownership of the buildings once the bonds were paid off). The bonds would not be direct obligations of the states, but the states would contribute one-half of a reserve fund for the servicing of the authority bonds. The other half would come from the federal government.

With this complicated apparatus, everyone's objectives, seemingly, would be served. The bond markets would be opened up to fund local school needs (through the borrowings by the school construction authorities). The states would not run up against constitutional debt limits, which they would if they were to issue their own bonds for the schools. The federal government would play a role, but one that would be neither obtrusive nor very expensive (its contribution to the reserve funds, in toto, would be a modest $150 million).

"It was a great program for a middle-of-the-road approach," says Perkins.

"It was completely consistent with the Eisenhower philosophy, and it was a way of harnessing a partnership of the federal government and private enterprise." Rockefeller wholeheartedly agreed; the Mitchell plan was exactly the masterstroke he was searching for. It emerged as the centerpiece of the President's long-awaited educational aid package—a program that would finance, through the state authorities, some $6 billion in school construction over three years.

But no sooner was the proposal announced than it was savaged, and for many of the same reasons that the health reinsurance plan was attacked. Like the reinsurance scheme, it was dismissed by one senator after another as a gimmicky halfway measure that would have little impact on the fundamental problem. Alabama's Lister Hill, the chairman of the Senate Labor and Public Welfare Committee, which would be taking up the legislation, charged that the plan offered only "interminable delay on the one hand or a meager dole on the other."

The decisive blow against the program came from the educators themselves, through the National Education Association. The NEA, at Senate hearings, denounced the "no state school authority–no aid" aspect of the plan, pointing out that unless those authorities were set up, the nation's poorest school districts would be denied any federal aid. The plan was just too complicated for the teachers, who wanted, instead, simply an outright grant of federal funds.

In the end, the clever school construction program pushed by Rockefeller met the same fate as his clever reinsurance scheme: an unceremonious burial by a derisive Congress. The stratagems, ingenious though they were, were plainly too convoluted, too cute, for their own good.

Although the program never saw the light of day, the school construction plan—and the man who formulated it—lingered in Rockefeller's memory, and would shadow his future.

The time would come, not very many years hence, when Rockefeller would summon up that blueprint: a blueprint for a public building authority issuing bonds that were, and weren't, guaranteed by the state. The time would come when he would use it to build and build, on a scale far grander than anything he envisioned while toiling for Eisenhower's HEW. And when he did, he would again call on the architect of the whole scheme, the pipe-puffing bond lawyer from Caldwell, Trimble & Mitchell.

John N. Mitchell would be there to help Rockefeller realize his dreams. And, not very long afterward, the poker-faced attorney would also be there to crush them.

In the early summer of 1954, when Rockefeller's breakneck agenda at HEW was at full gallop—with the reinsurance plan coming up before Congress, and the Social Security package on its way, and the school aid schemes in progress—he received word, while closeted with his aides in the conference room, that two visitors wanted to see him.

The two men, one trim and dashingly attired, the other portly and virtually bursting out of his business suit, were Tex McCrary and Bill Zeckendorf. They were surely among the most unlikely personages ever to step through the corridors of HEW: Zeckendorf, the grandiloquent real estate mogul and high priest of the cult of leverage, and McCrary, the public relations whiz, television and radio personality, and Stork Club habitué.

Both men were virtuoso promoters—of deals, of personalities, and, in McCrary's case, of Dwight Eisenhower's candidacy in 1952. And they were calling on Rockefeller to talk about their latest promotion: the nomination of Nelson Rockefeller as the Republican Party's candidate for New York governor in 1954.

Just a few weeks earlier, the word had gone out that Tom Dewey would not run for a fourth term. The party had to search for a new standard-bearer, and McCrary, after talking it over with his good friend Jock Whitney, decided that Rockefeller was the one. He mentioned the possibility to Zeckendorf, for whom he was doing p.r. work, and Zeckendorf thought it was a fabulous idea; so enthused was he that he offered to help McCrary make the approach to Rockefeller. "Boy, do I know how to sell a Rockefeller," he told McCrary. "Let me go down there with you."

McCrary, meanwhile, was working his White House contacts. He sent a note to Sherman Adams contending that Rockefeller was the only Republican in New York who could beat Franklin D. Roosevelt, Jr., then the front-runner for the Democratic nomination. Adams sent copies of the letter to GOP national chairman Leonard Hall, to White House press secretary James Hagerty, and to top Eisenhower political counselor Thomas Stephens. The only one of the three who responded was Hagerty, who advised Adams that a Rockefeller nomination would be a terrible mistake; Hagerty, who had previously worked for Dewey, didn't think Rockefeller had a glimmer of a chance.

Unfazed, McCrary and Zeckendorf resolved to pop in on Rockefeller anyway. Before they did, McCrary touched base with Oveta Culp Hobby, who had no objection to the approach; in fact, McCrary recalls, she was all for it.

The two men took their seats in Rockefeller's office and proceeded to brandish a yellow legal pad on which they had ticked off the reasons why Rockefeller should run. Not only could he beat FDR, Jr., they pointed out, but he could trounce Averell Harriman, whom the Democratic regulars, led by Tammany Hall boss Carmine De Sapio, were backing for the nomination. "Here is somebody as rich as you are," McCrary said. "Wealth would not be an issue." And McCrary and Zeckendorf were not shy about mentioning the exalted horizons for which the New York governorship would be a stepping-stone. Recalls McCrary, "I said to Nelson, 'If you win you'll be like Roosevelt, like Dewey. You'll be in the ball game for the big run.' "

Rockefeller sat and listened, keeping his own counsel. Afterward, McCrary heard from Hobby. Rockefeller had just talked to her about the overtures, and, said Hobby, "I urged him to do it."

Jock Whitney also chimed in. He, too, vigorously urged Rockefeller to consider a race.

Rockefeller, however, remained on the fence. And as the days slipped by, the ever-conniving Zeckendorf attempted one last ploy to force his hand.

Each Sunday evening, Zeckendorf knew, Governor Dewey met with the legislative leadership at the executive mansion in Albany. One day Zeckendorf phoned Dewey's counsel, George Shapiro. "George," he said, "at the next meeting I'd like to ask you to raise the issue of the candidacy for governor in November." Shapiro asked him what exactly he had in mind. Replied Zeckendorf, "I think I have a candidate that would be an easy winner, easy to work with, easy to live with." And who might that be? Shapiro inquired. "Nelson Rockefeller," said Zeckendorf.

"I reacted with a little bit of shock," remembers Shapiro. "For the Republicans, who had always been badgered as the party of the rich, to name Nelson Rockefeller seemed to me to be a very questionable bit of wisdom."

Nonetheless, Shapiro gave his word to Zeckendorf that he would at least bring it up. And so, at the next Sunday meeting, Shapiro delivered Zeckendorf's spiel for Rockefeller. When he got to the punch line—Nelson Rockefeller's name—one of the leaders let out a big, booming laugh. "For the Republican Party to nominate a Rockefeller would be *suicidal,*" this man chortled.

Relates Shapiro, "It was that laughter that really decided the issue for that meeting. Because his laughter made the whole idea sound silly." The prospect of a Rockefeller candidacy had effectively been laughed into oblivion. Zeckendorf's maneuver had backfired.

Whether it was because of this incident, or because his advisers, notably Anna Rosenberg, were adamantly against a 1954 run—or because he still had a full plate of unresolved issues at HEW—Rockefeller soon made it known to his prospective sponsors that he would not join the race. The nomination went to Dewey's handpicked choice, the solid but uninspiring Senator Irving Ives. His opponent would, in fact, be the Democrats' millionaire, Averell Harriman.

In November, despite Ives's lackluster campaign, the Democratic machine's solid grip on the New York City vote, and Harriman's stellar credentials, Ives lost by a mere 11,000 votes—the thinnest margin in the state's history. How Rockefeller might have fared is anyone's guess, but it would not be too far-fetched to assume—as Tex McCrary would always assume—that with his exuberant, if unpolished, political personality, Rockefeller could have won those 11,000 votes.

He may have blanched at a gubernatorial run that year, but Rockefeller did not mean to turn his back on Albany.

It so happened that shortly after the election, Dewey asked George Shapiro if he was free on a certain day. "I would like you to take Nelson Rockefeller through the state capitol," said the governor. "Show him around the place physically, and introduce him to as many people as you can." To Shapiro, it was not clear whether this was Rockefeller's idea or Dewey's. But in any case he agreed to be the escort.

"I took him around and introduced him," remembers Shapiro. "He was young, filled with vitality and good spirit, and he already had the 'Hiya, fella' bit of embracing you."

Afterward they went to lunch. "I've enjoyed this enormously," said Rockefeller. "Could I prevail upon you to do it again from time to time?"

Shapiro said he would be delighted. Then, in passing, he mentioned the constitutional convention the state was required to hold a few years hence, and the need to assemble a commission of eminent citizens to prepare for it.

It was something they could talk about the next time they had lunch.

Thirty-one

Nancy Hanks

Wherever Nelson Rockefeller went as HEW Undersecretary, whatever he did, his twenty-seven-year-old executive assistant, Nancy Hanks, was at his side.

"She was in on every meeting, practically," remembers Rod Perkins. "Taking notes. And she was damn good." Hanks, said Donna Mitchell, "was the person that people went to if they wanted to get through to Nelson. . . . She was almost an appendage to Nelson. The only place he ever went without her, I think, was to the bathroom. . . . He never had a meeting, as far as I can remember, with anybody, that Nancy wasn't there"—although "he would once in a while see Mrs. Hobby without Nancy."

When Hanks joined his office, Rockefeller told her he wanted her to "control all our mail" and cultivate contacts throughout the executive branch. This she did, but she also did much, much more. "She kept tabs on everything that was going on," said Mitchell. "She would attend all of the conferences, all of the strategy conferences at HEW." Working with Mitchell, Hanks would vet all the department's position papers before they reached Rockefeller's and Hobby's desks. As Rockefeller's eyes and ears, Hanks would shepherd legislative proposals through the HEW ranks, coordinating with "the program people, the assistant secretaries, all the way down to the budget and the legal staff," said Mitchell. And when Rockefeller took his proposals to Capitol Hill, buttonholing congressmen or staff members, or presenting testimony, Hanks was always hovering in the background, ready with the data or the chart that would clinch the sale.

"She could keep up with Nelson because her mind was absolutely first-rate," recalls Hal Haskell. "She understood the politics instantly." Her fluid competence and incisive intelligence brought to mind Rockefeller's New York assistant Louise Boyer. Yet unlike Boyer, whose haughty Auchincloss manner many found off-putting, Hanks displayed a shy self-effacement that charmed just about everyone with whom she came into contact. "She was really chief of staff, but she would make everybody else think they were her superior," says Haskell. "She was much smarter than I was, and yet she pretended to be secondary."

To excel, but to do it quietly, with a minimum of fuss, had always been Nancy Hanks's way. The daughter of a strong-willed attorney with a taste for speculative ventures, she learned to accommodate herself to her family's meandering lifestyle; in the course of her youth, the family moved from Miami, Florida, to Montclair, New Jersey, to Fort Worth, Texas, prompting friends to describe them as "nomads" and "professional visitors." The one element of stability in their lives was their summer retreat in the North Carolina mountain community of Cashiers; there, father Bryan Hanks assembled a six-hundred-acre spread of woods, ravines, and waterfalls where his children could roam.

Staying close to Cashiers, Nancy matriculated at Duke University, where she endeavored in every respect to fit into the norm. On one of her first jaunts through the campus with her freshman roommate, Nancy insisted that they "say hello to everybody" because the Duke handbook said "everyone says hello to everybody." Although hardly a great beauty, she was attractive enough, and her liveliness and vivacity won her election as a campus May Queen. Eager to join a sorority, she rushed them all and was energetically courted by them in return.

Hanks seemed well launched on the typical vector of the Duke coed circa 1950: a degree in some innocuous liberal arts field (in her case, botany), followed in very short order by marriage and children. But then a series of calamities set her off course. First, there was the death in a truck accident of her younger brother; with his son's passing, Bryan Hanks suddenly was intent on seeing his surviving child truly make something of herself. Then there was the sad denouement of her romance with a Boston physician, broken off over the thorny issue of her husband-to-be's staunch Catholicism. Adrift, she spent a summer in England, studying at Oxford, and then decided to find a position for herself in Washington.

Her father's not inconsiderable connections won Hanks a job at the Office of Defense Mobilization, run at the time by his old friend Charlie Wilson, the future Secretary of Defense. But the best Wilson could do for a botany major utterly lacking in secretarial skills was a receptionist's position. Congenitally buoyant, Hanks plugged away, never allowing her lowly role to dampen her joie de vivre. Virginia Read, with whom she shared an apartment, remembered her popping in the door each evening "with a bunch of flowers in her arms, ecstatic over their beauty. . . . At other times, she would fling open the door and parade around with a wild new hat or an umbrella. Or she would pile all her purchases on the couch and open them, one after another, for me to behold."

Then, in early 1953, a fresh, bracing breeze wafted through the stuffy corridors of the Office of Defense Mobilization, in the person of one Nelson A. Rockefeller. Looking for staff for his government reorganization panel, he pulled in various ODM people. And among those who were swept up by him—in more ways than one—was Nancy Hanks.

In March, she breathlessly wrote her parents, "Mr. R's comment when I said that the daffodils on my desk were just to brighten up this dreary day (it's raining): 'You're the brightest thing in this office.' . . . So you see, he is really a very thoughtful person. Always complimentary and appreciative."

Rockefeller appreciated Hanks's hitherto untapped organizational skills, her perky serenity—and her sparkling good looks. Dark-haired, blessed with an enviable figure ("she looked absolutely marvelous in her clothes, which were not in themselves very interesting," remembered her college roommate), Hanks radiated a wholesome charm that truly did brighten every room she entered. "She had something about her, all her life, that drew people to her, that I have yet to explain," observes her close friend Donna Mitchell. Perhaps, she opines, it was because Hanks "made them feel, not overtly but very subtly, like they were the most important people in the world."

Attracted to Hanks, Rockefeller soon took her into his confidence to a degree that transcended the normal boss-secretary relationship. He spoke with her about his decision to accept Hobby's job offer. "I was shocked and crushed when I first heard," Hanks reported to her parents, but she managed to persuade herself it was for the good of the country. "It surely is not a spectacular or an 'in the public eye' job," she said, "but I admire him more for going into one where he thinks that he can do the most good." By then, it almost went without saying that wherever Rockefeller went, Nancy Hanks would go, too.

"Very shortly after we went over to HEW on the first of June," recalled Mitchell, "she started to go out to Nelson's house for work sessions. There may have been other staff there, there may not have been, whatever it was, but they would work on papers all weekend, and sometimes in the evenings. They were both workhorses. They never let up."

At the same time, Mitchell couldn't help noticing that Hanks's previously active social life was shriveling to the negligible. "This revolving door of boyfriends, they would call, but she was too busy to see them. She really didn't date very much then. She was too dedicated to her work and to Nelson." To Mitchell, it was also apparent that Hanks's devotion to her job was of a different order than her own. "I would get all charged up about something, but Nancy never did," Mitchell noted. "I was dedicated to Nelson and to the issues," whereas "Nancy was more dedicated to Nelson than she was to the issues."

In her frequent missives to her parents in Fort Worth, Hanks was giving enough of a picture of her growing attachment to Rockefeller to send shivers down the fundamentalist spines of Bryan and Virginia Hanks. Within weeks of her start at HEW, Bryan saw fit to send his daughter the sternest of warnings about "keeping your relationship with those you are closely associated with on a *businesslike basis.* This does not mean you cannot be friendly; cannot have a happy time in your work; cannot have pleasure over 'this and that' in your work and working with others. BUT from experience, Nancy, I know how disaster can come to one's employment and/or its relationships by too much familiarity . . ."

To Nelson Rockefeller, of course, there was no such thing as "too much familiarity." His conception of what constituted a "businesslike basis" was, to say the least, rather elastic. This was, after all, the same man who had suggested to Joan Braden that "working together and sleeping together are the same thing. They're part of a whole."

With that postulate in mind, it was, perhaps, no coincidence that his liaison with Hanks was ripening at much the same time that he was experiencing a vexing change in his relationship with Braden.

Shortly after Braden came to work for him at HEW, Rockefeller sought out a new position for her: that of personal assistant to Secretary Hobby. In essence, she would be Hobby's Nancy Hanks. Ostensibly, he offered Braden to Hobby in the spirit of helpfulness: the secretary's staff, in his view, was deficient, and Hobby needed a strong right arm to organize her schedule and set her priorities. But Braden, and others, suspected some less altruistic motives. Braden believed the job was a Rockefeller attempt to keep her from fleeing to California to help her husband with his newly acquired newspaper. And it was hard not to surmise that by planting his good friend Braden in Hobby's inner circle, Rockefeller was assuring himself of one more lever of control over the department.

Hobby, though, seemed not to have harbored such suspicions and gave Braden the job. Braden was installed in what she describes as "this huge office, with two secretaries, a couch, and a White House telephone. Nelson thought this was very funny. He used to come in every day and laugh at me, it was so big."

But he wasn't laughing long. Now that she worked for Hobby, Braden saw the department pecking order from a different perspective; she prodded Hobby to take charge and not allow herself to be bulldozed by Rockefeller. Braden's campaign did not exactly endear her to her former boss, and his displeasure was magnified when Hobby, at Braden's urging, refused to allow Hanks to sit in for Rockefeller at meetings.

Clearly, Rockefeller's little gambit had backfired. A chill descended on his relationship with Braden. "In meetings," she says, "if I said the sun was shining, he'd say, no, it's raining." She had committed the cardinal sin in the Rockefeller camp—disloyalty. But while Rockefeller himself would come to shrug the whole thing off, Nancy Hanks refused to absolve Braden. "Joan, in her eyes, was not loyal to Nelson," notes Mitchell. "And if there was anything that Nancy would not forgive, it was disloyalty."

Total, unquestioning loyalty was what Rockefeller demanded, and total unquestioning loyalty was what Hanks gave him. And that, as far as Joan Braden was concerned, was what set her own situation with Rockefeller apart from Nancy Hanks's. "Nancy gave her life to him," she says, "and I never did."

Willingly, even ardently, Hanks had crossed over into the psychological terrain that Frank Jamieson and Wally Harrison and Louise Boyer had entered before her: the territory of complete thralldom to the whims and will of Nelson Rockefeller. It was terrain with which Donna Mitchell, who would work for Rockefeller for twenty-five years, would come to be very familiar. "He regarded his employees as his personal property," she explained. "You just didn't do anything around Nelson Rockefeller unless you talked to him first and made it clear why you had to do something. . . . He made you feel guilty if you wanted to do things your own way."

"He tried hard to understand how you lived, but it never made any difference. He'd say, 'I know you have a home, and I know you have a husband, but can't you work until midnight?' "

Still, as demanding as he was with her, Mitchell could see that his relationship with Hanks was governed by a whole other level of possessiveness. "He put her in a shrine. He enshrined her in his life. It was clear that he was doing this early on, that she was his personal property, like a beautiful Picasso. . . . She was his. He'd show her off. . . . She was a possession."

Other women might have bridled at this, but Hanks offered no resistance. She even joked about it. "NAR really sort of cute—he acts like a proud father when people talk to me and like me," she wrote her parents.

"At least Louise Boyer's attitude about him was a little more objective," says someone who worked with both Boyer and Hanks. "But in Nancy's case, it was sheer idolatry."

Rockefeller asserted his claim on Hanks in the long hours at HEW and the weekend work sessions at Foxhall Road. And he asserted it in more tangible ways as well.

Just before Thanksgiving, 1953, he told Hanks he was ordering an antique Chinese bench—and, while he was at it, he wanted to buy another one for her. "I thanked him sweetly," she related, "and *unfortunately* gave him as a reason, 'I just couldn't fit another piece of furniture in that little apartment.' " But the offers of artwork kept coming, and eventually she succumbed. He gave her drawings and etchings by Picasso and Degas ("I do think the Picasso is sweet," she told her parents) and a painting by Toulouse-Lautrec—all of which he came by to hang himself.

Then he began expressing his pique over the inadequacy of Hanks's government salary. To be sure, he voiced that concern about all his handpicked staff (it was one reason, he said, why he had so many women around the place; "you just can't get men to work at these salaries"). But in Hanks's case, he seemed especially determined to do something about it. "His stand now," she remarked at the time of the Chinese bench incident, "is that he just doesn't like inequities and he thinks my salary is one."

In short order, he came up with a particularly handsome remedy. He offered her $200,000 in blue-chip securities—more than $1 million worth in today's dollars. The stocks, aside from capital appreciation, figured to yield her over $12,000 a year in dividends, considerably more than she was making as a grade nine federal employee—allowing her to live in a far lusher lifestyle than her normal income would have permitted.

Hanks discussed with her parents whether to accept the gift, and managed to rationalize it this way: "I figure this money is just as much yours as it is mine. I figured he gave it to all of us so that we could have a more comfortable lifestyle." Her friend Mitchell, who knew all about the gift, could never understand Hanks's moralistic father, who was hardly a pauper, "allowing Nancy to take this money from Rockefeller. I just can't understand it. It's an enigma to me. But they did." Many of the stocks would remain in Hanks's portfolio for the rest of her life, tripling and quadrupling in value, making her a wealthy woman.

Still, even as Hanks accepted the securities, she wrestled with her conscience about what the gift denoted. In her communiqués to her parents, she struggled to come to grips with the nature of her involvement with her benefactor. "I am sure it is very obvious that I think very highly of him—and admire him a great deal," she wrote. "I think he also feels the same way about me. He likes to work with me, mostly because he knows that I'm frank and honest and will tell him exactly what I think, and he needs that. . . . We have developed what I would call more a comradeship between us. And it really is a wonderful thing."

But "comradeship" was not the word Hanks's intimates would use to describe the relationship. As Nadia Williams remarked, "She was like a wife to Nelson: accepting his dominance, filling in the areas in which he was weak; giving up a part of herself—in order to serve him."

There was, indeed, a curious note of domesticity to their relationship. She mended his socks. He bought her vitamins, and prescribed cures for her ailments. "This is Dr. Rockefeller calling," he would say over the phone. She fixed him dinner at her apartment for his birthday: "some shrimp which he liked, some chicken livers cooked with sherry (which were amazingly good), broiled tomatoes, peas and a birthday cake. Just made one from one of those mixes, and then made lemon icing and put coconut on top."

Hanks convinced herself that she was Rockefeller's entrée to the everyday world. "I think sometimes, though it's hard to believe, that he has rarely come into contact with down-to-earth people, and that it means a great deal to him," she reflected.

Once, she took him to a Giant supermarket in McLean, Virginia. Despite his IBEC investments in supermarkets, he had rarely ever been in one, and he prowled the aisles with juvenile abandon, loading up the shopping cart with a bizarre array of comestibles: jars of frozen shrimp cocktail, herring in sour cream, frozen soft-shell crabs, frozen candied sweet potatoes, cookies, lamb chops, watermelon, Sanka, blueberries, and an avocado. (To Rockefeller's glee, he got the avocado at half price because it was soft.) "He was perfectly delighted," said Hanks, "and would have bought the entire store if I had let him."

And while she was busy introducing him to the mundane, he was eagerly introducing her to the grandiose.

There were the frequent visits to Foxhall Road, working visits that often lasted through dinner and were sometimes interrupted by long walks. There was an invitation to Pocantico (which for some unexplained reason she declined) and an invitation to the house in Maine (which she accepted).

On more than one occasion, Rockefeller took Hanks up to New York with him. He showed her around the 810 Fifth Avenue triplex, and then brought her to 13 West 54th Street, to what she described as "the little 'club' that's across the street from the Modern Art Museum." Together, they spent a Saturday making the gallery rounds, just as Rockefeller once did with Joan Braden. "Went to the Dutch show, Egyptian, Japanese and then early American furniture," a dazzled Hanks reported to her parents. "From there to two small selling galleries . . ."

Rarely, in Hanks's detailed accounts of her peregrinations with Rockefeller, is there any reference to Tod Rockefeller.

Tod was not much seen in Washington, Mitchell recalled. "She'd come down if there was some function which she was expected to attend or if the children were going to be there or something like that, but she really wasn't in Washington very much of that time while we were down there."

But while Tod wasn't present, she was never far from her husband's thoughts. Like many another errant spouse, Nelson Rockefeller was acutely sensitive to the question of his whereabouts and what his wife knew of them—as Donna Mitchell learned to her regret.

"The only time that Nelson, in all the years I worked for him, ever got angry with me was when we were at HEW in 1954, and he had told me to do something that related to Mrs. Rockefeller," she related. "Somehow or other, she called me on the phone, and I said something to her, whatever it was, but whatever it was was wrong. I didn't know it was wrong, but I said it to her, that he's going to be in New York, or something innocuous. But it was not exactly what he had told me to say to her, not precisely. He came storming out and said, 'Don't you ever, ever change anything that I have ever said to Mrs. Rockefeller again. Don't you ever do that.' . . . Whatever I said caused him problems. That's the only time he ever got angry with me."

His concern about Tod notwithstanding, he continued to pursue Nancy Hanks impetuously, heedlessly, as though totally oblivious to consequences.

Like some overeager young swain, Rockefeller did not feel it was enough to win the lady; he had to win her parents as well. He offered them the use of his house in Pocantico (which Nancy, on her parents' behalf, declined) as well as the house on Foxhall Road (which they accepted). Hearing that Bryan Hanks was thinking of starting a "Mountain Museum," Rockefeller sent him some Early American tools as a Christmas present. During a trip to Nevada, Rockefeller picked up Indian artifacts for the Hankses.

His most munificent gesture occurred when he joined Nancy in a visit to her family's country home in Cashiers, North Carolina. As he and her father toured the property, he listened attentively as Bryan outlined his dream of someday damming a mountain stream to create a magnificent lake. On the spot, Rockefeller offered to pay for the dam.

Bryan was hesitant, but his daughter pressed him to accept. "He likes both of you very much—says he feels so much at home. . . . Has gotten it into his head that we are the most perfect family he has ever known. . . . He knows how much we love Cashiers and, I think, would, just for that reason, like to be a part of it. Money is really nothing to him except that it enables him to do things he'd like to do, and I think this is something he would like to do very much." It was only after the $5,000 check arrived that she admitted that "it certainly is hard to accept such a gift. We cannot feel obligated, however, as I have told you."

But accept it they did, just as they accepted the $200,000 in stock. The dam was built, and Bryan Hanks soon would have his splendid lake—as well as a new motorboat and canoe with which to navigate it, two more gifts from their friend in Washington.

Rockefeller insisted on flying down to Cashiers to personally inspect the work. He patiently listened to Bryan's yammering and stoically sat through Bryan and Virginia's bickering. Most of his time there he spent alone with Nancy: canoeing on Bear Lake, strolling among the rose bushes and rhododendrons, gazing across the valley from Mac's View. They photographed one another: he, breezy and casual in a tennis shirt, she, longing and sensual in a sports dress, bearing a sprig of roses. They adopted pet names for each other: Dr. and Mrs. Snail.

By the time Rockefeller returned to Washington, his conquest of the Hanks family was complete. Whatever moral scruples and reservations Bryan and Virginia had about his relationship with their daughter crumbled in the face of his incessant attentiveness and generosity. "This was pretty heady stuff for those two people from Texas," Mitchell remarked. "He completely buffaloed them. They thought he was God." Bryan sent him cloyingly reverent letters of appreciation, letters addressed "to you . . . the maker of such good things." The senior Hanks confessed to Nancy, "He does so much, I am fearful our expressions of appreciation will grow weak because said so often, but in our hearts they grow stronger."

As for Nancy, there was little question that her "comradeship" with Rockefeller had evolved into something else. Said Donna Mitchell, "It was very apparent to me that she was in love with Nelson." And Rockefeller, for his part, gave Nancy every reason to believe that he was equally smitten. "Nancy," he would write to her, "there is nothing more beautiful than our love."

No longer were they simply the undersecretary and his executive assistant. They were also Dr. and Mrs. Snail.

Thirty-two

Overt and Covert

By the fall of 1954 Nelson Rockefeller was at the pinnacle of his influence at HEW. He was master of the issues, master of the legislative process, and, for all intents and purposes, master of the department. But now that he had attained that state of governmental grace, he felt the old restlessness gnawing at him. He yearned for a seat at the cabinet table, but Hobby was not about to step aside so he could take it. For over sixteen months he had accepted his subservient position, playing the game, loyally deferring to a superior whom he, and everyone else in Washington, knew was hardly his equal in energy or ability. Clearly, he expected some payoff for this most arduous (for him) of exertions: the squelching of his ego. But there was no payoff at hand.

He had also come to recognize that in this administration, domestic policy—particularly matters of health, education, and welfare—was strictly a sideshow. With the Cold War in full swing, the main event was foreign affairs. Unable to secure a foreign policy role for himself in the initial go-round, Rockefeller nonetheless still nurtured the hope that somehow, somewhere, a place for him could be found.

By early November, Rockefeller had served notice on Hobby that he intended to leave to pursue something in the international field. Noticeably reluctant to lose his services, despite the evident strains in their relationship, she dropped hints that she might be departing soon herself. Rockefeller didn't believe it for a minute.

He cast his net over the executive branch, dredging for possibilities. An alluring one soon presented itself—a product, fortuitously, of his efforts at the government organization committee. Heeding the Rockefeller panel's warnings that the United States still lacked a coherent foreign economic program,

Eisenhower had asked his former budget director, Joseph Dodge, to study the question. Dodge, in turn, handed in a report urging the creation of a White House office of foreign economic policy—an office that would be the economic equivalent (and on a par with) the National Security Council. This, of course, was but the latest incarnation of the position Rockefeller had been angling for for years. He was no less eager now than he ever was to take it on.

It was with some anticipation, then, that Rockefeller arrived at the White House for a lunch with the President, at which this new office was to be discussed. Also at the luncheon were Milton Eisenhower and various lower-level White House aides. When the talk turned to the question of who might run the new office, Dodge's name was broached, and spoken of approvingly by all hands. Later, after Milton Eisenhower excused himself, the President raised the possibility that perhaps his brother, rather than Dodge, might do the job. Never, in the course of the lunch, was Rockefeller's name ever advanced—even though he was indisputably the author of the whole scheme they were discussing.

Rockefeller left the luncheon crestfallen, and decided, then and there, that the time for deference, for politely waiting his turn, was over. He stormed over to Sherman Adams' office and insisted he had to see the chief of staff at once. Adams kept him cooling his heels for a full two hours.

When Rockefeller was at last admitted into Adams' presence, he curtly informed the chief of staff that he had reached the end of his rope at HEW. His chief interest, he said, was in the international field. Unless the administration could find something for him in that area, he intended to return to the private sector.

The laconic, stone-faced Adams, whose power was such that reporters had taken to referring to him as the "Assistant President," was known as Eisenhower's no-man. In the words of one of the President's biographers, Peter Lyon, "He said no to cabinet secretaries and to congressmen, to journalists and to jobhunters; he said no short and sharp, without troubling to be polite about it." He didn't say no to Rockefeller, but what he did say was almost as deflating.

He wished, he said, that Rockefeller had said something about this before.

Rockefeller returned to his office at HEW with his hopes for a new position seemingly dashed. But as he prepared himself for yet another reluctant exit from public life, certain wheels in the Eisenhower administration began to turn. And the person turning those wheels was Oveta Culp Hobby.

On a Tuesday morning in mid-November, she summoned Rockefeller to her office and told him that after the cabinet meeting the previous Friday she had approached the President on Rockefeller's behalf. She had confided to Eisenhower that Rockefeller really wanted the foreign economic job, and, if that wasn't available, something else in the foreign field. Eisenhower, she reported, seemed glad to hear it.

The overture to the President was, she told Rockefeller, "really the only truly generous thing I've ever done in my life."

Rockefeller then phoned Sherman Adams, who informed him that a new job had indeed been found for him: special assistant to the President for psychological warfare. The position had been vacant for over six months, ever since the departure from government of C. D. Jackson, Eisenhower's guru on the subject. The job was Rockefeller's, if he wanted it.

What Hobby had not disclosed to Rockefeller—and what he only later learned from Jackson—was that just six weeks earlier the White House had floated Rockefeller's name for the Jackson position and had met with a firm rebuff from Hobby. She insisted she simply could not let her indispensable undersecretary go.

So Hobby's approach to the President was not exactly the spontaneous magnanimous gesture she made it out to be. She was simply withdrawing her veto of his move—withdrawing it in the face of the near-certainty that Rockefeller would depart from HEW in any case.

What's more, once he had the offer in hand, Hobby did her best to dissuade him from accepting it. The job, she warned somewhat cryptically, would ruin him politically.

Rockefeller, however, was determined to take it, particularly after a conversation he had with Joe Dodge. Dodge had raced over to see Rockefeller after a breakfast meeting with the President, at which Eisenhower and Dodge had discussed the foreign economic policy position. Dodge told the President he was willing to take the post to get it organized, but didn't want it permanently. That was fine, replied the President; once Dodge stepped down, he would appoint Rockefeller to take his place. (Eisenhower explained that he feared adverse public reaction if he were to tap his brother Milton.)

This added wrinkle left Rockefeller elated. He would have the job he wanted after all. In the meantime, he told aides he was delighted that Dodge was taking the position. Not only was he confident he could work with the former budget director, but at least at the outset Rockefeller felt he could accomplish more with the influential Dodge in place than he could if he held the post himself.

There was only one more element Rockefeller had to consider: the reaction of John Foster Dulles to his psychological warfare appointment. But Sherman Adams reassured him on that score. It had all been cleared with Dulles, Adams said, and Dulles had pronounced himself pleased.

The White House wanted Rockefeller to start immediately, but Hobby objected. She refused to release him until after the President's State of the Union message in mid-January. In the meantime, word of Rockefeller's appointment leaked, in a front-page *New York Times* story by Rockefeller's old confidant James Reston. "The White House," Nancy Hanks wrote her parents, "probably thinks he leaked the story." And well the White House might have, considering Reston's grandiose characterization of Rockefeller's new position.

"Secretary of State Dulles," he reported, "will, of course, remain the President's principal adviser on foreign affairs, but Mr. Rockefeller will work with him and with the other departments and agencies on the coordination of the Administration's 'cold war' strategy."

This sweeping construction of his new post was advanced by Rockefeller himself in his conversations with friends such as Adolf Berle. After lunching with Rockefeller shortly after the New Year, Berle recorded the following in his diary: "Dulles had asked Nelson to take this new job—Coordinator of International Programs—because Dulles understands perfectly that he is merely putting out fires—if he is putting them out—and is on the defensive everywhere. He himself has no time to think and feels something is lacking, and expects Nelson to supply the miraculous element."

This florid description of his role was patently a spectacular exercise in wishful thinking on Rockefeller's part. He was not "coordinator of international programs"—there was no such job. And the idea that Dulles, the domineering vizier of Eisenhower era foreign policy, would look to Nelson Rockefeller to "supply the miraculous element" was utterly ludicrous.

If nothing else, Rockefeller's wild exaltation of his mission underscored the inscrutability of the role he was taking on. Was his job to "coordinate Cold War strategy"? Was it to wage psychological warfare? Or was it the woolly formulation that Eisenhower cited in his letter appointing Rockefeller to the job: to render "advice and assistance in the development of increased understanding and cooperation among all peoples"?

The truth was, his mission was a strange amalgam of all three elements, and only one man fully comprehended how it was all supposed to work: Rockefeller's flamboyant predecessor, C. D. Jackson. Indeed, it would not be too much to say that the job was the creature of Jackson's idiosyncratic vision and of his grand strategy for the Cold War—a vision in which "international understanding" and "psychological warfare" were truly synonymous.

Charles Douglas Jackson was in many ways an American archetype: a bombastic, Barnum-like figure, a master salesman who ardently believed in the redemptive power of public relations. Tall, urbane, and Princeton-educated, Jackson had the mien of a Yankee aristocrat and the promotional pizzazz of a Tin Pan Alley song hustler.

Early in his career, Jackson latched on to a kindred soul, Henry Luce, and became one of the mainstays of Luce's Time-Life publishing empire (Jackson was the first general manager of *Life* magazine). But for Jackson, the broader canvas of world affairs always beckoned; in 1941, he established the Council for Democracy, "to combat all the Nazi, fascist, communist, pacifist" antiwar groups in the United States. With the American entry into the war, Jackson's considerable talents as a propagandist caught the eye of Dwight Eisenhower, and when Eisenhower was anointed supreme Allied commander, he tapped Jackson to spearhead his psychological warfare effort in anticipation of D-Day.

Psychological warfare—a fancy term for military propaganda aimed at friends, or foes, or both—was hardly a World War II development. It had been employed by the American armed forces as far back as the Revolutionary War, when Thomas Jefferson and Benjamin Franklin devised a plan to incite desertions by Hessian mercenaries through the distribution of propaganda handbills. But it was only under Eisenhower and Jackson's sponsorship that psychological warfare emerged from the shadows and was openly recognized as a vital element in America's war machine. With his radio broadcasts and his leaflets, Jackson roused support in occupied Europe for the Allied invaders; his efforts would win him the French Legion of Honor.

At war's end Jackson returned to Time-Life, becoming publisher of *Fortune.* But his true calling was as a propagandist, and the postwar years presented him with a ripe new psychological battlefield: the campaign against Communism. In early 1951, with the active support of the CIA, Jackson organized the National Committee for a Free Europe to pierce the Iron Curtain with the gospel of freedom. The committee's chief activity was Radio Free Europe, whose broadcasts permeated the Eastern bloc with a mixture of news, entertainment, and outright anti-Soviet propaganda. Always the showman, Jackson reveled in such NCFE stunts as a massive balloon bombardment of Poland and Czechoslovakia; the 11,000 balloons carried 13 million leaflets to "fortify spiritual resistance" until the "day of liberation" arrived. Jackson gleefully launched the first of the balloons himself.

His "American Crusade" attained singular prominence with the presidential candidacy of his old boss in 1952. Enlisted as a speechwriter, Jackson steered the campaign into unabashed advocacy of psychological warfare. In Eisenhower, Jackson saw a leader "who grasps the concept of political warfare" and who recognized that "it was just about the only way to win WW III without having to fight it." Installed in the White House as the new President's special assistant, Jackson savored the chance to make psychological warfare "the entire posture of the entire Government to the entire world."

He scored some quick coups. One was his adroit promotion of an important Eisenhower speech in April 1953 that opened the door to new peace initiatives in the wake of Joseph Stalin's death a month earlier. Jackson literally blanketed the globe with this speech: flooding Europe and Latin America with some 3 million copies, distributing 100,000 handbills in eight languages in New Delhi, India, flying out films and kinescopes of the President's address to television stations on three continents, broadcasting the speech hourly on every Radio Free Europe channel.

Another was Atoms for Peace, a presidential bid for international cooperation in the peaceful use of atomic energy. The idea was Eisenhower's, but it was left to Jackson to shepherd it through a resistant bureaucracy. When Eisenhower presented the plan in a speech to the United Nations in December 1953 (a speech that Jackson ended up rewriting thirty-two times), even the Communist representatives rose in applause.

But all too often Jackson found his quicksilver intellect grinding against the monumental intransigence of Dulles. "Foster Dulles hasn't got the faintest conception—and that is where everything gets off the rails and nothing gets done," Jackson observed in his diary. He sneered at State's "business-as-usual attitude" in the face of popular unrest in East Germany, and fumed at Dulles' negativism about the Atoms for Peace idea. He also found himself frustrated with Eisenhower, complaining about the lack of "command decisions" and, more specifically, about the President's refusal to take on Joe McCarthy.

By April 1954, Jackson had had enough of the White House and returned to Time-Life. His faith in psychological warfare, however, his belief that it held the key to victory in the Cold War, never wavered. What remained to be seen was whether Eisenhower still shared that faith, and who—if anyone—might be tapped to take Jackson's place.

When Jackson heard that Rockefeller was the man, he heaved a great sigh of relief. "As you can imagine," he wrote his successor, "I have been very concerned ever since I left Washington about who might fill that particular slot, and quite humanly couldn't help hoping it would be someone I would feel happy about.

"With Nelson R. in the job I am not only happy, but overjoyed."

Jackson had good reason to be jubilant, for Nelson Rockefeller was as close to a spiritual brother as Jackson was likely to find, inside or outside government.

They were both effervescent idea men with seemingly limitless self-confidence, and their ideas were remarkably congruent. Both men saw business expansion not as an end in itself, but as the ultimate bulwark against the Communist menace. Both perceived the Cold War as a clash on many fronts, not all of them military, a war that could be won with plows as well as with swords. "Defense, in and of itself, is not enough," Rockefeller had written in his Point Four report. "There must be a positive force as well." Those were precisely C. D. Jackson's views.

And, in his own way, Rockefeller was as much of an expert on psychological warfare as was Jackson. The coordinator's office, after all, could be regarded as just one big psychological warfare machine: disseminating propaganda, promoting cultural exchanges, winning the hearts and minds of the Latin American populace with health and sanitation measures and a pinch of Walt Disney. Much of what Jackson was talking about was merely the CIAA program writ large.

In short, Jackson had no need to proselytize his successor, because Rockefeller was as much of a true believer in the Jackson creed as Jackson himself. As Rockefeller wrote Jackson, shortly after accepting the job, "I am completely convinced of the absolute essentiality of the program you have been pushing." Now it would be up to Rockefeller to wage the war for the "minds and wills of men," to win the "victory without casualties" that was C. D. Jackson's great crusade.

Although he was now a presidential assistant, Rockefeller did not quite rate a White House office. Instead, he found himself back in the all too familiar confines of the Executive Office Building next door. Not that his quarters there were anything to complain about; he was assigned to the opulent corner suite that was once the office of the Secretary of State, with magnificent views of the White House south lawn, the Ellipse, and the Washington Monument. When Adolf Berle came to call, he asked Rockefeller if he saw ghosts, and well he might have, so rich was the chamber with personal associations for him. It was here that Rockefeller kowtowed to Cordell Hull, here that he bullied Edward Stettinius—and here that he was fired by Jimmy Byrnes.

He brought with him, from HEW, a full complement of assistants and secretaries, including Nancy Hanks, Donna Mitchell, and Hal Haskell. Appalled by how many people Rockefeller was adding to the White House payroll from his old unit, Sherman Adams cracked down, informing Rockefeller, "They will come at their present salaries. They will not get a raise." As Adams would later ruefully point out, "Jackson was pretty much a lone operator. But Rockefeller liked to have a lot of people around."

In fact, the HEW crew was merely the advance guard. A veritable army of aides followed in their wake, many of whom were presently employed by the Office of the Messrs. Rockefeller in New York. Stacy May was brought in as a three-day-a-week economics consultant, and was assisted by a full-time economist, Shaw Livermore, another New York import. Frank Jamieson agreed to spend two days a week in Washington helping his once and future boss. Then three more secretaries were brought down from Room 5600 to work directly for Rockefeller.

Realizing there was no way he could get the pinchpenny Adams to approve such an augmentation of the staff, Rockefeller did what he always did when budgetary exigencies got in the way of his plans.

He paid for all these people out of his own pocket.

He paid their salaries. And he paid their travel expenses; in cases where the government allowed them per diem reimbursements, he personally made up the difference between the modest per diem and their out-of-pocket costs. (The U.S. Treasury was not let totally off the hook, though. It footed part of the bill indirectly, when Rockefeller claimed, and won, a tax deduction for his share of the extra expense.)

Rockefeller's extravagance in his new position did not stop there. He wanted what he always had, wherever he worked in the government: his own chart room. But the White House—no doubt recalling the political flak the HEW room had engendered—said no. So he decided to pay for that, too, from his personal treasury. Not only would he pay for the remodeling of the room, but he made it known he would also buy the projectors and assume the printing expenses and all the other costs of preparing his elaborate presentations.

The financing, however, turned out to be only half the battle. Rockefeller wanted to set up his chart room in the West Wing of the White House, as close to the Oval Office as he could get, but there was no space large enough to accommodate it. He eyed the basement bowling alley, and the White House swimming pool, but Eisenhower was unwilling to part with either of those amenities for the sake of Rockefeller's picture shows. Rockefeller had no choice but to find something in the vast warrens of the Executive Office Building.

There, he happened upon one promising, albeit unorthodox space: the old State Department library on the top floor of the building. It was still fitted out as a Beaux Arts library, with old cast-iron shelving and small staircases between levels, with turreted study alcoves and a huge skylight bathing the room with a magisterial radiance. Rockefeller was swept away by the grandeur of the room—until the Secret Service and CIA came around and informed him that all those nooks and crannies would be impossible to secure. "My God," the CIA man said, "think of all the places to hide microphones."

Instead, Rockefeller found a smaller, more nondescript setting for his chart shows, the former Office of Defense Mobilization library on the Executive Office Building's fourth floor. And, as it turned out, it was just as well. Despite Rockefeller's best efforts to lure him, Eisenhower never showed up for a single one of his special assistant's multimedia displays.

By the time Rockefeller settled into his new job, the brief glimmer of hope that flared after Stalin's death and after Eisenhower's Atoms for Peace speech had long since been extinguished. The Cold War had deteriorated into a glacial impasse. U.S. foreign policy, under the stewardship of Eisenhower and Dulles, vaulted from one icy precipice to the next, the footing less sure with each leap.

The previous year, 1954, had seen the fall of the French stronghold at Dien Bien Phu and the final collapse of the French position in Vietnam. Amid talk of falling dominoes and a Red tide swarming over Southeast Asia, the United States contemplated stepping into the breach, but thought better of it. Grudgingly, the administration accepted the partition of the country negotiated with the Communist Vietminh in Geneva, while pledging support of the new regime of Ngo Dinh Diem in the south—and secretly dispatching a CIA paramilitary team, under Colonel Edward Lansdale, to Saigon.

Having stepped back from the brink in Vietnam, the United States was stepping toward it in China. Under pressure from the potent China lobby seeking the restoration of the Nationalist regime of Chiang Kai-shek—now in exile on the offshore island of Taiwan—the administration was backing Chiang's campaign of harassment and sabotage against the Red government. In November 1954 Beijing announced it had shot down a planeload of Americans trying to drop supplies to teams of saboteurs. The thirteen prisoners—eleven U.S. airmen and two CIA agents—were convicted of espionage and sentenced to terms ranging from four years to life.

By January 1955 Chiang's campaign was on the verge of escalating into all-out war. Seeking to retaliate against his trespasses, the Chinese launched attacks against several smaller islands occupied by the Nationalist forces. Eisenhower and Dulles, fearful that this might be a prelude to a Red invasion of Taiwan, determined, in the President's words, that "the time had come to draw the line." The question was where the line would be drawn: which islands would be defended, and at what cost. On January 24, Eisenhower went before the Congress and declared "our readiness to fight, if necessary, to preserve the vital stake of the free world in a free [Taiwan]." Suddenly, the rocky outcroppings of the Matsus and the obscure fishing ports of Quemoy were looming as potential tinderboxes of a third world war.

Brinkmanship—the term coined to describe Dulles' policy of calculated confrontation—was manifesting itself in Europe as well. The West alarmed the new Soviet leadership by bringing West Germany into NATO and urging the Germans to rearm. Then Dulles raised the ante at a NATO meeting in mid-December by pressing the Western allies to accept nuclear weapons on their soil—purely as a defensive measure, of course.

With the Soviets now possessing hydrogen bombs of their own, a fearsome stalemate existed: a "balance of terror," in Churchill's words, in which only the specter of nuclear annihilation kept the two sides in check.

In the minds of American policy makers, the doctrine of containment—the arresting of Communist influence and expansion by any means short of all-out war—still held sway. And the means included not only overt actions—strategic alliances and the like—but covert measures, too. The CIA, run by Dulles' younger brother Allen, was now arguably America's most potent foreign policy tool.

In 1953, CIA operatives in Iran orchestrated the overthrow of Prime Minister Mohammed Mossadegh, whose nationalization of British oil interests stirred fears he was moving into the Soviet camp. A year later, the agency was at it again, secretly choreographing the ouster of Guatemalan President Jacobo Arbenz Guzmán. Arbenz, like Mossadegh, had committed the cardinal sin of expropriating foreign property: in the Guatemalan's case, vast acreages belonging to the giant banana grower United Fruit. And, like Mossadegh,

Arbenz was seen as a potential Soviet ally (although the evidence, in both cases, was flimsy).

The success of these two operations—achieved, as one historian of the agency pointed out, with "a minimum of fuss, bloodshed, and time expended"—spurred a rapid proliferation of CIA covert activity around the globe. The agency was given a secret green light by the National Security Council to "create and exploit problems for international communism" through measures ranging from "propaganda and political action" to "sabotage" and "subversion against hostile states." Thus, the CIA was in the vanguard of the ongoing struggle for the "minds and wills of men"—a fact that was not lost on the new special assistant to the President for Cold War strategy.

From the start, Rockefeller understood that there were dimensions to his job that went well beyond the bland charter ("increased understanding and cooperation among all peoples") given to him by the President.

The line between psychological warfare and intelligence activity, if there was one, had always been indistinct. Bill Donovan's OSS, the predecessor of the CIA, had, after all, started out as an information agency. And C. D. Jackson's definition of his work encompassed endeavors—such as the bombardment of Eastern Europe with propaganda balloons—that might just as well have been thought up at CIA headquarters. Jackson's National Committee for a Free Europe was funded by the CIA, and at one point Jackson was moved to express his appreciation to CIA director Walter Bedell Smith: "We would never have been able to create these things . . . had it not been for the attitude that you and your organization had toward us."

In his White House position, Jackson conferred regularly with Allen Dulles and was one of the agency's most vociferous cheerleaders in the administration; he was, among other things, a forceful advocate of the action in Guatemala. More to the point, Jackson's job put him in the direct chain of oversight over CIA covert activities. He was the President's representative on the Operations Coordinating Board (OCB), a committee of the National Security Council whose other members were the Undersecretary of State, the Deputy Secretary of Defense, the director of the Foreign Operations Administration (Stassen), and the CIA director. The OCB's job was to oversee the "timely and coordinated execution of . . . policy and plans"; the "policy and plans" included clandestine actions.

In December 1954, just prior to Rockefeller's arrival on the scene, the CIA's charter for covert operations and the OCB's oversight of them were clarified by the National Security Council. The CIA was given a blanket authorization for the full gamut of covert activities, and the OCB was to be its watchdog, to be "advised in advance of major programs involving covert operations." Thus, the President retained some measure of control over the agency—while preserving his deniability if any of the operations were exposed or went awry.

When Rockefeller arrived, he took Jackson's seat on the OCB. Working with the CIA was nothing new for him. Soon after joining HEW, he was asked to address an internal CIA seminar on the role of the agency in a changing economic world. (His appearance was arranged by Joan Braden, obviously working her special connection to the CIA higher-ups through hubby Tom.) And according to a report that surfaced two decades later, while at HEW he was aware that his department was used as a cover for some of the CIA's most sensitive programs, code-named Artichoke and MK-Ultra: programs of experimentation with the new hallucinogenic drug LSD. Reportedly, Rockefeller knew—and Hobby didn't—that the CIA was funding some of its experiments through the HEW's National Institute of Mental Health.*

Rockefeller, with his unabashed enthusiasm for clandestine operations dating back to his coordinator days, was perfectly comfortable with the strong links to the CIA that his new position entailed. In fact, he was eager to make them even stronger, to formalize the relationship. He knew full well that in this administration the already blurred line between psychological warfare and covert activity was growing ever fainter. Close ties to the ascendant intelligence agency would undoubtedly magnify his effectiveness; a weak relationship would, just as surely, undermine it.

And so, in his first weeks on the job, the new special assistant sought to pull the CIA even more into his orbit. Using skills honed in numerous past turf battles, he endeavored to carve out a special role for himself in the agency's affairs.

In this, he found himself the beneficiary of Eisenhower's penchant for organization and planning. Believing that the administration's Cold War efforts—specifically, its economic, psychological, political warfare and foreign information activities—ought to be better coordinated, the President asked the Budget Bureau to pull together some proposals. The study conveniently coincided with Rockefeller's arrival on the scene; no sooner had he settled himself in than he began working vigorously to leave his stamp on the deliberations.

*Actually, as good as Rockefeller's relations were with the CIA, his brother David's were better. During the war David had served in Army intelligence in North Africa, and afterward he discreetly maintained his contacts with the intelligence community. "David kept in very close touch," recalls Tom Braden. "He was a friend and confidant of Allen Dulles, and in some instances furnished a front"—agreeing to finance a do-good foundation that was a CIA cover. "I remember briefing him, in great detail, about the work of the division that I headed in the CIA. Allen asked me to brief him, and I gave him a full briefing, so that he knew everything that I was doing. And I think he did it with the other division chiefs, too. He was close to intelligence work—much, much, much closer than Nelson was."

Rockefeller's intervention had its impact. Indeed, the report by budget director Rowland Hughes that landed on the President's desk in early March sounded very much like a typical Rockefeller manifesto. It spoke of the need for "dynamic, new and imaginative ideas" and "imaginative planning"; it cited the need to more effectively use "U.S. private organizations and foreign individuals and groups and foreign public and private organizations."

What was required to attain all this, Hughes concluded, was the creation of "a small, high-level group" that would "aid in developing planning in both overt and covert fields." This group would consist of the Undersecretary of State, the Deputy Secretary of Defense, and the director of the CIA—and its chairman would be special assistant Nelson Rockefeller.

The potential power of this new Planning Coordination Group would be considerable. On the overt side, it would "advise and assist the responsible operating agencies in the coordinated development of plans and programs" to carry out national security policies. As for the covert, it would "be advised in advance of major covert programs initiated by the Central Intelligence Agency . . . and should be the normal channel for giving policy approval for such programs." Thus, it would supplant the OCB as the CIA's White House overseer. The agency would have to go to the Planning Coordination Group, under Nelson Rockefeller, whenever it needed a green light.

There is no available record of the behind-the-scenes bureaucratic maneuvering that produced this proposal. The only documentation of what went on was the final Hughes memorandum to the President, once secret, now declassified. So it is impossible to precisely chart Rockefeller's role in pushing it through and the resistance he might have encountered in the process.

Nonetheless, the memo does make it clear that in the end he and Hughes obtained the necessary consensus from the powers that be in favor of the plan. The President's National Security Adviser, Robert Cutler, signed off on it, as did Allen Dulles, Undersecretary of State Herbert Hoover, Jr., and Deputy Defense Secretary Robert Anderson. The plan also had the persuasive concurrence of Walter Bedell Smith.

With these consents in hand, Rockefeller and Hughes presented the memo to the President on March 4. Always reassured by a show of unity among his advisers (unlike Franklin Roosevelt, who thrived on just the opposite), Eisenhower gave his approval. The Planning Coordination Group came into being, and Nelson Rockefeller had his coveted direct line into the clandestine workings of the CIA.*

* Rockefeller was proud of his CIA connection, and had no compunction about playing it up within the inner councils of the administration. When the White House that spring circulated a guide to the agencies for which various presidential aides were responsible, Rockefeller was aggrieved when the CIA was not listed under his name. At his insistence, "CIA (operations)" was added to the list. Source: Andrew Goodpaster to NAR, April 29, 1955, NAR Special Assistant Book 16, RAC.

Within weeks after this secret executive order, some new, unfamiliar faces began popping up in the office of the special assistant to the President. They were not the usual cast of economists, lawyers, and p.r. men that made up Rockefeller's entourage. To anyone who was unaware of the Planning Coordination Group, the arrival of these mysterious newcomers was ample indication that there was more on the special assistant's plate than forging "increased cooperation and understanding."

The first to arrive was William Kintner, a former U.S. Army colonel who had most recently been attached to the National Security Council's planning board. Kintner's background was in military intelligence, and the Army early on had singled him out for special training, sending him off to Georgetown University for a Ph.D. in international relations. Those who would come to work with him in Rockefeller's office knew Kintner as an astute judge of the Soviets, a broad-gauge thinker with impressive connections with the leading academic foreign policy theorists. What they might not have known—it was not exactly trumpeted—was that Kintner had worked in the CIA before coming to the NSC, and that from 1950 to 1952 he was chief planner of covert operations.

At Kintner's suggestion, Rockefeller brought in another military man, Brigadier General Theodore Parker, to serve as the Planning Coordination Group's chief of staff. Parker was on active military duty, with a particularly sensitive assignment—overseeing the emplacement of Nike antiaircraft missiles in the Chicago area—when the word came that Rockefeller wanted to see him. The general was decidedly reluctant to give up a prestigious command position for what he regarded as a Washington desk job, and told Rockefeller as much. "I explained to him that, if he didn't mind, I would just like to go back to where I was, and let it go at that. I was honored that he had asked me, but I was really not interested," relates Parker. "He nodded and smiled. Ten days later, I was in his office working."

If there was still any question about the direction in which Rockefeller was headed, it was dispelled by the identity of the third individual assigned to the PCG. He was one Richard D. Drain, and he came to Rockefeller's staff directly from the CIA. While Kintner was to be the PCG's thinker, and Parker its administrator, Drain's exact role was unclear. Perhaps he was meant to be Rockefeller's personal liaison with the CIA; perhaps, as his colleagues came to suspect, he functioned as an undisguised CIA mole in Rockefeller's office. ("Drain always felt he was a little responsible to his people back home," says Parker, "and I suppose for that reason we didn't include him quite as much in our discussions.")

"I've got my general," a beaming Rockefeller announced to his staff one day. "I've got my Soviet expert. And I've got my man from the CIA." He was ready to go to work—or, more precisely, to go to war.

Thirty-three

COLD WARRIOR

The war in which Rockefeller was enlisted was very much war the way his predecessor liked it: fought with propaganda salvos and booming public relations gestures and fusillades of shrewdly dispensed dollar bills, a war waged on the terrain of the mind and the will.

Although he had not devoted himself to the anti-Communist crusade with the same single-mindedness that Jackson had, Rockefeller unhesitatingly plunged into the fray. Eager to establish his bona fides as a Cold Warrior, Rockefeller, in his first months as a presidential assistant, presented himself as an implacable hard-liner—C. D. Jackson's true spiritual heir.

He proved it in his very first assignment. Chinese leader Zhou Enlai, at the height of the tensions over Taiwan and the offshore islands, had offered to allow the families of the captured U.S. airmen to visit the prisoners. Rockefeller was given the task of responding to this Chinese olive branch, and he concluded, after talking it over with State, Defense, and the CIA, that the visit would play right into China's hands. He and his confreres agreed that there was only one possible response: the Air Force should orchestrate a snub of the invitation by the families, with the President sending each of the families a personal letter of consolation.

A month later, Rockefeller was asked by Eisenhower to study another goodwill gesture: a proposal by Agriculture Secretary Ezra Taft Benson that the United States give some of its vast wheat surplus to the Soviet Union, which was facing a food shortage due to miserable harvests. All his past concerns about world hunger notwithstanding, Rockefeller urged rejection of the idea. His arguments were those of a true-blue psychological warrior: "The furnishing of agricultural commodities from the U.S. would have the direct effect of relieving the Soviet government of a political embarrassment. . . .

Agricultural shortages promise to create internal dissatisfaction which may be to our advantage to promote rather than to diminish." Eisenhower went along with his recommendation; there would be no gift of grain to the Soviets.

From Jackson, Rockefeller inherited a preoccupation with anti-Communist exiles and refugees. On a personal level, Jackson found these expatriates distasteful (he divided them into two groups: "the nice, honest, but slightly gaga" and the "conniving"). Nonetheless, he recognized their political utility as walking, talking defamers of the Soviet system. Among his first suggestions to Rockefeller was that he plant a prominent Hungarian exile, former Prime Minister Ferenc Nagy, at the upcoming conference of Afro-Asian nonaligned nations in Bandung, Indonesia. When the talk of the conference turned to colonialism, Nagy and his brethren would pop up "to give testimony regarding the new Soviet colonialism."

"The suggestion is terrific," enthused Rockefeller. Although the Bandung scenario never came to pass, Rockefeller continued to pursue ploys for exploiting the exiles. At one point, he pushed for a statement in the UN on the refugees, but was rebuffed by UN ambassador Henry Cabot Lodge, who thought it would be "highly disastrous."

One of Jackson's inspirations at his National Committee for a Free Europe was a Free University in Exile, which would prepare young Eastern European refugees "to take over the leadership of their liberated countries." The notion that the West should have a counterpart to the Kremlin's indoctrination of young Third World cadres was one of his favorite hobbyhorses. Rockefeller found himself caught up in those schemes as well. He was given responsibility for an ongoing program dubbed Militant Liberty, which, in its original conception, would train young "democratic leaders" around the world—"leaders from Indo-China would get top priority." The Pentagon, the CIA, the State Department, and the United States Information Agency all took a hand in the project, as a result of which, Nancy Hanks reported, there was "a general feeling of haziness on everyone's part as to what the project is." Militant Liberty fizzled into a vague propaganda initiative, but Rockefeller pushed it ahead anyway, and conferred with Admiral Arthur Radford, chairman of the Joint Chiefs of Staff, about launching a pilot program in an area of strategic importance to the United States: Iran, the Philippines, South Vietnam, or Guatemala.

When Militant Liberty stalled, Rockefeller looked for other ways to advance the concept of an anti-Communist academy. He latched on to a proposal put forth by Karl Harr, Jr., a partner at John Foster Dulles' old firm of Sullivan & Cromwell, for an Institute of Political Science. This institute would, in Harr's words, provide "training in the methods, techniques and objectives of political warfare, for the purpose of equipping foreign and domestic leaders, both governmental and private, to counter Communist activities on the international plane."

The institute, with its planned indoctrination of American businessmen overseas as well as foreign politicians, sounded very much like a CIA enterprise, which undoubtedly enhanced its appeal to Rockefeller. (In fact, the businessman angle was reminiscent of his network of intelligence-sniffing "coordinating committees" in Latin America during World War II.) He touted the idea to John Foster Dulles—"it seems to me to be a most interesting undertaking and one that could be of great value," Rockefeller advised the secretary. Dulles endorsed the proposal, as long as the institute's connection to the U.S. government was covered up; he insisted there should be no government funding, and no U.S. government personnel should be permitted to take the course, "at least in the beginning."

To conceal the government involvement, Rockefeller needed a front—and for that he turned to his brother David. They talked about setting up a separate incorporated vehicle to fund the institute—it would be called the Fund for International Freedom—and asking the Ford Foundation to provide the FIF's endowment. Rockefeller's instructions to David about the approach to the Ford official had the elliptical, sotto voce tone of a communiqué between secret agents: "Perhaps you could say to your friend at lunch next week that this had come to your attention, that it was known and favorably regarded by both the President and the Secretary of State, and that it had just occurred to you that we might be able to take hold of it and make it a reality because of its great intrinsic merit and significance to the future of our country." In addition, David should mention that Ford Foundation sponsorship of the fund "might have some positive offsetting values at this particular time"—a veiled reference to the ongoing attacks on the foundation by congressional conservatives who accused it of financing "un-American" subversive causes.

David's overtures—appealing both to the foundation's patriotism and to its self-interest—worked; the foundation indicated it was disposed to cooperate. All that was needed to clinch the sponsorship, his brother was told, was a direct pitch to the foundation by Nelson himself. But, mysteriously, just as the proposal was on the verge of being realized, Rockefeller backed away from it. "NAR does not feel he can do anything more on this," Hanks noted on the bottom of a memo appealing for his help on the plan. The anti-Communist institute was stillborn.

No explanation was ever given for Rockefeller's sudden case of cold feet. All that can be suggested are some educated surmises: that perhaps he was so caught up in his various internecine battles within the administration at the time that he simply had no energy left to expend on this scheme. Or that maybe he had a sudden attack of scruples about using the Ford Foundation in this way.*

* On the other hand, Rockefeller suffered from no such scruples when it came to tapping his own family's foundations for his enterprises. One of his ventures as special assistant was

As diligently as Rockefeller worked to present himself as a Cold War gladiator, his heart clearly was set on more benevolent means of winning the struggle. The spirit of IBEC, AIA, and Point Four had never left him; he was as convinced as ever that the most formidable weapons the West wielded against the Communists were economic. In his White House position, he tirelessly endeavored to brandish those weapons—with distinctly mixed results.

Seeking to temper the strident anticolonialist, anti-Western power rhetoric that was bound to emanate from the Afro-Asian conference in Bandung, he pushed, successfully, for an economic olive branch to the developing world. At Rockefeller's urging, the President on the eve of the conference promised a huge boost in aid to Southeast Asia. Adopting his aide's familiar Point Four rhetoric, Eisenhower spoke of "destroying the conditions under which totalitarianism grows—poverty, illiteracy, hunger and disease."

But more often than not, Rockefeller's attempts to dangle free world economic carrots were thwarted by others of a less munificent bent. The President's pledges notwithstanding, no major economic package for Southeast Asia ever materialized. Lowering his sights, Rockefeller tried to obtain favorable financing by the U.S. Export-Import Bank for construction of an Indian steel mill by the eminent Tata financial group of India. But Treasury Secretary George Humphrey refused to give Tata any breaks—even after Rockefeller lined up the support of Sherman Adams—and the Indians ended up going to the World Bank for funding instead.

Rockefeller's efforts at dollar diplomacy in the volatile Middle East met much the same fate. A charismatic new figure had emerged to roil the already turbulent politics of the region: Gamal Abdel Nasser, co-instigator of a military coup that deposed the corrupt King Farouk from the Egyptian throne three years earlier. As the undisputed leader of Egypt, and the putative leader of the Arab world, Nasser was eager to capitalize on the pivotal role he had overnight come to play in the region's affairs.

Rockefeller saw Nasser as Nasser wanted to be seen: as a neutralist leader who would not hesitate to turn to the Soviets for support if his demands of the West were not met. After meeting with Egyptian Foreign Minister Mahmoud Fawzi, Rockefeller pressed for stepped-up economic aid to Egypt. Dulles, however, balked at this. When Nasser appealed to Washington for tanks, planes, and artillery—and hinted that he would turn to the Soviet bloc if his demands were not met—Rockefeller was one of the few high officials who took the threat seriously, warning that it would open the way for a Soviet

---

an Institute for International Special Research, in which he employed two of his favorite public opinion experts from CIAA days, Hadley Cantril and Lloyd Free, to study "the dynamics of influence operating in France, Japan and Thailand." The financing of this institute came from the Rockefeller Brothers Fund. Source: NAR to Hadley Cantril, April 12, 1955, NAR Special Assistant Book 44, RAC.

beachhead in the Middle East. His concerns were borne out in September, when Nasser confirmed that he was indeed buying his arms from Communist Eastern Europe.

The arms deal made Dulles considerably more receptive to Rockefeller's pitch for another big Egyptian aid request: the financing of Nasser's great showcase project, the Aswan High Dam on the Nile. The dam, potentially the world's largest, promised to be an economic godsend for the parched, impoverished nation, adding a full third to Egypt's arable land and increasing its electric power resources eightfold. But not long after Dulles extended his helping hand, he yanked it back. A combination of congressional opposition and anger with Egypt's recognition of Red China caused him to rescind the offer in June 1956. An irate Nasser responded by nationalizing the Suez Canal and triggering one of the postwar era's greatest crises.

With Egypt, as with Southeast Asia, Rockefeller's position was driven by a single article of faith: that America's strategic interests could best be protected by America's largesse. And in no sphere did he believe this axiom more effectively applied than in the field of atomic energy.

The conviction that the atomic scourge that threatened mankind with annihilation could also be man's salvation had come to occupy a central position in Rockefeller's worldview. Like other starry-eyed proponents of the atomic age, Rockefeller envisioned a world in which the beneficent influence of Father Atom would usher in a new era of international cooperation and prosperity.

Key to encouraging this view was his friend and counsel Oscar Ruebhausen, who since World War II had been a fervent advocate of the peaceful uses of atomic power. In 1954 Ruebhausen helped organize the Fund for Peaceful Economic Development (of which David Rockefeller was a director), a nonprofit corporation dedicated to fostering benign atomic uses. Among the projects he discussed with Rockefeller was the possibility of IBEC developing and promoting nuclear electric plants in Latin America.

As special assistant, Rockefeller saw the President's Atoms for Peace plan not as a one-time propaganda coup (as some in the administration did) but as an ongoing commitment. "I can think of nothing that we can do as a nation today that would be more beneficial in building international confidence and good will for the United States in the face of the increasingly astute program of Soviet aggression," he wrote Atomic Energy Commission chairman Lewis Strauss.

Since its advancement by the President in his dramatic UN address in December 1953, Atoms for Peace had stalled. The Soviets, as expected, were leery of surrendering any part of their nuclear stockpiles to a UN-administered agency, particularly in view of America's overwhelming advantage (Eisenhower's experts had assured him that even if the United States reduced its stockpiles by triple the amount the Soviets did, America would still come out ahead). Nine months later, with the Soviets still resistant, Eisenhower announced that the free world would proceed without the Russians to develop a "new atomic technology for peaceful use." But he had no more success with the U.S. Congress than he had with the Russians; conservative elements shuddered at the prospect of an international nuclear pool over which the United States would have only limited control.

Rockefeller took it as his mission to breathe new life into the moribund Atoms for Peace initiative. In that regard, it certainly did not hurt that he had a long-standing relationship with Strauss, who, as a Kuhn, Loeb partner, had been one of the Rockefeller brothers' financial advisers, and who had later helped with the Point Four report. Strauss, a querulous man of deeply conservative—some would say McCarthyite—bent (he was a principal persecutor of nuclear guru J. Robert Oppenheimer, ostracized as a "security risk"), had been a reluctant draftsman of the Atoms for Peace proposal and noticeably tortoiselike about implementing its provisions. Nonetheless, under Rockefeller's prodding, Strauss began to come around.

With the concept of an international pool still in limbo, the focus of Atoms for Peace shifted to bilateral technology agreements with selected countries. The United States would share information and, in some cases, provide "research" atomic reactors and supplies of nuclear fuel. A number of these agreements—with Turkey, Brazil, Canada, the Philippines, and Switzerland—were pending, and Rockefeller pushed Strauss and State to move them along before Congress adjourned for the summer. As a result, the first pact, with Turkey, was signed on April 1, and seventeen more would be cleared by Congress in the months ahead.

Eyeing, as always, the propaganda benefits, Rockefeller saw the United States reaping a harvest of goodwill with these agreements. He targeted, in particular, the Far East. He tried, in vain, to secure an atomic reactor deal with the Philippines in time for the Bandung conference. Afterward, he discussed with Strauss the possibility of setting up a nuclear research center somewhere in Asia, with the United States providing a reactor free of charge.

By the early spring, Rockefeller had decided to move beyond the piecemeal. It was time, he decided, for the President to make another bold atomic offer to the world; it was time for Atoms for Peace II. The proposal Rockefeller had in mind was basic, and blunt: the United States would make a research reactor available, free, to any nation ready to train scientists in the peaceful uses of the atom.

Rockefeller formed an atomic energy study group—essentially, himself, Ruebhausen, and Stacy May—and began churning out memos to the President and to the State Department advocating his idea. Eisenhower, who saw the peaceful propagation of atomic energy as potentially one of his greatest achievements in office, was instantly enthusiastic. The ever wary Dulles, however, was much less so. Sharing his qualms in a phone call to the equally baleful Strauss, Dulles dismissed Rockefeller's plan as a gimmicky "give-away"; it sounded to him like "a half-price sale thing."

Strauss, in turn, described for the secretary a White House meeting on the proposal: "Nelson Rockefeller was there and did a selling job and the President bought it on the spot." Dulles sighed. "I don't think there is much we can do about it if the President has passed on it," he said.

Eisenhower decided to use his commencement speech at Pennsylvania State University in early June to publicly announce the new atomic initiative. It was an appropriate venue; Penn State was in the process of building the first atomic reactor on a university campus, and the President was expected to tour the facility. The speech drafting was left in the hands of Rockefeller, who gave the job to Ruebhausen.

Dulles grabbed at one last chance to modify the proposal. The least the beneficiaries of America's generosity could do, he told Strauss, was "show enough interest to put up some money themselves." The United States, he insisted, should only finance half the cost of the reactors; the rest should be borne by the recipient countries. Rockefeller, anxious to sidestep any eleventh-hour Dulles assault on his plan, agreed, calling the "fifty-fifty" idea an "excellent" one.

On June 11, the President stood before some 15,000 at Penn State and formally made his offer "to the people of free nations": not only to finance half the cost of the research reactors but to furnish all the fuel they needed as well. As a gambit of psychological warfare, Nelson Rockefeller's nuclear program was a spectacular *coup de théâtre,* an affirmation that the United States was committed to nonbelligerent use of the atom. But the coup was not without its costs, both for the world in the long term and for Rockefeller in the short run. By sprinkling reactors, nuclear fuel, and know-how around the globe, he helped launch the world into a dangerous new era of nuclear proliferation—for once that genie emerged from his bottle, his pacifism could never be guaranteed.

Of more immediate consequence was the shadow his momentary triumph cast on Rockefeller's dealings with Dulles. Up to then the two men had enjoyed a sort of wary coexistence, much in the way Dulles had coexisted with C. D. Jackson. But now that Rockefeller had shown that he could forge policy initiatives, *major* policy initiatives, out of his ideas, the secretary regarded the special assistant with mounting apprehension. Accustomed to absolute hegemony over the conduct of foreign affairs, Dulles could not see Rockefeller as anything but a threat. And against this threat, he would marshal all his formidable defenses.

"An autocrat, a self-centered autocrat," was the way Sherman Adams—no milquetoast himself—would come to describe John Foster Dulles. "It was rather difficult for Dulles to assimilate people who had aggressive, creative ideas. . . . Really Dulles was, in a sense, a one-man show." C. D. Jackson irritated Dulles. Walter Bedell Smith irritated Dulles. "In fact," said Adams, "most everybody irritated Dulles who had anything to do with high-level State Department and world affairs."

The dour, imperious Dulles was a man of commanding intellect and presence, and commanding idiosyncrasies. He routinely unnerved visitors and dinner companions with his bizarre personal habits: chewing candle grease, stirring and sucking whiskey with his fingers, sticking his pencil in his hair, nose, and ears.

These gaucheries were, in a sense, offshoots of his arrogance and his obtuse self-centeredness. One of his biographers, Townsend Hoopes, described him as "an intellectual loner—a man who relied not merely as the last resort, but almost exclusively in large matters and in small, on his own counsel." Dulles' smug certitude and self-righteous air (a product, in part, of his rigid Presbyterian upbringing) intimidated virtually all those with whom he dealt. "To cross him," muttered a young State Department underling, "was to cross the deity."

Yet for all his boundless contempt for those he deemed his inferiors (which was just about everyone with the exception of the President), there was, within the man, a perennial quiver of insecurity about his own position. In large measure, this was a legacy of his uncle Robert Lansing's experience when *he* was Secretary of State under Woodrow Wilson. Thwarted at every turn by the President's majordomo, Colonel Edward House, Lansing ultimately was forced to resign. "The history of the Lansing-Wilson thing was very vividly on his mind," recalled Dulles aide Robert Murphy. Dulles was "determined that this was not going to happen to him."

With Eisenhower, Dulles enjoyed a relationship that was "very much *à deux*," in the words of another Dulles deputy, Robert Richardson Bowie. Dulles was accustomed to sauntering into the Oval Office at will, without an appointment, and meeting with Eisenhower with no one else present (save occasionally Eisenhower's staff secretary Colonel Andrew Goodpaster). "There was no doubt that Mr. Dulles thought that it was his task to be the chief adviser on foreign affairs, and he asserted this role very strongly," said Bowie. "Mr. Dulles wasn't willing to accept a situation in which there seemed to be some other person who was coming between him and the President."

Rockefeller knew all too well about Dulles' regal sensitivities. Back in 1953, hearing that Dulles had vetoed a $300 million loan to Brazil pledged by the Truman administration, Rockefeller went to see Eisenhower about it. The President phoned Dulles and ordered him to reverse the decision. The outcome, Rockefeller would ruefully reflect years later, "was good for Eisenhower, good for the U.S., good for Brazil, but finished me with John Foster Dulles."

Nonetheless, eager to demonstrate that—contrary to reputation and past experience—he could indeed be a team player, special assistant Rockefeller went out of his way in his first few months to mollify the prickly Secretary of State.

With the utmost care, he scrupulously avoided doing anything that might be construed as meddling in his old Latin American turf. When, in his first weeks on the job, Rockefeller was contacted by Brazil's ambassador about the miserable state of U.S.-Brazil relations, Rockefeller dutifully reported the meeting to Dulles, along with the copious assurances he offered the Brazilian about the "wisdom, understanding and long experience" of the new U.S. ambassador.

A short while afterward, Rockefeller spurned an offer by his old aide Berent Friele to act as his eyes and ears in Brazil. As he explained to Friele, "I have been very assiduously trying to avoid in any situation interference with the normal flow of responsibility and action . . ."

Rockefeller's discretion extended to his press contacts. He avoided giving interviews, and when he did agree to the occasional article he proved to be an elusive subject. "What exactly is Rockefeller's job?" asked the Associated Press in a July profile. "He treats it as if it were an atomic secret."

C. D. Jackson, for one, felt Rockefeller was taking his press-shyness a bit too far. He sent a cautionary note to his successor:

> I have heard journalists' gossip (not from *Time*'s Washington news bureau) that you are much too incommunicado to the press, and that although they recognize that you cannot and should not become a weekly blabbermouth, at the same time your aloofness represents an exaggeration at the other end of the scale.
>
> I appreciate that this is a delicate and very personal subject for me to be writing you about, and I am only doing so because I would hate to see these fellows, who can turn into hyenas at the drop of a hat, close in on you . . .

Rockefeller took Jackson's advice—that he let selected Washington correspondents "come around and chew the fat"—under advisement. But, at least in the first few months, he remained one of the administration's most circumspect figures.

And to further prove his allegiance to Dulles, Rockefeller resorted to one of his time-tested gambits: fulsome flattery. "Your historic inter-American speech at noon today should have a tremendous effect throughout the hemisphere," he wrote the secretary in mid-April. "I feel that it will go down in history as one of the truly great speeches on United States inter-American policy."

Yet as much as he reduced his profile, and as much as he took pains to defer to Dulles and inform Dulles and flatter Dulles, Rockefeller could not help but be a burr in the secretary's flank. To a considerable degree, it was simply the nature of his job: there was no way a presidential assistant for psychological warfare or Cold War planning or however else it was described, someone whose mission was to find fresh new ways of waging the Cold War, could coexist happily for very long with a Secretary of State. And particularly not with *this* Secretary of State, a "self-centered autocrat" with an almost obsessive compulsion to control and with bitter memories of his uncle's fate.

If Dulles' personality made any rapprochement difficult, Nelson Rockefeller's irrepressible nature made it even more so. As strenuously as he might try to keep his dynamism, his ideas, and his ambitions in check—to cap the well—they all would sooner or later come gushing to the surface. It had happened at the coordinator's office. It had happened at HEW. And it would be impossible to believe it would not happen at the White House as well.

There was something else to consider: the more than passing resemblance John Foster Dulles had to another great authority figure in Rockefeller's life—another somber, steely autocrat in wire-rimmed spectacles spouting Christian homilies and propounding a Calvinist creed. In very many respects, Dulles might well have been a clone of John D. Rockefeller, Jr. (although Junior, to be sure, was a considerably humbler personality). And confronted with such an authority figure, Nelson fell almost reflexively into a mode of challenging and testing, even as he exhibited his well-oiled deference. All his life he had been under the thumb of a Dulles type, and all his life he had been rebelling. The clash with the Secretary of State would not just be a clash of wills or philosophies; it would be a repeat of a very old familial drama.

If Rockefeller had learned anything from his past government turf battles, it was that the most effective safeguard of his position was direct, unfettered access to the ultimate arbiter, the man in the Oval Office.

But access to Eisenhower was a far different affair than access to his past mentor, FDR. Whereas Roosevelt disdained chains of command and savored direct input from all levels of his government, Eisenhower, ex-general that he was, insisted on a rigid hierarchy and tightly controlled entrée to the top. More than any other postwar President, Eisenhower governed through his cabinet, and expected most of his input to come from them. Anyone wishing to see the President first had to contend with his glowering gatekeeper, Sherman Adams; the only exception to the rule was Dulles.

To cut through the hierarchy and maneuver around Adams, Rockefeller would have to establish a special, personal relationship with Eisenhower, much as he had a special relationship with FDR. And to accomplish that, he would need to resort to some familiar expedients: egregious sycophancy, complemented by a wide-open wallet.

The process had actually started when he was still at HEW, in the summer of 1954. From his own pocket, Rockefeller financed the reproduction and distribution of some twenty thousand official photographs of Eisenhower to U.S. government offices around the world "as a public service." Rockefeller's involvement was supposed to be kept secret from the President—but somehow Eisenhower found out. Although the President affected a show of modesty about the gesture, he was plainly flattered. "I hasten to say," he wrote Rockefeller, "that while I am appalled at the vision of any photograph of me distributed in such quantity, nevertheless in this one instance I must bow to the judgment of the experts. I am therefore gratified by your generosity in providing the material assistance necessary to carry out the project."

But that was merely the start of Rockefeller's "material assistance."

In 1954 Eisenhower and his wife, Mamie, had settled into their comfortable new retreat, a 190-acre farm near the Civil War battlefield of Gettysburg, Pennsylvania. The spread, including a brand-new main house and new barns (the old ones were torn down), radio-equipped tractors, and a herd of Black Angus cattle, was financed by a consortium of the President's well-heeled friends. But something more needed to be done about the landscaping, and at breakfast one day with Rockefeller, soon after the latter joined his staff, the President casually mentioned his problem to Rockefeller. Whether or not Eisenhower was dropping a hint, Rockefeller was not about to let the opportunity pass. He hired a favorite landscape architect, Zenon Schreiber, who had worked on the Foxhall Road estate, to look into the matter and plant some proper trees. In short order, a copious supply of trees—oaks, elms, pines, spruces, red maples, and sugar maples—arrived at Gettysburg, courtesy of Nelson Rockefeller.

The President, who evidently did not think such a luxuriant gift from a subordinate to a boss was at all unseemly, was extremely grateful. "Nothing could have pleased Mamie and me more than the trees you have so carefully and thoughtfully chosen to complete the landscaping at our Gettysburg home," he wrote Rockefeller on April 11. "I am still a little embarrassed that I should have mentioned the matter that morning at breakfast, but my embarrassment does not in the slightest detract from the great enjoyment we now have—and will continue to have—from these trees. Somehow or other they give a 'settled,' completely-at-home look to the farmhouse that I find at once relaxing and secure.

"There are no words to tell you of our deep appreciation."

But Rockefeller did not allow his involvement in the farm to end there. He also arranged for Schreiber to plant an array of Dutch tulip bulbs on the property. "I really think that the view from your terrace in the spring could be made to look like a magic carpet," Schreiber told the President. Rockefeller kept on top of the tulip bulb situation as assiduously as if it were a matter of high state policy. "I am going to see Mr. Schreiber this afternoon," he advised the President, "and will try to get from him more details concerning the bulbs—colors, types, etc.—and find out how far he has gotten to preparing his suggestions for the planting." Once again, Eisenhower was profoundly grateful; the "magic carpet" of tulips Rockefeller provided was all he could have wished.

Rockefeller involved himself as well in the adornment of the White House. He arranged for the loan of eleven paintings from MOMA and the Whitney Museum, including Rockwell Kent's "Evening Shadows" and T. L. Feininger's "Ghost of Engines." Eisenhower hung two of them in his office, and, from the leavings, Rockefeller selected four for his own quarters.

Eisenhower had only to express the vaguest wish, and Rockefeller would be ready, checkbook in hand, to satisfy it. Early in 1955, the President mentioned his interest in arranging a Congressional Medal for the recently retired Winston Churchill. After congressional leaders balked, Rockefeller took it upon himself to explore alternative possibilities, and came up with the idea of a special Presidential Medal. Unfortunately, the President would have to foot the cost of the medal himself, but that posed no problem. One day, Eisenhower found a letter on his desk from Rockefeller, advising him that Sir Winston's "friends and admirers have asked me to transmit to you the enclosed token of their high regard for him." The "token" was a check for $2,500, made out to Dwight D. Eisenhower, "to defray the expense incurred in having the medal prepared." In reality, there was only one "friend and admirer" involved. Nelson Rockefeller had paid for the medal himself.

But by far Rockefeller's most meaningful gift to Eisenhower touched on the President's illustrious military career. From Eisenhower's wartime headquarters, Stanwell House near London, Rockefeller acquired (for the not insignificant sum of $35,000) the eighteenth-century table and chairs—along with the Indian carpet on which they rested—at which the general planned the D-Day invasion. All these Rockefeller presented to Eisenhower to commemorate the tenth anniversary of V-E Day, "as a token of gratitude felt by so many throughout the world for what you have done and continue to do for your fellow man." Eisenhower was genuinely touched by the gesture. "You could not possibly have thought of a war memento of greater significance to me," he told his special assistant.

Not all of Rockefeller's efforts at ingratiation were quite as successful. He built a one-hole golf course at his Foxhall Road digs, in the hopes that he could lure the golf-mad President for a visit—but Eisenhower never came. And his lavish praise of the President's pronouncements—he regularly compared them to the utterances of Lincoln—must have made even the susceptible President blanch. "Some time ago," Rockefeller wrote the President, "I started a hobby of collecting your statements on various basic questions. It seemed to me that you expressed basic American beliefs on current issues with greater clarity and penetration than anyone since Lincoln." He had gone so far as to hire a researcher to organize the material, and he hoped that the President might want to arrange for the publication of this compilation. The

President, though, resisted the temptation, and nothing more was heard of Rockefeller's "hobby."

As Rockefeller continued to burrow his way into the President's favor, he was reminded that there were forces within this administration, potent forces, which did not look so kindly upon him.

In early May, Rockefeller was contacted by Defense Secretary Charles Wilson. Wilson, who had been an admirer of Rockefeller's ever since they had worked together on the defense reorganization plan, was looking for a deputy secretary to succeed Robert Anderson, who was returning to his Texas oil business (temporarily, as it turned out). He wanted to talk to Rockefeller about the job.

To someone who still aspired to a cabinet post, the position Wilson was offering glistened with promise. True, it was a number two job, and Rockefeller was not eager to resume the sort of subordinate role he had gladly shucked off five months earlier. But as number two at Defense, he was ideally situated to succeed the incumbent—and the conventional wisdom in Washington was that sooner or later Wilson would self-destruct.

In his previous position as president of General Motors, Wilson had achieved a reputation for irrepressible loquaciousness; it was Wilson who uttered the immortal line "What's good for General Motors is good for the country." (The joke was that Charlie Wilson invented the automatic transmission in order to have one foot to put in his mouth.) As Defense Secretary, Wilson was no less talkative ("preposterously opinionated" was how Sherman Adams regarded him), with a gift for the ill-advised bon mot ("I wouldn't give the Ethiopians anything but spears") and mindless digressions. "Damn it," Eisenhower exploded at one point, "how in hell did a man as shallow as Charlie Wilson ever get to be head of General Motors?"

Rockefeller's chance of settling into Wilson's Pentagon suite, in other words, was as close to a sure thing as anything he would happen upon in this administration.

On May 20, Rockefeller was summoned to the Oval Office. The President wanted to talk to him about Wilson's offer. Eisenhower revealed that he had given Wilson the go-ahead to approach Rockefeller—not because he wasn't pleased with the job his special assistant was doing, but because *both* jobs were important. He left it to Rockefeller to decide what he wanted to do. The only problem the President saw was that if he took the Defense job, Eisenhower would have to find a good replacement, because he realized every day now how much he needed someone in the psychological warfare role.

Afterward, Rockefeller polled his advisers. Wally Harrison and John Lockwood were in favor of accepting Wilson's offer; Louise Boyer and Frank Jamieson were against it. As for Nancy Hanks, "I lean toward his not doing so, but do not feel strongly," she confided to her parents. "Have always said that I would hate to work in the Pentagon. Maybe I should retire." Hanks's guess was that Rockefeller would take the job.

But then, when Rockefeller was on the verge of making up his mind, he heard again from Wilson. The secretary was very sorry, but he would have to withdraw the offer, because of "highly placed objections elsewhere in the administration." The secretary would not say more, nor would he identify where those "highly placed objections" came from.

It did not take Rockefeller long, though, to sniff out their source. He had been blackballed, he learned, by George Humphrey, the Secretary of the Treasury.

When Eisenhower's critics chided him for creating an administration dominated by big business tycoons, it was usually George Humphrey they were thinking of. The portly, bald-headed Humphrey, the former head of the Cleveland conglomerate M. A. Hanna & Co., walked and talked like the quintessential tycoon, right down to the pompous platitudes ("In business it's results that count" was one of his favorites). He and Eisenhower had not known one another before Humphrey's appointment to the cabinet, but from their very first encounter they found themselves simpatico. "If anyone talks to you about money," Humphrey is said to have instructed Ike at their first meeting, "you tell him to go see George." Eisenhower, who was bored and befuddled by the niceties of monetary and fiscal policy, was delighted to do just that.

Alone among the cabinet members, Humphrey achieved the status of a presidential alter ego. The President and his Treasury Secretary thought alike about most issues, shared the same gut reaction to problems, and even, the President joked, parted their hair the same way. Humphrey was the only cabinet member to enter the select circle of Eisenhower cronies; when the President needed a getaway, Humphrey would invite him down to his Georgia plantation for some quail hunting and skeet shooting.

Early on in his first term, Eisenhower praised Humphrey as "a man of splendid personality . . . persuasive in his presentations," and he never saw any reason to change his mind. (So highly did Eisenhower regard Humphrey that in early 1956 he suggested that if he didn't run for reelection he wanted Humphrey to take his place.) On almost any issue, if Humphrey objected, if Humphrey had reservations, those reservations nearly always carried the day.

And Humphrey clearly had his reservations about Nelson Rockefeller.

The two men had first crossed swords, indirectly, when Rockefeller persuaded the President to reverse Dulles' veto of the 1953 loan to Brazil. The decision had been Dulles', but it had been made at Humphrey's behest; the Treasury Secretary regarded the loan as "inflationary." During Rockefeller's days at HEW, Humphrey took a dim view of his schemes and "hit the ceiling" when he heard about his medical reinsurance idea; only the budget director's assurance that it would never get through Congress (and it didn't) caused the

Treasury Secretary to hold his fire. Later, when Rockefeller moved to the White House, he found himself at loggerheads with Humphrey over special financing for the Indian steel mill. Rockefeller could do little but seethe as the Treasury Secretary, for reasons of frugality, quashed the proposal.

Humphrey, the unreconstructed capitalist, regarded Rockefeller as that most contemptible of species: a "big spender" and big-government type. As a presidential assistant for psychological warfare, those proclivities didn't matter much—but as a prospective Secretary of Defense, in Humphrey's eyes, they did. "That was enough to kill him, in Humphrey's view," recalls fellow cabinet member Herbert Brownell.

So Rockefeller returned to his warren in the Executive Office Building, his path to advancement once again blocked. In George Humphrey, he found a bookend to his other great nemesis, John Foster Dulles. No one, in Eisenhower era Washington, could have faced more formidable adversaries.

To prevail in this administration, he would need more than a magic carpet of tulips. He would need a certain brazenness, and he would need guile—neither of which was a quality in which he was ever deficient.

Thirty-four

Open Skies

Day after day, in the first week of June 1955, word seeped through to Foggy Bottom about a massive mobilization at the Marine base in Quantico, Virginia: a mobilization not of bayonet-wielding Marines, but of academicians, intelligence experts, and leading lights from the nation's most eminent think tanks, all assembled in Quantico under the aegis of presidential special assistant Nelson A. Rockefeller. Monitoring this spectacle, John Foster Dulles became profoundly uneasy. "He seems to be building up a big staff," Dulles grumbled to Sherman Adams. "He's got them down at Quantico, and nobody knows what they're doing."

The jittery Secretary of State phoned his brother Allen, the CIA director, who, as it happened, had been invited by Rockefeller to join in the Quantico proceedings. Rockefeller, complained the secretary, had gone off on his own, "without prior consultation." The brothers assured each other that whatever Rockefeller was doing, nothing would probably come of it. Nonetheless, Allen, America's spymaster, offered to engage in a bit of personal espionage for his brother, reporting to John Foster on exactly what was happening down at Quantico.

The chronically distrustful John Foster Dulles had good reason, this time, for his suspicions. The mysterious Quantico exercise had been couched by Rockefeller, in a memo to the President, as a general brainstorming session—examining "the current international relations situation, with emphasis on, and attention to, the psychological factors involved." But, in fact, what it really was was a spectacular bureaucratic flanking maneuver, a mechanism with which Rockefeller could surreptitiously override Dulles' iron grip on American foreign policy.

His timing could not have been better. The Cold War had reached a particularly fluid juncture, with the rigid doctrine of containment giving way, at least momentarily, to a far more subtle array of policy options. Bowing to congressional and popular pressure, the administration had backed off from a confrontation with Red China over the offshore islands, and mainland leader Zhou Enlai was sounding a new conciliatory note, offering to sit down with the United States to "discuss the question of relaxing tension in the Far East." Eisenhower was guardedly receptive, although he adamantly ruled out any talks until the U.S. airmen held captive by the Chinese were released.

Pacific overtures were also sounded by the Soviet leadership. In mid-May the Russians ended their postwar military occupation of Austria, signing a treaty with the other Big Four powers guaranteeing an independent, democratic future for the country. The Austrian occupation had long been one of the principal East-West stumbling blocks, and an uncharacteristically ebullient Dulles, in Vienna for the emotional treaty signing, saw in the development "something contagious."

At the same time, the Soviets threw conventional diplomacy off balance by suddenly agreeing on May 10 to many of the West's earlier disarmament proposals, including reductions in both conventional and nuclear armaments. Eisenhower reacted cautiously. "The whole question is so confused . . . it is something that has to be studied," he told a press conference the next day. But there was little doubt that the Soviet peace initiative—whether it be sincere or simply a propaganda stunt—was forcing a rapid revision of the Cold War calculus. The United States would have to find some way to respond.

The Eisenhower administration's gesture toward conciliation was to finally agree to long-standing French and British calls for a four-power summit conference. Dulles had erected a barricade of arguments against the summit push: the West should wait until it could deal from a clear position of strength, the summit would accomplish nothing of substance, the conference would invoke shades of the Yalta "sellout" so despised by Republican right-wingers. But pressure from the Allies, particularly from Great Britain, whose new Prime Minister, Anthony Eden, had made the prospect of a summit a key element in his reelection campaign, eventually forced a U.S. turnaround.

Dulles, however, was resistant to the last. At one point he asked British Foreign Minister Harold Macmillan if the United States might send Vice President Richard Nixon to the summit instead of Eisenhower; Macmillan assumed Dulles was joking, but he wasn't. After the meeting was scheduled for late July in Geneva, Dulles suggested to Eisenhower that it be postponed—on the astonishing grounds that there were too many tourists in Switzerland in July. (An unimpressed Eisenhower rejected the secretary's appeal.)

The Secretary of State's grudging acceptance of the summit did not bode well for any prospective American initiatives. While others saw the parley as an opportunity—to win friends for the United States, if not to actually precipitate a Cold War breakthrough—Dulles regarded it as a minefield.

With East-West relations in so much flux, the times demanded creativity and flexibility in fashioning American policy. Yet creativity and flexibility were the least of John Foster Dulles' talents. Dulles could cobble together strategic alliances and play the game of brinkmanship with the best of them. A dynamic new approach, an approach that went beyond the grim pursuit of containment, was simply beyond him—beyond his capabilities and his scruples.

As summit preparations got underway, it was clear that if any new approaches were forthcoming, they would not be emanating from Foggy Bottom. An idea vacuum existed: the sort of vacuum that Nelson Rockefeller, who collected ideas with the same avidity with which he collected Mirós and Picassos, always stood ready to fill. Seeing his opportunity, he stepped swiftly, decisively, into the breach.

In this, he was egged on, as usual, by C. D. Jackson. "Something is happening inside the Soviet Union," Jackson wrote him on May 20. "We don't know whether it is for good or evil (but it surely isn't from strength). All we know is that whereas they always maintained complete maneuverability, we were pretty well frozen into certain positions. Now they have given us more maneuverability than we have had in a long time."

Jackson wasn't counting on any State Department initiatives. Instead, he suggested that Rockefeller and a handful of other administration officials "should go away somewhere for two or three days and dream up some screwy ones."

Jackson's notion of a brainstorming retreat to cook up ideas for the summit had enormous appeal to Rockefeller. Other advisers, notably his Planning Coordination Group deputy Bill Kintner, were pushing him in the same direction; Kintner said they should "get together some really smart guys and figure out what we should do." Still, certain of Rockefeller's aides, evidently fearful of the wrath of Dulles, counseled against such a move. His two top public relations advisers, Frank Jamieson and Donald Irwin, warned that it would mean "friction at best and conflict at worst. It should be shelved fast. . . . It would probably be well to give this idea the silent treatment."

But Rockefeller shrugged off such forebodings. For one thing, he knew that if he didn't churn out some fresh ideas someone else would, and that someone else might well be Harold Stassen. Until March, Stassen had headed the Foreign Operations Administration, the foreign aid-dispensing Point Four artifact that Rockefeller had once sought to run. When Eisenhower decided to fold the FOA, he offered a brand-new position to Stassen:

special assistant to the President for disarmament. Stassen, who still clung to a grandiose dream that he would oversee an Asian Marshall Plan, was expected to turn the vague new job down; instead, to everyone's surprise, he accepted it.

Despite his many career setbacks, Stassen's ponderous self-esteem had not diminished in the slightest. He still saw himself (even if others didn't) as a national figure and a presidential contender, and his new position became the latest vessel for his consuming ambition. "He grabbed the ball and ran very hard with it," recalled Robert Murphy. "He was determined that he was going to get a disarmament agreement to which the name of Harold Stassen would be attached." With the input of a distinguished advisory panel, Stassen began cranking out policy papers setting out possible disarmament strategies that could be broached at the Geneva summit.

Rockefeller and his aides tended to sneer at Stassen's self-important efforts. "We dubbed him the Prince of Peace," says Parker. Still, there was no denying that if there was a creative void in policy making, Stassen was ready and able to fill it. His activities only served to strengthen Rockefeller's resolve to go his own freewheeling way.

Over lunch with the President on May 25, Dulles expressed his apprehensions about Rockefeller's upcoming session at Quantico. Rockefeller, he grumbled, was trying to determine the policy the United States was to follow at the summit conference. But Eisenhower pooh-poohed Dulles' concerns; he assured his Secretary of State that "Nelson" had no such intention.

Nonetheless, to give Dulles an extra measure of reassurance, Eisenhower summoned Rockefeller after the lunch was over and Dulles had returned to State. Questioned by the President, Rockefeller insisted that his Quantico exercise had nothing to do with the summit. Eisenhower then phoned Dulles to relay Rockefeller's impassioned disclaimer. All that Rockefeller had done, said Eisenhower, was "appoint himself a consultative body to study foreign reactions to things. Heads of universities are on it. It advises on psychological warfare."

What Rockefeller told the President was, strictly speaking, true. But no one—not Rockefeller, not Dulles, not even Eisenhower—could have had any illusions about what this "consultative body" represented: an alternative source of strategic and tactical ideas, a source that the President could tap at his discretion. "Eisenhower was very much open to new ideas," notes Herbert Brownell, "especially in the field of foreign affairs, and he encouraged Nelson to come up with them." With Rockefeller, as with Stassen, Eisenhower had craftily provided himself with additional sources of counsel—while all the while professing his unfaltering faith in the judgment of his Secretary of State.

Bill Kintner had handpicked each of the members of Rockefeller's Quantico panel, and the group he put together was an elite corps of Cold War scholars and intelligence experts, men who made it their business to decode Communist intentions and propound stratagems for dealing with them. There were Sovietologists and Sinologists, leaders of Army and Air Force and private think tanks—and, from the Massachusetts Institute of Technology's Center of International Studies, Walt Whitman Rostow.

It was the energetic, incisive Rostow, not yet forty, who was tapped to be the group's chairman. He was the epitome of the globally minded Cambridge intellectual, a species that would achieve its full flowering in the Kennedy administration. Equally at home with military men (during World War II, Rostow had selected bombing targets for the Air Corps) and with footnote-wielding theoreticians, an avid self-promoter who published in such nonacademic journals as *The New York Times Magazine,* Rostow was precisely the sort of bubbly idea-spouter to whom Rockefeller had always been attracted. He was a geopolitical variant of Beardsley Ruml or Stacy May, someone whose natural affability, intellectual prowess, and talents as a synthesizer made him a logical choice to pull these diverse minds together.

Given the distinctly professorial bent of the panel, it was probably no accident that the final member of the group was the distinctly unprofessorial C. D. Jackson. The only Quantico participant (aside from Rockefeller) without a "Dr." in front of his name, and the only one (aside from Rockefeller) to have actually served in the upper reaches of government, Jackson would function as the Quantico group's house pragmatist: someone who would goad the Ph.D.s into turning their abstractions into action programs.

The whole group gathered in the lobby of the Executive Office Building late Sunday afternoon, June 5, and were whisked off in a fleet of official cars across the Potomac to Quantico. Ahead of them were five grueling days of activity, commencing with dinner that evening and going morning, afternoon, and night until Friday—five days of virtually nonstop discussions and draftsmanship. "I couldn't quite figure out when anybody was going to sleep," Jackson would relate.

Each evening, they would be joined for dinner by a sprinkling of high-ranking government guests: the guest list for the first dinner included Dillon Anderson of the NSC, Walworth Barbour of the State Department, Allen Dulles, and the CIA's chief of covert operations, Frank Wisner. "Nelson was adding to the guest list all the time," recalls Parker. "I finally said to him, 'We can't have that many. We can't afford it.' And he looked at me and said, 'Can't afford it? A Rockefeller?' "

By bringing in these outsiders, Rockefeller was not only attempting some intellectual cross-fertilization but also trying to defuse some of the ingrained suspicions and distrust of his Quantico think tank. (Typical of those attitudes was Wisner's peevish gibe, expressed over the phone to Jackson, that "some smart outside one-shot kibitzers will be able to suck out of their thumbs something that the professionals who work 365 days a year won't already have thought of, and probably discarded.")

Knowing his guests' attitudes (and perhaps suspecting that Allen Dulles would be faithfully reporting to his brother), Rockefeller, with Rostow at his side, began that opening dinner in the Quantico officers' mess by repeating his disclaimers about the Geneva conference. His group, he maintained, would be focusing on long-range concerns, and would not presume to suggest to the professionals what should happen at Geneva—on which they were already, he knew, working feverishly.

Then, as if to underscore those assurances, the evening's colloquy commenced, and rapidly degenerated into a semantic rhubarb among the professors over the definitions of such words as "peace." It was a faculty conference run amok, and left Jackson, for one, with a sinking feeling about what the ensuing days would produce. "It looked as though all five days would be spent arguing about definitions, with the losers sulking in corners," he later recounted. Jackson motored back to Washington that night with Dulles and Barbour "feeling very doubtful about the whole exercise."

Those who stayed also had reason to feel doubtful, and not solely because of the abstruseness of the dialogue. The Quantico Marine base was not exactly the Elysian grove most of them were accustomed to in their academic retreats. They slept on cots, three to a room, in the officers' club, and were given the princely per diem of eight dollars, out of which they were expected to reimburse the government for their meals, laundry, and dry cleaning. (Participants not employed by the government, however, were also paid consultant's fees.) It was as though Rockefeller was trying, via his spartan accommodations, to put these cloistered, deskbound thinkers on a war footing.

Rockefeller didn't spare himself; in fact, he seemed to derive a boyish pleasure in the Scout camp atmosphere. He shared a room with two others. ("We all snored in harmony," remembers one of his roommates, Kintner.) Each morning, he would join the rest in lining up to shave and use the meager bathroom facilities. "We all thought he was a pretty good Joe to take it as he did," says Parker. "After all, he could have stayed in Washington and helicoptered down each day. But he didn't. He stayed through the evening discussions, and went to bed with the rest of us."

On Monday morning, Rostow took charge of the discussion. Each panel member was given a chance to discourse on what he thought the group's report should contain. After they all had said their piece, Rostow outlined the modus operandi: over the next four days, they would come up with a terse set of recommendations on which they could all agree, buttressed by appendices and papers in which the participants could have their individual say. And, Rostow added, those recommendations would be geared toward the Geneva summit. Thus, the glib pretense that the Quantico session had nothing to do with the summit—a pretense that both Rockefeller and Rostow had affected as late as Sunday evening—was instantly shucked aside, like a molted carapace.

Rockefeller listened attentively to the presentations, but said little. He had, however, in a speech two weeks earlier, already laid out the underlying assumption that would govern the Quantico deliberations. Representing the President at the dedication of the Peace Arch in Blaine, Washington, on the U.S.-Canadian border, Rockefeller, in one of his few public utterances as special assistant, spoke caustically of the Soviets' recent peace overtures.

"Unfortunately, while the Communists talk of their desire for peace and reducing military tensions, through subversion they are intensifying their exploitation of this ferment of new hope. They seek to marshal these new forces under their leadership. . . . Exploiting new-born aspirations, they pose, with infinite cynicism and deceit, as 'merchants of hope.' "

Thus, the task of the United States was to challenge the Soviets and expose this "cynicism and deceit," to put the lie to the Communists' supposed "desire for peace."

This acerbic view of Soviet intentions was the prevailing gospel at Quantico. For the Quantico panel, the Geneva summit was not a place of peacemaking, but simply a new arena for the never-ending East-West struggle.

The position of the group was succinctly spelled out by Hans Speier of the Rand Corporation in a paper he submitted on Thursday:

> The current disposition of the Soviet leaders to sit down at the "summit" cannot be traced to a genuine interest on their part to ease any tensions for the sake of peace and harmony. It must be traced to a specific Communist interest in improving its position in the international struggle for power. . . . the Soviet leaders are interested in gaining time in order to achieve nuclear parity—a goal which they can hope to achieve, for all practical purposes, within three to five years. . . .
>
> The United States would play into the hands of the Soviet Union if it were to approach the conference with the hope to "ease tension." It should meet the Soviet leaders with the intention to force them to retreat. . . . the United States should seize the initiative by presenting the Soviet Union with heavy demands for major concessions on their part at a price that is tolerable to us.

Speier's analysis, taken literally word for word, would comprise the opening pages of the Quantico panel report.

About the strategic goals, there was no question. It was all now a matter of tactics.

The Geneva summit, as Rostow saw it, was a test—a "test of the seriousness of Soviet peaceful intentions." What the United States had to do was force the Soviets to run a gauntlet of concessions. If the Russians unexpectedly complied with most or all of those demands, the United States would solidify its dominant position and weaken the Soviets' hold on their satellites. If the Russians refused, then the United States would expose their peace initiative for the sham it really was.

The Quantico group came up with a series of "soft" proposals: expanded East-West trade, free and unhampered international communications, freer travel "for peaceful purposes," further exploration of the peaceful uses of atomic energy. But the proposals on which the panel lavished most of their attention were the "hard" ones, the ones the Soviets would find toughest to swallow. And those related to arms control.

Before there could be any meaningful move toward disarmament, the panelists agreed, an effective system of mutual inspection had to be established. In Jackson's words, "Any specific proposals for arms limitation without real inspection would be suicide." The Soviets, in their May 10 disarmament plan, had offered their version of an inspection system: one overseen by an international control body, with "control posts" at large ports, railway junctions, main highways, and airports. The United States had rejected this as inadequate in the nuclear age, when large arsenals of nuclear weapons could be stockpiled out of range of those "control posts."

For the Quantico group, the challenge was to come up with a new inspection wrinkle, one that went beyond the Soviet proposals. After much mulling, Rostow's MIT colleague Max Milliken spoke up; why not, he said, mutual aerial inspection?

The concept had long been bruited about in academic circles but had never surfaced as a formal government proposal. In the context of Geneva, it was potentially a masterstroke: a simple concept, understood by all, that would trump anything the Soviets could put on the table. If the Soviet Union was as serious about peacemaking as it professed to be, then it could not help but embrace such a plan. But if, as the Quantico panelists believed, the Russians were simply posturing, if they had something to hide, then they would reject the concept, and the United States would score a major propaganda coup.

The Quantico participants quickly embraced the idea—all except Hans Speier, who for some reason was visibly distressed by it. Pulling Rostow and Stefan Possony, the Viennese head of the U.S. Air Force think tank, aside, Speier darkly warned them that the plan was "dangerous" and that he felt it his duty to alert U.S. Air Force intelligence that the Quantico group was considering it. What sparked his agitation was his knowledge of the United States' pending plans for aerial reconnaissance, plans that included both balloons and a new supersonic spy aircraft, then under development by the CIA:

a plane with the code name U-2. Should the Russians actually accept the mutual inspection idea, the U.S. reconnaissance edge would be instantly eradicated.

But neither Rostow nor Possony were as apprehensive as Speier, perhaps because they were confident the Soviets would never accept the proposal in any case. Possony, who was in a position to know as much if not more about the U-2 than Speier, persuaded the overzealous academic to keep quiet. In return, Rostow and Possony agreed to insert a strange-sounding footnote in the section of the report broaching the mutual inspection plan, recommending that "this proposal be examined with particular skepticism by the Department of Defense."

The final draft of the panel's report highlighted a plan of action for the July summit; at the top of the list was the proposal of aerial inspection. The panel had little doubt about how the Soviets would react to the initiative: "It is not at all inconceivable that they would accept some form of inspection system, although we would probably have to insist on a system unacceptable to them. It is almost certain that they will reject the free overflight proposal."

The Quantico group, indeed, foresaw just about every eventuality at the Geneva conference *except* a meaningful breakthrough for peace. That much was clear in its disarmament game plan: "Proposal of a disarmament plan to the USSR; after rejection of the plan, the U.S. to make every effort to win the arms race as the safest way of forcing the Soviet Union to accept a satisfactory arms convention."

On Thursday evening, the group went over its recommendations with a large contingent of visiting officials, including Allen Dulles, White House staff secretary Andrew Goodpaster, and Harold Stassen. Pointedly, no one from State came; C. D. Jackson's last-minute efforts to get *someone* from the department met with a sulky rebuff.

When the aerial inspection idea was unveiled, the visitors reacted with surprise and some confusion. According to Rostow, Stassen "appeared to have some difficulty understanding the rationale for the concept." But the bigger surprise—particularly to those who sat in on the first night—was that the report as a whole was so coherent and straightforward, and not the foggy, hedge-ridden exegesis that might have been expected.

The next morning, Rostow placed the three-quarter-inch-thick mimeographed report in Rockefeller's hands and headed home to Cambridge. Rockefeller had what he wanted out of his Quantico panel: an agenda for the summit. The far harder slog—guiding the ideas past the bureaucratic snipers until they reached the Oval Office—was all now up to him.

The first thing he did was approach Jackson and ask if he would help sway the President and Dulles. Jackson was happy to oblige, and as soon as he returned to his office on Monday he penned a note to Eisenhower:

> Having just returned from Nelson Rockefeller's Quantico skull session, I wanted to send you this brief note to convey a personal reaction and a personal hope.
>
> I think that the meeting was a great success, and its findings could be of enormous value. Nelson deserves high praise for having carried it through in the face of quite an array of raised eyebrows, if not worse. And the fact that this group, containing an alarmingly large number of Ph.D.'s, was able to reach a dynamic consensus at the end of five days of argument, was to a great extent due to the atmosphere which Nelson created.
>
> Even though you will probably not have the time to work your way through the entire report and appendices, I do hope that you will be able to read the first section of the report, as it is the mood-setting section from which the possible action items flow.

Jackson's letter arrived on the President's desk the next day, at the very same time as a copy of the Quantico report that Rockefeller sent over. "I find much of value in the material he has sent me," Eisenhower wrote Jackson, "and I am delighted, of course, that you thought the meeting successful and helpful." He assured Jackson he would speak to Dulles about Quantico immediately.

Dulles, however, did his best to make believe that Quantico never happened. Later that week, he sent Eisenhower a briefing memo on Geneva that alluded to Soviet gestures toward disarmament: "We want to keep this discussion within the narrow and, theoretically, confidential confines of the United Nations Disarmament Subcommittee which is now dealing with it." Far from playing up the disarmament issue, as Rockefeller was suggesting, Dulles wanted to bury it. His memo made no reference at all to Quantico or any of the ideas spawned there.

At 12:08 P.M. on June 15 the shrill peal of sirens stirred the nation's capital, signaling the populace that a nuclear attack was imminent. The President, his cabinet, and other top government officials, including Rockefeller, hurried into waiting cars, buses, and helicopters for evacuation to a secret emergency command site, somewhere in the North Carolina mountains. There, at his "Emergency White House"—a large tent filled with small wooden desks and folding chairs—the President received word that New York, Washington, Chicago, and fifty other major cities had been demolished by nuclear warheads, leaving untold millions of casualties. From his wooded refuge, Eisenhower would have to do what he could to govern a shattered nation.

So went Operation Alert, the most far-ranging—and melodramatic—Civil Defense exercise ever staged in the United States. Throughout America, citizens evacuated the streets on cue, to simulate the devastation of a nuclear holocaust. In Washington, there was a mass exodus from every single government building—although most federal workers got no farther than their car doors before returning en masse to their desks. Cooperation with the simulation was virtually 100 percent, with the notable exception of John Foster Dulles, who refused to have anything to do with the exercise and stubbornly remained in his office while his colleagues fled to the mountains.

The intended message of Operation Alert was that the nation could sustain a nuclear strike and continue to function, that from those tents the President could go on governing. That much it showed, but its timing—a little more than a month before the summit—was unfortunate, to say the least. America appeared to be girding itself for the worst, while the rest of the world was caught up in the quest for peace.

Even Eisenhower could see the weirdness of it all. At an NSC meeting a month earlier, he openly questioned the wisdom of the whole operation. Was the President, he asked, to run out to a cave for a few days in what was essentially a war game, and then turn around and go to a Four Power conference? The whole thing seemed "queer and incongruous" to him.

But the schizoid national priorities inherent in Operation Alert were, in many ways, merely reflections of Eisenhower's own inscrutable attitudes toward war and peace—what one biographer would call "a disjunction between the elements of extrovert cheerfulness and self-protective caution." He could be just as suspicious of the Soviets as Dulles, just as warily watchful, telling Herbert Hoover, "You can't trust them, the Soviets, when they are talking nice and you can't trust them when they are talking tough." Yet he genuinely believed that peace was attainable and that some end could be, and must be, found to the pernicious nuclear arms race. He could send Dulles off to rattle his sabers and forge anti-Soviet alliances, yet at the same time press Harold Stassen to come up with new disarmament schemes.

Just five days after he waged a third world war from a tent in the Carolina mountains, Eisenhower the peacemaker reemerged. The occasion was the tenth anniversary of the United Nations, celebrated on the same San Francisco Opera House stage where the charter was signed. At Rockefeller's behest, C. D. Jackson had drafted a speech that would serve as a bold curtain-raiser for Geneva, including a "statement of principles" whose references to "unwillingly dependent peoples" was bound to offend the Soviets. Eisenhower, however, rejected Jackson's draft as too tough, and decided to handle the job himself.

Standing before the stage where more than forty of the original UN conference participants were gathered—including Rockefeller, Stassen, and Molotov—Eisenhower vowed that "the United States will leave no stone unturned to work for peace. We shall reject no method, however novel, that holds out any hope, however faint, for a just and lasting peace." He expressed the hope that "we can in time make unnecessary the vast armaments that—even when maintained only for security—still terrify the world with their devastating potentiality."

Those sentiments were not purely for public consumption either, as Eisenhower made clear at a meeting of the National Security Council on June 30. The NSC was taking up the latest disarmament proposals crafted by Stassen. This plan called for a nuclear freeze at current levels, rather than the outright ban of nuclear weaponry embodied in previous schemes. Policing the freeze would be an International Armaments Commission, "with the right to observe and inspect by land, sea, or air . . . all existing armaments." This sounded very much like the Quantico aerial inspection proposal, although the fact was that Stassen had first come up with his plan in late May, weeks before the Quantico group met.

At the NSC session, the chairman of the Joint Chiefs of Staff, Admiral Arthur Radford, denounced Stassen's design as "unworkable." If the United States pursued it, he warned, the country would eventually "reach a position of absolute military inferiority vis-à-vis the Soviet Union." But Eisenhower was visibly impatient with the military men's objections. So far as he could see, he snapped, Radford believed that the United States should proceed with the arms race "despite the fact that this was a mounting spiral toward war." He conceded Stassen's plan had its problems, but "at least it has the advantage of providing a basis for negotiating."

The ever calculating Dulles listened attentively to this dialogue. However rigid his worldview was, he was also scrupulously careful not to fall out of line with his chief; in his own way, he was a consummate courtier. Striking a newly dovish pose, Dulles interjected his belief that "this whole issue of arms limitation is of tremendous importance for the entire future of the United States." The United States, he said, "must certainly be prepared to make some positive move in the direction of disarmament." What's more, it could not afford to wait until all its political problems with the Soviets are solved before it moves ahead. (So much for relegating arms control to the "narrow" and "confidential" confines of a UN subcommittee—the position he had taken just twelve days earlier.)

Dulles' recommendation was that since effective arms control couldn't come about until an effective policing mechanism was established, the United States should start looking intensively into "the problem of inspection and policing."

This approach met with Eisenhower's approval. He directed Stassen to immediately study what sort of inspection system would work, so that a plan could be presented to the Soviets.

Rockefeller had been unable to attend that meeting, and sent Parker in his stead. But he and Parker were quick to comprehend just how big a breakthrough had occurred. By emphasizing the inspection issue, in his struggle to make the best of Eisenhower's disarmament inclinations, Dulles had played right into their hands. For inspection and policing was exactly what Rockefeller and his group were stressing in their Quantico report.

The only difference was that Dulles was talking about a proposal that would take months to formulate and that certainly would not be ready, in any shape, for the summit. Rockefeller, on the other hand, was solely focused on Geneva; he had a proposal he could deliver to the President *now*.

Shortly after noon on July 6, Rockefeller walked over to the White House west wing, a freshly crafted memo in hand. The memo urged the President to "offer at the forthcoming Big Four conference a proposal for future mutual inspection of military installations, forces and armaments, without any arms limitations provisions"—in other words, an inspection system that was not necessarily linked to specific arms control measures. Said Rockefeller, "I cannot see any aspect of it—even if the Soviets accept it, which is highly doubtful—which in any way jeopardizes our security. Instead, it would offer many advantages . . ."

Significantly, none of Rockefeller's "advantages" related to actual arms reduction. Instead, they all were in keeping with the militant spirit of Quantico. The inspection proposal, in his view, helps "bring down the Iron Curtain," "provides us with intelligence," "poses a difficult decision for the Soviets," "exposes the phoniness of the proposed Soviet inspection system"—and "demonstrates first hand to the Soviets our greater war potential."

Although the brief memo was hardly a disarmament blueprint, Eisenhower was clearly intrigued by Rockefeller's arguments, balancing, as they did, the President's desire to do something dramatic with his instinctive distrust of the Soviets. In essence, Rockefeller had sketched out for him a win-win scenario: even if the Russians rejected the proposal, the United States would still reap immense psychological dividends.

So captivated was Eisenhower that, with Rockefeller still in his office, he phoned Dulles. "Nelson is here," he said, "and he has got a tremendous idea." The United States would "develop a plan for immediately starting inspection of each other's armament." Dulles was quick to interject that that was *his* idea—in fact, he had told Stassen four days ago that that was the way to get started.

Well, said the President, as long as the secretary was thinking of it, he was satisfied.

Dulles, however, had said nothing about Geneva (and the President, for his part, had not mentioned it either). What's more, in his conversation with Stassen, Dulles had talked about taking two or three months to formulate inspection ideas. So even if Dulles sincerely did believe that mutual inspection was the way to go—and was not simply embracing it as a way of defusing the disarmament talk, as some might suspect—he was hardly assenting to Rockefeller's pitch that it be placed on the summit agenda.

Indeed, Dulles still clung tenaciously to his view that nothing good could come of this summit. He resisted putting substantive issues on the table and feared that the whole exercise was nothing but a propaganda circus that would prop up the struggling new Soviet regime. In a briefing memo to the President, he urged Eisenhower to avoid social meetings where he would be photographed with Soviet leaders, and to maintain "an austere countenance" on those occasions when photography was unavoidable.

Eisenhower, however, rejected such cautions; the closer he was coming to the summit date, the more he saw Geneva as a rare opportunity. "We are going there honestly to present our case in a conciliatory, in a friendly attitude," he told a press conference on July 6, "and we don't intend to reject anything from mere prejudice or truculence or any lesser motive of that kind." And at an NSC meeting the next day, he pointedly referred to United States Information Agency polls on Western European attitudes, which showed a strong sentiment for reduction of East-West tensions. Those results, he said, in the presence of a dubious Dulles and a glum Admiral Radford, could not be ignored.

"I am suddenly reminded that today you are celebrating your birthday anniversary," the President wrote Rockefeller on July 8. "At any rate, it gives me the opportunity to wish you the best of everything in the years to come, and at the same time to thank you for the many wonderful things you do for Mrs. Eisenhower and me." He then referred, in a postscript, to one of those "wonderful things," the gift of the World War II furniture: "I am anxiously awaiting the arrival of the table, chairs and carpet. Where do you think we should exhibit them in the White House?"

Such good wishes from the boss confirmed Rockefeller's sense that now was the time to press his advantage. Upon learning that the President planned to address the nation on television on the eve of his departure for Geneva, Rockefeller brought Rostow down to Washington to prepare a suggested draft. Addressing the disarmament issue, Rostow's draft asserted, "No system of controlled armaments can provide security unless it is backed by extensive and thorough measures of mutual inspection. . . . we shall lay before the forthcoming conference specific measures to this end." This certainly would have been news to John Foster Dulles and Harold Stassen. Rockefeller, it seemed, was using the speech to lock the President into a commitment to deliver "specific" inspection proposals to the summit.

He also was maneuvering for a place for himself at the conference. Back in May, when plans for the summit were first coming together, Eisenhower had told Dulles he wanted to "hold down to a minimum" the number of people in the U.S. entourage, and mentioned, to the secretary's evident pleasure, Rockefeller, Stassen, and Lodge as among those who would be left out. But by early July, Eisenhower had had second thoughts—which were not shared in the least by Dulles. The President felt compelled to call Stassen to his office and sheepishly confess, "Harold, Foster does not want you to be at the Geneva conference." But when Stassen protested his exclusion, Eisenhower came up with an expedient: perhaps Stassen could travel incognito to Paris, where he would be available for a presidential summons to Geneva when the need for his presence arose (and when Eisenhower had sufficiently stroked Dulles' ruffled feathers). Radford and Deputy Defense Secretary Anderson could join Stassen on standby alert.

Hearing of this arrangement, Rockefeller wasted no time letting the President know that he, too, should be part of the rump delegation in Paris. The President was agreeable, and at a White House meeting (at which Rockefeller sat in) he informed Dulles of his plans for the Paris foursome: they would come down to Geneva "when needed," but in any case he would invite each of them to Geneva for at least one evening in the course of the conference.

After the meeting Rockefeller hurried to arrange for his diplomatic passport and to book his suite at the Plaza-Athénée in Paris. Dulles, meanwhile, stewed about this latest unpleasant development in a conference he never wanted in the first place.

That evening, Dulles had C. D. Jackson over for dinner. Whatever their past policy differences, Dulles regarded Jackson as a confidant, someone with whom he could commiserate about the vicissitudes of life with Ike. With the secretary's wife, Janet, joining them, Dulles proceeded to unburden himself about the conference for which he would be leaving in just thirty-six hours.

"I am terribly worried about this Geneva conference," he began. He was worried about the French and he was worried about the British, but most of all he was worried about Eisenhower. "He is so inclined to be humanly generous, to accept a superficial tactical smile as evidence of inner warmth, that he might in a personal moment with the Russians accept a promise or a proposition at face value and upset the apple cart." He was especially concerned about the informal buffet dinners, where "the real work will be done," and where the Russians, he feared, "may get in their real work with the President."

"We have come such a long way by being firm, occasionally disagreeably firm," said Dulles, "that I would hate to see the whole edifice undermined in response to a smile."

At stake, he believed, was the entire foreign policy framework he had arduously labored for two and a half years to construct. "You know," he told Jackson, "I may have to be the Devil at Geneva, and I dread the prospect."

He put his dilemma in the starkest, most harrowing terms. "I am afraid that either something will go wrong in Geneva, some slip of the allies, some slip of the President's, which will put me in the position of having to go along with a kind of foreign policy for the U.S. which could be described as appeasement—no, appeasement is too strong a word, but you know what I mean—or, on the other hand, I may have to behave in such a way at Geneva that my usefulness as Secretary of State, both domestically and abroad, will come to an end."

As Jackson would recall, "This was said with a depth of emotion on his part such as I had never heard before, and I was quite rocked."

Jackson tried his best to boost Dulles' spirits, citing Dulles' vast prestige in the United States (a point with which Dulles, who had his Gallup poll approval ratings at his fingertips, readily agreed), reminding him of his foreign policy successes—and assuring him that the President "was no bubblehead."

"It was quite corny," Jackson later related, "and somewhat like a football coach between the halves, but it seemed to work, because as I then had to leave, he took me to the door, grabbed me by both arms, and said, 'I am so grateful to you for having come down.' "

The next morning, a still-overwrought Dulles arrived at his office to find an appointment with Nelson Rockefeller penciled in on his schedule.

Rockefeller arrived with another of his memos, this one entitled "Psychological Strategy at Geneva." He had given it to the President the previous day, and now, after the fact, he was sharing it with the Secretary of State.

In his memo, Rockefeller described the summit as a propaganda battleground. "The U.S.S.R. uses conferences more often to achieve psychological and propaganda advantage than to conduct serious diplomatic negotiations," he argued. "In view of the prolonged build-up and the widespread interest shown in the Four Power Conference, the propaganda stakes at Geneva may prove more significant than the actual conference results."

This perspective was very much in keeping with Dulles' view of the summit. But whereas Dulles used this cynicism to justify aloofness and inaction, Rockefeller employed it for exactly the opposite ends: as a rationale for a dynamic U.S. approach to the conference. "A basic U.S. aim at Geneva," he contended, "must be to capture the political and psychological imagination of the world."

"Since it is the Soviet practice to take the offensive at conferences, we can only assume that they will have bold propositions in hand," argued Rockefeller. "We need our own positive approach at Geneva if we are to capture the world's imagination."

Rockefeller then offered to the President "suggested guidelines" for handling ten potential conference issues.

Through his steel-rimmed spectacles Dulles glanced at the memo, and then cast the stoniest of gazes at its author sitting across from him. It was hard to say what made him angrier: the "suggested guidelines" and all the rest that completely contradicted his department's policies, or the fact that Rockefeller had not deigned to show him the memo before sending it off to the President.

In the chilling, metallic tones his subordinates had come to quietly dread, he addressed his visitor.

"I have grave question as to the propriety of the President getting this kind of advice from sources outside the State Department," he said. Dulles reminded his guest that the Secretary of State was supposed to be the President's principal adviser on foreign affairs. If the President was getting advice on the whole gamut of international issues from Mr. Rockefeller, that would put Mr. Rockefeller and the secretary in a competitive position—which, Dulles caustically noted, was not "good organization." Dulles allowed as to how there had been Presidents who did get much of their advice from "private advisers," ignoring the State Department—an obvious reference to his uncle's problems with Colonel House in the Wilson era. But that was not *his* idea of how things should work, nor was he "disposed to be Secretary of State under those conditions."

Rockefeller responded to this tongue-lashing with a great show of innocent befuddlement. He had never thought of the matter that way, he said, and he certainly could see the force of Dulles' arguments. But he professed to be bewildered as to what to do. He had this job, but he did not know how to do it other than the way he was doing it. Certainly, he would be happy to funnel his ideas through the State Department. Just how he could do so, however, eluded him.

Still, if the secretary thought there was no real role for Rockefeller to play in his present job, then he would be glad to give it up.

All Dulles would say, in response to that, was that he would give further thought as to how Rockefeller "might coordinate better with the State Department."

Rockefeller then asked whether he could get into the meeting of NATO ministers in Paris just prior to the summit. Dulles' reply was frosty: he already had sharply cut the list of participants, and he doubted whether he could work Rockefeller in.

Utterly unfazed, Rockefeller brought up another request: was there some way of keeping the Paris contingent informed of what was going on in Geneva? To this, Dulles stiffly replied that he thought it would be possible to send to the Paris group the same bulletin that was being sent to Vice President Nixon in Washington.

Thus rebuffed and rebuked by the Secretary of State, Rockefeller departed—leaving an anguished Dulles to wonder just where he would strike next.

He didn't have long to wait. The next morning, Drew Pearson's column reported that Rockefeller had hired former congressman Charles Kersten, a staunch anti-Communist crusader who, while in Congress, had called for an all-out political offensive against the Reds with rhetoric that was extreme even by Dulles' hard-line standards. Dulles' aide Roderick O'Connor broke the news to the chief, and added this worrisome note on Rockefeller's doings: "I know of at least two other people who have been hired on his staff and there is growing evidence that he is going into business in rather a big way. You will recall that C. D. Jackson operated without any staff at all."

Then O'Connor tossed in some more grist for Dulles' already overworked mill, with this handwritten postscript: "White House tells me *confidentially* that there are now 27 people working for Rockefeller (including secretaries) and still hiring—"

As soon as the secretary read O'Connor's missive, he was on the phone to his brother Allen. Had Allen known about Kersten? Allen, it turned out, had; the funds for Kersten's hiring, in fact, had come from the CIA. What's more, Kersten had been brought on after a good deal of talk with Vice President Nixon, who was evidently one of the congressman's sponsors.

The Secretary of State made it plain to his brother that he had serious objections—not to Kersten per se, but to the vast organization that Rockefeller seemed to be building up, a "high-power organization under him which is running competition with State." Trying to placate his brother, Allen assured him no one envisioned Rockefeller having such an apparatus. John Foster, however, continued to bristle. It was, he fumed, "the sort of thing that should not go on."

While Dulles seethed, Rockefeller methodically went about the business of cabling the Royal Monceau Hotel in Paris, to book rooms—rooms to be used by his staff. Ted Parker would be going to Paris, as would Bill Kintner and pollster Lloyd Free and Air Force intelligence expert Stefan Possony. And Nancy Hanks. Unbeknownst to Dulles, Rockefeller would have at his beck and call almost as large a personal entourage as the Secretary of State, ready to assist their chief when the summons to Geneva came. The "high-power organization" of Dulles' nightmares was set to bivouac in Paris.

At 8:15 P.M. on July 15, the nation's television and radio programming was interrupted for an address by the President of the United States. Less than an hour before his scheduled departure for Geneva, he wanted to talk to the people about his hopes and expectations for the summit.

The text he used was not the one provided him by Rockefeller. Instead, Eisenhower spoke off the cuff, without notes, with a fervor rarely found in his public utterances. To those cynics who wondered what another conference would accomplish, he replied, "Well, now, the first question I ask you, 'Do we want to do nothing? Do we want to sit and drift along to the inevitable end in such a contest of war or increased tensions?' "

He hoped, he said, to "change the spirit" of U.S.-Soviet relations. "I say to you, if we can change the spirit in which these conferences are conducted we will have taken the greatest step toward peace, toward future prosperity and tranquillity that has ever been taken in the history of mankind."

Then, waxing even more evangelical, Eisenhower spoke of "a terrific force to which I believe all the political leaders of the world are beginning to respond": the force of prayer. He urged all 165 million Americans to crowd into their places of worship on the next Sabbath day and offer a prayer for peace. "This," he assured them, "would be a mighty force."

Hearing these words, Dulles groaned.

That this would be a summit of spirit and of image as much as, if not more than, of substance was borne out from the moment the world leaders touched down at Cointrin Airport. Arriving with the First Lady and son John aboard the presidential plane *The Columbine,* Eisenhower was surrounded by a phalanx of Secret Service men who dogtrotted beside his limousine as it coasted into town, while helicopters searched the skies overhead. The Kremlin leaders' arrival the next day seemed positively carefree by comparison: no swarm of guards surrounded their Ilyushin 14, and they proceeded to the spartan residence of the Soviet consul general in an open touring car, *sans* helicopter escort, as though thumbing their noses at American paranoia.

The stiff, forbidding visage that the Russians customarily displayed at international meetings was also notably absent. True, the perdurable Molotov was there, as stone-faced as ever. But he was overshadowed by the new Kremlin masters, men who projected far more multihued personalities than the gray eminences of the Stalin era. Leading the delegation was Premier Nikolai Bulganin, a well-mannered, well-turned-out goateed man who reminded some of an opera impresario, others of a successful Kentucky horse breeder. Right behind him, exuding the swaggering self-confidence of the power behind the throne, was the First Secretary of the Communist Party, squat, bald-headed Nikita Khrushchev. With his earthy peasant style (causing one American diplomat to remark upon his "extraordinary table manners"), his air of plainspoken bonhomie (he told reporters that he subscribed to the doctrine of "live it up"), and his penchant for emotional vituperation, Khrushchev was the antithesis of the colorless, calculating apparatchik to which the world had become accustomed.

Compared to Khrushchev, the two leading Western figures, Eisenhower and Eden, came off as dull, shopworn personages. If one goal of the conferees was to capture the world's imagination, then the Soviets had the early lead.

When Churchill first called for a summit two years earlier, he had envisioned a parley "with a measure of informality and a still greater measure of privacy and seclusion." Nothing could have been further from Churchill's ideal than the scene in Geneva.

Some 1,200 newsmen descended on the city, forcing the statesmen to repair to their lakeside villas if they hoped for a scrap of seclusion. Spontaneity was circumscribed by the rigid agenda agreed to by the conferees, as well as by the setting of the proceedings: the Council Chamber of the Palais des Nations, the old League of Nations headquarters on the outskirts of Geneva. The conferees positioned themselves around four tables, drawn up in a rectangle with an opening in the middle; overlooking them behind a railing, on all sides, were a half dozen banked rows for aides and onlookers, making the participants feel like they were in the middle of a boxing ring. Everywhere they turned they were confronted by grotesque frescoes adorning the walls, showing subhuman beasts tossing babies down the muzzles of cannons—a sickening artistic allegory of the strife they were there to prevent. Said British Foreign Minister Macmillan, "I could conceive of no arrangement less likely to lead to intimate or useful negotiations."

A single large picture window, framing a view of the lake, offered the only note of placidity.

The Geneva summit formally opened in sweltering heat on the morning of July 18. Eisenhower, as chairman of the first session, led off with a discourse that revealed Dulles' fine hand: long on the elucidation of problems, short on solutions. The first issue he put on the table was "the problem of unifying Germany and forming an all-German government based on free elections." German unification was one of Dulles' most cherished causes, since he expected a democratic Germany to lodge itself firmly in the Western camp; for that very reason, the Soviets were in no great hurry to assent. It was not an issue on which much conference harmony could be expected.

Equally off-putting to the Russians was what Eisenhower had to say about international Communism. "Its activities are not confined to efforts to persuade. It seeks throughout the world to subvert lawful governments and to subject nations to an alien domination." Whatever the truth of those assertions might be, they were hardly the most politic words with which to open a summit.

Then the President turned to disarmament. He raised the issue of mutual inspection as "the foundation for real disarmament"—and as a means of preventing surprise attacks. But he offered no specifics on a possible inspection system, leaving the whole matter in the realm of vague rhetoric—which was exactly where his Secretary of State wanted it.

The other leaders, by contrast, seemed far more willing to chance new—albeit highly theoretical—initiatives in the opening round. France's premier

Edgar Faure offered a disarmament plan based on budgetary controls. Eden suggested a demilitarized area between Eastern and Western Europe. And Bulganin plumped for a "system of collective security" involving Russia, the United States, and all of Europe, a system that would replace NATO and the East's military alliances and would lead to the eventual withdrawal of all "foreign troops" from European soil.

Bulganin also brought to the conference table an olive branch: the Soviet Union would contribute to the Atoms for Peace pool Eisenhower had proposed eighteen months before.

That evening, Eisenhower hosted the Soviet delegation at his lakeside villa, the Château de Creux de Genthod, a miniature eighteenth-century French château lent to the President by its owner, a Swiss perfume magnate. It was Eisenhower's first chance to assess the Kremlin leaders up close; as he would later reflect in his memoirs, he found them "mechanical" men who "drank little and smiled much." Khrushchev made the strongest impression on the President: "rotund and amiable, but with a will of iron only slightly concealed." Eisenhower felt the dinner was "useful," not because of any interchange of ideas but because of his vivid impression of Russian intransigence. "I saw that the implacability of this quintet in a social situation would certainly be encountered in ensuing conferences," Eisenhower related, "and we would have to shape our own tactics accordingly."

In Paris, meanwhile, Rockefeller met up with the rest of the standby contingent—Anderson, Stassen, and Radford—at their hotel, the Crillon, opposite the Place de la Concorde. Awaiting the summons from Geneva, they all had time on their hands—a situation that Rockefeller vigorously took advantage of.

Commandeering a meeting room, he asked his pollster Lloyd Free to give the group a briefing on his latest surveys of European sentiment on such issues as disarmament and nuclear warfare: findings that were distinctly negative toward the United States. This led into a presentation by Rockefeller of the key Quantico proposals, which the others listened to politely, but with a certain degree of bored indifference. Radford, for one, doodled the whole time.

Obviously, they had not seen the point of his whole exposition, and so Rockefeller laid it on the line for them. It was essential, he said—as Free's surveys pointed up—that the President offer something dramatic at Geneva. But because of the State Department's reactive attitude, the President was bound to falter once the opening statements were disposed of. The U.S. side needed fresh ideas, and that was what the Quantico proposals offered.

At that juncture, Stefan Possony intervened. The Air Force intelligence expert felt it important that they focus on one Quantico suggestion in particular: the aerial inspection plan. As Possony hammered home the benefits of the proposal in his rich Hungarian accent, Radford sprang to life. "I see what you fellows are trying to do," he suddenly exclaimed. "You're trying to open up the Soviet Union."

It was the intelligence aspect of the plan that intrigued the Joint Chiefs chairman, rather than the peacemaking or propaganda value. The Soviet Union already knew practically all there was to know about the U.S. capabilities; with aerial inspection, the United States could equalize things. If the Russians actually accepted the proposal—and Radford personally doubted they would—America would achieve "a decided intelligence advantage," in Radford's view.

What especially sold Radford, as Kintner recalled, was that "we had, by far, a superiority in manned aircraft at that time, but we lagged behind the Soviets in intercontinental-range missiles. And that was one of the things that we wanted to find out about through this proposal."

Thus, by packaging the aerial inspection plan as an espionage opportunity, Rockefeller was able to bring Radford around. And the backing of Radford for the proposal was indispensable, points out Kintner: "Had the military opposed it, then Ike would not have gone through with it."

Late that night, Rockefeller had his top aide, Ted Parker, place a call to Eisenhower's staff secretary, Andrew Goodpaster, in Geneva. Goodpaster had agreed to serve as a liaison with the group in Paris, and Parker asked him how the first day's proceedings had gone. Venting his discomfort to a fellow Army officer, Goodpaster, who had just returned from the dinner with the Russians, described the sterility of the whole extravaganza, and painted a gloomy picture of the U.S. delegation's chances of a breakthrough. Parker then casually mentioned that the people in Paris might be able to provide some help, might be able to offer some ideas from their perch in the City of Light. Goodpaster, whose sole allegiance was to Eisenhower and who was plainly worried about the bind in which Dulles was putting his boss, encouraged Parker to give it a try.

When Rockefeller heard this, he immediately asked Kintner and Possony to draft something in plain language that the President could use in Geneva. What they produced was a "Presidential Statement on Disarmament" that highlighted the mutual inspection issue and called for "aerial observation" of "military establishments." Early the next afternoon, Rockefeller cabled the statement to Goodpaster, with this cover note: "From psychological and public opinion point of view President laid excellent foundation on subject of limitation of armaments in opening statement Monday. It appears highly desirable to expand on this foundation by explaining in greater detail what is meant by supervision and inspection. . . . This draft statement has been written in a conciliatory tone but in a manner to sharpen the issue."

At the same time, Radford and Anderson sent down to Dulles a rather muted memo calling for an "affirmative proposal" on "effective inspections." It pointedly did not mention the overflight idea, nor did it mention the statement Rockefeller was transmitting to Eisenhower. Thus, Dulles was formally kept in the loop—but with a certain calculated obfuscation of what was really going on behind his back.

As the conference moved into its second day, Dulles was fixated on a single issue: the reunification of Germany. Unless the summit moves in that direction, he told Eisenhower that morning, "our Conference here will, I think, be a failure." Despite the obstacles, he was optimistic that the principals would, at least, accept the principle of unification.

Following his Secretary of State's game plan, Eisenhower pressed the issue at that day's session. He sought to give the Russians all sorts of assurances that a reunited Germany would never again pose a military threat. But the Soviets were unmoved. Bulganin said he expected reunification to occur—but not for a very long time, and not by a simple wave of a statesman's hand.

The rejection left the summit at a stalemate. German unification, the United States' pet issue, was a nonstarter, as was Eden's plan for a European demilitarized zone and Faure's wild idea of budget-based disarmament. The Soviets, for their part, were still harping, to no avail, on the need for a grandiose European security system, which Eden warned would take years to accomplish. So frustrated were Eisenhower and Dulles that they seriously discussed walking out of the conference to protest Soviet intransigence.

The only bright note in the dour proceedings was an impromptu visit to a Geneva toy shop by Eisenhower prior to the session. The President spent the equivalent of twenty-one dollars on dolls and a toy plane for his grandchildren, as a swarm of reporters jammed the tiny store. When he emerged, onlookers asked him how the summit was progressing. He gave one of his patented ear-to-ear grins. "So far, very friendly," he said.

Later that evening, the word arrived at the Crillon: the President wanted Rockefeller and Stassen to come to Geneva at once.

The two men, accompanied by Rockefeller's sizable retinue, early the next morning boarded a military aircraft for Geneva. Upon their arrival, Goodpaster was there to greet them, and he drove Rockefeller and Stassen to their hotel, the Du Rhône, while the staff was left to scrounge up accommodations for themselves. (Unable to find anything in Geneva, they wound up in Lausanne, forty miles away.)

Rockefeller and Stassen barely had time to check in and leave their bags before Goodpaster hustled them off to the President's lakeside château.

When the threesome were ushered into the paneled library, they found the President eager to discuss the mutual inspection proposal. Not only had Eisenhower seen and digested Rockefeller's memo, but he had broached the idea to Eden over breakfast that morning; the British Prime Minister, he reported, had reacted enthusiastically. Before he went any further, though, Eisenhower wanted his military leaders in on the plan. He would summon Radford and Anderson from Paris, as well as NATO commander General Alfred Gruenther. They could all meet later that afternoon, after the day's formal discussions were over.

With three or four hours to kill, Rockefeller headed over to a buffet lunch Eden was hosting for the Russians. There he found himself approached by none other than Nikita S. Khrushchev. "So this is Mr. Rockefeller himself!" the Soviet boss exclaimed, playfully jabbing Rockefeller in the ribs; Rockefeller laughingly jabbed him right back. Relishing the opportunity to take the measure of the world's premier capitalist (to the Russians, all Rockefellers were *the* Rockefeller), Khrushchev jauntily invited him on the spot to visit the Soviet Union.

Taken aback, but endeavoring to play along, Rockefeller insisted that "I can't go by myself. I'd like to bring Carl McCardle," an Assistant Secretary of State. McCardle, standing within earshot of the conversation, protested, "But I've been to Russia." Khrushchev waved off the objection. "It doesn't make any difference," he said. "Let's all go. Things are different now."

Accustomed to stern Soviet visages, Rockefeller was not prepared for such spontaneous garrulousness. "Khrushchev," he observed afterward in a letter home to his daughter Mary, "has a very good sense of humor and is a tremendous extrovert, although he is only half-pint size. As a matter of fact, they [the Russians] are all very short." The Soviets, he noted, "were all smiles and friendliness—a tremendous change from the old days."

His close encounter, however, did not cause him to change his calculations; if anything, Khrushchev's gruff charm served in his mind to confirm the wisdom of the propaganda counteroffensive he wanted the President to pursue.

At a press conference that day, Dulles was asked, point-blank, "Will the United States present any plan or proposal on disarmament?" The Secretary of State replied that the United States would present its "broad philosophical approach," along the lines of the President's opening statement. But, he insisted, "there will be nothing in the way of a concrete proposal on a take-it-or-leave-it basis."

Dulles' misleading prediction may not in fact have been the exercise in dissembling it later appeared; even at that juncture, even after sitting in on Eisenhower's breakfast with Eden, he may not have put much stock in the mutual inspection proposal. In any case, all his assessment accomplished was to harden the perception, among the press at least, that Eisenhower was mainly involved in a vague bridge-building exercise at Geneva, hoping that somehow his lubricative personality would smooth the path to peace in much the same way it brought the Allied armies together in World War II.

The President's seeming determination to sail along on a sea of platitudes led reporters to readily accept the official explanations for the sudden arrival on the scene of Stassen, Rockefeller, Radford, and Gruenther. Stassen was there, it was said, to brief the President prior to the next day's discussion of disarmament. Rockefeller was supposedly there because of his concern with peaceful atomic energy development; the President had toured, that afternoon, an experimental nuclear reactor the United States put on display in the Palais des Nations as part of an upcoming "atoms for peace" conference. And the President summoned Gruenther, said the *Times*'s James Reston, "for the simple reason that he likes him and wanted to play bridge with him tonight."

At 6 P.M. the President gathered his advisers in the library of his villa. A round of bridge was not on the agenda. A mutual inspection plan was.

Eisenhower and Dulles sat in easy chairs by the fireplace, while the rest—Radford and Gruenther and Anderson, Stassen and Rockefeller and Goodpaster, along with Assistant Secretary of State Livingston Merchant and National Security Adviser Dillon Anderson—positioned themselves around the room. Stassen proceeded to hand out copies of a proposed presidential statement on disarmament that Eisenhower had asked him to draft that afternoon.

All was silent as the group perused Stassen's words, intended for delivery by the President at the next day's summit session.

> My government is ready in principle to permit trial inspection of units of our armed forces if other countries will do the same. My government is ready in principle to permit test aerial photographic inspection if other countries will do the same. . . . We are ready to proceed in the study and testing of a reliable system of inspections and reporting, and when that system is designed, then to reduce armaments . . .

Eisenhower pronounced himself "entirely in agreement" with the language of Stassen's draft—which was largely based on the statement Rockefeller had sent to Goodpaster the previous day.

Seeing that any attempt at dissuasion was hopeless, Dulles now hastened to climb aboard himself. From the standpoint of both drama and substance, he opined, the proposal was "very promising and should have a very great effect."

All that remained was the matter of tactics. Should the President include the proposal in his prepared opening statement on disarmament—or try to maximize its impact by dropping his bombshell "extemporaneously"? (The consensus favored the "extemporaneous" approach.) Should the British and French be notified in advance of exactly what Eisenhower was about to say? (To minimize leaks, it was decided to keep them in the dark, although Eden, at least, had a general idea of the President's intentions.)

And what about Congress? Robert Anderson argued that they should at least let the leadership in on their plans. Eisenhower agreed, and told Dulles he should have his people contact congressional leaders—while stressing the need for absolute secrecy.

Throughout the hour-and-a-half discussion, Rockefeller was conspicuously silent. He seemed content to let the others debate tactics, content, for once, to recede into the background. However the scenario played itself out, he had achieved precisely what he wanted. Now all he had to do was quietly wait less than twenty-four hours for the denouement.

The summit was called to order at 3:30 the next afternoon by Bulganin. Through the picture windows in the council chamber, masses of thunder-clouds could be seen enveloping the mountains. The delegates and their supporting casts took their places: directly behind Eisenhower and Dulles sat Rockefeller and Stassen, and behind them, Goodpaster and John Eisenhower, the President's son. John had been reluctant to attend the session, but earlier that day he had been waylaid by Rockefeller. "You ought to be here this afternoon," Rockefeller suggested. "Your dad's going to do a great thing. It's going to be great. You gotta be here."

The President drew doodles of Bulganin and Molotov as the Soviet leader droned on. Finally, Bulganin yielded the floor to the Americans.

As the storm clouds darkened behind him, Eisenhower launched into his prepared text. He spoke of the difficulties of achieving an agreement on disarmament and the overriding need for an adequate inspection system. Then he glanced up from his text and looked over at the Russians. Rockefeller leaned back and whispered to the President's son, "Hold your hat, here we go now!"

"Gentlemen," the President said, "since I have been working on this memorandum to present to this conference, I have been searching my heart and mind for something that I could say here that could convince everyone of the great sincerity of the United States in approaching this problem of disarmament.

"I should address myself for a moment principally to the delegates from the Soviet Union, because our two great countries admittedly possess new and terrible weapons in quantities which do give rise in other parts of the world, or reciprocally, to the fears and dangers of surprise attack."

He was speaking now, seemingly, extemporaneously, truly from the heart; what he was saying appeared nowhere in the prepared text. (In fact, the President's reading copy was marked with two bold carats, indicating the spot where the "spontaneous" material could be inserted.)

"I propose, therefore, that we take a practical step, that we begin an arrangement, very quickly, as between ourselves— immediately."

The arrangement, he said, would include exchanging "a complete blueprint of our military establishments, from beginning to end, from one end of our countries to the other." Next, it would involve providing "within our countries facilities for aerial photography to the other country." Through this step, he declared, the two powers would "convince the world that we are providing as between ourselves against the possibility of great surprise attack, thus lessening danger and relaxing tensions."

And all this, he assured his audience, "would be but a beginning," a first step toward an effective system of inspection and disarmament.

All eyes now turned to the Russians, who, in the words of a State Department official, "gave the appearance of having turned into stone."

Then, as the President gathered up his papers, a tremendous thunderclap resounded through the hall, and the room went dark. "Well," Eisenhower laughed, "I expected to make a hit, but not *that* much of one."

Although they had received no advance word of the President's proposals (except for the hint Eden was given over breakfast), both Faure and Eden spoke up in support of them. Bulganin, for his part, was reserved, but hardly disapproving. The proposals, he said, had real merit, and the Soviet delegation would have to study them carefully.

The meeting adjourned, and the participants headed off to an adjoining reception area for their daily ritual of postadjournment cocktails. On the way over, Khrushchev and his interpreter sidled across to Eisenhower. As they strolled side by side, Khrushchev muttered, with a grim smile, "I don't agree with the chairman."

When they arrived at the reception, the Soviet boss remained tethered to Eisenhower. Bulganin, Faure, Eden, Dulles, Rockefeller, Stassen, and almost everyone else in the room formed a ring around the principals, straining to hear what was said.

The President's proposals, Khrushchev sneered, were nothing but a bald espionage plot.

Eisenhower let Khrushchev fulminate, and then calmly fired back. If the NATO powers were the aggressors Khrushchev claimed them to be, and the Soviet Union such a peace-loving state, then, Eisenhower said, Mr. Khrushchev should welcome this opportunity to keep tabs on NATO's moves.

If the United States was so peace-loving, Khrushchev responded, then it should accept the Soviet disarmament plan of May 10. The President answered that he would be happy to accept that plan—if the Soviets would accept his.

Khrushchev offered no reply. Instead, he excused himself and walked away.

To Eisenhower, the brief, tempestuous exchange confirmed two things he and his advisers suspected: that it was Khrushchev, not Bulganin, who was calling the shots in the Soviet camp, and that this beefy boss was determined, at all costs, to keep the U.S.S.R. a closed society. As long as Khrushchev was in charge, there was only a hairbreadth chance that the mutual inspection schemes would go anywhere—which was exactly what Rockefeller and almost everyone else involved in framing the proposals expected.

At the same time, Khrushchev's edginess proved that the proposals had succeeded in throwing the Soviets into absolute disarray. For once, the United States had taken the disarmament initiative; for once, the Soviets, not the Americans, were pushed into reactive defensiveness.

Like the thunderclap that accompanied it, Eisenhower's plan—soon to be dubbed "Open Skies" by the press—startled and galvanized the Geneva summit. The world's reaction was overwhelmingly positive; even *Le Monde* of Paris, notoriously chary of praise for anything American, was moved to enthuse, "Eisenhower, whose personality has long been misunderstood, has emerged as the type of leader humanity needs today."

For Nelson Rockefeller, the acclaim was full and sweet vindication of his efforts. Convinced that the United States needed to risk a bold stroke at Geneva, he had packaged and repackaged his ideas, edging them along in the face of Dulles' ironbound resistance, until the culminating moment arrived: the moment when the President was ready to take the plunge. And the outcome was exactly what Rockefeller had predicted: a major psychological triumph for the United States and a stunning embarrassment for the Soviets, cornered by their own peacemaking rhetoric.

What had begun with a sputtering professorial debate at Quantico had ended in unalloyed triumph in Geneva. A grateful, elated Rockefeller immediately dispatched telegrams to all the Quantico participants: "You should be reading newspapers tonight with great pride and satisfaction. We are delighted to be expressing from Geneva our deep appreciation of your contribution to your country."

In his jubilation, he also remembered his overworked staff in Lausanne. Forgoing the formal round of summit dinners, he spent the evening with his Lausanne crew at a swank lakeside restaurant, La Perle du Lac. There the happy group—Hanks, Parker, Kintner, et al.—downed bottles of champagne and feasted on steaks and crêpes suzette as Rockefeller regaled them with his breathless account of the day's events.

By Saturday, July 23, the summit's last day, Rockefeller had good reason to believe that he had carved out for himself a special place among the President's counselors. He was invited to lunch at the Château de Creux de Genthod on that final day; Eisenhower's only other guests were his son and his wartime British military aide, Brigadier James Gault.

Afterward, the President asked Rockefeller to ride with him to the Palais des Nations. Seated beside the grinning Eisenhower in the rear of his open car, Rockefeller basked vicariously in the adulation showered on his chief: the excited throngs waving, hollering, jumping up and down for a better look. It was, he told Hanks afterward, "an inspiration."

He took his seat in the gallery as the closing remarks began, and listened to Eisenhower pronounce the summit a success. "In this final hour of our assembly, it is my judgment that the prospects of a lasting peace with justice, well-being, and broader freedom, are brighter. The dangers of modern war are less." The other leaders echoed these sentiments, with Bulganin declaring "the beginning of a new stage" in East-West relations.

The conference's final communiqué, however, showed that the summit was, as planned, more a triumph of sentiment than of substance. The issues of German unification and European security were left unresolved. As for disarmament, all the principals could agree on was that they would work through the UN's Disarmament Subcommittee to develop an acceptable system; there was no mention of blueprint exchanges or aerial surveillance.

Forty-three minutes after the Geneva summit was gaveled to a close, *The Columbine* lifted off for the long flight home.

Still buoyed by the outcome, Rockefeller and his staff prepared for a stopover in Paris before heading back to Washington.

The one complication was all the classified documents relating to Open Skies that were still in their possession. Throughout the meeting they had taken turns carrying around the satchel holding the papers; rather than lug it to Paris they decided to simply destroy the documents. Parker and Kintner tore them up and, for want of any safer means of disposal, flushed them down the toilet at the Lausanne hotel. But all those top-secret files overburdened the hotel's plumbing, and the staffers had to desperately summon a plumber before they found themselves awash in chewed-up, waterlogged memoranda.

With that mishap behind them, the group flew to Paris—and one more celebratory dinner. Rockefeller chose his favorite restaurant in the city, Laurent, off the Champs-Elysées, and as soon as they arrived he ordered up champagne and caviar. When all the caviar was gone, the waiters came to clear the table, but Rockefeller shooed them off; he wanted a second helping of caviar. "The waiters were dumbfounded," remembers Parker. And so a fresh service of caviar arrived on silver platters, accompanied by still more bottles of champagne: a Rockefeller toast, on a truly Rockefeller scale, to what he and his team had achieved in Geneva.*

*After Parker left Rockefeller's employ to rejoin the Army, he was assigned to duty in Paris. Rockefeller was excited when he heard the news. "How wonderful!" he said to Hanks. "Now Ted can eat at Laurent." Hanks gingerly informed Rockefeller that even a general couldn't afford Laurent. Source: Parker interview.

Rarely had any American President returned from a foreign mission to such an outpouring of praise and congratulations. Not only Republicans but Democrats as well enthusiastically hailed Eisenhower's performance in Geneva—particularly the Open Skies initiative. From his hospital bed, where he was recovering from a heart attack, Senate Majority Leader Lyndon Johnson called Open Skies "the daring, imaginative stroke for which a war-weary world has been waiting." In the wake of the summit, Eisenhower's approval rating in the polls soared to an astonishing 84 percent.

At home, and abroad, there was euphoria about the so-called Spirit of Geneva engendered at the summit: the commitment by the superpowers, despite their many differences, to a way out of the doomsday maze they had created.

Eisenhower, who had hoped to "change the spirit" of U.S.-Soviet relations through the conference, told the American people, in his nationally broadcast report on the summit, that his hopes had been fulfilled. "Each side assured the other earnestly and often," he said, "that it intended to pursue a new spirit of conciliation and cooperation in its contacts with the other."

Those who had witnessed Eisenhower's dialogue with Khrushchev might be hard pressed to recall what was so conciliatory and cooperative about the Soviets. Nonetheless, the President truly believed that the summit was a breakthrough of sorts. "At the moment, I can't possibly make an objective appraisal of the final results of Geneva," he wrote his brother Milton the day after his return. "There is no doubt in my mind that in the few days we were there I personally gained insight and understanding that I could never have achieved otherwise. I think, too, that the personal contacts—in some cases, like friendships—that were developed there alone made the trip worthwhile."

So fervently did Eisenhower believe this that he hastened to send Bulganin a letter expressing his satisfaction. "I personally feel that some of the world tensions, of which we so often spoke at Geneva, have been eased by the fact of our meeting face to face. . . . If we can continue along this line . . . eventually, a durable peace based on right and justice will be the monument to the work which we have begun."

His optimism extended to Open Skies. Rather than view it as a bald propaganda initiative (which was plainly how its framers, led by Rockefeller, saw it) or as an intelligence ploy (which was how the Joint Chiefs regarded it), Eisenhower now seemed deeply convinced that his proposals were exactly what he publicly described them to be: an epochal first step toward disarmament.

"To say that my plan has nothing to do with eventual disarmament is to miss the major purpose of the proposal," he wrote General Gruenther. ". . . If we assume that the kind of inspection to which I referred would eliminate the danger of devastating *surprise* attack, the agreement for such inspection and this result would yield an immense gain in mutual confidence and trust. This means that we would have established a truly realistic basis for studying disarmament."

Rockefeller and his Quantico cohorts saw the Open Skies idea as a prelude to an arms *buildup,* once the Russians rejected the proposal—which they felt was a foregone conclusion. But Eisenhower actually saw it as a prelude to arms reduction, and felt it was by no means certain that the Soviets wouldn't come around. As much as anyone who came under its spell, Eisenhower believed his own propaganda.

And because the President believed, Dulles, against all his instincts and experience, felt compelled to believe as well.

In contrast to his earlier bad-mouthing of the summit, the Secretary of State now had nothing but praise for the outcome. "Personally, I feel reasonably satisfied," he wrote C. D. Jackson upon his return. "You know how nervous I was. I think we have avoided the most dangerous pitfalls and came out with some pluses, of which the most conspicuous was the President's proposal on mutual aerial inspection."

At a news conference the next day, Dulles went so far as to describe Open Skies as "the most dramatic, and at the same time, most serious and sober peace proposal that history records." If the Soviets, he said, "have the genuine desire of peace which they indicated at Geneva, then I feel confident that positive results will come from President Eisenhower's proposal."

In the midst of the panegyrics, Dulles, who was nothing if not resourceful, actually sought to take some credit for fathering Open Skies. At a dinner party, someone asked him, "Foster, just how did that idea come up?" "Well," Dulles replied, "we all more or less thought of it at the same time."

To further prove his newfound zeal for aerial inspection, Dulles phoned Brownell and asked if the Attorney General could find out what U.S. laws needed to be changed to implement Open Skies. When Brownell inquired what the time schedule was, Dulles said there was no rush—a report in a week's time would be fine.

On August 4, speaking before the Supreme Soviet, Bulganin firmly and unequivocally rejected the U.S. proposals. The United States and the U.S.S.R., Bulganin argued, were so vast that no aerial inspection plan could preclude concealment; furthermore, Eisenhower's proposals did not provide for aerial inspection outside those two countries. The Soviet Premier contended that his country's May 10 proposals for inspection and disarmament were a "more realistic" way to proceed.

Perhaps because Bulganin refrained from denouncing Open Skies as an American espionage plot, Eisenhower was not noticeably disheartened by the news. At a National Security Council meeting, he told his advisers that the

Soviet rejection "did not necessarily mean anything." And Dulles chimed in that the Russians had for a long time rejected the President's Atoms for Peace proposal, only to finally accept it at Geneva.

But, in fact, the ensuing months would show that Bulganin's speech was, indeed, the last word on the subject. The Soviets would never accept Open Skies. And, lacking an agreement, the United States went ahead unilaterally to develop its own aerial reconnaissance capability: the U-2. It would be one of the Cold War's great ironies that the downing of one of those spy planes by the Soviets five years later would scuttle Eisenhower's next, and final, attempt to keep the spirit of Geneva alive through summitry.

Still, in the summer of 1955, by Nelson Rockefeller's reckoning, the Open Skies proposal had more than served its purpose, no matter what the Soviet response would be. As he noted, in a letter to his daughter Mary, it "made a tremendous impression around the world as to the sincerity of the President and the American people in their desire for peace." The pendulum of world opinion had swung decisively in the United States' direction, thanks to Open Skies. A Western European poll, which Rockefeller proudly forwarded to the President in early August, showed that 69 percent of the respondents believed Eisenhower was sincerely working for peace. Only 47 percent felt that way about the Soviets.

Open Skies had also served its purpose in Rockefeller's personal agenda. Its success was a dazzling validation of his efforts, from Quantico onward, to craft alternatives to Dulles' hidebound realpolitik. With his tenacity and his unerring opportunism, he had brought the President to his side—and, undoubtedly, earned the President's deepest appreciation and gratitude.

Yet as he basked in the glory of the moment, Rockefeller could not escape John Foster Dulles' withering stare, fixed steadily, ravenlike, upon him as he returned in triumph to official Washington.

Thirty-five

GROUNDING THE GADFLY

The post-Geneva euphoria did not diminish Dulles' anxieties in the slightest. In the end, it merely furnished a new justification for his eternal vigilance, a new pretext for his angst. "Geneva has certainly created problems for the free nations," he told his State Department minions in a policy paper he circulated upon his return. "For eight years they have been held together largely by a cement compounded of fear and a sense of moral superiority. Now the fear is diminished and the moral demarcation is somewhat blurred." That Dulles' own acerbic view of the Soviets had not changed one whit—he privately derided their peacemaking as a "classic" zigzag "Communist maneuver"—did not alter his conclusion that "we must re-think our basic strategy in order to meet this new situation," as he put it to the National Security Council on July 28.

The formerly hidebound Secretary of State now urged his subordinates to develop fresh approaches and new ideas—caustically reminding them that it was not the State Department that had produced the big Geneva breakthrough. "Honestly," he challenged one of his deputies, "can you think of an original idea that's come out of the department since I've been Secretary of State—a really, truly original idea?" When the assistant candidly admitted he couldn't, Dulles brought up Open Skies. "I don't know where it came from," he said. "It may have come from the meeting in Quantico. It may have come from a number of places, but it didn't come from here."

"We've got to get more original thinking in this building," demanded Dulles. "How can we stimulate some original thinking?"

He was a general firing up his officers to meet the advancing threat: a threat that came not so much from Moscow as from the third floor of the Executive Office Building.

Late in the afternoon of July 28 Rockefeller stopped by Dulles' office. The special assistant wanted to apologize for their misunderstandings prior to Geneva. He realized, he said, the necessity of coordination with the State Department.

Dulles reacted grumpily to this ex post facto bit of fence-mending. Once again, he lectured Rockefeller on how it was "very bad organization" to have projects in the foreign field going to the President before they had been vetted by State. He recognized that it could be annoying to see "brilliant ideas" scrapped through this process; nonetheless, only the State Department had the "global background" to view the situation "in its entirety."

As always, Rockefeller did not openly contest Dulles. He appreciated what the secretary was telling him, he said, and would "try to bear it in mind." His problem, he insisted, was that he did not have any really adequate channel into the State Department; perhaps, he suggested, Dulles' top aide Bob Murphy might be willing to serve in that role. Dulles seemed to be agreeable to this, and Rockefeller expressed himself as "very satisfied" with Murphy as liaison.

Rockefeller came away from this meeting, and another the same day with Allen Dulles, convinced that he had achieved détente with State. His talks with the Dulles brothers, he wrote Stacy May, were "excellent." "I feel that we are now in shape, both within our own group and within the government itself, to do a really effective job in the coming months."

So enthusiastic was Rockefeller about the outcome of his session with Dulles that he ebulliently assured Sherman Adams that "everything was settled" in his relations with the secretary. But Adams, dryly noting that "sometimes Mr. Rockefeller was more exuberant about the outcome of meetings than the facts warranted," decided to check the matter out with the other party to the conversation.

And, not surprisingly, Adams learned that everything was *not* settled as far as John Foster Dulles was concerned.

Dulles expounded at some length, and with some heat, to Adams on what *he* thought Rockefeller's role should be. As Dulles later recounted, he told Adams that "my conception of the proper job of someone like Rockefeller was to scrutinize the vast number of suggestions which flowed into the White House through letters and personal visits, out of which there were nuggets of value; that ideas which seemed to be of value should then be brought by Rockefeller to the attention of the agencies primarily concerned, which would usually be either State, AEC, or CIA, and then if after initial scrutiny in the organized agency, they still seemed to have value, to press them on to definitive consideration." Rockefeller, in other words, would serve as an idea clearinghouse, a neutral coordinator passing along "nuggets of value" to the proper departments.

What Dulles found unacceptable, he told Adams, was for "Nelson Rockefeller to build up a big staff of his own for the purpose of advising the President in the field of foreign relations." The Secretary of State was the President's principal foreign policy adviser; if he ceased to be, Dulles warned, "I would no longer be interested in being Secretary of State."

Adams assured Dulles that his conception of Rockefeller's job coincided largely with the secretary's, and promised to "try to see that it was kept in bounds." To this, Dulles replied, as he would later relate, that "some breaking of bounds was almost inevitable with a person of the temperament of Nelson Rockefeller, and I would be disposed to be tolerant of such exceptions, but it was another matter if the exception became the rule."

Dulles, the master of containment, was determined to contain Nelson Rockefeller.

Precisely the role Dulles had in mind for Rockefeller was pointed up in a phone conversation the two men had the day after their meeting.

Dulles brought up the President's pre-Geneva appeal to all Americans to flock to their houses of worship on the eve of the conference. Had Rockefeller seen any reports on exactly what effect Eisenhower's appeal had on churchgoing? He hadn't seen anything official, Rockefeller replied, but he heard the response was tremendous. Well, said Dulles, perhaps Rockefeller might undertake a spot check around the country, to determine exactly what the percentage increase in church attendance was. If they found there was a huge increase, then it would show the world how much Americans wanted peace.

Rockefeller agreed to undertake the survey. A week later, as if it was a matter of the greatest national urgency, the Secretary of State sent him a reminder: "Don't forget to let me know about the church attendance in the United States on the Sabbath immediately preceding the Conference."

To make matters worse for Rockefeller, Dulles had obtained, from the sympathetic Sherman Adams, a memo the special assistant had sent Adams on his staff requirements. Just what that memo proposed is not known (all extant copies seem to have disappeared), but it evidently called for a hefty augmentation of what was already, by almost any standard, a sprawling operation. Some indication of this is the amount of office space Rockefeller and his aides were to occupy in the EOB: from five rooms in early June, to twenty-three offices by mid-December.

For Dulles, the memo was proof positive that Rockefeller's empire building continued apace. It furnished him with all the justification he needed to bring the situation to a head.

Over lunch with the President on August 5, Dulles confided that "at this stage we are having a very difficult time working with Rockefeller." Dulles was trying to work the situation out, but "I am not at all sure that I will be successful in doing so." The Secretary of State then described to Eisenhower *his* concept of Rockefeller's function: "to screen the many ideas, written and oral, that came into the White House in the field of foreign affairs and to see to it that the worthwhile ones were put into proper government channels." But if Rockefeller built up a staff of his own—"as he appears to have every intention of doing"—then he became a bureaucrat himself and "defeated the whole purpose of the exercise."

To buttress this point, Dulles pulled out a copy of Rockefeller's memo on staffing. As Dulles would later relate, "the President expressed some surprise at the size and complexity of the proposed staff and said that he had been unaware of all these arrangements."

Eisenhower, whose worldwide prestige had been immeasurably enhanced by the efforts of Rockefeller and his staff, chose not to rise to his special assistant's defense. Rather, he seemed mainly intent on mollifying his aggrieved Secretary of State. After his session with Dulles, he sent off a memo to Rockefeller that largely parroted the secretary's line on Rockefeller's role.

"In the whole general subject of *psychological warfare,*" the President advised him, "the critical need of the President is for coordination. Hundreds of people have ideas affecting it. . . . The problem is to get the proper staff work of government—not of a special agency—on them, so that we may achieve true coordination." Eisenhower defined "the critical—the absolutely vital—mission of yourself and your office" as "the establishment of such splendid relationships with all concerned Departments that new ideas can be examined from every viewpoint and when necessary the result presented to me."

The notion that Nelson Rockefeller would actually function in this way—as a bureaucratic traffic cop whose main concern was establishing "splendid relationships" with his peers—was, on its face, completely absurd, as even Sherman Adams recognized when he chatted with Dulles on the phone that evening. Adams expressed doubts that Rockefeller would ever operate in this fashion. In the chief of staff's mind, the conundrum "raises the whole question of whether he should continue to serve in this capacity."

In the past—if the President involved was, say, Franklin Roosevelt—Rockefeller might have challenged this restrictive interpretation of his role. But knowing how much this President abhorred conflict among his aides, and knowing that, at the end of the day, Eisenhower would stand by his Secretary of State, Rockefeller held his fire. If "splendid relationships" were what the President desired, then Rockefeller would do his utmost to bring them about.

Henceforth, he would hew to the chain of command: all of his ideas, all of his memos, would be cleared with Dulles. "Pursuant to my discussion with the Secretary of State and also with Sherman Adams," he advised Eisenhower on August 27, "I have been sending brief memoranda setting forth ideas and suggestions to the Secretary. Some of these we discuss and others are processed in the Department and I receive formal comment. The procedure is very satisfactory." He added this humble postscript: "I look forward to the opportunity of discussing with you at some convenient time to what extent you would like to be kept informed as to the nature and character of these recommendations."

Far from exulting at Rockefeller's profuse shows of obeisance, Dulles found them annoying and irksome; plainly the last thing he expected was for Rockefeller to actually accede to his demands. The secretary found himself bombarded with memos from the solicitous special assistant, leading Dulles to complain to Adams about the "terrible drain" on his time created by Rockefeller and his ideas. He didn't know how much longer he could afford to take the time. Rockefeller, Dulles floridly declared, was "a cross" he had to bear.

Rockefeller had just informed him of some of his plans, and the secretary confided to Adams that "I am not awfully happy with it." Still, sighed Dulles, "I can live with it if it does not get any worse." He would go along until winter, and "see what happens."

The plans that Rockefeller shared with him, and that Dulles was grudgingly accepting, were for another brainstorming parley: a conference that Rockefeller and his aides were calling Quantico II.

The meeting's ostensible mission was to probe "psychological aspects of U.S. strategy" in the wake of the Geneva summit. But its true scope went well beyond the bounds of the "psychological," as Rockefeller's letter of invitation to prospective participants makes clear: "This study should develop the means and methods best calculated to achieve U.S. objectives, taking into consideration the necessity for an integrated national program within which long-term military, economic, technological, and ideological programs can be developed and financed."

Bill Kintner recalls some of the thinking behind it: "We felt, as a result of the first Geneva meeting, that we needed to have a somewhat different national strategy, and rarely have we had a national strategy. It's still one of our national problems."

Given its overarching purposes, the conference was bound to raise the hackles of Dulles and countless other administration figures. But with Quantico I's successful outcome still fresh in everyone's mind, no one of influence was about to stifle a repeat performance. Rockefeller scrupulously made the rounds of the powers that be: Dulles, Defense Secretary Wilson, CIA director Dulles, Radford of the Joint Chiefs. All signed off on the meeting.

Invitations were sent to all the participants in the first Quantico conference, and almost every one of them, including C. D. Jackson, accepted. But some new names also appeared on the invitation list, among them another, younger figure from the Cambridge academic circuit: one Henry Alfred Kissinger.

If Walt Rostow was the quintessential Cambridge scholar-cum-climber, Henry A. Kissinger, at thirty-two, was showing every sign of outdoing the master. Having emigrated from Nazi Germany as an adolescent, having assimilated himself into a strange new culture (mastering baseball and English at much the same time), having returned to his native land with a U.S. Army counterintelligence unit during the postwar occupation, Kissinger arrived at Harvard in the fall of 1947 as a twenty-four-year-old sophomore of relentless drive and consuming ambition. He poured much of his energy into his studies, where he distinguished himself as a prodigious scholar who could discourse with equal facility about Kant and Metternich, about Virgil and Bismarck; his Ph.D. thesis on the Congress of Vienna won a Sumner Prize for distinguished scholarly achievement. But he devoted himself with even greater assiduity to the art of networking.

While still a graduate student he organized the Harvard International Seminar, a summer program for young leaders from around the world that attracted such notable lecturers as Eleanor Roosevelt and Walter Reuther and funding from the Ford and Rockefeller foundations. Graduate student Kissinger also founded *Confluence,* a foreign affairs quarterly whose contributors would include Rostow, John Kenneth Galbraith, Reinhold Niebuhr, and Hannah Arendt. "When I met some of the contributors," he would later proudly note, "they were stunned to see how young I was." To his critics at Harvard—he was already enough of a presence to have some—the journal and the seminar were primarily enterprises, in one man's words, "designed to make Henry known to great people around the world."

Kissinger's advancement was immeasurably aided by his Harvard mentor, Professor William Yandell Elliott, a hulking former All-American tackle with a vast array of contacts in the loftiest strata of business and government. It was Elliott, more than any other individual, who introduced Kissinger to the limitless possibilities available to the well-connected academic, putting Kissinger in charge of the Harvard International Seminar. And it was Elliott who set the wheels in motion that would eventually secure Kissinger a place at Nelson Rockefeller's bounteous table.

The initial point of contact was Bill Kintner. As Kintner tells the story, "Bill Elliott was one of my consultants when I was in the CIA, from 1950 to 1952, and it was through Bill that I met Kissinger. He was a young graduate student at the time; he hadn't even gotten his Ph.D. yet." Kissinger had just returned from a trip to South Korea and Japan on assignment from the U.S. Army's intelligence think tank, the Operations Research Office. When Elliott mentioned the young man's mission, Kintner asked if he could send Kissinger down to the CIA for a briefing. During the rest of Kintner's tenure as the agency's chief covert operations planner, he recalls, he and Kissinger "saw a lot of each other, and became extremely close friends." The CIA, through a front organization, would help fund Kissinger's seminars—although Kissinger vehemently denied any knowledge of the agency's involvement when it came to light in 1967.

In assembling the team for Quantico II, Kintner remembered his old Harvard friend. At that point, Kissinger had left Harvard, after having been denied a tenured professorship there, and had resettled in New York to work for the Council on Foreign Relations as director of an elite study group on Cold War alternatives. Despite the demands of this study, Kissinger gladly accepted Kintner's invitation to come to Washington—perhaps because the scope of the work he would undertake for Nelson Rockefeller was not terribly different from what he was doing for the council.

Kissinger had never met Nelson Rockefeller before he arrived for the first Quantico session. His memory of his first encounter with Rockefeller, at the opening day of Quantico II on August 25, was a vivid one: "Rockefeller entered the room slapping the backs of the assembled academics, grinning and calling each by the closest approximation of his first name that he could remember." But if the intent was to ingratiate himself with the academics, Rockefeller's glad-handing had just the opposite effect on the morose, analytical Kissinger: he saw it as establishing his host's remoteness. "When everybody is called by his first name and with equal friendliness, relationships lose personal significance," Kissinger would later conclude. Yet it would not be long before this particular relationship would assume overwhelming personal significance for both men.

The initial organizing sessions of Quantico II were not in Quantico, but in the more accessible confines of Room 213 of the Executive Office Building. Rockefeller had cut his annual Maine vacation short to attend the early rounds, and he was there to welcome the group with praise for what their earlier work had accomplished in Geneva.

What they would be wrestling with now, he said, was the legacy of the hopes generated by that summit. There were three questions, in particular, he wanted them to consider: "What is to take the place of fear as a cohesive force in the Western alliance system?" "What about the loss of the moral stigma that the U.S.S.R. has carried all these years?" "How do we become identified in the minds of the peoples of other countries with their aspirations and hopes?"

In the ensuing discussion, the panelists delved not only into those questions but into the more practical issue of how their proposals might prevail over the objections of John Foster Dulles. But when the subject of Dulles was raised, the smile left Rockefeller's face and his eyes froze into the hooded slits that his associates had learned to dread. Plainly, the professors had ventured onto forbidden ground.

"I did not bring you gentlemen down here to tell me how to maneuver in Washington," Rockefeller interrupted. "That is my job. *Your* job is to tell me what is right."

With that warning, the panelists returned to the more politic terrain of arms policy and psychological warfare.

Nevertheless, the truce with Dulles continued to be an uneasy one. Try as they might to conceal their hostility, the Quantico participants couldn't help baiting Foggy Bottom. In the course of that first day's session, Assistant Secretary of State Douglas MacArthur 2nd (nephew and namesake of the general) arrived to give State's appraisal of the Geneva summit, along with a preview of the anticipated line for the upcoming follow-up meeting of Foreign Ministers. Rather than receive this wisdom with deferential courtesy, the panelists, led by Kissinger and Stefan Possony, went on the attack. As C. D. Jackson saw it, Kissinger and Possony "were partly to blame in that they were trying to pin MacArthur down much more than one should try to pin a diplomat. He bristled undiplomatically and the fight was on."

Dulles and MacArthur would have to tolerate Quantico II. But the fact remained that Rockefeller's conclave was merely an act of dispensation on the Secretary of State's part; the platform that the conference gave Rockefeller led nowhere. In every significant respect, the quarantine that Dulles was imposing on the bumptious special assistant held firm.

The chief enforcer of that quarantine was the scion of another famous name: the Undersecretary of State, Herbert Hoover, Jr. An engineer by training, like his father before him, Hoover had earned his spurs as Dulles' special petroleum adviser, reorganizing the West's oil interests in Iran after the CIA-backed overthrow of Prime Minister Mossadegh. As reward for his efforts, Hoover was tapped to succeed Walter Bedell Smith as State's number two in October 1954. Yet for all his acknowledged engineering talents, the younger Hoover was handicapped by a host of crippling traits: an unyielding, mulish rigidity, a paralytic indecisiveness, and a plodding, constricted worldview that bordered on the neo-isolationist. Even his much-maligned father seemed a model of broad-mindedness by comparison. Hoover, Jr., also suffered from a physical handicap, deafness, that some would say accounted for his chronic suspiciousness of his associates.

If Dulles were to construct, in a laboratory, a personality that would unnerve and unhinge Rockefeller, he could not have done better than Herbert Hoover, Jr.'s.

Hoover would come to serve as Dulles' proxy in upbraiding Rockefeller whenever the special assistant veered out of line. A Rockefeller subordinate once recalled how his boss "would come back from one of the tongue-lashings

Hoover gave him holding onto himself like grim death to keep from losing his temper."

Rockefeller found his economic proposals—for increased foreign aid, for more liberal Third World loans—landing on Hoover's desk, where they would promptly be entombed in the permafrost. Hoover became his principal State Department nemesis in Rockefeller's campaign for U.S. Export-Import Bank loans to India's Tata financial group; with the significant backing of Treasury Secretary Humphrey, Hoover was able to kill the scheme.

Although Hoover did not derail the Quantico II seminar, he left his imprint on the proceedings by insisting that Rockefeller drop several of the panel members—including Rostow—because they lacked the proper security clearance. The fact that Rostow, for one, had a top-secret classification from another government agency was of no account; Hoover judged him, for reasons he refused to enumerate, a security risk, and forced his removal from the panel.

But the domain where Hoover stymied Rockefeller the most was in the work of the Planning Coordination Group, the interagency body Rockefeller set up to oversee CIA covert actions and other anti-Communist activities. Hoover regarded the PCG as a potential threat to his department's prerogatives, in much the same way he had viewed the PCG's predecessor, the Operations Coordinating Board; C. D. Jackson, an OCB member, complained Hoover had turned it into an "ice-cold morgue" with his "bureaucratic pocket veto methods." Now he was applying those same methods to Rockefeller's creation.

Almost from the beginning Rockefeller found himself hamstrung in his efforts to make the PCG—and, by extension, himself as PCG chairman—the agency's chief covert watchdog. The opposition came not just from Hoover but from the CIA itself. Allen Dulles utterly ignored the committee, choosing to notify its members individually about secret activities in the pipeline. Any attempt Rockefeller might make to get on top of the projects was hampered by his staff's specific exclusion from the list of officials cleared to have knowledge of covert programs. And every time he tried to initiate a discussion of the PCG's role, he was rebuffed by the State-CIA coalition.

The treatment of the PCG showed that Hoover was, if nothing else, a master of the bureaucratic stall. When Rockefeller requested approval of the PCG's budget for the second half of 1955, Hoover insisted that Rockefeller first produce a paper on "how the PCG should function." The memo was delivered, but all that resulted from it was further inconclusive discussion. Finally, Rockefeller was forced to swallow a much-reduced budget.

In his frustration, Rockefeller decided to just pull the plug on the PCG. Without consulting Hoover or the other members, he sent a note to the budget director on September 23 recommending the abolishment of the PCG by year end, on the grounds that it "could not discharge its functions." When he finally informed Hoover of his plan three days later, the undersecretary—obdurately slow-moving to the last—simply said he would consider the recommendation.

Rockefeller's decision on the PCG came four days after he was forced to endure yet another slight at the hands of Dulles, Hoover, and company. On September 19 Dulles appointed former CIA deputy director William H. Jackson, now a partner of Jock Whitney, as his special assistant to coordinate U.S. positions on East-West contacts and cultural exchanges for the upcoming Foreign Ministers conference. For months now, Rockefeller had staked out East-West contacts as *his* bailiwick; it had been Rockefeller, not Dulles or anyone else from State, who had worked with the President on the U.S. proposals in those areas at the Geneva summit. Dulles' move seemed specifically aimed at squeezing Rockefeller out of the picture on that front as well.

Rockefeller's aides urged him to oppose the appointment, or, at the very least, push for an important role in the preconference planning. But by this point, Rockefeller seemed to have lost the stomach for another round of bureaucratic trench warfare. Across Ted Parker's memo urging him to assert his prerogatives, he slashed a big "X" and scrawled the words "No Go."

Quantico II, meanwhile, had mutated into an intellectual exercise seemingly unaffected by Rockefeller's tribulations (except for the brouhaha over Rostow's security clearance). The first round in late August had adjourned with the assignment of specific papers (on subjects ranging from arms control to the future of NATO) to the panelists. The meetings were scheduled to resume on September 25, and it would not be until sometime in October that a report would be prepared.

The sense of urgency that had propelled Quantico I was completely absent this time around. No one talked about producing proposals in time for the Foreign Ministers conference in Geneva, now slated for late October. The unstated assumption was that even if they did break their backs to formulate a plan of action, Dulles would only ignore it.

For over a month, since the middle of August, the President had been away from Washington, vacationing in Denver. Much of the time was spent at the Rocky Mountain ranch of a banker friend, where Eisenhower could fish for trout on the St. Louis Creek and take to a painter's easel. Back in Denver, he golfed: eighteen, twenty-seven, even thirty-six holes a day. Although Dulles frequently reached him on the phone—sometimes even on the sacrosanct links—he would actually devote no more than an hour or so each day to the affairs of state.

On Friday, September 23, after a robust round of twenty-seven holes (interrupted once by Dulles), Eisenhower returned to his mother-in-law's home in Denver, where he and his wife were staying, for a quiet dinner with friends. He retired at 10 P.M., but four and a half hours later he was awakened by an acute pain in his chest. His wife summoned the President's Army physician, who raced to the scene and found a pale, perspiring Eisenhower in the midst of a coronary thrombosis.

It was not until the next morning—after the press had been told the President had merely suffered a "digestive upset"—that Eisenhower was taken to the hospital. Only after Eisenhower was ensconced there, with an oxygen tent over half his body, was the world told the truth.

Despite the administration's determined efforts to mute the impact—Vice President Nixon announced that the "business of government will go on without delay," and Dulles and Humphrey unflappably flew off to Canada for a conference—the nation was propelled into near-panic by the news. When the stock market reopened on Monday, it suffered its most precipitous drop since the Great Depression. The crisis eased after the eminent Boston heart specialist Paul Dudley White examined the stricken President and concluded he would recover—although it would be months before he could resume his normal activities.

For the indeterminate future, then, the President would be convalescing at Fitzsimons General Hospital in Denver, with Sherman Adams in attendance as his sole link to the business of the United States government.

Rockefeller fell in line with the business-as-usual stance of the administration. The Quantico II meetings went on as scheduled that week at the Marine base hideaway, with only a brief, elliptical reference by Rockefeller, at the opening session on Sunday evening, to the "changed situation due to the President's illness."

Still, he couldn't help taking one nervy step that, he no doubt believed, would rally the President's spirits. Rockefeller began talking about nominating Eisenhower for the Nobel Peace Prize. "In view of his superb achievements in striving for the cause of world peace, which were nobly demonstrated at Geneva, it seems to me that such a nomination is very much in order." Adams responded favorably to the idea, although, he cautioned, "I am sure the President would not want us to initiate any campaign as such."

Yet even as he bravely indulged in one further act of ingratiation, even as he proceeded with the Quantico meetings as though nothing out of the ordinary had happened, Rockefeller was plunged into a rare (for him) malaise; Nancy Hanks found him "numb." The President's condition added an acute new twist to the growing sense of isolation he felt. Almost always, in the past, Rockefeller could overcome his opponents through a direct appeal to the chief executive. It had been that way with Roosevelt, and, as recently as the Geneva summit, it had been that way with Ike. But now, with the President out of commission for no one knew how long, that panacea was denied him.

And, as he looked around the cabinet room, past the President's vacant chair, Rockefeller saw two domineering figures, his two staunchest opponents, John Foster Dulles and George Humphrey, and no one in that room with the will or the clout to contest them.

Feeling cornered, Rockefeller could see no way out of the political and emotional impasse. There seemed, now, only one worthwhile path to pursue.

During the first days of October he met with his father and brothers at 30 Rockefeller Plaza to discuss yet another return to the family fold.

On October 10, Sherman Adams arrived at Fitzsimons Hospital with documents for the President's signature. Eisenhower was now feeling well enough to conduct some routine business—although his doctors shielded him from weightier decisions—and to banter with Adams about administration goings-on. On this day, Adams brought him some news about "the problem of Nelson Rockefeller."

"The thing has cured itself," Adams informed Eisenhower. Rockefeller had told him that he planned to terminate his governmental work by the end of the year. The decision, according to Rockefeller, was based on "family problems": he felt the need to give more time to his father, soon to turn eighty-two, and to help manage the family enterprises. The special assistant had also said, almost as an afterthought, that in his present assignment "things have not worked out very well."

Eisenhower expressed a certain wistful regret at the decision; he felt moved to voice some sympathy for Rockefeller's predicament. Several times in his own career, he said, he had been given assignments dealing, like Rockefeller's, with psychological intangibles, and he knew firsthand the difficulties. "You give a man the job of coordinating," reflected the President, "and he immediately starts initiating." He didn't think that was so bad. "Give me a gadfly now and then," Eisenhower told Adams. "Give me someone who will make sure certain things are not forgotten."

In that regard, the President felt Dulles had been hypersensitive. "I am astonished," said Eisenhower, "at the sensitivity of big people."

He conceded that Rockefeller was not perfect in his job, summing up what he felt to be Rockefeller's limitations pithily: "He is too used to borrowing brains instead of using his own."

Nonetheless, even though Adams reminded him that "Nelson was wearing Dulles down," the President made it plain that he, for one, was sorry to lose Nelson Rockefeller.

Among the few individuals who were immediately privy to Rockefeller's decision was Nancy Hanks. He had phoned her from New York to fill her in on his talks with his family, leading her to report to her parents that "I think the decision is just about as firm as it can possibly be." Yet struggle as she might to accept the reasonableness and inevitability of the move, Hanks quietly shuddered at what it portended. The dreamlike dollhouse world she and her patron had created, the world of Dr. and Mrs. Snail, was about to come to an aching end.

Up to then, their relationship had floated along, an idyllically self-contained entity. She had gone to Geneva with him, and shared the joy of his great breakthrough there, shared it with popped champagne corks and salvers of beluga. Upon their return, a still-jubilant Rockefeller offered her a Ford Thunderbird from his fleet (Hanks, however, wasn't sure she wanted the car, and insisted that if she did accept it, she would buy it from him). He even took Hanks with him for an early August visit with Eisenhower; what the President made of her appearance by his assistant's side was not recorded.

So naively confident was she of their relationship that she dropped her guard of prudence and began taking liberties that her friends feared bordered on the unseemly. In June she attended the wedding of Rockefeller's daughter Ann. Rather than fade discreetly into the woodwork, Hanks moved out front and center, greeting family members by their first names, ordering sluggard butlers around, and generally taking on the role, as Donna Mitchell recalled, of "Mrs. Full Charge."

"Nancy was making a fool out of herself," Mitchell related. "You would have thought she was Mrs. Rockefeller, the way she was behaving. She was going around and being with the guests, almost as though she was Mrs. Rockefeller. . . . She was going around doing things that Mrs. Rockefeller really should have been doing. She was the boss. . . . It was embarrassing."

The spectacle, to Hanks's friends, painfully revealed the self-delusion at the core of her relationship with Rockefeller. It was only a matter of time before the bubble was burst, either by Rockefeller's own hand or by someone else's. As it happened, the blow was only three months away, when Rockefeller revealed to Hanks his plans to return to New York.

"I have been worried or I should say rather numb about the future, etc.," Hanks confessed to her parents after she heard. "Don't have any feel for what is right or what I should do—and N has been numb for other reasons and rather unsettled situation has therefore existed."

Unwilling to address their intimacy, she and Rockefeller each retreated into an aggrieved sullenness, quarreling in the roundabout way of a couple on the brink of a major blowup, each accusing the other of failing to understand the other person's plight. "He allowed that it was my fault," reported Hanks, "and the reason he felt was that I refused to talk to him about my plans and that made me unable to understand, etc. (I had told him that I didn't want to talk to him because I felt that I didn't want to worry him with that now when he had so much on his mind. He apparently did not understand my reasoning.) Anyway I had allowed that it might be fifty percent me, but it was fifty percent him."

Shortly afterward, Rockefeller phoned and admitted Hanks had been right. "He just hadn't realized how upset, numb and withdrawn he had been. Poor thing," Hanks related. "Anyway, communication lines will probably be open again."

In the ensuing weeks, she gamely endeavored to once again subordinate her emotional needs to his. On November 3, she cheerily told her parents that "NAR seems to be feeling better and things are going better." Her own feelings, however, were quite another tale. As Hanks confessed at the time, "Depression is always a vicious circle and one that it is very hard to break out of."

Rockefeller's intention to quit was, for the time being, a closely guarded secret. Nothing in his demeanor or his actions gave away his plans; he appeared to be every bit as engaged by his work as he always was.

The Quantico II deliberations proceeded, and in mid-October a small group of panel members joined Kintner at West Point to hammer out the final report. The task of actually drafting the report fell to Kissinger, "probably because I had more time, at that time, than the others," he recalls. Because their work was deemed highly classified, the panel members were confined to a suite of rooms at the Hotel Thayer, where they took their meals in a cordoned-off section of the dining room. Whenever they left the hotel for some air, military guards followed along.

The group was given all of three days to complete the report, prompting Kissinger to half jokingly complain about writer's block due to his lack of military discipline. On October 18, on schedule, the work was finished. Still bearing the title "Psychological Aspects of U.S. Strategy," the report was weightier—both in style and in sheer bulk—than the Quantico I effort: the report itself was 41 pages, and the accompanying papers by panel members ran to 228.

When C. D. Jackson saw the finished product, he sent his congratulations to Rockefeller. "There is an awful lot of good stuff—important and concrete proposals—in those papers," said Jackson, "and I hope that you will be able to get this thinking into the official 'think-stream' of the Administration."

Rockefeller, however, was in no hurry to do so. Rather than risk having his proposals prematurely shot down by Dulles, Hoover, and Humphrey, he would hold on to the Quantico II report until the President's return to Washington. Only then—when he could count on a sympathetic arbiter in the cabinet room—would he take the wraps off his group's handiwork.

The wisdom of his strategy was validated by the goring he suffered at the hands of other administration officials in Eisenhower's absence.

One after another of his initiatives fell by the wayside, slashed to shreds by his peers. UN ambassador Lodge rebuffed his bid to have the issue of "Red

Colonialism" raised at the UN—pointing out that if the United States cited Estonia and Latvia, the Soviets would counter by mentioning Hawaii and Alaska. "Lodge's view is that in view of the current good will spirit he is putting this whole question in the 'ice box,'" Parker reported to Rockefeller. Another of Rockefeller's pet schemes—the appointment of a presidential panel to study U.S. involvement in international cultural relations—also was shunted off to administrative limbo.

The bureaucratic cross fire even frustrated Rockefeller's attempts to make further hay out of his one acknowledged policy coup, Open Skies. Rockefeller wanted to wring still more propaganda points out of the initiative by mounting an aerial inspection exhibit at the UN. But the mandarins at State pronounced his idea "over-propagandistic," and insisted that if the show was held at all, it be restricted to UN delegates only, with no publicity. They were particularly incensed when they heard about Rockefeller's most flamboyant publicity ploy: he had arranged with *Life* magazine to send a photographer aboard an Army plane flying from San Francisco to New York to demonstrate the potency of aerial reconnaissance. The plan was for the photographs to show up not only in the magazine but, blown up, at the UN exhibit.

After a month of hemming and hawing, Dulles allowed the exhibit to go forward—but vetoed the *Life* stunt as unseemly. The show, entitled "Open Skies for Peace," was eventually presented not at the UN, but at the nearby Carnegie International Center. It was opened to the public, after a private tour for UN delegates, and garnered a certain amount of press attention. But the hoopla that Rockefeller had hoped would accompany the exhibit was markedly absent.

Struggling to surmount his isolation during those last months at the White House, Rockefeller fastened on one high administration official he thought could be an ally, an official he deemed a kindred soul, at least philosophically.

The potential helper was the Vice President, Richard M. Nixon.

From the moment the dire announcements about the President's condition began issuing forth from Denver, the world's glaring scrutiny was focused on his number two. And while Nixon acquitted himself well enough—that is, with a low-key, circumspect dignity—during the crisis, there was a collective shudder at the thought that this inexperienced, Red-baiting Californian might soon be the leader of the free world. (The concern was shared at the White House, where Adams and press secretary James Hagerty scotched any consideration of delegating Eisenhower's powers to Nixon during the President's incapacity.)

But during that tense period Rockefeller made it clear to Nixon that if the world and the White House apparatchiks had their apprehensions, they were not shared by Nelson A. Rockefeller. "All of us in the Administration are proud indeed of the job you have done during these truly difficult days," he wrote the Vice President on October 22, "and are proud to be associated with you as the leader who is carrying on in the President's absence."

Never one to stint on ego massage, Rockefeller declared his admiration again two weeks later. Sending Nixon a copy of a speech he was about to give, he allowed that "it might have one or two ideas in it that could be useful to you, although from the speeches of yours that I have read you do such a superb job that I doubt it." And again, two weeks after that: "You were superb at the NSC meeting this afternoon. You have no idea what your understanding, integrity, courage and leadership mean to so many of us."

Such egregious flattery usually indicated that Rockefeller was making an investment in the recipient. And, in Nixon's case, the investment seemed well placed. Nixon's views on the worldwide Communist menace, and the need for aggressive U.S. countermeasures, paralleled Rockefeller's. Both men made much of "Red Colonialism" and other elements of subversion; it was with Nixon's hearty approval that Rockefeller brought on board the vituperative, rabidly anti-Soviet ex-congressman Charles Kersten. Both saw the war against the Communist threat as one that had to be waged on a multitude of fronts: political, psychological, military, and economic.

In private White House councils, Rockefeller's call for a dramatic expansion of foreign aid to counter Communist influence was echoed by the Vice President. Confronted by a dubious Dulles and a penny-pinching George Humphrey, Rockefeller knew that at least he could count on Richard Nixon.

On Friday, November 11, seven weeks after he was stricken, Dwight Eisenhower made his triumphant return to Washington, in a dramatic homecoming that was broadcast nationwide. Attired in his familiar tan polo coat and brown snap-brim hat, he was greeted by Nixon and a horde of other VIP well-wishers. "I am happy the doctors have given me at least a parole, if not a pardon," the President told the crowd.

He spent the weekend at the White House, attending to routine duties and showing off his recuperative powers by taking to the south lawn for some practice golf swings. But his stay in Washington was brief; on Monday morning Eisenhower and his wife repaired to their farm in Gettysburg to continue his convalescence. It was not until the following week that the President was fully back on the job—and even then, it was not at the White House, but at the presidential mountainside retreat, Camp David.

Perhaps to cheer the still-fragile chief executive, Rockefeller sent over a recent public opinion poll showing that an overwhelming 74 percent of Americans approved the way "officials in Washington are handling our affairs."

Privately, of course, Nelson Rockefeller was not among that overwhelming majority.

His grievances against Hoover, Humphrey, and other administration skinflints continued to fester. Rather than sedately wind up his affairs and tidy his desk, Rockefeller, in his last weeks on the job, worked frenetically to score points against his nemeses. His demeanor was not that of an outgoing executive, gracefully exiting the scene, but that of a quixotic striver, tilting at every windmill in his path.

He was still, against all odds, lobbying for the special loan to the Tata financial group of India. To Rockefeller, the loan had come to be a veritable litmus test of the administration's intentions toward the Third World. That he had twice failed to get anywhere with his appeals did not deter him in the slightest. He decided to go around Hoover and take the matter up directly with Dulles.

He phoned the Secretary of State and made his pitch, insisting that the loan needed Dulles' "personal attention." Dulles pleaded ignorance of the whole matter and promised to look into it. But the outcome, as Rockefeller must have known, was preordained; there was simply no way that Dulles would override his number two *and* George Humphrey to satisfy Nelson Rockefeller.

Rockefeller also took up the cause of the USIA. The agency was asking for a dramatic increase in its appropriation—from $85 million to $150 million—and running into the determined opposition of budget director Rowland Hughes, Humphrey, and other deficit-minded officials.

The USIA request was one of the first issues Rockefeller took to the President upon his return. Stepped-up spending, he argued, was warranted by the drastic change in the stratagems of the Cold War: "The world struggle is shifting more than ever from the arena of power to the arena of ideas and international persuasion," he told Eisenhower. "The Soviets have greatly intensified their efforts to woo the uncommitted areas of Asia and undermine the determination of the free areas in the Near East and Europe." The $150 million sum, he contended, was the rock-bottom minimum that was needed.

His pitch for the USIA had Nixon's backing, Stassen's, and, for once, the State Department's. But it put Eisenhower in the unsettling position of having to mediate between one set of his advisers and another. It was about the last thing Eisenhower wanted, or needed, so soon after his return to action.

Then, two days later, on Friday, December 2, Rockefeller sent over to the President the Quantico II report.

"I hope that you will have an opportunity to go over the report this weekend," he wrote Eisenhower. "I feel that the situation which the report highlights is not only of such importance, but also of such urgency, as to call for early positive action. In this regard, I will furnish you Monday morning a personal report including several recommendations for your consideration."

The document that landed in Eisenhower's briefcase was not exactly calculated to cheer the convalescing President. From beginning to end, the Quantico II report, as drafted by Kissinger, had the apocalyptic tone of biblical prophecy, conjuring scenarios that glistened with the fire and brimstone of geopolitical nightmare. Those who still basked in the benevolent Spirit of Geneva, who still thought of the United States and its allies as awash in unparalleled prosperity and military might, would scarcely recognize the picture painted by the report in its opening pages: "In the short-term, the Free World military situation is only partially satisfactory; the overall Western economic situation is spotty; though potentially strong, the political and economic situation in many areas, particularly in the underdeveloped regions, is precarious; and Free World military security and psychological unity are generally deteriorating."

It warned of the "false sense of security" engendered by Moscow's new foreign policy flexibility; the Soviets' means may have changed, but their ends—world domination—had scarcely altered. "Soviet tactics for the emerging phase of the struggle will continue to work toward the long-term objective of capturing the Eurasian-African land-mass piecemeal and by means short of a general war."

To stem the Red Tide, the Rockefeller panel urged the administration to immediately set in motion an all-out, coordinated program. Part of this program was military: finding the nation's defenses, and those of its allies, inadequate, the report called for a sweeping military buildup, on the order of a 10 to 20 percent increase in the Pentagon's budget. "We can and must afford to survive," the panel declared.

The other large component of the program was a multibillion-dollar developing world aid package. Once again, the ringing rhetoric of Point Four and Partners in Progress could be heard: "In order that the democratic way may survive, the aspirations of all classes and regions in each nation's society have to receive consideration."

But the Quantico II report was short on specifics on what this package would actually consist of. All in all, Rockefeller's report was more a call to arms than a blueprint, a polemic that warned of the most harrowing consequences should its jeremiad be ignored.

> If the United States confines itself to its present level of national effort, the somber prospect is that the Soviet Union may achieve military and technological superiority. The Soviet Union could exploit this superiority to shatter the cohesion of the Free World and reduce the United States to an encircled and isolated position. In such a position the U.S. might then be able to survive only at the cost of its way of life.

Such was the Gettysburg weekend reading that Nelson Rockefeller commended to the President.

That same Friday afternoon, Rockefeller went to see John Foster Dulles.

The time for cooperative gestures and palliative discourse between the two men had long since passed. Like the heads of two feuding clans, they eyed one another across a vast psychological chasm that neither had the will, or the means, or the desire to bridge.

Rockefeller did not bring with him a copy of the Quantico II report, perhaps fearing that Dulles would shoot it down before the President had a chance to digest it. Instead, he spoke with the secretary, in very general terms, about just one aspect of his proposals: the need for "greater flexibility on economic policy."

But Rockefeller found himself unable to talk about economic policy without bringing up Herbert Hoover, Jr. Neither Hoover nor John Hollister, the head of State's foreign aid arm, were very sympathetic to the foreign economic program, he complained. To this charge, Dulles bluntly replied that he and Hoover saw things very much alike, and then went on to excoriate Rockefeller for the bad relationship that existed between Rockefeller and Hoover—which Dulles attributed to Rockefeller's habit of going around the State Department and taking up matters directly with the President.

"That's happened only twice," Rockefeller insisted. But rather than parry Dulles' thrusts any further, he simply said that, in any case, he would be resigning as of the first of January—because his father needed him and because his White House job was "impossible."

Dulles, however, couldn't resist having the last word. He doubted, he said, whether any presidential assistant should operate the way Rockefeller did: "as a sort of free-lance, cutting across established procedures." It was regrettable, he added, that "the personal relationships which had developed here were such that a good many people were antagonized," leaving no doubt as to who was responsible for *that.*

With that riposte, the meeting came to an end. After eleven acrimonious months, Rockefeller and Dulles had finally done with each other.

On Monday morning, an official car bearing Rockefeller and Sherman Adams crunched along the Gettysburg farm's driveway, past the stands of trees that Rockefeller had bought for the President's pleasure.

The two men were ushered into the President's study and were greeted by a visibly restless Eisenhower. A thick fog had kept him housebound all day Sunday, and now that it was lifting, he found himself reluctantly confined to quarters by official business.

Sensing the President's edginess, Rockefeller came to the point quickly, handing the President a twenty-two-page memo—plus charts and annexes amounting to another forty-odd pages—entitled "Action Program for Free World Strength." Each page was stamped "Secret," on top and bottom. Rockefeller proceeded to walk the President and Adams through his proposals, which, he said in his cover letter, "reflect my own conclusions as to a sound course of action, both immediate and long range, necessary for developing the strength of the Free World."

The Action Program picked up where the Quantico II report left off, proposing specific measures the President could take to meet the Communist challenge. But if the underlying premises were the same, the Action Program's packaging was worlds apart from Kissinger's ominous presentation of the Quantico II agenda. The bleak assessments of Quantico II gave way, in Rockefeller's memo, to a sunnier report on the state of the nation: "At home, as a result of sound planning, we are enjoying peace, unparalleled prosperity and the prospect not only of a balanced budget but of surplus cash revenues." Abroad, "as things stand the first round of the political cold war under the Republican Administration has been won by the West." There were accolades for Dulles' "brilliant negotiations" and for the President's "magnificent" performance at Geneva. The memo, in short, seemed calculated to appeal to the President's rose-colored view of his administration's performance.

There was the requisite talk about "ruthless Soviet intentions" in this "new round in the cold war," but the prescriptions Rockefeller offered the President had a decidedly positive spin. He urged him to make a major foreign policy address unveiling a new "Free World Crusade," "lofty in aim but practical in concept, that would capture the hearts and the minds of men throughout the Free World."

The components of this Crusade were much the same elements that were broached in Quantico II. First, there was a program of economic development, and here Rockefeller resurrected one of his old Partners in Progress proposals: the creation of an International Development Authority, which would offer loans and grants for power, transportation, irrigation, and other major Third World projects. But whereas Partners in Progress talked about the IDA as an international venture, akin to the World Bank, Rockefeller now suggested it as a U.S. government entity. The initial price tag: $1 billion.

Then there was the matter of free world defense (although Rockefeller was careful to point out that "our present military position is basically sound," in sharp contrast to Quantico II's anxiety). He proposed beefed-up air defenses, and the creation of a "mobile ready force," to "put out brush-fire type wars and to prevent their spread into general war." (This idea was hatched by Kissinger, whose thesis of "limited wars" waged "with or without the use of tactical nuclear weapons" would soon germinate into an all-encompassing theory that would bring him his first international renown.) The cost of this buildup was put at $4 billion for the first eighteen months, and close to $2 billion a year thereafter.

The other great thrust of Rockefeller's Action Program was in the general area of psychological warfare. "The Communists are carrying on the battle for men's minds with full dedication, and with a highly organized and massively supported machine," he pointed out. "They have been particularly successful in penetrating universities and flooding the Free World with low-cost Communist literature. . . . It should be one of the aims of a Free World Crusade to correct this situation." He would correct it through overt measures—funding new universities around the world that would "teach the facts about Communism," distributing books that impart "important Free World ideas," expanding exchange programs. But he also suggested an "offensive against the Communist conspiracy" to be conducted "primarily through covert or otherwise unattributed channels." In that regard, Rockefeller brought up, once again, the idea of overseas "training centers" to cultivate "indigenous leaders" who would then "be able to cope successfully with the trained Communist cadres."

The cost of this information offensive, both overt and covert, was estimated at $420 million—and that was over and above the $150 million he was seeking for the USIA.

When all the numbers were added up, Rockefeller's Action Program would cost American taxpayers over $3 billion a year—or a grand total of up to $19 billion over its five-and-a-half-year lifetime.

Foreseeing the collective gasps and groans that those figures would induce—he was, after all, talking about an increase of up to 5 percent in the total federal budget—Rockefeller hastened to play down the impact on the economy. The United States, he insisted, could afford it, what with a $3 billion federal *surplus* expected in the current fiscal year and a $6 billion surplus in the next. "It clearly appears possible," he said, "to undertake these programs and still achieve the President's campaign pledge of a balanced cash budget."

There is no official record of how the President responded to Rockefeller's sweeping plans.

Four days after the Gettysburg meeting, Rockefeller told C. D. Jackson that his report had been "very well received all around." But this sanguine appraisal was belied by what Rockefeller reported to Rostow shortly afterward, when the two met for lunch in Cambridge at the MIT Faculty Club. According to Rostow's later account, Rockefeller told him that Eisenhower "clearly indicated that he would not act to implement the Quantico II budget recommendations."

The latter version was probably closer to the truth. For the fact was that after that December 5 meeting, the "Action Plan for Free World Strength" vanished from sight, never to be seen or heard from again for the duration of the Eisenhower administration.

After Rockefeller and Adams departed, Eisenhower picked up a copy of that morning's *New York Times*. There, atop the front page, was the headline "President Faces Dispute on Scope of Aid Programs."

The article described "a growing dispute within his Administration over foreign-aid programs" and noted, in the second paragraph, Rockefeller's visit to Gettysburg.

"The subject of the conference was not announced. It is understood, however, that Mr. Rockefeller plans, tomorrow or later, to give the President a detailed outline of his views on meeting the Russian threat of economic penetration." Rockefeller was "pressing for a bolder and somewhat bigger program of aid." The *Times* went on to depict the two camps: the Rockefeller supporters, including Nixon and Stassen, and the Rockefeller foes, the "4-H Club": Humphrey, Hoover, Hollister, and budget director Hughes.

Incensed by the leak about his meeting with Rockefeller—and doubly incensed because the article implied a rift in what he liked to believe was a totally harmonious inner circle—Eisenhower immediately dashed off a letter to his special assistant.

> After you left today, I saw a story in the "Times" to the effect that we were splitting up within the Cabinet and staff, and were practically having a "civil war." I know you understand how anxious I am that we always have full, free and thorough discussion and argument about the differing opinions within the official family circle. But it is exceedingly important that such issues not be turned over to the newspapers for trial and decision. I know that you will not be a party to putting any of this information in front of the newspapers, but I hope that in discussing it with others, you will warn them of the need for keeping this on a confidential basis.

An abashed Rockefeller promptly replied by recounting how "absolutely distressed" he was by the article. Without directly denying that he, or one of his advisers, was its source, he tried to explain it away by noting that "for many years I have worked for and been an active proponent of strong U.S. participation in an expanding world economy. I am afraid that this fact, which is well known, coupled with my enthusiasm for a dynamic long-range program has contributed to this most unfortunate situation."

Whether or not Eisenhower bought this modified mea culpa, his fury at the *Times* piece certainly did not help Rockefeller's cause.

The day after the Gettysburg meeting, Rockefeller received word that despite his pleas, the USIA would be getting $130 million in the next fiscal year, or $20 million less than the bare minimum he considered necessary. Furthermore, he was advised that "neither the President nor Governor Adams ever want to hear about the USIA budget again."

His expressed intention to resign notwithstanding, until early December Rockefeller had been operating in a very open-ended way about his planned departure from the government. His position on speaking invitations was the best indicator of this: as recently as December 2 he was still deflecting invitations for January and February, on the grounds that in his capacity as special assistant he was not making any speeches. It was as though he was grasping, to the end, at the slim hope that his Action Program would somehow sweep him back into a position of influence.

But upon his return from Gettysburg all that changed. Responding, later that same day, to a invitation from National Business Publications for a February address, he waffled. "It is impossible," Rockefeller said, "for me to make a definite commitment this far in advance. I wonder if I could get in touch with you at a later date?"

Ten days later, Rockefeller notified the President that "compelling personal responsibilities, which I have talked over with you, cause me with sincere regret to submit my resignation as your Special Assistant, effective December 31, 1955. Under the circumstances I deeply appreciate your unique understanding."

Eisenhower accepted the resignation with the usual regretful sentiments, couched in the same vague formulaic language he had used in appointing Rockefeller a year earlier. Rockefeller, said the President, had "effectively assisted" in the increase of "understanding and cooperation among all peoples." Eisenhower noted with satisfaction that Rockefeller would continue as a member of his advisory commission on government organization, "despite the other pressing demands on your time."

Then, as a private and personal going-away present, Eisenhower sent over to his departing art connoisseur one of his own paintings. For this gift, Rockefeller dispatched a gushing, handwritten letter of thanks: "Your painting has given so many people so much pleasure, and your thought in giving it is so typical of your qualities of human understanding for which people throughout the world love and trust you."

The parting from Dulles, meanwhile, was marked by both men with the most respectful of obsequies. "I have greatly enjoyed personally the association we have had," the secretary wrote, "and I appreciate the consideration which you have consistently shown me. . . .

"I am confident that you will not remain indefinitely in private life as there is great need for public servants who have the inspiration, energy and capability which you possess."

Rockefeller, in turn, offered this bouquet: "Of the lasting impressions that will go with me from Washington, none is stronger than the sense of confidence inspired by your wise and skillful stewardship over our affairs of state."

Retreating behind the walls of decorous politeness, neither official gave any hint of the animus that was the true cause of this whole turn of events.

It did not take long, though, for the more cynical members of the Washington press corps to poke holes in the tissue-thin layer of civility, and to figure out that there was more to the special assistant's departure than the principals were letting on. Perhaps the most brutally insightful was *Washington Post* columnist Roscoe Drummond. "There is no evidence that Rockefeller found that 'compelling personal' reasons were calling him back to private life until he found that compelling impersonal reasons had made him feel that, for the present at least, his usefulness in the Government had come to an end," wrote Drummond. "A Presidential adviser without operating authority, particularly a Presidential adviser who has no well-defined areas of policy responsibility, is likely to end up a pretty lonely person. Rockefeller could always know that he was working on his assigned duties because his assigned duties were so nebulously all-embracing that he couldn't possibly be off the subject.

"I think that what Rockefeller found was that he was so busy accomplishing so little that it was time to step aside."

This view of Rockefeller as an isolated, frustrated policy maker was recast in far more heroic terms the next day by Joseph and Stewart Alsop in their widely read and quoted syndicated column. The hawkish Alsops had for months been chiding the administration for what they deemed a lackadaisical response to the Communist menace; contending that the United States was rapidly losing its military edge over the Russians, they pushed for a huge increase in defense spending.

Correctly perceiving that they had at least one potential ally in the administration, in the person of Nelson Rockefeller, Joseph Alsop had met privately with Rockefeller three months earlier to press his views. But on that occasion at least, Rockefeller proved more of a team player than Alsop had bargained for. As Rockefeller would later recount the conversation, "I told him that I agreed with his basic premise that we must maintain our supremacy but that I thought he was wrong in his conclusion that every effort was not being made to do so."

Rockefeller's resignation served to confirm to the Alsops that they had been right about Rockefeller—and right about the Eisenhower administration's weak-kneed policies. The development gave the columnists, who evidently knew something about Rockefeller's Action Program, the opportunity for some high-styled hand-wringing, and they made the most of it. In a column entitled "Casualty Rockefeller," they called Rockefeller "the most important casualty to date of the peculiar policy-making process of the Eisenhower administration. . . . The fact remains that Rockefeller would never have left his key post as a Presidential adviser, if the advice he gave in the recent struggle over next year's budget had not proved unpalatably insistent and forthright."

"What wore out Rockefeller's usefulness," said the Alsops, "was his powerful insistence on a new order of national policy priorities. Balancing the budget and even cutting taxes must now yield pride of place, he declared. And he pleaded for giving an overriding first priority to meeting the double challenge of the enormous progress of the Kremlin arms program and the wide extension of the Kremlin's political offensive in the Middle and Far East. . . .

"If Rockefeller's factually justified forebodings prove correct . . . his departure from the government will later be remembered in the way men now remember the departures of British officials in the '30s, who got into hot water by insisting that it was dangerous to neglect the challenge of Adolf Hitler."

Thus, in one stroke, the Alsops had elevated Nelson Rockefeller to Churchillian stature. Others in the media followed suit. The notion that Rockefeller resigned over an issue of principle, rather than of power, as was actually the case, quickly took root, and soon proved impossible to supplant.

Rockefeller's friends and associates did their part to cultivate this assessment. In a letter to Rockefeller, Henry Kissinger—who by now felt secure enough to use the salutation "Dear Nelson"—lauded his sponsor's "willingness to stand up for what you thought important without considering what might be administratively easiest. I have no doubt that time will vindicate what you have stood for . . ."

Talking with C. D. Jackson about his resignation just before it was made public, Rockefeller expressed his fear that his departure would be linked to the budget debate, which, Jackson recorded, "he would deeply regret and which is not true." But untrue though it was, Rockefeller had little cause to regret the outcome. His resignation, sparked by his isolation and ineffectiveness in the administration's inner councils, had been transmuted into an act of high principle and moral courage. His allies sung his praises, and among the most effusive was Richard Nixon. "I think the position we have taken during the past few months is fundamentally sound and that history will vindicate most of what we have said and done," Nixon privately advised him. "I am sure that as the months go by the contribution you have made to the policies and programs of the Administration will loom even larger than they do today."

Instead of serving as monuments to his political impotence, the policy proposals of his final months now were potential foundation stones for Rockefeller's career to come: a platform on which he could build.

Although he could not say, in the tumult surrounding his resignation, where his career would lead, there was one thing that Rockefeller now knew for certain about it.

"I've learned one thing, Ted," he told Parker as he prepared to exit the capital. "You can't have influence in government if you haven't been elected."

On and off for the past fifteen years, he had pursued the path of appointed office: currying favor with Presidents, fending off his rivals, jockeying for a place at the cabinet table. There was much he had accomplished in that decade and a half: the World War II alliance with Latin America, the instigation of Point Four, the birth of HEW, Open Skies. But always, at the end, there was frustration and a sense of political ineffectuality. At the end, he was always at the mercy of other, often lesser figures: Stettinius and Byrnes, Harriman, Hobby and Dulles.

For an appointed official—any appointed official—legitimacy is elusive and evanescent, a prize that can crumble to dust in the faintest breeze. Only for the elected official, Rockefeller could see now, was legitimacy enduring and unassailable. He had pursued power in every corridor of official Washington, but now he knew there was only one place where it could truly be found: at the ballot box.

Part Seven

Running

Thirty-six

A Sense of Purpose

Not long after Rockefeller reentered the private sector, Adolf Berle pondered his old friend's dilemma. Rockefeller, reflected Berle, has "access to the Republican Administration: the ability to command any expert on anything: the question is what to do with his life; and with the most magnificent 'do it yourself' kit ever provided; only it has no plans or suggestions." Blessed with virtually limitless resources, commanding a personal brain trust that would be the envy of most Presidents, Rockefeller could impel his side-tracked career in any of a half dozen different directions. The choice was his to make—and, being Nelson Rockefeller, the temptation was to try them all. Yet he had no certainty that any of them would lead him where he wanted to go.

He returned to 30 Rockefeller Plaza in January 1956 like an exiled monarch come to retake his throne. His brothers—not without some reluctance—handed back to him the keys to the kingdom he had relinquished two and a half years before. Even though he had just spearheaded the expansion of the Rockefeller Center complex to the west of Sixth Avenue—the first element of which would be the projected new headquarters of Time, Inc.—Laurance dutifully surrendered the Center chairmanship to brother Nelson. John, meanwhile, turned over the presidency of the Rockefeller Brothers Fund, the philanthropic vehicle the brothers had organized before the war. Thanks to Junior's gift to the RBF, four years earlier, of his $58 million Rockefeller Center note, the RBF was now one of the nation's most formidable foundations. Nelson had big, albeit hazy, plans for the fund. As John noted in his diary, the view was that the RBF "should not just be an orthodox foundation but has a real opportunity to do something more."

Rockefeller also exercised his *droit du seigneur* over his other fiefdoms, regaining the chairmanship of the Museum of Modern Art and of IBEC and AIA.

His return to the family institutions coincided with a growing public recognition that this generation of Rockefellers was America's first family not only of wealth but also of power. In a two-part paean to the brothers published a year earlier, *Fortune* detailed how their impact "reaches into almost every area of life—cultural, economic, political, religious, scientific. For sheer diversity and excellence of intent, it has set these young men apart as the most unusual brothers of their generation." While attention inevitably was riveted on their wealth—each brother was said to be worth upward of $100 million—the focus was now shifting to the intricate filigrees of connections and influence that the brothers collectively were spinning.

There was John 3rd, at last coming out of his shell to emerge as a titan of philanthropy: combating the world's hunger and population problems by launching the Population Council, and furthering U.S.-Asian relations by creating first the Japan Society, then the Asia Society. Now he was taking on a new cause: an incipient performing arts complex on Manhattan's Upper West Side, dubbed Lincoln Square.

There was David, steadily making his way up the Chase Bank's corporate ladder; he had just been named vice chairman of what was, since its recent merger with the Manhattan Company, America's biggest bank. His ascension to the top was considered only a matter of time. And, along the way, he was also evolving into a New York civic figure of note, a potent champion of urban renewal.

There was Laurance, at forty-five one of America's foremost venture capitalists, with a portfolio of high-technology investments in aircraft companies, rocket engine makers, and the like. "We're not big business," he would insist, in a typical mock-folksy disclaimer. "We're just a seed-corn proposition." But the sprouting of those seeds (his holdings' value had quintupled over the past five years) was already making Laurance a force to be reckoned with in American capitalism, and his grandfather's one true spiritual heir. At the same time, he was emerging as a budding resort entrepreneur, building world-class getaways in Puerto Rico (the Dorado Beach Hotel) and the U.S. Virgin Islands (the Caneel Bay Plantation).

There was even Winthrop, who had finally, it seemed, found himself on Petit Jean Mountain in Arkansas. There, on his 900-acre estate, Winrock Farm, he raised prize-winning Santa Gertrudis cattle (the same breed Nelson had unsuccessfully tried to introduce in Venezuela), fostered innovative irrigation systems, and became the most visible exponent of the backward state's development possibilities. "This is my show," he exulted. "It doesn't have anything to do with any Rockefeller family project." His newfound sense of serenity extended to his domestic life: that year he would marry an attractive thirty-seven-year-old divorcée, Jeannette Edris, and settle down to a considerably less tempestuous scene than his previous marital go-round.

The brothers' individual accomplishments, grafted onto the already awesome power base of the Rockefeller family institutions, was fast transforming them into national icons, veritable incarnations of the confluence of wealth and influence in America.

To Junior, whose own accomplishments would be commemorated that year with the publication of Raymond Fosdick's biography and a *Time* cover story, this celebration of his sons was the ultimate affirmation of all he had striven for. Upon reading the *Fortune* pieces, he sent each of them a note expressing his unbounded pride. "To our family have come unprecedented opportunities," he said. "With the opportunities have come equally great responsibilities. Magnificently and modestly you boys are measuring up to those opportunities and responsibilities. . . .

"What you are doing for the well-being of mankind throughout the world is breathtaking."

It was the sort of note that, in the past, the patriarch would send only to Nelson. But now, all his sons, even Winthrop, were deemed worthy of the accolade.

The fifty-sixth floor still maintained the air of understated, almost antebellum gentility that was the hallmark of Junior's reign, right down to the courtly old southern black retainers who greeted visitors in the reception area. Employees who once labored for "Mr. Junior" now toiled for "Mr. Nelson," "Mr. David," or "Mr. John." "Room 5600 was a wonderful, genteel, white-gloved place," recalls reporter Deirdre Carmody, who went to work there as a secretary in the mid-1950s. "Going to the fifty-sixth floor was like going to your grandparents' formidable old house." Yet at the same time, she also sensed the vibrant undercurrent that coursed behind the decorous facade. "I was young, but I knew power when I saw it. I knew this was a place where power ricocheted off the walls—but in a discreet way."

As each brother's sphere of influence grew, each built his own entourage. But upon his return to Room 5600, Nelson could look around and note, with satisfaction, that his people still occupied the positions of power. John Lockwood, whose spindly, cranelike appearance made him look more and more like a Dickensian caricature, was still the family counsel, although Oscar Ruebhausen was increasingly a supplemental presence. Frank Jamieson, whose hair was now a shock of startling white, setting off his piercing blue eyes all the more, was still the family p.r. man. Wally Harrison, as laconic and bemused as ever, remained the family architect.

Although all supposedly served the entire family, there was never any question as to whom they owed their primary loyalty. As Lockwood points out, it was always assumed that "when Nelson came back, the office was his to take over."

And, as loyal vassals, all were fiercely protective of their relationship with the boss—a phenomenon that became more marked when he was once again an everyday presence at 5600. Jamieson's aide Kershaw Burbank noticed that "Frank didn't want anyone too close to Nelson. I know there were some people he worried about. He feared what advice they would give to Nelson."

As much as he prized Jamieson's counsel, Rockefeller often resented his aide's tendency to run interference for him. He vented his displeasure by ceasing to call Jamieson "Frankie"; "Jamie always knew when Nelson was mad at him, because it was then that he called him 'Frank,' " says Jamieson's wife, Linda. But the chill would never last very long. "Sometimes he doesn't like my advice," Jamieson would sigh, "and I don't get consulted for a couple of weeks. But sooner or later I get consulted again."

Harrison was, if anything, even more possessive of his special relationship with Rockefeller. Indisposed for months by a prostate problem, Harrison instructed his partner Max Abramovitz to deal with Rockefeller in his absence and "take care of anything Nelson wanted." But when he at last returned to the office, Harrison flew into a rage when he learned that Abramovitz had done exactly that. "He accused me of trying to move in on him, as far as Nelson was concerned," remembers Abramovitz. "I became furious, and we almost split up the partnership. From then on, I never attended any meeting between Wally and Nelson."

Harrison extended his turf to the entire Rockefeller family, as his fellow architect Philip Johnson learned in the mid-1950s when Blanchette Rockefeller, John 3rd's wife, asked Johnson to design a new outdoor pool for the Playhouse at Pocantico. "I worked on it for a few weeks," says Johnson, "and then the word came down from above that I wasn't to go on. It turned out that Wally got very, very jealous, and he said to Blanchette, 'I've always done all of that work. So why are you asking this young whippersnapper to take on something that I've always done for the family?' So they threw me off." Harrison got the commission, and finished the job. (The Playhouse pool was a Rockefeller family *cause célèbre* for other reasons as well. Junior was aghast at Harrison's free-form design in gleaming white marble—he complained that from Kykuit he could see the glint of all that marble—and at the old autocrat's insistence, the marble was pulled out and replaced with sky blue concrete.)

Hovering protectively around their patron, the Rockefeller court eyed warily any potential interloper who arrived in their midst. And for one particular newcomer to 5600 from Washington, this only made the transition to her new life that much more difficult, that much more painful.

It had not been very long after he made up his mind to leave Washington that Rockefeller began pressing Nancy Hanks to come back to New York with him. He considered her part of his permanent entourage now, and perfunctorily assumed that wherever he went, she would go, too. That there were, for her at least, serious emotional complications to the move, that she was confronted by the loss of the intimacy they had enjoyed for two and a half years, seems to have barely given him pause. He moved freely, unreservedly, between the twin spheres of his work and personal relations ("working together and sleeping together are the same thing") and he truly didn't understand why his counterparts couldn't do the same. As it was for Joan Braden, so it could be for Nancy Hanks.

Hanks, however, did not have Braden's emotional plasticity, the same easy ability to accept Nelson Rockefeller on whatever terms he came. Hanks sanctified the relationship; as Braden herself observed, "Nancy surrendered herself to Nelson. I never did." To see that special relationship transformed to the workaday was almost more than she could bear.

One day in November, during the denouement of Rockefeller's Washington tenure, Hanks emerged from his office with tears in her eyes. As her friend and co-worker Donna Mitchell recalled, it was "one of the few times in my life I ever saw Nancy show any kind of emotion." Mitchell asked her what the matter was, and Hanks mumbled something about trying to make up her mind about going to New York.

"Well, Nancy," Mitchell then asked, "do you want to get married ever?"

Yes, Hanks replied, she did. "More than anything else in this world, I want to get married and have a family."

"Well," said Mitchell, "my advice to you is don't go to New York."

But Hanks found herself tugged in the other direction by an even more persuasive force: her father. Tooling his motorboat (courtesy of Nelson Rockefeller) around his man-made lake at Cashiers (courtesy of Nelson Rockefeller), tending his daughter's portfolio of blue-chip stocks (courtesy of Nelson Rockefeller), Bryan Hanks was aghast at the thought that Nancy would spurn "the maker of such good things," in Bryan's reverential words. "Be not independent," he counseled his daughter. "New horizons are opening to you . . . beyond the dreams of everyone."

Lacking, at that point in her young life, the inner fiber to defy both the strong male figures in her life—and perhaps still clinging to some wishful visions of the future—Hanks finally acceded to Rockefeller's offer.

Yet, as if this act of surrender wasn't enough, Bryan Hanks continued to hound his daughter about the need for total submission to Rockefeller's whims. "If he suggests you live in a hotel, or some furnished apartment in NY for a time; keep your own apt. in D.C., and then look about in NY leisurely etc.," Bryan wrote her on the eve of her departure. "Do not, in my opinion, 'buck him' as to his suggestions about living situations in DC or NY. You have said 'yes'; he liked it; said you would not worry etc. . . . So take him 100% at his word, and follow along his desires; wishes; suggestions. Such is the wise thing to do; such is the appreciative thing to do; such is *the* thing to do from every viewpoint in my opinion."

She ended up buying an efficiency apartment at the Rockefeller Apartments on 54th Street. While it was Rockefeller who arranged the deal, Hanks insisted on paying the $10,000 purchase price herself (with some help from her parents).

Arriving for work at Room 5600, she found herself adrift, a stateless figure whose past was whispered about and whose future remained ill-defined. The Rockefeller inner circle "regarded Nancy as just another one of Nelson's girlfriends," said Mitchell, who joined her friend in the move from Washington. "They'd seen them come and go, come and go." They alternately gossiped about her behind her back and studiously ignored her, and the line of hostility began with the formidable Louise Boyer. "Mrs. Boyer could be a very, very overbearing person," said Mitchell. "Everybody stood in awe of her. You never crossed Mrs. Boyer."

Hanks silently endured it all, until one day she had had enough. "I don't have to take this from this staff around here," she seethed. "Even Mrs. Boyer I don't have to take." Said Mitchell, "It just really got to her. I don't know to this day whether she realized what it was, that these people were regarding her as just another one of Nelson's girlfriends."

Her letters home took on more and more of a resigned, disconsolate tone. She was reconciling herself to the fact, she said, that her future contact with Rockefeller "will be very minor. I will easily admit that I am not happy about that part, primarily because for at least three years I have been used to working hard, in exciting fields, where something was always going on, where you felt you could contribute. None of those are in the crystal ball as far as I can see. . . . Will just stick it out I suppose for a year and try to develop some enthusiasm for a condition of not being interested in my work or contributing anything at all."

But if Hanks was hoping to tap some reserve of consolation from the home front, she found soon enough that the well was dry. Rather than think so much of herself, advised Bryan, she should ponder Rockefeller's situation. "I am wondering if you fully appreciate what N has gone thru; how he must sit and think of the position in Government he had; of those who are responsible for the change; for him not moving on up and up, and how such is bound to effect the average man, much less as ambitious as he. . . . An appreciation of this, surely will make you, any sensible person as you, most understanding; most considerate; most overlooking of moodishness; of uncalled for 'jabs'; of hurts; of embarrassing situations. Time, and it may be short, can correct the things which do not seem right now, and bring about a happier situation."

In the meantime, he suggested, "Say a little prayer as you approach the office each morning, asking God to help you; to make you thoughtful; considerate; understanding; forgiving, and make it a GOOD day for you, Nelson and those about you."

Nancy, however, found the power of prayer insufficient to assuage her misery. "Very frankly am not sure that life is worth it to stay much longer," she wrote a month later. "I realize this is weak of me, but I never claimed to be the strongest person in the world."

Rockefeller had been thinking about moving some staff over to his townhouse at 13 West 54th Street to do some "international studies," and "if I can arrange it so that I can go over there too I think it might work out all right," she confided. "There is a chance that he will start some studies that will be worthwhile, and he has gotten his brothers interested in them apparently. I realize in my mind that this is purely a situation of being paid more and cut completely out of things that are interesting to me—i.e. things that interest NAR and I can advise him on. The international is a tenth of his interest at present, if that, and I don't have a chance to even talk about that, so . . ."

"Green paper," she ruefully observed, "sure isn't everything."

Hanks had difficulty accepting that what was past was past, but her patron had no such problem. Living, as always, in the present tense, Rockefeller had embarked on a dizzying new array of activities, rarely stopping long enough to acknowledge any of his associates' private travails. He was never one for brooding pauses or wistful reflection. A ravenous appetite for action defined his nature, and his response to the sudden disjuncture in his career path was simply to pile more and more upon his plate.

Soon after his return to New York, he expressed the hope that "now as we go on to the new work we can arrange things so that life will not be as hectic and that there will not be the pressure that we've had to meet during the past three years." But if some small part of his being yearned for respite, the rest of his nature spurned it. The engine could never go at half throttle.

Presiding over Rockefeller Center and the Rockefeller Brothers Fund and IBEC was not enough for him. There had to be other outlets for his energy, other projects he could tackle. He quickly found one at his alma mater, spearheading plans for a new creative arts center at Dartmouth to be named after his erstwhile mentor, president emeritus Ernest Hopkins.

At the same time, Rockefeller busied himself with plans for his own personal arts center in New York. This was the Museum of Primitive Art, a museum devoted to showing off the vast collection of pre-Columbian American art, African carvings, and the like that he had amassed over three decades, since his very first purchase, a Sumatran knife adorned with a sculptured head and human hair he acquired on his honeymoon.

In the course of his globe-trotting (he vacationed in Africa several times during the 1950s) Rockefeller had stockpiled some 1,500 pieces: Ivory Coast children's masks, pre-Columbian Peruvian wooden monkeys, New Guinea memorial totems. His interest was not anthropological; as he once confessed, "Don't ask me whether this bowl which I am holding is a household implement or a ritual vessel. I could not care less." Rather, he regarded the multicultural works as high art that could rank side by side with the Picassos and Gauguins they had so obviously inspired.

Rockefeller planned to house his museum in 15 West 54th Street, the twin of its next-door neighbor, number 13. Rockefeller had bought the building in the fall of 1953 to serve as offices for his Government Research Foundation. The transaction had been negotiated by the foundation's head, former lieutenant governor Frank Moore, and Moore's tale of how it transpired became a classic of Rockefeller lore: prima facie evidence of Rockefeller's unworldly extravagance in pursuit of his ends. The owner, it seemed, wanted the then-exorbitant sum of $880,000 for the building, and Moore told Rockefeller of the problem. "Well, Frank, you have to be tough," Rockefeller advised. "Don't pay him any more than a million dollars."

Other art ventures—equally expansive, and even more far-fetched—occupied Rockefeller's mind. Wally Harrison had told him of a tapestry version of Picasso's "Guernica," for which the artist himself had designed the maquette, chosen the yarns, and supervised the weaving. Rockefeller tracked it down and bought it immediately, to the disapproval of Alfred Barr, who objected to the way the tapestry, executed in softer tones, compromised Picasso's stark Spanish Civil War vision. Rockefeller had no such objections; in fact, so enraptured was he by this rendering that he tried to persuade Picasso to reproduce others of his classic works in yarn.

As a go-between, he contacted in Paris a Madame Marie Cuttoli, a former lover of the artist who had worked with him on past tapestries. To Rockefeller's delighted surprise, Picasso sent back word through Cuttoli that he was agreeable to the undertaking. Rockefeller would select the paintings, and Picasso would oversee the production of the tapestry reproductions by a French weaver, Madame J. de la Baume-Durrbach. In time, over twenty of the artists' greatest masterworks, including "Les Demoiselles d'Avignon," "Girl with a Mandolin," and "Night Fishing at Antibes," would be transformed into tapestries at the express order of Nelson Rockefeller. The collaboration between Picasso and Rockefeller went on until the artist's death almost two decades later.

Aside from the pleasure it gave him, the Picasso experiment cemented, in Rockefeller's mind, the belief that reproduced art—"the next best thing"—was a legitimate medium in its own right, worthy of patronage and propagation. There was more to be done in this field, and someday Rockefeller would do it.

On Mother's Day, 1956, three generations of Rockefellers gathered in the intimate Union Church of Pocantico Hills, the family house of worship, for the dedication of a memorial to the beloved matriarch, Abby Aldrich Rockefeller. Gazing above the altar, they saw it shimmering: a rose window of gold and yellow flames encircled by a leafy blue-green arabesque. The window, the last great work of Henri Matisse, was a singular filial tribute from Nelson Rockefeller to his mother.

It had been his idea, as early as a year after Abby's death, to commission the window from Matisse, and he had grittily persisted despite the reluctance of the aged, bedridden artist to take on the project. Finally, after numerous entreaties on Rockefeller's behalf by Alfred Barr, Matisse relented in late August 1954. "Fatigued at the beginning of the summer," he wrote Barr, "I have spent some weeks resting but now I want to tell you that I feel my spirit caught by this project." Throughout the early fall, plans, designs, and correspondence went back and forth between Matisse's studio in Vence in the South of France and New York, until on October 28 the artist notified Rockefeller that he was close to completion. The letter arrived on November 1. Two days later, the world learned that the master had died. A crestfallen Rockefeller contemplated the near-certainty that the final design of the rose window had died with him.

But later that day, an envelope arrived from Vence, dated November 1. It was from Matisse, perhaps the last letter he had ever written. "Thanks to the design of the full-size maquette," he advised, "I have been able to bring to a happy conclusion the work I had undertaken." In his final days, he had completed the rose window; all that remained was for his master glazier to finish the job.

And so, nineteen months later, Nelson brought the family and a few select guests (among them Barr and Wally Harrison) together to witness the dedication of Matisse's last masterwork, a stained-glass commemoration of the life of the maternal figure to whom they were all so devoted. The intense colors the window cast on the sanctuary brought to mind Abby's vibrant personality—or, perhaps, the flower-spangled hats of which she was so fond.

But never one to leave well enough alone—even in the case of such a sublime creation—Nelson decided the setting could be further improved upon. He arranged for the Pocantico gardeners to transplant a large white pine in front of the window outside the church. The tree was positioned to mute the flow of morning sunlight through the window, adding the natural rustle of foliage to the verdant ballet of Matisse's design. Thus, with the movement of a tree, Nelson Rockefeller added his own bit of artistic expression to that of Henri Matisse.

Rockefeller's appearance at the Union Church was a homecoming of sorts; he had been away most of the previous month in Latin America, for his first grand tour south of the border since his HEW appointment almost three years before. Much had changed in the political landscape in the interim: his old ally Getulio Vargas was dead, a suicide, and Juan Perón had finally been swept aside in Argentina. But what had not changed, for Rockefeller, was the enthusiasm with which he was greeted at every stop. For someone still smarting from his political bruises in Washington, the *abrazos* offered the best possible balm for his ego.

This swing through the continent, however, was notably devoid of the majestic promises and vaulting expectations of Rockefeller's earlier visits. The hard knocks of IBEC's early years had taken their toll. No longer was Rockefeller stirring the populace with dreams of economic rebirth; no longer was he a "Luke in the service of God." Dramatic new initiatives were markedly absent from his agenda.

Rather than create great new enterprises, Rockefeller now operated more like an old-fashioned *yanqui* plantation owner (albeit one with more advanced social attitudes than the norm). Much of his time in Latin America was spent looking in on his personal interests. He owned a banana farm in Ecuador, as well as a coffee plantation there, where he was attempting to cultivate a new variety of bean, *café robusto.*

Having acquired, in the earlier IBEC shakeout, the company's Venezuelan corn and potato farm in Monte Sacro, in the Andes foothills, he now began planning a sprawling hacienda for himself on the estate. He assigned the job to Wally Harrison, but Harrison, for once, balked, perhaps because he was less than thrilled about taking on a project on a remote Andean mountainside. He recommended, instead, that Rockefeller give the commission to a young Connecticut architect, Peter Ogden, who had experience in Latin America working on IBEC Housing's projects in El Salvador.

Ogden was faced with certain unique architectural obstacles, not the least of which was the fact that a cemetery occupied the commanding hilltop site Rockefeller had chosen for his house. Eventually, says Ogden, "we got permission to move the bones to another cemetery that we set up elsewhere." Taking advantage of the cooling breezes that wafted through the hills, Ogden designed a multi-wing structure surrounded by twelve-foot-wide covered walkways, a conception similar to what Harrison had come up with for the Avila Hotel. "It was sort of a natural air conditioning," says Ogden.

As a gift to the Chirgua Valley natives who watched this splendid edifice arise in their midst, Rockefeller, in the manner of a Renaissance prince, renovated the local church, which had fallen into serious disrepair. "We added the bell tower and we added some windows and put some doors on and fixed the rotting beams," says Ogden.

A year in the making, the hacienda at Monte Sacro became Rockefeller's

Latin American retreat, another spectacular residence to add to those he already possessed on Fifth Avenue, at Pocantico, on Foxhall Road, and in Seal Harbor. The young man who had come to Venezuela twenty years before burning with indignation about the isolation of Creole Petroleum's Americans was now living on a hilltop, a true grandee.

When Rockefeller last toured Latin America, before his Eisenhower administration stint, his IBEC venture was still a gasping enterprise, still struggling to overcome the trauma of its early years. But in his absence (and some cynics might say *because* of his absence) IBEC had experienced a dramatic turnaround. The IBEC that he now surveyed was vigorous, prosperous, in the black, and on its way to recouping all its losses of the previous ten years.

In part, this reversal of fortune could be attributed to the earlier shucking of such losers as the Venezuelan fisheries, the food wholesaler, and the farms. What was left were the potential winners: the milk companies and the supermarkets. The milk operation's fleet of giant Leche de Carabobo trucks was shipping 83,000 quarts a day, ten times its initial run. As for the supermarkets, what started as the single experimental store in Maracaibo, Todos, had sprouted into a chain, with seven in Venezuela, four more on the way there, and stores opening in Lima, Peru, and in Puerto Rico. The showpiece of the chain, opened in December 1954, was Automercado, Venezuela's first American-style shopping mall, a two-story glass-and-steel structure in the Caracas suburbs which included the country's largest supermarket. So successful were the Latin American marts that IBEC was even contemplating crossing the Atlantic and introducing the concept in Italy.

Meanwhile, IBEC Housing, after a stumbling start, was also starting to come to life. Its first full-blown development, Las Lomas in Puerto Rico, had just opened. Some two hundred of the mass-produced homes were already occupied, the first of 1,600 units IBEC Housing was putting up at the rate of six a day. Demand was so strong that speculators were already bidding up the cost of uncompleted dwellings by 25 percent over IBEC's asking price.

Not that everything was so successful. When Rockefeller had last involved himself with IBEC, he had voiced great hopes for the company's foray into investment banking, a joint Brazilian venture with brother David's Chase Bank. But in the interim, the undertaking had turned out to be a flop. There were simply not enough new stock issues to sustain the operation, and those few it did manage to underwrite performed badly. By the time of Rockefeller's 1956 swing through Latin America, the investment bank had folded.

But the dream of financial services as a magnificent leveraging device for IBEC's capital remained an idée fixe for Nelson. In the United States, the hot financial product now was mutual funds, and Rockefeller didn't see any reason why it couldn't catch on in Brazil as well. Fundo Crescinco it would be called, Brazil's first mutual fund, and its debut would be ballyhooed with banners in the streets of Rio and splashy newspaper ads touting this new form of people's capitalism.

Recruiting a distinctly populist sales force—from the manager of the steam bath at Rio's Hotel Glória to prostitutes in the coastal town of Recife—IBEC began peddling its shares, allowing investors to buy as few as ten shares, $15 worth, at a time. By mid-1957, sales would be running at $75,000 a month. By the admittedly diminutive standards of the Latin American capital market, Crescinco was a huge success.

To mastermind Crescinco, Rockefeller recruited Robert W. Purcell, a market-savvy attorney who had been a principal figure in one of the biggest of the U.S. mutual fund groups, Investors Diversified Services. Gruff and utterly driven by the bottom line, Purcell was completely bereft of the social improvement instincts that had driven his predecessors at IBEC. "When we are philanthropic," he was fond of saying, "it simply means that somebody has made a mistake."

"This confusion of business and philanthropy was there at IBEC all the time," Purcell would recall years later. "I had a number of discussions with Nelson, and Nelson told me to run it as a business." And Purcell did exactly that. Although most of Crescinco's assets were invested in Brazilian companies, a small core of its portfolio—some 6 percent—consisted of stakes in such U.S. giants as Sears, Roebuck and General Motors, ostensibly because they had operations in Brazil. Those U.S. holdings turned out to be the best-performing stocks in the fund and were a principal reason why Crescinco was so popular.

Asked to advise on IBEC's own holdings, Purcell suggested that earnings could be stabilized through some sound strategic investments—in U.S. companies. Consequently, in the course of 1956 IBEC acquired a Cleveland, Ohio, manufacturer of vegetable oil extracting machinery. Other U.S. investments—in an Akron hydraulic valve maker, in a Connecticut poultry breeder, and in a housing development near Pompano Beach, Florida—would follow.

"They were good investments," boasts Purcell. "There were times when they kind of kept IBEC alive." Still, while no one would gainsay their steadying effect on IBEC's earnings, these investments were a startling departure from IBEC's past raison d'être. After all, it was not to boost the economies of Cleveland and Akron, nor to house the needy of Pompano Beach, that Nelson Rockefeller had founded IBEC. His creation was fast becoming just another multinational conglomerate, whose principal contributions to Latin American development were a chain of supermarkets and a high-flying mutual fund.

Grateful that at least it was no longer a perpetual drain on his bank account, happy to be rid of the monumental distraction, Rockefeller uncomplainingly accepted IBEC's change of course. There were other enterprises, other missions, to preoccupy him now.

The Latin American ventures, the art and architecture projects, the tending of his family's interests: all these were, for Nelson Rockefeller, diversions, momentarily absorbing sideshows in which he could invest some portion of his formidable reserves of energy. Even as he threw himself into these activities, he kept his eye on the larger stage, the stage from which he was a temporary exile. Even as he acquired and invested and gallivanted around the world, he plotted his return.

He held on to his one continuing link to official Washington, his chairmanship of the seemingly never-ending President's Advisory Commission on Government Organization. PACGO gave him continuing entrée to Eisenhower, a chance to show up at the White House for luncheons and presidential stag dinners. It also gave him a justification to maintain the house on Foxhall Road—along with the elaborate antiwiretapping system the FBI had installed there at his insistence. When the bureau contacted Rockefeller after his departure as special assistant to find out when it might be convenient to remove the system, Rockefeller insisted that the devices had to remain—because of his involvement with PACGO.

Rockefeller was eager to revalidate his credentials as a Republican, and Eisenhower, loyalist of the first order. With the President, in early 1956, still uncertain whether to try for a second term, Rockefeller was among the faithful ardently encouraging him to run again. That January, he helped organize a "Salute to Eisenhower" at Madison Square Garden, a bald-faced replay of the "I Like Ike" rally that had helped clinch Eisenhower's decision in 1952 (and which a then-noncommittal Rockefeller had declined to finance).

Once the President made up his mind, Rockefeller stumped enthusiastically on his behalf, passionately defending the very foreign policy that, in private, he had so bitterly assailed. At the same time, he rallied to the side of his erstwhile ally in the administration wars, Richard Nixon, whose place on the ticket was by no means assured; Eisenhower himself, sobered by his illness, was said to have his doubts about his number two. Rockefeller, however, had none. In mid-March, after the New Hampshire primary, he wrote Sherman Adams expressing his delight with the outcome, "especially the write-in for Mr. Nixon."

Joined by his brothers, Rockefeller opened his wallet to the national campaign, financing, among other things, a gala birthday tribute to the President in late October. And when all the votes were counted, and another Eisenhower landslide was achieved, Rockefeller was the happy recipient of a presidential letter that testified to Eisenhower's gratitude.

"The Republican Party does have another opportunity—and I hope you will be in the forefront of those who help shape its destiny," the President wrote.

Yet it was one thing to earn the President's gratitude and goodwill, and quite another, as Rockefeller well knew, to translate it into the hard currency of power. No longer content to wait until the administration gods smiled on him, Rockefeller had already set in motion a formidable mechanism that would, he earnestly believed, secure him a platform and a power base independent of, and immune to, the machinations of the Humphreys and the Dulleses. And he attached to this exercise a certain evangelical component: what resulted, he was convinced, would be not only a boon for Nelson Rockefeller but a godsend for the nation and the world.

"Just before he left for South America last week, Nelson Rockefeller called up and asked if I would do a job for him," Adolf Berle recorded in his diary on April 4. " 'Tell me where we will be twenty years from now,' he said, 'and what the problems will be.' "

"I told him that no sane man would take an assignment like that. He said that was why he had asked me. I agreed to do the job."

Thus was born the Special Studies Project.

The concept of the project could be traced back directly to the Quantico exercises: Rockefeller's convocation of big-dome academics, military strategists, and policy makers, brought together to formulate new game plans for an idea-starved administration. But its true antecedents date back much earlier, to the Point Four Partners in Progress committee and, going back even further, to the prewar Greenwich Village townhouse meetings of The Group. Interminable brainstorming sessions—the sort of intellectual sparring matches that most other men of action shunned like the plague—were, for Nelson Rockefeller, sources of endless stimulation and sustenance. What other men derived from reading, Rockefeller, with his dyslexia and his impatience with the written word, derived from discussion. "The best way to read a book," he would say, "is to talk with the author."

"Nelson was always attracted by bright, articulate people," recalled a participant in several of those forums. "He loved to suck out of them what he could get." That this penchant was often mocked—even Eisenhower, after all, was moved to waspishly note that "Nelson is too used to borrowing brains instead of using his own"—and often, as in Partners in Progress and Quantico II, proved fruitless and futile, did not bother Rockefeller in the slightest. He had a permanent gusto for ideas, and an abiding, sometimes naive, belief in their power. He collected them with the same avidity with which he stormed through Caracas street markets—and often with less discernment. As one friend put it, "If Nelson has a major weakness, it is the lack of a sufficient critical faculty."

The first whiff of his new project came in January, just days after his return to private life. A memo, aptly entitled "What Is to Be Done?," author unknown, was circulated among his associates, proposing another take on Rockefeller's ill-fated Action Program of early December. It would meet the "total threat of Soviet Communism" through "research" that would study how to knit together "our military, political, psychological capabilities into a single strategic weapon."

To lay the groundwork for the project, Rockefeller brought in Franklin Lindsay, one of his legion of consultants on the Quantico seminars. Another example of that species of Cold War theoretician who could glide effortlessly between the worlds of intelligence and academia—he had worked, in turn, for the CIA and then the Ford Foundation—Lindsay was perfectly at home with political warfare concepts. Nonetheless, he thought a Rockefeller study group should move in a different direction.

"I was very much concerned with the coming elections," he recalls, "and that down the road, there should be developed a liberal Republican position on international affairs. I wrote a memorandum to Nelson, suggesting that he set up a Republican think group, and we had two or three talks about it. He took my idea and accepted it, but he changed it to make it a bipartisan group."

The more Rockefeller toyed with the idea, the broader and airier the concept became. His "think group" would plot out not only a diplomatic strategy for the nation but also a military one and an economic one. It would not examine these areas piecemeal, but as part of an integrated approach, a "basic U.S. posture." And its time frame would not be the next four years, but the next fifteen or twenty.

The project he envisioned was the sort of long-range, big-think exercise usually handled by the larger foundations. And it just so happened that he knew of a foundation that would be happy to fund it: the Rockefeller Brothers Fund, whose chairman was now Nelson A. Rockefeller.

There was the small matter of getting his brothers' assent, but none of them were inclined to stand in his way. They recognized, as Laurance put it, that "Nelson liked to look at the long term, the big picture." "We all agreed that it was a good idea," says David. "I was enthusiastic"—so much so that he offered to kick in some additional funds of his own to finance it.

The brothers accepted the fact that the study might serve as yet another vehicle for Nelson's personal ambition, but, David points out, they believed "it certainly was not done exclusively or specifically for that purpose. It was done because he saw a need."

Whatever his motives were for undertaking the study, it was hard not to see it redounding to Nelson Rockefeller's benefit. At worst, he was pouring his money and energy into a noble but ineffectual experiment. At best, he was charting new directions and husbanding new ideas for a nation, and a world, in flux, and emerging, in the process, as the most farsighted of political leaders. Ignored and scorned as a White House insider, he would recast himself as the most influential of outsiders.

But first he had to find someone to direct the study, someone with the intellectual firepower to fill in its vague contours. His first choice, Lindsay, turned down the job, because he had just accepted a position at the management consulting firm of McKinsey & Co.

It was then that Henry Kissinger's name came up. Over lunch at Washington's Hay-Adams Hotel, Rockefeller asked Bill Kintner and Bill Elliott, Kissinger's old Harvard mentor, whom they thought he should put in charge of the panel, and they unhesitatingly recommended Kissinger. Recalling the up-and-coming young academic's work for Quantico II, Rockefeller needed little persuading.

At the time he was approached, Kissinger was deep in work on his book on nuclear weapons and foreign policy, the product of his studies for the Council on Foreign Relations. To accept Rockefeller's offer meant stretching himself thin at a juncture when he needed all the intellectual concentration he could muster to complete his groundbreaking tome.

Nevertheless, he accepted. Anyone who knew anything about him expected he would. As Kintner points out, "Henry was very bright and very ambitious, and Nelson was a very good thing to latch on to."

Besides, Rockefeller had assured him that the whole project would take only six months, "at the outside." What's more, when Kissinger expressed some apprehension about having to write the report—he would be happy, he said, to offer general advice, but he didn't want the writing burden—Rockefeller told him not to worry, that was exactly the role he had in mind for him.

Neither promise, Kissinger would learn soon enough, amounted to very much.

To work with Kissinger, Rockefeller assigned Nancy Hanks. Officially, her job was to shoulder the project's administrative load; unofficially, it was to keep the mercurial Harvard man on track. Hanks was hardly thrilled with the assignment; she saw it as one more indication of her exile from Rockefeller's inner circle. Reluctantly, after a long morale-boosting talk with Rockefeller, she took on the job.

By early summer, when Rockefeller set off for a long African vacation with his family, the project had acquired an imposing title—it was now the Special Studies Project—and an ambitious superstructure that dwarfed any of Rockefeller's earlier study groups.

There would be one overall panel, along with six subpanels, each of which would examine a vast area of American policy. Military and security objectives would be the focus of one subpanel. Foreign policy would be examined by another. International economic strategy, U.S. economic policy, and human resources planning would all get separate subpanels. Finally, in a quasi-replication of Rockefeller's work on PACGO, the sixth subpanel would ponder possible changes in the structure of the American government.

To give some focus to these subgroups—so they would not, in Kissinger's words, "spend so much time arguing what it is they should argue about"—he and Rockefeller decided to commission papers from an army of experts in each field. By the time they were through handing out the assignments that spring, Rockefeller and Kissinger presided, at least temporarily, over the most far-reaching think tank America had ever seen. Topics ranging from colonialism to farm policy, from social welfare to guerrilla warfare, were studied by leading lights from Yale, Harvard, the University of Chicago, and the University of California at Berkeley. A grand total of ninety-eight papers were commissioned that spring. All were due by the panel's first meetings in the fall, and all had to be digested somehow by Henry Kissinger.

Rockefeller, meanwhile, was pulling together the membership of his overall panel. The group he assembled was a distinguished, middle-of-the-road lot, full of the respectable heavyweights who populated elite corporate boards across the country. He had big businessmen—Justin Dart, the president of Rexall Drug, Thomas McCabe, the president of Scott Paper, and Bell & Howell president Charles Percy, widely regarded as corporate America's brightest young star. He had ex-generals: former U.S. commander in Europe Lucius Clay and retired Air Force general James McCormack, Jr. He had media titans: Time-Life boss Henry Luce and RCA chief David Sarnoff. He had university presidents: Theodore Hesburgh of Notre Dame and John Dickey of Dartmouth. And he had foundation bosses: Dean Rusk, the president of the Rockefeller Foundation, and John Gardner, the president of the Carnegie Corporation.

Rockefeller also included in the group a fair sprinkling of faces from his past: Adolf Berle and Oveta Culp Hobby and Anna Rosenberg and clothing workers' union boss Jacob Potofsky. (Before asking Potofsky, however, Rockefeller was careful to clear it with George Meany.) And, from his family, both Laurance and John 3rd agreed to serve.

Mainstream to a fault, the closest Rockefeller's panel came to a wild-eyed left-winger was Berle. The only member who could lay claim to eclectic thinking was physicist Edward Teller, the archconservative father of the hydrogen bomb.

Only a few whom Rockefeller asked to serve voiced any doubts about the exercise; one who did was Chester Bowles, the former ambassador to India and governor of Connecticut, whose relationship with Rockefeller dated back to World War II. Disquieted by the conservative cast of characters, the liberal Bowles warned Rockefeller that "either you'll have a terribly namby-pamby report that won't say anything—in which case we'll all be embarrassed about it, and it will be a waste of time—or, if it does say anything, there'll be such violent disputes over everything that I'll have to spend the whole rest of the winter or summer writing my minority report. And I haven't got the time to do that."

"That won't happen," Rockefeller vehemently insisted. "The reports will be ones that you'll sign, and they'll be strong." He suggested that Bowles speak with Kissinger, who was equally insistent on that point. Kissinger said he had shared Bowles's concerns earlier on and had taken them up with Rockefeller, who had assured him "it was going to be a liberal report and he would see to it."

Bowles still had his reservations, but he signed on. He took Rockefeller at his word that the report would be strong, and "liberal."

The Special Studies group did not meet for the first time until November 20. In the meantime, much had happened in the world to justify the mammoth planning project Rockefeller was undertaking.

A full-blown global crisis had erupted in the Middle East when Nasser, in late July, nationalized the Suez Canal. After months of fruitless international wrangling, British, French, and Israeli forces jointly invaded Egypt. Breaking with its staunchest allies, the United States condemned the assault and demanded that the invading forces withdraw. Their capitulation, in the face of American pressure, marked, to some, a turning point in the Cold War, a breach of the hitherto impregnable Western alliance.

At the same time, events of equal gravity were rending the Iron Curtain. Civil unrest in Hungary had exploded into full-fledged revolution, with Soviet tanks set aflame and government buildings seized by insurgent forces. Alarmed that the fate of their satellite empire was at stake, Soviet leaders sent in the Red Army in the first week of November to crush the rebellion. Within days, thirty thousand Hungarians lay dead. Even though the United States, through the broadcasts of Radio Free Europe, had egged on the rebels, the Eisenhower administration, fearing the crisis could flare into a world war, drew back from direct intervention.

To Rockefeller and Kissinger, the squeamish, helter-skelter administration response to these twin crises pointed up the anomie at the heart of U.S. policy making. "What really seems to be lacking in us is a sense of mission," Kissinger wrote Adolf Berle. "Every decade, the experts are wrong precisely because they are unwilling to face the fact that without great goals it is impossible to achieve great things. . . . We never seem to be in a position to exploit an opening because we engage in endless debates about whether it is an opening or not and by the time we get ready to do something, the opportunity has passed us by.

"At the risk of being blasphemous, one might say that if Christ had been advised by a policy planning staff, he would never have mounted the Cross."

To forge "great goals," to create "a sense of mission": such was the mandate with which Rockefeller and Kissinger charged their Special Studies group.

The first convocation of Rockefeller's panel commenced at 5 P.M. sharp in the faux Baroque splendor of the Plaza Hotel's Crystal Room. Rockefeller welcomed them all on behalf of the Rockefeller Brothers Fund, and then launched into a grandiose discourse on what he hoped to accomplish. Referring to the "last few tragic weeks" (an allusion to the ill-fated Hungarian uprising), he spoke of a world "torn by revolutionary forces": some positive, such as the aspirations of the emerging colonial peoples, and others negative, namely a "Soviet-Communist bloc" bent on "the destruction of all the basic values that are our heritage." It was America's task to master those forces, and it could do so *only* if it had a "clear sense of purpose." That was where the Special Studies came in. Gazing out at the distinguished personages he had assembled, Rockefeller declared that "no group of men and women can contribute more to helping our nation plant its feet squarely on the road that leads to the common destiny of all."

He then left it to Kissinger—whom he introduced in the most glowing terms—to explain, via a slide show, the nuts and bolts of how the studies would work and the schedule.

All was organized with impeccable Room 5600 precision. After a very brief break for cocktails, the group reconvened for dinner, with the tables organized by subpanels. The gathering ran until past ten—and at nine-thirty the next morning, the participants were expected back at the Plaza to continue the subpanel deliberations and review the stack of academic papers that framed the key issues for them.

In every respect—in their brusque, no-nonsense pace, in their enthusiastic barreling ahead, with barely enough time for sleep—the panels perfectly reflected the style of their patron. At the same time, the pace revealed Kissinger's determination to keep the proceedings on a tight leash and to avoid the bombastic quagmires that such commissions were prone to sink into.

Rockefeller himself, after his opening remarks, said little, aside from reminding his panelists, every once in a while, of the need for "concepts"; it was the lack of "concepts," he said, that was responsible for the recent failures of U.S. foreign policy. In general, he seemed content—as was the case with his past study commissions—to let all the others have their say.

His willingness to hear everyone out was indicative not only of his skillful handling of egos but of his own lack of preconceptions, beyond certain broad parameters, as to what his reports would actually say. He wanted to shape national objectives and a national strategy, but he was fairly open-minded as to what that strategy should be. "He was educable," notes Oscar Ruebhausen, one of his advisers on the study, "and he was open, always, to new ideas, so that he didn't know precisely where he was going to come out. He was constantly growing, and everything was put through his own meat chopper, his own thinking process."

Nevertheless, as the months passed, and the panelists gathered in a succession of posh venues—the Arden House conference center in Westchester, the Sleepy Hollow Country Club, the Louis XIV Suite at the St. Regis—certain ideas moved to the forefront. It was no coincidence that those ideas were the closely related progeny of the two most forceful intellects connected with the Special Studies Project: Kissinger and Edward Teller. "Once in a while," Rockefeller would later gush, "I have encountered an individual of energy, dedication and genius so extraordinary as to mark him indelibly on my memory and leave me eternally in his debt for the services he has rendered mankind. One such person is Henry Kissinger. Another is Dr. Edward Teller."

Like Kissinger a European Jewish émigré (Budapest-born, Teller came to the United States in 1935), the forty-eight-year-old Teller had already reaped the rich harvest of controversy that his younger counterpart would experience two decades hence. That he was one of the preeminent physicists of the age was beyond question: an early participant in the Manhattan Project that developed the atomic bomb, Teller soon emerged as the principal theoretician behind the far more potent hydrogen bomb. As much as any individual, Teller unleashed the staggeringly destructive potential of thermonuclear weaponry. But it was not Teller's theories, but Teller's avid pursuit of them, that gave him his national notoriety. While other fathers of the nuclear age, such as J. Robert Oppenheimer, shuddered at the destructive powers they had wrought and brooded that, in Oppenheimer's words, they have now "known sin," Teller suffered from no such moral compunctions. Obsessed, as a scientist, with the development of his "Super" (the early nickname of the H-bomb), Teller openly derided the qualms of his peers. "The important thing in any science," he said, "is to do the things that can be done." He became, in the postwar years, the single most outspoken scientific proselytizer for the new weaponry, a saturnine, bushy-eyebrowed figure who could well have been, along with Kissinger, the inspiration for Stanley Kubrick's Dr. Strangelove.

The distaste for Teller among many of his confreres turned to outright revulsion after his testimony at Oppenheimer's AEC security hearing in 1954. Waffling on the issue of whether his old colleague was or wasn't a security risk, Teller finally suggested it "would be wiser not to grant clearance." When the government heeded Teller's advice, Teller found himself ostracized by fellow physicists who refused, in public encounters, to even shake the hand of the man they considered a scientific Judas.

Yet while he was subjected to constant opprobrium, Teller was also, in many circles, a figure of considerable esteem. The Cold War, and the Soviets' development of their own thermonuclear capability, served to validate his foresight; in an America committed to a vast nuclear stockpile, Teller was no longer a prophet without honor. Although he was fond of disparaging the broad moral pronunciamentos of fellow scientists ("There is a time for scientists and movie stars and people who have flown the Atlantic to restrain their opinions lest they be taken more seriously than they should be," he told an interviewer), Teller was hardly shy himself about sharing his wisdom on the affairs of the day with all who sought it.

Assigned to the subpanel on defense, Teller instantly asserted himself. Two weeks after the first meeting, he wrote the subpanel's chairman, General James McCormack, Jr., offering some "possible statements which our group might want to make." They were all blockbusters, and all perfect expressions of Teller's views on the nuclear era.

Among Teller's "possible statements" was this: "Atomic weapons will be used in future wars against the enemy's armed forces. Public opinion in our country and abroad must be adequately prepared for such use." And this: "Army planning should concentrate on the building of small, highly mobile, atomically armed units." Others might regard nuclear arms as unthinkable tools of mass destruction, to be unsheathed in only the most dire of circumstances; to Teller, they were simply alternative elements of America's arsenal. ("The distinction between nuclear warfare and conventional warfare, which is paramount in the public mind, leads to unrealistic policy decisions," he wrote McCormack.)

Considering nuclear warfare highly thinkable, Teller also considered it survivable—as long as the country prepared for the worst. He urged the Rockefeller panel to call for "deep underground mass shelters." It is, he argued, "technically and economically feasible to provide the majority of our crowded population with shelters which are safe against any eventuality except a direct hit by an H-bomb. . . . They should be equipped in such a way that people can stay in them for a time like two weeks." The United States' present civil defense effort, he complained, "is worse than useless."

Teller also urged a strong stance on disarmament: that is, a strong stance *against* it. "It is likely that nuclear weapons will be developed by an increasing number of nations," he contended. "Limitations of such development are not likely to work, and will cause resentment." Disarmament, he insisted, "leads to an unstable situation."

For the most part, Teller's views, extreme as they were, went unchallenged by Rockefeller and other members of the Special Studies group. There were a few cavils. "What about fallout?" Anna Rosenberg asked at one point. (Not to worry, Teller replied. The bigger warheads would soon have negligible fallout, and as for the smaller ones, they would "in the end produce considerable fallout but those fortunately will produce that fallout only locally.") And both Lucius Clay and Dean Rusk wondered if it might be "reckless" to assume, as Teller did, that his limited conflicts would not escalate into all-out nuclear confrontations. (Teller played down the risk—and, in any case, he said, "it happens that we live in a dangerous world.")

On the rare occasions when he was openly challenged, Teller was dismissive of his questioner, to the point of rudeness. When Adolf Berle began expounding on the dangers of nuclear radiation, Teller cut him off. "There is no more danger of radiation in those circumstances"—and here Teller yanked the watch off his wrist and tossed it down the table toward Berle—"than there is in this watch." Infuriated, Berle stormed out of the room, with Rockefeller at his heels, trying to calm him down.

Among the few with the intellectual prowess and arrogance to take Teller on head-to-head was Henry Kissinger. But Kissinger chose not to—because Kissinger, as it happened, agreed wholeheartedly with Teller's views. After hearing the physicist's exposition, Kissinger dropped him a note bubbling over with enthusiasm: "Having sat through two years of meetings on military policy, I can tell you that I have derived more new ideas from you than from anyone else." And this was hardly empty flattery. In a letter to General James Gavin, another outspoken critic of U.S. military preparedness, Kissinger described the initial meeting of the defense subpanel: "You know my views, of course, and I was very excited by Dr. Teller's. As you might suspect, we found ourselves in almost complete agreement."

Indeed, Kissinger at that very moment was putting the finishing touches on a book that vigorously advocated a nuclear policy virtually identical to Teller's. In *Nuclear Weapons and Foreign Policy,* based on his work for the Council on Foreign Relations, Kissinger would argue that "limited nuclear war represents our most effective strategy." And, by happy coincidence, when the book was published in the summer of 1957, the reviewer *The New York Times Book Review* assigned to it was none other than Edward Teller—who, of course, had nothing but praise for the work.

The book's surprising success—it was on the best-seller list for fourteen weeks and stirred a national debate on nuclear warfare that reached the highest levels of government—served to instantly legitimize the Teller-Kissinger thesis. Almost overnight, the concept of limited nuclear war moved from the far-out to the mainstream. That it would now figure as a prime tenet of the Rockefeller panel reports was a foregone conclusion.

In his voracious hunt for ideas, Nelson Rockefeller scooped up those of Kissinger and Teller and incorporated them into his worldview. Despite his congenital optimism, he fully agreed with their gloomy assessment of Cold War realities. Their militant views, after all, had been foreshadowed by the Quantico II report (authored by Kissinger) and the Action Program for Free World Strength—both of which Rockefeller had endorsed and sent on to the President. "On the basic approach," Kissinger would later say, "my view and Nelson's were essentially the same. I put it into a more strategic framework, but it was fundamentally the same view."

The idea of a winnable nuclear conflict—winnable through will and technology and the vast network of catacombs in which the populace would be shielded—was adopted by Rockefeller and made his own.

He was equally comfortable with other aspects of the plan his military subpanel was hatching.

After hearing alarming confidential CIA assessments of the metastasizing Soviet military machine—that as much as 15 percent of the U.S.S.R. gross national product was devoted to military programs—the group agreed that a counter buildup by the United States was in order. The current defense budget, they concluded, was at least 10 percent below what it should be, and that was not accounting for all the additional measures, such as fallout shelters, that Teller was advocating. America was rapidly losing its lead in the arms race—and it was time, the panel agreed, to go public and sound the alarm.

The sense of urgency, the sense, as the subpanel's chairman put it, that they were America's "conscience," was wholeheartedly shared by Rockefeller. The call for an arms buildup had been an essential element in all his previous reports—in Quantico I, Quantico II, and the Action Program—and he saw it as even more imperative now. The public, he told an early meeting of the Special Studies group, "was not really informed of the nature and character of the threat and what was necessary on their part in the way of sacrifices either in terms of the military or in terms of civil defense. It is essential that they be informed if we are going to do what is needed."

And so, a recitation of America's defense inadequacies, and a call for at least $3 billion a year to cure them, became a paramount element in the subpanel report.

As Rockefeller's panelists eagerly assented to this call to arms, Chester Bowles raised a lone voice in protest. "Aren't we going to deal with the biggest problem of all, which is arms control?" he asked. Teller, sitting directly across the table, was scornful. "Why should we?" he said. "It's totally unrealistic to even think about it and nonsense to even consider it." Nonetheless, the other participants—Rockefeller included—agreed that *something* should be said about disarmament, and something was: namely, a point-by-point analysis of why the quest for arms reduction was a fruitless chimera, a blistering bit of ratiocination that clearly bore the Kissinger-Teller stamp. "The illusion of security brought about by a spurious agreement to disarm would be a poor substitute for vigilance based on strength," the military subpanel concluded.

Meanwhile, the Special Studies group took on another of Rockefeller's pet causes: Defense Department reorganization. Four years earlier, Rockefeller had studied the department for the new administration, but had hesitated, for political reasons, to tackle the thorniest issues: interservice rivalry and the lack of a coherent, unified strategic framework at the Pentagon. But now, as outsiders, his Special Studies panel had no such reluctance. Concluding that the Pentagon's organization was hopelessly antique, wasteful, and inefficient, they decided it was time to unify the armed services under a single command structure, reducing the individual departments—the Army, the Navy, the Marines, and the Air Force—to mere recruitment and training vehicles.

It was a bold plan. Coming on top of the military panel's other recommendations—for an arms buildup and for fallout shelters and for the legitimacy of limited nuclear war—it guaranteed that Rockefeller would keep at least one of his promises about his Special Studies. The reports, he had vowed to a doubting Chester Bowles, "will be strong." Whether they would also be "liberal," as he also promised Bowles, depended on one's definition of liberalism.

Rockefeller's other commitments, notably the commitment to Kissinger and others that the whole project would be completed within six months, were not so easily kept.

The self-imposed deadline came and went with none of the subpanels even close to producing a finished report. Just before adjourning the work for the summer of 1957, Rockefeller spoke of completing all the panel reports by the end of the year, but no one, probably not even Rockefeller himself, believed it would happen. "We just have to keep our faith, and go forward," he enjoined his panelists before excusing them for the summer.

Despite Rockefeller's and Kissinger's determination to keep the discussions on course, the meetings inevitably drifted into the realm of the recondite. How could anyone, after all, possibly avoid mind-numbing abstractions if the topic at hand was, as in the case of Subpanel VII, "The Moral Framework of National Purpose"? At this panel's sessions, there was much quoting of Spinoza, much discussion of moral relativism, and much fretting about "Kantian blight."

The Special Studies participants were also caught up in considerable soul-searching about the potentially negative tone of their report: a not unnatural worry, in view of how the military study, at least, was coming out. As Charles Percy put it, "I would hate to have someone pick up and read the full report and say, oh my gosh, I don't want to live in these next fifteen years, they are going to be terrible!" Rockefeller tried to reassure him: "Well, I can't imagine this report ending up on a hopeless or negative tone . . . there are so damn many ideas and so much enthusiasm."

As the meetings ground on, concern was also voiced about the potential size of the report. Rockefeller must have sent shivers down Kissinger's spine with his response: "I was thinking in terms of *Reader's Digest* length." When someone pointed out that it might be tougher to draft ten thousand words out of all this material than a hundred thousand, Rockefeller blithely replied, "The *Reader's Digest* does it."

"Henry Kissinger is plumb worn out," Nancy Hanks observed—and *that* was in June 1956, when the Special Studies project was just getting off the ground.

As the months rolled by, as he sat through interminable discussions and waded through heaps of expert papers and contemplated emulating the *Reader's Digest,* the pallor became ever more noticeable—as was his petulance. Never the soul of equanimity to begin with, the high-strung Kissinger sulked and groused and seethed as he contemplated Nelson Rockefeller's demands.

Most of the time, he kept his fury bottled up, but his co-workers at Special Studies could see the signs of his inner tension: the chewed fingernails, the continual cleaning and recleaning of his spectacles, the perspiration that coursed across his brow and saturated his shirts. Every so often, he could contain himself no longer, and he would storm into Rockefeller's office and resign, or at least threaten to; by Kissinger's later count, he resigned at least five times in the course of the project. Each time, Rockefeller would drape a consoling arm around his aide's shoulder, offer the right soothing words, remind him of his indispensability, and send him back into the trenches.

Throughout, Kissinger displayed a certain ambivalence about his involvement in the project: thrilled and flattered by Rockefeller's patronage, excited by his proximity to the influential figures on the panel, yet discreetly disdainful of the whole exercise. As Kissinger himself recalls, "Nelson would listen to anything in these committees, and figure at the end he'd get to the essence. My tolerance level wasn't as high as his." Typically, Kissinger would listen respectfully during the panel discussions—and then later privately offer his colleagues in the Rockefeller office acid commentary on the proceedings. Kershaw Burbank remembers one panel meeting when Henry Luce held forth. Kissinger reacted obsequiously—"he was practically rolling over on the floor before him"—but afterward, in the safe confines of his office, was absolutely cutting. "Oh, what a stupid man," he muttered. "A stupid man."

Kissinger's japeries even extended to his patron. At least two eyewitnesses remember Kissinger privately mocking Rockefeller. Burbank relates that "he'd do some little Nelson gesture, or tell us, 'Well, Nelson didn't do his homework again.' It was belittling." And another old Special Studies hand recalls dinner parties where Kissinger would "make fun of Nelson. He'd make deprecating remarks about Nelson's naive view of the world, that sort of thing."

These little acts of rebellion, however, almost never extended to their face-to-face encounters. At panel meetings, he would be downright fawning in Rockefeller's presence, nodding in agreement whenever the boss had something to say, gazing at Rockefeller, one witness would observe, "with the same nervous intensity a child might show when expressing an idea to his teacher."

To the exasperation of his colleagues, Kissinger was utterly incapable of saying no to Rockefeller's demands—even as he privately stewed about them. "Henry has been saying that NAR maneuvers him into things," Hanks noted, "whereas in fact it is greatly HAK's [Henry Kissinger's] fault because he will not say to NAR what he will or will not do; therefore NAR just assumes he will do it and then everyone gets under pressure—mostly Henry moaning to me that he will not do it."

And Rockefeller, for his part, insulated himself from Kissinger's complaints by delegating his care and feeding to associates like Oscar Ruebhausen. It was Ruebhausen, for instance, who dealt with his salary. "Henry really fooled me. He would tell me, 'Oscar, I don't care about money. All I'm concerned with is my intellectual capital,' " relates Ruebhausen. "But then he'd go to Nelson and say, 'Oscar won't give me enough money. Either Oscar's going to go, or I'll go.' So then Nelson would call me and say, 'Henry's concerned about money, and I told him I'd referred it back to you.' So I increased his salary."

But the aide who bore the brunt of Kissinger's nonstop tantrums was Nancy Hanks. "Nancy was the buffer," remembers Donna Mitchell, who worked briefly for Kissinger in the early days of the project. "She was the one who kept the lid on Henry." Subjected to his volatile mood swings, she did her best to bring him back to earth. As Laurance Rockefeller recalled, "She would assure him that he was appreciated, that there was no reason for him to resign, that there was no way he could resign—it would be terrible."

Yet even Hanks was moved on occasion to throw up her hands. "HAK has for my money let me and everyone else down," she confided to her parents at one point. "He's just close to being a psychological case. . . . Really has been like a child and dropped all responsibility as far as directing the Project is concerned. Puts all the blame on NAR and Oscar—for silly things such as not keeping in touch with him, etc. . . . Oscar and NAR just plumb fed up with him."

The combustible situation reached its flash point when work commenced on drafting the panel reports. "*Nobody* edits my copy," Kissinger had declared, but Rockefeller ignored this dictum and sent copies of his drafts to various of his aides for comment. As Kissinger sardonically remembers, "He had a cast of characters who would sit around, none of whom would ever admit that they didn't know anything, and they'd start fixing a sentence here and a sentence there." One day, when Louise Boyer phoned with some suggested revisions, Kissinger blew up. "Why don't you tell Nelson," he snapped, "that he's wasting his money buying Picassos? Why doesn't he get somebody to draw pictures and then get a bunch of housepainters, let them pick the colors and throw them at the board?"

So incensed was Kissinger that, as he tells the story, he warned Rockefeller at a dinner gathering that "if he did something that I objected to, again, I'd leave. I forget what it was; probably something petty. But anyway, he did it. So I just turned my back on him at dinner and walked out."

The next day, Kissinger came in to clean out his desk and found Rockefeller in his office, calmly sipping a cup of tea. It was time to clear the air. "Look,

Henry," said Rockefeller, "you're a strong man and I'm a strong man. Now, we have two choices. We can try to destroy each other, or we can try to work together."

"Basically," recalls Kissinger, "he never accepted the proposition that I might leave. The only question was, how I would stay." So Kissinger stayed.

Deep down, neither man had any wish to sever the alliance. Climber that he was, Kissinger simply could not turn his back on a connection with America's most powerful family and that family's most dynamic figure. And Rockefeller could not afford to lose the intellectual mainspring of his vast Special Studies machine, the one person capable of giving coherent shape to the whole sprawling enterprise. He knew he had something special in the jowly, bespectacled whirlwind from Harvard, someone whose depth and virtuosity surpassed that of all the gurus—the Rumls, the Mays, the Warrens, the Rostows—who had gone before him, someone whose potential role transcended their current project. And if he ever forgot, there were plenty of admiring panel members—unaware of what Kissinger was saying about them behind their backs—to remind him.

Charles Percy, for one, no mean judge of talent himself, was positively rhapsodic in his praise of Kissinger. "He is the best listener I have ever known," he wrote Rockefeller. "He has the patience of Job. His attributes are all the more remarkable when it is recognized that he is essentially a doer, an original thinker as well as a conciliator. Whenever I get discouraged about the potential leadership we have in this country and where we are going to find men to give our nation a sense of direction, I think of Henry Kissinger and feel better."

Rockefeller's reply to this, though brief, spoke volumes about his admiration for his deputy. "I agree with you," he told Percy, "about Henry Kissinger . . ."

All around the world, one day in early October 1957, radio operators began picking up a sound: an eerie, intermittent croak mysteriously emanating from somewhere beyond the earth's atmosphere. The source of the strange noise was a 23-inch, 184-pound metal sphere, circling the planet at an altitude of 560 miles and at a speed of 18,000 miles per hour. This was Sputnik, the first man-made object ever launched into space, and its appearance in the heavens portended a seismic shift in the global balance of power.

While the Eisenhower administration pooh-poohed the Soviet triumph (Defense's Charlie Wilson derided the artificial satellite as a "useless hunk of iron"), the American press, the intelligentsia, and most of the public knew better. Not only had the Russians, in launching the space age, scored a shattering propaganda coup, justifying their braggadocio about the Communist system's superiority, but they now wielded a potentially decisive weapon in the nuclear arms race. In *The New York Times*'s blunt words, "The launching of Sputnik means that Russia is ahead of the U.S. in rocket development. That lends substance to the Soviet claim of having at least a prototype of the 'ultimate weapon'—the intercontinental ballistic missile."

A sense of alarm seized the nation, as a new fear, "the missile gap," entered the lexicon. In Congress, there were calls for an investigation and vehement denunciation of Eisenhower's pinchpenny approach to defense and technology. "We have not kept in step with the needs of our times," declared the Senate Majority Leader, Lyndon Johnson, who called for "bold new thinking in defense and foreign policy." Searching for the root cause of the debacle, critics pointed to alleged deficiencies in America's educational system. A hitherto obscure treatise, *Why Johnny Can't Read,* rocketed to the top of the best-seller list. Among those chiming in was Edward Teller: "We have suffered a very serious defeat in a field where at least some of the most important engagements are carried out: the classroom," he told a group of educators.

Beset by insecurity, the American colossus plunged into a rare postwar interval of self-examination. If ever there was an ideal moment for a study of the nation's future course—for the very study Nelson Rockefeller had presciently championed—this was it.

But in early October 1957, eleven months after it was launched, Nelson Rockefeller's study was not even close to completion. Many of the subpanels were still meeting, still debating, and a frazzled Kissinger was struggling to make sense of the verbiage.

There was one subpanel, however, where consensus was clear, and where a draft report could be hammered out. This was the military subpanel—whose focus was now at the forefront of the nation's concerns.

Rather than wait for the rest of his subpanels to finish their work—no one knew how long that would be—Rockefeller decided to grab the opportunity the "useless hunk of iron" had handed him. He would rush the military report into release. In a letter to the Special Studies group members, Rockefeller explained that "the world situation made it clear that if maximum usefulness is to be achieved from the panel work, we should publish certain reports as soon as possible."

And so, in the course of the last two months of the year, Rockefeller and Kissinger scrambled to prepare the subpanel report for publication. Working through the Christmas holiday, Kissinger had the final version of the report ready by New Year's Eve. Rockefeller's plan was to distribute copies of it to the media the day after the New Year, for release four days later. At the same time, Doubleday would go to press with a paperback edition of the report, for sale to the public at fifty cents a copy.

Before he went public with it, however, Rockefeller sought to wield the report's influence privately. In fact, even before he had the final draft in hand, Rockefeller was vigorously promoting his military proposals in the corridors of power. Focusing on the plans for defense reorganization, he had Kissinger prepare a quick memo summarizing the recommendations, and in mid-October, at the height of the Sputnik furor, Rockefeller took the memo to the President. He knew Eisenhower would be receptive, because that summer he and other PACGO members had talked with the President about a Pentagon study. Eisenhower had been hesitant then, because a new Defense Secretary, Neil McElroy, had just been brought in, but by October he was ready to move. McElroy, however, was in no hurry, and as the year wound down he stalled off Rockefeller's bid to bring defense reorganization to the forefront.

Undaunted, Rockefeller urged Sherman Adams to make reorganization a principal theme of the President's State of the Union message. The speech would be given on January 9, three days after the Rockefeller panel report was due to hit the headlines.

"Arms Rise Urged Lest Reds Seize Lead in 2 Years" boomed the front page of *The New York Times.* "U.S. Must Act Fast or Lose Arms Race, Study Group Warns" reported the banner headline in *The Washington Post.* The attention garnered by the first of Rockefeller's reports exceeded even his own most exuberant hopes. The *Times* not only put it atop page one but actually devoted a full page inside to a summary of the key points—a rare honor for a private, nongovernment document. The report's findings were debated on editorial pages throughout the nation, and in the halls of Congress. Far and away the most talked-about aspect of the study was its blunt words on the state of the arms race: that the United States "is rapidly losing its lead over the U.S.S.R. in the military race" and that only a crash $3 billion-a-year program could stave off disaster. House Appropriations Committee chairman Clarence Cannon announced his hearty approval of the proposal. "No amount is too high for defense," he declared. In the Senate, Majority Leader Johnson asked Rockefeller to appear before his Preparedness Subcommittee.

Far less attention was paid to the aspect of the Rockefeller report dearer to Eisenhower's heart: the proposed armed services shake-up. And the flurry of publicity barely touched on what was, arguably, the panel's most chilling conclusion, the brainchild of Teller and Kissinger: that "in order to deter aggression, we must be prepared to fight a nuclear war either all-out or limited." Preparedness was now the public's paramount concern, and preparedness, or the lack of it, was the overriding message of the Rockefeller report.

Just how responsive a chord that message struck with the American people was dramatically demonstrated the day after the report came out, when Rockefeller appeared on NBC's *Today* morning show. At Rockefeller's prompting, the show's host, Dave Garroway, offered to send free copies to any viewers who wanted it. "We figured we might have to give away a thousand, two thousand copies," remembers Burbank. But by week's end, five mail trucks were lined up outside 30 Rockefeller Plaza, carrying more than 200,000 requests. Doubleday went back to press to print 400,000 more copies; half to go to the *Today* viewers (the cost of which was totally borne by the Rockefeller Brothers Fund) and half to be sold at bookstores and newsstands.

For what was, after all, a private think-tank document, the Rockefeller report was having an unprecedented influence. And this fact did not go unnoticed by the embattled resident of 1600 Pennsylvania Avenue.

While most observers regarded the report as a stinging rebuke of the administration's defense policies, Eisenhower chose to view it otherwise. Right after the study appeared, he wrote Rockefeller, "Despite the fact that momentarily the press has 'accentuated the negative' in reporting on the content of the study, I don't doubt that over the long run it will prove its value as a contribution to better public understanding of these important questions." He was particularly pleased, he said, by the proposals on defense reorganization—which "paralleled so closely the views I have myself long held."

Indeed, the very next day Eisenhower went before Congress to deliver his State of the Union message and followed precisely the path Rockefeller had urged upon him. Warning that the new weaponry "cut across all services, involve all services and transcend all services," he demanded an end to interservice rivalry and promised a Pentagon reorganization that would promote "real unity in the Defense establishment," particularly in technology and strategic planning. The speech amounted to an out-and-out endorsement of the Rockefeller report's approach. Two weeks later, when McElroy assembled a five-man committee to help structure the reorganization, the only nonmilitary, non-Defense Department member was Nelson Rockefeller.

Later that month, Chuck Percy sat next to the President at a Republican fund-raising dinner in Chicago, and asked him what he thought of the Special Studies report. Eisenhower replied that he had enjoyed reading it, and considered it "an exceptionally fine job." His only qualm about it was its emphasis on a specific defense spending goal; in his opinion, there was still much fat in the defense budget that could be trimmed. "His general response to the report, however, was *extremely* favorable," Percy reported to Rockefeller.

Elated by the acclaim for his military report, and confident now that the man in the White House was listening, Rockefeller stepped up the efforts to complete the rest of his Special Studies. Kissinger spoke about finishing it all in two months, but despite a string of workdays running to midnight and 1 A.M. the best that could be accomplished was more piecemeal releases of the subpanel findings. In April the report on the U.S. economy was published; in June came the reports on education and world trade. It was perhaps no coincidence that these were the subjects in which Kissinger had the least interest. The panel report that most engrossed him, the one on foreign affairs, was nowhere in sight.

There were more headlines as each report came out. The economic study was front-page news because it called for a major tax cut to revitalize an economy mired in recession, the education report because it proposed a sweeping overhaul of American educational practices. None of these, however, had the aura of crackling immediacy, the galvanic public appeal of the first of the reports; there were no more mail trucks parked outside 30 Rockefeller Plaza.

The reports' early luster may have dimmed, but on the whole, even in their still-incomplete state, they had more than served their purpose. "The main thing," Rockefeller told an interviewer, "is to stimulate public interest and focus attention." That much they had done—stirring the very debate on national policy and objectives that Rockefeller had cited as the principal reason for undertaking his studies. The reports had surely focused attention: and not just on the issues, but also on Nelson Rockefeller.

Few connected with the Special Studies had any illusions that the latter was not as compelling an objective of the project as the former. As Rockefeller's old HEW aide Rod Perkins, who had returned to the fold to help out, puts it, "I think that everyone recognized that Nelson wouldn't be doing it if he hadn't had a long-term desire to participate in national policy making in some way or other." Yet, at the same time, the participants had convinced themselves that the public interest, and Rockefeller's own, were not at all incompatible. Reflected Charles Percy, three decades later, "Who could argue with the fact that what we did was certainly in the national interest? And if it got him better prepared, if it got him better known—well, there's nothing wrong with that, really, if the end result is something that's really good for the country."

Marshaling the country's best minds and his own formidable resources (in the first two years, the project had cost the Rockefeller Brothers Fund over half a million dollars), Rockefeller had given the nation a blueprint, and himself a political identity: a vehement hawk on military matters, an enlightened progressive on social programs, an ardent foe of the budget-balancing propensities of the current administration.

All in all, it was a considerable achievement—but, in the immediate thrust of Rockefeller's political career, it would pale in significance beside the simultaneous efforts of a bushy-haired, hatchet-nosed politico from Ticonderoga, New York, an operator who would sooner attend a luncheon of the Plattsburgh Rotary than a splendiferous think tank at the Plaza.

For while Rockefeller was erecting the most magnificent of platforms for himself, exchanging great ideas with the likes of Henry Luce and Henry Kissinger, L. Judson Morhouse—unintellectual, unreflective, and unconcerned about the great issues of the day—was venturing forth from his dairy farm, hard by the shores of Lake George, to craft a candidacy.

Thirty-seven

Cram Course

"Breezy" was the nickname Jud Morhouse's classmates fastened on him at Middlebury College, and two decades later the tag was just as apt. A beefy, voluble six-footer, Morhouse glad-handed his way across the landscape of New York State, heartily clapping the backs of Republican functionaries at ten-dollar-a-plate fund-raisers, merrily swapping yarns with wizened county clerks over coffee and apple cobblers at the local café. It was all part of a day's work for him, as chairman of the New York State Republican Party. And, by most accounts, few had ever been better at the job.

He had been an unlikely and obscure choice when Tom Dewey had tapped him to take over the party reins back in 1954—a forty-year-old journeyman political hand of no special distinction or prominence. His climb had been of a backcountry variety that many thought had gone out of style with Abraham Lincoln: after dropping out of Middlebury, he clerked at a Ticonderoga law firm, studying nights for his bar exam. Morhouse's first foray into politics was a run, at age twenty-three, for town justice of the peace; he lost, but four years later ran again and won. Following World War II Army service (where he rose from private to first lieutenant) Morhouse returned to Ticonderoga and was elected to the first of three uneventful terms as state assemblyman for Essex County.

He left the Assembly in the early 1950s to become executive director of the Good Roads Association, a trade association of contractors eager to cash in on the era's mega-project, the New York State Thruway. And, oddly, it was in his work as a lobbyist, rather than as a legislator, that Morhouse caught Dewey's eye. The thruway was to be the crowning glory of Dewey's final years as governor, and Morhouse's tireless, and effective, campaigning on the project's behalf impressed the usually unimpressionable chief executive. Hurriedly seeking a new party chairman when his previous handpicked choice, Dean Taylor, stepped down near the end of the 1954 campaign, and looking for someone who was unaligned with the various contending party factions, Dewey turned to Morhouse. "We were at a ribbon cutting for a section of the thruway," remembers Dewey aide R. Burdell Bixby. "Jud would always be there for the ribbon cuttings, and I said to Dewey, 'Hey, you just found your answer. Let's get Jud Morhouse.' "

It was not the best of times to assume the party chairmanship. With Dewey declining to run for a fourth term, the GOP's standard-bearer that year was Senator Irving M. Ives, who despite a sterling reputation was edged out for the governorship by a man with even more enviable credentials: W. Averell Harriman. There was some consolation for the Republicans in the thinness of the victor's margin (a mere 11,000 votes, the smallest edge in state history) and in their retention of control of both houses of the legislature. Nonetheless, for the first time in a dozen years the GOP had to cope with the loss of gubernatorial power—and all the patronage and perquisites that went with it.

In the face of this debacle, the new chairman labored mightily to pull the party out of its postelection malaise and lay the groundwork for its comeback. Crisscrossing the state in his chartered four-seat plane, he touched down in every one of the sixty-two counties, hustling through an endless round of party rallies, farm barbecues, and Kiwanis lunches. "In my first eight months as chairman," Morhouse recalled, "I guess I managed to spend about twenty days with my family." As one newspaper commentator observed, "Under Dewey many of the leaders had not only grown older but cynical as well. They set back to watch the young man do his stuff. What they have seen has amazed them. . . . No meeting is too small for his attention, no meeting is too distant and he uses airplanes as most folks use automobiles."

Morhouse laid out a five-point program to revitalize the state GOP: "Have good candidates . . . Take the right side of the issues . . . Raise the dough . . . Get good public relations . . . And build that organization." Seeking to inject some youthful vigor into the sclerotic party, he persuaded county chairmen to designate young Republicans between twenty-one and thirty as "alternates" to the county committees. And, to get a handle on where the party was weakest, he had his Albany research staff produce an election-by-election breakdown of every one of the state's ten thousand election districts.

His emphasis on public relations paid off when he brought in a veteran Associated Press hand, Harry O'Donnell, to head his Albany "news bureau." Thanks to the wily O'Donnell, the party out of power—and Jud Morhouse—enjoyed unprecedented media coverage. "Harry was the best press person I ever saw," says veteran political reporter Jack Germond, who cut his journalistic teeth covering the Albany scene in the mid-1950s. "He knew how to play the wire services, and the wire services were very important back then. On every story they put out on Harriman, Harry would somehow get Morhouse into the second or third paragraph. He made Morhouse into an equal time vehicle." Ready to hammer the governor at every opportunity (O'Donnell was known to carry two press releases in his pocket, one if Harriman went one way on an issue, one if he went the other), O'Donnell "built this image of Harriman as a vacillating, weak figure," remembers Germond. "He kept using this theme, that Harriman was weak, until it crystallized in people's minds."

Less than two years after he took over, Morhouse's bravura performance was gaining raves from the GOP elite. "Morhouse is doing a tremendous job in New York," Dewey told the party's national campaign director, Robert Humphreys. "He has a political sixth sense."

The most vaunted recognition of Morhouse's achievements came when Vice President Nixon asked him to second his nomination at the 1956 national convention at the Cow Palace in San Francisco. As *Newsday* noted, "Morhouse will stand before the convention and the nationwide television audience for only two minutes. But the simple fact that he is there—in one of the convention's most prominent spots—indicates his growing political stature."

The newspaper went on to observe that "Morhouse's political future is riding on two elections—the presidential voting of 1956 and the gubernatorial balloting of 1958. If Morhouse can put the GOP over the top both times, his political future, as a state leader or as a party candidate, seems unbounded."

The first part was easy. With Eisenhower still at the peak of his popularity, New York went for the Republican ticket by a margin that dwarfed even the landslide figures of 1952.

The true test of Morhouse's performance, the reconquest of the Governor's Mansion in 1958, lay ahead. All that he was doing now—the endless circuits of the state aboard his prop-driven Stinson Voyager, the barrage of press releases pounding away at Harriman, the arduous district-by-district canvassing—were pointed toward that one end. "Jud Morhouse," reported veteran Albany correspondent Arvis Chalmers in the summer of 1956, "has scheduled each step of the way from this fall's elections to the next state election in 1958."

And the first step, the most essential step, was to find a winning candidate.

The paths of Jud Morhouse and Nelson Rockefeller had first crossed late in 1955, when Rockefeller was still at the White House. They met at a gathering at the Knickerbocker Club to discuss the state party's finances. Strolling out to the street together afterward, they stood on the corner while Morhouse searched for a cab. As they gazed at the traffic speeding up and down Fifth Avenue, they fell to talking some more about the future of the GOP in New York. A full half hour passed as they stood there on the windswept curb animatedly chatting about Republican politics, each man finding his restlessness mirrored by the other's.

The conversation convinced Morhouse that Rockefeller was a potentially hot political property. There was so much about him that Morhouse found attractive: his dynamism, his physical presence, and, not least, his financial resources. To the chairman of a party out of power scrambling to keep his state machine solvent, the latter was an especially potent lure.

Morhouse decided, then and there, that Rockefeller was a quarry worth pursuing—and one that might respond to the right political bait. A few months later, when Rockefeller had returned to private life, Morhouse sounded him out about a run for the U.S. Senate. Rockefeller, however, declined; he was temperamentally unsuited, he told Morhouse, to be a legislator. (Frank Jamieson confided to a colleague that their boss was "elaborately disinterested in this type of service.") Instead, Rockefeller joined Jock Whitney in backing the Senate bid of New York's attorney general, Jacob Javits.

For the enterprising Morhouse, the setback was merely transitory. Rockefeller might not be ready for the Senate in 1956—but the governorship in 1958 could be quite another story. Having glommed on to Rockefeller, the chairman was determined now to nudge him, somehow, into the New York political arena.

And it was not long before he came up with exactly the vehicle to do it.

Every twenty years, by law, the voters of New York State were asked whether a convention should be held to revise the state's constitution. The question was next due to appear on the ballot in November 1957. To lay the groundwork for the possible convention, the state legislature in the past had created a temporary commission to study and report on the possible constitutional changes that might come before the convention. Early in 1956, the legislature followed tradition and created just such a commission in anticipation of the November 1957 referendum.

There were to be fifteen members of the temporary commission: five appointed by Governor Harriman, five by Senate Majority Leader Walter Mahoney, and five by Assembly Speaker Oswald Heck. Since the Republicans controlled both houses, this gave the GOP two-thirds of the seats. Nonetheless, the commission was ostensibly intended to be a bipartisan undertaking, and to assure this bipartisan flavor, the commission chairman would be named jointly by Harriman, Mahoney, and Heck. The chairman would be a Republican—but a Republican acceptable to Averell Harriman.

Various distinguished names were bruited about—Attorney General Herbert Brownell, state Court of Appeals judge David Peck—but Harriman summarily rejected them all. When he got wind of the deadlock, Morhouse told Mahoney to put a new possibility in the hopper: Nelson A. Rockefeller.

"Oh, *Nelson,*" Harriman said, when Rockefeller's name was first advanced. "I know Nelson. That would be all right. I'd go for Nelson."

As far as Harriman was concerned, Rockefeller was an inspired choice. "In Harriman's mind," observed his biographer, Rudy Abramson, "the convention was so supremely in the public interest that it transcended personal ambition, partisanship, and State House politics. And who was there in all New York better suited to lead a great civic movement for political reform than the most public-spirited and energetic of John D. Rockefeller's five grandsons?"

That Rockefeller might use the position not as a springboard for a "great civic movement," but for a great personal one—namely, a move to the Governor's Mansion on January 1, 1959—seemed to have only barely permeated the labyrinthine recesses of Averell Harriman's lofty mind.

But not the minds of his political advisers. The top political operative on Harriman's staff, Milton Stewart, had a very good idea of what Rockefeller's appointment might portend, and bluntly warned his boss of the consequences: Rockefeller, he said, was "the very son-of-a-bitch we are going to have to beat. The guy is not anybody to fool around with."

Harriman might shrug off the jitters of a staff member like Stewart. But the concerns of Carmine Gerard De Sapio were something else again.

He was the boss of Tammany Hall, the great kingmaker, wielding "more influence in the Democratic party than the Governor of the state and the Mayor of its largest city combined," in the words of *The New York Times.* Tall, wavy-haired, impeccably groomed and attired, given to soft-spoken, erudite public utterances, the forty-nine-year-old De Sapio seemed the utter antithesis of his cigar-chomping, saloon-keeping predecessors. He was the first political boss in memory to engage a personal p.r. man, to lecture civics groups, to write for the *Harvard Law Review,* and to appear on television panel shows. He regularly startled his interlocutors by speaking not in the "dese and dose" cadences of the street, but with "a precise and faultless English that would do credit to Groton, Harvard and the Village literati," as one commentator put it.

Withal, he was still the boss of Tammany (or "the Bishop," as his compatriots called him), master of one of the nation's most formidable, and most frequently reviled, political machines. In counterpoint to his faultless diction and Hart Schaffner & Marx suits were his trademark tinted eyeglasses (worn because of a longtime eye affliction), which, in the public mind, served to underscore the vague pall of the sinister that clung to De Sapio's well-tailored shoulders. There were frequent whispers about his connections to Mafia kingpin Frank Costello, long reputed to be a silent partner in Tammany's affairs. There was the notorious matter of the Scotch-taped envelope, found one day in the backseat of a taxi in which De Sapio had just been riding; when the cabbie opened it, he discovered some $11,000 in fifty- and hundred-dollar bills. (De Sapio denied that the cash was his.)

His reputation may have been murky, but Carmine De Sapio's power was unquestioned. Far from shrinking from his presence, New York politicos vied for his favor. He could literally make or break them, as he proved by engineering the election of Robert Wagner as New York City mayor in 1953—and then, a year later, switching his support from Franklin Roosevelt, Jr., to Averell Harriman for the governorship.

Without De Sapio's backing, Harriman would never have been governor, and once he was elected, the governor took pains to keep the Tammany boss in his inner circle. De Sapio, in fact, claims that "during Harriman's term all the political decisions were handled by me. I handled everything."

Harriman would routinely go over his potential appointments to various state commissions with De Sapio. And so it was that in the early summer of 1956 the question of the chairmanship of the Temporary Commission on the Constitutional Convention arose.

As De Sapio would recall, "Harriman said to me, 'I have a good friend who would be right for that.' I asked Harriman who his friend was, and he said, 'Nelson Rockefeller.' I couldn't believe it. I said to Harriman, 'Governor, do you realize what you're doing? You're giving this man the keys to every agency in the state. He'll know what's happening in the state inside and out. And if he runs for governor, he'll end up using it against you.' And Harriman said, 'Oh, Nelson would never do that. He'd never run against me.' And I said to him, 'What makes you so sure?' And Harriman says, 'Because he and I are old friends. We're like *this.*' "

To be sure, there was some legitimate cause for Harriman's trust and confidence in Rockefeller. Harriman could take some comfort in his memory of the wrangling over Point Four, when Harriman, as Rockefeller's administration patron, was able to "control" him and, ultimately, best him in the bureaucratic turf wars. Unquestionably, Harriman's image of Rockefeller—as a sincere, eager-to-please, and not particularly guileful go-getter—was shaped by that Point Four experience.

And then there was the input Harriman was getting from his trusted aide-de-camp, Jonathan Bingham, the executive secretary to the governor. At the time Rockefeller's name was first bandied about, Bingham happened to run into him at the Washington airport. Chatting at the airport, and later on the flight up to New York, they talked about the constitutional convention, and the opportunity it offered to revitalize state government. Bingham came away convinced that Rockefeller and the governor were on precisely the same wavelength about the commission and the chairmanship.

Not long afterward, Bingham sent a memo to Harriman: "I told him [Rockefeller] that we had heard that he was interested and that the Governor was delighted at the prospect, since the Governor had complete confidence that he, Nelson Rockefeller, would follow his own conscience and judgment on the questions that came up rather than follow the dictates of any party line. He expressed his gratification at this . . ."

Thus, Harriman appeared to have Rockefeller's word that he would not turn the commission into a partisan stomping ground. And, according to one eyewitness, he also had his word on something else.

Daniel Patrick Moynihan was Bingham's assistant at the time, occupying an increasingly important position in the gubernatorial hierarchy. He remembers being present in Harriman's office when Rockefeller came by to finally accept his appointment to the commission. Recollects Moynihan: "As they shook hands, Nelson said, 'Don't worry, Averell, I'll never run against you.' "

Years later, another commission appointee, Joseph Carlino, the Assembly Majority Leader at the time, pronounced this verdict on Harriman's gullibility: "He was a very fine gentleman, well bred with a tremendous background, but he didn't know shit from shinola about politics."

Openly scornful of the concerns about his old friend Nelson, Harriman took to joking about the "monster" he had supposedly created. The following spring, at the annual Legislative Correspondents Association dinner spoofing the state's politicos, Harriman closed the festivities by pointing out that the reporters had touched on all his prospective gubernatorial rivals except "the most likely of all, Nelson Rockefeller—stand up and take a bow, Nelson." Rockefeller rose to acknowledge the applause, while De Sapio and the rest of Harriman's men simply rolled their eyes in disbelief.

Ironically, Rockefeller's advisers were as wary as Harriman's of the opportunity the governor was offering.

The aide Rockefeller would turn to first in such matters was Frank Moore, president of his Government Affairs Foundation. Despite its civic mission, the foundation's main value for Rockefeller was the ongoing access it gave him to the political counsel of the former lieutenant governor of New York. Moore had to be discreet about offering his advice; were it to become too overt, it might jeopardize the foundation's tax-exempt status. Nonetheless, offer it he did.

Moore's advice now on the constitutional commission was succinct: don't do it. "His attitude," Frank Jamieson reported to Rockefeller, "is that it would involve a great deal of work and not any opportunity for achievement because of no great need for constitutional revision." And Moore had reason to know; he had served on the previous such commission in 1937. What particularly worried him was the political booby trap he saw lurking in the commission's work: namely, the volatile issue of reapportionment. The Republican leadership feared a constitutional convention because of the opportunity it offered the Democrats to put reapportionment on the table—and, potentially, undermine the GOP's control of the state legislature. (They feared it because that was exactly what *they* did to the Democrats in 1937.)

Almost anything the commission did, Moore warned, would play into the

Democrats' hands. As he explained, "If the commission says there are possible changes that should be considered for the constitution, it is then recommending a convention. If it mentions the changes that should be considered, it would then have to mention reapportionment, a hot political issue—the Democrats' only hope of controlling the legislature."

Moore's deep misgivings about the enterprise were fully shared by Rockefeller's most trusted adviser, Jamieson. "I confess," he wrote Rockefeller, "certain intuitive instincts against it—even though I recognize that there are positive aspects in favor of it." Among those "positive aspects," he acknowledged, were the "opportunity to become well known and figure prominently at a state level." But arguing against the appointment, he said, were the risks of becoming embroiled in the reapportionment mess and other controversies—which might, in turn, actually torpedo any political hopes Rockefeller had.

Rockefeller pondered Jamieson's objections and Moore's. Persuasive though they were, he decided to go ahead anyway. He would accept Averell Harriman's offer.

In Rockefeller's restless mind, the rewards more than outweighed the risks; somehow, he would figure out a way to handle the whole reapportionment business. Other than that thorny little problem, there was little else on the horizon to dissuade him. Unlike an outright run for office, the position was not much of a reach. Indeed, the commission seemed organically related to many of his other current activities: the Government Affairs Foundation, the President's reorganization committee, even the Special Studies.

To serve as chairman of the commission seemed an eminently public-spirited thing to do, well within the civic-minded tradition of his father before him. Yet, at the same time, there is every indication that Rockefeller was fully aware of the personal ramifications of the appointment and its potential impact on his future. As one of his aides would note, "The job was a cram course in the mechanics of state government." And, just as Morhouse had hoped, Rockefeller was eager to go to school.

The first thing he did, appropriately enough, was to seek out a professor.

Rockefeller wanted someone who could serve as an intellectual fulcrum for the commission, playing much the same role Kissinger played in the Special Studies; someone who was as erudite about state government as Kissinger was about geopolitics; someone who had the same sure grasp of realpolitik that Kissinger had.

He asked Frank Moore whom he would recommend, and Moore came up with one name: William J. Ronan, the forty-three-year-old dean of New York University's Graduate School of Public Administration.

Although no one would mistake the burly, six-foot-two-inch Ronan for Henry Kissinger, there was much about him that was indeed reminiscent of the Harvard man. Like Kissinger, he possessed an impeccable academic reputation. And, like Kissinger, Ronan was eager to escape the ivory tower and test his mettle in the rough-and-tumble world of public affairs. As much as Henry Kissinger was, William J. Ronan was an intellectual moonlighter, a venturesome soul who never met a consultantship he didn't like.

Born in Buffalo, the son of a lawyer turned businessman, Ronan was always precociously enterprising: at sixteen, he landed his first job, as assistant to the curator of the city's Museum of Science. With the help of a succession of similar jobs, he put himself through Syracuse University, where he switched from the study of mathematics and physics to international law and diplomacy. After postgraduate work abroad, and a year at Harvard, he was hired by NYU as an instructor in 1938. Settling in on the Washington Square campus, he obtained his Ph.D., married one of his students, and shifted his specialty from international affairs to the far more wide-open field of American government—specifically, government on the state and local level.

After a three-year wartime hitch in the Navy (conveniently spent based in New York) Ronan continued his rise up the NYU ladder, becoming dean of the public affairs school in 1953, at age forty. But at the same time he assiduously trolled for opportunities outside the campus walls, snapping up whatever consulting assignments came his way. He served as research director of a New York State version of the Hoover Commission under Governor Dewey, and later ran the staff of a special state commission looking into public authorities. The latter assignment showed Ronan to be no shrinking violet, as he openly challenged the practices of New York's all-powerful authorities czar, Robert Moses.

By the summer of 1956, Ronan had decided to leave academia entirely, and accepted an offer to become first deputy city administrator in the regime of Robert F. Wagner. But no sooner had he settled into City Hall than the call came from Nelson A. Rockefeller.

Rockefeller invited him to stop by Room 5600 for a chat. As Ronan would recall the scene, they sat down for coffee, "and the young lady serving some goodies along with it came over with a tray that had a Danish pastry and one glazed doughnut. It was passed to me and I took the glazed doughnut. When I did, I thought she was going to drop the tray. The next day, when I appeared for the second conversation, there were two glazed doughnuts on the tray. This was the beginning of my association with Nelson Rockefeller." Henceforth, Ronan would never again approach Rockefeller's lair so incautiously.

From their first encounters, Rockefeller could see that Ronan was his kind of academic: a man of ideas, but an aficionado, as well, of the art of the possible. Edward Kresky, who studied with Ronan at NYU and would later become one of his closest associates, describes that aspect of Ronan this way: "He was always a man I felt very much at ease in what C. P. Snow would call 'matters of affairs,' whether they be in business or in politics. His notions of politics were not the notions of a typical Harvard faculty person who cannot tolerate compromise. Ronan lived in the world of realpolitik, of accomplishing what is doable."

At the same time, there was a silken smoothness to Ronan, a polish and an effortless erudition, that Rockefeller also found appealing. A connoisseur of fine food and wine and a collector of antiques, Ronan seemed more like a prosperous business executive—someone who might show up at one of Rockefeller's Fifth Avenue soirees—than a woolly academic specialist from south of 14th Street. Says Kresky, "Bill Ronan was very worldly, extremely well read, very knowledgeable about history, about foreign affairs. He was a mannered, poised person. Very cultured. He was a perfect fit with the Nelson A. Rockefeller of Pocantico Hills and 810 Fifth Avenue and Foxhall Road and a ranch in Venezuela and an estate in Maine.

"And," adds Kresky, "it was a fit that Ronan liked. Ronan liked that type of social milieu."

For Bill Ronan, a position with Rockefeller was a passport: a passport not just to the world of affairs but to the world of candlelight and Spode and Lafite-Rothschild.

The City Hall job, the job he had eagerly accepted from Mayor Wagner just a few months before, was forgotten. Ronan was going to work for Nelson Rockefeller.

For Averell Harriman and his handlers, Rockefeller's hiring of the well-credentialed William Ronan as his commission's executive director was hardly cause for alarm, hardly cause to question Rockefeller's good faith and bipartisanship. But it was not so with the other key staff member Rockefeller brought aboard, the man he chose to be the commission counsel: George A. Hinman.

Not that there was anything about Hinman as a personality that ruffled anyone. On the contrary, every nuance of Hinman's courtly persona seemed calculated to render him as neutral and invisible as possible. A universally respected Binghamton attorney, he presided over the best-connected, most prestigious law practice in the "southern tier," the deeply conservative group of New York counties west of the Catskills and abutting the Pennsylvania border. Lean, thin-lipped, and grandfatherish in his wire-rimmed spectacles, Hinman was a dignified figure whose natural habitat was the boardroom and the executive suite; among the prestigious companies whose boards he served on were IBM (which had its roots in the Binghamton area) and New York Telephone. He served, as well, as a regent of the State University of New York.

What was provocative about Hinman was his political pedigree. His father, Harvey Hinman, was a Republican powerhouse in southern New York, a state senator and lieutenant governor who had spearheaded the impeachment of a Democratic governor back in 1913, the only such event in the state's history.

The law firm Harvey founded, and to which George succeeded, was as known for its political clout as for its fine legal work. While lacking his father's appetite for controversy, George Hinman nonetheless preserved—and, in his own quiet way, augmented—his family's impressive GOP connections.

By retaining Hinman as the commission counsel, Rockefeller was not just bringing in someone with a deep understanding of western New York—he was also building an important bridge to one of the state's staunchest Republican strongholds. To the Democrats on the commission, it was a telling indication that the chairman had in mind something other than a disinterested review of the constitution.

From what Charles Poletti could see, Rockefeller's true intentions were evident from the very first commission meeting.

Poletti was a savvy old Democratic standby: lieutenant governor of the state under the last Democratic governor, Herbert Lehman, and, very, very briefly (twenty-nine days), governor himself when Lehman resigned to do war work. More to the point, he had chaired the last constitutional commission, in 1937, and was a principal player at the subsequent convention. From that experience, Poletti put great stock in what a convention could accomplish.

Dubious from the start about Rockefeller's appointment as chairman (Poletti had been one of those who warned Harriman he was making a big mistake), Poletti agreed to serve as commission vice chairman to counterbalance the Republican chairman. Sitting in a Room 5600 conference room for that first meeting, Poletti could barely contain a smirk as Rockefeller outlined his plans—plans that included holding public hearings in Albany, Buffalo, and New York. That, to Poletti, was the tip-off. As far as he was concerned, a series of forums at which irate citizens and pressure groups could vent their spleens was not any way to rewrite a constitution. "Well, I mean, you are either after publicity or you are after serious study and reform," he would later say, and "it was obvious" to him that by taking the process on the road, Rockefeller was more inclined to the latter than the former.

Poletti's suspicions were well founded. As choreographed by Ronan, these hearings would not be sedate, closed-door affairs, but full-blown events, heralded by a steady drumbeat of media attention. Early on, Ronan circulated an internal memo urging that "contact should be made with the press to insure coverage, the spotting of photographers, any radio or television coverage." He laid out a program of press releases and follow-up contacts, and insisted that ample facilities for newsmen be provided at each of the hearings. Even at this early date, Ronan was displaying more of the instincts of a political spin master than those of a public administration professor.

Not that there wasn't a substantive side to the commission's deliberations. The panel contracted for reports by some seventy consultants on virtually every area of state concern: housing and urban renewal, water supply, health and welfare, budgeting, highway finance, higher education. In essence, Rockefeller and Ronan turned the commission into a New York State version of the Special Studies Project. "Within a short period of time, they had every goddamn question briefed and catalogued," recalls Carlino. "There were whole volumes in this office at 30 Rockefeller Plaza."

It was, in short, the greatest assemblage of information on the workings of New York State outside the state capitol. And, as in the Special Studies, it was hard not to discern a dimension of personal education in the process. Among the reports commissioned by Rockefeller and Ronan was one entitled "The Governor as Chief Executive."

The great lightning rod of controversy, in those early months, was not Rockefeller, but Ronan. The unforgiving Robert Moses, enraged by Ronan's previous attacks on his public authority powers, sent intermediaries to Rockefeller to voice his displeasure with Ronan's appointment and to express his concern that Rockefeller's panel might adopt some of his nemesis's recommendations. To deflect Moses' potent anger, Rockefeller issued this statement: "The Rockefeller Commission is charged with the power to study and present the pros and cons—not to recommend. Therefore, there can be no influence exerted by the Executive Director." Moses, however, was barely mollified, and he continued to launch broadsides against his presumed antagonist.

Inside Room 5600, there was a similar concern about Ronan; far from exerting "no influence," it was feared that he was exerting all too much. Both Hinman and Moore worried about his imperious tendencies, and suspected that he was seeking to dominate the proceedings, making the commission members little more than figureheads signing off on a staff report. They conveyed their apprehensions to Rockefeller's longtime assistant Vera Goeller, who in turn relayed them to Rockefeller. "Now certainly is the time to clear the air," she suggested, "and I wonder if you would want to include Frank Moore and George in your meeting with Bill this week."

"I am beginning to wonder," she added, "if your weekly meetings with Bill should not include counsel and occasionally associate counsel."

It was starting to dawn upon his colleagues that the ways of William J. Ronan were not those of the typical NYU professor.

Try as Rockefeller might to paper over the political differences, the deliberations of his commission soon enough became a partisan tinderbox—just as Frank Moore had predicted. And, just as he had foreseen, the core issue was whether there should even *be* a constitutional convention, with the two parties bitterly divided on the question. The Democrats wanted one, because of the possibilities it offered for reapportionment; the Republicans, for the same reason, were against it.

The battle lines were drawn even as the commission prepared for its first hearing in Buffalo. In that conservative stronghold, the fiefdom of Senate Majority Leader Walter Mahoney, commission staffers found many local officials reluctant to testify—for fear that their mere appearance at the hearing would be construed as advocating a convention. Local newspapers railed against the convention, and the uproar grew so intense that the Buffalo Bar Association canceled the luncheon it planned for commission members. As a Rockefeller aide explained, "It is believed that they are afraid that their entertaining of the Commission would be interpreted as giving approval to the holding of a convention."

With the anticonvention forces boycotting the hearing, the twenty-two speakers who did show up at the Statler Hotel ballroom all (with just one exception) spoke up in favor of a convention. The same scenario played out the next day, when the commission moved its road show to Albany. There, at least, the luncheon went on as scheduled—because the venue was the Governor's Mansion, and the host was Averell Harriman.

Afterward, the governor led his guests on a tour of the mansion. Never known for his wit, Harriman nonetheless couldn't resist needling Rockefeller. "Take a good look around, Nelson," he said, "because it's the only chance you'll have to see this place."

Everyone laughed, Rockefeller most of all.

His jocular twitting notwithstanding, Harriman still took for granted that Rockefeller was a bipartisan figure. And he took for granted that the chairman of the Temporary Commission on the Constitutional Convention would be in favor of having a constitutional convention (although, to be sure, Rockefeller had never expressly said that he was, and Harriman had never asked).

Very soon, Harriman would learn how mistaken he was.

At the September 11 commission meeting, with the referendum on the convention question less than two months away, someone asked whether the commission was planning to take a position on whether a convention should be held. Rockefeller was ready with his reply. According to the minutes, "The chairman said he felt that the Commission was not charged with that responsibility and further, on the basis of discussions of this question at previous meetings, there was a general understanding that the Commission would not get into the question." With the Republican-selected members firmly in the majority, Rockefeller's position of neutrality stood unchallenged.

Meanwhile, outside the commission chambers, the GOP hue and cry against the convention was mounting. Assembly Speaker Heck said that from what he could see, the Rockefeller commission hearings had not brought out any "urgent need for constitutional change" that could not be accomplished through the legislature. Tom Dewey urged a "no" vote, decrying the convention as "an outmoded, unwieldy instrument" which "would be a waste of the people's money." And Jud Morhouse chimed in, too, denouncing the convention as a Democratic "once-in-a-lifetime gamble to turn control of the state legislature over to Tammany Hall."

With the prospect of a convention clearly in jeopardy, the Harriman administration made one last effort to bring Rockefeller around—to get the chairman of the convention commission to at least come out in favor of the convention he was supposedly preparing for. In the last week of October, Rockefeller agreed to issue a statement, but it wasn't exactly what the administration had in mind. Rockefeller offered to merely recite the commission's functions: to "study proposals" for constitutional changes and to "collect and compile" information useful for the delegates—if the convention ever took place. As for the prospect of a convention itself, the commission had decided to "refrain from making any recommendations."

Poletti sent over a copy of the press release to Harriman aide Milton Stewart with this comment: "Milt: This is the best we could get Nelson to do!"

Two weeks later, the Republicans prevailed at the polls, as the voters rejected the proposition of a constitutional convention in 1959. And three days after that, the temporary commission met, and unanimously adopted a resolution that "constitutional revision and simplification are both desirable and feasible."

This was too much for Harriman. Forwarded a copy of the resolution by Rockefeller, he fired off a tart response to the chairman: "Thank you for sending me the resolution unanimously adopted on November 8th by the Temporary State Commission on the Constitutional Convention. I am gratified to note that the Commission is convinced 'constitutional revision and simplification are both desirable and feasible.' It seems unfortunate that this conviction was not expressed publicly prior to November 5th."

Much too late, Harriman realized that what Carmine De Sapio had warned him about Nelson Rockefeller was true. Rockefeller was neither a friend nor some Olympian bipartisan figure. He was, really, just another politician.

With the defeat of the convention question, Rockefeller's commission was, technically, out of business. Harriman, however, sought to call his Republican rivals' bluff; in the course of their campaign against the convention, they had talked about creating a "permanent constitutional commission" in lieu of the temporary commission. Now, he said, it was time for them to put up or shut up. The legislature's response was to establish a "Special Legislative Commission on the Revision and Simplification of the Constitution." But this was not the independent body Harriman had envisioned. Rather it was merely the Rockefeller commission redux, still Republican-dominated, still under the chairmanship of Nelson Rockefeller.

Rockefeller dutifully accepted this appointment, even though, from his personal point of view, his commission work had already more than served its purpose. Through its studies and hearings he had become thoroughly conversant with a subject at which he was heretofore a novice: the subject of New York State, its governance and its problems. He had identified himself, in the public mind, with reform and change, even though he had managed not to take a particular stand on anything, except his desire not to take a stand. What's more, the commission work had brought into his circle of advisers two sagacious characters, Ronan and Hinman, who would be ideal handmaidens to his ambitions.

And there was this added dividend: he had begun to prove, to the Republican leadership, that he was someone they could count on.

It was a message that Jud Morhouse, in his own way, was conveying as well.

While Rockefeller was boning up on the state of the state—thanks to the position that Morhouse had arranged for him—the state chairman, in the course of his regular excursions around the state in his puddle-jumping Stinson Voyager, was spreading the word to the party's power brokers, the county chairmen: don't commit yourselves to a gubernatorial candidate until you've looked over Nelson Rockefeller.

"Jud had gotten himself pretty well tied in with Rockefeller," recalls Guy Graves, Morhouse's executive assistant at the time, who often joined him on his rounds. "We went to nearly every county in the state. We did everything except go by horseback to some of these meetings, trying to promote Rockefeller."

Among those who received the gospel was John Walsh, the young acting chairman in Fulton County, a region of small factories and scenic lakes on the southern border of the Adirondacks. One day, in the late summer of 1957, Walsh was asked to meet Morhouse in Glens Falls, forty miles away, at Alfonso's Restaurant. As they dug into their lunch, recollects Walsh, "Jud asked me a very pointed question: who would Fulton County support for the nomination? I very carefully indicated it would be our home area local candidate, Ozzie Heck. And then Jud asked me, 'What would your Fulton County people think of Nelson Rockefeller as a candidate?' And I said, 'Well, I haven't even thought of it, and I'm sure they haven't.' That was my first indication that Jud was quite obviously behind Nelson Rockefeller."

It was, at the time, a truly daring step for the state chairman to take. This, after all, was the same Nelson Rockefeller whose prospective candidacy for the governorship four years earlier had been derisively laughed into oblivion by the party elders. So far down the pecking order was Rockefeller that at the state GOP's annual dinner in June, he was neither invited to speak nor even asked to sit on the dais; Rockefeller was simply another face in the crowd, sitting with Tod at table thirty.

What's more, in touting Rockefeller, Morhouse was well aware he was playing a dangerous game. The state chairman was supposed to be a neutral figure in these matters. By maneuvering behind the scenes for Rockefeller, Morhouse was not only violating his supposed neutrality but risking the formidable wrath of the powerful state figures who were putative candidates themselves: Assembly Speaker Heck, Senate Majority Leader Mahoney, and former Republican national chairman Leonard Hall. In quietly advancing Rockefeller's cause, Morhouse was, quite literally, putting his job and his whole future on the line.

His son, Sanford, recalls his father's quandary: "His personal agenda was to get Nelson Rockefeller to be the Republican nominee. But his role as state chairman precluded him from supporting a candidate, so he was walking something of a tightrope." But his father, in the end, was confident that the cause was worth the considerable risk: "He was an absolute convert to the faith that Nelson Rockefeller could do it."

Morhouse's initial test of that faith came earlier that summer of 1957. The New York Federation of Women's Republican Clubs was holding its summer conference in the sylvan surroundings of the late health faddist Bernarr Macfadden's Castle on the Hill in Dansville, New York. Morhouse was invited to speak, and so was Rockefeller.

It was a humid, sweltering day, and as Rockefeller took his turn at the podium he gazed down upon a sea of Republican women desperately fanning themselves with whatever papers and brochures were available. His subject was the budgetary policy of the Eisenhower administration, a tedious topic that was hardly likely to take his audience's mind off the oppressive heat. And, as Rockefeller launched into his speech, he did little to help his cause with his mechanical, uninflected delivery of the text. Despite two decades in public life, and despite the best efforts of speech coaches and speechwriters, Rockefeller remained a wooden, soporific orator. An uneasy truce existed between Rockefeller and the written word, owing partly to his dyslexia and partly to his utter indifference to the art of public speaking. As a later speechwriter, Joseph Persico, would observe, "He took no pleasure in language, lacked delight in the well-crafted phrase and the satisfaction of moving people through the power of speech."

Rockefeller droned on about the Eisenhower budget, enveloping the room in a mist of torpor and boredom. Watching this inept performance, watching the bobbing heads of Republican women nodding off, Jud Morhouse was plunged into despondency.

Afterward, when the meeting had broken, Morhouse trailed Rockefeller as he waded through the audience. A small knot of women had gathered around him, and Morhouse saw, suddenly, a different Rockefeller emerge: bantering, parrying questions with an effortless charm, disarming the throng with his boyish grin and his glistening blue-gray eyes that seemed to establish an instant intimacy with each of them. The crowd was rapt, the atmosphere electric.

Morhouse's spirits soared. In an instant, Rockefeller had transformed himself from a stick figure behind a lectern to a vibrant, crackling presence. Gazing at the cluster of women growing ever larger, Morhouse experienced a political epiphany of sorts. Nelson Rockefeller, he saw now, was more than just the sum total of his résumé and his bank account; he had that most ineffable and elusive of qualities for a candidate, sex appeal.

If the party was to regain the governor's mansion in 1958, Morhouse knew, it had to make a special effort to woo female voters; he was fond of pointing out, to all who would listen, that "women are the most powerful single voting bloc." And here before him was a candidate—trim, zestful, radiating charisma—who could capture that vote.

Jud Morhouse had arrived at the Castle on the Hill with his fingers crossed. He left absolutely certain that his great leap of faith in Nelson Rockefeller truly would be rewarded.

And yet, at that moment, there was still no certainty that Rockefeller would run for the governorship in 1958, or anything else.

Again and again, over the last four years, he had rebuffed all entreaties to enter the political arena. In 1953, he had been mentioned for the New York mayoralty; in 1954, Bill Zeckendorf and Tex McCrary had tried to coax him into a run for governor; in 1956, there was talk about a U.S. Senate race. Most recently, in early 1957, Manhattan County GOP boss Thomas Curran had floated his name again as a mayoral prospect. Each time, Rockefeller had let it be known that he wasn't interested.

He always had his reasons, and most of the time they were perfectly sound. In 1953 and again in 1954, he was intent on making his mark in the new Republican administration in Washington. He considered himself temperamentally unsuited to be a legislator; hence his decision in 1956 not to run for the U.S. Senate.

Still, for a man who had left Washington vowing never to return except as an elected official, he seemed remarkably ambivalent about pursuing his goal. Rather than actively plot his political future, Rockefeller plunged himself into the Special Studies Project. While it was hard not to read a certain amount of personal calculation into that project, and to see it furnishing its sponsor with a political platform, Special Studies remained, at bottom, a think-tank exercise—for the most part, a rather squishy stepping-stone.

Aggressively decisive about almost every other aspect of his life, Rockefeller was plagued with a Hamlet-like indecision about his political career. It was a trait that would bedevil him time and time again in the future, often with disastrous consequences, to the total bewilderment of both his supporters and his foes. But, at least in the run-up to 1958, it was still possible to discern some plausible reasons for his behavior.

Laurance Rockefeller would later say of his brother's involvement in politics, "Philosophically, psychologically, emotionally it was a continuous life process. And it wasn't a crossroad or a sudden thing. It was a lifestyle." But it was equally true that for Nelson, as for the rest of his family, being a Rockefeller was also a lifestyle, philosophically, psychologically, and emotionally. And, in weighing where he would take his life, that Rockefeller heritage—a heritage he doted on more than any of his siblings—factored heavily.

From their earliest youth, Nelson and his brothers had been taught to value public service as the highest of callings. But that concept of public service was the public service of John D. Rockefeller, Jr.: great philanthropic undertakings that would deploy the family's immense wealth in the interests of the commonweal. It was Nelson who first expanded the boundaries by accepting a position in Washington, without any real objection from Junior; indeed, Nelson's work was a source of immense pride for his father, who saw his accomplishments burnishing the family name. Similarly, Nelson's later positions—the Point Four board, PACGO, HEW Undersecretary, White House special assistant—were generally regarded in the family as laudable, public-spirited activities. "We have a responsibility," he once said, "to participate to the extent that we can in local, state and national affairs. It's as simple as that." By and large, the family had agreed.

But elective office was something else again. To shill for votes, to *sell* oneself in public: it all ran counter to the deeply ingrained reticence that was as much a Rockefeller birthright as the shares of Standard Oil.

This reticence was not a matter of shyness (although it certainly was in the case of Junior and his eldest son); it was a question of self-preservation. Ever sensitive to the issue of concentration of wealth that dogged the first John D., his heirs had always been careful not to be seen to be *too* voracious in the pursuit of power. Although their influence on American life was ubiquitous and profound, it was almost always exerted behind the scrim of corporations and foundations. To bring that influence front and center was simply beyond the pale.

Earlier in the 1950s, Nelson had had firsthand experience with his family's sensitivities on that score. In 1955, around the time he arrived at the White House, he and his brothers were approached about buying the foundering flagship of New York Republicanism, the *New York Herald Tribune*. The Reid family, the *Trib*'s longtime owner, was desperate to unload the money-losing property, and the Rockefellers, staunch New York Republicans that they were, seemed likely candidates. In fact, *Trib* matriarch Helen Reid thought she had a commitment from the brothers, until, at the last moment, the

Rockefellers backed off—in large measure because of Frank Jamieson's cautionary counsel.

"Frank's concern," remembers his aide Kerk Burbank, "was that the family already had so much power that if they went into anything in newspapers or magazines or radio or television, they would be asking for trouble." (Eventually, Reid did find a buyer, and one who was, ironically, a far more reticent character than Nelson Rockefeller: his old friend and colleague Jock Whitney.)

The *Tribune* affair was still fresh in Rockefeller's mind when, soon after his return to private life, another, even more alluring media prospect presented itself. The idea came from his Dartmouth classmate Sylvester "Pat" Weaver, who in the years since he worked for Rockefeller in the coordinator's office had come into his own as one of the most innovative forces in the nascent medium of television. As president of the National Broadcasting Company, Weaver had expanded TV's horizons with such breakthroughs as the *Today* and *Tonight* programs.

Having less than complete respect for David Sarnoff, the autocrat who controlled NBC—Weaver considered him "a real idiot"—Weaver tried, on several occasions, to arrange a buyout of the network. When Sarnoff indicated once that he might consider such a deal, "I went to the elevator to see if I could get Nelson and the boys interested," recalls Weaver.

"They were very interested, and they talked about it. Nelson was very receptive." But shortly afterward, Weaver received word from 5600 that Rockefeller involvement was out of the question. He was told, he said, that "it was absolutely against the basic family policy, because of course television had this tremendous influence on people. That's what really killed it."

So as Rockefeller mulled his political moves, he had good reason to wonder how much of a backlash he might encounter within his own family. And there was a more intimate element to this as well: namely, the reaction of his wife, Tod.

It was plain to all who knew her that she despised public life, and her minimal tolerance for its demands grew ever feebler the longer her husband spent in government. During his last stint in Washington she had barely gone through the motions, choosing to spend most of her time away from her husband, in New York and Pocantico. The skittish bride who had snapped at photographers on her wedding day was now a sharp-tongued matron who was every bit as intemperate as she ever was about incursions on her privacy. She had absolutely no use for the media, and was completely baffled when her feisty cousin Eleanor Clark French became women's editor of *The New York Times*.

With flinty determination, Tod had managed to raise her five children away from the glare that enveloped their father. A run for office, however, would shatter that cocoon instantly and permanently. She and her children would have to submit themselves to all the prying eyes; she and they would become as much public property as her husband.

That she would ultimately adjust to those demands, there was never any doubt; when called upon, she could still play the part of the loyal helpmate. But her own preference in the matter was clear.

Rockefeller would encounter, as well, an equally lukewarm reaction from his most trusted adviser, Frank Jamieson.

Despite his Runyonesque swagger, deep within Jamieson beat the heart of a corporate attorney. He was fiercely protective of Nelson Rockefeller, and unwaveringly dubious about many of his schemes. A wartime rival had denounced Jamieson as a "holder-backer," and over the years the enterprises from which he essayed to hold Rockefeller back—sometimes successfully, sometimes not—were legion. He talked Rockefeller out of supporting a CIA front operation in the early 1950s. He argued against his joining HEW. He vociferously opposed the *Herald Tribune* purchase. And, most recently, he was distinctly negative about the constitutional convention appointment.

"Jamie was definitely not a yes-man," recalls his wife, Linda. "He would fight, really fight Nelson on something that Nelson might be doing that he, Jamie, thought he shouldn't be doing. He would fight him on the telephone, he'd fight him in person."

No other Rockefeller retainer ever guarded the family's reputation so zealously. And it was this protectiveness that at least partly accounted for Jamieson's wariness about his boss's entry into politics. He had feared the repercussions for the family of the *Tribune* deal, and, says Burbank, "he had the same feeling about getting into politics. There was just too much power there. He felt that this would be a concentration that would really damage the family in the long run."

But there was more to Jamieson's cautiousness than that. His unstinting fealty to Rockefeller masked a deep-seated ambivalence about the man. "Jamie had a great deal of admiration for Nelson," says his wife, "but he also had very mixed feelings about him, too. There were some personality traits that perhaps he didn't admire so much." Jamieson worried about Rockefeller's impetuousness, and his malleability—his tendency to latch on to faddish advisers like Kissinger and Teller and parrot their views. "Frank knew that Nelson fed on advice from people," explains Burbank, "and he was concerned about what would happen if a new group came into his inner circle."

"I think Frank actually was a little afraid of Nelson," Burbank adds. "Not afraid of him personally, but afraid of what power would do to him."

Impelled by his misgivings, but keeping them well camouflaged, Jamieson tried to talk Rockefeller out of a gubernatorial bid on substantive grounds. Nineteen fifty-eight promised to be a Democratic year; unseating a prestigious incumbent such as Harriman might be well-nigh impossible. He passed along to Rockefeller Frank Moore's view that "if Harriman runs again for governor in 1958 with Wagner as a candidate for senator in the same election, it would be the strongest ticket the Democrats could present in New York State and the Democrats, of course, must realize it." Jamieson's counsel was to wait.

An even more gloomy prognosis was offered to Rockefeller by the past master of state politics, Mr. New York Republican himself, Thomas E. Dewey.

One day in 1956, Dewey lunched with David Rockefeller at the Chase Bank (Dewey's law firm represented Chase). When the talk turned to Nelson's political aspirations, the former governor was openly scornful. "He made the flat statement," David recalled, "that clearly no member of our family could ever be elected to office, because of the family name."

Undaunted by David's experience, Nelson decided to seek out Dewey himself. There are varying accounts of this meeting. According to one, Dewey condescendingly suggested to Rockefeller that a slow slog was in order: if Nelson was really interested in politics, Dewey could arrange to have him appointed New York postmaster—after which he might be able to run for Congress, and "then later, maybe then, you could run for governor."

Rockefeller's own account of Dewey's reaction was a bit more colorful. "He slapped my knee and laughed out loud and said, 'Nelson, you're a great guy, but you couldn't get elected dogcatcher in New York.' "

Fueling Dewey's skepticism was his certitude that the GOP, long castigated as the party of the rich, simply could not win with a Rockefeller as its nominee. As the governor's aide and law partner R. Burdell Bixby explains, "There was a feeling among Republicans in New York that nobody who had as much money as Herbert Lehman [Lehman came from one of New York's wealthiest investment banking families] could be elected on the Republican ticket." It was Dewey's view that only if Rockefeller earned his spurs at a lower level would he have any sort of a shot at the governorship. Says Bixby, "Dewey properly felt he had been elected governor because he had established himself as a heroic prosecutor of bad guys. He was not elected because he was a Republican but because of his record as prosecutor."

With his name, not his record, as his political capital, Nelson Rockefeller didn't, in Tom Dewey's opinion, stand a chance.

There was, of course, one way around the conundrum posed by Dewey. And that was to become a Democrat.

There was much to be said for a party switch. Wealth did not seem to pose the same problems for New York Democrats as it did for Republicans, as evidenced by the elections of FDR, Lehman, and Harriman. Furthermore, most of Rockefeller's friends and advisers—Jamieson, Harrison, Berle, Rosenberg, Ruebhausen—were Democrats. (Rockefeller once walked into a meeting in Room 5600, looked around the room, and chuckled. "My goodness," he said, "do you realize I'm the only Republican here?")

Pat Weaver remembers bringing up the possibility with Rockefeller in 1957, when Rockefeller was pondering his political future. "I told him, 'Nelson, there's one thing you should face right away. You should do just exactly what all the other guys in your position have always done, Lehman, Franklin Roosevelt, Harriman. You should turn your back on your people, become a Democrat, and embrace the masses.' "

Rockefeller, however, didn't even want to discuss it. "Forget it," he snapped at Weaver. "Forget it."

To those who pressed him on the point, Rockefeller would speak about his family's deep Republican roots, not only on the Rockefeller side but on the Aldrich side as well. Turning his back on this tradition was, for him, simply unthinkable.

And there was another reason for his resistance, which he spoke about years later to one of his gubernatorial aides, Harry Albright. They were having lunch at Rockefeller's 54th Street hideaway, when Albright noticed on a table a small photograph of FDR. "What a guy," said Rockefeller, practically genuflecting at the photo, and he proceeded to reminisce about Roosevelt's periodic attempts to cajole Rockefeller into changing parties. The reason he never succumbed, he said, was a matter of philosophy. "I used to play tennis at Foxhall Road with [Henry] Wallace and [Rexford] Tugwell," Rockefeller said, "and I was always uncomfortable with their very leftish views. The way I saw it, if I became a Democrat, I'd always be in the position of holding the party back, whereas if I stayed a Republican, I'd be pushing the party forward"—and pushing forward was a position far more suited to his temperament.

And so, for better or worse, Rockefeller would stake his future on the Republican Party—pushing forward, not pulling back.

He pondered Dewey's words, and Jamieson's, and took into account all the family misgivings. He hesitated, but not for very long.

This time, at least, Rockefeller let his hunger and impetuousness rule the day. He would not be New York postmaster. He would not change parties. He would not worry about the family complications.

He wasn't rushing into the race, but he was determined to start laying the groundwork for it. He would aim for 1958, and he would aim for Harriman's chair. The time of watchful waiting, of biding his time, was over. "His philosophy," his brother Laurance had said, "was, well, let's start, and nine times out of ten, you'll find a way." Shrugging off all the perceived drawbacks and impediments, Rockefeller took his first considered steps toward a candidacy.

First, he did what came most naturally: he commissioned some more studies.

Evidently judging that the seventy-odd papers for his constitutional convention commission were not sufficient for his purposes, Rockefeller approached his former HEW deputy Roswell Perkins, now a partner in Ruebhausen's law firm. "He basically wanted to have the kind of analytical studies done pointing up policy issues, the pros and cons, of the type that I did for him in Washington," recalls Perkins. "He wanted to get himself wrapped around some of the issues relating to New York." Perkins ended up retaining a whole new bushel of consultants to get the job done.

If Rockefeller's initial gambit was eminently predictable, his next was anything but. In fact, it quite literally came out of left field.

He was going to lead a crusade to keep the Brooklyn Dodgers in Brooklyn.

For the proud citizens of Brooklyn, and indeed for all New Yorkers, a tragedy had been unfolding that summer of 1957 in Ebbets Field, a tragedy played out not on the field but in the corporate office of Dodger owner Walter O'Malley. Tired of the meager financial returns offered by that bandbox of a ballpark, the cheroot-chomping O'Malley was entertaining a lucrative offer by the city fathers of Los Angeles to move the club out West.

Coming on the heels of the Giants' decision to desert the Polo Grounds and relocate to San Francisco, the Dodgers' exodus would deal a devastating blow to the city's spirit. Yet New York officials seemed totally unable to structure a counteroffer that might change O'Malley's mind. Truly a *deus ex machina* was needed if Brooklyn was to have any hope of holding on to its team.

Enter Nelson Rockefeller.

This unexpected move was Frank Jamieson's idea. Having failed to dissuade Rockefeller from a gubernatorial bid, Jamieson, consummate pro that he was, was now doing everything in his power to advance his chief's political fortunes. With his usual shrewdness, he perceived the Dodger situation as an ideal means to catapult Rockefeller front and center in the public consciousness. Rockefeller's intervention would be seen as a great public-spirited gesture, of a piece with his maneuvers a decade earlier to keep the United Nations in New York. "You don't have to buy the team," he assured Rockefeller. "You just have to make a bid, to show your interest."

Yet if Jamieson had searched for a hundred years, he couldn't have come up with a cause less likely to fire up Rockefeller's enthusiasm. Rockefeller had absolutely no interest in spectator sports, including the national pastime; his utter ignorance of a game that so preoccupied his fellow Americans was a constant source of wonderment to his subordinates. On the infrequent occasions when Louise Boyer (who was herself a great fan) actually persuaded him to attend a Yankee World Series game, he had to be coached in advance on when to cheer. At the ballpark, his boredom and bewilderment were transparent. "He didn't like it a bit," says John Lockwood, "and he'd get on television looking like a sour apple. Jamieson would tell him, 'Goddamnit, don't go if you can't look like you're having fun.' "

Nevertheless, even as benighted a soul as Nelson Rockefeller could see the surefire promotional possibilities of the Dodger affair. He met with O'Malley and baseball commissioner Ford Frick, and then issued a statement proclaiming his interest in the matter. "I share the feeling of so many New Yorkers that every effort should be made to keep National League baseball in New York. Certainly the greatest city in the world should have two baseball teams. It has proved that it can support them."

Noting that the big stumbling block seemed to be O'Malley's demand for a new 50,000-seat stadium in downtown Brooklyn, Rockefeller and his aides crafted a plan whereby Rockefeller would offer some package of financial aid to move the stadium along. Then he and his entourage went down to City Hall to present Mayor Wagner with the proposal. "Nelson was going to have a car take us down," remembers Burbank, "but Frank said, 'No, you're going on the subway.' And he went." Not having ventured much underground, Rockefeller was positively dazzled by the trip. "Hey, these subways are neat!" he exclaimed. "I don't know why people complain about them." "Of course," relates Burbank, "this was about ten-thirty in the morning, when it was all deserted and clean." (On another, later occasion, when he happened onto the subway, Rockefeller was equally impressed by the conditions. "Does every car have a rest room?" he asked, not realizing that the little nook he was pointing to was the conductor's cab.)

Wagner was receptive to Rockefeller's ideas, and the two went on to offer the plan to O'Malley. Oscar Ruebhausen remembers the meeting at the mayor's residence, Gracie Mansion, and the pungent aroma of O'Malley's "big fat cigar" as he listened to Rockefeller's pitch. Afterward, O'Malley told reporters that the proposal "has merit" and that he would defer any final decision on the move until Wagner had a chance to meet with the city's Board of Estimate.

Ruebhausen, for one, saw through the Dodger owner's posturing. "All Walter was doing, after we offered him this or that, was turn around and call the mayor of Los Angeles and say, 'They're offering me such and such, and such and such. What can you do?' " But Rockefeller was not nearly so skeptical. Caught up now in the chase, thrilled by the headlines it was engendering, he believed he had a real shot at bringing O'Malley around. "Nelson is like a little boy with the baseball thing," Nancy Hanks related to her parents. "Really excited." So engrossed was Rockefeller that when he heard about Los Angeles' counteroffer, he began furiously making plans to up his bid—until an alarmed Frank Jamieson stepped in. "By this point," recalls Burbank, "Frank was saying to him, 'Let it go! You don't really want it.' "

Reluctantly, Rockefeller finally gave up. Unable to meet O'Malley's escalating demands, the city of New York sadly bade goodbye to the Brooklyn Dodgers.

Just as Frank Jamieson had anticipated, Brooklyn's loss turned out to be Nelson Rockefeller's gain. Although packaged as a gesture of civic pride, everyone around him knew what his headline-grabbing bid signified. On his first visit to Washington after the Dodger affair, staffers at the reorganization advisory committee greeted him with "Hello, Governor." Even Averell Harriman got into the act. Recalling for reporters his "nomination" of Rockefeller for governor at the legislative correspondents' dinner six months before, he jocularly expressed satisfaction that it might have resulted in a new stadium for the Brooklyn Dodgers.

Day after day, New York newspapers had breathlessly chronicled the saga of Rockefeller's eleventh-hour mission. The capstone was the *Times*'s profile of him on September 11, as its "Man in the News." Rather than ascribe his effort to political aspirations, the *Times* bought the party line put out by Room 5600: that it was Rockefeller's "United Nations mood" coming to the fore, a reference to his role in keeping the UN in New York. It quoted a Rockefeller friend: "Whenever the community of New York begins to lose something, the family gets interested."

He was described in that profile as "a resolute, aggressive and boundlessly energetic man of 49 who enjoys rare gifts of salesmanship. He is bursting with an optimism that can find an outlet only in action."

The Nelson Rockefeller who was girding himself, at forty-nine, for his first political campaign seemed indeed barely different than Nelson Rockefeller at thirty-nine or twenty-nine. He was four times a grandfather now, but the typical ravages of middle age barely grazed him: his face was virtually unlined, his hair full and brown, his five-foot-nine-inch (or five-ten; no one was quite sure which was right) physique as trim as a young midshipman's. The only tip-off that he was verging on fifty was the reading glasses, which he was still not enough of a politician to abjure in his public appearances.

His adrenal level was as astounding as ever, the array of his activities a kaleidoscopic whirl that would have left most mortals reeling. For starters, he was still fully immersed, at the moment, in the Special Studies Project, the first report of which had still not appeared. He chaired the state constitutional convention commission. He headed the President's reorganization committee, and was in the midst of a study, at Eisenhower's behest, of the foreign policy apparatus—a study that contemplated possibly kicking John Foster

Dulles upstairs to a senior advisory role.* Soon, in the wake of Sputnik, he would start studying, as well, a possible Defense Department reorganization.

He had just opened his Museum of Primitive Art on 54th Street. He was overseeing the new Dartmouth arts center. He continued as chairman of the Museum of Modern Art, of Rockefeller Center, and of IBEC. And somehow, he also found plenty of time to travel: to Africa, to Iran, to Korea.

So sprawling were his activities now, and so copious the staff needed to attend to them, that Rockefeller found his existing offices inadequate to accommodate it all. In 1956 he had acquired the two townhouses on West 55th Street that backed into the twins he already owned on West 54th Street, with an eye toward future expansion of his primitive art museum. But it wasn't long before the Beaux Arts structures were crammed not with Congolese artifacts but with the desks of Rockefeller staff members. In the shadow of his father's great monument, Rockefeller Center, a mini Nelson Rockefeller complex was taking shape.

There were those who wondered how Rockefeller kept up this frenetic pace, how he raced from meeting to meeting and project to project without ever slackening or falling ill. Part of the explanation was simply glandular; one wag called him "the male equivalent of Eleanor Roosevelt." Then, too, he had the cushion of his energetic and talented staff; with the equanimity of the super-rich, he could sail serenely through a day that left Kissinger or Hanks frazzled and overwhelmed.

But there was another answer as to how he did it, an answer that August Heckscher stumbled upon when he was working on the Special Studies Project. Heckscher, the director of the Twentieth Century Fund (and grandson and namesake of the realtor who tangled with the Rockefellers in the early days of Rockefeller Center), had been asked to rewrite the foreign policy report. With no other office available, and Rockefeller away, Nancy Hanks told him he could use Rockefeller's. One day, in search of a paper clip, Heckscher happened to open the desk drawer—and there, to his astonishment, he encountered "hundreds of little boxes and bottles of pills." Says Heckscher, "It was enough to suggest to me that a man who seemed so well balanced and happy was really under enormous strain and stress."

This was Rockefeller's private little treasure trove: the cornucopia of pills that he stuffed into his desk drawer and carried in a satchel wherever he

* Under the proposal, Dulles would become "First Secretary of the Government," overseeing foreign affairs policy making, while "a younger man," in Eisenhower's words, would take over as Secretary of State. In boosting this plan, Rockefeller would appear to be exacting a measure of revenge against his old rival, but it was actually Eisenhower's idea. The President's handling of it was typical of his somewhat devious dealings with his Secretary of State: while Rockefeller's memos on the plan date back to the fall of 1956, it was not until January 1958 that Eisenhower authorized Rockefeller to fill in Dulles. Sources: Ann Whitman Diary, January 1958, DDEL; "Minutes—Foreign Affairs Reorganization," NAR PACGO Box 51, RAC.

went. What he did with them all, and where he obtained them, was always a mystery, but he was more than willing to share his stash with anyone with a complaint. "He was always taking pills," remembers his Washington aide Bill Kintner. "And he was always giving them out, too." When Nancy Hanks was tired, Rockefeller slipped her vitamin pills. When Rod Perkins, in the HEW days, was bedridden with the flu, Rockefeller arrived at his house with his bag of pills and, says Perkins, "insisted to my wife that she administer some of these to me." Perkins thought they were penicillin, but he never knew for sure.

Most of the time, Rockefeller's eager ministrations were appreciated, but not always. During a trip to Africa, he was visiting with the fabled missionary doctor Albert Schweitzer. Just before joining the good doctor for lunch, Rockefeller decided to offer the natives some medical help of his own, and stood outside Schweitzer's ward handing out sulfasuxidine, an antidysentery drug. When Schweitzer came along, he was appalled. "It is not necessary here," he berated Rockefeller in French. ("I was terribly embarrassed," Rockefeller would confess when he told the story later. "Schweitzer, imagine!")

There were plenty of antibiotics in Rockefeller's pill collection, and painkillers, and vitamins, and medications for his troublesome sinuses (what Lockwood referred to as "liquid dynamite" for the nose). And there were also a goodly number of tranquilizers.

Rockefeller freely admitted taking them. In fact, in one interview, he waxed enthusiastic to a sympathetic reporter about "the whole Miltown field." Tranquilizers, he said, had helped him over many tense moments.

His Miltown habit was one indication of the inner tension that coiled like an overwound watch spring beneath the surface. Another was the continued omnipresence of his favorite osteopath, Kenneth Riland. So frequently did Rockefeller need Riland's services that he set up an office for him just downstairs from Room 5600.

Given the velocity of Rockefeller's life, there was abundant cause for the strain and for the assuagement he sought from Miltowns and the osteopath's table. But far and away the chief cause in the fall of 1957, as he prepared for the electoral test to come, was his marriage to Tod.

Since the war, their relationship had come to more and more resemble the frigid marriage of Charles Foster Kane and his society wife in *Citizen Kane*: one marked by ever widening distances, physically and emotionally, between the partners. During Rockefeller's stint in Washington under Eisenhower—with Tod declining to join him in the capital—they had seen little of one another, leaving Rockefeller free to indulge in what amounted to a double life with a new young consort, Nancy Hanks. With Hanks, he behaved like a footloose young swain, sharing dinners at Foxhall Road and her apartment, visiting her family's North Carolina homestead, lavishing her with gifts—in general, acting as though his marriage to Tod did not exist.

Tod's intimates have little doubt that she was aware of her husband's peregrinations. But, in the manner of many an upper-class doyenne, she seemed willing to overlook his wayward ways, in the interest of home and hearth, the children and grandchildren.

Not much changed upon his return to the New York office in 1956. The breach between Nelson and Tod was, by then, an irreparable fact of life. Not long afterward, a young Norwegian housemaid, Anne-Marie Rasmussen, came to work for the Rockefellers, and quickly noticed something odd about their domestic arrangements at Pocantico: while Mr. Rockefeller would spend considerable time with his family at their Colonial home, Hawes House, each night he would repair to the guest house Wally Harrison had designed for him in the 1930s. "As far as I knew," she would relate, "he never slept in the main house with his family."

This arrangement was, in fact, nothing new; it had been in force for at least a decade, dating back to the late 1940s. One of Steven Rockefeller's most vivid childhood memories is of greeting his father in the late afternoon, upon his arrival from his New York office: "I would take his briefcase and proudly march up the hill with him"—the hill leading from Hawes House to the guest house. "After he and Mother stopped sharing a bedroom," Steven recalled, "Father stayed up on that hill when in Pocantico."

Both husband and wife seemed acclimated to this state of affairs. But now, facing the prospect of a very public campaign, with countless family photographs and countless family interviews, Nelson Rockefeller inwardly shuddered. What had been tolerable for so long was, quite suddenly, intolerable.

Now, as he came to grips with the most monumental decision of his career, he suddenly lurched toward another decision. He would seek a divorce from Tod.

In the course of a long, meandering car ride he told Frank Jamieson of his plans. Jamieson was appalled that Rockefeller would consider such a precipitous step on the eve of a major campaign, and made no bones about the consequences: it would be political suicide. "Frank felt it would be the end for Nelson politically," his wife, Linda, would recall. "Nelson knew it too, but Frank had to work very hard to change his mind." Finally, after much hammering by Jamieson, Rockefeller backed off. For the sake of his future in politics, he would maintain the charade of his marriage.

Shortly after this was settled, Rockefeller was waiting for his private plane at Westchester County Airport with George Hinman when he spotted a gorgeous red Ferrari. "That's really what I'd like to have," he said as he ogled the vehicle.

"Well," retorted the laconic Hinman, "you can take your choice. You can have the sports car or you can be a governor—you can't do both."

For the time being, in the interests of his ambitions, he would keep his impulses in check. But the beckoning sheen of the red Ferrari was never far from Nelson Rockefeller's mind.

Thirty-eight

Travels with Malcolm

The setting was the Roxy Rothafel suite at Radio City Music Hall, now appropriated by Nelson Rockefeller, the Music Hall's landlord, for his most private political conversations. There, seated in the plush gilt fabric armchairs, dwarfed by the twenty-foot-high cherry-wood walls and softly illuminated by the Deskey torchères, were Rockefeller and two guests: Thomas E. Dewey and Dewey's longtime confidant and counsel, George Shapiro.

Rockefeller had asked Dewey to come by because, he said, he was close to making up his mind about the governorship and wanted the former governor's advice on how he might go about securing the nomination.

Somehow, the three men managed to set aside Dewey's conviction that Rockefeller could not be elected dogcatcher and focused instead on the mechanics of the Republican nomination. The system had not changed since Dewey's first quest for the nomination: there was no gubernatorial primary, but rather a race to win the allegiance of delegates to the party convention. Since those delegates were largely handpicked by the county chairmen, the paramount concern of an aspiring nominee was to gain the support of the chairmen. As Warren Moscow observed in his 1948 study, *Politics in the Empire State,* "The delegates are just a list of names who will vote in the convention as they are told by the bosses."

It was these bosses—chief among them Kenneth Simpson of New York County, Edwin Jaeckle of Buffalo, and J. Russel Sprague of Nassau—who gave Dewey his nomination. And it would be the bosses again—many of the same characters, in fact—to whom Rockefeller would have to turn for his.

Dewey recalled that he won their support not in a smoke-filled room, but by journeying from county to county, pressing the flesh of the local party gentry. That, he suggested, was what Rockefeller would have to do as well.

So entranced was Rockefeller with the ex-governor's dissertation that, remembers Shapiro, "he postponed an airplane flight he was supposed to take that afternoon until later in the evening." Resorting to his stock of superlatives, he told Dewey his advice was "superb" and he would do all he could to follow it.

What Dewey was urging was, of course, what Jud Morhouse had been doing surreptitiously on Rockefeller's behalf for months.

Morhouse's latest ploy was to circulate a poll showing voter preference among various possible GOP gubernatorial nominees. The number one choice was Thomas E. Dewey, who plainly would not be running. Number two, finishing ahead of all the familiar GOP stalwarts, including Heck and Mahoney, was Nelson Rockefeller. What's more, the poll showed that Rockefeller had the broadest appeal to independent and Democratic voters—an essential element if the Republicans were to regain the Governor's Mansion.

Morhouse was less than forthcoming about his poll's provenance and its methodology, leading those on the losing end to wonder about its legitimacy. "He has declined to say publicly how many persons were sampled, what questions were asked, who paid for the poll, how much it cost, or what were the specific results," complained the conservative *National Review*. "He has also not made it clear whether the 'Rockefeller' recognized by the respondents is the founder of the Standard Oil Company, the builder of Rockefeller Center, the divorced husband of Bobo, Bobo herself, one of the foundations, the owner of the dog which won first prize in a showing two weeks ago, or Nelson."*

Whether or not the survey was for real, Morhouse's circulation of the results in late 1957 more than accomplished his purpose. His aim was to simply leave an impression with the county leaders, an impression that Rockefeller was not some overeager, bumptious millionaire, but an electable commodity. The poll, dubious though it may have been, was Morhouse's calling card, and with it he would open the doors, county by county, to a Rockefeller candidacy.

His candidate, meanwhile, was starting to open a few doors on his own.

One afternoon that September, Rockefeller and his wife flew to Binghamton for a dinner party at George Hinman's house. Dinners in that stolid southern tier city on the banks of the Susquehanna River not being part of their normal fall social calendar, there had to be something special drawing

*Later, after the election, it would be alleged that Morhouse's polls in fact had been undertaken and financed by Rockefeller. No conclusive evidence, however, has surfaced to confirm this. See Stewart Alsop, *Nixon and Rockefeller*, p. 108.

them there. And there was: the only other guest, a slight, courtly octogenarian by the name of William H. Hill.

For close to half a century now, any Republican who aspired to statewide prominence had to pass Billy Hill's way. His dominance of the political scene in the southern tier of New York was complete. Not only was Hill the region's former congressman and, for as long as anyone could remember, the Republican chairman of Broome County; he was also publisher of the area's leading paper, the Binghamton *Sun.* His editorials dictated policy; his handpicked local officials, who all owed their positions to him, implemented it.

Like any absolute monarch, Hill had his regular ritual of obeisance. Each Sunday morning, Republican factotums, young and old, would arrive at Hill's home in Endicott, just west of Binghamton. Greeted by a maid in a well-starched uniform, they would be ushered through the fusty parlor, with its tasseled lampshades and its plump armchairs of faded chintz, past the grand piano with the photograph of Hill on it, and onto the porch. There they would take their places around the old man in the wicker chair, offering up tidbits of political gossip for his consumption as the maid came around with coffee and doughnuts.

Under Hill's regency, the southern tier counties had remained an ironclad Republican stronghold and an indispensable element in any potential statewide victory. The road to GOP victory in November had always run past Billy Hill's porch.

Thus it was that Rockefeller presented himself at Hinman's house, with Tod in tow, for his first audience with the genteel local pasha. Hill had apparently been well primed by Hinman; he greeted Rockefeller warmly and, when the talk turned to the 1958 race, he was surprisingly encouraging. A curious reversal of their expected roles took place: Rockefeller was the one who was coy and noncommittal, while Hill was the enthusiast.

That Rockefeller was several degrees more liberal than the southern tier's rock-solid conservative constituency seemed to be of little interest to Hill. What counted, as Hill later put it, was that Rockefeller was "a winner," someone capable of harvesting the independent votes needed to unseat Harriman.

Hill's positive comments were more than Rockefeller could have hoped for. Late in his political career, Rockefeller would exalt his memories of that dinner. Hill and Hinman, he would say, "were the first to vocalize the fact that maybe it would not be a bad idea if I considered running for governor. Well, you know, if you've got something you're thinking about and didn't dare mention and somebody says that, you are particularly grateful."

At the time, though, Rockefeller kept his gratitude well hidden. He seemed intent on adhering to his neutral, testing-the-waters stance, even when they talked about how a Rockefeller campaign might be launched. So unencouraging was Rockefeller that Hinman wondered afterward if he was really interested in pursuing the race.

Rockefeller's circumspection, however, may have been more for his wary wife's consumption than for the politicos'. He was interested, and he showed it two months later, turning up once again in Binghamton—this time without Tod—for another private get-together with Billy Hill. By then, Rockefeller knew for certain he had acquired, in one of the state's most conservative bastions, a critical ally.

And it was not long before he picked up another; someone who, in the long run, would play an even more pivotal role in his ascension than even Billy Hill.

In January 1958 Rockefeller was invited to speak at the annual gala fund-raiser of the Westchester County Republican Committee at the Hotel Commodore in New York City. As the county's wealthiest Republican residents, the Rockefellers had for decades been the committee's financial mainstays. For that January 30 dinner alone, Nelson contributed $1,000, buying up a table of ten.

Hence, if there was one county chairman whose backing Rockefeller could surely count on, it was the veteran Westchester boss, Herbert Gerlach. In the course of the dinner, Rockefeller took Gerlach aside. "A lot of people have been talking to me about running for governor," he said. "I'd like to get your views on it."

Gerlach glanced over at the head table, in the direction of the evening's other featured speaker, longtime Yonkers assemblyman Malcolm Wilson. "We might have a candidate already," he informed Rockefeller. "You know, Malcolm Wilson hasn't made up his mind what he's going to do."

"Let's talk to him," Rockefeller snapped.

The next day Gerlach phoned Wilson and arranged for the three of them to meet at Gerlach's White Plains law office the following Sunday evening.

"The reason I asked you here," Gerlach told Wilson when they all sat down on Sunday, "is because Mr. Rockefeller indicated to me that he was considering the possibility of seeking the Republican nomination for governor. And he asked me, if he did, whether he would have the support of the Westchester County Republican Committee. And I told him that if you, Malcolm Wilson, sought the nomination, you would have our support. Otherwise, he would have it."

Wilson spoke right up. "Sometime," he said, "I would like to be governor, but I would not aspire to the nomination this year. I think Mr. Rockefeller would be a fine nominee. And if he makes up his mind that he wants to seek the nomination, I know how he can get it."

Rockefeller thanked Wilson for his offer, but refrained from taking him up on it. Perhaps this was because he was still focused on his principal objective that evening: obtaining the Westchester committee's support. It was only much later, weeks after that meeting, that Rockefeller came to realize that the truly significant event that night was that Malcolm Wilson had proffered his help.

He was only forty-three, but 1958 would mark twenty years since Wilson first took his seat in the Assembly. In his early days in the legislature, his mellifluous baritone and ready command of Latin epigrams (a prodigious reader, Wilson was all of nineteen when he graduated from Fordham) earned him the tag "the boy orator of the Assembly." But what truly distinguished Wilson, among colleagues who were not exactly known for their monastic ways, was his implacable piety.

Wilson boasted that nary a drop of alcohol—beer, wine, or whiskey—had ever passed his lips, and no one had any reason to challenge his claim. Half Irish, he had been raised in an ardently Catholic Yonkers household (his father, a patent lawyer, was actually born a Protestant but converted) and educated solely in Catholic schools. Once he was in Albany, the church's moral compass never left his pocket. He pushed legislation banning "obscene movie advertising" and became the legislature's principal opponent of divorce law liberalization, going so far as to introduce bills that would set up additional barriers for those seeking annulments.

His conservatism was striking even by the standards of GOP diehards. He steadfastly fought against extending unemployment insurance, and as chairman of the powerful Codes Committee he single-handedly killed bills that would have raised benefits to keep up with inflation. He voted against public housing legislation ("the hard-pressed taxpayer shouldn't be forced to pay for it," he said) and against efforts to bar discrimination in private housing. ("There are many people who feel that they may do with their property what they wish to do," he explained.) And Wilson managed an unsuccessful attempt to impose residency requirements on those seeking welfare.

Dogmatic though he was, Wilson also gained a reputation as one of the capital's canniest, most effective legislators. A brilliant parliamentarian, Wilson had a consummate mastery of the highways and byways of the legislative process. "When he was in the Assembly," says someone who served with him there, "he not only could keep track of all of his own legislation, but of everyone else's, and what they were really trying to push. He was the type that if he played chess, he'd want to play five games at once."

His effectiveness was due, in large measure, to his uniquely encyclopedic command of virtually every one of the sixty-two counties of New York State. Over the years, Wilson had made it his business to travel the length and breadth of the state, and with his unusually retentive memory he could call up at will the details of nearly every one of those trips. The tales of his prowess abounded. Typical was this one told by Betsy Kaplan, the Republican chairman of St. Lawrence County: "Malcolm was up here one time for a rally, and a man was in the audience, and he was fussing with his finger. Malcolm stopped his speech and said, 'What did you do to your finger?' And the man told him he had some farm accident. Then, a couple of years later, Malcolm was visiting the county fair here, and the same fellow came up to him, wanting to shake his hand, and Malcolm said, 'Well, hi. How's your finger?' The guy nearly dropped dead."

While Wilson's facility may have earned him the warm feelings of town clerks in every snowbound hamlet, it was not enough to advance him to a higher political plateau. Time after time, he found himself stymied in his attempts to move up. In 1957, when Jacob Javits left the attorney generalship to become a U.S. senator, Wilson was passed over as his successor by the GOP hierarchy in favor of Louis J. Lefkowitz. Hoping to be named Assembly Majority Leader, Wilson was thwarted when Speaker Heck bowed to the wishes of the powerful Nassau County boss, J. Russel Sprague, and named Sprague's protégé, Joseph Carlino.

Wilson, in short, was in a political cul-de-sac when Gerlach and Rockefeller approached him in January 1958. A run for governor was out of the question. "I had no power base at all," he would explain. "I had an awful lot of friends but I didn't have money."

It would be hard to think of two political figures who were further apart ideologically, or, for that matter, in personality, than the pietistic archconservative from Yonkers and the bouncy liberal-minded do-gooder from Pocantico Hills. Yet, at that particular time, an immediate symbiosis existed between them. Stalled in his career, Wilson desperately required a jump start, and an alliance with Rockefeller could well provide it. And Rockefeller, for his part, badly needed Wilson's imposing array of local contacts and his intimate county-by-county, ward-by-ward grasp of the state—not to mention his ties to the party's right wing, for whom Rockefeller was undoubtedly the least preferred candidate.

Potentially, Wilson's support was a turning point, as F. Clifton White, the savvy campaign manager for gubernatorial hopeful Walter Mahoney, was quick to foresee. "Malcolm had a huge reservoir of IOUs upstate, and he was a terribly tough guy to attack," notes White. "Malcolm also had a tremendous amount of credibility, which you needed to sell Nelson Rockefeller. After all, what the hell had Nelson Rockefeller ever done for the party?"

For White, the only puzzle was why Wilson would align himself with Rockefeller rather than his ideological soul brother, Mahoney. So he phoned Wilson to ask him. Wilson was apologetic, and asked over and over, "Cliff, Walter really isn't going to run, is he?" White assured him he was. And at that point, as White recalls, Wilson confided his real rationale for supporting Rockefeller. "Cliff," he said, "it's a bad year for Republicans. It doesn't look like we can win, and we need somebody who can raise the money and put up the money to run a campaign."

This may simply have been a convenient bit of rationalization to placate Mahoney, but it certainly reflected the prevailing view of the cognoscenti as the 1958 race took shape. At the same time that Morhouse's polls were touting Rockefeller's candidacy, other surveys were showing that no Republican—Rockefeller included—could beat Averell Harriman.

It was not that Harriman had done such a splendid job; Al Smith, or FDR, or even Herbert Lehman, he wasn't. As tightfisted with the state budget as he was with his personal finances (he was given to referring to the voters as "stockholders"), Harriman kept a lid on any programs that might necessitate a dreaded tax increase. "The price for his stolid, conservative handling of the New York purse," concluded his biographer, Abramson, "was an unremarkable record as a leader."

To be sure, much of the Albany stagnation was not his fault, but rather the product of the impasse between a conservative Republican legislature and a liberal Democratic executive. "The legislature gave him *nothing,*" says Moynihan. Unable to get his own limited agenda through, Harriman made sure the Republicans didn't get theirs, vetoing more than 1,200 of the nearly 5,000 bills sent to his desk.

And Harriman's unexceptional record was certainly not the result of any lassitude on his part. He thoroughly savored being "the Guv," as he called himself, and poured every ounce of his energies into the job. "As governor he worked. God, how he worked," remembers Moynihan. "Fourteen-hour days. Endless working over his speeches. Endless!" He was the epitome of the hands-on administrator, setting up an alert system to flash him word of every forest fire, jailbreak, train wreck, or wildcat strike. After hours, he would join legislators for dinner at the Ten Eyck Hotel, or spar with journalists over drinks at their favorite hangout, Yenties.

His tirelessness had paid off in one very important respect. More than any other Democratic governor in memory, he had courted the traditional GOP bastions of upstate New York. Wherever there was a ribbon to be cut, a festival to be rung open, or a cornerstone to be laid, Harriman was there. His administration squeezed its limited budget to fund upstate road and school building, and it showed its sensitivity to the plight of the state's farmers by launching a pilot antipoverty program for the struggling small farmers of Oneida County.

As a result of these efforts, the Democrats for the first time were making inroads in GOP hegemony. Upstate Democratic registration increased by 40 percent, and the party captured a slew of local positions: village mayors, sheriffs, councilmen.

In view of the Democrats' domination of the New York City vote, the upstate swing augured ill for the Republican prospects in November. And there were far larger forces at work to dampen the GOP's hopes, not just in

New York but nationally. The uproar over the state of American preparedness—a national debate touched off by Sputnik and abetted, ironically enough, by the Rockefeller report issued that January—was at its peak, swamping the Eisenhower administration in a deluge of negative publicity. America's foreign policy, under the stewardship of the ill, visibly aging John Foster Dulles, seemed calcified and increasingly inept; the calls for Dulles' resignation were mounting. Worst of all, the country was mired in a full-blown recession, with plummeting farm prices and lengthening unemployment lines.

Small wonder, then, that Carmine De Sapio was confidently predicting that Harriman not only would be returned to office but would win by as much as 500,000 votes "if the international climate persists." And there were more than a few Republicans who privately agreed with him—including, perhaps, Malcolm Wilson.

Despite the glum prognostications, there was no shortage of GOP gubernatorial contenders as 1958 began.

To begin with, there was the venerable leader of the Assembly, Oswald D. Heck. Speaker now for two decades, the portly Heck had spent most of that time dutifully carrying water for Tom Dewey. He might, with good reason, feel it was now his turn to shine—but, as a somewhat moth-eaten insider, he seemed an unlikely choice to inspire anyone but the oldest of the party's old guard.

Next, Walter Mahoney. With the visage of a bull mastiff and a panatela never far from his lips, Mahoney was everyone's idea of the backroom Irish pol. And he was every bit as pugnacious as he looked; Mahoney had a reputation for eating governors for breakfast, starting with the governor from his own party, Tom Dewey. But when he chose to, he could also deploy a hearty, backslapping charm, and his memory of names was rivaled only by Malcolm Wilson's. He was a sly, effective Majority Leader, who enjoyed the absolute loyalty of his fellow GOP senators. Whether he could command the loyalties of the voters, however, particularly in view of his doctrinaire conservatism, was another matter.

Finally, there was Leonard Hall. Of all Rockefeller's prospective rivals, this former eight-term congressman from Oyster Bay and Republican national chairman posed the most credible challenge. A burly 225-pounder with a ready smile, Hall was, in the words of one national magazine, a "bald and bouncy gladhander as carefree as a prankster at an American Legion convention." Hall was the perennial jovial uncle: an amateur magician, a composer of comic lyrics, cabinetmaker, and gardener. Yet behind the happy-go-lucky facade was the native shrewdness and drive of a ring-tested politician who had bobbed and weaved through thirty years of public life.

If Nelson Rockefeller represented the Republican Party's haves, then Leonard Hall was the quintessence of its striving have-nots. The one advantage with which he started out in life was that his father was Teddy Roosevelt's coachman at TR's Sagamore Hill estate—but Roosevelt never paid his father more than $100 a month, and Hall grew up with seven siblings in a home without electricity or a bathroom. Hall was forced to work his way through his night classes at Georgetown Law School by holding down a $50-a-month bookkeeping job at Potomac Electric. Determined to make a career in politics, he climbed his way up rung by rung: state assemblyman, Nassau County sheriff, and finally member of Congress.

Though a GOP loyalist, Hall was hardly a cast-iron conservative. He crossed party lines to support draft extension, lend-lease, and the Marshall Plan. "You must vote your conscience," he said, "on questions of war and peace." Above all, Hall was a wily political operator, a talent he put to maximum use as Republican national chairman: he was instrumental in persuading Eisenhower to run for a second term, and single-handedly defused Harold Stassen's drive to have Nixon dumped from the 1956 ticket.

He stepped down as party chairman in 1957 with Eisenhower's support in his pocket. "If Leonard Hall is going to run for governor of New York," declared the President, "he is going to have one booster in me." Having paid the dues that he had, having cultivated the party hierarchy at every possible level, Hall felt that the nomination was practically his as of right. "Len felt that he *deserved* it," says White.

Significantly, in Morhouse's polls it was Hall who finished first among those voters who identified themselves as Republicans. And as Rockefeller took stock of his chances, Hall's impressive appeal to the party faithful weighed heavily. "Hall had all the rock-ribbed New York Republicans in his corner," recalls one of Rockefeller's aides. "He was really seen as more of a problem than Harriman."

Rockefeller, though, already had some inkling that the support for Hall was not all that it seemed—starting, in fact, with Hall's supposed number one "booster," Dwight D. Eisenhower. In mid-October, Rockefeller had visited the White House to talk to the President about his prospective run for governor. Far from reiterating his pro-Hall position, Eisenhower was downright encouraging to Rockefeller, suggesting that he speak with his political aide Tom Stephens about the run.

Afterward, Ike confided to his secretary, Ann Whitman, that he felt it was time for some "fresh faces in the political picture." Leonard Hall had many sterling qualities, but a fresh face was definitely not one of them.

Throughout the winter of 1958 and right on into the early spring, Rockefeller was publicly coy about his prospective candidacy. "I'm not a candidate for anything," he told reporters after a late January meeting in Albany with party leaders, including Heck, Mahoney, and Javits. "All I want to do is get out the Rockefeller report."

His demurral was at least partly sincere. He truly was preoccupied at the time with the Rockefeller reports—the first and most controversial of which, on national defense, had just appeared—and was eager to aim the spotlight on his handiwork, rather than on his aspirations.

But an interview he gave to the *New York Post* in late March offered another clue as to why he was so noncommittal. When the writer, Irwin Ross, asked him if he might talk to Tod, Rockefeller replied, "There's not a chance. We've had a long family tradition about keeping the children and the home out of the press. Perhaps that's one reason why we all developed as normally as we did." No amount of persuasion, Ross found, could secure a session with Mrs. Nelson Rockefeller.

"It's not me you have to convince," Rockefeller said. "My wife just has very strong views on the subject."

So how did Rockefeller propose to sequester her from the press if he ran for governor? The unavowed candidate grinned. "I'll cross that bridge when I come to it," he said.

Yet even as he recoiled from a firm commitment, Rockefeller himself did not exactly shy from the political limelight. Not only did he gladly appear at Herb Gerlach's Westchester County GOP gala, but he was the principal speaker at the New York Young Republican Club's "Salute to Eisenhower" on January 19 at the Waldorf-Astoria.

Unfortunately, the Waldorf appearance once again exposed Rockefeller's abysmal speechmaking skills. He praised the President in his usual Lincolnesque terms—"like Lincoln he leads our nation in time of trial"—and he spoke so haltingly and mechanically that one guest wondered, as she recalled, "if he'd even seen the speech before. I was thinking, 'Gosh, and they talk about maybe this man running for *governor.*' "

Such performances, however, did not in the least dampen the enthusiasm of the growing band of supporters who were unofficially talking up his candidacy. On their own, members of the Women's National Republican Club—some of whom, no doubt, had been present for his speech before the Republican women the previous summer—were plotting a Citizens for Rockefeller Committee. And Tex McCrary was at it again, starting up anew his "Draft Rockefeller" bandwagon and urging Eisenhower to jump aboard.

Even Richard Nixon made a pitch for Rockefeller's candidacy. Speaking in late January at the annual luncheon of that same Women's National Republican Club, Nixon mentioned that he knew of many "fine men" whom he would rather see as governor than Averell Harriman. But he singled out only one:

Nelson Rockefeller. The tumultuous applause by the women almost drowned out Nixon's words, while Rockefeller, just two seats away, smiled broadly.

Also beating the drums for Rockefeller, in its own way, was the *Herald Tribune*. Virtually every uptick in Rockefeller's fortunes was accorded front-page coverage, capped by this page one banner headline on March 9: "Nelson A. Rockefeller Is Strongest Republican in Poll for Governorship." The poll, undertaken by the *Tribune,* was of the 1,274 delegates to the 1954 state GOP convention, and it showed Rockefeller barely edging out Hall, 23 percent to 21 percent, as the delegates' first choice. As prognostication, the best that could be said about this survey was that it was of dubious value, in view of Rockefeller's paper-thin margin, which hardly justified such grandiose billing. But as promotion—whether intentional or otherwise—the *Tribune*'s much-trumpeted survey gave an added lift to the Rockefeller boomlet.

Then, on April 25, a man who hitherto had no known connection to Nelson Rockefeller stood before reporters and announced he was opening "Draft Rockefeller for Governor" headquarters at the Hotel Bedford on East 40th Street. The organizer was John Roosevelt, FDR's youngest son, who years earlier had broken with his family's Democratic tradition to support Dwight Eisenhower. Roosevelt may have had ideological reasons for backing Rockefeller, but undoubtedly there were pragmatic ones as well: seeking to build a power base for himself in the New York City Republican Party, Roosevelt was immersed in an ongoing feud with New York county boss Tom Curran. To preserve his preconvention leverage, Curran was supporting a "favorite son" for governor, U.S. attorney Paul Williams; by lining up early behind Rockefeller, Roosevelt was hoping to paint Curran into a corner.

Whatever his motives, Roosevelt was quickly able to raise some $27,000 for his "Draft Rockefeller" movement, tapping such well-heeled contributors as Twentieth Century–Fox boss Spyros Skouras, socialite Peggy Woodward, Bill Zeckendorf, and, naturally, Tex McCrary. With this war chest, he hoped to establish a network of "Draft Rockefeller" clubs around the state. To all who asked, Roosevelt made it plain that Rockefeller himself had nothing to do with his initiative.

And, for his part, Rockefeller remained the picture of coyness. "As matters stand, I'm not a candidate for governor," he told his questioners on TV's *Meet the Press.* His obfuscatory phraseology would have made the master of fog-speak, Dwight Eisenhower, proud: "The situation is developing and moving very rapidly in the state, and my relation to it is a matter of question which, frankly, I haven't got the basis for an answer today."

Early one afternoon that April, the phone rang in Malcolm Wilson's law office in White Plains. Nelson Rockefeller, he was told, was on the line.

"Remember when we had our meeting with Herb?" asked Rockefeller.

Wilson said he did. "Well," said Rockefeller, "I would like to talk to you about that. Could I come over and see you?" Sure, replied Wilson. "I'm at 30 Rockefeller Plaza now," said Rockefeller, "and I'll be leaving soon for Pocantico. I could stop by on the way. How about four o'clock?"

It was, in fact, not until five that Rockefeller arrived at Wilson's unprepossessing quarters atop a 1920s office building in White Plains. Settling into a green vinyl armchair, Rockefeller explained his reason for coming.

"Last January," he began, "in Gerlach's office you said that if I wanted to be the nominee you'd know how to get the nomination. Well, I think I've made up my mind that I'm going to seek it. So what did you have in mind?"

Wilson, however, was reluctant to divulge any secrets until they had a talk, first, about Rockefeller's supposedly liberal ideology—a subject they had never quite gotten around to in January. "All I know," said Wilson, "is what I read in the papers, and they've got you out in left field waving the liberal flag."

Seeking to allay Wilson's concerns, Rockefeller insisted that he had been misunderstood by the media: that while he was a liberal on social issues like civil rights, he was thoroughly conservative about economic matters. This explanation satisfied Wilson, who saw himself in much the same terms (although anyone perusing his voting record might have cause to wonder just how "liberal" he was on social concerns).

Thus reassured, Wilson proceeded to unveil his game plan. To secure the nomination, he said, Rockefeller had to appeal not just to the county chairmen but to the rank and file beneath them, since few county bosses would willfully defy the preferences of their troops. And it was essential, given his liberal reputation, that Rockefeller concentrate his efforts on the conservative upstate districts. Rockefeller did not know the upstate party faithful, but Wilson did; indeed, he knew practically every one of them by name, by occupation, and by next of kin. So, to make this plan work, Wilson would make the rounds with Rockefeller, county by county, dinner by dinner, across the length and breadth of New York State. (This was much the same strategy that Dewey had suggested, the key difference being that Dewey made no offer to accompany Rockefeller.)

Their pilgrimage, said Wilson, would be a quiet one, without ballyhoo and balloons. "There will be no spear carriers, no sycophants, no acolytes, no baggage handlers. Just the two of us." Furthermore, Wilson was insistent that "neither you, nor your brothers, nor your father is to pay a farthing for this trip." To head off any rumblings that Rockefeller was buying the nomination, all the bills would be picked up by Wilson, who would be reimbursed by Gerlach's county organization. (Wilson's scruples notwithstanding, the arrangement was a bit of a sham since, as Wilson was well aware, it was the Rockefellers who bankrolled Gerlach's committee in the first place.)

The would-be candidate was impressed. Of course, he pointed out to Wilson, "if you do this, it's going to take a lot of your time. I don't know how they'd handle that around here," he said, looking around Wilson's law office. Wilson knew what Rockefeller was driving at. As he would recall, "I think Nelson fully expected to hear, 'Well, your family has legal matters here in Westchester County, and . . .' "

Rockefeller may have expected a pitch for a quid pro quo; he certainly was prepared to offer it. But Wilson did not rise to the bait. "Well," he told his guest, "I will just do it."

Rockefeller confided that he planned to toss his hat in the ring at the end of June. In the meantime, he wanted Wilson to join the little group of trusted advisers who were already plotting the campaign.

The group gathered once a week in the Roxy suite at Radio City Music Hall. "We mainly talked about issues and reviewed proposed position papers," Wilson remembered. The regulars included the usual old standbys: Lockwood, Jamieson, Stacy May, Rod Perkins, and Nancy Hanks. There were the two New York gurus, Bill Ronan and George Hinman. And, as well, there was a new face, a trim, sprightly blonde who had suddenly popped up in Rockefeller's entourage. She was introduced to everyone as one of his assistants, Mrs. James S. Murphy.

Even before Rockefeller and Wilson hit the hustings, Frank Moore was out in the field taking soundings. And the reports he came back with gave Rockefeller the last bit of encouragement he needed to enter the race.

Moore had met in Buffalo with the former state chairman, Ed Jaeckle, who in the Dewey years had been the GOP's premier power broker. Although no longer the almighty force he once was, Jaeckle was still as well wired as anyone in the party, and as he and Moore drove in from the airport together, Jaeckle remarked, with his usual bluntness, "It looks like your boyfriend can have the nomination if he wants it."

Moore reminded Jaeckle that a year earlier, when they had chatted about the governorship, the old boss had told him that Rockefeller didn't have a chance. But now, in a single sentence, Jaeckle dismissed Mahoney, Heck, and Hall as all losers. "They tell me that Rockefeller is quite a nice guy," said Jaeckle. "I think he would have a better chance [against Harriman] than any of the others that have been mentioned."

Jaeckle's was not the last word on the subject. But it was a telling indication that the support Hall and Mahoney were counting on from the party regulars would not be there when they needed it.

What Jaeckle was saying privately, another of the old party barons, Billy Hill, was now saying publicly.

On May 6, in a rare signed editorial in his newspaper, the Binghamton *Sun,* Hill came out foursquare for Nelson Rockefeller for governor. He described Rockefeller in the most adulatory terms: "His new, fresh, vigorous leadership has caught the imagination of the people. . . . He has personality—one of the warmest we have seen. He has brains. He has tireless energy. . . . He is a winner, a rising star of the first magnitude.

"The Republican party owes it to the people of the state—and to itself—to nominate Nelson Rockefeller for Governor."

To guarantee that his appeal gained maximum press coverage, Hill sent copies of the editorial to the state's major news organs two days before it was published in his own paper. The *Herald Tribune* ran the story on page one—"Movement to Draft Rockefeller Gaining" was the headline—and on its inside pages reprinted the editorial verbatim, as though the pronouncement of the Broome County Republican boss was a major address by a head of state.

Hill's pronunciamento quickly had its intended effect on its target audience. The day it broke, Frank Moore received a call from Ogden Bush, the longtime chairman of Delaware County in the Catskill region. Excited about Hill's endorsement, Bush told Moore that none of Rockefeller's rivals had a chance. Not only was Bush enthusiastically for Rockefeller, but he believed that the chairmen of two other Catskill counties, Sullivan and Greene, were as well.

Despite these developments, Jud Morhouse was worried. At least ten upstate counties had come out early in support of Mahoney, and Hall had been endorsed by his home county of Nassau as well as neighboring Suffolk. By Morhouse's own reckoning, Hall and Mahoney each had actual or potential commitments from a quarter of the 1,170 delegates, while Rockefeller could probably count on another quarter. Morhouse stewed about the possibility of a Hall-Mahoney coalition that would stop Rockefeller's bid dead in its tracks.

To stem the tide, Morhouse resorted to his favorite ploy: his polls. In meetings with upstate leaders, he revealed the results of his latest soundings, showing Rockefeller faring better than any of his rivals against Harriman. When he arrived in New York City the first week of June for the state party's annual fund-raising gala, he took his polls with him, playing them up in closed-door sessions with county bosses prior to the big dinner. Then, the day after the dinner, he upped the ante even further in a meeting with a dozen leaders. "Either you guys support me while I pick the best candidate," Morhouse sniped, "or you will get yourselves some chowderhead and get this election all messed up."

"I say that the organization has got to go for Rockefeller—and if it doesn't, I will step down as state chairman."

Morhouse's threat and his blatant stumping for Rockefeller outraged Hall and Mahoney backers. No longer was there the slightest pretense about his "neutrality."

There was no turning back now for Jud Morhouse. He had staked all he had, his whole future in politics, on Nelson Rockefeller. He could only hope that his noncandidate candidate would finally drop the pose of coyness and step into the ring.

And at long last, on the thirtieth of June, Nelson Rockefeller obliged.

Summoning reporters to Room 5600, Rockefeller stood in the small library there, before a bronze bust of his grandfather Rockefeller, and announced his candidacy for the governorship. Peering through his reading glasses, he read from a prepared statement.

"With so much that must and can be done," he said, "I would welcome the opportunity of accepting the challenge should the Republican Party choose me as its nominee."

Rather than recite his own qualifications, Rockefeller chose to blood himself for the wars by launching an all-out attack on the administration of his old friend Averell. He ran down a litany of the woes of the day: juvenile delinquency, organized crime, run-down streets and roads, and, above all, economic decline. "New York State is faced with serious financial and social problems," he warned. "Its income is unequal to the outgo. And the delayed reckoning will confront the state next year."

"What we need," he said, "is a transfusion of political courage."

The newsmen asked the obvious questions, and Rockefeller offered the obvious pat answers. Did he think his wealth would hamper him as a candidate? "I must say that I think the voter judges the man," he replied. How did his family feel? "They've been very enthusiastic—a fact which I appreciate greatly." Did he see the governorship as a stepping-stone to the White House in 1960? "My interests are concentrated on the problems of the state of New York."

He was then asked about a telegram he had just received from Len Hall, welcoming him into the field and inviting him to a series of debates around the state à la Lincoln-Douglas. Rockefeller said he was "complimented" by the challenge, and he thought debates were useful—but he would not commit himself until he learned more about what Hall had in mind.

Thanking the reporters, Rockefeller made it known he had to be going. He and Malcolm Wilson were expected in Kinderhook, New York, that very evening, and they had a long drive ahead of them up the Taconic Parkway.

"Nelson always liked to say that he drove around the state with Malcolm in his old Buick," Wilson would recall thirty years later. "Well, it wasn't an old Buick. It was a *new* Buick." Whatever the car's vintage, the fact remained that it was just Wilson and Rockefeller, sharing the front seat in a vehicle that Rockefeller, whose taste in Buicks ran to 1930s roadsters, would not normally be caught dead in.

On the way up the Taconic Parkway that afternoon, they happened to pass an immense Rolls-Royce driven by an elderly woman, with an even more elderly man beside her. "Why, that's Father," Rockefeller gasped. They slowed and pulled over and signaled to the Rolls to do the same. Astonished to see his son in such a nondescript vehicle, Junior asked where he was going. "To Kinderhook," Nelson replied, an answer that undoubtedly astonished Junior all the more.

Kinderhook was a tidy little Hudson River valley town whose one claim to fame was that it was the home of the first New York governor to become President, Martin Van Buren. (The choice of this site for Rockefeller's maiden campaign stop was quite deliberate, Wilson would later say.) There, at the Dutch Inn on the Post Road, Rockefeller and Wilson were to meet with the Columbia County Republican Committee.

"Columbia County was as rural and conservative a county as any you'd find in New York State," Wilson would say. It wasn't really—there were a good many other counties in the state that surpassed it on both counts—but it was rural and conservative enough to suit Wilson's purposes. The chairman was a woman with the euphonious name of Myrtie Tinklepaugh, and it so happened that she was both a staunch conservative *and* an admirer of Nelson Rockefeller. Years earlier, Tinklepaugh had asked Rockefeller to participate in a local debate at Chatham High School; to her delight and eternal gratitude, he accepted. So Tinklepaugh was more than happy to have her county committee be the first to host the new gubernatorial candidate.

At Wilson's insistence, the tables were arranged in a hollow square, to avoid a head-table arrangement that would have ruffled someone's feathers. When Rockefeller and Wilson arrived, they shook hands all around, and it was then Wilson noticed something special about Rockefeller: "During the five or ten seconds that you and he were talking, it was as if there was nobody else in the world except you and him. He just focused on the person. Never had I seen anything like it in any public figure."

After dinner, the former county chairman stood up and praised Rockefeller, and then Tinklepaugh rose and praised Rockefeller some more. Finally, it was Rockefeller's turn. He said little of substance, but it didn't seem to matter. "He just charmed everyone," recalls Wilson. Tinklepaugh asked Wilson to take Rockefeller over to the bar; two minutes later, she called them back into the room. "I just want you to know," she said, "that our six delegates have just endorsed Nelson Rockefeller."

It was exactly as Wilson had planned. The next morning, when the New York papers reported Rockefeller's entry into the race, they also reported that that same evening he won the support of conservative Columbia County's six delegates.

"Nelson thought he knew New York State, because as chairman of this constitutional commission he'd been to Buffalo, Rochester, Syracuse, Binghamton, and Albany," says Wilson. "But he didn't know the state at all. Hardly anybody really knows it, knows that you can drive one hundred miles southwest of Buffalo and still not be out of the state. Or that the town of Dunkirk in Chautauqua County is closer to Chicago than it is to New York City. It's a hell of a big state."

For the next eight weeks Wilson would be giving Rockefeller a firsthand education. Zipping along in Wilson's Buick, they rolled through the Catskills, traversed the Mohawk Valley west of Albany, and passed through the vast undulant terrain of farm country at the state's heart. They took in the splendor of the Finger Lakes, the pristine isolation of the Adirondacks, and the sallow grittiness of the struggling factory towns.

To be sure, they were the most mismatched of traveling companions: the impulsive, hyperenergetic multimillionaire and the calculating, often ponderous Yonkers assemblyman. Not since Franklin D. Roosevelt and his trusted adviser Louis Howe had there been an unlikelier political duo, but just as Roosevelt had found an ideal political complement in Howe, so, too, did Rockefeller find one in Wilson: someone who, set down at random on any acre of New York State, could find his way to the local county committeeman's house.

Not that Rockefeller accepted Wilson's approach with total serenity. "Riding in the car was pure torture for him," says Wilson. "He would have preferred to fly." At one point, he had had enough. After finishing a meeting in Utica, Rockefeller climbed back in the Buick and asked Wilson where they were going next. Told they had to be in Massena, on the St. Lawrence River, for a lunch the next day, Rockefeller pulled out a map and gazed at it with a pained expression. "It's a long way from Utica to Massena," he sighed. "I think we'd better fly. There's an airport around here, and I can have a plane take us up there tomorrow morning." Wilson gasped (he had never flown before and was scared to try), but Rockefeller was adamant. "There's nothing like it," he assured Wilson. "You'll enjoy it."

To ease the driving burden, Rockefeller began bringing along his son Steven, who had just graduated from Princeton. "Stevie's the real political pro in the family," he would joke. "He was elected president of the Princeton student council." Steven, indeed, proved a game helper, hoisting beers with the party pros after hours while his father and Wilson went upstairs to rest (although one pol sardonically observed, "Now I know why the Rockefellers are so rich. Steven didn't buy a single round of drinks all night").

Following Wilson's prescription, there was no entourage, no caravan of limousines—just the lone Buick. Arriving once for a lunch at the Cortland County American Legion post, the Rockefellers and Wilson were greeted by a cordon of policemen who had cleared curb space for the expected convoy of vehicles. To the cops' bewilderment, the Buick pulled up, and nothing else. "When we would arrive at a hotel, we would carry our own bags in," recalled

Wilson. "It was part of our effort to get people to understand what sort of a person Nelson Rockefeller was: that he was a man and a real man."

Never had Rockefeller made more of a determined effort to play down his wealth. To well-wishers, he never said "Thanks a million"; it was always "Thanks a thousand."

What was equally an element of Wilson's game plan was that the candidate, in his appearances, say as little of substance as possible. Left behind at Rockefeller Plaza were the position papers, the policy analyses—anything that might taint the campaign with the dreaded stamp of liberalism. "I would never let Nelson speak about anything," says Wilson. "No issues. Nothing. *Nothing.* He'd say hello to people, and say some high-level stuff. 'We've got to be sure we have a Republican governor' and so on. But that was it."

What Wilson was selling—the "merchandise," as he put it—was not Rockefeller's policies but his personality. And no matter how weary he was from his rambling, Rockefeller never failed to deliver. Grinning broadly, grabbing arms, Rockefeller bounded around the room, enveloping the faithful in his high-voltage charm. Even the crustiest of old soldiers succumbed. They would gape, slack-jawed, as the candidate, not content to confine his sunshine to the party workers, suddenly barged into the kitchen to pump the hands of cooks and busboys.

Nearly everyone who encountered him was caught up in the vortex. He was an irresistible presence, with his insouciant affability, with his square-jawed good looks, and, not least, with the magical aura of the Rockefeller name. All the elements worked in tandem, and produced a reaction not unlike what would have happened if Clark Gable had suddenly shown up at the Oneida Kiwanis Club's annual barbecue. The difference was that Nelson Rockefeller was no unapproachable demigod, but a super-rich celebrity who was as eager to ingratiate as a Fuller Brush Man.

The press covering the campaign got their first exposure to the phenomenon when Rockefeller showed up at the annual Savannah, New York, Potato Festival. Without anyone prompting him, Rockefeller shucked off his coat and tie, unbuttoned his collar, rolled up his sleeves, and mounted one of the tractors. A crowd gathered around, and as the farmers gawked at the sight of a Rockefeller on a tractor, Rockefeller climbed down and began engaging them, one by one, in earnest conversation—much to the astonishment of the reporters covering this scene. Says Jack Germond, "I can remember one guy telling him about the problem he was having with some state law that required lights on their manure spreaders. He must have talked with this guy ten or fifteen minutes." Rockefeller was not just going through the motions; "he really wanted to talk to these people," says Germond. "It was just so different from what we were used to with Harriman. Harriman was always shaking one hand and looking ahead to the next voter, just like any politician. But Rockefeller got into these long conversations. He spent the whole day there." For the state's political press, it was their first realization that there was more to Nelson Rockefeller than policy papers and a nine-figure bank account.

Word of Rockefeller's barnstorming performances soon spread, sending shivers of apprehension down the spines of county chairmen who had already aligned themselves with his rivals. The last thing they wanted was Rockefeller ingratiating himself in their territory, and several made it known to Wilson that his man would not be welcome. "No, no, no, Malcolm, he can't come into my county," bellowed the chairman of Cattaraugus County, who was supporting Mahoney. Wilson got the same message from another Mahoney backer, Joseph Rubinstein in Chautauqua County—but in that case Wilson employed a ruse to smuggle in Rockefeller. Wilson accepted a standing invitation to speak at the annual luncheon of the Women's Republican Club, and asked the organizers if it was all right if he brought along Nelson Rockefeller, who just happened to be traveling with him. The women were delighted. Then Wilson phoned Rubinstein. "Joe," he said, "I'm here at the White Hotel in Dunkirk, and I'll be speaking at the women's luncheon today. Now I have Nelson Rockefeller with me, but I want you to know that I am not violating your rules. All I want to know is, do you want me to tell him that he's going to have to stay in his room here while I go and speak at the lunch?"

"You son of a bitch," snarled Rubinstein. The county boss headed over to the hotel, in time to catch Rockefeller greeting well-wishers on the porch, while a photographer from the local paper snapped away. Prudently, Rubinstein gave in and let Rockefeller speak—and, while he was at it, squeezed himself into some of the pictures.

By August 4, a little more than a month after he had entered the race, Rockefeller had visited all but seven of the state's sixty-two counties. "I never worked so hard for anything," he would recall, "as I did for that nomination."

And it was equally true that Malcolm Wilson had never worked so hard for anything, either. "I have this memory of Malcolm," recounted Steven Rockefeller. "I'd get up in the morning and go into Malcolm's room and there he would be at 7 A.M., a cigarette in his mouth, the phone cocked under the side of his head, talking softly to someone, making arrangements and taking notes. At the end of the day, it would be the same thing . . . The truth of the matter is that without Malcolm Wilson, Father's nomination probably could not have been pulled off."

While Rockefeller was roaming around the state, his chief rival, Len Hall, was not exactly standing still. He, too, was making a grand tour of the Empire State, visiting with most of the same county committees that were receiving Rockefeller. But the reception accorded this pillar of Republicanism was far different than what Rockefeller was experiencing. There was much respect, but zero adulation.

Hall had no illusions about what he was up against. As he would later ruefully remark, "Nelson would go upstate and smile and shake hands with some leader's wife, and she'd get all watery at the knees, like he was a prince or something." But Hall still felt he had a chance, still believed he could puncture the Rockefeller bubble if he could only engage his rival in a one-on-one debate. Rockefeller, however, refused to bite, rebuffing Hall's entreaties by falling back on that trusty old prop, "party unity." He was "ready to fight the Democratic incumbent," he declared, but he would not fight his fellow Republicans.

In his frustration with his elusive opponent, Hall erupted. In a television appearance, he lambasted Rockefeller as a "silent" candidate whose managers were "keeping him under glass."

Rockefeller beatifically ignored Hall's taunts. A little more than a week later, he appeared with Hall and the other GOP gubernatorial hopefuls at the Orange County Republican Committee's "Rally for Victory" dinner. His rivals devoted their speeches to fierce excoriations of the Harriman administration. Rockefeller, on the other hand, spent his time at the podium lavishing praise on his adversaries, most especially Len Hall. "The fact that a man of the caliber of Len Hall, who has devoted his life to public service, is presenting himself as a candidate," he said, "is a great tribute to the party and shows the confidence he has in this great state." Hall could only smile, and wave, and acknowledge the applause, while inwardly he seethed.

All along, Len Hall had counted on the party's old guard, the wizened pros with whom he had joshed, connived, and swapped yarns all these years, to deliver him the nomination. But now, one by one, they were defecting to the Rockefeller camp. And what Hall didn't realize was that the ultimate act of betrayal had come from his very own camp, his home county of Nassau—and that the Judas was the county leader, the formidable J. Russel Sprague.

Sprague, an old intimate of Tom Dewey's and master of arguably the state party's most efficient county apparatus, had done all the right things by Hall. Promptly declaring Hall the county party's favorite son, he lined up the Nassau delegation solidly behind him. So Hall felt it was perfectly reasonable to call on the old boss and ask him if he might borrow Sprague's protégé, Assembly Majority Leader Joe Carlino, to do for him what Wilson was doing for Rockefeller.

Sprague agreed it was a good idea—but there was one problem. Heck, the Assembly Speaker, was still nominally a candidate: "Unless Ozzie gives Joe clearance, it will look like a betrayal of his own Speaker." This didn't bother Hall, who was an old ally of Heck's (he had been one of those instrumental in making him Speaker twenty years earlier); he offered to visit Heck at his law firm in Schenectady, with Carlino in tow, to ask Heck's permission.

Recalls Carlino, "We called Ozzie up right then and there, and we got him in his office, and Russ said, 'Ozzie, Len Hall and Joe would like to come up and speak to you about something.' And Heck said okay, and fixed the time. We even got a private plane from Grumman or somebody to take us up there. Len was all beaming, and he left.

"So then old Russ said to me, 'Sit down. Wait a few minutes.' He waited until Len had left the building, and then he picked up the phone and got to Ozzie Heck again. And he said, 'Ozzie, here's what they're coming up to talk to you about. But I don't want you to do that. Say you can't do it, that it would be embarrassing to you.'

"So Len and I fly up to see Heck, and Ozzie says to him, 'Gee, Len, you know, I'd love to do something for you,' because when Heck had been elected Speaker, Hall was one of his supporters. 'I'd love to do it, but it would be very embarrassing to me. The members would probably resent it, because here's their Majority Leader traveling with Hall when their Speaker is still a declared candidate. You can understand that, can't you, Len?' "

Hall said he understood, and left, without the assist from Carlino that he so desperately needed. Carlino chortles as he tells the tale. "Len," he says, "never realized what a screwing he got from Russ Sprague on the way up there."

That Sprague might pull the rug out from under Hall would not have come as a total shock to party insiders. There had been bad blood between the two men since 1948, when Hall openly criticized the management of Dewey's presidential campaign; it was only in the last twelve months that they had buried the hatchet.

Nonetheless, ill will alone did not fully explain why the ever calculating Sprague would turn on Hall and insidiously boost Rockefeller. Nor, for that matter, would Rockefeller's charisma alone explain why so many of Sprague's counterparts throughout the state were abandoning party stalwarts like Hall and Mahoney in favor of the newcomer.

A better, fuller explanation was offered candidly years later by someone in a position to know: Malcolm Wilson. "I always had the feeling," he says, "although the leaders there never articulated it to me, that I was able to get the support of many of the small upstate counties not necessarily out of a conviction on the part of the leaders that Nelson Rockefeller would be elected, but because they felt that if he was on the ticket, there would be adequate funding of the campaign, including the candidates below him."

Rockefeller himself made much the same assumption. "When I decided to run for office in 1958," he told an interviewer in 1975, "the party was bust. Harriman was governor. I have to assume that one of the reasons the party let in an independent—and I was an independent—was because they figured nobody could win, and here was somebody who could probably finance his own campaign, and therefore what's wrong with that?"

Hayward "Red" Plumadore, the leader of the Adirondack county of Franklin at the time, confirms that that was exactly what happened. "I said to myself, 'Our party treasury is broke. Let's at least get a guy who can run and pay his own way.' "

In later years, one of Rockefeller's rivals for the nomination would charge, anonymously, that Rockefeller money not only influenced the party leaders but influenced them in a far more sinister way. "A lot of small towns are run by bankers, and a lot of Republican chairmen are close to those bankers," he told Michael Kramer and Sam Roberts, co-authors of the 1976 investigative biography of Rockefeller, *"I Never Wanted to Be Vice President of Anything!"* "In some cases, the bankers and the county GOP chairmen are the same people. Three men I thought loyal to me came to me and said that their financial survival depended on their switching to Rockefeller. I told them to switch. Some things aren't worth the fight." (When Wilson is asked about this allegation, he snarls, "That is the most asinine thing. Whoever said that doesn't have any brains.")

Whether the power of Rockefeller wealth was brought to bear directly, as this adversary charges, or indirectly, through the covetous eyes of the party leaders, there was little question, then or in the future, that it played an important role in the 1958 outcome. As a disheartened Walter Mahoney told his campaign manager, Clifton White, "Cliff, you can't beat that kind of money."

Nelson Rockefeller did not buy his first gubernatorial nomination. But the awesome weight of his fortune—particularly going into a contest against another megamillionaire, Harriman—acted as decisively as if he did.

As they fell in, one by one, behind Rockefeller, few of the party's movers and shakers bothered to unravel the skein of platitudes that camouflaged the candidate's political philosophy. There were no ideological litmus tests; the leaders simply accepted at face value Wilson's assurances that Rockefeller was not a New Deal liberal. "I've talked to him. I know what he is," Wilson would say. "Do you think I'd want him to be governor unless I was sure?"

Nonetheless, a small but vocal element of hard-core conservatives refused to be taken in by Wilson's seal of approval. To them, Rockefeller was an interloper with suspiciously liberal leanings and a suspiciously liberal circle of acquaintances. He may be a Republican, but what manner of Republican was he?

Among the first to sound the alarm was the influential conservative journal *National Review*. In its issue of August 2, the publication castigated the party leadership for its uncritical acceptance of Rockefeller's vague credentials. Rockefeller, the journal complained, "has been shielded from questions and has ducked debate. His campaign has consisted entirely of his publicized reports, grandiose claims of delegate support, the emission of pleasantries—

and the circularization of Mr. Morhouse's poll proving that Rockefeller is a well-known name. . . .

"Between now and the Convention, the delegates to the Republican Convention may want to know just where Rockefeller *does* stand politically. They may even want to discover the nature of that brand of politics which Liberal journalists are hailing as 'Rockefeller Republicanism.' "

Then, two weeks later, a group calling itself the "Committee for Republican Victory" issued a broadside from its headquarters at the Hotel McAlpin on West 34th Street in Manhattan. In a letter to Republican delegates, it attacked Rockefeller as "a liberal posing as a Republican" and "a New Deal lackey, faithfully supporting Roosevelt and Truman." The committee even brought up the registration of Rockefeller's "socialite wife" in "New York's socialistic Liberal Party."

Rockefeller's candidacy, it warned, "would cause hundreds of thousands of Republicans to sit on their hands, to refuse to vote on election day or, in utter disgust, to vote for Harriman in protest."

The tirades were impassioned, vitriolic—and, in the end, utterly ineffectual. In their haste to climb aboard Rockefeller's hurtling bandwagon, few of the party bosses could be bothered with such ideological purism, and fewer still pondered the import of these right-wing attacks. In the summer of 1958, hardly anyone recognized these salvos for what they really were: the first fusillade of a bitter and enduring battle for the soul of the Republican Party.

"Hall is just about finished," an aide to Walter Mahoney remarked in early August. The old GOP stalwart's delegate count was stuck at 163, less than half of what Rockefeller commanded. Gamely, Hall stuck in the race, aiming a few more barbs in Rockefeller's direction. His only hope was a floor fight at the convention. But Hall now knew there wouldn't be one—and even if there was, he would lose it.

Wearily deciding it was pointless to postpone the inevitable, Hall sent a three-paragraph statement to the media on August 17, eight days before the convention was to open. "I have always been a realist in politics," it said. "I am therefore withdrawing my name as a candidate for governor."

Mahoney, for his part, had been issuing brave proclamations of his intentions. "We are in this for the long haul," he told party workers. As late as the first week of August, he and Cliff White still believed he had a chance. The linchpin of their hopes was Queens County boss Frank Kenna, who controlled the single largest bloc of uncommitted delegates: 109 votes that were still there for the taking. If they could swing Kenna to their side, they could come to the convention with strength rivaling Rockefeller's.

And Mahoney believed, based on past discussions with Kenna, that he could count on the Queens leader. But when he tried contacting Kenna, in the three weeks prior to the convention, the Queens boss was nowhere to be found. "Walter couldn't get him on the phone for two weeks," recalls White.

"Then when Walter finally got to Kenna, maybe a week before the convention, Kenna said he couldn't support him, for reasons which I never found acceptable. Our belief was that he was bought off, if you want to know the real, hard truth. He was promised all kinds of things, in some way or other."

On Wednesday, August 20, five days before the convention was to open in Rochester, Mahoney phoned White. "Cliff," he said, "I've got to go before the Erie County delegation tonight. I've never led these people down a primrose path. We aren't going to make it, are we?"

"Not if we haven't got Kenna, we aren't going to make it," White replied.

"Well, then," sighed Mahoney, "I'm going to tell the Erie delegation tonight that I'm going to drop out." And so Mahoney did.

Attired in a rumpled gray glen plaid suit, his hair in need of cutting, and flashing a smile that bared all thirty-two teeth, Nelson Rockefeller stepped off a private plane at Rochester–Monroe County Airport at 4 P.M. on Friday, August 22, and exultantly plunged into the blaring rituals of his first state political convention.

As he stepped down the gangway, accompanied by Tod, Steven, and Mary, Rockefeller was greeted by the Rockettes—not the dancers from Radio City Music Hall, but a dozen pretty local girls clad in blue capes and military shakos emblazoned with Rockefeller slogans. After pumping the hands of the mayor and other local dignitaries, the Rockefeller party was hustled in a screaming police motorcade to their lodgings in the Sheraton Hotel.

Then it was on to Red Wing Stadium, for a night game of the town's minor league team. Rockefeller paraded to the pitcher's mound and, employing an exaggerated windup that displayed to one and all his total unfamiliarity with the game, he flung the first ball at the catcher, wildly bouncing it into the ground. "I didn't have a warm-up," he explained to reporters on his way back to his seat.

Most of his time, before, during, and after the game, was spent shaking hands. The accent, throughout, was on humility. Utterly unnecessarily, he would introduce himself to people. "I'm Nelson Rockefeller," he said, "and I'm running for governor." When one well-wisher was so bold as to call him "Governor," Rockefeller adroitly corrected him: "I don't answer to that yet." At one point, the mayor leaned over to Rockefeller and whispered, "You're doing all right." "Thanks," Rockefeller answered, "but I still have a lot to learn about this business."

"It all added up," commented the Rochester *Democrat & Chronicle,* "to an appearance of a 'regular guy.' "

At her husband's side at every one of his public appearances, smartly dressed in a cotton print suit, low-heeled black kid slippers, and a brimmed hat of natural straw, was Tod. The woman who five months before had balked at even the briefest interview was now, incredibly, every inch the poised political wife. She shook almost as many hands as her husband ("and appeared to be enjoying it," one reporter noted), called out greetings to the GOP women's group leaders she recognized, and gratefully accepted a bouquet of prize-winning flowers from the 4-H Club and an autographed baseball from the Red Wings catcher. She even found time to meet with newsmen at her hotel, and thoroughly charmed them. Asked about her Democratic cousin, Senator Joseph Clark of Pennsylvania, she spoke of her "respect and esteem" for him, then added, with a twinkle in her eye, "but he flew the coop." She didn't blanch when asked about political issues ("I'd say that one of the great issues in all government is integrity") and even did not rule out making speeches on her own. "Maybe I will if I can be of any help," she said. "But I'm not very experienced."

"Both Nelson and I are in it together," Tod emphasized. "I want to give it every bit I have. I wouldn't want to be anything but effective to the very end."

The next day, in between glad-handing appearances (e.g., the annual picnic of the Eighteenth Ward Republican Club), Rockefeller repaired to his suite on the fourth floor of the Sheraton to deliberate with the party elders on the one pressing bit of unfinished business at hand: the makeup of the rest of the state ticket.

The only automatic nominee, other than Rockefeller, was the incumbent attorney general, Louis Lefkowitz; all the rest of the slate—lieutenant governor, comptroller, U.S. senator to replace the ailing Irving Ives—was still to be determined. On one thing, every leader, including Rockefeller, agreed: the lieutenant governor candidate should be someone wise in the ways of the legislature, someone who could compensate for Rockefeller's greenness. As they mulled the prospects, one name came to everyone's lips: that of Joe Carlino. He was young (forty-one), attractive, articulate, with all the necessary experience; what's more, he was Italian, giving the ticket the ethnic balance (white Anglo-Saxon Protestant, Italian, Jew) then thought indispensable to statewide victory. (Harriman's lieutenant governor, after all, was another Italian-American, George De Luca.)

There was only one small problem: J. Russel Sprague. The Nassau County boss was grooming Carlino for big things, and serving as Nelson Rockefeller's lieutenant governor was not one of them. It was the speakership of the Assembly that Sprague prized, the chance to wrest control of the lower house from his upstate brethren. And with Heck known to be in failing health, with diabetes and other ailments, that prize could fall into Carlino's hands, and Sprague's, very, very soon. Sprague had no desire to sacrifice it for a mostly meaningless position that entailed little more than presiding over the Senate and making the occasional speech.

"When we got to the convention," Carlino recalls, "Nelson was putting the heat on me, and Dewey was putting the heat on Sprague, to make me take it [the lieutenant governorship]." But neither Carlino nor Sprague would budge. Rockefeller would have to look elsewhere.

With Carlino out of the picture, Rockefeller turned to Walter Mahoney. Cliff White had warned Mahoney, when they arrived in Rochester, that he would be offered the number two spot on the ticket. And Mahoney, the unquestioned ruler of the Senate, had no more interest in the job than Carlino and Sprague; as he put it, "I *tell* the lieutenant governor what to do." Mahoney asked White how he should handle it, and White suggested that he boost for the job the man who deserved it more than anyone else: Malcolm Wilson.

Sure enough, on that Saturday, Rockefeller made the offer, and Mahoney turned it down, proposing Malcolm Wilson instead. "But we can't do that," Rockefeller had insisted. "We're from the same county." Mahoney persuaded him that that really didn't matter. Then the Senate leader went off to a Young Republicans luncheon, where, for the first time, he publicly touted Wilson for lieutenant governor. The next morning, newspapers reported that Wilson was a "virtual certainty" for the nomination.

Wilson's own recollection of what happened is a bit different. He was not, he says, Rockefeller's third choice, after Carlino and Mahoney; actually, he says, he had been first approached about the position by Rockefeller several weeks earlier, during one of their meetings in the Roxy suite. Wilson recalls that he balked at accepting. "I told him I didn't want it, that I was happy where I was." He raised the ticket-balancing concerns. "You should have an upstate Catholic running with you," he told Rockefeller. "I'm a Catholic, but I have a Scotch Presbyterian name." But Rockefeller persisted, and Wilson eventually gave in, after Rockefeller promised him he would be a "full working partner" in the administration.

However it came about, Rockefeller's choice of Wilson as his running mate was instantly viewed as an act of supreme political sagacity, an olive branch to conservative elements leery of the gubernatorial candidate. At the same time, it was regarded as a gesture of supreme gratitude to the man who had done more than anyone, save Jud Morhouse, to gain Rockefeller the nomination.

The U.S. Senate nomination, meanwhile, was a tougher slog. Also-ran Leonard Hall had been seen as an obvious fence-mending choice, but he took himself out of contention. "I have spent eighteen years in Washington and that's enough," he said. (Rockefeller, still infuriated by Hall's attacks, was expected to veto him anyway.) Rockefeller asked Carlino, but the assemblyman, his spine stiffened by Sprague and his designs, refused. That left one live possibility: the quiet but well-regarded veteran congressman from Rochester, Kenneth B. Keating.

Reluctant to give up his hard-earned House seniority (he was ranking minority member of the Judiciary Committee), Keating, too, declined. But Rockefeller was not about to let him slide off the hook. He called Keating up to his Sheraton suite and, with Morhouse, Wilson, and Javits assisting, spent five hours pressuring the congressman. Then, as the coup de grace, Rockefeller put into play his old Washington contacts, phoning Vice President Nixon and asking him to see what he could do about exerting some White House pressure on Keating. Nixon obliged, sending Keating word—from a phone in the Oval Office—that it was the President's wish, and his own, that he not decline the nomination. Faced with this edict from on high, the loyal Keating backed down. He would join Nelson Rockefeller's team.

The final piece of the puzzle—the nominee for comptroller, the state's top fiscal officer—was a lot easier to put into place. He would be James A. Lundy, the former borough president of Queens. An Irishman, he would add an extra element of ticket balancing. (Although Wilson, too, was of Irish descent, his name didn't sound it.) But more than Lundy's background, what may have commended him to Rockefeller's attention was that he was a longtime ally of Frank Kenna. This, perhaps, was Kenna's reward for having dodged his old friend Walter Mahoney's calls for two weeks.

Rockefeller was still hours away from his nomination, but, as his decisive role in the selection of his running mates showed, he was already swiftly seizing control of the state party apparatus. The party platform, supposedly left to the devices of a committee of upstate legislators led by James A. FitzPatrick of Plattsburgh, was in fact vetted by Rockefeller and his aides. As *The New York Times* reported, "The extensive research and counseling staffs of various Rockefeller foundations played a leading role in the writing of both the platform and Mr. Rockefeller's acceptance speech." (Actually, it was George Shapiro, Dewey's old counsel, who did the initial platform drafting, at Rockefeller's behest.)

While most of what the upstaters wanted in the platform went through, one key provision didn't: the call for a one-year residency requirement for welfare recipients. Rockefeller was dead set against it, and it was duly expunged from the platform—yet another indication, for anxious conservatives, that their brand of Republicanism and Rockefeller's were not one and the same.

At 9:30 P.M. on Monday, August 25, Malcolm Wilson stood before the 2,340 delegates and in one of the briefest nominating speeches on record—a speech whose brevity (especially for the loquacious Wilson) was evidently dictated by the demands of live television coverage—placed the name of Nelson A. Rockefeller in nomination. The convention hall erupted.

As Lionel Hampton's orchestra, augmented by the Rochester Park Band, belted out "Hail, Hail, the Gang's All Here" and "For He's a Jolly Good Fellow," multicolored streamers filled the air, the delegates blew their noisemakers and bobbed their placards (bearing such slogans as "Roll with Rock," "Go Far with N.A.R.," and "Win the Day with Nelson A."), and the Rockettes paraded around the auditorium, their cheerleader costumes emblazoned with letters that spelled out "We Can Win with Rockefeller!" All over the convention floor jubilant delegates were snake-dancing to the music. The cacophony lasted a full twenty-five minutes before order was restored for the balloting.

Then, a half hour later, after Rockefeller had won his first-ballot nomination, it started all over again.

Five thousand balloons were released from the rafters. A giant eight-by-ten-foot portrait of Rockefeller was unfurled. The Rockettes bounced around the stage. The bands blared "For He's a Jolly Good Fellow."

Led by marching sidemen from Lionel Hampton's band, and accompanied by a delegation that included Hall, Heck, and Mahoney, Rockefeller made his way through the throng to the stage. As Tod, their five children, and Rodman's wife, Barbara, joined the nominee, Hampton launched into "Happy Days Are Here Again"—until someone nudged him and pointed out that FDR's theme song was not an appropriate anthem for a Republican convention. (Hampton switched back to "For He's a Jolly Good Fellow.")

Reaching over to Tod, Rockefeller raised her arm in a champion's victory flourish. Finally, the crowd quieted.

Looking out at the ten thousand expectant faces, Rockefeller thanked them all "from the bottom of my heart. You have offered me the greatest challenge of my life and the highest opportunity to serve the people of our Empire State.

"I proudly accept your nomination."

Then, alluding to the weeks he spent bouncing around in Malcolm Wilson's Buick, he declaimed, "I don't need to tell you I was not drafted for this nomination. I worked and fought from one end of the state to the other to get your support, and you can be sure that in the weeks ahead I will work twice as hard to win a smashing victory in November."

The stupefying prolixity of his previous speaking efforts was notably absent from this, the most important speech of his life. With the television cameras homing in on him for the first time, Rockefeller was terse, vigorous, and pugnacious. The gloves were off now, as he lashed into "the dismal record of vacillation and veto of the Harriman administration.

"The box score of these last four years has been: no hits, no runs, and what errors."

One by one, he ticked off all the Harriman miscues. "His floundering," he charged, "is rapidly leading us into a fiscal crisis."

As for his own program, Rockefeller offered few surprises. He would "stop the flight of industry from New York" and "aggressively attract new business."

He would help to "solve the problems of expanding, improving, and financing our schools and colleges." He would "march against the menace of organized crime" and tackle "the heartbreaking and frightening problems of juvenile delinquency." And he pledged to "restore financial soundness, prudence, efficiency, economy, and businesslike management to our government."

In years to come, some of what he promised that evening would prove prophetic, and some of it ironic. But at the time, there was little in Rockefeller's words that was very different from what other politicians, including Averell Harriman, were saying.

It was not the message he was delivering that inspired the GOP faithful, hungry after four years for a return to power. Rather, it was the virile, youthful messenger. As the worshipful *Herald Tribune*—in an editorial entitled "A New Champion Is Born"—put it, "There was in the spirit of Nelson Rockefeller's speech and in the manner of the crowd's repeatedly ardent response something that expressed a good deal more than a speech tailored to the brevity of his radio and TV time. . . . It was in the obvious conviction of his audience that in him—young, vigorous, progressive, eager to seek 'bold but practical solutions' to the problems of a swiftly changing world—they had found a new leader and a champion who could carry his party to victory."

The convention adjourned at 11:30, but the partying at the Sheraton went on for most of the night. Hustling from one smoke-filled suite to the next—with Lionel Hampton's band heralding his every arrival—Rockefeller pounded backs and accepted bilious congratulations from one and all. And with him every step of the way, navigating the tangle of beer-swilling politicos, was Tod Rockefeller.

In the convention hall she had sat through all the speeches, pronouncing the moment "the most exciting experience that could happen to my family" and showing what a trouper she was by clipping an oversized Rockefeller button to her black cherry-print dress. She had stood side by side with her husband onstage, sharing his moment of jubilant victory. And now, in the raucous aftermath, she briskly made the rounds with him, accepting the greetings and salutations of florid-faced county chairmen reeking of Genesee beer and Pall Malls.

One county boss who observed her that evening remembers that "she seemed very uncomfortable with the noise and the tumult and the people. Nelson relished it, but she—I mean, you could see right there that she was not going to be comfortable on any campaign trail."

For the most part, though, she kept her disquietude well hidden from view. Only once in that endless evening did Tod let on her true feelings about this dramatic new phase in her life; only once did the genteel smiles melt away to reveal the core of stoic acceptance within. And that was when a reporter approached her, in the midst of the late-night revelries, and asked her how she felt about abandoning her discreetly private existence for all this hurly-burly.

Her reply was crisp, as crisp as the Maine mornings she had forsaken to be there.

"This," she simply said, "is what Nelson wants to do."

Thirty-nine

ELECTED

While the Republicans' festivities ended in a paroxysm of good feeling and harmony, the same could not be said of the Democrats' proceedings some seventy-five miles to the west.

At the very same moment that Rockefeller was presiding over a newly united party, Averell Harriman, at the Democratic state convention in Buffalo, was trying to hold together a deeply divided one. And the schism was largely his own doing.

For months now, Harriman had vacillated about his candidate for his ticket's choicest available plum, the U.S. Senate nomination. The likeliest possibility seemed to have been Mayor Wagner of New York, who was long thought to have coveted the Senate seat that his late father had held, with much distinction, in the Roosevelt era. (His earlier bid for the Senate, in 1956, had been thwarted by Jacob Javits and the Eisenhower landslide.) But Harriman, wagging his finger under De Sapio's nose one day, had said flat out, "I don't want that Wagner on the ticket." Harriman muttered something about scandals in the city administration, but the scandals, such as they were, were penny-ante high jinks that were hardly likely to disqualify the mayor. The true reason for Harriman's animus toward Wagner, it was believed, was Harriman's national ambitions: a Wagner victory would make him a serious rival for a slot in a new administration, should the Democrats prevail in 1960.

Meeting with Wagner that summer at the governor's summer house in Sands Point, Long Island, Harriman lowered the boom, albeit in the most diplomatic terms. As Wagner would recall, Harriman advised him that the mayor was "at one of those dips in popularity that we all go through. He just thought I couldn't be helpful to him."

Exactly who Harriman thought *could* be helpful was, however, impossible to divine. And, in the absence of strong direction from the governor, the vying party factions, which had grudgingly coexisted with each other for years, promoted their own candidates. The liberal wing, led by such revered figures as Eleanor Roosevelt and former governor and U.S. senator Herbert Lehman, was pushing Thomas K. Finletter, a stalwart New York City reformer who had been Air Force Secretary in the Truman administration and a key figure in Adlai Stevenson's two failed bids for the presidency. Meanwhile, the party regulars, led by De Sapio and fellow city bosses Charles Buckley of the Bronx and Joseph Sharkey of Brooklyn, were lining up behind Manhattan district attorney Frank Hogan.

In the weeks leading up to the convention, Harriman continued to waffle. At times he would talk up Finletter; on other occasions, he would muse about a Wagner candidacy. Rather than take a stand, Harriman contrived to toss one more name into the ring: Thomas E. Murray, a wealthy upstate industrialist and inventor who had served for seven years on the Atomic Energy Commission. Eyeing Murray as a suitable Irish Catholic alternative to Hogan, the governor arranged for the five New York City county leaders to meet his new prospect at De Sapio's office across from City Hall. The get-together was a disaster. "The guy looked like death on vacation," Wagner, who sat in, recalled. "He was so pale and thin that all of the leaders came out saying, 'Jesus, he won't live through the convention.' "

On the Friday before the convention was to open, Harriman was dining with some aides in Albany when a call came through from De Sapio. The Tammany boss was emphatic: Finletter would not do, and neither would Murray. The Democratic regulars wanted Hogan, and only Hogan.

Unwilling to stand up to De Sapio and the party machine, but reluctant to offend the party's influential liberal wing, Harriman was a victim of his own equivocation, berated and bullied by both sides. No less a figure than Eleanor Roosevelt privately warned him, in brutally frank terms, of the dire consequences of his inaction. "Many liberal Democrats in this election," she wrote, "are weighing the question of whether they will vote for you or for Nelson Rockefeller—both of you suffer under the same difficulty, that of not really knowing the game sufficiently well to play it on the level of the bosses. [She obviously did not know Rockefeller very well.] . . . From what I hear it might be quite possible that Democratic liberals, not wanting to vote for the Democratic candidate for the U.S. Senate, will shed also the Democratic governorship because they will think the responsibility is yours."

As for her own position, she made it plain that "it would be hard to work for you if I felt that the party was guided by De Sapio and not by you."

By the time the governor arrived in Buffalo, he had decided that the only way out of his box was to draft Wagner after all. Harriman phoned the mayor—only to learn that Wagner had gone off with his wife and sons to Niagara Falls for the day. Then, having convinced himself that Wagner would not agree unless Hogan first stepped aside, Harriman summoned the district attorney to his suite and asked Hogan to drop out of the race for the good of the party. Hogan replied that he would rather put a bullet through his brain.

With his nomination for the governorship now just hours away, Harriman had time for one last, decisive blunder. Had he chosen to, he could have brought De Sapio and the regulars to heel at that point by threatening to refuse the nomination unless his choice for the Senate was accepted. It was a ploy that Al Smith, back in 1922, and Herbert Lehman, in 1938, had used with great success. But Harriman, eager for the salve of adulation that would be his that evening, refused to go that route. When he stepped to the podium at 9:30 and, arms raised, soaked up the thunderous acclaim of the delegates, he surrendered the last bit of leverage that he had.

The next morning's newspapers were rife with speculation that Wagner would accede to a draft and join the ticket. But as he sat down to breakfast with the mayor, Harriman learned otherwise. Still smarting from his treatment at Sands Point, Wagner crisply informed Harriman that he would stay where he was. "You didn't want me on the ticket three months ago," the mayor snapped. "I don't see how you need me now."

By then, De Sapio had lined up all the support he needed to put the nomination of Hogan over the top. As insurance, he cut a deal with the Erie County chairman, Peter Crotty, agreeing, in exchange for Crotty's backing of Hogan, to give the Erie boss the attorney general nomination. Thus, not only would Hogan's candidacy be shoved down Harriman's patrician throat, but so would Crotty's.

Infuriated as he was with this denouement, Harriman felt himself helpless to unravel it. The best he could do was try to hold his fractured coalition together. He phoned Alex Rose, leader of the Liberal Party, the Democrats' longtime partner in statewide elections. The Liberals had already endorsed Finletter for the Senate, although Finletter would soon withdraw and the party would come around to Hogan. Harriman asked Rose if he couldn't see a way to back Crotty.

No, Rose replied, he couldn't—not under any circumstances.

That evening, a drained, sulking Averell Harriman reluctantly dragged himself to the convention hall to witness De Sapio's triumph. Mounting the stage, the governor held up Frank Hogan's hand in the ritual victory gesture. Harriman would later describe it as the lowest moment of his life.

He was exposed to all the world as a political eunuch, in thrall to the dark-lensed wizard of Tammany. As *The New York Times* proclaimed on its front page the next day, "Carmine G. De Sapio established himself at the convention as the boss of the Democratic party in New York State, stronger than Governor Harriman and Mayor Wagner together."

The pithiest epitaph on De Sapio's accomplishment was uttered by the governor's wife, Marie, who despite her well-heeled upbringing had a particularly earthy tongue. "Yeah," said the state's first lady, "they gave ole Ave a real Philadelphia rat-fucking."

Harriman was no fool. He understood as well as anyone what the events in Buffalo meant. The next morning he summoned his counsel, Daniel Gutman, to his suite. Stepping out of the bathroom, where he was shaving, Harriman said, "Dan, do you know what last night cost me?" "Plenty, Governor," replied Gutman, "but I can't estimate it in votes."

"I'm going to tell you," said Harriman. "It cost me a million votes, and we can't make it up. You divide it in two, and you've got the figure by which I'm going to lose."

In the Rockefeller camp, wrapping up their far happier show in Rochester, the dispatches from Buffalo were avidly consumed, and by no one more avidly than Frank Jamieson.

"There's your issue," he announced. " 'Tammany is back in the saddle.' "

Others in the Rockefeller brain trust groaned. "We said to ourselves, 'Oh no, not again,' " Malcolm Wilson would recall. "We'd been beating Tammany to death for as long as we could remember and where had it got us? If Jamie was going to push that, we'd have our work cut out for us."

But Jamieson was adamant. He knew all about the potency of the bossism issue. Long before he had come to work for Rockefeller, Jamieson had helped his brother, a New Jersey state senator, take on the imposing Jersey City boss, Frank "I am the law" Hague. What had worked against Hague would work against Harriman and De Sapio. He was sure of it.

Left unsaid by Jamieson (and no one else was about to bring it up) was that in raising the banner of bossism, Rockefeller would be guilty of the grossest hypocrisy. After all, he would never have won his own nomination if it hadn't been for the support of bosses: Kenna in Queens, Gerlach in Westchester, Sprague in Nassau, Hill in Binghamton. There were as many smoke-filled-room sessions (maybe even more) at the Sheraton in Rochester as there were at the Statler Hilton in Buffalo. Indeed, veteran political reporter Warren Moscow described the Rochester convention as essentially "the most boss-ridden in party history." And Rockefeller was no more willing to tangle with the party leaders than Harriman was—as witness his kowtowing to Russel Sprague on Carlino's prospective Senate candidacy.

The difference was that Rockefeller and *his* bosses achieved a unanimity of view on all the key matters before them. There was a willingness by almost everyone concerned (Sprague excepted) to subordinate their private agendas to the greater goal of victory in November. The same, assuredly, could not be said of De Sapio, Crotty, and their brethren.

Thus, by virtue of his intraparty squabbles, Harriman was vulnerable to the bossism charge, while Rockefeller was not. The real issue, as Jud

Morhouse was quick to point out, was the governor's weakness: "If a governor obviously has so little power and influence in his own political organization, it is not difficult to judge how little power and influence he must have in the administration of the state government itself."

It was an issue that Rockefeller, who couldn't wait to get in the ring with his opponent, warmed to immediately. At a press conference in his Rockefeller Center office two days after his return from Rochester, he was positively sarcastic, suggesting that Harriman might "like to drop out" and let De Sapio be the candidate for governor. After all, said Rockefeller, De Sapio was "sort of running the place as it is."

Time after time now, at every stop, he would hammer on the theme Jamieson had scripted for him. The message hit home, especially with the New York City liberals who had been some of the governor's staunchest supporters. As Harriman backer Adolf Berle complained in his diary, "I think De Sapio and Tammany Hall by their high-riding arrogance are doing their best to elect Nelson Rockefeller. He really hadn't much of an issue until they handed him this one."

Other than that issue, there really was little difference between the two candidates.

"The voters of New York State are being asked to choose between a couple of extremely rich Siamese twins," concluded Stewart Alsop in *The Saturday Evening Post.* Both men were avid internationalists who were far more comfortable opining about the direction of the Cold War than about the direction of milk prices in Otsego County. Both were devout, dyed-in-the-wool capitalists, but capitalists who observed a common liberal creed: strong on activist government, strong on civil rights.

And both candidates, it was assumed, viewed the governorship not as an end in itself, but as a launch pad for a far more ambitious national agenda. Harriman had tried for the Democratic presidential nomination in 1952 and 1956; were he to win reelection in New York, he was expected to make another bid in 1960—or, at least, have a major say in who did get the nod. As for Rockefeller, even though his political career was barely two months old, his name was already bandied around as possible GOP presidential timber—assuming, of course, he won in 1958. "If he bucks the odds to win," predicted Alsop, "he will be a towering figure in the Republican Party—so towering that he could represent a danger to the candidacy of Vice President Richard Nixon."

Their other great common denominator was, of course, their immense fortunes, the fruit of the labors of their robber baron forebears. To the extent that the mega-wealth was an electoral liability, it was a liability for both; to the extent that it was seen as an asset, giving the possessor the virtue of incorruptibility, it was an asset for both. ("One thing you got to say about this

Rockefeller," remarked an upstate GOP county chairman, "we don't have to worry about him being on the take.")

Given the philosophical and aristocratic kinship of the two candidates, it was easy to see why a certain smug complacency about the race had set in among the Democratic regulars—even allowing for that unpleasant bit of business that had just occurred in Buffalo. After all, Rockefeller didn't seem to bring anything to the table that their man didn't bring in spades, and Harriman had the considerable advantage of incumbency to boot. As his top political aide, Milton Stewart, exulted to an interviewer, Harriman was "the champ. He gets things done. Nelson Rockefeller may be a good guy to be chairman of a conference, but what's he done?"

The events in Buffalo may have rattled Harriman and the Roosevelt-Lehman liberal wing, but the party pros saw no great cause for alarm. "The wounds are not wide nor deep," proclaimed De Sapio, "and they will soon heal."

Only a few Democratic insiders dared burst the bubble. One was Eleanor Clark French, the vice chairman of the party's state committee. As Tod Rockefeller's first cousin and erstwhile traveling companion, and as the spouse of John French, Nelson Rockefeller's friend and college roommate, French knew better than most the nature of the opponent Harriman was taking on in November. Speaking at a breakfast meeting of the Democratic faithful in Buffalo the morning after Harriman's nomination, French warned them of what lay ahead. "All of us Democrats have to get together and work as hard as we can, because we have a tough row to hoe," she said. "The Republicans have nominated a wonderful person, and he's going to be a very tough opponent."

After the meeting broke up, French recalls, "I saw Carmine De Sapio and Mike Prendergast, who was then the state chairman, waiting for me. They took me aside and said, 'Ellie, don't you know that you never say anything good about your opponent?' And I said, 'Well, it's the truth, and everybody there realized that. Harriman's in for a tough fight, and he'd better face it.' . . .

"They didn't appreciate Nelson: his personality and his power," she says. "They just didn't appreciate it."

The complacency that benumbed Harriman's forces did not afflict the Rockefeller camp.

It was not that Rockefeller considered Harriman, per se, such a formidable rival. In fact, he could be caustically dismissive when discussing his adversary, openly questioning Harriman's staying power—an attitude that sprang from the two men's work together on the Point Four program. "When Averell loses his enthusiasms he just disappears," he said. "He's like a submarine, he submerges, he just isn't there anymore."

Nevertheless, Rockefeller knew as well as anyone that unseating a Democratic incumbent in what was already conceded to be a Democratic year would require every ounce of his formidable energies, every aspect of his equally formidable resources. From day one, he and his supporters would have to go at full throttle.

Republican leaders who were hoping for a quick getaway after the Rochester convention adjourned found themselves summoned instead to an all-day strategy session in Rockefeller's suite. Among the items discussed was the formation of a Citizens for Rockefeller Committee to attract the independent vote. A week later, Rockefeller complained to an aide that he had been driving all around midtown Manhattan and had spotted only two locations where Citizens Committee banners were flying and campaign literature was handed out. "Well, it takes a little time to get started," the assistant meekly replied.

"We haven't got a little time," Rockefeller barked. "I want to see those Citizens signs all over town. Everywhere you go."

By the end of the following week, some twenty vacant stores had been taken over and transformed into Citizens for Rockefeller outposts.

The driving sense of urgency was palpable at the new campaign headquarters at the Roosevelt Hotel, a block from Grand Central Station. Rockefeller's staff—hitherto housed in the 20 West 55th Street townhouse—occupied the entire seventh floor of the cavernous hotel: in all, some eighty bedrooms. (To clear space for the offices, the beds were stacked on end in the bathtubs). The atmosphere at the Roosevelt, with gruff-voiced men slamming phones and disheveled aides scurrying down the corridors with sheafs of paper fresh from the mimeograph, was akin to that of a particularly frenetic betting parlor.

Unless they were out on the campaign trail with the candidate or his running mates, those inhabiting the Roosevelt rarely left; time with wives and families was out of the question. "During the campaign Dad was gone for four whole months," recalls Jud Morhouse's son Sandy. "He lived at the Roosevelt. I don't think he was home once until the election was over."

Despite its helter-skelter appearance, the Roosevelt operation was organized, as one reporter put it, "on the lines of a major industrial sales program"—complete with organization chart. There were five divisions—media promotion and publicity; headquarters; research; special groups; and organization—and the heads of each were expected to meet daily with Morhouse to coordinate.

What's more, the resources at hand would have been the envy of most industrial sales programs. "It was startling," says John Terry, a north country attorney brought in to work on upstate scheduling. "Whatever you needed was there and available. Telephones, mimeograph machines, the works." Those who worked there were constantly reminded that this was, after all, not just another campaign headquarters, but an appendage of the Greater Rockefeller Empire. Travel arrangements, for instance, were made by Room 5600's in-house travel bureau. "If you needed four buses or three airplanes, there was a gal there who could get it," says Terry. "You didn't have to fool around getting competitive bids, because she knew what was the lowest price around." Even Room 5600's varied idiosyncrasies were faithfully replicated at the Roosevelt—including the man in the white doctor's coat who would make the rounds daily unscrewing the telephone mouthpieces and spraying them with antiseptic to prevent the spread of colds.

Like most Nelson Rockefeller enterprises, the Roosevelt operation smelled strongly of the think tank. A team of researchers diligently churned out position papers on everything from juvenile delinquency to the state of rural roads, assembling them in thick blue binders for the candidate's perusal. (When he hit the campaign trail, Rockefeller would take along as many as eighteen of these reports to study between stops.) Under the leadership of Rockefeller's longtime in-house economist, Stacy May, the staff produced a staggeringly detailed breakdown of the condition of New York's economy—the better to skewer the incumbent governor with. The study, indeed, was far more extensive than anything the state's own Department of Commerce had produced. Looking over the Rockefeller team's output, commerce commissioner Edward T. Dickinson sheepishly admitted, "We just don't have the manpower to do the same job that Rockefeller has done."

Ensconced now in the offices-cum-bedrooms at the Roosevelt were many of the old familiar faces: Jamieson (although he was functioning more as a private *consigliere* to the candidate than as a day-to-day manager), Lockwood, Rod Perkins, May. Lloyd Free and Hadley Cantril, whose public opinion work for Rockefeller dated back to the CIAA, were on board as the candidate's private pollsters. And assuming greater and greater prominence by the day was the duo from the constitutional commission: Bill Ronan (who oversaw the speechwriting and research) and George Hinman (who served as an overall strategist and contact man). Already they seemed like venerable Rockefeller hands.

At the same time, some significant new faces were popping up in the stable of Rockefeller advisers and operatives. One was R. Burdell Bixby, the Dewey aide (and now the ex-governor's law partner) who had handled the scheduling and logistics for the Dewey gubernatorial campaigns. Bixby was a walking Baedeker of New York State; "he knew where the Shenango River crossed Route 11, as well as what restaurants were on the corner of 42nd Street and Broadway," says Terry, who worked for him. His encyclopedic command of New York State made Bixby an indispensable addition to a team that, with the exception of Wilson and Morhouse, was notably short on statewide savvy.

Rockefeller badly needed Bixby, as Bixby saw for himself the very first time they sat down together at the Roosevelt. "He knew nothing about the state's geography," Bixby recalls. "He didn't know, for instance, where Painted Post was, or Watkins Glen, or Owego. He had never charted where he was going to go, which counties and which cities. With Governor Dewey, I had to justify every stop: why here, why not here, and so on. So it was a great surprise to me when I took a schedule in to Nelson and he said, 'If you say that's where I have to go, I'll go. I don't have to know the details.' " Accustomed from his earliest days to cushioning himself with expertise, and well aware of what a novice he was at state politics, Rockefeller was willing, at least this first time around, to entrust his fate to wiser heads.

That was the case, as well, with another important addition to the Rockefeller camp: his Dartmouth classmate, former NBC president Pat Weaver. It would be Weaver's job to introduce Rockefeller to the vast possibilities of the electronic media, particularly television, which in 1958 was still a nascent political tool. "Being in the business, it was obvious to me how powerful this would be," says Weaver. Under Weaver's tutelage, and with the help of the candidate's considerable means, the Rockefeller campaign would usher in a new era of electronic electioneering.

The rental of the Roosevelt Hotel space would cost upward of $90,000, not including meals and all the other add-ons. (Accustomed to a Rockefelleresque budget, the staff nestled in the hotel was not inclined to stint, leading one wag to joke that the most immortal line uttered in the course of the campaign was "Room Service.") The television time would cost untold hundreds of thousands of dollars, as would the salaries of all the speechwriters, researchers, pollsters, and schedulers in the candidate's employ. Just before the Democratic convention, for instance, Rockefeller lured *The New York Times*'s top local political hand, Richard Amper, to his public relations team with a five-year contract at a princely $25,000 a year, probably two to three times what Amper was making at the paper.

There was no question that the Rockefeller run for governor was looming as the most expensive state campaign in history.

And there was also no question that he could afford every penny.

By law, a candidate for governor could not spend more than $20,000 on his own campaign. But that did not prevent a cornucopia of contributions from family members (including spouses) and friends, contributions whose impact was camouflaged by their disbursement into a stupefying array of different campaign committees. Thus, there might be—and was—a gift to Friends of Rockefeller and Wilson, and another to Citizens for Rockefeller-Keating, and another to the United Republican Finance Committee (an organ of Morhouse's state committee), and another to Democrats for Rockefeller. Furthermore, the election law—which was hardly policed in any case—did not cover other tools at a wealthy candidate's disposal, such as guarantees of bank loans. Nor did it foresee a situation which was uniquely Rockefeller's: namely, that a vast empire of experts and factotums, from p.r. men to travel agents, would already be in place, an empire whose upkeep was shouldered by the family office and foundations.

Practically speaking, then, there were really no limits on what Nelson Rockefeller and his family could spend on his political career.

Nevertheless, the family and its advisers—hypersensitive as always to their public image, wary of charges that they were "buying" a public office—were not without inhibitions of their own. While Junior had always been a generous political contributor, particularly to Tom Dewey and to the Westchester County committee, he was always careful not to tip the scales too far. "He felt that in a democracy it was somehow *wrong* for rich people to dominate campaigns with large contributions," notes one family aide. His children, to varying degrees, adhered to those self-imposed constraints.

Now, even with one of their own running, there was still a certain reluctance to open the coffers too widely, to put the Rockefeller wealth fully into play. On the other hand, Nelson needed the money. "We are caught between a series of cross currents on this problem," Lockwood confessed to John 3rd after a meeting early in the campaign with Nelson and Jamieson.

> The first is the desire to have family contributions not out of proportion to total contributions.
>
> The second is the problem that most of the money-raisers think that this is not a very good money-raising year.
>
> The third is the fact that many people seem to feel that with a Rockefeller as a candidate there is no need for anyone to contribute. (In fact, I have received letters of contribution already in which the donor practically apologizes for being so presumptuous.)
>
> The fourth is the fact that as communication media get more expensive, campaign costs go up (I have in mind, particularly, television).
>
> And fifth is the general expectation that a campaign between a Rockefeller and a Harriman would tend to run a little more expensive than some other campaigns. . . .

The solution that Nelson and his advisers came up with was to ask each of the siblings to contribute $18,000 to the various committees. "The resulting aggregate," wrote Lockwood, "would represent an acceptable percentage of the presently estimated total."

By and large, the family members complied, although the burden sharing was not as even as Lockwood envisioned. In fact, the totals probably reflected the varying levels of enthusiasm for Nelson's candidacy among his siblings. By one unofficial tally, Nelson and Tod would lead the way with total contributions of $41,600, following by Laurance and wife's $27,700, and David and wife's $18,950. (There was no indication of Winthrop's contributions, but by all indications he followed Lockwood's guidelines.) Pulling up the rear, with $15,000 apiece, were the intensely private elder sister, Abby Mauzé, and John 3rd, who among the brothers was said to have the greatest misgivings about Nelson's entry into the political limelight.

As for Junior, he and wife Martha would reportedly give a total of $19,350: a respectable but hardly overwhelming sum. Whatever reservations the patriarch might have felt about his son's run for public office were kept to himself. When Nelson first told him of his plans, Junior simply asked him if he believed he could be of service to his country; if Nelson thought he could, then he would have his blessing.

With the family placing a cap on its contributions, Nelson's campaign organization looked beyond the confines of Pocantico to fill the gap. As Lockwood pointed out, persuading people to give to a Rockefeller campaign was no mean feat, given the tendency to view such contributions as superfluous, if not downright presumptuous. To oversee the fund-raising, Rockefeller turned to his old friend William A. M. Burden, a socially prominent investor and fellow MOMA trustee, who had once worked for Rockefeller in the early days of the coordinator's office. Using his superb Rolodex, Burden opened every possible financial spigot. As his assistant, a young banker named James Helmuth, recalls, "Burden raised money from friends of Rockefeller, from good Republicans, from liberals who were unhappy with the Democrats, and from Democrats who were unhappy with the Democrats."

Mostly, Burden raised it from well-heeled aristocrats like himself. Therein lay another of Rockefeller's inestimable advantages: the ability to call upon the network of super-rich contemporaries with whom he had consorted his whole life. Other candidates might have to bow and scrape before the upper crust; Rockefeller and Burden merely had to invoke the ties of old friendships. The roster of Rockefeller donors looked like the index of the Social Register: Vincent Astor, Pierre Du Pont, Harvey Firestone, Amory Houghton. And the biggest contributors of all were Jock Whitney and his wife, who wrote checks totaling $62,000, and Whitney's sister and brother-in-law, Mr. and Mrs. Charles Shipman Payson, who gave a whopping $136,900.

The other great source of funds was bank loans. Some $800,000—nearly half of what the Rockefeller campaign was reported to have spent in 1958—came from loans to the New York State Republican Committee. No further record of these loans exists, so it is impossible to say for certain that Rockefeller guaranteed them. But given the state committee's creditworthiness—it was perpetually squeezed for funds throughout the 1950s—it is impossible to conceive how such substantial loans could have been secured without some guarantee, explicit or implicit, from the candidate or those close to him.

After all, what had helped Rockefeller win over the Republican powers that be was the impression that even if he didn't win, he at least would pay his own way. In that respect, among others, he was not letting his supporters down.

The contest was billed as "The Battle of the Millionaires," an epic struggle of dueling billfolds. But it was fast playing out as a one-sided tussle.

Harriman had always been a classic pinchpenny, given to stiffing aides on restaurant tabs and taxi fares, and his stint as governor had not loosened his iron grip on the purse strings one iota. Eleanor Clark French would tell the story of the time Harriman invited her to fly down with him from Albany to New York. "We'll have lunch on the plane," he told her. Relates French: "I got out to the airport expecting, you know, a DC-3 or something like that, but all there was was this shabby little Army plane. I got on board, and there was no window by my seat at all, and then they brought lunch—in a little paper bag. It was absolutely awful, but Averell was perfectly happy. It didn't bother him at all."

"The only time he ever spent money on himself," recalls his aide Philip Kaiser, "was when he ran for President in 1952 and 1956." His gubernatorial races, however, were another story. At the outset of the 1954 race, his aide Ted Tannenwald handed him $5,000 in cash, suggesting he use it for tips, meals, and whatever useful causes presented themselves in the course of his travels. At the end of the campaign, Harriman returned $4,900 of it—and Tannenwald could see that the bills were the exact same ones he had given him to start with.

"He has the most defensive attitude about his money," said another adviser, James Loeb. "He'd give two hundred fifty dollars, five hundred dollars to some of these senatorial candidates, thinking, you know, that they would be indebted to him for life, and it was like you or me giving a quarter."

Even now, confronted by an opponent who was spending like the Aga Khan, Harriman held fast to the keys to the vault. "He felt that he had been a good governor," explains Kaiser, "and therefore the good Democratic people of the state should supply the money to reelect him."

Instead of aggressively raising funds through an array of committees, as Rockefeller was doing, Harriman simply chose to rely on the existing party apparatus: the machine whose throttles were under the thumb of Carmine De Sapio. Once again, the incumbent was playing right into his challenger's hands.

The Rockefeller campaign strategy was based on one undisputed fact of New York electoral life: no Republican could win statewide office solely with the support of the GOP faithful. There just were not enough Republicans; in 1954, enrolled Democrats had outnumbered enrolled Republicans by over 200,000. To prevail, a GOP candidate had to start with his solid base of upstate Republicans, and then layer on top of it a thick helping of swing voters—Liberals, independents, disaffected Democrats—from New York City and its suburbs.

It was a given that Harriman would carry the downstate vote. For Rockefeller, the task was to hold down that victory margin, to make enough dents in the Democratic-Liberal coalition to deny his opponent the 600,000 or so majority he would need to overcome the Republican's upstate advantage.

That was why the debacle in Buffalo was such a godsend. By one reckoning, Rockefeller would have to capture as much as a quarter of the Democratic and Liberal Party voters to have a chance. The brouhaha over the Senate nomination gave angry doctrinaire Liberals and antiboss Democrats all the reason they needed to cross over to the Republican line.

From here on in it would be up to Rockefeller, in the course of the two-month campaign, not to give them any reason to switch back again. And that would mean a quick shift in the game plan that had gained him the Republican nomination. In his quest for that nomination, he had fudged the issue of his liberalism. Now, with the emphasis not on persuading old-line Republicans but on swaying left-of-center Democrats, he would have to adopt a whole new coloration—what the *National Review* crowd suspected were his true colors anyway. It was time to reassert his progressive credentials.

Sitting down to an interview with Theodore H. White for *Life* magazine, Rockefeller offered several liberal-sounding tidbits that, in White's estimation, would "murder him with his fellow Republicans" if they ever appeared. Afterward, White gave Rockefeller a chance to back away from them, but Rockefeller stood by the statements. He made it plain, as White would recall, that "he intended to go all out on the liberal line."

There were, at the campaign's inception, a few perfunctory nods to GOP hard-liners, such as an egregiously Red-baiting ad run in upstate newspapers: "How, Governor Harriman, can you condone Communists in public housing? . . . Your softness towards Communists is something the people will *Remember in November.*" But after that, Rockefeller largely turned his back on orthodox Republicanism, offering positions on the major social welfare issues of the day that were virtually identical to Harriman's. The term "Republican," in fact, was virtually banished from the lexicon, rarely showing up in his speeches, his literature, or his advertising.

His independent tack thoroughly confounded Harriman's strategists. "We will of course link Rockefeller to the Republican record in the state," Loeb opined in a memo to the governor, "but we have a difficult strategic task in the sense that to show the difference between Rockefeller and the Republicans may make the GOP look bad, but can also make Rockefeller look good."

From the campaign's opening gun, the efforts of the Rockefeller team were largely dedicated to driving wedges in the already fractious Democratic coalition. And that would involve more than just strident Tammany-bashing by the candidate. His confidant Oscar Ruebhausen organized a Democrats for Rockefeller Committee, lining up behind the candidate various distinguished Democrats, including Rudolf Sonneborn, husband of Dorothy Schiff, the publisher of the impeccably liberal *New York Post.*

Rockefeller was also not shy about taking aim at one of the coalition's most essential components: organized labor. Recognizing that it was too much to expect labor to turn its back on a Democratic governor, Rockefeller tried a subtler approach. He had his veteran Rockefeller Center aide Victor Borella, a past master at cultivating good relations with the unions, invite a select group of labor leaders to a mid-September off-the-record lunch. Among those in attendance were American Federation of Labor Central Trades boss Harry Van Arsdale; Building Service Union chief David Sullivan; and Peter Brennan, the new head of the construction trades union, described by the astute labor reporter Victor Riesel as "a silent but upcoming man to watch."

Rockefeller did not ask the union bosses for their support in the coming election; in fact, he said, he expected them to buck him. All he wanted to do, he said, was let them know that they should come back to him after the election and "we'll get busy with projects," which would help both their membership and the state.

The promise of "projects" after four years of Harriman inactivity intrigued the labor leaders. They would continue to back the governor, but a certain ambivalence now crept into their thinking about the election—leading Riesel to report, on September 15, that despite their official endorsements of the governor, the unions "are not going to campaign directly against Mr. Rockefeller."

The ambivalence was especially pronounced among the labor leaders who had the most long-standing ties to Rockefeller. And, happily for Rockefeller, these same leaders were the bulwarks of New York liberalism. One was Jacob Potofsky, the boss of the Amalgamated Clothing Workers. Another was David Dubinsky, chief of the International Ladies' Garment Workers' Union and co-founder (with milliners union boss Alex Rose) of the Liberal Party. Of late, Dubinsky had a particularly good reason to feel allied with Rockefeller: the Puerto Rican housing that Rockefeller's IBEC was building was co-sponsored by the ILGWU (whose membership was increasingly coming from the island).

Thus, it came as no surprise that, at the Liberal Party's 1958 Labor Day dinner, an occasion when the Republican candidate would normally be lambasted by the union bosses, Dubinsky, Potofsky, et al. were conspicuously silent on the subject of Nelson A. Rockefeller. And that reserved approach would last for the duration of the campaign. The unions endorsed Harriman—to do otherwise would be utter heresy—but their support was half-hearted at best.

Since the onset of the New Deal, the Democrats in New York had always counted on the unions, and they had always counted on the support of Jews and blacks and Puerto Ricans. But just as Rockefeller's largesse, past and future, had upset the old labor equation, so, too, did it turn topsy-turvy all the assumptions about those racial and ethnic blocs.

Each of those groups, after all, had a special reason to feel grateful to the Republican candidate. To the Jewish community, Rockefeller was one of its most dependable and generous Gentile supporters, a mainstay of the UJA's fund-raising campaigns (most recently, in March 1958, he chaired its "person to person" fund-raising drive) who had come up with the idea of a separate nonsectarian campaign to solicit the help of non-Jews. The Puerto Ricans could look to his IBEC home-building efforts, as well as such goodwill gestures as the sponsorship of the San Juan Little League by one of his IBEC companies (Rockefeller personally footed the bill for a Bronx Little League team to visit Puerto Rico for Christmastime exhibition games).

As for black voters, their debt to Rockefeller and his family was perhaps the most profound. With a commitment that dated back to their forebears' involvement in the Underground Railroad, the Rockefellers had been the philanthropic backbone of a host of Negro causes, most especially education in the South through their General Education Board. In the past twenty years alone, it was estimated they had given over $50 million to black education. Although Harriman had a sound record on equal rights issues, and he enjoyed the support of such eminent black personages as baseball great Jackie Robinson, the allegiance to Rockefeller in the black leadership ran far deeper. Early on, the governor was warned that he was in for some trouble there. A campaign aide sent him this telegram: "I have regretfully learned from a number of Negro leaders that the Urban League and the NAACP people, if not the NAACP, are considering supporting Rockefeller."

Unlike Rockefeller, the parsimonious Harriman had no great reservoir of philanthropic goodwill to fall back on. His problems were summed up by a single bon mot crafted at Rockefeller headquarters: "Ever hear of a Harriman Foundation?"

What the incumbent was up against was articulated by a black housewife in Brooklyn. "When I was a little girl in the West Indies," she said, "the Rockefeller family gave us food, clothing and shelter after a hurricane nearly ruined our island. I've never voted for a Republican in my life but I'm going to now."

The Rockefellers, in all their giving, had never asked for quid pro quos. But in that election year of 1958, it was as if, all the same, they had a stack of due bills ready for cashing.

"If Nelson makes it," a friend of his remarked, "he'll be the first man to ride to high office on a tide of philanthropy."

Speeding through the night from one upstate gathering to the next in the early days of his campaign, Rockefeller tried to explain to journalist Teddy White what his political goals were. "There's a Spanish phrase politicians use in Latin America that I like," he said. "It's *auténtico representante de pueblo.* It means 'the authentic representative of the people.' That's the way I feel about this campaign."

In those first forays on the hustings, however, the larger-than-normal crowds were there to gawk at the authentic representative of Standard Oil and Rockefeller Center. In Gloversville, a depressed factory town in the Mohawk Valley whose principal industry was, appropriately enough, leather goods, a spectator listening to Rockefeller's spiel from a sound truck remarked, "I wish some of his money would rub off on me." Later, another man getting Rockefeller's autograph cracked, "Put it on a check." In Herkimer, an eight-year-old boy asked him, "How much money have you got, Mr. Rockefeller?" "I've got a pocketful of dimes," Rockefeller replied, an allusion to his spindly grandfather's penchant for handing them out to youngsters.

But if they initially turned out to see that rara avis, a Rockefeller in the flesh, they were soon enough lured by another element: Rockefeller's megawatt personality. "No man I ever knew," says Burdell Bixby, "could charm more people per square inch than Nelson Rockefeller."

Meeting FDR for the first time, Winston Churchill once said, was like opening your first bottle of champagne. So it was, as well, with Nelson Rockefeller. His natural exuberance, his zest for life, his contagious joie de vivre were in full flower on the campaign trail. At Alfred University he popped a blue college beanie on his head to the huzzahs of 2,000 students. In Salamanca he picked up a baton and directed the high school band, then grabbed a Hula-Hoop and tossed it around his neck. At the Rensselaer County Fair he trotted around the racetrack in a sulky, beaming and waving all the while. In Olean he strode into W. T. Grant to pump the hands of astonished shoppers and buy a nickel's worth of green taffy. In Batavia early one morning he shook up the bleary breakfast regulars at Victor's Open Kitchen: bounding in with an ear-to-ear smile, ducking behind the counter to greet the cook, the counterman, the waitresses, and the busboy before joining a table of sleepy Batavians for poached eggs and coffee. "Hello," he introduced himself. "I'm Nelson Rockefeller. I'm running for governor."

Appearing at Colgate University, Rockefeller delivered his set speech, then literally leapt off the stage to greet the cheering students. "It turned into a full-fledged rally," recalls Joseph Boyd, the president of the Colgate Young Republicans. Boyd found himself swept up in more ways than one. Afterward the candidate asked him if he'd like to head Students for Rockefeller. Boyd said he'd be happy to. "Fine," said Rockefeller. "Get on the bus." Remembers Boyd, "I had no clothes, not even a toothbrush. At the first stop I walked into an Army and Navy store and got some clothes." Days later, when the bus trip ended, Boyd was driven back to the campus in a siren-screaming, rooflight-flashing Oneonta police squad car. For the bedazzled young man, it was the start of a long association with Nelson Rockefeller.

Rockefeller seemed, for all the world, to have been at the business of politics for years, rather than a mere three months. No one ever had to prompt him to shake hands; he grabbed at every opportunity to wrap his beefy arms around the electorate. (Watching his father go overboard as usual at a country filling station, Steven Rockefeller was heard to mutter, "Let's get him out of here before he starts shaking hands with the gas pumps.")

"God," said one awed old pro, "must have meant Nelson to be a politician." Yet those who had long been close to him, who had watched him mount tractors in the Mato Grasso and exchange *abrazos* in Caracas, were not at all surprised by his performance. In many respects, he had been a politician all his life. It was a craft that came naturally to him.

And, as a campaigner, Rockefeller had that rarest of gifts: the ability not only to win over the crowd but to completely disarm those he encountered one-on-one. It was the same talent that FDR had, an ability to ensnare every person he met in the force field of his presence.

The magnetism was especially potent with members of the opposite sex. ("He's stealing our women," a Democratic leader was heard to complain.)

Flying in his Convair on a swing through the state's remote north country with the local state senator, Robert McEwen, Rockefeller peered out the window when they landed in Plattsburgh and asked McEwen to identify the receiving party. "Who's that girl standing over there by herself?" Rockefeller asked. McEwen told him it was his wife—an unreconstructed Walter Mahoney supporter, he might add, who still was a skeptic about Rockefeller's chances.

"The door to the Convair opened up," remembers McEwen, "and Nelson Rockefeller went right down those steps, and he had my wife locked in eyeball-to-eyeball. He went right over and threw his arms around her, and made her feel as though there was no one in the world who was as important as she was. I swear to God, from that point on she forgot Walter Mahoney's name."

This intensity was not reserved for politicians' wives either. Eager to be seen as "the authentic representative of the people," he applied his solicitude to the humblest of voters. At the opening of the Democrats for Rockefeller headquarters in midtown Manhattan, Rockefeller let the assembled bigwigs cool their heels while he talked for minutes on end with the cleaning woman. When an aide tried to pull him away, Rockefeller snapped, "Just a minute. I haven't finished with this woman yet."

Aboard the Staten Island Ferry one day, Rockefeller assiduously chatted up the bootblack while having his shoes shined. Two days later the man opened his mailbox and found a photo autographed to "my good friend Tony" and a personal note from Rockefeller inquiring whether Tony might be available to work on his shoes again when the candidate made a return trip to Staten Island the following week. Rockefeller's attentiveness paid off big: it not only swayed Tony but also Tony's many friends in Staten Island's Italian community, which accounted for more than 40 percent of the borough's vote.

Again and again, the essential contradiction embodied in Rockefeller's style—the idea that this crown prince of America's monied ruling class could be so concerned, so "sincere," so "normal"—resonated with the voters.

Adding to the "regular guy" effect was Rockefeller's heedlessness about his personal appearance. He wore the same creased, mud-spattered, food-stained trench coat wherever he went, the same tired homburg. Though he was never a fashion plate to begin with, his clothes seemed to droop more and more on his frame as the campaign wore on.

He appeared totally oblivious to matters of personal comfort and safety. At a rain-swept rally in the town of Stony Point in Rockland County, he spoke from atop a wooden plank suspended between two oil drums. (When the beam started tottering, he joked, "I hope my platform is stronger than this plank.") Later, as the rains kept coming, he gamely pumped hands at a sodden, sparsely attended gathering in New City. The local Republican worker who was escorting him remembered thinking to himself, "Here's Nelson A. Rockefeller, in the dark and in the rain in New City—what's he doing this for? But boy, did he get into it."

In a matter of weeks he had toured thirty-five of the state's sixty-two counties. In the process he lost six pounds, his palms were heavily callused from shaking as many as 2,000 hands a day, his untrimmed hair curled over his shirt collar (somehow, he couldn't find time for a haircut). Yet at the end of another eighteen-hour day he could still look out over a street-corner gathering of all of fifty people and chirp, "This is terrific. Really wonderful!"—and sound as if he really, truly meant it.

The quintessential event in Rockefeller's first campaign—the event that solidified the image of him, in the media and in the minds of countless New Yorkers, as a hustling, man-of-the-people multimillionaire—was his visit on October 2 to New York City's Lower East Side, in the company of Louis J. Lefkowitz.

Rockefeller could not have found a better tour guide than the fifty-four-year-old attorney general. The grimy, vibrant tenement neighborhood was where Lefkowitz was born (at 718 East 6th Street, in a tiny flat with the bathtub in the kitchen), the son of a garment center vest maker; where he was educated (at PS 188); where, to help provision his struggling family, he scavenged coal that fell off delivery trucks and ice chunks left by icemen on the East Houston Street docks; and where he achieved his first political success (running for the State Assembly in 1927 at age twenty-three). He had come a long way since, but almost everything about the wiry, balding, bespectacled Lefkowitz—his broad New York accent, his mile-a-minute speech pattern, his abundant nervous energy—still bespoke the pushcart-cluttered cobblestone streets from which he had sprung.

Lefkowitz was a throwback to the style of politics of a fellow Lower East Sider, Al Smith: someone whose roots were in the party clubhouse (in Lefkowitz's case, the Federal Club on Avenue C), where judgeships were proffered through a haze of blue-gray smoke; someone who could stroll down every street in the old neighborhood and rattle off—walk-up building by walk-up building, apartment by apartment—the names of every constituent who once lived there, and maybe still did. Over the years, his career had as many ups and downs as an East 3rd Street pool hustler (two judicial appointments and as many lost elections), but Lefkowitz never lost faith that the party for which he so loyally toiled would come through for him. Sure enough, in January 1957 it did, when Javits stepped down as attorney general to take his U.S. Senate seat and the Republican legislature tapped Lefkowitz to fill his unexpired term.

The 1958 race was Lefkowitz's first statewide election, and he was champing at the bit to make his mark. But the Rockefeller handlers who controlled his schedule weren't quite sure what to make of this streetwise, fast-talking pol and at the outset strictly rationed his appearances.

Rockefeller's jaunt through the Lower East Side was Lefkowitz's chance to at last show his stuff. This was his turf. No one in New York politics knew it better.

Rockefeller, on the other hand, had never before set foot in that part of the city, as he readily confessed when he arrived with his son Steven on the appointed day. Despite the pouring rain, the group, which included Manhattan GOP chairman Bernard Newman, another born-and-bred Lower East Sider, made its way through the soggy streets. Wearing his by now trademark battered hat and spattered trench coat, Rockefeller waylaid pedestrians and introduced himself. "You're kidding!" one woman gasped.

Then the party headed over to Ratner's, a locally famous Jewish dairy restaurant on Delancey Street. As waiters and startled patrons gathered around, Lefkowitz insisted that Rockefeller try the specialty of the house, cheese blintzes. Biting into one, his first blintz ever, Rockefeller pronounced it "wonderful, absolutely delicious, terrific." As reporters scribbled and photographers flashed, he ambled around the restaurant, autographing waiter's checks, paper napkins, and menus, and advising patrons, "I recommend the blintzes."

The next stop was Max Weitzman's Kosher Delicatessen, a short stroll down Delancey Street. There, Rockefeller munched on a corned beef on rye, donned an apron, posed for pictures with a two-foot salami, and made the acquaintance of a counterman named Ben. Expressing an interest in the salami, Rockefeller asked Weitzman how much it cost. "Five dollars," the proprietor replied, "but I'll sell it to you wholesale, three dollars." One of Weitzman's regulars was not amused. "For Rockefeller, he gives discounts," the customer grumbled.

It was a day for photo opportunities and autographs, not for political discourse. The closest the visitors came was when an elderly widow with a kerchief, babushka style, on her head complained to Rockefeller that she couldn't find a decent apartment at an affordable rent. In reply, Rockefeller offered an earnest treatise on housing policy, mentioning two $100 million bond issues then under consideration. "If we can get that passed," he told the woman, "it will help relieve the shortage of apartments for elderly people who live alone like you."

"I should live so long," the widow said with a shrug.

The pictures—of Rockefeller toting his two-foot salami, of Rockefeller and Lefkowitz hoisting their corned beef sandwiches—were plastered the next day in newspapers all over the state. Above all, there was the one indelible image: that of the grandson of the world's greatest oil tycoon and son of the world's premier philanthropist happily wolfing down an oozing cheese blintz on Delancey Street.

It was the most cornball of campaign poses, but its impact was incalculable, cementing the impression of him in the public mind as a millionaire who would go anywhere and eat anything for a vote. As James Reston asked in *The New York Times* the morning after, "When in the political history of the great Republic has a real, live Rockefeller been seen eating cheese blintzes on the Lower East Side of Manhattan with the resident voters of that district?"

No longer was he Nelson Rockefeller, scion of Standard Oil. From now on he was Rocky, eater of blintzes.

Armed with this gleaming new product, Rockefeller's campaign apparatus made sure that no opportunity was left unexploited, and no dime was left unspent, to keep it in the public eye.

A top-flight adman, Thomas Losee of McCann-Erickson, had joined the Roosevelt Hotel team to work with Weaver on marketing the candidate, and together they came up with a strategy geared to making the most of what was clearly the candidate's greatest strength: his interaction with the common folk. A film and sound crew would follow Rockefeller everywhere, and the best bits would be edited into commercials. Recalls Weaver, "I told Nelson that what we have to do with our commercials is, you go out and you meet the average people, and just talk to them, because you know how to do that. It'll be you in the gas station, you in the restaurant eating all that awful ethnic food. And he liked that approach."

This innovative person-to-person approach had something else going for it:

it largely spared Weaver and the other handlers the horror of watching the dyslexic Rockefeller stumble through a speech on a Teleprompter. But even on that front, Rockefeller was showing signs of improvement. In his first extended TV ad—a mock interview in which an on-screen moderator asked him rehearsed questions—he hardly ever flubbed. "He handled cards and flip charts very professionally," wrote *The New York Times*'s television reviewer, "and managed much of the time not to look at a Teleprompter. For a beginner it was quite a professional job."

Professionalism—a mark of the level of expertise, in Weaver and Losee, that Rockefeller had in his corner—was one element that distinguished Rockefeller's TV and radio blitz. The other was a seemingly bottomless pool of media dollars. Although no precise figures on his spending are available, his campaign was later said to have spent more than two and a half times what Harriman's did on TV time alone. "All this," observed *New York Daily News* political columnist Edward O'Neill, "marks at least a partial abandonment of the initial Rockefeller strategy of play down the money, make him just another guy. The money has to show, because you don't pay for all that advertising with cigar wrappers."

O'Neill saw the Rockefeller ad barrage as a harbinger of campaigns to come: "Look for many future elections to take on the new look, with the candidate's public relations firm replacing the clubhouse."

This mammoth effort was starting to pay off.

Prior to the two party conventions, polls had shown Harriman with a commanding 60–40 lead. But in early October, Rockefeller's pollster called the race dead even, with a full 20 percent undecided. Two weeks later, Jud Morhouse said his surveys were showing Rockefeller pulling ahead, 44–42.

Beyond the poll numbers, there was a sense in the Rockefeller camp that they were piloting a steamroller. *Time* magazine captured the feeling—and to some extent certainly contributed to it—in putting Rockefeller on its October 6 cover. The race, said *Time,* "is turning from a Democratic walkaway into a neck-and-neck sprint."

The switchboard operator at the state Republican committee in Albany could see that something big was happening. One day in early October her board began lighting up—and it stayed lit. She knew then and there, she told a co-worker, that "we had a winner."

The reporters covering the campaign could see it, too. Jack Germond recalls going on back-to-back trips through the southern tier counties—first with Harriman, then with Rockefeller. The two candidates made virtually the same stops. As soon as he got back in early October from the second trip, Germond called his Albany bookmaker. "What's the line on the governorship?" Nine to five on Harriman, he was told. "Well, bet me fifty dollars on Rockefeller," said Germond.

For Germond, it was an open-and-shut case. Rockefeller had "captured the imagination of the people." Averell Harriman hadn't.

Harriman was, in his own right, an indefatigable campaigner; his schedule was every bit as backbreaking as Rockefeller's. Yet even as he tossed off his jacket and waded into crowds in shirtsleeves, Harriman could not seem to overcome the starchiness of his persona. He was the perfect foil for Rockefeller: an aristocrat who truly looked and sounded like one. Where Rockefeller spoke with a vaguely New Yorkish honk that was getting more plebeian by the day, Harriman's accent was strictly Grotonian. Where Rockefeller clapped backs and, at a loss to remember names, greeted one and all with a hearty "Hi ya, fella," Harriman primly shook hands and said, "Hello, stranger." Where Rockefeller delighted in the raucous rituals of an American political campaign, the band leading and the headdress wearing, Harriman could barely conceal his distaste for it. Presented with a handmade bibelot by a youthful admirer, Harriman declared that he'd "cherish it always." Then, when the youth had gone, Harriman turned around and handed it to his bodyguard, saying within earshot of reporters, "Here, Eddie, cherish it for me."

Harriman also seemed curiously averse to denigrating his opponent. Rather than take on Rockefeller directly, he chose to launch salvos against the Eisenhower administration, blaming the White House's "tight money policies" for the recession, excoriating its foreign policy, all by way of raising in the gubernatorial campaign the issue of guilt by association. His opponent, he said, "can't divorce himself from the Republican Party"; he was "their candidate." He described Rockefeller as "this young man who is going around the state and trying to cover up the Eisenhower recession."

With the general downturn in the national administration's fortunes, there did appear to be some sound reasons for taking this tack; what's more, it certainly would not hurt to remind all those disaffected liberals that Rockefeller was, after all, a Republican. Nevertheless, by fixating on national and international issues, Harriman created the impression that he couldn't care less about the state's problems. As one county leader groused, "If instead of devoting the last three years to a campaign against President Eisenhower he had been campaigning for Averell Harriman, he would be unbeatable."

His toothless campaign thoroughly disheartened Democratic Party workers who, in past years, would have enthusiastically rallied around the incumbent. One local captain from Manhattan's Upper East Side was so distraught that he wrote the governor directly. "I want to see you and Mr. Hogan elected, but there is little encouragement for me in the air," he told Harriman. "Where are all the Harriman and Hogan posters, banners and buttons? Why is it that all one hears and sees is Rockefeller, Rockefeller ad nauseam? . . . Where is the fire in your campaign?"

The fire, if truth be told, had been tamped down to just a few scattered embers, not just by the candidate's aloofness and miscalculations but by the infighting and mismanagement that was rampant in his campaign organization. "Between the undercutting and the back-sniping and all the other nonsense that went on," recalled Harriman's counsel, Daniel Gutman, "you had a very disjointed piece of business in the Harriman campaign." The handling of the Democratic heartland, the five boroughs of New York City and its adjoining suburbs, was especially botched. "Nothing seemed to be happening in New York City," said Gutman. There was no great crescendo of pro-Harriman rallies and speeches; in fact, the city's number one Democrat, Mayor Wagner, was never asked to make a single speech in support of the ticket.

Harriman was largely leaving the management of his downstate effort in the hands of De Sapio and the regulars, but the regulars were proving to be almost as unenthusiastic about the campaign as the reformers. The party leaders were said to be infuriated that Harriman, desperate to prove his independence from the machine, had publicly made it known he intended to appoint a reform-wing stalwart, Franklin Adams, as Hogan's successor as Manhattan DA. The announcement may have been good public relations, but it thoroughly embittered the county leaders—at precisely the moment that Harriman needed them most.

"You must talk to Carmine," one of Harriman's aides beseeched the governor in mid-October. "The fact that the Rockefeller people have beat us out with foreign language press and radio advertising, with stores, with literature, with posters, has not mattered up to now—but in the closing two weeks it makes a difference."

It was not that De Sapio was shying from combat; on the contrary, the Tammany boss was quite willing—more willing, in fact, than his gubernatorial candidate—to publicly lash out at Rockefeller. Rockefeller's daily denunciations of him were clearly getting under De Sapio's skin, leading De Sapio to finally step out from the shadows and accuse the Republican of "smear" and "gutter tactics." There was true passion and indignation in his voice as he described how he, "the son of an immigrant family," had become, for want of any better target, Rockefeller's "whipping boy, his target, a symbol of everything that his own background and upbringing had taught him to hate and despise."

He reminded the voters that Rockefeller was no man of the people, but "the candidate of Standard Oil, Du Pont, and the Chase Manhattan Bank." He was "the product of oil cartels, the descendant of one of America's most notorious financial dynasties, the present day disciple of the cynical theory that, politically, if a little money can go a long way—then a lot of money can perhaps go all the way to the White House, via Albany."

Using vituperation that Harriman, himself the descendant of a notorious financial dynasty, would never dare employ, De Sapio produced easily the most cutting remarks of the Democratic campaign. Their one drawback was that they cast the race exactly as Rockefeller and his handlers wanted it to be cast: as a contest between Nelson Rockefeller and Carmine G. De Sapio.

On top of all its other woes, the Harriman campaign was hit by a true hammer blow on October 15: *The New York Times*'s decision to endorse Nelson Rockefeller for governor.

It was bad enough that the *Times* rhapsodized about Rockefeller's attributes: "He has the qualities of character, the breadth of business, administrative and governmental expertise, the vigor and the strength of conviction to make a good chief executive of New York State and possibly a great one." What was especially galling to the incumbent was how contemptuous the paper was of Harriman's four years in office: "He has given the state a pedestrian performance, disappointing in achievement and, we believe, unpromising of improvement in the future."

While Harriman may not have expected a *Times* endorsement—the paper had not supported him in 1954 either—he certainly had no reason to expect such a dismissive editorial. Yet even the shock of the *Times* editorial was not enough to stir Harriman to reappraise his campaign strategy. The day after the *Times* blockbuster, he challenged Rockefeller to a debate—"any place, any time, on any subject. On state, national or foreign issues." One evening in Watertown, he spotted a group of reporters dining in an Italian restaurant and went over to their table to voice his enthusiasm for the prospective debate. "If I can get Nelson on foreign policy," he told them, "I'll demolish him."

But Rockefeller was not about to let his opponent get him on foreign policy or anything else that might tie him to the Republican administration in Washington. After initially accepting Harriman's offer, he backed off when it was clear that the governor would put national and international issues on the table. Instead, Rockefeller charged that his rival's "insistence on bringing national and international affairs into a debate . . . is a patent effort to run out on a reckoning with the voters."

Rockefeller was proving himself a maddeningly elusive target. Most of his campaign rhetoric was confined to a core of catchphrases, what in a later era would be called "sound bites." The Harriman administration, he would say over and over, was one of "do nothing and drift." "If my opponent is re-elected," he declared, in one egregious non sequitur, "we're liable to go over Niagara Falls, not in a barrel, but in a Hula-Hoop." And always, there was, like a mantra, the invocation of Tammany. "The basic issue in this campaign is bossism." "I have never been bossed by anybody and I never shall be." "What a tragic thing to see a great governor rolled under by the powerful Tammany machine."

He also made political hay out of the headline-making state police raid on a powwow of Mafia kingpins in the hamlet of Apalachin, outside Binghamton, a year earlier. Well aware of the whispers linking De Sapio with organized crime, Rockefeller brought up Apalachin constantly, insinuating that the meeting was facilitated by a lax Albany attitude toward the mob. "Organized crime," he declared, "has found New York State a good place to do business under the Harriman administration."

This was no genteel amateur dabbling in the electoral process; this was a thorough pro ruthlessly seizing every opening his adversary gave him, eagerly slamming his foe at every turn. In one speech about Tammany that questioned Harriman's courage, Rockefeller crossed out the word "courage" and substituted "guts." His advisers thought that went a bit far, and successfully persuaded him to change it back to "courage."

Obscured in the billowy smoke of Rockefeller's rhetorical barrage was his program. Still, if one looked really hard one could begin to discern the faint outline of his plans for the governorship. He talked about offering a medical insurance plan that would protect wage earners against the "big bills" of catastrophic illnesses—a new version of the reinsurance scheme he had unsuccessfully tried to launch at HEW. He spoke of expanding the State University and the state's college scholarship and loan programs. And, after warning that the state was entering into "its most serious financial crisis in a generation," he promised "long range fiscal planning with the development of a real capital budget plan," and a return to the "pay as you go" policies of the Dewey years—rather than a dependence on borrowed funds for financing public works. (It was a promise that would, soon enough, be ripe with irony.)

These excursions into the land of policy, however, were few and far between. What governed this race, as it headed into the homestretch, was one ineluctable fact: Nelson Rockefeller was a white-hot political property, and what he said about budgets or education or housing was almost beside the point.

The reception Rockefeller was getting around the state was rapidly assuming Elvis-like proportions.

In Coney Island, Rockefeller was mobbed by a surging, cheering horde that overwhelmed the four policemen assigned as an escort. Sixteen more officers were summoned to handle the crush. Greeting some of the voters in Spanish, and others in French, Rockefeller inched his way over to Nathan's for a hot dog with Jacob Javits in tow. When Rockefeller emerged from the tumult an hour later, to board a BMT subway back to Manhattan, he proudly bore the scars of battle: rumpled suit, scuffed shoes, mussed hair, and a mustard stain on his jacket sleeve.

In Spanish Harlem five days later, cheers of "Viva Rockefeller" rang out as thousands of Puerto Rican New Yorkers jammed a raucous block party for the Republican candidate. Tossing away his prepared remarks, Rockefeller adlibbed for twenty minutes in Spanish, pausing only to ask the crowd "*¿Cómo* *se dice?"* (How do you say?) when he was at a loss to translate such terms as "seven hundred thousand substandard homes." He promised to hold the line on the fifteen-cent "soobway" fare; when one man shouted out that it should be less, Rockefeller shouted back, *"Mira, hombre* [Look, man], one thing at a time."

When he was finished Rockefeller vaulted from the stage and was swallowed up by the swaying, dancing crowd. Seconds later he reemerged, hoisted aloft on shoulders like a triumphant matador. "We're losing the candidate. He'll break a leg," one worried assistant groaned. But there was no stopping this jubilant tide, nor the candidate who bobbed along exultantly in their embrace.

A policeman eyeing this scene threw up his hands in disgust. "He's mad, mad, mad," he said.

On that evening, as well as at so many of her husband's other appearances, Tod Rockefeller was in attendance, looking owlishly bemused at the goings-on. As natural as this nonstop carnival was for him, it was thoroughly unnatural for her, and the adjustment to its demands was still wrenching. "Political stumping was very hard for her," says her nephew James Wallis. "She wasn't particularly accustomed to sharing niceties and small talk with people she didn't know. She's really not a small talk person. It was all quite foreign to her."

Her trepidation about her appearances on the stump was, to a great extent, shared by Rockefeller's counselors—but, oddly, not because of fears of what she wouldn't say, but because of fears of what she would. Tact and diplomacy were never her great strength; in the Rockefeller inner circle, many were the tales of Tod's waspish tongue. What no doubt set off alarms were recollections of her swings through Latin America with her husband, tours that in many ways resembled campaign hops. During one visit, their party was forced to spend the whole night at the airport. "What a rathole," she proclaimed, in a voice loud enough for the whole airport to hear.

She had no patience for the flamboyant gestures that were part and parcel of such junkets—and in which her husband indulged so shamelessly. Seeking to promote his milk-retailing ventures, Rockefeller spoke often of his love for chocolate milk. Each time he visited his Venezuelan ranch, he made sure there was plenty of chocolate milk on hand. Tod watched the shipments with barely concealed disgust, and finally berated her husband. "Nelson," she said, "you never drink *chocolate milk.* What do you want with all that?"

Still, as much as Rockefeller's handlers might have wanted to cloister Tod for the duration of the 1958 campaign, and as much as she might have welcomed it, there was no way to hide her for two-plus months. Her early performances on the campaign circuit, however, were not encouraging. During a rainy day swing by the candidate through Rockland County, Tod sat in the limousine the whole time. Jay Coral, who spearheaded the Rockefeller volunteer effort in Rockland, remembers going over to her and trying to draw her out. "I mentioned to her that I had met her daughter Mary at the campaign headquarters in New York, and all she said was 'Oh, yes, Mary is very interested.' It was very hard to make conversation with her. She was completely aloof from the whole process."

"She became almost physically ill at the thought of having to go up on a podium and talk," recalls Arthur Richardson, who accompanied her for a good part of the campaign. It was not until October 21, seven weeks into the contest, that Tod ventured forth on her own to campaign. In one whirlwind "Meet Mary Rockefeller" day in Manhattan, she posed with seamstresses in the garment center, toured a new, integrated public school on the Upper West Side, dined on manicotti at Leone's restaurant in midtown, and braved firecrackers and confetti at the Jefferson Houses block party in Spanish Harlem. It was a jam-packed day worthy of her hyperenergetic husband—but it would not be repeated.

She was, to be sure, no Eleanor Roosevelt. Caustic, blunt, she was incapable of camouflaging her hauteur or muzzling her acid tongue. One morning, during a tour of western New York, she and Richardson went to a local diner for breakfast. Such a stop might be an occasion for garrulous glad-handing for her husband, but not so for Tod. Settling in on a counter stool, she was greeted by the cook, a gnarled fellow in a food-begrimed apron. "What'll you have?" he asked her. "Well," Tod sniffed, "the first thing I'll have is a clean apron on you, my man."

Her encounters with the press were models of brusqueness. One reporter, trying to ascertain how much political background she had, asked her, "Have you ever been to Albany?" "No," she tartly shot back. "Have you?"

On the rare occasions when she tried to build bridges to the press, she found herself hopelessly out of synch. Once, when the campaign bus was traveling through Letchworth State Park near the Finger Lakes, Tod ventured to the back, where the newsmen were busily typing away. "Oh, look at that fall foliage out there," she said. "It is absolutely gorgeous." Harry O'Donnell, the old Albany newshound who was now the state GOP p.r. whiz, peered up from his papers and gave a brief glance out the window. "Mrs. Rockefeller," he said, "when you've seen one tree, you've seen them all."

"That," says Richardson, "was the last time she came to the back of the bus."

As the race picked up steam, one familiar female in the Rockefeller entourage was notably missing in action: Nancy Hanks.

There were perfectly understandable reasons for her absence. With the Special Studies reports still being ground out, Hanks was needed to shepherd the project to its completion—and to keep the increasingly ornery Henry

Kissinger in line. Now that the project's sponsor and driving force had moved on to more pressing matters, Hanks's involvement was more crucial than ever.

Nevertheless, as plausible as this explanation was, there were whispers in the Rockefeller camp that something else was behind her invisibility: that Hanks had been directed to make herself scarce, possibly by Frank Jamieson, to fend off any unwanted rumors.

The irony, points out Hanks's friend Donna Mitchell, was that "by that time Nancy and Nelson's relationship had distanced itself to such an extent that there was no reason for anybody to say anything. The press could have done something a couple of years before that, but not in 1958. . . .

"When 1958 came along," Mitchell crisply notes, "he was already involved with other women."

With Hanks gone from view, another woman soon stepped forward to take Hanks's place in the Rockefeller coterie, a woman who since the early strategy-making days in the Roxy suite had become as much a fixture in the entourage as Hanks once was: Mrs. James S. Murphy, known to one and all as "Happy."

Mrs. Murphy had more in common with Rockefeller's Room 5600 majordomo, Louise Boyer, than she did with Nancy Hanks. Her breeding and social connections were akin to Boyer's: Murphy had a sound Main Line Philadelphia background, and her husband, a researcher at the Rockefeller Medical Institute, came from an equally prominent family with long-standing ties to the Rockefellers. But unlike the commanding, supremely self-possessed Boyer, Murphy seemed adrift; her precise duties were unclear. "She was sort of an office manager," remembers Kerk Burbank. "She didn't have too much experience, but she did a good job." What impressed most people about her, aside from her coltish blond good looks, was her sunny personality; she fully lived up to her nickname. "She was bright, cheerful, and totally unimpressed by titles or things," says Burbank. "I think the staff welcomed her after Nancy. Nancy was a bit of a slave driver. She worked seven days a week, and expected everyone else to work with her seven days a week. Happy, on the other hand, had a different approach."

Not everyone was so keen on Mrs. Murphy. At the Roosevelt, some questioned her intelligence; some even called her "scatterbrained." She was regarded at the headquarters as an omnipresent busybody who was constantly poking her nose into every aspect of the campaign, even the areas about which she plainly knew nothing. "She was all over the place," says June Martin, a policy aide and speechwriter, "but we couldn't figure out what her function was. She didn't have a title. She didn't have a role. I'd be going from my office to Ronan's to work on a speech, and she'd intercept me and ask, 'How's that speech coming?' Well, you didn't know whether she knew what kind of a speech you were working on or not. Then she'd say, 'Don't go away. I want to talk to you.' But I was supposed to report to Ronan. Happy had nothing to do with it. It was all very, very strange."

On one thing everyone who dealt with Mrs. Murphy was agreed: she seemed to have a rather special access to the candidate. One day, a group of Rockefeller aides gathered in Ronan's office after a brief campaign appearance in New York by the President. "Happy walked in," remembers Martin, "and sat on the table—I can still picture her—and started talking about Eisenhower. 'Didn't he look awful? That *awful* flush.' She said several derogatory things about him. And there just wasn't a question in my mind that she wasn't saying this herself. She was quoting." Quoting, it appeared, from the private thoughts of Nelson A. Rockefeller.

Ever since the race's opening gun on Labor Day, all the momentum had been Rockefeller's. But as the contest entered its final week and a half, the pendulum finally seemed to be swinging in Averell Harriman's direction.

The Democratic Party's old warhorses, largely silent for most of the campaign, at long last started to weigh in. Harry Truman, reacting to Rockefeller ads highlighting the candidate's Point Four work for Truman, issued a statement saying he was shocked to find that "as part of Nelson Rockefeller's campaign of sham and deceit, he has been implying in his campaign literature that he has my endorsement as a candidate for Governor of New York."

Eleanor Roosevelt set aside her postconvention bitterness and, in a five-minute radio broadcast, zeroed in on the distinctly nonliberal record of Rockefeller's running mate, Malcolm Wilson: "He voted against all the liberal housing bills advocated by Governor Harriman. . . . He voted for the anti-labor bills vetoed by Governor Harriman."

Herbert Lehman, like Truman, complained about foul play in Rockefeller ads that cited laudatory comments the ex-governor made about Rockefeller at the time of the latter's HEW appointment. "Mr. Rockefeller," said Lehman, "did not . . . justify my expression of complimentary confidence. . . . He showed neither courage nor independence of mind while he was in that office."

The most stinging assault on Rockefeller came from Harlem's redoubtable Democratic congressman, the Reverend Adam Clayton Powell, Jr. Indicted for income tax evasion, assailed as a political turncoat (he endorsed Eisenhower in 1956), pilloried in the press for his all too frequent absences from Congress, the fiery preacher nonetheless had an iron grip on his constituency. When the Democratic machine, earlier in 1958, tried to deny him renomination, he trounced its handpicked candidate in a primary by a three-to-one margin.

Despite Republican hopes that they could win Powell's support in the 1958 gubernatorial race, and despite the GOP's cross-endorsement of him in the congressional contest, Powell decided to stand with Harriman. Making peace, for the time being, with Tammany, the ever pragmatic reverend cut a deal with De Sapio that assured Powell of the Manhattan leader's backing in his campaign to become the first black chairman of a congressional committee. Thus conciliated, Powell proceeded to lash Rockefeller as only Adam Clayton Powell could. Speaking at the Greater New York Baptist Ministers Conference, he charged that Rockefeller was "campaigning on the basis of his philanthropy, doing nothing more than a mass production method of trying to buy the vote." He sneered that Rockefeller family funding of southern black education amounted to nothing more than millions for "Jim Crow colleges" and that the Rockefellers had only meagerly supported the National Association for the Advancement of Colored People.

But his most graphic accusation was that the Republicans had tried to "buy" his backing in the statewide race. A national GOP figure, Powell said, had approached him with the offer. "If they [the Republicans] deny it, I will name the names and dates where they sent people to me." Shortly afterward, Powell did name the "national figure": he was Charles Willis, a former deputy to Sherman Adams in the White House, who had been the principal administration go-between in securing Powell's endorsement in 1956. "I wouldn't say it was an attempt to bribe me," said Powell, "because no specific amount was mentioned to me by Willis—only that he had a bundle for me."

Willis adamantly denied this: "Adam Powell was never offered any money by me at any time in behalf of the Republican Party or for any other reason."

"No verifiable paper trail is available on these discussions," notes Powell's biographer, Charles V. Hamilton. Furthermore, even if Willis did make the cash offer, no connection was ever established between Willis and Nelson Rockefeller. They certainly knew one another from White House days, but Willis was never identified as an active Rockefeller supporter or adviser in that 1958 race.

Be that as it may, Powell's allegations—spurious or not—hit home. The Rockefellers had always taken pride in their support of black education and civil rights, cherishing like family heirlooms the tales of their involvement in the Underground Railroad and the General Education Board. Coming as close as he would come, in the course of that campaign, to losing his composure, Rockefeller devoted two consecutive precious evenings in the final fortnight of the campaign to answering the charges (at least, some of them) in speeches before Harlem audiences. About the supposed cash offer, he said nothing, but about the insinuations about his support of Negro causes, he said much. He found it "especially shocking to be charged with philanthropy to buy votes." Regarding Powell's crack about "Jim Crow colleges," he proudly pointed out that his family had given some $55 million over the decades "to aid Negro education." As for his support of the NAACP, he said his family had contributed since 1928, and that he personally had contributed to the NAACP's legal defense fund in 1951 and 1956. "If anyone challenges this," said Rockefeller, "they can ask Thurgood Marshall," the organization's chief counsel. (Marshall confirmed that Rockefeller had given some $5,000.)

His rebuttal won him reams of press coverage, but few converts among the Powell faithful. A gala Rockefeller rally on Seventh Avenue in Harlem brought out thousands to see such headline entertainers as the Count Basie band, Cab Calloway, and comedian Nipsy Russell. When Rockefeller, his family (including brother Winthrop), and his running mates took the stage, however, the applause was anemic and perfunctory—easily the most lackluster reception of his whole campaign. Powell couldn't resist adding some salt to the wound by mocking the whole affair as one more Rockefeller attempt to buy Harlem's votes with "souvenirs, gifts and jazz for all."

The Democrats managed to hit another Rockefeller hot button in the contest's closing days: the issue of rent control.

The regulation of apartment rents—first introduced as a wartime measure—was the most hallowed of political sacred cows. No aspirant to statewide office dared breathe a word against it, certainly no one who had the slightest designs on the New York City vote. Of the two million rent-controlled units in the state, 90 percent were in New York City; in all, some 4.5 million city residents—more than half the city's population—lived in apartments covered by the regulation.

In their hunt for issues on which Rockefeller might be vulnerable, Democratic strategists seized on rent control—not because Rockefeller had ever said anything about it, but because upstate Republicans, from time to time, had talked about curbing its scope.

Grasping this rather slender reed, Harriman charged that rent control would be in jeopardy if Rockefeller was elected. The Republicans, he asserted, had tried "to end rent control in '55 and '57, and then tried to sabotage it, to scuttle it by crippling amendments." Voters, he warned, would be running a grave risk by pulling the GOP lever. "If I were a tenant, I wouldn't take a chance on it," he said.

For the first time in the campaign, Harriman had his opponent on the defensive. In a television interview, Rockefeller deplored this "misrepresentation." For six weeks, he insisted, he had been saying that "I'd keep rent control and strengthen the law and see that it was enforced." Just two days earlier, he had met with Republican leaders of the legislature and "all were in complete agreement this must be kept."

The denials were followed up by an all-out ad barrage on television, radio, even the sports pages of newspapers, aimed at setting the record straight and neutralizing this scare issue. The sledgehammer quality of the ads ("Rockefeller for *Rent Control*," they read, in big bold type) was indicative of just how worried Rockefeller's people were.

"Rockefeller has been the life of the party this fall," columnist Mary Mc-

Grory quipped in the *Washington Star,* "but he is desperately hoping the voters won't remember which party." Indeed, as the race headed into the homestretch it was this concern—the fear that all those swing voters would be reminded that Rockefeller was, after all, a Republican—that, even more than rent control, elevated blood pressures on the seventh floor of the Roosevelt Hotel.

For the most part, Rockefeller had adroitly finessed the issue, expunging any references to the Grand Old Party in his ads and campaign materials and keeping campaign appearances by the likes of Tom Dewey and Walter Mahoney to a minimum. When President Eisenhower flew into New York to participate in Columbus Day festivities, Rockefeller met with him for two hours, but the visit was largely apolitical; at a wreath-laying ceremony in Columbus Circle, both gubernatorial candidates were in attendance.

But then, on October 23, a day of reckoning arrived. Richard M. Nixon came to town.

Stumping the country on behalf of his party's candidates, the Vice President—apparently without consulting Rockefeller—decided to include New York in his itinerary. He accepted an invitation to appear at a Theodore Roosevelt centennial dinner in Garden City, Long Island, organized by Leonard Hall; before the dinner he would also make a statewide address in support of the GOP ticket.

A Nixon drop-in was the last thing that Rockefeller's strategists needed. Still seen as the Red-baiting persecutor of Alger Hiss, Nixon was thoroughly despised by the liberal swing voters whose support was considered essential for a Rockefeller victory. An appearance by the candidate with the Vice President was certain to yank the issue of Rockefeller's Republicanism back into the open, at the very moment when he and his team were going all out to bury it.

A mere three years earlier, Rockefeller regarded Nixon as his closest administration ally. Just two months before, he had thought nothing of enlisting Nixon's help in pressuring Keating to take the senatorial nomination. Now, though, that old friendship was an albatross that might well destroy Rockefeller's political ambitions.

Conveniently, Rockefeller was winding up a swing in Buffalo when Nixon arrived at the Waldorf Towers on the twenty-third. And just as conveniently, Rockefeller would be returning to Manhattan that evening, for a reception at the Hotel St. Moritz, at almost the exact same time Nixon was leaving for the Garden City dinner. Thus, if all went according to plan, he and Nixon would never be within twenty-five miles of one another.

But while Rockefeller might evade the Vice President, he couldn't evade the press. Quickly picking up on the remarkable divergence in the two politicians' schedules, reporters read into it a deliberate snub of the Vice President. As soon as he touched down at Newark Airport, Rockefeller phoned Jamieson, who informed him that trouble was brewing. They agreed that the only proper course of action was to contact Nixon at once. When he reached the Vice President's suite at the Waldorf Towers, however, Rockefeller was curtly informed that Nixon was working on his speech and couldn't be disturbed. Evidently, the Vice President was every bit as miffed at Rockefeller's treatment of him as the reporters thought he would be.

Nevertheless, Nixon went on to the TV studio and made his pitch for the entire Republican ticket, specifically praising Rockefeller's "dynamic leadership." Rockefeller phoned again when he had finished, to thank him; this time, Nixon took the call. The two agreed to meet the following morning for breakfast in Nixon's suite.

And so, the next morning, Rockefeller found himself doing what he probably least wanted to do to start the day: posing self-consciously for photographers with Richard Nixon over his ham and eggs, and denying to newsmen afterward that he had been avoiding the Vice President. "A lot of bunk . . . sheer bunk . . . absolute fabrication . . . absolutely nothing to it," he sputtered. Nixon, for his part, insisted he had not felt "snubbed"; of a possible rift between him and Rockefeller, he said, "There is none and never has been one."

Drifting over the proceedings was the inescapable specter of the 1960 presidential race—in the words of the *Times*'s William Lawrence, "the possible rivalry for the Republican presidential nomination in 1960 that many expect between the two men if Mr. Rockefeller is elected Governor." Nixon, though, didn't even want to discuss it. And Rockefeller asserted that a presidential run was the furthest thing from his mind. "Honestly and truly," he said, "all that I am interested in is becoming Governor."

Harriman and company were quite willing to take the duo's word that there was no rift between them. As far as the Democrats were concerned, the Waldorf breakfast proved exactly what they had been saying all along: that Rockefeller and Nixon were comrades-in-arms. Harriman went so far as to suggest that the breakfast proved there was a "deal" or "understanding" between them about 1960.

Pouncing on Rockefeller's discomfiture, the party blanketed New York City newspapers with a new series of ads. "The Only Answer to the Republican Party of Rockefeller and Nixon!" they read. "Vote the Harriman Ticket."

The Rockefeller-Nixon entente was apparently enough to tip the scales at the *New York Post,* the voice of New York liberalism. As late as October 23, the day of Nixon's visit, the *Post* had declared itself unable to endorse one candidate or the other. But all that changed with the fateful breakfast. Likening it to Eisenhower's historic Morningside Heights meeting with archconservative Robert Taft in 1952, a *Post* editorial on October 30 said it raised the question whether "Rockefeller is ready and eager to do battle with the powerful right wing of his party. . . .

"We cannot support a candidate by pretending we know what he thinks when he doesn't say it aloud and by reading large significance into his public silences," the paper declared. "We favor Harriman's reelection."

Buoyed by these developments as his campaign headed into its final days, Harriman spoke with a new, almost Trumanesque directness and vigor, and no longer had any hesitancy about slamming Rockefeller head-on. He picked apart Rockefeller's promises, claiming that they would cost the state $1.5 billion and require a 50 percent boost in state income taxes. He charged that if Rockefeller was elected, "the state would go back into the control of the reactionaries of the Republican Party." And he denounced Rockefeller for his lavish campaign expenditures, adding, "I think it is boomeranging. People resent the fact that this fellow is trying to buy the election."

Brimming with pugnacity, Harriman appeared on Barry Gray's New York radio interview program late in the evening of October 30. It had been a long day for the governor; he had just come from the annual Alfred E. Smith dinner at the Waldorf. Clearly fighting fatigue, but not wanting to miss one more chance to go on the offensive, Harriman began rambling about Suez and the Middle East and Rockefeller's role in the administration's policy there. "When the first appeasement of Nasser took place, he was in the White House—and was, I am told, an adviser to the President on foreign affairs. . . . The Arabs took that as a green light for them to move ahead. . . . if he had been firm, the President had been firm . . . we wouldn't be in the difficulty we are in now."

"There is no doubt in my mind," he continued, "that the big business—the oil interests—have had a great deal of influence on the—President Eisenhower's and Dulles' foreign policy has been the oil interests."

Harriman's incoherent late-night diatribe would have passed totally into the oblivion of the airwaves had a *New York Post* reporter not been listening. The *Post* included an account in its coverage the next day, but even then, hardly anyone paid any attention; Rockefeller didn't even bother to respond. Unluckily for Harriman, among the few people who did take note of his little discourse was one of the few people he dared not alienate: the publisher of the *Post,* Dorothy Schiff.

Imperious, elitist, and headstrong, Dorothy Schiff shared a common heritage with Averell Harriman. Both owed their fortunes to the robber baron era—in Schiff's case to her grandfather, investment banker Jacob Schiff, whose backing helped Harriman's father consolidate his control of much of the nation's railroads. And, like Harriman, Schiff had abandoned her family's staid Republicanism in favor of the New Deal Democratic Party. But whereas Harriman's party switch would always have a careerist tinge, Schiff's allegiance had a true ideological base: she was a veritable high priestess of the cult of liberalism, and she turned her *New York Post* into the movement's foremost clarion.

Her paper's indecision about the gubernatorial race reflected her own ambivalence. A rabid foe of De Sapio, Schiff had been thoroughly disgusted with Harriman's Buffalo cave-in. In Nelson Rockefeller, whom she knew personally and liked, she saw a sound alternative with impeccable liberal instincts. As she described her feelings in a "Dear Reader" column published the day after the *Post*'s endorsement of Harriman, "It was true that Nelson Rockefeller was a Republican and . . . he had chosen as his closest running mate a Republican reactionary. However, Nelson's reputation was so magnificent that perhaps he would be able to overwhelm these tremendous liabilities." The Waldorf performance, however, caused her to question whether he could. She sent word to her editor, James Wechsler, that he now had her okay to come out for Harriman.

But then, the day after the endorsement, came the news from the Barry Gray show. Schiff spent the weekend in Baltimore. When she returned to the office on Monday, less than twenty-four hours before the election, she sent a one-paragraph statement down to Wechsler. Her instructions were to print it in that afternoon's final edition—not just print it, but make it the whole of page one.

It would be addressed, in the biggest headline type the editors could find, "To Post Readers":

> Gov. Harriman's recent snide insinuation that Nelson Rockefeller is pro-Arab and anti-Israel should not be condoned by any fair-minded person. Rockefeller, far from being anti-Israel, has been a liberal contributor to the United Jewish Appeal for twelve years. It is deplorable but true that in political campaigns lower echelons on both sides indulge in vile demagoguery. But when the head of the ticket repeats such libels, he should be punished by the voters. If you agree with me, do not vote for Averell Harriman tomorrow.
>
> DOROTHY SCHIFF,
> Publisher

A startled Wechsler tried to talk Schiff out of this unprecedented page one appeal from the publisher. But Schiff would not budge.

And so, for that last "Final Blue" edition of the paper, the presses were stopped, the front page (with the headline "Heiress Tries Suicide") ripped out, and the newly composed front page stripped in. One more remade page was also sent down: the editorial page, which contained the list of "The Post's Election Choices." Harriman's name had been at the top of the page, and his photograph was the page's centerpiece. Now both name and photo had been expunged. Instead, the *Post* indicated it had no preference in the gubernatorial race.

Harriman was pumping hands that afternoon in Jackson Heights, Queens, when a reporter raced over to him with word of what the *Post* had done. The governor was visibly shaken, but quickly regained his composure. "I have never said he was pro-Arab or anti-Israel," he told the newsmen who had gathered around. "I said the spirit of Geneva was phony and I held Mr. Rockefeller responsible because he was one of the President's advisers." Harriman then stepped into his open car, and his motorcade resumed, only to be halted after half a block when the governor got out and walked back to the press car to talk some more about what he had said. "I have simply stated the facts of the case, the change from pro-Israel to a neutrality position," he protested. "That's the fact."

His opponent, meanwhile, was also in New York City, getting in one last big rally at Herald Square, when he heard the news. Elated, Rockefeller told reporters that "I appreciate her statement very much indeed. The facts are accurate and I admire her courage in saying them." Of course, he added, Schiff could have said even more. "She could have added this business of misrepresentation on rent control which is one that really burns me up. I don't care how much a man wants to win. I'd like to win, too, but I'm not going to do it by being dishonest."

Later, Rockefeller sent off a telegram to Schiff: "Your courageous statement is a significant contribution to the cause of honest political campaigning and good government."

The *Post* about-face was easily the campaign's most stunning single development—especially coming, as it did, on the very eve of the election and addressed, as it was, to the New York liberal constituency that both candidates saw as the key swing bloc in the election. In view of all that, more than a few political observers wondered whether it was really the spontaneous expression of indignation that Schiff made it out to be. Democratic state chairman Michael Prendergast, for one, asked the publisher in a telegram, "Was your switch planned for effect and made so late that you hoped it could not be answered before election?"

Schiff would vehemently maintain then, and later, that there was nothing so calculated in her decision. As she explained to *Post* readers in her column three days after the election, "Time was running out. No one else had dared or cared to refute Harriman's unfair insinuation that Rockefeller was hostile to Israel. As the deadline arrived, I stopped the presses and tried to correct what seemed to me to have been a shocking injustice done to a dedicated humanitarian."

Still, there are less drastic ways of righting a "shocking injustice" than stopping the presses and remaking the front page. Did Harriman's barely comprehensible jumble of late-night radio remarks really justify a dramatic, last-minute intervention that might well turn the tide of the election?

Schiff herself, in a 1975 interview with writers Michael Kramer and Sam Roberts, conceded that her motives were far more complex than she made them out to be at the time—that, in fact, she had a long-standing grudge against Harriman. "I'd been for Franklin Roosevelt, Jr., for governor in 1950," she explained. "I spoke to Carmine De Sapio and he said, 'Not this time but next time you can have it for Frank.' Of course, Harriman got it and then tried to take the presidential nomination away from Adlai Stevenson in 1956. I was adamantly pro-Stevenson. Then, in 1958, at the convention, I was for Finletter for the Senate and they gave it to Hogan."

She was also affected, she said, by thoughts of the next presidential race. "The big menace was Nixon in 1960. I wanted a 1960 alternative to Nixon. I wanted to nip him in the bud, in his own party."

As candid as that explanation sounds, there would be those, over the years, who would suggest that far more elemental motivations were at work. It did not, for instance, escape anyone's notice that Schiff's husband at the time (she would have four), industrialist Rudolf Sonneborn, was co-chairman of Democrats for Rockefeller—and that her ex-husband, real estate heir George Backer, was Harriman's closest political confidant. (Backer, in fact, had been publisher of the *Post* during their marriage.)

Then there was the explanation ventured by Harriman's top aide, Milton Stewart. "I have always felt that it was personal," he said, "that somehow the governor had offended Mrs. Schiff."

Harriman came to believe that was what did him in. Schiff, he said, felt snubbed because he had excluded her from social events at the Governor's Mansion—an exclusion that had come about because private remarks at those affairs had a tendency to make it into print whenever she was around.

Though it seems far-fetched, the theory does have a core of truth in it. Schiff did harbor a deep personal grudge against Harriman, a grudge that might well have driven her to turn on him at the moment he needed her most.

Harriman, however, was wrong about the source of it. Schiff's grievance dated back a good deal further than he could possibly have imagined.

Late one evening, having had one too many drinks, Schiff told her dinner companions the story. It seemed that when they were both young she had a crush on the tall, dashing, much-sought-after Harriman. One summer they found themselves in Paris at the same time, and Harriman came by to ask Schiff for a date. Schiff delightedly accepted, only to learn that Averell's idea of a date was to have her watch him play tennis in the suburb of St.-Cloud for three hours. She sat there on the sideline, thoroughly bored, until another young man she knew approached and asked her if she would like to watch her father's horses race at Longchamps. The high-spirited Schiff bolted in a flash, leaving Harriman to pound his tennis balls without an audience.

That evening, Schiff was supposed to meet Harriman for dinner. As she was dressing at her hotel, the room buzzer rang. She opened the door to find, not her date, but a bellhop bearing a note from Averell, angrily canceling their dinner. Accompanying the note was a single dead orchid.

Schiff never forgot that orchid. Thirty-odd years later, she may have finally found a way to get even.

The morning after the *Post*'s front-page message from Dorothy Schiff—the morning of election day—liberal precincts throughout the city were blanketed with reproductions of the *Post* front page, reproductions produced and distributed by volunteers for Rockefeller.

The skies were clear, the air crisply autumnal in the city that election day morn. Thirty miles to the north, in Pocantico Hills, Nelson and Tod arrived at the village's fire station at 9:30 A.M. to cast their votes. For the first time in five months, the candidate looked tired and drawn as he bantered with reporters. Since the day of his nomination he had logged over 8,000 miles, had made 135 speeches in 103 communities, and had toured every single one of the state's sixty-two counties (the last, remote Hamilton County, he visited by seaplane near the very end of the campaign). It had been a grinding, relentless expedition, and now his pallor finally indicated its effects.

Although the newsmen sensed he was on edge, he insisted he was free of any anxiety. "I've tried to keep myself in balance," he said, "so whatever way it goes, I'm relaxed."

In the afternoon, he drove down to the city with Tod and son Steven, making a brief stop at the Roosevelt before repairing to the Fifth Avenue apartment for dinner. Whatever tension he felt soon vanished when the word came from the Roosevelt: a landslide was in the making.

Harriman had forged ahead early, by 30,000 votes, but the lead proved as short-lived as one of his smiles. By 9 P.M., two hours after the polls closed, it was clear that Rockefeller was going to win and win big, with a margin of upward of half a million votes.

Returning to the Roosevelt, Rockefeller closeted himself with Jamieson to scan the returns and await Averell Harriman's concession of defeat.

With patrician graciousness, Harriman did not keep him waiting long. At 10:40 P.M. the governor appeared before reporters at his Biltmore Hotel headquarters and, gazing down at a yellow legal pad, read them the telegram of congratulations he was sending to his rival. The strain that had been written on his face since the Buffalo convention was gone; he looked relieved that the whole ordeal was over.

When word of Harriman's concession came, Rockefeller turned to Jamieson, the ever loyal, ever dependable handmaiden of his ambitions for almost two decades, and, without saying a word, shook his hand.

Downstairs a great exultant roar came up from the two thousand supporters who were jammed elbow to elbow in the ballroom. The seven-piece band swung into "Happy Days Are Here Again"; no one gave a damn any longer that it was a Democratic anthem they were swaying to.

Tod, dressed in an orchid-bedecked powder-blue damask gown, stood alongside the platform with her five children, one daughter-in-law, and one son-in-law—all seemingly frozen in fear at the spectacle before them. They dared not mount the stage until the paterfamilias arrived, but he remained on the seventh floor, having decided that he would not come down to claim victory until it was clear that Keating, too, had won.

"I just saw Nelson," a friend shouted to Tod. "But where *is* he?" Tod shouted back. Then someone held aloft a morning tabloid, hot off the press: "ROCKY WINS," the headline screamed. All Tod was heard to say was "Good" before she scurried off to a side room, where, for a brief moment, the mask of stoicism disappeared: she was seen wiping tears from her eyes.

Finally, at twenty-two minutes past eleven, the victor arrived. Clad in a brown flannel suit and sporting a grin that creased every inch of his blocky countenance, he inched his way through the horde to the bouncy strains of "Sweet Georgia Brown," reputed to be his favorite tune. As he approached the platform, Tod reemerged and, instructing her brood to "hold hands and keep together," held fast to eldest son Rod as the family snaked its way through the crush and onto the stage.

"What is she wearing?" one Rockefeller worker asked another when Tod took her place beside her arm-flailing husband. "A fixed smile," the other worker replied.

After a ten-minute ovation the crowd silenced itself to hear the man who was now governor-elect. His remarks were very brief. He accepted this victory, he said, "with a great sense of humility and with great appreciation." He was confident, he added, "that the entire ticket will be elected with me." (It would turn out that he spoke too soon; comptroller candidate James Lundy, nominated as a payoff to Queens boss Frank Kenna, ended up losing to the incumbent, Arthur Levitt.)

Thanking everyone for their efforts on his behalf, Rockefeller left them with a single promise for the future: "We'll give it everything we've got."

The magnitude of his triumph was truly staggering. Rockefeller won by 557,000 votes, the second-biggest victory margin ever in a New York gubernatorial contest (thus proving that Harriman was, if nothing else, a superb prognosticator; in the grim aftermath of the Buffalo convention he had predicted that Rockefeller would win by half a million). And Rockefeller did it at a time when, virtually everywhere else in the nation, Republicans were being swept from power. In a massive repudiation of the President's party, the Democrats that evening would pick up thirteen U.S. Senate seats, forty-seven House seats, and have a net gain of four governorships. The scythe did not leave New York unscathed: the GOP would lose three congressional seats and six in the state legislature. But somehow, in the midst of this debacle, Nelson Rockefeller emerged as the victor of victors, not only accomplishing his own stunning triumph but pulling in Ken Keating besides.

To win, he needed to knife into Harriman's margins in New York City, and Rockefeller did just that. The Democrat would carry the city, but only by 300,000 votes—half of what Harriman needed to overcome the GOP's upstate electoral advantage. Rockefeller carried Queens and Staten Island, cut Harriman's margin in Brooklyn from the two-and-a-half-to-one edge of four years earlier to three-to-two, and did astonishingly well in Manhattan, losing the borough by a mere 80,000 votes. In the state's other urban areas he also performed superbly, winning Buffalo, Rochester, and Utica, all of which had gone for Harriman in 1954.

The linchpin of Rockefeller's victory was exactly what the Roosevelt Hotel strategists thought it would be: the anti-De Sapio independents and liberals, many of whom were Jewish, and many of whom, it turned out, were *New York Post* readers. Harriman's aide-de-camp, Milton Stewart, would later say, "It seems to me that the defection . . . came where a Democrat can least afford to lose it, from the hard-core, well-educated, middle-income, liberal Jewish community in New York and middle-income in the suburbs."

Clearly, the centerpiece of Rockefeller's strategy—an all-out, incessant attack on De Sapio, coupled with a deliberate obfuscation of his own Republican identity—paid off. But there were other reasons why he had so thoroughly plastered the incumbent in what was supposed to be, and largely was, a Democratic year.

Organization certainly played a part in it, not only the range and depth of expertise he commanded but the relative harmony in which those experts worked, in marked contrast to the backbiting and factionalism of the Harriman camp.

Advertising unquestionably played its part as well, particularly the candidate's tapping of the still largely unfathomed potential of television, introducing the public not just to his positions but to his personality. Primitive though his efforts might seem by today's standards, they were potent, even revolutionary stuff in the black-and-white world of 1958.

And, of course, there was the money. The official totals, at the end of the campaign, showed that the Rockefeller campaign spent just shy of $1.8 million versus Harriman's $1.1 million. No candidate for statewide office had ever spent more, yet Democratic aides, with some justification, claimed that the Rockefeller figures were in fact grossly understated. In the final weeks of the campaign, according to these officials, Rockefeller was spending as much as

$50,000 a day on TV and radio ads alone; the Harriman camp, on the other hand, anted up a total of $59,000 for the whole of the last week. The *real* Rockefeller outlay, the Democrats would say, was a staggering $4 million.*

Finally, there was sheer luck: that the Democrats were so riven by internal strife, that Harriman was so inept and indecisive, that De Sapio was such a ripe target, and that the *Post,* for the flimsiest of reasons, pulled its endorsement at the eleventh hour.

All of these elements—the resources, the ad blitz, the brain trust, the good fortune—went into the victory, but there was one more factor, a factor that was probably the most decisive of all. Tom Dewey put it best, when a reporter stopped him in a Roosevelt Hotel corridor and asked him what he thought accounted for Rockefeller's triumph. "Nelson Rockefeller," Dewey shot back.

Pumping hands, pounding backs, straddling tractors, and leaping off stages, Rockefeller had ignited the New York political scene with his impetuousness and gusto. Even Harry Truman, who had seen just about everything in politics, was forced to admit that this was something different: a "new personality" that "catches popular imagination à la Elvis Presley style and sweeps everything before it." There was no denying Rockefeller's charismatic power, a heady admixture of immense wealth, youthful vitality, and potent sex appeal.

This was indeed something new in American politics: a phenomenon that, very soon, would permanently change the country's political landscape.

It escaped no one that evening that this was more than just another gubernatorial election. New York, traditional breeding ground of presidential candidates, had just hatched another one.

When he finally broke away from the ballroom mayhem and returned to the seventh floor, Rockefeller headed straight into a press conference. What the newsmen there wanted to know, more than how he felt about his victory, more than his plans for the governorship, was what he intended to do in 1960.

Rockefeller dismissed the speculation out of hand. "That has absolutely no meaning to me. I have no other interests than to be governor of this state. . . . I have no other intention but to serve out my term."

However, the next day, when he met with reporters again, Rockefeller thought it prudent to modify his disclaimer. It was not, he said, "a promise." He did not want, he said, "to try and cross bridges ahead."

*So profligate was the Rockefeller effort that it found itself strapped for funds as the campaign drew to a close, despite the deep pockets supposedly at its disposal. The Rockefeller-Keating committee, for one, found itself $70,000 in the red as of October 20, and was forced to hold a last-minute reception at the "21" Club to scrounge for financing. Source: Bernard Katzer to Kenneth Keating, Keating Papers Series VI, Box 23, Rochester.

At 12:30 A.M. that election night, the wife of the governor-elect held a press conference of her own. Expecting a certain formality, the reporters were put at ease when, upon entering the conference room, Tod noticed there weren't enough chairs and offered to surrender her own and sit on the floor. (That wouldn't be necessary, she was told.)

All in all, she was poised, unruffled, but hardly bubbling over with excitement. Again and again, she resisted attempts to elicit an emotional gush. Asked how she felt, she answered, "I'm fine, fine. We're feeling very happy."

Would she call this a high moment in her life? Tod paused and considered her words carefully. "I would say," she finally replied, "this is a very high moment in Nelson's career."

Did she look forward to her life in the limelight?

Again, she measured her words as meticulously as she measured spoons of plant food for her zinnias. "I expect it to be a very interesting life," she said. "I expect it to be very challenging and very busy."

Among the millions rooted to their television screens, taking in the spectacular changing of the guard in New York, was a wizened, frail eighty-four-year-old man, seated erectly in the dim amber light of the study in his Park Avenue apartment, his doting wife at his side. Except for his relatively modest financial contributions, John D. Rockefeller, Jr., had been invisible throughout the campaign, his innate reticence compounded by the increasing disabilities of age. Now, in the hushed, almost sepulchral confines of his abode, he watched the raucous goings-on at the Roosevelt and took stock of the realization that one of his boys had been elected by the people of New York to be their governor.

"Mr. Rockefeller was absolutely stunned," recalls John Lockwood. Despite his professions of faith in Nelson, deep down he never believed that he would actually win, that he would ever overcome the stigma that, in Junior's mind at least, still shadowed the family.

But as the news sank in, the astonishment gave way to the flush of quiet elation. To the well-wishers who flooded his office with congratulatory telegrams in the days ahead, Junior would write, "We are naturally very proud of Nelson. What joy and pride his election would bring to his mother also!"

For Junior, the salient fact in his son's victory was not Nelson's political skills or charisma, but something George O'Neill, the spouse of his granddaughter Abby, pointed to in a letter to the patriarch at Christmas that year. "I thought it was most significant that the opposition was not able to bring up an issue against the family," said O'Neill. "This shows that you and your family have built up by your wonderful deeds a respect from the people."

Nelson's triumph at the polls was a climactic vindication, the capstone of a half century's struggle to efface the robber baron past. Through an avalanche of good deeds, through the creation of the greatest philanthropic edifice the country had ever known, through such enduring monuments as Rockefeller Center, the United Nations, and the Cloisters, John D. Junior had wiped away every speck of tarnish from the family name. That the name was not a drag on his son's chances, that it actually immeasurably helped them, was proof, if any further was needed, of the wondrous feat that Junior had accomplished.

It seemed, for so long, inconceivable that a Rockefeller, any Rockefeller, could be an "authentic representative of the people." But now, amazingly, Nelson was.

And so, as his son breathlessly prepared to write a whole new chapter in his career, John D. Rockefeller, Jr., could, with infinite satisfaction and no little sense of wonderment, close the final pages of his own.

Acknowledgments

"Writing a long and substantial book," Winston Churchill once said, "is like having a friend and companion at your side, to whom you can always turn for comfort and amusement." Such has certainly been my experience with Nelson Rockefeller. Never, in the more than eight years I have devoted to the study of his life, has he bored me or wearied me; never has he ceased to enthrall and surprise. And so my list of thanks must begin with my subject, for living such a life.

This work is not, and never has been, an authorized biography. No member of the Rockefeller family asked me to undertake it, and the reaction of the family can best be described as nonpartisan: neither actively encouraging nor discouraging my pursuit. Some individual family members, including Rockefeller's wife Happy, his brothers David and Laurance, and his oldest son Rodman were cooperative, and I am very grateful for their help. But others chose not to cooperate, or to cooperate to only a very limited extent. This checkered pattern was, to me, one more piece of evidence that in this generation the Rockefeller monolith has ceased to exist.

Still, as I point out in my source notes, there is no question that this biography owes much to my access to the family archives. (It should be noted that I was given no special consideration in this that would not have been granted to any other qualified scholar.) For their innumerable acts of kindness and aid in helping me navigate that imposing repository, I am indebted to the Rockefeller Archive Center's director, Darwin H. Stapleton, and his staff. I would especially like to cite the help given me by Harold Oakhill, the archive's authority on Nelson Rockefeller; it is impossible to say enough about his professionalism, good cheer, and patience in the face of my endless inquiries over the years.

I am also grateful to Peter Johnson of the Rockefeller family office: for his own past scholarship, which had a significant impact on my overview of the family, for his encouragement dating back to the project's inception, and for his assistance in matters large and small. And I am indebted, as well, to Judge Harold Tyler, who, acting as a family intermediary, was consistently helpful and supportive in his uniquely laconic way; and to the judge's partner and my dear friend Marilyn Friedman for putting in a well-timed good word on the author's behalf.

As indispensable as these inside resources were, my work on this volume has relied equally on a host of outside archival sources. I particularly wish to thank Ronald J. Grele and his staff at the Columbia University Oral History Collection; James Leyerzapf of the Dwight D. Eisenhower Library in Abilene, Kansas; Dennis Bilger of the Harry S. Truman Library in Independence, Missouri; Sharon Estes Knapp of the Duke University Library; and the staff of the New York Public Library's Cooperative Services Division.

Many, many people who knew Nelson Rockefeller shared their insights and recollections with me, and adequately thanking them all would be a book in itself. But a few are worth singling out for their help with the material covered in this volume: Ellen Harrison, Wallace Harrison's wife, for the impromptu (and probably illegal) tour she gave me of the Seal Harbor home her husband designed for Rockefeller; the late Charles Widmayer, Dartmouth '30, my indispensable guide to the college and his and Nelson's classmates, and Ort Hicks, for introducing me to Widmayer; Donna Mitchell, whose recollections brought the Nancy Hanks chapter to life; James Wallis and the late Eleanor Clark French, for their invaluable reminiscences about the Clark family; Kershaw Burbank, for the many hours spent detailing the dynamics of the Rockefeller family office in the 1940s and 1950s; Malcolm Wilson, whose memory, in our meetings, certainly lived up to its vaunted reputation; William Alton, who knew Nelson Rockefeller longer than anyone outside his immediate family, yet whose unique recollections have amazingly gone untapped until now.

And I might add a special note of gratitude to the late Meade H. Esposito, for arranging one of the most memorable moments of my eight year odyssey: a lunch at Patsy's on West 56th Street with "the bosses," Meade and Carmine De Sapio. Never have I dined in such legendary company; it was a privilege to be stuck with the tab.

As anyone who has ever undertaken a large-scale biography knows, the quality of the work depends less on great flashes of insight than on the grubby gathering of details: endless scrutiny of documents, old newspapers and oral histories, the relentless pursuit of obscure individuals' whereabouts, the checks and cross-checks of leads and references and dimly remembered anecdotes. For her tireless and fruitful labors in this, the decidedly unglamorous aspect of the biography business, I am truly grateful to my research assistant, Elisabeth Mason Corsaro. Her contribution to this project over a four-year period may be invisible to the reader, but it was quite palpable to me every single grinding day of the research process. I am grateful as well to my friend Jill Filler, who shared with me her considerable expertise in navigating the National Archives.

In the course of my travels, I was the beneficiary of numerous gestures of hospitality. For lodging me during my frequent trips to Washington, I thank Jill Filler and family, and my friends William and Deborah Meyers; for putting me up in San Francisco, my friends Ross and Rosemary Matthews. I am especially indebted to certain old associates of Rockefeller's who offered me a room *and* reminiscences: George and Barbara Dudley in Rensselaerville, New York, and Nadia Williams of Rockport, Massachusetts.

The interviews for this volume, and the one to follow, produced more than a thousand hours of tape. The transcription of all this was handled by George Macy, and, in the later stages, by Kathy and Jeff Honeyman; I am most appreciative of their efforts.

From the moment, back in the summer of 1987, that I first contemplated spending the next several years with Nelson Rockefeller, I had the all-out support and encouragement of my agent, Elaine Markson. My most profound thanks to her for that, and for her devoted and diligent representation of my interests all these years. My thanks, as well, to my friend and attorney, Mark Levine, for his tenacious efforts on my behalf.

Although many of the faces at Doubleday have changed since the inception of this book, the one constant, happily, has been the house's enthusiasm for the project and its steadfast support of the author. This climate was created, at the outset, by Nancy Evans and Patrick Filley; I will always be grateful for their belief in this book, and in me. The enthusiasm was then sustained by Herman Gollob. Everyone told me Herman was one of the great editors in the business, and, in my time with him, I began to understand why. My one regret was that Herman retired before he could complete the editing of the book.

That regret, however, was soon tempered by my experience with Bill Thomas. Herman assured me that Bill was wise beyond his years; exactly how wise, I have only just begun to appreciate. If the qualities of a world-class editor are sensitivity, acuity, and judgment, then Bill, in my estimation, has already attained such stature.

Many thanks, also, to those others at Doubleday who helped in the home stretch: to managing editor Janet Hill and assistant managing editor Stephen Bottum, art director Mario Pulice, and Bill Thomas's assistant, Jacqueline LaPierre.

It was not very long after I had begun work on this biography that a rather formidable challenge presented itself, one that, potentially, could have derailed the whole project. For his inestimable aid in surmounting that hurdle, and for his words of support at a decisive moment, I am deeply grateful to Edmund Morris.

It is one thing to write a big book. It is quite another to find words that can even begin to depict the solace, the support, the understanding, the joy provided by my partner in life. Suffice it to say that nothing I have achieved here would have been possible without Karen at my side.

Finally, my affectionate thanks to our son, Jeremy, who, to paraphrase something David McCullough once wrote about his children, at age six cannot remember when his father was not working on a book about Nelson Rockefeller.

Notes

Just across the road from the main gate of the Rockefeller property in Pocantico Hills is a fieldstone Palladian mansion that seems, from its hilltop perch, to glower like a disapproving dowager at the comings and goings of the estate down below. Despite its venerable aspect, the mansion, dubbed Hillcrest, dates only to 1963, when it was built as a new country seat for Martha Baird Rockefeller, second wife and widow of John D. Rockefeller, Jr., after stepson Nelson took over the estate's main house, Kykuit. But no sooner had its deluxe fittings—including an enormous fully loaded kitchen that would be the envy of most Manhattan restaurants—been set into place than Martha decided she really wouldn't be comfortable there; she was said to have never spent a single night at Hillcrest.

The mansion remained unoccupied for over a decade, until the Rockefellers, looking for a more permanent and commodious home for the family's overflowing archives than the storerooms at 30 Rockefeller Plaza, decided to move the archives there. Thus was born the Rockefeller Archive Center, a unit of the Rockefeller University, a facility as superbly equipped and as well staffed as any private repository in the world. While researchers toil upstairs in the airy rooms designed for Martha and her guests, ten full-time archivists patrol a three-story underground bunker, deep beneath the house's foundations, where forty-foot-long walls of shelves on rails hold a century and a half of Rockefelleriana.

Within this awesome subterranean facility, Nelson Rockefeller looms as large as he did in life. Behind an orange door in Room 202 of the subbasement are his collected papers, in sheer volume exceeding those of any other family member: in all, a staggering 3,427 cubic feet, filling the whole of the thirty-by-fifty-foot room from floor to ceiling. And yet, when work on this biography was begun, in April 1988—nine years after Rockefeller's death—almost none of these 3,400 cubic feet were open to researchers. It has only been in the ensuing eight years—in response, perhaps, to the inquisitiveness of this author and others—that a portion of these files, amounting to about a third of the total, have been processed and opened. The newly opened files, however, include very few from the most prominent aspects of Rockefeller's public life: his gubernatorial and presidential campaigns and his fifteen-year tenure as New York's governor. Some of these will be processed and released over the next five years, but some—including the gubernatorial papers, amounting to a full third of the total corpus—will remain sealed for the foreseeable future.

Clearly, what is going on here is something endemic to any family archive (and some public ones, notably the John F. Kennedy Presidential Library): a certain skittishness about releasing any material that might potentially embarrass or offend the archive subject's survivors. For that reason, every single page must be vetted before it is opened to outside researchers—even if that process means, as it does in this case, that something approaching a full archive documenting Nelson Rockefeller's life will not be available until well into the twenty-first century.

The defensiveness about Rockefeller's papers has made for some bizarre and contradictory twists. Correspondence between Junior and Abby and Nelson, for instance, is freely open for perusal if the letters are in Junior or Abby's files; but if the letters happened to have landed in Nelson's files, they are sealed. And the original gubernatorial papers remain sealed even though most of them can be inspected, both at the Rockefeller Archive Center and at the State Library in Albany, on microfilm. (A good explanation for this anomaly was given to me by the family's longtime principal archivist, Joseph Ernst, who pointed out that one of Rockefeller's secretaries reviewed all the documents prior to filming, and pulled those she deemed "troublesome." Thus, the microfilm is an expurgated version of the papers, the complete contents of which will remain under lock and key indefinitely.)

Nevertheless, for all these frustrating cul-de-sacs, the road to the Rockefeller Archive Center remains the one indispensable route to a complete understanding of Nelson Rockefeller's life and career. This volume has been immensely enriched by the material made available in the last eight years—much of which has made its way into print for the first time in the preceding pages. And this history has benefited in equal measure from files that have been open all along but whose riches have been largely untapped: such as the documents revealing the spectacular coup d'état that made Nelson, before the age of thirty, the master of Rockefeller Center.

"If we don't open this stuff up now, nobody will care about it when we finally *do* open it up": that, apparently, is Laurance Rockefeller's attitude, as conveyed to me by Ernst. Hopefully, before long, those views will infect others in the family—and their often overly protective agents—as well.

Two other archival sources deserve special mention here. One is Columbia University's oral history project. Close to two hundred of the oral histories at Columbia deal in some way with Nelson Rockefeller, and all were reviewed for this book. All told, they represent an invaluable supplement to the interviews undertaken by the author—as evidenced by the ubiquitousness of the abbreviation COHP in the source notes.

The other is the files of the Federal Bureau of Investigation in Washington, D.C. Various of these files were opened to the author pursuant to a Freedom of Information Act request, and they shed light on some hitherto unrevealed aspects of Nelson Rockefeller—including his close ties to FBI director J. Edgar Hoover. In terms of "bang for the buck"—the amount of useful material yielded per hour of research—nothing in the author's experience came close to the days he spent in the spartan, windowless confines of the FBI reading room in Washington.

Inevitably, in probing Nelson Rockefeller's career, one has to run the gauntlet of national security classification. Fortunately, most of the relevant documents generated during his tours of duty as a federal official have been declassified, including the report of his first Quantico panel, which resulted in the "Open Skies" proposal. However, there were some notable exceptions from the period (1955) when Rockefeller was assistant to the President for psychological warfare.

Despite their continued "secret" status, several of these vital documents were privately furnished to the author by individuals who had worked with Rockefeller. William Kintner, his Cold War strategist (and the man who brought Henry Kissinger into Rockefeller's orbit), provided me with a copy of the report of the second Quantico panel. Another of his aides gave me the illuminating "History of the Planning Coordination Group," which details Rockefeller's futile attempt to gain oversight over the CIA's covert activities, and the "Action Program for Free World Strength," his spurned big-ticket Cold War program.

While federal officials might object to such unauthorized document disclosure, it should be pointed out that Rockefeller himself in his later, postgovernment years took a rather cavalier attitude toward the secret documents in his possession. In one instance, he took his copy of the Action Program memo, crossed out all the "secret" markings, and scribbled on the top page: "Declassified by NAR"—an imprimatur he no doubt believed overrode any petty official bureaucratic objections.

In his lifetime Nelson Rockefeller cooperated with several authorized biographers—whose work, not at all coincidentally, was published at the time of one or another of his runs for the presidency. In each instance, the appellation "authorized" was very much an understatement; not only did Rockefeller public relations minions actively assist in the research and assembly of documents, but in the case of at least one of the three books—and, quite probably, in all three cases—vetted and "corrected" the manuscript prior to publication. (The first of these books, in fact, was dedicated to the recently deceased head of the family p.r. effort.)

Given these books' provenance, it would be reasonable to discount them as hagiographic junk (despite the fact that all three of the authors were not hacks but well-respected veteran journalists) and pay them no further mind. But, at least with the first, Joe Alex Morris' *Nelson Rockefeller: A Biography,* that would be a huge mistake. Not that Morris is any less worshipful than the others; the closest he comes to a criticism of his subject is to accuse him of having "a residue of arrogance." Nonetheless, the Morris book offers some unique insights, owing largely to the fact that the author had Rockefeller's cooperation—thus giving us Rockefeller's own version of critical events in his life—as well as apparently unfettered access to letters and other family documents. Some of these letters are no longer available to outside researchers, either because they ended up in Rockefeller's restricted files or because they have simply been lost. In those instances, in the following notes, Morris' book (or his earlier *Those Rockefeller Brothers*) is cited as the primary source.

Rockefeller also cooperated with two other authorized accounts that were never published. The first was written in the late 1950s by Donald Irwin, one of his old Washington p.r. operatives, apparently as a prospective campaign biography. It offers some useful background, particularly on Rockefeller's Eisenhower administration work, and the author is grateful to Donna Mitchell, another longtime Rockefeller assistant, for lending me her copy.

The later, and much stranger, book was a biography undertaken by Rockefeller's aide and adviser Wallace K. Harrison, the world-renowned architect. Sometime in the mid-1970s, Harrison began work on the book, combining his own reminiscences with extensive interviews with Rockefeller. Harrison was apparently very secretive about this effort—so secretive that even his wife confessed to me that she knew nothing about it. The memoir-cum-biography never saw the light of day, even though it was largely completed (admittedly in a rather sketchy, hole-ridden draft). However, the chapter drafts—and, more importantly, the taped interviews upon which they were based—can now be found in Harrison's papers at Columbia University's Avery Library. Even in its patchwork state, Harrison's account provides much valuable first-hand material.

As to why Harrison, who was already past eighty, might undertake such a project in his declining years . . . that is a tale to be told in the next volume of this saga.

Abbreviations

AAA	Archives of American Art, Smithsonian Institution
AAR	Abby Aldrich Rockefeller
AIA	American International Association
CIAA	Coordinator of Inter-American Affairs
COHP	Columbia University Oral History Project
DDE	Dwight D. Eisenhower
DDEL	Dwight D. Eisenhower Library, Abilene, Kan.
DOS	U.S. State Department (RAC designation)
DR	David Rockefeller
FBI Files	Files of Federal Bureau of Investigation, Washington, D.C.
FDR	Franklin D. Roosevelt
FDRL	Franklin D. Roosevelt Library, Hyde Park, N.Y.
FRUS	*Foreign Relations of the United States* (published State Department compilation of documents)
HST	Harry S. Truman
HSTL	Harry S. Truman Library, Independence, Mo.
IBEC	International Basic Economy Corporation
IDAB	International Development Advisory Board
JDR3	John D. Rockefeller 3rd
Jr.	John D. Rockefeller, Jr.
LBJL	Lyndon B. Johnson Library, Austin, Tex.
LC	Library of Congress, Washington, D.C.
LSR	Laurance S. Rockefeller
NA	National Archives, Washington, D.C.
NAR	Nelson A. Rockefeller
NYHT	*New York Herald Tribune*
NYT	*New York Times*
OF	Official File (Presidential Papers Designation)
OIAA	Records of the Office of Inter-American Affairs, National Archives, Suitland, Md.
PACGO	Presidential Advisory Committee on Government Organization
PPF	President's Personal File (Presidential Papers Designation)
PSF	President's Secretary's File (Presidential Papers Designation)
R	Rockefeller
RAC	Rockefeller Archive Center, Pocantico Hills, N.Y.
SCOGO	Special Committee on Government Organization
SD	U.S. State Department (NA Designation)
Sr.	John D. Rockefeller, Sr.

SUNY	State University of New York
WHCF	White House Confidential File (Presidential Papers Designation)
WR	Winthrop Rockefeller

Introduction

xi. "He irritated": William Rusher interview.

xii. "If he should get": *NYT,* October 3, 1995.

xii. "I would think": Joseph E. Persico, *The Imperial Rockefeller* (New York: Simon & Schuster, 1982), p. 162.

xiii. "Nothing stands": Richard Reeves, "The Nationwide Search for Nelson Rockefeller," *New York,* September 2, 1974.

xiii. Kissinger would complain: Henry Kissinger interview.

xiii. Yellow Rolls-Royce: Joseph Canzeri interview.

xiii. Mount Rushmore: Gerald Benjamin and T. Norman Hurd, eds., *Rockefeller in Retrospect* (Albany, N.Y.: Nelson A. Rockefeller Institute of Government, 1984), p. 65.

xiv. Metropolitan Museum: Craig Thorne interview.

xiv. Earl of Mountbatten: Happy Rockefeller interview.

xiv. "Only Nelson": Clay Felker interview.

xiv. "Because of a guilt complex": Persico, *Imperial Rockefeller,* p. 162.

xiv. "How's it feel": *New Yorker,* November 5, 1960.

xv. "A tool": NAR TV interview with David Frost, July 20, 1971.

xv. "He had none of the hangups": Steven Rockefeller interview, done by NAR aide Hugh Morrow shortly after NAR's death. It is hereafter referred to as Steven Rockefeller–Morrow interview. The author is grateful to Steven Rockefeller for furnishing him with a copy.

xvi. "The last great moment": Daniel Moynihan interview.

xvi. "He wasn't a liberal": Joseph Persico interview.

xvii. "Been President": Helen Dudar, "Nelson Now," *New York,* September 25, 1978.

xvii. "Ever since I was a kid": Michael Kramer and Sam Roberts, *"I Never Wanted to Be Vice-President of Anything!"* (New York: Basic Books, 1976), p. 3.

xviii. "Mr. Churchill": William Manchester, *The Last Lion* (New York: Dell, 1983), p. 21.

1. July 1908

3. Senator Nelson Aldrich: Nathaniel Wright Stephenson, *Nelson W. Aldrich: A Leader in American Politics* (New York: Scribners, 1930); David Graham Phillips, *The Treason of the Senate* (Chicago: Quadrangle Books, 1964; a reprint of the *Cosmopolitan* series); Nelson W. Aldrich, Jr., *Old Money* (New York: Alfred A. Knopf, 1988). The latter is notable for its especially caustic view of the author's forebear.

4. Employees in the Capitol: *NYT,* November 2, 1908.

4. He talked of leaving: Ibid.

4. John D. Rockefeller, Sr.: John Ensor Harr and Peter J. Johnson, *The Rockefeller Century* (New York: Scribners, 1988); Peter Collier and David Horowitz, *The Rockefellers* (New York: Holt, Rinehart and Winston, 1976). These books, in turn, made extensive use of Allan Nevins, *Study in Power: John D. Rockefeller, Industrialist and Philanthropist* (New York: Scribners, 1953).

5. Standard's attorneys: *NYT,* July 3, 1908.

5. "Thus, the chief exploiter": Phillips, *Treason of the Senate,* p. 82.

6. Junior's courtship of Abby: Mary Ellen Chase, *Abby Aldrich Rockefeller* (New York: Macmillan, 1950); Raymond B. Fosdick, *John D. Rockefeller, Jr.: A Portrait* (New York: Harper & Bros., 1956).

6. The senator was said: Collier & Horowitz, *The Rockefellers,* p. 95.

6. Junior-Abby love letters: JDR Jr. Personal, Box 55, RAC.

6. The Rockefellers in Bar Harbor: Jr. letter to the editor of the *Bar Harbor Times,* May 1, 1941.

6. Bar Harbor life: Louise Dickinson Rich, *The Coast of Maine: An Informal History* (New York: Thomas Y. Crowell, 1956); Marian L. Peabody, "Old Bar Harbor Days," in *Only in Maine* (Barre, Mass.: Barre Publishers, 1969).

7. Junior spent much: Jr. Personal, Box 55, RAC.

7. John D. Rockefeller had celebrated: *NYT,* July 9, 1908.

8. The next day, he even did: *NYT,* July 10, 1908.

2. *The Family Foundation*

9. Junior's breakdowns: Harr & Johnson, *Rockefeller Century,* p. 85; Collier & Horowitz, *The Rockefellers,* pp. 82–83, 156; *NYT,* October 31, 1922.

9. "He was constantly": Fosdick, *John D. Rockefeller, Jr.,* p. 415.

9. Cettie Rockefeller: Ibid., pp. 35, 43; Collier & Horowitz, *The Rockefellers,* pp. 77–81; Harr & Johnson, *Rockefeller Century,* pp. 38–41.

10. Junior took the pledge: Harr & Johnson, *Rockefeller Century,* p. 39.

10. "I am so glad my son": Ellen Harrison interview.

10. "Practicing the violin": Collier & Horowitz, *The Rockefellers,* p. 81.

10. "He taught us everything": Fosdick notes for his biography of Jr., RAC.

10. "I took responsibility early": Fosdick notes.

10. Junior at Brown: Fosdick, *John D. Rockefeller, Jr.,* pp. 45–82.

10. "My one thought": Fosdick notes.

11. "Father never said a word": "Recollections of My Father," speech by Jr., August 1920, RAC.

11. Bargaining with J. P. Morgan: Fosdick, *John D. Rockefeller, Jr.,* p. 105.

11. "Gates was the brilliant dreamer": Ibid., pp. 111–12.

12. Ludlow massacre: Ibid., Chapters 8 and 9; Collier & Horowitz, *The Rockefellers,* Chapter 8; Harr & Johnson, *Rockefeller Century,* Chapter 7.

13. "I have never squandered money": Jr. to Sr., February 1, 1915, RAC.

13. The doctor's Rolls-Royce: William Alton interview.

13. "There was a kind of formality about him": Fosdick, *John D. Rockefeller, Jr.,* p. 421.

13. Aldrich as connoisseur: Stephenson, *Nelson W. Aldrich,* p. 408.

14. "I gave it away": Chase, *Abby Aldrich Rockefeller,* p. 26.

14. "I won't!": Ibid., p. 28.

14. "Do you know, John": Ibid.

14. "Your father is afraid": Ibid., p. 33.

14. Bible verses: Alvin Moscow, *The Rockefeller Inheritance* (New York: Doubleday, 1977), p. 36.

14. Solace in Abby's sitting room: Harr & Johnson, *Rockefeller Century,* p. 94.

15. Abby's economies: Chase, *Abby Aldrich Rockefeller,* p. 36.

15. NAR and the weeds: Tom Pyle, *Pocantico* (New York: Duell, Sloan and Pearce, 1964), p. 83.

15. 54th Street house: Description is from Chase, *Abby Aldrich Rockefeller,* p. 35, and Harr & Johnson, *Rockefeller Century,* p. 99.

15. The Eyrie: Harr & Johnson, *Rockefeller Century,* p. 98, and an ad in the *Bar Harbor Times,* January 28, 1963, detailing the house and offering "any and all" portions of the Eyrie for sale prior to its demolition.

16. Kykuit: Pyle, *Pocantico,* pp. 76–77.

16. "The world is full of Sham": Grace Goulder, *John D. Rockefeller: The Cleveland Years* (Middletown, Conn.: Western Reserve Historical Society, 1973).

17. Babs's rebellion: Moscow, *Rockefeller Inheritance,* p. 49; interview with Babs by her niece, Laura Chasin, November 10, 1973, cited in Harr & Johnson, *Rockefeller Century,* pp. 101–2.

17. "She gave my mother": Abby O'Neill interview.

17. John 3rd and his sailboat: Joe Alex Morris, *Those Rockefeller Brothers* (New York: Harper & Bros., 1953), p. 22.

17. "He is such a taciturn boy": Harr & Johnson, *Rockefeller Century,* p. 102.

3. *A Most Unruly Little Boy*

18. Lunchroom story: Edward Warburg interview.

18. Food throwing: LSR interview; Moscow, *Rockefeller Inheritance,* p. 51.

18. "Nelson is so full of life": Florence Scales to AAR, September 4, 1921, RAC.

18. Marksmanship lessons: Pyle, *Pocantico,* p. 122.

19. Learning the cello: AAR to Babs, October 19, 1920, RAC.

19. "Nelson is having great struggles": Scales to AAR, November 16, 1915, RAC.

19. Christmas lists: Scales to AAR, November 14, 1916, RAC.

19. Nelson would clown around: Scales to AAR, November 3, 1916, RAC.

19. "I have been going to dancing school": Joe Alex Morris, *Nelson Rockefeller: A Biography* (New York: Harper & Bros., 1960), pp. 23–24. Henceforth referred to as Morris, *NR.*

20. "You can count": Kelly to AAR, January 28, 1921.

20. Nelson was moved: Morris, *NR,* p. 13.

20. Junior's rubber band: Ibid.

20. "We looked to God": LSR speech at the Woodrow Wilson School, Princeton University, February 16, 1991.

20. Singing off-key: Abby O'Neill interview; Moscow, *Rockefeller Inheritance,* p. 51.

20. Rabbit in the muff: Ibid.

20. Children's allowances: John Cushman Fistere, "The Rockefeller Boys," *Saturday Evening Post,* July 16, 1938; Moscow, *Rockefeller Inheritance,* p. 41.

20. David's classmate: Pyle, *Pocantico,* p. 84.

21. Nelson's contract: AAR letters, RAC.

21. "They were a very severe business": Ellen Harrison interview.

21. Five cents a mouse: Moscow, *Rockefeller Inheritance,* p. 42.

21. Junior's antismoking offer: LSR Princeton speech; Morris, *NR,* p. 22.

21. Nelson catching rose bugs: Pyle, *Pocantico,* p. 84.

21. "You had better come back soon": Morris, *NR,* p. 24.

21. NAR's rabbit-breeding business: LSR interview; LSR Princeton speech; Morris, *Those Rockefeller Brothers,* p. 26.

22. "We were taught to be self-reliant": Morris, *NR,* pp. 20–21.

22. The cabin in the Maine woods: Harr & Johnson, *Rockefeller Century,* p. 237; Morris, *NR,* p. 22; Moscow, *Rockefeller Inheritance,* pp. 58–59.

22. "It was a big project for us": Morris, *NR,* p. 22.

22. The western rail trip: Harr & Johnson, *Rockefeller Century,* pp. 232–34 (the authors base their account on JDR3's diary); Morris, *NR,* p. 19.

23. "One of us paid the bills": Fistere, "The Rockefeller Boys."

23. Haggling with the superintendent: Horace Albright oral history, COHP.

23. "We had two rooms": David Frost interview with NAR, July 20, 1971.

24. Alton's memory of the Eyrie: William Alton interview.

24. Stark's dinner with NAR: Sheldon Stark interview.

24. NAR's rifle accident: *NYT,* July 11, 1922.

25. 54th Street watchman: LSR interview.

25. Junior kept a pistol: File of family pistol permits, RAC.

25. "Certainly the thought that bodyguards": WR, *A Letter to My Son,* a privately printed memoir available at RAC.

25. "My mother and father were very apprehensive": James Flexner interview.

25. NAR and Vanderbilt visit to Prideaux: Tom Prideaux interview.

25. Victory gardens and Red Cross: Moscow, *Rockefeller Inheritance,* pp. 42–43; Collier & Horowitz, *The Rockefellers,* p. 183.

26. Abby's volume on Junior's war work: AAR's introduction, December 25, 1922, JDR3 Box 3 Confidential File, RAC.

26. Nelson could recall: Chapter 1 of Wallace K. Harrison's unpublished biography of NAR, December 1, 1975, in Harrison's papers at Columbia University's Avery Library. Henceforth this biography will be referred to as Harrison-NAR.

26. Senior and his grandchildren: Moscow, *Rockefeller Inheritance,* pp. 59–60; Collier & Horowitz, *The Rockefellers,* p. 186; Morris, *Those Rockefeller Brothers,* p. 12; Frost interview.

27. "I can always get a dollar": Moscow, *Rockefeller Inheritance,* p. 49.

27. "We look to you": Sr. to JDR3, December 1921, quoted in Harr & Johnson, *Rockefeller Century,* p. 105.

27. "I am eager": AAR to NAR, February 21, 1923, RAC.

27. "I had Nelson read": Scales to AAR, November 19, 1915, RAC.

27. "Nelson will have to do some good work": Scales to AAR, February 7, 1923, RAC.

27. "The best thing that can happen": Lillian M. Kline to AAR, February 13, 1923, RAC.

27. Chess with Laurance: Alta Albertson to AAR, February 13, 1923, RAC.

28. Fiddling with his wireless: Alta Albertson to AAR, March 19, 1923, RAC.

28. "Perhaps there is a little bit too much Aldrich": Chase, *Abby Aldrich Rockefeller,* p. 44.

28. "Nelson dances very well": JDR3's diary, quoted in Harr & Johnson, *Rockefeller Century,* p. 247.

28. John's rope-climbing accident: Harr & Johnson, *Rockefeller Century,* p. 247.

29. "Bill" and "Dick": There are numerous accounts of how the two came to use those nicknames. NAR's version appears in Kramer & Roberts, *"I Never Wanted to Be Vice-President of Anything!,"* p. 35.

29. "He could always put the rapier": Morris, *NR,* p. 14.

29. Bars in the window: Moscow, *Rockefeller Inheritance,* pp. 53–54.

29. John 3rd joined in: Scales to AAR, November 19, 1916, RAC.

29. NAR's tormenting of Winthrop: WR, *A Letter to My Son.*

29. "I believe that the teasing": Ibid.

30. Winthrop took his guest: George Dudley interview.

30. The decision against Browning: Harr & Johnson, *Rockefeller Century,* p. 229.

30. Flexner's concept of Lincoln School: *NYT,* January 20, 1917; Flexner speech, June 2, 1939, R Family Educational Interests, Box 61, RAC.

4. *Lincoln's Lessons*

32. The Lincoln School: Lawrence Cremin, *The Transformation of the School: Progressivism in American Education, 1876–1957* (New York: Alfred A. Knopf, 1961); Raymond Fosdick, *Adventure in Giving: The Story of the General Education Board* (New York: Harper & Row, 1962).

32. Lincoln School's Jewish quota: Otis Caldwell to Charles Heydt, October 1, 1925; Heydt to Caldwell, October 2, 1925, R Family Educational Interests, Box 61, RAC.

33. No blacks in NAR's class: *The Lincolnian,* NAR's senior class yearbook, 1926; interviews with NAR's and Laurance's classmates. The black girl's brief appearance was recalled by Laurance's classmate Pauline Falk.

33. The vast middle tier: The middle-class character of the Lincoln student body was testified to by NAR's classmates.

33. "Try anything once": Cremin, *Transformation of the School,* p. 282.

33. Interdisciplinary approach: Ibid., pp. 283–86. A fascinating chart, evidently prepared by the Lincoln faculty, on the third-grade boat project appears on pp. 284–85.

34. Lincoln's grading system: Correspondence between Jr. and Caldwell about the school's grading system can be found in R Family Educational Interests, Box 61, RAC.

34. Guinea pigs: James Flexner interview.

34. Roller-skating to school: LSR interview. NAR refers to skating to 93rd Street in an unpublished interview his aide Hugh Morrow did with him about his dyslexia problem; a crude transcript of the interview can be found in the Joseph Persico Papers, State University of New York at Albany. It is hereafter referred to as NAR-Morrow interview.

34. He performed gamely: A description of the performance, along with a photo of NAR in the role, can be found in the 1926 *Lincolnian.*

34. He wrote a short story: Scales to AAR, April 16, 1921, RAC.

34. "A jolly, noisy little boy": Virginia Derby interview.

34. "I don't have a very high IQ": Geoffrey Hellman, "Best Neighbor," Part II, *New Yorker,* April 18, 1942, p. 22.

34. He had great difficulty adding: NAR-Morrow interview.

35. He excelled in a host: "Nelson Rockefeller Record in Achievement Tests Made in Lincoln School," chart kept by physical education instructor Colba F. "Chief" Gucker, R Family Educational Interests, Box 61, RAC. Gucker noted that NAR's overall scores in a combined series of events set a school record.

35. Abby's report: AAR to JDR3, February 18, 1922, R Family Educational Interests, Box 61, RAC.

35. NAR as a soccer player: William Alton, Sheldon Stark interviews.

36. At the end of the school day: Pauline Falk interview.

36. Weekends at Pocantico: Linda Storrow interview.

36. Details on how the Rockefellers took Alton under their wing are from the author's interviews with Alton.

37. NAR and Sheldon Stark: Stark interview.

37. The closest he came: Flexner interview; Stark interview.

38. Nelson's one great foray: NAR to AAR, April 22, 1920, RAC; Frank Gervasi, *The Real Rockefeller* (New York: Atheneum, 1964), p. 55.

38. "Nelson . . . is changing": Scales to AAR, January 26, 1923, RAC.

38. He began to show an interest: Lillian M. Kline to AAR, April 18, 19, 1923.

38. "Red bugs": LSR interview; WR, *A Letter to My Son.*

38. He once earned: Stark interview.

39. Nelson's Ford: AAR to Babs, July 16, 1925, RAC.

39. He cited frugality: NAR to AAR, October 25, 1925, RAC.

39. A certain show-off quality: AAR to Babs, July 16, 1925, RAC.

39. Abby saw these qualities: Harr & Johnson, *Rockefeller Century,* p. 247.

39. NAR's motorcycle escort: NAR to JDR3, July 14, 1925, cited in ibid.

40. Geraldine Chittolini: Prideaux, Storrow, Flexner, Falk, Stephen Duggan, Stark, Betsy Lawton interviews; 1926 *Lincolnian.* Details on her background come from her obituary, *NYT,* July 6, 1983. As Geraldine Souvaine, she went on to some renown as producer of the popular intermission features for the Texaco–Metropolitan Opera radio broadcasts.

40. "Gerry and I": NAR to AAR, October 25, 1925, RAC.

40. There were even whispers: Falk, Flexner interviews. (Flexner: "I heard that force majeure had to be used to stop him from marrying her.")

41. "I guess the affair": NAR to AAR and Jr., November 7, 1925, RAC.

41. The one explanation: NAR-Morrow interview.

42. "I covet for my boys": Harr & Johnson, *Rockefeller Century,* p. 252.

42. NAR's mediocre grades: Charles W. Finley to Jr., December 19, 1924, RAC ("These marks can not be certified for college"), R Family Educational Interests, Box 61, RAC.

42. To document this: Jr. to Finley, December 26, 1924, R Family Educational Interests, Box 61, RAC.

42. "The record does not indicate": Jr. to Caldwell, May 20, 1925, R Family Educational Interests, Box 61, RAC.

42. "Nelson's work was such": Caldwell to Charles Heydt, October 7, 1925, R Family Educational Interests, Box 61, RAC.

43. Nelson agreed that the best course: NAR to AAR and Jr., November 21, 1925, RAC. In the same letter NAR reported on playing the Riverdale School in "scouker," indicating that more than his poor command of Spanish was keeping him out of Princeton.

43. "I was told": NAR-Morrow interview.

43. Junior's enthusiasm for Hopkins and Dartmouth: Charles E. Widmayer, *Hopkins of Dartmouth* (Hanover, N.H.: Dartmouth College, 1977), pp. 133–34, 145. Widmayer relates that Junior once offered Hopkins a piece of property near the Rockefeller estate in Seal Harbor, but Hopkins refused it.

43. Junior had prodded John 3rd: Harr & Johnson, *Rockefeller Century,* pp. 251–53.

43. Hopkins had come to know Nelson: Widmayer, *Hopkins,* p. 145.

43. Nelson's initial visit to Hanover: Stark interview.

44. "The only times I ever felt shy": Morris, *NR,* p. 16.

5. *Prince of Hanover*

45. Nelson's plan, and Junior's response: Jr. to Caldwell, December 22, 1925, JDR3 Papers, Box 18, RAC.

45. Details of the trip: JDR3 Papers, Box 18, RAC.

46. The speeding ticket incident: Morris, *NR,* pp. 29–30.

46. "Everybody rushed about": Morris, *NR,* p. 30.

47. Tracking down the taxi driver: JDR3 Papers, Box 18, RAC.

48. "You have come": *The Dartmouth,* September 22, 1926, Dartmouth College Library.

48. Under Hopkins' iron rule: Charles Widmayer interview.

48. The local bootlegger: Widmayer interview; Francis Horn interview.

48. The college whore: Horn interview.

48. The Winter Carnival: *The Dartmouth,* February 9, 1928.

49. Freshman-sophomore rush: *The Dartmouth,* September 25, 1926; Albert Inskip Dickerson, "Hail and Farewell," 1930 *Aegis* (Dartmouth yearbook); Horn interview.

49. Calling on Hopkins: Morris, *NR,* p. 32.

49. Delta Alpha: Lane Dwinell interview; Widmayer interview; Morris, *NR,* p. 33.

49. Green beanies: John Minary interview.

49. Freshman rules: *The Dartmouth,* September 24, 1926.

49. Hazing rituals: Dickerson, "Hail and Farewell": Widmayer interview; Robert Keene interview; Morris, *NR,* p. 33.

50. Nelson was summoned more often: NAR Dartmouth classmate reminiscences in Stewart Alsop, *Nixon and Rockefeller: A Double Portrait* (New York: Doubleday, 1960), p. 205.

50. "I haven't had six hours": Morris, *NR,* p. 33.

50. "It would make a very bad impression": AAR to NAR, October 6, 1926, AAR Box 12, RAC.

50. Abby sent him Chinese carpets: AAR to NAR, October 6, 1926, AAR Box 12, RAC.

50. John French: John French reminiscence in *Dartmouth Alumni Magazine,* October 1974; Morris, *NR,* p. 31; Eugene Zagat interview.

51. "There is only one thing": AAR to NAR, September 19, 1926, AAR Box 12, RAC.

51. Arising at 7: Morris, *NR,* p. 35.

51. Nelson would underline: Ibid., p. 65.

51. "As soon as we get well started": Ibid., p. 40.

52. "He was a real smoothie": Churchill Lathrop interview.

52. "We are still rejoicing": AAR to NAR, April 1927, AAR Box 12, RAC.

52. "I've lost my feeling": Morris, *NR,* p. 37.

52. Fraternity rushes: Dickerson, "Hail and Farewell": Morris, *NR,* pp. 38–39.

52. French-NAR letter: *The Dartmouth,* March 30, 1927; French reminiscence, *Dartmouth Alumni Magazine,* October 1974.

53. Nelson's attire: Lee Chilcote interview; William Alton interview; Horn interview; Alsop, *Nixon and Rockefeller,* p. 206.

53. Hard up for cash: Chilcote interview; Morris, *NR,* p. 36.

53. The scuttlebutt: Widmayer interview.

53. "He was always": "Nelson Rockefeller: A Post Portrait," *New York Post,* March 25, 1958.

54. Taking the picture unframed: Alsop, *Nixon and Rockefeller,* p. 204.

54. Nelson as a waiter: Ibid., p. 207; Morris, *NR,* p. 36.

54. Expensive camera equipment: Zagat interview; Kirt Meyer interview.

54. Meeting Laurance with a sleigh: LSR interview.

54. Nelson and the Outing Club: Keene interview.

54. Retrieving duck hawk eggs: Hermann N. Sander reminiscence in *Dartmouth Alumni Magazine,* October 1974.

54. "He majored": Keene interview.

54. Brawl with freshmen: *Boston Herald,* April 13, 1928; *The Dartmouth,* April 13, 1928; Morris, *NR,* p. 41; Stark interview.

54. White River Junction flood: *The Dartmouth,* November 11, 1927; Keene, Widmayer, Fred Scribner, Horn, Stark interviews.

55. Not partaking of vices: Horn, Chilcote, Keene interviews.

55. The Nugget: Minary interview.

55. French thought the flowers: Harrison-NAR, Chapter 1, p. 5.

55. Walking with the Sunday-school girls: Harrison-NAR, Chapter 1, page 5.

55. Abstaining from football weekends: Morris, *NR,* p. 36.

56. Nelson spotted Hopkins: Morris, *NR,* p. 38.

56. Hopkins invited Nelson: Lathrop interview.

56. "A man becomes": Morris, *NR,* p. 40.

56. French as a shield: Keene interview.

57. NAR continued to shine: Junior to Caldwell, March 16, 1928, Jr. Educational Interests, Box 61, RAC.

57. "I have always realized": AAR to NAR, February 19, 1928, AAR Box 12, RAC.

57. "This is just a little note": Undated letter, NAR to Jr., on SS *Olympic* stationery, AAR Box 12, RAC.

58. "My chief regret": Jr. to NAR, July 8, 1927, in Morris, *NR,* p. 60.

58. "I feel more ashamed than ever": NAR to Jr., July 15, 1927, AAR Box 12, RAC.

59. "I think this time": NAR to Jr., January 4, 1928, AAR Box 12, RAC.

59. Nelson's overdrawn account: AAR to NAR, January 29, 1928, AAR Box 12, RAC.

59. "I was thinking": Morris, *NR,* pp. 43–44.
59. "It was thrilling!": NAR to parents, February 7, 1929, AAR Box 12, RAC.
60. Nelson's Standard Oil thesis: The thesis is in the Dartmouth College Library.
61. "He never went to class": NAR-Morrow interview.
61. "I really carried him socially": NAR-Morrow interview.
61. Hopkins' senior fellowship program: Widmayer, *Hopkins,* pp. 98–100; *The Dartmouth,* April 11, 1929; Widmayer interview.
61. Nelson's selection raised eyebrows: Horn, Keene, Scribner, Widmayer interviews.
62. Junior's support of Dartmouth's honors program: Widmayer, *Hopkins,* p. 98.
62. "The common remark": Morris, *NR,* p. 52.

6. *Arts and Craft*

63. The Grenfell expedition: LSR interview; Harr & Johnson, *Rockefeller Century,* p. 275; Morris, *NR,* pp. 80–81.
63. "They just sit around": Morris, *NR,* p. 80.
64. "I feel as if": NAR to AAR, January 2, 1928, AAR Box 12, RAC.
64. "I would like to have": NAR school papers, RAC.
64. "We could have such good times": AAR to NAR, January 7, 1928, AAR Box 12, RAC.
64. Picking out the originals: Morris, *NR,* p. 74.
64. Carpenter Hall: Lathrop interview.
64. Nelson at Carpenter: Lathrop interview; NAR, "The Use of Leisure," *Dartmouth Alumni Magazine,* June 1930, p. 522.
65. "I am glad": Morris, *NR,* pp. 74–75.
65. "With the responsibilities": NAR oral history for the AAA, July 24, 1972.
66. Transformation of *The Pictorial:* Copies from the NAR era and before are at the Dartmouth College Library.
66. "Mr. Rockefeller . . . is certainly off to a fine start": *The Dartmouth,* June 15, 1929.
66. The Arts in disrepute: 1930 *Aegis;* "The Use of Leisure."
66. Nelson began a lecture series: 1930 *Aegis;* "The Use of Leisure"; John French, Jr., "Trends," in 1930 *Aegis;* Morris, *NR,* p. 55.
66. Constant aide and companion: Horn, Lathrop interviews.
67. "It would be hard": "The Use of Leisure."
67. Russell's lecture: *The Dartmouth,* October 9, 1929. (Among the pithier Russell aphorisms that Nelson heard: "A cynic is a man conscious of ideals but not influenced by them.")
67. Reproductions of masterworks: "The Use of Leisure."
67. The Arts poetry anthology: *The Dartmouth,* June 16, 1930.
67. Walter Chrysler: Horn, Lathrop, Keene interviews.
68. The sumptuous presentation: *The Dartmouth,* April 26, 1930.
68. Nelson and Millay: Horn interview.
68. Play in the *Times: NYT,* June 14, 1930.
69. Publishing stock quotes: *The Dartmouth,* October 15, 1929.
69. "The Crash made very little impression": Alsop, *Nixon and Rockefeller,* p. 209.
70. Invitation to Pocantico: Morris, *NR,* p. 55.

70. Cane carving: James Wiggin interview; Horn interview. Both Wiggin and Horn proudly displayed their "Rocky"-inscribed canes to the author.

70. Junior's $80,000 gift: *The Dartmouth,* November 27, 1929.

70. Junior's speech: *The Dartmouth,* June 17, 1930.

7. *A Main Line Wedding*

71. "I didn't know the road": Morris, *NR,* p. 78.

71. Trip to France: Ibid.

72. Tod's family background: David Loth, *Pencoyd and the Roberts Family,* privately printed volume circa 1960. The author is grateful to James Wallis, Tod Rockefeller's nephew, for furnishing him with a copy of this volume as well as copies of the Roberts and Clark family trees.

72. The Main Line owed: Ibid., p. 50.

72. Description of Willoughby: James Wallis interview.

72. "We grew up": Eleanor Clark French, *A Happy Childhood,* privately printed volume circa 1969, p. 14. The author is grateful to the late Mrs. French for providing him with a copy.

73. "A sunny fog": Margaret Parton, "Mr. and Mrs. Nelson Rockefeller," *Ladies' Home Journal,* November 1959, p. 158.

73. The young Clarks were hustled off: French, *A Happy Childhood,* p. 25.

73. Everything about Tod's upbringing: Wallis interview; French interview.

73. Year at the Sorbonne: French interview; "A Fourth Home to Manage," *NYT,* November 7, 1958, p. 18; Morris, *NR,* p. 96.

73. Upon her return: "Cynwyd Girl Wed to Scion of Rockefeller," *Philadelphia Inquirer,* June 24, 1930, p. 1.

73. She had a gift for mimicry: Bob Considine, "Portrait of a Lady," *Cosmopolitan,* April 1962, p. 79.

73. She and older sister Miriam: Wallis interview.

73. Tod in *Snow White:* Parton, "Mr. & Mrs. Nelson Rockefeller," p. 158.

73. Northeast Harbor summers: Harold Haskell, Wallis, French, William Alton interviews.

74. Tod's sense of showmanship: Wallis interview; Considine, "Portrait of a Lady," p. 79; Haskell interview.

74. Camping out with the Clarks: AAR to WR, August 14, 1925, AAR Box 12, RAC.

75. "She is always full of good fun": Morris, *NR,* p. 79.

75. He invited Tod: Ibid.

75. "I do so want to know": Ibid.

75. "You don't know how glad I was": NAR to AAR and Jr., January 13, 1929, AAR Box 12, RAC.

75. "In my own life I have found": AAR to NAR, February 15, 1929, AAR Box 12, RAC.

76. "All of a sudden I realize": NAR to AAR, March 1, 1929, AAR Box 12, RAC.

76. He cautioned his parents: Morris, *NR,* p. 80.

76. "I'm beginning to think": NAR to AAR and Jr., July 8, 1929, AAR Box 12, RAC.

77. "It means so much": NAR to AAR, September 1, 1929, AAR Box 12, RAC.

77. "I still am thrilling": NAR to AAR, November 25, 1929, AAR Box 12, RAC.

77. "Nelson and I not only hope": Mary Clark to Jr., November 29, 1929, AAR Box 12, RAC.

78. "Maybe it was the difference": Bernice Kert, *Abby Aldrich Rockefeller* (New York: Random House, 1993), p. 292.

78. Nelson and Tod's wedding: "Cynwyd Girl Wed to Scion of Rockefeller," *Philadelphia Inquirer,* June 24, 1930, p. 1; "Miss Clark Becomes Bride of Nelson A. Rockefeller," *Philadelphia Public Ledger,* June 24, 1930, p. 1; "N. A. Rockefeller Weds Mary Clark," *NYT,* June 24, 1930, p. 1; French, Alton, Stark, Prideaux interviews.

80. Senior's gift: Jr. to Sr., March 14, 1930, Jr. Personal, Box 22, RAC.

80. They stayed at the Eyrie: Morris, *NR,* p. 24.

80. "We're off on a little trip": Zagat interview.

80. Round-the-world trip: Morris, *NR,* pp. 84–90; AAR to JDR3, August 15, 1930, AAR Box 12, RAC; Geoffrey Hellman, "Best Neighbor," Part II, *New Yorker,* April 18, 1942, p. 24.

81. "We haven't even had a meal alone": Morris, *NR,* p. 85.

81. "You look fairly bursting with health": AAR to NAR, February 21, 1931, AAR Box 12, RAC.

81. Packhorse trip in the Himalayas: Morris, *NR,* p. 86.

82. The meeting with Gandhi: Harrison-NAR, Chapter 2, pp. 2–3; Hellman, "Best Neighbor—II," p. 24; Morris, *NR,* pp. 89–90.

82. "It gave me the Indian point of view": Hellman, "Best Neighbor," Part II, p. 24.

82. There were other times: Morris, *NR,* pp. 86–88.

83. "Tell Pa": Quoted in Harr & Johnson, *Rockefeller Century,* p. 308.

84. Nelson only spent half: JDR3 to Jr., March 13, 1931, JDR3 Confidential, Box 3, RAC.

84. "Do you not suppose": Jr. to JDR3, March 20, 1931, JDR3 Confidential, Box 3, RAC.

84. John told his father: JDR3 to Jr., March 31, 1931, Jr. Personal, Box 30, RAC.

84. Ordering a new car: Harr & Johnson, *Rockefeller Century,* p. 308.

84. Redecorating Hawes House: AAR to NAR, January 17, 1931; February 12, 1931, AAR Box 12, RAC.

8. Ventures and Misadventures

89. "I only hope": Morris, *NR,* p. 59.

89. "Frankly, I don't relish": Ibid., p. 50.

89. "Unless I have some definite goal": Samuel E. Bleecker, *The Politics of Architecture* (New York: Rutledge Press, 1981).

90. "There are so many fine things": Morris, *NR,* p. 74.

90. "So long as you earn your living": Ibid., p. 50.

90. "The thought of having you": Ibid.

90. "I'm sorry to say": Ibid., p. 91.

90. Reporting to Junior: JDR3 to Jr., February 1931, RAC.

90. That spring the office: Jr.'s activities in the late 1920s and early 1930s are chronicled in Harr & Johnson, *Rockefeller Century,* Part II, "The Liberal Vision."

91. Rockefeller Center's origins: Carol Herselle Krinsky, *Rockefeller Center* (New York: Oxford University Press, 1978); Harr & Johnson, *Rockefeller Century,*

pp. 317–34; Victoria Newhouse, *Wallace K. Harrison, Architect* (New York: Rizzoli, 1989), pp. 34–55; "Rockefeller Center," *Fortune,* December 1936, p. 139.

92. Junior's advisers: Harr & Johnson, *Rockefeller Century,* pp. 159–63; Collier & Horowitz, *The Rockefellers,* pp. 139–42.

92. The dark, forbidding chamber: Jr.'s office furniture is tucked away in a little-noticed side room at the RAC.

92. "Either before I went abroad": Jr. to JDR3, September 28, 1936, JDR3 Confidential File, RAC.

92. "I have not been working": Harr & Johnson, *Rockefeller Century,* p. 316.

92. John would dryly recall: Collier & Horowitz, *The Rockefellers,* p. 196.

92. Nelson's first months on the job: NAR to Jr., August 22, 1931; October 14, 1931; July 14, 1932, Jr. Personal, RAC.

93. Nelson and the Cloisters: Jr. to NAR, March 1, 1933; March 10, 1933, Jr. Personal, RAC.

93. All hell broke loose: Jr. to JDR3 and NAR, August 4, 1933, JDR3 Confidential File, RAC.

93. "I realize that I am taking": Morris, *NR,* p. 92.

94. Turck & Co.: All material on the company is from the Special Work File, R Family Business Interests, Boxes 137–38, RAC.

94. "His temperament is such": Jr. to Sr., February 11, 1932, Jr. Personal, Box 22, RAC.

94. "The old gentleman got the idea": Hellman, "Best Neighbor," Part II, p. 25.

95. Details on Turck & Co.'s client base are in "History of Turck & Co. Now Special Work, Inc.," Special Work File, RAC.

95. "Influence brought to bear": "History of Turck & Co.," p. 6.

95. "Efforts have been made": Ibid.

96. Turck & Co.'s rent-free office: Ibid., p. 4.

96. Johns-Manville: NAR to Turck, January 27, 1933, Special Work File, RAC.

96. "Apparently the contract": "History of Turck & Co.," p. 6.

96. "It is a perfect spot here": Turck to NAR, October 17, 1932, Special Work File, RAC.

96. Turck & Co.'s reorganization: "History of Turck & Co.," pp. 7–9.

96. Turck thought he was underpaid: Thomas Debevoise to George A. Wilson (Turck's attorney), November 17, 1932, Special Work File, RAC.

96. Renegotiating the contracts: "History of Turck & Co.," pp. 9–11.

97. New relationship with Chase: "History of Special Work, Inc.," a report to Special Work directors on the year 1933, Special Work File, RAC.

97. Socony-Vacuum and Colorado Fuel and Iron: "History of Special Work, Inc.," p. 1.

97. Nelson closed twenty-one leases: Report to Special Work directors from Edwin K. Simpson, April 1934, Special Work File, RAC.

98. Chase lease dispute: The controversy is detailed in correspondence between Jr., Heydt, Aldrich, and Robertson, all in R Family Business Interests, Box 91, RAC.

99. "Conditions have not been ideal": Report to Rockefeller Center board from Lawrence A. Kirkland, March 17, 1933, R Family Business Interests, Box 91, RAC.

99. Sarnoff's offer: NAR to Jr., May 26, 1933, R Family Business Interests, Box 91, RAC.

100. Assuming the lease burdens: The Centroc arrangement is detailed in an

unpublished history prepared by Rockefeller Center, Chapter 19, "Outside Spaces." Jr. Business Interests, Box 83, RAC. The arrangement is further discussed in Geoffrey T. Hellman's profile of John R. Todd, "The Man Behind Prometheus," Part II, *New Yorker,* November 21, 1936.

100. Heckscher suit: *NYT, NYHT,* January 11, 1934; Krinsky, *Rockefeller Center,* p. 76.

100. A feisty old entrepreneur: August Heckscher (the first August's grandson) interview.

101. National Health Council inducements: Undated memo in Special Work File, RAC.

101. Heckscher's last years: Heckscher interview.

101. Consolidated Oil: Unpublished Rockefeller Center history, p. 94, R Family Business Interests, Box 83, RAC. Rockefeller Center did the same for U.S. Rubber.

101. Museum of Modern Art: The best source on the museum's history is Russell Lynes, *Good Old Modern* (New York: Atheneum, 1973). Also highly useful is Alice Goldfarb Marquis, *Alfred H. Barr, Jr.: Missionary for the Modern* (New York: Contemporary Books, 1989).

102. "I showed Papa": AAR to NAR, May 1, 1929, AAR Box 25, RAC.

102. Appointing NAR chairman: Conger Goodyear to AAR, June 14, 1930; AAR to Goodyear, June 20, 1930, AAR Box 25, RAC.

102. "Every time I see": AAR to NAR, February 12, 1931, AAR Box 25, RAC.

102. Junior Advisory Committee: Elizabeth Bliss Parkinson Cobb interview; Edward Warburg interview; Lynes, *Good Old Modern,* pp. 74–76.

103. Kirstein's idea: W. McNeil Lowry, "Conversations with Kirstein," Part II, *New Yorker,* December 22, 1986, p. 52; Cobb interview; Warburg interview. Within the next decade, Kirstein would turn on MOMA and become one of its most strident critics. In an October 1948 article in *Harper's,* he attacked the museum as "a modern Abstract Academy," propagating "improvisation method, deformatism as a formula, and painting . . . as an amusement manipulated by interior decorators and high pressure salesmen."

103. Todd underwrote the catalogue: Alan R. Blackburn, Jr., to NAR, May 27, 1932, R Family Cultural Interests, Box 21 (138.6), RAC.

103. Murals uproar: Cobb interview; Lynes, *Good Old Modern,* pp. 99–101.

103. "I cannot help feeling": Clark to NAR, April 18, 1932, R Family Cultural Interests, Box 21 (138.6), RAC.

103. Nelson offered to remove the pictures: NAR to Stephen Clark, April 19, 1932, R Family Cultural Interests, Box 21 (138.6), RAC.

103. The artists were adamant: NAR to Abbott Lawrence Lowell, April 28, 1932, R Family Cultural Interests, Box 21, RAC.

104. "The point which Nelson thinks insignificant": Jr. to Debevoise, April 17, 1932, R Family Cultural Interests, Box 21, RAC.

104. Junior told Nelson: Ibid.

104. Nelson called on Morgan: NAR to Abbott Lawrence Lowell, April 28, 1932, R Family Cultural Interests, Box 21, RAC.

104. "We have been caught": Ibid.

104. Clark, Goodyear approved the exhibition: NAR telegram to Jr., April 29, 1932, R Family Cultural Interests, Box 21, RAC.

104. The critics were far from kind: Lynes, *Good Old Modern,* p. 101.

104. "Many of the pictures are scarcely worth sending": Barr to John S. Ankeney, May 23, 1932, R Family Cultural Interests, Box 21, RAC.

105. A more upbeat line with Nelson: Barr to NAR, May 11, 1932, R Family Cultural Interests, Box 21, RAC.

105. Nelson pushed the trustees: NAR to AAR, May 31, 1932, R Family Cultural Interests, Box 21, RAC.

105. "It seems to me": Ibid.

105. Luncheon with Barr and Woods: NAR to Barr, June 28, 1932, R Family Cultural Interests, Box 21, RAC.

105. Diego Rivera: Bertram D. Wolfe, *The Fabulous Life of Diego Rivera* (New York: Stein & Day, 1963); Irene Herner de Larrea, *Diego Rivera: Paradise Lost at Rockefeller Center* (Mexico City: Edicupes, 1987); Geoffrey T. Hellman, "Enfant Terrible," *New Yorker,* May 20, 1933, p. 21; Anita Brenner, "Diego Rivera: Fiery Crusader of the Paint Brush," *NYT,* April 2, 1933; Frank Getlein, "Diego Rivera—Artist in Rebellion," *Milwaukee Journal,* December 26, 1957.

105. She asked Rivera to make a copy: Hellman, "Diego Rivera."

105. Abby's dealings with Rivera: Frida Kahlo to AAR, January 1932; Rivera to AAR, February 6, 1932 (thanking her for allowing him to store paintings in her garage); Kahlo to AAR, January 24, 1933, R Family Business Interests, Box 95 (205.14A), RAC.

106. Nelson began promoting him: NAR to Clifford Wight, September 23, 1932, R Family Business Interests, Box 94, RAC. "I feel this is perhaps the most important piece in the development and that he is, without question, the man to do it," NAR wrote.

106. Hood's idea: Krinsky, *Rockefeller Center,* p. 77.

106. Wooing Matisse and Picasso: Hood to Jr., October 7, 1932, R Family Business Interests, Box 94, RAC. Apropos of Picasso, Hood remarked, "He is a whimsical fellow who goes away from time to time leaving no trace of himself."

106. "Although I do not personally care": Jr. to Hood, October 12, 1932, R Family Business Interests, Box 94, RAC.

106. Rivera accepted: Rivera to Hood, October 7, 1932; NAR to Rivera, October 13, 1932, R Family Business Interests, Box 94, RAC.

106. Rivera's description: Wolfe, *The Fabulous Life,* pp. 320–22.

106. Todd, Hood, and Junior approved: Ibid., p. 323.

107. Hood glanced at it only cursorily: The source for this, as well as for much else about the Rivera RCA Building saga, is Lucienne Bloch's excellent memoir, "On Location with Diego Rivera," *Art in America,* February 1986. Based on the extensive diary notes Bloch kept as Rivera's assistant, the Bloch article is by far the most vivid and definitive contemporaneous account of the controversy.

107. The Detroit storm: Wolfe, *The Fabulous Life,* pp. 312–313.

107. Nelson spoke up: Holger Cahill oral history, COHP.

107. "Diego had been expelled": Bloch, "On Location," p. 114.

107. Rivera consulted: Brenner, "Diego Rivera: Fiery Crusader."

107. Abby climbed the scaffold: Bloch, "On Location," p. 114.

108. Tod and Nelson would show up: Hellman, "Enfant Terrible," p. 21.

108. *World-Telegram* article: Wolfe, *The Fabulous Life,* pp. 324–25; Bloch, "On Location," p. 115.

108. "All of us . . . begged him": *Flint* (Michigan) *Journal,* March 22, 1959.

108. Rivera's letter from NAR: NAR to Rivera, May 4, 1933, R Family Business Interests, Box 95, RAC.

109. Rivera's reply: Wolfe, *The Fabulous Life,* pp. 326–27.

109. Rivera's dismissal: Bloch, "On Location," p. 118; Morris, *NR,* pp. 103–4. Rivera offered his own, somewhat hyperbolic account of the scene in his introduction to *Portrait of America,* a survey of his American murals. (New York: Courici, Friede, 1934).

109. A crowd of protesters: "Rockefellers Ban Lenin in RCA Mural and Dismiss Rivera," *NYT,* May 10, 1933; "Rivera Ousted as Rockefeller Center Painter," *NYHT,* May 10, 1933.

109. Columbus Circle rally: Bloch, "On Location," p. 120.

109. National Association of Manufacturers: John E. Edgerton to NAR, May 16, 1933, R Family Business Interests, Box 95, RAC.

109. E. B. White doggerel: "I Paint What I See," *New Yorker,* May 20, 1933, p. 25.

110. Showing the mural at MOMA: John Todd to NAR, December 15, 1933; NAR to Todd, December 16, 1933; NAR to Alan Blackburn, December 16, 1933, R Family Cultural Interests, Box 95, RAC.

110. Bloch and Dimitroff's stroll: Bloch, "On Location," p. 123.

110. "An act of cultural vandalism": *NYT,* February 13, 1934.

111. "The picture was obscene": Jr. to Sr., February 17, 1934, Jr. Personal, Box 22, RAC.

111. A chastened Nelson: In the years to come, Nelson would blame the whole affair on Rivera's wife, Frida Kahlo. "She got him incorporating the most unbelievable subjects into this mural," he remarked at a 1967 lecture at the New School for Social Research. "I had pretty well thrashed this out, I thought, but Frida was peeking in and out of the door to keep check on developments." But as Bloch's account, buttressed by Dimitroff, makes clear, Frida had nothing to do with it.

9. *Power Play*

112. "Your great-grandson": NAR to Sr., April 24, 1932, Jr. Personal, Box 22, RAC.

112. "It seems difficult": Jr. to Sr., April 25, 1932, Jr. Personal, Box 22, RAC.

112. "We went to Grandfather's": NAR to Jr., August 1, 1932, Jr. Personal, Box 22, RAC.

113. "My chief desire": NAR to AAR, July 25, 1934, AAR Personal, Box 5, RAC.

113. "Johnny is showing": NAR to AAR, April 15, 1934, AAR Personal, Box 5, RAC.

113. Winthrop's progress: NAR to AAR, July 25, 1934, AAR Personal, Box 5.

113. Nelson and Blanchette: Blanchette told the story to a Rockefeller family source, who related it to the author.

114. "One of those men": Kert, Abby Aldrich Rockefeller, p. 290.

114. Nelson's letter to Abby and Abby's reply: NAR to AAR, March 21, 1933; AAR to NAR, March 23, 1933, AAR Box 12, RAC.

117. Meeting with Boss Ward: *Tarrytown News,* June 13, 1958; NAR to W. L. Ward, December 14, 1932, R Family Civic Interests, Box 51, RAC; *NYT,* February 1, 1976.

117. Declining to visit the health center: NAR to Matthias Nicoll, July 22, 1933, R Family Civic Interests, Box 51, RAC.

118. Selling souvenirs: Philip Johnson interview.

118. Restaurant-café: NAR to Jr., April 27, 1933; Jr. to NAR, May 1, 1933; R Family Business Interests, Box 96, RAC.

118. "Realizing the general feeling": NAR to John D. Kennedy, August 25, 1933, R Family Business Interests, Box 96, RAC.

118. "I have just emerged": Morris, *NR,* p. 98.

119. NAR and Consolidation Coal: NAR to Robert C. Hill, December 21, 1933, Special Work File, RAC.

119. Contract with Harrison: NAR to Harrison, January 26, 1933, Special Work File, RAC.

119. Harrison had come a long way: The definitive account of Harrison's life and work is Newhouse's *Wallace K. Harrison, Architect.* Also see Bleecker, *The Politics of Architecture.*

119. Harrison and Rockefeller Center: Newhouse, *Harrison,* Chapters 6 and 7; Krinsky, *Rockefeller Center,* pp. 38–39.

120. Nelson and Harrison's meeting: Newhouse, *Harrison,* p. 46; Harrison-NAR, Chapter 2, p. 4.

120. The two would meet: Taped interview with Harrison, Harrison Papers, Columbia University, Tape 1-B, p. 2.

121. "To work with great people": Newhouse, *Harrison,* p. 47.

121. The siblings' letter: JDR3 to Jr., May 1, 1933, JDR3 Confidential File, RAC.

122. Gift of Socony-Vacuum stock: Jr. to JDR3, December 20, 1933, JDR3 Confidential File, RAC.

122. The 1934 trusts: The most authoritative account of the trusts, both in their extent and how they work, is in Harr & Johnson, *Rockefeller Century,* pp. 354–61.

122. John saw his annual income rise: JDR3 1935 financial statement, October 22, 1936, JDR3 Confidential File, RAC.

122. Harrison's redesign of the apartment: Newhouse, *Harrison,* p. 56.

123. "My own feeling": AAR to NAR, July 6, 1935, AAR Box 4, RAC.

123. "If you start to cultivate": AAR to NAR, January 7, 1928, AAR Box 12, RAC.

124. NAR's early collecting: NAR lecture at New School for Social Research, March 15, 1967; NAR interview at AAA, July 24, 1972.

124. Lillie Bliss collection: Marquis, *Alfred Barr,* pp. 115–16; Cobb interview.

125. A hard-bitten powerhouse: Geoffrey T. Hellman, "The Man Behind Prometheus," *New Yorker,* November 14, 1936 (Part I), and November 21, 1936 (Part II).

125. "In spite of almost insuperable": Jr. to John Todd, September 8, 1933, R Family Business Interests, Box 79, RAC.

125. Nelson's preliminary report: NAR to Jr., August 29, 1933, Family and Friends, Box 137, RAC.

126. "The time has come": Jr. to Debevoise, September 8, 1933, R Family Business Interests, Box 79, RAC.

126. He found both places: NAR to Jr., "Study of Office and Estate Management," October 19, 1933, Homes Box 28, RAC.

126. "From your reaction": JDR3 and NAR to Jr., December 18, 1933, JDR3 Confidential File, RAC.

126. "All the money in the world": Jr. to JDR3 and NAR, December 20, 1933, JDR3 Confidential File, RAC.

127. In early August: NAR to Jr., August 6, 1934, R Family Business Interests, Box 98, RAC.

127. "There has been so much talk": Debevoise to Todd, October 24, 1934, R Family Business Interests, Box 98, RAC.

127. "They have done a stupendous job": Debevoise, "Memorandum in re Rockefeller Center, Inc.," October 29, 1934, R Family Business Interests, Box 98, RAC.

127. Nelson's western Chase trip: Jr. to Sr., November 30, 1934, RAC.

127. The imperial lifestyle: Morris, *NR,* p. 100; Jr. to Sr., July 30, 1935, August 20, 1935, RAC.

128. Phoning Edsel Ford: Morris, *NR,* p. 100.

128. Lunch with John: Harr & Johnson, *Rockefeller Century,* pp. 376–77.

128. They found their father unyielding: Ibid., p. 377.

128. Debevoise's complaints about Todd: Debevoise to NAR, May 7, 1935, R Family Business Interests, Box 79, RAC.

128. Debevoise was wondering aloud: Debevoise to NAR, January 2, 1936, R Family Business Interests, Box 79, RAC.

129. Debevoise convinced Junior: Debevoise to Jr., February 18, 1936, R Family Business Interests, Box 79.

129. Squeezing Todd: NAR to Executive Committee, "Re: Renewal of Managers' Contract," March 10, 1936, R Family Business Interests, Box 79, RAC.

129. Todd put into play: NAR to Jr., March 20, 1936, R Family Business Interests, Box 79, RAC.

129. Nelson's new setup: Memoranda to Rockefeller Center Committees, January 8, 1937, R Family Business Interests, Box 98, RAC.

129. He sat down: Harr & Johnson, *Rockefeller Century,* p. 378.

130. The managers' severance agreements: Unpublished history of Rockefeller Center, pp. 40–41, R Family Business Interests, Box 83, RAC.

10. *The Ruler of Rockefeller Center*

131. East River Savings Bank: Charles Heydt to NAR, March 5, 1937, R Family Business Interests, Box 91, RAC; "Two Rockefeller Sons Lead Trek to New Bank," *N.Y. Post,* March 15, 1937.

131. "You have caught the snake": "Rockefeller Center," *Fortune,* December 1936, p. 148.

132. "Open bunny gardens": Hellman, "Best Neighbor," Part II, p. 26.

132. Radio address: Text in Real Estate Box 36, RAC.

132. Nelson and Robert Moses: NAR to Robert Moses, June 4, 1936, Real Estate Box 36, RAC.

132. Sidewalk Superintendents Club: R Family Business Interests, Box 80, RAC.

133. Squelching the *Today* profile: NAR to Vincent Astor, July 27, 1936, Real Estate Box 36, RAC.

133. Nelson quietly acceded: R Family Business Interests, Box 95 (Sert file); Krinsky, *Rockefeller Center,* p. 147.

133. "I should say frankly": NAR to Jr., September 22, 1938, R Family Business Interests, Box 80, RAC.

134. U.S. Rubber ploy: Unpublished Rockefeller Center history, p. 95, R Family Business Interests, Box 83, RAC; Krinsky, *Rockefeller Center,* pp. 98–99.

134. Parking garage: NAR to Robert Straus, December 22, 1939, R Family Business Interests, Box 80, RAC.

134. Rockefeller Apartments: Real Estate Box 36, RAC; Newhouse, *Harrison,* pp. 68–72.

135. John's opposition: JDR3 to Jr., October 19, 1936, October 24, 1936, Real Estate Box 36, RAC.

135. La Guardia's municipal art center: Krinsky, *Rockefeller Center,* pp. 85–87; *Collier's,* January 27, 1951 (for NAR's recollection of the obstinacy of "21").

136. Nelson and Selznick: Harold Bruckner to NAR, July 24, 1937, R Family Business Interests, Box 90, RAC.

136. Nelson and "art diver" Jane Fauntz: R Family Business Interests, Box 96, [File 205.19], RAC.

137. Labor unrest at Rockefeller Center: NAR's file on the crisis, including a copy of the flyer, is in R Family Business Interests, Box 101, RAC. See also *NYT,* February 17–22, 27, 1938.

138. Junior's antiquated paternalism: Jr. to Hugh S. Robertson, March 10 and March 29, 1938, R Family Business Interests, Box 100, RAC.

139. Anna Rosenberg: "The 'Buffalo Plan,'" *Time,* September 27, 1943, p. 84; "Sentence for Anna," *Time,* March 6, 1944, pp. 80–82; "Outgoing Directrix," *New Yorker,* September 15, 1945, pp. 20–21; "The Woman—What a Woman!—Who Bosses the Men," *Newsweek,* February 26, 1951, pp. 20 ff.; "Busiest Woman in U.S.," *Life,* January 21, 1952, pp. 79 ff.; Lynn Hudson, "The Confident Confidante," *Fifty Plus,* August 1981, pp. 56 ff.; Anna Rosenberg Hoffman obituary, *NYT,* May 10, 1983.

139. "There never was a story": William Benton oral history, COHP.

139. He took his dilemma to Anna Rosenberg: NAR to Jr., June 8, 1938, R Family Business Interests, Box 101, RAC.

140. "You were very wise": Jr. to NAR, June 27, 1938, R Family Business Interests, Box 101, RAC.

140. George Meany: Victor Borella to Barton Turnbull and Lawrence Kirkland, January 19, 1942, R Family Business Interests, Box 102. For some years now, books about Nelson Rockefeller have asserted that it was Meany, not Tom Murray, with whom Rockefeller negotiated. (An oral history in COHP with union leader Nelson Cruikshank is the source for this assertion.) However, there is no evidence that Rockefeller ever bargained with Meany in the 1930s.

141. Rosenberg and Ronald Reagan: Thomas Rosenberg interview.

141. He put Rosenberg on retainer: Special Work File, RAC.

141. Last-rivet ceremony: *Rockefeller Center Magazine,* December 1939, pp. 25 ff.; R Family Business Interests, Box 81, RAC.

142. "Radio City has become": *Forbes,* August 1, 1939.

11. Playing Politics

143. Gala opening of the new building: Lynes, *Good Old Modern,* pp. 203–9; "President Praises U.S. Art Freedom," *NYT,* May 11, 1939; "Beautiful Doings," *Time,* May 22, 1939, pp. 82–89.

144. "I learned about politics": Lynes, *Good Old Modern,* p. 151.

145. He came up with a scheme: NAR to AAR, April 22, 1933, AAR Box 25, RAC.

145. Building the endowment: NAR to H. E. Winlock, January 10, 1934; Winlock to NAR, January 11, 1934; A. Conger Goodyear to NAR, January 12, 1934, R Family Cultural Interests, Box 20, RAC.

145. "This is not a traditional museum": Marquis, *Alfred H. Barr,* p. 137.

146. "Why is Mr. Barr": James Flexner interview.

146. Barr and Goodyear: Alan Blackburn to Alfred Barr, May 15, 1933, Alfred Barr Papers, Roll 2165, AAA; Marquis, *Alfred H. Barr,* pp. 197–98.

147. Nelson and Abby's exchange on the MOMA presidency: NAR to AAR, April 22, 1933; AAR to NAR, April 26, 1933, May 1, 1933, AAR Box 12, RAC.

147. Nelson approached Goodyear: NAR to Goodyear, May 9, 1933, R Family Cultural Interests, Box 20, RAC.

147. "It does not seem wise": AAR to Goodyear, December 16, 1937, AAR Box 25, RAC.

148. Rockefeller family financing of the building: Memo for Jr. on Museum of Modern Art Building Fund, 1942, R Family Cultural Interests, Box 23, RAC.

148. Goodwin was apoplectic: Thomas Mabry to Barr, June 18, 1936, Barr Papers, Roll 2165, AAA.

148. "One day I overheard Wally Harrison": Lynes, *Good Old Modern,* p. 192.

148. "I do not believe that Nelson": Barr to AAR, July 2, 1936, Barr Papers, Roll 2165.

149. "When I left New York": Barr to Goodyear, July 6, 1936, Barr Papers, Roll 2165.

149. Goodyear's reply: Goodyear to Barr, July 7, 1936, Barr Papers, Roll 2165.

149. A livid Barr wired Nelson: Barr to NAR, July 7, 1936, Barr Papers, Roll 2165.

149. "Sometimes his mother": Lynes, *Good Old Modern,* p. 202.

149. Barr sulked: Marquis, *Alfred H. Barr,* p. 172.

150. "Alfred had not foreseen the consequences": Margaret Scolari Barr, "Our Campaigns," *New Criterion,* Summer 1987.

150. The firings: Lynes, *Good Old Modern,* p. 214.

150. "Profoundly shocked": Barr to AAR, July 15, 1939, AAR Box 8, RAC.

150. "Executive Committee voted": AAR to Barr, July 17, 1939, AAR Box 8, RAC.

150. "He didn't have any power": Lynes, *Good Old Modern,* p. 214.

150. McAndrew's dismissal: Barr, "Our Campaigns"; Lynes, *Good Old Modern,* p. 220.

151. Barr's personal relationship with Nelson: Marquis, *Alfred H. Barr,* pp. 328–30.

151. "Nelson needs art": Alfred H. Barr, Jr., "On Nelson Rockefeller and Modern Art," essay in *The Nelson A. Rockefeller Collection: Masterpieces of Modern Art* (New York: Hudson Hills Press, 1981).

151. The villain in his eyes: Margaret Scolari Barr, "Our Campaigns"; Dorothy Miller interview; Cobb interview.

152. Matisse and Léger murals: Nelson A. Rockefeller, Introduction to *The Nelson A. Rockefeller Collection;* Newhouse, *Harrison,* pp. 56–57.

152. Guest house: Newhouse, *Harrison,* pp. 68–69.

152. Seal Harbor house: Ibid., pp. 99–101; Harmon Goldstone interview; James Wallis interview; Ellen Harrison interview; author's visit to house, December 1988.

153. Junior's letter: Morris, *NR,* p. 76.

153. Nelson's boat-buying syndicate: Boats File, R Family Homes, Boxes 63–64, RAC; Wallis interview; Harold Haskell interview.

154. The media took notice: John Cushman Fistere, "The Rockefeller Boys,"

Saturday Evening Post, July 16, 1938; Samuel T. Williamson, "The Rockefeller Boys," *NYT Magazine,* April 9, 1939.

155. Tossed out of Yale: Harr & Johnson, *Rockefeller Century,* p. 390.

155. "My chief desire": NAR to AAR, July 25, 1934, RAC.

155. "I can honestly say": Fistere, "The Rockefeller Boys," p. 36.

156. Rockefeller Brothers Fund: DR interview; Harr & Johnson, *Rockefeller Century,* pp. 392–93.

156. Junior began musing aloud: Harr & Johnson, *Rockefeller Century,* p. 393, pp. 477–78; Moscow, *Rockefeller Inheritance,* p. 166.

156. "Nelson presented his point of view": Harr & Johnson, *Rockefeller Century,* p. 393.

157. Teachers College deficits: "Mr. J. B. C. Woods' Reports to parents," p. 12, R Family Educational Interests, Box 61, RAC.

157. Lincoln School battle: A detailed blow-by-blow account of the battle, and Nelson Rockefeller's involvement in it, was privately prepared by his attorneys and the family office—possibly with an eye toward the litigation that ensued. This untitled account will be referred to as "5600 report." It is in R Family Educational Interests, Box 62, RAC.

158. Debevoise approached: John Lockwood interview.

158. Flexner's speech: R Family Educational Interests, Box 61, RAC.

158. Woods warned Nelson: Woods to NAR, October 22, 1939, R Family Educational Interests, Box 61, RAC.

158. Teachers College "bears no legal obligation": *Report of the Informal Advisory Committee on the Lincoln School,* p. 8, R Family Educational Interests, Box 61, RAC.

158. Woods insisted that Nelson could solve the problem: 5600 report, p. 38.

158. He summoned Russell and Del Manzo to his office: Ibid., p. 36.

159. Nelson ripped the draft to shreds: Ibid., p. 48.

159. "I don't want to let Mr. Rockefeller down": Ibid., p. 95.

159. Too many Jewish students: Ibid., pp. 47, 59–60.

159. Nelson had worked out a deal: Ibid., pp. 64–70.

159. Nelson was pilloried by parents: Ibid., pp. 79–81.

159. "Groups to Watch Out For": R Family Educational Interests, Box 62, RAC.

160. The resignation letter: R Family Educational Interests, Box 62, RAC.

161. "The point is that Rockefeller believed": Morris, *NR,* p. 239.

162. Jack Woods's politics: Arthur Bullowa, Mary Woods, John Woods, Jr., interviews.

162. The Lincoln School battle was a turning point: Morris, *NR,* pp. 239–40.

12. *El Príncipe de Gasolina*

165. The Group: Harrison-NAR, Chapter 2, p. 9; Morris, *NR,* pp. 125–26; Hellman, "Best Neighbor," Part II, p. 28.

165. Beardsley Ruml: Harr & Johnson, *Rockefeller Century,* pp. 186–87; Collier & Horowitz, *The Rockefellers,* p. 213.

166. Nelson dispatched Flexner: James Flexner interview.

166. Nelson and pre-Columbian art: NAR oral history, AAA; NAR lecture at New School for Social Research, March 15, 1967.

167. Investing in Creole: Moscow, *Rockefeller Inheritance,* p. 154; Morris, *NR,* p. 112.

167. 1937 trip: Eleanor Clark French interview; Morris, *NR,* pp. 111–15.

168. "Nelson loved the Latin Americans": Harrison interview in Claude Curtis Erb, "Nelson Rockefeller and United States–Latin American Relations, 1940–45," Ph.D. Thesis, Clark University, 1982 (hereafter cited: Erb, Ph.D. Thesis).

168. Creole camps: Morris, *NR,* pp. 116–17; Collier & Horowitz, *The Rockefellers,* p. 209.

169. Addressing the Standard managers: Morris, *NR,* p. 115.

169. Proudfit and Linam: Ibid., p. 119.

169. "The old days were over": "Creole Petroleum: Business Embassy," *Fortune,* February 1949, pp. 91 ff.

169. Changes at Creole: Ibid.; Morris, *NR,* pp. 120–21; Collier & Horowitz, *The Rockefellers,* pp. 210–11.

169. Nelson chatted with the drillers: Morris, *NR,* pp. 119–20.

169. Betancourt's denunciation: Ibid., pp. 118–19.

170. Meeting with Cárdenas: NAR memo on the meeting, October 14–15, 1939, NAR Country Files, Box 52, RAC.

170. Contreras lamented: Harrison-NAR, Chapter 2, p. 8; Morris, *NR,* p. 126.

171. "Contribute to the general good will": NAR to Henry Linam, September 20, 1939, Business Interests, Box 99, RAC.

171. Only 16 percent: Memo on "Compañía Anónima Hotelera Venezolana," June 24, 1942, Business Interests, Box 110, RAC.

171. David wanted to join: Barton Turnbull to Thomas Debevoise, August 27, 1940, Business Interests, Box 109, RAC.

171. One of Laurance's advisers: John Green to LSR, November 1940, Business Interests, Box 99, RAC.

171. "Opportunism characterizes": Carl Spaeth to NAR, March 18, 1940, Business Interests, Box 109, RAC.

172. "If we were having any difficulty: Edward Robbins to NAR, March 20, 1940, Business Interests, Box 109, RAC.

172. Harrison's design: Max Abramovitz interview; Newhouse, *Harrison,* pp. 95–96; Bleecker, *Politics of Architecture,* p. 109.

172. Fomento could be of assistance: NAR to Herman Schneebeli, May 9, 1940, Business Interests, Box 109, RAC.

172. "Almost every day": Spaeth to NAR, June 10, 1940, Business Interests, Box 109, RAC.

13. The Way In

174. Ruml's note: Beardsley Ruml to Harry Hopkins, December 28, 1937, Hopkins Papers, Box 97, FDRL.

175. Rosenberg assured Roosevelt: Memo, OF 4025, FDRL.

175. Contribution to Landon: Harr & Johnson, *Rockefeller Century,* p. 398.

175. Rosenberg phoned the White House again: Memo, OF 4025, FDRL.

176. "We have had so many enthusiastic": NAR to FDR, May 29, 1939, NAR Coordinator of Inter-American Affairs File (henceforth CIAA), Box 9, RAC.

176. Nelson on the WPA: NAR to FDR, June 1, 1939; FDR to NAR, June 6, 1939, PPF 6035, FDRL.

176. Hopkins expressed a general interest: Hopkins to Ruml, January 4, 1939, Hopkins Papers, Box 97, FDRL.

176. "Tommy the Cork": Ted Morgan, *FDR: A Biography* (New York: Simon & Schuster, 1985), pp. 425–26; Robert Caro, *The Years of Lyndon Johnson: The Path to Power* (New York: Alfred A. Knopf, 1983), pp. 448, 460.

176. "Smart people": Alva Johnston, "White House Tommy," *Saturday Evening Post,* July 31, 1937.

176. Hay-Adams meeting: NAR to Thomas Corcoran, March 3, 1939, Corcoran Papers, Box 211, LC.

177. "If we go down": Frank Freidel, *Franklin D. Roosevelt: A Rendezvous with Destiny,* (New York: Little, Brown, 1990), p. 338.

177. Pro-Nazi sympathizers: Alton Frye, *Nazi Germany and the Western Hemisphere* (New Haven: Yale University Press, 1967).

177. "We must concentrate": Marshall memo to War Plans Division cited in Erb, Ph.D. Thesis, p. 16.

178. Rockefeller and Ruml's meeting with Hopkins: NAR to Carl Spaeth, July 1, 1940, NAR CIAA Box 1, RAC; Morris, *NR,* pp. 128–30.

178. Rockefeller's memo: A copy is in NAR CIAA Box 9, RAC.

179. Roosevelt dictated a letter: *History of the Office of the Coordinator of Inter-American Affairs* (Washington, D.C.: U.S. Government Printing Office, 1947), hereafter *CIAA History,* p. 279.

180. The cabinet members gathered: Henry Wallace Journals, p. 1160, COHP.

180. Rockefeller was distressed: NAR to Spaeth, July 1, 1940, NAR CIAA Box 1, RAC.

180. Cabinet joint program: *CIAA History,* p. 6.

180. Rosenberg's meeting with FDR: NAR to Rosenberg, June 19, 1940, NAR CIAA Box 4, RAC; NAR to Spaeth, July 1, 1940, NAR CIAA Box 1, RAC.

180. "It is simply tragic": NAR to Spaeth, July 1, 1940, NAR CIAA Box 1, RAC.

181. James Forrestal: Townsend Hoopes and Douglas Brinkley, *Driven Patriot: The Life and Times of James Forrestal* (New York: Alfred A. Knopf, 1992); Walter Millis, ed., *The Forrestal Diaries* (New York: Viking, 1951).

181. Would Rockefeller be willing: NAR to Spaeth, July 10, 1940, NAR CIAA Box 1, RAC.

182. "Frankly, my reaction was": Ibid.

182. "I went around town": Paul Nitze interview.

182. Nitze drew up the outline: Nitze interview.

182. Interdepartmental scheme: *CIAA History,* pp. 6–7.

183. Who would get the job: Nitze interview (Nitze was briefed by Forrestal after his meeting with FDR); Paul H. Nitze, *From Hiroshima to Glasnost* (New York: Grove Weidenfeld, 1989), pp. 10–11; Paul Nitze oral history, COHP.

183. Clayton would later insist: William Clayton oral history, COHP.

183. The third name down: In his memoir, *As It Happened* (Garden City, N.Y.: Doubleday, 1979), CBS chairman William Paley claims that it was he who suggested Rockefeller to Forrestal, after Forrestal unsuccessfully offered the job to Paley. Nitze, however, did not recall such an offer to the CBS chief, and said Rockefeller's name had come up through other means.

183. Rockefeller had given $25,000: Nitze interview.

183. Rockefeller support of Willkie: LSR to Willkie Volunteer Mailing Committee, May 27, 1940, Civic Interests, Box 37, RAC.

183. Willkie forces sent the checks back: Oren Root, *Persons and Persuasions* (New York: Norton, 1974), p. 134.

184. Forrestal felt Rockefeller was too young: Nitze interview.

184. Dinner with Forrestal at the F Street Club: NAR to Spaeth, July 10, 1940, NAR CIAA Box 1, RAC.

185. Checking Forrestal out: George S. Franklin to NAR, July 18, 1940, NAR CIAA Box 1, RAC.

185. "George Franklin": "Franklin's" telegrams to Willkie's secretary and others are in Civic Interests, Box 37, RAC.

185. "I went up the back way": "Nelson Rockefeller: A Record to Fit the Times," *Fortune,* June 1, 1967.

186. "It would be very unfortunate": NAR to Spaeth, July 1, 1940, NAR CIAA Box 1, RAC.

186. "If I were President": Morris, *NR,* p. 132.

186. The game plan had changed: NAR to Forrestal, July 26, 1940, NAR CIAA Box 6, RAC.

186. "I'm not worried": Morris, *NR,* p. 132.

187. "As yet the situation has not": NAR to Edward Robbins, August 2, 1940, Business Interests, Box 109, RAC.

187. Forrestal submitted the final plan: Forrestal to Hopkins, August 14, 1940, Hopkins Papers (Sherwood Collection), Box 311, FDRL.

187. "Forrestal asked me to inquire": Edwin Watson to FDR, August 15, 1940, OF 4512, FDRL.

187. "I got the job": James Desmond, *Nelson Rockefeller* (New York: Macmillan, 1964), p. 74.

187. "Most of the things": Kramer & Roberts, *"I Never Wanted to Be Vice-President of Anything!,"* p. 50.

188. "Now, Anna": Thomas Rosenberg interview.

14. Go-getter

189. Prewar Washington: Scott Hart, *Washington at War: 1941–1945* (Englewood Cliffs, N.J.: Prentice-Hall, 1970); David Brinkley, *Washington Goes to War* (New York: Alfred A. Knopf, 1988).

190. Junior's letter: CIAA Box 4, RAC. On top of the copy in the file is written: "Not used—original destroyed."

190. CIAA cast of characters: *CIAA History,* pp. 148–50.

190. John Hay Whitney: E. J. Kahn, Jr., *Jock: The Life and Times of John Hay Whitney* (Garden City, N.Y.: Doubleday, 1981).

190. Advisory committee: *CIAA History,* p. 150.

191. "Lockwood was very sharp": Collier & Horowitz, *The Rockefellers,* p. 682.

191. Frank Jamieson: Francis Jamieson oral history, COHP; Linda Storrow interview; Jamieson obituary, *NYT,* January 31, 1960; "Daily Closeup," *New York Post,* December 8, 1958; "Key Figure in Rockefeller Victory," *Newark News,* November 9, 1958.

192. "I quake at the thought": Storrow interview.

192. "Washington is shocked daily": "Pan-American Powerhouse," *Cosmopolitan,* May 1941.

193. "A reorientation": Minutes of meeting, August 27, 1940, Box 543 OIAA.

193. Foxhall Road house guests: Nitze interview; Hellman, "Best Neighbor," Part I.

193. "While you have": Morris, *NR,* p. 144.

194. Pearson's memo: Pearson to NAR, November 28, 1940, Drew Pearson Personal Papers, G85-2083, LBJL.

194. J. Edgar Hoover: Curt Gentry, *J. Edgar Hoover: The Man and the Secrets* (New York: Norton, 1991).

195. Rockefeller's meeting with Foxworth: P. E. Foxworth to J. Edgar Hoover, August 23, 1940, FBI Files.

195. War's effect on Latin markets: FDR to Cabinet, September 27, 1940, Official File, FDRL; Clyde C. Hall, "Preservation of Democracy," *Dartmouth Alumni Magazine,* January 1941; "A Rockefeller Swings into Action," *The Pan American,* November 1940.

195. He met with Roosevelt: *CIAA History,* p. 12; James Reston, "Second Line of Defense," *NYT Magazine,* June 25, 1941.

196. Jesse Jones: Bascom N. Timmons, *Jesse H. Jones: The Man and the Statesman* (New York: Henry Holt, 1956); Freidel, *Franklin D. Roosevelt,* p. 353; Otis L. Graham, Jr., and Meghan Robinson Wander, eds., *Franklin D. Roosevelt: His Life and Times* (Boston: G. K. Hall, 1985), pp. 220–22.

196. Rockefeller and Jones: Morris, *NR,* p. 164.

197. Letter to Forrestal: *CIAA History,* p. 29.

197. Taking the issue to FDR: Ibid.

197. The consequences: Annex A to Memorandum for NAR, July 21, 1941, Box 144 OIAA.

197. Ineffectual OPM: Brinkley, *Washington Goes to War,* p. 63.

197. FDR directed Knudsen: FDR to Knudsen, April 5, 1941, Box 147 OIAA.

197. Rockefeller and Acheson at loggerheads: Notes on meetings of Committee on Essential Requirements of the Other American Republics, July 3, 1941, July 11, 1941, Box 147 OIAA.

198. Ten-cent stores: NAR to FDR, February 18, 1941, CIAA Box 9, RAC.

198. "Your reelection yesterday": NAR to FDR, November 6, 1940, PPF 6035, FDRL.

198. "Deeply moved": NAR to FDR, March 16, 1941, PPF 6035, FDRL.

198. Roosevelt Scholarships: Edward Robbins to Grace Tully, July 23, 1941, OF 4512, FDRL.

198. Speaking to the National Police Academy: *NYHT,* March 30, 1941.

199. Foxworth's participation: Foxworth to J. Edgar Hoover, August 23, 1940, September 5, 1940, September 14, 1940, FBI Files.

199. Fact-finding mission: Lockwood interview.

199. Adolf Berle: Jordan Schwarz, *Liberal: Adolf A. Berle and the Vision of an American Era* (New York: Free Press, 1987); Morgan, *FDR,* pp. 345–346.

199. His early impression: Berle Papers, Box 212, FDRL.

199. Rockefeller wanted to go public: Rockefeller to Berle, January 8, 1941, Berle Papers, Box 7, FDRL.

200. "U.S. Firms' Agents": *NYT,* January 9, 1941.

200. 1,700 letters: *CIAA History,* p. 17.

200. "Hundreds of undesirable": *NYT,* May 20, 1941.

200. General Motors: Adolf Berle to Alfred P. Sloan, Jr., May 9, 1941, Berle Papers, Box 57, FDRL; Sloan to Summer Welles, May 19, 1941, NAR to Sloan, June 6, 1941, CIAA Box 1, RAC; Morris, *NR,* pp. 173–74.

201. "Here's at least": James Forrestal to NAR, July 21, 1941, James Forrestal Papers, Box 55, Princeton University.

201. Rockefeller's office: Shelby Cullom Davis, "Remember South America," *Current History,* April 1941; Hellman, "Best Neighbor," Part I; *Time,* June 9, 1941.

202. The chart room: Harmon Goldstone, George Dudley, Nadia Williams interviews.

203. Sumner Welles: Obituary, *NYT,* September 25, 1961; Freidel, *Franklin D. Roosevelt,* pp. 213, 329; Morgan, *FDR,* pp. 510–21, 677–84.

204. Rockefeller's first encounter with Welles: Morris, *NR,* pp. 154–55.

204. He was particularly scornful: *CIAA History,* p. 182.

204. Rockefeller steered his own course: Ibid., pp. 182–83.

204. "We finished up": Rockefeller to Hoover, October 18, 1940, FBI Files.

204. Rockefeller's observers: *CIAA History,* p. 245.

204. Berent Friele: Erb, Ph.D. Thesis, p. 100; Collier & Horowitz, *The Rockefellers,* p. 260.

205. Ad fiasco: *CIAA History,* pp. 242–43; Erb, Ph.D. Thesis, p. 96; Jamieson oral history, COHP; Berle to NAR, March 11, 1941, Berle Papers, Box 57, FDRL.

205. "It was his chance": Morris, *NR,* p. 156.

205. Welles took his case to Roosevelt: Erb, Ph.D. Thesis, pp. 96–97; *CIAA History,* pp. 85–86.

206. Visit with FDR: Morris, *NR,* pp. 157–58.

207. Liaison procedures: *CIAA History,* p. 186.

207. "We've worked out": Hellman, "Best Neighbor," Part I.

207. "We now need": Memo on meeting between Welles and NAR, July 2, 1941, NAR CIAA Box 12, RAC.

207. Welles was pleased: *CIAA History,* p. 184.

208. Douglas Fairbanks mission: Douglas Fairbanks, Jr., *Salad Days* (New York: Doubleday, 1988); *NYT,* April 27, 1941; June 3, 1941; June 9, 1941; *Life,* June 2, 1941; *CIAA History,* p. 82; Spruille Braden oral history, COHP.

208. Robbins' memo: Robbins to NAR, June 6, 1941, PSF Box 96, FDRL.

208. Getting FDR's sponsorship: *CIAA History,* pp. 246–47.

208. "Hutch would slay me": FDR to Welles, July 21, 1941, PSF Box 96, FDRL.

15. Going to War

210. Sunday evening at Foxhall Road: Spruille Braden oral history, COHP.

211. Henry Wallace: Edward L. and Frederick H. Schapsmeier, *Henry A. Wallace of Iowa: The Agrarian Years, 1910–1940* (Ames, Iowa: Iowa State University Press, 1968) and *Henry A. Wallace and the War Years* (Ames, Iowa: Iowa State University Press, 1970); J. Samuel Walker, *Henry A. Wallace and American Foreign Policy* (Westport, Conn.: Greenwood Press, 1976).

212. Tennis partners: Morris, *NR,* pp. 141–42; Schapsmeier, *Henry A. Wallace and the War Years,* p. 6.

212. "I am overwhelmed": Wallace to NAR, December 31, 1941, Henry Wallace Papers, Correspondence, Reel 23-128, University of Iowa.

213. Visit with Wallace: Philip Dunne, *Take Two* (New York: McGraw-Hill, 1980), pp. 155–56.

213. Rockefeller's frustration: Erb, Ph.D. Thesis, pp. 40–45; "Priorities Threatening Good-Neighbor Policy," *NYT,* October 19, 1941.

214. "Confidentially": CIAA Executive Committee meeting minutes, November 21, 1941, quoted in *CIAA History,* p. 207.

214. Merger with EDB: *CIAA History,* pp. 207–8

215. MOMA exhibition: Minutes of CIAA Cultural Relations division meeting, July 8, 1941, NAR CIAA Box 1, RAC.

215. Moe Berg: Nicholas Dawidoff, "Scholar, Catcher, Soldier, Spy," *Sports Illustrated,* March 23, 1992; *CIAA History,* p. 98.

216. "Process shots, gentlemen": Kahn, *Jock,* p. 136.

216. *Down Argentine Way:* NAR to Wallace, "Program of the Communications Division," April 1, 1941, p. 7, Henry Wallace Papers, FDRL.

216. CIAA censorship: Ibid.

216. Films based on Latin American themes: Ibid.

216. Walt Disney contract: Contract No. NDCar-110, August 5, 1941, Box 216, OIAA.

217. Parsons contacted Rockefeller: W. A. Swanberg, *Citizen Hearst* (New York: Scribners, 1961), p. 497; Frank Brady, *Citizen Welles* (New York: Scribners, 1989), pp. 281–82.

217. Defamatory article about Senior: Robert L. Carringer, *The Making of Citizen Kane* (Berkeley: University of California Press, 1985).

217. Rockefeller offered to subsidize: Brady, *Citizen Welles,* p. 334.

217. Cost overruns: Ibid., pp. 338–40.

217. Uproar over *favelas:* Ibid., p. 342.

218. Rockefeller asserted: *CIAA History,* p. 79; Brady, *Citizen Welles,* pp. 347–48.

218. "I thought he was the one": Barbara Leaming, *Orson Welles: A Biography* (New York: Viking, 1985), pp. 340–41.

219. "Nobody was ever more cowardly": Ibid., p. 252.

219. Welles's revenge: Ibid., pp. 340–41.

219. MOMA contract: *CIAA History,* p. 71; "Column 'Hoot' at 'Cultural Relations' Draws Reply," *Motion Picture Herald,* January 31, 1942; Erb, Ph.D. Thesis, pp. 117–18.

220. "A nation of flag pole sitters": *CIAA History,* p. 74.

220. Rockefeller offered them a deal: Ibid., p. 76.

220. "The American newsreels": Erb, Ph.D. Thesis, p. 121.

220. *En Guardia:* Jamieson oral history, COHP; *CIAA History,* pp. 46–49.

221. "Imitation is the highest form": NAR to FDR, June 3, 1942, OF 4512, FDRL.

221. Don Francisco's report: *CIAA History,* p. 58.

221. William Paley's trip: Paley, *As It Happened,* p. 142; Sally Bedell Smith, *In All His Glory* (New York: Simon & Schuster, 1990), pp. 201–2.

222. World Wide Broadcasting Foundation: *CIAA History,* pp. 58–59.

222. He told Frank Jamieson: Jamieson oral history, COHP.

222. Donovan: Anthony Cave Brown, *The Last Hero: Wild Bill Donovan* (New York: Times Books, 1982); Corey Ford, *Donovan of OSS* (Boston: Little, Brown, 1970); Richard Dunlop, *Donovan, America's Master Spy* (Chicago: Rand McNally, 1982).

224. "The topsy-turvy": Morgan, *FDR,* p. 551.

224. He phoned Rosenberg: Memo of conversation, July 15, 1941, NAR CIAA Box 5, RAC.

224. Dinner meeting: "How the Donovan Arrangement Finally Evolved" (internal memo), October 24, 1941, NAR CIAA Box 5, RAC.

224. Donovan invited: John Lockwood remarks re Donovan (internal memo), September 4, 1941, NAR CIAA Box 5, RAC.

224. Spaeth's meeting: Spaeth to NAR, September 5, 1941, NAR CIAA Box 5, RAC.

225. "It won't work": Joseph Barnes to Donovan, October 5, 1941, NAR CIAA Box 5, RAC.

225. Both men dug in their heels: "Main Points Made by Colonel Donovan" (internal memo), October 7, 1941, NAR CIAA Box 5, RAC.

225. Meeting with Welles: "How the Donovan Arrangement Finally Evolved," op. cit.; Welles to NAR, October 10, 1941, NAR CIAA Box 5, RAC.

225. The budget office was leery: Bernard Gladieux oral history, pp. 270–74, COHP.

225. Donovan's letter: Donovan to NAR, October 9, 1941, NAR CIAA Box 5, RAC.

226. Meeting with Donovan and James Roosevelt: "Donovan's Office" (internal CIAA memo), October 29, 1941, NAR CIAA Box 5, RAC.

226. He began working his contacts: Ibid.

227. Anna Rosenberg meets with FDR: Ibid.

227. Donovan exploded: Ibid.; FDR to Harold Smith, October 24, 1941, OF 4512, FDRL.

228. Rio conference: Laurence Duggan, *The Americas: The Search for Hemisphere Security* (New York: Henry Holt, 1949).

228. "Our moral leadership": Beatrice Bishop Berle and Travis Beal Jacobs, eds., *Navigating the Rapids 1918–1971* (New York: Harcourt Brace Jovanovich, 1973), p. 398.

228. Hull was furious: Ibid.; Cordell Hull, *Memoirs* (New York: Macmillan, 1948), Vol. II, p. 1149.

228. Rockefeller's pep talk: *CIAA History,* p. 165.

228. "The other American republics": Erb, Ph.D. Thesis, p. 131.

229. The CIAA began bombarding: *CIAA History,* p. 86.

229. "I hate to think": Spruille Braden oral history, COHP.

229. Lunch with FDR: NAR, "Memorandum Concerning Lunch with the President," August 13, 1942, NAR CIAA Box 5, RAC.

16. No Limits

230. "Is it wise": Shelley Tracy to NAR, February 19, 1942, NAR CIAA Box 1, RAC.

230. *Life* article: Noel F. Busch, "Nelson A. Rockefeller," *Life,* April 27, 1942.

230. *New Yorker* articles: Hellman, "Best Neighbor," Parts I and II.

231. OWI threat: Samuel B. Hand, *Counsel and Advice: A Political Biography of Samuel I. Rosenman* (New York: Garland, 1979), pp. 160–61; *CIAA History,* pp. 198–200; Bernard Gladieux oral history, COHP; "All Our News Thro [sic] One Channel" (internal CIAA memo), NAR CIAA Box 5, RAC.

232. Caucus with aides: Morris, *NR,* pp. 167–68.

232. "While I recognize": NAR to Watson, March 7, 1942, NAR CIAA Box 9, RAC.

232. "If this decision sticks": Morris, *NR,* p. 169.

232–33. Cabinet members dragged in: Francis Biddle to FDR, April 22, 1942; Sumner Welles to FDR, May 13, 1942; NAR to Harold Smith, May 13, 1942, OF 4512, FDRL.

233. "A coordinator is someone": Wallace Diaries, December 16, 1942, COHP.

233. A little empire of his own: Morris, *NR,* p. 180.

234. "Certain differences in emphasis": *CIAA History,* p. 209.

234. Rockefeller had offered: NAR to Spaeth, March 25, 1942, NAR CIAA Box 7, RAC.

234. Rockefeller sent Spaeth a check: NAR to Spaeth, April 9, 1942, NAR CIAA Box 1, RAC.

234. Spaeth's CPD plans: *CIAA History,* pp. 219–20.

234. Spaeth's memo: Spaeth to Duggan, June 19, 1942, quoted in internal CIAA memo, "PERSPECTV," July 4, 1942, NAR CIAA Box 5, RAC.

234. "In my opinion": NAR to Duggan, June 29, 1942, quoted in above memo.

234. He went even further: "PERSPECTV," p. 2.

234–35. "A review of our unpleasant meeting": Spaeth to NAR, July 1, 1942, NAR CIAA Box 1, RAC.

235. Spaeth's son's illness: Spaeth to NAR, February 2, 1943, NAR CIAA Box 1, RAC.

235. Lockwood's stomach pain: George Dudley interview.

236. Commerce's plan: Wayne Taylor to NAR, June 11, 1942, NAR CIAA Box 11, RAC.

236. Rockefeller talked of building: "Progress Report on Wooden Sailing Vessels," June 15, 1942, NAR CIAA Box 11, RAC.

236. FDR's suggestions: NAR to FDR, August 18, 1942, OF 4512, FDRL.

236. A great wooden armada: Spruille Braden oral history, COHP.

236. Program's problems: "History, Organization and Function of the Inter-American Navigation Corporation," June 30, 1943, OF 4512-2, FDRL.

236. Jesse Jones's powers: Timmons, *Jesse H. Jones;* Jesse H. Jones, *Fifty Billion Dollars: My Thirteen Years with the R.F.C.* (New York: Macmillan, 1951).

237. Appropriations Act clause: Public Law 678, approved July 25, 1942, cited in *CIAA History,* p. 235.

237. Mexican railways: Lockwood interview; *CIAA History,* pp. 32–36.

238. Prencinradio and Mexican moviemaking: "Annual Report of Prencinradio Incorporated," June 1943, OF 4512-2, FDRL.

238. *Wall Street Journal* story: *Wall Street Journal,* May 18, 1944.

238. Public works program: War Plans Division memos, November 13, 17, 24, WPD 4115-63, NA.

238. Rockefeller's black book: Dudley interview; Goldstone interview.

239. Program for Hopkins: NAR to Hopkins, December 29, 1941, Hopkins Papers (Sherwood Collection), Box 311, FDRL.

239. Hopkins took it to FDR: Morris, *NR,* p. 177.

239. Welles's resolution: NAR to Welles, January 1, 1942, Hopkins Papers (Sherwood Collection), Box 311, FDRL.

239. Rockefeller called on Marshall: NAR to Hopkins, January 20, 1942, ibid.

239. "If any hint": Welles to NAR, March 26, 1942, NAR CIAA Box 12, RAC.

240. It fell to Henry Wallace: Wallace Diaries, August 26, 1942, COHP.

240. 1942 trip: Itineraries and memoranda in NAR CIAA Boxes 1 and 12, RAC.

241. Institute operations: 1942–43 Annual Report, Basic Economy Department, Office of the Coordinator of Inter-American Affairs, OF 4512-2, FDRL; *CIAA History,* Chapters 10–12.

241. *Servicio* concept: *CIAA History,* pp. 234–37.

241. Fighting yaws: Erb, Ph.D. Thesis, pp. 179–80.

242. Rockefeller's visit to the clinic: Morris, *NR,* pp. 182–83.

242. El Oro relief: 1942–43 Annual Report, Basic Economy Department, op. cit., pp. 10–11.

242. Guayaquil earthquake: NAR to FDR, May 14, 1942, OF 4512-2, FDRL.

242. Inland waterway: *CIAA History,* pp. 36–37.

242. Llama shortage: Harrison-NAR, Tape 3-b, p. 9.

242. "Some of their ideas": John Cabot oral history, HSTL.

243. Rockefeller invoked the specter: *CIAA History,* p. 36.

243. "Too much credit": NAR CIAA Box 4, RAC.

243. "In his handling": "Capitol Stuff," *N.Y. Daily News,* November 26, 1943.

243. Hugh Butler: *NYT* obituary, July 2, 1954.

243. Butler's report: "Our Deep Dark Secrets in Latin America," *Reader's Digest,* December 1943.

244. McKellar's defense: "McKellar Assails Butler Facts," *N.Y. Sun,* December 13, 1943.

244. He issued a statement: NAR CIAA Box 10, RAC.

244. "It was his own belief": Jamieson oral history, COHP.

17. *Pull and Haul*

245. Meetings upon meetings: *CIAA History,* pp. 223–24.

246. Rosenberg and FDR: Anna Rosenberg Hoffman Papers, Box 1, Schlesinger Library, Radcliffe College.

246. "He drove as if he were piloting": Morris, *NR,* p. 137.

246. "Nelson has lost thirty pounds": AAR to WR, April 20, 1944, AAR-WR correspondence, RAC.

247. "After breakfast we settled down": AAR to WR, May 24, 1944, AAR-WR correspondence, RAC.

247. "Laurance puts you off": AAR to DR, December 31, 1943, AAR-DR correspondence, RAC.

247. "I can't tell you how badly": NAR to Jr., December 27, 1942, NAR-Jr. correspondence, RAC.

248. The children's time was measured out: Morris, *NR,* p. 142; Rodman Rockefeller interview.

248. Maine summers: Rodman Rockefeller interview.

248. Tod was always there: Beatrice Berle, Eleanor Clark French, Rodman Rockefeller interviews.

249. Janet Barnes: Richard Aldrich interview.

250. State's distrust: Merwin L. Bohan oral history, HSTL.

250. State memorandum: Quoted in *CIAA History,* p. 254.

250. McClintock memo: McClintock to NAR, June 10, 1942, NAR CIAA Box 4, RAC.

250. "They have very definite ideas": Collier & Horowitz, *The Rockefellers,* p. 233.

251. "Whenever anybody had a new idea": Morris, *NR,* p. 146.

251. Takeover of telephone companies: Report of Interdepartmental Committee on Hemispheric Communications, January 30, 1942. Welles to NAR, April 2, 1942, NAR CIAA Box 4, RAC.

251. Ambitious ten-year plan: CIAA summary report, OF 5300, FDRL.

251. Irate reaction: Draft interagency memo on U.S. economic development policy in the Americas (with NAR's markings), August 26, 1944, NAR CIAA Box 5, RAC.

251. George Messersmith: Jesse H. Stiller, *George S. Messersmith: Diplomat of Democracy* (Chapel Hill: University of North Carolina Press, 1987).

252. "Nelson is not a very clear thinker": Duggan to Messersmith, June 10, 1943, 103.9161/4251, SD-NA.

252. "I have just had a letter": Messersmith to Duggan, July 19, 1943, 103.9161/4467, SD-NA.

252. He formed his own: Stiller, *Messersmith,* p. 182.

252. "Either we are going to run our own": Morris, *NR,* p. 160.

252. A compromise was worked out: Jamieson oral history, COHP.

252. Conflict with Agriculture: *CIAA History,* pp. 210–17; Erb, Ph.D. Thesis, pp. 198–204.

253. Le Cron resignation: James Le Cron oral history, COHP; *NYT,* September 4, 1943.

253. Rockefeller quickly backtracked: *CIAA History,* pp. 216–17.

253. Difficulties with State: Le Cron oral history, COHP; Erb, Ph.D. Thesis, p. 212.

254. A volatile conjunction: Morgan, *FDR,* pp. 677–86.

254. "I cut the s.o.b.'s throat": Ibid., p. 394.

254. Ingratiating himself with Hull: NAR to Hull, April 27, 1943; NAR to Hull, November 13, 1943, NAR CIAA Box 6, RAC.

254. Edward Stettinius: Thomas M. Campbell and George C. Herring, eds., *The Diaries of Edward Stettinius* (New York: New Viewpoints, 1975); Graham & Wander, *Franklin D. Roosevelt,* p. 403.

255. Rockefeller urged him to write a letter: CIAA memo (author unknown), October 11, 1941, NAR CIAA Box 1, RAC.

255. Wallace's conflicts with Jones: Schapsmeier, *Henry A. Wallace and the War Years,* pp. 50–51.

256. Babies were named after him: *NYT,* March 28, 1944.

256. "Today, for the first time": Irwin F. Gellman, *Good Neighbor Diplomacy: United States Policies in Latin America 1933–1945* (Baltimore: Johns Hopkins University Press, 1979), p. 171.

256. Economic development department: *CIAA History,* p. 191.

257. "In no instances": Ibid., p. 171.

257. "The wealth of manpower and experience": NAR to Stettinius, January 7, 1944, NAR CIAA Box 11, RAC.

257. Stettinius made it plain: Stettinius to NAR, January 22, 1944, NAR CIAA Box 11, RAC.

257. McClintock was greeted: NAR to Stettinius, February 9, 1944, NAR CIAA Box 11, RAC.

257. Interdepartmental committee: *CIAA History,* p. 192.

258. IADC conference: Erb, Ph.D. Thesis, pp. 250–53.

258. Bill Benton announced: William Benton oral history, COHP.

258. "Each and every one of them told me": AAR to WR, May 24, 1944, AAR-WR correspondence, RAC.

258. "When you started on this work": Morris, *NR,* pp. 181–82.

259. "Personally, I think two weeks": AAR to WR, June 21, 1944, AAR-WR correspondence, RAC.

259. Letter to Hull: NAR to Hull, September 5, 1944, NAR CIAA Box 11, RAC.

259. He talked about leaving: Chester Bowles to NAR, December 8, 1944, NAR Department of State (DOS) Files, Box 18, RAC.

259. "Rather than have someone": Leon Pearson interview with NAR for International News Service, November 14, 1944, in OF 4512-2, FDRL.

259. "Tired of intrigue": Graham & Wander, *Franklin D. Roosevelt,* p. 194.

260. It was clear he wanted; Friedel, *Franklin D. Roosevelt,* p. 569.

260. Marshall's support: Wallace Diaries, January 7, 1944, COHP.

260. "It was the boss": Morris, *NR,* p. 184.

260. "The trouble is": FDR to Henry Morgenthau, March 7, 1944, Morgenthau Diaries Book 5, FDRL.

18. Changing Course

265. Swearing-in ceremony: Dean Acheson, *Present at the Creation* (New York: Norton, 1969), pp. 90–91.

266. Latin American reaction: "Propaganda analysis," December 5, 1944, NAR Department of State (DOS) Files, Box 18, RAC.

266. Caracas dinner party: Frank P. Corrigan to NAR, December 6, 1944, Corrigan Papers, Box 8, FDRL.

266. "It is very pleasant": AAR to WR, January 15, 1945, AAR-WR correspondence, RAC.

266. Liquidation talk dropped: *CIAA History,* pp. 172–73.

267. Rockefeller's salary: NAR to Lockwood, January 30, 1945, NAR DOS Box 18, RAC.

267. Avra Warren: Obituary, *NYT,* January 24, 1957; Henry L. Feingold, *The Politics of Rescue* (New York: Holocaust Library, 1970); Frank L. Israel, ed., *The War Diary of Breckinridge Long* (Lincoln: University of Nebraska Press, 1966); Collier & Horowitz, *The Rockefellers,* pp. 236–37; Frank Jamieson oral history, COHP; Spruille Braden, *Diplomats and Demagogues* (New Rochelle, N.Y.: Arlington House, 1971), p. 320.

268. Rockefeller intimated to Berle: Berle & Jacobs, *Navigating the Rapids,* p. 512.

268. Helping Braden: Braden to NAR, January 5, January 12, February 14, 1945, Braden Papers, Box 35, Columbia University.

268–69. Confrontation with Messersmith: Messersmith's account is in "Inadequacies of Stettinius as Secretary of State," George Messersmith Papers, University of Delaware.

270. Rockefeller vs. MacLeish: MacLeish to Stettinius, February 26, 1945, MacLeish Papers, Box 21, LC.

270–71. Argentina during the war: Randall Bennett Woods, *The Roosevelt Foreign Policy Establishment and the "Good Neighbor"* (Lawrence: Regents Press of Kansas, 1979); Joseph A. Page, *Perón: A Biography* (New York: Random House, 1983); Ysabel F. Rennie, *The Argentine Republic* (New York: Macmillan, 1945); Gellman, *Good Neighbor Diplomacy,* pp. 190–97.

271. Hull and Argentina: Hull, *Memoirs,* Vol. II, p. 1406.

271. Juan Domingo Perón: Page, *Perón;* Frank Owen, *Perón: His Rise and Fall* (London: Cresset Press, 1957).

271–72. Hull's reaction to Perón: Hull, *Memoirs,* Vol. II, pp. 1402–6.

272. "If Argentina goes on": C. W. Gray memo to Stettinius, August 5, 1944, Cordell Hull Papers, Reel 32, Folder 261, LC.

272. "You make a bad face": Morgan, *FDR,* p. 711.

272. He impishly enjoyed: Sumner Welles, *Seven Decisions That Shaped History* (New York: Harper, 1950), p. 105.

272. He fully backed Hull's measures: "Statement by President Roosevelt with Regard to Argentina," September 30, 1944, Hull Papers, Reel 32, Folder 261, LC.

272. "I do not see": Churchill to FDR, July 1, 1944, Hull Papers, Reel 25, LC.

272. Padilla's conference proposal: His original concept is in George Messersmith to Hull, June 8, 1944, Hull Papers, Box 25, LC.

272. Padilla background: *NYHT,* March 5, 1945.

272. "Argentina can go to hell!": Sumner Welles, *Where Are We Heading?* (New York: Harper, 1946), p. 205.

273. Wallace pushed for sanctions: Gellman, *Good Neighbor Diplomacy,* pp. 192–93.

273. Rockefeller's early hard line: Wallace Diaries, January 7, 1944, COHP.

273. Staff paper on boycott: CIAA research division report, July 1944, NAR CIAA Box 2, RAC.

273. Carrot-and-stick approach: Morris, *NR,* p. 185.

273–74. Rockefeller's new thinking: NAR to Hull, September 7, 1944, NAR CIAA Box 6, RAC.

274. Nonrecognition as "negative": Rafael Oreamuno to NAR, August 8, 1944, NAR CIAA Box 2, RAC.

274. He wrote to Hull again: NAR to Hull, September 7, 1944, NAR CIAA Box 6, RAC.

274. Latin American division on the meeting: "Reasons for a Meeting of Foreign Ministers," September 7, 1944, Hull Papers, Reel 25, LC.

274. Rockefeller urged Hull to accept: NAR to Stettinius, October 31, 1944, NAR CIAA Box 11, RAC.

275. "Until there is a real turnover": Stettinius to FDR, November 21, 1944, PSF Box 75, FDRL.

275. Lunch with ambassadors: Morris, *NR,* p. 190.

275–76. Rockefeller's meetings with FDR: Gellman, *Good Neighbor Diplomacy,* pp. 199–200; Morris, *NR,* pp. 191–93.

276. Two memos: Both, with initialed OK's by FDR, are in NAR CIAA Box 8, RAC.

277. Stettinius had reaffirmed: Stettinius circular telegram to embassies, November 12, 1944, Hull Papers, Reel 26, LC.

277. He hoped to send an emissary: Harrison-NAR, Chapter 3, p. 16, Harrison Papers, Columbia; Gellman, *Good Neighbor Diplomacy,* p. 200.

277. Roosevelt held on: Handwritten notation on top of copy of the memo, PSF Box 23, FDRL.

277. River Plate division refusal: Memo, January 3, 1945, 711.35 NA.

277. "My instructions": Morris, *NR,* p. 194.

277. Meeting with Santos: "Memorandum of Conversation," January 9, 1945, NAR CIAA Box 9, RAC; Eduardo Santos, "My Interviews with President Roosevelt and the Plans of Inter-American Military Organization," *La Democracia Liberal,* March 1947; Harrison-NAR interview, Harrison Papers, Columbia University; Morris, *NR,* pp. 193–94.

278. James Miller letter: James I. Miller to NAR, January 5, 1945, Spruille Braden Papers, Box 2, Columbia University.

279. Change in economic policy: Joseph Grew to FDR, "Economic Policy Toward Argentina," January 12, 1945, NAR DOS Box 19, RAC.

279. Stettinius edict on war declarations: Edward Stettinius Diaries, January 10, 1945, NA.

279. "Neutral" countries' assistance: Norman Armour to Hull, September 18, 1944, Hull Papers, Reel 26, LC.

279. FDR was insistent: State Department memorandum of conversation, November 15, 1944, Pasvolsky Papers, Box 5, LC.

280. "Ed Stettinius made up his mind": Joseph E. Johnson oral history, HSTL.

280. Proposed Mexico City agenda: Stettinius Diaries, January 19, 1945, NA.

280. FDR approved the agenda: NAR to FDR, January 22, 1945, NAR DOS Box 19, RAC.

280. Rockefeller's bombshell: Stettinius Diaries, January 19, 1945, NA.

280. He elaborated on his thinking: NAR to Messersmith, January 19, 1945, *FRUS* 1945, Vol. IX, pp. 11–12.

281. Meeting with Iramain: Drew Pearson, "Washington Merry-Go-Round," *Washington Post,* February 21, 1945.

281. Iramain's report: *NYT,* February 17, 1945.

281. Berle's visit: Berle & Jacobs, *Navigating the Rapids,* p. 521.

282. Yalta and Argentina: Diane Shaver Clemens, *Yalta* (New York: Oxford University Press, 1970); Jim Bishop, *FDR's Last Year* (New York: Morrow, 1974), p. 430.

282. Perón's measures: Erb, Ph.D. Thesis, pp. 326–27; Woods, *Roosevelt Foreign Policy Establishment,* p. 180.

282. Oreamuno's meeting with Perón: Oreamuno cable to NAR, February 18, 1945, NAR DOS Box 19, RAC.

283. Hoover's dossier: J. Edgar Hoover to Harry Hopkins, February 22, 1945, Hopkins Papers, Container 140, FDRL. Hoover furnished a summary of his findings to Hopkins, possibly to impress Hopkins and FDR about the job the FBI was doing in Latin America.

19. Chapultepec

284. Flight to Mexico City: Dudley Bonsal interview.

284. Dr. Kenneth Riland: Susan Herter interview.

284–85. Leo Pasvolsky: Joseph Johnson oral history, HSTL; Gellman, *Good Neighbor Diplomacy,* p. 202.

285. Stettinius and Vargas: Campbell & Herring, *Stettinius Diaries,* pp. 263–65; Stettinius telegram to FDR, February 20, 1945, PSF Box 76, FDRL.

286. Playing poker: Herter interview.

286. Reston and Stettinius: James Reston, *Deadline* (New York: Random House, 1991).

286. Rockefeller's dinner at the embassy: March 14, 1945, secret memo in Leo Pasvolsky Papers, Box 10, LC.

287. Pasvolsky was willing: Pasvolsky's draft account of Mexico City meeting, March 13, 1945, Pasvolsky Papers, Box 11, LC.

287. Stettinius' arrival: Edward Stettinius "Calendar Notes" (diaries), February 20, 1945, Stettinius Papers, Boxes 285–286, University of Virginia. Henceforth referred to as CN.

287. Hotel Genève: T. Philip Terry, *Terry's Guide to Mexico* (Boston and New York: Houghton Mifflin, 1935).

287. Meeting in Stettinius' suite: CN, February 20, 1945.

288. Chapultepec Castle: Terry, *Guide to Mexico,* p. 379; Henry Albert Phillips, *New Designs for Old Mexico* (New York: McBride, 1939).

289. Steering committee scene: *NYT,* February 23, 1945.

289. Opening ceremonies: CN, February 21, 1945; *NYT,* February 23, 1945.

290. Perón-Santos talks: State Department memo on meeting, February 20, 1945, in Stettinius CN files.

291. "The Argentines seem prepared": Text of cable in Stettinius CN files.

291. Approach through Gallagher: Morris, *NR,* p. 195.

291. "The test": "Haunted Castle," *Time,* February 26, 1945.

292. Rockefeller and FBI in Mexico City: Unpublished magazine serialization excerpt of Wallace K. Harrison memoir of NAR, Chapter V, Harrison Papers, Columbia University; Morris, *NR,* pp. 194–95.

292. Monthly FBI sweep of Rockefeller's home: S. S. Alden to D. M. Ladd, January 10, 1945, FBI Files.

293. Quiver of foreboding: "Minutes of Meeting, Hotel Reforma, February 24, 1945," in Stettinius CN files.

293. "The sweep of the Red Army": Duggan, *The Americas,* pp. 116–17.

293. "The Latin American oligarchs": Ibid.

293. Joint Chiefs' endorsement: "Minutes of Meeting, Hotel Reforma, February 24, 1945"; CN, February 24, 1945; Berle & Jacobs, *Navigating the Rapids,* p. 471.

294. Warren Austin: George T. Mazuzon, *Warren P. Austin at the UN* (Kent, Ohio: Kent State University Press, 1977).

294. Austin's fury: Minutes of meeting of U.S. Group on Committee III, February 27, 1945, in Stettinius CN files.

295. "If you're going to work against": Morris, *NR,* p. 197.

295. "E" area lukewarm: Merwin Bohan oral history, HSTL.

295. "Some disappointment": CN, February 27, 1945.

295. "A good speech made by Theodore Roosevelt": Stiller, *Messersmith,* p. 217.

296. Attacks on Pasvolsky: Pasvolsky's notes of February 28, 1945, meeting, Pasvolsky Papers, Box 10, LC.

297. "It's in the bag": Morris, *NR,* p. 196.

297. Wallace on Connally: John Blum, ed., *The Price of Vision* (Boston: Houghton Mifflin, 1973).

297. "Don't try to rush me": Morris, *NR,* p. 196.

297. He begged Reston: Ibid.

298. Senators work on formula: *NYHT,* March 2, 1945.

298. Cable to the President: Top Secret Stettinius to President, March 1, 1945, Stettinius CN files.

298. "Completely beyond his depth": Messersmith memo, "Inadequacies of Stettinius as Secretary of State," Messersmith Papers, University of Delaware.

299. "His cheerful ignorance": Berle & Jacobs, *Navigating the Rapids,* p. 473.

299. "Just a few lines": NAR to Stettinius, February 28, 1945, NAR CIAA Box 11, RAC.

299. Rockefeller's cable to Santos: Santos, "My Interviews with President Roosevelt."

299. "Stettinius' Aides Lauded": *NYT,* March 5, 1945.

300. "You won't believe this": Harrison-NAR, Chapter 3, p. 18.

300. Pasvolsky's backroom negotiations: Pasvolsky account of Mexico City meeting, Pasvolsky Papers, Box 11, LC.

300. Padilla's formula: *NYT,* March 6, 1945.

301. Lleras Camargo grabbed a typewriter: Morris, *NR,* p. 197.

301. "I don't believe you should": Morris, *NR,* p. 198.

302. U.S. delegation meeting: "Notes on Delegation Meeting—March 7, 1945" (Hayden Raynor memo, plus original handwritten notes), in Stettinius CN files.

302. Stettinius at steering committee: "Notes on the Steering Committee Meeting, March 7, 1945," in Stettinius CN files.

303. Rockefeller press conference: Transcript is in Stettinius CN files.

303. Ameghino's statement: *NYT,* March 8, 1945, p. 10.

303–4. Scene at closing of conference: Stettinius' vivid description is in "Notes on Plenary Session, 5:00, March 7, 1945," in Stettinius CN files.

304. Delegates' mood: Erb, Ph.D. Thesis, p. 354.

304. "The most successful meeting": *NYT,* March 10, 1945.

304. "Beyond all doubt": Erb, Ph.D. Thesis, p. 354.

304. "The Act of Chapultepec will provide": Barnet Nover, "Chapultepec and Dumbarton Oaks," *Washington Post,* March 6, 1945.

305. Rockefeller paid tribute: *NYHT,* March 11, 1945.

20. *Welcoming the Pariah*

306. "You have been through a long strain": Stettinius to Rockefeller, March 13, 1945, NAR CIAA Box 11, RAC.

306. Meeting with García: "Argentina Commitment Ignored After F.D.R. Died," *New Bedford* (Mass.) *Standard-Times* series, December 1959.

307. Blair House meeting: Ibid.; "Chronology of Events in the Argentine Situation Since October 1944," Spruille Braden Papers, Box 35, Columbia University.

308. Rockefeller was shocked: "Argentina Commitment"; Morris, *NR,* p. 200.
308. Rockefeller's memorandum: A copy, with FDR's "OK" scrawled on top, is in NAR CIAA Box 9, RAC.
308. He and Tod at the dinner: Bishop, *FDR's Last Year,* p. 682.
308. Bohlen's charge: Charles E. Bohlen, *Witness to History* (New York: Norton, 1973), pp. 206–7.
309. Yalta agreements re Argentina: Clemens, *Yalta,* pp. 235–36; Hull, *Memoirs,* Vol. II, p. 1408.
309. Oliver letter: NAR DOS Box 19, RAC.
310. Feelers were sent out: "Chronology of Events," Braden Papers.
310. "The decision has been taken": UP dispatch, March 27, 1945.
310. Reaction in Argentina: "Entry in War Brings Crisis to Argentina," *NYHT,* April 22, 1945.
311. He gained Stettinius' assent: Stettinius to U.S. Diplomatic Corps in Latin America, March 31, 1945, *FRUS* 1945, Vol. IX, pp. 372–73.
311. Rockefeller's radio broadcast: "Chronology of Events"; Erb, Ph.D. Thesis, p. 370.
311. Berle's telegram: Berle & Jacobs, *Navigating the Rapids,* p. 525.
311. "I am firmly convinced": Reed to Stettinius, April 2, 1945, *FRUS* 1945, Vol. IX, p. 451.
311–12. Argentina's measures: Stettinius to American Diplomats in Latin America, April 4, 1945, ibid., pp. 374–75.
312. Stettinius was insistent: Stettinius CN, April 3, 1945, NA.
312. "He has definitely committed himself": Stettinius CN, April 8, 1945, NA.
312. A buoyant Nelson Rockefeller: Stettinius CN, April 9, 1945, NA.
313. Ameghino summons Reed: Reed to Stettinius, April 13, 1945, *FRUS* 1945, Vol. IX, p. 377.
313. McClintock memo: McClintock to Rockefeller, April 13, 1945, NAR DOS 20, RAC.
314. Fiore confided: Paul Wallin memorandum, April 16, 1945, *FRUS* 1945 Vol. IX, pp. 454–56.
314–15. Avra Warren mission: Warren's full report is in NAR DOS 20, RAC.
315. Oreamuno's conversations with Perón: "Summary of Conversations with Vice President Perón" (attachment to Warren report), April 24, 1945, NAR DOS 20, RAC.
315. "The situation in Argentina": Stettinius CN, April 18, 1945, NA.
316. Rockefeller's memorandum: Stettinius CN, April 17, 1945, NA.
316. "It was the most fascinating meeting": Harrison-NAR Chapter 4, p. 3.
316. "A terrific handshaker": Gellman, *Good Neighbor Diplomacy,* p. 211.
316–17. "There is a commitment": Stettinius CN, April 18, 1945, NA.
317. Memo to Truman: NAR DOS 20, RAC.
317. Truman's reaction: Stettinius CN, April 21, 1945, NA.
318. Stettinius, Eden, and Cadogan: Ibid.
318. Perón's arrests: *NYT,* April 24, 1945.
318. "If we had kept our shirts on": Berle & Jacobs, *Navigating the Rapids,* pp. 530–31.
319. "Nelson's a goner": Lockwood interview.
319. Jamieson's misgivings: Jamieson oral history, pp. 159–63, COHP.

319–20. The "steel shutter look": Susan Herter interview.
320. Reporters surrounded Rockefeller: *NYT*, April 21, 1945.

21. Nineteen Votes

321. Conference scene: *NYHT, NYT*, April 26, 1945.

321–22. Rockefeller's suite: Herter interview; Harry Frantz to Jr., June 13, 1945, NAR DOS Box 21, RAC.

322. Doing the Latins' laundry: Harold Train oral history, COHP.

322. FBI's main function: W. A. Branigan to W. C. Sullivan, January 16, 1964, FBI Files.

322. He made it clear to Tamm: Branigan to Sullivan; Edward Tamm to J. Edgar Hoover, April 28, 1945, FBI Files.

322. "If this works out": Tamm to Hoover, April 28, 1945, FBI Files.

322. "It was anticipated": Ibid.

322–23. Getting a ticket to Rockefeller: Tamm to Hoover, June 4, 1945, FBI Files.

323. Opening ceremonies: *NYT, NYHT*, April 26, 1945; Stettinius CN, April 25, 1945, NA.

324. "Aggressive to the point": Alger Hiss, *Recollections of a Life* (New York: Seaver Books/Henry Holt, 1988), p. 134.

324. "In real life": Walter Lippmann oral history, COHP.

324. "He had small": Stettinius CN, April 30, 1945.

324. Molotov meeting with Truman: David McCullough, *Truman* (New York: Simon & Schuster, 1992), pp. 374–76.

325. "Throughout these days": Stettinius CN, April 26, 1945.

325. "I would have to go home": *FRUS* 1945, Vol. I, p. 383.

326. Delegation's first meeting: *FRUS* 1945, Vol. I, pp. 388–401; Hamilton Fish Armstrong diary, Hamilton Fish Armstrong Papers, Box 173, Princeton University.

326. "He'll just mess everything up": Alger Hiss oral history, COHP.

327. Delegation evening meeting: *FRUS* 1945, Vol. I, pp. 408–13.

328. Truman's reaction: Hamilton Fish Armstrong diary, April 26, 1945; *FRUS* 1945, Vol. I, p. 483.

328. Steering committee meeting: Armstrong diary, April 27, 1945; *NYT*, April 28, 1945.

329. Stettinius' call to Hull: *FRUS* 1945, Vol. I, p. 484; Hull, *Memoirs*, Vol. II, p. 1407.

329. Rockefeller's reminder: *FRUS* 1945, Vol. I, p. 485.

330. Penthouse meeting: "Memorandum of Conversation," April 28, 1945, Pasvolsky Papers, Box 10, LC.

330. Monday's meetings: Stettinius message to the President, May 1, 1945, Hull Papers, Reel 52, LC; *NYT*, May 1, 1945; Stettinius CN, April 30, 1945; Armstrong diary, April 30, 1945; *FRUS* 1945, Vol. I, pp. 500–2.

332. "We've had a great tussle": AAR to WR, May 1, 1945, AAR-WR Correspondence, RAC.

332. *Washington Post* blasts: *Washington Post*, May 1 and May 2, 1945.

332. Lippmann criticism: Walter Lippmann, "Today and Tomorrow," *NYHT*, May 3, 1945.

332. "I remember being there": Walter Lippmann oral history, COHP.

332. Within the U.S. delegation: *NYT,* May 1, 1945.

333. Arthur Vandenberg: Reston, *Deadline;* Ronald Steel, *Walter Lippmann and the American Century* (Boston: Little, Brown, 1980).

333. "This is the best news in months": Arthur H. Vandenberg, Jr., ed., *The Private Papers of Senator Vandenberg* (Boston: Houghton Mifflin, 1952), p. 176.

333. "I don't know whether": Ibid.

333. Vandenberg on Molotov: David Green, *The Containment of Latin America* (Chicago: Quadrangle Books, 1971), p. 221.

333. "Our only friends": *FRUS* 1945, Vol. I, pp. 501–4.

334. "Anything that pleased Mr. Rockefeller": Ibid., p. 504.

334. "Nelson Rockefeller undoubtedly": Stettinius CN, April 27, 1945.

334. Minister's reply: *Washington Post,* May 6, 1945.

334. Lleras Camargo's remark: Allan Dawson to Spruille Braden, October 15, 1945, Spruille Braden Papers, Box 35, Columbia University.

334. Wallace's visit to Hull: Wallace Diaries, May 3, 1945, COHP.

334–35. Dinner with Stevenson: Ibid.

335. Rockefeller's testimony: Wallace Diaries, May 7, May 8, 1945; Richard V. Gilbert to Harry Hopkins, May 8, 1945, Hopkins Papers (Sherwood Collection), Box 338, FDRL.

336. "Rockefeller . . . will provoke": Wallace Diaries, May 7, 1945, COHP.

337. Meeting with Truman: *NYT,* May 4, 1945.

337. Stettinius blew up: "Memorandum of Conversation," Grew and Stettinius, May 4, 1945, Spruille Braden Papers, Box 35, Columbia University.

337–38. Buenos Aires on V-E Day: Joseph Newman, "Blood in Buenos Aires," *Collier's,* July 28, 1945.

338. Braden was surprised: Braden, *Diplomats and Demagogues,* p. 319.

338. Telegram to Rockefeller: Berle and McClintock to NAR, May 1, 1945, 711.35 NA.

338. "I have discussed": NAR to Berle, May 5, 1945, 711.35 NA.

22. *In Self-defense*

339. Latins' meeting with Pasvolsky: Memorandum of conversation, May 5, 1945, Pasvolsky Papers, Box 11, LOC.

340. Rockefeller-Vandenberg dinner: Vandenberg, Jr., *Private Papers,* pp. 187–88; Harrison-NAR, Chapter 4, pp. 5–6; Susan Herter interview (Herter was the secretary present at the dinner); Morris, *NR,* pp. 216–18.

341. Stettinius phoned Rockefeller: Summary of phone conversations, May 6, 1945, Stettinius Papers, Box 292, University of Virginia.

341–42. Dulles' fury: Harrison-NAR, Chapter 4, p. 6; Morris, *NR,* p. 218.

342. Meeting in Bowman's room: Memorandum, May 6, 1945, Armstrong Papers, Box 51, Princeton University.

342. May 7 delegation meeting: *FRUS* 1945, Vol. I, pp. 617–26; Armstrong diary; Stettinius diary.

343. May 8 meeting with ministers: Stettinius diary; Armstrong diary.

344. "He'll get me in the same trap": Harrison-NAR, Chapter 4, p. 6; Harrison interview with NAR.

344. "This way we'll find out": Harrison interview with NAR.

344. Dinner with Stassen: Harold Stassen interview; Harrison interview with NAR; Morris, *NR,* pp. 219–20.

344. Stassen memo: NAR DOS Box 21, RAC.

345. "It's interesting": *FRUS* 1945, Vol. I, p. 660.

345. Lippmann column: *NYHT,* May 10, 1945.

345. *Washington Post* editorial: May 11, 1945.

345. Vandenberg on Stettinius: Vandenberg, Jr., *Private Papers,* pp. 191–92.

345–46. "Vandenberg came in": Off-the-record conversation on origins of Cold War, May 31, 1967, Averell Harriman Papers, Box 869, LC.

346. "One of the most underrated": Ibid.

346. A U.S. delegate felt humiliated: James Reston to Arthur Krock (n.d.), Arthur Krock Papers, Book 1, Princeton University.

346. "What'll I do?": Escott Reid, *On Duty: A Canadian at the Making of the United Nations 1945–46* (Kent, Ohio: Kent University Press, 1983), p. 41.

346. "He is a total misfit": Memoirs of the San Francisco conference, Charles Darlington Papers, Box 5, HSTL.

346. "The time has arrived": Stettinius diary, May 11, 1945; *FRUS* 1945, Vol. I, p. 666.

347–48. Lockwood's meetings: Unidentified Special Agent to Edward Tamm (internal FBI memo), May 11, 1945, FBI Files.

348. "Several times recently": Stanley Tracy to J. Edgar Hoover, June 21, 1945, FBI Files.

349. Remarks to Peruvians: Wallace Harrison unpublished magazine article, "The Battle of San Francisco," pp. 12–13; Morris, *NR,* pp. 223–24.

350. Vandenberg had concluded: Armstrong diary, May 14, 1945; *FRUS* 1945, Vol. I, p. 708.

350. Meeting with Latin Americans: Stettinius diary, May 14, 1945; memorandum on meeting, May 14, 1945, Pasvolsky Papers, Box 10, LC; *FRUS* 1945, Vol. I, pp. 712–19.

351. May 15 U.S. delegation meeting: Stettinius diary; Armstrong diary; *FRUS* 1945, Vol. I, pp. 719–25.

352. Call to Oval Office: Campbell & Herring, *Stettinius Diaries,* pp. 368–70.

352. May 15 meeting with Latin Americans: Stettinius diary; Armstrong diary; *FRUS* 1945, Vol. I, pp. 730–36.

353. Meeting with Big Five: Memorandum of meeting, May 15, 1945, Pasvolsky Papers, Box 10, LC.

353–54. Dulles on Article Fifty-one: John Foster Dulles, *War or Peace* (New York: Macmillan, 1950), p. 92.

354. "I owe you an apology": Morris, *NR,* p. 227.

354. 1949 Vandenberg letter: Vandenberg to NAR, April 28, 1949, Vandenberg Collection, University of Michigan.

23. *Endgame*

355. Dinner for Padilla: Transcript in NAR DOS Box 21, RAC.

355. Rockefeller whispered to Armstrong: Armstrong diary, May 20, 1945, Armstrong Papers, Princeton.

355. Rockefeller phoned his mother: AAR to WR, May 21, 1945, RAC.

355–56. Whispering instructions to Belt: Morris, *NR,* p. 208.

356. "Cracking the whip": Allan Dawson to Spruille Braden, October 15, 1945, Braden Papers, Box 35, Columbia University.

356. Costa Rican minister: Ibid.

356. "The 'veto' is bad enough": Vandenberg, Jr., *Private Papers,* p. 196.

357. "We're up against a buzz saw": *FRUS* 1945, Vol. I, p. 842; Stettinius diaries, May 22, 1945.

357. Memo on veto: NAR to Stettinius, May 22, 1945, NAR DOS 21, RAC.

357. Stettinius asked him point-blank: Stettinius diary, May 26, 1945.

357. An anxious Stettinius wanted to know: *FRUS* 1945, Vol. I, pp. 1246–47.

358. Rockefeller-Stettinius exchange: Ibid.

358. Rockefeller and Warren joined in: Edward Tamm to J. Edgar Hoover, May 19, 1945, FBI Files.

358. Stettinius phoned him: Summary of phone conversation, May 7, 1945, Stettinius Papers, Box 292, University of Virginia.

359. Original draft of Stettinius speech: Archibald MacLeish to Spruille Braden, May 24, 1945, MacLeish Papers, Box 21, LC.

359. Rockefeller's memos to Stettinius: NAR DOS Box 22, RAC.

360. Hull's meeting with Krock: Krock private memorandum, May 26, 1945, Krock Papers, Book I, pp. 158–59, Princeton.

360. Stettinius phoned Grew: Green, *Containment of Latin America,* pp. 237–38.

361. Rockefeller and Warren's FBI getaway: D. M. Ladd to E. A. Tamm, June 5, 1945, FBI Files.

362. Rockefeller's private intelligence: John McClintock to NAR, June 8, 1945, NAR DOS Box 20, RAC.

362. Brazilians were incensed: Berle & Jacobs, *Navigating the Rapids,* p. 538.

362. Martins collared Rockefeller: Ibid., p. 537.

363. "My personal feeling": NAR to Stettinius, June 21, 1945, NAR DOS Box 20, RAC.

363. Rockefeller's party: Harry W. Frantz to Kathleen Frantz, June 19, 1945, NAR DOS Box 21, RAC.

363. Carmen Miranda stormed in: Susan Herter interview.

364. He offered the use of Foxhall Road: AAR to WR, July 7, 1945, RAC.

364. No room on the plane: Summary of phone conversation, June 22, 1945, Stettinius Papers, Box 245, University of Virginia.

364. Allen's visit: Campbell & Herring, *Stettinius Diaries,* pp. 398–401.

365. Were he a free agent today: Armstrong diaries, June 25, 1945, Armstrong Papers, Box 53, Princeton.

365. "He's a fellow": Armstrong diaries, June 27, 1945, Armstrong Papers, Box 53, Princeton.

366. "It is said": Acheson, *Present at the Creation,* p. 110.

366. He confessed to his mother: AAR to WR, July 2, 1945, RAC.

366. "He was simply exhausted": AAR to WR, July 10, 1945.

366. "Young Nelson Rockefeller": *New Republic,* July 2, 1945, pp. 9–11.

367. Braden and Perón: *FRUS* 1945, Vol. IX, pp. 508–11; Braden, *Diplomats and Demagogues,* pp. 328–30.

368. "You are instructed": *FRUS* 1945, Vol. IX, pp. 513–14.

368. "Simply delighted": Transcript of phone conversation, July 6, 1945, NAR DOS Box 20, RAC.

368. "I told him": AAR to WR, July 25, 1945, RAC.

369. Approach to Hull: Alsop, *Nixon and Rockefeller,* p. 89.

369. "There are many things": NAR to Grew, August 1, 1945, 711.35 NA.

369–70. Meeting with businessman: Memorandum of meeting, August 3, 1945, 835.00 NA.

370. Push for Rockefeller on Capitol Hill: *NYT,* August 14, 1945.

370. Acheson's talk with Byrnes: Acheson, *Present at the Creation,* p. 119.

371. "I have just gotten word": NAR to MacLeish, August 17, 1945, MacLeish Papers, Box 6, LC.

371. "Events in Argentina": NAR to Byrnes, August 21, 1945, 711.35 NA.

371. Meeting with Byrnes: Morris, *NR,* p. 230; Alsop, *Nixon and Rockefeller,* p. 90.

371–72. Rockefeller's speech: NAR DOS Box 20, RAC.

372. "Last diplomatic backflip": *The Inter-American,* October 1945.

372. Meeting with Truman: Desmond, *Nelson Rockefeller,* p. 132.

372. "I feel as though a great burden": AAR to WR, August 28, 1945, RAC.

373. "Poor dear": AAR to WR, September 4, 1945, RAC.

24. The Next Conspiracy

377. He lent the house to Benton: Sidney Hyman, *The Lives of William Benton* (Chicago: University of Chicago Press, 1969), p. 316.

377. Helping Winthrop: AAR to WR, September 6, 1945, RAC.

378. Letters to Rockefeller: NAR DOS Box 18, RAC.

378. Forrestal letter: Forrestal to Jr., September 7, 1945, James Forrestal Papers, Box 64, Princeton.

379. "I'm a great believer": "What Makes Rockefeller Run?" *American Weekly,* November 1, 1959.

379. Pinnacle of the free world: Jan Morris, *Manhattan '45* (New York: Oxford University Press, 1987).

379. Nelson's return to 5600: Moscow, *Rockefeller Inheritance,* pp. 7–11.

380. "They descended on the office": Ibid., p. 7.

380. "We have done everything possible": NAR to Jr., June 14, 1946, RAC.

380. "Gee, Pa": Moscow, *Rockefeller Inheritance,* p. 17.

381. They agreed to act: Harr & Johnson, *Rockefeller Century,* p. 423.

381. "As you can well imagine": Turnbull to NAR, January 4, 1946, Business Interests, Box 70, RAC.

381. Victory Clothing Committee: Vera Goeller interview.

381. UJA committee: Edward Warburg interview; Goeller interview.

381. "I am glad to see": Morris, *NR,* p. 6.

382. Repudiating Rockefeller's legacy: Braden, *Diplomats and Demagogues,* pp. 356–58.

383. "I felt pretty well informed": "Nelson Now," *New York,* September 25, 1978.

383. Medal of Merit campaign: Anna Rosenberg Hoffman Papers, Box 1, Folder 56, Schlesinger Library, Radcliffe College.

383. "I learned my lesson": "Nelson Now."

383. United Nations site: John Lockwood interview; Jamieson oral history, COHP; Harrison-NAR, Chapter 5, pp. 7–14; DR interview; George Dudley interview; Gilmor Clark oral history, COHP; Wallace Harrison profile, *New Yorker,* December 4, 1954; "How the U.N. Found Its Home at Last," *Reader's Digest,* May 1947; Raymond Fosdick conversations with Jr., RAC; William Zeckendorf with Edward McCreary, *Zeckendorf* (New York: Holt, Rinehart and Winston, 1970), pp. 65–71; Robert Moses, *Public Works: A Dangerous Trade* (New York: McGraw-Hill, 1970), pp. 483–91; Robert Caro, *The Power Broker* (New York: Vintage, 1975), pp. 771–74; Newhouse, *Harrison,* pp. 104–13; Harr & Johnson, *Rockefeller Century,* p. 432.

387. "I just couldn't imagine": Harold Haskell interview.

388. Rebuffed by Gumbel: Kershaw Burbank interview.

388. "Mr. Rockefeller, Jr., was like a sun": Collier & Horowitz, *The Rockefellers,* p. 246.

388. "The public relations position": Ibid., p. 259.

388. Lockwood's appointment: Lockwood interview.

389. Junior's gifts: Harr & Johnson, *Rockefeller Century,* pp. 472–73.

389. "The matter we discussed": NAR to Jr., October 24, 1942, RAC.

389. Junior's new willingness: DR interview; LSR interview; Harr & Johnson, *Rockefeller Century,* pp. 479–80.

390. Nelson tried to boost its value: Harr & Johnson, *Rockefeller Century,* p. 482.

392. Winthrop and Mary Martin: Tex McCrary interview.

392. Winthrop and Bobo: Moscow, *Rockefeller Inheritance,* pp. 206–10; Harr & Johnson, *Rockefeller Century,* p. 474.

394. "We all did push-ups": Steven Rockefeller–Morrow interview.

394. "Our lives were actually": Collier & Horowitz, *The Rockefellers,* p. 520.

394. "If they wanted extra money": "Mr. and Mrs. Nelson Rockefeller," *Ladies' Home Journal,* November 1959.

395. "She has got into her mind": AAR to NAR, August 4, 1941, RAC.

395. Steven once disappeared: Pyle, *Pocantico,* p. 168.

395. Michael and the servants: AAR to WR, June 28, 1944, RAC.

395. Rodman in the school play: *New York Post,* February 12, 1941.

395. Kidnapping threat: E. E. Conroy to J. Edgar Hoover, November 26, 1945, FBI Files.

395. Training his daughters: L. B. Nichols to Clyde Tolson, January 23, 1953, FBI Files.

396. Bringing Rodman along: Rodman Rockefeller interview.

396. "I don't think": Eleanor Harris, "What Makes Rockefeller Run?" *American Weekly,* November 1, 1959.

396. "His presence was always": Steven Rockefeller–Morrow interview.

396–97. Tod and Bellevue School of Nursing: Morris, *NR,* p. 97.

397. She drove herself around town: E. E. Conroy to J. Edgar Hoover, November 26, 1945, FBI Files.

397. "Dressmakers stick pins in you": "Mr. and Mrs. Nelson Rockefeller."

397. She enrolled in the Liberal Party: Hearst Columnist Westbrook Pegler reported on November 27, 1959, that Tod, through her secretary, admitted to him in writing that she had so registered in 1946. "Previously and subsequently," the secretary wrote, "Mrs. Rockefeller registered as a member of the Republican Party."

397. Wedding anniversary celebration: James Wallis interview.

397. She took the dance floor: Francis Horn interview.

397. "People can really get close to each other": "Mr. and Mrs. Nelson Rockefeller."

397–98. Tod's tangles with Junior: Pyle, *Pocantico,* pp. 169–74.

398. "You couldn't change her mind": Nadia Williams interview.

398. "No one in the entire family": Pyle, *Pocantico,* p. 166.

399. Harrison's appointment: Memo of Harrison talk with *Architectural Record,* March 5, 1947, Harrison Papers, Columbia; Newhouse, *Harrison,* p. 113.

399. "One good thing about Wally": Max Abramovitz interview.

399. "Let's go ahead with it": Harmon Goldstone interview.

399. "In this world": Harrison profile, *New Yorker,* November 20, 1954.

399. Two sides of Harrison: Goldstone interview.

400. Harrison's apartment: NAR to Harrison, May 21, 1948, Harrison Papers, Columbia.

400. Trust fund for Sarah: Oscar Ruebhausen interview; Newhouse, *Harrison,* p. 259.

400. "Bill, I want to tell you": Anna Rosenberg Hoffman Papers, Box 1, Schlesinger Library, Radcliffe College.

400. Anna Rosenberg's work for Rockefeller: Thomas Rosenberg interview.

400. Smuggling in booze: Ibid.

401. Rosenberg an irritant: Oscar Ruebhausen interview.

401. Rockefeller and Tom Braden: Thomas Braden interview.

402. "I learned": Ruebhausen interview.

402. Louise Robbins Boyer: Obituary, *NYT,* July 4, 1974; Susan Herter, Kershaw Burbank, William Alton, Vera Goeller interviews.

404. "Nelson Rockefeller gave you the feeling": Persico, *The Imperial Rockefeller,* p. 110.

25. *Miraculous Mandarin*

405. Rockefeller's visit to Rio: *Brazilian Bulletin,* December 1, 1946; *Business Week,* January 4, 1947; Martha Dalrymple, *The AIA Story* (New York: American International Association, 1968), pp. 31–32.

406. Concept of AIA: Frank Corrigan to NAR, November 21, 1944; July 21, 1945; NAR to Corrigan, November 17, 1945, AIA-IBEC Files, Box 1, RAC.

407. "He is generally favorably inclined": NAR to Corrigan, September 26, 1945, AIA-IBEC Box 1, RAC.

407. Rockefeller sketched out a program: His original jottings on a legal pad are in AIA-IBEC Box 1, RAC.

407. Statement of principles: Lockwood to NAR, April 8, 1946, AIA-IBEC Box 1, RAC.

407. Letter to Junior: NAR to Jr., April 27, 1946, AIA-IBEC Box 11, RAC.

408. "He said that he was himself": Quoted in Harr & Johnson, *Rockefeller Century,* p. 434.

408. "You have to realize": Lockwood interview.

408. Flap with deputy secretary of state: Wayne G. Broehl, Jr., *The International Basic Economy Corporation* (New York: National Planning Association, 1968).

409. They sneered: John W. Brice memo (undated), AIA-IBEC Box 1, RAC.

409. Venezuelan coup: John V. Lombardi, *Venezuela: The Search for Order, the Dream of Progress* (New York: Oxford University Press, 1982), pp. 221–24.

409. Betancourt and the oil companies: Edwin Lieuwen, *Venezuela* (London: Oxford University Press, 1969), pp. 69–98.

409. A sound business move: Memo on December 17, 1946, meeting in NAR's office, AIA-IBEC Box 1, RAC.

409. "Greater security": Undated memo from Standard of New Jersey foreign marketing department, AIA-IBEC Box 1, RAC.

410. Rockefeller was looking for: December 17, 1946, memo, op. cit.

410. The oil companies attached: Broehl, *IBEC,* p. 18.

410. Malnutrition in Venezuela: Ibid., p. 16.

410. Rampant inflation: *NYT,* December 14, 1945.

411. Stacy May's report: Lockwood interview.

411. "Increasing the supply": Outline of IBEC-AIA program in Venezuela, AIA-IBEC Box 11, RAC.

411. "Sound paying basis": NAR handwritten comments on draft memo of IBEC purposes, March 15, 1947, AIA-IBEC Box 11, RAC.

411. "It's got to pay": *St. Louis Post-Dispatch,* June 8, 1947.

412. Faced with bankruptcy: Jr. to Philip Keebler, May 7, 1942; Jr. to NAR, May 26, 1942, Business Interests, Box 110, RAC.

412. He extracted a commitment: NAR to Jr., July 1, 1942, Business Interests, Box 110, RAC.

412. Nelson balked: NAR to Jr., May 29, 1944, Business Interests, Box 110, RAC.

412. Creole intervened: William Coles memorandum, July 28, 1944, Business Interests, Box 110, RAC.

412. Junior forced to eat: Jr. memorandum, January 24, 1947; Barton Turnbull to NAR, January 24, 1947, Business Interests, Box 110, RAC.

413. Meeting with Betancourt: NAR's full account of his trip, evidently jotted while it was going on or just after his return, is in AIA-IBEC Box 9, RAC.

414. Details of IBEC's early Venezuelan operations are in Broehl, *IBEC,* pp. 26–41.

416. He even talked about retiring: AAR to WR, October 14, 1947, RAC.

416. Joint venture with Kleberg: John Camp interview.

416. "Who is silly enough": Quoted in Morris, *NR,* p. 259.

416. Rockefeller's trip to Venezuela: Harold Haskell interview; Morris, *NR,* pp. 254–56; Morris, *Those Rockefeller Brothers,* pp. 220–22.

418. "If VBEC can pay": H. T. Galey to Chester Crabbe, August 21, 1947, AIA-IBEC Box 11, RAC.

418. "They reflected very much": NAR to John Camp, September 15, 1947, AIA-IBEC Box 11, RAC.

418. Alton's report: AIA-IBEC Box 1, RAC; Alton interview.

419. He promised: NAR to Camp, September 15, 1947.

419. IBEC Housing start-up: George Dudley interview; Newhouse, *Harrison,* pp. 77–78.

420. Brazilian start-ups: Broehl, *IBEC,* pp. 50–73.

420. Pig iron: December 1, 1947, memo, AIA-IBEC Box 11, RAC.

420. Dry ice plant: December 5, 1947, memo, AIA-IBEC Box 11, RAC.

420. "Zeckendorf had a new idea": Oscar Ruebhausen interview.

420. Migration scheme: Alton interview.

421. "Nelson Rockefeller is having more fun": *Newsweek,* March 15, 1948.

26. A Bigger Program

422. Drive up with Nelson: Chase, *Abby Aldrich Rockefeller,* p. 157.

422. Weekend at Pocantico: Ibid., pp. 157–58.

423. Early the next morning: JDR3 diary entry cited in Harr & Johnson, *Rockefeller Century,* p. 468.

423. "Father was terribly hard hit": Ibid.

423. "It was as though": Kert, *Abby Aldrich Rockefeller,* p. 472.

423. "I can remember": Steven Rockefeller–Morrow interview.

424. Abby's burial: Moscow, *Rockefeller Inheritance,* p. 209.

424. He invited the staff: Collier & Horowitz, *The Rockefellers,* p. 335.

424. Presents to grandchildren: Moscow, *Rockefeller Inheritance,* p. 209.

424. "The lovely calla lilies": Jr. to JDR3 and Blanchette Rockefeller, April 11, 1950, JDR3 Box 3 Confidential File, RAC.

424. Trip to Brazil: DR interview; Walther Moreira Salles interview.

425. Genesis of ACAR: Dalrymple, *The AIA Story,* pp. 40–44; Elizabeth Anne Cobbs, "Good Works at a Profit: Private Development and U.S.–Brazil Relations, 1945–1966," Ph.D. Thesis, Stanford University, 1988, pp. 118–21.

425. New Deal parallels: Robert Hudgens oral history, COHP.

426. "He is genuinely interested": James Le Cron to Robert Hudgens, August 8, 1947, Robert Hudgens Papers, Box 18, Duke University.

426. The man, the girl, the jeep: Harry Bagley interview; Dalrymple, *The AIA Story,* p. 43.

426. ACAR's broader concerns: Cobbs, "Good Works," pp. 123–24.

426. Every loan was repaid: Dalrymple, *The AIA Story,* p. 43.

426. ACAR's success: Cobbs, "Good Works," pp. 132–34.

426. Kubitschek and ACAR: Dalrymple, *The AIA Story,* pp. 56–58.

427. John's help: NAR to JDR3, December 31, 1948, Economic Interests, Box 1, RAC.

427. Meeting with Coca-Cola: Hudgens oral history, COHP.

427. Note to Truman: NAR to Truman, November 4, 1948, PPF 689, HSTL.

428. Hardy's meetings with Rockefeller: Morris, *NR,* p. 271.

428. Hardy's intervention: Clark Clifford, *Counsel to the President* (New York: Random House, 1991), pp. 248–50; Ken Hechler, *Working with Truman* (New York: Putnam, 1982), pp. 115–17.

428. Hardy memo: "Use of U.S. Technological Resources as a Weapon in the Struggle with International Communism," December 15, 1948, IDAB Box 39, RAC.

429. "I'm not sure": Hechler, *Working with Truman,* p. 116.

429. "One reading convinced me": Clifford, *Counsel,* p. 250.

429. Truman's reaction: Hechler, *Working with Truman,* p. 118; Harry S. Truman, *Memoirs,* Vol. II (New York: Doubleday, 1956), pp. 231–33; Margaret Truman, *Harry S. Truman* (New York: Morrow, 1973).

430. Acheson pronounced: Clifford, *Counsel,* p. 251.

431. "Your inauguration speech": NAR to Truman, January 24, 1949, PPF 200, HSTL.

431. "He certainly has done": Note scribbled on top of Jamieson memo re Hardy memo, November 17, 1950, IDAB Box 39, RAC.

431. "I can't tell you": Truman, *Memoirs,* Vol. II, p. 231.

432. NAR's meeting with Truman: Eben Ayers to Matthew Connally, February 2, 1949, Truman to NAR, February 17, 1949, PPF Box 1460, HSTL; Morris, *NR,* p. 272.

432. Praise of Point Four: *NYT,* October 1, 1949; CIAA Box 8, RAC.

432. Rockefeller and the new regime: NAR to Walter J. Donnelly, July 13, 1949, AIA-IBEC Box 5, RAC.

433. Rockefeller identified Moses: George Dudley interview.

433. Moses was willing: Caro, *The Power Broker,* p. 1060.

433. He distributed the money: Ibid., p. 1070.

433. "To buy other men": Ibid., p. 812.

433. Receiving the minister: Dudley interview.

433. Caracas report: Moses, *Public Works,* pp. 791–94.

433. Problems of highway: Documented in various memoranda in AIA-IBEC Box 5, RAC.

434. Plan for São Paulo: Moses, *Public Works,* pp. 797–805; Moses report to IBEC, January 20, 1950, AIA-IBEC Box 5, RAC.

434. "Mr. Moses should be watched": Minutes of meeting, September 22, 1950, AIA-IBEC Box 22, RAC.

434. Norfolk construction: *Life,* October 10, 1949; Dudley interview; Broehl, *IBEC,* p. 205; Newhouse, *Harrision,* p. 78; Morris, *Those Rockefeller Brothers,* p. 178.

435. IBEC plagues: Alton interview; Broehl, *IBEC,* p. 29.

435. Floods: Had Rockefeller done his homework, he would have learned that such climatic extremes in that region were the norm. The vast grassy plains were "flooded in the wet months and bone dry the rest of the year." William Russell, *The Bolivar Countries* (New York: Coward-McCann, 1949), p. 223.

436. "If the Venezuelan papers": Jamieson oral history, COHP.

436. Venezuelan corruption: John Camp interview; Edward Kimball interview.

436. Fishermen's scam: Kimball interview; Broehl, *IBEC,* p. 34.

437. Finicky consumers: Alton interview; Broehl, *IBEC,* p. 31.

437. Retailers kept the profits: Broehl, *IBEC,* p. 38.

437. Machold's report: Machold to NAR, July 1, 1949, AIA-IBEC Box 10, RAC.

438. Lockwood appointment: NAR to Berent Friele, July 27, 1949, AIA-IBEC Box 24, RAC.

438. "Coles is a persistent amateur": Lockwood to NAR, November 22, 1949, AIA-IBEC Box 24, RAC.

439. Reporting to Junior: Lockwood interview.

439. Political pressures: Broehl, *IBEC,* p. 42.

439. Rockefeller flew to Venezuela: Ibid., p. 30.

440. INLACA success: Kimball interview; *Caracas Journal,* April 23, 1955.

440. Supermarket opening: *Journal of Commerce,* January 5, 1950; *Christian Science Monitor,* September 23, 1952; Kimball interview; Broehl, *IBEC,* pp. 88–89.

440. Hybrid corn: Broehl, *IBEC,* pp. 52–53; Cobbs, "Good Works," pp. 182–83.

440. Venezuelans wanted out: Broehl, *IBEC,* p. 42.

440. Fomento's stake, Rockefeller's exposure: Figures cited in Jr. to NAR, February 24, 1950, Economic Interests, Box 2, RAC.

441. Letter to father: NAR to Jr., February 7, 1950, Economic Interests, Box 2, RAC.

442. Junior's response: Jr. to NAR, February 24, 1950, Economic Interests, Box 2, RAC.

443. When he recounted: Joan Braden interview.

443. He applied for a bank loan: Memo of meeting, March 15, 1950, AIA-IBEC Box 22, RAC; NAR to Lockwood, October 10, 1950, AIA-IBEC Box 24, RAC.

443. Lockwood's talks: Lockwood to NAR, March 18, 1950, AIA-IBEC Box 24, RAC.

444. Rockefeller's optimistic reports: NAR to Robert G. Fulton, Jr., July 13, 1950; NAR to Lockwood, August 30, 1950, AIA-IBEC Box 10, RAC.

27. *Debacle*

445. Dinner at Rockefeller's: Appointment File, W. Averell Harriman Papers, Box 279, LC; Memo on dinner, IDAB Box 26, RAC; Jamieson agenda, IDAB Box 27, RAC; Morris, *NR,* p. 274.

445. Averell Harriman: Rudy Abramson, *Spanning the Century: The Life of W. Averell Harriman 1891–1986* (New York: Morrow, 1992).

447. "He was not inconsiderate": Ibid., p. 271.

447. "We were really making a lot": Dean Acheson oral history, HSTL.

447. "It seems to me": Clifford, *Counsel,* p. 253.

448. "No action": Quoted in "Effect of the Reported Point IV Appropriations Cut," July 7, 1950, Harriman Papers, Box 309, LC.

448. Contemplating shutting AIA: NAR to Lockwood, August 30, 1950, AIA-IBEC Box 24, RAC.

448. "This field is a government field": Ibid.

448. Meeting with Truman: Eben Ayers memo, July 14, 1950, OF 87, HSTL; Morris, *NR,* p. 273.

448. Acheson deflected the suggestion: Memorandum of conversation, July 24, 1950, Dean Acheson Papers, HSTL.

448. "Memorandum on Groups": IDAB Box 38, RAC.

450. Rockefeller prepared himself: "Things to Discuss with the President," October 10, 1950, IDAB Box 35, RAC.

450. Truman was agreeable: Theodore Tannenwald, Jr., to Donald Dawson, November 20, 1950, OF 87, HSTL; Oscar Ruebhausen to NAR, November 21, 1950, IDAB Box 35, RAC.

451. "Very quiet": NAR memo, October 10, 1950, IDAB Box 38, RAC.

452. Lubell received $5,000. Jamieson to NAR, February 2, 1951, IDAB Box 31, RAC.

452. Ruebhausen's link: Oscar Ruebhausen interview.

453. Lubell snapped: Ibid.

454. Rockefeller's key points: Minutes of meeting, November 16, 1950, IDAB Box 27, RAC.

455. "Political, psychological": NAR handwritten outline of report, IDAB Box 31, RAC.

455. Jamieson warned: Minutes of meeting, November 16, 1950, IDAB Box 27, RAC.

455. "We should tone down": Minutes of meeting, December 13, 1950, IDAB Box 29, RAC.

455. "In November–early December": R. N. Johnson to Harriman, February 16, 1951, IDAB Box 31, RAC.

456. TCA official's question: Minutes of IDAB meeting April 16, 1951, IDAB Box 29, RAC.

456. Savage's reports: NAR to John Savage, January 26, 1951, IDAB Box 25, RAC.

456. He prodded his task forces: Minutes of meeting, November 14, 1950, IDAB Box 27, RAC.

457. "I think the time has come": NAR to Jamieson, December 20, 1950, IDAB Box 30, RAC.

457. "NAR without question is": Fred Gardner to Jamieson, December 4, 1950, IDAB Box 30, RAC.

457. Rockefeller's Washington visits: Morris, *NR*, p. 277.

457. "We might be helpful to the cause": Ruebhausen to Jamieson, December 22, 1950, IDAB Box 35, RAC.

458. Ruebhausen's draft: IDAB Box 27, RAC.

458. Meeting with Truman: NAR to Harvey Firestone, January 18, 1951; NAR to Lewis Hines, January 18, 1951, IDAB Box 25, RAC.

458–59. Johnson hectored Rockefeller: Summary of remarks at February 10, 1951, IDAB meeting, IDAB Box 29, RAC.

459. "Economic offensive": Johnson to Harriman, February 16, 1951, IDAB Box 31, RAC.

459. "I gave this to Averell": Johnson to NAR, February 20, 1951, IDAB Box 31, RAC.

459. "Bright ideas": Lincoln Gordon to Harriman, February 23, 1951, Harriman Papers Box 310, LC.

459. He warned the President: NAR reported on the meeting at the March 2, 1951, IDAB meeting, IDAB Box 28, RAC.

459. All-night session: Ruebhausen interview.

460. "Good report": Johnson to Harriman, March 8, 1951, Harriman Papers, Box 310, LC.

460. Rockefeller's choreography: David Lloyd to Charles Murphy, February 28, 1951, OF 20-U, HSTL; Ruebhausen to Lloyd, March 5, 1951, David Lloyd Files, Box 5, HSTL.

460. Jamieson warned Rockefeller: Jamieson to NAR, March 7, 1951, IDAB Box 35, RAC.

460. Harriman intervened: Morris, *NR,* p. 278.

461. Citizen's Committee: Memos on its creation are in IDAB Box 25, RAC.

461. Simon & Schuster deal: Jamieson to Tom Braden, March 28, 1951, IDAB Box 27, RAC; Jamieson to NAR, June 1, 1951, IDAB Box 34, RAC.

461. Rockefeller ended up buying: Rockefeller office memo, April 28, 1954, IDAB Box 34, RAC.

461. "I have heard nothing but": Harriman to NAR, April 9, 1951, IDAB Box 33, RAC.

461. Meeting with Thorp: Memo on meeting, April 16, 1951, IDAB Box 29, RAC.

462. Sawyer's letter: Charles Sawyer to HST, March 16, 1951, OF 20-U, HSTL.

462. "I think your analysis": HST to Sawyer, March 26, 1951, OF 20-U, HSTL.

463. His aides urged him: Lincoln Gordon to Harriman, May 2, 1951, Harriman Papers, Box 310, LC.

463. He barnstormed the country: Details of the trip are in IDAB Box 38, RAC. Also see José Figueres Ferrer oral history, HSTL.

463. He spoke extemporaneously: Stanford University address, June 19, 1951, IDAB Box 38, RAC.

464. He appeared as a private citizen: NAR to IDAB members, July 27, 1951, IDAB Box 27, RAC.

464. Its true motivation: *NYT,* August 3, 1951.

464. Military-economic aid link: *NYT,* July 18, 1951; NAR to Stringfellow Barr, July 25, 1951, IDAB Box 27, RAC.

465. Totally compatible with Harriman's: Mark Chadwin interview with Lincoln Gordon (for Harriman's memoirs), Harriman Papers, Box 868, LC.

465. He phoned Potofsky: Jacob Potofsky oral history, COHP.

466. Lockwood dissuaded him: Lockwood to NAR, October 16, 1951.

28. *Diversions*

468. 13 West 54th Street: Harr & Johnson, *Rockefeller Century,* pp. 97–98.

468. "A very homey place": Raymond Fosdick, "Conversations with John D. Rockefeller, Junior," RAC.

469. Nelson wrote his father: NAR to Jr., June 27, 1946, Jr. Real Estate Investments, Box 29, RAC.

469. "Mr. Nelson Rockefeller": Richard J. Cronan to Lester Abberley, July 11, 1947, Jr. Real Estate Investments, Box 29, RAC.

469. Dining room: Berle & Jacobs, *Navigating the Rapids,* p. 599.

470. His guest confessed: Joan Braden, *Just Enough Rope* (New York: Villard Books, 1989), p. 42.

470. Joan Ridley's background: Kathy Stroud, "The Bradens' Washington Salon: The Politics of Their Parties," *New York,* February 17, 1975; Braden, *Just Enough Rope,* pp. 10–14.

470. First meeting with Rockefeller: Joan Braden interview.

471. Rockefeller phoned her: Ibid.

472. "I thought he was quite moral": Nadia Williams interview.

473. Rockefeller in the shower: Braden, *Just Enough Rope,* p. 43.

473. "Joanie, I want you to know": Ibid.

475. "She became a problem": Kershaw Burbank interview.

475. Braden tried to involve Rockefeller: Thomas Braden interview.

475. Newspaper purchase: *NYT,* November 20, 1974; Thomas Braden interview.

475. Private picnic: Joan Braden interview.

475. "Why did Tom": Ibid.

476. "Men assume": Braden, *Just Enough Rope,* pp. 195–96.

476. Rockefeller's art shopping: Dorothy Miller oral history, AAA.

476. Visit with Janis: James R. Mellow, "Rocky as a Collector," *NYT Magazine,* May 18, 1969.

477. Barr and the Braque: Marquis, *Alfred H. Barr,* p. 254.

477. He acquired seven of the paintings: Ibid., p. 255.

477. "I like strong, simple painting": NAR oral history, AAA.

478. *Nirvana:* James Wallis, Harold Haskell interviews.

478. *Dragon Lady:* Rodman Rockefeller, Dorothy Wodell interviews.

479. Raised floor: Eleanor Harris, "What Makes Rockefeller Run?" *American Weekly,* November 1, 1959.

479. Knickerbocker Club: Oscar Ruebhausen interview. Title to the clubhouse was eventually passed on to Nelson Jr.

479. Potofsky was appalled: Potofsky oral history, COHP.

480. *Dragon Lady*'s voyage: LSR interview; Stewart Alsop, "The Rockefeller Nobody Knows," *Saturday Evening Post,* July 25, 1959; Morris, *Those Rockefeller Brothers,* p. 56.

481. "The trouble with Nelson": Barbara Dudley interview.

481. "He goes a little like a mad man": Morris, *Those Rockefeller Brothers,* p. 199.

481. "He never stopped": Haskell interview.

481. "Nelson's philosophy": LSR interview.

482. Bill Zeckendorf: Cary Reich, *Financier: The Biography of André Meyer* (New York: Morrow, 1983), pp. 130–34.

482. Rockefeller and Zeckendorf: Ruebhausen interview.

482. Saks Fifth Avenue: Robert Fulton to NAR, July 14, 1953, AIA-IBEC Box 10, RAC.

483. Chrysler pullout: Ruebhausen interview.

483. IBEC losses: Memo on accumulated deficits, September 18, 1952, AIA-IBEC Box 10, RAC.

484. Avila Oil Company: AIA-IBEC Box 17, RAC.

484. "Too much too soon": *Christian Science Monitor,* September 23, 1952.

484. "Money honestly spent": *Christian Science Monitor,* October 18, 1952.

484. Expansion talk: VBEC memo, April 2, 1953, AIA-IBEC Box 10, RAC.

485. Did not justify the belief: Charles Pineo to NAR, March 27, 1952, AIA-IBEC Box 10, RAC.

485. Junior's buyout of the oil companies: Lockwood interview.

486. Martha Baird Allen: Harr & Johnson, *Rockefeller Century,* p. 469; Collier & Horowitz, *The Rockefellers,* p. 335.

486. "There was no jealousy": Harr & Johnson, *Rockefeller Century,* pp. 469–70.

487. Much on Junior's mind: Thomas Debevoise to Jr., June 4, 1948, Homes Box 28, RAC.

487. The only way to avoid: Harr & Johnson, *Rockefeller Century,* p. 524.

487. Junior's lawyers had formulated: George C. Williams to Phillip Keebler, April 29, 1949, Homes Box 28, RAC.

487. When the transaction stalled: NAR to Thomas Debevoise, August 8, 1950, Homes Box 28, RAC.

487. Nelson added some wrinkles: Ibid.

488. He asked Debevoise: Debevoise to NAR, June 28, 1951, Homes Box 28, RAC.

488. "I presume I should make": Quoted in Collier & Horowitz, *The Rockefellers,* p. 252.

488. Astonishingly low sum: Harr & Johnson, *Rockefeller Century,* p. 528.

489. Pocantico's assessed value: George C. Williams to Phillip Keebler, April 29, 1949, Homes Box 28, RAC.

489. Purchase of the Park: Harr & Johnson, *Rockefeller Century,* p. 528.

489. Rockefeller Center transaction: Ibid., pp. 534–35.

490. Junior's memo: Jr. to Sons, December 29, 1952, JDR3 Box 3, RAC.

29. Back Inside

493. Whitney and GOP politics: Kahn, *Jock,* pp. 205–13.

493–94. "He did not seek": Stephen E. Ambrose, *Eisenhower,* Vol. I (New York: Simon & Schuster, 1983), p. 490.

494. "I don't know why": Ibid., p. 516.

494. Clark's mission: William Bragg Ewald, Jr., *Eisenhower the President* (Englewood Cliffs, N.J.: Prentice-Hall, 1981), pp. 38–41.

495. Aldrich and Dewey: Richard Norton Smith, *Thomas E. Dewey and His Times* (New York: Touchstone/Simon & Schuster, 1982).

495. Aldrich and Eisenhower: Ambrose, *Eisenhower,* Vol. I, p. 516.

495. McCrary approached him: Tex McCrary interview.

495. In one speech: NAR to National Conference on International Economic and Social Development, Washington, D.C., April 7, 1952.

496. "Just back from convention": NAR to Galo Plaza, July 23, 1952, NAR Country Files, Box 29, RAC.

496. Rockefeller tried to carve out: Smith, *Thomas E. Dewey,* p. 624. In an interview with the author, Smith identified his source as John Burton.

496–97. "I got him some of the best": *Nomination of Nelson A. Rockefeller of New York to be Vice President of the United States: Hearings before the Committee on Rules and Administration, U.S. Senate,* p. 65.

497. Eisenhower expressed thanks: DDE to NAR, November 5, 1952, WHCF Box 2649, DDEL.

497. May's memo: NAR SCOGO Box 51, RAC.

497. Returning to his old position: *NYT,* November 20, 1952.

498. Meeting with Brownell: Herbert Brownell interview; Herbert Brownell, *Advising Ike* (Lawrence: University Press of Kansas, 1993), p. 136.

499. Temple studies: *Washington Post,* December 1, 1952; unpublished campaign biography of NAR by Donald Irwin, Chapter VIII, p. 4; memo on SCOGO antecedents, February 25, 1953, NAR SCOGO Box 45, RAC.

499. Eisenhower had confidentially asked him: Bernard L. Gladieux oral history, Ford Foundation Oral History Project.

500. Rockefeller himself dictated: NAR to Jamieson, Lockwood, May, November 10, 1952, NAR PACGO Box 51, RAC.

500. Gladieux had always thought: Gladieux oral history.

500. "A second-string job": Berle to Rockefeller, December 1, 1952, Berle Papers, Box 84, FDRL.

500–1. "Rockefeller has never allowed": *Newsweek,* December 22, 1952.

501. Bedell Smith reaction: Thomas Braden interview.

501. Rockefeller passed the loyalty check: FBI memo, March 20, 1953, FBI Files.

501. Gladieux controversy: Gladieux oral history.

501. Loyalty commission: SCOGO to Eisenhower, December 21, 1952, NAR SCOGO Box 46. See Robert J. Donovan, *Eisenhower: The Inside Story* (New York: Harper, 1956), pp. 286–87, for a discussion of the administration's response.

502. "Avoid publicity at all times": December 3, 1952, memo, NAR SCOGO Box 50, RAC.

502. Blueprint for chief of staff: Sherman Adams, *Firsthand Report* (New York: Harper, 1961), pp. 52–53.

502. Offered the use of Foxhall Road: NAR to Adams, December 15, 1952, Adams to NAR, December 19, 1952, WHCF Box 2649, DDEL.

503. Eisenhower assured Hobby: Dwight D. Eisenhower, *Mandate for Change* (Garden City, N.Y.: Doubleday, 1963), p. 92.

503. FSA plans moved to the top of the stack: Ruth Tillinghast to NAR, December 11, 1952, NAR SCOGO Box 49, RAC.

503. "They are, in the main": Dulles to Harvard Alumni Association, June 19, 1952.

503. "I don't think I really": Townsend Hoopes, *The Devil and John Foster Dulles* (Boston: Atlantic Monthly Press, 1973), p. 137.

503. "Supracabinet" post: Ibid.

503. Rockefeller relayed Dulles' wish: Minutes of SCOGO meeting, December 21, 1952, NAR SCOGO Box 48, RAC.

503–4. "Department of International Cooperation": NAR memo, November 3, 1952, NAR SCOGO Box 51, RAC.

504. "When these changes": Draft of recommendations, April 18, 1953, NAR SCOGO Box 50, RAC.

504. He made the most of it: "Outline of Report to President-Elect and Cabinet Designees," January 13, 1953, NAR SCOGO Box 50, RAC.

504. Sat down with Dulles: Minutes of Foreign Affairs Reorganization, NAR PACGO Box 51, RAC.

505. Meetings were very informal: Frederick W. Babbell oral history, COHP.

505. "It was suggested": PACGO minutes, February 14, 1953, NAR PACGO Box 51, RAC.

506. Rockefeller's defense study: Irwin, Chapter VI, pp. 1–9.

506. The most influential member was Lovett: Ibid., pp. 4–5.

506. Rockefeller's moderate course: Ibid., pp. 6–9.

506. "Now, Nelson": Morris, *NR*, p. 286.

507. Even Rockefeller recognized: Irwin, Chapter VI, p. 12.

507. AMA was placated: Ibid., Chapter VIII, pp. 16–17.

507. Hoover observed: Herbert Hoover to NAR, April 16, 1953, NAR SCOGO Box 46, RAC.

507. Eisenhower's note: DDE to NAR, April 23, 1953, NAR SCOGO Box 46, RAC.

508. FOA director subordinate to Secretary of State: *NYT*, June 1, 1953.

508. Government Research Foundation and Frank Moore: *NYT*, April 24, 1953; Lawrence Murray interview.

510. Mayoral run: The offer was revealed in an exchange of letters between NAR and Berle after the fact: May 29, 1953, and June 2, 1953, Berle Papers, Box 84, FDRL.

511. Brain trust advised him against it: Donna Mitchell interview.

511. "This is something": Nancy Hanks to parents, May 26, 1953, Nancy Hanks Papers, Box 237, Duke University.

511. "I'm responsible": Ibid.

511. It was vital: Morris, *NR,* p. 289; Donna Mitchell oral history, Nancy Hanks Papers, Duke University.

511. "Harry Emerson Fosdick": James Cannon, "Rocky: He Who Runs Least Runs Best," *Newsweek,* December 18, 1967.

512. "Of course, this leaves a hole": Berle to NAR, May 29, 1953, Berle Papers, Box 84, FDRL.

512. "I feel in a way": NAR to Berle, June 2, 1953, Berle Papers, Box 84, FDRL.

512. "I have always thought": Benton to NAR, June 3, 1953, NAR HEW Box 57, RAC.

30. *The Acting Secretary*

513. One of the town's ten most powerful: George Fuermann, *Houston: Land of the Big Rich* (Garden City, N.Y.: Doubleday, 1951), pp. 78–80.

513. Hobby's iron resolve: *Time,* May 4, 1953, pp. 24–27.

514. Hobby molded the WACs: Mattie F. Treadwell, *United States Army in World War II Special Studies: The Women's Army Corps* (Office of the Chief of Military History, Department of the Army, Washington, D.C., 1956); *Time,* May 4, 1953, pp. 24–27.

514. "WACs as officers": Treadwell, *Women's Army Corps,* p. 73.

514. "They're in the Army": Ibid., p. 182.

515. Hobby's efforts for Eisenhower: Brownell, *Advising Ike,* p. 112; Herbert S. Parmet, *Eisenhower and the American Crusades* (New York: Macmillan, 1972), p. 76.

515. Hobby style: *Life,* April 27, 1953, pp. 36–39; *Time,* May 4, 1953, pp. 24–27.

515. "She was very feminine in her appearance": Nelson Cruikshank oral history, COHP.

515. First press conference: *Newsweek,* May 11, 1953, p. 62.

516. "Mrs. Hobby was extremely timid": William L. Mitchell oral history, COHP.

517. "A growing concern today": *U.S. News & World Report,* December 26, 1952, p. 44.

517. "I am amazed": Stephen E. Ambrose, *Eisenhower,* Vol. II (New York: Simon & Schuster, 1984), p. 115.

517. "She couldn't exercise her power": Mitchell oral history, COHP.

518. "I guess that means I'm in": Nancy Hanks to parents, May 29, 1953, Hanks Papers, Box 237, Duke.

518. "Countermeasure devices": R. R. Roach to A. N. Belmont, December 29, 1955, FBI Files.

519. Chart room: Nadia Williams interview; Rufus Miles interview; *NYT,* June 5, 1954.

519. "We just weren't used": Katheryn Goodwin oral history, COHP.

519. Rockefeller summoned Miles: Miles interview; Harr & Johnson, *Rockefeller Century,* p. 547.

519. Hiring Joan Braden: Joan Braden interview; Braden, *Just Enough Rope,* pp. 55–56.

520. "Well, I'll tell you": Donna Mitchell interview.

520. "I have never liked to have a man assistant": Nancy Hanks to parents, May 29, 1953, Hanks Papers, Box 237, Duke.

520. Roswell Perkins: Roswell Perkins interview.

521. Haskell's job: Harold Haskell interview; Nadia Williams interview; *NYT,* August 15, 1953.

522. "The unusual thing about Nelson Rockefeller": Kevin McCann oral history, COHP.

522. Pressure for patronage: Donovan, *Eisenhower: The Inside Story,* pp. 96–100

522. Curtis' list: Wilbur Cohen oral history, DDEL.

522. "The heads just had to roll": Katheryn Goodwin oral history, COHP.

522. Rockefeller and Mitchell: Mitchell oral history, COHP.

523. Wilbur Cohen: Martha Derthick, *Policymaking for Social Security* (Washington, D.C.: The Brookings Institution, 1979).

523. Cohen refused: Cohen oral history, COHP.

523. Meany's meeting with Rockefeller: Nelson Cruikshank oral history, COHP; Joseph C. Goulden, *Meany* (New York: Atheneum, 1972), p. 215.

523. Calling Cruikshank: Cruikshank oral history, COHP.

525. Tramburg and Mitchell's retention: Mitchell oral history, COHP.

525. Cohen permitted to stay on: Cohen oral history, COHP.

525. "The Eisenhower administration, in my book": Archie Robinson, *George Meany and His Times* (New York: Simon & Schuster, 1981), p. 208.

526. Conservative attacks: Derthick, *Policymaking for Social Security,* pp. 132–57.

526. "If they were going to persuade": Roswell Perkins oral history, COHP.

527. White House visit: Donovan, *Eisenhower: The Inside Story,* pp. 172–74.

527. He met with Reed: Perkins interview.

527. "In strictly human terms": *NYT,* September 2, 1954.

527. "For the first time": Cohen oral history, DDEL.

528. Ten dollars for every dollar: Irwin, Chapter II, p. 8.

528. "Every one of these people": Haskell interview.

528. "Rockefeller instituted a revolution": Irwin, Chapter I, pp. 3–4.

528. "He amazed me": Samuel Brownell oral history, COHP.

528–29. Contrast with Hobby: Dorothy West interview.

529. Bow tie and beanie: Hanks to parents, May 10, 1954, Hanks Papers, Box 237, Duke.

529. Pumpkin-carving contest: Michael Straight, *Nancy Hanks: An Intimate Fortrait* (Durham, N.C.: Duke University Press, 1988), pp. 43–44.

529. "There was a standoffishness": Mitchell oral history, Hanks Papers, Duke.

530. Insurance inadequacies: NAR testimony to Senate Labor and Public Welfare Committee, April 13, 1954.

530. Interest in health care: Irwin, Chapter II, p. 15.

531. "It was impossible": Oscar Ruebhausen interview.

531. "He hit the ceiling": Marion Folsom oral history, COHP.

531. "I think he assumed": Ibid.

531. AMA position: *NYT,* April 6, 1954.

532. Sam Rayburn and the reinsurance bill: Cruikshank oral history, COHP; Cohen oral history, DDEL.

533. School inadequacies: *NYT,* March 7, 1954; September 13, 1954; December 6, 1954.

534. Brownell's view: *NYT,* October 9, 1954.

534. Dodge memo: Dodge to Hobby, January 8, 1954, Oveta Culp Hobby Papers, Box 19, DDEL.

534. Rockefeller went along with Brownell: NAR to Sherman Adams, April 7, 1954, Oveta Culp Hobby Papers, Box 19, DDEL.

535. John Mitchell: *Current Biography,* June 1969; *Wall Street Journal,* January 17, 1969.

535. Mitchell denied the idea: Francis Maloney interview.

535. Mitchell's proposal: Roswell Perkins interview; "Statement of Financing Plan," attached to Hobby to DDE, January 25, 1955.

536. Senators savaged the plan: *NYT,* February 10, 1955.

536. NEA opposition: *NYT,* February 18, 1955.

537. McCrary and Zeckendorf visit: Tex McCrary interview.

537. Note to Sherman Adams: Tex McCrary to Sherman Adams, July 9, 1954, WHCF Box 2649, DDEL.

538. Zeckendorf and Shapiro: George Shapiro interview.

538. Dewey asked: Shapiro interview.

31. Nancy Hanks

540. "The person that people went to": Donna Mitchell oral history, Nancy Hanks Papers, Duke.

540. "She kept tabs": Ibid.

541. Hanks background: Straight, *Hanks,* pp. 3–25.

541. ODM job: Ibid., pp. 34–39.

541. "A bunch of flowers in her arms": Ibid., p. 39.

542. "Mr. R's comment": Hanks to parents, March 18, 1953, Hanks Papers, Box 236, Duke.

542. "She looked absolutely marvelous": Straight, *Hanks,* p. 19.

542. "I was shocked and crushed": Hanks to parents, May 26, 1953, Hanks Papers, Box 237, Duke.

542. "Very shortly after": Mitchell oral history, Hanks Papers, Duke.

543. "Keeping your relationship": Bryan Hanks to Nancy Hanks, June 12, 1953, Hanks Papers, Box 237, Duke.

543. Offer of Braden: Joan Braden interview; Donna Mitchell interview.

544. "He regarded his employees": Mitchell oral history, Hanks Papers, Duke.

544. "He put her in a shrine": Ibid.

544. "NAR really sort of cute": Straight, *Hanks,* p. 50.

544. Offer of Chinese bench: Hanks to parents, November 24, 1953, Hanks Papers, Box 237, Duke.

544. He gave her drawings: Hanks to parents, April 1954, Hanks Papers, Box 237, Duke.

545. "His stand now": Ibid.

545. Gift of securities: Donna Mitchell oral history; Bryan Hanks to Nancy Hanks, March 1956, Hanks Papers, Box 239, Duke.

545. "I figure this money": Mitchell oral history, Hanks Papers, Duke.

545. "I am sure it is very obvious": Straight, *Hanks,* p. 50.

545. "She was like a wife": Ibid., pp. 49–50.

545. "This is Dr. Rockefeller calling": Hanks to parents, March 8, 1954, Hanks Papers, Box 237, Duke.

545. Birthday dinner: Hanks to parents, Hanks Papers, Box 237, Duke.

546. "I think sometimes": Straight, *Hanks,* p. 50.

546. Visit to supermarket: Hanks to parents, August 8, 1954, Hanks Papers, Box 237, Duke.

546. Visit to New York: Hanks to parents, July 5, 1954, Hanks Papers, Box 237, Duke.

546. Making gallery rounds: Hanks to parents, November 2, 1954, Hanks Papers, Box 237, Duke.

546. "She'd come down": Mitchell oral history, Hanks Papers, Duke.

546. "The only time": Ibid.

547. Gifts to Hanks's parents: Bryan Hanks to NAR, April 19, 1955, Hanks Papers, Box 238, Duke.

547. "He likes both of you": Hanks to parents, September 21, 1954, Hanks Papers, Box 237, Duke.

547. "It certainly is hard": Hanks to parents, October 3, 1954, Hanks Papers, Box 237, Duke.

547. Motorboat and canoe: Straight, *Hanks,* p. 51.

547. Rockefeller's visit to Cashiers: Ibid., pp. 51–52.

548. "This was pretty heady stuff": Mitchell oral history, Hanks Papers, Duke.

548. Bryan Hanks's reverent letters: Bryan Hanks to NAR, April 19, 1955; Bryan Hanks to Nancy Hanks, April 19, 1955, Hanks Papers, Box 238, Duke.

548. "It was very apparent to me": Mitchell oral history, Hanks Papers, Duke.

548. "Nancy, there is nothing more beautiful": Quoted in Straight, *Hanks,* p. 47.

32. *Overt and Covert*

549. Rockefeller served notice: Nancy Hanks to parents, November 6, 1954, Hanks Papers, Box 237, Duke.

550. Lunch with President: Nancy Hanks to parents, November 25, 1954, Hanks Papers, Box 237, Duke.

550. He stormed over: Ibid.

550. "He said no": Peter Lyon, *Eisenhower: Portrait of the Hero* (Boston: Little, Brown, 1974), p. 502.

550. Hobby approached the President: Nancy Hanks to parents, November 25, 1954, Hanks Papers, Box 237, Duke.

551. What Hobby had not disclosed: Nancy Hanks to parents, November 27, 1954, Hanks Papers, Box 237, Duke.

551. Conversation with Dodge: Nancy Hanks to parents, November 25, 1954, Hanks Papers, Box 237, Duke.

551. Adams reassured him: Ibid.

551. "The White House probably thinks": Nancy Hanks to parents, December 10, 1954, Hanks Papers, Box 237, Duke.

552. "Secretary of State Dulles": *NYT,* December 8, 1954.

552. "Dulles had asked Nelson": Berle & Jacobs, *Navigating the Rapids,* p. 644.

552. C. D. Jackson: H. W. Brands, Jr., *Cold Warriors: Eisenhower's Generation and American Foreign Policy* (New York: Columbia University Press, 1988), pp. 118–36; Blanche Wiesen Cook, "First Comes the Lie: C. D. Jackson and Political Warfare," *Radical History Review,* No. 31 (1984), pp. 42–70; "The Careers of C. D. Jackson Come to an End," *NYHT,* September 20, 1964.

553. Eisenhower and psychological warfare: William E. Daugherty, *A Psychological Warfare Casebook* (Baltimore: Operations Research Office, Johns Hopkins University Press, 1958), pp. 27–30.

553. Jackson blanketed the globe: Donovan, *Eisenhower: The Inside Story,* p. 75.

553. Atoms for Peace: Adams, *Firsthand Report,* pp. 109–12.

554. "Foster Dulles hasn't got the faintest": Ewald, *Eisenhower the President,* p. 71.

554. "Business as usual": Ibid., p. 228.

554. Frustrated with Eisenhower: Adams, *Firsthand Report,* pp. 112, 135.

554. "As you can imagine": C. D. Jackson to NAR, December 20, 1954, C. D. Jackson Papers, Box 75, DDEL.

555. "I am completely convinced": NAR to C. D. Jackson, December 23, 1954, C. D. Jackson Papers, Box 75, DDEL.

555. Berle asked him: Berle & Jacobs, *Navigating the Rapids,* p. 650.

555. Adams cracked down: Donna Mitchell oral history, Hanks Papers, Duke.

555. "Jackson was pretty much": Sherman Adams oral history, COHP.

555. Paid for out of his own pocket: Details of the expenditures are in a letter from Weston Vernon, Jr., of Milbank, Tweed, to the Commissioner of Internal Revenue, May 12, 1955, requesting deductibility of the expenses, NAR Special Assistant Box 59, RAC.

556. He paid for the chart room: Ibid.

556. Locating the chart room: Nadia Williams interview; Morris, *NR,* p. 295.

556. Eisenhower administration foreign policy: Lyon, *Eisenhower: Portrait of the Hero,* pp. 579–81, 593–96, 600–11, 614–39; Ewald, *Eisenhower the President,* pp. 105–20; Donovan, *Eisenhower: The Inside Story,* pp. 259–60, 300–10; Hoopes, *The Devil and John Foster Dulles,* pp. 284 ff.

557. Emergence of the CIA: David Wise and Thomas B. Ross, *The Invisible Government* (New York: Random House 1964); John Ranelegh, *The Agency: The Rise and Decline of the CIA* (New York: Touchstone/Simon & Schuster, 1987); Gregory F. Treverton, *Covert Action* (New York: Basic Books, 1987); William R. Corson, *The Armies of Ignorance* (New York: Dial Press, 1977); Lyon, *Eisenhower: Portrait of the Hero,* pp. 548–54, 588–92, 611–14.

558. "We would never have been able": Quoted in Cook, "First Comes The Lie."

558. A forceful advocate: Brands, *Cold Warriors,* p. 122.

558. Operations Coordinating Board: Corson, *Armies of Ignorance,* pp. 342–43; Treverton, *Covert Action,* p. 75.

559. Addressing CIA seminar: Robert Scheer, "Nelson Rockefeller Takes Care of Everybody," in *Thinking Tuna Fish, Talking Death* (New York: Hill and Wang, 1988), p. 214.

559. LSD experiments: Tad Szulc, "Why Rockefeller Tried to Cover Up the CIA Probe," *New York,* September 5, 1977. For a complete account of MK-Ultra's mind control experiments, see John D. Marks, *The Search for the "Manchurian Candidate"* (New York: Times Books, 1979).

559. Budget Bureau report: Hughes to President, March 3, 1955, NSC memos, March 3, 1955, March 4, 1955, Office of Special Assistant for National Security Affairs, Box 2, DDEL; "History of the Planning Coordination Group" [secret report prepared for NAR], January 23, 1956. A Rockefeller aide, who declined to be identified, furnished the author with a copy of this report.

561. Kintner background: William Kintner interview.

561. Parker's arrival: Theodore Parker interview.

561. Richard Drain: Theodore Parker to NAR, October 13, 1955, NAR Special Assistant Book 16, RAC; Parker interview.

561. "I've got my general": Nadia Williams interview.

33. *Cold Warrior*

562. Imprisoned airmen: NAR memo on January 25, 1955, meeting, NAR Special Assistant Book 16, RAC.

562. Wheat to Russia: NAR to DDE, March 1, 1955, NAR Special Assistant Book 43, RAC.

563. Jackson on exiles: Brands, *Cold Warriors,* p. 127.

563. Nagy idea: Jackson to NAR, January 11, 1955, C. D. Jackson Papers, Box 75, DDEL.

563. UN statement: Donna Mitchell to NAR, October 25, 1955, NAR Special Assistant Book 44, RAC.

563. Militant Liberty: NAR Special Assistant Book 18, RAC.

563. Institute of Political Science: NAR Special Assistant Book 16, RAC; Karl Harr interview.

565. Bandung aid: Irwin, Chapter V-3, pp. 100–1.

565. Tata aid: Ewald, *Eisenhower the President,* p. 235; Gervasi, *Real Rockefeller,* pp. 183–84.

565. Aid to Egypt: Irwin, Chapter V-3, pp. 96–98.

566. Ruebhausen and atomic power: NAR Special Assistant Book 15, RAC.

566. "I can think of nothing": Ibid.

566. Atoms for Peace had stalled: Donovan, *Eisenhower: The Inside Story,* pp. 191–92.

567. Rockefeller and bilateral agreements: Irwin, Chapter VII, pp. 1–2.

568. Report to President: "International Peaceful Atomic Development," June 13, 1955, NAR Special Assistant Book 44, RAC.

568. Dulles' doubts: Dulles phone conversation with Strauss, June 8, 1955, Dulles Telephone Conversation Memoranda, Box 4, Folder 6, DDEL.

568. Dangerous era of proliferation: David Fischer, *Stopping the Spread of Nuclear Weapons* (London: Routledge, 1992), pp. 45–46; Robert L. Beckman, *Nuclear Non-Proliferation* (Boulder: Westview Press, 1985), pp. 97–98; Jed C. Snyder and Samuel F. Wells, eds., *Limiting Nuclear Proliferation* (Cambridge, Mass.: Ballinger, 1985), pp. 185–86, 257–59.

568. "An autocrat": Ewald, *Eisenhower the President,* p. 217.

568. "It was rather difficult": Sherman Adams oral history, COHP.

569. Dulles' idiosyncrasies: Hoopes, *The Devil and John Foster Dulles,* p. 40, 144.

569. "An intellectual loner": Ibid., p. 38.

569. "To cross him": Ibid., p. 35.

569. "The history of the Lansing-Wilson thing": Brands, *Cold Warriors,* p. 4.

569. Dulles and Eisenhower: Robert Richardson Bowie oral history, COHP.

569. Reversing Dulles' veto: Ewald, *Eisenhower the President,* p. 235.

570. Reporting Brazil meeting to Dulles: NAR to Dulles, January 31, 1955, NAR Special Assistant Book 44, RAC.

570. "I have been very assiduously": NAR to Berent Friele, March 21, 1955, NAR Special Assistant Book 44, RAC.

570. "I have heard journalists' gossip": Jackson to NAR, March 16, 1955, C. D. Jackson Papers, Box 75, DDEL.

570. "Your historic inter-American speech": NAR to Dulles, April 14, 1955, Dulles Papers, Box 97, Princeton.

571. Rigid Eisenhower hierarchy: Herbert Brownell interview.

572. "I hasten to say": DDE to NAR, August 10, 1954, WHCF Box 2649, DDEL.

572. Gettysburg farm: Lyon, *Eisenhower: Portrait of the Hero,* pp. 512–13.

572. Rockefeller and Gettysburg farm: NAR Special Assistant Book 16, RAC.

573. Loan of paintings: NAR Special Assistant Box 59, RAC.

573. Churchill medal: NAR to DDE, May 9, 1955, NAR Special Assistant Book 23, RAC; NAR to John Foster Dulles, August 27, 1955, NAR Special Assistant Book 44, RAC; NAR to DDE, November 30, 1955, Ann Whitman Files, Administration Series, Box 30, DDEL.

573. Gift of furniture: NAR Special Assistant Box 59, RAC.

573. Golf course at Foxhall Road: Stewart Alsop, *Nixon and Rockefeller,* p. 97.

573. "Some time ago": NAR to DDE, November 10, 1955, NAR Special Assistant Book 23, RAC.

574. Wilson's offer: Nancy Hanks to parents, May 20, 1955, Hanks Papers, Box 238, Duke. Joe Alex Morris and subsequent NAR biographers dated this offer to the late summer or early fall, but Hanks's letter makes clear it was earlier.

574. "Damn it": Ewald, *Eisenhower the President,* p. 192.

574. Eisenhower revealed: Nancy Hanks to parents, May 20, 1955, Hanks Papers, Box 238, Duke.

575. Withdrawal of offer: Morris, *NR,* pp. 303–4; Gervasi, *Real Rockefeller,* p. 186.

575. George Humphrey: Brownell, *Advising Ike,* p. 135; Ewald, *Eisenhower the President,* p. 65; Piers Brendon, *Ike: His Life and Times* (New York: Harper & Row, 1986), p. 231; Lyon, *Eisenhower: Portrait of the Hero,* p. 467.

575. Humphrey and Rockefeller: Brownell interview; Ewald, *Eisenhower the President,* pp. 235–36; Morris, *NR,* p. 303.

34. Open Skies

577. "He seems to be building": Adams, *Firsthand Report,* p. 91.

577. Dulles phoned Allen: J. F. Dulles to Allen Dulles, June 9, 1955, Dulles Telephone Conversation Memoranda, Box 4, DDEL.

577. Memo to President: NAR to DDE, June 3, 1955, Ann Whitman Files, Administration Series, Box 31, DDEL.

578. Zhou's offer: Lyon, *Eisenhower: Portrait of the Hero,* p. 643.

578. "Something contagious": Hoopes, *The Devil and John Foster Dulles,* p. 294.

578. Dulles' objections to summit: Ibid., p. 287, 290; Lyon, *Eisenhower,* pp. 648–49.

578. Sending Nixon: Hoopes, *The Devil and John Foster Dulles,* p. 293.

578. Too many tourists: Memo of conversation, May 14, 1955, Ann Whitman Files, Ann Whitman Diary Series, Box 5, DDEL.

579. "Something is happening": C. D. Jackson to NAR, May 20, 1955, C. D. Jackson Papers, Box 75, DDEL.

579. "Friction at best": Don Irwin to NAR, May 20, 1955, NAR Special Assistant Book 44, RAC.

579. Harold Stassen: Harold Stassen and Marshall Houts, *Eisenhower: Turning the World Toward Peace* (St. Paul: Merrill/Magnus, 1990), pp. 275–305; Brands, *Cold Warriors,* pp. 138–43.

580. Dulles' lunch with Eisenhower: Ann C. Whitman Diary, May 25, 1955, Whitman Diary, Box 5, DDEL.

580. Rockefeller insisted: DDE to Dulles, Dulles Telephone Conversation Memoranda, Box 10, DDEL.

581. Walt Rostow: David Halberstam, *The Best and the Brightest* (New York: Random House, 1972), pp. 156–57.

581. The group gathered: "Administrative Arrangements for Quantico Panel Discussions," Hans Speier Papers, SUNY Albany.

581. "I couldn't quite figure out": C. D. Jackson, "From Quantico to Geneva—June & July 1955," C. D. Jackson Papers, Box 56, DDEL.

582. "Some smart outside one-shot kibitzers": Ibid.

582. First night's discussions: Ibid.; W. W. Rostow, *Open Skies* (Austin: University of Texas Press, 1982), pp. 27–28.

582. Quantico living arrangements: William Kintner interview; Theodore Parker interview; "Administrative Arrangements for Quantico."

582. Rostow outlined: Rostow, *Open Skies,* p. 28.

583. Blaine, Washington, speech: Irwin, Chapter V, p. 99.

583. Hans Speier paper: Hans Speier, "U.S. Strategy at the Forthcoming Conferences," June 9, 1955, Speier Papers, SUNY Albany.

584. "A test of the seriousness": Rostow, *Open Skies,* p. 29.

584. Max Milliken spoke up: Ibid., p. 30; Jackson, "From Quantico to Geneva."

584. Speier warned: Rostow, *Open Skies,* p. 30; Jackson, "From Quantico to Geneva."

585. "It is not at all inconceivable": "Report of the Quantico Vulnerabilities Panel," Appendix B, p. 6.

585. "Proposal of a disarmament plan": Ibid., Summary of Recommendations, p. 2.

585. Thursday evening: Rostow, *Open Skies,* p. 32; Jackson, "From Quantico to Geneva."

586. Jackson's letter to Eisenhower and Eisenhower reply: C. D. Jackson to DDE, June 13, 1955, Administration Series, Box 22, DDEL.

586. Dulles' briefing memo: Dulles to DDE, June 18, 1955, Dulles Papers, White House Memoranda Series, Box 3, DDEL.

587. Operation Alert: *NYT,* June 16, 1955; Ambrose, *Eisenhower,* p. 256; John Kennedy to NAR, June 10, 1955, NAR Special Assistant Book 44, RAC.

587. Eisenhower openly questioned: NSC meeting May 19, 1955, memorandum of discussion, *FRUS* 1955, Vol. V, pp. 182–89.

587. "A disjunction between the elements": Brendon, *Ike,* p. 306.

587. Jackson's draft: Jackson, "From Quantico to Geneva," C. D. Jackson Papers, DDEL.

588. June 30 NSC meeting: Ann Whitman Files, NSC Series, Box 7, DDEL.

589. Rockefeller's memo: Reprinted in Rostow, *Open Skies,* pp. 133–35.

589. Eisenhower phoned Dulles: Memorandum of phone conversation July 6, 1955, Dulles Telephone Conversation Memoranda, Box 10, DDEL.

589. Two or three months: Dulles memorandum of conversation with Harold Stassen, July 2, 1955, John Foster Dulles Papers, Chronological Series, Box 12, DDEL.

590. Avoid social meetings: State Department paper on U.S. goals at Geneva, July 1, 1955, Dulles Papers, Box 92, Princeton.

590. USIA polls: NSC meeting July 7, 1955, memorandum of discussion, *FRUS* 1955, Vol. V, pp. 268–83.

590. "I am suddenly reminded": DDE to NAR, July 8, 1955, Ann Whitman Files, Administration Series, Box 30, DDEL.

590. Rostow's draft: Rostow, *Open Skies,* pp. 177–83.

590. Rockefeller was using the speech: Ibid., p. 51.

590–91. Eisenhower wanted to hold down the number: Memorandum of meeting with the President, May 20, 1955, Dulles White House Memoranda, Box 3, DDEL.

591. The President called Stassen: Stassen & Houts, *Eisenhower,* pp. 321–23.

591. They would come down to Geneva: Andrew Goodpaster memo of conference with President, July 11, 1955, Ann Whitman Files, International Meetings Series, Box 1, DDEL.

591. Rockefeller hurried: NAR Special Assistant Book 44, RAC.

591. Jackson's dinner with Dulles: C. D. Jackson log entry, July 11, 1955, C. D. Jackson Papers, Box 56, DDEL.

592. "Psychological Strategy at Geneva": NAR to President, July 11, 1955, *FRUS* 1955, Vol. V, pp. 298–301.

592. Dulles' reaction: Dulles memorandum of conversation, July 12, 1955, Dulles Papers, Box 50, DDEL.

594. "I know of at least two": Roderick O'Connor to Dulles, July 13, 1955, Dulles Papers, Box 6, DDEL.

594. Dulles phoned Allen: Memo of conversation, July 13, 1955, Dulles Telephone Conversation Memoranda, Box 4, DDEL.

594. Cabling Royal Monceau: NAR Special Assistant Book 44, RAC.

594. Rockefeller's text: Rostow, *Open Skies,* pp. 169–83.

595. Dulles groaned: Ambrose, *Eisenhower,* p. 261.

595. Contrast in arrivals: Richard Rovere, *Affairs of State* (New York: Farrar, Straus & Cudahy, 1956), pp. 287–88.

595. Bulganin and Khrushchev: Ibid., pp. 281–82.

595. "Extraordinary table manners": Livingston T. Merchant, "Recollections of the Summit Conference, Geneva 1955," John Foster Dulles Papers, Box 92, Princeton.

595. "Live it up": Rovere, *Affairs of State,* p. 281.

596. Grotesque frescoes: Hoopes, *The Devil and John Foster Dulles,* p. 296.

596. Eisenhower's opening statement: Eisenhower, *Mandate for Change,* pp. 515–16.

596–97. Other leaders' proposals: *NYT,* July 19, 1955.

597. Eisenhower's impressions of the Soviets: Eisenhower, *Mandate for Change,* pp. 517–18.

597. Meeting at the Crillon: Jackson, "From Quantico to Geneva"; Kintner interview; Rostow, *Open Skies,* pp. 52–53.

598. Parker's call to Goodpaster: Rostow, *Open Skies,* p. 54.

598. "Presidential Statement on Disarmament": Ibid., pp. 136–40. In his book on Eisenhower, and in an interview with the author, Stassen claimed that *he* was the author of this statement, and that the aerial inspection proposal came out of the work of his advisory panel on disarmament. But Rockefeller's memo to Goodpaster from Paris, reproduced in *Open Skies,* merely stated that the draft "contains Stassen's specific suggestions and has his endorsement."

Exactly who deserved the credit—Stassen or Rockefeller—for the proposal would continue to be hotly debated for years to come. Rockefeller "did not have a major role," Stassen told the author. "Neither did his committee." Stassen and Rostow would go so far as to write whole books to assert their claims of authorship and disparage the other side. While both parties marshaled some persuasive documentation—and, it should be noted, were also guilty of some significant omissions—the author has concluded that the preponderance of evidence supports the argument that Rockefeller, rather than Stassen, was the proposal's prime mover.

598. Radford and Anderson's memo: Ibid., p. 135.

599. Dulles memo on unification: Quoted in Stassen & Houts, *Eisenhower,* pp. 348–49.

599. They considered walking out: Eisenhower, *Mandate for Change,* p. 524.

599. Visit to toy shop: *NYT,* July 20, 1955.

599. Meeting with the President: Andrew Goodpaster's "random notes" of Geneva trip, Ann Whitman Files, International Meetings Series, Box 1, DDEL.

600. Encounter with Khrushchev: Strobe Talbott, ed., *Khrushchev Remembers* (Boston: Little, Brown, 1970), p. 399; *NYHT,* July 21, 1955.

600. "Khrushchev has a very good sense of humor": NAR to Mary Rockefeller, July 30, 1955, Nancy Hanks Papers, Duke.

601. Meeting in the library: Andrew Goodpaster, Dillon Anderson memos for the record, Ann Whitman Files, International Meetings Series, Box 1, DDEL.

602. "You ought to be here": John S. D. Eisenhower oral history, COHP.

602. Two bold carats in the reading copy: The copy is in Ann Whitman Files, International Meeting Series, Box 2, DDEL.

603. The Russians "gave the appearance": Merchant, "Recollections."

603. "I expected to make a hit": Ambrose, *Eisenhower,* p. 265.

603. Khrushchev's response: Eisenhower account at July 28, 1955, NSC meeting, Ann Whitman Files, NSC Series, Box 6, DDEL; Eisenhower, *Mandate for Change,* pp. 521–22.

604. Rockefeller telegram: NAR to C. D. Jackson, July 21, 1955, C. D. Jackson Papers, Box 75, DDEL.

604. Dinner at lakeside restaurant: Nancy Hanks to parents, July 31, 1955, Nancy Hanks Papers, Box 238, Duke.

604. Rockefeller's lunch with President: President's appointments calendar, July 22, 1955, Ann Whitman Files, International Meetings Series, Box 1, DDEL.

605. Rockefeller basked vicariously: Nancy Hanks to parents, July 31, 1955, Nancy Hanks Papers, Box 238, Duke.

605. Clogged toilet: Ibid.

605. Dinner at Laurent: Theodore Parker interview.

606. "At the moment": DDE Diary, July 25, 1955, DDE Diary Series, Box 11, DDEL.

606. Letter to Bulganin: Quoted in Stassen & Houts, *Eisenhower,* pp. 353–54.

606. "To say that my plan": DDE Diary, July 25, 1955, DDE Diary Series, Box 11, DDEL.

607. "Personally, I feel reasonably satisfied": Dulles to C. D. Jackson, July 25, 1955, C. D. Jackson Papers, Box 56, DDEL.

607. Dulles at dinner party: Harold Stassen interview.

607. Phoned Brownell: Dulles to Brownell, July 26, 1955, Dulles Telephone Conversation Memoranda, Box 4, DDEL.

607. Bulganin rejection: Minutes of August 4, 1955, NSC meeting, Ann Whitman Files, NSC Series, Box 7, DDEL.

35. *Grounding the Gadfly*

609. "Geneva has certainly created problems": "United States Post-Geneva Policy," August 15, 1955, Dulles Papers, Box 92, Princeton.

609. "Honestly, can you think of": William B. Macomber oral history, John Foster Dulles Oral History Project, Princeton.

610. July 28 meeting with Dulles: "Memorandum of Conversation with Nelson Rockefeller," Dulles Papers, Chronological Series, Box 12, DDEL.

610. "I feel that we are now in shape": NAR to Stacy May, July 29, 1955, NAR Special Assistant Book 44, RAC.

610. "Everything was settled": J. F. Dulles, "Memorandum of Conversation with Governor Adams," July 30, 1955, Dulles Papers, Subject Series, Box 6, DDEL.

610. "Sometimes Mr. Rockefeller": Ibid.

611. Church attendance: Dulles Telephone Conversation Memoranda, July 29, 1955, Telephone Memoranda Box 10; Dulles to NAR, August 5, 1955, Dulles Papers, Subject Series, Box 6, DDEL.

611. Dulles lunch with President: Dulles memo, August 5, 1955, Dulles Papers, White House Memoranda Series, Box 3, DDEL.

612. Adams' chat with Dulles: Dulles memo, August 5, 1955, Dulles Telephone Memoranda Box 10, DDEL.

612. "Pursuant to my discussion": NAR to DDE, August 27, 1955, NAR Special Assistant Book 44, RAC.

613. "Terrible drain": Dulles memo, August 11, 1955, Dulles Telephone Memoranda Box 10, DDEL.

613. "This study should develop": NAR letter of invitation, August 16, 1955, NAR Special Assistant Book 44, RAC.

614. Kissinger background: Marvin Kalb and Bernard Kalb, *Kissinger* (Boston: Little, Brown, 1974); Walter Isaacson, *Kissinger* (New York: Simon & Schuster, 1992).

614. Harvard activities: Isaacson, *Kissinger,* pp. 70–73.

614. Elliott: Ibid., pp. 62–63; Enrique Hank Lopez, *The Harvard Mystique* (New York: Macmillan, 1979), pp. 63–64.

614. Elliott and Kissinger: Kintner interview.

615. CIA funding: Lopez, *The Harvard Mystique,* pp. 64–65.

615. "Rockefeller entered the room": Henry A. Kissinger, *The White House Years* (Boston: Little, Brown, 1979), p. 4.

615. Quantico meetings: Minutes of each day's sessions are in C. D. Jackson Papers, Box 74, DDEL.

616. "I did not bring you gentlemen": Kissinger, *The White House Years,* p. 4.

616. MacArthur confrontation: C. D. Jackson log, August 25, 1955, C. D. Jackson Papers, Box 56, DDEL.

616. Herbert Hoover, Jr.: Lyon, *Eisenhower: Portrait of the Hero,* p. 553; Herman Finer, *Dulles Over Suez* (Chicago: Quadrangle Books, 1964), pp. 398–99.

616–17. "Would come back from": James Poling, *The Rockefeller Record* (New York: Thomas Y. Crowell, 1960), p. 12.

617. Hoover and Rostow: "History of the Planning Coordination Group"; Rostow, *Open Skies,* p. 67; Theodore Parker interview.

617. Jackson complained: Jackson to Henry Luce, August 29, 1955, C. D. Jackson Papers, Box 56, DDEL.

617. Rockefeller found himself hamstrung: "History of the Planning Coordination Group."

617. Note to budget director: Ibid.

618. Parker's memo: Parker to NAR, September 9, 1955, NAR Special Assistant Book 44, RAC.

619. Eisenhower stricken: Donovan, *Eisenhower: The Inside Story,* pp. 358–67.

619. Rockefeller and Nobel Peace Prize: NAR to Sherman Adams, September 30, 1955, NAR Special Assistant Book 44, RAC.

619. Hanks found him "numb": Hanks to parents, September 25, 1955, Hanks Papers, Box 238, Duke.

620. Meeting with father and brothers: Nancy Hanks to parents, October 4, 1955, Hanks Papers, Box 238, Duke.

620. "The problem of Nelson Rockefeller": DDE diary entry, October 10, 1955, DDE Diary Series, Box 9, DDEL.

620. "I think the decision": Nancy Hanks to parents, October 4, 1955, Hanks Papers, Box 238, Duke.

621. Ford Thunderbird: Nancy Hanks to parents, July 31, 1955, Hanks Papers, Box 238, Duke.

621. Hanks at Ann's wedding: Donna Mitchell oral history, Hanks Papers, Duke.

621. "I have been worried": Hanks to parents, September 25, 1955, Hanks Papers, Box 238, Duke.

621. "He allowed that it was my fault": Ibid.

622. "Depression is always a vicious circle": Nancy Hanks to parents, November 3, 1955, Hanks Papers, Box 238, Duke.

622. Drafting the report: Henry Kissinger interview; Nadia Williams interview. Williams did the report's graphics and was one of those interned.

622. "There is an awful lot of good stuff": Jackson to NAR, November 10, 1955, C. D. Jackson Papers, Box 56, DDEL.

622–23. Lodge's rebuff: Theodore Parker to NAR, September 30, 1955, Nancy Hanks to Parker, October 17, 1955, NAR Special Assistant Book 44, RAC.

623. Cultural panel: NAR to DDE, July 11, 1955, NAR Special Assistant Book 59, RAC; Theodore Streibert to NAR, October 28, 1955, NAR Special Assistant Book 21, RAC.

623. Open Skies exhibit: Don Irwin to NAR, October 14, 1955, NAR Special Assistant Book 44, RAC; Nadia Williams interview.

623. The concern was shared: Lyon, *Eisenhower: Portrait of the Hero,* pp. 668–69.

623. "All of us in the Administration": NAR to Richard Nixon, October 22, 1955, NAR Special Assistant Book 44, RAC.

624. "It might have one or two ideas": NAR to Nixon, November 3, 1955, NAR Special Assistant Book 44, RAC.

624. "You were superb": NAR to Nixon, November 21, 1955, NAR Special Assistant Book 44, RAC.

624. Eisenhower's homecoming: Donovan, *Eisenhower: The Inside Story,* p. 385.

625. He phoned the Secretary of State: Dulles memo, November 22, 1955, Dulles Telephone Conversation Memoranda, Box 4, DDEL.

625. USIA request: NAR to DDE, November 30, 1955, NAR Special Assistant Book 23, RAC.

625. Quantico II letter: NAR to DDE, December 2, 1955, Ann Whitman Files, Administration Series, Box 30, DDEL.

625. Quantico II report: A copy of the secret report was furnished to the author by William Kintner.

627. Meeting with Dulles: "Memorandum of Conversation with Nelson Rockefeller," December 2, 1955, Dulles Papers, Subject Series, Box 6, DDEL.

627. "Action Program for Free World Strength": A Rockefeller aide provided the author with one of the original copies of the report, bearing the blue "Secret" stamps. A copy is also available at the RAC, NAR Special Assistant Box 59.

629. "Very well received all around": NAR to C. D. Jackson, December 9, 1955, NAR Special Assistant Book 44, RAC.

629. Rockefeller told Rostow: Rostow, *Open Skies,* p. 67.

630. "After you left today": DDE to NAR, December 5, 1955, Ann Whitman Files, Administration Series, Box 30, DDEL.

630. Rockefeller tried to explain: NAR to DDE, December 7, 1955, Ann Whitman Files, Administration Series, Box 30, DDEL.

630. USIA budget: Nancy Hanks to NAR, December 6, 1955, NAR Special Assistant Book 44, RAC.

631. Speaking invitation: NAR to National Business Publications, December 5, 1955, NAR Special Assistant Book 44, RAC.

631. NAR resignation letter, Eisenhower response: *NYT,* December 20, 1955.

631. "Your painting has given": NAR to DDE, January 1, 1955, NAR Special Assistant Book 23, RAC.

631. "I have greatly enjoyed": John Foster Dulles to NAR, December 20, 1955, Dulles Papers, Box 97, Princeton.

631–32. "Of the lasting impressions": NAR to Dulles, December 21, 1955, Dulles Papers, Subject Series, Box 6, DDEL.

632. Drummond column: *Washington Post,* December 25, 1955.

632. Alsop met with Rockefeller: NAR memo, September 20, 1955, NAR Special Assistant Book 44, RAC.

632. Alsops' column: *Washington Post,* December 26, 1955.

633. Others in the media followed suit: See *NYT* editorial, "Exit Rockefeller," December 25, 1955; *U.S. News & World Report,* December 30, 1955, pp. 73–74; *Time,* January 2, 1956, pp. 11–12.

633. Kissinger lauded: Henry Kissinger to NAR, December 21, 1955, NAR Special Assistant Book 44, RAC.

633. Rockefeller expressed his fear: C. D. Jackson log, December 19, 1955, C. D. Jackson Papers, Box 56, DDEL.

633. "I think the position we have taken": Nixon to NAR, December 31, 1955, NAR Special Assistant Book 44, RAC.

634. "I've learned one thing, Ted": Parker interview. Rockefeller said much the same thing to Rostow at the time. See Rostow, *Open Skies,* p. 67.

36. A Sense of Purpose

637. Berle pondered: Berle & Jacobs, *Navigating the Rapids,* pp. 667–68.

637. "Should not just be an orthodox": John Ensor Harr and Peter J. Johnson, *The Rockefeller Conscience* (New York: Scribners, 1991), p. 202.

638. *Fortune* articles: Richard Austin Smith, "The Rockefeller Brothers," *Fortune,* February and March 1955.

639. "To our family": Quoted in Collier & Horowitz, *The Rockefellers,* p. 333.

640. "Frankie": Linda Storrow interview.

640. "Sometimes he doesn't like": Ibid.

640. Harrison flew into a rage: Max Abramovitz interview.

641. "One of the few times": Donna Mitchell oral history, Hanks Papers, Duke.

641. "Be not independent": Quoted in Straight, *Hanks,* p. 54.

641–42. "If he suggests": Bryan Hanks to Nancy Hanks, December 28, 1955, Hanks Papers, Box 238, Duke.

642. "Just another one": Donna Mitchell oral history, Hanks Papers, Duke.

642. She was reconciling herself: Hanks to parents, March 17, 1956, Hanks Papers, Box 239, Duke.

642. "I am wondering": Bryan Hanks to Nancy Hanks, March 1956, Hanks Papers, Box 239, Duke.

643. "Very frankly": Nancy Hanks to parents, April 30, 1956, Hanks Papers, Box 239, Duke.

643. "Now as we go on": NAR to Bryan Hanks, January 1956, Hanks Papers, Box 239, Duke.

643. Dartmouth project: *NYT,* February 9, 1956; Newhouse, *Harrison,* pp. 210–11.

643. Museum of Primitive Art: *NYT,* December 18, 1954; "A Prime Accumulation of Primitive Art," *Life,* May 6, 1957.

644. Moore's tale: Alton Marshall interview.

644. Picasso tapestries: NAR interview, July 24, 1972, AAA; William Kennedy interview with NAR (transcript), July 27, 1972, Joseph Persico Papers, SUNY Albany; NAR introduction to *The Nelson A. Rockefeller Collection: Masterpieces of Modern Art,* pp. 16–18.

644. The experiment cemented: Dorothy Miller interview.

645. Matisse window: Alfred Barr essay in *The Nelson A. Rockefeller Collection: Masterpieces of Modern Art,* p. 22; program of dedication of window, Religious Interests, Box 29, RAC.

645. Transplanting the white pine tree: *Boston Globe,* January 25, 1959.

646. Personal interests in Latin America: NAR to Galo Plaza, June 20, 1956, NAR Country Files, Box 29, RAC.

646. Monte Sacro hacienda: Peter Ogden interview; *NYT,* November 13, 1958.

647. IBEC turnaround: *Barron's,* September 2, 1957; *Business Week,* September 10, 1955, April 27, 1957.

647. Investment banking flop: Cobbs, "Good Works at a Profit," pp. 199–200.

647. Fundo Crescinco: Ibid., pp. 200–6; Broehl, *IBEC,* pp. 166–72; Richard Aldrich interview.

648. "When we are philanthropic": *Barron's,* September 2, 1957.

648. "This confusion of business and philanthropy": Robert Purcell interview.

649. Antiwiretapping: R. R. Roach to A. N. Belmont, December 29, 1955, FBI Files.

649. "Salute to Eisenhower": NAR General 1956–60 File, Public Relations, Box 16, RAC.

649. Passionately defending the very foreign policy: Speech at Middlesex Club's Lincoln Night dinner, Boston, February 13, 1956, NAR HEW Vol. II, RAC.

649. Standing by Nixon: NAR to Sherman Adams, March 14, 1956, WHCF Box 2649, DDEL.

649. "The Republican Party": DDE to NAR, November 9, 1956, WHCF Box 2649, DDEL.

650. "Just before he left for South America": Berle & Jacobs, *Navigating the Rapids,* pp. 667–68.

650. "What Is to Be Done?": Harrison Papers, Columbia.

651. Brought in Lindsay: Franklin Lindsay interview.

651. "Nelson liked to look": Laurance Rockefeller interview.

652. Lunch at Hay-Adams: William Kintner interview.

652. Rockefeller had assured him: Kissinger remarks to opening session of "Critical Choices," December 3, 1973, Hanks Papers, Duke.

653. "Spend so much time arguing": Kissinger to Max Milliken, June 20, 1956, Special Studies Box 8, RAC.

653. Bowles warned Rockefeller: Chester Bowles oral history, COHP.

654. "What really seems to be lacking": Kissinger to Berle, December 19, 1956, Special Studies Box 1, RAC.

655. First meeting of panel: NAR Notes, Special Studies Box 54, RAC.

656. "Once in a while": Stanley A. Blumberg and Gwinn Owens, *Energy and Conflict: The Life and Times of Edward Teller* (New York: Putnam, 1976), p. 1.

656. Edward Teller: Ibid.; "The Tangled Drama and Private Hells of Two Famous Scientists," *Life,* December 13, 1963; Richard Rhodes, *The Making of the Atomic Bomb* (New York: Simon & Schuster, 1986), pp. 106–13.

656. "The important thing": Quoted in Rhodes, *Making of the Atomic Bomb,* p. 770.

656. "There is a time": Ibid.

657. "Possible statements": Edward Teller to James McCormack, Jr., December 10, 1956, Special Studies Box 13, RAC.

657. Teller's views went unchallenged: Minutes of meeting of March 19–20, 1957, Special Studies Box 54, RAC.

657–58. Berle and Teller: Oscar Ruebhausen interview.

658. "Having sat through": Kissinger to Edward Teller, January 25, 1957, Special Studies Box 13, RAC.

658. "You know my views": Kissinger to General James Gavin, November 30, 1956, Special Studies Box 13, RAC.

658. "On the basic approach": Henry Kissinger interview.

659. Time to sound the alarm: See transcript of meeting May 6–8, 1957, Special Studies Box 55, RAC.

659. The public "was not really informed": Transcript of second overall panel meeting, Special Studies Box 54, RAC.

659. Bowles's protest: Chester Bowles oral history, COHP.

660. "We just have to keep our faith": Transcript of third overall panel meeting, Special Studies Box 55, RAC.

660. "I would hate to have someone": Transcript of fourth overall panel meeting, Special Studies Box 55, RAC.

660. *Reader's Digest* length: Ibid.

661. Kissinger's petulance: Kershaw Burbank, Donna Mitchell, Oscar Ruebhausen interviews.

661. Inner tension: Kershaw Burbank written reminiscence on Henry Kissinger, September 20, 1988.

661–62. "Henry has been saying": Nancy Hanks to parents, March 15, 1958, Hanks Papers, Box 241, Duke.

662. "Henry really fooled me": Ruebhausen interview.

662. "She would assure him": Straight, *Hanks,* p. 57.

662. "HAK has for my money": Nancy Hanks to parents, April 20, 1958, Hanks Papers, Box 241, Duke.

662. "*Nobody* edits my copy": Burbank interview.

662. "He had a cast of characters": Kissinger interview.

662. He warned Rockefeller: Ibid.

663. "He is the best listener": Charles Percy to NAR, July 2, 1958, Special Studies Box 42, RAC.

663–64. Sputnik: *Life,* October 14, 1957; *NYT,* October 13, 1957, November 5, 1957, November 17, 1957; David Halberstam, *The Fifties* (New York: Villard Books, 1993), pp. 624–26.

664. "We have suffered": *U.S. News & World Report,* November 15, 1957.

664. "The world situation made it clear": NAR to Chester Bowles, December 2, 1957, Chester Bowles Papers, Folder 0561, Yale. Interestingly, the files on this decision to rush out the military report are missing from the otherwise complete Special Studies record in the RAC.

664. Rockefeller was promoting his proposals: Irwin, Chapter VI, pp. 14–24; Gervasi, *Real Rockefeller,* pp. 191–95.

665. Banner headlines: *NYT, Washington Post,* January 6, 1958.

665. Congressional reaction: *Washington Post,* January 7, 1958.

665. Appearance on *Today:* Burbank interview; Nancy Hanks to William Kintner, January 9, 1958, Special Studies Box 14, RAC; *Time,* January 20, 1958; NAR to Chester Bowles, January 24, 1958, Bowles Papers, Folder 0561, Yale.

666. "Despite the fact": DDE to NAR, January 8, 1958, Ann Whitman Files, Administration Series, Box 30, DDEL.

666. Eisenhower's talk with Percy: Percy to NAR, January 22, 1958, Special Studies Box 42, RAC.

667. "The main thing": *U.S. News & World Report,* January 17, 1958.

667. "Who could argue": Charles Percy interview.

37. *Cram Course*

668. Jud Morhouse: Guy Graves interview; R. Burdell Bixby interview; Sanford Morhouse interview; obituary, *NYT,* March 23, 1982; *N.Y. World-Telegram & Sun,* August 21, 1956; *Newsday,* August 21, 1956; Albany *Knickerbocker News,* August 21, 1956.

669. The new chairman labored mightily: Albany *Knickerbocker News,* August 18, 1955, August 21, 1956; *Newark Sunday News,* September 18, 1955; Syracuse *Post-Standard,* August 23, 1956; *Newsday,* August 21, 1956.

669. "Under Dewey many of the leaders": *Newark Sunday News,* September 18, 1955.

669. Harry O'Donnell: Jack Germond, Burdell Bixby, Warren Weaver interviews.

670. "Morhouse is doing a tremendous job": *Newsday,* August 21, 1956.

670. They met at the Knickerbocker Club: Gervasi, *Real Rockefeller,* pp. 204–5.

671. Morhouse found attractive: Sanford Morhouse interview.

671. Morhouse sounded him out: Morris, *NR,* p. 310.

671. Various distinguished names: Joseph Carlino interview.

671. Morhouse told Mahoney: Morris, *NR,* p. 311; Gervasi, *Real Rockefeller,* p. 205.

672. "Oh, *Nelson*": Carlino interview.

672. "In Harriman's mind": Abramson, *Spanning the Century,* p. 543.

672. "The very son-of-a-bitch": Ibid., p. 545.

672. Carmine De Sapio: Leo Egan, "The How and Why of De Sapio," *NYT Magazine,* September 14, 1958; *Newsweek,* September 8, 1958; *The Nation,* October 31, 1959; Warren Moscow, *The Last of the Big-Time Bosses* (New York: Stein & Day, 1971).

673. De Sapio's recollection: Carmine De Sapio interview.

673. Bingham happened to run into him: Abramson, *Spanning the Century,* pp. 544–45.

673. "I told him": Bingham memorandum July 2, 1956, Averell Harriman Papers, Box 1410, Syracuse University.

674. Moynihan remembers: Daniel P. Moynihan interview.

674. "He was a very fine gentleman": Carlino interview.

674. "His attitude is that it would involve": Jamieson to NAR, June 21, 1956, Public Relations, Box 17, RAC.

675. "If the commission says": Memorandum on Constitutional Convention Commission, Public Relations, Box 17, RAC.

675. "I confess certain intuitive instincts": Jamieson to NAR, June 25, 1956, Public Relations, Box 17, RAC.

675. Moore recommended Ronan: Lawrence Murray interview; Edward Kresky interview.

675. William Ronan: Fred C. Shapiro, "The Wholly Ronan Empire," *NYT Magazine,* May 17, 1970; *NYT,* November 19, 1974.

676. He openly challenged Moses: *NYT,* January 18, 1957, January 25, 1957.

676. Ronan's chat with Rockefeller: *Senate Hearings,* pp. 924–25.

677. George Hinman: F. Clifton White, Robert MacCrate, Robert Douglass, Edward Kresky, James Helmuth interviews.

678. From what Charles Poletti could see: Charles Poletti oral history, COHP.

678. "Contact should be made with the press": Jane Magee to Frank Jamieson, March 5, 1957, Public Relations, Box 17, RAC.

679. Moses voiced his displeasure: Jane Magee to Frank Jamieson, March 6, 1957, Public Relations, Box 17, RAC.

679. Both Hinman and Moore worried: Vera Goeller to NAR, April 1, 1957, Public Relations, Box 17, RAC.

680. Reluctant to testify: Jane Magee to Frank Jamieson, April 26 and 29, 1957, Public Relations, Box 17, RAC.

680. "Take a good look around": Carlino interview.

680. September 11 meeting: Minutes, Harriman Papers, Box 1410, Syracuse.

680. Heck denunciation: *NYT,* September 21, 1957.

681. One last effort to bring Rockefeller around: Poletti note, Rockefeller statement, October 23, 1957, Harriman Papers, Box 1535, Syracuse.

681. "Thank you for sending me": Harriman to NAR, November 15, 1957, Harriman Papers, Box 729, Syracuse.

682. Morhouse was spreading the word: Guy Graves, John Walsh interviews.

683. Speech to New York Federation: Morris, *NR,* p. 312; Gervasi, *Real Rockefeller,* p. 208.

683. "He took no pleasure in language": Persico, *The Imperial Rockefeller,* p. 233.

685. "Philosophically": Kramer & Roberts, *"I Never Wanted to Be Vice-President of Anything!"* p. 65.

685. "We have a responsibility": *NYT,* September 11, 1957.

685. *Tribune* purchase: Burbank interview; March 4, 1955, entry, DDE Diary Series, Box 9, Phone Calls, DDEL.

686. Weaver's buyout: Sylvester "Pat" Weaver interview.

686. Tod and public life: Eleanor Clark French interview; Morris, *NR,* p. 315.

687. Jamieson's advice: Linda Storrow interview; Burbank interview; Collier & Horowitz, *The Rockefellers,* p. 330; Frank Moore to Frank Jamieson, October 19, 1956, Public Relations, Box 13, RAC.

688. "He made the flat statement": David Rockefeller interview.

688. Slow slog: Morris, *NR,* p. 310.

688. "He slapped my knee": Smith, *Thomas E. Dewey and His Times,* p. 624.

688. "There was a feeling": R. Burdell Bixby interview.

688. Party switch: Pat Weaver interview; Harry Albright interview.

690. Brooklyn Dodgers: *NYT, NYHT,* September 11, 1957, September 18, 1957; Oscar Ruebhausen interview; Kershaw Burbank interview; John Lockwood interview; Nancy Hanks to parents, September 8, 1957, Hanks Papers, Box 240, Duke.

692. "Hello, Governor": Donna Mitchell interview.

693. Heckscher's discovery: August Heckscher interview.

694. Albert Schweitzer incident: *New York Post,* March 24, 1958.

694. "The whole Miltown field": Ibid.

695. Rasmussen's discovery: Anne-Marie Rasmussen, *There Was Once a Time* (New York: Harcourt Brace Jovanovich, 1975), p. 32.

695. "I would take his briefcase": Steven Rockefeller–Morrow interview.

695. Car ride with Jamieson: Storrow interview; Collier & Horowitz, *The Rockefellers,* p. 346.

695. Red Ferrari: Kramer & Roberts, *"I Never Wanted to Be Vice-President of Anything!,"* pp. 72–73.

38. *Travels with Malcolm*

697. Meeting with Dewey: George Shapiro interview.

697. "The delegates are just a list of names": Warren Moscow, *Politics in the Empire State* (Westport, Conn.: Greenwood Press, 1979), p. 60.

698. Morhouse poll: *NYT,* January 13, 1958.

698. "He has declined to say publicly": *National Review,* August 2, 1958.

699. Billy Hill: Warren Anderson, Robert MacCrate, Collins Lyden interviews; Warren Moscow, *Politics in the Empire State,* p. 146.

699. Meeting with Hill: Morris, *NR,* p. 313.

699. What counted: Binghamton *Sun,* May 5, 1958.

699. Rockefeller would exalt his memories: Speech before Broome County Republican Committee, March 5, 1970.

700. "A lot of people": Desmond, *Nelson Rockefeller,* pp. 157–58.

700. Meeting with Wilson: Malcolm Wilson interview.

701. Malcolm Wilson: *N.Y. Post,* September 28, 1958; Rochester *Democrat & Chronicle,* August 24, 1958; *NYT Magazine,* October 27, 1974; *NYT,* December 12, 1973; Albany *Times-Union,* December 23, 1973; "Malcolm Wilson's Voting Record on Major Issues," Harriman Papers, Box 1663, Syracuse; Douglas Barclay, Robert McEwen, Betsy Kaplan interviews.

702. "I had no power base": Transcript of interview with Malcolm Wilson by Hugh Morrow. A copy of the transcript was furnished to the author by Wilson.

702. He phoned Wilson: F. Clifton White interview.

703. "The price for his stolid": Abramson, *Spanning the Century,* p. 520.

703. Harriman as governor: W. Averell Harriman oral history, COHP; Abramson, *Spanning the Century,* Chapter 20; Daniel Moynihan interview; *Life,* September 22, 1958.

704. Leonard Hall: *Newsday,* May 27, 1958; Syracuse *Herald-Journal,* May 5, 1958; F. Clifton White interview.

705. Eisenhower was encouraging: Ann Whitman Diary, October 18, 1957, entry, Ann Whitman Diary Series, Box 9, DDEL.

706. Interview with *New York Post: N.Y. Post,* March 26, 1958.

706. One guest wondered: Jean McKee interview.

707. John Roosevelt efforts: *NYT,* April 25, May 1, 1958; Kramer & Roberts, *"I Never Wanted to Be Vice-President of Anything!,"* p. 197; "Draft Rockefeller" telegram to Ogden Reid, May 15, 1958, Ogden Reid Papers, Series II, Box 47, Yale.

707. "As matters stand": *Meet the Press,* April 20, 1958.

708. Meeting with Wilson: Malcolm Wilson interview; Hugh Morrow interview with Wilson.

709. Frank Moore and Jaeckle: Moore to NAR, May 6, 1958, *Public Relations,* Box 16, RAC.

710. Moore's call from Bush: Ibid.

710. Morhouse was worried: *NYT,* June 8, 1958.

710. Morhouse's meetings: *NYT,* June 8, June 9, 1958; *Newsday,* June 9, 1958; *Time,* October 6, 1958; Morris, *NR,* p. 317.

711. Rockefeller's announcement: *NYT, NYHT,* July 1, 1958.

711. "Nelson always liked to say": Malcolm Wilson interview.

712. Running into Junior: Ibid.

712. Myrtie Tinklepaugh: Interview with Marianne Fish (Tinklepaugh's daughter).

712. Meeting at the Dutch Inn: Malcolm Wilson, Marianne Fish, Albert Callan interviews.

713. Travels with Wilson: Malcolm Wilson interview.

713. "Stevie's the real political pro": Jay Coral interview.

713. "Now I know why": John Vandervoort interview.

714. Rockefeller never failed to deliver: Malcolm Wilson interview; Jay Coral interview; *Life,* September 22, 1958; *Glens Falls Times,* July 30, 1958.

714. Potato Festival: Malcolm Wilson, Jack Germond, Warren Weaver interviews.

715. Several made it known to Wilson: Malcolm Wilson interview.

715. "I never worked so hard for anything": NAR interviewed on *Between the Lines,* WNEW-TV, September 7, 1958.

715. "I have this memory": Steven Rockefeller–Morrow interview.

716. "Nelson would go upstate": Alsop, *Nixon and Rockefeller,* p. 39.

716. Hall lambasted Rockefeller: *NYT,* July 28, 1958.

716. Orange County GOP dinner: *NYT,* August 10, 1958.

716. Sprague: Moscow, *Politics in the Empire State,* p. 138.

716. Sprague's betrayal of Hall: Joseph Carlino interview.

717. "When I decided to run": Kramer & Roberts, *"I Never Wanted . . . ,"* p. 202.

718. "I said to myself": Hayward Plumadore interview.

718. "A lot of small towns": Kramer & Roberts, *"I Never Wanted . . . ,"* p. 200.

718. "You can't beat that kind of money": F. Clifton White interview.

718. *National Review* sounded the alarm: *National Review,* August 2, 1958.

719. "Committee for Republican Victory": A copy of the letter is in Harriman Papers, Box 1702, Syracuse.

719. "Hall is just about finished": *NYT,* August 7, 1958.

719. Hall's withdrawal: Rochester *Democrat & Chronicle, NYT,* August 18, 1958.

719. "We are in this": John Vandervoort interview.

719. Mahoney and Kenna: F. Clifton White interview.

720. Arrival in Rochester: Rochester *Democrat & Chronicle,* August 23, 1958.

721. Courting of Carlino: Joseph Carlino interview.

722. Approach to Mahoney: F. Clifton White interview.

722. Wilson's version: Malcolm Wilson interview.

722. Search for Senate nominee: Kenneth Keating oral history, COHP; Joseph Carlino interview; Rochester *Democrat & Chronicle,* August 22 through August 27, 1958; *NYHT,* August 25 and 26, 1958; *NYT,* August 25, 1958.

723. Call to Nixon: Rochester *Democrat & Chronicle,* August 27, 1958; *NYHT,* August 27, 1958.

723. Lundy's nomination: James Desmond, in his 1964 authorized NAR biography, says flatly that Lundy's selection was a payoff to Kenna. See p. 173.

723. Platform vetted: *NYT,* August 26, 1958; George Shapiro interview.

723. Rockefeller's nomination: *NYT, NYHT, N.Y. Post,* Rochester *Democrat & Chronicle,* August 26, 1958.

725. *Herald Tribune* editorial: *NYHT,* August 27, 1958.

725. "She seemed very uncomfortable": Manley Thaler interview.

726. "This is what Nelson wants to do": *N.Y. Post,* August 26, 1958.

39. *Elected*

727. "I don't want that Wagner": Moscow, *The Last of the Big-Time Bosses,* p. 144.

727. The true reason: Abramson, *Spanning the Century,* p. 556.

727. Harriman advised him: Ibid.

728. "The guy looked like death on vacation": Abramson, *Spanning the Century,* p. 557.

728. Call from De Sapio: Mark Chadwin interview with Daniel Gutman, Harriman Papers, Box 868, LC.

728. "Many liberal Democrats": Abramson, *Spanning the Century,* pp. 558–59.

729. Hogan's meeting with Harriman: Mark Chadwin interview with Milton Stewart, Harriman Papers, Box 870, LC.

729. "You didn't want me on the ticket": Moscow, *The Last of the Big-Time Bosses,* p. 150.

729. Rose said he couldn't: Mark Chadwin interview with Daniel Gutman, Harriman Papers, Box 868, LC.

729. The lowest moment: Abramson, *Spanning the Century,* p. 563.

730. "They gave ole Ave": Ibid.

730. "Dan, do you know": Mark Chadwin interview with Daniel Gutman, Harriman Papers, Box 868, LC.

730. "Tammany is back in the saddle": Malcolm Wilson interview.

730. "Oh no, not again": Desmond, *Nelson Rockefeller,* p. 177.

730. "The most boss-ridden": Moscow, *The Last of the Big-Time Bosses,* p. 156.

731. "If a governor": *NYT,* September 2, 1958.

731. Harriman might "like to drop out": *NYT,* August 29, 1958.

731. "I think De Sapio": Berle & Jacobs, *Navigating the Rapids,* p. 688.

731. "The voters of New York State": "Battle of the Millionaires", *Saturday Evening Post,* October 25, 1958.

732. Harriman was "the champ": "A Voters' Choice of Millionaires," *Life,* September 22, 1958.

732. "The wounds are not wide nor deep": "Battle of the Millionaires."

732. "All of us Democrats": Eleanor Clark French interview.

732. "When Averell loses his enthusiasms": "A Voters' Choice of Millionaires."

733. All-day strategy session: Manley Thaler interview.

733. "Well, it takes a little time": Morris, *NR,* p. 323.

733. Roosevelt Hotel atmosphere: *New Yorker,* October 4, 1958; Morris, *NR,* pp. 322–23; John Terry interview.

733. Organization at headquarters: June Martin interview; *The Reporter,* October 30, 1958.

734. "We just don't have the manpower": *NYHT,* October 17, 1958.

735. "Being in the business": Sylvester "Pat" Weaver interview.

736. "We are caught between a series of cross currents": Lockwood to JDR3, August 5, 1958, Rockefeller Family Civic Interests, Box 32, RAC.

736. Unofficial tally: List of major Republican contributors in Harriman Papers, Box 386, LC. Also see Rockefeller Family Civic Interests, Box 27 and Box 33, RAC, for WR and Abby Mauzé contributions.

737. Bank loans: *NYT,* November 26, 1958.

738. French story: Eleanor Clark French interview.

738. "The only time": Philip Kaiser interview.
738. Ted Tannenwald handed him: Abramson, *Spanning the Century,* p. 509.
738. "He has the most defensive attitude": James Loeb oral history, HSTL.
739. Liberal tidbits: James Loeb to Harriman, July 30, 1958, Harriman Papers, Box 1700, Syracuse.
739. "We will of course": James Loeb to Harriman, July 12, 1958, Harriman Papers, Box 729, Syracuse.
740. Off-the-record lunch: Victor Riesel column, *N.Y. Mirror,* September 15, November 14, 1958.
741. "I have regretfully learned": Frank Karelsen to Harriman, August 21, 1958, Harriman Papers, Box 729, Syracuse.
741. "When I was a little girl": *NYT,* October 26, 1958.
742. "There's a Spanish phrase": "A Voters' Choice of Millionaires."
742. "I wish some of his money": *N.Y. Post,* September 12, 1958.
742. Exuberant campaigning: *Time,* October 6, 1958; Joseph Boyd interview.
743. "Let's get him out of here": *N.Y. Post,* November 5, 1958.
743. "Who's that girl": Robert McEwen interview.
743. Talking with the cleaning woman: Linda Storrow interview.
743. Staten Island Ferry bootblack: Moscow, *The Last of the Big-Time Bosses,* p. 157.
744. "What's he doing this for?": Clinton Dominick interview.
744. Louis Lefkowitz: *NYT,* September 15, 1958; *New Yorker,* October 4, 1958; Louis Lefkowitz interview; Bernard Newman interview.
745. Lower East Side visit: *NYT, NYHT,* October 2, 1958; Louis Lefkowitz interview; Bernard Newman interview.
746. "When in the political history": *NYT,* October 2, 1958.
746. Television strategy: Pat Weaver interview.
747. "He handled cards": *NYT,* September 30, 1958.
747. Spent two and a half times what Harriman's did: Edward Chester, *Radio, Television and American Politics* (New York: Sheed & Ward, 1969), p. 108.
747. "All this marks": *N.Y. Daily News,* October 26, 1958.
747. Switchboard operator at the state committee: Jean McKee interview.
747. Germond's bet: Jack Germond interview.
748. "Cherish it for me": June Martin interview.
748. "If instead of devoting": *NYT,* October 26, 1958.
748. "I want to see you and Mr. Hogan elected": Jonathan S. Liebowitz to Harriman, October 8, 1958, Harriman Papers, Box 730, Syracuse.
749. "Between the undercutting and the back-sniping": Mark Chadwin interview with Daniel Gutman, Harriman Papers, Box 868, LC.
749. Fury over Franklin Adams: Ibid.
749. "You must talk to Carmine": Memo, author unknown, to Harriman, Harriman Papers, Box 733, Syracuse.
749. "Whipping boy": *NYT,* October 19, 1958.
750. "If I can get Nelson on foreign policy": Jack Germond interview.
751. Coney Island horde: *NYHT, NYT,* October 20, 1958.
751. Spanish Harlem rally: *N.Y. Post,* October 26, 1958, *NYT,* October 25, 1958.
752. "What a rathole," chocolate milk: Edward Kimball interview.
752. Tod sat in the limousine: Jay Coral interview.

753. "The first thing I'll have": Arthur Richardson interview.

753. "Have you ever been to Albany?": Morris, *NR*, p. 326.

753. "When you've seen one tree": Arthur Richardson interview.

754. Whispers about Hanks: Donna Mitchell interview.

756. Powell cut a deal: Charles V. Hamilton, *Adam Clayton Powell, Jr.: The Political Biography of an American Dilemma* (New York: Atheneum, 1991), pp. 311–12.

756. Powell's charges: *NYHT, NYT,* October 22, 1958; *N.Y. Post,* October 23, 1958.

756. Willis' offer: Hamilton, *Adam Clayton Powell,* pp. 310–11.

757. The applause was anemic: *N.Y. Post,* October 21, 1958.

757. Rent control charges: *NYT,* October 12, October 30, 1958, among other dates.

758. Nixon visit and aftermath: *N.Y. Post, NYT, NYHT,* October 24, 1958; *NYT, NYHT,* October 25, 1958; Morris, *NR,* pp. 328–29; Desmond, *Nelson Rockefeller,* p. 182.

760. Harriman on Barry Gray: A transcript is in Harriman Papers, Box 386, LC.

760. Dorothy Schiff: Jeffrey Potter, *Men, Money & Magic: The Story of Dorothy Schiff* (New York: Coward, McCann & Geoghegan, 1976).

761. Schiff's switch: *N.Y. Post,* November 3, 4, 7, 1958; *NYHT, NYT,* November 4, 1958.

762. The governor was visibly shaken: *NYHT,* November 4, 1958.

763. "I'd been for Franklin Roosevelt, Jr.": Kramer & Roberts, *"I Never Wanted to Be Vice-President of Anything!,"* pp. 207–8.

763. "I have always felt that it was personal": Mark Chadwin interview with Milton Stewart, Harriman Papers, Box 870, LC.

763. Harriman came to believe: Abramson, *Spanning the Century,* p. 568.

764. Dead orchid story: Clay Felker interview; Potter, *Men, Money & Magic,* pp. 72–73.

764. The candidate looked tired and drawn: Desmond, *Nelson Rockefeller,* p. 191.

764. Election night at the Roosevelt: *NYT, NYHT, N.Y. Post,* November 5, 1958; Morris, *NR,* pp. 329–30.

766. "It seems to me": Mark Chadwin interview with Milton Stewart, Harriman Papers, Box 870, LC.

766. Democratic aides claimed: *N.Y. Post,* October 27 and 31, 1958.

767. "A new personality": Orville Freeman to Harriman (quoting phone conversation with Truman), November 7, 1958, Harriman Papers, Box 399, LC.

767. Rockefeller's disclaimers: *NYHT,* November 5 and 6, 1958.

768. Tod's press conference: *N.Y. Post,* November 5, 1958.

768. "We are naturally very proud": Jr. to Kenneth Chorley, November 7, 1958, Jr. Box 27, RAC.

768. "I thought it was most significant": George O'Neill to Jr., Christmas 1958, Jr. Box 27, RAC.

Interviews

The following interviews conducted by the author figured in the making of this volume. Some are cited in the source notes; some are not. In addition to those individuals mentioned below, others were interviewed on a not-for-attribution basis.

The interviewees are identified by their connections to Nelson Rockefeller or to someone in his inner circle or by their official positions at the time they interacted with Rockefeller.

Max Abramovitz (Wallace Harrison partner)
Harry Albright (gubernatorial aide)
Meade Alcorn (Dartmouth classmate; Republican national chairman)
Richard Aldrich (cousin; IBEC aide)
William Alton (friend; IBEC aide)
Warren Anderson (N.Y. State Senator)
Harry Bagley (AIA-IBEC aide)
Douglas Barclay (N.Y. State Senator)
Beatrice Berle (Adolf Berle's wife)
Peter Berle (Adolf Berle's son)
R. Burdell Bixby (campaign aide)
Dudley Bonsal (CIAA aide)
Joseph Boyd (campaign aide)
Joan Braden (friend; family aide)
Thomas Braden (friend; family aide)
Herbert Brownell (U.S. Attorney General)
Arthur Bullowa (Lincoln classmate)
Kershaw Burbank (campaign, family aide)
Albert Callan (Columbia County Republican leader)
Virginia Callan (gubernatorial aide)
Llewelyn Callaway (Dartmouth classmate)
John Camp (AIA-IBEC aide)
Joseph Canzeri (gubernatorial, family aide)
Joseph Carlino (New York State Assembly Majority Leader)
Deirdre Carmody (family aide)
Lee Chilcote (Dartmouth classmate)
Elizabeth Bliss Parkinson Cobb (MOMA trustee)
Joy Coral (Republican worker)
Edward Costikyan (Democratic leader)
Paul Curran (son of Republican leader Thomas Curran)
Ernest Curto (Niagara County Republican official)
Jerry Danzig (campaign aide)
Virginia Derby (Lincoln classmate)
Carmine De Sapio (Democratic leader)
Clinton Dominick (local Republican official)
Robert Douglass (gubernatorial aide)
Barbara Dudley (Albany society figure)
George Dudley (gubernatorial aide)
Stephen Duggan (Lincoln classmate)
Lane Dwinell (Dartmouth schoolmate)
Pauline Falk (Lincoln schoolmate)
Justin Feldman (Democratic official)
Clay Felker (journalist)
Marianne Fish (Myrtie Tinklepaugh's daughter)
Arnold Fisher (Republican official)

James Flexner (Lincoln classmate)
Lloyd Free (pollster)
Eleanor Clark French (Tod Rockefeller cousin)
Jack Germond (journalist)
Roswell Gilpatric (Special Studies panelist)
Vera Goeller (family aide)
Harmon Goldstone (Lincoln friend; Harrison associate)
Guy Graves (New York Republican official)
Robert Grimm (Erie County Republican leader)
Karl Harr (Sullivan & Cromwell partner)
Ellen Harrison (Wallace Harrison's wife)
Harold Haskell (HEW aide)
August Heckscher (Special Studies consultant)
James Helmuth (campaign aide)
Susan Herter (CIAA, State Department, family aide)
Ort Hicks (Dartmouth alumnus)
Alger Hiss (State Department official)
Francis Horn (Dartmouth classmate)
John Innes (Republican county chairman)
Philip Johnson (architect)
Philip Kaiser (Harriman aide)
Betsy Kaplan (Republican county leader)
Robert Keene (Dartmouth classmate)
Edward Kimball (IBEC aide)
William Kintner (White House aide)
Henry Kissinger
Edward Kresky (gubernatorial aide)
Churchill Lathrop (Dartmouth teacher)
Betsy Lawton (Lincoln classmate)
Louis Lefkowitz (New York attorney general)
Franklin Lindsay (White House consultant)
Margo Lindsay (Franklin Lindsay's wife)
John Lockwood (family aide)
Collins Lyden (campaign aide)
Robert MacCrate (gubernatorial aide)
Francis Maloney (John Mitchell partner)
Alton Marshall (gubernatorial aide)
June Martin (campaign aide)
Arthur Massolo (journalist)
Tex McCrary (television personality)
Porter McCray (MOMA aide)
Robert McEwen (upstate Republican leader)
Jean McKee (Republican women's leader)
Kirt Meyer (Dartmouth classmate)
Rufus Miles (HEW aide)
Dorothy Miller (art aide)
John Minary (Dartmouth schoolmate)
Donna Mitchell (HEW, White House aide)

Beth Moore (friend)
Sanford Morhouse (L. Judson Morhouse's son)
Daniel Moynihan (Harriman aide)
Lawrence Murray (Frank Moore's deputy)
Bernard Newman (Republican leader)
Paul Nitze (CIAA aide)
Peter Ogden (architect)
Abby O'Neill (niece)
Theodore Parker (White House aide)
Charles Percy (Special Studies panelist)
Roswell Perkins (HEW, campaign aide)
Joseph Persico (gubernatorial aide)
Hayward Plumadore (Republican leader)
Tom Prideaux (Lincoln classmate)
Robert Purcell (IBEC aide)
Ogden Reid (newspaper publisher)
Arthur Richardson (campaign aide)
Laurance Roberts (Tod Rockefeller's cousin)
David Rockefeller
Happy Rockefeller
John D. Rockefeller 4th
Laurance Rockefeller
Rodman Rockefeller
Wilma Rogalin (Republican women's official)
Thomas Rosenberg (Anna Rosenberg's son)
Oscar Ruebhausen (friend; counsel)
William Rusher (magazine publisher)
Walther Moreira Salles (Latin American investor)
Fred Scribner (Dartmouth classmate)
George Shapiro (Dewey aide)
Carlton Sprague Smith (CIAA aide)
Carl Spad (campaign aide)
Sheldon Stark (Lincoln, Dartmouth classmate)
Harold Stassen (UN delegate; White House official)
Linda Storrow (Frank Jamieson's wife)
William St. Thomas (Republican county leader)
Edward Teller (Special Studies panelist)
John Terry (campaign official)
Manley Thaler (Republican county leader)
Craig Thorne (campaign aide)
John Vandervoort (campaign aide)
Robert Wagner (New York City mayor)
James Wallis (nephew)
John Walsh (Republican county leader)
Edward Warburg (friend; MOMA trustee)
Sylvester Weaver (Dartmouth classmate; campaign aide)
Warren Weaver (journalist)
Dorothy West (HEW aide)

F. Clifton White (Walter Mahoney aide)
Ann Whitman (Eisenhower assistant)
Charles Widmayer (Dartmouth classmate)
James Wiggin (Dartmouth classmate)
Nadia Williams (CIAA, HEW aide)
Malcolm Wilson (lieutenant governor)
Dorothy Wodell (friend)
John Woods, Jr. (son of Lincoln School foe)
Mary Woods (daughter of Lincoln School foe)
Eugene Zagat (Dartmouth classmate)

INDEX